Contents

Article   *Page*

Chapter 5. Special Occupancies . . . .

Chapter 6. Special Equipment . . . .

Chapter 7. Special Conditions . . . .

Chapter 8. Communications Systems . . . .

Chapter 9. Tables and Examples . . . .

Article   *Page*

Appendix . . . .

Foreword

The National Electrical Code, as its name implies, is a nationally accepted guide to the safe installation of electrical wiring and equipment.

This *NFPA Handbook of the National Electrical Code* is designed to aid those concerned with electrical safety in understanding the scope and intent of the 1975 Edition of the Code. Included is a verbatim reproduction of the official 1975 National Electrical Code as published by its sponsor, the National Fire Protection Association, and as approved by the American National Standards Institute (formerly the United States of America Standards Institute, and prior to that the American Standards Association). Added, where necessary or considered desirable, are comments, diagrams, and illustrations, supplied by the author, to facilitate understanding of the Code rules.

The author wishes it clearly understood that the National Electrical Code is prepared by the cooperative effort of representatives of every segment of the electrical industry with the sole purpose of safeguarding the public in its utilization of its great servant—electricity. The development of this Handbook is likewise a cooperative effort incorporating the knowledge and ideas of the over 300 members of the National Electrical Code Committee, and the guidance given herein taps experience in the application and interpretation of the Code developed over the more than half a century since it first appeared.

The McGraw-Hill Book Company has been publishing a Handbook on the National Electrical Code since 1932. Originally developed by Arthur L. Abbott in that year and carried on in seven successive editions until the time of his death in 1952, each subsequent issue has been authored by the Electrical Field Specialist of the National Fire Protection Association. The late Charles L. Smith prepared the editions based on the 1953 and 1956 Codes while he served as the NFPA Electrical Specialist. Frank Stetka took on the responsibility upon assuming the position and edited the Handbooks based on the 1959, 1962, 1965, and 1968 Codes. Mr. Merwin M. Brandon, Chairman of the National Electrical Code Committee from 1950 to 1961, assisted in a previous Handbook (based on the 1965 Code). Following the retirement of Mr. Stetka at the end of 1968, John Watt assumed the position of Electrical Field Engineer for the NFPA. The present edition has been prepared by Mr. Wilford I. Summers, based on the 1975 National Electrical Code, following Mr. Watt's untimely death in December 1973.

This edition of the *NFPA Handbook of the National Electrical Code* replaces the edition published in 1972 by the McGraw-Hill Book Company.

The author wishes to give particular acknowledgment to the assistance of Mr. Richard L. Lloyd, Chairman of the National Electrical Code Committee; to the author's assistant, Arel Sessions; and to the chairmen of the various Code-Making Panels of the National Electrical Code Committee, many of whom were consulted by the author in the preparation of this Handbook. The contributions of the manufacturers who provided illustrations and information about their products are greatly appreciated. The aid and assistance given by the staff of the McGraw-Hill Book Company made this book possible, and their cooperative attitude assisted the author in overcoming many technical problems in connection with the preparation of this text.

National Electrical Code

This *NFPA Handbook of the National Electrical Code* is based on the 1975 Edition of the National Electrical Code as developed by the National Electrical Code Committee of the American National Standards Institute (ANSI), sponsored by the National Fire Protection Association (NFPA). The National Electrical Code is identified by the designation NFPA No. 70-1975 and ANSI C 1-1975. The NFPA adopted this 1975 Code at the NFPA Annual Meeting held in Miami, Florida, May 20–24, and approval was given by ANSI on April 17, 1975.

The National Electrical Code, as its name implies, is a nationally accepted guide to the safe installation of electrical wiring and equipment. The committee sponsoring its development includes all parties of interest having technical competence in the field, working together with the sole objective of safeguarding the public in its utilization of electricity. The procedures under which the Code is prepared provide for the orderly introduction of new developments and improvements in the art, with particular emphasis on safety from the standpoint of its end use. The rules of procedure under which the National Electrical Code Committee operates are published in each official edition of the Code and in separate pamphlet form so that all concerned may have full information and free access to the operating procedures of the sponsoring committee. The Code has been a big factor in the growth and wide acceptance of the use of electrical energy for light and power and for heat, radio, television, signaling, and other purposes from the date of its first appearance (1897) to the present.

The National Electrical Code is primarily designed for use by trained electrical people and is necessarily terse in its wording. As a consequence, some sections are clearer if explained from the standpoint of the background intent of the Code writers, and giving these explanations is the first purpose of this *NFPA Handbook of the National Electrical Code.*

The sponsoring National Electrical Code Committee is composed of a Correlating Committee and 22 Code-Making Panels, each responsible for one or more Articles in the Code. Each Panel is composed of experienced men representing balanced interests of all segments of the industry and the public concerned with the subject matter. The present Chairman of the National Electrical Code Committee is Richard L. Lloyd, Assistant to the President, Codes and Standards of the Underwriters' Laboratories, Inc. Wilford Summers, author of this Handbook, has been the Secretary of the National Electrical Code Committee and Electrical Field Specialist of the NFPA since April 1974. The internal operations of the sponsoring committee are guided by a *Manual of Procedure for Code-Making Panels.* This Manual is published in pamphlet form, and copies are available from the NFPA, 470 Atlantic Avenue, Boston, Massachusetts 02210.

The National Fire Protection Association also has organized an Electrical Section to provide the opportunity for NFPA members interested in electrical safety to become better informed and to contribute to the development of NFPA electrical standards. This new Handbook reflects the fact that the National Electrical Code was revised in 1974, requiring an updating of the previous Handbook which was based on the 1971 Edition of the Code. The established schedule of the National Electrical Code Committee contemplates a new edition of the National Electrical Code every three years. The "Timetable for the National Electrical Code" has been announced and is published in all official copies of the 1975 National Electrical Code as well as in this volume. Provision is made under the rules of procedure for handling urgent emergency matters through a Tentative Interim Amendment Procedure. The Committee also has established rules for rendering Official Interpretations. Two general forms of findings for such Interpretations are recognized: (1) those making an interpretation of literal text and (2) those making an interpretation of the intent of the National Electrical Code when a particular rule was adopted. All Tentative Interim Amendments and Official Interpretations are published by the NFPA as they are issued, and notices are sent to all interested trade papers in the electrical industry.

Those interested in further details on the processing of each new edition of the National Electrical Code should be advised that the schedule includes a final date for receipt of proposals for changes from the public. For the 1978 Code, this date is December 1, 1975. In July of 1976, following processing of all proposals received, the Association will issue the "Proposed Amendments for the 1978 National Electrical Code." Public announcement will be made of the issuance of this document, and a period of study is included so that all interested persons may comment on the Proposed Amendments. In April 1977, the Association will issue the final agreed-upon Proposed 1978 National Electrical Code (with revisions to the 1975 Code indicated), which will be presented at the Annual Meeting of the Association in that year (now scheduled for May 16–21 at the Washington Hilton Hotel, Washington, D.C.) for action. All interested persons may attend this meeting and participate in any discussions on the proposed 1978 Code that are pertinent to the adoption procedures. Further details with regard to procedures are available from the Association upon request.

The National Electrical Code had its origin in 1897 as a result of united efforts of various insurance, electrical, architectural, and allied interests. The original Code, prepared by the National Conference on Standard Electrical Rules, was issued in successive editions until the National Conference was disbanded in 1911. Since then the National Fire Protection Association has been the sponsor. The text for editions up to 1947 was prepared by the NFPA Electrical Committee. In 1949 the NFPA Electrical Section was organized and the National Electrical Code Committee created.

The National Electrical Code is purely advisory as far as the National Fire Protection Association is concerned but is very widely used as the basis of law and for legal regulatory purposes. The Code is administered by various local inspection agencies, whose decisions govern the actual application of the National Electrical Code to individual installations. Local inspectors are largely members of the International Association of Electrical Inspectors, 802 Busse Highway, Park Ridge, Illinois 60068. This organization, the National Electrical Manufacturers Association, the National Electrical Contractors Association, the Edison Electric Institute, the Underwriters' Laboratories, Inc., the International Brotherhood of Electrical Workers, governmental groups, and independent experts all contribute to the development and application of the National Electrical Code.

Determination of the suitability of devices and materials for installation in accordance with the National Electrical Code is the responsibility of the electrical inspection authority, which, under the terms of the Code, must approve the devices and materials used. Many such "approvals" are based upon tests and listings of Underwriters' Laboratories, Inc. This nationally recognized testing laboratory maintains facilities for testing electrical equipment and checking manufacturers' production to assure maintenance of proper standards, evidenced by a label or reexamination marker on each individual product. Underwriters' Laboratories, Inc., publishes annually (with bimonthly supplements) three pamphlets, indicating electrical appliances and materials which have been examined and listed by them, entitled "Electrical Appliance and Utilization Equipment

List," "Electrical Construction Materials List," and "Hazardous Location Equipment List." These Lists may be secured from local representatives of the Laboratories in principal cities of the United States. Standards for design and testing of various types of electrical equipment developed by Underwriters' Laboratories, Inc., may be obtained from their main office at 207 East Ohio Street, Chicago, Illinois 60611.

Brief History of the
National Electrical Code

The National Electrical Code was originally drawn in 1897 as a result of the united efforts of various insurance, electrical, architectural, and allied interests. The original Code was prepared by the National Conference on Standard Electrical Rules, composed of delegates from various interested national associations. Prior to this, acting on an 1881 resolution of the National Association of Fire Engineers' meeting in Richmond, Virginia, a basis for the first Code was suggested to cover such items as identification of the white wire, the use of single disconnect devices, and the use of insulated conduit.

In 1911, the National Conference of Standard Electrical Rules was disbanded, and since that year, the National Fire Protection Association (NFPA) has acted as sponsor of the National Electrical Code. Beginning with the 1920 edition, the National Electrical Code has been under the further auspices of the American National Standards Institute (and its predecessor organizations, United States of America Standards Institute, and the American Standards Association), with the NFPA continuing in its role as Administrative Sponsor. Since that date, the Committee has been identified as "ANSI Standards Committee C1" (formerly "USAS C1" or "ASA C1").

Major milestones in the continued updating of successive issues of the National Electrical Code since 1911 appeared in 1923, when the Code was rearranged and rewritten; in 1937, when it was editorially revised so that all the general rules would appear in the first chapters followed by supplementary rules in the following chapters; and in 1959, when it was editorially revised to incorporate a new numbering system under which each Section of each Article is identified by the Article Number preceding the Section Number.

For many years the National Electrical Code was published by the National Board of Fire Underwriters (now American Insurance Association), and this public service of the National Board helped immensely in bringing about the wide public acceptance which the Code now enjoys. It is recognized as the most widely adopted Code of standard practices in the U.S.A. Over 500,000 copies of the 1975 Code were printed to fill orders within the first three months of issue. The National Fire Protection Association first printed the document in pamphlet form in 1951 and has, since that year, supplied the Code for distribution to the public through its own office and through the American National Standards Institute. The National Electrical Code also appears in Volume 6 of the National Fire Codes, issued annually by the National Fire Protection Association.

It has been the practice of the NFPA as sponsor of the National Electrical Code to include in each edition a list of the personnel of the Committee, and each NFPA edition of the Code carries this roster. Also in each printing of the text of the National Electrical Code and in the Appendix of this Handbook, the Rules of Procedure for the NFPA Electrical Section and for the National Electrical Code Committee are published, together with the Time Schedule for the next edition of the Code. To further facilitate improvements in the Code, the Appendix contains a special section on the "Method of Submitting a Proposal to Revise the National Electrical Code." The publication of this information is consistent with the operating procedures of the American National Standards Institute and the National Fire Protection Association to assure that all interested parties may participate in the work of the sponsoring committee and that there is an orderly procedure for processing the many changes that flow from the expanding use of electricity and the many new materials, methods, and systems that characterize the growth of the electrical industry.

Principal Tables

Resume of Code Changes

The following list indicates deletions, revisions, and new Sections that are reflected in the 1975 National Electrical Code through changes to the 1971 Edition. Also included, but not specifically indicated, are the results of editorial revisions to convert the Code to mandatory statements. The section numbers used in this resume correlate with the editorial rewrite contained in Preprint Part I; therefore, the cross references which follow this resume must be used.

Art. 90. New. (1) 90-4 Enforcement second paragraph.
Revised. (1) 90-7.
Art. 100. New. (1) Scope second paragraph; **(2)** Approved for the purpose; **(3)** Bonding; **(4)** Conduit Body; **(5)** Enclosure; **(6)** Labeled; **(7)** Listed; **(8)** Neutral Conductor; **(9)** Premises Wiring System; **(10)** Power Outlet; **(11)** Service-Entrance Conductors, Sub-sets; **(12)** Voltage, Nominal; **(13)** Part B, Over 600 Volts, Nominal.
Revised. (1) Askarel; **(2)** Branch-Circuit; **(3)** Circuit Breaker; **(4)** Conductor; **(5)** Disconnecting Means; **(6)** Enclosed; **(7)** Sealed (Hermetic Type) Motor Compressor; **(8)** AC General-Use Snap Switch; **(9)** AC-DC General-Use Snap Switch; **(10)** Voltage of a Circuit; **(11)** Weatherproof.
Art. 110. New. (1) 110-13(b); **(2)** Part B.
Revised. (1) 110-1; **(2)** 110-2; **(3)** 110-3; **(4)** 110-4; **(5)** 110-14(a); **(6)** 110-14(a) Exception; **(7)** 110-16(a)(3) Ex. No. 1 and Ex. No. 2.

Art. 200. Revised. (1) 200-1; (2) 200-2; (3) 200-3.

Art. 210. New. (1) 210-8(a) second paragraph; (2) 210-8(b) Ex.; (3) 210-25(b) Paragraph 5, 6, and 10; (4) 210-26.
Revised. (1) 210-4; (2) 210-5(c); (3) 210-5(c) Ex. No. 1 and Ex. No. 2; (4) 210-6(d) Ex. No. 2; (5) 210-8(b); (6) 210-19(a); (7) 210-25(b) Paragraph 1.
Deleted. (1) 210-5 FPN; (2) 210-23 (d).

Art. 215. Revised. (1) 215-1; (2) 215-2 FPN; (3) 215-4; (4) 215-5 FPN.

Art. 220. New. (1) 220-33; (2) 220-19 Table Note 5.
Revised. (1) 220-2 Ex. No. 2; (2) 220-2(c) Ex. No. 2; (3) 220-3(b)(1) Ex.; (4) 220-3(d) FPN; (5) 220-10(b) Ex.; (6) 220-11; (7) 220-11 Table; (8) 220-13; (9) 220-15 Ex. No. 2; (10) 220-19 Note 3 to Table; (11) 220-30; (12) Table 220-30; (13) 220-31; (14) 220-32(a)(3).
Deleted. (1) 220-2 FPN; (2) 220-3(d) FPN; (3) 220-19 FPN; (4) 220-30 last paragraph; (5) Table 220-32 FPN.

Art. 225. (Formerly Article 730). **New.** (1) 225-6(d).
Revised. (1) 225-7(c); (2) 225-11; (3) 225-19(c).
Deleted. 225-21.

Art. 230. New. (1) 230-45; (2) 230-79(a); (3) 230-95 third paragraph; (4) 230-95 fifth paragraph; (5) 230-208; (6) 230-209; (7) 230-10; (8) 230-211.
Revised. (1) 230-2 Ex. No. 4; (2) 230-30 Ex. No. 4; (3) 230-40 Ex.; (4) 230-41(b)(3) Ex. No. 1, No. 2, and No. 3; (5) 230-46 Ex. No. 2; (6) 230-48; (7) 230-49 (a), b, and (c) moved to 300-5; (8) 230-72; (9) 230-72(d); (10) 230-75; (11) 230-78 Ex.; (12) 230-82 Ex. No. 5; (13) 230-83 Ex.; (14) 230-84(a); (15) 230-94; (16) 230-95; (17) 230-98 (was 230-97); (18) 230-205.
Deleted. (1) 230-63(b); (2) 230-202(b) second paragraph.

Art. 240. New. (1) 240-3 Ex. No. 2; (2) 240-81 second paragraph; (3) Part H.
Revised. (1) 240-1; (2) 240-3 Ex. No. 1; (3) 240-4; (4) 240-6; (5) 240-8; (6) 240-11; (7) 240-20(a); (8) 240-21 Ex. No. 2; (9) 240-30 Ex. No. 1; (10) 240-40 Ex. No. 2; (11) 240-80; (12) 240-82.

Art. 250. New. (1) 250-3 (Ex. No. 3), (2) 250-3 Ex. No. 4; (3) 250-3 Ex. No. 5; (4) 250-5(c). ((c) is now (d)); (5) 250-6; (6) 250-23 Ex. No. 4; (7) 250-23 Ex. No. 5; (8) 250-57(b) Ex. No. 1 and Ex. No. 2; (9) 250-61(b) Ex. No. 3 and Ex. No. 4; (10) 250-74 Ex. No. 3 and Ex. No. 4; (11) 250-91(b) Ex. No. 3; (12) 250-91(c); (13) 250-91(b)(9); (14) 250-94(a) Ex. No. 2; (15) 250-95 third paragraph; (16) 250 Part N.
Revised. (1) 250-3(a) and (b); (2) 250-5(b); (3) 250-23; (4) 250-23(b); (5) 250-24; (6) 250-25; (7) 250-26(a); (8) 250-26(b); (9) 250-42(f) Ex. No. 3; (10) 250-44(d) Ex.; (11) 250-45(c)(2); (12) 250-45(c)(3) Ex.;

(13) 250-45(d)(5) Ex. No. 1; (14) 250-53(b); (15) 250-53 FPN; (16) 250-56; (17) 250-57(b) Ex. No. 1 and Ex. No. 2; (18) 250-60; (19) 250-71(e); (20) 250-73; (21) 250-74 Ex. No. 2; (22) 250-80; (23) 250-83(b); (24) 250-83(b)(2); (25) 250-84; (26) 250-86 FPN; (27) 250-91(a) Ex. No. 1 and Ex. No. 2; (28) 250-94(a) and Ex. No. 1, (29) 250-95 Ex. No. 1; (30) 250-99; (31) 250-115; (32) 250-131; (33) 250-132.
Deleted. (1) 250-3(b) FPN; (2) 250-23(a) FPN; (3) 250-94(b); (4) Table 250-94(b).

Art. 280. Revised. (1) 280-30; (2) 280-32.
Deleted. (1) 280-31.

Art. 300. New. (1) 300-4 (formerly 300-8); (2) 300-5; (3) 300-15 Ex. No. 4 and Ex. No. 5; (4) 300-19(a) Ex. No. 2; (5) 300-19(b)(4); (6) 300-22(c) Ex. No. 1 and Ex. No. 2; (7) 300-22(d); (8) Part B.
Revised. (1) 300-1(b); (2) 300-15(a) Ex. No. 1; (3) 300-19(b); (4) 300-19(b)(1); (5) 300-20; (6) 300-20 FPN; (7) 300-21(1) and (2); (8) 300-22(c).
Deleted. (1) 300-8(a) and (b) (now 300-4).

Art. 305. New. (1) 305-4(g); (2) Part B.
Revised. (1) 305-2(c).

Art. 310. New. (1) 310-4 FPN; (2) 310-11(b)(3)e; (3) Note 3 and Note 14 (to Tables 310-16 through 310-19); (4) Part C.
Revised. (1) 310-3; (2) 310-5; (3) 310-6; (4) 310-7; (5) 310-10(b) and (c), 310-11(b)(1); (6) 310-13; (7) Table 310-13; (8) Tables 310-16 through 310-19; (9) Note 7 combined with Note 13 (Notes to Tables 310-16 through 310-19); (10) Note 8; (11) Table to Note 13 (Correction Factors).
Deleted. (1) Note 10 FPN (Notes to Tables 310-16 through 310-19); (2) 310-20; (3) 310-21, Table 310-21(c), and Table 310-21.

Art. 318. Cable Trays (Formerly Continuous Rigid Cable Supports) complete re-write.

Art. 320. Revised. (1) 320-3; (2) 320-15; (3) 320-16.
Deleted. (1) 320-4.

Art. 324. Revised. (1) 324-3; (2) 324-6 Ex.; (3) 320-11(a).

Art. 330. Revised. (1) 330-11; (2) 330-13; (3) 330-14.

Art. 331. Revised. (1) 331-11; (2) 331-12; (3) 331-13; (4) 331-14.

Art. 332. New. (Copper-Sheathed Cable).

Art. 334. Revised. (1) 334-1; (2) 334-2; (3) 334-4(a); (4) 334-8(a) and (b); (5) 334-12.

Art. 336. New. (1) 336-3(b)(9).
Revised. (1) 336-2(a) and (b); (2) 336-3(a) and (b); (3) 336-5 Ex.; (4) 336-7; (5) 336-8; (6) 336-12.

Art. 337. New. 337-7.
Revised. (1) 337-2; (2) 337-8 (Formerly 337-7).

Art. 338. Complete re-write.

Art. 339. Revised. (1) 339-1; (2) 339-2(a)(1) and (3).

Art. 340. New. (Power and Control Tray Cable).

Art. 342. Revised. (1) 342-8.

Art. 345. New. (Intermediate Metal Conduit).

Art. 346. New. (1) 346-14; **(2)** 346-15(d), (formerly 346-14).
Revised. (1) 346-4; **(2)** 346-6; **(3)** 346-10 Ex.; **(4)** Table 346-12 (Ex. No. 1 and Ex. No. 2); **(5)** 346-15(a), (formerly 346-14).

Art. 347. New. (1) 347-2(a)(6); **(2)** 347-16; **(3)** 347-17(d), (formerly 347-16).
Revised. (1) 347-2; **(2)** 347-11.

Art. 348. New. (1) 348-14.
Revised. (1) 348-4; **(2)** 348-5; **(3)** 348-6; **(4)** 348-9 Ex.; **(5)** 348-14(a).

Art. 350. New. (1) 350-6.
Revised. (1) 350-2; **(2)** Table 350-3; **(3)** 350-5 Ex.

Art. 351. Revised. (1) 351-3; **(2)** 351-4(a) and (b); **(3)** 351-6; **(4)** 351-7.

Art. 352. Revised. (1) 352-2 Ex. No. 2; **(2)** 352-8; **(3)** 352-22.

Art. 353. Revised. (1) 353-1; **(2)** 353-2; **(3)** 353-3.

Art. 354. New. (1) 354-3(d).
Revised. (1) 354-3(c); **(2)** 354-5; **(3)** 354-6 FPN; **(4)** 354-9; **(5)** 354-13; **(6)** 354-14; **(7)** 354-15.
Delete. (1) 354-11; **(2)** 354-12.

Art. 356. Revised. (1) 356-5; **(2)** 356-6 FPN; **(3)** 356-8; **(4)** 356-9; **(5)** 356-10; **(6)** 356-11.

Art. 357. Delete. (Structural Raceways).

Art. 358. Revised. (1) 358-3; **(2)** 358-5; **(3)** 358-6; **(4)** 358-7; **(5)** 358-9; **(6)** 358-11.

Art. 363. New. (1) Part B.
Revised. (1) 363-6.

Art. 364. Revised. (1) 364-2; **(2)** 364-3; **(3)** 364-4; **(4)** 364-10; **(5)** 364-11.
Delete. (1) 364-13 FPN.

Art. 365. New. (1) 365-6 Ex.
Revised. (1) 365-1; **(2)** 365-2 second paragraph.

Art. 366. New. (Electrical Floor Assemblies).

Art. 370. New. (1) 370-6(d); **(2)** 370-18(a)(2) Ex.; **(3)** Part D.
Revised. (1) 370-1; **(2)** 370-4; **(3)** 370-5; **(4)** 370-6(a), (b) and (c); **(5)** Table 370-6(a); **(6)** Table 370-6(a)(2); **(7)** 370-12; **(8)** 370-14; **(9)** 370-18; **(10)** 370-19.
Delete. (1) 370-20(a) FPN.

Art. 373. Revised. (1) 373-2 FPN; **(2)** 373-6(b); **(3)** 373-10(a).

Art. 380. Revised. (1) 380-1; **(2)** 380-2; **(3)** 380-3; **(4)** 380-8; **(5)** 380-11; **(6)** 380-13(c).
Delete. (1) 380-16 FPN.

Art. 384. New. (1) 384-3(e) and (f); **(2)** 384-10; **(3)** 384-16(d); **(4)** 384-26 Ex. No. 2; **(5)** 384-27 Ex.
Revised. (1) 384-3(a), (c), and (d); **(2)** 384-4; **(3)** 384-6; **(4)** 384-21.
Delete. (1) Table 384-26 FPN.

Art. 390. (Now Manufactured Building, Art. 545).

Art. 400. New. (1) Note 2 (Notes to Table 400-4).
Revised. (1) Table 400-4; **(2)** Note 1 and Note 8 (Notes to Table 400-4); **(3)** 400-6;

(4) 400-7; **(5)** Table 400-5; **(6)** 400-9; **(7)** 400-22(b) Ex.; **(8)** 400-22(e).
Delete. Note 2 (Notes to Table 400-4).

Art. 402. Revised. (1) Table 402-3; **(2)** 402-4; **(3)** 402-5; **(4)** 402-8 incorporated with 402-5.
Delete. (1) Table 402-5.

Art. 410. New. (1) 410-16(b) and (c); **(2)** 410-18 (formerly 410-92); **(3)** 410-20 (formerly 410-94); **(4)** 410-30(d); **(5)** 410-31 Ex. No. 2 FPN; **(6)** 410-56(a) Ex.; **(7)** 410-56(e); 410-69(b).
Revised. (1) 410-4 FPN; **(2)** 410-21; **(3)** 410-31 Ex. No. 2, a and b; **(4)** 410-32; **(5)** 410-37 and Ex.; **(6)** 410-36; **(7)** 410-56(d); **(8)** 410-57(c); **(9)** 410-58(c); **(10)** 410-66; **(11)** 410-69; **(12)** 410-73(a); **(13)** 410-74; **(14)** 410-76; **(15)** 410-76 FPN; **(16)** 410-77(c); **(17)** 410-78; **(18)** 410-82.
Delete. (1) 410-32 FPN (Formerly 410-27)

Art. 422. New. (1) 422-14(b); **(2)** 422-27(e) Ex.
Revised. (1) 422-3 (second paragraph); **(2)** 422-16 (second paragraph); **(3)** 422-23(c) FPN; **(4)** 422-24(b); **(5)** 422-27(a) Ex.; **(6)** 422-27 (c); **(7)** Part F (Moved to Part G, Article 440).

Art. 424. New. (1) 424-22(c) Ex. No. 2; **(2)** 424-41(f) Ex.; **(3)** Part G; **(4)** Part H.
Revised. (1) 424-3(a) and Ex.; **(2)** 424-19; **(3)** 424-22(c) and (d); **(4)** 424-42; **(5)** 424-43(a) and b); **(6)** 424-63; **(7)** 424-66.
Delete. (1) 424-22; **(2)** 424-45 FPN; **(3)** 424-63 FPN.

Art. 426. Revised. (1) 426-3; **(2)** 426-21(c) 426-25(e).

Art. 427. New. (Fixed Electric Heating Equipment for Pipelines and Vessels).

Art. 430. New. (1) 430-2; **(2)** 430-6(a) Ex. No. 2; **(3)** 430-6(c); **(4)** 430-7(a)(10); **(5)** 430-7(a) Ex. No. 4 and Ex. No. 5; **(6)** 430-21 Ex.; **(7)** 430-25 Ex.; **(8)** 430-28; **(9)** 430-52 Ex. (e) and (f); **(10)** 430-71 (third paragraph); **(11)** 430-102 Ex.
Revised. (1) 430-3 Ex.; **(2)** 430-7 Ex. No. 2; **(3)** 430-8; **(4)** 430-12(b); **(5)** Table 430-12(b); **(6)** 430-12(d); **(7)** 430-31 (fourth paragraph); **(8)** 430-32 (a)(1); **(9)** 430-32(c)(1); **(10)** 430-32 (make last paragraph FPN); **(11)** 430-34; **(12)** 430-35(a), 430-40 Ex. No. 1; **(13)** 430-51 (second paragraph); **(14)** 430-52 (second paragraph), Ex, a., c., and last paragraph; **(15)** 430-53(c)(1), (3), (4), (5), and (6); **(16)** 430-72; **(17)** 430-74; **(18)** 430-82(a); **(19)** 430-83 Ex. No. 2; **(20)** 430-84 Ex.; **(21)** 430-109 Ex. No. 3 c.; **(22)** 430-110(a) and (b); **(23)** 430-111(2) and last paragraph; **(24)** 430-112 Ex.; **(25)** 430-123, 430-124 and 430-126 are rewritten as 430-122 through 430-127; **(26)** 430-133 FPN; **(27)** 430-142(2) and last paragraph; **(28)** Table 430-147; **(29)** Table 430-150; **(30)** Table 430-151; **(31)** Table 430-152.
Delete. (1) Table 430-22(a) Ex. (second FPN); **(2)** 430-39 FPN; **(3)** 430-59; **(4)** 430-62 FPN; **(5)** 430-111(3) FPN; **(6)** 430-133 FPN; **(7)** 430-143 (second FPN).

Art. 440. New. (1) 440-1 (Second paragraph); **(2)** 440-3(b) Ex. No. 2; **(3)** 440-14; **(4)** 440-33 Ex. No. 2; **(5)** 440-52(b) Ex.; **(6)** 440-55; **(7)** 440 Part G.
Revised. (1) 440-3(a); **(2)** 440-3(b); **(3)** 440-3(c); **(4)** 440-12(a)(1) and (2); **(5)** 440-12(b)(1) and (2); **(6)** 440-33; **(7)** 440-52(a)(3); **(8)** 440-52(b)(3); **(9)** 440-53 and Ex.; **(10)** 440-54.
Delete. (1) 440-22(b)(2) Ex.; **(2)** 440-52(a)(3) Ex.

Art. 445. Revised. (1) 445-1; **(2)** 445-2; **(3)** 445-3, **(4)** 445-4(a), **(3)** 445-5, **(6)** 445-7.

Art. 450. New. (1) 450-4.
Revised. (1) 450-1 Ex. No. 3; **(2)** 450-3; **(3)** 450-8; **(4)** 450-10; **(5)** 450-21; **(6)** 450-22; **(7)** 450-25 (paragraphs one and three); **(8)** 450-42; **(9)** 450-43(a); **(10)** 450-47.
Delete. (1) 450-6 FPN.

Art. 460. New. (1) 460-10 Ex.; **(2)** 460-2; **(3)** Part B.
Revised. (1) 460-1 (second paragraph); **(2)** 460-6(a); **(3)** 460-6(b); **(4)** 460-8(c) Ex.; **(5)** 460-9.
Delete. (1) 460-1 Ex.; **(2)** 460-2; **(3)** 460-3; **(4)** 460-4; **(5)** 460-5; **(6)** 460-6(b) (last sentence); **(7)** 460-11.

Art. 470. New. (1) 470-1; **(2)** 470-3; **(3)** 470-7 Ex.; **(4)** Part B.
Revised. (1) 470-2 (formerly 470-1).
Delete. (1) 470-3; **(2)** 470-4; **(3)** 470-5; **(4)** 470-6.

Art. 480. Rewrite.

Art. 500. New. (1) 500-2(b) Ex. No. 2.
Revised. (1) Title (Hazardous (Classified) Locations); **(2)** 500-1 (second paragraph); **(3)** 500-1 FPN (FPN No. 3 and No. 5); **(4)** 500-2; **(5)** 500-2 (make second paragraph a FPN); **(6)** 500-2 Group F; **(7)** 500-2(b) FPN; **(8)** 500-2(c) (make second sentence FPN); **(9)** Table 500-2.

Art. 501. New. (1) 501-4(b) (second paragraph and Ex.); **(2)** 501-5(d); **(3)** 501-11 Ex.
Revised. (1) 501-3(b)(1) Ex. c; **(2)** 501-3(b)(4); **(3)** 501-4(b); **(4)** 501-5 FPN; **(5)** 501-5(a); **(6)** 501-5(a) FPN; **(7)** 501-5(b); **(8)** 501-5(c); **(9)** 501-6(b)(1); **(10)** 501-6(b)(2); **(11)** 501-6(b)(4); **(12)** 501-6(b) FPN; **(13)** 501-7(b)(3); **(14)** 501-8(a); **(15)** 501-9(b)(2); **(16)** 501-10(b)(1); **(17)** 501-14(b)(1) Ex. c.
Delete. (1) 501-6(b)(1) FPN.

Art. 502. New. (1) 502-1 FPN.
Revised. (1) 502-4(a)(1); **(2)** 502-4(a)(2); **(3)** 502-5; **(4)** 502-6(a)(1); **(5)** 502-7(b)(2); **(6)** 502-9; **(7)** 502-9(a); **(8)** 502-9(b); **(9)** 502-14(a)(5).

Art. 503. New. (1) 503-1 FPN.
Revised. (1) 503-3(a); **(2)** 503-7 (second paragraph).
Delete. (1) 503-13(d) FPN; **(2)** 503-14.

Art. 510. New. Title (Hazardous (Classified) Locations).
Delete. (1) 510 (last sentence); **(2)** 510-2 FPN.

Art. 511. Rewrite.

Art. 512. Delete.

Art. 513. Revised. (1) 513-2(d); **(2)** 513-4(a); **(3)** 513-8; **(4)** 513-9 (first and second paragraphs); **(5)** 513-11(c).
Delete. (1) 513-10(b) FPN.

Art. 515. Revised. (1) 515-4.
Delete. (1) 515-2(c) FPN.

Art. 516. New. (1) 516-3 (Figures 1, 2, and 3); **(2)** 516-6 FPN.
Revised. (1) 516-1 FPN; **(2)** 516-2(b); **(3)** 516-3(d); **(4)** 516-4; **(5)** 516-4(c); **(6)** 516-4(d); **(7)** 516-4(e); **(8)** 516-4(f); **(9)** 516-4(g); **(10)** 516-4(h); **(11)** 516-4(i); **(12)** 516-5(a); **(13)** 516-5(c); **(14)** 516-5(d); **(15)** 516-6; **(16)** 516-6(a); **(17)** 516-6(d); **(18)** 516-6(d)(2) and (3); **(19)** 516-7(a).

Art. 517. New. (1) 517-2 Definitions (Critical System, Patient Grounding Point, Patient Vicinity, Reference Grounding Point, and Room Grounding Point); **(2)** Part C (Rewrite); **(3)** Part D (Rewrite); **(4)** 516-62(f).
Revised. (1) 517-1; **(2)** Diagram 517-1; **(3)** 517-2 Definitions (Anesthetizing-Location Receptacle, and Life Support Branch); **(4)** 517-60; **(5)** 517-61(d); **(6)** 517-62(a); **(7)** 517-62(e); **(8)** 517-63(a); **(9)** 517-63(d); **(10)** 517-63(e); **(11)** 517-64(f) (second paragraph).
Delete. (1) 517-2 Definitions (Electrically Susceptible Patient, Electrically Susceptible Patient Area, Probable Failure, and Reference Grounding Bus, Patient, and Reference Grounding Bus Room); **(2)** Figure 517-2(a); **(3)** Figure 517-2(b); **(4)** 517-63(d) FPN.

Art. 518. New. Places of Assembly.

Art. 520. New. (1) Title (Theaters and Similar Locations); **(2)** 520-26; **(3)** 520-27.
Revised. (1) 520-1; **(2)** 520-4; **(3)** 520-4 Ex. No. 2 (formerly Ex. No. 3); **(4)** 520-6; **(5)** 520-23; **(6)** 520-25(b); **(7)** 540-43(b); **(8)** 540-44(b); **(9)** 520-45; **(10)** 520-49.
Delete. (1) 520-4 Ex. No. 2 and FPN; **(2)** 520-25(b) FPN; **(3)** 520-53(j) (second sentence, (1) and (2)).

Art. 530. Revised. (1) 530-1 FPN; **(2)** 530-14; **(3)** 530-16; **(4)** 530-18(b); **(5)** 530-19(a); **(6)** 530-41; **(7)** 530-63.

Art. 540. New. (1) 540-1 FPN.
Delete. (1) 540-18; **(2)** 540-22.

Art. 545. Rewrite. (Manufactured Building).

Art. 550. New. (1) 550-3(f) FPN' **(2)** Figure 550-3(f); **(3)** 550-4(a) FPN; **(4)** 550-5(c)(4) FPN; **(5)** 550-6(a)(1) FPN; **(6)** 550-8(1).
Revised. (1) 550-1(c); **(2)** 550-3(f); **(3)** 550-3(g); **(4)** 550-3(k)(1) and (2); **(5)** 550-4; **(6)** 550-4(a) (third paragraph); **(7)** 550-4(b) (third paragraph); **(8)** 550-4(d); **(9)** 550-6(c); **(10)** 550-8(e); **(11)** 550-8(f); **(12)** 550-8(g)(1); **(13)** 550-9(a)(2); **(14)** 550-9(c)(4); **(15)** 550-11; **(16)** 550-11(c) and Table; **(17)** 550-12(a) and (c); **(18)** 550-23(a), (b) and (c).
Delete. (1) 550-12(c).

Art. 551. New. (1) Definitions (Low Voltage, Travel Trailer, Motor Home, and Truck Camper); (2) 551-3(b) (5) Ex.; (3) 551-3(f) and FPN; (4) 551-5(f); (5) 551-7(d); (6) 551-8(c); (7) 551-10(d) Ex. No. 2; (8) 551-13(c)(1) FPN; (9) 551-13(c)(2) FPN; (10) 551-13(c)(3) FPN; (11) 551-13(c)(4) FPN; (12) Figure 551-13(c); (13) 551-41 Definition (Recreational Vehicle Park); (14) 551-42 FPN; (15) 551-51(b) FPN.

Revised. (1) 551-3; (2) 551-3(c); (3) 551-3(c)(2); (4) 551-3(d); (5) 551-3(e)(1); (6) 551-3(e)(2); (7) 551-3(e)(3); (8) 551-4(b); (9) 551-4(e); (10) 551-6(b); (11) 551-8; (12) 551-9; (13) 551-13(c)(1); (14) 551-13(c)(2), (3) and (4); (15) 551-13(e) Ex.; (16) 551-14(g), (k), and (n); (17) 551-15(a); (18) 551-17; (19) 551-23(e) FPN; (20) 551-25(a); (21) 551-25(b); (22) 551-41 Definition (Recreational Vehicle Lot Electric Supply Equipment); (23) 551-42; (24) 551-47(a), (b) and (c); (25) 551-48 Title; (26) 551-52.

Delete. (1) 551-26.

Art. 555. New. (1) 555-9; (2) 555-11.

Revised. (1) 555-1; (2) 555-3; (3) 555-4; (4) 555-6 FPN; (5) 555-8.

Art. 600. New. (1) 600-4; (2) 600-6(a) and (b); (3) 600-9; (4) 600-10; (5) 600-32(f) and (g); (6) 600-36; (7) 600-37.

Revised. (1) 600-2; (2) 600-3; (3) 600-6; (4) 600-8(a); (5) 600-21(a); 600-21(d); (6) 600-21(e); 600-22; (7) 600-31(a) and (d); (8) 600-32(e); (9) 600-34(d); (10) 600-34(i).

Delete. (1) 600-3 FPN; (2) 600-21(e); (3) 600-31(d) and (g).

Art. 610. New. (1) 610-43; (2) 610-55; (3) 610-53; (4) 610-57; (5) 610-61.

Revised. (1) 610-1; (2) 610-2; (3) 610-11 Ex. No. 1, Ex. No. 3, and Ex. No. 4; (4) 610-12; (5) 610-13; (6) 610-14(a), (b), (c), and (d); (7) Table 610-14(a); (8) 610-21; (9) 610-31; (10) 610-32; (11) 610-33; (12) 610-41; (13) 610-42; (14) 610-51.

Art. 620. New. (1) 620-22; (2) 620-101.

Revised. (1) 620-13 FPN; (2) 620-51; (3) 620-53.

Art. 640. Revised. (1) 640-5; (2) 640-12.

Art. 645. Revised. (1) 645-2(c) and Ex.; (2) 645-3.

Art. 660. Revised. (1) 660-1 FPN; (2) 660-4(b); (3) 660-6; (4) 660-7; (5) 660-48.

Delete. (1) Figure 660-4(b); (2) 660-22.

Art. 665. New. (1) 665-2 Definitions (Dead Front); (2) 665-10.

Revised. (1) Part B (Title); (2) 665-46.

Art. 675. New. Electrically Driven or Controlled Irrigation Machines.

Art. 680. New. Title (Swimming Pools, Fountains and Similar Installations); (2) 680-21(e); (3) 680-23; (4) 680-25(d) Ex. No. 4; (5) 680-31 FPN; (6) Part D.

Revised. (1) 680-1; (2) 680-2; (3) 680-4(d); (4) 680-5(b) Ex.; (5) 680-6; (6) 680-20(a)(1); (7) 680-20(b)(1); (8) 680-21(d); (9) 680-22(a) and (c); (10) 680-24; (11) 680-25(a) (1); (12) 680-25(a)(2) Ex. No. 2; (13) 680-25(d) and Ex. No. 3; (14) 680-31.

Delete. (1) 680-4 Definition (Permanently Installed Swimming or Wading Pool).

Art. 700. New. (1) 700-4 (e).

Revised. (1) 700-1; (2) 700-6(a), (b), (c), (d), and (e); (3) 700-11; (4) 700-14 FPN; (5) 700-15(2); (6) 700-17.

Art. 710. New. (1) Title (Over 600 Volts, Nominal—General); (2) 710-6; (3) 710-9; (4) 710-10; (5) 710-14; (6) 710-20; (7) 710-23; (8) Part E; (9) Part F.

Revised. (1) 710-3(b); (2) 710-4; (3) 710-8; (4) 710-21(b)(3); (5) 710-22 FPN; (6) 710-31 (second paragraph); (7) 710-34(a); (8) 710-34(c).

Deleted. (1) 710-5 and Table 710-5 (Now in 310 Part C); (2) 710-6; (3) 710-22 FPN.

Art. 720. Delete. (1) 720-3.

Art. 725. Re-write (Class 1, Class 2, Class 3 Remote-Control, Signaling, and Power-Limited Circuits).

Art. 730. (Now Article 225).

Art. 750. Revised. (1) 750-1; (2) 750-7 FPN; 750-9.

Delete. (1) 750-4; (2) 750-5.

Art. 760. New. (Fire Protective Signaling Systems).

Art. 800. New. (1) 800-3(d).

Revised. (1) 800-2; (2) 800-3(c); (3) 800-11(a)(1) and (b) Ex.; (4) 800-11(c)(3); (5) 800-21(b); (6) 800-31(b)(7).

Delete. (1) 800-1 FPN; (2) 800-31(b) (7) FPN.

Art. 810. Revised. (1) 810-13 (second paragraph); (2) 810-14; (3) 810-20(a) Ex.; (4) 810-21(b).

Delete. (1) 810-14 FPN; (2) 810-21(i) FPN; (3) Table 810-52 FPN; (4) 810-71(b) FPN.

Art. 820. Revised. (1) 820-11(a); (2) 820-13(d) FPN; (3) 810-22(g) and (h); (4) 820-23.

Delete. (1) 820-22(g) FPN.

Chap. 9. New. (1) Note 5 (to Table 1); (2) Examples 1, 1(a), 1(b), 1(c), and 4(a) (Neutral loads).

Revised. (1) Table 2; (2) Table 3A; (3) Table 3B; (4) Table 3C; (5) Table 4; (6) Table 5; (7) Table 6—Note; (8) Varnished Cambric, Type V (Paragraph); (9) Table 8 (Last Note); (10) Example No. 1 (C).

Cross References

(Old to New)		(New to Old)	
1971 NEC	1975 NEC	1975 NEC	1971 NEC
90-4 (Deleted)		90-4	90-7
90-5 (Deleted)		90-5	90-6
90-6	90-5	90-6	90-8
90-7	90-4	90-7	90-9
90-8	90-6		
90-9	90-7		
90-10 (Deleted)			

ARTICLE 110

(Old to New)		(New to Old)	
1971 NEC	1975 NEC	1975 NEC	1971 NEC
110-1 (Deleted)		110-1	110-3
110-3	110-1	110-3(1) thru (6)	110-4(a) thru (f)
110-4(a) thru (f)	110-3(1) thru (6)	110-4	110-5
110-5	110-4	110-5	110-7
110-7	110-5	110-7	110-20
110-20	110-7		

ARTICLE 200

(Old to New)		(New to Old)	
1971 NEC	1975 NEC	1975 NEC	1971 NEC
200-2	200-2, 200-7 (Part)	200-2	200-2, 200-7 (Part)
200-4	210-9	200-6(c) (New)	
200-5(a)	210-10, 215-7	200-7	200-7, 200-2 (Part)
200-5(b), (c) (Deleted)			
200-6(c)	215-8		
200-7	200-7, 200-2 (Part)		

ARTICLE 210

(Old to New)		(New to Old)	
1971 NEC	1975 NEC	1975 NEC	1971 NEC
210-6(a), Ex. 5	210-6(b)	210-6(b)	210-6(a), Ex. 5
210-6(b)	210-6(c)	210-6(c)	210-6(b)
210-6(c)	210-6(d)	210-6(d)	210-6(c)
210-6(d)	210-19(a) FPN	210-7	210-7, 210-21(b)
210-7 (3rd paragraph)	210-8	210-8	210-7, 210-22(d)
210-8	210-21(a)	210-9	200-4
210-21(b)	210-7, 210-21(b)	210-10	200-5(a)
210-22	210-25	210-19	210-6(d), 210-19
210-22(d)	210-8	210-21	210-8, 210-21
210-23	210-22	210-22	210-23
210-24	210-23	210-23	210-24
210-25	210-24	210-24	210-25
Table 210-25	Table 210-24	210-25	210-22
		Table 210-24	Table 210-25

ARTICLE 215

(Old to New)		(New to Old)	
1971 NEC	1975 NEC	1975 NEC	1971 NEC
215-3	215-2(c) FPN	215-2	215-2, 215-3
215-4	215-3	215-3	215-4
215-5	215-4	215-4	215-5
215-6	215-5	215-5	215-6
215-7	215-6	215-6	215-7
215-8	215-9	215-7	200-5(a)
		215-8	200-6(c)
		215-9	215-8

ARTICLE 220

(Old to New)		(New to Old)	
1971 NEC	1975 NEC	1975 NEC	1971 NEC
220-2	220-2(a)	220-2(a)	220-2
220-2(a)	220-2(b), (c)	220-2(b)	220-2(a)
Table 220-2(a)	Table 220-2(b)	Table 220-2(b)	Table 220-2(a)
220-2(b)	220-2(c)	220-2(c)	220-2(b), (c)
220-2(c)	220-2(c)	220-3(a) thru (d)	220-3(a) thru (c)
220-3(a) thru (c)	220-3(a) thru (d)	220-10(a)	220-4 (Part)
220-4	220-10(a), 220-32(a)	220-10(b)	220-4(a)
220-4(a)	220-10(b)	220-11	220-4(b)
220-4(b)	220-11	Table 220-11	Table 220-4(b)
Table 220-4(b)	Table 220-11	220-12	220-4(c)
220-4(c)	220-12	220-13	220-4(h)
220-4(d)	220-14	220-14	220-4(d)
220-4(e)	220-22	220-15	220-4(f)
220-4(f)	220-15	220-16	220-4(i)
220-4(g)	220-21	220-17	220-4(k)
220-4(h)	220-13	220-18	220-4(o)
220-4(i)	220-16(a), (b)	Table 220-18	Table 220-6(b)
220-4(j)	220-19	220-19	220-4(j)

220-4(k)	220-17	Table 220-19	Table 220-5
220-4(l)	220-21	220-20	Table 220-5, Note 3
220-4(m)	220-40	Table 220-20	Table 220-6(a)
Table 220-4(m)	Table 220-40	220-21	220-4(g), (1)
220-4(n)	220-41, Table 220-41	220-22	220-4(e)
220-4(o)	220-18	220-30	220-7
Table 220-5	Table 220-19	Table 220-30	Table 220-7
Table 220-6(a)	Table 220-20	220-31	220-8
Table 220-6(b)	Table 220-18	220-32	220-9
220-7	220-30	Table 220-32	Table 220-9
Table 220-7	Table 220-30	220-40	220-4(m)
220-8	220-31	Table 220-40	Table 220-4(m)
220-9	220-32	220-41	220-4(n)
Table 220-9	Table 220-32	Table 220-41	220-4(n)

ARTICLE 225 (formerly 730)
(New to Old)

1975 NEC	1971 NEC
225-1	730-1
225-2	730-2
225-3	730-3
225-4	730-4
225-5	730-5
225-6	730-6
225-7	730-7
225-8	730-8
225-9	730-9(a), (b)
225-10	730-10
225-11	730-11
225-12	730-12
225-13	730-13
225-14(a)	730-14(a), (b)
225-14(b), (c), (d)	730-14(c), (d), (e)
225-15	730-15
225-16	730-16
225-17	730-17
225-18	730-18
225-19	730-19
225-20	730-20
225-21	730-22
225-22	730-23
225-23	730-24
225-25	730-25
225-26	730-26

ARTICLE 230

(Old to New)		(New to Old)	
1971 NEC	1975 NEC	1975 NEC	1971 NEC
230-2, Ex. 7	230-45		
230-21	230-2	230-2	230-2, 21, 31(c)
230-23	230-21, 23	230-21	230-23

230-25	230-29	230-28	230-26
230-26	230-26, 28	230-29	230-25
			230-2, Ex. 7
230-31(a), (b)	230-31	230-31	230-31(a), (b), 230-2
		230-45	
230-31(c)	230-2	230-46	230-42
230-32	230-49	230-47	230-43
230-33	230-48	230-48	230-33
230-42	230-46	230-49	230-32
230-43	230-47	230-50	230-46
230-46	230-50	230-51(a), (b)	230-50
230-47	230-51(c)	230-51(c)	230-47, 48
230-48	230-51(c)	Table 230-51(c)	230-47, 48
230-49	230-52	230-52	230-49
230-50	230-51	230-53	230-52
230-51	230-54	230-54	230-51
230-52	230-53	230-55	230-53
230-53	230-55	230-70	230-70(a), (c), 60
230-60	230-70	230-71	230-70(g)
230-61	230-72	230-72	230-61, 70(b)
230-63(b) Delete)		230-73	230-70(b)
230-70(a), (c)	230-70	230-74	230-70(h)
230-70(g)	230-71	230-75	230-70(i)
230-70(b)	230-72(c), (d), 73	230-76	230-70(d)
230-70(h)	230-74	230-77	230-70(f)
230-70(i)	230-75	230-78	230-70(e)
230-70(d)	230-76	230-79	230-71(a)
230-70(f)	230-77	230-80	230-71(b)
230-70(e)	230-78	230-81	230-72
230-71(a)	230-79	230-82	230-73
230-71(b)	230-80	230-83	230-74
230-72	230-81	230-84	230-76
230-73	230-82	230-200	230-100
230-74	230-83	230-201	230-100
230-76	230-84	230-202	230-101
230-100	230-200, 201	230-203	230-102
230-101	230-202	230-204	230-104
230-102	230-203	230-205	230-103
230-103	230-205, 206	230-206	230-103
230-104	230-204	230-207	230-105
230-105	230-207	230-208	230-106
230-106	230-208	230-209	230-107
230-107	230-209		

ARTICLE 240

(Old to New)		(New to Old)	
1971 NEC	1975 NEC	1975 NEC	1971 NEC
240-1	240-1	240-1	240-1
240-2	240-1 (FPN)	240-1 (FPN)	240-2
240-3	240-2	240-2	240-3
240-5(a), Ex. 1, 3, 4, 5, 6	240-3	240-3	240-5(a), Ex. 1, 3, 4, 5, 6
240-5(a), Ex. 2	240-4	240-4	240-5(a), Ex. 2
240-5(b)	240-6	240-6	240-5(b)
240-6(a)	240-50(a)	240-8	240-14

240-6(b)	240-60(a)	240-9	240-8
240-6(c)	240-50(e)	240-10	240-30
240-8	240-9	240-11	240-27
240-11	240-20	240-20	240-11
240-12	240-22	240-21	240-15
240-13	240-23	Ex. 1	Ex. 2
240-14	240-8	Ex. 2	Ex. 5
240-15	240-21	Ex. 3	Ex. 6
Ex. 1	Ex. 4	Ex. 4	Ex. 1
Ex. 2	Ex. 1	Ex. 5	Ex. 3
Ex. 3	Ex. 5	Ex. 6	Ex. 4
Ex. 4	Ex. 6, 7	Ex. 7	Ex. 4
Ex. 5	Ex. 2	Ex. 8	Ex. 7
Ex. 6	Ex. 3	240-22	240-12
Ex. 7	Ex. 8	240-23	240-13
240-16	240-24	240-24	240-16
240-17(a)	240-30	240-30	240-17(a)
240-17(b)	240-32	240-32	240-17(b)
240-17(c)	240-33	240-33	240-17(c)
240-18	240-40	240-40	240-18
240-19	240-41	240-41	240-19, 240-25(b)
240-20(a)	240-51(a)	240-50(a)	240-6(a)
240-20(b)	240-50(d)	240-50(b)	240-22(h)
240-20(c)	240-50(c) Except	240-50(c)	240-20(c), 22(i)
	last Paragraph)	240-50(d)	240-20(b)
240-21	240-52	240-50(e)	240-6(c)
240-22	240-53	240-51	240-20(a), (c)
240-22(a)	240-53(a)	240-52	240-21
240-22(b)	240-53(b)	240-53	240-22(a), (b), (c), (g)
240-22(c)	240-53(b), 54(b)	240-54(a)	240-22(f) last 2 lines
240-22(d)	240-54(d)	240-54(b)	240-22(c)
240-22(e)	240-54(c)	240-54(c)	240-22(e)
240-22(f)	240-54(a), (e)	240-54(d)	240-22(d)
240-22(g)	240-53	240-54(e)	240-22(f) first 2 lines
240-22(h)	240-50(b)	240-60(a)	240-6(b)
240-22(i)	240-50(c)	240-60(b)	240-23(b)
240-23(a)(1)	240-61(a)	240-60(c)	240-23(c)
240-23(a)(2)	240-61(b)	240-61(a)	240-23(a)(1)
240-23(b)	240-60(b)	240-61(b)	240-23(a)(2)
240-23(c)	240-60(c)	240-80	240-25(a)
240-25(a)	240-80	240-81	240-25(c)
240-25(b)	240-41(a)	240-82	240-25(d)
240-25(c)	240-81	240-83(a)	240-25(e)
240-25(d)	240-82	240-83(b)	240-25(e)
240-25(e)	240-83	240-83(c)	240-25(e)
240-27	240-11		
240-30	240-10		

ARTICLE 250

(Old to New)		(New to Old)	
1971 NEC	1975 NEC	1975 NEC	1971 NEC
250-45(b)(1)	250-45(b), Ex. 1	250-23(a)	250-52
250-45(b)(2)	250-45(b), Ex. 2	250-45(b), Ex. 1	250-45(b)(1)
250-52	250-23(a)	250-45(b), Ex. 2	250-45(b)(2)

250-57(a)	250-57		250-57	250-57(a)
250-57(b)(1)	250-57(b)		250-57(b)	250-57(b)(1)
250-57(b)(2)	250-57(b)		250-57(b)	250-57(b)(2)
250-57(b)(3)	250-57(c)		250-57(c)	250-57(b)(3)
250-83(b)	250-83(c)		250-82(c)	250-82(b)
250-83(c)	250-83(b)(1)		250-83(b)(1)	250-83(c)
250-83(d)	250-83(b)(2)		250-83(b)(2)	250-83(d)
250-83(e)	250-83(b)(3)		250-83(b)(3)	250-83(e)
			250-83(c)	250-83(b)

ARTICLE 280

(Old to New) | | (New to Old)

1971 NEC	1975 NEC		1975 NEC	1971 NEC
280-1	280-10		280-1	
280-2	280-11		280-10	280-1
280-3	280-12		280-11	280-2
280-11	280-20		280-12	280-3
280-21	280-30		280-20	280-11
280-23	280-32		280-30	280-21
280-24	280-33		280-32	280-23
280-25	280-34		280-33	280-24
280-26	280-35		280-34	280-25
			280-35	280-26

ARTICLE 300

(Old to New)

1971 NEC	1975 NEC
300-5	300-6
300-6	300-7
300-7	300-5
300-8	300-4

ARTICLE 310

(Old to New) | | (New to Old)

1971 NEC	1975 NEC		1975 NEC	1971 NEC
310-1(a)	310-1		310-1	310-1(a), (c)
310-1(b)	310-2		310-2	310-1(b)
310-1(c)	310-1		310-3	310-9
310-2(a)	310-12		310-4	310-10
310-2(b)	310-13		310-5	310-8
Table 310-2(a)	Table 310-13, Table 402-3		310-7	310-5
			310-8	310-7
Table 310-2(b)	Table 310-13		310-9	310-4
310-2(c)	310-10(a)		310-10(a)	310-2(c)
310-2(d)	310-10(c)		310-10(b)	Copied from 210-5(b)
310-2(e)	310-14		310-10(c)	310-2(d)
Table 310-2(e)(1)	Table 310-14(a)		310-11	310-12
Table 310-2(e)(2)	Table 310-14(b)		310-12	310-2(a)
Table 310-2(e)(3)	Table 310-14(c)		310-13	310-2(b)

Table 310-2(e)(4)	Table 310-14(d)	Table 310-13	Tables 310-2(a) & (b)
310-3	310-12, 310-13	310-14	310-2(e)
310-4	310-9	Table 310-14(a)	Table 310-2(e)(1)
310-5	310-7	Table 310-14(b)	Table 310-2(e)(2)
310-7	310-8	Table 310-14(c)	Table 310-2(e)(3)
310-8	310-5	Table 310-14(d)	Table 310-2(e)(4)
310-9	310-3	310-15	310-11
310-10	310-4	Table 310-16	Table 310-12
310-11	310 15	Table 310-17	Table 310-13
310-12	310-11, 400-6, 402-10	Table 310-18	Table 310-14
Table 310-12	Table 310-16	Table 310-19	Table 310-15
Table 310-13	Table 310-17		
Table 310-14	Table 310-18		
Table 310-15	Table 310-19		

ARTICLE 320

(Old to New)		(New to Old)	
1971 NEC	1975 NEC	1975 NEC	1971 NEC
320-2(a)	320-3	320-2	320-3
320-2(b)	320-4	320-3	320-2(a)
320-3	320-2	320-4	320-2(b)
320-4	320-5	320-5	320-4
320-5(a), (b)	320-6	320-6	320-5(a), (b)
320-5(c)	320-7	320-7	320-5(c)
320-6	320-9	320-9	320-6
320-7	320-10	320-10	320-7
320-9	320-11	320-11	320-9
320-10	320-12	320-12	320-10, 11
320-11	320-12	320-13	320-14
320-12	320-14	320-14	320-12
320-13	320-15	320-15	320-13
320-14	320-13	320-16	320-15
320-15(a), (b)	320-16		

ARTICLE 324

(Old to New)		(New to Old)	
1971 NEC	1975 NEC	1975 NEC	1971 NEC
324-2	324-3, 4	324-2	324-3
324-3	324-2	324-3	324-2
324-4	324-5	324-4	324-2
324-5	324-6, 7	324-5	324-4
324-6	324-8	324-6	324-5
324-7	324-9, 10	324-7	324-5
324-8	324-11	324-8	324-6
324-9	324-13	324-9	324-7
324-10	324-14	324-10	324-7
324-11	324-12	324-11	324-8
		324-12	324-11
		324-13	324-9
		324-14	324-10

ARTICLE 330

(Old to New)		(New to Old)	
1971 NEC	1975 NEC	1975 NEC	1971 NEC
330-2	330-3, 4	330-2	330-3
330-3	330-2	330-3	330-2
330-4	330-12	330-4	330-2
330-5	330-11	330-10	330-6
330-6	330-10	330-11	330-5
330-7	330-13	330-12	330-4
330-8	330-15	330-13	330-7
330-9	330-14	330-14	330-9
330-11(a)	330-20	330-15	330-8
330-11(b)	330-21	330-20	330-11(a)
330-11(c)	330-22	330-21	330-11(b)
		330-22	330-11(c)

ARTICLE 331

(Old to New)		(New to Old)	
1971 NEC	1975 NEC	1975 NEC	1971 NEC
331-2	331-3, 4	331-2	331-3
331-3	331-2	331-3	331-2
331-4	331-12	331-4	331-2
331-5	331-11	331-10	331-6
331-6	331-10	331-11	331-5
331-7	331-13	331-12	331-4
331-8	331-14	331-13	331-7
331-9(a)	331-20	331-14	331-8
331-9(b)	331-21	331-20	331-9(a)
331-9(c)	331-22	331-21	331-9(b)
331-9(d)	331-23	331-22	331-9(c)
		331-23	331-9(d)

ARTICLE 337
(Old to New)

1971 NEC	1975 NEC
337-1 (Deleted)	
337-2	337-1
337-3	337-2
337-4	337-3
337-5	337-4
337-6	337-5
337-7	337-6

ARTICLE 338
(Old to New)

1971 NEC	1975 NEC
338-1(a)	338-1(1)
338-1(b)	338-1(2)

ARTICLE 339
(Old to New)

1971 NEC	1975 NEC
339-3(a)	339-3(a)(1)
339-3(b)	339-3(a)(2)
339-3(c)	339-3(a)(3)
339-3(d)	339-3(a)(4)
339-3(e)	339-3(b)

ARTICLE 346
(Old to New)

1971 NEC	1975 NEC
346-14	346-15

ARTICLE 347
(Old to New)

1971 NEC	1975 NEC
347-2(b)	347-2(a)(1)
347-2(c)	347-2(a)(2)
347-2(d)	347-2(a)(3)
347-2(e)	347-2(a)(4)
347-2(f)	347-2(a)(5)

ARTICLE 348
(Old to New)

1971 NEC	1975 NEC
348-14	348-15

ARTICLE 363
(Old to New)

1971 NEC	1975 NEC
363-1 (Deleted)	
363-2	363-1
363-3	363-2
363-4	363-3
363-5	363-4
363-6	363-5
363-7	363-6
363-8	363-7
363-9	363-8
363-10	363-9
363-11	363-10
363-12	363-11
363-13	363-12
363-14	363-13
363-15	363-14
363-16	363-15
363-17	363-16
363-18	363-17

363-19	363-18
363-20	363-19
363-21	363-20

ARTICLE 370
(Old to New)

1971 NEC	1975 NEC
370-6(a) (2nd paragraph)	370-6(a)(1)
370-6(b)	370-6(a)(2)
370-6(c)	370-6(b)

ARTICLE 373
(Old to New)

1971 NEC	1975 NEC
373-6(a)(1)	373-6(b)
373-6(b)	373-6(c)
373-7(a)	373-7
373-11(a)(3) (Deleted)	
373-11(a)(4)	373-11(a)(3)

ARTICLE 380
(Old to New)

1971 NEC	1975 NEC
380-1	380-2(b)

ARTICLE 390
(Changed to Article 545 with new title)

ARTICLE 400

(Old to New)		(New to Old)	
1971 NEC	1975 NEC	1975 NEC	1971 NEC
400-1	400-3	400-1 (New Scope)	
400-2	400-4	400-2 (New)	
400-3	400-7	400-3	400-1
400-4	400-8	400-4	400-2
400-5	400-9	Table 400-4	400-15, Table 400-11
400-6	400-11	400-5	Paragraph before Table
400-7	400-12		400-9(b)
400-8	400-21	Table 400-5	Table 400-9(b)
400-9	400-13	400-6	310-12(b)(3)
Table 400-9(b)	400-5, Table 400-5	400-7	400-3
Table 400-11	Table 400-4	400-8	400-4
400-12	400-20	400-9	400-5
400-13	400-22	400-11	400-6
400-14	400-23	400-12	400-7
400-15	Table 400-4	400-13	400-9
400-16	400-24	400-20	400-12
		400-21	400-8
		400-22	400-13
		400-23	400-14
		400-24	400-16

ARTICLE 402

(Old to New)		(New to Old)	
1971 NEC	1975 NEC	1975 NEC	1971 NEC
402-1	402-2, 402-11, 402-12	402-1 (New Scope)	
402-2	402-6	402-2	402-1
402-3(a)	402-4	402-3 (New)	
402-3(b)	402-8	Table 402-3	Table 402-6,
Table 402-4	Table 402-5		Table 310-2(a)
402-5	402-13	402-4	402-3(a)
Table 402-6	Table 402-3	402-5 (New)	
	402-5 (New)	Table 402-5	Table 402-4
	402-8 (New)	402-6	402-2
	402-9 (New)	402-8	402-3(b)
	402-10 (New)	402-9	310-2(c), 400-13
	402-11 (New)	402-10	310-12(b)
	402-12 (New)	402-11	402-1
		402-12	402-1
		402-13	402-5
		402-5 (New)	
		402-8 (New)	
		402-9 (New)	
		402-10 (New)	
		402-11 (New)	
		402-12 (New)	

ARTICLE 410

(Old to New)		(New to Old)	
1971 NEC	1975 NEC	1975 NEC	1971 NEC
410-91	410-17	410-17	410-91
410-92	410-18	410-18	410-92
410-94	410-19	410-19	410-94
410-96	410-21	410-21	410-96
410-17	410-22	410-22	410-17
410-18	410-23	410-23	410-18
410-19	410-24	410-24	410-19
410-20	410-25	410-25	410-20
410-21	410-26	410-26	410-21
410-22	410-27	410-27	410-22
410-23	410-28	410-28	410-23
410-24	410-29	410-29	410-24
410-25	410-30	410-30	410-25
410-26	410-31	410-31	410-26
410-27	410-32	410-32	410-27
410-28	410-34	410-34	410-28
410-29	410-35	410-35	410-29
410-30	410-36	410-36	410-30
410-31	410-37	410-37	410-31
410-32	410-38	410-38	410-32
410-33	410-39	410-39	410-33
410-34	410-40	410-40	410-34
410-35	410-41	410-41	410-35
410 36	410-42	410-42	410-36
410-37	410-43	410-43	410 37
410-38	410-44	410-44	410-38

410-39	410-45	410-45	410-39
410-40	410-46	410-46	410-40
410-41	410-47	410-47	410-41
410-42	410-48	410-48	410-42
410-43	410-49	410-49	410-43
410-44	410-50	410-50	410-44
410-45	410-51	410-51	410-45
410-46	410-52	410-52	410-46
410-49	410-53	410-53	410-49
410-50	410-54	410-54	410-50
410-51	410-55	410-55	410-51
410-52	410-56	410-56	410-52
410-54	410-57	410-57	410-54
410-55	410-58	410-58	410-55
410-57	410-59	410-59	410-57
410-58	410-60	410-60	410-58
410-59	410-61	410-61	410-59
410-60	410-62	410-62	410-60
410-61	410-63	410-63	410-61
410-62	410-64	410-64	410-62
410-63	410-65	410-65	410-63
410-64	410-66	410-66	410-64
410-65	410-67	410-67	410-65
410-66	410-68	410-68	410-66
410-67	410-69	410-69	410-67
410-68	410-70	410-70	410-68
410-69	410-71	410-71	410-69
410-70	410-72	410-72	410-70
410-71	410-73	410-73	410-71
410-72	410-74	410-74	410-72
410-73	410-75	410-75	410-73
410-74	410-76	410-76	410-74
410-75	410-77	410-77	410-75
410-76	410-78	410-78	410-76
410-77	410-79	410-79	410-77
410-78	410-80	410-80	410-78
410-79	410-81	410-81	410-79
410-80	410-82	410-82	410-80
410-81	410-83	410-83	410-81
410-82	410-84	410-84	410-82
410-83	410-85	410-85	410-83
410-84	410-86	410-86	410-84
410-85	410-87	410-87	410-85
410-86	410-88	410-88	410-86
410-87	410-89	410-89	410-87
410-88	410-90	410-90	410-88
410-89	410-91	410-91	410-89
410-90	410-92	410-92	410-90

ARTICLE 422
(Old to New)

1971 NEC	1975 NEC
422-40	440-60
422-41	440-61

422-42	440-62
422-43	440-63
422-44	440-64

ARTICLE 424
(Old to New)

1971 NEC	1975 NEC
424-22(c)	424-22(b)
424-22(c), third paragraph	424-22(c)
424-22(c), last paragraph	424-22(d)

ARTICLE 430

(Old to New) & (New to Old)

1971 NEC	1975 NEC	1975 NEC	1971 NEC
Diagram 430-1(a)	Diagram 430-1	Diagram 430-1	Diagram 430-1(a)
430-21(a)	430-21	430-21	430-21(a)
430-31(a)	430-31	430-28	430-59
430-31(b)	430-31	430-31	430-31(a)
430-59	430-28	430-31	430-31(b)
430-86(a)	430-86(1)	430-86(1)	430-86(a)
430-86(b)	430-86(2)	430-86(2)	430-86(b)
430-111(a)	430-111(1)	430-111(1)	430-111(a)
430-111(b)	430-111(2)	430-111(2)	430-111(b)
430-111(c)	430-111(3)	430-111(3)	430-111(c)
430-124(a)	430-124(1)	430-132(1)	430-132(a)
430-124(b)	430-124(2)	430-132(2)	430-132(b)
430-124(c)	430-124(3)	430-132(3)	430-132(c)
430-132(a)	430-132(1)	430-132(4)	430-132(d)
430-132(b)	430-132(2)	430-142(1)	430-142(a)
430-132(c)	430-132(3)	430-142(2)	430-142(b)
430-132(d)	430-132(4)	430-142(3)	430-142(c)
430-142(a)	430-142(1)	430-142(4)	430-142(d)
430-142(b)	430-142(2)		
430-142(c)	430-142(3)		
430-142(d)	430-142(4)		

ARTICLE 445
(Old to New)

1971 NEC	1975 NEC
445-1	445-2
445-2	445-3

ARTICLE 470
(Old to New)

1971 NEC	1975 NEC
470-1	470-2
470-7	470-4

ARTICLE 480
(Old to New)

1971 NEC	1975 NEC
480-4	480-5

ARTICLE 500
(Old to New)

1971 NEC	1975 NEC
Table 500-2(c)	Table 500-2

ARTICLE 501
(Old to New)

1971 NEC	1975 NEC
501-3(b)(1)	501-3(b)(1), Ex. a
501-3(b)(2)	501-3(b)(1), Ex. b
501-3(b)(3)	501-3(b)(1), Ex. c
501-5(a)(3)	501-5(a)(4)
501-5(d)	501-5(f)

ARTICLE 503
(Old to New)

1971 NEC	1975 NEC
503-15	503-14
503-16	503-15
503-17	503-16

ARTICLE 516
(Old to New)

1971 NEC	1975 NEC
516-4(g)	516-4(f)
516-4(h)	516-4(g)
516-4(i)	516-4(h)

ARTICLE 551
(Old to New)

1971 NEC	1975 NEC
551-8	551-7
551-7	551-8
551-10	551-9
551-11	551-10
551-9	551-11

ARTICLE 555

(Old to New)		(New to Old)	
1971 NEC	1975 NEC	1975 NEC	1971 NEC
555-2 (Deleted)	555-2 (New Material)	555-2 (New Material)	
555-7(a), last sentence	555-7(b)	555-7(b)	555-7(a), last sentence
555-7(b)	555-7(c)		
555-7(c)	555-7(d)	555-7(c)	555-7(b)
555-7(d)	555-7(e)	555-7(d)	555-7(c)
		555-7(e)	555-7(d)

ARTICLE 600
(Old to New)

1971 NEC	1975 NEC
600-2	600-2(a)
600-2(a)	600-2(b)
600-2(b)	600-3
600-21(f)	600-21(e)
600-31(f)	600-31(e)
600-31(h)	600-31(f)
600-31(i)	600-31(g)

ARTICLE 660

(Old to New)		(New to Old)	
1971 NEC	1975 NEC	1975 NEC	1971 NEC
660-1 (Definitions)	660-2	660-2	660-1(Definitions)
660-2	660-3	660-3	660-2
660-3	660-4	660-4	660-3
660-4	660-5	660-5	660-4
660-5	660-6	660-6	660-5
660-6	660-7	660-7	660-6
660-7	660-8	660-8	660-7
660-8	660-9	660-9	660-8
660-9	660-10	660-10	660-9
660-10	660-20	660-20	660-10
660-11	660-21	660-21	660-11
660-12	660-22	660-22	660-12
660-13	660-23	660-23	660-13
660-14	660-24	660-24	660-14
660-15	660-35	660-35	660-15
660-16	660-47	660-36	660-16
660-17	660-37	660-47	660-17
660-18	660-48	660-48	660-18

ARTICLE 665

(Old to New)		(New to Old)	
1971 NEC	1975 NEC	1975 NEC	1971 NEC
665-22	665-20	665-20	665-22
665-23	665-21	665-21	665-23
665-24	665-22	665-22	665-24
665-25	665-23	665-23	665-25

665-26	665-24		665-24	665-26
665-27	665-25		665-25	665-27
665-28	665-26		665-26	665-28
665-29	665-27		665-27	665-29
665-5	664-40		665-40	665-5
665-10	665-45		665-45	665-10
665-6	665-41		665-41	665-6
665-7	665-42		665-42	665-7
665-8	665-43		665-43	665-8
665-9	665-44		665-44	665-9
665-11	665-46		665-46	665-11
665-12	665-47		665-47	665-12
665-13	665-60		665-60	665-13
665-14	665-61		665-61	665-14
665-15	665-62		665-62	665-15
665-16	665-63		665-63	665-16
665-17	665-64		665-64	665-17
665-19	665-66		665-66	665-19
665-20	665-67		665-67	665-20
665-21	665-68		665-68	665-21
665-30	665-80		665-80	665-30
665-31	665-81		665-81	665-31
665-32	665-82		665-82	665-32
665-33	665-83		665-83	665-33
665-34	665-84		665-84	665-34

ARTICLE 680
(Old to New)

1971 NEC	1975 NEC
680-22(b)	680-22(c)
680-23	680-24
680-24	680-25

ARTICLE 700
(Old to New)

1971 NEC	1975 NEC
700-7	700-6(a)
700-8	700-6(b)
700-9	700-6(c)
700-10	700-6(d)
700-22	700-6(e)

ARTICLE 710
(Old to New)

1971 NEC	1975 NEC
710-5	Delete
Table 710-5	Tables 310-33 and 310-34
710-10	710-11
710-11	710-12
710-12	710-13

ARTICLE 810

(Old to New) | | (New to Old)

1971 NEC	1975 NEC	1975 NEC	1971 NEC
810-20	810-20(a), (b)	810-20(a), (b)	810-20
810-21	810-21(a)	810-21(a)	810-21
810-22	810-21(b)	810-21(b)	810-22
810-23	810-22(c)	810-22(c)	810-23
810-24	810-22(d)	810-22(d)	810-24
810-25	810-22(e)	810-22(e)	810-25
810-26	810-22(f)	810-22(f)	810-26
810-27	810-22(g)	810-22(g)	810-27
810-28	810-22(h)	810-22(h)	810-28
810-29	810-22(i)	810-22(i)	810-29
810-58	810-58(a)	810-58(a)	810-58
810-59	810-58(b)	810-58(b)	810-59
810-60	810-58(c)	810-58(c)	810-60

ARTICLE 820

(Old to New) | | (New to Old)

1971 NEC	1975 NEC	1975 NEC	1971 NEC
820-3	820-7	820-7	820-3
820-4	820-11	820-11	820-4
820-5	820-12	820-12	820-5
820-6	820-13	820-13	820-6
820-7(a)	820-18	820-14	820-10
820-8(a)(1)	820-22(a)	820-18	820-7(a)
820-8(a)(2)	820-22(b)	820-22(a)	820-8(a)(1)
820-8(a)(3)	820-22(c)	820-22(b)	820-8(a)(2)
820-8(a)(4)	820-22(d)	820-22(c)	820-8(a)(3)
820-8(a)(5)	820-22(e)	820-22(d)	820-8(a)(4)
820-8(a)(6)	820-22(f)	820-22(e)	820-8(a)(5)
820-8(a)(7)	820-22(g)	820-22(f)	820-8(a)(6)
820-8(a)(8)	820-22(h)	820-22(g)	820-8(a)(7)
820-9	820-23	820-22(h)	820-8(a)(8)
820-10	820-14	820-23	820-9

NFPA Handbook of the
National Electrical Code

National Electrical Code

NFPA No. 70

ARTICLE 90. INTRODUCTION

90-1. Purpose.

(a) The purpose of this Code is the practical safeguarding of persons and property from hazards arising from the use of electricity.

▲ This is a clear-cut statement of the intent of the Code and is of particular importance wherever enforcement of the Code is made mandatory by law.

(b) This Code contains provisions considered necessary for safety. Compliance therewith and proper maintenance will result in an installation essentially free from hazard, but not necessarily efficient, convenient, or adequate for good service or future expansion of electrical use.

Hazards often occur because of overloading of wiring systems by methods or usage not in conformity with this Code. This occurs because initial wiring did not provide for increases in the use of electricity. An initial adequate installation and reasonable provisions for system changes will provide for future increases in the use of electricity.

(c) This Code is not intended as a design specification nor an instruction manual for untrained persons.

▲ The National Electrical Code contains provisions considered necessary for safety, but does not provide information of a design nature and should not be used to ensure adequate or efficient forms of installation. These latter features should be obtained from design manuals or through the services of a competent consulting engineer or electrical contractor.

90-2. Scope.

(a) Covered. This Code covers:

(1) Electric conductors and equipment installed within or on public and private buildings or other structures, including mobile homes and recreational vehicles; and

other premises such as yards, carnival, parking and other lots, and industrial substations.

(2) Conductors that connect the installations to a supply of electricity.

(3) Other outside conductors on the premises.

(b) Not Covered. It does not cover:

(1) Installations in automotive vehicles, other than mobile homes and recreational vehicles, ships, watercraft, railway rolling stock, or aircraft.

(2) Installations underground in mines.

(3) Installations of railways for generation, transformation, transmission, or distribution of power used exclusively for operation of rolling stock or installations used exclusively for signaling and communication purposes.

(4) Installations of communication equipment under the exclusive control of communication utilities, located outdoors or in building spaces used exclusively for such installations.

(5) Installations under the exclusive control of electric utilities for the purpose of communication, or metering; or for the generation, control, transformation, transmission, and distribution of electric energy located in buildings used exclusively by utilities for such purposes or located outdoors on property owned or leased by the utility or on public highways, streets, roads, etc., or outdoors by established rights on private property.

(c) Special Permission. The authority having jurisdiction for enforcing this Code may grant exception for the installation of conductors and equipment, not under the exclusive control of the electric utilities and used to connect the electric utility supply system to the service entrance conductors of the premises served, provided such installations are outside a building or terminate immediately inside a building wall.

90-3. Code Arrangement. This Code is divided into nine Chapters. Chapters 1, 2, 3, and 4 apply generally; Chapters 5, 6, and 7 apply to special occupancies, special equipment, or other special conditions. These latter Chapters supplement or modify the general rules. Chapters 1 through 4 apply except as amended by Chapters 5, 6, and 7 for the particular conditions.

Chapter 8 covers communications systems and is independent of the other Chapters except where they are specifically referenced therein.

Chapter 9 consists of tables and examples.

90-4. Enforcement. This Code is intended to be suitable for mandatory application by governmental bodies exercising legal jurisdiction over electrical installations and for use by insurance inspectors. The authority having jurisdiction of enforcement of the Code will have the responsibility for making interpretations of the rules, for deciding upon the approval of equipment and materials, and for granting the special permission contemplated in a number of the rules.

In industrial establishments and research and testing facilities, the authority having jurisdiction may waive specific requirements in this Code or permit alternate methods, where it is assured that equivalent objectives can be achieved by establishing and maintaining effective safety and maintenance procedures.

▲ The local authority having jurisdiction is responsible for the enforcement of Code requirements and is charged with making any interpretations that may be necessary in regard to specific installations or rules.

Even where there may be no enforcement by a local authority, an installer should be concerned as to his legal liability in any construction which may present a fire or accident hazard. Compliance with the latest edition of the Code will minimize the risk of legal actions.

90-5. Formal Interpretations. To promote uniformity of interpretation and application of the provisions of this Code, the National Electrical Code Committee has established interpretation procedures.

See Part D of the Appendix.

▲ Official interpretations of the National Electrical Code are based on specific sections of specific editions of the Code. In most cases such official interpretations apply to the stated conditions on given installations. Accordingly, they would not necessarily apply to other situations that vary slightly from the statement on which the official interpretation was issued.

As official interpretations of each edition of the Code are issued they are published in the NFPA Fire News and press releases are sent to interested trade papers.

All official interpretations issued on a specific code edition are reviewed by the appropriate code-making panel during the period when the specific code edition is being revised. In reviewing an interpretation a code panel may agree with the interpretation findings and clarify the code text to avoid further misunderstanding of intent, or the panel may reject the findings of the interpretation and alter the code text to clarify the code panel's intent. On the other hand, the code panel may not recommend any change in the code text because of the special conditions described in the official interpretation. For these reasons the NFPA does not catalog official interpretations issued on previous editions of the Code. And in reviewing all previous interpretations it can be stated that practically none of them would apply to the present edition of the Code because of revised code wording that materially changes the intent.

If anyone feels that a past interpretation applies to the present text they should submit it in the form of a proposed code change when revisions for the next edition of the Code are being considered.

With the wide adoption of the Code throughout the country the authority having jurisdiction has the prime responsibility of interpreting code rules in its area, and disagreements on the intent of particular code rules should be resolved at the local level if at all possible. There is no guarantee that the authority having jurisdiction will accept the findings of an official interpretation processed in accordance with Part D in the Appendix of the Code in this Handbook.

90-6. Examination of Equipment for Safety. For specific items of equipment and materials covered by this Code, examinations for safety made under standard conditions will provide a basis for approval where the record is made generally available through promulgation by organizations properly equipped and qualified for experimental testing, inspections of the run of goods at factories, and service-value determination through field inspections. This avoids the necessity for repetition of examinations by different examiners, frequently with inadequate facilities for such work, and the confusion that would result from conflicting reports as to the suitability of devices and materials examined for a given purpose.

It is the intent of this Code that factory-installed internal wiring or the construction of equipment need not be inspected at the time of installation of the equipment, except to detect alterations or damage, if the equipment has been listed by an electrical testing laboratory that is nationally recognized as having the facilities described above and which requires suitability for installation in accordance with this Code.

See Examination of Equipment, Section 110-3.
See definition of "Listed," Article 100.

▲ It is not the intent of the National Electrical Code to include the detailed requirements for electrical equipment. Such information is usually contained in individual standards for the equipment concerned.

The last sentence does not intend to take away the authority of the local inspector to examine and approve equipment, but rather to indicate that the requirements of the National Electrical Code did not generally apply to the internal construction of devices which had been listed by a nationally recognized electrical testing laboratory.

90-7. Wiring Planning.

(a) Plans and specifications that provide ample space in raceways, spare raceways, and additional spaces will allow for future increases in the use of electricity. Distribution centers located in readily accessible locations will provide convenience and safety of operation. See Sections 110-16 and 240-24 for clearances and accessibility.

(b) It is elsewhere provided in this Code that the number of wires and circuits confined in a single enclosure be varyingly restricted. Limiting the number of circuits in a single enclosure will minimize the effects from a short-circuit or ground fault in one circuit.

▲ Space should always be provided for the equipment required for future extensions of the wiring installation. Failure to provide this space is short-sighted economy for the user.

CHAPTER ONE
General

ARTICLE 100. DEFINITIONS

Scope. Only definitions of terms peculiar to and essential to the proper use of this Code are included. In general, only those terms used in two or more Articles are defined in Article 100. Other definitions are included in the Article in which they are used but may be referenced in Article 100.

Part A of this Article contains definitions intended to apply wherever the terms are used throughout this Code. Part B contains definitions applicable only to the Parts of Articles covering specifically installations and equipment operating at over 600 volts, nominal.

A. General

AC General-Use Snap Switch: See under "Switches."

AC-DC General-Use Snap Switch: See under "Switches."

Accessible: (As applied to wiring methods.) Capable of being removed or exposed without damaging the building structure or finish, or not permanently closed in by the structure or finish of the building. (See "Concealed" and "Exposed.")

▲ See comments following "Concealed: (As applied to wiring methods.)"

Accessible: (As applied to equipment.) Admitting close approach because not guarded by locked doors, elevation, or other effective means. (See "Readily Accessible.")

Ampacity: Current-carrying capacity of electric conductors expressed in amperes.

Anesthetizing Location: See Section 517-2.

Appliance: Utilization equipment, generally other than industrial, normally built in standardized sizes or types, which is installed or connected as a unit to perform one or more functions such as clothes washing, air conditioning, food mixing, deep frying, etc.

Appliance, Fixed: An appliance which is fastened or otherwise secured at a specific location.

Appliance, Portable: An appliance which is actually moved or can easily be moved from one place to another in normal use.

Appliance, Stationary: An appliance which is not easily moved from one place to another in normal use.

Appliance Branch Circuit: See "Branch Circuit, Appliance."

Approved: Acceptable to the authority having jurisdiction.

▲ There are several new definitions contained in the Code to overcome confusion in the usage of the term *approved*. These new definitions are "approved for the purpose," "listed," and "labeled" (which are already defined in the NFPA Regulations Governing Technical Committees). The term "approved" has formerly been used to mean "acceptable to the authority enforcing the Code," as well as an acceptable wiring method and in some cases devices and materials which should be "listed" or "labeled." These new definitions should be very helpful to those in the field whose job it is to determine the acceptability of wiring methods and materials.

Approved for the Purpose: Approved for a specific purpose, environment, or application described in a particular Code requirement.

▲ See the comments following the definition of "Approved."

Askarel: A generic term for a group of nonflammable synthetic chlorinated hydrocarbons used as electrical insulating media. Askarels of various compositional types are used. Under arcing conditions the gases produced, while consisting predominantly of noncombustible hydrogen chloride, can include varying amounts of combustible gases depending upon the askarel type.

Attachment Plug (Plug Cap) (Cap): A device which, by insertion in a receptacle, establishes connection between the conductors of the attached flexible cord and the conductors connected permanently to the receptacle.

Automatic: Self-acting, operating by its own mechanism when actuated by some impersonal influence, as for example, a change in current strength, pressure, temperature, or mechanical configuration. (See "Nonautomatic.")

Bare Conductor: See under "Conductor."

Block (City, Town, or Village): See Section 800-2.

Bonding: The permanent joining of metallic parts to form an electrically conductive path which will assure electrical continuity and the capacity to conduct safely any current likely to be imposed.

Bonding Jumper: A reliable conductor to assure the required electrical conductivity between metal parts required to be electrically connected.

Bonding Jumper, Circuit: The connection between portions of a conductor in a circuit to maintain required ampacity of the circuit.

Bonding Jumper, Equipment: The connection between two or more portions of the equipment grounding conductor.

Bonding Jumper, Main: The connection between the grounded circuit conductor and the equipment grounding conductor at the service.

Branch Circuit: The circuit conductors between the final overcurrent device protecting the circuit and the outlet(s).

See Section 240-9 for thermal cutouts, thermal relays, and other devices.

Branch Circuit, Appliance: A branch circuit supplying energy to one or more outlets to which appliances are to be connected; such circuits to have no permanently connected lighting fixtures not a part of an appliance.

Branch Circuit, General Purpose: A branch circuit that supplies a number of outlets for lighting and appliances.

Branch Circuit, Individual: A branch circuit that supplies only one utilization equipment.

▲ *Example:* Only one heater, as a single unit, may be placed on an individual branch circuit. Where more than a single unit is used on a branch circuit, the circuit needs to conform with the requirements of Sec. 210-23. See also Sec. 424-3.

An individual branch circuit supplying a receptacle may only supply a "single" receptacle.

A branch circuit supplying two or more single receptacles or one or more duplex receptacles needs to conform to Sec. 210-23.

A duplex receptacle without a split bus is actually two devices (receptacles) on the same yoke and is not intended to be used on an individual branch circuit. See the definition of "Receptacle" in this Article.

Branch Circuit, Multiwire: A branch circuit consisting of two or more ungrounded conductors having a potential difference between them, and an identified grounded conductor having equal potential difference between it and each ungrounded conductor of the circuit and which is connected to the neutral conductor of the system.

Branch-Circuit Selection Current: See Section 440-3(c), Definition.

Building: A structure which stands alone or which is cut off from adjoining structures by fire walls with all openings therein protected by approved fire doors.

▲ Most areas have building codes to establish the requirements for buildings, and such codes should be used as a basis for deciding the use of the definition given in the National Electrical Code. The use of the term "fire walls" in this definition has resulted in differences of opinions among electrical inspectors and others, and a request for a clarification has been frequently proposed. Since the definition of a fire wall may differ in each jurisdiction, the processing of an interpretation of a "fire wall" has been studiously avoided in the National Electrical Code because this is a function of Building Codes and not a responsibility of the National Electrical Code.

Cabinet: An enclosure designed either for surface or flush mounting, and provided with a frame, mat, or trim in which swinging doors are hung.

▲ The door of a cabinet is hinged to a trim covering, wiring space, or gutter; the door of a cutout box is hinged directly to the side of the box. Cabinets usually contain panelboards, while cutout boxes contain cutouts, switches, or miscellaneous apparatus.

Cell (As Applied to Raceways):   See Sections 356-1 and 358-1.

Circuit Breaker: A device designed to open and close a circuit by nonautomatic means and to open the circuit automatically on a predetermined overcurrent without injury to itself when properly applied within its rating.

See definition in Part B of this Article for definition applying to circuits and equipment over 600 volts, nominal.

ADJUSTABLE: (As Applied to Circuit Breakers.) A qualifying term indicating that the circuit breaker can be set to trip at various values of current and/or time within a pre-determined range.

INSTANTANEOUS TRIP: (As Applied to Circuit Breakers.) A qualifying term indicating that no delay is purposely introduced in the tripping action of the circuit breaker.

INVERSE TIME: (As Applied to Circuit Breakers.) A qualifying term indicating there is purposely introduced a delay in the tripping action of the circuit breaker, which delay decreases as the magnitude of the current increases.

NONADJUSTABLE: (As Applied to Circuit Breakers.) A qualifying term indicating that the circuit breaker does not have any adjustment to alter the value of current at which it will trip or the time required for its operation.

SETTING: (Of Circuit Breaker.) The value of current and/or time at which an adjustable circuit breaker is set to trip.

Communication Circuit: See Section 800-1.

Concealed: Rendered inaccessible by the structure or finish of the building. Wires in concealed raceways are considered concealed, even though they may become accessible by withdrawing them. [See "Accessible—(As applied to wiring methods)".]

▲ Wires run in an unfinished basement or an accessible attic on knobs or through tubes are not "rendered inaccessible by the structure or finish of the building," and are therefore considered as open work rather than knob-and-tube work, which is a concealed type of wiring.

Conductor:

BARE: A conductor having no covering or electrical insulation whatsoever. (See "Conductor, Covered.")

COVERED: A conductor encased within material of composition or thickness that is not recognized by this Code as electrical insulation. (See "Conductor, Bare.")

INSULATED: A conductor encased within material of composition and thickness that is recognized by this Code as electrical insulation.

Conduit Body: A separate portion of a conduit or tubing system that provides access through a removable cover(s) to the interior of the system at a junction of two or more sections of the system or at a terminal point of the system.

▲ Conduit bodies have been commonly referred to in the electrical trade as LB, LL, LR, C, and T conduit fittings. This definition clearly indicates that conduit bodies are not fittings, but rather, a portion of the conduit or tubing system. The rules for usage of conduit bodies are contained in Secs. 300-15, 346-14, 346-15, 347-16, 348-14, 348-15, 370-1, 370-6(c), and 370-18(a) Exception.

Connector, Pressure (Solderless): A device that establishes a connection between two or more conductors or between one or more conductors and a terminal by means of mechanical pressure and without the use of solder.

Continuous Duty: See under "Duty."

Continuous Load: A load where the maximum current is expected to continue for three hours or more.

Control Circuit: See Section 430-71.

Controller: A device or group of devices that serves to govern, in some predetermined manner, the electric power delivered to the apparatus to which it is connected. See also Section 430-81(a).

▲ See "Motor Controllers," Art. 430, Part G.

Cooking Unit, Counter-Mounted: A cooking appliance designed for mounting in or on a counter and consisting of one or more heating elements, internal wiring, and built-in or separately mountable controls. (See "Oven, Wall-Mounted.")

Covered Conductor: See under "Conductor."

Current-Limiting Overcurrent Protective Device: (See Section 240-11.)

Cutout Box: An enclosure designed for surface mounting and having swinging doors or covers secured directly to and telescoping with the walls of the box proper. (See "Cabinet.")

Damp Location: See under "Location."

Demand Factor: The ratio of the maximum demand of a system, or part of a system, to the total connected load of a system or the part of the system under consideration.

Device: A unit of an electrical system which is intended to carry but not utilize electric energy.

▲ Switches, fuses, circuit breakers, controllers, receptacles, and lampholders are "devices."

Disconnecting Means: A device, or group of devices, or other means by which the conductors of a circuit can be disconnected from their source of supply.

See definition in Part B of this Article for definition applying to circuits and equipment over 600 volts, nominal.

▲ Manually operable switches and circuit breakers are examples, and under certain conditions (see Arts. 422, 424, 430, and 440) branch-circuit overcurrent devices or attachment plugs can serve as the disconnecting means.

Dry Location: See under "Location."

Dust-Ignition-Proof: See Section 502-1.

Dustproof: So constructed or protected that dust will not interfere with its successful operation.

Dust-tight: So constructed that dust will not enter the enclosing case.

Duty:

CONTINUOUS DUTY: Operation at a substantially constant load for an indefinitely long time.

INTERMITTENT DUTY: Operation for alternate intervals of (1) load and no load; or (2) load and rest; or (3) load, no load and rest.

PERIODIC DUTY: Intermittent operation in which the load conditions are regularly recurrent.

SHORT TIME DUTY: Operation at a substantially constant load for a short and definitely specified time.

VARYING DUTY: Operation at loads, and for intervals of time, both of which may be subject to wide variation.

See Table 430-22(a) Exception for illustration of various types of duty.

▲ See also Sec. 430-33.

Duty Cycle (Welding): See Section 630-31(b), Fine Print Note.

Electric Sign: A fixed, stationary, or portable self-contained, electrically illuminated utilization equipment with words or symbols designed to convey information or attract attention.

Enclosed: Surrounded by a case, housing, fence or walls which will prevent persons from accidentally contacting energized parts.

Enclosure: The case or housing of apparatus, or the fence or walls surrounding an installation to prevent personnel from accidentally contacting energized parts, or to protect the equipment from physical damage.

Equipment: A general term including material, fittings, devices, appliances, fixtures, apparatus, and the like used as a part of, or in connection with, an electrical installation.

Equipment Grounding Conductor: See "Grounding Conductor, Equipment."

Explosion-Proof Apparatus: Apparatus enclosed in a case that is capable of withstanding an explosion of a specified gas or vapor which may occur within it and of preventing the ignition of a specified gas or vapor surrounding the enclosure by sparks, flashes, or explosion of the gas or vapor within, and which operates at such an external temperature that a surrounding flammable atmosphere will not be ignited thereby.

Exposed: (As applied to live parts.) Capable of being inadvertently touched or approached nearer than a safe distance by a person. It is applied to parts not suitably guarded, isolated, or insulated. (See "Accessible" and "Concealed.")

Exposed: (As applied to wiring methods.) On or attached to the surface or behind panels designed to allow access. [See "Accessible—(As applied to wiring methods)".]

Externally Operable: Capable of being operated without exposing the operator to contact with live parts.

Feeder: All circuit conductors between the service equipment, or the generator switchboard of an isolated plant, and the final branch-circuit overcurrent device.

Festoon Lighting: See Section 225-6(b).

Fitting: An accessory such as a locknut, bushing, or other part of a wiring system that is intended primarily to perform a mechanical rather than an electrical function.

Fixed Appliance: See "Appliance, Fixed."

Garage: A building or portion of a building in which one or more self-propelled vehicles carrying volatile flammable liquid for fuel or power are kept for use, sale, storage, rental, repair, exhibition, or demonstrating purposes, and all that portion of a building which is on or below the floor or floors in which such vehicles are kept and which is not separated therefrom by suitable cutoffs.

See Section 511-1.

General-Purpose Branch Circuit: See "Branch Circuit, General Purpose."

General-Use Snap Switch: See under "Switches."

General-Use Switch: See under "Switches."

Ground: A conducting connection, whether intentional or accidental, between an electrical circuit or equipment and the earth, or to some conducting body that serves in place of the earth.

Grounded: Connected to earth or to some conducting body that serves in place of the earth.

Grounded (Effectively Grounded Communication System): See Section 800-2(c) (1).

Grounded Conductor: A system or circuit conductor that is intentionally grounded.

Grounding Conductor: A conductor used to connect equipment or the grounded circuit of a wiring system to a grounding electrode or electrodes.

Grounding Conductor, Equipment: The conductor used to connect noncurrent-carrying metal parts of equipment, raceways, and other enclosures to the system grounded conductor at the service and/or the grounding electrode conductor.

Grounding Electrode Conductor: The conductor used to connect the grounding electrode to the equipment grounding conductor and/or to the grounded conductor of the circuit at the service.

▲ This definition takes the place of the two former definitions of common main and main grounding conductors. Accordingly, it applies to the grounding conductor that extends to a grounding electrode for either grounded or ungrounded systems. See Table 250-94.

Guarded: Covered, shielded, fenced, enclosed, or otherwise protected by means of suitable covers, casings, barriers, rails, screens, mats, or platforms to remove the likelihood of approach or contact by persons or objects to a point of danger.

▲ See Arts. 110, 430, 450, and 710.

Hazardous Locations: See Article 500.
Header: See Sections 356-1 and 358-1.
Hermetic Refrigerant Motor-Compressor: See Section 440-1.
Hoistway: Any shaftway, hatchway, well hole, or other vertical opening or space in which an elevator or dumbwaiter is designed to operate.

▲ See Art. 620.

Identified: Identified, as used in this Code in reference to a conductor or its terminal, means that such conductor or terminal is to be recognized as grounded. See Article 200.

Individual Branch Circuit: See "Branch Circuit, Individual."
Insulated Conductor: See under "Conductor."
Intermittent Duty: See under "Duty."
Isolated: Not readily accessible to persons unless special means for access are used.

▲ See Secs. 110-31 and 710-22. Oil circuit breakers and switches should be isolated from other electrical apparatus where practicable.

Labeled: Equipment or materials having a label, symbol, or other identifying mark of a nationally recognized testing laboratory, inspection agency, or other organization concerned with product evaluation that maintains periodic inspection of production of labeled equipment or materials and by whose labeling is indicated compliance with nationally recognized standards or tests to determine suitable usage in a specified manner.

▲ See the comments that follow the definition of "Approved."

Lighting Outlet: An outlet intended for the direct connection of a lampholder, a lighting fixture, or a pendant cord terminating in a lampholder.
Listed: Equipment or materials included in a list published by a nationally recognized testing laboratory, inspection agency, or other organization concerned with product evaluation that maintains periodic inspection of production of listed

equipment or materials, and whose listing states either that the equipment or material meets nationally recognized standards or has been tested and found suitable for use in a specified manner.

The means for identifying listed equipment may vary for each testing laboratory, inspection agency, or other organization concerned with product evaluation, some of which do not recognize equipment as listed unless it is also labeled. The authority having jurisdiction should utilize the system employed by the listing organization to identify a listed product.

▲ **See the comments that follow the definition of "Approved."**

Location:

DAMP LOCATION: Partially protected locations under canopies, marquees, roofed open porches, and like locations, and interior locations subject to moderate degrees of moisture, such as some basements, some barns, and some cold-storage warehouses.

DRY LOCATION: A location not normally subject to dampness or wetness. A location classified as dry may be temporarily subject to dampness or wetness, as in the case of a building under construction.

WET LOCATION: Installations underground or in concrete slabs or masonry in direct contact with the earth, and locations subject to saturation with water or other liquids, such as vehicle washing areas, and locations exposed to weather and unprotected.

Low-Energy Power Circuit: A circuit that is not a remote-control or signaling circuit but has its power supply limited in accordance with the requirements of Class 2 and Class 3 circuits. (See Article 725.)

Multioutlet Assembly: A type of surface or flush raceway designed to hold conductors and receptacles, assembled in the field or at the factory.

▲ **Multioutlet assemblies may be metallic or nonmetallic. They are intended for surface mounting except that the metal type may be surrounded by the building finish or recessed so long as the front is not covered, and the nonmetallic type may be recessed in baseboards. (See Art. 353.)**

Multiwire Branch Circuit: See "Branch Circuit, Multiwire."

Neutral Conductor: See Note 10 to Tables 310-16 to 310-19.

Nonautomatic: Action requiring personal intervention for its control. (See "Automatic.")

As applied to an electric controller, nonautomatic control does not necessarily imply a manual controller, but only that personal intervention is necessary.

Outlet: A point on the wiring system at which current is taken to supply utilization equipment.

Outline Lighting: An arrangement of incandescent lamps or electric discharge tubing to outline or call attention to certain features such as the shape of a building or the decoration of a window.

▲ **See Art. 600.**

Oven, Wall-Mounted: An oven for cooking purposes designed for mounting in or on a wall or other surface and consisting of one or more heating elements, internal wiring, and built-in or separately mountable controls. (See "Cooking Unit, Counter-Mounted.")

Panelboard: A single panel or group of panel units designed for assembly in the form of a single panel; including buses, automatic overcurrent devices, and with or without switches for the control of light, heat, or power circuits; designed to be placed in a cabinet or cutout box placed in or against a wall or partition and accessible only from the front. (See "Switchboard.")

Periodic Duty: See under "Duty."

Portable Appliance: See "Appliance, Portable."

Power Outlet: An enclosed assembly which may include receptacles, circuit breakers, fuseholders, fused switches, buses and watt-hour meter mounting means; intended to supply and control power to mobile homes, recreational vehicles or boats, or to serve as a means for distributing power required to operate mobile or temporarily installed equipment.

Premises Wiring (System):   That interior and exterior wiring, including power, lighting, control, and signal circuit wiring together with all of its associated hardware, fittings, and wiring devices, both permanently and temporarily installed which extends from the load end of the service drop, or load end of the service lateral conductors to the outlet(s). Such wiring does not include wiring internal to appliances, fixtures, motors, controllers, motor control centers, and similar equipment.

Projector, Nonprofessional: See Section 540-30.

Projector, Professional: See Section 540-10.

Qualified Person: One familiar with the construction and operation of the equipment and the hazards involved.

Raceway: Any channel for holding wires, cables, or busbars that is designed expressly for, and used solely for, this purpose.

Raceways may be of metal or insulating material, and the term includes rigid metal conduit, rigid nonmetallic conduit, intermediate metal conduit, flexible metal conduit, electrical metallic tubing, underfloor raceways, cellular concrete floor raceways, cellular metal floor raceways, surface raceways, wireways, and busways.

Rainproof: So constructed, protected, or treated as to prevent rain from interfering with successful operation of the apparatus.

Raintight: So constructed or protected that exposure to a beating rain will not result in the entrance of water.

▲ **In Secs. 225-22 and 230-53 "Raintight" is applied to raceways on the exterior of buildings.**

Rated-Load Current: See Section 440-3(a) Definition.

Readily Accessible: Capable of being reached quickly for operation, renewal, or inspections, without requiring those to whom ready access is requisite to climb over or remove obstacles or to resort to portable ladders, chairs, etc. (See "Accessible.")

▲ **The term *readily accessible* implies a need for performing promptly an indicated act, for example, to reach quickly a disconnecting switch or circuit breaker without the use of ladders, chairs, etc. The installation of such a switch or circuit breaker at a height above 7 ft from a standing level is not considered "readily accessible."**

Receptacle: A receptacle is a contact device installed at the outlet for the connection of a single attachment plug.

A single receptacle is a single contact device with no other contact device on the same yoke. A multiple receptacle is a single device containing two or more receptacles.

▲ **Only a single receptacle can be served by an individual branch circuit. See Secs. 210-21(b) and 555-3.**

Receptacle Outlet: An outlet where one or more receptacles are installed.

Remote-Control Circuit: Any electric circuit that controls any other circuit through a relay or an equivalent device.

Sealable Equipment: Equipment enclosed in a case or cabinet that is provided with a means of sealing or locking so that live parts cannot be made accessible without opening the enclosure. The equipment may or may not be operable without opening the enclosure.

Service: The conductors and equipment for delivering energy from the electricity supply system to the wiring system of the premises served.

Service Cable: Service conductors made up in the form of a cable.

Service Conductors: The supply conductors that extend from the street main or from transformers to the service equipment of the premises supplied.

▲ **In an overhead distribution system, the service conductors begin at the line pole where connection is made. If a primary line is extended to transformers installed outdoors on private property, the service conductors to the building proper begin at the secondary terminals of the transformers. See Sec. 230-200.**

Where the supply is from an underground distribution system, the service conductors begin at the point of connection to the underground street mains.

In every case the service conductors terminate at the service equipment.

Service Drop: The overhead service conductors from the last pole or other aerial support to and including the splices, if any, connecting to the service-entrance conductors at the building or other structure.

Service-Entrance Conductors, Overhead System: The service conductors between the terminals of the service equipment and a point usually outside the building, clear of building walls, where joined by tap or splice to the service drop.

Service-Entrance Conductors, Sub-sets: See Section 230-2 Exception No. 3(b).

Service-Entrance Conductors, Underground System: The service conductors between the terminals of the service equipment and the point of connection to the service lateral.

Where service equipment is located outside the building walls, there may be no service-entrance conductors, or they may be entirely outside the building.

Service Equipment: The necessary equipment, usually consisting of a circuit breaker or switch and fuses, and their accessories, located near the point of entrance of supply conductors to a building or other structure, or an otherwise defined area, and intended to constitute the main control and means of cutoff of the supply.

▲ **A meter is not considered a part of the service equipment.**

Service Lateral: The underground service conductors between the street main, including any risers at a pole or other structure or from transformers, and the first point of connection to the service-entrance conductors in a terminal box or meter or other enclosure with adequate space, inside or outside the building wall. Where there is no terminal box, meter, or other enclosure with adequate space, the point of connection shall be considered to be the point of entrance of the service conductors into the building.

Service Raceway: The raceway that encloses the service-entrance conductors.

Setting: (Of Circuit Breaker.) The value of the current at which it is set to trip.

Short-Time Duty: See under "Duty."

Show Window: Any window used or designed to be used for the display of goods or advertising material, whether it is fully or partly enclosed or entirely open at the rear and whether or not it has a platform raised higher than the street floor level.

Sign: See "Electric Sign."

Signaling Circuit: Any electric circuit that energizes signaling equipment.

Special Permission: The written consent of the authority having jurisdiction.

▲ **See paragraphs entitled "Formal Interpretation" (Sec. 90-5) and "Enforcement" (Sec. 90-4) in the Introduction of the Code.**

Stationary Appliance: See "Appliance, Stationary."

Switches:

GENERAL-USE SWITCH: A switch intended for use in general distribution and branch circuits. It is rated in amperes, and it is capable of interrupting its rated current at its rated voltage.

GENERAL-USE SNAP SWITCH: A form of general-use switch so constructed that it can be installed in flush device boxes or on outlet box covers, or otherwise used in conjunction with wiring systems recognized by this Code.

AC GENERAL-USE SNAP SWITCH: See Section 380-14(a).

AC-DC GENERAL-USE SNAP SWITCH: See Section 380-14(b).

ISOLATING SWITCH: A switch intended for isolating an electric circuit from the source of power. It has no interrupting rating, and it is intended to be operated only after the circuit has been opened by some other means.

MOTOR-CIRCUIT SWITCH: A switch, rated in horsepower, capable of interrupting the maximum operating overload current of a motor of the same horsepower rating as the switch at the rated voltage.

Switchboard: A large single panel, frame, or assembly of panels on which are mounted, on the face or back or both, switches, overcurrent and other protective devices, buses, and usually instruments. Switchboards are generally accessible from the rear as well as from the front and are not intended to be installed in cabinets. (See "Panelboard.")

▲ **In most modern installations switchboards are completely enclosed in metal.**

Thermal Cutout: An overcurrent protective device that contains a heater element in addition to and affecting a renewable fusible member which opens the circuit. It is not designed to interrupt short-circuit currents.

Thermally Protected: (As applied to motors.) The words "Thermally Protected" appearing on the nameplate of a motor or motor-compressor indicate that the motor is provided with a thermal protector.

Thermal Protector: (As applied to motors.) A protective device for assembly as an integral part of a motor or motor-compressor and which, when properly applied, protects the motor against dangerous overheating due to overload and failure to start.

The thermal protector may consist of one or more sensing elements integral with the motor or motor-compressor and an external control device.

Utilization Equipment: Equipment which utilizes electric energy for mechanical, chemical, heating, lighting, or similar purposes.

Varying Duty: See under "Duty."

Ventilated: Provided with a means to permit circulation of air sufficient to remove an excess of heat, fumes, or vapors.

Volatile Flammable Liquid: A flammable liquid having a flash point below 38°C (100°F) or whose temperature is above its flash point.

Voltage (Of a Circuit): The greatest root-mean-square (effective) difference of potential between any two conductors of the circuit concerned.

Some systems, such as 3-phase 4-wire, single-phase 3-wire, and 3-wire direct-current may have various circuits of various voltages.

▲ On a three-phase four-wire wye system or on any DC or single-phase three-wire system there are two voltages. If the "circuit concerned" is a feeder including all the conductors of the system, the *voltage of the circuit* is the highest voltage between any two of the conductors. A two-wire subfeeder or branch circuit supplied by such a system may have only the lower voltage between the two conductors, in which case this lower voltage is the voltage of the circuit. (See Sec. 110-4.)

Voltage, Nominal: A nominal value assigned to a circuit or system for the purpose of conveniently designating its voltage class (as 120/240, 480Y/277, 600, etc.).

The actual voltage at which a circuit operates can vary from the nominal within a range that permits satisfactory operation of equipment.

See "Voltage Ratings for Electric Power Systems and Equipment (60 Hz)," ANSI C84.1-1970 and supplement C84.1a-1973.

Voltage to Ground: For grounded circuits, the voltage between the given conductor and that point or conductor of the circuit that is grounded; for ungrounded circuits, the greatest voltage between the given conductor and any other conductor of the circuit.

▲ The voltage to ground on a three-phase, three wire 480-V undergrounded supply system would be 480 V. The term *circuit* means the entire system—not merely *branch* circuits.

Watertight: So constructed that moisture will not enter the enclosure.

Weatherproof: So constructed or protected that exposure to the weather will not interfere with successful operation.

Rainproof, raintight, or watertight equipment can fulfill the requirements for weatherproof where varying weather conditions other than wetness, such as snow, ice, dust, or temperature extremes, are not a factor.

Welder, Electric:
RATED PRIMARY CURRENT: See Section 630-31(b).
ACTUAL PRIMARY CURRENT: See Section 630-31(b).
Wet Location: See under "Location."
X-ray:
LONG TIME RATING: See Section 660-2.
MOMENTARY RATING: See Section 660-2.

B. Over 600 Volts, Nominal

Whereas the preceding definitions are intended to apply wherever the terms are used throughout this Code, the following ones are applicable only to the Parts of Articles covering specifically installations and equipment operating at over 600 volts, nominal.

Circuit Breaker: (See "Switching Devices.")
Cutout: (See "Switching Devices.")
Disconnect (Isolator): (See "Switching Devices.")
Disconnecting Means: (See "Switching Devices.")
Fuse: An overcurrent protective device with a circuit opening fusible part that is heated and severed by the passage of overcurrent through it.

A fuse comprises all the parts that form a unit capable of performing the prescribed functions. It may or may not be the complete device necessary to connect it into an electrical circuit.

EXPULSION FUSE UNIT (EXPULSION FUSE): A vented fuse unit in which the expulsion effect of gases produced by the arc and lining of the fuse-holder, either alone or aided by a spring, extinguishes the arc.

POWER FUSE UNIT: A vented, nonvented or controlled vented fuse unit in which the arc is extinguished by being drawn through solid material, granular material, or liquid, either alone or aided by a spring.

VENTED POWER FUSE: A fuse with provision for the escape of arc gases, liquids, or solid particles to the surrounding atmosphere during circuit interruption.

NONVENTED POWER FUSE: A fuse without intentional provision for the escape of arc gases, liquids, or solid particles to the atmosphere during circuit interruption.

CONTROLLED VENTED POWER FUSE: A fuse with provision for controlling discharge circuit interruption such that no solid material may be exhausted into the surrounding atmosphere. The discharge gases shall not ignite or damage insulation in the path of the discharge, nor shall these gases propagate a flashover to or between grounded members or conduction members in the path of the discharge when the distance between the vent and such insulation or conduction members conforms to manufacturer's recommendations.

Grounded, Effectively: Permanently connected to earth through a ground connection of sufficiently low impedance and having sufficient ampacity that ground fault current which may occur cannot build up to voltages dangerous to personnel.

Interrupter Switch: (See "Switching Devices.")
Multiple Fuse: An assembly of two or more single-pole fuses.
Oil (Filled) Cutout: (See "Switching Devices.")
Power Fuse: (See "Fuse.")
Regulator Bypass Switch: (See "Switching Devices.")

Switching Device: A device designed to close and/or open one or more electric circuits.

Switching Devices:

CIRCUIT BREAKER: A switching device capable of making, carrying, and breaking currents under normal circuit conditions, and also making, carrying for a specified time, and breaking currents under specified abnormal circuit conditions, such as those of short circuit.

CUTOUT: An assembly of a fuse support with either a fuseholder, fuse carrier, or disconnecting blade. The fuseholder or fuse carrier may include a conducting element (fuse link), or may act as the disconnecting blade by the inclusion of a non-fusible member.

DISCONNECTING (OR ISOLATING) SWITCH (DISCONNECTOR, ISOLATOR):   A mechanical switching device used for isolating a circuit or equipment from a source of power.

DISCONNECTING MEANS: A device, group of devices, or other means whereby the conductors of a circuit can be disconnected from their source of supply.

INTERRUPTER SWITCH: A switch capable of making, carrying, and interrupting specified currents.

OIL CUTOUT (OIL-FILLED CUTOUT):   A cutout in which all or part of the fuse support and its fuse link or disconnecting blade are mounted in oil with complete immersion of the contacts and the fusible portion of the conducting element (fuse link), so that arc interruption by severing of the fuse link or by opening of the contacts will occur under oil.

OIL SWITCH: An oil switch is a switch having contacts which operate under oil (or askarel or other suitable liquid).

REGULATOR BYPASS SWITCH: A specific device or combination of devices designed to bypass a regulator.

ARTICLE 110. REQUIREMENTS FOR ELECTRICAL INSTALLATIONS

A. General

110-1. Mandatory Rules and Explanatory Material.   Mandatory rules of this Code are characterized by the use of the word, "shall." Explanatory material is in the form of fine print notes.

110-2. Approval.   The conductors and equipment required or permitted by this Code shall be acceptable only when approved.

See Examination of Equipment for Safety, Section 110-3. See definitions of "Approved," "Approved for the purpose," "Labeled," and "Listed."

▲ The definition of "approved" states that this term means "acceptable to the authority enforcing this Code," such authority usually being a municipal, state, or Federal inspection department or an Underwriters' inspection or rating bureau. In most cases it is assumed that the approval of the inspection department will be based upon listings by Underwriters' Laboratories, Inc., where there are UL standards for specific equipment.

Since by definition the term "equipment" includes all the materials, devices, and apparatus used in an electrical installation, the effect is to require that only approved material, devices, and apparatus shall be used.

110-3. Examination, Installation and Use of Equipment.

(a) Examination. In judging equipment, considerations such as the following shall be evaluated:

(1) Suitability for installation and use in conformity with the provisions of this Code. Suitability of equipment may be evidenced by listing or labeling.

(2) Mechanical strength and durability, including, for parts designed to enclose and protect other equipment, the adequacy of the protection thus provided.

(3) Electrical insulation.

(4) Heating effects under normal conditions of use and also under abnormal conditions likely to arise in service.

(5) Arcing effects.

(6) Classification by type, size, voltage, current capacity, specific use.

(7) Other factors which contribute to the practical safeguarding of persons using or likely to come in contact with the equipment.

(b) Installation and Use. Listed or labeled equipment shall be used or installed in accordance with any instructions included in the listing or labeling.

110-4. Voltages. Throughout this Code the voltage considered shall be that at which the circuit operates.

▲ See definitions "Voltage (of a circuit)" and "Voltage to Ground."

110-5. Conductors. Conductors normally used to carry current shall be of copper unless otherwise provided in this Code. Where the conductor material is not specified, the sizes given in this Code shall apply to copper conductors. Where other materials are used, the size shall be changed accordingly.

For aluminum and copper-clad aluminum conductors, see Tables 310-18 and 310-19.

110-6. Conductor Sizes. Conductor sizes are expressed in American Wire Gage (AWG) or in circular mils.

▲ In this country, the American Wire Gage is the standard for copper wire and for aluminum wire used for electrical conductors. The American Wire Gage is the same as the Brown & Sharpe (B. & S.) gage. The largest gage size is No. 0000; above this size the sizes of wires and cables are stated in circular mils.

The circular mil is a unit used for measuring the cross-sectional area of the conductor, or the area of the end of a wire which has been cut square across. One circular mil (commonly abbreviated CM or cmil) is the area of a circle 1/1,000 in. in diameter. The area of a circle 1 in. in diameter is 1,000,000 CM; also, the area of a circle of this size is 0.7854 sq in.

To convert square inches to circular mils, multiply the square inches by 1,273,200.

To convert circular mils to square inches, divide the circular mils by 1,273,200 or multiply the circular mils by 0.7854 and divide by 1,000,000.

In interior wiring the gage sizes 14, 12, and 10 are usually solid wire; No. 8 and larger conductors in raceways are required to be stranded. (See Sec. 310-3.)

A cable (if not larger than 1,000,000 CM) will have one of the following numbers of strands; 7, 19, 37, or 61. In order to make a cable of any standard size, in nearly every case the individual strands cannot be any regular gage number but must be some special odd size. For example, a No. 00 cable must have a total cross-sectional area of 133,100 CM and is usually made up of 19 strands. No. 12 has an area of 6,530 CM and No. 11, an area of 8,234 CM; therefore each strand must be a special size between Nos. 12 and 11.

110-7. Insulation Integrity. All wiring shall be so installed that when completed the system will be free from short circuits and from grounds other than as permitted in Article 250.

▲ Previous editions of the Code (e.g., 1965) contained *recommended* values for testing insulation resistance. It was found that those values were incomplete and not sufficiently accurate for use in modern installations, and the recommendation was deleted from the Code. However, basic knowledge of insulation-resistance testing is important.

Measurements of insulation resistance can best be made with a megohmmeter insulation tester. As measured with such an instrument, insulation resistance is the resistance to the flow of direct current (usually at 500 or 1,000 V for systems of 600 V or less) through or over the surface of the insulation in electrical equipment. The results are in ohms or megohms, but insulation readings will be in the megohm range.

The insulation resistance test is nondestructive, quite different from a high-voltage or *breakdown* test. It is made with direct current rather than alternating current, and is not a measure of dielectric strength as such. However, insulation-resistance tests assist greatly in determining when and where not to apply high voltage.

In general, insulation resistance decreases with increased size of a machine or length of cable, because there is more insulating material in contact with conductors and frame, ground, or sheath.

Insulation resistance usually increases with higher voltage rating of apparatus because of increased thickness of insulating material.

Insulation-resistance readings are not only *quantitative*, but are *relative* or *comparative* as well, and since they are influenced by moisture, dirt, and deterioration, they are reliable indicators of the presence of those conditions.

Cable and conductor installations present a wide variation of conditions from the point of view of the resistance of the insulation. These conditions result from the many kinds of insulating materials used, the voltage rating or insulation thickness, and the length of the circuit involved in the measurement. Furthermore, such circuits usually extend over great distances, and may be subject to wide variations in temperature, which will have an effect on the insulation resistance values obtained. The terminals of cables and conductors will also have an effect on the test values unless they are clean and dry, or guarded.

It is important to understand the correct use of insulation testers. The use of an insulation tester is not complicated. However, temperature correction, humidity, temporary dampness during construction, types of conductor insulation, lengths of runs, and the proper *interpretation* of readings are major factors that must be considered. The important thing is to make an insulation test and to record the results for immediate and future attention.

Excellent manuals on this subject are available from instrument manufacturers, such as the James G. Biddle Co., Plymouth Meeting, Pa., and thorough knowledge in the use of insulation testers is essential if the test results are to be meaningful.

See Fig. 110-1 for a typical megohmmeter insulation tester.

FIG. 110-1. Multivoltage multirange insulation tester. (*James G. Biddle Co.*)

110-8. Wiring Methods. Only wiring methods recognized as suitable are included in this Code. The recognized methods of wiring shall be permitted to be installed in any type of building or occupancy, except as otherwise provided in this Code.

▲ See Art. 300.

110-9. Interrupting Capacity. Devices intended to break current shall have an interrupting capacity sufficient for the voltage employed and for the current that must be interrupted.

110-10. Circuit Impedance and Other Characteristics. The overcurrent protective devices, the total impedance, and other characteristics of the circuit to be protected shall be so selected and coordinated as to permit the circuit protective devices used to clear a fault without the occurrence of extensive damage to the electrical components of the circuit. This fault shall be assumed to be either between two or more of the circuit conductors, or between any circuit conductor and the grounding conductor or enclosing metal raceway.

▲ It is the intent of Secs. 110-9 and 110-10 that overcurrent devices have interrupting capacity (IC) ratings not less than the short-circuit current available at the line terminals of each overcurrent device. See Secs. 240-60(c) and 240-83(c) for common IC ratings of fuses and circuit breakers (up to 10,000 A).

If overcurrent devices with a specific IC rating are inserted at a point on a wiring system where the available short-circuit current exceeds the IC rating of the device, a resultant downstream solid short circuit between conductors or between one ungrounded conductor and ground (in grounded systems) could cause serious damage to life and property.

Since each electrical installation is different, the selection of overcurrent devices with proper IC ratings is not always a simple task. To begin with, the amount of available short-circuit current at the service equipment must be known. Such short-circuit current depends upon the capacity rating of the utility primary supply to the building, transformer impedances, and service conductor impedances. Most utilities will provide this information.

Downstream from the service equipment IC ratings of overcurrent devices may be reduced to lower than those at the service, depending on lengths and sizes of feeders, line impedances, and other factors. However, large motors and capacitors, while in operation, will feed additional current into a fault, and this must be considered when calculating short-circuit currents.

Manufacturers of overcurrent devices have excellent literature on figuring short-circuit currents, including graphs, charts, and one-line-diagram layout sheets to simplify the selection of proper overcurrent devices.

See comments on Sec. 230-95, which concerns ground-fault protection of 480Y/277-V systems.

110-11. Deteriorating Agents. Unless approved for the purpose, no conductors or equipment shall be located in damp or wet locations; where exposed to gases, fumes, vapors, liquids, or other agents having a deteriorating effect on the conductors or equipment; nor where exposed to excessive temperatures.

See Section 300-6 for protection against corrosion.

Control equipment, utilization equipment, and busways approved for use in dry locations only shall be protected against permanent damage from the weather during building construction.

110-12. Mechanical Execution of Work. Electric equipment shall be installed in a neat and workmanlike manner.

▲ This statement has been the source of many conflicts because opinions differ as to what is a neat and workmanlike manner.

The Code places the responsibility for determining what is acceptable on the authority having jurisdiction and how it is applied in the particular jurisdiction. This basis in most areas is the result of:

1. Competent knowledge and experience of installation methods;

2. What has been the established practice by the qualified journeyman in the particular area;

3. What has been taught in the trade schools having certified electrical training courses for apprentices and journeymen.

There should be an understanding that individual inspectors will not make an arbitrary ruling of their own but will apply in a uniform manner the practice established by the organization having responsibility for enforcement of electrical requirements.

Examples which generally would not be considered as "neat and workmanlike" include nonmetallic cables installed with kinks or twists; unsightly exposed runs; wiring improperly trained in enclosures; slack in cables between supports; flattened conduit bends; or improvised fittings, straps, or supports.

110-13. Mounting and Cooling of Equipment.

(a) Mounting. Electric equipment shall be firmly secured to the surface on which it is mounted. Wooden plugs driven into holes in masonry, concrete, plaster, or similar materials shall not be used.

(b) Cooling. Electrical equipment which depends upon the natural circulation of air and convection principles for cooling of exposed surfaces shall be installed so that room air flow over such surfaces is not prevented by walls or by adjacent installed equipment. For equipment designed for floor mounting, clearance between top surfaces and adjacent surfaces shall be provided to dissipate rising warm air.

Electrical equipment provided with ventilating openings shall be installed so that walls or other obstructions do not prevent the free circulation of air through the equipment.

110-14. Electrical Connections. Because of different characteristics of copper and aluminum, devices such as pressure terminal or pressure splicing connectors and soldering lugs shall be suitable for the material of the conductor and shall be properly installed and used. Conductors of dissimilar metals shall not be intermixed in a terminal or splicing connector where physical contact occurs between dissimilar conductors (such as copper and aluminum, copper and copper-clad aluminum, or aluminum and copper-clad aluminum), unless the device is suitable for the purpose and conditions of use. Materials such as solder, fluxes, inhibitors, and compounds, where employed, shall be suitable for the use and shall be of a type which will not adversely affect the conductors, installation, or equipment.

(a) Terminals. Connection of conductors to terminal parts shall insure a thoroughly good connection without damaging the conductors and shall be made by means of pressure connectors (including set-screw type), solder lugs, or splices to flexible leads.

Exception: Connection by means of wire binding screws or studs and nuts having upturned lugs or equivalent shall be permitted for No. 10 or smaller conductors.

Terminals for more than one conductor and terminals used to connect aluminum shall be of a type approved for the purpose.

(b) Splices. Conductors shall be spliced or joined with splicing devices suitable for the use or by brazing, welding, or soldering with a fusible metal or alloy. Soldered splices shall first be so spliced or joined as to be mechanically and electrically secure without solder and then soldered. All splices and joints and the free ends of conductors shall be covered with an insulation equivalent to that of the conductors or with an insulating device suitable for the purpose.

▲ Proper electrical connections at terminals and splices are absolutely essential to ensure a safe installation. Improper connections are the causes of many failures of wiring devices, equipment burndowns, and electrically oriented fires.

Many years ago soldered splices and lugs were widely used in the electrical industry, but in modern practice such methods have been replaced with solderless-type lugs, terminals, and splicing devices. These modern solderless devices have overcome most of the flaws inherent in soldered splices and lugs. However, solderless devices are only as good as they are selected and used, and misapplications or poor workmanship account for many failures.

Proper connections for all types of solderless devices can be assured if suitable wire combinations, types of conductor material (copper, copper-clad aluminum or aluminum), and proper torque-tightening of screws are used with specific devices. In general, approved pressure-type wire splicing lugs or connectors bear no marking if approved for only copper wire. If approved for copper, copper-clad aluminum, and/or aluminum they are marked "AL-CU"; and if approved for aluminum only they are marked "AL." Devices listed by Underwriters' Laboratories, Inc., indicate the range or combination of wire sizes for which such devices have been listed.

Where solderless terminals are not suitable for aluminum (or copper-clad aluminum) conductors, a short piece of copper wire can be attached to the terminal, and the other end is then connected to the aluminum wire with a pressure-type splicing device approved for joining copper and aluminum (straight types for larger conductors and pigtail types for smaller conductors). In such cases consideration must be given to available space in enclosures.

Reports have been made of field failures where aluminum conductors have been connected to the screw terminals of wiring devices. These failures have been largely due to poor workmanship and the use of minimum-quality wiring devices.

Terminals of 15- and 20-A receptacles not marked "CO/ALR" are for use with copper and copper-clad aluminum conductors only. Terminals marked "CO/ALR" are for use with aluminum, copper, and copper-clad aluminum conductors.

Screwless pressure terminal connectors of the conductor push-in type are for use only with copper and copper-clad aluminum conductors.

Terminals of receptacles rated 30 A and above not marked "AL-CU" are for use with copper and copper-clad aluminum conductors only. Terminals of receptacles rated 30 A and above marked "AL-CU" are for use with aluminum, copper, and copper-clad aluminum conductors.

For New Installations

The following was prepared by the *Ad Hoc* Committee on Aluminum Terminations: Comply with Sec. 110-14(a) of the 1975 *National Electrical Code* (*NEC*) when aluminum wire is used in new installations.

New Materials and Devices

a. For direct connection use only 15-amp and 20-amp receptacles and switches marked "CO/ALR" and connected as described under "Installation Method."

The "CO/ALR" marking is on the device mounting strap. The "CO/ALR" marking means the devices have been tested to stringent heat cycling requirements to determine their suitability for use with UL-labeled aluminum, copper, or copper-clad aluminum wire.

Note: Pigtailing, either field or factory-wired, as illustrated in Figure 110-2, is recognized by the *NEC.*

b. Use solid aluminum wire, No. 12 or 10 AWG marked with the Underwriters' Laboratories' new aluminum insulated wire label, as shown below. Follow the installation instructions packaged with the wire.

Conductor bearing this UL label is judged under the requirements for the chemistry, physical properties, and processing of the conductor which became effective September 20, 1972.

Installation Method

1. Wrap the freshly stripped end of the wire $\frac{2}{3}$ to $\frac{3}{4}$ of the distance around the wire-binding screw post, as shown in Step A of Fig. 110-3.

The loop is made so that rotation of the screw in tightening will tend to wrap the wire around the post rather than unwrap it.

2. Tighten the screw until the wire is snugly in contact with the underside of the screw head, and with the contact plate on the wiring device, as shown in Step B of Fig. 110-3.

3. Tighten the screw an additional $\frac{1}{2}$ turn, thereby providing a firm connection. Where torque screwdrivers are used, tighten to 12 pound-inches. See Step C of Fig. 110-3.

4. Position the wires behind the wiring device so as to decrease the likelihood of the terminal screws loosening when the device is positioned into the outlet box.

Figure 110-4 illustrates incorrect methods for connection and should *not* be used.

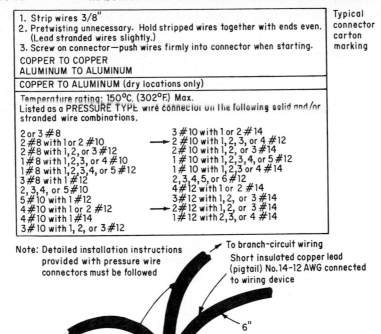

1. Strip wires 3/8"
2. Pretwisting unnecessary. Hold stripped wires together with ends even. (Lead stranded wires slightly.)
3. Screw on connector—push wires firmly into connector when starting.

COPPER TO COPPER
ALUMINUM TO ALUMINUM

COPPER TO ALUMINUM (dry locations only)

Temperature rating: 150°C. (302°F.) Max.
Listed as a PRESSURE TYPE wire connector on the following solid and/or stranded wire combinations.

2 or 3 #8	3 #10 with 1 or 2 #14
2 #8 with 1 or 2 #10	2 #10 with 1, 2, 3, or 4 #12
2 #8 with 1, 2, or 3 #12	2 #10 with 1, 2, or 3 #14
1 #8 with 1, 2, 3, or 4 #10	1 #10 with 1, 2, 3, 4, or 5 #12
1 #8 with 1, 2, 3, 4, or 5 #12	1 #10 with 1, 2, 3 or 4 #14
3 #8 with 1 #12	2, 3, 4, 5, or 6 #12
2, 3, 4, or 5 #10	4 #12 with 1 or 2 #14
5 #10 with 1 #12	3 #12 with 1, 2, or 3 #14
4 #10 with 1 or 2 #12	2 #12 with 1, 2, or 3 #14
4 #10 with 1 #14	1 #12 with 2, 3, or 4 #14
3 #10 with 1, 2, or 3 #12	

Typical connector carton marking

Note: Detailed installation instructions provided with pressure wire connectors must be followed

To branch-circuit wiring

Short insulated copper lead (pigtail) No.14–12 AWG connected to wiring device

6"

From branch circuit wiring

Aluminum wire No. 12–10 AWG

U.L. listed CU/AL insulated wire connector provided in carton marked "FOR DRY LOCATIONS ONLY" and for the aluminum-to-copper combinations for which it is suitable

FIG. 110-2. Pigtailing copper to aluminum conductor.

Existing Inventory

When UL-labeled solid aluminum wire No. 12 and 10 AWG not bearing the new aluminum wire label is used, it should be used with wiring devices marked "CO/ALR" and connected as described in "Installation Method." This is the preferred and recommended method for using such wire.

Note: Pigtailing, either field or factory-wired, as illustrated in Figure 110-2 is recognized by the NEC.

In the following types of devices the terminals shall *not* be directly connected to aluminum conductors but may be used with UL-labeled copper or copper-clad conductors:
Receptacles and snap switches marked "AL-CU"
Receptacles and snap switches having no conductor marking
Receptacles and snap switches having backwired terminals or screwless terminals of the push-in type

For Existing Installations

If examination discloses overheating or loose connections the recommendations described under "For New Installations—Existing Inventory" should be followed.

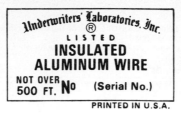

Correct method of terminating
aluminum wire at wire-binding-
screw terminals of receptacles
and snap switches

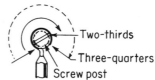

Two-thirds
Three-quarters
Screw post

Step A: Strip and wrap wire

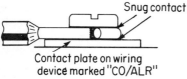

Snug contact

Contact plate on wiring
device marked "CO/ALR"

Step B: Tighten screw to full contact

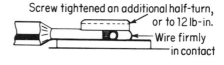

Screw tightened an additional half-turn,
or to 12 lb-in.
Wire firmly
in contact

Step C: Complete connection

FIG. 110-3. Correct method of terminating aluminum wire at wirebinding screw terminals of receptacles and snap switches.

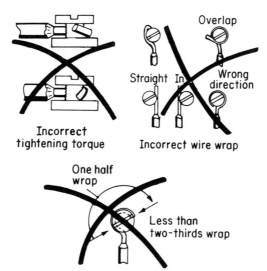

Overlap

Straight In   Wrong
               direction

Incorrect
tightening torque   Incorrect wire wrap

One half
wrap

Less than
two-thirds wrap

FIG. 110-4. Incorrect methods of terminating aluminum
wire at wire-binding screw terminals of receptacles and
snap switches.

110-16. Working Space About Electric Equipment (600 Volts or Less, Nominal).
Sufficient access and working space shall be provided and maintained about all electric equipment to permit ready and safe operation and maintenance of such equipment.

(a) Working Clearances. Except as elsewhere required or permitted in this Code, the dimension of the working space in the direction of access to live parts operating at 600 volts or less and likely to require examination, adjustment, servicing, or maintenance while alive, shall not be less than indicated in Table 110-16(a). In

Table 110-16(a). Working Clearances

Voltage to Ground		Minimum clear distance (feet)		
	Condition:	1	2	3
0–150		$2\frac{1}{2}$	$2\frac{1}{2}$	3
151–600		$2\frac{1}{2}$	$3\frac{1}{2}$	4

addition to the dimensions shown in Table 110-16(a), the work space shall not be less than 30 inches wide in front of the electric equipment. Distances shall be measured from the live parts if such are exposed or from the enclosure front or opening if such are enclosed. Concrete, brick, or tile walls shall be considered as grounded.
Where the "Conditions" are as follows:

1. Exposed live parts on one side and no live or grounded parts on the other side of the working space, or exposed live parts on both sides effectively guarded by suitable wood or other insulating materials. Insulated wire or insulated busbars operating at not over 300 volts shall not be considered live parts.
2. Exposed live parts on one side and grounded parts on the other side.
3. Exposed live parts on both sides of the work space (not guarded as provided in Condition 1) with the operator between.
Exception No. 1: Working space shall not be required in back of assemblies, such as dead-front switchboards or motor control centers where there are no renewable or adjustable parts such as fuses or switches on the back and where all connections are accessible from locations other than the back.
Exception No. 2: By special permission smaller spaces may be permitted where it is judged that the particular arrangement of the installation will provide adequate accessibility.

(b) Clear Spaces. Working space required by this Section shall not be used for storage. When normally enclosed live parts are exposed for inspection or servicing, the working space, if in a passageway or general open space, shall be suitably guarded.

(c) Access and Entrance to Working Space. At least one entrance of sufficient area shall be provided to give access to the working space about electric equipment.

(d) Front Working Space. In all cases where there are live parts normally exposed on the front of switchboards or motor control centers, the working space in front of such equipment shall not be less than 3 feet.

(e) Illumination. Illumination shall be provided for all working spaces about switchboards and motor control centers.

(f) Headroom. The minimum headroom of working spaces about switchboards or motor control centers where there are live parts exposed at any time shall be $6\frac{1}{4}$ feet.

For higher voltages, see Article 710.

As used in this Section, a motor control center is an assembly of one or more enclosed sections having a common power bus and principally containing motor control units.

110-17. Guarding of Live Parts. (600 volts or less, nominal)

(a) Except as elsewhere required or permitted by this Code, live parts of electric equipment operating at 50 volts or more shall be guarded against accidental contact by approved cabinets or other forms of approved enclosures or by any of the following means:

(1) By location in a room, vault, or similar enclosure that is accessible only to qualified persons.

(2) By suitable permanent, substantial partitions or screens so arranged that only qualified persons will have access to the space within reach of the live parts. Any openings in such partitions or screens shall be so sized and located that persons are not likely to come into accidental contact with the live parts or to bring conducting objects into contact with them.

(3) By location on a suitable balcony, gallery, or platform so elevated and arranged as to exclude unqualified persons.

(4) By elevation of 8 feet or more above the floor or other working surface.

(b) In locations where electric equipment would be exposed to physical damage, enclosures or guards shall be so arranged and of such strength as to prevent such damage.

(c) Entrances to rooms and other guarded locations containing exposed live parts shall be marked with conspicuous warning signs forbidding unqualified persons to enter.

For motors, see Sections 430-132 and 430-133. For over 600 volts, see Section 110-34.

▲ Live parts of equipment should in general be protected from accidental contact by complete enclosure; i.e., the equipment should be "dead-front." Such construction is not practicable in some large control panels, and in such cases the apparatus should be isolated or guarded as required by these rules.

110-18. Arcing Parts. Parts of electric equipment, which in ordinary operation produce arcs, sparks, flames, or molten metal, shall be enclosed or separated and isolated from all combustible material.

For hazardous locations, see Articles 500 through 517. For motors, see Section 430-14.

▲ The same considerations apply here as in the case covered in Sec. 110-17. Full enclosure is preferable, but where this is not practicable, all combustible material must be kept well away from the equipment.

110-19. Light and Power from Railway Conductors. Circuits for lighting and power shall not be connected to any system containing trolley wires with a ground return.

Exception: Car houses, power houses, or passenger and freight stations operated in connection with electric railways.

110-21. Marking. The manufacturer's name, trademark, or other descriptive marking by which the organization responsible for the product may be identified shall be placed on all electric equipment. Other markings shall be provided giving voltage, current, wattage, or other ratings as are specified elsewhere in this Code. The marking shall be of sufficient durability to withstand the environment involved.

▲ The marking required in Sec. 110-21 should be done in a manner which will allow inspectors to examine such marking without removing the equipment from a permanently installed position.

110-22. Identification of Disconnecting Means. Each disconnecting means required by this Code for motors and appliances, and each service, feeder, or branch circuit at the point where it originates shall be legibly marked to indicate its purpose unless located and arranged so the purpose is evident. The marking shall be of sufficient durability to withstand the environment involved.

B. Over 600 Volts, Nominal

110-30. General. Conductors and equipment used on circuits exceeding 600 volts, nominal, shall comply with all applicable provisions of the preceding Sections of this Article and with the following Sections, which supplement or modify the preceding Sections. In no case shall the provisions of this Part apply to equipment on the supply side of the service conductors.

110-31. Enclosure for Electrical Installations. Electrical installations in a vault, room, or closet or in an area surrounded by a wall, screen, or fence, access to which is controlled by lock and key or other approved means, shall be considered to be accessible to qualified persons only. The type of enclosure used in a given case shall be designed and constructed according to the nature and degree of the hazard(s) associated with the installation.

A wall, screen, or fence less than 8 feet in height shall not be considered as preventing access unless it has other features that provide a degree of isolation equivalent to an 8-foot fence.

Article 450 covers minimum construction requirements for transformer vaults.
Isolation by elevation is covered in paragraph (b) of this Section and in Section 110-34.

(a) Indoor Installations.

(1) In Places Accessible to Unqualified Persons. Indoor electrical installations that are open to unqualified persons shall be made with metal-enclosed equipment or shall be enclosed in a vault or in an area access to which is controlled by a lock. Metal-enclosed switchgear, unit substations, transformers, pull boxes, connection boxes, and other similar associated equipment shall be marked with appropriate caution signs. Openings in ventilated dry-type transformers or similar openings in other equipment shall be designed so that foreign objects inserted through these openings will be deflected from energized parts.

(2) In Places Accessible to Qualified Persons Only. Indoor electrical installations considered accessible to qualified persons only in accordance with this Section shall comply with Sections 110-34, 710-32, and 710-33.

(b) Outdoor Installations.

(1) In Places Accessible to Unqualified Persons. Outdoor electrical installations that are open to unqualified persons shall comply with Article 225.

For clearances of conductors over 600 volts, see National Electrical Safety Code (ANSI C2-1973).

(2) In Places Accessible to Qualified Persons Only. Outdoor electrical installations having exposed live parts shall be accessible to qualified persons only in accordance with the first paragraph of this Section and shall comply with Sections 110-34, 710-32, and 710-33.

(c) Metal-Enclosed Equipment Accessible to Unqualified Persons.
Ventilating or similar openings in equipment shall be so designed that foreign objects inserted through these openings will be deflected from energized parts. When exposed to physical damage from vehicular traffic suitable guards shall be provided. Metal-enclosed equipment located outdoors accessible to the general public shall be designed so that exposed nuts or bolts cannot be readily removed, permitting access to live parts. If installed so that the bottom of the enclosure is less than 8 feet above the floor, the door or cover shall be kept locked.

110-32. Workspace about Equipment.
Sufficient space shall be provided and maintained about electric equipment to permit ready and safe operation and maintenance of such equipment. Where energized parts are exposed, the minimum clear workspace shall not be less than $6\frac{1}{2}$ feet high (measured vertically from the floor or platform), or less than 3 feet wide (measured parallel to the equipment). The depth shall be as required in Section 110-34(a). In all cases, the workspace shall be adequate to permit at least a 90-degree opening of doors or hinged panels.

110-33. Entrance and Access to Workspace.
(a) At least one entrance not less than 24 inches wide and $6\frac{1}{2}$ feet high shall be provided to give access to the working space about electric equipment. On switchboard and control panels exceeding 48 inches in width, there shall be one entrance at each end of such board where reasonably practicable. Where bare energized parts at any voltage or insulated energized parts above 600 volts are located adjacent to such entrance, they shall be suitably guarded.

(b) Permanent ladders or stairways shall be provided to give safe access to the working space around electric equipment installed on platforms, balconies, mezzanine floors, or in attic or roof rooms or spaces.

110-34. Work Space and Guarding.
(a) Working Space. The minimum clear working space in front of electric equipment, such as switchboards, control panels, switches, circuit breakers, motor controllers, relays, and similar equipment shall not be less than specified in Table 110-34(a) unless otherwise specified in this Code. Distances shall be measured from

Table 110-34(a). Minimum Depth of Clear Working Space in Front of Electric Equipment

Nominal Voltage to Ground	Conditions		
	1	2	3
	(Feet)	(Feet)	(Feet)
601–2500	3	4	5
2501–9000	4	5	6
9001–25,000	5	6	9
25,001–75 kV	6	8	10
Above 75 kV	8	10	12

the live parts if such are exposed, or from the enclosure front or opening if such are enclosed.

Where the "Conditions" are as follows:

1. Exposed live parts on one side and no live or grounded parts on the other side of the working space or exposed live parts on both sides effectively guarded by suitable wood or other insulating materials. Insulated wire or insulated busbars operating at not over 300 volts shall not be considered live parts.

2. Exposed live parts on one side and grounded parts on the other side. Concrete, brick, or tile walls will be considered as grounded surfaces.

3. Exposed live parts on both sides of the work space (not guarded as provided in condition 1) with the operator between.

Exception: Working space is not required in back of equipment such as dead-front switchboards or control assemblies where there are no renewable or adjustable parts (such as fuses or switches) on the back and where all connections are accessible from other locations than the back.

(b) Separation from Low-Potential Equipment. Where switches, cutouts, or other equipment operating at 600 volts nominal, or less are installed in a room or enclosure where there are exposed live parts or exposed wiring operating at over 600 volts nominal, the high-potential equipment shall be effectively separated from the space occupied by the low-potential equipment by a suitable partition, fence, or screen.

Exception: Switches or other equipment operating at 600 volts or less, nominal, and serving only equipment within the high-voltage vault, room, or enclosure may be installed in the high-voltage enclosure, room, or vault if accessible to qualified persons only.

(c) Locked Rooms or Enclosures. The entrances to all buildings, rooms, or enclosures containing exposed live parts or exposed conductors operating at over 600 volts, nominal, shall be kept locked.

Exception: Where such entrances are under the observation of a qualified person at all times.

(d) Illumination. Adequate illumination shall be provided for all working spaces about electrical equipment. The lighting outlets shall be so arranged that persons changing lamps or making repairs on the lighting system will not be endangered by live parts or other equipment.

The points of control shall be so located that persons are not likely to come in contact with any live part or moving part of the equipment while turning on the lights.

(e) Elevation of Unguarded Live Parts. Unguarded live parts above working space shall be maintained at elevations not less than required by Table 110-34(e).

Table 110-34(e). Elevation of Unguarded Energized Parts above Working Space

Nominal Voltage Between Phases	Elevation
601–7500	8' 6"
7501–35000	9'
Over 35 kV	9' + 0.37" per kV above 35

CHAPTER TWO

Wiring Design and Protection

ARTICLE 200. USE AND IDENTIFICATION OF GROUNDED CONDUCTORS

200-1. Scope. This Article provides requirements for: (1) identification of terminals; (2) grounded conductors in premises wiring systems; and (3) identification of grounded conductors.

See Article 100 for definitions of "Grounded Conductor" and "Grounding Conductor."

200-2. General. All premises wiring systems shall have a grounded conductor that is identified in accordance with Section 200-6.

Exception: Circuits and systems exempted or prohibited by Sections 210-10, 215-7, 250-3, 250-5, 250-7, 503-13, and 517-63.

The grounded conductor, when insulated, shall have insulation which is suitable, other than color, for any ungrounded conductor of the same circuit.

▲ Ungrounded circuits are required in anesthetizing locations such as hospital operating rooms. (See Sec. 517-63.) Such circuits must be connected to a system which is provided with a line isolation monitor. (See NFPA No. 56A-1973, Inhalation Anesthetics Standard.)

200-3. Connection to Grounded System. Premises wiring shall not be electrically connected to a supply system unless the latter contains, for any grounded conductor of the interior system, a corresponding conductor which is grounded.

For the purpose of this Section, "electrically connected" shall mean connection capable of carrying current as distinguished from connection through electromagnetic induction.

▲ The interior wiring grounded conductor and the system grounded conductor must be connected together, in order to assure a completely grounded system.

200-6. Means of Identifying Grounded Conductors.

(a) Sizes No. 6 or Smaller. An insulated grounded conductor of No. 6 or smaller shall be identified by a continuous white or natural gray outer finish along its entire length.

Exception: The grounded conductor of a mineral-insulated metal-sheathed cable shall be identified at the time of installation by distinctive marking at its terminations.

(b) Sizes Larger Than No. 6. An insulated grounded conductor larger than No. 6 shall be identified either by a continuous white or natural gray outer finish along its entire length or at the time of installation by a distinctive white marking at its terminations.

(c) Flexible Cords. An insulated conductor intended for use as a grounded conductor, where contained within a flexible cord, shall be identified by a white or natural gray outer finish or by methods permitted by Section 400-22.

▲ The general requirements on identification of conductors are contained in Art. 200 of the Code and concern primarily the grounded circuit conductor which is required to be the identified conductor. Where a system consists of a four-wire three-phase delta with midpoint of one phase grounded, Sec. 215-8(c) requires that the phase having the higher voltage to ground be orange in color or be identified by tagging or other effective means at any point where a connection is to be made if the neutral is present. The *high leg* of a 120/240-V, four-wire, three-phase delta system is 208 V to ground and to neutral (120 V × 1.73).

For many years, it has been the practice to use black-colored conductors for large feeders, with only the neutral grounded conductor identified. Although plastic insulation is now available in colors, even in the larger sizes, there is no requirement for the use of such color coding for feeders other than for the neutral, which is to be identified by white or natural gray. The color coding mentioned in Sec. 210-5 concerns branch circuits and not feeders. Definitions for "branch circuits" and for "multiwire branch circuits" are given in Art. 100.

200-7. Use of White or Natural Gray Color. A continuous white or natural gray covering on a conductor or a termination marking of white or natural gray color shall be used only for the grounded conductor.

Exception No. 1: An insulated conductor with a white or natural gray finish shall be permitted as an ungrounded conductor where permanently reidentified to indicate its use, by painting or other effective means at its termination and at each outlet where the conductor is visible and accessible.

Exception No. 2: A cable containing an insulated conductor with a white or natural gray outer finish shall be permitted for single-pole 3-way, or 4-way switch loops where the white or natural gray conductor is used for the supply to the switch, but not as a return conductor from the switch to the switched outlet. In these applications, reidentification of the white or natural gray conductor shall not be required.

Exception No. 3: A flexible cord for connecting a portable or stationary appliance having one conductor identified with a white or natural gray outer finish or by any other means permitted by Section 400-22, shall be permitted whether or not the outlet to which it is connected is supplied by a circuit having a grounded conductor.

Exception No. 4: A white or natural gray conductor of circuits of less than 50 volts shall be required to be grounded only as required by Section 250-5(a).

200-9. Means of Identification of Terminals. The identification of terminals to which a grounded conductor is to be connected shall be by means of a metallic plated coating substantially white in color, such as nickel or zinc, or the terminal material shall be substantially white in color. The other terminals shall be of a readily distinguishable different color.

200-10. Identification of Terminals.

(a) Device Terminals. All devices provided with terminals for the attachment of conductors and intended for connection to more than one side of the circuit shall have terminals properly marked for identification.

Exception No. 1: Where the electrical connection of a terminal intended to be connected to the grounded conductor is clearly evident.

Exception No. 2: Single-pole devices to which only one side of the line is connected.

Exception No. 3: The terminals of lighting and appliance branch-circuit panelboards.

Exception No. 4: Devices having a normal current rating of over 30 amperes other than polarized attachment plugs and polarized receptacles for attachment plugs as required in (b) below.

(b) Plugs, Receptacles, and Connectors. Receptacles, polarized attachment plugs and cord connectors for plugs and polarized plugs shall have the terminal intended for connection to the grounded (white) conductor identified by a metal or metal coating substantially white in color.

If the terminal for the grounded conductor is not visible, the conductor entrance hole for the connection shall be marked with the word "white."

The terminal for the connection of the equipment grounding conductor shall be identified by: (1) A green-colored, not readily removable terminal screw with a hexagonal head; (2) A green-colored hexagonal, not readily removable terminal nut; or (3) A green-colored pressure wire connector. If the terminal for the grounding conductor is not visible, the conductor entrance hole shall be marked with the word "green" or otherwise identified by a distinctive green color.

Exception: Two-wire attachment plugs shall not be required to have their terminals marked for identification.

(c) Screw-Shells. For devices with screw-shells, the terminal for the grounded conductor shall be the one connected to the screw-shell.

(d) Screw-Shell Devices with Leads. For screw-shell devices with attached leads, the conductor attached to the screw-shell shall have a white or natural gray finish. The outer finish of the other conductor shall be of a solid color that will not be confused with the white or natural gray finish used to identify the grounded conductor.

(e) Fixed Appliances. Marking of terminals for fixed appliances to indicate the proper connection to the grounded conductor shall not be required.

Exception: Where a single-pole switch forms an integral part, then the terminal connected to the switch shall be the terminal for the ungrounded conductor.

(f) Portable and Stationary Appliances. Identification marking of terminals for portable and stationary appliances shall not be required.

ARTICLE 210. BRANCH CIRCUITS

A. General Provisions

210-1. Scope. The provisions of this Article apply to branch circuits supplying lighting or appliance loads or combinations of both. Where motors or motor-operated appliances are connected to any branch circuit that also supplies lighting or other appliance loads, the provisions of both this Article and Article 430 shall apply. Article 430 applies where a branch circuit supplies motor loads only.

210-2. Other Articles for Specific-Purpose Branch Circuits. Branch circuits shall comply with this Article and also with the applicable provisions of other Articles of this Code. The provisions for branch circuits supplying equipment in the following list amend or supplement the provisions in this Article and shall apply to branch circuits referred to therein:

210-3. Classifications. Branch circuits recognized by this Article shall be classified in accordance with the maximum permitted ampere rating or setting of the over-current device. The classification for other than individual branch circuits shall be: 15, 20, 30, 40, and 50 amperes. Where conductors of higher ampacity are used for any reason, the ampere rating or setting of the specified overcurrent device shall determine the circuit classification.

▲ The size of conductor does not determine the circuit rating. For example: A circuit with 30-A conductors protected by 15-A fuses or circuit breakers is still a 15-A circuit. For the 15-, 20-, 30-, 40-, and 50-A circuits referred to above, see Sec. 210-23.

210-4. Multiwire Branch Circuits. Branch circuits recognized by this Article shall be permitted as multiwire circuits. Multiwire branch circuits shall supply only line to neutral load.

Exception No. 1: A multiwire branch circuit supplying a single appliance.

Exception No. 2: Where all ungrounded conductors of the multiwire branch circuit are opened simultaneously by the branch circuit overcurrent device.

▲ Multiwire branch circuits are most commonly three-wire circuits taken from a three-wire single-phase system.

The advantages of three-wire circuits are, first, that only three wires are required to supply a load that would require four wires if two-wire circuits were used; and, second, that, other conditions being the same, the percentage voltage drop is only one-half as great in a three-wire as in a two-wire circuit.

Three-wire circuits may be used to good advantage in simple wiring layouts in large spaces, where each circuit supplies only a few outlets. In most localities three-wire circuits are commonly used in house wiring but, where this practice is followed, special care must be taken to see that the circuits are properly balanced.

Three-phase four-wire circuits and two-phase five-wire circuits are also permissible. In a four-wire circuit the neutral wire can never be called on to carry a current heavier than the heaviest current carried by any one of the outside or phase wires, and therefore all four wires may be of the same size. In a three-wire two-phase circuit the neutral must have a carrying capacity of at least 1.41 times the ampere rating of the circuit.

It is the intent of this Code rule to require two-pole or three-pole circuit breakers or switches to disconnect loads which are hooked up line to line. It is possible to have hazardous conditions when 120-V loads are used with a line-to-line load (240 V) and such appliances are separate units. If one fuse or a single-pole circuit breaker opens, a hazardous condition is created through a series circuit of the two loads. Under these conditions all 240-V loads are subjected to 120 V. Workmen have been injured when working on circuits which were thought to be de-energized.

210-5. Color Code for Branch Circuits.

(a) Grounded Conductor. The grounded conductor of a branch circuit shall be identified by a continuous white or natural gray color. Where conductors of different systems are installed in the same raceway, box, auxiliary gutter, or other types of enclosures, one system neutral, if required, shall have an outer covering of white or natural gray. Each other system neutral, if required, shall have an outer covering of white with an identifiable colored stripe (not green) running along the insulation or other and different means of identification.

Exception: The grounded conductors of mineral-insulated metal-sheathed cable shall be identified by distinctive marking at the terminals during the process of installation.

(b) Grounding Conductor. The grounding conductor of a branch circuit shall be identified by a continuous green color or a continuous green color with one or more yellow stripes unless it is bare.

Exception No. 1: As permitted in Section 250-57(b).

Exception No. 2: The use of conductor insulation having a continuous green color or a continuous green color with one or more yellow stripes shall be permitted for internal wiring of equipment if such wiring does not serve as the lead wires for connection to branch-circuit conductors.

(c) Ungrounded Conductor. Ungrounded conductors of different voltages shall be of different color or identified by other means.

▲ Section 210-5 divides color coding of branch-circuit conductors into three categories: (a) grounded conductor; (b) grounding conductor; and (c) ungrounded conductor. The major item in paragraph (a) is the requirement concerning the use of two grounded neutral conductors from different systems in the same enclosure, such as a conduit containing a 480Y/277-V circuit and a 208Y/120 or similar lower voltage circuit. In such instances one system would use the conventional white or natural gray color for the neutral, while the other system neutral would have to be identified by the use of a white color with a colored stripe (not green) or other suitable and different means (such as labels).

This section no longer recommends the use of black, red, and blue for phase conductors of a circuit. Where there is only one system voltage the phase conductors may be any color other than green, white, or natural gray, i.e., all black conductors for the phase wires. Where there is more than one system voltage, such as 208Y/120-V and 480Y/277-V circuits, one of the systems could be identified with all black conductors. However, the other system conductors would have to be of a different color.

210-6 Maximum Voltage.

(a) Voltage to Ground. Branch circuits supplying lampholders, fixtures, or standard receptacles rated 15 amperes or less shall not exceed 150 volts to ground.

Exception No. 1: The voltage shall not exceed 300 volts to ground on branch circuits in industrial establishments where all the following conditions are met:

a. The conditions of maintenance and supervision assure that only competent individuals will service the lighting fixtures.

b. The branch circuits supply only lighting fixtures that are equipped with mogul-base screw-shell lampholders or with lampholders of other types approved for the purpose.

c. The fixtures are mounted not less than 8 feet above the floor.

d. The fixtures do not have switch control as an integral part of the fixture.

Exception No. 2: The voltage shall not exceed 300 volts to ground on branch circuits in industrial establishments, stores, health care facilities, office buildings, schools, or public and commercial areas of other buildings, such as hotels or transportation terminals, where all of the following conditions are met:

a. The branch circuits supply only the ballasts for electric-discharge lamps mounted in permanently installed fixtures.

b. The fixtures do not have manual switch control as an integral part of the fixture.

c. Electric-discharge lampholders of the screw-shell type are mounted not less than 8 feet above the floor.

Exception No. 3: For lampholders of infrared industrial heating appliances as provided in Section 422-15(c).

Exception No. 4: The railway properties as described in Section 110-19.

▲ In other than residential occupancies, 230- or 208-V two-wire circuits may be used to supply lampholders of all standard types if the circuits are taken from a 115/230-V single-phase three-wire system or a 208Y/120-V three-phase four-wire system having a grounded neutral. In industrial establishments, office buildings, schools and stores, and public and commercial areas of other buildings such as hotels or transportation terminals, the voltage to ground of lighting circuits may be as much as 300 V. This permits the use of electric-discharge ballasts at line-to-line or line-to-neutral voltages (254 to 277 V) of a three-phase four-wire 480Y/277-V system, and makes it unnecessary to use separate transformers to supply the lighting load.

Exception 1. Where the inspection authority having jurisdiction is satisfied that all repairs and maintenance of fixtures will be performed by qualified persons, fixtures approved for the application may be installed on 480Y/277-V circuits, provided they are at least 8 ft from the floor and are controlled by switches entirely separate and apart from the fixtures, i.e., by panelboard or wall switches. Fixtures approved for the application could include medium-base lampholders.

Exception 2. This permits the use of electric-discharge lamps, other than screw-shell types, on a 480Y/277-V system at less than 8 ft from the floor, provided that the fixtures are controlled by switches entirely separate and apart from the fixtures, i.e., by panelboard or wall switches.

(b) Voltage between Conductors—Poles, Tunnels, and Similar Structures. The voltage shall not exceed 500 volts between conductors on branch circuits supplying only the ballasts for electric-discharge lamps mounted in permanently installed fixtures as provided in Section 225-7(d) where the fixtures are mounted as follows:

(1) Not less than a height of 22 feet on poles or similar structures for the illumination of outdoor areas, such as highways, roads, bridges, athletic fields, or parking lots.

(2) Not less than a height of 18 feet on other structures, such as tunnels.

(c) Voltage between Conductors—Dwellings. The voltage shall not exceed 150 volts between conductors on branch circuits supplying screw-shell lampholders, receptacles, or appliances in dwelling occupancies.

Exception No. 1: Permanently connected appliances.

Exception No. 2: Portable and stationary appliances of more than 1380 watts.

Exception No. 3: Portable motor-operated appliances of $\frac{1}{4}$ horsepower or greater rating.

▲ In residential occupancies 230-V two-wire circuits may be used to supply lampholders of other than the screw-shell type, permanently connected appliances, or portable appliances of more than 1,380 W rating. Since the lampholders for fluorescent lamps are not of the screw-shell type, 230-V lamps of this type may be used in residential occupancies.

(d) Voltage Between Conductors—Nondwelling Occupancies. The voltage shall not exceed 150 volts between conductors on branch circuits supplying one or more medium-base, screw-shell lampholders in nondwelling occupancies.

See Exception No. 1 to (a) above for 300-volt limitation for mogul-base screw-shell lampholders under specific conditions in industrial establishments.

210-7. Receptacles and Cord Connectors.

(a) Grounding Type. Receptacles installed on 15- and 20-ampere branch circuits shall be of the grounding type. Grounding-type receptacles shall be installed only on circuits of the voltage class and current for which they are rated, except as provided in Tables 210-21(b)(2) and (b)(3).

Exception: Grounding-type receptacles of the type that reject nongrounding-type attachment plugs or which are of the locking type shall be permitted for specific purposes or in special locations. Receptacles required in Sections 517-61(d) and 517-62(e) shall be considered as meeting the requirements of this Section.

(b) To Be Grounded. Receptacles and cord connectors having grounding contacts shall have those contacts effectively grounded.

(c) Methods of Grounding. The grounding contacts of receptacles and cord connectors shall be grounded by connection to the equipment grounding conductor of the circuit supplying the receptacle or cord connector.

The branch circuit or branch-circuit raceway shall include or provide a grounding conductor to which the grounding contacts of the receptacle or cord connector shall be connected.

Section 250-91(b) describes acceptable grounding means.

Exception: Only for extensions of existing branch circuits that do not have an equipment grounding conductor, the grounding contact of a grounding-type receptacle shall be permitted to be grounded to a grounded cold water pipe near the equipment.

(d) Replacements. Grounding-type receptacles shall be used as replacements for existing nongrounding types and shall be connected to a grounding conductor installed in accordance with (c) above.

Exception: If it is impractical to reach a source of ground, a nongrounding-type receptacle shall be used.

▲ In all cases where a grounding-type receptacle is installed, it shall be grounded. For nonmetallic-sheathed cable the grounding conductor is run with the branch-circuit conductors. The armor of Type AC metal-clad cable, the sheath of ALS cable, and certain metallic raceways are acceptable as grounding means.

The purpose here is to make certain that grounding-type receptacles are used and grounded where a ground is available, and nongrounding-type receptacles are used where grounding is impractical so that no one will be deceived as to the availability of a grounding means for appliances.

In order to prevent the improper interpretation of the intent of this requirement, some explanatory wording was included, which reads, "the installation of grounding-type outlets shall not be used as a requirement that all portable equipment be of the grounding type."

There are some appliances, such as a toaster, in which grounding of the enclosure could introduce an additional hazard. For example, where a fork is used to retrieve a small-diameter bread slice or English muffin that cannot easily be lifted out by hand, the possibility is present that the "live" element may be contacted, and if the person and the enclosure are not grounded, no shock or electrical fault will result. If the enclosure is grounded, the possibility of a shock or burn from a fault becomes substantial.

This approach to providing adequate grounding only where needed is based on the recommendations of a technical subcommittee of the National Electrical Code Committee made up of a membership representing all of the major segments of the electrical industry.

One of the major problems in reducing electric-shock accidents is the education of users of electrical equipment to understand the causes of electric shock, the functioning of a grounding conductor, and the need to maintain its integrity. Misuse of electrical equipment is one of the leading causes of electric shock.

(e) Portable Equipment. The installation of grounding-type receptacles shall not be used as a requirement that all portable equipment be of the grounded type.

See Section 250-45 for type of portable equipment to be grounded.

▲ It should be recognized that the replacement of an attachment plug or flexible cord on a grounded-type portable appliance necessitates a knowledge of the conductor identification in order to avoid connections that create a shock hazard rather than provide the intended protection.

Section 250-45 indicates the conditions under which cord-connected equipment needs to be grounded.

The obvious purpose is to have grounding-type receptacles conveniently located for general use so that any appliance which needs to be grounded can be grounded by simply connecting the attachment plug to the receptacle. It is realized that there are millions of receptacles in current use which are not of the grounded type and that it will take a long time to arrive at the point where even most of the general-use receptacles on 15- and 20-A circuits are of the grounded type. In the interim, it will be necessary to use an adapter or other means to achieve grounding of a cord-connected appliance which is supplied from a nongrounded-type receptacle.

Double-insulated tools and appliances, and ground-fault protection for personnel, offer a high degree of protection from shock hazards.

(f) Noninterchangeable Types. Receptacles connected to circuits having different voltages, frequencies, or types of current (AC or DC) on the same premises shall be of such design that the attachment plugs used on these circuits are not interchangeable.

210-8. Ground-Fault Circuit Protection.

(a) Residential Occupancies. For residential occupancies all 120-volt, single-phase, 15- and 20-ampere receptacle outlets installed outdoors and in bathrooms shall have ground-fault circuit protection for personnel.

Such ground-fault circuit protection may be provided for other circuits, locations, and occupancies, and where used, will provide additional protection against line-to-ground shock hazard.

See Section 215-9 for feeder protection.

		15 ampere		20 ampere		30 ampere		50 ampere		60 ampere	
		Receptacle	Plug	Receptacle	Plug	Receptacle	Plug	Receptacle	Plug	Receptacle	Plug
2-pole 2-wire	[1] 125V		1-15P*								
	[2] 250V		2-15P	2-20R	2-20P	2-30R	2-30P				
	[3] 277V AC	(Reserved for future configurations)									
	[4] 600V	(Reserved for future configurations)									
2-pole 3-wire grounding	[5] 125V	5-15R	5-15P	5-20R	5-20P	5-30R	5-30P	5-50R	5-50P		
	[6] 250V	6-15R	6-15P	6-20R	6-20P	6-30R	6-30P	6-50R	6-50P		
	[7] 277V AC	7-15R	7-15P	7-20R	7-20P	7-30R	7-30P	7-50R	7-50P		
	[8] 480V AC	(Reserved for future configurations)									
	[9] 600V AC	(Reserved for future configurations)									
3-pole 3-wire	[10] 125/250V			10-20R	10-20P	10-30R	10-30P	10-50R	10-50P		
	[11] 3∅ 250V	11-15R	11-15P	11-20R	11-20P	11-30R	11-30P	11-50R	11-50P		
	[12] 3∅ 480V	(Reserved for future configurations)									
	[13] 3∅ 600V	(Reserved for future configurations)									
3-pole 4-wire grounding	[14] 125/250V	14-15R	14-15P	14-20R	14-20P	14-30R	14-30P	14-50R	14-50P	14-60R	14-60P
	[15] 3∅ 250V	15-15R	15-15P	15-20R	15-20P	15-30R	15-30P	15-50R	15-50P	15-60R	15-60P
	[16] 3∅ 480V	(Reserved for future configurations)									
	[17] 3∅ 600V	(Reserved for future configurations)									
4-pole 4-wire	[18] 3∅Y 120/208V	18-15R	18-15P	18-20R	18-20P	18-30R	18-30P	18-50R	18-50P	18-60R	18-60P
	[19] 3∅Y 277/480V	(Reserved for future configurations)									
	[20] 3∅Y 347/600V	(Reserved for future configurations)									
4-pole 5-wire grounding	[21] 3∅Y 120/208V	(Reserved for future configurations)									
	[22] 3∅Y 277/480V	(Reserved for future configurations)									
	[23] 3∅Y 347/600V	(Reserved for future configurations)									

* Represents configuration number.

FIG. 210-1. Configuration chart for general-purpose nonlocking plugs and receptacles; taken from ANSI C73 Standard.

			15 ampere		20 ampere		30 ampere	
			Receptacle	Plug	Receptacle	Plug	Receptacle	Plug
2-pole 2-wire	125 V	L1	L1-15R	L1-15P				
	250 V	L2			L2-20R	L2-20P		
	277 V AC	L3	F	U	T	U	R	E
	600 V	L4	F	U	T	U	R	E
2-pole 3-wire grounding	125 V	L5	L5-15R	L5-15P	L5-20R	L5-20P	L5-30R	L5-30P
	250 V	L6	L6-15R	L6-15P	L6-20R	L6-20P	L6-30R	L6-30P
	277 V AC	L7	L7-15R	L7-15P	L7-20R	L7-20P	L7-30R	L7-30P
	480 V AC	L8			L8-20R	L8-20P	L8-30R	L8-30P
	600 V AC	L9			L9-20R	L9-20P	L9-30R	L9-30P
3-pole 3-wire	125/250 V	L10			L10-20R	L10-20P	L10-30R	L10-30P
	3φ 250 V	L11	L11-15R	L11-15P	L11-20R	L11-20P	L11-30R	L11-30P
	3φ 480 V	L12			L12-20R	L12-20P	L12-30R	L12-30P
	3φ 600 V	L13					L13-30R	L13-30P
3-pole 4-wire grounding	125/250 V	L14			L14-20R	L14-20P	L14-30R	L14-30P
	3φ 250 V	L15			L15-20R	L15-20P	L15-30R	L15-30P
	3φ 480 V	L16			L16-20R	L16-20P	L16-30R	L16-30P
	3φ 600 V	L17					L17-30R	L17-30P
4-pole 4-wire	3φ 208Y/120 V	L18			L18-20R	L18-20P	L18-30R	L18-30P
	3φ 480Y/277 V	L19			L19-20R	L19-20P	L19-30R	L19-30P
	3φ 600Y/347 V	L20			L20-20R	L20-20P	L20-30R	L20-30P
4-pole 5-wire grounding	3φ 208Y/120 V	L21			L21-20R	L21-20P	L21-30R	L21-30P
	3φ 480Y/277 V	L22			L22-20R	L22-20P	L22-30R	L22-30P
	3φ 600Y/347 V	L23			L23-20R	L23-20P	L23-30R	L23-30P

FIG. 210-2. Configuration chart for specific-purpose nonlocking plugs and receptacles; taken from ANSI C73 Standard.

(b) Construction Sites. All 120-volt single phase 15 and 20 ampere receptacle outlets which are not a part of the permanent wiring of the building or structure, shall have ground-fault circuit-interrupters for personnel protection.

Exception: Receptacles on a portable generator rated not more than 5 kW, where the circuit conductors of the generator are insulated from earth and the generator frame is insulated from earth and all grounded surfaces.

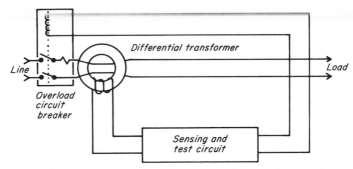

Fɪɢ. 210-3. Circuit arrangement of a typical ground-fault circuit-interrupter for personnel protection. (*Pass & Seymour, Inc.*)

▲ Figure 210-3 shows a typical arrangement of a personnel ground-fault circuit-interrupter (GFCI). The incoming two-wire circuit is connected to a two-pole, shunt-trip overload circuit breaker. The load-side conductors pass through a differential transformer. As long as the current in both load wires is equal, the circuit functions normally. If one of the conductors becomes in contact with a grounded condition or passes through a person's body to ground, an unbalanced current is established. This unbalanced current is picked up by the differential transformer, and a circuit is established through the sensing circuit to energize the shunt trip of the overload circuit breaker and quickly open the main circuit. Present settings are set to operate when line-to-ground currents reach 5 mA ($\pm$ 1), which is in line with present standards of Underwriters' Laboratories, Inc. (5 mA $\pm$ 1, i.e., 4 to 6 mA). Even at trips of 5 mA, it should be clearly understood that instantaneous current will be higher and any shock during the time the fault is being cleared will not feel comfortable. A shock at 5 mA is not pleasant either. The advantage of GFCI is the time-current characteristic. Trip-out time is about $\frac{1}{40}$ of a second (25 milliseconds) when the fault reaches or exceeds 5 mA. It should also be understood that the GFCI does not operate on phast-to-phase faults. Experience has shown that certain precautions must be taken to aid the efficient operation of GFCIs on construction sites. The principle of operation of a GFCI dictates that current to a load on the "hot" conductor must return to ground by returning on the "neutral" conductor, with less than 5 mA current returning by a different parallel path. Tests have shown that 500 ft of wire (250 ft out and 250 ft back) subjected to swimming pool conditions would probably be sufficient to trip a "Class A GFCI" (5-mA trip). Most appliances listed by Underwriters' Laboratories, Inc., have 0.5-mA leakage or less under normal operating conditions; however, moisture and improper maintenance on portable hand-held tools can create conditions under which GFCIs can be expected to trip. Portable cords with standard cap and connector connections when dropped in casual water, such as puddles on construction sites, can be expected to cause leakage currents (100 to 300 mA or greater) far in excess of GFCI trip currents. Motors with dirty brushes, carbon-tracking on commutators, or moisture in the windings contribute to leakage current. A common-sense approach to using and maintaining GFCI circuits would do much toward eliminating the so-called "nuisance tripping." Tripping under any of the above conditions is not "nuisance tripping," but proper performance of the device. It has been shown that moisture is the major culprit in current leakage on wiring and equipment. Panelboards, receptacles, and cord caps and connectors intended for dry locations should not be subjected to moisture. Construction receptacles should be centrally located to enable cords of 150 ft or less to be used, with a sufficient number of circuits used to keep the number of tools on a circuit to a minimum. Receptacles should not be on the same circuit as lighting or other uses. Maintenance of all motors used on construction sites should be performed periodically.

Figures 210-5 and 210-6 show receptacles and branch-circuit breakers with built-in ground-fault protection. Current UL-listed GFCIs are presently available in the units shown in Figs. 210-4, 210-5 and 210-6. Such units contain a *test switch* so that the unit can be checked periodically to ensure continued safety.

210-9. Circuits Derived from Autotransformers.   Branch circuits shall not be supplied by autotransformers.

Exception No. 1: Where the system supplied has a grounded conductor that is electrically connected to a grounded conductor of the system supplying the autotransformer.

Exception No. 2: An autotransformer used to extend or add an individual branch

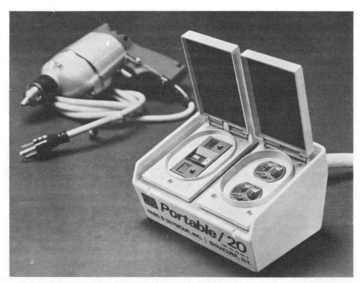

FIG. 210-4. A ground-fault circuit-interrupter for personnel protection. See Fig. 210-3 for circuit arrangement. (*Pass & Seymour, Inc.*)

FIG. 210-5. Duplex receptacle, rated 15 amps, 125 volts, with built-in ground-fault circuit-interrupter. Load wires are also protected by GFCI. (*Pass & Seymour, Inc.*)

FIG. 210-6. Plug-in circuit breaker (15-, 20-, or 30-amp single pole) with built-in ground-fault circuit-interrupter. Jumper lead connects to neutral bar in panelboard. (*Square D Co.*)

circuit in an existing installation for an equipment load without the connection to a similar identified grounded conductor when transforming from a nominal 208 volts to a nominal 240-volt supply or similarly from 240 volts to 208 volts.

An autotransformer is a transformer in which a part of the winding is common to both primary and secondary circuits.

▲ Figure 210-7 shows how a 110-V system for lighting may be derived from a 220-V system by means of an autotransformer. The 220-V system either may be single phase or may be one leg of a three-phase system.

In Fig. 210-8 an autotransformer is used to derive a three-wire 110/220-V system for lighting from a 220-V system.

In both of the cases illustrated by Figs. 210-7 and 210-8 the "supplied" system has a grounded wire solidly connected to a grounded wire of the "supplying" system; 220-V single-phase systems with one conductor grounded and 220-V, three-phase, three-wire systems with one conductor grounded are not commonly used; hence it is not often possible to make use of either one of the arrangements shown in the figures.

Autotransformers are commonly used to supply reduced voltage for starting induction motors.

The exception permits the use of an autotransformer in existing installations for

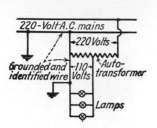

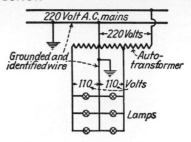

Fig. 210-7. Autotransformer used to derive a two-wire 110-V system for lighting from a 220-V power system.

Fig. 210-8. Autotransformer used to derive a three-wire 110/220-V system for lighting from a 220-V system.

an individual branch circuit without connection to a similar identified grounded conductor where transforming from 208 to 240 V or vice versa. Typical applications are with cooking equipment, heaters, motors, and air-conditioning equipment. For such applications *buck or boost* transformers are commonly used.

Buck or boost transformers are designed for use on single- or three-phase circuits to supply 12/24- or 16/32-V secondaries with a 120/240-V primary. When connected as autotransformers the kVA load they will handle is large in comparison to their physical size and relative cost. Figures 210-9 and 210-10 show typical autotransformer connections for single- and three-phase loads. As shown in Fig. 210-9, a 5-kVA buck or boost transformer will handle equipment rated up to 32 kVA. For open-delta

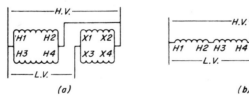

Fig. 210-9. Typical buck or boost transformers connected as autotransformers for changing 240 V single phase to 208 V or vice versa.

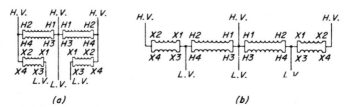

Fig. 210-10. Typical buck or boost transformers connected in three-phase open delta as autotransformers for changing 240 to 208 V or vice versa.

connections, as shown in Fig. 210-10, two 5-kVA buck or boost transformers will handle equipment rated up to 56 kVA.

Complete information on buck or boost transformers may be obtained from manufacturers of such equipment.

210-10. Ungrounded Conductors Tapped from Grounded Systems. Two-wire dc circuits and ac circuits of two or more ungrounded conductors shall be permitted to be tapped from the ungrounded conductors of circuits having a grounded neutral conductor. Switching devices in each tapped circuit shall have a pole in each ungrounded conductor. All poles of multipole switching devices shall manually switch together where such switching devices also serve as a disconnecting means as required by Sections 422-21(b) and 422-23(b) for an appliance: 424-20 for a fixed electric space heating unit; 426-21 for electric de-icing and snow melting equipment; 430-85 for a motor controller; and 430-103 for a motor.

▲ This permits the use of two-wire branch circuits tapped from the outside conductors of any of the following systems, where the neutral is grounded: three-wire DC or single-phase, four-wire three-phase, and five-wire two-phase systems.

Figures 210-11 and 210-12 illustrate the use of unidentified two-wire branch circuits to supply small motors, the circuits being tapped from the outside conductors of a three-wire DC or single-phase system (Fig. 210-11) and a four-wire three-phase wye system (Fig. 210-12).

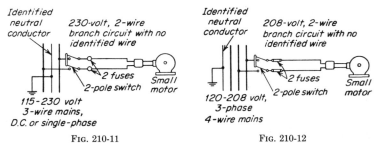

FIG. 210-11   FIG. 210-12

FIGS. 210-11 and 210-12. Unidentified branch circuits tapped from the outside conductors of multiwire systems.

All poles of the disconnecting means used for branch circuits supplying stationary appliances shall be operated at the same time. This requirement applies where the circuit is supplied by either circuit breakers or switches.

In the case of fuses and switches, when a fuse blows in one pole, the other pole may not necessarily open and the requirement to "manually switch together" involves only the manual operation of the switch. Similarly, when a pair of circuit breakers is connected with handle ties, an overload on one of the conductors with the return circuit through the neutral may open only one of the circuit breakers; but the manual operation of the pair when used as a disconnecting means will open both poles. The words "manually switched together" should be considered as "operating at the same time," that is, during the same operating interval, and apply to the equipment used as a disconnecting means and not as an overcurrent protective device. While there may be some slight difference in the opening instant for circuit breakers connected by handle ties, this is of no consequence; and even where a two-pole breaker may have a common trip, both poles may not open at exactly the same instant.

Circuit breakers with handle ties are, therefore, considered as providing the disconnection required by this section.

The requirement in paragraph (a) to "manually switch together" can be achieved by a "master handle" or "handle tie" since the operation is intended to be effected by manual operation. The intent was not to require a common trip for the switching device but to require that it have the ability to disconnect ungrounded conductors by one movement of the hand. For service disconnecting means see Sec. 230-71.

B. Specific Requirements

210-19. Conductors—Minimum Ampacity and Size.

(a) General. Branch-circuit conductors shall have an ampacity of not less than the rating of the branch circuit and not less than the maximum load to be served. Cable assemblies with the neutral conductor smaller than the ungrounded conductors shall be so marked.

See Tables 310-16 through 310-19 for ampacity ratings of conductors.
See Part B of Article 430 for minimum rating of motor branch-circuit conductors.
Conductors for branch circuits as defined in Article 100, sized to prevent a voltage drop exceeding 3 percent at the farthest outlet of power, heating, and lighting loads, or combinations of such loads and where the maximum total voltage drop on both feeders and branch circuits to the farthest outlet does not exceed 5 percent, will provide reasonable efficiency of operation. See Section 215-2(c) for voltage drop on feeder conductors.

(b) Household Ranges and Cooking Appliances. Branch-circuit conductors supplying household ranges, wall-mounted ovens, counter-mounted cooking units, and other household cooking appliances shall have an ampacity not less than the rating of the branch circuit and not less than the maximum load to be served. The minimum size shall not be smaller than No. 8 for ranges of $8\frac{3}{4}$ kW or more rating.

Exception No. 1: The neutral conductor of a 3-wire branch circuit supplying a household electric range, a wall-mounted oven, or a counter-mounted cooking unit shall be permitted to be smaller than the ungrounded conductors where the maximum demand of a range of $8\frac{3}{4}$ kW or more rating has been computed according to Column A of Table 220-19, but shall have an ampacity of not less than 70 percent of the ampacity of the ungrounded conductors and shall not be smaller than No. 10.

▲ The maximum demand for a range of 12 kW rating or less may be considered as 8 kW. 8,000 W divided by 230 V is approximately 35 A. Therefore, No. 8 conductors may be used for the range branch circuit. On modern ranges the heating elements of surface units are controlled by five-heat unit switches. The surface-unit heating elements will not draw current from the neutral unless the unit switch is in one of the low-heating positions. This is also true to a greater degree as far as the oven-heating elements are concerned, so that the maximum current in the neutral of the range circuit seldom exceeds 20 A. Exception 1 permits a smaller-size neutral than the ungrounded conductors, but not smaller than No. 10.

Exception No. 2: Tap conductors supplying electric ranges, wall-mounted electric ovens, and counter-mounted electric cooking units from a 50-ampere branch circuit shall have an ampacity of not less than 20 and shall be sufficient for the load to be served. The taps shall be no longer than necessary for servicing the appliance.

▲ This would permit a 50-A branch circuit to be run to counter-mounted electric cooking units and wall-mounted electric ovens. The tap to each unit must be as short as possible and should be made in a junction box immediately adjacent to each unit. The words "no longer than necessary for servicing the appliance" mean that it should be necessary only to move the unit to one side in order that the splices in the junction box be accessible.

(c) Other Loads. Branch-circuit conductors supplying loads other than cooking appliances as covered in (b) above and as listed in Section 210-2 shall have an ampacity sufficient for the loads served and shall not be smaller than No. 14.

Exception No. 1: Tap conductors for such loads shall have an ampacity not less than 15 for circuits rated less than 40 amperes and not less than 20 for circuits rated at 40 or 50 amperes and only where these tap conductors supply any of the following loads:

a. Individual lampholders or fixtures with taps extending not longer than 18 inches beyond any portion of the lampholder or fixture.

b. A fixture having branch-circuit terminal connections operating at a temperature in excess of 60° C having tap conductors not longer than 6 feet as provided in Section 410-67(b) (2).

c. Individual outlets with taps not over 18 inches long.

d. Infrared lamp industrial heating appliances.

e. Nonheating leads of de-icing and snow melting cables and mats.

▲ No. 14 wire, not longer than 18 in., may be used to supply an outlet unless the circuit is a 40- or 50-A branch circuit, in which event the minimum size of the tap conductor must be No. 12.

Exception No. 2: Fixture wires and cords as permitted in Section 240-4.

210-20. Overcurrent Protection.

(a) General. Branch-circuit conductors and equipment shall be protected by overcurrent protective devices having a rating or setting (1) not exceeding that specified in Section 240-3 for conductors; (2) not exceeding that specified in the applicable Articles referenced in Section 240-2 for equipment; and (3) as provided for outlet devices in Section 210-21.

Exception: Tap conductors, fixture wire, and cords as permitted in Section 210-19(c) shall be considered as being protected by the circuit overcurrent device.

See Section 240-1 for the purpose of overcurrent protection and Sections 210-22 and 220-2 for continuous loads.

210-21. Outlet Devices. Outlet devices shall have an ampere rating not less than the load to be served and shall comply with (a) and (b) below.

(a) Lampholders. Where connected to a branch circuit having a rating in excess of 20 amperes, lampholders shall be of the heavy-duty type. A heavy-duty lampholder shall have a rating of not less than 660 watts if of the admedium type and not less than 750 watts if of any other type.

▲ The intent is to limit the rating of lighting branch circuits supplying fluorescent fixtures to 20 A. The ballast is connected to the branch circuit rather than the lamp, but by controlling the lampholder rating, a 20-A limit is established for the ballast circuit. Most lampholders manufactured and intended for use with electric-discharge lighting for illumination purposes are rated less than 750 W, and are not classified as heavy-duty lampholders.

(b) Receptacles.

(1) A single receptacle installed on an individual branch circuit shall have an ampere rating of not less than that of the branch circuit.

See definition of Receptacle in Article 100.

(2) Where connected to a branch circuit supplying two or more receptacles or outlets, a receptacle shall not supply a total portable and/or stationary appliance load in excess of the maximum specified in Table 210-21(b) (2).

Table 210-21(b)(2). Maximum Portable and/or Stationary Appliance Load to Receptacle

Circuit Rating Amperes	Receptacle Rating Amperes	Maximum Load Amperes
15 or 20	15	12
20	20	16
30	30	24

(3) Where connected to a branch circuit supplying two or more receptacles or outlets, receptacle ratings shall conform to the values listed in Table 210-21(b) (3).

(4) It shall be acceptable to base the ampere rating of a range receptacle on a single range demand load specified in Table 220-19.

210-22. Maximum Loads. The total load shall not exceed the rating of the branch circuit, and it shall not exceed the maximum loads specified in (a) through (c) below under the conditions specified therein.

(a) Motor-Operated and Combination Loads. Where a circuit supplies only

Table 210-21(b)(3). Receptacle Ratings for Various Size Circuits

Circuit Rating Amperes	Receptacle Rating Amperes
15	Not over 15
20	15 or 20
30	30
40	40 or 50
50	50

motor-operated loads, Article 430 shall apply. Where a circuit supplies only air conditioning and/or refrigerating equipment, Article 440 shall apply. For circuits supplying loads consisting of motor-operated appliances of other than the portable or stationary type having a motor larger than $\frac{1}{8}$ hp in combination with other loads, the total computed load shall be based on 125 percent of the largest motor load plus the sum of the other loads.

(b) Inductive Lighting Loads. For circuits supplying lighting units having ballasts, transformers, or autotransformers, the computed load shall be based on the total ampere ratings of such units and not on the total watts of the lamps.

(c) Other Loads. Continuous loads, such as store lighting and similar loads, shall not exceed 80 percent of the rating of the branch circuit.

Exception No. 1: Motor loads having demand factors computed in accordance with Article 430.

Exception No. 2: Circuits that have been derated in accordance with Note 8 to Tables 310-16 through 310-19.

Exception No. 3: Circuits supplied by an assembly together with its overcurrent devices that is listed for continuous operation at 100 percent of its rating.

It shall be acceptable to apply demand factors for range loads in accordance with Table 220-19, including Note 4.

▲ Where the load of a branch circuit is expected to be continuous, such as in stores, hotel lobbies, and places of public gathering, such loads must not exceed 80 percent of circuit rating unless Exception No. 3 is applied. The term "Continuous Load" is defined as three hours or more in Art. 100, Definitions.

210-23. Permissible Loads. In no case shall the load exceed the branch-circuit ampere rating. It shall be acceptable for an individual branch circuit to supply any load for which it is rated. A branch circuit supplying two or more outlets shall supply only the loads specified according to its size in (a) through (c) below and summarized in Section 210-24 and Table 210-24.

(a) 15- and 20-Ampere Branch Circuits. A 15- or 20-ampere branch circuit shall be permitted to supply lighting units, appliances, or a combination of both. The rating of any one portable or stationary appliance shall not exceed 80 percent of the branch-circuit ampere rating. The total rating of fixed appliances shall not exceed 50 percent of the branch-circuit ampere rating where lighting units, portable or stationary appliances, or both are also supplied.

Exception: The small appliance branch circuits required in dwellings by Section 220-3(b) shall supply only the receptacle outlets specified in that Section.

▲ *Example:* 50 percent of a 15-A branch circuit = 7.5 A. A room-air-conditioning unit fastened in place, with a rating not in excess of 7.5 A may be installed on a 15-A circuit having two or more outlets. Such units may not be installed on one of the small-appliance branch circuits required in Sec. 220-3(b).

(b) 25- and 30-Ampere Branch Circuits. A 25- or 30-ampere branch circuit shall be permitted to supply fixed lighting units with heavy-duty lampholders in other than dwelling occupancies or appliances in any occupancy. The rating of any one portable or stationary appliance shall not exceed 80 percent of the branch circuit ampere rating.

(c) 40- and 50-Ampere Branch Circuits. A 40- or 50-ampere branch circuit shall be permitted to supply fixed lighting units with heavy-duty lampholders or infrared heating units in other than dwelling occupancies, or fixed cooking appliances in any occupancy.

The term "fixed" as used in this Section recognizes cord connections where otherwise permitted.

▲ Except as permitted in Sec. 660-4 for portable, mobile, and transportable medical x-ray equipment, branch circuits having two or more outlets may supply only the loads specified in each of the above categories. It should be noted that any other circuit is not permitted to have more than one outlet and would be an individual branch circuit.

210-24. Branch-Circuit Requirements—Summary. The requirements for circuits having two or more outlets, other than the receptacle circuits of Section 220-3(b) as specifically provided for above, are summarized in Table 210-24.

▲ Table 210-24 summarizes the requirements for the size of conductors where two or more outlets are supplied. The asterisk note also indicates that these ampacities are for copper conductors where derating is not required. Where more than three

Table 210-24. Summary of Branch-Circuit Requirements

(Type FEP, FEPB, RUW, SA, T, TW, RH, RUH, RHW, RHH, THHN, THW, THWN, and XHHW conductors in raceway or cable.)

CIRCUIT RATING	15 Amp	20 Amp	30 Amp	40 Amp	50 Amp
CONDUCTORS: (Min. Size)					
Circuit Wires*	14	12	10	8	6
Taps	14	14	14	12	12
Fixture Wires and Cords			Refer to Section 240-4		
OVERCURRENT PROTECTION	15 Amp	20 Amp	30 Amp	40 Amp	50 Amp
OUTLET DEVICES:					
Lampholders Permitted	Any Type	Any Type	Heavy Duty	Heavy Duty	Heavy Duty
Receptacle Rating**	15 Max. Amp	15 or 20 Amp	30 Amp	40 or 50 Amp	50 Amp
MAXIMUM LOAD	15 Amp	20 Amp	30 Amp	40 Amp	50 Amp
PERMISSIBLE LOAD	Refer to Section 210–23(a)	Refer to Section 210–23(a)	Refer to Section 210–23(b)	Refer to Section 210–23(c)	Refer to Section 210–23(c)

* These ampacities are for copper conductors where derating is not required. See Tables 310–16 through 310–19.
** For receptacle rating of cord-connected electric-discharge lighting fixtures see Section 410-14.

conductors are contained in a raceway or a cable, Note 8 to Tables 310-16 through 310-19 specifies the derating factors to apply for the number of conductors involved. A 20-A branch circuit is required to have conductors which have an ampacity of 20 A after derating and also must have the overcurrent protection rated 20 A where the branch circuit supplies two or more outlets. If four of these branch-circuit conductors are placed in a conduit they would need to have an ampacity of 20 A after derating. Thus, 4 No. 10 AWG type TW copper conductors derated to 80 percent would have a rating of 24 A and be acceptable for the 20-A multioutlet branch circuit.

Where an individual branch circuit supplies only one load, the conductors can be selected on the basis that the maximum allowable load current after derating is not exceeded. Thus, if four branch-circuit conductors supplying individual loads are placed in a conduit, the maximum allowable load current of each conductor could not exceed 16 A. If the maximum load was 16 A or less, it would then be permissible to use No. 12 AWG Type TW with a 20-A overcurrent device.

210-25. Receptacle Outlets Required. Receptacle outlets shall be installed where specified in (a) through (c) below.

A cord connector that is supported by a permanently connected cord pendant shall be considered a receptacle outlet.

(a) General. Where flexible cords are used.

Exception: Where flexible cords are specifically permitted to be permanently connected, and are so connected in boxes or fittings approved for the purpose, it shall be acceptable to omit receptacles on such equipment.

See Article 400 for use and installation of flexible cords.

▲ Plugging a portable cord into a lampholder is not permissible. See Sec. 410-47.

(b) Dwelling-Type Occupancies. In every kitchen, family room, dining room, breakfast room, living room, parlor, library, den, sun room, bedroom, recreation room, or similar rooms, receptacle outlets shall be installed so that no point along the floor line in any wall space is more than 6 feet, measured horizontally, from an outlet in that space, including any wall space 2 feet or more in width and the wall space occupied by sliding panels in exterior walls. The wall space afforded by fixed room dividers, such as free-standing bar-type counters, shall be included in the 6-foot measurement.

In kitchen and dining areas a receptacle outlet shall be installed at each counter space wider than 12 inches. Counter top spaces separated by range tops, refrigerators, or sinks shall be considered as separate counter top spaces. Receptacles rendered inaccessible by the installation of stationary appliances shall not be considered as these required outlets.

Receptacle outlets shall, insofar as practicable, be spaced equal distances apart. Receptacle outlets in floors shall not be counted as part of the required number of receptacle outlets unless located close to the wall.

At least one wall receptacle outlet shall be installed in the bathroom adjacent to the basin location.

For a one-family dwelling, at least one receptacle outlet shall be installed outdoors.

▲ In determining the location of a receptacle outlet, the measurement is to be made along the floor line of the wall and is to continue around corners of the room, but is not to extend across doorways, archways, fireplaces, passageways, or other space unsuitable for having a flexible cord extended across it.

At least one receptacle outlet shall be installed in each basement and attached garage.

Outlets in other sections of the dwelling for special appliances, such as laundry equipment, shall be placed within 6 feet of the intended location of the appliance.

At least one receptacle outlet shall be installed for the laundry.

Exception No. 1: In a dwelling unit that is an apartment or living area in a multifamily building where laundry facilities are provided on the premises that are available to all building occupants, a laundry receptacle shall not be required.

Exception No. 2: In other than single-family dwellings where laundry facilities are not to be installed or permitted, a laundry receptacle shall not be required.

Exception No. 3: A dwelling that is a unit in a hotel, motel, motor court, or motor hotel, a laundry receptacle shall not be required.

▲ The location of outlets for special appliances within 6 ft of the appliance does not affect the spacing of general-use convenience outlets but merely adds a requirement for special-use outlets.

Figure 210-13 shows two wall sections 9 ft and 3 ft wide extending from the same

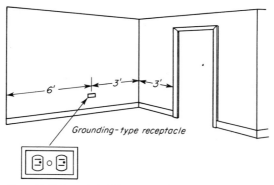

Grounding-type receptacle

Fig. 210-13. Location of the receptacle as shown will permit the plugging in of a lamp or appliance located 6 ft on either side of the receptacle.

corner of the room. The receptacle shown located in the wider section of the wall will permit the plugging in of a lamp or appliance located within 6 ft of either side of the receptacle. The same rule would apply to the other wall shown.

Receptacle outlets shall be provided for all wall space within the room except individual isolated sections which are less than 2 ft in width. For example, a wall space 23 in. wide and located between two doors would not need a receptacle outlet.

Sliding panels in exterior walls are counted the same as regular wall space, and a floor-type receptacle can be used to meet the required spacing.

It is considered more desirable and safer to have an outlet at these locations than to run extension cords which may in many instances have to cross a passageway used in connection with the sliding glass door or panel.

The reference to "sliding panels" in exterior walls is not based on whether or not the structure is called a wall, but rather on the less-defined term *wall space*. This was intended to convey the thought of locations wherein portable lamps and other electrical appliances might be used in normal occupancy conditions where these lamps or appliances could be connected by means of the normally supplied 6-ft flexible cord without requiring the use of extension cords.

In residential bathrooms a wall receptacle outlet must be installed adjacent to the wash basin. Fixtures that contain a receptacle are not considered to be a "wall receptacle outlet."

Receptacles installed behind stationary appliances, such as refrigerators or freezers, are inaccessible to the user, and they are not counted as one of the *required* receptacles in determining the minimum number in a given room.

As used in this Section a "wall space" shall be considered a wall unbroken along the floor line by doorways, fireplaces, and similar openings. Each wall space two or more feet wide shall be treated individually and separately from other wall spaces within the room. A wall space shall be permitted to include two or more walls of a room (around corners) where unbroken at the floor line.

The purpose of this requirement is to minimize the use of cords across doorways, fireplaces, and similar openings.

The receptacle outlets required by this Section shall be in addition to any receptacle that is part of any lighting fixture or appliance, located within cabinets or cupboards, or located over $5\frac{1}{2}$ feet above the floor.

(c) Guest Rooms. Guest rooms in hotels, motels, and similar occupancies shall have receptacle outlets installed in accordance with (b) above.

Exception: In rooms of hotels and motels, receptacle outlets may be located convenient for the permanent furniture layout.

(d) Show Windows. At least one receptacle outlet shall be installed directly above a show window for each 12 linear feet or major fraction thereof of show window area measured horizontally at its maximum width.

▲ The requirement for receptacles in show windows is to accommodate portable signs and similar displays. A show window measuring 32 ft along the horizontal base would require three receptacles (32/12 = 2.66 or 3), spaced not more than 12 linear ft apart directly above the show window.

210-26. Lighting Outlets Required. Lighting outlets shall be installed where specified in (a) and (b) below:

(a) Dwelling-Type Occupancies. At least one wall switch controlled lighting outlet shall be installed in every habitable room; in hallways, stairways, and attached garages; and at outdoor entrances.

At least one lighting outlet shall be installed in an attic, underfloor space, utility room and basement where used for storage or containing equipment requiring servicing.

Exception No. 1: In habitable rooms, other than kitchens or bathrooms, one or more receptacles controlled by a wall switch shall be permitted in lieu of lighting outlets.

Exception No. 2: In hallways, stairways, and at outdoor entrances remote, central, or automatic control of lighting shall be permitted.

▲ In applying this exception, care should be taken to ensure that the original intent of this Code requirement is met. The intent of the requirements for lighting outlets in dwelling-type occupancies is to ensure the safe movement of occupants through livable areas of an occupancy. Accidents are caused by persons groping around in the dark, and it is essential that paths of illumination be provided. In multifamily dwellings it is sometimes impractical to install switches in hallways, stairways, and outdoor entrances because of pranksters who turn the switches off. Under these conditions it is necessary to install the control switches so as to be accessible only to the party responsible for keeping these areas illuminated. In the case of single-family dwellings, it is necessary that switches be installed at all of these points in order to meet the original intent of providing illumination.

(b) Guest Rooms. At least one wall switch controlled lighting outlet or wall switch controlled receptacle shall be installed in guest rooms in hotels, motels, or similar occupancies.

ARTICLE 215. FEEDERS

215-1. Scope. This Article covers the installation requirements and minimum size and ampacity of conductors for feeders supplying branch-circuit loads as computed in accordance with Article 220. The requirements of Section 215-8 shall apply to feeders and other applications where identification is equally necessary.

▲ This article deals with the determination of the minimum sizes of feeder conductors necessary for safety. Overloading of conductors may result in insulation breakdowns due to overheating; overheating of switches, bus-bars, and terminals; the blowing of fuses and consequent overfusing; excessive voltage drop and excessive copper losses. Thus the overloading will in many cases create a fire risk and is sure to result in very unsatisfactory service.

The actual maximum load on a feeder depends upon the total load connected to the feeder and the demand factor. If at certain times the entire connected load is in operation, the demand factor is 100 percent; i.e., the maximum load, or maximum demand, is equal to the total connected load. If the heaviest load ever carried is only one-half the total connected load, the demand factor is 50 percent. The actual load on a feeder can best be determined by a recording ammeter.

A feeder must not be smaller than No. 10 under any of the following conditions:

Feeder	Branch circuits supplied
Two-wire	Two or more two-wire circuits
Three-wire	Three or more two-wire circuits
Three-wire	Two or more three-wire circuits

Nominal Voltage

For uniform application of the provisions of Arts. 210 and 220, a nominal voltage of 115 and 230 V shall be used in computing the ampere loads on conductors.

There are two steps in the process of predetermining the maximum load that a feeder will be required to carry: first, a reasonable estimate must be made of the probable connected load; and, second, a reasonable value for the demand factor must be assumed. From a survey of a large number of buildings, the average connected loads and demand factors have been ascertained for lighting and small-appliance loads in buildings of the more common classes of occupancy, and these data are presented in Sec. 220-2 and Part B of Art. 220 as minimum requirements.

The load is specified in terms of watts per square foot for certain occupancies. These loads are here referred to as standard loads, because they are minimum standards established by the Code in order to provide that the feeders and branch circuits shall have sufficient carrying capacity for safety.

Feeder loads may consist of lamps, motors, appliances that are not motor-driven, or any combination of such loads.

In addition to lighting loads, standard loads are set up for small appliances in dwelling occupancies. These small appliances are, in general, those that may be supplied by the 20-A branch circuits described in Art. 220.

In the case of large appliances and motors that are not incorporated in appliances, it is assumed that the number of appliances or motors and the current rating of each are definitely known before the wiring is installed, and the feeder sizes are to be based upon these definitely known loads, termed in the Code "specific" loads.

215-2. Minimum Rating and Size. Feeder conductors shall have an ampacity not lower than required to supply the load as computed in Parts B, C, and D of Article 220. The minimum sizes shall be as specified in (a) and (b) below under the conditions stipulated.

(a) For Specified Circuits. The feeder conductors shall not be smaller than No. 10 where the load supplied consists of the following number and types of circuits: (1) Two or more 2-wire branch circuits supplied by a 2-wire feeder; (2) More than two 2-wire branch circuits supplied by a 3-wire feeder; (3) Two or more 3-wire branch circuits supplied by a 3-wire feeder.

(b) Ampacity Relative to Service-Entrance Conductors. The feeder conductor ampacity shall not be lower than that of the service-entrance conductors where the feeder conductors carry the total load supplied by service-entrance conductors No. 6 or smaller.

(c) Overloaded Feeders. Where at any time feeder conductors are or will be overloaded the feeder conductors shall be increased in ampacity to accommodate the actual load served.

See Examples 1 through 8 in Chapter 9.

Conductors for feeders as defined in Article 100, sized to prevent a voltage drop exceeding 3 percent at the farthest outlet of power, heating, and lighting loads, or combinations of such loads and where the maximum total voltage drop on both feeders and branch circuits to the farthest outlet does not exceed 5 percent, will provide reasonable efficiency of operation.

See Section 210-19(a) for voltage drop for branch circuits.

▲ This section indicates not more than 3 percent for feeders supplying power, heating, or lighting loads. It also provides for a maximum drop of 5 percent for the conductors between the service entrance equipment and the connected load. If the feeders have an actual voltage drop of 3 percent, then only 2 percent is left for the branch circuits. If a lower voltage drop is obtained in the feeder, then the branch circuit has more voltage drop available, provided that the total drop does not exceed 5 percent. For any one load, the total voltage drop is made up of the voltage drop in the one or more feeders plus the voltage drop in the branch circuit supplying that load.

The values stated in Sec. 215-2(c) FPN are recommended values and are not intended to be enforced as a requirement.

Convenient voltage-drop tables and slide calculators are available from various electrical-equipment manufacturers. Voltage-drop calculations will vary according to the actual circuit parameters, e.g., AC or DC, single or multiphase, power factor, circuit impedance, line reactance, types of enclosures (nonmetallic or metallic), length and size of conductors, and conductor material (copper, copper-clad aluminum, or aluminum).

The following voltage-drop formula can be used to provide fairly accurate results for most applications.

$$VD = \frac{2K \times L \times I}{CM}$$

$$CM = \frac{2K \times L \times I}{VD}$$

where VD = voltage drop
CM = area of conductor in circular mils (see Table 8, Chap. 9)
I = current in amperes
L = length one way of circuit in feet
K = resistivity of conductor material in ohms per ft per cm-ft = 12 for copper and 18 for aluminum or copper-clad aluminum

This formula is for two-wire AC (when inductance can be neglected) and DC circuits. On three-wire single-phase or DC systems with balanced loads, measure voltage drop across the outside wires (e.g., 230 V instead of 115 V). For three-phase, three- or four-wire systems, multiply the voltage drop in the two-wire formula by 0.866.

Example: 230-V two-wire heating circuit. Load is 24 A. Circuit size is No. 10 AWG copper, and the one-way circuit length is 200 ft.

$$VD = \frac{24 \times 200 \times 24}{10,380} = \frac{115,200}{10,380} = 11$$

An 11-V drop on a 230-V circuit is about a 5 percent drop (11/230 = 0.0478). No. 8 AWG copper conductors would be needed to reduce the voltage drop to 3 percent on the branch circuit and allow 2 percent more on the feeder.

215-3. Overcurrent Protection. Feeders shall be protected against overcurrent in accordance with the provisions of Part A of Article 240.

215-4. Feeders with Common Neutral.

(a) Feeders with Common Neutral. Feeders containing a common neutral shall be permitted to supply two or three sets of 3-wire feeders, or two sets of 4-wire or 5-wire feeders.

(b) In Metal Raceway or Enclosure. Where installed in a metal raceway or other metal enclosure, all conductors of all feeders using a common neutral shall be enclosed within the same raceway or other enclosure as required in Section 300-20.

▲ The neutral conductor of a feeder is one of the conductors of the circuit, and for an AC system all of the conductors, including the neutral, must be contained in the same metal raceway. With a three-phase four-wire system, a single feeder is often used to supply a combination lighting and motor load. Assume 208Y/120 V and a load of 200 A for motors and 100 A for lighting. The total load on the feeder is 300 A. None of the motor load will cause current in the neutral conductor. Therefore the maximum current that the neutral will carry is 100 A, and the neutral conductor can be sized accordingly.

Where a feeder supplies only a lamp load on a three-wire DC, three-wire single-phase, or four-wire three-phase, the neutral conductor must be of such a size as to carry the maximum current on any one of the outside conductors, except that if this current is in excess of 200 A, the neutral must have a carrying capacity of only 200 A plus 70 percent of the excess over 200 A. There may, however, be no reduction in neutral capacity for any portion of the load supplying electric-discharge lighting. See Sec. 220-22 and Example 4 in Chap. 9.

Inasmuch as the maximum current in the neutral of a range is generally much less than the current in the ungrounded conductors, the branch-circuit neutral is permitted to have a minimum ampacity of only 70 percent of that of the ungrounded conductors, except that it shall not be smaller than No. 10.

If two three-wire feeders use a common neutral, the opening of a fuse in one of the supply conductors would force the current of both feeders through the common neutral; so theoretically the neutral should be large enough to carry the total current of both feeders. The likelihood of having this condition with both feeders fully loaded is remote, so the Code permits a demand factor of 70 percent to that portion of the possible load in excess of 200 A. Thus, if the maximum possible load were 400 A, the neutral would need to be only large enough to carry 200 A plus 70 percent of 200 A, or 340 A.

215-5. Diagrams of Feeders. If required by the authority having jurisdiction, a diagram showing feeder details shall be provided prior to the installation of the feeders. Such a diagram shall show the area in square feet of the building or other structure supplied by each feeder, the total connected load before applying demand factors, the demand factors used, the computed load after applying demand factors and the size and type of conductors to be used.

215-6. Feeder Conductor Grounding Means. Where a feeder supplies branch circuits in which grounding conductors are required, the feeder shall include or provide a grounding means to which the grounding conductors of the branch circuits shall be connected.

215-7. Ungrounded Conductors Tapped from Grounded Systems. Two-wire DC circuits and AC circuits of two or more ungrounded conductors may be tapped from the ungrounded conductors of circuits having a grounded neutral conductor. Switching devices in each tapped circuit shall have a pole in each ungrounded conductor.

▲ See comments following Sec. 210-10.

215-8 Means of Identifying Conductor with the Higher Voltage to Ground. On a 4-wire, delta-connected secondary where the midpoint of one phase is grounded to supply lighting and similar loads, the phase conductor having the higher voltage to ground shall be identified by an outer finish that is orange in color or by tagging or other effective means. Such identification shall be placed at any point where a connection is made if the neutral conductor is also present.

▲ See comments following Sec. 200-6.

215-9. Ground-Fault Personnel Protection. Feeders supplying 15- and 20-ampere receptacle branch circuits may be protected by a ground-fault circuit-interrupter approved for the purpose in lieu of the provisions for such interrupters as specified in Section 210-8.

▲ A ground-fault circuit-interrupter may be located in the feeder and protect all branch circuits connected to that feeder. In such cases the provisions of Sec. 210-8 will be satisfied and additional *downstream* ground-fault protection would not be required. It should be mentioned, however, that downstream ground-fault protection is more desirable than ground-fault protection in the feeder because less equipment will be de-energized when the ground-fault circuit-interrupter opens the supply in response to a line-to-ground fault.

ARTICLE 220. BRANCH-CIRCUIT AND FEEDER CALCULATIONS

A. General

220-1. Scope. This Article provides requirements for determining the number of branch circuits required and for computing branch-circuit and feeder loads.

220-2. Computation of Branch Circuits. Branch-circuit loads shall be computed as shown in (a) through (d) below.

(a) Continuous Loads. The continuous load supplied by a branch circuit shall not exceed 80 percent of the branch-circuit rating.

Exception No. 1: Where branch-circuit conductors have been derated in accordance with Note 8 to Tables 310-16 through 310-19.

Exception No. 2: Where the assembly, including overcurrent devices, is listed for continuous operation of 100 percent of its rating.

(b) Lighting Load for Listed Occupancies. A unit load of not less than that specified in Table 220-2(b) for occupancies listed therein shall constitute the minimum lighting load for each square foot of floor area. The floor area for each floor shall be computed from the outside dimensions of the building, apartment, or other area involved. For dwelling occupancies, the computed floor area shall not include open porches, garages, or unused or unfinished spaces not adaptable for future use.

The unit values herein are based on minimum load conditions and 100 percent power factor, and may not provide sufficient capacity for the installation contemplated.

(c) Other Loads—Occupancies Not Listed. For lighting and appliance loads not covered in (b) above and not used for general illumination or for general-use receptacles in the occupancies listed in Table 220-2(b), a unit load of not less than the following shall constitute the minimum load for each outlet, the loads shown being based on nominal branch-circuit voltages.

(1) Outlet for a specific appliance or other load except for a motor load . . . .
Ampere rating of appliance or load served

(2) Outlet for motor load . . . . See Sections 430-22 and
430-24 and Article 440.

(3) Outlet for heavy-duty lampholder . . . . 600 volt-amperes

Table 220-2(b). General Lighting Loads by Occupancies

Type of Occupancy	Unit Load per Sq. Ft. (Watts)
Armories and Auditoriums	1
Banks	5
Barber Shops and Beauty Parlors	3
Churches	1
Clubs	2
Court Rooms	2
*Dwellings (Other Than Hotels)	3
Garages—Commercial (storage)	½
Hospitals	2
*Hotels and Motels, including apartment houses without provisions for cooking by tenants	2
Industrial Commercial (Loft) Buildings	2
Lodge Rooms	1½
Office Buildings	5
Restaurants	2
Schools	3
Stores	3
Warehouses Storage	¼

In any of the above occupancies except single-family dwellings and individual apartments of multifamily dwellings:
    Assembly Halls and Auditoriums
    Halls, Corridors, Closets
    Storage Spaces
	
	1
	½
	¼

* All receptacle outlets of 20-ampere or less rating in single-family and multifamily dwellings and in guest rooms of hotels and motels [except those connected to the receptacle circuits specified in Section 220-3(b)] shall be considered as outlets for general illumination, and no additional load calculations shall be required for such outlets.

(4) *Other outlets . . . . 180 volt-amperes
per outlet.

For receptacle outlets, each single or multiple receptacle shall be considered at not less than 180 volt-amperes.

* This provision shall not be applicable to receptacle outlets connected to the circuit specified in Section 220-3(b) nor to receptacle outlets provided for the connection of stationary equipment as provided for in Section 400-7.

Exception No. 1: Where fixed multioutlet assemblies are employed, each 5 feet or fraction thereof of each separate and continuous length shall be considered as one outlet of not less than $1\frac{1}{2}$ ampere capacity, except in locations where a number of appliances are likely to be used simultaneously, when each one foot or fraction thereof shall be considered as an outlet of not less than $1\frac{1}{2}$ amperes. The requirements of this Section shall not apply to dwellings or the guest rooms of hotels or motels.

Exception No. 2: Table 220-19 shall be considered as an acceptable method of computing the load for a household electric range.

Exception No. 3: A load of not less than 200 watts per linear foot of show window, measured horizontally along its base, shall be permitted instead of the specified unit load per outlet.

Exception No. 4: The loads of outlets serving switchboards and switching frames in telephone exchanges shall be waived from the computations.

(d) Loads for Additions to Existing Installations.

(1) Dwelling Occupancies. Loads for structural additions to an existing dwelling occupancy or to a previously unwired portion of an existing dwelling occupancy, either of which exceeds 500 square feet, shall be computed in accordance with (b) above. Loads for new circuits or extended circuits in previously wired dwelling occupancies shall be computed in accordance with either (b) or (c) above.

(2) Other Than Dwelling Occupancies. Loads for new circuits or extended circuits in other than dwelling occupancies shall be computed in accordance with either (b) or (c) above.

220-3. Branch Circuits Required. Branch circuits for lighting and for appliances, including motor-operated appliances, shall be provided to supply the loads computed in accordance with Section 220-2. In addition, branch circuits shall be provided for specific loads not covered by Section 220-2 where required elsewhere in this Code; for small appliance loads as specified in (b) below; and for laundry loads as specified in (c) below.

(a) Number of Branch Circuits. The minimum number of branch circuits shall be determined from the total computed load and the size or rating of the circuits used. In all installations the number of circuits shall be sufficient to supply the load served. In no case shall the load on any circuit exceed the maximum specified by Section 210-22.

(b) Small Appliance Branch Circuits—Dwelling Occupancies.

(1) In addition to the number of branch circuits determined in accordance with (a) above, two or more 20-ampere small appliance branch circuits shall be provided for all receptacle outlets specified by Section 210-25(b) for the small appliance loads, including refrigeration equipment, in the kitchen, pantry, breakfast room, dining room, and family room of dwelling occupancies. Such circuits, whether two or more are used, shall have no other outlets.

Exception: A receptacle installed solely for the electric supply to and support of an electric clock in any of these stipulated rooms or outdoor receptacle outlets shall be supplied either by a small appliance branch circuit or by a general purpose branch circuit.

(2) Receptacle outlets installed in the kitchen shall be supplied by not less than two small appliance branch circuits, either or both of which shall also be permitted to supply receptacle outlets in the other rooms specified in (1) above. Additional small appliance branch circuits shall be permitted to supply receptacle outlets in such other rooms.

▲ This provision is intended to require that at least two appliance receptacle circuits be installed in the kitchen. They may be installed on the circuits which also supply the receptacles in the pantry, family room, dining room, and breakfast room or on separate appliance circuits. The important point is that there be receptacle outlets on each of two appliance branch circuits in the kitchen.

It should be noted that all of the rooms listed are areas in dwelling occupancies where cooking or food-preparing appliances may be expected to be used.

(c) Laundry Branch Circuits—Dwelling Occupancies. In addition to the number of branch circuits determined in accordance with (a) and (b) above, at least one additional 20-ampere branch circuit shall be provided to supply the laundry receptacle(s) required by Section 210-25(b).

(d) Load Evenly Proportioned Among Branch Circuits. Where the load is computed on a watts-per-square-foot basis, the load, insofar as practical, shall be evenly proportioned among the branch circuits according to their capacities.

See Examples 1, 1(a), 1(b), 1(c), and 4, Chapter 9.

B. Feeders

220-10. General.

(a) Ampacity and Computed Loads. Feeder conductors shall have sufficient ampacity to supply the load served. In no case shall the computed load of a feeder be less than the sum of the loads on the branch circuits supplied as determined by Part A of this Article after any applicable demand factors permitted by Parts B, C, or D have been applied.

See Examples 1 through 8, Chapter 9. See Section 210-22(b) for maximum load in amperes permitted for lighting units operating at less than 100 percent power factor.

(b) Continuous and Noncontinuous Loads. Where a feeder supplies continuous loads or any combination of continuous and noncontinuous load, neither the ampere rating of the overcurrent device nor the ampacity of the feeder conductors shall be less than the noncontinuous load plus 125 percent of the continuous load.

Exception: Where the assembly including the overcurrent devices protecting the feeder(s) are listed for operation at 100 percent of their rating, neither the ampere rating of the overcurrent device nor the ampacity of the feeder conductors shall be less than the sum of the continuous load plus the noncontinuous load.

220-11. General Lighting. The demand factors listed in Table 220-11 shall apply to that portion of the total branch-circuit load computed for general illumination. They shall not be applied in determining the number of branch circuits for general illumination.

See Sections 220-16 for application of demand factors to small appliance and laundry loads in dwellings.

220-12. Show-Window Lighting. For show-window lighting, a load of not less than 200 watts shall be included for each linear foot of show window, measured horizontally along its base.

See Section 220-2(c), Exception No. 3 for branch circuits supplying show windows.

220-13. Receptacle Loads—Nondwelling Occupancies. In other than dwelling occupancies, the use of the demand factors for lighting loads in Table 220-11 shall

Table 220-11. Lighting Load Feeder Demand Factors

Type of Occupancy	Portion of Lighting Load to Which Demand Factor Applies (wattage)	Demand Factor Percent
Dwelling—Other Than Hotels	First 3000 or less at	100
	Next 3001 to 120,000 at	35
	Remainder over 120,000 at	25
*Hospitals	First 50,000 or less at....................	40
	Remainder over 50,000 at	20
*Hotels and Motels—Including Apartment Houses without Provision for Cooking by Tenants	First 20,000 or less at....................	50
	Next 20,001 to 100,000 at	40
	Remainder over 100,000 at	30
Warehouses (Storage)	First 12,500 or less at....................	100
	Remainder over 12,500 at	50
All Others	Total Wattage	100

*The demand factors of this Table shall not apply to the computed load of feeders to areas in hospitals, hotels, and motels where the entire lighting is likely to be used at one time; as in operating rooms, ballrooms, or dining rooms.

be permitted for receptacle loads computed at not more than 180 volt-amperes per outlet in accordance with Section 220-2(c) (4).

220-14. Motors. Motor loads shall be computed in accordance with Sections 430-24, 430-25, and 430-26.

220-15. Fixed Electric Space Heating. Fixed electric space heating loads shall be computed at 100 percent of the total connected load.

Exception No. 1: Where reduced loading of the conductors results from units operating on duty-cycle, intermittently, or from all units not operating at one time, the authority having jurisdiction may grant permission for feeder conductors to have an ampacity less than 100 percent, provided the conductors have an ampacity for the load so determined.

Exception No. 2: The use of the optional calculations in Sections 220-30 and 220-31 shall be permitted for fixed electric space heating loads in a single-family dwelling or an individual apartment of a multifamily dwelling. In a multifamily dwelling the use of the optional calculation in Section 220-32 shall be permitted.

220-16. Small Appliance and Laundry Loads—Dwellings.

(a) Small Appliance Circuit Load. In each single-family dwelling, each apartment of multifamily dwellings having cooking facilities, and each hotel or motel suite having cooking facilities or a serving pantry, the feeder load shall be computed at 1500 watts for each 2-wire small appliance branch circuit required by Section 220-3(b) for portable appliances supplied by 15- or 20-ampere receptacles on 20-ampere branch circuits in the kitchen, pantry, dining room, breakfast room, and family room. Where the load is subdivided through two or more feeders, the computed load for each shall include not less than 1500 watts for each 2-wire branch circuit for small appliances. These loads shall be permitted for the general lighting load and subjected to the demand factors permitted in Table 220-11 for the general lighting load.

(b) Laundry Circuit Load. A feeder load of not less than 1500 watts shall be included for each 2-wire laundry branch circuit installed as required by Section 220-3(c). It shall be permissible to include this load with the general lighting load and subjected to the demand factors provided in Section 220-11.

220-17. Fixed Appliance Load—Dwelling. It shall be permissible to apply a demand factor of 75 percent to the nameplate-rating load of four or more fixed appliances served by the same feeder in a single-family or multifamily dwelling.

Exception: This demand factor shall not be applied to electric ranges, clothes dryers, space heating equipment, or air conditioning equipment.

▲ *Example:* 115/230-V service, single-family dwelling.

Water heater	2,500 W	230 V =	11.0 A
Kitchen disposal	½ hp	115 V = 6.5 A + 25 percent =	8.1 A
Furnace motor	¼ hp	115 V =	4.6 A
Attic fan	¼ hp	115 V = 4.6 A	0.0 A
Water pump	½ hp	230 V =	3.7 A

Load in amperes on each ungrounded leg of feeder = 27.4 A

To comply with Sec. 430-24, 25 percent is added to the full-load current of the ½-hp 115-V motor because it is the highest-rated motor in the group. Since it is assumed that the load on the 115/230-V feeder will be balanced and each of the ¼-hp motors will be connected to different ungrounded conductors, only one is counted in the above calculation. Except for the 115-V motors, all the other appliance loads are connected to both ungrounded conductors and are automatically balanced. Since there are four or more fixed appliances in addition to a range, clothes dryer, etc., a demand factor of 75 percent may be applied to the total load of these appliances. 75 percent of 27.4 = 20.5 A, which is the current to be added to that computed for the lighting and other loads to determine the total current to be carried by the ungrounded (outside) service-entrance conductors.

The above demand factor may also be applied to similar loads in multifamily dwellings.

220-18. Electric Clothes Dryers—Dwellings. The load for household electric clothes dryers in dwellings shall be 5000 watts or the nameplate rating, whichever is larger, for each dryer served. The use of the demand factors in Table 220-18 shall be permitted.

▲ Section 220-18 prescribes a *minimum* demand of 5 kW for 120/240-V electric clothes dryers in determining branch-circuit and feeder sizes. Feeder demands are subject to Table 220-18. This rule is helpful because the ratings of electric clothes dryers are not usually known in the planning stages when feeder calculations must be determined.

220-19. Electric Ranges and Other Cooking Appliances—Dwellings. The feeder demand load for household electric ranges, wall-mounted ovens, counter-mounted

Table 220-18. Demand Factors for Household Electric Clothes Dryers

Number of Dryers	Demand Factor Percent
1.	100
2.	100
3.	100
4.	100
5.	80
6.	70
7.	65
8.	60
9.	55
10.	50
11–13	45
14–19	40
20–24	35
25–29	32.5
30–34	30
35–39	27.5
40 & over	25

cooking units, and other household cooking appliances individually rated in excess of $1\frac{3}{4}$ kW shall be permitted to be computed in accordance with Table 220-19. Where two or more single-phase ranges are supplied by a 3-phase 4-wire feeder, the total load shall be computed on the basis of twice the maximum number connected between any two phases.

See Example 7, Chapter 9.

▲ The load for one or more household electric ranges or other household cooking appliances which are individually rated at more than 1.75 kW and are all of the same rating may be calculated in accordance with the following:

For ranges individually rated at 8.75 kW or more but not more than 12 kW, the load on the feeder may be considered as the maximum demand value specified in column A in Table 220-19 for the given number of ranges.

For range, wall-mounted oven, or counter-mounted cooking unit branch circuits, see Note 4 of Table 220-19.

For commercial ranges see Table 220-20.

Note 1. Over 12 kW through 27 kW ranges all of same rating. For ranges, individually rated more than 12 kW but not more than 27 kW, the maximum demand in Column A shall be increased 5 percent for each additional kW of rating or major fraction thereof by which the rating of individual ranges exceeds 12 kW.

Note 2. Over 12 kW through 27 kW ranges *of unequal ratings.* For ranges individually rated more than 12 kW and of different ratings but none exceeding 27 kW an average value of rating shall be computed by adding together the ratings of all ranges to obtain the total connected load (using 12 kW for any range rated less than 12 kW) and dividing by the total number of ranges; and then the maximum demand in Column A shall be increased 5 percent for each kW or major fraction thereof by which this average value exceeds 12 kW.

Table 220-19. Demand Loads for Household Electric Ranges, Wall-Mounted Ovens, Counter-Mounted Cooking Units, and Other Household Cooking Appliances over $1\frac{3}{4}$ kW Rating. Column A to be used in all cases except as otherwise permitted in Note 3 below.

	Maximum Demand (See Notes)	Demand Factors Percent (See Note 3)	
NUMBER OF APPLIANCES	COLUMN A (Not over 12 kW Rating)	COLUMN B (Less than $3\frac{1}{2}$ kW Rating)	COLUMN C ($3\frac{1}{2}$ kW to $8\frac{3}{4}$ kW Rating)
1	8 kW	80%	80%
2	11 kW	75%	65%
3	14 kW	70%	55%
4	17 kW	66%	50%
5	20 kW	62%	45%
6	21 kW	59%	43%
7	22 kW	56%	40%
8	23 kW	53%	36%
9	24 kW	51%	35%
10	25 kW	49%	34%
11	26 kW	47%	32%
12	27 kW	45%	32%
13	28 kW	43%	32%
14	29 kW	41%	32%
15	30 kW	40%	32%
16	31 kW	39%	28%
17	32 kW	38%	28%
18	33 kW	37%	28%
19	34 kW	36%	28%
20	35 kW	35%	28%
21	36 kW	34%	26%
22	37 kW	33%	26%
23	38 kW	32%	26%
24	39 kW	31%	26%
25	40 kW	30%	26%
26-30	{ 15 kW plus 1 kW for each range }	30%	24%
31-40		30%	22%
41-50		30%	20%
51-60	{ 25 kW plus $\frac{3}{4}$ kW for each range }	30%	18%
61 & over		30%	16%

Note 3. Over $1\frac{3}{4}$ kW through $8\frac{3}{4}$ kW. In lieu of the method provided in Column A, it shall be permissible to add the nameplate ratings of all ranges rated more than $1\frac{3}{4}$ kW but not more than $8\frac{3}{4}$ kW and multiply the sum by the demand factors specified in Column B or C for the given number of appliances.

Note 4. Branch-Circuit Load. It shall be permissible to compute the branch-circuit load for one range in accordance with Table 220-19. The branch-circuit load for one wall-mounted oven or one counter-mounted cooking unit shall be the nameplate rating of the appliance. The branch-circuit load for a counter-mounted cooking unit and not more than two wall-mounted ovens, all supplied from a single branch circuit and located in the same room, shall be computed by adding the nameplate rating of the individual appliances and treating this total as equivalent to one range.

Note 5. This table also applies to household cooking appliances rated over $1\frac{3}{4}$ kW and used in instructional programs.

See Table 220-20 for commercial cooking equipment.

▲ The likelihood of one range having all the surface units and ovens on simultaneously for any length of time is small. As the number of ranges increases, the likelihood of full loading of all of them decreases. This was checked by recording meters for range installations over wide areas and formed the basis for the diversity factors included in the Code.

▲ Where a counter-mounted cooking unit and not more than two wall-mounted ovens are installed on one branch circuit in the same room, the last sentence in Note 4 requires that the nameplate ratings of the individual appliances be added together and this total be treated as equivalent to one range.

Example:

1 counter-mounted cooking unit . . . . .7 kW
1 wall-mounted oven . . . . .6 kW
1 wall-mounted oven . . . . .5 kW
                                                                  ————
Total . . . . 18 kW

From column A, the maximum demand for one range of 12 kW rating is 8 kW.
18 kW exceeds 12 kW by 6 (see Note 1).
5 percent × 6 = 30 percent (5 percent increase for each kilowatt in excess of 12).
8 kW × 30 percent = 2.4 kW increase.
8 kW + 2.4 kW = 10.4 kW—value to be used in selection of branch circuit.
10,400 W ÷ 230 V = 45 A.

220-20. Kitchen Equipment—Other Than Dwelling.   It shall be permissible to compute the load for commercial electric cooking equipment, dishwasher booster heaters, water heaters, and other kitchen equipment in accordance with Table 220-20.

**Table 220-20. Feeder Demand Factors
for Commercial Electric Cooking
Equipment; Including Dishwasher
Booster Heaters, Water Heaters, and
Other Kitchen Equipment**

Number of Units of Equipment	Demand Factors Percent
1	100
2	100
3	90
4	80
5	70
6 & over	65

220-21. Noncoincident Loads. Where it is unlikely that two dissimilar loads will be in use simultaneously, it shall be permissible to omit the smaller of the two in computing the total load of a feeder.

220-22. Feeder Neutral Load. The feeder neutral load shall be the maximum unbalance of the load determined by this Article. The maximum unbalanced load shall be the maximum connected load between the neutral and any one ungrounded conductor, except that the load thus obtained shall be multiplied by 140 percent for 5-wire, 2-phase systems. For a feeder supplying household electric ranges, wall-mounted ovens, and counter-mounted cooking units, the maximum unbalanced load shall be considered as 70 percent of the load on the ungrounded conductors, as determined in accordance with Table 220-19. For 3-wire DC or single-phase AC, 4-wire, 3-phase, and 5-wire, 2-phase systems, a further demand factor of 70 percent shall be permitted for that portion of the unbalanced load in excess of 200 amperes. There shall be no reduction of the neutral capacity for that portion of the load which consists of electric-discharge lighting.

See Examples 1, 1(a), 1(b), 1(c), 2, 3, 4, and 5, Chapter 9.

C. Optional Calculations for Computing Feeder and Service Loads

220-30. Optional Calculation—Single-Family Dwelling or Individual Apartment in Multifamily Dwellings. For a single-family dwelling or an individual apartment in a multifamily dwelling having the total connected load served by a single 3-wire 115/230-volt or 120/208 volt set of service-entrance or feeder conductors with an ampacity of 100 or greater, it shall be permissible to compute the feeder and service loads in accordance with Table 220-30 instead of the method specified in Part B

Table 220-30. Optional Calculation for Single-Family Dwelling or Individual Apartment of Multifamily Dwelling

Load (in kW or kVA)	Demand Factor Percent
Air conditioning and cooling, including heat pump compressors..............	100
Central electric space heating...	65
Less than four separately controlled electric space heating units	65
First 10 kW of all other load..	100
Remainder of other load	40

of this Article. Feeder and service-entrance conductors whose demand load is determined by this optional calculation shall be permitted to have the neutral load determined by Section 220-22. The loads identified in Table 220-30 as "other load" and as "Remainder of other load" shall include the following:

(1) 1500 watts for each 2-wire, 20-ampere small appliance branch circuit and each laundry branch circuit specified in Section 220-16.

(2) 3 watts per square foot for general lighting and general-use receptacles.

(3) The nameplate rating of all fixed appliances, ranges, wall-mounted ovens, counter-mounted cooking units, and including four or more separately controlled space heating units.

(4) The nameplate ampere or kva rating of all motors and of all low-power-factor loads.

(5) When applying Section 220-21 use the largest of the following: (1) Air-conditioning load; (2) The 65 percent diversified demand of the central electric space heating load; (3) The 65 percent diversified demand of the load of less than four separately-controlled electric space heating units; (4) The connected load of four or more separately-controlled electric space heating units.

▲ This optional method of calculations is restricted to a single-family residence or an individual apartment of a multifamily dwelling.

Examples of how these calculations are applied are also given in Chap. 9 in Examples (b) and (c).

220-31. Optional Calculation for Additional Loads in Existing Single-Family Dwelling Occupancy.   For an existing single-family dwelling occupancy presently being served by an existing 115/230 volt or 120/208, 3-wire, 60-ampere service, it shall be permissible to compute load calculations as follows:

Load (in kW or kVA)	Percent of Load
First 8 kW of load at	100%
Remainder of load at	40%

Load calculation shall include lighting and portable appliances at 3 watts per square foot; 1500 watts for each 20-ampere appliance circuit; range or wall-mounted oven and counter-mounted cooking unit, and other fixed or stationary appliances, at nameplate rating.

If air conditioning equipment or electric space heating equipment is to be installed the following formula shall be applied to determine if the existing service is of sufficient size.

Air conditioning equipment* 100%
Central electric space heating* 100%
Less than four separately controlled space heating units* 100%
First 8 kW of all other load 100%
Remainder of all other load 40%

Other loads shall include:
1500 watts for each 20-ampere appliance circuit.
Lighting and portable appliances at 3 watts per sq. ft.
Household range or wall-mounted oven and counter-mounted cooking unit.
All other fixed appliances including four or more separately controlled space heating units, at nameplate rating.

* Use larger connected load of air conditioning and space heating, but not both.

▲ The purpose of Sec. 220-31 is to permit the maximum possible load on an existing 60-A service. The calculations are based on numerous load surveys and tests made by local utilities throughout the country. This optional method would seem to be particularly advantageous when *smaller* loads such as window air conditioners or bathroom heaters are to be installed in a dwelling with an existing 60-A service. If there is an existing electric range, say 12 kW (and no electric water heater), it would not be possible to add any load of substantial rating. The total *gross load* that can be connected to an existing 115/230-V 60-A service would be 22,500 W (X), based on the formula: 13,800 W (230V $\times$ 60A) = 8,000 + 0.4(X — 8000).

Thus, an existing 1,000-sq ft dwelling with a 12-kW electric range, two 20-A appliance circuits, a 750-W furnace circuit and a 60-A service would have a gross load of:

	Watts
1000 sq ft $\times$ 3 W/sq ft	3,000
Two 20-A appliance circuits	
@ 1500 W each	3,000
One electric range @	12,000
Furnace circuit @	750
Gross watts	18,750

Since the *maximum* permitted gross load is 22,500 W, an appliance not exceeding 3,750 W could be added to this existing 60-A service. However, Section 220-31 lists air conditioning equipment, central space heating, and less than four separately controlled space heating units at 100 percent demands, and if the appliance to be added is one of these, then it would be limited to 1,500 W. From the 18,750-W gross load we have 8,000 W @ 100 percent demand + [10,750 W (18,750 — 8000) $\times$ 0.40] or 12,300 W. Then, 13,800 W (60A $\times$ 230V) — 12,300 W = 1,500 W for an appliance listed at 100 percent demand.

220-32. Optional Calculation—Three or More Multifamily Dwelling Units.

(a) It shall be permissible to compute the feeder or service load of a multifamily dwelling having three or more units in accordance with Table 220-32 instead of Part B of this Article where all the following conditions are met:

(1) No individual dwelling unit is supplied by more than one feeder.

(2) Each dwelling unit is equipped with electric cooking equipment.

Exception: When the computed load for multifamily dwellings under this Section without electric cooking exceeds that computed under this Section for the identical load plus electric cooking (based on 8 kW per unit), the lesser of the two loads may be used.

(3) Each dwelling unit is equipped with either electric space heating or air conditioning or both.

Feeders and service-entrance conductors whose demand load is determined by this optional calculation shall be permitted to have the neutral load determined by Section 220-22.

(b) House loads shall be computed in accordance with Part B of this Article and shall be in addition to the dwelling unit loads computed in accordance with Table 220-32.

(c) The connected load to which the demand factors of Table 220-32 apply shall include the following:

(1) 1500 watts for each 2-wire 20-ampere small appliance branch circuit and each laundry branch circuit specified in Section 220-16.

(2) 3 watts per square foot for general lighting and general-use receptacles.

(3) The nameplate rating of all fixed and stationary appliances, ranges, wall-mounted ovens, counter-mounted cooking units, clothes dryers, water heaters, and space heaters.

If water heater elements are so interlocked that all elements cannot be used at

Table 220-32. Optional Calculation—Demand Factors for Three or More Multifamily Dwelling Units

Number of Dwelling Units	Demand Factor Percent
3–5	45
6–7	44
8–10	43
11	42
12–13	41
14–15	40
16–17	39
18–20	38
21	37
22–23	36
24–25	35
26–27	34
28–30	33
31	32
32–33	31
34–36	30
37–38	29
39–42	28
43–45	27
46–50	26
51–55	25
56–61	24
62 & over	23

the same time, the maximum possible load shall be considered the nameplate load.

(4) The nameplate ampere or kVA rating of all motors and of all low-power-factor loads.

(5) The larger of the air conditioning load or the space heating load.

220-33. Optional Method—Schools. The calculation of a feeder or service load for schools shall be permitted in accordance with Table 220-33 in lieu of Part B of this Article where equipped with electric space heating, or air conditioning, or both. The connected load to which the demand factors of Table 220-33 apply shall

Table 220-33. Optional Method—Demand Factors for Feeders and Service-Entrance Conductors for Schools

Connected Load Watts Per Sq. Ft.	Demand Factors Percent
Connected load up to and including 3, plus	100
Connected load over 3 and including 20, plus	75
Connected load over 20 at	25

include interior and outdoor lighting, power, water heating, cooking, other loads, and the larger of the air conditioning load or space heating load.

Feeders and service entrance conductors whose demand load is determined by this optional calculation shall be permitted to have the neutral load determined by Section 220-22.

D. Method for Computing Farm Loads

220-40. Farm Loads—Buildings and Other Loads.

(a) Dwellings. The feeder or service load of a farm dwelling shall be computed in accordance with the provisions for dwellings in Part B or C of this Article.

(b) Other Than Dwellings. For each farm building or load supplied by two or more branch circuits the load for feeders, service-entrance conductors, and service equipment shall be computed in accordance with demand factors not less than indicated in Table 220-40.

See Section 230-21 for overhead conductors from a pole to a building or other structure.

Table 220-40. Method for Computing Farm Loads for Other Than Dwellings

Ampere Load At 230 Volts	Demand Factor Percent
Loads expected to operate without diversity, but not less than 125 percent full-load current of the largest motor and not less than the first 60 amperes of load	100
Next 60 amperes of all other loads	50
Remainder of other load	25

220-41. Farm Loads—Total.

The total load of the farm for service-entrance conductors and service equipment shall be computed in accordance with the farm dwelling load and demand factors specified in Table 220-41. Where there is equipment in two or more farm equipment buildings or for loads having the same function, such loads shall be computed in accordance with Table 220-40 and may be combined as a single load in Table 220-41 for computing the total load.

See Section 230-21 for overhead conductors from a pole to a building or other structure.

Table 220-41. Method for Computing Total Farm Load

Individual Loads Computed in Accordance with Table 220-40	Demand Factor Percent
Largest load	100
Second largest load	75
Third largest load	65
Remaining loads	50

To this total load, add the load of the farm dwelling computed in accordance with Part B or C of this Article.

ARTICLE 225. OUTSIDE BRANCH CIRCUITS AND FEEDERS

225-1. Scope. This Article covers electric equipment and wiring for the supply of utilization equipment located on or attached to the outside of public and private buildings, or run between buildings, other structures or poles on other premises served.

For additional information on wiring over 600 volts, see the National Electrical Safety Code (ANSI C2-1973).

225-2. Other Articles. Application of other Articles, including additional requirements to specific cases of equipment and conductors, are as follows:

225-3. Calculation of Load.

(a) Branch Circuits. The load on outdoor branch circuits shall be as determined by Section 220-2.

(b) Feeders. The load on outdoor feeders shall be as determined by Part B of Article 220.

225-4. Conductor Covering. Where within 10 feet of any building or other structure, open wiring on insulators shall be insulated or covered. Conductors in cables or raceways, except Type MI cable, shall be of the rubber-covered type or thermoplastic type and in wet locations shall comply with Section 310-7. Conductors for festoon lighting shall be of the rubber-covered or thermoplastic type.

225-5. Size of Conductors. The ampacity of outdoor branch-circuit and feeder conductors shall be in accordance with Tables 310-16 through 310-19 based on loads as determined under Section 220-2 and Part B of Article 220.

225-6. Minimum Size of Conductor.

(a) Overhead Spans. Overhead conductors shall not be smaller than the following: (1) for 600 volts or less, No. 10 for spans up to 50 feet in length and No. 8 for longer spans; (2) for over 600 volts, No. 6 where open individual conductors and No. 8 where in cable.

(b) Festoon Lighting. Overhead conductors for festoon lighting shall not be smaller than No. 12.

Exception: Where supported by messenger wires.

See Section 225-25 for outdoor lampholders.
DEFINITION: Festoon lighting is a string of outdoor lights suspended between two points more than 15 feet apart.

225-7. Lighting Equipment on Poles or Other Structures.

(a) General. For the supply of lighting equipment installed on a single pole or structure, the branch circuits shall comply with Article 210 and (c) below.

(b) Common Neutral. It shall be permissible to use a multiwire branch circuit consisting of the neutral and not more than 8 ungrounded conductors. The ampacity of the neutral conductor shall not be less than the calculated sum of the currents in all ungrounded conductors connected to any one phase of the circuit.

▲ In installations for the lighting of outdoor athletic fields a large number of floodlights may be mounted on one structure. For example, at one stadium for major-league baseball games there are two structures on each of which 264 floodlights are mounted, constituting for each structure a load of approximately 475 kW. The lamps used are commonly of 1,500 W rating and are usually operated at 10 percent overvoltage to provide increased light output, in which case the actual watts per lamp are about 1,800, and at 130 V the current per lamp is approximately 15 A.

(c) Voltage to Ground. Branch circuits supplying lamp holders or lighting fixtures mounted on the outside of buildings or on poles or structures for area illumination of residential, commercial, or industrial property shall not exceed 150 volts to ground.

Exception: The voltage shall not exceed 300 volts to ground on branch circuits supplying lighting fixtures for illumination of outdoor areas of industrial establishments, office buildings, schools, stores, and other commercial or public buildings where all of the following conditions are met:

1. The fixtures are mounted on the outside of buildings or out-of-doors on poles or other structures.

2. The fixtures are not less than 8 feet above grade or other surface accessible to individuals other than those charged with fixture maintenance and supervision.

3. The fixtures are not less than 3 feet from windows, platforms, fire escapes, and the like.

(d) Voltage Between Conductors. The voltage between conductors on branch circuits supplying only the ballast for permanently installed electric-discharge fixtures for area illumination shall be in accordance with Section 210-6(b).

225-8. Disconnection. The disconnecting means for branch-circuit and feeder fuses shall be in accordance with Section 240-40.

225-9. Overcurrent Protection. Overcurrent protection shall be in accordance with Section 210-20 for branch circuits and Part A of Article 240 for feeders.

225-10. Wiring on Buildings. The installation of outside wiring on surfaces of buildings shall be permitted for circuits of not over 600 volts as open wiring on insulators, as multiconductor cable approved for the purpose, as aluminum-sheathed cable, as Type MI cable, in rigid metal conduit, in intermediate metal conduit, in busways as provided in Article 364, or in electrical metallic tubing. Circuits of over 600 volts shall be installed as provided for services in Section 230-202. Circuits for sign and outline lighting shall be installed in accordance with Article 600.

225-11. Circuit Exits and Entrances. Where outside branch and feeder circuits leave or enter a building, the requirements of Section 230-43, 230-52 and 230-54 shall apply.

225-12. Open-Conductor Supports. Open conductors shall be supported on glass or porcelain-knobs, racks, brackets, or strain insulators.

225-13. Festoon Supports. In spans exceeding 40 feet, the conductors shall be supported by a messenger wire; and the messenger wire shall be supported by strain insulators. Conductors or messenger wires shall not be attached to any fire escape, downspout, or plumbing equipment.

▲ Messenger wires are needed for long strings in order to support the weight and relieve the conductors from strain.

Where the span is over 40 ft long and a messenger wire is used, the wire must be insulated at every point of support by means of a strain insulator, and where no messenger wire is used the wires of the festoon must be secured to their supports through strain insulators.

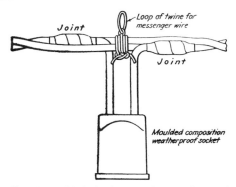

Fig. 225-1. Method of connecting weatherproof socket for festoon lighting.

A downspout does not as a rule provide a sufficiently secure means of support for a festoon. A festoon attached to a fire escape would be accessible; the metal of the fire escape would probably be grounded, and an "unqualified person" standing on the fire escape and tampering with the wire or sockets might receive a severe shock.

225-14. Open-Conductor Spacings.

(a) **600 Volts or Less.** Conductors of 600 volts or less shall comply with the spacings provided in Table 230-51(c).

(b) **Over 600 Volts.** Conductors of over 600 volts shall comply with the spacings provided in Part D of Article 710.

(c) Separation From Other Circuits. Open conductors shall be separated from open conductors of other circuits or systems by not less than 4 inches.

(d) Conductors on Poles. Conductors on poles shall have a separation of not less than one foot where not placed on racks or brackets. Conductors supported on poles shall provide a horizontal climbing space not less than the following:

```
Power conductors, below communication
  conductors . . . . . . . . . . . . . . . . . . . . . . . . . . . . . . . . . . . . . . . . . . 30 inches
Power conductors alone or above communication conductors:
  300 volts or less . . . . . . . . . . . . . . . . . . . . . . . . . . . . . . . . . . . . 24 inches
  Over 300 volts . . . . . . . . . . . . . . . . . . . . . . . . . . . . . . . . . . . . . . 30 inches
Communication conductors below power
  conductors . . . . . . . . . . . . . . . . . . . . . . . . . . . . . . same as power conductors
Communication conductors alone . . . . . . . . . . . . . . . . . . . . . . no requirement
```

▲ The climbing space is the distance between the two crossarm pins nearest to the pole that are used to carry wires. Ample climbing space is needed in order to avoid danger to linemen and disturbance of the lower set of wires in climbing through them to reach the upper wires.

225-15. Supports Over Buildings. Supports over a building shall be in accordance with Section 230-29.

225-16. Point of Attachment to Buildings. The point of attachment to a building shall be in accordance with Section 230-26.

225-17. Means of Attachment to Buildings. The means of attachment to a building shall be in accordance with Section 230-27.

225-18. Clearance From Ground. Open conductors of not over 600 volts shall conform to the following:

10 feet—above finished grade, sidewalks, or from any platform or projection from which they might be reached.

12 feet—over residential driveways and commercial areas such as parking lots and drive-in establishments not subject to truck traffic.

15 feet—over commercial areas, parking lots, or agricultural or other areas subject to truck traffic.

18 feet—over public streets, alleys, roads, and driveways on other than residential property.

Note: For clearances of conductors of over 600 volts, see National Electrical Safety Code (ANSI C2-1973).

225-19. Clearances From Buildings for Conductors of Not Over 600 Volts.

(a) Over Roofs. Open conductors shall have a clearance of not less than 8 feet from the highest point of roofs over which they pass.

Exception No. 1: Where the voltage between conductors does not exceed 300 and the roof has a slope of not less than 4 inches in 12 inches, a reduction in clearance to 3 feet shall be permitted.

Exception No. 2: Where the voltage between conductors does not exceed 300, a reduction in clearance over the roof to 18 inches shall be permitted if:

a. They do not pass over more than 4 feet of the overhang portion of the roof; and

b. They are terminated at a (through-the-roof) raceway or approved support.

(b) Horizontal Clearances. Open conductors not attached to a building shall have a minimum horizontal clearance of 3 feet.

(c) Final Spans. Final spans of feeders or branch circuits to a building they supply or from which they are fed shall be permitted to be attached to the building, but they shall be kept 3 feet from windows, doors, porches, fire escapes, or similar locations.

Conductors run above the top level of a window shall be considered out of reach from that window.

(d) Zone for Fire Ladders. Where buildings exceed three stories or 50 feet in height, overhead lines shall be arranged, where practicable, so that a clear space (or zone) at least 6 feet wide will be left either adjacent to the buildings or beginning not over 8 feet from them to facilitate the raising of ladders when necessary for fire fighting.

Note: For clearance of conductors over 600 volts, see National Electrical Safety Code (ANSI C2-1973).

225-20. Mechanical Protection of Conductors. Mechanical protection of conductors on buildings, structures, or poles shall be as provided for services in Section 230-50.

225-21. Multiconductor Cables on Exterior Surfaces of Buildings. Multiconductor cables on exterior surfaces of buildings shall be as provided for service cable in Section 230-51.

225-22. Raceways on Exterior Surfaces of Buildings. Raceways on exterior surfaces of buildings shall be made raintight and suitably drained.

▲ Condensation of moisture is very likely to take place in conduit or tubing located outdoors. The conduit or tubing should be considered suitably drained when it is so installed that any moisture condensing inside the raceway or entering from the outside cannot accumulate in the raceway or fittings. This requires that the raceway shall be installed without "pockets," that long runs shall not be truly horizontal but shall always be pitched, and that fittings at low points be provided with drainage openings.

In order to be raintight, all conduit fittings should be provided with threaded hubs, and the joints and connections to fittings must be made up wrench-tight. Couplings and connectors used with electrical metallic tubing shall be of the raintight type. See Sec. 348-8.

225-23. Underground Circuits. Underground circuits shall meet the requirements of Section 300-5.

225-24. Outdoor Lampholders. Where outdoor lampholders are attached as pendants, the connections to the circuit wires shall be staggered. Where such lampholders have terminals of a type that puncture the insulation and make contact with the conductors, they shall be attached only to conductors of the stranded type.

▲ This section applies particularly to lampholders used in festoons. Where "pigtail" lampholders are used, the splices should be staggered as shown in Fig. 225-1 in order to avoid the possibility of short circuits, in case the taping for any reason should become ineffective.

According to the UL Standard for Edison-Base Lampholders, "pin-type" terminals shall be employed only in lampholders for temporary lighting or decorations, signs, or specifically approved applications.

225-25. Location of Outdoor Lamps. Locations of lamps for outdoor lighting shall be below all live conductors, transformers, or other electrical equipment:

Exception No. 1: Where clearances or other safeguards are provided for relamping operations.

Exception No. 2: Where equipment is controlled by a disconnecting means that can be locked in the open position.

▲ In some types of outdoor lighting it would be difficult to keep all electrical equipment above the lamps and hence a disconnecting means may be required. A disconnecting means should be provided for the equipment on each individual pole, tower, or other structure if the conditions are such that lamp replacements may be necessary while the lighting system is in use. It may be assumed that grounded metal conduit or tubing extending below the lamps would not constitute a condition requiring that a disconnecting means must be provided.

ARTICLE 230. SERVICES

A. General

230-1. Scope. This Article covers service conductors and equipment for control and protection of services; the number, types, and sizes of services and service equipment; and the installation requirements.

230-2. Number of Services. A building or other structure served shall be supplied by only one set of service drop or service lateral conductors.

Exception No. 1: For fire pumps where a separate service is required.

Exception No. 2: For emergency electrical systems where a separate service is required.

Exception No. 3: Multiple-Occupancy Buildings.

a. By special permission, in multiple-occupancy buildings where there is no available space for service equipment accessible to all the occupants.

b. Buildings of multiple occupancy shall be permitted to have two or more separate sets of service-entrance conductors which are tapped from one service drop or lateral, or two or more sub-sets of service-entrance conductors shall be permitted to be tapped from a single set of main service-entrance conductors.

DEFINITION: Sub-sets of service-entrance conductors are taps from main service conductors run to service equipment.

▲ The granting of special permission is a responsibility of the local authority having jurisdiction as covered by Sec. 90-4.

Exception No. 4: Capacity Requirements. Two or more services shall be permitted:

a. Where the capacity requirements are in excess of 3000 amperes at a supply voltage of 600 volts or less; or

b. Where the load requirements of a single-phase installation are greater than the serving agency normally supplies through one service; or

c. By special permission.

▲ It is permissible to install two or more services where the serving utility cannot supply the load requirements of large single-phase installations. The serving utility is in the best position to judge how much capacity it can make available to supply the load through one service. For example, if a customer has requested a 240-V 3,000-A single-phase service for a multiple-occupancy building, it becomes impossible to supply this load through only one service. In most cases, the serving utility would use distribution transformers of 50 to 200 kVA with a secondary rating of less than 1,000 A. Therefore, two or more services shall also be allowed where the capacity of standard available equipment is exceeded.

Exception No. 5: Buildings of Large Area. By special permission, for a single building or other structure sufficiently large to make two or more services necessary.

Exception No. 6: For different characteristics, such as for different voltages, frequencies, or phases, or for different uses, such as for different rate schedules.

▲ It is generally the rule that a small building be supplied through one service.

Because of the type or size of occupancy or the need for different classes of use, it is sometimes necessary to supply a building with more than one set of service conductors.

Example: Exceptions 1 and 2 recognize additional separate services to supply fire pumps or emergency lighting. Each separate service is limited to not more than six disconnecting means, as described in Sec. 230-71. This would mean that the service could consist of the regular service equipment with six two- or three-pole circuit breakers or switches and separate service equipment to supply a fire pump, emergency lighting, etc.

Exception No. 3 pertains to multiple-occupancy buildings, and 3(a) requires special permission. The provisions of 3(b) permit two or more sub-sets of service-entrance conductors to be tapped from a single set of main service-entrance, and this rule should be coordinated with Sec. 230-72(d).

Exception No. 4 allows two or more services without special permission where a calculated service load exceeds 3,000 A. For lesser loads special permission is required to install more than one service.

Exception No. 5 requires special permission to install more than one service to buildings of *large area*. Examples of large-area buildings are high-rise buildings, shopping centers, and major industrial plants. In granting special permission the authority having jurisdiction must examine the availability of utility supplies for a given building, load concentrations within the building, and the ability of the utility to supply more than one service. Any of the special permission clauses in the exceptions in Sec. 230-2 require close cooperation and consultation between the authority having jurisdiction and the serving utility.

Exception No. 6 pertains to different classes of service some of which are described in Figs. 230-2 and 230-4.

230-3. One Building or Other Structure Not to Be Supplied Through Another.

Service conductors supplying a building or other structure shall not pass through the interior of another building or other structure.

Exception: Where the buildings or other structures served are under single occupancy or management.

See Section 230-44 for masonry-encased conductors considered outside of a building.

▲ A building as defined in Art. 100 is a structure which stands alone or is cut off from adjoining structures by fire walls with all openings therein protected by approved fire doors. A building divided into four units by such fire walls may be supplied by four separate service drops, but a similar building without the fire walls may be supplied by only one service drop except as permitted in Sec. 230-2.

A commercial building may be a single building but may be occupied by two or more tenants whose quarters are separate, in which case it might be undesirable to supply the building through one service drop. Under these conditions special permission may be given to install more than one service drop.

Some of the applications of service drops are shown in Figs. 230-1 through 230-4.

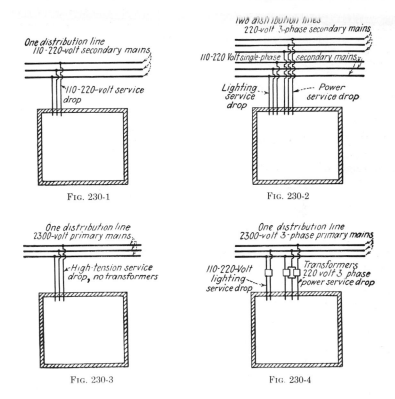

FIG. 230-1   FIG. 230-2

FIG. 230-3   FIG. 230-4

A secondary lighting main and a secondary power main run on the same pole line should be considered as different classes of use, so conductors from each main may be carried into one building. If the distribution line consists only of a high-voltage primary as in Fig. 230-4, two service drops, one for light and one for power, may be run to one building if the lighting service drop and the power service drop are supplied through different transformers.

B. Insulation and Size of Service Conductors

230-4. Insulation of Service Conductors. Service conductors shall normally

withstand exposure to atmospheric and other conditions of use without detrimental leakage of current.

For Service Drops—See Section 230-22.
For Underground Services—See Section 230-30.
For Service-Entrance Conductors—See Section 230-40.

▲ **It is not necessary to insulate the neutral conductor, because it is solidly tied to the service conduit, tubing, or cable armor at the service-equipment enclosure.**

230-5. Size of Service Conductors.   Service conductors shall have adequate ampacity to conduct safely the current for the loads supplied without a temperature rise detrimental to the insulation or covering of the conductors, and shall have adequate mechanical strength.

Minimum sizes are given in the following references:
For Service Drops--See Section 230-23.
For Underground Service Conductors—See Section 230-31.
For Service-Entrance Conductors—See Section 230-41.
For Farmstead Service Conductors—See Part D of Article 220.

C. Overhead Services

230-21. Overhead Supply.   Overhead conductors to a building or other structure from another building or other structure (such as a pole) on which a meter or disconnecting means is installed shall be considered as a service drop and installed accordingly.

Example: Farm loads in Part D of Article 220.

230-22. Insulation or Covering.
(a) **Cable.**   Individual conductors of multiconductor cable shall be insulated or covered with thermoplastic, rubber or other vulcanizable material.
Exception: A grounded conductor shall be permitted to be bare.
(b) **Open Wiring.**   Individual conductors shall be insulated or covered.

Service-drop conductors with an extruded covering have an ampacity equal to that of covered conductors of the same size as listed in Tables 310-17 and 310-19.

230-23. Size and Rating.   Conductors shall have sufficient ampacity to carry the load. They shall have adequate mechanical strength and shall not be smaller than No. 8 copper, No. 6 aluminum or copper-clad aluminum.
Exception: For installations to supply only limited loads of a single branch circuit such as small polyphase power, controlled water heaters and the like, they shall not be smaller than No. 12 hard-drawn copper or equivalent.
The grounded conductor shall not be less than the minimum size required by Section 250-23(b).
230-24. Clearances.   Service-drop conductors shall not be readily accessible and shall comply with (a) through (c) below for services not over 600 volts.
(a) **Over Roofs.**   Conductors shall have a clearance of not less than 8 feet from the highest point of roofs over which they pass.
Exception No. 1: Where the voltage between conductors does not exceed 300 and

*the roof has a slope of not less than 4 inches in 12 inches, a reduction in clearance
to 3 feet shall be permitted.*

▲ The intent of Exception 1 is that where the roof has a slope greater than 4 in.
in 12 in. it is considered difficult to walk upon and the height of conductors could
then be less than 8 ft from the highest point over which they pass but in no case
less than 3 ft except as permitted in Exception 2. See Figs. 230-5 and 230-6.

*Exception No. 2: Where the voltage between conductors does not exceed 300,
a reduction in clearance over the roof to not less than 18 inches shall be permitted
if (1) they do not pass over more than 4 feet of the overhang portion of the roof,
and (2) they are terminated at a through-the-roof raceway or approved support.*

See Section 230-28 for mast supports.

▲ See Figs. 230-5 and 230-6.

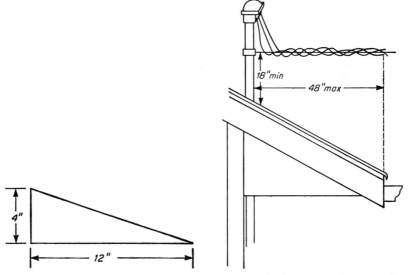

Fig. 230-5. Roof having a slope of not less
than 4 in. in 12 in.

Fig. 230-6. Service-drop conductors passing
over the overhang portion of the roof. Sec.
230-24, Exception No. 2.

(b) Clearance From Ground.   Service-drop conductors when not in excess of 600
volts, shall have the following minimum clearance from ground:

10 feet—above finished grade, sidewalks or from any platform or projection from which
   they might be reached;

12 feet—over residential driveways and commercial areas such as parking lots and drive-in
   establishments not subject to truck traffic;

15 feet—over commercial areas, parking lots, agricultural or other areas subject to truck
   traffic;

18 feet—over public streets, alleys, roads and driveways on other than residential property.

(c) Clearance from Building Openings. Conductors shall have a clearance of not less than 3 feet from windows, doors, porches, fire escapes, or similar locations. Conductors run above the top level of a window shall be considered out of reach from that window.

▲ The intent here is to provide the clearance specified and to prevent mechanical damage to and accidental contact with service conductors.

230-26. Point of Attachment. The point of attachment of conductors to a building or other structure shall provide the minimum clearances as specified in Section 230-24. In no case shall this point of attachment be less than 10 feet above finished grade.

▲ The clearances required in Secs. 230-24, 230-26 and 230-29 are based on safety-to-life considerations in that wires are required to be kept a reasonable distance from people who stand, reach, walk, or drive under service-drop conductors.

230-27. Means of Attachment. Multiconductor cables used for service drops shall be attached to buildings or other structures by fittings approved for the purpose. Open conductors shall be attached to fittings approved for the purpose or to noncombustible, nonabsorbent insulators securely attached to the building or other structure.

▲ See Sec. 230-51 for support of cable.

230-28. Service Masts As Supports. Where a service mast is used for the support of service-drop conductors, it shall be of adequate strength or be supported by braces or guys to withstand safely the strain imposed by the service drop. Where raceway-type service masts are used, all raceway fittings shall be approved for the purpose.

230-29. Supports Over Buildings. Service-drop conductors passing over a roof shall be securely supported by substantial structures. Where practicable, such supports shall be independent of the building.

D. Underground Services.

230-30. Insulation. Service lateral conductors shall be insulated for the applied voltage.

Exception: A grounded conductor shall be permitted as follows:
  1. *Bare copper used in a raceway.*
  2. *Bare copper for direct burial where bare copper is judged to be suitable for the soil conditions.*
  3. *Bare copper for direct burial without regard to soil conditions where part of an approved cable assembly with a moisture- and fungus-resistant outer covering.*
  4. *Aluminum or copper-clad aluminum without individual insulation or covering used in a raceway or for direct burial when part of a cable assembly approved for the purpose and having a moisture- and fungus-resistant outer covering.*

230-31. Size and Rating. Conductors shall have sufficient ampacity to carry the load. They shall not be smaller than No. 8 copper or No. 6 aluminum or copper-clad aluminum. The grounded conductor shall not be less than the minimum size required by Section 250-23(b).

Exception: For installations to supply only limited loads of a single branch circuit such as small polyphase power, controlled water heaters and the like, they shall not be smaller than No. 12 copper or No. 10 aluminum or copper-clad aluminum.

E. Service-Entrance Conductors

230-40. Insulation of Service-Entrance Conductors.

(a) Service-entrance conductors entering buildings or other structures shall be insulated. Where only on the exterior of buildings or other structures the conductors shall be insulated or covered.

Exception: A grounded conductor shall be permitted as follows:

1. *Bare copper used in a raceway or part of a service cable assembly.*
2. *Bare copper for direct burial where bare copper is judged to be suitable for the soil conditions.*
3. *Bare copper for direct burial without regard to soil conditions where part of an approved cable assembly with a moisture- and fungus-resistant outer covering.*
4. *Aluminum or copper-clad aluminum without individual insulation or covering used in a raceway or for direct burial when part of a cable assembly approved for the purpose and having a moisture- and fungus-resistant outer covering.*

(b) Open individual conductors which enter the building or other structure shall be rubber-covered or thermoplastic-covered.

230-41. Size and Rating.

(a) General. Conductors shall be of sufficient size to carry the loads as computed in accordance with Article 220. Ampacity shall be determined from Tables 310-16 through 310-19 and all applicable notes to these Tables.

(b) Ungrounded Conductors. Ungrounded conductors shall not be smaller than:

(1) 100-ampere, 3-wire, for a single-family dwelling with six or more 2-wire branch circuits.

(2) 100-ampere, 3-wire, for a single-family dwelling with an initial computed load of 10 kW or more.

(3) 60 amperes for other loads.

Exception No. 1: For loads consisting of not more than two 2-wire branch circuits, No. 8 copper or No. 6 aluminum or copper-clad aluminum.

Exception No. 2: By special permission, for loads limited by demand or by the source of supply, No. 8 copper or No. 6 aluminum or copper-clad aluminum.

Exception No. 3: For limited loads of a single branch circuit, No. 12 copper or No. 10 aluminum or copper-clad aluminum, but in no case smaller than the branch-circuit conductors.

(c) Grounded Conductors. The grounded (neutral) conductor shall not be less than the minimum size as required by Section 250-23(b).

F. Installation of Service Conductors

230-43. Wiring Methods for 600 Volts or Less. Service-entrance conductors shall be installed in accordance with the applicable requirements of this Code covering the type of wiring method used and limited to the following methods: (1) open wiring

on insulators; (2) rigid metal conduit; (3) electrical metallic tubing; (4) service-entrance cables; (5) wireways; (6) busways; (7) auxiliary gutters; (8) rigid non-metallic conduit; (9) cablebus; or (10) mineral-insulated metal-sheathed cable.

230-44. Conductors Considered Outside of Building. Conductors shall be considered outside of a building or other structure under any of the following conditions: (1) where installed under not less than 2 inches of concrete beneath a building or other structure, or (2) where installed within a building or other structure in a raceway that is enclosed by concrete or brick not less than 2 inches thick.

230-45. Separate Enclosures. Where two to six service disconnecting means in separate enclosures supply separate loads from one service drop or lateral, one set of service-entrance conductors shall be permitted to supply each or several such service equipment enclosures.

▲ This section permits two to six disconnecting means to be supplied from a single service drop or lateral where each disconnecting means supplies separate loads. Examples would be services to multifamily dwellings where six 400-A service entrances could be used in lieu of a single main 2,400-A entrance. Another application would be in a single-occupancy building where up to six subdivided loads can extend from a single drop or lateral, and in such cases, doughnut-type CT's would be installed at the service drop where single metering is required. This same approach can be used in subdividing service entrances into smaller load blocks to avoid the use of the equipment ground-fault circuit protection indicated in Sec. 230-95. The real importance of this rule is to avoid "paralleling" conductors with large-capacity services where this is desired. Another benefit concerns services added to an existing installation, and would allow a new additional service entrance in many instances without replacing the original one.

230-46. Unspliced Conductors. Service-entrance conductors shall not be spliced.

Exception No. 1: Clamped or bolted connections in metering equipment enclosures shall be permitted.

Exception No. 2: Where service-entrance conductors are tapped to supply two to six disconnecting means grouped at a common location.

Exception No. 3: At a properly enclosed junction point where an underground wiring method is changed to another type of wiring method.

▲ An underground service conduit usually terminates at the inside of the building wall unless the building has no basement. A metal conduit or a service cable may terminate at this point or may be run directly to the service equipment, as shown in Fig. 230-7.

From the terminal box, the conductors are run to the service equipment in rigid metal conduit or electrical metallic tubing or in an auxiliary gutter, and may terminate at any suitable point behind the switchboard. If the conductors are lead-covered, the end of the conduit or tubing is to be fitted with an ordinary bushing. If the conductors are not lead-covered, an insulating bushing must be used.

Exception No. 4: A connection shall be permitted where service conductors are extended from a service drop to an outside meter location and returned to connect to the service-entrance conductors of an existing installation.

▲ Where the meter is placed on the line side of the service equipment, splices are

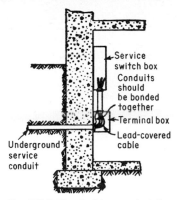

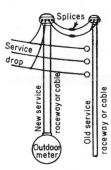

FIG. 230-7. Terminal box used at the end of an underground service conduit.

FIG. 230-8. Splices in service-entrance conductors where an outdoor meter is installed in place of an indoor meter for an existing installation.

necessary in order to connect the meter, and the forms of connections used in the meter base shown in Fig. 230-16 are satisfactory.

Where an underground service conduit terminates in a terminal box as shown in Fig. 230-7, the service conductors may be spliced in the box, provided the run is continued in a different type of raceway or as a suitable type of cable.

Figure 230-8 shows a form of construction sometimes employed where the inside meter of an existing installation is removed and an outdoor meter is installed. New service-entrance conductors are connected to the service drop and are carried down to a meter fitting in raceway or cable. From the meter, the outside service conductors return in the raceway or cable and are spliced to the old service-entrance conductors. These splices are permitted by Exception No. 4.

230-47. Other Conductors in Raceway or Cable. Conductors other than service conductors shall not be installed in the same service raceway or service-entrance cable.

Exception No. 1: Grounding conductors.

Exception No. 2: Time switch conductors having overcurrent protection.

▲ See Fig. 230-9.

230-48. Raceway Seal. Where a service raceway enters from an underground distribution system, it shall be sealed in accordance with Section 300-5. Spare or unused raceways shall also be sealed.

▲ This is not a requirement for a sealing fitting but for merely a puttylike compound stuffed into the end of the raceway.

230-49. Protection Against Damage—Underground. Underground service conductors shall be protected against physical damage in accordance with Section 300-5.

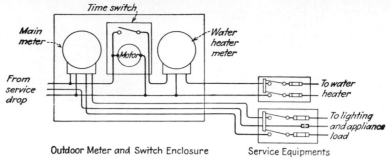

Outdoor Meter and Switch Enclosure   Service Equipments

FIG. 230-9. A time switch with its control circuit connected on the supply side of the service equipment.

230-50. Protection of Open Conductors and Cables Against Damage—Above Ground. Service-entrance conductors installed above ground shall be protected against physical damage as specified in (a) or (b) below.

(a) Service-Entrance Cables. Service-entrance cables, where subject to physical damage, such as where installed in exposed places near driveways or coal chutes, or where subject to contact with awnings, shutters, swinging signs, or similar objects, shall be protected in any of the following ways: (1) by rigid metal conduit; (2) by rigid nonmetallic conduit suitable for the location; (3) by electrical metallic tubing; or (4) by other approved means.

(b) Other Than Service-Entrance Cable. Individual open conductors and cables other than service-entrance cables shall not be installed within 8 feet of grade level or where exposed to physical damage.

230-51. Mounting Supports. Cables or individual open service conductors shall be supported as specified in (a), (b), or (c) below.

(a) Service-Entrance Cables. Service-entrance cables shall be supported by straps or other approved means within 12 inches of every service head, gooseneck, or connection to a raceway or enclosure and at intervals not exceeding $4\frac{1}{2}$ feet.

(b) Other Cables. Cables that are not approved for mounting in contact with a building or other structure shall be mounted on insulating supports installed at intervals not exceeding 15 feet and in a manner that will maintain a clearance of not less than 2 inches from the surface over which they pass.

(c) Individual Open Conductors. Individual open conductors shall be installed in accordance with Table 230-51(c). Where exposed to the weather, the conductors shall be mounted on insulators or on insulating supports attached to racks, brackets, or other approved means. Where not exposed to the weather, the conductors shall be mounted on glass or porcelain knobs.

230-52. Individual Conductors Entering Buildings or Other Structures. Where individual open conductors enter a building or other structure, they shall enter through roof bushings or through the wall in an upward slant through individual, noncombustible, nonabsorbent insulating tubes. Drip loops shall be formed on the conductors before they enter the tubes.

230-53. Raceways to Drain. Where exposed to the weather, raceways enclosing service-entrance conductors shall be raintight and arranged to drain. Where embedded in masonry, raceways shall be arranged to drain.

Table 230-51(c). Supports and Clearances for Individual Open Service Conductors

Maximum Volts	Maximum Distance In Feet Between Supports	Minimum Clearances In Inches	
		Between Conductors	From Surface
000	9	6	2
600	15	12	2
300	4½	3	2
600*	4½*	2½*	1*

*Where not exposed to weather.

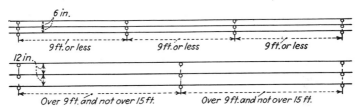

Fig. 230-10. Either of the above arrangements may be employed in supporting outside service conductors exposed to the weather.

▲ It is difficult to keep water vapor from entering metal raceways, but most of the trouble from this source can be prevented by avoiding low points in the raceway where water can collect.

230-54. Connections at Service Head.

(a) Service raceways shall be equipped with a raintight service head.

(b) Service cables, either (1) unless continuous from pole to service equipment or meter, shall be equipped with a raintight service head, or (2) formed in a gooseneck and taped and painted or taped with a self-sealing weather-resistant thermoplastic.

(c) Service heads and goosenecks in service-entrance cables shall be located above the point of attachment of the service-drop conductors to the building or other structure.

Exception: Where it is impracticable to locate the service head above the point of attachment, the service head location shall be permitted not farther than 24 inches from the point of attachment.

(d) Service cables shall be held securely in place by connection to service-drop conductors below the gooseneck or by a fitting approved for the purpose.

(e) Service heads shall have conductors of opposite polarity brought out through separately bushed holes.

(f) Drip loops shall be formed on individual conductors. To prevent the entrance of moisture, service-entrance conductors shall be connected to the service-drop conductors either (1) below the level of the service head, or (2) below the level of the termination of the service-entrance cable sheath.

(g) Service-drop conductors and service-entrance conductors shall be arranged so that water will not enter service raceway or equipment.

▲ See Fig. 370-1 for service head.

Where no service head is used at the upper end of a service cable, the cable should be bent over so that the individual conductors leaving the cable will extend in a downward direction and the end of the cable should be carefully taped and painted to exclude moisture.

Figure 230-11 shows a service cable terminating in a gooseneck above the service drop. The connections to the conductors of the service drop tend to hold the gooseneck in shape.

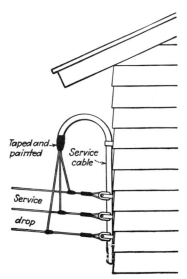

Fig. 230-11. Service-entrance cable terminating in a gooseneck.

Fig. 230-12. Fitting for use with service-entrance cable. (*Kwikon Co.*)

By using the fitting shown in Fig. 230-12 the gooseneck is held in place securely without depending upon the connections to the service-drop conductors.

Where the pole connection is higher than the connection of the service-entrance conductors at the service head, the connections at the pole should be made in such a manner that moisture will not enter the conductor.

In many cases the connection at the utility pole is higher than the connection at the building. Any stranded service-drop conductors act as a hose and the moisture is forced up through the service-entrance conductors by this head pressure and down into the meter or service equipment.

230-55. Termination at Service Equipment. Any service raceway or cable shall terminate at the inner end in a box, cabinet, or equivalent fitting that effectively encloses all live metal parts.

Exception: Where the service disconnecting means is mounted on a switchboard having exposed busbars on the back, a raceway shall be permitted to terminate at a bushing.

G. Service Equipment—Guarding and Grounding

230-62. Service Equipment—Enclosed or Guarded. Live parts of service equipment shall be enclosed as specified in (a) below, or guarded as specified in (b) below.

(a) Enclosed. Live parts shall be enclosed so that they will not be exposed to accidental contact or guarded as in (b) below.

(b) Guarded. Live parts that are not enclosed shall be installed on a switchboard, panelboard, or control board and guarded in accordance with Sections 110-17 and 110-18. Such an enclosure shall be provided with means for locking or sealing doors giving access to live parts.

230-63. Grounding and Bonding. Service equipment, raceways, cable armor, cable sheaths, etc., and any service conductor that is to be grounded shall be grounded in accordance with the following parts of Article 250.

Part B. Circuit and System Grounding.

Part C. Location of System Grounding Connections.

Part D. Enclosure Grounding.

Part F. Methods of Grounding.

Part G. Bonding.

Part H. Grounding Electrodes.

Part J. Grounding Conductors.

Exception: Service equipment shall not be required to be grounded where the voltage does not exceed 150 volts to ground and such enclosures are (1) isolated from conducting surfaces, and (2) unexposed to contact by persons or materials that could also be in contact with other conducting surfaces.

H. Service Equipment—Disconnecting Means

230-70. General. Means shall be provided to disconnect all conductors in a building or other structure from the service-entrance conductors. Each such disconnecting device shall be permanently marked to identify it as a service disconnecting means and shall be of a type that is suitable for use as service equipment under prevailing conditions. Service equipment installed in hazardous locations shall comply with the requirements of Articles 500 through 517.

230-71. Maximum Number of Disconnects.

(a) General. The service disconnecting means for each set or for each sub-set of service-entrance conductors shall consist of not more than six switches or six circuit breakers mounted in a single enclosure, in a group of separate enclosures, or in or on a switchboard.

(b) Single-Pole Units. Two or three single-pole switches or breakers, capable of individual operation, shall be permitted on multiwire circuits, one pole for each ungrounded conductor, as one multipole disconnect provided they are equipped with "handle ties" or a "master handle" to disconnect all conductors of the service with no more than six operations of the hand.

See Section 384-16(a) for service equipment in panelboards.

▲ The special or emergency service equipments permitted by Sec. 230-2 do not have to be grouped with the regular service equipment. It should also be noted that Sec. 700-6(c) requires emergency services to be widely separated from the other services.

The service equipment should be identified on the enclosures by such designations as "Light—115/230 Volts" and "Power—220 Volts."

The intent of this section is to limit to six operations of the hand the disconnection of all conductors of the service. The limitation is applicable to all of the service disconnecting means located in one place or "grouped" as required in Sec. 230-72. It does not include the "separate" services for fire pumps, emergency lighting, etc., which are recognized in Sec. 230-2 as being separate services for specific purposes.

See comments following Sec. 210-10. The cross reference to Sec. 384-16(a) calls attention to the requirement of over 20 A rating for service-disconnect means and overcurrent protection.

230-72. Grouping of Disconnects.

(a) Sets of Disconnects. Where supplied by one service drop or service lateral, the two to six service disconnecting means permitted in Section 230-71 shall be grouped and each marked to indicate the load it serves.

Exception: Services as permitted in Section 230-2.

(b) Emergency or Fire Pump Services. The one or more additional service disconnecting means for fire pumps or for emergency services shall be installed sufficiently remote from the one to six service disconnecting means for normal services to minimize the possibility of simultaneous interruption of supply.

See Sections 700-6(c) and 700-6(d) for emergency system services.

(c) Location. The service disconnecting means shall be installed either inside or outside of a building or other structure at a readily accessible location nearest the point of entrance of the service-entrance conductors.

▲ This paragraph states that the disconnecting means shall be located at a readily accessible point nearest to where the service conductors enter the building. No specific distance is stated, and approval of a specific installation is based on many existing factors and is a responsibility of the local inspection authority, as indicated in Sec. 90-4 of the Code.

The reason for keeping service conductors to a minimum length is that they do not have overcurrent protection and thus could become badly overheated in the event of an electrical breakdown or fault. The interior of the building presents more readily ignitible material than the outside, greater delay in the detecting of a fire, and greater life hazard to persons within the building in the event of a fire. For these and other reasons, the run of service conductors within the building should be kept to a minimum. See comments following Sec. 230-90(a).

(d) In a multiple-occupancy building, each occupant shall have access to his disconnecting means. A multiple-occupancy building having individual occupancy above the second floor shall have service equipment grouped in a common accessible location.

The disconnecting means shall consist of not more than six switches or six circuit breakers.

Multiple-occupancy buildings that do not have individual occupancy above the second floor shall be permitted to have service conductors run to each occupancy in accordance with Section 230-2, Exception No. 3 and each such service may have not more than six switches or six circuit breakers.

▲ The use of "individual occupancy" means any space such as an office or living apartment that is independent of any other occupancy in the building. Generally each such space is supplied through a separate meter.

Each apartment intended for use as living quarters by one family is an individual occupancy. Each apartment might be supplied through a separate meter, or all might be supplied through one meter.

It should be noted that the access for each occupant as required by paragraph (d) would not apply where the building was under the management of a building superintendent or the equivalent and where electrical service and maintenance was furnished. See Sec. 240-24(b), Exception.

Where there is individual occupancy above the second floor, the disconnecting means shall be located in a commonly accessible place, as shown in Fig. 230-14.

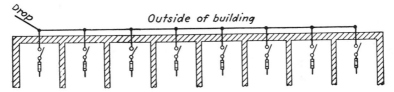

FIG. 230-13. Multiple-occupancy building having eight occupancies but no individual occupancy above the second floor. The service equipment for each occupancy may consist of any number of fusible switches or circuit breakers not exceeding six.

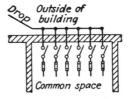

FIG. 230-14. Multiple-occupancy building having one or more individual occupancies above the second floor.

Where there is *no* individual occupancy above the second floor, a separate set of service-entrance conductors may be run to each occupancy, as shown in Fig. 230-13. In order to comply with Sec. 230-72(c), the conductors should either be run on the outside of the building to each occupancy or, if run inside the building, be encased in 2 in. of concrete or masonry in accordace with Sec. 230-44. In either case the service equipment should be located "nearest to the entrance of the conductors inside the building," and each occupant would have access to his disconnecting means.

Any desired number of sets of service-entrance conductors may be tapped from the service drop or lateral, or two or more subsets of service-entrance conductors may be tapped from a single set of main service conductors.

230-73. Working Space. Sufficient working space shall be provided in the vicinity of the service disconnecting means to permit safe operation, inspection, and repairs. In no case shall this be less than that specified by Section 110-16.

230-74. Simultaneous Opening of Poles. Each disconnecting means shall simultaneously disconnect all ungrounded conductors.

230-75. Disconnection of Grounded Conductor. Where the service disconnecting means does not disconnect the grounded conductor from the premises wiring, other means shall be provided for this purpose in the service equipment. A terminal or bus to which all grounded conductors can be attached by means of pressure connectors shall be permitted for this purpose.

▲ In this section the other means for disconnecting the grounded conductor from the interior wiring may be a screw or bolted lug on the neutral terminal block.

The grounded conductor must not be run straight through the service switch box with no means of disconnection.

230-76. Manually or Power Operable. The disconnecting means for ungrounded conductors shall consist of either (1) a manually operable switch or circuit breaker equipped with a handle or other suitable operating means, or (2) a power-operated switch or circuit breaker provided the switch or circuit breaker can be opened by hand in the event of a power supply failure.

230-77. Indicating. The disconnecting means shall plainly indicate whether it is in the open or closed position.

230-78. Externally Operable. An enclosed service disconnecting means shall be externally operable without exposing the operator to contact with live parts.

Exception: A power-operated switch or circuit breaker shall not be required to be externally operable by hand to the closed position.

▲ If a switch can be opened and closed without exposing the operator to contact with live parts, it is an externally operable switch, even though access to the switch handle requires opening the door of a cabinet. The exception pertains to electrically operated switches and circuit breakers.

230-79. Rating of Disconnect. The service disconnecting means shall have a rating not less than the load to be carried, determined in accordance with Article 220. In no case shall the rating be lower than specified in (a), (b), (c) or (d) below.

(a) One-Circuit Installation. For installations to supply only limited loads of a single branch circuit, the service disconnecting means shall have a rating of not less than 15 amperes.

(b) Two-Circuit Installations. For installations consisting of not more than two 2-wire branch circuits, the service disconnecting means shall have a rating of not less than 30 amperes.

(c) Single-Family Dwelling. For a single-family dwelling, the service disconnecting means shall have a rating of not less than 100 amperes, 3-wire under either of the following conditions: (1) where the initial computed load is 10 kW or more, or (2) where the initial installation consists of six or more 2-wire branch circuits.

▲ See Examples 1(b) and (c), Chap. 9.

(d) All Others. For all other installations the service disconnecting means shall have a rating of not less than 60 amperes.

230-80. Combined Rating of Disconnects. Where the service disconnecting means consists of more than one switch or circuit breaker, as permitted by Section 230-71, the combined ratings of all the switches or circuit breakers used shall not be less than the rating required for a single switch or circuit breaker.

230-81. Connection to Terminals. The service conductors shall be connected to the service disconnecting means by pressure connectors, clamps, or other approved means. Connections that depend upon solder shall not be used.

230-82. Equipment Connected to the Supply Side of Service Disconnect. Equipment shall not be connected to the supply side of the service disconnecting means.

Exception No. 1: Service fuses.

Exception No. 2: Fuses and disconnecting means or circuit breakers, in meter pedestals, connected in series with the ungrounded service conductors and located away from the building supplied.

Exception No. 3: Meters nominally rated not in excess of 600 volts, provided all metal housings and service enclosures are grounded in accordance with Article 250.

Exception No. 4: Instrument transformers (current and potential), high-impedance shunts, surge-protective capacitors, time switches, and lightning arresters.

Exception No. 5: Taps used only to supply time switches, circuits for emergency systems, stand-by power systems, fire pump equipment, and fire and sprinkler alarms if provided with service equipment and installed in accordance with requirements for service-entrance conductors.

▲ Emergency-lighting circuits, surge protective capacitors, and fire alarm and other protective signaling circuits, when placed ahead of the regular service disconnecting means, must have separate disconnects and overcurrent protection.

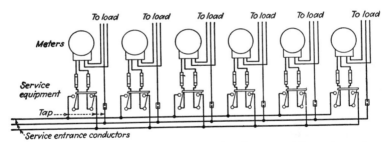

FIG. 230-15. Service equipment grouped at the point of entrance of the service conductors. No main switch is required. This could consist of six sets of fuses and switches or six circuit breakers as shown in Fig. 230-16. They could be in one enclosure or in separate enclosures.

230-83. Emergency Transfer Equipment. Where an emergency source is used as an alternate supply to the same load conductors supplied by the normal source, transfer equipment for shifting from one source to the other shall open all ungrounded conductors of one source before connection is made to the other.

Exception: Where parallel operation is used and suitable automatic control equipment is provided.

▲ This is intended to prevent an on-site generating plant for emergency service from feeding back into the utility company's supply.

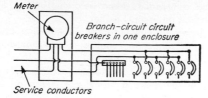

Fig. 230-16. Six circuit breakers in one enclosure suitable for use as service equipment.

Figures 230-15 and 230-16 comply with Secs. 230-71 and 230-90(a) Exception 3, which provide that any number of circuit breakers or fusible switches up to and including six may be used as the service equipment.

230-84. More Than One Building or Other Structure.

(a) Disconnect Required for Each. Where more than one building or other structure is on the same property and under single management, each building or other structure served shall be provided with means for disconnecting all ungrounded conductors.

See Sections 230-72(c) and (d) for location.

(b) Suitable for Service Equipment. The disconnecting means specified in (a) above shall be suitable for use as service equipment.

Exception: For garages and outbuildings on residential property, a snap switch or a set of 3-way or 4-way snap switches suitable for use on branch circuits shall be permitted as the disconnecting means.

▲ Applications of this rule to two buildings under single management and to three buildings under single management are shown in Figs. 230-17 and 230-18.

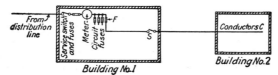

Fig. 230-17. With two buildings under single management, a switch, *S*, must be installed to control conductors *C*. This switch may be in building No. 1 if that building is adjacent to building No. 2.

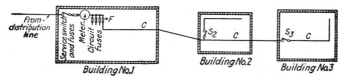

Fig. 230-18. Three buildings under single management. A switch S_2 must be provided to control the wiring in building No. 2, and a switch S_3 to control the wiring in building No. 3. Switch S_3 may be in either building No. 1 or building No. 2 if these buildings are adjacent to building No. 3.

Where outlets in a detached garage are supplied from a dwelling on the same premises, the garage circuit must be controlled by a switch; this may be a snap switch and may be either in the house or in the garage. (Three-way switches would provide greater convenience.) Disconnecting means must be provided for the wiring in each farm building.

J. Service Equipment—Overcurrent Protection

230-90. Where Required. Each ungrounded service-entrance conductor shall have overcurrent protection.

(a) Ungrounded Conductor. Such protection shall be provided by an overcurrent device in series with each ungrounded service conductor having a rating or setting not higher than the allowable ampacity of the conductor.

▲ The intent in paragraph (a) is to assure that the overcurrent protection required in the service-entrance equipment protects the service-entrance conductors from "overload." It is obvious that these overcurrent devices cannot provide "fault" protection for the service-entrance conductors if the fault occurs in the service-entrance conductors, but can protect them from overload where so selected as to have proper rating. Conductors on the load side of the service equipment are considered as feeders or branch circuits and are required by the Code to be protected as described in Arts. 210, 215, and 240.

Assume that the load of a building computed in accordance with Art. 220 is 255 A. Under Sec. 240-3(g), Exception 1, a 300-A fuse or circuit breaker may be considered as the proper-size overcurrent protection for service conductors rated between 255 and 300 A.

If the load could be separated in such a manner that six circuit breakers could be used instead of a single service disconnect means, total rating of the circuit breakers should be as near the ampacity of the service-entrance conductors as practicable based on standard ampere rating. See Sec. 240-3 and comments for Sec. 230-90(a), Exception 3.

Example: Six feeders supplied by six circuit breakers. If copper service-entrance conductors are 250,000-CM Type THW (255 A), six 50-A circuit breakers with a total rating of 300 A would be considered reasonable. This applies also to fused switches. It will be noted that the requirement is based on the fuse in the switch and not the rating of the switch; for example, for the above purpose a 60-A switch with a 50-A fuse is counted the same as a 50-A circuit breaker. In all the above cases the ungrounded service-entrance conductors are considered as being properly protected in accordance with Sec. 230-90(a).

Exception No. 1: For motor-starting currents, ratings in conformity with Sections 430-52, 430-62, or 430-63 shall be permitted.

▲ For motor branch circuits and feeders, Arts. 220 and 430 permit the use of overcurrent devices having ratings or settings higher than the capacities of the conductors. Article 230 makes similar provisions for services where the service supplies a motor load or a combination load of both motors and other loads.

Exception No. 2: Fuses and circuit breakers with a rating or setting in conformity with Section 240-3, Exception No. 1, and Section 240-6.

Exception No. 3: Not more than six circuit breakers or six sets of fuses shall be considered as the overcurrent device.

▲ For residential occupancies, the most widely accepted interpretation of Exception 3 by authorities having jurisdiction is to compute the total load of the building according to Art. 220. This will provide the minimum size of the service-entrance conductors. Then, if multiple overcurrent devices (two to six sets of fuses or circuit breakers) are used, the total rating of the multiple overcurrent devices need *not* match the ampacities of the service-entrance conductors within the limits of Exception 2. The logic to this interpretation is the nature of loads in residential occupancies where basic laws of diversity will prevent any serious or prolonged overload on the service-entrance conductors.

Exception No. 4: In a multiple-occupancy building each occupant shall have access to his overcurrent protective devices. A multiple-occupancy building having individual occupancy above the second floor shall have service equipment grouped in a common accessible location. The overcurrent protection shall consist of not more than six circuit breakers or six sets of fuses.

Multiple-occupancy buildings that do not have individual occupancy above the second floor shall be permitted to have service conductors run to each occupancy and each such service shall not have more than six circuit breakers or six sets of fuses.

Exception No. 5: Fire Pumps. Where the service to the fire pump room is judged to be outside of buildings, these provisions shall not apply. Service equipment for fire pump services shall be selected or set to carry locked-rotor current of the motor(s) indefinitely (see NFPA No. 20—1972, Standard for Centrifugal Fire Pumps).

▲ In the interest of fire protection, fire-pump motors are permitted to have much larger overcurrent protection than normal motor applications since the purpose of fire pumps is to aid in putting out fires. It should also be noted that Sec. 430-31 does not require motor-running protection for fire pumps for this same reason.

A set of fuses shall be considered all the fuses required to protect all the ungrounded conductors of a circuit. Single-pole circuit breakers, grouped in accordance with Section 230-71(b), shall be considered as one protective device.

▲ See comments following Sec. 230-72(c).

(b) Not in Grounded Conductor. No overcurrent device shall be inserted in a grounded service conductor except a circuit breaker which simultaneously opens all conductors of the circuit.

(c) More Than One Building. In a property comprising more than one building under single management, the ungrounded conductors supplying each building served shall be protected by overcurrent devices, which may be located in the building served or in another building on the same property, provided they are accessible to the occupants of the building served.

230-91. Location. The service overcurrent device shall be an integral part of the service disconnecting means or shall be located immediately adjacent thereto, unless located at the outer end of the entrance.

▲ The overcurrent devices, if inside the building, shall be close to the point at which the service conductors enter the building, because the service conductors are not fully protected against overcurrent and any run of service conductors inside a building is more or less hazardous and hence should be as short as possible. If the disconnecting means and overcurrent device are installed outside the building, it is not of great importance, from a safety standpoint, that this equipment be mounted close to the point at which the load-side conductors enter the building.

230-92. Location of Branch-Circuit Overcurrent Devices. Where the service overcurrent devices are locked or sealed, or otherwise not readily accessible, branch-circuit overcurrent devices shall be installed on the load side, shall be mounted in an accessible location, and shall be of lower rating than the service overcurrent device.

230-93. Protection of Specific Circuits. Where necessary to prevent tampering, an automatic overcurrent device protecting service conductors supplying only a specific load, such as a water heater, shall be permitted to be locked or sealed where located so as to be accessible.

230-94. Relative Location of Overcurrent Device and Other Service Equipment. The overcurrent device shall protect all circuits and devices.

Exception No. 1: The service switch shall be permitted on the supply side.

Exception No. 2: High-impedance shunt circuits, lightning arresters, surge protective capacitors, instrument transformers (current and potential), shall be permitted to be connected and installed on the supply side of the service disconnecting means as permitted in Section 230-82.

Exception No. 3: Circuits for emergency supply and time switches shall be permitted to be connected on the supply side of the service overcurrent device where separately provided with overcurrent protection.

Exception No. 4: Circuits used only for the operation of fire alarm, other protective signaling systems, or the supply to fire pump equipment shall be permitted to be connected on the supply side of the service overcurrent device where separately provided with overcurrent protection.

Exception No. 5: Meters nominally rated not in excess of 600 volts, provided all metal housings and service enclosures are grounded in accordance with Article 250.

Exception No. 6: Where service equipment is power operable, the control circuit shall be permitted to be connected ahead of the service equipment if suitable overcurrent protection and disconnecting means are provided.

230-95. Ground-Fault Protection of Equipment. Ground-fault protection of equipment shall be provided for solidly grounded wye electrical services of more than 150 volts to ground, but not exceeding 600 volts phase-to-phase for each service disconnecting means rated 1000 amperes or more.

(a) The ground-fault protection shall operate to cause the service disconnecting means to open all ungrounded conductors of the faulted circuit. The maximum setting of the ground-fault protection shall be 1200 amperes.

(b) If a switch and fuse combination is used, the fuses employed shall be capable of interrupting any current higher than the interrupting capacity of the switch during a time when the ground-fault protective system will not cause the switch to open.

As used in this Section, the rating of the Service Disconnecting Means is considered to be the rating of the largest fuse that can be installed or the highest trip setting for which the actual overcurrent device installed in a circuit breaker is rated or can be adjusted.

It is recognized that ground-fault protection is desirable for service disconnecting means rated less than 1000 amperes on solidly grounded systems having more than 150 volts to ground, not exceeding 600 volts phase-to-phase.

As used in this Section, solidly grounded means that the grounded conductor (neutral) is grounded without inserting any resistor or impedance device.

Ground-fault protection that functions to open the service disconnecting means will not protect service conductors or the service disconnecting means but will limit the damage to conductors and equipment on the load side of the ground-fault protection.

This added protective equipment at the service equipment will make it necessary to review the overall wiring system for proper selective overcurrent protection coordination. Additional installations of ground-fault protective equipment will be needed on feeders and branch circuits where maximum continuity of electrical service is necessary.

▲ Section 230-95 is aimed mainly at 480Y/277-V services. The purpose is to prevent *burndowns* of such services where line-to-ground faults occur on the load side of any service disconnecting means rated 1,000 A or more. Any disconnecting means rated less than 1,000 A, such as the use of five 800-A disconnecting means in lieu of a single 4,000-A disconnect, would not require ground-fault protection as described in this Section.

Data have shown that arcing to ground from an ungrounded conductor of a 480Y/277-V system is sustained at voltages from 70 to 140 V.

With larger conventional fuses and circuit breakers the line-to-ground arc is seen only as a moderate *load* current. Hence, such devices may not operate and serious burndowns and fires may result. Voltages below 150 V to ground generally do not sustain line-to-ground arcs because the arc voltage is low. Higher voltage systems, such as 4,160Y/2,400 V, will usually provide enough ground-fault current in line-to-ground arcing faults to clear conventional overcurrent devices used with such systems, and this is the major reason why ground-fault equipment protection is not required for systems of over 600 V phase to phase.

The selection of ground-fault equipment protection for 480Y/277-V systems requires a careful analysis of each particular installation—much the same as short-circuit studies to determine the interrupting capacity of overcurrent devices throughout a given installation (see comments following Sec. 110-9 and 110-10).

Figures 230-19 and 230-20 show two basic types of ground-fault equipment protectors presently available. The ground-fault sensor in Fig. 230-19 encircles all circuit conductors (phase conductors and the neutral). Under normal conditions the sum of all currents flowing through the circuit conductors will be zero. However, if one un-grounded conductor arcs to ground downstream from the ground fault sensor, such as to metallic conduits or cabinets, a *stray* current will return to the neutral bar through the metallic enclosures. This sets up a flux in the ground-fault sensor toroid in proportion to the amount of current in the grounding conductor. When this current exceeds the trip rating of the unit the circuit breaker shunt trip will operate and open the ungrounded conductors.

The ground-fault sensor shown in Fig. 230-20 is placed only over the bonding jumper (from the metal enclosure to the insulated neutral bar) and directly measures the line-to-ground current in the grounding conductor. When this current exceeds the

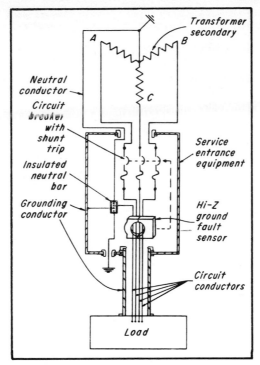

Fig. 230-19. Ground-fault sensor installed around all
conductors. (*O. Z. Electrical Mfg. Co., Inc.*)

trip rating of the unit it will operate the circuit breaker trip unit as explained in the
description of Fig. 230-19.

The 1,200-A value mentioned in Sec. 250-95 is the *maximum* trip setting to clear
ground-faults. Lower settings are permitted, and there are no minimum or maximum
time values because of differing needs for each installation. If ground-fault settings
are too low, an unnecessary outage may occur.

The fine print notes in Sec. 230-95 outline the basic considerations in selecting the
number and locations of ground-fault protectors. Manufacturers of such equipment
provide excellent literature on this subject, and consultation with these manufacturers
will avoid costly misapplications.

The following approach can be used in subdividing service entrances into smaller
load blocks to avoid the use of the equipment ground-fault circuit protection as
indicated in Sec. 230-95. An example would be a service to a multifamily dwelling
where six 400-A service entrances could be used in lieu of a single main 2,400-A
entrance. Another application would be in a single-occupancy building where up to
six subdivided loads can extend from a single drop or lateral, and in such cases,
donut-type CTs would be installed at the service drop where single metering is
required.

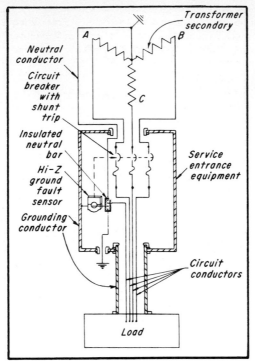

FIG. 230-20. Ground-fault sensor installed around the grounding-conductor bonding jumper only. (*O. Z. Electrical Mfg. Co., Inc.*)

230-96. Working Space. Sufficient working space shall be provided in the vicinity of the service overcurrent devices to permit safe operation, replacements, inspection, and repairs. In no case shall this be less than that specified by Section 110-16.

230-98. Available Short-Circuit Current. Service equipment shall be suitable for the short circuit current available at its supply terminals.

▲ See comments following Secs. 110-9 and 110-10.

K. Services Exceeding 600 Volts, Nominal

230-200. General. Service conductors and equipment used on circuits exceeding 600 volts shall comply with all applicable provisions of the preceding Sections of this Article and with the following Sections, which supplement or modify the preceding Sections. In no case shall the provisions of the Article apply to equipment on the supply side of the service conductors.

230-201. Classification of Service Conductors.

(a) Secondary Conductors. The secondary conductors shall constitute the service conductors where the step-down transformers are located as follows: (1) outdoors;

(2) in a separate building from the building or other structure served; (3) inside the building or other structure served where in a vault complying with Part C of Article 450; or (4) inside the building or other structure served where in a locked room or other locked enclosure and accessible to qualified persons only.

(b) Primary Conductors. In all other cases, the primary conductors shall be considered the service conductors.

▲ In the cases shown in Figs. 230-21 through 230-24, the secondary conductors are considered as the service conductors. The transformers in vaults are assumed to be accessible only to qualified persons.

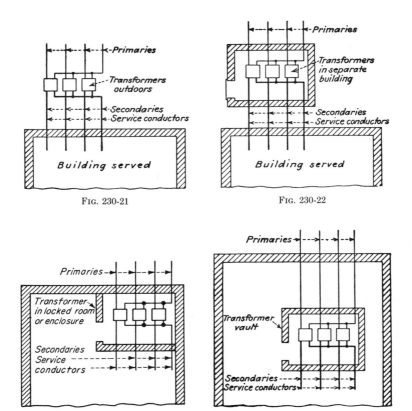

FIG. 230-21   FIG. 230-22

FIG. 230-23   FIG. 230-24

230-202. Service-Entrance Conductors. Service-entrance conductors to buildings or enclosures shall be installed to conform to the following:

(a) Conductor Size. Service conductors shall be not smaller than No. 6 unless in cable. Conductors in cable shall be not smaller than No. 8.

(b) Wiring Methods. Service-entrance conductors shall be installed by means of one of the following wiring methods: (1) in rigid metal conduit; (2) in rigid nonmetallic conduit where encased in not less than 2 inches of concrete: (3) as multiconductor cable approved for the purpose; (4) as open conductors where supported on insulators approved for the purpose and where either accessible only to qualified persons or where effectively guarded against accidental contact; or (5) in cablebus. Underground service-entrance conductors shall conform to Section 710-3(b).

See Section 310-51 for shielding of solid dielectric insulated conductors.

(c) **Open Work.**   Open wire services over 600 volts shall be installed in accordance with the provisions of Article 710, Part D.

(d) **Supports.**   Service conductors and their supports, including insulators, shall have strength and stability sufficient to insure maintenance of adequate clearance with abnormal currents in case of short circuits.

(e) **Guarding.**   Open wires shall be guarded to make them accessible only to qualified persons.

(f) **Service Cable.**   Where cable conductors emerge from a metal sheath or raceway, the insulation of the conductors shall be protected from moisture and physical damage by a pothead or other approved means.

(g) **Draining Raceways.**   Unless conductors specifically approved for the purpose are used, raceways embedded in masonry, or exposed to the weather, or in wet locations shall be arranged to drain.

(h) **Over 15,000 Volts.**   Where the voltage exceeds 15,000 volts between conductors they shall enter either metal-enclosed switchgear or a transformer vault conforming to the requirements of Sections 450-41 through 450-48.

(i) **Conductor Considered Outside Building.**   Conductors placed under at least 2 inches of concrete beneath a building, or conductors within a building in conduit or duct and enclosed by concrete or brick not less than 2 inches thick shall be considered outside the building.

230-203. Warning Signs.   High-voltage signs with the words "High Voltage" shall be posted where unauthorized persons might come in contact with live parts.

230-204. Isolating Switches.

(a) **Where Required.**   Where oil switches or air or oil circuit breakers constitute the service disconnecting means, an air-break isolating switch shall be installed on the supply side of the disconnecting means and all associated service equipment.

Exception: Where such equipment is mounted on removable truck panels or metal-enclosed switchgear units, which cannot be opened unless the circuit is disconnected, and which, when removed from the normal operating position, automatically disconnect the circuit breaker or switch from all live parts.

(b) **Fuses As Isolating Switch.**   Where fuses are of the type that can be operated as a disconnecting switch, a set of such fuses shall be permitted as the isolating switch where: (1) the oil disconnecting means is a nonautomatic switch, and (2) the set of fuses disconnect the oil switch and all associated service equipment from the service-entrance conductors.

(c) **Accessible to Qualified Persons Only.**   The isolating switch shall be accessible to qualified persons only.

(d) **Grounding Connection.**   Isolating switches shall be provided with a means for readily connecting the load side conductors to ground when disconnected from the source of supply.

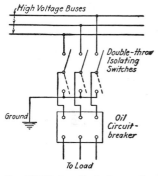

FIG. 230-25. High-voltage fuses (with "fire" condensers) and isolating switches. (*Westinghouse Electric Corp.*)

FIG. 230-26. A method of grounding the load side of isolating switches while the switches are open.

A means for grounding the load side conductors need not be provided for any duplicate isolating switch installed and maintained by the electric supply company.

230-205. Disconnecting Means. The service disconnecting means shall simultaneously disconnect all ungrounded conductors and shall be capable of being closed on a fault within the maximum interrupting rating of the overcurrent protection.

230-206. Overcurrent Devices As Disconnecting Means. Where the circuit breaker or alternative for it specified in Section 230-208 for service overcurrent devices meets the requirements specified in Section 230-205, they shall constitute the service disconnecting means.

230-207. Equipment in Secondaries. Where the primary service equipment supplies one or more transformers whose secondary windings connect to a single set of mains, and the primary load-interrupter switch or circuit breaker is capable of being opened and closed from a point outside the transformer vault, the disconnecting means and overcurrent protection shall not be required in the secondary circuit if the primary fuse or circuit breaker is rated or set to protect the secondary circuit.

230-208. Overcurrent Protection Requirements. Service-entrance conductors shall have a short circuit protective device in each ungrounded conductor, on the load side of, or as an integral part of the service-entrance switch. The protective device shall be capable of detecting and interrupting all values of current in excess of its trip setting or melting point, which can occur at its location. A fuse rated in continuous amperes not to exceed three times the ampacity of the conductor, or a circuit breaker with a trip setting of not more than six times the ampacity of the conductors shall be considered as providing the required short circuit protection.

See Tables 310-39 through 310-50 for ampacity of high voltage conductors.

Overcurrent devices shall conform to the following:

(a) In Vault or Consisting of Metal-Enclosed Switchgear. Where the service equipment is installed in a transformer vault meeting the provisions of Sections 450-41 through 450-48, or consists of metal-enclosed switchgear, the overcurrent protection and disconnecting means shall be one of the following:

(1) A nonautomatic oil switch, oil fuse cutout, air load-interrupter switch, or other switch approved for the purpose shall be permitted with suitable fuses. The interrupting rating of this switch shall equal or exceed the continuous current rating of the fuse.

(2) An automatic trip circuit breaker of suitable current-carrying and interrupting capacity.

(3) A switch capable of interrupting the no-load current of the transformer supplied through the switch and suitable fuses shall be permitted provided the switch is interlocked with a single switch or circuit breaker on the secondary circuit of

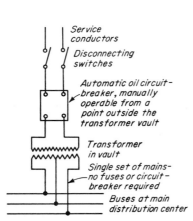

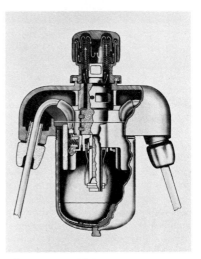

Fig. 230-27. Where a transformer supplies only one set of secondary mains, these mains may be connected direct to the buses at the distribution center without a switch or overload protection. The primary breaker must be set to protect the secondary circuit.

Fig. 230-28. Oil-fuse cutout. (*General Electric Co.*)

the transformer so that the primary switch cannot be opened when the secondary circuit is closed.

(b) Not in Vault or Not Consisting of Metal-Enclosed Switchgear. Where the service equipment is not in a vault or metal-enclosed switchgear, the overcurrent protection and disconnecting means shall be either of the following:

(1) An air load-interrupter switch or other switch approved for the purpose capable of interrupting the rated circuit load shall be permitted with suitable fuses on a pole or elevated structure outside the building provided the switch is operable by persons using the building.

(2) An automatic-trip circuit breaker of suitable ampacity and interrupting capacity. The circuit breaker shall be located outside the building as near as practicable to where the service conductors enter the building. The location shall be permitted on a pole, roof, foundation or other structure.

(c) Fuses. Fuses shall have an interrupting rating no less than the maximum available short-circuit current in the circuit at their supply terminals.

(d) Circuit Breakers. Circuit breakers shall be free to open in case the circuit is closed on an overload. This can be accomplished by means such as trip-free circuit breakers. A service circuit breaker shall indicate clearly whether it is open or closed,

Fig. 230-29. Group-operated interrupter-switch and power-fuse combination for use in metal-enclosed switchgear. Shown in open position. Switch rating: 13.8 kV, 600 A continuous and interrupting, 40,000 A momentary, 40,000 A fault closing. Fuse rating: 400 E A max continuous, 40,000 A RMS asym. interrupting. (*S & C Electric Company.*)

and shall have an interrupting rating no less than the maximum available short-circuit current at its supply terminals.

Overcurrent relays shall be furnished in connection with current transformers in one of the following combinations:

(1) Three overcurrent relays operated from current transformers in each phase.

(2) Two overcurrent relays operated by current from current transformers in any two phases and one overcurrent relay sensitive to ground-fault current that is operated by the sum of the currents from current transformers in each phase.

(3) Two overcurrent relays operated by current from current transformers in any two phases and one overcurrent relay sensitive to ground-fault current that is operated from a current transformer which links all three phase conductors and the grounded circuit conductor (neutral), if provided.

(e) Enclosed Overcurrent Devices. The restriction to 80 percent of rating for an enclosed overcurrent device on continuous loads shall not apply to overcurrent devices installed in services operating at over 600 volts.

▲ *Suitable ampacity* as mentioned in Sec. 230-208(b)(2) is the ability of the circuit breaker to carry the connected load without overheating.

230-209. Surge Arresters (Lightning Arresters). Surge arresters installed in accordance with the requirements of Article 280 shall be placed on each ungrounded

FIG. 230-30. Exploded view of indoor solid-material (SM) power fuseholder (boric-acid arc-extinguishing type). Shows spring and cable assembly, refill unit, holder, and snuffler. Rated 14.4 kV, 400 E A max., 40,000 A RMS asym. interrupting. (*S & C Electric Company.*)

overhead service conductor on the supply side of the service equipment, when called for by the authority having jurisdiction.

230-210. Service Equipment-General Provisions. Service equipment including instrument transformers shall conform to Article 710, Part B.

230-211. Metal-Enclosed Switchgear. Metal-enclosed switchgear shall consist of a substantial metal structure and a sheet metal enclosure. Where installed over a wood floor, suitable protection thereto shall be provided.

ARTICLE 240. OVERCURRENT PROTECTION

240-1. Scope. Parts A through G of this Article provide the general requirements for overcurrent protection and overcurrent protective devices not more than 600 volts, nominal. Part H covers overcurrent protection over 600 volts, nominal.

Overcurrent protection for conductors and equipment is provided to open the circuit if the current reaches a value that will cause an excessive or dangerous temperature in conductors or conductor insulation. See also Sections 110-9 and 110-10 for requirements for interrupting capacity and protection against fault currents.

A. General

240-2. Protection of Equipment. Equipment shall be protected against overcurrent in accordance with the Article in this Code covering the type of equipment as specified in the following list.

240-3. Protection of Conductors—Other Than Flexible Cords and Fixture Wires.
Conductors, other than flexible cords and fixture wires, shall be protected against overcurrent in accordance with their ampacities as specified in Tables 310-16 through 310-19 and all applicable notes to these Tables.

Exception No. 1: Next Higher Overcurrent Protective Device Rating. Where the ampacity of the conductor does not correspond with the standard ampere rating of a fuse or a circuit breaker without overload trip adjustment above its rating (but which may have other trip or rating adjustments), the next higher standard device rating shall be permitted only if this rating does not exceed 800 amperes.

▲ As indicated in Sec. 240-1, Art. 240 provides the general requirements for overcurrent protection and overcurrent protective devices.

Sec. 210-19(a) requires that branch-circuit conductors shall have an ampacity of not less than the rating of the branch circuit and not less than the maximum load to be served. In this case, Sec. 210-19(a) is a specific requirement and has precedence over Sec. 240-3, Exception No. 1, only where it applies to multioutlet branch circuits. See Sec. 210-3 and the asterisk note to Table 210-24.

Exception No. 2: Tap Conductors. Tap conductors as permitted in Sections 210-19(c); 240-21, Exception Nos. 2, 3, 5, and 8; 364-9 and 364-10; and Part D of Article 430.

Exception No. 3: Motor and Motor-Control Circuits. Motor and motor-control circuit conductors protected in accordance with Parts C, D, E, and F of Article 430. Motor-operated appliance circuit conductors protected in accordance with Parts B and D of Article 422. Air-conditioning and refrigerating equipment circuit conductors protected in accordance with Parts C and F of Article 440.

Exception No. 4: Remote-Control Circuits. Where not in the same cable with communication circuits, as provided in Section 725-5, conductors of remote-control circuits other than motor-control circuits shall be considered as protected by overcurrent devices that are rated or set at not more than 300 percent of the ampacity of the remote-control conductors.

Exception No. 5: Transformer Secondary Conductors. Conductors supplied by the secondary side of a single-phase transformer having a 2-wire (single-voltage) secondary shall be considered as protected by overcurrent protection provided on the primary (supply) side of the transformer, provided this protection is in accordance with Section 450-3 and does not exceed the value determined by multiplying the secondary conductor ampacity by the secondary-to-primary transformer voltage ratio.

▲ *Example:* A 10-kVA dry-type transformer has a two-wire 480-V primary and a two-wire 240-V secondary (a 2:1 ratio). The full-load primary current is 20.8 A. The full-load secondary current is 41.6 A. The primary conductors are No. 10 AWG copper conductors, Type TW. The secondary conductors are No. 6 AWG copper conductors,

Type TW, which extend to a 10-kW heater. Primary protection consists of two 25-A fuses. This arrangement satisfies Exception 5 in that (1) the primary of the transformer is protected to satisfy Sec. 450-3(b)(1), since 20.8 A × 125% is more than 25 A; (2) the No. 10 primary conductors have an ampacity of 30 A and are properly protected; (3) the No. 6 secondary conductors have an ampacity of 55 A, which times $\frac{1}{2}$ (the secondary-to-primary voltage ratio) = 27.5 A and is properly protected by the 25-A primary fuse. Accordingly, no overcurrent protection is required in the secondary, and the length of secondary conductors is not limited.

For other than two-wire to two-wire transformations complying with Exception 5, secondary conductors must be protected on the secondary side, except as permitted for limited tap lengths in Exceptions 2 and 8 of Sec. 240-21.

Where transformers have more than two wires on the secondary, unbalanced currents in the secondary will cause an overload on part of the secondary circuit and transformer winding and go unnoticed by the primary overcurrent device.

If, in the previous example, the secondary was three-wire, 120/240-V, one secondary transformer winding could carry 100 A (line-to-neutral with no load on the other 120-V winding). In this case the 25-A primary fuse sees the 100-A secondary load as only 25 A as the result of a 4:1 ratio (480:120), and one 120-V secondary winding and two of the three No. 6 secondary conductors would be seriously overloaded.

Main secondary protection will protect against such unbalances, except for a line-to-ground fault that could occur between the transformer secondary connection and the secondary overcurrent devices; however this risk is inherent in the 10- and 25-ft tap rule exceptions of Sec. 240-21.

240-4. Protection of Fixture Wires and Cords. Fixture wire or flexible cord, size No. 16 or No. 18, and tinsel cord shall be considered as protected by 20-ampere overcurrent devices. Fixture wires of the sizes permitted for taps in Section 210-19(c) shall be considered as protected by the overcurrent protection of the 30-, 40-, and 50-ampere branch circuits of Article 210. Flexible cord approved for use with specific appliances shall be considered as protected by the overcurrent device of the branch circuit of Article 210 when conforming to the following:

20-ampere circuits, No. 18 cord and larger.
30-ampere circuits, cord of 10-ampere capacity and over.
40-ampere circuits, cord of 20-ampere capacity and over.
50-ampere circuits, cord of 20-ampere capacity and over.

240-6. Standard Ampere Ratings. The standard ampere ratings for fuses and inverse time circuit breakers shall be considered 15, 20, 25, 30, 35, 40, 45, 50, 60, 70, 80, 90, 100, 110, 125, 150, 175, 200, 225, 250, 300, 350, 400, 450, 500, 600, 700, 800, 1000, 1200, 1600, 2000, 2500, 3000, 4000, 5000, and 6000.

240-8. Fuses or Circuit Breakers in Parallel. Fuses, circuit breakers, or combinations thereof shall not be connected in parallel.

Exception: Circuit breakers assembled in parallel that are tested and approved for the purpose.

240-9. Thermal Devices. Thermal cutouts, thermal relays, and other devices not designed to open short circuits shall not be used for the protection of conductors against overcurrent due to short circuits or grounds but the use of such devices shall be permitted to protect motor-branch-circuit conductors from overload if protected in accordance with Section 430-40.

▲ Thermal cutouts and thermal and magnetic relays are used to protect the motors as well as the motor-circuit conductors against excessive overloads, but they must be backed up by fuses or circuit breakers that provide short-circuit protection.

240-10. Supplementary Overcurrent Protection. Where supplementary overcurrent protection is used for lighting fixtures, appliances, and other equipment or for internal circuits and components of equipment, it shall not be used as a substitute for branch-circuit overcurrent devices or in place of the branch-circuit protection specified in Article 210. Supplementary overcurrent devices shall not be required to be readily accessible.

240-11. Definition of Current-Limiting Overcurrent Protective Device. A current-limiting overcurrent protective device is a device which, when interrupting currents in its current-limiting range, will reduce the current flowing in the faulted circuit to a magnitude substantially less than that obtainable in the same circuit if the device were replaced with a solid conductor having comparable impedance.

▲ This paragraph is more in the form of a definition than a requirement and has to do with the requirement for marking of current limitation under Sec. 240-60. It concerns fuses which can open the circuit during the first half cycle before the current reaches its expected short-circuit peak. See comments on Secs. 110-9 and 110-10.

B. Location

240-20. Ungrounded Conductors.

(a) Overcurrent Device Required. A fuse or an overcurrent trip unit of a circuit breaker shall be connected in series with each ungrounded conductor. A combination of a current transformer and overcurrent relay shall be considered equivalent to an overcurrent trip unit.

For motor circuits, see Parts C, D, F, and J of Article 430.

(b) Circuit Breaker As Overcurrent Device. Circuit breakers shall open all ungrounded conductors of the circuit.

Exception: Individual single-pole circuit breakers shall be acceptable as the protection for each conductor of ungrounded 2-wire circuits, each ungrounded conductor of 3-wire direct-current or single-phase circuits, or for each ungrounded conductor of lighting or appliance branch circuits connected to 4-wire 3-phase systems or 5-wire 2-phase systems, provided such lighting or appliance circuits are supplied from a system having a grounded neutral and no conductor in such circuits operates at a voltage greater than permitted in Section 210-6.

240-21. Location in Circuit. An overcurrent device shall be connected at the point where the conductor to be protected receives its supply.

Exception No. 1: Smaller Conductor Protected. Where the overcurrent device protecting the larger conductor also protects the smaller conductor in accordance with Tables 310-16 through 310-19.

Exception No. 2: Feeder Taps Not Over 10 Feet Long. For conductors tapped to a feeder or transformer secondary where all of the following conditions are met:

a. The length of the tap conductors does not exceed 10 feet.

b. The ampacity of the tap conductors is: (1) not less than the combined computed loads on the circuits supplied by the tap conductors, and (2) not less than the ampere rating of the switchboard, panelboard, or control device supplied by the tap conductors unless they are terminated in an overcurrent protective device not exceeding the ampacity of the tap conductors.

c. The tap conductors do not extend beyond the switchboard, panelboard, or control devices they supply.

d. Except at the point of connection to the feeder, the tap conductors are enclosed in a raceway, which shall extend from the tap to the enclosure of an enclosed switchboard, panelboard, or control devices, or to the back of an open switchboard.

See Section 384-16(a) for lighting and appliance branch-circuit panelboards.

Exception No. 3: Feeder Taps Not Over 25 Feet Long. For conductors tapped to a feeder where all of the following conditions are met:

a. The length of the tap conductors does not exceed 25 feet.

b. The ampacity of the tap conductors is not less than ⅓ that of the feeder conductors from which they are supplied.

c. The tap conductors terminate with a single circuit breaker or a single set of fuses that will limit the load to the ampacity of the tap conductors. This single overcurrent device shall be permitted to supply any number of additional overcurrent devices on its load side.

d. The tap conductors are suitably protected from physical damage.

Exception No. 4: Service Conductors. For service-entrance conductors where protected in accordance with Section 230-91.

Exception No. 5: Branch-Circuit Taps. Taps to individual outlets and circuit conductors supplying a single household electric range shall be considered as protected by the branch-circuit overcurrent devices when in accordance with the requirements of Sections 210-19, 210-20, and 210-24.

Exception No. 6: Motor Circuit Taps. For motor-branch-circuit conductors where protected in accordance with Sections 430-28 and 430-53.

Exception No. 7: Busway Taps. For busways where protected in accordance with Sections 364-9 through 364-13.

Exception No. 8: Transformer Feeder Taps with Primary Plus Secondary Not Over 25 Feet Long. Where all of the following conditions are met:

a. The conductors supplying the primary of a transformer have an ampacity at least ⅓ that of the conductors or overcurrent protection from which they are tapped, and

b. The conductors supplied by the secondary of the transformer have an ampacity that, when multiplied by the ratio of the secondary-to-primary voltage, is at least ⅓ the ampacity of the conductors or overcurrent protection from which the primary conductors are tapped, and

c. The total length of one primary plus one secondary conductor, excluding any portion of the primary conductor that is protected at its ampacity, is not over 25 feet, and

d. The primary and secondary conductors are suitably protected from physical damage, and

e. The secondary conductors terminate in a single circuit breaker or set of fuses which will limit the load to that allowed in Tables 310-16 through 310-19.

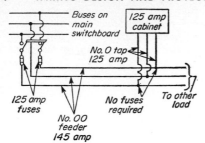

FIG. 240-1. Feeder tap where the tap
conductors are protected by the feeder
fuses.

▲ Exception 1 is illustrated by Fig. 240-1. A No. 00 feeder is run from a main
switchboard where it is protected by 125-A fuses. No. 0 conductors are tapped to the
feeder conductors.

Exception 2 concerns a 10-ft feeder or transformer tap to a switchboard, panelboard,
single fusible switch or single circuit breaker. If the tap extends to a switchboard
or panelboard the tap must have an ampacity not less than the switchboard or
panelboard rating unless terminated in an overcurrent device not exceeding the
ampacity of the tap conductors. Furthermore if the panelboard is a lighting and
appliance type (see definition in Sec. 384-14) the tap must terminate in an overcurrent
device complying with Sec. 384-16(a). Taps to a fusible switch or circuit breaker must
be sized not less than the calculated load supplied by the switch or breaker, in which
case, the tap would be of a size not less than the load conductors of the switch or
breaker.

In extending to equipment the tap must be enclosed in a raceway.

In the case of transformers, the 10-ft tap can be applied to the secondary conductors
if the primary overcurrent devices conform to Sec. 450-3(a)(1) or (b)(1) and the primary
conductors are properly protected by the primary overcurrent devices. In such
instances, the previously mentioned general considerations would also apply.

Exception 3 is illustrated in Fig. 240-2.

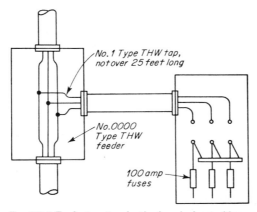

FIG. 240-2. Feeder taps terminating in a single set of fuses.
See Exception 3.

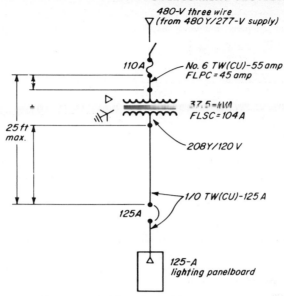

Taps protected from physical damage.
Secondary-to-primary voltage ratio = 208:480 = 1:2.3

FIG. 240-3. Example of Sec. 240-21, Exception 8, which also conforms with Secs. 384–16(a) and 450-3(b).

Exception 8 is a 25-ft-feeder-tap rule specifically for transformer applications other than specified in Sec. 240-3, Exception 5, and Sec. 240-21, Exception 2 (as previously described).

In all cases the provisions of Secs. 450-3 (transformer overcurrent protection) and 384-16(a) (panelboard overcurrent protection) must be satisfied. The example in Fig. 240-3 complies with Exception 8 and with Secs. 384-16(a) and 450-3(b).

240-22. Grounded Conductors. No overcurrent device shall be connected in series with any conductor that is intentionally grounded.

Exception No. 1: Where the overcurrent device opens all conductors of the circuit, including the grounded conductor, and is so designed that no pole can operate independently.

Exception No. 2: Where required by Sections 430-36 and 430-37 for motor running (overload) protection.

▲ Many years ago fused neutrals were in use, but it was found that damage resulted from an unbalanced voltage when only the neutral fuse opened.

240-23. Change in Size of Grounded Conductor. Where a change occurs in the size of the ungrounded conductor, a similar change may be made in the size of the grounded conductor.

▲ In effect, this recognizes the fact that if the neutral is the same size as the ungrounded conductor, it will be protected wherever the ungrounded conductor is protected. One of the most obvious places this is encountered is in a distribution center where a small grounded conductor may be connected directly to a large grounded feeder conductor.

240-24. Location in or on Premises.

(a) Readily Accessible. Overcurrent devices shall be readily accessible.

Exception No. 1: For services as provided in Section 230-91.

Exception No. 2: For busways as provided in Section 364-11.

Exception No. 3: For supplementary overcurrent protection as described in Section 240-10.

(b) Occupant to Have Ready Access. Each occupant shall have ready access to all overcurrent devices protecting the conductors supplying his occupancy.

Exception: In a multiple-occupancy building where electric service and electrical maintenance are provided by the building management and where these are under continuous building management supervision, the service overcurrent devices and feeder overcurrent devices supplying more than one occupancy shall be permitted to be accessible to authorized management personnel only.

(c) Not Exposed to Damage. Overcurrent devices shall be located where they will not be exposed to physical damage.

(d) Not in Vicinity of Easily Ignitible Material. Overcurrent devices shall not be located in the vicinity of easily ignitible material.

C. Enclosures

240-30. General. Overcurrent devices shall be enclosed in cabinets or cutout boxes.

Exception No. 1: Where a part of an assembly that provides equivalent protection.

Exception No. 2: Where mounted on open-type switchboards, panelboards, or control boards that are in rooms or enclosures free from dampness and easily ignitible material and accessible only to qualified personnel.

Exception No. 3: The operating handle of a circuit breaker shall be permitted to be accessible without opening a door or cover.

▲ Protective devices are intended to open the circuit in the event of disturbances on the line so that abnormal conditions are limited to a small area. It is in consideration of this fact that every precaution is taken to see that malfunctioning of the protective device or its associated equipment will not create a hazard in that vicinity. This is the basis for the requirements in Secs. 240-24 and 240-30. Sec. 384-4 requires that all switchboards having exposed live parts shall be located where accessible only to qualified persons.

240-32. Damp or Wet Locations. Enclosures for overcurrent devices in damp or wet locations shall be of a type approved for the purpose and shall be mounted so there is at least $\frac{1}{4}$-inch air space between the enclosure and the wall or other supporting surface.

240-33. Vertical Position. Enclosures for overcurrent devices shall be mounted in a vertical position unless in individual instances this is shown to be impracticable.

▲ The requirement in Sec. 240-33 is to prevent the mounting of enclosures on ceilings and floors where poor operation of the enclosed equipment may result.

D. Disconnecting and Guarding

240-40. Disconnecting Means for Fuses and Thermal Cutouts. Disconnecting means shall be provided on the supply side of all fuses or thermal cutouts in circuits of over 150 volts to ground and cartridge fuses in circuits of any voltage, where accessible to other than qualified persons, so that each individual circuit containing fuses or thermal cutouts can be independently disconnected from the source of electric energy.

Exception No. 1: Where fuses are permitted on the supply side of the service disconnecting means as provided by Section 230-82.

Exception No. 2: A single disconnecting means shall be permitted on the supply side of more than one set of fuses as provided by Section 430-112 for group operation of motors and in Section 424-22 for fixed electric space heating equipment.

▲ Whenever cartridge fuses are accessible to other than qualified persons, a disconnect switch must be provided for each circuit.

240-41. Arcing or Suddenly Moving Parts. Arcing or suddenly moving parts shall comply with (a) and (b) below.

(a) Location. Fuses and circuit breakers shall be so located or shielded that persons will not be burned or otherwise injured by their operation.

(b) Suddenly Moving Parts. Handles or levers of circuit breakers, and similar parts which may move suddenly in such a way that persons in the vicinity are liable to be injured by being struck by them, shall be guarded or isolated.

▲ Section 240-41 is intended to apply to switchboards and control panels located in spaces where full enclosure is not required. (See Sec. 240-30 and comments.) Such equipment should be accessible to qualified operators only, but qualified operators should be protected from unnecessary hazards.

E. Plug Fuses, Fuseholders, and Adapters

240-50. General.

(a) Maximum Voltage. Plug fuses and fuseholders shall not be used in circuits exceeding 125 volts between conductors.

Exception: In circuits supplied by a system having a grounded neutral and having no conductor at over 150 volts to ground.

(b) Marking. Each fuse, fuseholder, and adapter shall be marked with its ampere rating.

(c) Hexagonal Configuration. Plug fuses of 15-ampere and lower rating shall be identified by a hexagonal configuration of the window, cap, or other prominent part to distinguish them from fuses of higher ampere ratings.

(d) No Live Parts. Plug fuses, fuseholders, and adapters shall have no exposed live parts after fuses or fuses and adapters have been installed.

(e) Screw-Shell. The screw-shell of a plug-type fuseholder shall be connected to the load side of the circuit.

240-51. Edison-Base Fuses.

(a) Classification. Plug fuses of the Edison-base type shall be classified at not over 125 volts and 0 to 30 amperes.

(b) Replacement Only. Plug fuses of the Edison-base type shall be used only for replacements in existing installations where there is no evidence of overfusing or tampering.

240-52. Edison-Base Fuseholders. Fuseholders of the Edison-base type shall be installed only where they are made to accept Type S fuses by the use of adapters approved for the purpose.

240-53 Type S Fuses. Type S fuses shall be of the plug type and shall comply with (a) and (b) below.

(a) **Classification.** Type S fuses shall be classified at not over 125 volts and 0 to 15 amperes, 16 to 20 amperes, and 21 to 30 amperes.

(b) **Noninterchangeable.** Type S fuses of an ampere classification as specified in (a) above shall not be interchangeable with a lower ampere classification. They shall be so designed that they cannot be used in any fuseholder other than a Type S fuseholder or a fuseholder with a Type S adapter inserted.

240-54. Type S Fuses, Adapters, and Fuseholders.

(a) **To Fit Edison-Base Fuseholders.** Type S adapters shall fit Edison-base fuseholders.

(b) **To Fit Type S Fuses Only.** Type S fuseholders and adapters shall be so designed that either the fuseholder itself or the fuseholder with a Type S adapter inserted cannot be used for any fuse other than a Type S fuse.

(c) **Nonremovable.** Type S adapters shall be so designed that once inserted in a fuseholder, they cannot be removed.

(d) **Nontamperable.** Type S fuses, fuseholders, and adapters shall be so designed that tampering or shunting (bridging) would be difficult.

(e) **Interchangeability.** Dimensions of Type S fuses, fuseholders, and adapters shall be standardized to permit interchangeability regardless of the manufacturer.

F. Cartridge Fuses and Fuseholders

240-60. General.

(a) **Maximum Voltage—300-Volt Type.** Cartridge fuses and fuseholders of the 300-volt type shall not be used in circuits of over 300 volts between conductors.

Exception: In circuits supplied by a system having a grounded neutral and having no conductor at over 300 volts to ground.

(b) **Noninterchangeable—0-6000 Ampere Cartridge Fuseholders.** Fuseholders shall be so designed that it will be difficult to put a fuse of any given class into a fuseholder that is designed for a current lower, or voltage higher, than that of the class to which it belongs. Fuseholders for current-limiting fuses shall not permit insertion of fuses that are not current limiting.

(c) **Marking.** Fuses shall be plainly marked, either by printing on the fuse barrel or by a label attached to the barrel, showing the following: (1) Ampere rating; (2) Voltage rating; (3) Interrupting rating where other than 10,000 amperes; (4) "Current Limiting" where applicable; (5) The name or trademark of the manufacturer.

Exception: Interrupting rating marking shall not be required on fuses used for supplementary protection.

240-61. Classification.

(a) **0 through 600 Amperes.** Cartridge fuses and fuseholders of 0 through 600 amperes shall be classified as follows:

Not over 250 Volts Amperes	Not over 300 Volts Amperes	Not over 600 Volts Amperes
0– 30	0–15	0– 30
31– 60	16–20	31–60
61–100	21–30	61–100
100–200	31–60	101–200
201–400	–	201–400
401–600	–	401–600

(b) 601 through 6000 Amperes. Cartridge fuses and fuseholders of 601 through 6000 amperes shall be classified as follows:

Not over 600 Volts
Amperes

601– 800	1601–2000	3001–4000
801–1200	2001–2500	4001–5000
1201–1600	2501–3000	5001–6000

There are no 250-volt fuses with current ratings over 600 amperes, but the use of 600-volt fuses and fuseholders shall be permitted for lower voltages.

G. Circuit Breakers

240-80. Method of Operation. Circuit breakers shall be trip free and capable of being closed and opened by manual operation. Their normal method of operation by other than manual means such as electrical or pneumatic shall be permitted if means for manual operation is also provided.

240-81. Indicating. Circuit breakers shall clearly indicate whether they are in the open (off) or closed (on) position.

Where circuit breaker handles on switchboards are operated vertically rather than rotationally or horizontally, the up position of the handle shall be the ON position.

240-82. Nontamperable. A circuit breaker shall be of such design that any alteration of its trip point (calibration) or the time required for its operation will require dismantling of the device or breaking of a seal for other than intended adjustments.

240-83. Marking.

  (a) Durable and Visible. Circuit breakers shall be marked with their rating in a manner that will be durable and visible after installation. Such marking shall be required to be visible after removal of a trim or cover.

  (b) Location. Circuit breakers rated at 100 amperes or less and 600 volts or less shall have the ampere rating molded, stamped, etched, or similarly marked into their handles or escutcheon areas.

  (c) Interrupting Rating. Every circuit breaker having an interrupting rating other than 5000 amperes shall have its interrupting rating shown on the circuit breaker.

  Exception: Interrupting rating marking shall not be required on circuit breakers used for supplementary protection.

▲ Sections 240-60(c) and 240-83 concern the marking of fuses and circuit breakers as to interrupting capacity (IC) ratings.

The most generally used cartridge fuses (250 and 600 V, 600 A and less) are designated as Class H types and have IC ratings of 10,000 A. According to Sec. 240-60 such fuses need not contain an IC rating on the fuse label. Such a marking, however, is required on Class L, K, R, J, or G cartridge fuses, which have IC ratings over 10,000 A. The exception in Sec. 240-60 concerns small fuses where it is impractical to imprint the IC rating on the fuse even though such fuses may have IC ratings less than 10,000 A.

Common circuit breakers, rated at having other than 5,000-A IC ratings as indicated in Sec. 240-83, are not required to have a marked IC rating on the breaker or its label. The exception to Sec. 240-83 applies to circuit breakers used for supplemental protection.

H. Overcurrent Protection Over 600 Volts, Nominal

240-100. Feeders. Feeders shall have a short circuit protective device in each ungrounded conductor. The protective device(s) shall be capable of detecting and interrupting all values of current which can occur at their location in excess of their trip setting or melting point. A fuse rated in continuous amperes not to exceed three times the ampacity of the conductor or a breaker having a trip setting of not more than six times the ampacity of the conductor shall be considered as providing the required short circuit protection. See Tables 310-39 through 310-50 for ampacities of high voltage conductors.

240-101. Branch Circuits. Branch circuits shall have a short circuit protective device in each ungrounded conductor. The protective device(s) shall be capable of detecting and interrupting all values of current which can occur at their location in excess of their trip setting or melting point. See Tables 310-39 through 310-50 for ampacities of high voltage conductors.

ARTICLE 250. GROUNDING

A. General

250-1. Scope. This Article covers general requirements for grounding and bonding of electrical installations, and specific requirements in (a) through (g) below.

(a) Systems, circuits, and equipment required, permitted, or not permitted to be grounded.

(b) Circuit conductor to be grounded on grounded systems.

(c) Location of grounding connections.

(d) Types and sizes of grounding and bonding conductors and electrodes.

(e) Methods of grounding and bonding.

(f) Conditions under which guards, isolation, or insulation may be substituted for gounding.

(g) Connections for lightning arresters.

Circuits are grounded to limit excessive voltages from lightning, line surges, or unintentional contact with higher voltage lines and to limit the voltage to ground during normal operation.

Conductive materials enclosing electric conductors or equipment, or forming part of such equipment, are grounded for the purpose of preventing a voltage above ground on these materials.

Circuits and enclosures are grounded to facilitate overcurrent device operation in case of insulation failure or ground faults. See Section 110-10.

▲ The fine print notes accurately describe the purposes of grounding.

250-2. Application of Other Articles. In other Articles, applying to particular cases of installation of conductors and equipment, there are requirements that are in addition to those of this Article or are modifications of them:

	Article	Section
Appliances		422-16
Branch Circuits		210-5
		210-6
		210-7
Cablebus		365-9
Circuits and Equipment Operating at Less Than 50 Volts . .	720	
Class 1, Class 2, and Class 3 Circuits		725-20
		725-42
Communications Circuits	800	
Community Antenna Television and Radio Distribution Systems		820-7
		820-22
		820-23
Conductors	310	
Conductors (Grounded)	200	
Cranes and Hoists	610	
Data Processing Systems		645-4
Electrically Driven or Controlled Irrigation Machines		675-8
		675-9
		675-10
		675-11
Electrical Floor Assemblies		366-14
Electric Signs and Outline Lighting	600	
Elevators, Dumbwaiters, Escalators, and Moving Walks . . .	620	
Fire Protective Signaling Systems		760-6
Fixed Electric Heating Equipment for Pipeline and Vessels .		427-26
Fixed Electric Space Heating Equipment		424-14
Fixed Outdoor Electric De-Icing and Snow Melting Equipment		426-28
Fixtures and Lighting Equipment		410-17
		410-18
		410-19
		410-20
		410-21
Flexible Cords		400-22
		400-23
Generators		445-8
Grounding-Type Receptacles (Outlets)		210-7
Hazardous Locations	500–517	
Health Care Facilities	517	
Induction and Dielectric Heating Equipment	665	
Lighting Fixtures, Lampholders, Lamp Receptacles, and Rosettes	410	
Marinas and Boatyards		555-7
Metalworking Machine Tools	670	
Mobile Homes and Mobile Home Parks	550	
Motion Picture Studios and Similar Locations		530-20
		530-66

B. Circuit and System Grounding

250-3. Direct-Current Systems.

(a) Two-Wire Direct Current Systems. Two-wire DC systems supplying premises wiring shall be grounded.

Exception No. 1: A system equipped with a ground detector and supplying only industrial equipment in limited areas.

Exception No. 2: A system operating at 50 volts or less between conductors.

Exception No. 3: A system operating at over 300 volts between conductors.

Exception No. 4: A rectifier derived DC system supplied from a grounded AC system.

Exception No. 5: DC Fire Protective Signaling Circuits having a maximum current of 0.030 amperes as specified in Article 760, Part C.

(b) Three-Wire Direct-Current Systems. The neutral conductor of all 3-wire DC systems supplying premises wiring shall be grounded.

▲ It should be noted that DC systems are not permitted to be grounded at individual services or elsewhere on interior wiring. See Sec. 250-22.

250-5. Alternating-Current Circuits and Systems to Be Grounded. AC circuits and systems shall be grounded as provided for in (a), (b), (c), or (d) below. Other circuits and systems shall be permitted to be grounded.

(a) Alternating-Current Circuits of Less Than 50 Volts. AC circuits of less than 50 volts shall be grounded under any of the following conditions:

(1) Where supplied by transformers if the transformer supply system exceeds 150 volts to ground.

(2) Where supplied by transformers if the transformer supply system is ungrounded.

(3) Where installed as overhead conductors outside of buildings.

(b) Alternating-Current Systems of 50 Volts to 1000 V. AC systems of 50 volts to 1000 volts supplying premises wiring and premises wiring systems shall be grounded under any of the following conditions:

(1) Where the system can be so grounded that the maximum voltage to ground on the ungrounded conductors does not exceed 150 volts.

(2) Where the system is nominally rated 480Y/277-volt, 3-phase, 4-wire in which the neutral is used as a circuit conductor.

(3) Where the system is nominally rated 240/120-volt, 3-phase, 4-wire in which the midpoint of one phase is used as a circuit conductor.

(4) Where a service conductor is uninsulated in accordance with Section 230-4.

Exception No. 1: Electric systems used exclusively to supply industrial electric furnaces for melting, refining, tempering, and the like.

Exception No. 2: Separately derived systems used exclusively for rectifiers supplying only adjustable speed industrial drives.

The proper use of suitable ground detectors on ungrounded systems can provide additional protection.

(c) Alternating-Current Systems of 1 KV and Over. AC systems of 1 kV and over supplying portable equipment shall be grounded. Where supplying other than portable equipment, such systems shall be permitted to be grounded. Where such systems are grounded, they shall comply with the applicable provisions of this Article.

(d) Separately Derived Systems. A premises wiring system whose power is derived from generator, transformer, or converter windings that have no direct electrical connection to supply conductors originating in another supply system, if required to be grounded as in (a) or (b) above, shall be grounded as specified in Section 250-26.

250-6. Portable and Vehicle Mounted Generators.

(a) Portable Generators. The frame of a portable generator shall not be required to be grounded under the following conditions:

(1) The generator supplies only equipment mounted on the generator and/or cord and plug connected equipment through receptacles mounted on the generator, and

(2) The non-current carrying metal parts of equipment and the equipment grounding conductor terminals of the receptacles are bonded to the generator frame.

(b) Vehicle Mounted Generators. Under the following conditions the frame of a vehicle shall be permitted to serve as the grounding electrode for a system supplied by a generator located on the vehicle:

(1) The frame of the generator is bonded to the vehicle frame, and

(2) The generator supplies only equipment located on the vehicle and/or cord and plug connected equipment through receptacles mounted on the vehicle or on the generator, and

(3) The system complies with all other provisions of this Article.

(c) Neutral Conductor Bonding. A neutral conductor shall be bonded to the generator frame. The bonding of any conductor other than a neutral within the generator to its frame shall not be required.

For grounding of portable generators supplying fixed wiring systems, see Section 250-5(d).

250-7. Circuits Not to Be Grounded. The following circuits shall not be grounded:

(a) Circuits for electric cranes operating over combustible fibers in Class III locations, as provided in Section 503-13.

(b) Circuits as provided in Article 517.

▲ See Sec. 517-63.

C. Location of System Grounding Connections

250-21. Objectionable Current over Grounding Conductors.

(a) Arrangement to Prevent Objectionable Current. The grounding of electric systems, circuit conductors, lightning arresters, and conductive noncurrent-carrying materials and equipment shall be installed and arranged in a manner that will prevent an objectionable flow of current over the grounding conductors or grounding paths.

(b) Alterations to Stop Objectionable Current. If the use of multiple grounding connections results in an objectionable flow of current, one or more of the following alterations shall be made:

(1) Discontinue one or more such grounding connections.

(2) Change the locations of the grounding connections.

(3) Interrupt the continuity of the conductor or conductive path interconnecting the grounding connections.

(4) Take other suitable remedial action satisfactory to the authority having jurisdiction.

(c) Temporary Currents Not Classified As Objectionable Currents. Temporary currents, resulting from accidental conditions, such as ground-fault currents, that occur only while the grounding conductors are performing their intended protective functions shall not be classified as objectionable current for the purposes specified in (a) and (b) above.

▲ If because of an accidental cross, a current flows through the neutral to the ground, the neutral will be raised to a voltage above ground, this voltage being equal to the current times the resistance of the path to ground. Sometimes a relatively poor ground on one installation will result in a continuous flow of current in the grounding conductor of another installation. This would constitute an objectionable flow of current as mentioned in Sec. 250-21.

250-22. Point of Connection for Direct-Current Systems. DC systems to be grounded shall have the grounding connection made at one or more supply stations. A grounding connection shall not be made at individual services nor at any point on premises wiring.

250-23. Grounding Connections for Alternating-Current Systems.

(a) An AC system that is grounded on the premises shall have a grounding electrode conductor connected to a grounding electrode at each service. Such supply

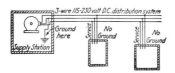

Fig. 250-1. On a three-wire DC distribution system, the neutral is shown grounded at the supply station only. On a two-wire DC system, grounding would be accomplished in the same manner.

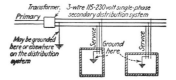

Fig. 250-2. On a two-wire or three-wire single-phase AC secondary distribution system, the neutral is grounded at each individual service and at least one other point.

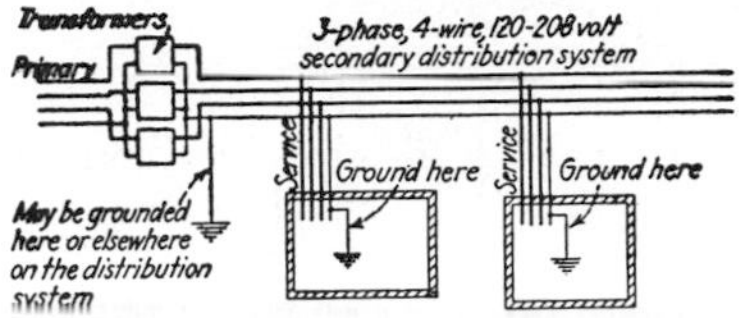

FIG. 250-3. On a four-wire three-phase 208Y/120-V secondary distribution system, the neutral is grounded at each individual service and at least one other point. When a three-wire three-phase service equipment is installed for power purposes on such a distribution system, the grounded (neutral) conductor must run to the service equipment. See comments following paragraph (b) of Section 250-23.

systems that originate outside the building shall have at least one additional grounding connection made to a grounding electrode on the secondary side of the transformer supplying the system, either at the transformer or elsewhere. The grounding electrode conductor shall be connected to the AC system on the supply side of the service disconnecting means at any convenient, accessible point on the premises, preferably within the enclosure for the service disconnecting means. Grounding connections shall not be made on the load side of the service disconnecting means.

Exception No. 1: A grounding conductor shall be connected to each separately derived system as provided in Section 250-26.

Exception No. 2: A grounding conductor connection shall be made at each separate building where required by Section 250-24.

Exception No. 3: For ranges, counter-mounted cooking units, wall-mounted ovens, clothes dryers and meter enclosures as permitted by Section 250-61.

Exception No. 4: For services that are dual fed (double ended) in a common enclosure or grouped together in separate enclosures and employing a secondary tie, a single grounding electrode connection to the tie point of the grounded circuit conductors from each power source shall be permitted.

▲ Center-point neutral grounding and omission of all other secondary grounding is necessary for selective ground-fault protection schemes to work for dual-power-source systems with secondary ties. Dual-power-source systems are utilized for maximum service continuity. Without selectivity, both sources would be shut down by any ground fault.

(b) Grounded Conductor Brought to Service Equipment. Where an AC system operating at 1000 volts or less is grounded at any point, the grounded conductor shall be run to each service. This conductor shall be routed with the phase conductors and shall not be smaller than the required grounding electrode conductor specified in Table 250-94 and, in addition, for service phase conductors larger than 1100 MCM, the grounded conductor shall not be smaller than 12½ percent of the area of the largest phase conductor.

Exception: The grounded conductor shall not be required to be larger than the largest ungrounded service conductor.

▲ It is the intent of this requirement that line-to-ground fault currents which develop on the premises return to the grounded conductor at the service equipment rather than returning to the transformer or system ground by means of the earth. In other words, a path of low impedance is provided to facilitate the operation of fuses or circuit breakers at buildings in accordance with Sec. 250-51(c).

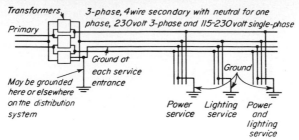

FIG. 250-4. On a four-wire three-phase 230-V secondary system with a neutral from one transformer to provide for three-wire 115/230-V service from one phase for lighting, the neutral is grounded at each individual service and at least one other point. When a three-wire three-phase service equipment is installed for power purposes on such a distribution system, the grounded (neutral) conductor must be run to the service equipment. On a three-wire three-phase 220-V distribution system where there is no neutral, but one of the phase wires is grounded, that phase wire must be grounded at each individual service.

It should be noted that paragraph (b) applies only where the secondary is grounded. Some AC systems need not be grounded. See Sec. 250-5 and 250-7.

In addition to applying the requirements of paragraph (b), it is necessary also to apply those of Sec. 250-53, which requires that a grounding electrode conductor be used to ground both the system (neutral) conductor and the service enclosure (and connecting raceway). This is intended to ensure that the neutral of the system and the service-equipment enclosure are interconnected and that the same grounding conductor is used to connect them both to the grounding electrode. This grounding conductor is to be installed in accordance with the requirements of Sec. 250-112.

Example: Assume a 115/230-V single-phase service. Each ungrounded leg consists of three 500,000 CM THW (CU) conductors in parallel.

Since the three 500,000 CM conductors in parallel provide an area of 1,500,000 CM, the *minimum* size of the grounded neutral conductor back to the transformer would be: $12\frac{1}{2}$ percent of 1,500,000 = 187,500 CM or 4/0 (CU). However, there will be many instances where the neutral service-entrance conductor will have to be *larger* than 4/0 (CU), depending upon the load conditions. See Sec. 220-22.

For "individual service," see Figs. 250-6 and 250-7.

250-24. Two or More Buildings Supplied from Single Service Equipment.

(a) Grounded Systems: Where two or more buildings are supplied by a grounded system from a single service equipment, each building shall have a grounding electrode connected to the AC system grounded circuit conductor on the supply side of the building disconnecting means.

(b) Ungrounded Systems: Where two or more buildings are supplied by an ungrounded system from a single service equipment, each building shall have a grounding electrode connected to the metal enclosure of the building disconnecting means.

Exception for (a) and (b) above: A grounding electrode at a separate building shall not be required where the conditions of either (1) or (2) below are met:

(1) Only one branch circuit is supplied and there is no equipment in the building that requires grounding.

(2) No livestock is housed in the building, an equipment grounding conductor is run with the circuit conductors for grounding any noncurrent carrying equipment, interior metal piping systems or building metal frames and the equipment grounding conductor is bonded to grounding electrodes described in Sections 250-81, 82, and 83 which exist at the building.

▲ When a grounding electrode is required, it shall be located "at such building." This would mean that the water pipe in one building would not be suitable as the grounding electrode for another building unless the water pipe extended to the other building.

Figure 250-5 shows three buildings served by a single service.

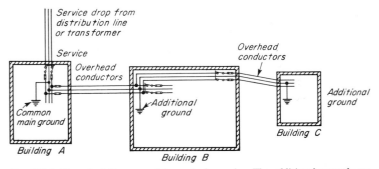

FIG. 250-5. Three buildings served by a single service. The additional grounds are required in most cases under the conditions described in Sec. 250-24. See Exception 2 for an alternate method.

On many farm properties the electric service is brought to a centrally located pole. Service drops are run from the pole to service equipment at each building. See Sec. 230-23. The neutral conductor and service equipment are grounded at each building. Another method would be to mount service equipment on the pole, in which case the conductors to the buildings are still treated as service drops and under the conditions described in Sec. 250-24, for grounding purposes, the disconnecting means in each building are treated as service equipment. See Fig. 250-5 for single service drop to a main building. See also comments following Sec. 250-54.

Paragraph (b) exception 1 indicates an instance when a grounding electrode is not required at a separate building. An example would be a small residential garage with a single lighting outlet or switch with no *metal* boxes, faceplates, or lighting fixtures within 8 ft vertically or 5 ft horizontally from a grounded condition.

Exception 2 actually provides an alternate method to achieve grounding in a separate building (other than one housing livestock). If the circuits supplying the separate building contain properly sized equipment grounding conductors, neither a separate grounding electrode nor grounding of the neutral is *required* at that building. However, if the separate building contains an approved grounding electrode, metal

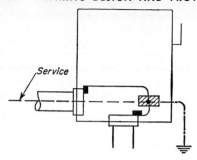

FIG. 250-6. Individual service showing grounding and bonding.

frames, or interior metal piping, these components must be bonded to the equipment grounding conductor.

250-25. Conductor to Be Grounded—Alternating-Current Systems. For AC premises wiring systems, the conductor to be grounded shall be as specified in (a) through (e) below.

(a) Single-phase, 2-wire: the identified conductor.

(b) Single-phase, 3-wire: the identified neutral conductor.

(c) Multiphase systems having one wire common to all phases: the identified common conductor.

(d) Multiphase systems having one phase grounded: the identified conductor.

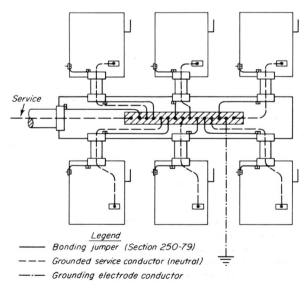

FIG. 250-7. Individual service showing grounding and bonding for six service switches.

(e) Multiphase systems in which one phase is used as in (b) above: the identified neutral conductor.

See Article 200 for means of identification.

▲ See Fig. 250-21 for tapping grounding electrode conductor.

250-26. Grounding Separately Derived Alternating-Current Systems. A separately derived AC system that is required to be grounded by Section 250-5 shall be grounded as specified in (a) through (d) below.

(a) A bonding jumper, sized in accordance with Section 250-79(c) for the derived phase conductors, shall be used to connect the system noncurrent-carrying equipment enclosures to the system circuit conductor that is to be grounded. Except as permitted by Exception No. 4 of Section 250-23(a), this connection shall be made on the supply side of the separately derived system and ahead of any system disconnecting means or overcurrent device.

(b) A grounding conductor, sized in accordance with Section 250-94 for the derived phase conductors, shall be used to connect the circuit conductor of the system that is to be grounded to the grounding electrode as specified in (c) below. Except as permitted by Exception No. 4 of Section 250-23(a), this connection shall be made on the supply side of the separately derived system and ahead of any system disconnecting means or overcurrent device.

(c) The grounding electrode shall be as near as practicable to and preferably in the same area as the grounding conductor connection to the system. The grounding electrode shall be: (1) The nearest available effectively grounded structural metal member of the structure; or (2) The nearest available effectively grounded metal water pipe; or (3) Other electrodes as specified in Sections 250-82 and 250-83 where electrodes specified by (1) or (2) above are not available.

(d) In all other respects, grounding methods shall comply with requirements prescribed in other parts of this Code.

▲ A separately derived AC wiring system is a source derived from an on-site generator (emergency or standby), a battery-inverter, or the secondary supply of a transformer. Any such AC supplies required to be grounded by Sec. 250-5 must comply with Sec. 250-26.

The most common applications of Sec. 250-26 are transformers installed in buildings, such as at load-center unit substations or individual transformers used to transform 480-V supplies to 120/240-V single phase or 208Y/120 V. The purpose of the requirements is to assure proper bonding and grounding so that line-to-ground faults from ungrounded conductors will open overcurrent devices through a *low impedance* grounding circuit to the grounded conductor of the grounded system.

Figure 250-8 shows a typical arrangement where a 480-V three-wire primary supplies a dry-type transformer, and a 208Y/120-V secondary is provided. The *most important* connection is the bonding jumper between the neutral of the 208Y/120-V secondary and the metal enclosure of the transformer *or* main secondary circuit breaker. Without such a bonding jumper secondary overcurrent devices would be unable to operate on line-to-ground faults that occur on the load side of such devices. The bonding jumper must be sized according to Sec. 250-79(c). The preferred connection of the bonding jumper is within the transformer between the metal enclosure and the secondary

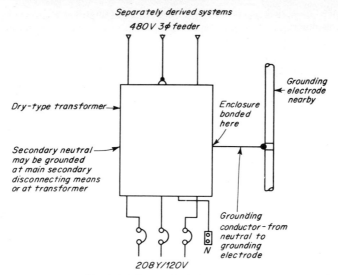

FIG. 250-8. Separately derived system.

conductor to be grounded. Such an arrangement overcomes the objection of neutral load currents flowing in parallel with conduits if the bonding jumper is located downstream from the transformer at the secondary main shown in Fig. 250-8.

The grounding conductor, extending to the grounding electrode from the secondary grounded conductor, is sized according to Sec. 250-94. See Sec. 250-26(b) for basic requirements.

Section 250-26(c) describes the various types of acceptable grounding electrodes. In many instances properly securing a transformer to a grounded, structural, metal-building-member, and installing the bonding jumper according to paragraph (a) will satisfy the requirements of Sec. 250-26.

D. Enclosure Grounding

250-32. Service Raceways and Enclosures. Metal enclosures for service conductors and equipment shall be grounded.

250-33. Other Conductor Enclosures. Metal enclosures for other than service conductors shall be grounded.

Exception No. 1: Metal enclosures for conductors added to existing installations of open wire, knob-and-tube wiring, and nonmetallic-sheathed cable, if in runs of less than 25 feet, if free from probable contact with ground, grounded metal, metal lath, or other conductive material; and if guarded against contact by persons shall not be required to be grounded.

Exception No. 2: Metal enclosures used to protect cable assemblies from physical damage shall not be required to be grounded.

▲ Exception 1 permits the installation of short runs as extensions from existing open wiring, knob-and-tube work, or nonmetallic-sheathed cable without grounding where there is little likelihood of an accidental connection to ground or of a person touching both the conduit, raceway, or armor and any grounded metal or other grounded surface at the same time.

E. Equipment Grounding

250-42. Fixed Equipment, General. Exposed noncurrent-carrying metal parts of fixed equipment likely to become energized under abnormal conditions shall be grounded under any of the conditions specified in (a) through (f) below.

(a) Where within 8 feet vertically or 5 feet horizontally of ground or grounded metal objects and subject to contact by persons.

(b) Where located in a wet or damp location and not isolated.

(c) Where in electrical contact with metal.

(d) Where in a hazardous location as covered by Articles 500 through 517.

(e) Where supplied by a metal-clad, metal-sheathed, or metal-raceway wiring method, except as permitted by Section 250-33 for short sections of raceway.

(f) Where equipment operates with any terminal at over 150 volts to ground.

Exception No. 1: Enclosures for switches or circuit breakers used for other than service equipment and accessible to qualified persons only.

Exception No. 2: Metal frames of electrically heated devices, exempted by special permission, in which case the frames shall be permanently and effectively insulated from ground.

Exception No. 3: Distribution apparatus, such as transformer and capacitor cases, mounted on wooden poles, at a height exceeding 8 feet above ground or grade level.

250-43. Fixed Equipment—Specific. Exposed, noncurrent-carrying metal parts of the kinds of equipment described in (a) through (i) below, regardless of voltage, shall be grounded:

(a) Switchboard frames and structures supporting switching equipment.

Exception: Frames of DC, single-polarity switchboards where effectively insulated.

(b) Generator and motor frames in an electrically operated organ.

Exception: Where the generator is effectively insulated from ground and from the motor driving it.

(c) Motor frames, as provided by Section 430-142.

(d) Enclosures for motor controllers.

Exception: Lined covers of snap switches.

(e) Electric equipment for elevators and cranes.

(f) Electric equipment in garages, theaters, and motion picture studios.

Exception: Pendant lampholders supplied by circuits not over 150 volts to ground.

(g) Electric signs and associated equipment.

Exception: Where insulated from ground and from other conductive objects and accessible only to authorized persons.

(h) Motion picture projection equipment.

(i) Equipment supplied by Class 1 and Class 2 remote-control and signaling circuits where required to be grounded by Part B of this Article.

250-44. Nonelectrical Equipment. The metal parts of nonelectrical equipment described in (a) through (e) below shall be grounded.

(a) Frames and tracks of electrically operated cranes.

(b) Frames of nonelectrically driven elevator cars to which electric conductors are attached.

(c) Hand-operated metal shifting ropes or cables of electric elevators.

(d) Metal partitions, grill work, and similar metal enclosures around equipment of over 750 volts between conductors except substations or vaults under the sole control of the supply company.

(e) Mobile homes and recreational vehicles as required in Articles 550 and 551.

Where extensive metal in or on buildings may become energized and is subject to personal contact, adequate bonding and grounding will provide additional safety.

250-45.   Equipment Connected by Cord and Plug.   Under any of the conditions described in (a) through (d) below, exposed noncurrent-carrying metal parts of cord- and plug-connected equipment likely to become energized, shall be grounded.

(a) In hazardous locations (see Articles 500 through 517).

(b) Where operated at over 150 volts to ground.

Exception No. 1: Motors, where guarded.

Exception No. 2: Metal frames of electrically heated appliances exempted by Section 422-16.

(c) In residential occupancies: (1) refrigerators, freezers, and air conditioners: (2) clothes-washing, clothes-drying, dish-washing machines, sump pumps, and electrical aquarium equipment; (3) portable, handheld, motor-operated tools and appliances of the following types: drills, hedge clippers, lawn mowers, wet scrubbers, sanders, and saws.

Exception: Listed portable tools and appliances protected by a system of double insulation, or its equivalent, shall not be required to be grounded. Where such a system is employed, the equipment shall be distinctively marked.

Portable tools or appliances not provided with special insulating or grounding protection are not intended to be used in damp, wet, or conductive locations.

(d) In other than residential occupancies: (1) refrigerators, freezers, and air conditioners; (2) clothes-washing, clothes-drying, dish-washing machines, and sump pumps; (3) portable, hand-held, motor-operated tools and appliances of the following types: drills, hedge clippers, lawn mowers, wet scrubbers, sanders, and saws; (4) cord- and plug-connected appliances used in damp or wet locations or by persons standing on the ground or on metal floors or working inside of metal tanks or boilers; and (5) portable tools likely to be used in wet and conductive locations.

Exception No. 1: Portable tools likely to be used in wet and conductive locations shall not be required to be grounded where supplied through an isolating trans-former with an ungrounded secondary of not over 50 volts.

Exception No. 2: Listed portable tools and appliances protected by an approved system of double insulation, or its equivalent, shall not be required to be grounded. Where such a system is employed, the equipment shall be distinctively marked.

▲ Except when supplied through an isolating transformer as permitted in paragraph (d) of this section, the frames of portable tools should be grounded by means of an equipment-grounding conductor in the cord or cable through which the motor is supplied.

Portable hand lamps used inside boilers or metal tanks should preferably be supplied through isolating transformers having a secondary voltage of 50 V or less, with the secondary ungrounded.

Code-recognized double-insulated tools and appliances may be used in all types of occupancies other than hazardous locations, in lieu of required grounding.

250-46. Spacing From Lightning Rods. Metal raceways, enclosures, frames, and other noncurrent-carrying metal parts of electric equipment shall be kept at least 6 feet away from lightning rod conductors, or they shall be bonded to the lightning rod conductors.

See Sections 250-86 and 800-31(b)(5) For further information see the Lightning Protection Code (NFPA No. 78—1968. ANSI C5.1—1969) which contains detailed information on grounding lightning protection systems.

▲ Lightning discharges with their steep wave fronts build up tremendous voltages to metal near the lightning rods, so the 6-ft separation or bonding is to prevent flashover with its attendant hazard.

F. Methods of Grounding

250-50. Equipment Grounding Connections. The grounding connection for metal noncurrent-carrying equipment shall be made on the supply side of the service disconnecting means or as outlined in Section 250-5(d) if for a separately derived system.

(a) For Grounded System. The connection shall be made by bonding the equipment grounding conductor to the grounded circuit conductor and the grounding electrode conductor.

(b) For Ungrounded System. The connection shall be made by bonding the equipment grounding conductor to the grounding electrode conductor.

Exception for (a) and (b) above: For branch-circuit extensions only in existing installations that do not have a grounding conductor in the branch circuit, the grounding conductor of a grounding-type receptacle outlet shall be permitted to be grounded to a grounded cold water pipe near the equipment.

250-51. Effective Grounding Path. The path to ground from circuits, equipment, and conductor enclosures shall:

(a) Be permanent and continuous.

(b) Have capacity to conduct safely any fault current likely to be imposed on it.

(c) Have sufficiently low impedance to limit the voltage to ground and to facilitate the operation of the circuit protective devices in the circuit.

▲ *Example:* A single-phase 115/230-V service is to supply a load of 100 A. The service-entrance conductors are three No. 3 Type THW conductors. The size of the grounding electrode conductor is based on the size of the largest service-entrance conductor. See Table 250-94. This table permits a No. 8 copper grounding electrode conductor for a No. 3 service. For connection and installation methods, see Secs. 250-81, 250-92, and 250-112. See also comments following Sec. 250-79.

250-53. Grounding Path to Grounding Electrode.

(a) Grounding Electrode Conductor. A grounding electrode conductor shall be used to connect the equipment grounding conductors, the service-equipment enclosures and, where the system is grounded, the grounded conductor to the grounding electrode.

(b) Main Bonding Jumper. For a grounded system, an unspliced main bonding jumper shall be used to connect the equipment grounding conductor and the service-equipment enclosure to the grounded conductor of the system within the service equipment or within the service conductor enclosure. A main bonding jumper shall be a wire, bus, screw, or similar suitable conductor.

▲ On a system having a grounded neutral, the neutral conductor is bonded to the box or cabinet enclosing the service equipment and to the service raceway so that a single grounding electrode conductor serves to ground both the system and the equipment.

250-54. Common Grounding Electrode. Where an AC system is connected to a grounding electrode in or at a building as specified in Sections 250-23 and 250-24, the same electrode shall be used to ground conductor enclosures and equipment in or on that building.

Two or more electrodes that are effectively bonded together shall be considered as a single electrode in this sense.

▲ In any building housing livestock, all piping systems, metal stanchions, drinking troughs, and other metalwork with which animals might come in contact should be bonded together and to the grounding electrode used to ground the wiring system in the building. See Sec. 250-81.

250-55. Underground Service Cable. Where served from a continuous underground metal-sheathed cable system, the sheath or armor of underground service cable metallically connected to the underground system, or underground service conduit containing a metal-sheathed cable bonded to the underground system, shall not be required to be grounded at the building and shall be permitted to be insulated from the interior conduit or piping.

250-56. Short Sections of Raceway. Isolated sections of metal raceway or cable armor, where required to be grounded, shall be grounded in accordance with Section 250-57.

▲ Where grounding is required, bonding jumpers connected to grounded runs of conduit, raceway, or armor, if available, should be used.

250-57. Fixed Equipment Grounding. Metal noncurrent-carrying equipment where required to be grounded shall be grounded by one of the methods indicated in (a), (b), or (c) below.

(a) By any of the grounding means permitted by Section 250-91(b).

(b) By an equipment grounding conductor contained within the same raceway, cable, or cord or otherwise run with the circuit conductors. An insulated equipment grounding conductor shall be permitted, but if individually covered shall have a continuous outer finish that is either green, or green with one or more yellow stripes.

Exception No. 1: An insulated grounding conductor larger than No. 6 shall, at the time of installation be permitted to be suitably identified as a grounding conductor at each end and at every point where the conductor is accessible. Identification shall be accomplished by one of the following:

a. Stripping the insulation from the entire exposed length,

b. Coloring the exposed insulation green, or

c. Marking the exposed insulation with green colored tape or green colored adhesive labels.

Exception No. 2: For direct-current circuits only, the equipment grounding conductor shall be permitted to be run separately from the circuit conductors.

(c) By special permission, other means for grounding fixed equipment may be used.

See Section 400-7 for use of cords for fixed equipment.

▲ See comments following Sec. 250-91(b).

250-58. Equipment Considered Effectively Grounded. The following noncurrent-carrying equipment, under the conditions specified in (a) and (b) below, shall be considered effectively grounded:

(a) Equipment Secured to Grounded Structural Metal. Electric equipment secured to, and in metallic contact with, the grounded structural metal frame of a building.

(b) Metal Car Frames. Metal car frames supported by metal hoisting cables attached to or running over metal sheaves or drums of grounded elevator machines.

250-59. Cord- and Plug-Connected Equipment. Noncurrent-carrying metal parts of cord- and plug-connected equipment, where required to be grounded, shall be grounded by one of the methods indicated in (a), (b), or (c) below.

(a) By means of the metal enclosure of the conductors supplying such equipment if grounding-type attachment plug with one fixed grounding contact is used for grounding the metal enclosure, and if the metal enclosure of the conductors is secured to the attachment plug and to equipment by connectors approved for the purpose.

Exception: A self-restoring grounding contact shall be permitted on grounding-type attachment plugs used on the power supply cord of portable hand-held, hand-guided, or hand-supported tools or appliances.

(b) By means of a grounding conductor run with the power supply conductors in a cable assembly or flexible cord properly terminated in grounding-type attachment plug with one fixed grounding contact. An uninsulated grounding conductor shall be permitted but, if individually covered, the covering shall have a continuous outer finish that is either green or green with one or more yellow stripes.

Exception: A self-restoring grounding contact shall be permitted on grounding-type attachment plugs used on the power supply cord of portable hand-held, hand-guided, or hand-supported tools or appliances.

▲ See Fig. 250-10.

(c) By means of a separate flexible wire or strap, insulated or bare, protected as well as practicable against physical damage, where part of an approved portable equipment, or by special permission.

▲ The proper method of grounding portable equipment is through an extra conductor in the supply cord. Then if the attachment plug and receptacle comply with the requirements of Sec. 250-59, the grounding connection will be completed when the plug is inserted in the receptacle.

Figure 250-9 shows a duplex receptacle and an attachment plug intended for use where it is desired to provide for grounding the frames of small portable appliances. These devices are rated 15 A, 125 V. The receptacle will receive standard two-pole attachment plugs, so grounding is optional with the user. The grounding contacts in the receptacle are electrically connected to the supporting yoke so that when the box is surface-mounted the connection to ground is provided by a direct metal-to-metal contact between the device yoke and the box. When the box is installed in the wall,

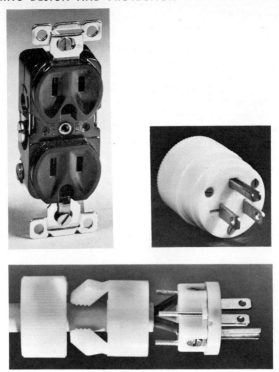

FIG. 250-9. Grounding-type receptacle and attachment plug. (*Bryant Electric Co.*)

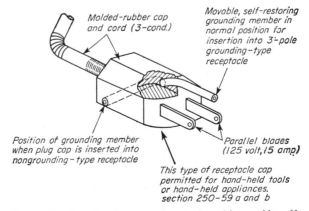

FIG. 250-10. Grounding-type attachment plug with movable, self-restoring grounding member.

a jumper or an approved contact device between the outlet box and the receptacle grounding terminal is required. See Sec. 250-74.

250-60. Frames of Ranges and Clothes Dryers. Frames of electric ranges, wall-mounted ovens, counter-mounted cooking units, and clothes dryers shall be grounded in the manner specified by Section 250-57 or 250-59; or except for mobile homes or travel trailers shall be permitted to be grounded to the grounded circuit conductor if all of the conditions indicated in (a) through (d) below are met.

(a) The supply circuit is 120/240-volt, single-phase, 3-wire; or 120/208-volt derived from a 3-phase, 4-wire, wye-connected system.

(b) The grounded conductor is not smaller than No. 10.

(c) The grounded conductor is insulated; or the grounded conductor is uninsulated and part of a service entrance cable and the branch circuit originates at the service equipment.

(d) Grounding contacts of receptacles furnished as part of the equipment are bonded to the equipment.

▲ Under the conditions stated in Sec. 250-60 the frame of an electric range, wall-mounted oven, or counter-mounted cooking unit may be grounded by direct connection to the grounded circuit conductor and thus may be supplied by a three-wire pigtail and range receptacle irrespective of whether or not the conductor to the receptacle contains a separate grounding conductor.

The reason for permitting these appliances to be grounded by connecting them to the circuit neutral is that the circuit is usually short and the grounding conductor is large enough to provide against its being broken. On such equipment, if the neutral were broken the equipment would usually become inoperative and it would be necessary to have repairs made before operation could be resumed.

Where SE cable with an uninsulated neutral supplies these appliances, the circuit must be initiated from the service equipment to avoid multiple neutral grounding which would occur if connected at downstream panelboards.

250-61. Use of Grounded Circuit Conductor for Grounding Equipment.

(a) Supply-Side Equipment. A grounded circuit conductor shall be permitted to ground noncurrent-carrying equipment on the supply side of the service disconnecting means, such as meter enclosures, service raceways, etc., and on the supply side of the main disconnecting means of separate buildings and of separately derived systems as provided in Sections 250-24 and 250-26 respectively.

(b) Load-Side Equipment. A grounded circuit conductor shall not be used for grounding noncurrent-carrying equipment on the load side of the service disconnecting means or on the load side of a separately derived system disconnecting means or the overcurrent devices for a separately derived system not having a main disconnecting means.

Exception No. 1: The frames of ranges, wall-mounted ovens, counter-mounted cooking units, and clothes dryers under the conditions specified by Section 250-60.

Exception No. 2: As permitted in Section 250-24 for separate buildings.

Exception No. 3: It shall be permissible to ground meter enclosures by connection to the grounded circuit conductor on the load-side of the service disconnect if:

a. No service ground-fault protection is installed; and

b. All meter enclosures are located near the service disconnecting means.

Exception No. 4: By special permission as provided in Section 250-57(c).

▲ The use of a neutral-to-ground panelboard or other equipment (other than specified in the exceptions) on the load side of service equipment would be extremely hazardous if the neutral became loosened or disconnected. In such cases any line-to-neutral load would energize all metal components connected to the neutral, creating a dangerous potential above ground. Hence, the prohibition of such a practice.

Where a meter housing is mounted outdoors, and the service equipment is mounted separately, with the meter on the supply side of the service equipment, the arrangements shown in Figs. 250-11 and 250-12 are permitted.

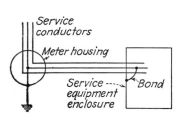

FIG. 250-11. Ground at meter housing, service equipment enclosure grounded to grounded service conductor.

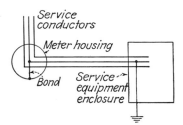

FIG. 250-12. Ground at service equipment, meter housing grounded to grounded service conductor.

In some areas the utilities and inspection departments will not permit the arrangement shown in Fig. 250-11 because the connecting lug in the meter housing is not always accessible for inspection and testing purposes.

250-62. Multiple Circuit Connections. Where an installation of fixed or portable equipment is supplied by separate connection to more than one circuit or grounded interior wiring system, a means for grounding shall be provided for each such connection as specified in Sections 250-57 and 250-59.

G. Bonding

250-70. General. Bonding shall be provided where necessary to assure electrical continuity and the capacity to conduct safely any fault current likely to be imposed.

250-71. Bonding Service Equipment. The metal noncurrent-carrying equipment indicated in (a), (b), and (c) below shall be effectively bonded together.

(a) Except as permitted in Section 250-55, the service raceways or service cable armor or sheath.

(b) All service equipment enclosures containing service-entrance conductors, including meter fittings, boxes, or the like, interposed in the service raceway or armor;

(c) Any conduit or armor that forms part of the grounding conductor to the service raceway.

250-72. Method of Bonding Service Equipment. Electrical continuity at service equipment shall be assured by one of the methods specified in (a) through (e) below.

(a) Bonding equipment to the grounded service conductor in a manner provided in Section 250-113.

(b) Threaded couplings and threaded bosses on enclosures with joints shall be made up wrenchtight where rigid conduit is involved.

FIG. 250-13. Grounding bushing for connecting a copper
jumper or grounding wire to
a conduit. (*Crouse-Hinds
Co.*)

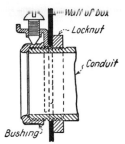

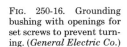

FIG. 250-14   FIG. 250-15

FIGS. 250-14 and 250-15. Grounding wedge lug for making
suitable electrical connection between a conduit and a
box. (*The Thomas & Betts Co.*)

FIG. 250-16. Grounding
bushing with openings for
set screws to prevent turning. (*General Electric Co.*)

(c) Threadless couplings made up tight for rigid metal conduit and electrical
metallic tubing.

(d) Bonding jumpers meeting the other requirements of this Article. Bonding
jumpers shall be used around concentric or eccentric knockouts that are punched
or otherwise formed so as to impair the electrical connection to ground.

(e) Other devices, such as bonding-type locknuts and bushings, approved for the
purpose.

▲ **Bonding jumpers must be used around concentric or eccentric knockouts in service
equipment.**

250-73. Metal Armor or Tape of Service Cable. The metal covering of service
cable having an uninsulated grounded service conductor in continuous electrical
contact with its metallic armor or tape, the metal covering shall be considered to
be grounded.

250-74. Connecting Receptacle Grounding Terminal to Box. An equipment
bonding jumper shall be used to connect the grounding terminal of a grounding-type
receptacle to a grounded box.

Exception No. 1: Where the box is surface-mounted, direct metal-to-metal contact between the device yoke and the box shall be permitted to ground the receptacle to the box.

Exception No. 2: Contact devices or yokes designed and listed for the purpose shall be permitted in conjunction with the supporting screws to establish the grounding circuit between the device yoke and flush-type boxes.

▲ The first paragraph requires that a jumper be used when the outlet box is installed in the wall. Since boxes installed in walls are very seldom found to be perfectly flush with the wall, direct contact between device yokes and boxes is seldom achieved. Screws and yokes currently in use were designed solely for the support of devices rather than as part of the grounding circuit.

Figure 250-17 illustrates a grounding device which is intended to provide the electrical grounding continuity between the receptacle yoke and the box on which it is mounted and serves the dual purpose of both a mounting screw and a means of providing electrical grounding continuity in lieu of the required bonding jumper.

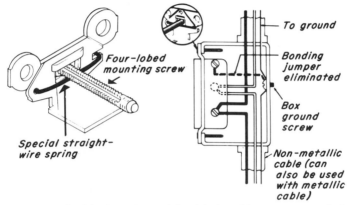

Fig. 250-17. Special wire springs and four-lobed machine screws are part of a receptacle designed for use without a bonding jumper to box. Complies with Sec. 250-74, Exception 2. (*Slater Electric, Inc.*)

Exception No. 3: Floor boxes designed for and listed as providing satisfactory ground continuity between the box and the device.

Exception No. 4: Where required for the reduction of electrical noise (electromagnetic interference) on the grounding circuit, a receptacle in which the grounding terminal is purposely insulated from the receptacle mounting means shall be permitted. The receptacle grounding terminal shall be grounded by an insulated equipment grounding conductor run with the circuit conductors. This grounding conductor shall be permitted to pass through one or more panelboards without connection to the panelboard grounding terminal as permitted in Section 384-27 Exception, so as to terminate directly at the applicable derived system or service grounding terminal.

▲ Exception No. 4 allows the use of a receptacle with an isolated grounding terminal (no connection between the receptacle grounding terminal and the yoke). Sensitive electronic equipment that is grounded normally through the building ground is often adversely affected by pickup of transient signals which cause an imbalance in the delicate circuits. This is particularly true with highly technical medical and communications equipment, which often pick up unwanted currents, even of very low magnitude.

The use of an isolated grounding receptacle allows a "pure" path to be established back to the system grounding terminal, in the service disconnecting means, without terminating in any other intervening panelboard.

See comments that follow Sec. 384-27 Exception.

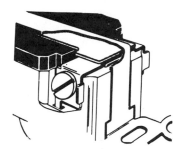

FIG. 250-18. A cutaway of an isolated grounding receptacle showing the insulation between the grounding screw and the yoke. (*Harvey Hubbell Inc.*)

250-75. Bonding Other Enclosures. Metal raceways, cable armor, cable sheath, enclosures, frames, fittings, and other metal noncurrent-carrying parts that are to serve as grounding conductors shall be effectively bonded where necessary to assure electrical continuity and the capacity to conduct safely any fault current likely to be imposed on them. Any nonconductive paint, enamel, or similar coating shall be removed at threads, contact points, and contact surfaces or be connected by means of fittings so designed as to make such removal unnecessary.

250-76. Bonding for Over 250 Volts. For circuits of over 250 volts to ground, the electrical continuity of metal raceways and cables with metal sheaths that contain any conductor other than service conductors shall be assured by one or more of the methods specified for services in Section 250-72(b) through (e); or by (a) or (b) below.

(a) Threadless fittings made up tight, with conduit or metal-clad cable.

(b) Two locknuts, one inside and one outside of boxes and cabinets.

▲ Where good electrical continuity is desired on installations of rigid metal conduit, two locknuts are specified so that the metal of the box can be solidly clamped between the locknuts, one being on the outside and one on the inside. The reason for not relying on the bushing in place of the inside locknut is that both conduit and box may be secured in place and if the conduit is placed so that it extends into the box to a greater distance than the thickness of the bushing, the bushing will not make contact with the inside surface of the box.

250-77. Bonding Loosely Jointed Metal Raceways. Expansion joints and telescoping sections of raceways shall be made electrically continuous by equipment bonding jumpers or other means approved for the purpose.

▲ Provision must be made for possible expansion and contraction due to temperature changes by installing expansion joints in long runs of raceways. See Sec. 300-7(b).

250-78. Bonding in Hazardous Locations. Regardless of the voltage of the electrical system, the electrical continuity of metal noncurrent-carrying equipment in any hazardous location as defined in Article 500 of this Code shall be assured by any of the methods specified for services in Section 250-72(b) through (e) that are approved for the wiring method used.

▲ In a Class I, Division 1 location, the wiring method must be rigid metal conduit with threaded explosionproof joints and fittings (see Fig. 501-3) or Type MI cable with termination fittings approved for the location (see Fig. 330-4).

In other hazardous locations where threaded hubs or MI termination fittings are not used, bonding jumpers must be used.

250-79. Main and Equipment Bonding Jumpers.

(a) Material. Main and equipment bonding jumpers shall be of copper or other corrosion-resistant material.

(b) Attachment. Main and equipment bonding jumpers shall be attached in the manner specified by the applicable provisions of Section 250-113 for circuits and equipment and by Section 250-115 for grounding electrodes.

(c) Size—Equipment Bonding Jumper on Supply Side of Service and Main Bonding Jumper. The bonding jumper shall not be smaller than the sizes given in Table 250-94 for grounding electrode conductors. Where the service-entrance phase conductors are larger than the sizes given in Table 250-94, the bonding jumper shall have an area not less than 12½ percent of the area of the largest phase conductor. Where the service-entrance conductors are paralleled in two or more raceways, the size of the bonding jumper for each raceway shall be based on the size of service conductors in each raceway.

(d) Size—Equipment Bonding Jumper on Load Side of Service. The equipment bonding jumper on the load side of the service overcurrent devices shall not be smaller than the sizes listed by Table 250-95 for equipment grounding conductors.

▲ Bonding-jumper size is based on the size of wire that would be required for the corresponding grounding conductor.

Example: In Fig. 250-7, if the No. 1 switch is rated 100 A and the required supply-conductor ampacity is 85 A (No. 4 THW), according to Table 250-94 the required grounding conductor would be No. 8. The bonding-jumper size would also be No. 8. If switch No. 2 is rated 200 A and the conductors supplying it are rated 175 A (No. 2/0 THW), the required grounding conductor and bonding jumper would be No. 4.

In other words, for bonding-jumper purposes each switch should be treated as a separate service equipment and Table 250-94 would be applicable to the bonding-jumper size instead of the grounding conductor.

It will be noted that the bonding jumper shown between the incoming service conduit and the neutral terminal block would be the same size as the "grounding electrode conductor" shown between the neutral terminal block and the cold water pipe.

Example: Largest service-entrance conductor 500,000 CM would require a No. 0 bonding jumper (see Table 250-94).

250-80. Bonding of Piping Systems. All interior metal water and gas piping that may become energized shall be bonded together and made electrically continuous. An equipment bonding jumper sized in accordance with Table 250-95 shall be connected between the bonded piping system(s) and the grounding electrode conductor at the service disconnecting means.

Bonding to sewer piping and metal air ducts within the premises will provide additional safety.

H. Grounding Electrodes

250-81. Water Pipe Electrode. Where available on the premises, a metal underground water pipe shall always be used as the grounding electrode, regardless of its length and whether supplied by a community or a local underground water piping system or by a well on the premises. Where the buried portion of the water pipe (including any metal well casing effectively bonded to the pipe) is less than 10 feet long or where the water pipe is or is likely to be isolated by insulated sections or joints so that the effectively grounded portion is less than 10 feet long, it shall be supplemented by the use of an additional electrode of a type specified by Section 250-82 or 250-83. The interior metal cold water piping system shall always be bonded to the service-equipment enclosure, the grounded conductor at the service, the grounding electrode conductor where of sufficient size, or to the one or more grounding electrodes used.

Expanding use of nonmetallic piping for water systems and insulating couplings on metal water systems makes it more important that water piping within a building be adequately grounded without depending on connections to an outside piping system.

▲ Perhaps the most significant feature of Art. 250 is contained in Sec. 250-81, where it is specified that a metallic underground water-piping system shall always be used as the grounding electrode where such a piping system is available on the premises. There has been so much misunderstanding over this point between electrical people and water-works people that some years ago a committee consisting of all interested parties was formed to issue an authoritative report on the subject. As a result, there was issued what was called the "Interim Report of the American Research Committee on Grounding," which recorded the unanimous opinion that grounding to water-piping systems has no deleterious effect on either the water or the piping but it does furnish the best available grounding means for the electrical system and thus contributes to the safe use of electricity in buildings. The International Association of Electrical Inspectors published this report in January 1944, and had reprints made in March 1949.

It is desirable to avoid the use of dissimilar metals in the soil in close proximity because of the electrolytic action that can be caused by them in wet soil.

On DC systems, the flow of current through the grounding electrode can cause displacement of metal, depending on the direction of flow. This does not appear to be a problem on AC systems. The National Bureau of Standards in Washington, D.C., has conducted a survey for many years of the corrosion of metals in the soil and has published a number of reports on the results of this work.

Any local water-piping system on the premises, if including 10 ft or more of buried pipe, is considered as an acceptable grounding electrode. If there is buried water piping less than 10 ft long, this piping must still be used as a grounding electrode but must be supplemented by one or more of the electrodes described in Secs. 250-82 and 250-83.

250-82. Other Available Electrodes. Where a water system as described in Section 250-81 is not available, the grounding connection shall be made to any of the electrodes specified in (a) through (d) below, where available.

(a) The metal frame of the building, where effectively grounded.

(b) Concrete-encased steel reinforcing bar or rod systems of underground footings or foundations where the total rod length, diameter, and depth below earth surface are not less than 50 feet, $\frac{3}{8}$ inch, and $2\frac{1}{2}$ feet respectively. The required length shall be made up of one or more rods.

(c) An electrically continuous metal underground gas piping system that is uninterrupted with insulating sections or joints and without an outer nonconductive coating, and then only if acceptable to and expressly permitted by both the serving gas supplier and the authority having jurisdiction.

(d) Other local metal underground systems or structures, such as piping systems and underground tanks.

▲ Although the word "available" is not defined in the Code, its use in Secs. 250-81, 250-82, and 250-83 is usually interpreted to mean at or within the building concerned. Unusual conditions should, of course, be subject to individual judgment by the authority having jurisdiction.

Paragraph (b) recognizes concrete-encased steel reinforcing bar or rod systems of underground footings or foundations as an approved grounding electrode where the water piping system, described in Sec. 250-81, is not available. The 50-ft length includes one rod or bar or the total of several (none less than $\frac{3}{8}$-in. diameter) bonded together.

250-83. Made Electrodes. Where none of the electrodes specified in Sections 250-81 and 250-82 is available, one or more of the electrodes specified in (a), (b), or (c) below shall be used. Where practicable, electrodes shall be embedded below permanent moisture level. Where more than one electrode is used (including those used for signaling or communication circuits, radio or television installations, or lightning rods), each electrode shall not be less than 6 feet from any other electrode.

Two or more electrodes that are effectively bonded together are to be treated as a single electrode in this sense.

(a) **Concrete-Encased Electrodes.** Not less than 20 feet of (1) bare copper conductor not smaller than No. 4, or (2) steel reinforcing bar or rod encased by at least 2 inches of concrete and located within and near the bottom of a concrete foundation footing that is in direct contact with the earth.

(b) **Rod and Pipe Electrodes.** Rod and pipe electrodes shall not be less than 8 feet in length and shall consist of the following materials, and shall be installed in the following manner:

▲ Paragraph (a) (1) and (2) recognizes two types of made electrode, which can be used where electrodes specified in Secs. 250-81 and 250-82 are not available. This method, known as the "Ufer system" (see Fig. 250-19), has particular merit in new construction where the bare copper conductor or steel reinforcing bar or rod can be used. Installations of this type using a bare copper conductor have been installed as far back as 1940, and subsequent tests have proved this system to be highly effective.

The intent of "bottom of the concrete foundation" is to completely encase the electrode within the concrete, in the footing near the bottom. The footing shall be in direct contact with the earth, which means that dry gravel or polyethylene sheets between the footing and the earth are not permitted.

It may be advisable to provide additional corrosion protection in the form of plastic tubing or sheath at the point where the grounding electrode leaves the concrete foundation.

(1) Electrodes of pipe or conduit shall not be smaller than ³⁄₄-inch trade size and, where of iron or steel, shall have the outer surface galvanized or otherwise metal coated for corrosion protection.

(2) Electrodes of rods of steel or iron shall be at least ⅝ inch in diameter. Nonferrous rods or their equivalent shall be listed and shall be not less than ½ inch in diameter.

(3) Where rock bottom is not encountered, the electrode shall be driven to a depth of 8 feet. Where rock bottom is encountered at a depth of less than 4 feet, electrodes not less than 8 feet long shall be buried in a trench. All electrodes shall be free from nonconductive coatings, such as paint or enamel.

(c) Plate Electrodes. Each plate electrode shall expose not less than 2 square feet of surface to exterior soil. Electrodes of iron or steel plates shall be at least ¼ inch in thickness. Electrodes of nonferrous metal shall be at least 0.06 inch in thickness.

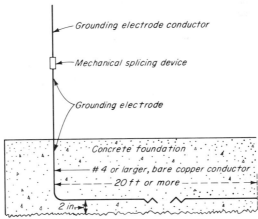

Fɪɢ. 250-19. The Ufer grounding system.

▲ As a general rule, if a water-piping system or other approved electrode is not available, a driven rod or pipe is used as the electrode. A rod or pipe driven in the ground does not always provide as low a ground resistance as is desirable, particularly where the soil becomes very dry. In some cases where several buildings are supplied, grounding at each building reduces the ground resistance. (See Sec. 250-24.)

Where it is necessary to bury more than one pipe or rod in order to lower the resistance to ground, they should be placed at least 6 ft apart. If they are placed closer together there would be little improvement.

Where two driven or buried electrodes are used for grounding two different systems that should be kept entirely separate from one another, such as a wiring system for light and power and a lightning rod, care must be taken to guard against the condition of low resistance between the two electrodes and high resistance from each electrode to ground.

If two driven rods or pipes are located 6 ft apart, the resistance between the two is sufficiently high and cannot be greatly increased by increasing the spacing.

250-84. Resistance of Made Electrodes. A single electrode consisting of a rod, pipe, or plate which does not have a resistance to ground of 25 ohms or less shall be augmented by one additional electrode of any of the types specified in Section 250-83.

▲ Insofar as made electrodes are concerned, there is a wide variation of resistance to be expected, and the present requirements of the National Electrical Code concerning the use of such electrodes do not provide for a system that is in any way comparable to that which can be expected where a good underground metallic piping can be utilized.

It is recognized that some types of soil may create a high rate of corrosion and will result in a need for periodic replacement of grounding electrodes.

It will also be noted that the intimate contact of two dissimilar metals, such as iron and copper, when subjected to wet conditions can result in electrolytic corrosion.

Under abnormal conditions, when a cross occurs between a high-tension conductor and one of the conductors of the low-tension secondaries, the electrode may be called upon to conduct a heavy current into the earth. The voltage drop in the ground connection, including the conductor leading to the electrode and the earth immediately around the electrode, will be equal to the current multiplied by the resistance. This results in a difference of potential between the grounded conductor of the wiring system and the ground. It is therefore important that the resistance be as low as practicable.

Where made electrodes are used for grounding interior wiring systems, resistance tests should be conducted on a sufficient number of electrodes to determine the conditions prevailing in each locality. The tests should be repeated several times a year to determine whether the conditions have changed due to corrosion of the electrodes or drying out of the soil.

Figure 250-20 shows how a ground tester is used for measuring the ground resistance of a driven electrode. Two auxiliary rod or pipe electrodes are driven to a depth of 1 or 2 ft, the distances A and B in the figure being 50 ft or more. Connections are made as shown between the tester and the electrodes, then the crank is turned to generate the necessary current, and the pointer on the instrument indicates the resistance to earth of the electrode being tested. In place of the two driven electrodes, a water-piping system, if available, may be used as the reference ground, in which case terminals P and C are to be connected to the water pipe.

It should be noted that where two made electrodes are used, it is not necessary to take a resistance reading, as would be the case of fulfilling the requirement of 25 ohms to ground for one made electrode.

250-86. Use of Lightning Rods. Lightning rod conductors and driven pipes, rods, or other made electrodes used for grounding lightning rods shall not be used in lieu of the made grounding electrodes required by Section 250-83 for grounding wiring

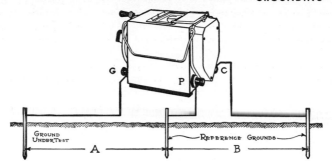

FIG. 250-20. Method of using a ground tester for measuring the resistance to ground of a driven electrode. (*James G. Biddle Co.*)

systems and equipment. This provision shall not prohibit the bonding together of grounding electrodes of different systems.

See Sections 250-46, 800-31(b)(7), and 820-22(h).
Bonding together of all separate electrodes will limit potential differences between them and between their associated wiring systems.

▲ There are cases where fires and shocks have been caused by a potential difference between separate ground electrodes and the neutral of AC electrical circuits.

J. Grounding Conductors

250-91. Material. The material for grounding conductors shall be as specified in (a) and (b) below.

(a) Grounding Electrode Conductor. The grounding electrode conductor shall be of copper, aluminum, or other corrosion-resistant material. The material selected shall be resistant to any corrosive condition existing at the installation or shall be suitably protected against corrosion. Where not of copper, its electrical resistance per linear foot shall not exceed that for copper of the size required by Table 250-94. The conductor shall be solid or stranded, insulated, covered, or bare and shall be installed in one continuous length without a splice or joint.

Exception No. 1: Splices in busbars shall be permitted.

Exception No. 2: Where a service consists of more than a single enclosure as permitted in Section 230-45, it shall be permissible to connect taps to the grounding electrode conductor. Each such tap conductor shall extend to the inside of each such enclosure.

▲ The taps to the common grounding electrode conductor shall be sized from Table 250-94 and shall be based on the size of the conductors that feed each disconnect. The size of the conductors feeding each disconnect is based on computed load and therefore the size may be derived from Table 250-94. This requirement should alleviate some of the problems of attempting to loop the grounding electrode conductor from one enclosure to the other. See Fig. 250-21.

(b) Types of Equipment Grounding Conductors. The equipment grounding conductor run with or enclosing the circuit conductors shall be one or more or a

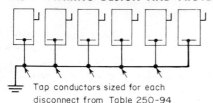

Tap conductors sized for each
disconnect from Table 250-94

FIG. 250-21. Grounding electrode tapped to
each enclosure to eliminate difficulties encountered in *looping*.

combination of the following: (1) a copper or other corrosion-resistant conductor. This conductor shall be solid or stranded; insulated, covered, or bare; and in the form of a wire or a busbar of any shape; (2) rigid metal conduit; (3) intermediate metal conduit; (4) electrical metallic tubing; (5) flexible metal conduit approved for the purpose and installed with fittings approved for the purpose; (6) armor of Type AC metal-clad cable; (7) the sheath of mineral-insulated metal-sheathed cable; (8) the sheath of Type ALS cable; (9) cable trays as permitted in Sections 318-2(c) and 318-6; (10) the sheath of Type CS copper-sheathed cable; (11) other raceways specifically approved for grounding purposes.

Exception No. 1: Flexible metal conduit shall be permitted for grounding if all the following conditions are met:

a. The length does not exceed 6 feet.

b. The circuit conductors contained therein are protected by overcurrent devices rated at 20 amperes or less.

c. The conduit is terminated in fittings approved for the purpose.

Exception No. 2: Liquidtight flexible metal conduit shall be permitted for grounding in the 1¼-inch and smaller trade sizes if the length is 6 feet or less and the conduit is terminated in fittings approved for the purpose.

Exception No. 3: For direct-current circuits only, the equipment grounding conductor shall be permitted to be run separately from the circuit conductors.

▲ Section 250-91(b) describes the various types of conductors and metallic cables or raceways that are considered suitable for use as equipment grounding conductors.

Exception 1 recognizes a flexible metal conduit with termination fittings "approved for the purpose" as a grounding means (without a separate equipment grounding wire) if the length of the flex is not over 6 ft and the contained circuit conductors are protected by overcurrent devices rated at 20 A or less.

Exception 2 recognizes a liquidtight flexible metal conduit with termination fittings "approved for the purpose" as a grounding means in sizes not over 1¼ in. and lengths not over 6 ft.

The term "approved for the purpose," as applied to termination fittings, will require the authority having jurisdiction to evaluate the grounding capabilities of fittings used with these short conduit lengths. See also Secs. 350-5 and 351-7.

(c) Supplementary Grounding. Supplementary grounding electrodes shall be permitted to augment the equipment grounding conductors specified in Section 250-91(b), but the earth shall not be used as the sole equipment grounding conductor.

250-92. Installation. Grounding conductors shall be installed as specified in (a) and (b) below.

(a) Grounding Electrode Conductor. A grounding electrode conductor or its enclosure shall be securely fastened to the surface on which it is carried. A No. 4 or larger conductor shall be protected if exposed to severe physical damage. A No. 6 grounding conductor that is free from exposure to physical damage shall be permitted to be run along the surface of the building construction without metal covering or protection where it is rigidly stapled to the construction; otherwise, it shall be in conduit, electrical metallic tubing, or cable armor. Grounding conductors smaller than No. 6 shall be in conduit, electrical metallic tubing, or cable armor.

Metal enclosures for grounding conductors shall be electrically continuous from the point of attachment to cabinets or equipment to the grounding electrode, and shall be securely fastened to the ground clamp or fitting. Metal enclosures that are not physically continuous from cabinet or equipment to the grounding electrode shall be made electrically continuous by bonding each end to the grounding conductor. Where rigid metal conduit or steel pipe is used as protection for a grounding conductor, the installation shall comply with the requirements of Article 346. Where electrical metallic tubing is used, the installation shall comply with the requirements of Article 348.

Aluminum or copper-clad aluminum grounding conductors shall not be used where in direct contact with masonry or the earth or where subject to corrosive conditions. Where used outside, aluminum or copper-clad aluminum grounding conductors shall not be installed within 18 inches of the earth.

(b) Equipment Grounding Conductor. An equipment grounding conductor shall be installed as follows:

(1) Where it consists of a raceway, cable armor, or cable sheath or where it is a wire within a raceway or cable, it shall be installed in accordance with the applicable provisions in this Code using fittings for joints and terminations approved for use with the type raceway or cable used. All connections, joints, and fittings shall be made tight using suitable tools.

(2) Where it is a separate grounding conductor as provided in Section 210-7 or by special permission as provided in Section 250-57(c), it shall be installed in accordance with (a) above in regard to restrictions for aluminum and also in regard to protection from physical damage.

Exception: Sizes smaller than No. 6 shall not be required to be enclosed in a raceway or armor where run in the hollow spaces of a wall or partition or where otherwise installed so as not to be subject to physical damage.

▲ If a steel conduit or tubing is used for mechanical protection of the grounding conductor, it needs to be bonded to the grounding conductor where it enters and where it leaves the protecting steel conduit in order to keep the impedance of the grounding circuit at an acceptable level. See Fig. 250-26.

250-93. Size of Direct-Current System Grounding Conductor. The size of the grounding conductor for a DC system shall be as specified in (a) through (c) below.

(a) Where the DC system consists of a 3-wire balancer set or a balancer winding with overcurrent protection as provided in Section 445-4(d), the grounding conductor shall not be smaller than the neutral conductor.

(b) Where the DC system is other than as in (a) above, the grounding conductor shall not be smaller than the largest conductor supplied by the system.

(c) In no case shall the grounding conductor be smaller than No. 8.

▲ See Fig. 445-2 for balancer set diagram.

250-94. Size of Alternating-Current Grounding Electrode Conductor. The size of the grounding electrode conductor of a grounded or ungrounded AC system shall not be less than given in Table 250-94.

Exception No. 1: Grounded Systems. Where connected to made electrodes (as in Section 250-83), that portion of the grounding electrode conductor which is the sole connection between the grounding electrode and the grounded system conductor shall not be required to be larger than No. 6 copper wire or its equivalent in ampacity.

Exception No. 2: Ungrounded Systems. Where connected to made electrodes (as in Section 250-83) that portion of the grounding electrode conductor which is the sole connection between the grounding electrode and the service equipment shall not be required to be larger than No. 6 copper wire or its equivalent in ampacity.

Table 250-94. Grounding Electrode Conductor for AC Systems

Size of Largest Service-Entrance Conductor or Equivalent for Parallel Conductors		Size of Grounding Electrode Conductor	
Copper	Aluminum or Copper-Clad Aluminum	Copper	*Aluminum or Copper-Clad Aluminum
2 or smaller	0 or smaller	8	6
1 or 0	2/0 or 3/0	6	4
2/0 or 3/0	4/0 or 250 MCM	4	2
Over 3/0 thru 350 MCM	Over 250 MCM thru 500 MCM	2	0
Over 350 MCM thru 600 MCM	Over 500 MCM thru 900 MCM	0	3/0
Over 600 MCM thru 1100 MCM	Over 900 MCM thru 1750 MCM	2/0	4/0
Over 1100 MCM	Over 1750 MCM	3/0	250 MCM

Where there are no service-entrance conductors, the grounding electrode conductor size shall be determined by the equivalent size of the largest service-entrance conductor required for the load to be served.
* See installation restrictions in Section 250-92(a).
See Section 250-23(b).

▲ For copper wire, a minimum size of No. 8 is specified in order to provide sufficient carrying capacity to ensure an effective ground and sufficient mechanical strength to be permanent.

Where one of the service conductors is a grounded conductor, the same grounding electrode conductor is used for grounding both the system and the equipment. Where the service is from an ungrounded three-phase power system, a grounding electrode conductor of the size given in Table 250-94 is required at the service.

Table 250-94 is based on the largest service-entrance conductor whether made up of a single conductor or paralleled conductors. Thus the total area of the paralleled conductors is to be used in arriving at the size listed in the table. The current rating of the conductors has no bearing on the use of these tables and should not be used.

For example, where two 500 MCM service conductors are used in parallel, the total area is 1,000 MCM, and this value should be used in sizing the grounding electrode conductor, and for copper, the grounding conductor would be 2/0.

250-95. Size of Equipment Grounding Conductors. The size of copper, aluminum, or copper-clad aluminum equipment grounding conductors shall not be less than given in Table 250-95.

Where conductors are run in parallel in multiple raceways, as permitted in Section 310-4, the equipment grounding conductor, where used, shall be run in parallel. Each parallel equipment grounding conductor shall be sized on the basis of the ampere rating of the overcurrent device protecting the circuit conductors in the raceway in accordance with Table 250-95.

When conductors are adjusted in size to compensate for voltage drop, grounding conductors, where required, shall be adjusted proportionately in size.

Exception No. 1: An equipment grounding conductor not smaller than No. 18 copper and not smaller than the circuit conductors if an integral part of a listed flexible cord assembly shall be permitted for grounding cord-connected equipment where the equipment is protected by overcurrent devices not exceeding 20-ampere rating.

Exception No. 2: The equipment grounding conductor shall not be required to be larger than the circuit conductors supplying the equipment.

▲ In general, nonmetallic raceways must contain an equipment grounding conductor. When two or more such raceways contain paralleled conductors (see Sec. 310-4), each such conduit must contain an equipment grounding conductor, sized in accordance with Table 250-95.

Example: Three $3\frac{1}{2}$-in. nonmetallic conduits each contain four 500,000 CM THW copper conductors. The conductors are connected in parallel and are protected by 1,200-A Class L fuses. From Table 250-95 a No. 3/0 copper equipment grounding conductor (bare or insulated) is required. Therefore, *each* $3\frac{1}{2}$-in. conduit must contain such a 3/0 conductor, and the three 3/0 conductors must be connected in parallel.

Enclosing metal raceways, which satisfy the provisions of Sec. 250-91(b), may serve as the equipment grounding conductor.

Exception 2 states that the equipment grounding conductor need not be larger than the circuit conductors. The main application for this exception is for motor circuits where motor starting overcurrent devices are usually considerably larger than the motor branch-circuit-conductor ampacity. Also, a circuit consisting of No. 10 aluminum conductors (with an ampacity of 25) can utilize a *No. 10* aluminum equipment grounding conductor according to Exception 2.

Exception No. 3: Where a raceway or a cable armor or sheath is used as the equipment grounding conductor, as provided in Sections 250-57(a) and 250-91(b).

▲ See comments following Sec. 250-95.

250-97. Outline Lighting. Isolated noncurrent-carrying metal parts of outline lighting systems shall be permitted to be bonded together by a No. 14 conductor protected from physical damage, where a conductor complying with Section 250-95 is used to ground the group.

250-98. Grounding Conductor in Common Raceway. A grounding conductor shall

Table 250-95. Size of Equipment Grounding Conductors for Grounding Raceway and Equipment

Rating or Setting of Automatic Overcurrent Device in Circuit Ahead of Equipment, Conduit, etc., Not Exceeding (Amperes)	Size	
	Copper Wire No.	Aluminum or Copper-Clad Aluminum Wire No.*
15	14	12
20	12	10
30	10	8
40	10	8
60	10	8
100	8	6
200	6	4
400	3	1
600	1	2/0
800	0	3/0
1000	2/0	4/0
1200	3/0	250 MCM
1600	4/0	350 "
2000	250 MCM	400 "
2500	350 "	500 "
3000	400 "	600 "
4000	500 "	800 "
5000	700 "	1000 "
6000	800 "	1200 "

*See installation restrictions in Section 250-92(a).

be permitted in the same raceway or enclosure with other conductors of the system to which it is connected.

250-99. Grounding Conductor Continuity.

(a) Separable Connections.   Separable connections such as those provided in draw-out equipment or attachment plugs and mating connectors and receptacles shall provide for first-make, last-break of the equipment grounding conductor.

Exception: Interlocked equipment, plugs, receptacles and connectors which preclude energization without grounding continuity.

(b) Switches.   No automatic cutout or switch shall be placed in the grounding conductor of a premises wiring system.

Exception: Where the opening of the cutout or switch disconnects all sources of energy.

K. Grounding Conductor Connections

250-111. To Raceway or Cable Armor.   The point of connection of the grounding conductor to interior metal raceways, cable armor, and the like shall be as near as practicable to the source of supply and shall be so chosen that no raceway or cable armor is grounded through a run of smaller size than is called for in Section 250-95.

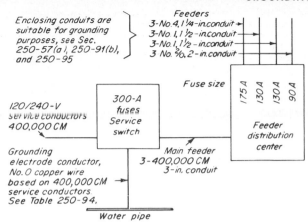

FIG. 250-22. Diagram of a service and feeder system showing application of rules for equipment grounding conductors to ground the various sizes of conduits.

▲ Figure 250-22 represents a service entrance, service switch, a short main feeder from the switch box to a feeder distribution center, and four feeders running from the distribution center to branch-circuit distribution centers in various parts of the building.

250-112. To Grounding Electrode. The grounding connection of a grounding conductor to a grounding electrode shall be made at a point and in a manner that will assure a permanent and effective ground. Where necessary to assure this for a metal piping system used as a grounding electrode, effective bonding shall be provided around insulated joints and sections and around any equipment that is likely to be disconnected for repairs or replacement.

▲ As a practical matter, grounding connections at grounding electrodes should be accessible where this can be readily accomplished. Exceptions to this recommendation are where connections are made in concrete [see Sec. 250-82(b)] or connections in earth to driven electrodes. In most other applications it is no hardship to provide grounding connections at electrodes where they can be conveniently inspected.

250-113. To Conductors and Equipment. Required grounding conductors and bonding jumpers shall be connected by pressure connectors, clamps, or other approved means. Connection devices or fittings that depend on solder shall not be used.

▲ Figures 250-23 through 250-27 show some of the methods for connecting a conductor to rigid metal conduit, electrical metallic tubing, and outlet boxes.

250-114. Continuity and Attachment of Branch-Circuit Equipment Grounding Conductors to Boxes. Where more than one equipment grounding conductor of a branch circuit enters a box, all such conductors shall be in good electrical contact with each other and the arrangement shall be such that the disconnection or removal

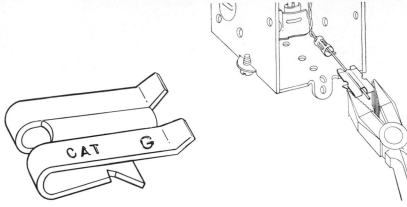

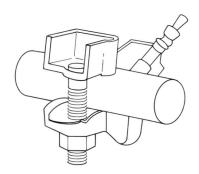

Fig. 250-23. Grounding clip for connecting grounding conductor to box. This clip is intended for use with copper conductors only. (*Steel City Electric Co.*)

Fig. 250-24. Installation of grounding clip. (*Steel City Electric Company.*)

Fig. 250-25. Ground clamp for use with No. 8 armored or No. 6 or No. 4 bare grounding conductor. (*Crouse-Hinds Co.*)

of a receptacle, fixture, or other device fed from the box will not interfere with or interrupt the grounding continuity.

(a) Metal Boxes. A connection shall be made between the one or more equipment grounding conductors and a metal box by means of a grounding screw which shall be used for no other purpose, or an approved grounding device.

(b) Nonmetallic Boxes. One or more equipment grounding conductors brought into a nonmetallic outlet box shall be so arranged that a connection can be made to any fitting or device in that box requiring grounding.

250-115. Connection to Electrodes. The grounding conductor shall be connected to the grounding fitting by suitable lugs, pressure connectors, clamps, or other approved means. Connections depending on solder shall not be used. Ground clamps shall be suitable for the materials of the grounding electrode and the grounding electrode conductor. Not more than one conductor shall be connected to the

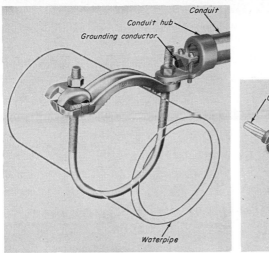

Fig. 250-26   Fig. 250-27

Figs. 250-26 and 250-27. Heavy-duty ground clamps. Clamps are available for all pipe sizes from $1\frac{1}{4}$ to 12 in. consisting of steel U-bolt and bronze saddle. One end of the saddle clamps the grounding wire, sizes Nos. 4 through 4/0. The other end is toothed to fit conduit hubs for use when the grounding wire is to be run in conduit. (*The Thomas & Betts Co., Inc.*)

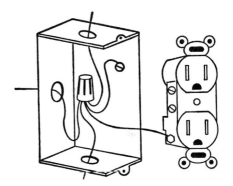

Fig. 250-28. The equipment grounding conductor may be attached to the box by a screw as shown or by other approved means, one of which is shown in Figs. 250-23 and 250-24.

grounding electrode by a single clamp or fitting unless the clamp or fitting is approved for the use. One of the methods indicated in (a), (b), (c), or (d) below shall be used.

(a) An approved bolted clamp of cast bronze or brass or plain or malleable iron.

(b) A pipe fitting, pipe plug, or other approved device screwed into a pipe or pipe fitting.

(c) A sheet-metal-strap type ground clamp having a rigid metal base that seats on the electrode and having a strap of such material and dimensions that it is not likely to stretch during or after installation.

(d) An equally substantial approved means.

250-117. Protection of Attachment. Ground clamps or other fittings shall be approved for general use without protection or shall be protected from ordinary physical damage as indicated in (a) or (b) below.

(a) Installations where they are not likely to be damaged.

(b) Enclosing in metal, wood, or equivalent protective covering.

250-118. Clean Surfaces. Nonconductive coatings (such as paint, lacquer, and enamel) on equipment to be grounded shall be removed from threads and other contact surfaces to assure good electrical continuity.

L. Instrument Transformers, Relays, etc.

250-121. Instrument Transformer Circuits. Secondary circuits of current and potential instrument transformers shall be grounded where the primary windings are connected to circuits of 300 volts or more to ground, and where on switchboards, shall be grounded irrespective of voltage.

Exception: Circuits where the primary windings are connected to circuits of 750 volts or less with no live parts or wiring exposed or accessible to other than qualified persons.

250-122. Instrument Transformer Cases. Cases or frames of instrument transformers shall be grounded where accessible to other than qualified persons.

Exception: Cases or frames of current transformers, the primaries of which are not over 150 volts to ground and which are used exclusively to supply current to meters.

250-123. Cases of Instruments, Meters, and Relays—Operating at 750 Volts or Less. Instruments, meters, and relays operating with windings or working parts at 750 volts or less shall be grounded as specified in (a), (b), or (c) below.

(a) **Not on Switchboards.** Instruments, meters, and relays not located on switchboards, operating with windings or working parts at 300 volts or more to ground, and accessible to other than qualified persons, shall have the cases and other exposed metal parts grounded.

(b) **On Dead-Front Switchboards.** Instruments, meters, and relays (whether operated from current and potential transformers, or connected directly in the circuit) on switchboards having no live parts on the front of the panels shall have the cases grounded.

(c) **On Live-Front Switchboards.** Instruments, meters, and relays (whether operated from current and potential transformers, or connected directly in the circuit) on switchboards having exposed live parts on the front of panels shall not have their cases grounded. Mats of insulating rubber or other suitable floor insulation, shall be provided for the operator where the voltage to ground exceeds 150.

250-124. Cases of Instruments, Meters, and Relays—Operating Voltage over 750. Where instruments, meters, and relays have current-carrying parts over 750 volts to ground, they shall be isolated by elevation or protected by suitable barriers, grounded metal or insulating covers or guards. Their cases shall not be grounded.

Exception: Cases of electrostatic ground detectors where the internal ground segments of the instrument are connected to the instrument case and grounded and the ground detector is isolated by elevation.

250-125. Instrument Grounding Conductor. The grounding conductor for secondary circuits of instrument transformers and for instrument cases shall not be smaller than No. 12 copper or equivalent. Cases of instrument transformers, instruments, meters, and relays which are mounted directly on grounded metal surfaces of enclosures or grounded metal switchboard panels shall be considered to be grounded and no additional grounding conductor will be required.

M. Connecting Lightning Arresters

250-131. Services of Less Than 1000 Volts. Where a lightning arrester is installed on a service of less than 1000 volts, the connecting conductors shall be as short and straight as practicable and of copper not smaller than No. 14 or of equivalent corrosion-resistant material. Bends, especially sharp bends, shall be avoided where practicable. The arrester grounding conductor shall be connected to one of the following:

(a) The grounded service conductor.

(b) The grounding electrode conductor.

(c) The grounding electrode for the service.

▲ The three methods of grounding the ground terminals of lighting arresters at service entrances are shown in Figs. 250-29, 250-30 and 250-31.

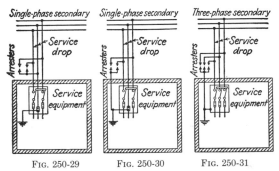

FIG. 250-29   FIG. 250-30   FIG. 250-31

FIG. 250-29. Arrester connected to neutral service conductor. FIG. 250-30. Arrester connected to a grounding electrode conductor. FIG. 250-31. Arrester connected to a grounding electrode conductor of an ungrounded system.

250-132. On Circuits of 1 KV and Over. The grounding conductor of a lightning arrester protecting a transformer that supplies a secondary distribution system shall be permitted to be interconnected as specified in (a), (b), or (c) below.

  (a) Metallic Interconnection. A metallic interconnection shall be permitted to be made to the secondary neutral provided that, in addition to the direct grounding connection at the arrester:

  (1) The grounded conductor of the secondary has elsewhere a grounding connection to a continuous metal underground water piping system. However, in urban water-pipe areas where there are at least four water-pipe connections on the neutral and not less than four such connections in each mile of neutral, the metallic interconnection shall be permitted to be made to the secondary neutral with omission of the direct grounding connection at the arrester.

(2) The grounded conductor of the secondary system is part of a multigrounded neutral system of which the primary neutral has at least four ground connections in each mile of line in addition to a ground at each service.

(b) Through Spark Gap. Where the secondary is not grounded as in (a) above, but is otherwise grounded as in Sections 250-82 and 250-83, such interconnection, where made, shall be through a spark gap having a 60-Hertz breakdown voltage of at least twice the primary circuit voltage but not necessarily more than 10 kV, and there shall be at least one other ground on the grounded conductor of the secondary not less than 20 feet distant from the lightning arrester grounding electrode.

(c) By Special Permission. An interconnection of the arrester ground and the secondary neutral, other than as provided in (a) and (b) above, may be made only by special permission.

▲ If the grounding conductor of lightning arresters is connected to the secondary neutral the likelihood of flashover between the transformer primary and secondary is reduced.

N. Grounding of Systems and Circuits of 1 KV and Over (High Voltage)

250-150. General. Where high-voltage systems are grounded, they shall comply with all applicable provisions of the preceding Sections of this Article and with the following Sections which supplement and modify the preceding Sections.

250-151. Derived Neutral Systems. A system neutral derived from a grounding transformer shall be permitted to be used for grounding a high-voltage system.

250-152. Solidly Grounded Neutral Systems.

(a) Neutral Conductor. The neutral of a solidly grounded neutral system shall comply with (1) and (2) below:

(1) The minimum insulation level for neutral conductors of solidly grounded systems shall be 600 V.

Exception No. 1: Bare copper conductors shall be permitted to be used for the neutral of service entrances and the neutral of direct buried portions of feeders.

Exception No. 2: Bare conductors shall be permitted for the neutral of overhead portions installed outdoors.

(2) The neutral grounding conductor shall be permitted to be a bare conductor if isolated from phase conductors and protected from physical damage.

(b) Multiple Grounding. The neutral of a solidly grounded neutral system shall be permitted to be grounded at more than one point for:

(1) Services.

(2) Direct buried portions of feeders employing a bare copper neutral.

(3) Overhead portion installed outdoors.

250-153. Impedance Grounded Neutral Systems. Impedance grounded neutral systems shall comply with the provisions of (a) through (d) below:

(a) The grounding impedance shall be inserted in the grounding conductor between the grounding electrode of the supply system and the neutral point of the supply transformer or generator.

(b) Where the neutral conductor of an impedance grounded neutral system is used, it shall be identified, as well as fully insulated with the same insulation as the phase conductors.

(c) The system neutral shall not be connected to ground, except through the neutral grounding impedance.

(d) Equipment grounding conductors shall be permitted to be bare and shall be connected to the ground bus and grounding electrode conductor at the service-entrance equipment and extended to the system ground.

250-154. Grounding of Systems Supplying Portable Equipment. Systems supplying portable high-voltage equipment, other than substations installed on a temporary basis, shall comply with (a) through (f) below:

(a) Portable high-voltage equipment shall be supplied from a system having its neutral grounded through an impedance. Where a delta-connected high-voltage system is used to supply portable equipment, a system neutral shall be derived.

(b) Exposed noncurrent-carrying metal parts of portable equipment shall be connected by an equipment grounding conductor to the point at which the system neutral impedance is grounded.

(c) The voltage developed between the portable equipment frame and ground by the flow of maximum ground fault current shall not exceed 100 volts.

(d) Ground-fault detection and relaying shall be provided to automatically de-energize any high-voltage system component which has developed a ground fault. The continuity of the equipment grounding conductor shall be continuously monitored so as to de-energize automatically the high-voltage feeder to the portable equipment upon loss of continuity of the equipment grounding conductor.

(e) The grounding electrode to which the portable equipment system neutral impedance is connected shall be isolated from and separated in the ground by at least 20 feet from any other system or equipment grounding electrode, and there shall be no direct connection between the grounding electrodes, such as buried pipe, fence, etc.

(f) High-voltage trailing cables and couplers for interconnection of portable equipment shall be of a type approved for the purpose.

See Article 400.

250-155. Grounding of Equipment. All noncurrent-carrying metal parts of fixed and portable equipment and associated fences, housings, enclosures, and supporting structures shall be grounded.

Exception No. 1: Where isolated from ground and located so as to prevent any person who can make contact with ground from contacting such metal parts when the equipment is energized.

Exception No. 2: Pole mounted distribution apparatus as provided in Section 250-42, Exception No. 3.

Grounding conductors not an integral part of a cable assembly shall not be smaller than No. 6.

ARTICLE 280. LIGHTNING ARRESTERS

A. General

280-1. Scope. This Article covers general requirements, location requirements, and installation methods for lightning arresters.

B. Industrial Stations

280-10. Where Required. Lightning arresters shall be provided in industrial stations in locations where thunderstorms are frequent and adequate protection against lightning is not otherwise provided.

For lightning arresters in hazardous locations, see Articles 500 through 517.

▲ The term *station* means either a generating station or a substation. An industrial station is a generating station or substation serving principally a single industrial plant or factory, as distinguished from a station serving several customers of a public utility corporation.

280-11. Number Required. A lightning arrester shall be connected to each ungrounded overhead conductor entering or leaving the station.

Exception: Where there is more than one circuit, a single set of arresters shall be permitted to be installed on the station bus where means are provided to protect circuits that may remain disconnected from the bus.

▲ A double-throw switch which disconnects the outside circuits from the station generator and connects these circuits to ground would satisfy the condition for a single set of arresters for a station bus.

280-12. Where Connected. The arrester shall be connected on the line side of all connected station apparatus.

C. Other Occupancies

280-20. Utilization Equipment. Lightning arresters installed for the protection of utilization equipment shall be installed either inside or outside the building or enclosure containing the equipment to be protected. Arresters shall be isolated by elevation or made otherwise inaccessible to unqualified persons, or they shall be enclosed. Where the operating voltage of the circuit exceeds 750 volts between conductors, they shall be inaccessible to unqualified persons.

Secondary lightning protection devices may reduce damage to wiring and equipment caused by lightning disturbances. (See Section 502-3.)

D. Installation

280-30. Location. Arresters installed indoors shall be located well away from other equipment, passageways, and combustible parts of buildings.

280-32. Arrester Conductors—Size and Material. The conductor between the arrester and the line wire or bus and between the arrester and the grounding connection shall be: (1) copper wire or cable or the equivalent; (2) not smaller than No. 6, except as provided for services in Section 250-131 for services of 750 volts or less; and (3) as short and straight as practicable, avoiding unnecessary bends and especially sharp bends and turns.

▲ Bends and turns enormously increase the impedance to lightning discharges and therefore tend to nullify the effectiveness of a grounding conductor.

280-33. Insulation. Lightning-protection accessories, such as gap electrodes and choke coils where used, shall have an insulation from ground or from other conductors at least equal to the insulation required at other points of the circuit.

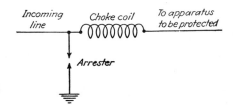

FIG. 280-1. Position of a choke coil where used with a lightning arrester.

280-34. Switch for Isolating Arrester. Where isolating switches or disconnecting devices are used, they shall withstand, in full open position, a voltage test between live parts 10 percent in excess of the maximum voltage test they will withstand to ground.

▲ Switches used to disconnect lightning arresters should be so mounted that when they are open, a lightning discharge will go to ground rather than jump to another switch or another part of the conductor system.

280-35. Grounding. Lightning arresters shall be grounded in the manner specified in Article 250. Grounding conductors shall not be run in metal enclosures unless bonded to both ends of such enclosures.

CHAPTER THREE

Wiring Methods and Materials

ARTICLE 300. WIRING METHODS

A. General Requirements

300-1. Scope.

(a) The provisions of this Article shall apply to all wiring installations.

Exception No. 1: Class 1, Class 2, and Class 3 circuits as provided for in Article 725.

Exception No. 2: Fire Protective Signaling circuits as provided for in Article 760.

Exception No. 3: Communication systems as provided in Article 800.

(b) The provisions of this Article are not intended to apply to the conductors which form an integral part of equipment, such as motors, controllers, motor control centers, or factory-assembled control equipment.

300-2. Voltage Limitations. Wiring methods specified in Chapter 3 shall be used for voltages not exceeding 600 where not specifically limited in some Section of Chapter 3. They shall be permitted for voltages over 600 where specifically permitted elsewhere in this Code.

300-3. Conductors of Different Systems.

(a) Conductors of light and power systems of 600 volts or less shall be permitted to occupy the same enclosure, without regard to whether the individual circuits are alternating current or direct current, where all conductors are insulated for the maximum voltage of any conductor within the enclosure.

▲ The conductors of a 115/230-V system may be run in the same enclosure with conductors of any system of not over 600 V, provided that all the conductors are insulated for 600 V. For Code purposes conductors of light and power systems of over 600 V are generally considered medium or high voltage.

(b) Conductors of light and power systems of over 600 volts shall not occupy the same enclosure with conductors of light and power systems of 600 volts or less.

(c) Secondary wiring to electric-discharge lamps of 1000 volts or less, if insulated for the secondary voltage involved, shall be permitted to occupy the same fixture enclosure as the branch-circuit conductors.

(d) Primary leads of electric discharge lamp ballasts, insulated for the primary voltage of the ballast, when contained within the individual wiring enclosure, shall be permitted to occupy the same fixture enclosure as the branch-circuit conductors.

(e) Excitation, control, relay, and ammeter conductors used in connection with any individual motor or starter shall be permitted to occupy the same enclosure as the motor circuit conductors.

(f) Conductors of signaling or radio systems shall not occupy the same enclosure with conductors of light or power systems.

Exception No. 1: As permitted for elevators in Section 620-36.

Exception No. 2: For sound recording in Section 640-6.

Exception No. 3: As permitted for Class 1, Class 2, and Class 3 circuits in Sections 725-15 and 725-38.

Exception No. 4: As permitted for communication system in Sections 800-3 and 800-21.

Exception No. 5: As permitted for Fire Protective Signaling circuits in Sections 760-15 and 760-28.

▲ Section 300-3(c) applies to an installation of fluorescent lamps where a 115- or 230-V circuit from the panelboard to the ballast is considered as the branch circuit. The ballast, the secondary wiring, and the lamps are considered as being supplied by the branch circuit; i.e., the branch circuit ends at the ballast. The "enclosure" in this case would usually be the housing for the ballast, and it may contain both the branch-circuit wires and the high-voltage secondary wires.

There is always a possibility that the wires in one raceway or box may become crossed with one another. In nearly all cases, a hazardous condition would exist if the conductors of a light and power system should become crossed with radio or signaling conductors.

The conductors of different light and power systems may be installed in the same raceway or other enclosure, provided that the different systems all operate at a voltage of less than 600 between conductors, and provided that all conductors are insulated for the highest voltage at which any conductor in the enclosure operates. Thus, the conductors of a single-phase 115/230-V system may be run in the same conduit or may be contained in the same box or cabinet with the conductors of a three-phase 220-, 440-, or 550-V system. Systems of over 600 V would usually be systems operating at 2,300 V or more. It is obvious that a hazard would be created by installing conductors of such systems in the same enclosures with conductors of low-voltage (600 V or less) systems.

300-4. Protection Against Physical Damage. Where subject to physical damage, conductors shall be adequately protected.

(a) Cables Through Wood Framing Members.

(1) Bored Holes. In both exposed and concealed locations, where a cable or raceway type wiring method is installed through bored holes in joists, rafters, or similar structural wood members, holes shall be bored at the approximate center of the face of the member. Holes in studs for cable type wiring methods shall be bored at the approximate center of the face of the member but not less than one and one-half inches from the nearest edge or shall be protected from nails and screws by either a steel plate or bushing at least $\frac{1}{16}$ inch thick and of appropriate length and width installed to cover the area through which nails or screws might penetrate the installed cable.

▲ Paragraph (a)(1) indicates that the requirements can be met by boring a hole in the approximate center of a stud or not less than $1\frac{1}{2}$ in. from the nearest edge. The intent in (a)(2) is that the cable shall be so installed as not to reduce below allowable limits the strength of a building or structure, or any part thereof.

(2) Notches in Wood.   Where there is no objection because of weakening the building structure, in both exposed and concealed locations, cables shall be permitted to be laid in notches in wood studs, joists, rafters or other wood members where the cable at those points is projected against nails or screws by a steel plate at least $\frac{1}{16}$ inch thick installed before the building finish is applied.

(b) Cables Through Metal Framing Members.   In both exposed and concealed locations where nonmetallic-sheathed cables pass through either factory or field punched, cut or drilled slots or holes in metal members, the cable shall be protected by bushings or grommets approved for the purpose securely fastened in the opening. Where nails or screws are likely to penetrate the cable, a steel sleeve not less than $\frac{1}{16}$ inch in wall thickness shall be used to protect the nonmetallic cable.

Exception: When the slots or holes are so formed that no metal edge can cut or tear cable insulation, bushings or grommets shall not be required.

300-5. Underground Installations.

(a) Minimum Cover Requirements.   Direct buried cable or conduit or other raceways approved for the purpose or duct shall be installed to meet the minimum cover requirements of Table 300-5.

Exception No. 1: The minimum cover requirements shall be permitted to be reduced by six inches for installations where a two-inch thick concrete pad or equivalent in physical protection is placed in the trench over the underground installation.

Exception No. 2: Areas subject to heavy vehicular traffic, such as thoroughfares, gasoline service stations, or commercial parking areas, shall have a minimum cover of 24 inches.

Exception No. 3: Residential branch circuits rated 300 volts or less and provided with overcurrent protection of not more than 30 amperes shall be permitted with a cover requirement of 12 inches.

Exception No. 4: Lesser depths are permitted where cables and conductors rise for terminations or splices or where access is otherwise required.

▲ A degree of judgment must be exercised in applying Exception No. 4, as some locations would still require protection from physical damage. See Fig. 300-1.

Exception No. 5: In airport runways, including adjacent defined areas where trespass is prohibited, cable shall be permitted to be buried not less than 18 inches deep and without raceways, concrete encasement or equivalent.

Exception No. 6: Ducts and raceways installed in solid rock shall be permitted to be buried at a lesser depth when covered by two inches or more of concrete over the installation and extending down to the rock surface.

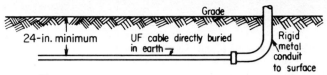

① UF cable without supplemental protection

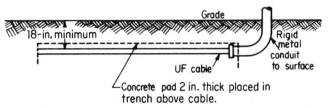

② UF cable with supplemental protective coverings

Fig. 300-1. Underground or direct burial of Type UF cable that complies with Sec. 300-5.

(b) Grounding. Metallic shielding, sheath, or metallic conduit shall be effectively grounded at terminations and meet the requirements of Section 250-51.

(c) Underground Cables Under Buildings. Underground cable installed under a building shall be in a raceway that is extended beyond the outside walls of the building.

(d) Protection From Damage. Conductors emerging from the ground shall be enclosed in enclosures or raceways approved for the purpose. Raceways installed

Table 300-5. Minimum Cover Requirements, 0 to 600 Volts

(Cover is defined as the distance between the top surface of direct buried cable, conduit, or other raceways approved for the purpose or duct and the finished grade.)

Wiring Method	Minimum Burial (inches)
Direct Buried Cables	24
Rigid Metal Conduit	6
Rigid Non-Metallic Conduit Approved for Direct Burial without Concrete Encasement	18
Other Approved Raceways*	18

* Note: Raceways approved for burial only when concrete encased shall require a concrete envelope not less than two inches thick.

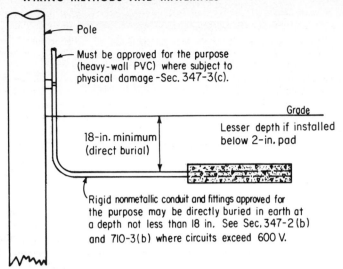

Pole

Must be approved for the purpose (heavy-wall PVC) where subject to physical damage –Sec. 347-3(c).

Grade

18-in. minimum (direct burial)

Lesser depth if installed below 2-in. pad

Rigid nonmetallic conduit and fittings approved for the purpose may be directly buried in earth at a depth not less than 18 in. See Sec. 347-2(b) and 710-3(b) where circuits exceed 600 V.

FIG. 300-2. Typical application of PVC rigid nonmetallic conduit that complies with Sec. 300-5.

on poles shall be of rigid metal conduit, PVC Schedule 80, or equivalent. The enclosures or raceways shall extend from below the ground line up to a point eight feet above finished grade. Conductors entering a building shall be protected by an approved enclosure or raceway from below the ground line to the point of entrance.

▲ See Fig. 300-2.

(e) Splices and Taps. Underground cables in trenches shall be permitted to be spliced or tapped without the use of splice boxes. The splices or taps shall be made by methods and with material approved for the purpose.

(f) Backfill. Backfill containing large rock, paving materials, cinders, large or sharply angular substance, or corrosive material, shall not be placed in an excavation where materials may damage ducts, cables, or other substructures or prevent adequate compaction of fill or contribute to corrosion of ducts, cables or other substructures.

(g) Raceway Seals. Conduits or raceways through which moisture may contact energized live parts shall be sealed or plugged at either or both ends.

(h) Bushing. A bushing shall be used at the end of a conduit which terminates underground where cables leave the conduit as a direct burial wiring method. A seal incorporating the physical protection characteristics of a bushing shall be permitted to be used in lieu of a bushing.

(i) Single Conductors. All conductors of the same circuit including the grounding conductor where required shall be installed in the same raceway or shall be installed in close proximity in the same trench.

300-6. Protection Against Corrosion. Metal raceways, cable armor, boxes, cable sheathing, cabinets, elbows, couplings, fittings, supports, and support hardware shall be of materials suitable for the environment in which they are to be installed.

(a) Ferrous raceways, cable armor, boxes, cable sheathing, cabinets, metal elbows, couplings, fittings, supports, and support hardware shall be suitably protected against corrosion inside and outside (except threads at joints) by a coating of approved corrosion-resistant material such as zinc, cadmium, or enamel. Where protected from corrosion solely by enamel, they shall not be used out of doors or in wet locations as described in (c) below. When boxes or cabinets have an approved system of organic coatings and are marked "Raintight" or "Outdoor Type," they shall be permitted out of doors.

(b) Unless made of materials judged suitable for the condition, or unless corrosion protection approved for the condition is provided, ferrous or nonferrous metal raceways, cable armor, boxes, cable sheathing, cabinets, elbows, couplings, fittings, supports and support hardware shall not be installed in concrete or in direct contact with the earth, or in areas subject to severe corrosive influences.

(c) In portions of dairies, laundries, canneries, and other indoor wet locations, and in locations where walls are frequently washed or where there are surfaces of absorbent materials, such as damp paper or wood, the entire wiring system, including all boxes, fittings, conduits, and cable used therewith, shall be mounted so that there is at least $\frac{1}{4}$-inch air space between it and the wall or supporting surface.

In general, areas where acids and alkali chemicals are handled and stored may present such corrosive conditions, particularly when wet or damp. Severe corrosive conditions may also be present in portions of meat-packing plants, tanneries, glue houses, and some stables; installations immediately adjacent to a seashore and swimming pool areas; areas where chemical de-icers are used; and storage cellars or rooms for hides, casings, fertilizer, salt, and bulk chemicals.

▲ Aluminum conduits should not be used in concrete without specific approval of the authority having jurisdiction. All metal raceways used for direct burial in earth should be protected by coatings of asphalt compounds or plastic sheaths to avoid deterioration.

300-7. Raceways Exposed to Different Temperatures.

(a) Sealing. Where portions of an interior raceway system are exposed to widely different temperatures, as in refrigerating or coldstorage plants, circulation of air from a warmer to a colder section through the raceway shall be prevented.

▲ If the air is allowed to circulate from the warmer to the colder section of the raceway, moisture in the warm air will condense in the cold section of the raceway. This can usually be eliminated by sealing the raceway just outside the cold rooms so as to prevent the circulation of air. Sealing may be accomplished by stuffing a suitable compound in the end of the pipe.

(b) Expansion Joints. Raceways shall be provided with expansion joints where necessary to compensate for thermal expansion and contraction.

300-9. Grounding Metal Enclosures. Metal raceways, boxes, cabinets, cable armor, and fittings shall be grounded as required in Article 250.

300-10. Electrical Continuity of Metal Raceways and Enclosures. Metal raceways, cable armor, and other metal enclosures for conductors shall be metallically joined together into a continuous electric conductor, and shall be so connected to all boxes, fittings, and cabinets as to provide effective electrical continuity. Raceways and cable assemblies shall be mechanically secured to boxes, fittings, cabinets, and other enclosures, except as provided for nonmetallic boxes in Section 370-7(c).

▲ Metal raceway, cable armor, and outlet boxes and fittings, must form a continuous path to ground of low resistance. In case of an accidental contact between an ungrounded conductor and such metal enclosures, the metal will not be raised to any potential more than a few volts above ground, and sufficient current will flow to ground through the metal enclosure to operate the overcurrent device.

In Fig. 300-3, outlet boxes B, C, and D depend upon the locknut-bushing connections at box A for their electrical connection to the cabinet and through the cabinet to ground.

FIG. 300-3. Locknut-bushing connections between conduit and outlet boxes.

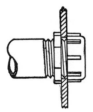  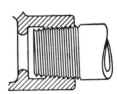

| FIG. 300-4. Locknut-bushing connection to a box or cabinet. | FIG. 300-5. Double-locknut and bushing type of connection to a box or cabinet. | FIG. 300-6. Threaded connection to a fitting. (*Crouse-Hinds Co.*) |

Figures 300-3 and 300-4 show the locknut-bushing type of connection.

Figure 300-5 shows the double-locknut type of connection. This is considered more reliable than the locknut-bushing type.

The threaded connection shown in Fig. 300-6 makes a very effective electrical connection, and is considered to be mechanically stronger.

300-11. Secured in Place. Raceways, cable assemblies, boxes, cabinets, and fittings shall be securely fastened in place, unless otherwise provided for specific purposes elsewhere in this Code.

See Article 318 for cable trays.

300-12. Mechanical Continuity—Raceways and Cables. Metal or nonmetallic raceways, cable armors, and cable sheaths shall be continuous between cabinets, boxes, fittings, or other enclosures or outlets.

300-13. Mechanical and Electrical Continuity—Conductors.

(a) Conductors shall be continuous between outlets, devices, etc., and there shall be no splice or tap within a raceway itself.

Exception No. 1: As provided in Section 374-8 for auxiliary gutters.
Exception No. 2: As provided in Section 362-6 for wireways.
Exception No. 3: As provided in Section 300-15(a), Exception No. 1 for boxes or fittings.
Exception No. 4: As provided in Section 352-7 for metal surface raceways.

(b) In multiwire circuits the continuity of an identified grounded conductor shall not be dependent upon device connections, such as lampholders, receptacles, etc., where the removal of such devices would interrupt the continuity

▲ Paragraph (b) in Sec. 300-13 prohibits splicing of neutral conductors at the terminals of receptacles or other wiring devices where circuits are of the multiwire types (three-wire or four-wire). This is to prevent the establishment of unbalanced voltages if a neutral conductor of such circuits is opened when changing a receptacle or similar device on energized circuits. In such cases, downstream line-to-neutral connections could cause a considerably higher voltage on one part of a multiwire circuit and damage equipment with the neutral "open" if the downstream line-to-neutral loads are appreciably unbalanced. This paragraph does not apply to two-wire circuits or to other circuits that do not contain a grounded neutral conductor.

300-14. Length of Free Conductors at Outlets and Switch Points. At least 6 inches of free conductor shall be left at each outlet and switch point for splices or the connection of fixtures or devices.

Exception: Conductors that are not spliced or terminated at the outlet or switch point.

▲ Wires looping through the box and intended for connection to outlets at the box need have only sufficient slack so that any connections can be made easily.

300-15. Boxes or Fittings—Where Required.
(a) Box or Fitting. A box or fitting shall be installed at each conductor splice connection point, outlet, switch point, junction point, or pull point for the connection of conduit, electrical metallic tubing, surface raceway, or other raceways.

Exception No. 1: A box or fitting shall not be required for a conductor splice connection in surface raceways, wireways, header ducts, multioutlet assemblies, and auxiliary gutters, cable trays and conduit bodies having removable covers which are accessible after installation.

Exception No. 2: As permitted in Section 410-31 where a fixture approved for the purpose is used as a raceway.

(b) Box Only. A box shall be installed at each conductor splice connection point, outlet, switch point, junction point, or pull point for the connection of metal-clad cable, mineral-insulated metal-sheathed cable, aluminum-sheathed cable, copper-sheathed cable, nonmetallic-sheathed cable, or other cables, at the connection point between any such cable system and a raceway system and at each outlet and switch point for concealed knob-and-tube wiring.

Exception No. 1: As permitted by Section 336-11 for insulated outlet devices supplied by nonmetallic-sheathed cable.

Exception No. 2: As permitted by Section 410-62 for rosettes.

Exception No. 3: Where accessible fittings approved for the purpose are used for straight-through splices in mineral-insulated metal-sheathed cable.

Exception No. 4: Where cables enter or exit from conduit or tubing which is used to provide cable support or protection against physical damage.

Exception No. 5: A device approved for the purpose having brackets that securely fasten the device in walls or ceilings of frame construction for use with nonmetallic-sheathed cable, shall be permitted without a separate box.

See Sections 336-5 Exception No. 2, 336-11, 545-10, 550-8(j), and 551-15(a) Exception.

▲ An outlet box provides an enclosure for the circuit wires where they are brought out for connection to a fixture or other device.

So-called Type T or Type L fittings (conduit bodies), shown in Figs. 300-7 and 300-8, actually become a part of the conduit or tubing and should not contain more conductors than permitted for the raceway. Conduit bodies shall not contain splices, taps, or devices unless having provisions for more than two conduit entries. See Sec. 370-6(c).

Where the wiring method requires threaded hub fittings, junction and outlet boxes are available for such use. For conductors No. 4 or larger see Sec. 370-18(a).

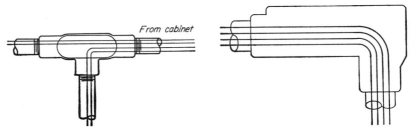

From cabinet

FIG. 300-7. ½-in. Type T fitting with four No. 14 conductors.

FIG. 300-8. ½-in. Type L fitting with four No. 14 conductors.

300-16. Raceway or Cable to Open or Concealed Wiring.

(a) A box or terminal fitting having a separately bushed hole for each conductor shall be used wherever a change is made from conduit, electrical metallic tubing, nonmetallic-sheathed cable, metal-clad cable, aluminum-sheathed cable, or mineral-insulated metal-sheathed cable and surface raceway wiring to open wiring or to concealed knob-and-tube wiring. A fitting used for this purpose shall contain no taps or splices and shall not be used at fixture outlets.

(b) A bushing shall be permitted in lieu of a box or terminal fitting at the end of a conduit or electrical metallic tubing where the raceway terminates behind an open (unenclosed) switchboard or at an unenclosed control and similar equipment. The bushing shall be of the insulating type for other than lead-sheathed conductors.

▲ Where the wires are run in conduit, tubing, metal raceway, or armored cable, and are brought out for connection to open wiring or concealed knob-and-tube work, a fitting such as is shown in Fig. 300-9 may be used. (See also Fig. 300-10.)

Where the terminal fitting is an accessible outlet box, the installation may be made as shown in Fig. 300-11.

300-17. Number and Size of Conductors in Raceway.   The number and size of conductors in any raceway shall not be more than will permit dissipation of the

FIG. 300-9. Terminal fitting for use at end of a run of rigid metal conduit.

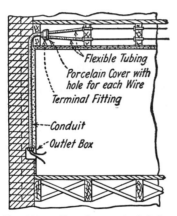

FIG. 300-10. Use of a terminal fitting where a change is made from concealed knob-and-tube work to rigid conduit.

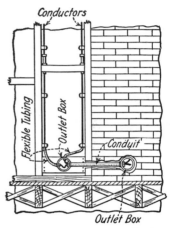

FIG. 300-11. Use of an outlet box where a change is made from concealed knob-and-tube work to rigid conduit.

heat and ready installation or withdrawal of the conductors without damage to the conductors or to their insulation.

See the following Sections of this Code: conduit, Sections 345-7 and 346-6; electrical metallic tubing, 348-6; flexible metal conduit, 350-3; liquid-tight flexible metal conduit, 351-4; surface raceways, 352-4 and 352-25; underfloor raceways, 354-5; cellular metal floor raceways, 356-5; cellular concrete floor raceways, 358-9; wireways, 362-5; auxiliary gutters, 374-5; fixture wire, 402-7; theaters, 520-5; signs, 600-21(d); elevators, 620-33; sound recording, 640-3 and 640-4; Class 1, Class 2, and Class 3 circuits, Article 725; and fire protective signaling circuits, Article 760.

300-18. Inserting Conductors in Raceways.

(a) Raceways shall first be installed as a complete raceway system without conductors.

Exception: Exposed raceways having a removable cover or capping.

(b) Where possible, conductors shall not be inserted until the interior of the building has been physically protected from the weather, and all mechanical work on the building which is likely to injure the conductors has been completed.

(c) Pull wires, if to be used, shall not be installed until the raceway system is in place.

(d) Cleaning agents or materials used as lubricants that might have a deleterious effect on conductor coverings shall not be used.

300-19. Supporting Conductors in Vertical Raceways.

(a) Spacing Intervals—Maximum. Conductors in vertical raceways shall be supported. One cable support shall be provided at the top of the vertical raceway or as close to the top as practical, plus a support for each additional interval of spacing as specified in Table 300-19(a).

Table 300-19(a). Spacings for Conductor Supports

			Conductors	
			Aluminum or Copper-Clad Aluminum	Copper
No. 18	to No. 8................	Not greater than........	100 feet	100 feet
No. 6	to No. 0................	" " "	200 feet	100 feet
No. 00	to No. 0000............	" " "	180 feet	80 feet
211,601 CM	to 350,000 CM........	" " "	135 feet	60 feet
350,001 CM	to 500,000 CM........	" " "	120 feet	50 feet
500,001 CM	to 750,000 CM........	" " "	95 feet	40 feet
	Above 750,000 CM........	" " "	85 feet	35 feet

Exception No. 1: If the total vertical riser is less than 25 percent of the spacing specified in Table 300-19(a), no cable support shall be required.

Exception No. 2: Steel wire armor cable shall be supported at the top of the riser with a cable support that clamps the steel wire armor. A safety device shall be permitted at the lower end of the riser to hold the cable in the event there is slippage of the cable in the wire armored cable support. Additional wedge type supports shall be permitted to relieve the strain on the equipment terminals caused by expansion of the cable under load.

(b) Support Methods. One of the following methods of support shall be used:

(1) By clamping devices constructed of or employing insulating wedges inserted in the ends of the conduits. Where clamping of insulation does not adequately support the cable, the conductor also shall be clamped.

(2) By inserting boxes at the required intervals in which insulating supports are installed and secured in a satisfactory manner to withstand the weight of the conductors attached thereto, the boxes being provided with covers.

(3) In junction boxes, by deflecting the cables not less than 90 degrees and carrying them horizontally to a distance not less than twice the diameter of the cable, the cables being carried on two or more insulating supports, and additionally secured thereto by tie wires if desired. When this method is used, cables shall be supported at intervals not greater than 20 percent of those mentioned in the preceding tabulation.

(4) By a method of equal effectiveness.

▲ **Long vertical runs of conductors should not be supported by the terminal to which**

Galvanized   Split taper
malleable   bushings of
iron inserts   hard fiber

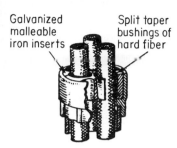

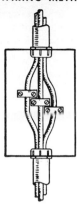

FIG. 300-12. Conductor-support bushing screwed on end of conduit at a
cabinet, pull box, or conductor-
support box. (*Russell & Stoll.*)

FIG. 300-13. Conductor-support box
with single-wire cleats to clamp conductors.

they are connected. Supports as shown in Figs. 300-12 and 300-13 may be used to comply with Sec. 300-19(a).

Example: A vertical raceway contains 4/0 copper conductors. One cable support—at or near the top of the run—would be required if the vertical run is from 20 to 80 ft. If the vertical run in this example is less than 20 ft, no cable support would be required.

300-20. Induced Currents in Metal Enclosures or Metal Raceways. Where conductors carrying alternating current are installed in metal enclosures or metal raceways, they shall be so arranged as to avoid heating the surrounding metal by induction. To accomplish this, all phase conductors and, where used, the neutral and all equipment grounding conductors shall be grouped together.

Exception: As permitted in Section 250-50, Exception for equipment grounding connections.

When a single conductor of a circuit passes through metal with magnetic properties the inductive effect shall be minimized by:

(1) Cutting slots in the metal between the individual holes through which the individual conductors pass, or

(2) Passing all the conductors in the circuit through an insulating wall sufficiently large for all of the conductors of the circuit.

Exception: In the case of circuits supplying vacuum or electric-discharge lighting systems or signs, or X-ray apparatus, the currents carried by the conductors are so small that the inductive heating effect can be ignored where these conductors are placed in metal enclosures or pass through metal.

Because aluminum is not a magnetic metal, there will be no heating due to hysteresis; however, induced currents will be present. They will not be of sufficient magnitude to require grouping of conductors or special treatment in passing conductors through aluminum wall sections.

300-21. Prevention of Fire Spread. Electrical installations shall be so made that the possible spread of fire or products of combustion through fire-rated, fire-resistant or fire-stopped walls, partitions, ceilings and floors; hollow spaces; vertical shafts; and ventilating or air-handling ducts will not be substantially increased.

▲ **Electric wiring shall not be installed in such a manner as to interfere with provisions that have been made to prevent fire from being carried from one space to another.**

300-22. Wiring in Ducts, Plenums, and Other Air Handling Spaces. The provisions of this Section apply to the installation and uses of electric wiring and equipment in ducts, plenums, and other air handling spaces.

See Article 424 Part F for Electric Duct Heaters.

(a) Ducts for Dust, Loose Stock, or Vapor Removal. No wiring systems of any type shall be installed in ducts used to transport dust, loose stock or flammable vapors. No wiring system of any type shall be installed in any duct, or shaft containing only such ducts, used for vapor removal or for ventilation of commercial-type cooking equipment.

(b) Ducts or Plenums Used for Environmental Air. Wiring systems of mineral-insulated metal-sheathed cable, aluminum-sheathed cable, copper-sheathed cable, electrical metallic tubing, intermediate metal conduit, or rigid metal conduit shall be permitted to be installed in ducts or plenum chambers used to transport environmental air. Flexible metal conduit and liquid tight flexible metal conduit shall be permitted, in lengths not to exceed 4 feet, to connect physically adjustable equipment and devices permitted to be in these ducts and plenum chambers. The connectors used with flexible metal conduit shall effectively close any openings in the connection. Equipment and devices shall be permitted within such ducts or plenum chambers only if necessary for their direct action upon, or sensing of, the contained air. Where equipment or devices are installed and illumination is necessary to facilitate maintenance and repair, enclosed gasketed-type fixtures shall be permitted.

(c) Hollow Spaces Used As Ducts or Plenums for Environmental Air. Hollow spaces used as ducts or plenum chambers for environmental air, other than those described in paragraph (b) above, may contain mineral-insulated metal-sheathed cable, aluminum-sheathed cable, copper-sheathed cable, electrical metallic tubing, intermediate metal conduit, rigid metal conduit, metal surface raceway with metal covers where accessible, flexible metal conduit, liquidtight flexible metal conduit in lengths not exceeding six feet, or metal-clad cables, and other electric equipment that is permitted within the concealed spaces of such structures if the wiring materials, including fixtures, are suitable for the expected ambient temperature to which they will be subjected.

Exception No. 1: The above provisions shall not apply to integral fan systems specifically approved for the purpose.

Exception No. 2: This Section does not include habitable rooms or areas of buildings, the prime purpose of which is not air handling.

(d) Data Processing Systems. Electric wiring in air handling areas beneath raised floors for data processing systems shall comply with Article 645.

▲ **The term** *environmental air* **is used by the air conditioning industry in talking about the air that people breathe.**

Paragraph (b) describes the types of wiring which may be installed in ducts and plenum chambers specifically constructed to transport environmental air.

Paragraph (c) describes the methods to be used as wiring in the hollow spaces of buildings such as the spaces over a hung ceiling which are also used for return or discharge air-handling purposes.

Where a "hung type" ceiling is suspended below the regular ceiling and the space in between is used as a passageway for air (return or discharge) to or from the space below, it is considered as being used for air handling. Whether it is considered as an air-handling duct or a plenum chamber, it would be judged under the requirements of Sec. 300-22(c).

Exception No. 1 recognizes the installation of motors and control equipment in air-handling ducts where such equipment has been specifically approved for the purpose. Equipment of this type is listed by Underwriters' Laboratories, Inc., and may be found in the "Electrical Appliance and Utilization Equipment List" under the heading "Heating and Ventilating Equipment." This pamphlet may be obtained by writing to Underwriters' Laboratories, Inc.

Exception No. 2 is intended to exclude from the requirements those areas which may be occupied by people. Hallways and habitable rooms are being used today as portions of air-return systems, and while having air of a heating or cooling system passing through them, the prime purpose of these spaces is obviously not air-handling.

In paragraph (c) the purpose of restricting wiring methods to specific metallic types is to minimize products of combustion or flame spread in such areas. Use of metallic systems reduces the products of combustion and fuel contribution during a fire. See Sec. 300-21.

B. Requirements For Over 600 Volts, Nominal

300-31. Covers Required. Suitable covers shall be installed on all boxes, fittings, and similar enclosures to prevent accidental contact with energized parts or physical damage to parts or insulation.

300-32. Conductors of Different Systems. Conductors of high-voltage and low-voltage systems shall not occupy the same wiring enclosure or pull and junction boxes.

Exception No. 1: In motors, switchgear and control assemblies and similar equipment.

Exception No. 2: In manholes, if low-voltage conductors are separated from high-voltage conductors.

300-33. Inserting Conductors in Raceways. Raceways, except those used for exposed work and having a removable cover, shall first be installed as a complete raceway system without the conductors. Pull wires, if used, shall not be installed until the raceway system is in place. Approved pulling compound may be used as a lubricant in inserting conductors in raceways. Cleaning agents or lubricants having a deleterious effect on conductor coverings shall not be used.

300-34. Conductor Bending Radius. The conductor shall not be bent to a radius less than 8 times the overall diameter for nonshielded conductors or 12 times the diameter for shielded or lead-covered conductors during or after installation.

300-35. Protection Against Induction Heating. Metallic ducts and associated conductors shall be so arranged as to avoid heating of the raceway by induction.

300-36. Grounding. Wiring and equipment installations shall be grounded in accordance with the applicable provisions of Article 250.

ARTICLE 305. TEMPORARY WIRING

A. 600 Volts, Nominal or Less

305-1. Scope. The provisions of this Article apply to temporary electrical power and lighting wiring methods which may be of a class less than would be required for a permanent installation. Except as specifically modified in this Article, all other requirements of this Code for permanent wiring shall apply to temporary wiring installations.

(a) Temporary electrical power and lighting installations shall be permitted during the period of construction, remodeling, or demolition of buildings, structures, equipment, or similar activities.

(b) Temporary electrical power and lighting installations shall be permitted for a period not to exceed 90 days for Christmas decorative lighting, carnivals, and similar purposes, and for experimental or development work.

305-2. General.

(a) Services. Services shall be installed in conformance with Article 230.

(b) Feeders. Feeders shall be protected as provided in Article 240. They shall originate in an approved distribution center. The conductors shall be permitted within multi-conductor cord or cable assemblies or where not subject to mechanical injury, they shall be permitted to be run as open conductors on insulators not more than 10 feet apart.

(c) Branch Circuits. All branch circuits shall originate in an approved power outlet or panelboard. Conductors shall be permitted within multi-conductor cord or cable assemblies or as open conductors. All conductors shall be protected by overcurrent devices at their rated ampacity. When run as open conductors they shall be fastened at ceiling height every 10 feet. No conductor shall be laid on the floor. Each branch circuit that supplies receptacles or fixed equipment shall contain a separate equipment grounding conductor when run as open conductors.

(d) Receptacles. All receptacles shall be of the grounding-type. Unless installed in a complete metallic raceway all branch circuits shall contain a separate equipment grounding conductor and all receptacles shall be electrically connected to the grounding conductor.

See Section 210-8 for receptacles installed on construction sites.

FIG. 305-1. Power outlet units provide flexibility of electrical distribution in locations where temporary power is required. Receptacle outlets provide a variety of necessary configurations together with ground-fault protection, as required. (*Daniel Woodhead Co.*)

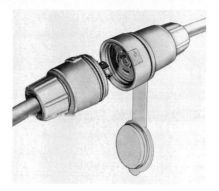

Fig. 305-2. Special watertight plugs and connectors provide insurance against nuisance tripping caused by weather conditions on construction sites. (*Daniel Woodhead Co.*)

(e) Earth Returns. No bare conductors nor earth returns shall be used for the wiring of any temporary circuit.

(f) Disconnecting Means. Suitable disconnecting switches or plug connectors shall be installed to permit the disconnection of all ungrounded conductors of each temporary circuit.

(g) Lamp Protection. All lamps for general illumination shall be protected from accidental contact or breakage. Protection shall be provided by elevation of at least 7 feet from normal working surface or by a suitable fixture or lampholder with a guard.

305-3. Grounding. All grounding shall conform with Article 250.

Fig. 305-3. Commercial lighting strings provide illumination where required. Splice enclosure is equipped with integral support means. A variety of lamp-guard styles provide protection for lamp bulbs. (*Daniel Woodhead Co.*)

B. Over 600 Volts, Nominal

305-10. Use. Temporary wiring over 600 volts shall be permitted during periods of construction, tests, experiments, or emergency. A less permanent class of wiring and equipment shall be permitted than would be required for permanent installations.

305-11. Guarding. Suitable fencing, barriers, or other effective means shall be provided to prevent access of other than authorized and qualified personnel to temporary wiring.

305-12. Temporary wiring over 600 volts shall be removed immediately upon completion of construction or purpose for which the wiring was installed.

305-13. Grounding of Equipment. Equipment shall be grounded in accordance with Section 250-42.

ARTICLE 310. CONDUCTORS FOR GENERAL WIRING

A. General

310-1. Scope. This Article covers general requirements for conductors and their type designations, insulations, markings, mechanical strengths, ampacity ratings, and uses. These requirements do not apply to conductors that form an integral part of equipment, such as motors, motor controllers, and similar equipment, or to conductors specifically provided for elsewhere in this Code.

For flexible cords and cables, see Article 400. For fixture wires, see Article 402.

310-2. Conductors to Be Insulated. Conductors shall be insulated.

Exception: Where covered or bare conductors are specifically permitted elsewhere in this Code.

310-3. Stranded Conductors. Where installed in raceways, conductors of size No. 8 and larger shall be stranded.

Exception No. 1: When used as busbars or in mineral-insulated metal-sheathed cable.

Exception No. 2: Bonding conductors as required in Section 680-22(a).

310-4. Conductors in Parallel. Aluminum, copper-clad aluminum, or copper conductors of size 1/0 and larger, comprising each phase or neutral, shall be permitted to be connected in parallel (electrically joined at both ends to form a single conductor) only if all of the following conditions are met: All of the parallel conductors shall be of the same length, of the same conductor material, circular-mil area, same insulation type and terminated in the same manner. Where run in separate raceways or cables, the raceways or cables shall have the same physical characteristics.

When metallic equipment grounding conductors are used with conductors in parallel, they shall comply with the requirements of this Section except that they shall be sized as per Section 250-95.

When conductors are used in parallel, space in enclosures shall be given consideration (See Articles 370 and 373). Conductors installed in parallel shall be subject to ampacity reduction factors as required in Note 8 to Tables 310-16 through 310-19.

▲ This section recognizes the use of conductors in sizes 1/0 and larger for use in parallel under the conditions which are stated. This provision is intended to allow a practical means of installing large-capacity feeders and services. Paralleling of conductors relies on a number of factors to ensure equal division of current, and thus all these factors must be satisfied in order to ensure that none of the individual conductors will become overloaded. There does not appear to be any practical need to parallel conductors in sizes smaller than 1/0, and such a practice would not be recognized under the requirements of the National Electrical Code.

Where large currents are involved, it is particularly important that the separate phase conductors be located close together to avoid excessive voltage drop and ensure equal division of current. It is also essential that each phase and the neutral, and grounding wires, if any, be run in each conduit even where the conduit is of non-metallic material.

The reason for the last sentence of the first paragraph is to provide for the same type of raceway or enclosure for conductors in parallel in separate enclosures. The impedance of the circuit in a nonferrous raceway will be different from the same circuit in a ferrous raceway or enclosure. See Sec. 300-20.

Except where the conductor size is governed by conditions of voltage drop, it is seldom economical to use in raceways conductors of sizes larger than 1,000,000 CM, because above this size the increase in ampacity is very small in proportion to the increase in the size of the conductor. Thus, for a 50 percent increase in the conductor size, i.e., from 1,000,000 to 1,500,000 CM, the ampacity of a Type THW conductor increases only 80 A or less than 15 percent, and for an increase in size from 1,000,000 to 2,000,000 CM, a 100 percent increase, the ampacity increases only 120 A or about 20 percent. In any case where single conductors larger than 500,000 CM would be required, it is worthwhile to compute the total installation cost using single conductors and the cost using two (or more) conductors in parallel.

310-5. Minimum Size of Conductors. Whether solid or stranded, conductors shall not be smaller than No. 14 copper or No. 12 aluminum or copper-clad aluminum.

Exception No. 1: For flexible cords as permitted by Section 400-12.

Exception No. 2: For fixture wire as permitted by Section 410-23.

Exception No. 3: For fractional hp motors as permitted by Section 430-22.

Exception No. 4: For cranes and hoists as permitted by Section 610-14.

Exception No. 5: For elevator control and signaling circuits as permitted by Section 620-12.

Exception No. 6: For Class 1, Class 2 and Class 3 circuits as permitted by Sections 725-16, 725-33, and 725-40.

Exception No. 7: For fire protective signaling circuits as permitted by Sections 760-16 and 760-30.

310-6. Underground Conductors. Cables of one or more conductors for direct burial in the earth or in underground raceways shall be of a type approved for the purpose and use.

Where necessary to prevent physical damage to the conductors from rocks, slate, or similar materials, or from vehicular or similar traffic, direct buried conductors shall be provided with supplementary protection, such as sand, sand and suitable running boards, suitable sleeves, or other approved means.

See Section 339-3 for Type UF cable.

310-7. Wet Locations.

(a) Insulated Conductors. Insulated conductors used in wet locations shall be (1) lead-covered; (2) Types RHW, RUW, TW, THW, THWN, XHHW; or (3) of a type approved for the purpose.

(b) Cables. Cables of one or more conductors used in wet locations shall be of a type approved for the purpose and use.

Such conductors shall not be used for direct burial in the earth unless of a type approved for the purpose.

310-8. Corrosive Conditions. Conductors exposed to oils, greases, vapors, gases, fumes, liquids, or other substances having a deleterious effect upon the conductor or insulation shall be of a type approved for the purpose.

310-9. Temperature Limitation. No conductor shall be used under such conditions that its operating temperature will exceed that specified for the type of insulation involved.

▲ This requirement is extremely important and is the basis of safe operation of insulated conductors. As shown in Table 310-13, conductors have various ratings— 60°C, 75°C, 90°C, etc.

Since Tables 310-16 through 310-19 are based on an assumed ambient (surrounding) temperature of 30°C (86°F) conductor ampacities are based on the ambient temperature plus the heat (I^2R) produced by the conductor (wire) while carrying current. Therefore, the type of insulation used on the conductor determines the maximum permitted conductor ampacity.

Example: A No. 3/0 THW copper conductor for use in a raceway has an ampacity of 200 according to Table 310–16. In a 30°C ambient the conductor is subjected to this temperature when it carries *no* current. Since a THW-insulated conductor is rated at 75°C this leaves 45°C (75-30) for increased temperature due to current flow. If the ambient temperature exceeds 30°C, the conductor ampacity must be reduced proportionally (see Note 13 to Tables 310-16 through 310-19) so that the *total* temperature (ambient plus conductor temperature rise due to current flow) will not exceed the temperature rating of the conductor insulation (60°C, 75°C, etc.). For the same reason conductor ampacities are derated where more than three conductors are contained in a raceway or cable (see Note 8 to Tables 310-16 through 310-19).

While it can be shown that smaller conductors such as Nos. 14 and 12 60°C-insulated conductors will not reach 60°C at their assigned ampacities (Table 310-16) in a 30°C ambient, ampacities beyond those listed in Tables 310-16 through 310-19 would create excessive voltage drop (*IR* drop) and would not be compatible with most termination devices.

Although conductor ampacities increase with the rating of conductor insulation, it should be noted that most terminations are designed only for 60°C or 75°C maximum temperatures (ambient plus current). Accordingly, the higher rated ampacities for conductors of 90°C, 110°C, etc., cannot be utilized unless the terminations have comparable ratings.

To find the temperature in degrees Fahrenheit (F) where the temperature is given in degrees Celsius (C), apply the formula

$$\text{Degrees F} = \tfrac{9}{5} \times \text{degrees C} + 32$$

Thus, the maximum operating temperature for Type T insulation is 60°C. $\frac{9}{5} \times 60° = 108°$. $108° + 32° = 140°$, which is the same temperature on the Fahrenheit scale as 60 degrees on the Celsius scale.

Reversing the process, where the temperature is given in degrees F_1

$$\text{Degrees C} = (\text{degrees F} - 32) \times \frac{5}{9}$$

The maximum operating temperature for Type THW insulation is 167°F

$$167° - 32° = 135°$$

$135° \times \frac{5}{9} = 75°$, the corresponding temperature in degrees C.

310-10. Conductor Identification.

(a) Grounded Conductors. Insulated conductors of No. 6 or smaller, intended for use as grounded conductors of circuits, shall have an outer identification of a white or natural gray color. Multiconductor flat cable No. 4 or larger shall be permitted to employ an external ridge on the grounded conductor.

Exception No. 1: Multiconductor varnished-cloth-insulated cables.

Exception No. 2: Fixture wires as outlined in Article 402.

Exception No. 3: Mineral-insulated metal-sheathed cable.

Exception No. 4: A conductor identified as required by Section 210-5(a) for branch circuits.

For aerial cable the identification shall be as above, or by means of a ridge so located on the exterior of the cable as to identify it.

Wires having their outer covering finished to show a white or natural gray color but having colored tracer threads in the braid, identifying the source of manufacture, shall be considered as meeting the provisions of this Section.

For identification requirements for conductors larger than No. 6, see Section 200-6.

(b) Grounding Conductors. An insulating equipment grounding conductor shall be permitted, but if individually covered shall have a continuous outer finish that is either green, or green with one or more yellow stripes.

Exception: An insulated grounding conductor larger than No. 6 shall, at the time of installation, be permitted to be suitably identified as a grounding conductor at each end and at every point where the conductor is accessible. Identification shall be accomplished by one of the following means:

1. Stripping the insulation from the entire exposed length.

2. Coloring the exposed insulation green, or

3. Marking the exposed insulation with green colored tape or green colored adhesive labels.

(c) Ungrounded Conductor. Conductors which are intended for use as ungrounded conductors, whether used as single conductors or in multi-conductor cables, shall be finished to be clearly distinguishable from grounded and grounding conductors. Ungrounded conductors shall be distinguished by colors other than white, natural gray, or green; or by a combination of color plus distinguishing marking.

Distinguishing markings shall also be in a color other than white, natural gray, or green, and shall consist of a stripe or stripes or a regularly spaced series of identical marks. Distinguishing markings shall not conflict in any manner with the surface markings required by Section 310-11(b)(1).

310-11. Marking.

(a) Required Information.   All conductors and cables shall be marked to indicate the following information using the applicable method described in (b) below.

(1) The maximum working voltage for which the conductor was tested or approved.

(2) The proper type letter or letters for the type of wire or cable as specified elsewhere in this Article, in Table 310-13 and in Articles 336, 337, 338, 339, and 340.

(3) The manufacturer's name, trademark, or other distinctive marking by which the organization responsible for the product can be readily identified.

(4) The AWG size or circular-mil area.

(b) Method of Marking.

(1) Surface Marking.   The following conductors and cables shall be durably marked on the surface at intervals not exceeding 24 inches:

(a) Single- and multiconductor rubber- and thermoplastic-insulated wire and cable.

(b) Nonmetallic-sheathed cable.

(c) Service-entrance cable.

(d) Underground feeder and branch-circuit cable.

(e) Tray cable.

(f) Irrigation cable.

(2) Marker Tape.   Metal-covered multiconductor cables shall employ a marker tape located within the cable and running for its complete length.

Exception No. 1: Mineral-insulated metal-sheathed cable.

Exception No. 2: Type AC metal-clad cables.

Included in the group of metal-covered cables are: aluminum-sheathed cable, Type ALS (Article 331); copper-sheathed cable, Type CS (Article 332); Type MC metal-clad cable (Article 334) and lead-sheathed cable.

(3) Tag Marking.   The following conductors and cables shall be marked by means of a printed tag attached to the coil, reel, or carton:

(a) Mineral-insulated, metal-sheathed cable.

(b) Switchboard wires.

(c) Metal-covered single-conductor cables.

(d) Conductors having outer surface of asbestos.

(e) Type AC metal-clad cable.

(4) Optional Marking of Wire Size.   For the following multiconductor cables, the information required in (a) (4) above shall be permitted to be marked on the surface of the individual insulated conductors:

(a) Type MC metal-clad cable.

(b) Tray cable.

(c) Irrigation cable.

(d) Type ALS aluminum-sheathed cable.

(e) Type CS copper-sheathed cable.

(c) Suffixes to Designate Number of Conductors.   A type letter or letters used alone shall indicate a single insulated conductor. The following letter suffixes shall indicate the following:

D—for two insulated conductors laid parallel within an outer nonmetallic covering.

M—for an assembly of two or more insulated conductors twisted spirally within an outer nonmetallic covering.

B. Conductors 600 Volts, Nominal or Less

310-12. Conductor Application. Insulated conductors listed in Table 310-13 shall be permitted for use with any of the wiring methods recognized by Chapter 3 as specified in the Table.

Thermoplastic insulation may stiffen at temperatures colder than minus 10°C (plus 14°F), requiring care be exercised during installation at such temperatures. Thermoplastic insulation may also be deformed at normal temperatures where subjected to pressure, requiring care be exercised during installation and at points of support.

310-13. Conductor Construction. Insulated conductors for use at 600 volts or less shall comply with Table 310-13.

Rubber insulations include those made from natural and synthetic rubber, and other vulcanizable materials.

▲ Conductors intended for general wiring under the requirements of the National Electrical Code need to be one of the recognized types listed in the following tables and not smaller than No. 14 AWG. The National Electrical Code does not contain detailed requirements for insulated conductors as these are covered in separate standards such as those of Underwriters' Laboratories, Inc.

"Dry locations" in this case would mean for "general use" in dry locations. It should be noted that "dry locations only" following "Asbestos A" permits such wire to be used in raceways only for leads to or within apparatus.

Table 310-13 permits maximum operating temperatures of 90°C (194°F) in dry locations for Types FEP, FEPB, RHH, XHHW, and THHN wire, but the ampacities for Nos. 14, 12, and 10 copper conductors and Nos. 12, 10, and 8 aluminum conductors are limited to those permitted for 75°C (167°F) insulated conductors. See footnote to Tables 310-16 through 310-19. The reason is that the wiring devices which are commonly connected by these sizes of conductors are not suitable for conditions encountered in the 90°C application. Also, the terminals in most switches, panelboards, etc., have not been tested for maximum insulation temperatures in excess of 75°C.

Terminals of 15- and 20-A receptacles not marked "CO/ALR" are for use with copper and copper-clad aluminum conductors only. Terminals marked "CO/ALR" are for use with aluminum, copper, and copper-clad aluminum conductors. Screwless pressure terminal connectors of the conductor push-in type are for use only with copper and copper-clad aluminum conductors.

Terminals of receptacles rated 30 A and above not marked "AL-CU" are for use with copper and copper-clad aluminum conductors only. Terminals of receptacles rated 30 A and above marked "AL-CU" are for use with aluminum, copper, and copper-clad aluminum conductors.

Newest of the conductor material being used in this country is copper-clad aluminum. This material is made from a metallurgical materials system—using a core of aluminum with a bonded outer skin of copper. There is 10 percent copper by volume (the outer skin) and 26.8 percent by weight. Terminations for copper-clad aluminum conductors should be marked "AL-CU" except where listings by Underwriters' Laboratories indicate otherwise. See comments following Sec. 110-14.

The following table compares the characteristics of copper-clad aluminum with copper and aluminum conductors.

Conductor Characteristics

	Copper	Cu/Al	Aluminum
Density LBS/IN³	0.323	0.121	0.098
Density GM/CM³	8.91	3.34	2.71
Resistivity OHMS/CMF	10.37	16.08	16.78
Resistivity Microhm-CM	1.724	2.673	2.790
Conductivity (IACS%)	100	61–63	61
Weight % Copper	100	26.8	....
Tensile K PSI-Hard	65.0	30.0	27.0
Tensile KG/MM²-Hard	45.7	21.1	19.0
Tensile K PSI-Annealed	35.0	17.0	17.0 °
Tensile KG/MM²-Annealed	24.6	12.0	12.0
Specific Gravity	8.91	3.34	2.71

° Semi-annealed.

310-15. Ampacity. The maximum continuous ampacities for copper, aluminum, and copper-clad aluminum conductors shall be as specified in Tables 310-16 through 310-19 and accompanying Notes 1 through 14.

Notes To Tables 310-16 through 310-19

Ampacity. The maximum, continuous, ampacities of copper conductors are given in Tables 310-16 and 310-17. The ampacities of aluminum and copper-clad aluminum conductors are given in Tables 310-18 and 310-19.

1. Explanation of Tables. For explanation of Type Letters, and for recognized size of conductors for the various conductor insulations, see Sections 310-12 and 310-13. For installation requirements, see Sections 310-1 through 310-9, and the various Articles of this Code. For flexible cords see Tables 400-4 and 400-5.

2. Application of Tables. For open wiring on insulators and for concealed knob-and-tube wiring, the allowable ampacities of Tables 310-17 and 310-19 shall be used. For all other recognized wiring methods, the allowable ampacities of Tables 310-16 and 310-18 shall be used, unless otherwise provided in this Code.

3. Three-Wire Single-Phase Residential Services. For 3-wire, single-phase residential services, allowable ampacity of Types RH, RHH, RHW, THW, and XHHW copper service-entrance conductors shall be for sizes No. 4-100 Amp., No. 3-110 Amp., No. 2-125 Amp., No. 1-150 Amp., No. 1/0-175 Amp., and No. 2/0-200 Amp., and the allowable ampacity of Types RH, RHH, RHW, THW, and XHHW aluminum and copper-clad aluminum service-entrance conductors shall be for sizes No. 2-100 Amp., No. 1-110 Amp.,

No. 1/0-125 Amp., No. 2/0-150 Amp., No. 3/0-175 Amp. and No. 4/0-200 Amp.

4. Aluminum and Copper-Clad Aluminum Conductors. For aluminum and copper-clad aluminum conductors the allowable ampacities shall be in accordance with Tables 310-18 and 310-19.

5. Bare Conductors. Where bare conductors are used with insulated conductors, their allowable ampacities shall be limited to that permitted for the insulated conductors of the same size.

6. Mineral-Insulated, Metal-Sheathed Cable. The temperature limitation on which the ampacities of mineral-insulated, metal-sheathed cable is based is determined by the insulating materials used in the end seal. Termination fittings incorporating unimpregnated, organic, insulating materials are limited to 85°C operation.

7. Ultimate Insulation Temperature. In no case shall conductors be associated together in such a way with respect to the kind of circuit, the wiring method employed, or the number of conductors, that the limiting temperature of the conductors will be exceeded.

Table 310-13. Conductor Application and Insulations

Trade Name	Type Letter	Max. Operating Temp.	Application Provisions	Insulation	AWG or MCM	Thickness of Insulation Mils	Outer Covering
Heat-Resistant Rubber	RH	75°C 167°F	Dry locations.	Heat-Resistant Rubber	**14–12 10 8–2 1–4/0 213–500 501–1000 1001–2000	30 45 50 50 65 110 125	*Moisture-resistant, flame-retardant, non-metallic covering
Heat-Resistant Rubber	RHH	90°C 194°F	Dry locations.				
Moisture and Heat-Resistant Rubber	RHW	75°C 167°F	Dry and wet locations. For over 2000 volts insulation shall be ozone-resistant.	Moisture and Heat Resistant Rubber	14–10 8–2 1–4/0 213–500 501–1000 1001–2000	45 50 50 65 110 125	*Moisture-resistant, flame-retardant, non-metallic covering
Heat-Resistant Latex Rubber	RUH	75°C 167°F	Dry locations.	90% Unmilled, Grainless Rubber	14–10 8–2	18 25	Moisture-resistant, flame-retardant, non-metallic covering

*Outer covering shall not be required over rubber insulations which have been specifically approved for the purpose.

**For 14–12 sizes RHH shall be 45 mils thickness insulation.

For insulated aluminum and copper-clad aluminum conductors, the minimum size shall be No. 12. See Tables 310-18 and 310-19.

Table 310-13 (Continued)

Trade Name	Type Letter	Max. Operating Temp.	Application Provisions	Insulation	AWG or MCM	Thickness of Insulation Mils	Outer Covering
Moisture-Resistant Latex Rubber	RUW	60°C 140°F	Dry and wet locations.	90% Unmilled, Grainless Rubber	14–10 8–2	18 25	Moisture-resistant, flame-retardant, non-metallic covering
Thermoplastic	T	60°C 140°F	Dry locations.	Flame-Retardant, Thermoplastic Compound	14–10 8 6–2 1–4/0 213–500 501–1000 1001–2000	30 45 60 80 95 110 125	None
Moisture-Resistant Thermoplastic	TW	60°C 140°F	Dry and wet locations.	Flame-Retardant, Moisture-Resistant Thermoplastic	14–10 8 6–2 1–4/0 213–500 501–1000 1001–2000	30 45 60 80 95 110 125	None
Heat-Resistant Thermoplastic	THHN	90°C 194°F	Dry locations.	Flame-Retardant Heat-Resistant Thermoplastic	14–12 10 8–6 4–2 1–4/0 250–500 501–1000	15 20 30 40 50 60 70	Nylon Jacket

Insulation	Type Letter	Max. Operating Temperature	Application Provisions	Insulation	AWG MCM Thickness	Outer Covering
Moisture- and Heat-Resistant Thermoplastic	THW	75°C 167°F 90°C 194°F	Dry and wet locations. Special applications *within* electric discharge lighting equipment. Limited to 1000 open-circuit volts or less. (Size 14-8 only as permitted in Section 410-26.)	Flame-Retardant, Moisture- and Heat-Resistant Thermoplastic	14-10......45, 8-2......60, 1-4/0......80, 213-500......95, 501-1000......110, 1001-2000......125	None
Moisture- and Heat-Resistant Thermoplastic	THWN	75°C 167°F	Dry and wet locations.	Flame-Retardant, Moisture- and Heat-Resistant Thermoplastic	14-12......15, 10......20, 8-6......30, 4-2......40, 1-4/0......50, 250-500......60, 501-1000......70	Nylon Jacket
Moisture- and Heat-Resistant Cross-Linked Synthetic Polymer	XHHW	90°C 194°F 75°C 167°F	Dry locations. Wet locations.	Flame-Retardant Cross-Linked Synthetic Polymer	14-10......30, 8-2......45, 1-4/0......55, 213-500......35, 501-1000......30, 1001-2000......35	None
Moisture-, Heat- and Oil-Resistant Thermoplastic	MTW	60°C 140°F 90°C 194°F	Machine Tool Wiring in wet locations as permitted in NFPA Standard No. 79 (See Article 670). Machine Tool Wiring in dry locations as permitted in NFPA Standard No. 79 (See Article 670).	Flame-Retardant, Moisture-, Heat- and Oil-Resistant Thermoplastic	(A) (B); 22-12......30 15; 10......30 20; 8......45 30; 6......60 30; 4-2......60 40; 1-4/0......80 60; 213-500......95 60; 501-1000......110 70	(A) None (B) Nylon jacket

For insulated aluminum and copper-clad aluminum conductors, the minimum size shall be No. 12. See Tables 310-18 and 310-19.

Table 310-13 (Continued)

Trade Name	Type Letter	Max. Operating Temp.	Application Provisions	Insulation	AWG or MCM	Thickness of Insulation	Mils	Outer Covering
Extruded Polytetrafluoroethylene	TFE	250°C 482°F	Dry locations only. Only for leads within apparatus or within raceways connected to apparatus, or as open wiring. (Nickel or nickel-coated copper only.)	Extruded Polytetrafluoroethylene	14–10 ......20 8–2 ....30 1–4/0 45			None
Thermoplastic and Asbestos	TA	90°C 194°F	Switchboard wiring only.	Thermoplastic and Asbestos	14–8 .... 6–2 .... 1–4/0	Th'pl'. 20 30 40	Asb. 20 25 30	Flame-retardant, non-metallic covering
Thermoplastic and Fibrous Outer Braid	TBS	90°C 194°F	Switchboard wiring only.	Thermoplastic	14–10 ...... 8 .... 6–2 .... 1–4/0	30 45 60 80		Flame-retardant, non-metallic covering
Synthetic Heat-Resistant	SIS	90°C 194°F	Switchboard wiring only.	Heat-Resistant Rubber	14–10 ...... 8 .... 6–2 .... 1–4/0	30 45 60 80		None
Mineral Insulation (Metal Sheathed)	MI	85°C 185°F 250°C 482°F	Dry and wet locations. For special application.	Magnesium Oxide	16–10 ...... 9–4 .... 3–250	36 50 55		Copper

Trade Name	Type Letter	Max. Operating Temperature	Application Provisions	Insulation	AWG Thickness	Outer Covering
Underground Feeder & Branch-Circuit Cable-Single Conductor. (For Type UF cable employing more than one conductor see Article 339)	UF	60°C 140°F / 75°C** 167°F	See Art, 339	Moisture-Resistant / Moisture- and Heat-Resistant	14-10.....60, 8-2.....80, 1-4/0.....95	Integral with insulation
Underground Service Entrance Cable-Single Conductor. (For Type USE cable employing more than one conductor see Article 338)	USE	75°C 167°F	See Art, 338	Heat- and Moisture-Resistant	12-10.....45, 8-2.....60, 1-4/0.....80, 213-500.....95, 501-1000.....110, 1001-2000.....125	Moisture-resistant nonmetallic covering See 338-1 (2)
Silicone-Asbestos	SA	90°C 194°F / 125°C 257°F	Dry locations. / For special application.	Silicone Rubber	14-10.....45, 8-2.....50, 1-4/0.....80, 213-500.....95, 501-1000.....110, 1001-2000.....125	Asbestos or glass

* Includes integral jacket.
** For ampacity limitation, see 339-1(a).
The nonmetallic covering over individual rubber-covered conductors of aluminum-sheathed cables and of lead-sheathed or multiconductor cable shall not be required to be flame retardant. For metal-clad cable, see Section 334-4. For nonmetallic-sheathed cable, see Section 336-2. For Type UF cable, see Section 339-1. For aluminum-sheathed cable, see Section 331-23.
For insulated aluminum and copper-clad aluminum conductors, the minimum size shall be No. 12. See Tables 310-18 and 310-19.

Table 310-13 (Continued)

Trade Name	Type Letter	Max. Operating Temp.	Application Provisions	Insulation	AWG or MCM	Thickness of Insulation — Mils	Outer Covering
Fluorinated Ethylene Propylene	FEP or FEPB	90°C 194°F 200°C 392°F	Dry locations. Dry locations—special applications.	Fluorinated Ethylene Propylene	14-10 8-2	.......20 30	None
				Fluorinated Ethylene Propylene	14-8 6-2	.......14 14	Glass braid Asbestos braid
Varnished Cambric	V	85°C 185°F	Dry locations only. Smaller than No. 6 by special permission.	Varnished Cambric	14-8 6-2 1-4/0 213-500 500-1000 1001-2000	......45 ......60 ......80 ......95 .....110 125	Nonmetallic covering or lead-sheath
Asbestos and Varnished Cambric	AVA	110°C 230°F	Dry locations only.	Impregnated Asbestos and Varnished Cambric		AVA: 1st Asb. / VC / 2nd Asb.; AVL: 2nd Asb.	AVA-asbestos braid or glass
Asbestos and Varnished Cambric	AVL	110°C 230°F	Dry and wet locations.	Impregnated Asbestos and Varnished Cambric			AVL-lead sheath

Thickness of Insulation — Mils (for AVA / AVL):

AWG or MCM	AVA 1st Asb.	VC	AVA 2nd Asb.	AVL 2nd Asb.
14-8 (solid only)	—	30	20	25
14-8	10	30	15	25
6-2	15	30	20	25
1-4/0	20	30	30	30
213-500	25	40	40	40
501-1000	30	40	40	40
1001-2000	30	50	50	50

Insulation	Trade Designation	Max. Operating Temperature	Application Provisions	Insulation	Thickness of Insulation	Outer Covering
Asbestos and Varnished Cambric	AVB	90°C 194°F	Dry locations only.	Impregnated Asbestos and Varnished Cambric	VC / Asb. 18–8 ... 30 / 20 6–2 ... 40 / 30 1–4/0 ... 40 / 40 Asb. / VC / 2nd Asb. 14–8 ... 10 / 30 / 15 6–2 ... 15 / 30 / 20 1–4/0 ... 20 / 30 / 30 213–500 ... 25 / 40 / 40 501–1000 ... 30 / 40 / 40 1001–2000 ... 30 / 50 / 50	Flame-retardant, cotton braid (switchboard wiring) Flame-retardant, cotton braid
Asbestos	A	200°C 392°F	Dry locations only. Only for leads within apparatus or within raceways connected to apparatus. Limited to 300 volts.	Asbestos	14 ... 30 12–8 ... 40	Without asbestos braid
Asbestos	AA	200°C 392°F	Dry locations only. Only for leads within apparatus or within raceways connected to apparatus or as open wiring. Limited to 300 volts.	Asbestos	14 ... 30 12–8 ... 30 6–2 ... 40 1–4/0 ... 30	With asbestos braid or glass
Asbestos	AI	125°C 257°F	Dry locations only. Only for leads within apparatus or within raceways connected to apparatus. Limited to 300 volts.	Impregnated Asbestos	14 ... 30 12–8 ... 40	Without asbestos braid

For insulated aluminum and copper-clad aluminum conductors, the minimum size shall be No. 12. See Tables 310-18 and 310-19.

Table 310-13 (Continued)

Trade Name	Type Letter	Max. Operating Temp.	Application Provisions	Insulation	AWG or MCM	Thickness of Insulation		Outer Covering
						Sol.	Str.	
Asbestos	AIA	125°C 257°F	Dry locations only. Only for leads within apparatus or within raceways connected to apparatus or as open wiring.	Impregnated Asbestos	14............	30	30	With asbestos braid or glass
					12–8............	30	40	
					6–2............	40	60	
					1–4/0............	60	75	
					213–500............		90	
					501–1000		105	
Paper		85°C 185°F	For underground service conductors, or by special permission.	Paper				Lead sheath

For insulated aluminum and copper-clad aluminum conductors, the minimum size shall be No. 12. See Tables 310-18 and 310-19.

Table 310-16. Allowable Ampacities of Insulated Copper Conductors

Not More than Three Conductors in Raceway or Cable or Direct Burial
(Based on Ambient Temperature of 30°C. 86°F.)

Size	Temperature Rating of Conductor. See Table 310-13							
AWG MCM	60°C (140°F)	75°C (167°F)	85°C (185°F)	90°C (194°F)	110°C (230°F)	125°C (257°F)	200°C (392°F)	250°C (482°F)
	TYPES RUW (14-2), T, TW, UF	TYPES RH, RHW, RUH (14-2), THW, THWN, XHHW, USE	TYPES V, MI	TYPES TA, TBS, SA, AVB, SIS, FEP, FEPB, RHH, THHN, XHHW**	TYPES AVA, AVL	TYPES AI (14-8), AIA	TYPES A (14-8), AA, FEP* FEPB*	TYPE TFE (Nickel or nickel-coated copper only)
18	...	...	...	21	...	...	...	...
16	...	...	22	22	...	...	...	...
14	15	15	25	25†	30	30	30	40
12	20	20	30	30†	35	40	40	55
10	30	30	40	40†	45	50	55	75
8	40	45	50	50	60	65	70	95
6	55	65	70	70	80	85	95	120
4	70	85	90	90	105	115	120	145
3	80	100	105	105	120	130	145	170
2	95	115	120	120	135	145	165	195
1	110	130	140	140	160	170	190	220
1/0	125	150	155	155	190	200	225	250
2/0	145	175	185	185	215	230	250	280
3/0	165	200	210	210	245	265	285	315
4/0	195	230	235	235	275	310	340	370
250	215	255	270	270	315	335	...	...
300	240	285	300	300	345	380	...	...
350	260	310	325	325	390	420	...	...
400	280	335	360	360	420	450	...	...
500	320	380	405	405	470	500	...	...
600	355	420	455	455	525	545	...	...
700	385	460	490	490	560	600	...	...
750	400	475	500	500	580	620	...	...
800	410	490	515	515	600	640	...	...
900	435	520	555	555	...	...	...	...
1000	455	545	585	585	680	730	...	...
1250	495	590	645	645	...	...	...	...
1500	520	625	700	700	785	...	...	...
1750	545	650	735	735	...	...	...	...
2000	560	665	775	775	840	...	...	...

* Special use only. See Table 310-13.
** For dry locations only. See Table 310-13.
These ampacities relate only to conductors described in Table 310-13.
† The ampacities for Types FEP, FEPB, RHH, THHN, and XHHW conductors for sizes 14, 12, and 10 shall be the same as designated for 75°C conductors in this Table.
For ambient temperatures over 30°C, see Correction Factors, Note 13.

Table 310-17. Allowable Ampacities of Insulated Copper Conductors

Single Conductor in Free Air
(Based on Ambient Temperature of 30°C. 86°F.)

Size				Temperature Rating of Conductor. See Table 310-13				
AWG MCM	60°C (140°F)	75°C (167°F)	85°C (185°F)	90°C (194°F)	110°C (230°F)	125°C (257°F)	200°C (392°F)	250°C (482°F)	
	TYPES RUW (14-2), T, TW	TYPES RH, RHW, RUH (14-2), THW, THWN, XHHW	TYPES V, MI	TYPES TA, TBS, SA, AVB, SIS, FEP, FEPB, RHH, THHN, XHHW**	TYPES AVA, AVL	TYPES AI (14-8), AIA	TYPES A (14-8), AA, FEP* FEPB*	TYPE TFE (Nickel or nickel-coated copper only)	Bare and Covered Conductors
18	...	...	...	25	...	...	...	...	...
16	...	...	27	27	...	...	...	...	...
14	20	20	30	30†	40	40	45	60	30
12	25	25	40	40†	50	50	55	80	40
10	40	40	55	55†	65	70	75	110	55
8	55	65	70	70	85	90	100	145	70
6	80	95	100	100	120	125	135	210	100
4	105	125	135	135	160	170	180	285	130
3	120	145	155	155	180	195	210	335	150
2	140	170	180	180	210	225	240	390	175
1	165	195	210	210	245	265	280	450	205
1/0	195	230	245	245	285	305	325	545	235
2/0	225	265	285	285	330	355	370	605	275
3/0	260	310	330	330	385	410	430	725	320
4/0	300	360	385	385	445	475	510	850	370
250	340	405	425	425	495	530	...	...	410
300	375	445	480	480	555	590	...	...	460
350	420	505	530	530	610	655	...	...	510
400	455	545	575	575	665	710	...	...	555
500	515	620	660	660	765	815	...	...	630
600	575	690	740	740	855	910	...	...	710
700	630	755	815	815	940	1005	...	...	780
750	655	785	845	845	980	1045	...	...	810
800	680	815	880	880	1020	1085	...	...	845
900	730	870	940	940	...	...	...	...	905
1000	780	935	1000	1000	1165	1240	...	...	965
1250	890	1065	1130	1130	...	...	...	...	...
1500	980	1175	1260	1260	1450	...	...	...	1215
1750	1070	1280	1370	1370	...	...	...	...	...
2000	1155	1385	1470	1470	1715	...	...	...	1405

* Special use only. See Table 310-13.
** For dry locations only. See Table 310-13.
These ampacities relate only to conductors described in Table 310-13.
† The ampacities for Types FEP, FEPB, RHH, THHN, and XHHW conductors for sizes 14, 12, and 10 shall be the same as designated for 75°C conductors in this Table.
For ambient temperatures over 30°C, see Correction Factors, Note 13.

Table 310-18. Allowable Ampacities of Insulated Aluminum and Copper-Clad Aluminum Conductors

Not More than Three Conductors in Raceway or Cable or Direct Burial
(Based on Ambient Temperature of 30°C. 86°F.)

Size AWG MCM	Temperature Rating of Conductor. See Table 310-13						
	60°C (140°F)	75°C (167°F)	85°C (185°F)	90°C (194°F)	110°C (230°F)	125°C (257°F)	200°C (392°F)
	TYPES RUW (12-2), T, TW, UF	TYPES RH, RHW, RUH (12-2), THW THWN XHHW, USE	TYPES V, MI	TYPES TA, TBS, SA, AVB, SIS, RHH THHN XHHW*	TYPES AVA, AVL	TYPES AI (12-8), AIA	TYPES A (12-8), AA
12	15	15	25	25†	25	30	30
10	25	25	30	30†	35	40	45
8	30	40	40	40	45	50	55
6	40	50	55	55	60	65	75
4	55	65	70	70	80	90	95
3	65	75	80	80	95	100	115
2	75	90	95	95	105	115	130
1	85	100	110	110	125	135	150
1/0	100	120	125	125	150	160	180
2/0	115	135	145	145	170	180	200
3/0	130	155	165	165	195	210	225
4/0	155	180	185	185	215	245	270
250	170	205	215	215	250	270	...
300	190	230	240	240	275	305	...
350	210	250	260	260	310	335	...
400	225	270	290	290	335	360	...
500	260	310	330	330	380	405	...
600	285	340	370	370	425	440	...
700	310	375	395	395	455	485	...
750	320	385	405	405	470	500	...
800	330	395	415	415	485	520	...
900	355	425	455	455	...	...	...
1000	375	445	480	480	560	600	...
1250	405	485	530	530	...	...	...
1500	435	520	580	580	650	...	...
1750	455	545	615	615	...	...	...
2000	470	560	650	650	705	...	...

These ampacities relate only to conductors described in Table 310-13.
* For dry locations only. See Table 310-13.
† The ampacities for Types RHH, THHN, and XHHW conductors for sizes 12 and 10 shall be the same as designated for 75°C conductors in this Table.
For ambient temperatures over 30°C, see Correction Factors, Note 13.

Table 310-19. Allowable Ampacities of Insulated Aluminum and
Copper-Clad Aluminum Conductors

Single Conductor in Free Air
(Based on Ambient Temperature of 30°C. 86°F.)

Size	Temperature Rating of Conductor. See Table 310-13							
AWG MCM	60°C (140°F)	75°C (167°F)	85°C (185°F)	90°C (194°F)	110°C (230°F)	125°C (257°F)	200°C (392°F)	
	TYPES RUW (12-2), T, TW	TYPES RH, RHW, RUH (12-2), THW THWN XHHW	TYPES V, MI	TYPES TA, TBS, SA, AVB. SIS, RHH, THHN, XHHW*	TYPES AVA, AVL	TYPES AI (12-8), AIA	TYPES A (12-8), AA	Bare and Covered Conductors
12	20	20	30	30†	40	40	45	30
10	30	30	45	45†	50	55	60	45
8	45	55	55	55	65	70	80	55
6	60	75	80	80	95	100	105	80
4	80	100	105	105	125	135	140	100
3	95	115	120	120	140	150	165	115
2	110	135	140	140	165	175	185	135
1	130	155	165	165	190	205	220	160
1/0	150	180	190	190	220	240	255	185
2/0	175	210	220	220	255	275	290	215
3/0	200	240	255	255	300	320	335	250
4/0	230	280	300	300	345	370	400	290
250	265	315	330	330	385	415	. . .	320
300	290	350	375	375	435	460	. . .	360
350	330	395	415	415	475	510	. . .	400
400	355	425	450	450	520	555	. . .	435
500	405	485	515	515	595	635	. . .	490
600	455	545	585	585	675	720	. . .	560
700	500	595	645	645	745	795	. . .	615
750	515	620	670	670	775	825	. . .	640
800	535	645	695	695	805	855	. . .	670
900	580	700	750	750	. . .	. . .	. . .	725
1000	625	750	800	800	930	990	. . .	770
1250	710	855	905	905	. . .	. . .	. . .	. . .
1500	795	950	1020	1020	1175	. . .	. . .	985
1750	875	1050	1125	1125	. . .	. . .	. . .	. . .
2000	960	1150	1220	1220	1425	. . .	. . .	1165

These ampacities relate only to conductors described in Table 310-13.
*For dry locations only. See Table 310-13.
†The ampacities for Types RHH, THHN, and XHHW conductors for sizes 12 and 10 shall be the same as designated for 75°C conductors in this Table.
For ambient temperatures over 30°C, see Correction Factors, Note 13.

8. More Than 3 Conductors in a Raceway or Cable. Where the number of conductors in a raceway or cable exceed 3, the maximum allowable load current of each conductor shall be reduced as shown in the following table:

Number of Conductors	Percent of Values in Tables 310-16 and 310-18
4 thru 6	80
7 thru 24	70
25 thru 42	60
43 and above	50

Where single conductors or multiconductor cables are stacked or bundled without maintaining spacing and are not installed in raceways, the maximum allowable load current of each conductor shall be reduced as shown in the above table.

Exception No. 1: When conductors of different systems, as provided in Section 300-3, are installed in a common raceway as provided the derating factors shown above shall apply to the number of power and lighting (Articles 210, 215, 220, and 230) conductors only.

Exception No. 2: The derating factors of Sections 210-22(c), 220-2(a) and 220-10(b) shall not apply when the above derating factors are also required.

Exception No. 3. For conductors installed in cable trays, the provisions of Section 318-10 shall apply.

9. Overcurrent Protection. Where the standard ratings and settings of overcurrent devices do not correspond with the ratings and settings allowed for conductors, the next higher standard rating and setting shall be permitted.

Exception: As limited in Section 240-3.

10. Neutral Conductor. (a) A neutral conductor which carries only the unbalanced current from other conductors, as in the case of normally balanced circuits of 3 or more conductors, shall not be counted in determining ampacities as provided for in Note 8.

(b) In a 3-wire circuit consisting of two phase wires and the neutral of a 4-wire, 3-phase wye-connected system, a common conductor carries approximately the same current as the other conductors and shall be counted in determining ampacities as provided in Note 8.

(c) On a 4-wire 3-phase wye circuit where the major portion of the load consists of electric-discharge lighting there are harmonic currents present in the neutral conductor and the neutral shall be considered to be a current-carrying conductor.

11. Voltage Drop. The allowable ampacities in Tables 310-16 through 310-19 are based on temperature alone and do not take voltage drop into consideration.

12. Aluminum-Sheathed Cable or Copper-Sheathed Cable. The ampacities of Type ALS and Type CS cables are determined by the temperature limitation of the insulated conductors incorporated within the cable. Hence the ampacities of aluminum-sheathed cable or copper-sheathed cable may be determined from the columns in Tables 310-16 and 310-18 applicable to the type of insulated conductors employed within the cable.

13. Use of Conductors With Higher Operating Temperatures. Where the room temperature is within 10 degrees C of the maximum allowable operating temperature of the insulation, it is desirable to use an insulation with a higher maximum allowable operating temperature; although insulation can be used in a room temperature approaching its maximum allowable operating temperature limit if the current is reduced in accordance with the correction factors for different room temperatures as shown in the correction factor table, Table 13.

▲ Note 5 provides that, if an uninsulated conductor is used with insulated conductors in a raceway or cable, its size shall be the size that would be required for a conductor having the same insulation as the insulated conductors and having the required ampacity.

Example: Two No. 6 Type THW conductors and one bare No. 6 conductor in a raceway or cable. The ampacity of the bare conductor would be 65 A.

If the insulated conductors were Type TW, the ampacity of the bare conductor would be 55 A.

The purpose of Exception No. 2 in Note 8 is to indicate that while the pyramiding of derating factors is not required, the greatest factor must always be used. Normally the requirements of Note 8 are equal to or greater than that stated in Secs. 210-22(c), 220-2(a), and 220-10(b); but in no case may a continuous load exceed 80 percent of branch-circuit or feeder overcurrent-device ratings except where the overcurrent devices and associated assemblies are approved for continuous operation at 100 percent of their ratings.

14. Type MTW Machine Tool Wire. The ampacities of Type MTW wire are specified in Table 200-B of the Electrical Standard for Metalworking Machine Tools 1973 (NFPA Publication No. 79).

Table 13. Correction Factors Ambient Temps. Over 30°C. 86°F.

C.	F.	60°C (140°F)	75°C (167°F)	85°C (185°F)	90°C (194°F)	110°C (230°F)	125°C (257°F)	200°C (392°F)	250°C (482°F)
40	104	.82	.88	.90	.91	.94	.95	...	...
45	113	.71	.82	.85	.87	.90	.92	...	...
50	122	.58	.75	.80	.82	.87	.89	...	...
55	131	.41	.67	.74	.76	.83	.86	...	...
60	140	...	.58	.67	.71	.79	.83	.91	.95
70	158	...	.35	.52	.58	.71	.76	.87	.91
75	167	...	...	.43	.50	.66	.72	.86	.89
80	176	...	...	.30	.41	.61	.69	.84	.87
90	194	...	...	...	...	.50	.61	.80	.83
100	212	...	...	...	...	...	.51	.77	.80
120	248	...	...	...	...	...	...	.69	.72
140	284	...	...	...	...	...	...	.59	.59
160	320	...	...	...	...	...	...	...	.54
180	356	...	...	...	...	...	...	...	.50
200	392	...	...	...	...	...	...	...	.43
225	437	...	...	...	...	...	...	...	.30

C. Conductors Over 600 Volts, Nominal

310-30. General. In addition to the generally applicable provisions of Part A of this article, the following rules shall apply.

310-31. Construction of Conductors For Over 600 Volts. Insulated Conductors for use over 600 volts, nominal shall comply with Table 310-31 through 310-37.

310-38. Ampacity. The maximum continuous ampacities for copper and aluminum solid dielectric insulated conductors rated 2001 to 15000 volts shall be as given in Tables 310-39 through 310-50 and accompanying notes, while for conductors rated 601 to 2000 volts the maximum continuous ampacities shall be as given in Tables 310-16 through 310-19 and their accompanying notes.

Notes To Tables 310-39 Through 310-50

Ampacities calculated in accordance with the following Notes 1 and 2 will require reference to AIEE/IPCEA "Power Cable Ampacities" Vols. I and II (IPCEA PUB. No. P-46-426) and "The References" therein for availability of all factors and constants.

Table 310-31. Conductor Application and Insulation

Trade Name	Type Letter	Maximum Operating Temperature	Application Provision	Insulation	Outer Covering
Medium voltage solid dielectric	MV-75 MV-85 MV-90	75C 85C 90C	Dry or wet locations rated 2001 volts and higher	Thermoplastic or Thermosetting	Jacket, Sheath or Armor

Table 310-32. Thickness Of Insulation For 601-2000 Volt Non-Shielded Types RHH and RHW, In Mils

Conductor Size AWG-MCM	A	B
14–10*	80	60
8	80	70
6–2	95	70
1–2/0	110	90
3/0–4/0	110	90
213–500	125	105
501–1000	140	120

Note: Column A insulations are limited to natural, SBR, and butyl rubbers.

Note: Column B insulations are those specifically approved for the purpose, such as cross-linked polyethylene and ethylene propylene rubber.

* Note: No. 12 shall be the minimum conductor size for aluminum and copper-clad aluminum.

1. Ambients Not in Tables. Ampacities at ambient temperatures other than those shown in the Tables shall be determined by means of the following formula:

$$I_2 = I_1 \sqrt{\frac{TC - TA_2 - DELTA\ TD}{TC - TA_1 - DELTA\ TD}}$$

Where,

I_1 = Ampacity from Tables at ambient TA_1
I_2 = Ampacity at desired ambient TA_2
TC = Conductor temperature in degrees C
TA_1 = Surrounding ambient from Tables in degrees C
TA_2 = Desired ambient in degrees C
$DELTA\ TD$ = Dielectric loss temperature rise

2. Applications Not Covered by Tables. Ampacities for cable insulations, cable configurations, voltage levels, or thermal resistivities not included in the Tables shall be permitted to be calculated, under engineering supervision, by means of the following general formula:

$$I = \sqrt{\frac{TC - (TA + DELTA\ TD)}{RDC\ (1 + YC)\ RCA}}$$

TC = Conductor temperature in degrees C
TA = Ambient temperature in degrees C
$DELTA\ TD$ = Dielectric loss temperature rise
RDC = D-c resistance of conductor at temperature TC
YC = Component a-c resistance resulting from skin effect and proximity effect
RCA = Effective thermal resistance between conductor and surrounding ambient.

3. Grounded Shields—Ampacities shown in Tables 310-39 and 310-45 are for cable with shields grounded at one point only.

4. Duct Bank Configuration—Ampacities shown in Tables 310-43, 310-44, 310-49 and 310-50 shall apply only when the cables are located in the outer ducts of the duct bank. Ampacities for cables located in the inner ducts of the duct bank will have to be determined by special calculations.

310-51. Shielding. Solid dielectric insulated conductors operated above 2000 volts in permanent installations shall have ozone resistant insulation and shall be shielded. Shielding shall be for the purpose of confining the voltage stresses to the insulation.

(*Continued on page 211.*)

Table 310-33. Thickness of Insulation and Jacket for Nonshielded Solid Dielectric Insulated Conductors Rated 2001 to 8000 Volts in Mils

Conductor Size AWG-MCM	2001–5000 Volts						5001–8000 Volts 100 Percent Insulation Level Wet or Dry Locations		
	Dry Locations Single Conductor			Wet or Dry Locations					
	Without Jacket	With Jacket		Single Conductor		Multi-Conductor*	Single Conductor		Multi-Conductor*
	Insulation	Insulation	Jacket	Insulation	Jacket	Insulation	Insulation	Jacket	Insulation
8	110	90	30	125	80	90	180	80	180
6	110	90	30	125	80	90	180	80	180
4–2	110	90	45	125	80	90	180	95	180
1–2/0	110	90	45	125	80	90	180	95	180
3/0–4/0	110	90	65	125	95	90	180	110	180
213–500	120	90	65	140	110	90	210	110	210
501–750	130	90	65	155	125	90	235	125	235
751–1000	130	90	65	155	125	90	250	140	250

*Note: Under a common overall covering such as a jacket, sheath or armor.

Table 310-34. Thickness of Insulation for Shielded Solid Dielectric Insulated Conductors Rated 2001 to 15000 Volts, In Mils

Conductor Size AWG-MCM	2001–5000 Volts	5001–8000		8001–15000	
		100* Percent insulation level	133* Percent insulation level	100* Percent insulation level	133* Percent insulation level
8	90	—	—	—	—
6–4	90	115	140	—	—
2	90	115	140	175	—
1–1000	90	115	140	175	215

DEFINITIONS:

100 Percent Insulation Level. Cables in this category shall be permitted to be applied where the system is provided with relay protection such that ground faults will be cleared as rapidly as possible, but in any case within 1 minute. While these cables are applicable to the great majority of cable installations which are on grounded systems, they shall be permitted to be used also on other systems for which the application of cables is acceptable provided the above clearing requirements are met in completely de-energizing the faulted section.

133 Percent Insulation Level. This insulation level corresponds to that formerly designated for ungrounded systems. Cables in this category shall be permitted to be applied in situations where the clearing time requirements of the 100 percent level category cannot be met, and yet there is adequate assurance that the faulted section will be de-energized in a time not exceeding 1 hour. Also they shall be permitted to be used when additional insulation strength over the 100 percent level category is desirable.

Table 310-35. Thickness of Varnished-Cambric Insulation for Single-Conductor Cable, in Mils

Conductor Size AWG or MCM	For Voltages Not Exceeding				
	1000	2000	3000	4000	5000
14	60	..	..	..	..
12	60	80	..	..	..
10	60	80	95	..	..
8–2	60	80	95	110	140
1–4/0	80	95	95	110	140
213–500	95	95	110	125	155
501–1000	110	110	110	125	155
1001–2000	125	125	125	140	155

Table 310-36. Thickness of Varnished-Cambric Insulation for Multiconductor Cable, in Mils

Conductor Size AWG or MCM	For Voltages Not Exceeding									
	1000		2000		3000		4000		5000	
	C	B	C	B	C	B	C	B	C	B
14	60	0	..	..	..	..	..	..	..	..
12	60	0	80	0	..	..	..	..	..	..
10	60	0	80	0	80	30	..	..	..	..
8-2	60	0	80	0	80	30	95	45	95	60
1-4/0	80	0	95	0	95	30	95	45	95	60
213-500	95	0	95	0	95	30	95	45	110	60
501-1000	95	30	95	30	95	45	95	60	110	60
1001-2000	110	30	110	30	110	45	110	60	110	80

The thickness given in columns headed "C" are for the insulation on the individual conductors. Those given in the columns headed "B" are for the thickness of the over-all belt of insulation.

Table 310-37. Thickness of Asbestos and Varnished-Cambric Insulation for Single-Conductor Cable, Types AVA, AVB, and AVL, in Mils

Conductor AWG or MCM	1st Wall Asbestos	Varnished Cambric					Asbestos 2nd Wall
		For Voltages Not Exceeding					
	1000–5000	1000	2000	3000	4000	5000	1000–5000
14-2	15	45	60	80	100	120	25
1-4/0	20	45	60	80	100	120	30
213-500	25	45	60	80	100	120	40
501-1000	30	45	60	80	100	120	40
1001-2000	30	55	75	95	115	140	50

Table 310-39. Allowable Ampacities for Insulated Single Copper Conductor Isolated in Air (Based on Conductor Temperature of 90°C and Ambient Air Temperature of 40°C)

Conductor Size AWG-MCM	2001–5000 Volts Ampacity	5001–15,000 Volts Ampacity
8	83	—
6	110	110
4	145	150
2	190	195
1	225	225
1/0	260	260
2/0	300	300
3/0	345	345
4/0	400	400
250	445	445
350	550	550
500	695	685
750	900	885
1000	1075	1060
1250	1230	1210
1500	1365	1345
1750	1495	1470
2000	1605	1575

Table 310-40. Allowable Ampacities of an Insulated Three Conductor Copper Cable, Isolated in Air (Based on Conductor Temperature of 90°C and Ambient Air Temperature of 40°C)

Conductor Size AWG-MCM	2001–5000 Volts Ampacity	5001–15,000 Volts Ampacity
8	59	—
6	79	93
4	105	120
2	140	165
1	160	185
1/0	185	215
2/0	215	245
3/0	250	285
4/0	285	325
250	320	360
350	395	435
500	485	535
750	615	670
1000	705	770

Table 310-41. Allowable Ampacities of an Insulated Triplexed or Three Single Conductor Copper Cables in Isolated Conduit in Air (Based on Conductor Temperature of 90°C and Ambient Air Temperature of 40°C)

Conductor Size AWG-MCM	2001–5000 Volts Ampacity	5001–15,000 Volts Ampacity
8	55	—
6	75	83
4	97	110
2	130	150
1	155	170
1/0	180	195
2/0	205	225
3/0	240	260
4/0	280	295
250	315	330
350	385	395
500	475	480
750	600	585
1000	690	675

Table 310-42. Allowable Ampacities of An Insulated Three Conductor Copper Cable in Isolated Conduit in Air (Based on Conductor Temperature of 90°C and Ambient Air Temperature of 40°C)

Conductor Size AWG-MCM	2001–5000 Volts Ampacity	5001–15,000 Volts Ampacity
8	52	—
6	69	83
4	91	105
2	125	145
1	140	165
1/0	165	195
2/0	190	220
3/0	220	250
4/0	255	290
250	280	315
350	350	385
500	425	470
750	525	570
1000	590	650

Table 310-43. Allowable Ampacities of An Insulated Triplexed or Three Single Conductor Copper Cables in Underground Ducts [Based on Conductor Temperature of 90°C, Ambient Earth Temperature of 20°C, 100% Load Factor and Thermal Resistance (RHO) of 90]

One Circuit Size AWG-MCM	2001–5000 Volts Ampacity	5001–15,000 Volts Ampacity
8	64	—
6	85	90
4	110	115
2	145	155
1	170	175
1/0	195	200
2/0	220	230
3/0	250	260
4/0	290	295
250	320	325
350	385	390
500	470	465
750	585	565
1000	670	640
Three Circuit Size		
8	56	—
6	73	77
4	95	99
2	125	130
1	140	145
1/0	160	165
2/0	185	185
3/0	210	210
4/0	235	240
250	260	260
350	315	310
500	375	370
750	460	440
1000	525	495
Six Circuit Size		
8	48	—
6	62	64
4	80	82
2	105	105
1	115	120
1/0	135	135
2/0	150	150
3/0	170	170
4/0	195	190
250	210	210
350	250	245
500	300	290
750	365	350
1000	410	390

Table 310-44. Allowable Ampacities of An Insulated Three Conductor Copper Cable In Underground Ducts [Based on Conductor Temperature of 90°C, Ambient Earth Temperature of 20°C, 100% Load Factor and Thermal Resistance (RHO) of 90]

One Circuit Size AWG-MCM	2001–5000 Volts Ampacity	5001–15,000 Volts Ampacity
8	59	—
6	78	88
4	100	115
2	135	150
1	155	170
1/0	175	195
2/0	200	220
3/0	230	250
4/0	265	285
250	290	310
350	355	375
500	430	450
750	530	545
1000	600	615
Three Circuit Size		
8	53	—
6	69	75
4	89	97
2	115	125
1	135	140
1/0	150	160
2/0	170	185
3/0	195	205
4/0	225	230
250	245	255
350	295	305
500	355	360
750	430	430
1000	485	485
Six Circuit Size		
8	46	—
6	60	63
4	77	81
2	98	105
1	110	115
1/0	125	130
2/0	145	150
3/0	165	170
4/0	185	190
250	200	205
350	240	245
500	290	290
750	350	340
1000	390	380

Table 310-45. Allowable Ampacities For Insulated Single Aluminum Conductor Isolated in Air (Based On Conductor Temperature of 90°C and Ambient Air Temperature of 40°C)

Conductor Size AWG-MCM	2001–5000 Volts Ampacity	5001–15,000 Volts Ampacity
8	64	—
6	85	87
4	115	115
2	150	150
1	175	175
1/0	200	200
2/0	230	235
3/0	270	270
4/0	310	310
250	345	345
350	430	430
500	545	535
750	710	700
1000	855	840
1250	980	970
1500	1105	1085
1750	1215	1195
2000	1320	1295

Table 310-46. Allowable Ampacities of An Insulated Three Conductor Aluminum Cable Isolated In Air (Based On Conductor Temperature of 90°C and Ambient Air Temperature of 40°C)

Conductor Size AWG-MCM	2001–5000 Volts Ampacity	5001–15,000 Volts Ampacity
8	46	—
6	61	72
4	81	95
2	110	125
1	125	145
1/0	145	170
2/0	170	190
3/0	195	220
4/0	225	255
250	250	280
350	310	345
500	385	425
750	495	540
1000	585	635

Table 310-47. Allowable Ampacities of Insulated Triplexed Or Three Single Conductor Aluminum Cables in isolated Conduit in Air (Based on Conductor Temperature of 90°C and Ambient Air Temperature of 40°C)

Conductor Size AWG-MCM	2001–5000 Volts Ampacity	5001–15,000 Volts Ampacity
8	43	—
6	58	65
4	76	84
2	100	115
1	120	130
1/0	140	150
2/0	160	175
3/0	190	200
4/0	215	230
250	250	255
350	305	310
500	380	385
750	490	485
1000	580	565

Table 310-48. Allowable Ampacities of an Insulated Three Conductor Aluminum Cable in Isolated Conduit in Air (Based on Conductor Temperature of 90°C and Ambient Air Temperature of 40°C)

Conductor Size AWG-MCM	2001–5000 Volts Ampacity	5001–15,000 Volts Ampacity
8	41	—
6	53	64
4	71	84
2	96	115
1	110	130
1/0	130	150
2/0	150	170
3/0	170	195
4/0	200	225
250	220	250
350	275	305
500	340	380
750	430	470
1000	505	550

Table 310-49. Allowable Ampacities of Insulated Triplexed or Three Single Conductor Aluminum Cables in Underground Ducts [Based on Conductor Temperature of 90°C, Ambient Earth Temperature of 20°C, 100% Load Factor and Thermal Resistance (RHO) of 90]

One Circuit Size AWG-MCM	2001–5000 Volts Ampacity	5001–15,000 Volts Ampacity
8	50	—
6	66	70
4	86	91
2	115	120
1	130	135
1/0	150	155
2/0	170	175
3/0	195	200
4/0	225	230
250	250	250
350	305	305
500	370	370
750	470	455
1000	545	525
Three Circuit Size		
8	44	—
6	57	60
4	74	77
2	96	100
1	110	110
1/0	125	125
2/0	145	145
3/0	160	165
4/0	185	185
250	205	200
350	245	245
500	295	290
750	370	355
1000	425	405
Six Circuit Size		
8	38	—
6	48	50
4	62	64
2	80	80
1	91	90
1/0	105	105
2/0	115	115
3/0	135	130
4/0	150	150
250	165	165
350	195	195
500	240	230
750	290	280
1000	335	320

Table 310-50. Allowable Ampacities of an Insulated Three Conductor Aluminum Cable in Underground Ducts [Based on Conductor Temperature of 90°C, Ambient Earth Temperature of 20°C, 100% Load Factor and Thermal Resistance (RHO) of 90]

One Circuit Size AWG-MCM	2001–5000 Volts Ampacity	5001–15,000 Volts Ampacity
8	46	—
6	61	69
4	80	89
2	105	115
1	120	135
1/0	140	150
2/0	160	170
3/0	180	195
4/0	205	220
250	230	245
350	280	295
500	340	355
750	425	440
1000	495	510
Three Circuit Size		
8	41	—
6	54	59
4	70	75
2	90	100
1	105	110
1/0	120	125
2/0	135	140
3/0	155	160
4/0	175	180
250	190	200
350	230	240
500	280	285
750	345	350
1000	400	400
Six Circuit Size		
8	36	—
6	46	49
4	60	63
2	77	80
1	87	90
1/0	99	105
2/0	110	115
3/0	130	130
4/0	145	150
250	160	160
350	190	190
500	230	230
750	280	275
1000	320	315

Exception: Non-shielded insulated conductors listed by a nationally recognized testing laboratory and approved for the purpose shall be permitted for use up to 8000 volts under the following conditions:

a. Conductors shall have insulation resistant to electric discharge and surface tracking, or the insulated conductor(s) shall be covered with a material resistant to ozone, electric discharge and surface tracking.

b. Where used in wet locations the insulated conductor(s) shall have an overall nonmetallic jacket or a continuous metallic sheath suitable for the purpose,

c. Where operated at 5001 to 8000 volts, the insulated conductor(s) shall have a nonmetallic jacket over the insulation. The insulation shall have a specific inductive capacity no greater than 3.6 and the jacket shall have a specific inductive capacity no greater than 10 and no less than 6.

d. Insulation and jacket thicknesses shall be in accordance with Table 310-33.

▲ In a solid dielectric insulated conductor, if a slight amount of moisture is present, some moisture will be absorbed by the outer jacket, which then becomes to some extent a conductor. The metal conductor, the insulation, and the jacket then form a capacitor, with the conductor and the jacket as the two electrodes. When a voltage to ground is impressed upon one electrode of a capacitor, a voltage of opposite sign will appear on the other electrode, and if this electrode is connected to ground, a current will flow to ground. Thus when a voltage is impressed upon the conductor, a voltage will appear upon the jacket if it has become partially conducting by absorbing some moisture.

If the cable is in a grounded metal conduit, the voltage appearing on the jacket will discharge to ground at the points where the jacket is in contact with the conduit; in other words, there is a charging current flowing between the conductor and the ground. If the voltage is high enough, the discharge will cause the air to be ionized and ozone will be formed. Ozone is oxygen in such form that it is extremely active in combining with any oxidizable substance. It will attack the jacket and the jacket insulation, and this action may eventually break down the insulation.

The discharge and the consequent formation of ozone can be prevented by surrounding the insulation with a metallic or semiconducting shield which is grounded. Instead of the jacket, the shield then becomes one electrode of the capacitor. Being grounded by a metallic connection to ground, the shield is kept at ground potential and no voltage above ground can appear on the jacket outside of the shield, hence there is no discharge from the jacket and no ionization of the air takes place.

A metallic shield usually consists of a thin ribbon or tape of tinned copper about $7/8$ in. or 1 in. wide, wrapped spirally around the insulation. The "semiconducting" shield may consist of conducting fibrous tape, conducting paint, certain types of asbestos coverings, metalized paper, graphite compounds, or similar materials.

Figure 310-1 shows a single-conductor shielded cable and a three-conductor shielded cable.

A stress cone consists of an application of insulating tape in conical form, over which the shielding is continued, the purpose being to build up the thickness of the insulation at the point where the shielding ends. The insulating tape may be varnished cambric. The shielding is continued over the cone of tape by means of a spiral wrapping of braided copper tinsel tape which is soldered to the shield on the cable.

Table 310-33 is for 2,001- to 8,000-V conductors, listed by a nationally recognized testing laboratory, referred to in the Exception to Sec. 310-51. Table 310-34 covers

Fig. 310-1. Single-conductor and three-conductor shielded rubber-insulated cable. (*The Okonite Co.*)

the conductors referred to in the first paragraph of Sec. 310-51. The requirements of Table 310-32, which describe the insulation requirements for rubber-covered types from 601 to 2,000 V, govern the construction of such cables. Accordingly, where single-conductor rubber-covered cables (including natural, SBR, and butyl rubbers, and cross-linked polyethylene and ethylene-propylene rubber) are used in other than multiconductor cables with a common overall covering at over 2 kV, shielding is required, unless conductors of the type referred to in Sec. 310-51 Exception are used. This should help to prevent failures if shielded 5-kV single-conductor cables for a 4,160-V system are installed in raceways. In the past, unshielded single-conductor 5-kV cable resulted in numerous failures.

Figures 310-2 and 310-3 show a stress cone formed on a single-conductor cable terminating without a pothead and a stress cone inside a pothead. In Fig. 310-2 the shield is grounded by means of a sheet-copper ground clamp which is soldered to the shield. In Fig. 310-3 a clamping ring is provided inside the pothead, and the end of the copper tape is turned out and clamped under the ring, thus grounding the tape and shield to the metallic base of the pothead.

Before proceeding with the installation of any type of high-voltage cable, complete instructions for installation should always be obtained from the manufacturer of the cable. Proper training for making high-voltage terminations is absolutely essential.

ARTICLE 318. CABLE TRAYS

318-1. Scope. A cable tray system is a unit or assembly of units or sections, and associated fittings, made of metal or other noncombustible materials forming a rigid structural system used to support cables. Cable tray systems include ladders, troughs, channels, solid bottom trays, and other similar structures.

It is not the intent of this Article to require that cables be installed in cable tray systems or to recognize the use of all conductors described in Article 310 in cable tray systems for general wiring.

318-2. Uses Permitted.

(a) The following shall be permitted to be installed in cable tray systems under the conditions described in the Article for each:

1. Mineral-insulated metal-sheathed cable, (Article 330); 2. aluminum-sheathed cable, (Article 331); 3. copper-sheathed cable, (Article 332); 4. metal-clad cable,

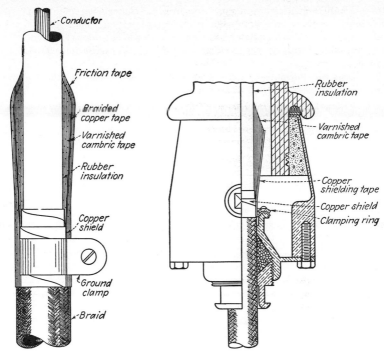

FIG. 310-2. Stress cone on a single-conductor shielded cable terminating without a pothead.

FIG. 310-3. Stress cone on a single-conductor shielded cable terminating in a pothead.

(Article 334); 5. nonmetallic-sheathed cable, (Article 336); 6. shielded nonmetallic-sheathed cable, (Article 337); 7. multiple-conductor service-entrance cable, (Article 338); 8. multiple-conductor underground feeder and branch-circuit cable, (Article 339); 9. power and control tray cable, (Article 340); 10. other factory-assembled, multiple-conductor control, signal, or power cables, which are specifically approved for installation in cable trays; or 11. any approved conduit or raceway with its contained conductors.

(b) In industrial establishments only, where conditions of maintenance and supervision assure that only competent individuals will service the installed cable tray system, any of the following sizes and types of cables shall be permitted to be installed in ladder, ventilated trough, or 4-inch ventilated channel-type cable trays:

(1) Single Conductor. Sizes 250 MCM and larger, Types RHH and RHW without outer braids, Types MV, USE, THW, and other types which are specifically approved for installation in cable trays. Where exposed to direct rays of the sun, cables shall be sunlight-resistant.

(2) Multiconductor. Type MV cables, (Article 310) where exposed to direct rays of the sun, cables shall be sunlight-resistant.

(c) The metal in cable trays, as defined in Table 318-6(b)(2), shall be permitted to be used as equipment grounding conductors in commercial and industrial establishments only, where continuous maintenance and supervision assure that only competent individuals will service the installed cable tray system.

(d) Cable tray systems shall be permitted to be used in hazardous locations where the contained cables are specifically approved for such use. See Sections 501-4, 502-4, and 503-3.

318-3. Uses Not Permitted. Cable tray systems shall not be used in hoistways or where subjected to severe physical damage.

318-4. Construction Specifications. Cable trays shall be approved for the purpose and shall comply with the following:

(a) Shall have suitable strength and rigidity to provide adequate support for all contained wiring.

(b) Shall not present sharp edges, burrs or projections injurious to the insulation or jackets of the wiring.

(c) If made of metal, shall be adequately protected against corrosion or shall be made of corrosion-resistant material.

(d) Shall have side rails or equivalent structural members.

(e) Shall include fittings or other suitable means for changes in direction and elevation of runs.

318-5. Installation.

(a) Cable trays shall be installed as a complete system. Field bends or modifications shall be so made that the electrical continuity of the cable tray system and support for the cables shall be maintained.

(b) Each run of cable tray shall be completed before the installation of cables.

(c) Supports shall be provided to prevent stress on cables where they enter another raceway or enclosure from cable tray systems.

Fig. 318-1. A cable tray trough. (*Husky Ventrib.*)

Fig. 318-2. A cable tray ladder. (*Husky Steel Ventray.*)

(d) In portions of runs where additional protection is required, noncombustible covers or enclosures providing the required protection shall be used.

(e) Installations involving different electrical systems shall comply with Section 300-3. Where barriers are required to separate cables of different systems in cable trays, the barriers shall be solid and noncombustible.

(f) Cable trays shall be permitted to extend transversely through partitions and walls or vertically through platforms and floors in wet or dry locations where the installations, complete with installed cables, are made in accordance with the requirements of Section 300-21.

(g) Cable trays shall be exposed and accessible except as permitted by Section 318-5(f).

(h) Sufficient space shall be provided and maintained about cable trays to permit adequate access for installing and maintaining the cables.

318-6. Grounding.

(a) Metallic cable trays which support electrical conductors shall be grounded as required for conductor enclosures in Article 250.

(b) Where steel or aluminum cable tray systems are used as equipment grounding conductors, all of the following provisions shall be complied with:

(1) The cable tray sections and fittings shall be approved for the purpose.

(2) The minimum cross-sectional area of cable trays shall conform to the requirements in Table 318-6(b) (2).

(3) All cable tray sections and fittings shall be legibly and durably marked to show the cross-sectional area of metal in channel-type cable trays or cable trays of one-piece construction, and the total cross-sectional area of both side rails for ladder or trough-type cable trays.

(4) Cable tray sections, fittings and connected raceways shall be bonded in

FIG. 318-3. A typical cable tray installation. (*Husky Trough and Ladder.*)

accordance with Section 250-75 using bolted mechanical connectors approved for the purpose or bonding jumpers sized and installed in accordance with Section 250-79.

318-7. Cable Installation.

(a) Cable splices made and insulated by approved methods shall be permitted to be located within a cable tray provided they are accessible and do not project above the side rails.

Table 318-6(b) (2). Metal Area Requirements for Cable Trays Used as Equipment Grounding Conductors

Ampere Rating or Setting of Largest Automatic Overcurrent Device Protecting Any Circuit in the Cable Tray System	Minimum Cross-Sectional Area of Metal* in Square Inches	
	Steel Cable Trays	Aluminum Cable Trays
0–60	0.20	0.20
61–100	0.40	0.20
101–200	0.70	0.20
201–400	1.00	0.40
401–600	1.50**	0.40
601–1000	—	0.60
1001–1200	—	1.00
1201–1600	—	1.50
1601–2000	—	2.00**

*Total cross-sectional area of both side rails for ladder or trough-type cable trays; or the minimum cross-sectional area of metal in channel type cable trays or cable trays of one-piece construction.

**Steel cable trays shall not be used as equipment grounding conductors for circuits protected above 600 amperes. Aluminum cable trays shall not be used for equipment grounding conductors for circuits protected above 2000 amperes.

(b) In other than horizontal runs, the cables shall be fastened securely to transverse members of the cable trays.

(c) A box shall not be required where cables or conductors are installed in bushed conduit used for support or for protection against physical damage.

(d) Where single conductor cables comprising each phase or neutral of a circuit are connected in parallel as permitted in Section 310-4, the conductors shall be installed in groups consisting of not more than one conductor per phase or neutral, to prevent current unbalance in the paralleled conductors due to inductive reactance.

Single conductors shall be securely bound in circuit groups to prevent excessive movement due to fault current magnetic forces.

Exception: Where single conductors are twisted together, such as triplexed assemblies.

318-8. Number of Multiple-Conductor Cables in Cable Trays. The number of multiple-conductor cables permitted in a single cable tray shall not exceed the requirements of this Section.

(a) Where ladder or ventilated trough cable trays contain multiple-conductor power or lighting cables, or any mixture of multiple-conductor power, lighting, control, and signal cables, the maximum number of cables shall conform to the following:

(1) Where all of the cables are 4/0 AWG or larger, the sum of the diameters of all cables shall not exceed the cable tray width, and the cables shall be installed in a single layer.

(2) Where all of the cables are smaller than 4/0 AWG, the sum of the cross-sectional areas of all cables shall not exceed the maximum allowable cable fill area in Column 1 of Table 318-8, for the appropriate cable tray width.

Table 318-8. Allowable Cable Fill Area for Multiple-Conductor Cables in Ladder, Ventilated Trough, or Solid Bottom Cable Trays

	Maximum Allowable Fill Area in Square Inches for Multiple-Conductor Cables			
	Ladder or Ventilated Trough Cable Trays, Section 318-8(a)		Solid Bottom Cable Trays, Section 318-8(c)	
Inside Width of Cable Tray (Inches)	Column 1 Applicable for Section 318-8(a) (2) Only (Square Inches)	Column 2* Applicable for Section 318-8(a) (3) Only (Square Inches)	Column 3 Applicable for Section 318-8(c) (2) Only (Square Inches)	Column 4* Applicable for Section 318-8(c) (3) Only (Square Inches)
6	7	7—(1.2 Sd)**	5.5	5.5—Sd**
12	14	14—(1.2 Sd)	11.0	11.0—Sd
18	21	21—(1.2 Sd)	16.5	16.5—Sd
24	28	28—(1.2 Sd)	22.0	22.0—Sd
30	35	35—(1.2 Sd)	27.5	27.5—Sd
36	42	42—(1.2 Sd)	33.0	33.0—Sd

*The maximum allowable fill areas in Columns 2 and 4 shall be computed. For example, the maximum allowable fill, in square inches, for a 6 inch wide cable tray in Column 2 shall be: 7 minus (1.2 multiplied by Sd).

**The term Sd in Columns 2 and 4 is equal to the sum of the diameters, in inches, of all 4/0 AWG and larger multiple-conductor cables in the same cable tray with smaller cables.

(3) Where 4/0 AWG or larger cables are installed in the same cable tray with cables smaller than 4/0 AWG, the sum of the cross-sectional areas of all cables smaller than 4/0 AWG shall not exceed the maximum allowable fill area resulting from the computation in Column 2 of Table 318-8, for the appropriate cable tray width. The 4/0 AWG and larger cables shall be installed in a single layer and no other cables shall be placed on them.

(b) Where a ladder or ventilated trough cable tray, having a usable inside depth of 6 inches or less, contains multiple-conductor control and/or signal cables only, the sum of the cross-sectional areas of all cables at any cross section shall not exceed 50 percent of the interior cross-sectional area of the cable tray. A depth of 6 inches shall be used to compute the allowable interior cross-sectional area of any cable tray which has a usable inside depth of more than 6 inches.

(c) Where solid bottom cable trays contain multiple-conductor power or lighting cables, or any mixture of multiple-conductor power, lighting, control, and signal cables, the maximum number of cables shall conform to the following:

(1) Where all of the cables are 4/0 AWG or larger, the sum of the diameters of all cables shall not exceed 90 percent of the cable tray width, and the cables shall be installed in a single layer.

(2) Where all of the cables are smaller than 4/0 AWG, the sum of the cross-sectional areas of all cables shall not exceed the maximum allowable cable fill area in Column 3 of Table 318-8, for the appropriate cable tray width.

(3) Where 4/0 AWG or larger cables are installed in the same cable tray with cables smaller than 4/0 AWG, the sum of the cross-sectional areas of all cables smaller than 4/0 AWG shall not exceed the maximum allowable fill area resulting from the computation in Column 4 of Table 318-8, for the appropriate cable tray width. The 4/0 AWG and larger cables shall be installed in a single layer and no other cables shall be placed on them.

(d) Where a solid bottom cable tray, having a usable inside depth of 6 inches or less, contains multiple-conductor control and/or signal cables only, the sum of the cross-sectional areas of all cables at any cross section shall not exceed 40 percent of the interior cross-sectional area of the cable tray. A depth of 6 inches shall be used to compute the allowable interior cross-sectional area of any cable tray which has a usable inside depth of more than 6 inches.

(e) Where ventilated channel-type cable trays contain multiple-conductor cables of any type, the combined cross-sectional area of all cables shall not exceed 1.3 square inches in 3-inch wide channel trays, or 2.5 square inches in 4-inch wide channel trays.

Exception: Where only one multiple-conductor cable is installed in a ventilated channel-type tray the cross-sectional area of the cable shall not exceed 2.3 square inches in a 3-inch wide channel tray, or 4.5 square inches in a 4-inch wide channel tray.

▲ **It is not expected that inspectors or contractors compute the various combinations of cable tray fill in the field. Installations handbooks are available from various manufacturers.**

318-9. Number of Single Conductor Cables in Cable Trays.   The number of single conductor cables permitted in a single cable tray section shall not exceed the requirements of this section. The single conductors, or conductor assemblies, shall be evenly distributed across the cable tray.

(a) Where ladder or ventilated trough cable trays contain single conductor cables, the maximum number of single conductors shall conform to the following:

(1) Where all of the cables are 1000 MCM or larger, the sum of the diameters of all single conductor cables shall not exceed the cable tray width.

(2) Where all of the cables are smaller than 1000 MCM, the sum of the cross-sectional areas of all single conductor cables shall not exceed the maximum allowable cable fill area in Column 1 of Table 318-9, for the appropriate cable tray width.

(3) Where 1000 MCM or larger single conductor cables are installed in the same cable tray with single conductor cables smaller than 1000 MCM, the sum of the cross-sectional areas of all cables smaller than 1000 MCM shall not exceed the maximum allowable fill area resulting from the computation in Column 2 of Table 318-9, for the appropriate cable tray width.

(b) Where 4-inch wide ventilated channel-type cable trays contain single conductor cables, the sum of the diameters of all single conductors shall not exceed the inside width of the channel.

Table 318-9. Allowable Cable Fill Area for Single Conductor Cables in Ladder or Ventilated Trough Cable Trays

	Maximum Allowable Fill Area in Square Inches for Single Conductor Cables in Ladder or Ventilated Trough Cable Trays	
Inside Width of Tray Cable (Inches)	Column 1 Applicable for Section 318-9(a) (2) Only (Square Inches)	Column 2* Applicable for Section 318-9(a) (3) Only Square Inches
6	6.50	6.50—(1.1 Sd)**
12	13.0	13.0—(1.1 Sd)
18	19.5	19.5—(1.1 Sd)
24	26.0	26.0—(1.1 Sd)
30	32.5	32.5—(1.1 Sd)
36	39.0	39.0—(1.1 Sd)

*The maximum allowable fill areas in Column 2 shall be computed. For example, the maximum allowable fill, in square inches, for a 6 inch wide cable tray shall be: 6.5 minus (1.1 multiplied by Sd).

**The term Sd in Column 2 is equal to the sum of the diameters, in inches, of all 1000 MCM and larger single conductor cables in the same ladder or ventilated trough cable tray with smaller cables.

318-10. Ampacity of Cables in Cable Trays.

(a) Multiple-Conductor Cables. The ampacity of multiple-conductor cables installed according to the requirements of Section 318-8 shall comply with the allowable ampacities of Tables 310-16 and 310-18.

Exception: Where cable trays are continuously covered for more than six feet with solid unventilated covers, not more than 95 percent of the allowable ampacities of Tables 310-16 and 310-18 shall be permitted for multiple-conductor cables.

(b) Single Conductor Cables. The ampacity of single conductor cables, or single conductors twisted together, shall comply with the following:

(1) Where installed according to the requirements of Section 318-9, the ampacities for 600 MCM and larger single conductor cables in uncovered cable trays shall not exceed 75 percent of the allowable ampacities in Tables 310-17 and 310-19. Where cable trays are continuously covered for more than six feet with solid unventilated covers, the ampacities for 600 MCM and larger cables shall not exceed 70 percent of the allowable ampacities in Tables 310-17 and 310-19.

(2) Where installed according to the requirements of Section 318-9, the ampacities for 250 MCM through 500 MCM single conductor cables in uncovered cable trays shall not exceed 65 percent of the allowable ampacities in Tables 310-17 and 310-19. Where cable trays are continuously covered for more than six feet with solid unventilated covers, the ampacities for 250 MCM through 500 MCM cables shall not exceed 60 percent of the allowable ampacities in Tables 310-17 and 310-19.

(3) Where single conductors are installed in a single layer in uncovered cable trays, with a maintained space of not less than one cable diameter between individual conductors, the ampacity of 250 MCM and larger cables shall not exceed the allowable ampacities in Tables 310-17 and 310-19.

ARTICLE 320. OPEN WIRING ON INSULATORS

320-1. Definition. Open wiring on insulators is an exposed wiring method using cleats, knobs, tubes, and flexible tubing for the protection and support of single insulated conductors run in or on buildings, and not concealed by the building structure.

▲ Conductors for open wiring may be any of the general-use types listed in Table 310-13 for "dry" locations and "dry and wet" locations such as RH, T, TW, etc.

The conductors are secured to and supported by insulators, of porcelain, glass, or other composition materials. In modern wiring practice open wiring is used for high-tension work in transformer vaults and substations; it is very commonly used for temporary work and is used occasionally for runs of heavy conductors for feeders and power circuits. See Art. 305.

320-2. Other Articles. Open wiring on insulators shall comply with this Article and also with the applicable provisions of other Articles in this Code, especially Articles 225 and 300.

320-3. Uses Permitted. Open wiring on insulators shall be permitted on systems of 600 volts, nominal or less for industrial or agricultural establishments, indoors or outdoors, in wet or dry locations, where subject to corrosive vapors, and for services.

320-5. Conductors.

(a) Type. Conductors shall be of a type specified by Article 310.

(b) Ampacity. The ampacity shall comply with Tables 310-17 and 310-19 and all applicable notes to those Tables.

320-6. Conductor Supports. Conductors shall be rigidly supported on noncombustible, nonabsorbent insulating materials and shall not contact any other objects.

Supports shall be installed as follows: (1) within 6 inches of each side of each tap or splice; (2) within 12 inches of a dead-end connection to a rosette, lampholder, or receptacle; (3) at intervals not exceeding $4\frac{1}{2}$ feet and at closer intervals sufficient to provide adequate support where likely to be disturbed.

Exception No. 1: Supports for conductors No. 8 or larger installed across open spaces shall be permitted up to 15 feet apart if noncombustible, nonabsorbent insulating spacers are used at least every $4\frac{1}{2}$ feet to maintain at least $2\frac{1}{2}$ inches between conductors.

Exception No. 2. Where not likely to be disturbed in buildings of mill construction, No. 8 and larger conductors shall be permitted to be run across open spaces if supported from each wood cross member on approved insulators maintaining 6 inches between conductors.

320-7. Mounting of Conductor Supports. Where nails are used to mount knobs, they shall not be smaller than 10 penny. Where screws are used to mount knobs, or where nails or screws are used to mount cleats, they shall be of a length sufficient to penetrate the wood to a depth equal to at least one-half the height of the knob and fully the thickness of the cleat. Cushion washers shall be used with nails.

▲ Mill construction is generally understood to mean the type of building in which the floors are supported on wooden beams spaced about 14 to 16 ft apart. Wires not smaller than No. 8 may safely span such a distance where the ceilings are high and the space is free from obstructions.

Methods of dead-ending open cable runs are shown in Figs. 320-1 and 320-2.

Where heavy AC feeders are run as open wiring, the reactance of the circuit is reduced and hence the voltage drop is reduced by using a small spacing between the conductors. Up to a distance of 15 ft between supports the $2\frac{1}{2}$-in. spacing may be used if spacers are clamped to the conductors at intervals not exceeding $4\frac{1}{2}$ ft. A spacer consists of the three porcelain pieces of the same form as used in the support, with a metal clamping ring.

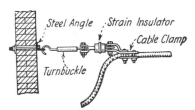

FIG. 320-1. Method of dead-ending heavy conductors used in open wiring.

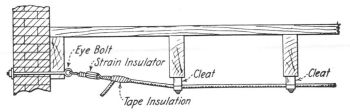

FIG. 320-2. Method of dead-ending heavy conductors used in open wiring.

Table 320-9. Minimum Clearances—Open Wiring on Insulators

Voltage Between Conductors	Distance in Inches Between Conductors	Distance in Inches From Surface Wired Over
300 or less	2½	½ (dry locations)
300 or less	2½	1 (damp or wet locations)
301–600	4	1 (damp, wet, or dry locations)

320-8. Tie Wires. No. 8 or larger conductors supported on solid knobs shall be securely tied thereto by tie wires having an insulation equivalent to that of the conductor.

320-9. Conductor Clearances. Conductors shall have clearances not less than specified in Table 320-9.

320-10. Flexible Nonmetallic Tubing. In dry locations where not exposed to severe physical damage, conductors shall be permitted to be separately enclosed in flexible nonmetallic tubing. The tubing shall be in continuous lengths not exceeding 15 feet and secured to the surface by straps at intervals not exceeding 4½ feet.

320-11. Through Walls, Floors, Wood Cross Members, Etc. Open conductors shall be separated from contact with walls, floors, wood cross members, or partitions through which they pass by tubes or bushings of noncombustible, nonabsorbent insulating material. Where the bushing is shorter than the hole, a waterproof sleeve of noninductive material shall be inserted in the hole and an insulating bushing slipped into the sleeve at each end in such a manner as to keep the conductors absolutely out of contact with the sleeve. Each conductor shall be carried through a separate tube or sleeve.

▲ Figure 320-3 illustrates a method for the support of No. 14, No. 12, and No. 10 conductors. For conductors of larger size, solid knobs with tie wires or single-wire cleats should be used.

320-12. Clearance From Piping, Exposed Conductors, Etc. Open conductors shall be separated at least 2 inches from metal conduit, piping, or other conducting material, and from any exposed lighting, power, or signaling conductor, or shall be separated therefrom by a continuous and firmly fixed nonconductor in addition to the insulation of the conductor. Where any insulating tube is used, it shall be secured

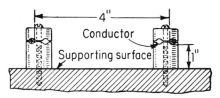

Fig. 320-3. Split knobs for supporting small wires used in open wiring or concealed knob-and-tube work.

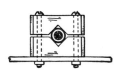

Fig. 320-4. Single-wire cleat for supporting large conductors used in open wiring.

at the ends. Where practicable, conductors shall pass over rather than under any piping subject to leakage or accumulations of moisture.

▲ The additional insulation on the wire is to prevent the wire from coming in contact with the adjacent pipe or other metal.

320-13. Entering Spaces Subject to Dampness, Wetness, or Corrosive Vapors. Conductors entering or leaving locations subject to dampness, wetness, or corrosive vapors shall have drip loops formed on them and shall then pass upward and inward from the outside of buildings, or from the damp, wet, or corrosive location, through noncombustible, nonabsorbent insulating tubes.

See also Section 230-52.

320-14. Protection From Physical Damage. Conductors within 7 feet from the floor shall be considered exposed to physical damage. Where open conductors cross ceiling joists and wall studs and are exposed to physical damage, they shall be protected by one of the following methods:

(1) By guard strips not less than ⅞ inch in thickness and at least as high as the insulating supports, placed on each side of and close to the wiring.

(2) By a substantial running board at least ½ inch thick back of the conductors with side protections. Running boards shall extend at least one inch outside the conductors, but not more than 2 inches, and the protecting sides shall be at least 2 inches high and at least ⅞ inch thick.

(3) By boxing made as above and furnished with a cover kept at least one inch away from the conductors within. Where protecting vertical conductors on side walls, the boxing shall be closed at the top and the holes through which the conductors pass shall be bushed.

(4) By rigid metal conduit or electrical metallic tubing, in which case the rules of Article 346 or 348 shall apply; or by metal piping, in which case the conductors shall be encased in continuous lengths of approved flexible tubing. The conductors passing through metal enclosures shall be so grouped that current in both directions is approximately equal.

320-15. Unfinished Attics and Roof Spaces. Conductors in unfinished attics and roof spaces shall comply with (a) or (b) below.

(a) Accessible by Stairway or Permanent Ladder. Conductors shall be installed along the side of or through bored holes in floor joists, studs, or rafters. Where run through bored holes, conductors in the joists and in studs or rafters to a height of not less than 7 feet above the floor or floor joists shall be protected by substantial running boards extending not less than one inch on each side of the conductors. Running boards shall be securely fastened in place. Running boards and guard strips shall not be required for conductors installed along the sides of joists, studs, or rafters.

(b) Not Accessible by Stairway or Permanent Ladder. Conductors shall be installed along the sides of or through bored holes in floor joists, studs, or rafters.

Exception: In buildings completed before wiring is installed and having head room at all points of less than 3 feet.

320-16. Switches. Surface-type snap switches shall be mounted in accordance with Section 380-10(a), and boxes shall not be required. Other type switches shall be installed in accordance with Section 380-4.

ARTICLE 324. CONCEALED KNOB-AND-
TUBE WIRING

324-1. Definition. Concealed knob-and-tube wiring is a wiring method using knobs, tubes, and flexible nonmetallic tubing for the protection and support of single insulated conductors concealed in hollow spaces of walls and ceilings of buildings.

▲ Conductors for concealed knob-and-tube work may be any of the general-use types listed in Table 310-13 for "dry" locations and "dry and wet" locations such as RH, T, TW, etc.

324-2. Other Articles. Concealed knob-and-tube wiring shall comply with this Article and also with the applicable provisions of other Articles in this Code, especially Article 300.

324-3. Uses Permitted. Concealed knob-and-tube wiring shall be permitted to be used only for extensions of existing installations and elsewhere only by special permission under the following conditions:

(1) In the hollow spaces of walls and ceilings.

(2) In unfinished attic and roof spaces as provided in Section 324-11.

324-4. Uses Not Permitted. Concealed knob-and-tube wiring shall not be used in commercial garages, theaters and similar locations, motion picture studios, or hazardous locations.

324-5. Conductors.

(a) Type. Conductors shall be of a type specified by Article 310.

(b) Ampacity. The ampacity shall comply with Tables 310-17 and 310-19 and all applicable notes to those Tables.

324-6. Conductor Supports. Conductors shall be rigidly supported on noncombustible, nonabsorbent insulating materials and shall not contact any other objects. Supports shall be installed as follows: (1) within 6 inches of each side of each tap or splice, and (2) at intervals not exceeding $4\frac{1}{2}$ feet.

Exception: If it is not practicable to provide supports in dry locations it shall be permissible to fish conductors through hollow spaces if each conductor is individually enclosed in flexible nonmetallic tubing. The tubing shall be in continuous lengths between supports, between boxes, or between a support and a box.

324-7. Tie Wires. Where solid knobs are used, conductors shall be securely tied thereto by tie wires having insulation equivalent to that of the conductor.

324-8. Conductor Clearances. Where practicable, conductors shall be run singly on separate joists, studs, or rafters. A clearance of not less than 3 inches shall be maintained between conductors and of not less than one inch between the conductor and the surface over which it passes.

Exception: Where space is too limited to provide the above minimum clearances, such as at meters, panelboards, outlets, and switch points, the conductors shall be individually enclosed in flexible nonmetallic tubing, which shall be in continuous lengths between the last support or box and the terminal point.

324-9. Through Walls, Floors, Wood Cross Members, Etc. Conductors shall comply with Section 320-11 where passing through holes in structural members. Where passing through wood cross members in plastered partitions, conductors shall be protected by noncombustible, nonabsorbent, insulating tubes extending not less than 3 inches beyond the wood member.

▲ The additional tube is to protect the wire from contact with the plaster that is likely to accumulate on any horizontal cross timber in a plastered wall.

324-10. Clearance from Piping, Exposed Conductors, Etc. Conductors shall comply with Section 320-12 for clearances from other exposed conductors, piping, etc.

324-11. Unfinished Attics and Roof Spaces. Conductors in unfinished attics and roof spaces shall comply with (a) or (b) below.

(a) Accessible by Stairway or Permanent Ladder. Conductors shall be installed along the side of or through bored holes in floor joists, studs, or rafters. Where run through bored holes, conductors in the joists and in studs or rafters to a height of not less than 7 feet above the floor or floor joists shall be protected by substantial running boards extending not less than one inch on each side of the conductors. Running boards shall be securely fastened in place. Running boards and guard strips shall not be required where conductors are installed along the sides of joists, studs, or rafters.

(b) Not Accessible by Stairway or Permanent Ladder. Conductors shall be installed along the sides of or through bored holes in floor joists, studs, or rafters.

Exception: In buildings completed before wiring is installed and having head room at all points of less than 3 feet.

▲ Where wires are run on knobs or through tubes in a closed-in and inaccessible attic or roof space, the wiring is concealed knob-and-tube work, but if the attic or roof space is accessible the wiring is open wiring on insulators. Both cases are covered by the foregoing rules.

Where the wiring is installed at any time after the building is completed, in a roof space having less than 3 ft headroom at any point, the wires may be run on knobs across the faces of the joists, studs, or rafters or through or on the sides of the joists, studs, or rafters. Such a space would not be used for storage purposes and the wiring may be considered as concealed knob-and-tube work.

An attic or roof space is considered accessible if it can be reached by means of a stairway or a permanent ladder. In any such attic or roof space wires run through the floor joists where there is no floor must be protected by a running board and wires run through the studs or rafters must be protected by a running board if within 7 ft from the floor or floor joists. These two cases are shown in Fig. 324-1.

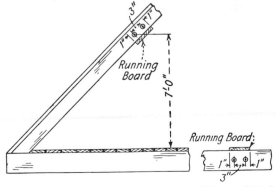

FIG. 324-1. Open wiring in an accessible attic. Wires run through rafters, and wires run through joists where there is no floor.

324-12. Splices. Splices shall be soldered unless approved splicing devices are used. In-line or strain splices shall not be used.

324-13. Boxes. Outlet boxes shall comply with Article 370.

324-14. Switches. Switches shall comply with Sections 380-4 and 380-10(b).

ARTICLE 330. MINERAL-INSULATED METAL-SHEATHED CABLE

Type MI

A. General

330-1. Definition. Type MI mineral-insulated metal-sheathed cable is a factory assembly of one or more conductors insulated with a highly compressed refractory mineral insulation and enclosed in a liquidtight and gastight continuous copper sheath.

330-2. Other Articles. Type MI cable shall comply with this Article and also with the applicable provisions of other Articles in this Code, especially Article 300.

▲ Mineral-insulated 600-V power and control wiring is a system in which the conductors are spaced and insulated by a densely compressed mineral insulation encased in a seamless metallic tube.

The original intent was to provide a wiring material which would be completely noncombustible, thus eliminating the fire hazards resulting from faults or excessive overloads on electrical circuits. To accomplish this, it is constructed entirely of inorganic materials. The conductors, sheath, and protective armor are of metal. The insulation is highly compressed magnesium oxide, which is extremely stable at high temperatures (fusion temperature of 2,800°C).

Mineral-insulated metal-sheathed cable is manufactured in a single-conductor construction from No. 16 AWG through No. 4/0 AWG, two- and three-conductor from No. 16 AWG through No. 4 AWG, four-conductor from No. 16 AWG through No. 6 AWG, and seven-conductor Nos. 16, 14, 12, and 10 AWG. The standard length in which any size is furnished depends on the final diameter of the cable. The smallest cable, 1/C No. 16 AWG, has a diameter of 0.216 in. and can be furnished in lengths of approximately 1,900 ft. Cables of larger diameter have proportionally shorter lengths. The cable is shipped in paper-wrapped coils ranging in diameter from 3 to 5 ft.

The terminating of this cable incorporates both the sealing and the insulating of the cable ends. (See Figs. 330-1 through 330-3. See also Mineral-Insulated Cable Fittings for Use in Hazardous Locations, Fig. 330-4.)

330-3. Uses Permitted. Type MI cable shall be permitted as follows: (1) for services, feeders, and branch circuits; (2) in dry, wet, or continuously moist locations; (3) indoors or outdoors; (4) where exposed or concealed; (5) embedded in plaster, concrete, fill or other masonry, whether above or below grade; (6) in any hazardous location; (7) where exposed to oil and gasoline; (8) where exposed to corrosive conditions not deteriorating to its sheath; (9) in underground runs where suitably protected against physical damage and corrosive conditions.

▲ Section 330-3 describes the general usage of mineral-insulated metal-sheathed cable, designated Type MI. Briefly, it includes, basically, general use as services, feeders,

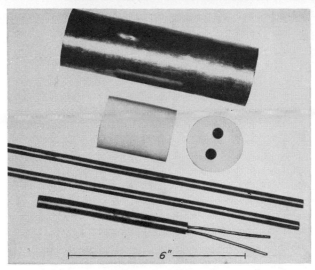

Fig. 330-1. Component parts and finished cable, No. 14 AWG, two-conductor.

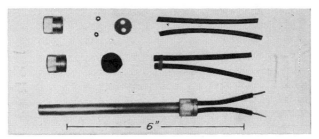

Fig. 330-2. Cable seal termination. Component parts of assembly (top); neoprene tubing mounted in insulating cap and sealing compound; and (bottom) completed cable-seal termination.

and branch circuits in exposed and concealed work, in dry and wet locations, for underplaster extensions and embedded in plaster, masonry, concrete, or fill, for underground runs, or where exposed to weather, continuous moisture, oil, or other conditions not having a deteriorating effect on the metallic sheath. It may be installed where exposed to gasoline when used with termination fittings approved for Class 1 locations. See Fig. 330-4. The maximum permissible operating temperature for general use is 85°C (determined by present standard terminations). The cable itself, however, is recognized for 250°C in special applications. Permissible current ratings will be those given in Table 310-16. Type MI cable in its many sizes and constructions is suitable for all power and control circuits up to 600 V.

330-4. Uses Not Permitted. Type MI cable shall not be used where exposed to destructive corrosive conditions.

Exception: Where protected by materials suitable for the conditions.

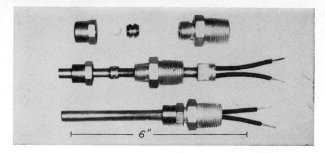

FIG. 330-3. Cable seal termination and gland. Component parts of gland (top); gland in place before tightening; and (bottom) gland locked in finished position.

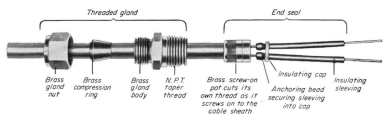

FIG. 330-4. Mineral-insulated cable fittings for use in hazardous locations. (*General Cable Corp.*)

B. Installation

330-10. Wet Locations. Where installed in wet locations, Type MI cable shall comply with Section 300-6(c).

330-11. Through Joists, Studs, or Rafters. Type MI cable shall comply with Section 300-4 where installed through studs, joists, rafters, or similar wood members.

330-12. Supports. Type MI cable shall be securely supported at intervals not exceeding 6 feet by straps, staples, hangers, or similar fittings so designed and installed as not to damage the cable.

Exception: Where cable is fished in.

330-13. Bends. Bends in Type MI cable shall be so made as not to damage the cable. The radius of the inner edge of any bend shall not be less than 5 times the cable diameter.

330-14. Fittings. Fittings approved for the purpose and conditions of use shall be used for connecting Type MI cable to boxes, cabinets, or other equipment. Where single-conductor cables enter ferrous metal boxes or cabinets, the installation shall comply with Section 300-20 to prevent inductive heating.

330-15. Terminal Seals. Where Type MI cable terminates, an approved seal shall be provided immediately after stripping to prevent the entrance of moisture into the insulation. The conductors extending beyond the sheath shall be individually provided with an approved insulating material.

C. Construction Specifications

330-20. Conductors. Type MI cable conductors shall be of solid copper with a cross-sectional area corresponding to standard AWG sizes.

330-21. Insulation. The conductor insulation in Type MI cable shall be a highly compressed refractory mineral that will provide proper spacing for the conductors.

330-22. Outer Sheath. The outer sheath shall be of a continuous copper construction to provide mechanical protection, a moisture seal, and an adequate path for grounding purposes.

ARTICLE 331. ALUMINUM-SHEATHED CABLE

Type ALS

A. General

331-1. Definition. Type ALS aluminum-sheathed cable is a factory assembly of one or more conductors, each individually insulated and enclosed in a liquidtight and gastight close-fitting and continuous aluminum sheath.

▲ This is a self-contained wiring system in which one or more insulated conductors are enclosed in an impervious, continuous, closely fitting seamless tube of aluminum.

It may be used in both exposed and concealed work, in dry or wet locations. The insulated conductors are protected by the sheath which also provides a means of grounding outlet boxes, fixtures, and other equipment.

331-2. Other Articles. Type ALS cable shall comply with this Article and also with the applicable provisions of other Articles in this Code, especially Article 300.

331-3. Uses Permitted. Type ALS cable shall be permitted as follows: (1) in dry or wet locations; (2) where exposed or concealed; (3) in underground runs where suitably protected against physical damage and corrosive conditions.

331-4. Uses Not Permitted. Type ALS cable shall not be used where exposed to destructive corrosive conditions, such as direct burial in the earth, in concrete, or where exposed to cinder fills, strong chlorides, caustic alkalis, or vapors of chlorine or of hydrochloric acids.

Exception: Where protected by materials suitable for the condition.

B. Installation

331-10. Wet Locations. Where installed in wet locations, Type ALS cable shall comply with Section 300-6.

331-11. Through Joists, Studs, or Rafters. Type ALS cable shall comply with Section 300-4 where installed through studs, joists, rafters, or similar wood members.

331-12. Supports. Type ALS cable shall be securely supported at intervals not exceeding 6 feet by straps, staples, hangers, or similar fittings so designed and installed as not to damage the cable.

Exception: Where cable is fished in.

331-13. Bends. All bends shall be so made that the cable will not be damaged and the radius of the curve on the inner edge of any bend shall not be less than:

(a) Ten times the external diameter of the sheath for cable not more than $\frac{3}{4}$ inch in external diameter.

(b) Twelve times the external diameter of the sheath for cable more than $\frac{3}{4}$ inch but not more than $1\frac{1}{2}$ inches in external diameter; and

(c) Fifteen times the external diameter of the sheath for cable more than $1\frac{1}{2}$ inches in external diameter.

Exception: On cables employing a corrugated aluminum sheath, the radius of the curve on the inner edge of any bend shall not be less than 7 times the external diameter of the sheath.

331-14. Fittings. Fittings approved for the purpose and conditions of use shall be used for connecting Type ALS cable to boxes, cabinets, or other equipment. Where single-conductor cables enter ferrous metal boxes or cabinets, the installation shall comply with Section 300-20 to prevent inductive heating.

C. Construction Specifications

331-20. Conductors. The conductors shall be of copper, copper-clad aluminum, or of electrical-conductor-grade aluminum, solid or stranded.

331-21. Insulation. The insulated conductors of Type ALS cable shall be of a type listed in Table 310-13.

331-22. Insulation Covering. The covering over the insulated conductors shall be the same as permitted for lead-sheathed or multiconductor cable.

331-23. Outer Sheath. The outer sheath shall be of a continuous, closely fitting tube of aluminum to provide mechanical protection, a moisture seal, and an adequate path for equipment grounding purposes and shall conform with provisions of Sections 331-3 and 331-4 for uses. The sheath shall not be used as a current-carrying conductor.

ARTICLE 332. COPPER-SHEATHED CABLE

TYPE CS

A. General

332-1. Definition. Type CS copper-sheathed cable is a factory assembly of one or more conductors, each individually insulated and enclosed in a liquidtight and gastight close-fitting and continuous copper or bronze sheath.

332-2. Other Articles. Type CS cable shall comply with this Article and also with the applicable provisions of other Articles in this Code, especially Article 300.

332-3. Uses Permitted. Type CS cable shall be permitted to be used as follows:

(1) In wet or dry locations.

(2) Where exposed or concealed.

(3) In corrosive locations where protected by materials suitable for the conditions.

B. Installations

332-10. Wet Locations. Where installed in wet locations, Type CS cable shall comply with Section 300-6.

332-11. Through Joists, Studs or Rafters. Where installed through joists, studs or rafters, Type CS cable shall comply with Section 300-4.

332-12. Supports. Type CS cable shall be securely supported at intervals not exceeding 6 feet by straps, staples, hangers or similar fittings so designed and installed as not to damage the cable.

Exception: Where the cable is fished in.

332-13. Bends. All bends shall be so made that the cable will not be damaged and the radius of the curve on the inner edge of any bend shall not be less than:

(a) Ten times the external diameter of the sheath for cable not more than ¾ inch in external diameter.

(b) Twelve times the external diameter of the sheath for cable more than ¾ inch but not more than 1½ inches in external diameter; and

(c) Fifteen times the external diameter of the sheath for cable more than 1½ inches in external diameter.

Exception: On cables employing a corrugated copper sheath, the radius of the curve on the inner edge of any bend shall not be less than seven times the external diameter of the sheath.

332-14. Fittings. Fittings approved for the purpose and conditions of use shall be used for connecting Type CS cable to boxes, cabinets or other equipment. Where single conductor cables enter ferrous metal boxes or cabinets, the installation shall comply with Section 300-20 to prevent inductive heating.

C. Construction Specifications

332-20. Conductors. The conductors shall be of copper, copper-clad aluminum, or electrical conductor grade aluminum, solid or stranded.

332-21. Insulation. The insulated conductors of Type CS cable shall be of a type listed in Table 310-13.

332-22. Insulation Covering. The covering over the insulated conductors shall be the same as permitted for lead-sheathed or multi-conductor cable.

332-23. Outer Sheath. The outer sheath shall be of a continuous, closely fitting tube of copper or bronze to provide mechanical protection, a moisture seal and an adequate path for equipment grounding purposes and shall conform with provisions of Section 332-3. The sheath shall not be used as a current-carrying conductor.

ARTICLE 334. METAL-CLAD CABLE

Type MC and AC Series

334-1. Definition. A metal-clad cable is a fabricated assembly of insulated conductors in a flexible metallic enclosure. See Section 334-4.

See Section 334-4 for construction of cable.

334-2. Other Articles. Metal-clad cable shall comply with this Article and also with the applicable provisions of other Articles in this code, especially Article 300.

Type MC cable shall be permitted for systems in excess of 600 volts. See Section 300-2.

334-3. Marking. The provisions of Section 310-11 shall apply, except that Type AC cable shall have ready identification of the maker by distinctive external markers in the cable sheath throughout its entire length.

334-4. Construction. Metal-clad cable shall be an approved cable of Type MC or AC Series, with acceptable metal covering. The insulated conductors shall conform with Section 334-5.

(a) **Type MC.** Type MC cables are power and control cables in the size range from No. 14 and larger for copper and No. 12 and larger for aluminum and copper-clad aluminum. For conductor sizes and insulation thickness of Type MC cables rated over 600 volts, see Article 310, Part C. The metal enclosures shall be either a covering of interlocking metal tape, or an impervious, close fitting, corrugated tube. Supplemental protection of an outer covering of corrosion-resistant material shall be required where such protection is needed. The cables shall provide adequate path for grounding purposes.

See Section 300-6 for protection against corrosion.

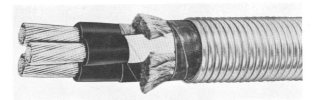

Fig. 334-1. Type MC cable.

▲ Type MC series employs rubber, varnished cloth, or composite varnished-cloth-thermoplastic-insulated conductors. A marker tape reading "Type MC cable" and indicating the type designation of the insulated conductor is included in the cable under the armor.

(b) **Type AC.** Type AC cables are branch-circuit and feeder cables with armor of flexible metal tape. Cables of the AC type, except ACL, shall have an internal bonding strip of copper or aluminum, in intimate contact with the armor for its entire length.

334-5. Conductors. Conductors for metal-clad cable shall comply with (a) and (b) below.

(a) **Type MC.** For cables of Type MC, insulated conductors shall be of a type listed in Table 310-13 for rubber, thermoplastic, varnished cloth, asbestos-varnished cloth, or of a type especially approved for the purpose.

(b) **Type AC.** For cables of Type AC, insulated conductors shall be of a type listed in Table 310-13. In addition, the conductors shall have an over-all moisture-resistant and fire-retardant fibrous covering. For Type ACT, a moisture-resistant fibrous covering shall be required only on the individual conductors.

334-6. Use. Except where otherwise specified elsewhere in this Code, and where not subject to physical damage, metal-clad cable shall be permitted for branch circuits and feeders in both exposed and concealed work as in (a) and (b) below.

FIG. 334-2. Metal-clad cable, Type AC. (*General Electric Co.*)

(a) Type MC. This type of cable shall be permitted in partially protected areas, such as in cable trays and the like, in dry locations, and when any of the following conditions are met, it shall be permitted in wet locations:

(1) The metallic covering is impervious to moisture.

(2) A lead sheath or moisture impervious jacket is provided under the metal covering.

(3) The insulated conductors under the metallic covering are approved for use in wet locations.

See Section 300-6 for protection against corrosion.

(b) Type AC. Metal-clad cable of the AC type shall be permitted in dry locations; for underplaster extensions as provided in Article 344; and embedded in plaster finish on brick or other masonry, except in damp or wet locations. It shall be permissible to run or fish this cable in the air voids of masonry block or tile walls; where such walls are exposed or subject to excessive moisture or dampness or are below grade line, Type ACL cable shall be used. This cable shall contain lead-covered conductors (Type ACL) if used where exposed to the weather or to continuous moisture; for underground runs in duct or raceway and embedded in masonry, concrete or fill in buildings in course of construction; or where exposed to oil, or other conditions having a deteriorating effect on the insulation.

Type AC metal-clad cable shall not be used where prohibited elsewhere in this Code, including (1) in theaters and similar locations, except as provided in Article 518, Places of Assembly; (2) in motion-picture studios; (3) in any hazardous locations; (4) where exposed to corrosive fumes or vapors; (5) on cranes or hoists, except as provided in Section 610-11 Exception No. 3; (6) in storage battery rooms; (7) in hoistways or on elevators, except as provided in Section 620-21; or (8) commercial garages where prohibited in Article 511.

Type ACL cable shall not be used for direct burial in the earth.

FIG. 334-3. Metal-clad cable with lead sheath, Type ACL. (*General Electric Co.*)

334-8. Supports. Metal-clad cable shall be secured by approved staples, straps, hangers or similar fittings so designed and installed as not to injure the cable.

(a) Type MC cable shall be secured at intervals not exceeding 6 feet, and within 2 feet from every box or fitting, except where cable is fished. Installation of this cable shall be permitted on metal racks, trays, troughs, or cable trays grounded as required by Article 250. The cables shall be separated from each other by a distance of not less than one-quarter of a cable diameter. There shall be no more than one layer of cables on a rack or other support member; each cable so installed shall be supported at intervals not exceeding 6 feet and within 2 feet from every box or fitting, and each cable shall be attached to the support at intervals of not more than 10 feet horizontally and 2 feet vertically.

(b) Type AC cable shall be secured at intervals of not exceeding $4\frac{1}{2}$ feet and within 12 inches from every outlet box or fitting.

Exception No. 1: Where cable is fished.

Exception No. 2: Lengths of not more than 2 feet at terminals where flexibility is necessary.

▲ See Figs. 334-4 and 334-5.

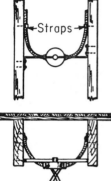

Fig. 334-4. Strap for securing cable in place.

Fig. 334-5. Staple for securing cable in place.

Fig. 334-6. Method of securing cable at outlets.

▲ **In exposed work, both as a precaution against physical damage and to ensure a workmanlike appearance, fastenings should be spaced not more than 24 to 30 in. apart. In concealed work in new buildings the cable should be supported at intervals of not over $4\frac{1}{2}$ ft for Type AC and 6 ft for Type MC, so as to keep it out of the way of possible injury by mechanics of other trades. In either exposed work or concealed work, the cable should be securely fastened in place within 1 ft of each outlet box or fitting for Type AC and 2 ft for Type MC, so that there will be no tendency for the cable to pull away from the box connector. The method of securing the cable at outlets in concealed work is shown in Fig. 334-6.**

334-9. Bends. All bends shall be so made that the cable will not be injured, and the radius of the curve of the inner edge of any bend shall not be less than 7 times the diameter of Type MC cable nor 5 times the diameter of Type AC cable.

334-10. Boxes and Fittings.

(a) At all points where Type MC metal-clad cable terminates, suitable fittings designed for use with the particular wiring cable and the conditions of service shall be used.

(b) At all points where the armor of AC cable terminates, a fitting shall be provided to protect wires from abrasion, unless the design of the outlet boxes or fittings is such as to afford equivalent protection, and in addition, an approved insulating bushing or its equivalent approved protection shall be provided between the conductors and the armor. The connector or clamp by which the metal-clad cable is fastened to boxes or cabinets shall be of such design that the insulating bushing or its equivalent will be visible for inspection. This bushing shall not be required with lead-covered cables where so installed that the lead sheath will be visible for inspection. Where change is made from metal-clad cable to other cable or raceway wiring methods, a box shall be installed at junction point as required in Section 300-15.

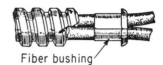

Fiber bushing

Fig. 334-7. Box connector for Type AC cable. (*General Electric Co.*)

Fig. 334-8. Fiber bushing to protect the conductors in Type AC cable from the sharp edges of the armor.

▲ A standard type of box connector for securing the cable to outlet boxes and cabinets is shown in Fig. 334-7.

A fiber bushing as shown in Fig. 334-8 can be inserted between the armor and the conductors. The fiber bushing, which can be seen through slots in the connector after installation, prevents the sharp edges of the armor from cutting into the insulation on the conductors and so grounding the copper wire.

The box shown in Fig. 334-9 is equipped with clamps to secure Type AC cables, making it unnecessary to use separate cable connectors such as shown in Fig. 334-7.

The box shown in Fig. 334-10 is similar to the other but has the cable clamps outside, thus permitting one more conductor in the box. See Sec. 370-6(a)(1).

334-11. Through Studs, Joists and Rafters. Metal-clad cable shall comply with Section 300-4 where installed through studs, joists, rafters, or similar wood members.

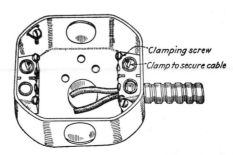

Clamping screw
Clamp to secure cable

Fig. 334-9. Outlet box with clamps for Type AC cable. (*National Electric Div., H. K. Porter Co., Inc.*)

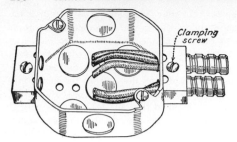

FIG. 334-10. Outlet box with clamps for Type AC cable. (*Allsteel Equipment Co.*)

334-12. Exposed Work.   Exposed runs of cable shall closely follow the surface of the building finish or of running boards.

Exception No. 1: Lengths of not more than 24 inches at terminals where flexibility is necessary.

Exception No. 2: Where suitably supported in accordance with Section 334-8(a).

▲ **Exception No. 1 refers to a length not over 24 in. to a motor or a range where some flexibility is necessary.**

Exception No. 3: On the underside of floor joists in basements where supported at each joist and so located as not to be subject to physical damage.

334-13. In Accessible Attics.   Type AC cables in accessible attics or roof spaces shall be installed as specified in (a) and (b) below.

(a) Where run across the top of floor joists, or within 7 feet of floor or floor joists across the face of rafters or studding, in attics and roof spaces which are accessible, the cable shall be protected by substantial guard strips which are at least as high as the cable. Where this space is not accessible by permanent stairs or ladders, protection shall only be required within 6 feet of the nearest edge of scuttle hole or attic entrance.

(b) Where cable is carried along the sides of rafters, studs or floor joists, neither guard strips nor running boards shall be required.

▲ **In many cases an accessible attic is used for storage, and care should be taken to protect the wiring properly.**

ARTICLE 336. NONMETALLIC-SHEATHED CABLE

Types NM and NMC

336-1. Definition.   Nonmetallic-sheathed cable is a factory assembly of two or more insulated conductors having an outer sheath of moisture-resistant, flame-retardant, nonmetallic material.

▲ **This type of wiring may be used either for exposed or for concealed wiring. It may be regarded as a substitute for concealed knob-and-tube work and open wiring** on insulators, and has the advantages that continuous protection is provided over the entire length of the conductor in addition to the insulation applied to ordinary rubber-covered or thermoplastic wire, and, as in the case of armored cable, no insulating supports are required and only one hole need be bored where the cable passes through a timber. Insulating bushings or grommets shall be used where the cable passes through holes in metal studs or similar members.

336-2. Construction. Nonmetallic sheathed cable shall be an approved Type NM or NMC in sizes No. 14 through 2 with copper conductors and in sizes No. 12 through 2 with aluminum or copper-clad aluminum conductors. In addition to the insulated conductors, the cable may have an approved size of insulated or bare conductor for equipment grounding purposes only.

Conductors of Types NM and NMC shall be one of the types listed in Table 310-13 which is suitable for branch-circuit wiring or one which is approved for the purpose. The ampacity of Types NM and NMC cable shall be that of 60°C (140°F) conductors in Tables 310-16 and 310-18.

(a) Type NM. The overall covering shall have a flame-retardant and moisture-resistant finish.

(b) Type NMC. The overall covering shall be flame-retardant, moisture-resistant, fungus-resistant, and corrosion-resistant.

(c) Marking. In addition to the provisions of Section 310-11, the cable shall have a distinctive marking on the exterior for its entire length specifying the cable type.

336-3. Uses Permitted or Not Permitted. Type NM and Type NMC Cables shall be permitted to be used in one and two family dwellings, or multi-family dwellings and other structures not exceeding three floors above grade.

(a) Type NM. This type of nonmetallic sheathed cable shall be permitted to be installed for both exposed and concealed work in normally dry locations. It shall be permissible to install or fish type NM cable in air voids in masonry block or tile walls where such walls are not exposed or subject to excessive moisture or dampness.

Type NM cable shall not be installed where exposed to corrosive fumes or vapors: nor shall it be imbedded in masonry, concrete, fill, or plaster; nor run in a shallow chase in masonry or concrete and covered with plaster or similar finish.

(b) Type NMC. Type NMC cable shall be permitted for both exposed and concealed work in dry, moist, damp, or corrosive locations, and in outside and inside walls of masonry block or tile.

(c) Uses Not Permitted for Either Type NM or NMC. Types NM and NMC cables shall not be used as: (1) service-entrance cable, (2) in commercial garages, (3) in theaters and similar locations, except as provided in Article 518, places of assembly, (4) in motion-picture studios, (5) in storage battery rooms, (6) in hoistways, (7) in any hazardous location, (8) embedded in poured cement, concrete, or aggregate.

▲ Where temperatures of 0°F or below are frequently experienced during the winter, the ordinary types of nonmetallic-sheathed cable, where installed in dairy barns and similar farm buildings, have in some cases deteriorated rapidly, due to the growth of fungus or mold. Type NMC cable has proved very helpful in these locations.

The cable may be made with an equipment grounding wire as a part of the assembly. (See Sec. 250-57 and Table 250-95.)

336-4. Other Articles. In addition to the provisions of this Article, installations of nonmetallic-sheathed cable shall comply with the other applicable provisions of this Code, especially Article 300.

336-5. Supports. Nonmetallic-sheathed cable shall be secured by staples, straps, or similar fittings so designed and installed as not to injure the cable. Cable shall be secured in place at intervals not exceeding $4\frac{1}{2}$ feet and within 12 inches from every cabinet, box, or fitting.

Exception No. 1: For concealed work in finished buildings or finished panels for prefabricated buildings where such supporting is impracticable, it shall be permissible to fish the cable between access points.

Exception No. 2: A wiring device approved for the purpose, without a separate outlet box, incorporating an integral cable clamp shall be permitted when the cable is secured in place at intervals not exceeding $4\frac{1}{2}$ feet and within 12 inches from the wiring device wall opening, and there shall be at least a 12 inch loop of unbroken cable or 6 inches of a cable end available on the interior side of the finished wall to permit replacement.

▲ In concealed work the cable should if possible be so installed that it will be out of reach of nails. Care should be taken to avoid wherever possible the parts of a wall where the trim will be nailed in place, e.g., door and window casings, baseboards, and picture moldings. See Sec. 300-4.

336-6. Exposed Work—General. In exposed work, except as provided in Sections 336-8 and 336-9, the cable shall be installed as specified in (a) and (b) below.

(a) To Follow Surface. The cable shall closely follow the surface of the building finish or of running boards.

(b) Protection From Physical Damage. The cable shall be protected from physical damage where necessary by conduit, pipe, guard strips, or other means. Where passing through a floor the cable shall be enclosed in rigid metal conduit or metal pipe extending at least 6 inches above the floor.

336-7. Through Studs, Joists, and Rafters. The cable shall comply with Section 300-4 where installed through studs, joists, rafters, and similar members.

336-8. In Unfinished Basements. Where the cable is run at angles with joists in unfinished basements, it shall be permissible to secure cables not smaller than two No. 6 or three No. 8 conductors directly to the lower edges of the joists. Smaller cables shall either be run through bored holes in joists or on running boards. Where run parallel to the joists, cable of any size shall be secured to the sides or faces of the joists.

336-9. In Accessible Attics. The installation of cable in accessible attics or roof spaces shall also comply with Section 334-13.

336-10. Bends. Bends in cable shall be so made, and other handling shall be such, that the protective coverings of the cable will not be injured, and no bend shall have a radius less than 5 times the diameter of the cable.

336-11. Devices of Insulating Material. Switch, outlet, and tap devices of insulating material shall be permitted to be used without boxes in exposed cable wiring, and for rewiring in existing buildings where the cable is concealed and fished. Openings in such devices shall form a close fit around the outer covering of the cable, and the device shall fully enclose that part of the cable from which any part of the covering has been removed.

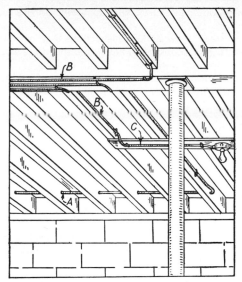

FIG. 336-1. Methods of installing nonmetallic-sheathed cable in an unfinished basement. *A*, through joists; *B*, on side or face of joist or beam; *C*, on running board.

Where connections to conductors are by binding-screw terminals, there shall be available as many terminals as conductors.

Exception: Where cables are clamped within the structure, and terminals are of a type approved for multiple conductors.

336-12. Boxes of Insulating Material. Nonmetallic outlet boxes shall be permitted as provided in Section 370-3.

▲ **By using nonmetallic outlet and switch boxes a completely "nonmetallic" wiring system is provided. Such a system has certain advantages in locations where corrosive vapors are present. See Sec. 370-5.**

ARTICLE 337. SHIELDED NONMETALLIC-SHEATHED CABLE

Type SNM

337-1. Definitions. Type SNM, shielded nonmetallic-sheathed cable, is a factory assembly of two or more insulated conductors in an extruded core of moisture-resistant, flame-resistant nonmetallic material, covered with an overlapping spiral metal tape and wire shield and jacketed with an extruded moisture-, flame-, oil-, corrosion-, fungus-, and sunlight-resistant nonmetallic material.

337-2. Other Articles. In addition to the provisions of this Article, installation of Type SNM cable shall conform to other applicable provisions, such as Articles 300, 318, 501, and 502.

337-3. Uses Permitted. Type SNM cable shall be used only as follows:

(1) Where operating temperatures do not exceed the rating marked on the cable.

(2) In cable trays or in raceways.

(3) In hazardous locations where permitted in Articles 500 through 516.

337-4. Bends. Bends in Type SNM cable shall be so made as not to damage the cable or its covering. The radius of the inner edge shall not be less than 5 times the cable diameter.

337-5. Handling. Type SNM cable shall be handled in such a manner as not to damage the cable or its covering.

337-6. Fittings. Fittings for connecting Type SNM cable to enclosures or equipment shall be approved for the purpose.

337-7. Bonding. The wire shield shall be bonded to the frame or enclosure of the utilization equipment and to the ground bus or connection at the power supply point. This bonding shall be accomplished using fittings (Section 337-6) or by other Code-approved bonding methods (Section 501-16(b)).

337-8. Construction. The conductors of Type SNM cable shall be Type TFN, TFFN, THHN or THWN in sizes No. 18 through No. 2 copper and No. 12 through No. 2 in aluminum or copper-clad aluminum. Conductor sizes may be mixed in individual cables. The flat overlapping metal tapes shall be spiraled with a long lay. The shield wires shall have a total cross-sectional area as required by Article 250 and not less than the largest circuit conductor in the cable.

The outer jacket shall be water-, oil-, flame-, corrosion-, fungus-, and sunlight-resistant, and suitable for installation in cable trays.

337-9. Marking. Type SNM cable shall have a distinctive marking on its exterior surface for its entire length indicating its type and maximum operating temperature. It shall comply with the general marking requirements of Section 310-11.

The conductors shall each be numbered for identification from each other by durable marking on two sides 180° apart every 6 inches of length, with alternate legends inverted to facilitate reading from both sides.

▲ **Type SNM cable is primarily designed for use in cable tray supports or raceways in Class I, Division 2 and Class II, Division 2 hazardous locations. The cable features an overlapping spiral metal tape and wire shield with an outer jacket. Figure 337-1 shows a cutaway view of a typical cable, and Fig. 337-2 shows fittings for connecting the cable to a rigid metal conduit.**

ARTICLE 338. SERVICE-ENTRANCE CABLE

Types SE and USE

338-1. Definition. Service-entrance cable is a single conductor or multiconductor assembly provided with or without an overall covering, primarily used for services and of the following types:

(1) Type SE, having a flame-retardant, moisture-resistant covering, but not required to have inherent protection against mechanical abuse.

(2) Type USE, recognized for underground use, having a moisture-resistant covering, but not required to have a flame-retardant covering or inherent protection

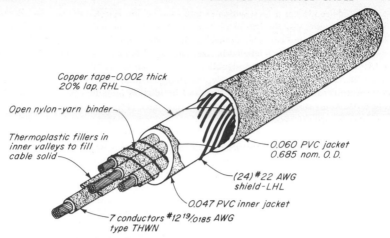

Copper tape—0.002 thick
20% lap. RHL

Open nylon-yarn binder

Thermoplastic fillers in
inner valleys to fill
cable solid

0.060 PVC jacket
0.685 nom. O.D.

(24)#22 AWG
shield-LHL

0.047 PVC inner jacket

7 conductors #12 ¹⁹/₀₁₈₅ AWG
type THWN

FIG. 337-1. Cutaway view of a seven-conductor No. 12 Type SNM cable.

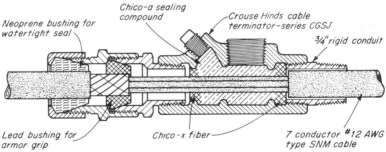

Chico-a sealing
compound

Crouse Hinds cable
terminator—series CGSJ

Neoprene bushing for
watertight seal

¾" rigid conduit

Lead bushing for
armor grip

Chico-x fiber

7 conductor #12 AWG
type SNM cable

FIG. 337-2. Drawing shows fittings used where Type SNM cable enters ¾-in. rigid metal
conduit in Class I and II, Division 2 hazardous locations.

against mechanical abuse. Single-conductor cables having rubber insulation specifically approved for the purpose do not require an outer covering.

Cabled single-conductor Type USE constructions recognized for underground use
may have a bare copper conductor cabled with the assembly. Type USE single,
parallel, or cabled conductor assemblies recognized for underground use may have
a bare copper concentric conductor applied. These constructions do not require an
outer overall covering.

See Section 230-40, Exception (2).

(3) If Type SE or USE cable consists of two or more conductors, one shall be
permitted to be uninsulated.

▲ The Code contains no specifications for the construction of this cable; it is left
to Underwriters' Laboratories, Inc., to determine what types of cable should be
approved for this purpose. The types listed by the Laboratories at the present time

are multiple-conductor cables, with all conductors insulated or having an uninsulated neutral conductor, usually with a steel tape armor and a saturated braid over the armor to protect it from the corrosive action of the atmosphere.

Service-entrance cable is labeled in sizes No. 12 AWG and larger. The temperature rating or the conductor-type designation may be marked on the outside surface of the cable. If no such markings appear, the rating shall be considered to be 75°C.

Type USE cable is listed for underground installation including burial directly in the earth. Many single-conductor cables are dual-rated (Type USE or RHW or RHH) and may be used in raceways.

338-2. Uses Permitted As Service-Entrance Conductors. Service-entrance cable used as service-entrance conductors shall be installed as required by Article 230.

338-3. Uses Permitted As Branch Circuits or Feeders.

(a) Grounded Conductor Insulated. Type SE service-entrance cables shall be permitted in interior wiring systems where all of the circuit conductors of the cable are of the rubber-covered or thermoplastic type.

(b) Grounded Conductor Not Insulated. Type SE service-entrance cables without individual insulation on the grounded circuit conductor shall not be used as a branch circuit or as a feeder within a building, except a cable that has a final nonmetallic outer covering and is supplied by alternating current at not over 150 volts to ground shall be permitted: (1) As a branch circuit to supply only a range, wall-mounted oven, counter-mounted cooking unit, or clothes dryer as covered in Section 250-60, or (2) as a feeder to supply only other buildings on the same premises.

Service-entrance cable shall be permitted for interior use where the fully insulated conductors are used for circuit wiring and the uninsulated conductor is used for equipment grounding purposes.

(c) Temperature Limitations. Type SE service-entrance cable used to supply appliances shall not be subject to conductor temperatures in excess of the temperature specified for the type of insulation involved.

▲ Where a group of buildings is supplied by a single service, such as in farm wiring, where a distribution center is installed inside one building, this type of cable may be used from the distribution center to the outside of the building for feeders or branch circuits supplying other buildings, and may also be used for such feeders or branch circuits from the outsides of the other buildings to the main cutoff switches.

Paragraph (b) permits the use of service-entrance cable with an uninsulated grounded conductor for the neutral to supply a range, wall-mounted oven, counter-mounted cooking unit, or a clothes dryer. Section 250-60 permits the use of this conductor for grounding these appliances, except in mobile homes and recreational vehicles.

338-4. Installation Methods.

(a) In addition to the provisions of this Article, Type SE service-entrance cable used for interior wiring shall comply with the applicable provisions of Article 300.

(b) Unarmored cable shall be installed in accordance with the applicable provisions of Article 336.

(c) Cables shall comply with Section 300-4 where installed through studs, joists, rafters, or similar members.

338-5. Marking. Service-entrance cable shall be marked as required in Section 310-11. Cable with the neutral conductor smaller than the ungrounded conductors shall be so marked.

ARTICLE 339. UNDERGROUND FEEDER AND BRANCH-CIRCUIT CABLE

Type UF

339-1. Description and Marking.

(a) Description. Underground feeder and branch-circuit cable shall be an approved Type UF cable in sizes No. 14 through No. 4/0. The conductors of Type UF shall be one of the moisture-resistant types listed in Table 310-13 which is suitable for branch-circuit wiring or one which is approved for the purpose. The ampacity of Type UF cable shall be that of 60°C (140°F) conductors in Tables 310-16 and 310-18. In addition to the insulated conductors, the cable shall be permitted to have an approved size of insulated or bare conductor for equipment grounding purposes only. The overall covering shall be flame-retardant, moisture-resistant, fungus-resistant, corrosion-resistant, and suitable for direct burial in the earth.

(b) Marking. In addition to the provisions of Section 310-11, the cable shall have a distinctive marking on the exterior for its entire length specifying the cable type.

339-2. Other Articles. In addition to the provisions of this Article, installations of underground feeder and branch-circuit cable (Type UF) shall comply with other applicable provisions of this Code, especially Article 300 and Section 310-13.

▲ This type of cable may be used underground, including direct burial in the earth, as feeder or branch-circuit cable when provided with overcurrent protection not in excess of the rated ampacity of the individual conductors. If single-conductor cables are installed, all cables of the feeder circuit, subfeeder or branch circuit, including the neutral circuit, must be run together in close proximity in the same trench or raceway. It may be necessary in some installations to provide additional mechanical protection, such as a covering board, concrete pad, raceway, etc., when required by the authority enforcing the Code. Multiple-conductor Type UF cable may also be used for interior wiring when complying with the provisions of Art. 336 of the Code, and may be used in wet locations.

Single-conductor Type UF cable embedded in poured cement, concrete, or aggregate may be used for nonheating leads of fixed electric space heating cables; see Sec. 339-3(a)(4) Exception.

339-3. Use.

(a) Uses Permitted.

(1) Type UF cable shall be permitted for use underground, including direct burial in the earth, as feeder or branch-circuit cable where provided with overcurrent protection of the rated ampacity as required in Section 339-4.

(2) Where single-conductor cables are installed, all cables of the feeder circuit, sub-feeder circuit, or branch circuit, including the neutral conductor, if any, shall be run together in the same trench or raceway.

(3) For underground requirements, see Section 300-5.

(4) Type UF cable shall be permitted for interior wiring in wet, dry, or corrosive locations under the recognized wiring methods of this Code, and where installed as nonmetallic-sheathed cable, the installation shall comply with the provisions of Article 336 and shall be of the multiconductor type.

Exception: Single conductor cables shall be permitted as the non-heating leads for heating cables as provided in Section 424-43.

Type UF cable supported by cable trays shall be of the multiconductor type.

(b) Uses Not Permitted. Type UF cable shall not be used: (1) as service-entrance cables; (2) in commercial garages; (3) in theaters; (4) in motion-picture studios; (5) in storage battery rooms; (6) in hoistways; (7) in any hazardous location; (8) embedded in poured cement, concrete, or aggregate, except where embedded in plaster as nonheating leads as provided in Article 424; (9) where exposed to direct rays of the sun, unless approved for the purpose.

339-4. Overcurrent Protection. Overcurrent protection shall be provided in accordance with provisions of Section 240-3.

339-5. Rated Ampacity. The ampacities of conductors in Type UF cable shall be according to Tables 310-16 and 310-18.

▲ Cables suitable for exposure to direct rays of the sun are indicated by tag marking and marking on the surface of the cable with the designation "sunlight resistant."

ARTICLE 340. POWER AND CONTROL
TRAY CABLE

Type TC

340-1. Definition. Type TC power and control tray cable is a factory assembly of two or more insulated conductors, with or without associated bare or covered grounding conductors under a nonmetallic sheath, approved for installation in cable trays, in raceways, or where supported by a messenger wire.

340-2. Other Articles. In addition to the provisions of this article, installations of Type TC tray cable shall comply with other applicable articles of this Code, especially Articles 300 and 318.

340-3. Construction. The insulated conductors of Type TC tray cable shall be in sizes 18 AWG through 1,000 MCM copper and sizes 12 AWG through 1,000 MCM aluminum or copper-clad aluminum. Insulated conductors of size 14 AWG and larger copper and size 12 AWG and larger aluminum or copper-clad aluminum shall be one of the types listed in Table 310-13, which is suitable for branch circuit and feeder circuits or one which is approved for the purpose. Insulated conductors of size 18 and 16 AWG copper shall be in accordance with Article 725-16. The outer sheath shall be a flame-retardant, nonmetallic material. Where installed in wet locations, Type TC cable shall be resistant to moisture and corrosive agents.

340-4. Use Permitted. Type TC tray cable shall be limited to use in industrial establishments where the conditions of maintenance and supervision assure that

GENERAL ELECTRIC TRAY CABLE (UL)

FIG. 340-1. Cutaway view of a three-conductor tray cable. (*General Electric.*)

Fig. 340-2. Cutaway view of a nine-conductor tray cable. *(General Electric.)*

only competent individuals will service the installation. It shall be permitted to be used:

(1) For power, lighting, control and signal circuits.

(2) In cable trays, or in raceways, or where supported in outdoor locations by a messenger wire.

(3) In cable trays in hazardous locations where the cable is specifically approved for the use as permitted in Articles 318 and 501.

340-5. Uses Not Permitted. Type TC tray cable shall not be:

(1) Installed where they will be exposed to physical damage.

(2) Installed as open cable on brackets or cleats.

(3) Used where exposed to direct rays of the sun, unless approved for the purpose.

340-6. Marking. The cable shall be marked in accordance with Section 310-11.

340-7. Ampacity. The ampacities of the conductors of Type TC tray cable shall be determined from Table 400-5 and Section 318-10.

ARTICLE 342. NONMETALLIC EXTENSIONS

342-1. Definition. Nonmetallic extensions are an assembly of two insulated conductors within a nonmetallic jacket or an extruded thermoplastic covering. The classification includes both surface extensions, intended for mounting directly on the surface of walls or ceilings, and aerial cable, containing a supporting messenger cable as an integral part of the cable assembly.

342-2. Other Articles. In addition to the provisions of this Article, nonmetallic extensions shall be installed in accordance with the applicable provisions of this Code.

342-3. Uses Permitted. Nonmetallic extensions shall be permitted only where all of the following conditions are met:

(1) The extension is from an existing outlet on a 15- or 20-ampere branch circuit in conformity with the requirements of Article 210.

(2) The extension is run exposed and in a dry location.

(3) For nonmetallic surface extensions, the building is occupied for residential or office purposes.

(4) For aerial cable, the building is occupied for industrial purposes, and the nature of the occupancy requires a highly flexible means for connecting equipment.

▲ A nonmetallic extension is an assembly of two conductors without a metallic envelope, designed specially for a 15- or 20-A branch circuit as an extension from an existing outlet. Surface extensions are limited to residences and offices. Aerial extensions are limited to industrial purposes where it has been determined that the nature of the occupancy would require such wiring for connecting equipment.

342-4. Uses Not Permitted.   Nonmetallic extensions shall not be used:

(1) As aerial cable to substitute for one of the general wiring methods specified by this Code.

(2) In unfinished basements, attics, or roof spaces.

(3) Where the voltage between conductors exceeds 150 volts for nonmetallic surface extension and 300 volts for aerial cable.

(4) Where subject to corrosive vapors.

(5) Where run through a floor or partition, or outside the room in which it originates.

342-5. Splices and Taps.   Extensions shall consist of a continuous unbroken length of the assembly, without splices, and without exposed conductors between fittings. Taps shall be permitted where approved fittings completely covering the tap connections are used. Aerial cable and its tap connectors shall be provided with an approved means for polarization. Receptacle-type tap connectors shall be of the locking-type.

342-6. Fittings.   Each run shall terminate in a fitting that covers the end of the assembly. All fittings and devices shall be of a type approved for the purpose.

342-7. Installation.   Nonmetallic extensions shall be installed as specified in (a) and (b) below.

(a) Nonmetallic Surface Extensions.

(1) One or more extensions shall be permitted to be run in any direction from an existing outlet, but not on the floor or within 2 inches from the floor.

(2) Nonmetallic surface extensions shall be secured in place by approved means at intervals not exceeding 8 inches.

Exception: Where connection to the supplying outlet is made by means of an attachment plug, the first fastening shall be permitted 12 inches or less from the plug.

There shall be at least one fastening between each two adjacent outlets supplied. An extension shall be attached only to woodwork or plaster finish, and shall not be in contact with any metal work or other conductive material other than with metal plates on receptacles.

(3) A bend that reduces the normal spacing between the conductors shall be covered with a cap to protect the assembly from physical damage.

(b) Aerial Cable.

(1) Aerial cable shall be supported by its messenger cable, securely attached at each end with approved clamps and turnbuckles. Intermediate supports shall be provided at not more than 20-foot intervals. Cable tension shall be adjusted to eliminate excessive sag. The cable shall have a clearance of not less than 2 inches from steel structural members or other conductive material.

(2) Aerial cable shall have a clearance of not less than 10 feet above floor areas accessible to pedestrian traffic, and not less than 14 feet above floor areas accessible to vehicular traffic.

(3) Cable suspended over work benches, not accessible to pedestrian traffic, shall have a clearance of not less than 8 feet above the floor.

(4) Aerial cables shall be permitted as a means to support lighting fixtures when the total load on the supporting messenger cable does not exceed that for which the assembly is intended.

(5) The supporting messenger cable, when installed in conformity with the applicable provisions of Article 250 and when properly identified as an equipment grounding conductor, shall be permitted to ground equipment. The messenger cable shall not be used as a branch-circuit conductor.

342-8. Marking. Nonmetallic extensions shall be marked in accordance with Section 110-21.

ARTICLE 344. UNDERPLASTER EXTENSIONS

344-1. Use. An underplaster extension installed as permitted by this Article shall be permitted only for extending an existing branch circuit in a building of fire-resistive construction.

▲ Such extensions are permitted in order to provide a suitable means of extending from existing outlets to new outlets without excessive expense, where there are no open spaces in walls or floors that will permit fishing from one outlet to another. In installing this work, the plaster is channeled and the conduit, cable, raceway, or tubing is secured to the concrete or tile and then plastered over.

344-2. Materials. Such extension shall be run in rigid or flexible conduit, Type AC metal-clad cable, electrical metallic tubing, Type MI cable, or metal raceways approved for the purpose. Standard sizes of conduit, cable, tubing, and raceways shall be used.

Exception: For a single conductor only, conduit or tubing having not less than $\frac{5}{16}$ inch inside diameter, single-conductor Type AC metal-clad cable, or single conductor Type MI cable shall be permitted.

344-3. Boxes and Fittings. Boxes and fittings shall comply with the applicable provisions of Article 370.

344-4. Installation. An underplaster extension shall be laid on the face of masonry or other material and buried in the plaster finish of ceilings or walls. The methods of installation of the raceway or cable for such extension shall be as specified elsewhere in this Code for the particular type of material used.

344-5. Extension to Another Floor. No such extension shall extend beyond the floor on which it originates unless installed in a standard size of rigid metal conduit, intermediate metal conduit, electrical metallic tubing, Type AC metal-clad cable, or Type MI cable.

▲ Such wiring is an expedient permitted for the purpose of avoiding an excessive amount of channeling and drilling of walls and floors. It is an expensive method, and from the standpoint of permanence, safety, and reliability the standard types of wiring are much to be preferred. For these reasons, underplaster extensions are limited to the floor within which they originate. In practice, the use of this method generally is, and should be, limited to short runs feeding not more than two or three additional outlets from one existing outlet.

ARTICLE 345. INTERMEDIATE METAL CONDUIT

A. General

345-1. Definition. Intermediate metal conduit is a metal raceway of circular cross section with integral or associated couplings, connectors and fittings approved for the installation of electrical conductors.

▲ Intermediate metal conduit is a lightweight rigid steel conduit which requires about 25 percent less steel than heavy-wall rigid conduit. Acceptance into the Code was based on a UL fact-finding report which showed through research and comparative tests that IMC performs as well as rigid steel conduit in many cases and surpasses rigid aluminum and EMT in most cases. The threading methods are completely interchangeable with standard rigid conduit fittings. IMC is satisfactory to use in most locations that rigid metal conduit is used with the exception of hazardous areas, where it has limited application.

345-2. Other Articles. Installations for intermediate metal conduit shall comply with the provisions of the applicable Sections of Article 300.

345-3. Uses Permitted. Use of intermediate metal conduit shall be permitted under all atmospheric conditions and occupancies. Where practicable, dissimilar metals in contact anywhere in the system shall be avoided to eliminate the possibility of galvanic action. Intermediate metal conduit shall be permitted as an equipment grounding conductor.

See Section 250-91.

345-4. Uses Not Permitted.

(a) Intermediate metal conduit shall not be used in hazardous locations.

(b) Unless made of material judged suitable for the condition, or unless corrosion protection is provided, intermediate metal conduit, elbows, couplings, and fittings shall not be installed in concrete or in direct contact with the earth, or in areas subject to severe corrosive influences.

(c) Intermediate metal conduit, unless approved for the purpose, shall not be used in or under cinder fill where subject to permanent moisture unless protected on all sides by a layer of non-cinder concrete not less than two inches thick or unless the conduit is not less than 18 inches under the fill.

B. Installation

345-5. Wet Locations. All supports, bolts, straps, screws, etc. shall be of corrosion resistant materials or protected against corrosion by corrosion resistant materials approved for the purpose.

See Section 300-6 for protection against corrosion.

345-6. Size.

(a) Minimum. Conduit smaller than $\frac{1}{2}$ inch electrical trade size shall not be used.

(b) Maximum. Conduit larger than four inch electrical trade size shall not be used.

345-7. Number of Conductors in Conduit. The number of conductors in a single conduit shall not exceed that permitted by the percentage fill specified in Table 1, Chapter 9, using the conduit dimensions of Table 4, Chapter 9.

345-8. Reaming and Threading. All cut ends of conduit shall be reamed to remove rough edges. Where conduit is threaded in the field, an electrical conduit thread cutting die with a taper shall be used.

345-9. Couplings and Connectors.

(a) Threadless couplings and connectors used with conduit shall be made tight. Where buried in masonry or concrete, they shall be the concrete-tight type. Where installed in wet locations, they shall be the raintight type.

(b) Running threads shall not be used on conduit for connection at couplings.

345-10. Bends—How Made. Bends of intermediate metal conduit shall be so made that the conduit will not be injured, and that the internal diameter of the conduit will not be effectively reduced. The radius of the curve of the inner edge of any field bend shall not be less than indicated in 346-10.

Exception: For field bends for conductors without lead sheath and made with a single operation (one shot) bending machine designed for the purpose, the minimum radius shall not be less than that indicated in Table 346-10 Exception.

345-11. Bends—Number in One Run. A run of conduit between outlet and outlet, between fitting and fitting, or between outlet and fitting, shall not contain more than the equivalent of 4 quarter bends (360 degrees, total), including those bends located immediately at the outlet or fitting.

345-12. Supports. Intermediate metal conduit shall be installed as a complete system as provided in Article 300 and shall be securely fastened in place. Conduit shall be firmly fastened within three feet of each outlet box, junction box, cabinet, or fitting. Conduit shall be supported at least every ten feet.

345-13. Boxes and Fittings. See Article 370.

345-14. Splices and Taps. Splices and taps shall be made only in junction, outlet boxes or conduit bodies. Conductors, including splices and taps, shall not fill a conduit body to more than 75 percent of its cross sectional area at any point. All splices and taps shall be made by approved methods.

345-15. Bushings. Where a conduit enters a box or fitting, a bushing shall be provided to protect the wire from abrasion unless the design of the box or fitting is such as to afford equivalent protection. See Section 373-6(c) for the protection of conductors at bushings.

C. Construction Specifications

345-16. General. Intermediate metal conduit shall comply with (a) through (c) below.

(a) Intermediate metal conduit as shipped shall be in standard lengths of ten feet including coupling, one coupling to be furnished with each length. For specific applications or use, it shall be permissible to ship lengths shorter or longer than ten feet, with or without couplings.

(b) Nonferrous conduit of corrosion-resistant material shall have suitable markings.

(c) Marking. Each length shall be clearly and durably identified at $2\frac{1}{2}$ foot intervals with the letters IMC. Each length shall be marked as required in the first sentence of Section 110-21.

ARTICLE 346. RIGID METAL CONDUIT

Note: Where conduit is threaded in the field it is assumed that a standard cutting die providing $\frac{3}{4}$ inch taper per foot will be employed.

346-1. Use. The use of rigid metal conduit shall be permitted under all atmospheric conditions and occupancies subject to the following:

(a) Ferrous raceways and fittings protected from corrosion solely by enamel shall be permitted only indoors and in occupancies not subject to severe corrosive influences.

(b) Where practicable, dissimilar metals in contact anywhere in the system shall be avoided to eliminate the possibility of galvanic action.

(c) Unless made of a material judged suitable for the condition, or unless corrosion protection approved for the condition is provided, ferrous or nonferrous metal conduit, elbows, couplings, and fittings shall not be installed in concrete, in direct contact with the earth, or in areas subject to severe corrosive influences.

▲ The above requirement was inserted into the Code on the basis of unsatisfactory performance of aluminum conduit in concrete which presumably had chloride additives that contributed to the high rate of corrosion. See comments following Sec. 300-6(c).

346-2. Other Articles. Installations of rigid metal conduit shall comply with the applicable provisions of Article 300.

A. Installation

346-3. Cinder Fill. Conduit shall not be used in or under cinder fill where subject to permanent moisture.

Exception No. 1: Where of corrosion-resistant material suitable for the purpose.

Exception No. 2: Where protected on all sides by a layer of non-cinder concrete at least 2 inches thick.

Exception No. 3: Where the conduit is at least 18 inches under the fill.

▲ Cinders usually contain sulfur, and if there is much moisture sulfuric acid is formed, which attacks steel conduit. A cinder fill outdoors should be considered as "subject to permanent moisture." In such a place conduit runs should be buried in the ground at least 18 in. below the fill. This would not apply if cinders were not present.

346-4. Wet Locations. All supports, bolts, straps, screws, etc., shall be of corrosion-resistant materials or protected against corrosion by corrosion-resistant materials approved for the purpose.

See Section 300-6 for protection against corrosion.

346-5. Minimum Size. Conduit smaller than $\frac{1}{2}$ inch electrical trade size shall not be used.

Exception No. 1: For underplaster extensions as permitted in Section 344-2.

Exception No. 2: For enclosing the leads of motors as permitted in Section 430-145(b).

346-6. Number of Conductors in Conduit. The number of conductors permitted in a single conduit shall not exceed the percentage fill specified in Table 1, Chapter 9.

▲ Conduit fill is based on the percentages specified in Table 1, Chapter 9, and applies equally to new and old work and concealed or exposed work.

346-7. Reaming. All cut ends of conduits shall be reamed to remove rough edges.

346-8. Bushings. Where a conduit enters a box or other fitting, a bushing shall be provided to protect the wire from abrasion unless the design of the box or fitting is such as to afford equivalent protection.

See Section 373-6(c) for the protection of conductors at bushings.

346-9. Couplings and Connectors.

(a) Threadless couplings and connectors used with conduit shall be made tight. Where buried in masonry or concrete, they shall be of the concrete-tight type. Where installed in wet locations, they shall be of the raintight type.

(b) Running threads shall not be used on conduit for connection at couplings.

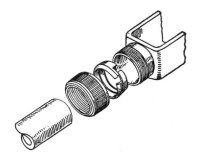

Fig. 346-1. Threadless connection to a fitting. (*Appleton Electric Co.*)

▲ Figure 346-1 is effective both mechanically and electrically if any nonconducting coating is removed from the conduit.

A running thread is considered mechanically weak and has poor electrical conductivity.

Where two lengths of conduit must be coupled together but it is impossible to screw both lengths into an ordinary coupling, the Erickson coupling shown in Fig. 346-2 may be used. This makes a rigid joint which is both mechanically and electrically effective. Also, bolted split couplings are available.

It is not intended that conduit threads be treated with paint or other materials in order to assure water tightness. It is assumed that the conductors are approved for the location and that the prime purpose of the conduit is for protection from physical damage and easy withdrawal of conductors for replacement.

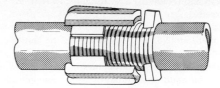

FIG. 346-2. Erickson couplings. (*The Thomas & Betts Co., Inc.*)

346-10. Bends—How Made. Bends of rigid metal conduit shall be so made that the conduit will not be injured, and that the internal diameter of the conduit will not be effectively reduced. The radius of the curve of the inner edge of any field bend shall not be less than shown in Table 346-10.

▲ *Field bend* means any bend made by workmen during the installation of the conduit.

346-11. Bends—Number in One Run. A run of conduit between outlet and outlet, fitting and fitting, or outlet and fitting shall not contain more than the equivalent of four quarter bends (360 degrees, total), including those bends located immediately at the outlet or fitting.

▲ Conduit runs should be so installed that the conductors can be pulled in without injuring the insulation or stretching small wires, and so that the conductors can be withdrawn easily.

Table 346-10. Radius of Conduit Bends (Inches)

Size of Conduit (In.)	Conductors Without Lead Sheath (In.)	Conductors With Lead Sheath (In.)
$\frac{1}{2}$	4	6
$\frac{3}{4}$	5	8
1	6	11
$1\frac{1}{4}$	8	14
$1\frac{1}{2}$	10	16
2	12	21
$2\frac{1}{2}$	15	25
3	18	31
$3\frac{1}{2}$	21	36
4	24	40
$4\frac{1}{2}$	27	45
5	30	50
6	36	61

Exception: For field bends for conductors without lead sheath and made with a single operation (one shot) bending machine designed for the purpose, the minimum radius shall not be less than indicated in Table 346-10 Exception.

346-12. Supports. Rigid metal conduit shall be installed as a complete system as provided in Article 300 and shall be securely fastened in place. Conduit shall be firmly fastened within 3 feet of each outlet box, junction box, cabinet, or fitting. Conduit shall be supported at least every 10 feet.

Exception No. 1: If made up with threaded couplings, it shall be permissible to support straight runs of rigid metal conduit in accordance with Table 346-12, provided such supports prevent transmission of stresses to termination where conduit is deflected between supports.

Exception No. 2: The distance between supports may be increased to 20 feet for exposed vertical risers from machine tools and the like, provided the conduit is made up with threaded couplings, is firmly supported at the top and bottom of the riser, and no other means of intermediate support is readily available.

346-13. Boxes and Fittings. Boxes and fittings shall comply with the applicable provisions of Article 370.

346-14. Splices and Taps. Splices and taps shall be made only in junction, outlet boxes or conduit bodies. Conductors, including splices and taps, shall not fill a

Table 346-10 Exception. Radius of Conduit Bends (Inches)

Size of Conduit (In.)	Radius to Center of Conduit (In.)
$\frac{1}{2}$	4
$\frac{3}{4}$	$4\frac{1}{2}$
1	$5\frac{3}{4}$
$1\frac{1}{4}$	$7\frac{1}{4}$
$1\frac{1}{2}$	$8\frac{1}{4}$
2	$9\frac{1}{2}$
$2\frac{1}{2}$	$10\frac{1}{2}$
3	13
$3\frac{1}{2}$	15
4	16
$4\frac{1}{2}$	20
5	24
6	30

Table 346-12. Supports for Rigid Metal Conduit

Conduit Size (Inches)	Maximum distance between rigid metal conduit supports (Feet)
$\frac{1}{2}$–$\frac{3}{4}$	10
1	12
$1\frac{1}{4}$–$1\frac{1}{2}$	14
2–$2\frac{1}{2}$	16
3 and larger	20

conduit body to more than 75 percent of its cross sectional area at any point. All splices and taps shall be made by approved methods.

B. Construction Specifications

346-15. General. Rigid metal conduit shall comply with (a) through (d) below.

(a) Rigid metal conduit as shipped shall be in standard lengths of 10 feet including coupling, one coupling to be furnished with each length. Each length shall be reamed and threaded on each end. For specific applications or uses, it shall be permissible to ship lengths shorter or longer than 10 feet, with or without couplings.

(b) Nonferrous conduit of corrosion-resistant material shall have suitable markings.

(c) Each length shall be clearly and durably identified in every 10 feet as required in the first sentence of Section 110-21.

(d) Conduit bodies shall have a cross sectional area at least twice that of the largest conduit to which they are connected.

ARTICLE 347. RIGID NONMETALLIC
CONDUIT

347-1. Description. This Article shall apply to a type of conduit and fittings of suitable nonmetallic material that is resistant to moisture and chemical atmospheres. For use aboveground, it shall also be flame retardant, resistant to impact and crushing, resistant to distortion from heat under conditions likely to be encountered in service, and resistant to low temperature and sunlight effects. For use underground, the material shall be acceptably resistant to moisture and corrosive agents and shall be of sufficient strength to withstand abuse, such as by impact and crushing, in handling and during installation. Where intended for direct burial, without encasement in concrete, the material shall also be capable of withstanding continued loading that is likely to be encountered after installation.

Materials that have been recognized as having suitable physical characteristics when properly formed and treated include fiber, asbestos cement, soapstone, rigid polyvinyl chloride and high-density polyethylene for underground use, and rigid polyvinyl chloride for use aboveground.

▲ All approved rigid nonmetallic conduits are suitable for underground installations. Some types are approved for direct burial in the earth while other types must be encased in concrete for underground applications. Listings by Underwriters' Laboratories, Inc., include such information.

The only nonmetallic conduit approved for use aboveground at the present time is rigid polyvinyl chloride (PVC Schedule 40, or Schedule 80). Since not all PVC conduits are suitable for use aboveground the UL label in each conduit length will indicate if the conduit is suitable for such use. For use of Schedule 80, see Secs. 300-5(d) and 710-3(b)(1).

347-2. Uses Permitted. The use of rigid nonmetallic conduit and fittings approved for the purpose shall be permitted under the following conditions:

(a) Where the potential is 600 volts or less.

(1) In walls, floors, and ceilings.

(2) In locations subject to severe corrosive influences as covered in Section 300-6 and where subject to chemicals for which the materials are specifically approved.

(3) In cinder fill.

(4) In portions of dairies, laundries, canneries or other wet locations and in locations where walls are frequently washed, the entire conduit system including boxes and fittings used therewith shall be so installed and equipped as to prevent water from entering the conduit. All supports, bolts, straps, screws, etc., shall be of corrosion-resistant materials or be protected against corrosion by approved corrosion-resistant materials.

(5) In dry and damp locations not prohibited by Section 347-3.

(6) For exposed work where not subject to physical damage if approved for the purpose.

(b) Where the potential is over 600 volts, rigid nonmetallic conduit shall be encased in not less than 2 inches of concrete.

(c) For underground installations see Section 300-5 and 710-3(b).

347-3. Uses Not Permitted. Rigid nonmetallic conduit shall not be used:

(a) In hazardous locations, except as covered in Sections 514-8 and 515-5.

(b) For the support of fixtures or other equipment.

(c) Where subject to physical damage unless approved for the purpose.

(d) Where subject to ambient temperatures exceeding those for which the conduit is approved.

(e) For conductors whose insulation temperature limitations would exceed those for which the conduit is approved.

▲ It should be noted that nonmetallic conduit is not permitted in ducts, plenums and other air-handling spaces. See Sec. 300-22. Also, such conduits or other nonmetallic materials should not be used in hollow spaces in buildings of fire-resistant construction because PVC conduits are combustible and add products of combustion and fuel contribution in the event of fire. See Sec. 300-21 and the comments following Sec. 300-22.

347-4. Other Articles. Installation of rigid nonmetallic conduit shall comply with the applicable provisions of Article 300. Where equipment grounding is required by Article 250, a separate equipment grounding conductor shall be installed in the conduit.

A. Installations

347-5. Trimming. All cut ends shall be trimmed inside and outside to remove rough edges.

347-6. Joints. All joints between lengths of conduit, and between conduit and couplings, fittings, and boxes shall be made by a method approved for the purpose.

347-8. Supports. Rigid nonmetallic conduit shall be supported as required in Table 347-8. In addition, there shall be a support within 4 feet of each box, cabinet, or other conduit termination.

▲ In regard to the spacing requirements in Table 347-8, where conductors are rated more than 60°C, the maximum spacing between supports is substantially reduced to compensate for slight sags that occur in PVC conduits at elevated temperatures.

It seems logical, however, that the phrase, "Conductors Rated More Than 60°C,"

Table 347-8. Support of Rigid Nonmetallic Conduit

Conduit Size (Inches)	Maximum Spacing between Supports (Feet)	
	Conductors Rated 60°C and Below	Conductors Rated More Than 60°C
½–¾	4	2
1–2	5	2½
2½–3	6	3
3½–5	7	3½
6	8	4

would not apply when such conductors (75°C or 90°C) are protected by overcurrent devices rated or set not greater than the ampacities listed in the 60°C column in Tables 310-16 and 310-18. For example, Type THW conductors are rated at 75°C and THHN conductors are rated at 90°C. For sizes 14 to 10 in Table 310-16, and sizes 12 and 10 in Table 310-18, Types THW and THHN have the same ampacities as 60°C conductors such as Type TW. Accordingly, there would be no reason why such conductors should not be considered as 60°C conductors in determining the spacing requirements in Table 347-8.

347-9. Expansion Joints. Expansion joints for rigid nonmetallic conduit shall be provided where required to compensate for thermal expansion and contraction.

▲ Where conduits are subject to constantly changing temperatures and the runs are long, expansion and contraction of PVC conduit must be considered. In such instances an expansion coupling should be installed near the fixed end of the run to take up any expansion or contraction that may occur. Available expansion couplings have a normal expansion range of 6 in. The coefficient of linear expansion of PVC conduit can be obtained from manufacturers' data.

Expansion couplings are normally used where conduits are exposed. In underground or slab applications such couplings are seldom used because expansion and contraction can be controlled by *bowing* the conduit slightly or by immediate burial. After the conduit is buried, expansion and contraction are not a problem. Conduits left exposed for an extended period of time during widely variable temperature conditions should be examined to see if contraction has occurred.

347-10. Minimum Size. No conduit smaller than ½-inch electrical trade size shall be used.

347-11. Number of Conductors. The number of conductors permitted in a single conduit shall not exceed the percentage fill specified in Table 1, Chapter 9.

▲ See comments following Sec. 346-6.

347-12. Bushings. Where a conduit enters a box or other fitting, a bushing or adapter shall be provided to protect the wire from abrasion unless the design of the box or fitting is such as to provide equivalent protection.

See Section 373-6(c) for the protection of conductors at bushings.

347-13. Bends, How Made. Bends of rigid nonmetallic conduit shall be so made that the conduit will not be injured and that the internal diameter of the conduit will not be effectively reduced. Field bends shall be made only with bending equipment intended for the purpose and the radius of the curve of the inner edge of such bends shall not be less than shown in Table 346-10.

347-14. Bends, Number in One Run. A run of conduit between outlet and outlet, fitting and fitting, or outlet and fitting shall not contain more than the equivalent of four quarter bends (360 degrees, total), including those bends located immediately at the outlet or fitting.

347-15. Boxes and Fittings. Boxes and fittings shall comply with the applicable provisions of Article 370.

347-16. Splices and Taps. Splices and taps shall be made only in junction, outlet boxes or conduit bodies. Conductors, including splices and taps, shall not fill a conduit body to more than 75 percent of its cross sectional area at any point. All splices and taps shall be made by approved methods.

B. Construction Specifications

347-17. General. Rigid nonmetallic conduit shall comply with (a) through (c) below.

(a) Rigid nonmetallic polyvinyl chloride conduit as shipped shall be in standard lengths of 10 feet including couplings, one coupling to be furnished with each length. For specific applications or uses, it shall be permissible to ship lengths shorter or longer than 10 feet with or without couplings.

(b) High-density polyethylene conduit as shipped shall be in standard lengths of 10 feet. One threaded coupling shall be furnished with each threaded length of high-density polyethylene conduit. For specific applications or uses, it shall be permissible to ship lengths shorter or longer than 10 feet with or without couplings.

(c) Each length of nonmetallic conduit shall be clearly and durably marked at least every 10 feet as required in the first sentence of Section 110-21. The type of material shall also be included in the marking unless it is visually identifiable. For conduit recognized for use aboveground these markings shall be permanent. For conduit limited to underground use only, these markings shall be sufficiently durable to remain legible until the material is installed.

(d) Conduit bodies shall have a cross sectional area at least twice that of the largest conduit to which they are connected.

ARTICLE 348. ELECTRICAL METALLIC
TUBING

348-1. Use. The use of electrical metallic tubing shall be permitted for both exposed and concealed work. Electrical metallic tubing shall not be used: (1) where during installation or afterward, it will be subject to severe physical damage; (2) where protected from corrosion solely by enamel; (3) in cinder concrete or cinder fill where subject to permanent moisture unless protected on all sides by a layer of noncinder concrete at least 2 inches thick or unless the tubing is at least 18 inches under the fill. Where practicable, dissimilar metals in contact anywhere in the system shall be avoided to eliminate the possibility of galvanic action.

Unless made of a material judged suitable for the condition, or unless corrosion protection approved for the condition is provided, ferrous or nonferrous electrical metallic tubing, elbows, couplings, and fittings shall not be installed in concrete, in direct contact with the earth, or in areas subject to severe corrosive influences.

348-2. Other Articles. Installations of electrical metallic tubing shall comply with the applicable provisions of Article 300.

A. Installation

348-4. Wet Locations. All supports, bolts, straps, screws, etc. shall be of corrosion-resistant materials or protected against corrosion by corrosion-resistant metals approved for the purpose.

See Section 300-6 for protection from corrosion.

348-5. Size.

(a) Minimum. Tubing smaller than $\frac{1}{2}$-inch electrical trade size shall not be used.

Exception No. 1: For underplaster extensions as permitted in Section 344-2.

Exception No. 2: For enclosing the leads of motors as permitted in Section 430-145(b).

(b) Maximum. The maximum size of tubing shall be the 4-inch electrical trade size.

348-6. Number of Conductors in Tubing. The number of conductors permitted in a single tubing shall not exceed the percentage fill specified in Table 1, Chapter 9.

348-7. Threads. Tubing shall not be coupled together nor connected to boxes, fittings, or cabinets by means of threads in the wall of the tubing, except by fittings approved for the purpose. Threads shall not be of the standard pipe-thread dimensions.

348-8. Couplings and Connectors. Threadless couplings and connectors used with tubing shall be made up tight. Where buried in masonry or concrete, they shall be concrete-tight type. Where installed in wet locations, they shall be of the raintight type.

▲ Couplings of the raintight type are required wherever electrical metallic tubing is used on the exteriors of buildings. (See Secs. 225-22 and 230-53.)

Sec. 370-7 requires that conductors entering a box, cabinet, or fitting be protected from abrasion. The end of a connector projecting inside a box, cabinet, or fitting must have smooth, well-rounded edges so that the covering of the wire will not be abraded while the wire is being pulled in. Where ungrounded conductors of size No. 4 or larger enter a raceway in a cabinet, etc., see Sec. 373-6(c).

348-9. Bends—How Made. Bends in the tubing shall be so made that the tubing will not be injured and that the internal diameter of the tubing will not be effectively reduced. The radius of the curve of the inner edge of any field bend shall not be less than shown in Table 346-10.

Exception: For field bends made with a bending machine designed for the purpose, the minimum radius shall not be less than indicated in Table 346-10 Exception.

348-10. Bends—Number in One Run. A run of electrical metallic tubing between outlet and outlet, fitting and fitting, or outlet and fitting shall not contain more than the equivalent of four quarter bends (360 degrees, total), including those bends located immediately at the outlet or fitting.

▲ See comment following Sec. 346-11.

348-11. Reaming. All cut ends of electrical metallic tubing shall be reamed to remove rough edges.

348-12. Supports. Electrical metallic tubing shall be installed as a complete system as provided in Article 300 and shall be securely fastened in place at least every 10 feet and within 3 feet of each outlet box, junction box, cabinet, or fitting.

348-13. Boxes and Fittings. Boxes and fittings shall comply with the applicable provisions of Article 370.

348-14. Splices and Taps. Splices and taps shall be made only in junction, outlet boxes or conduit bodies. Conductors, including splices and taps, shall not fill a conduit body to more than 75 percent of its cross sectional area at any point. All splices and taps shall be made by approved methods.

B. Construction Specifications

348-15. General. Electrical metallic tubing shall comply with (a) through (c) below.

(a) Cross Section. The tubing, and elbows and bends for use with the tubing, shall have a circular cross section. Conduit bodies shall have a cross sectional area at least twice that of the largest conduit to which they are connected.

(b) Finish. Tubing shall have such a finish or treatment of outer surfaces as will provide an approved durable means of readily distinguishing it, after installation, from rigid metal conduit.

(c) Connectors. Where the tubing is coupled together by threads, the connector shall be so designed as to prevent bending of the tubing at any part of the thread.

ARTICLE 350. FLEXIBLE METAL CONDUIT

350-1. Other Articles. Installations of flexible metal conduit shall comply with the applicable provisions of Articles 300, 334, and 346.

350-2. Use. Flexible metal conduit shall not be used: (1) in wet locations, unless conductors are of the lead-covered type or of other type approved for the specific conditions; (2) in hoistways, other than provided in Section 620-21; (3) in storage-battery rooms; (4) in any hazardous location other than permitted in Sections 501-4(b), 502-4, and 503-3; (5) where rubber-covered conductors are exposed to oil, gasoline, or other materials having a deteriorating effect on rubber; nor (6) underground or embedded in poured concrete or aggregate.

350-3. Minimum Size. Flexible metal conduit less than $\frac{1}{2}$-inch electrical trade size shall not be used.

Exception No. 1: For underplaster extensions as permitted in Section 344-2.

Exception No. 2: For enclosing the leads of motors as permitted in Section 430-145(b).

**Table 350-3. Maximum Number of Insulated Conductors in $\frac{3}{8}$ In.
Flexible Metal Conduit.***
Col. A = With fitting inside conduit.
Col. B = With fitting outside conduit.

Size AWG	Types RFH-2, SF-2		Types TF, T, XHHW, AF, TW, RUH, RUW		Types TFN, THHN, THWN		Types FEP, FEPB, PF, PGF	
	A	B	A	B	A	B	A	B
18	..	3	3	7	4	8	5	8
16	..	2	2	4	3	7	4	8
14	..	..	..	4	3	7	3	7
12	..	..	..	3	..	4	..	4
10	..	..	..	..	..	2	..	3

* In addition one uninsulated grounding conductor of the same AWG size shall be permitted.

Exception No. 3: Flexible metal conduit of $\frac{3}{8}$-inch nominal trade size shall be permitted in lengths not in excess of 72 inches as a part of an approved assembly or for lighting fixtures.

350-4. Supports. Flexible metal conduit shall be secured by an approved means at intervals not exceeding $4\frac{1}{2}$ feet and within 12 inches on each side of every outlet box or fitting.

Exception No. 1: Where flexible metal conduit is fished.

Exception No. 2: Lengths of not more than 3 feet at terminals where flexibility is necessary.

Exception No. 3: Lengths of not more than 6 feet from a fixture terminal connection for tap connections to lighting fixtures as required in Section 410-67(b)(2).

▲ Straps or other means of securing the conduit in place should be spaced much closer together for flexible conduit than is necessary for rigid conduit. Every bend should be rigidly secured so that it will not be deformed when the wires are being pulled in, thus causing the wires to bind.

350-5. Grounding. Flexible metal conduit shall be permitted as a grounding means where both the conduit and the fittings are approved for the purpose.

Exception: Flexible metal conduit shall be permitted as a grounding means if the length is 6 feet or less, the conduit is terminated in fittings approved for the purpose, and the circuit conductors contained therein are protected by overcurrent devices rated at 20 amperes or less.

▲ This means that where flexible metal conduit and fittings have not been specifically approved as a grounding means, a separate grounding conductor (insulated or bare) shall be run inside the conduit and bonded at each box or similar equipment to which the conduit is connected.

In regard to the Exception, see comments following Sec. 250-91(b).

350-6. Bends in Concealed Work. A run of conduit for concealed raceway, between outlet and outlet, fitting and fitting, or outlet and fitting, shall not contain more than the equivalent of four quarter bends (360° total), including those bends located immediately at the outlet or fitting.

Angle connectors shall not be used for concealed raceway installations.

ARTICLE 351. LIQUIDTIGHT FLEXIBLE METAL CONDUIT

351-1. Scope. This Article covers a type of flexible metal conduit having an outer liquidtight nonmetallic sunlight-resistant jacket.

Fig. 351-1. Grounding bushing for use where liquidtight flexible conduit is terminated. (*American Brass Co.*)

Fig. 351-2. Liquidtight flexible conduit. (*American Brass Co.*)

▲ Liquidtight flexible metal conduit is approved for use in wet locations and where exposed to mineral oil, both at a maximum temperature of 60°C. It is not for use where exposed to gasoline or similar light-petroleum solvents. It is being widely used in the wiring of machine tools. It is similar in construction to the common type of flexible metal conduit, but is covered with an outer sheath of thermoplastic material. Figure 351-1 shows a grounding bushing designed to be slipped inside each end of a length of conduit to ensure an adequate grounding connection, and Fig. 351-2 shows the construction of the conduit. The use of the bushing makes it unnecessary to remove any burrs or sharp edges where the conduit has been cut. This conduit can be terminated at any connector or other fitting of suitable size that is designed to receive unthreaded rigid conduit.

351-2. Use.

(a) The use of liquidtight flexible metal conduit shall be permitted for both exposed and concealed work:

(1) Where conditions of installation, operation, or maintenance require flexibility or protection from liquids, vapors, or solids.

(2) As permitted by Sections 501-4(b), 502-4, and 503-3, and in other hazardous locations where specifically approved.

(b) Liquidtight flexible metal conduit shall not be used:

(1) Where subject to physical damage.

(2) Where any combination of ambient and/or conductor temperature will produce an operating temperature in excess of that for which the material is approved.

351-3. Size.

(a) Minimum. Liquidtight flexible metal conduit smaller than ½-inch electrical trade size shall not be used.

Exception: ⅜-inch size shall be permitted as covered in Section 350-3.

(b) Maximum. The maximum size of liquidtight flexible metal conduit shall be the 4-inch trade size.

351-4. Number of Conductors.

(a) The number of conductors permitted in a single conduit, ½ through 4 inch trade sizes, shall not exceed the percentage of fill specified in Table 1, Chapter 9.

(b) The number of conductors permitted in ⅜-inch liquidtight flexible metal conduit shall not exceed that permitted in Table 350-3.

351-5. Fittings. Liquidtight flexible metal conduit shall be used only with terminal fittings approved for the purpose.

351-6. Supports. Where liquidtight flexible metal conduit is installed as a fixed raceway, it shall be secured at intervals not exceeding 4½ feet and within 12 inches on each side of every outlet box or fitting.

Exception: Where the conduit is fished.

351-7. Grounding. Liquidtight flexible metal conduit shall be permitted as a grounding conductor where both the conduit and the fittings are approved for the purpose.

Exception: Liquidtight flexible metal conduit shall be permitted as a grounding means in the 1¼ inch and smaller trade sizes if the length is 6 feet or less and the conduit is terminated in fittings approved for the purpose.

▲ **In regard to the Exception, see comments following Sec. 250-91(b).**

ARTICLE 352. SURFACE RACEWAYS

A. Metal Surface Raceways

352-1. Use. The use of surface raceways shall be permitted in dry locations. They shall not be used: (1) where subject to severe physical damage unless approved for the purpose; (2) where 300 volts or more between conductors unless the metal has a thickness of not less than .040 inch; (3) where subject to corrosive vapors; (4) in hoistways; (5) in any hazardous location; nor (6) concealed except as follows:

Exception No. 1: Metal surface raceways approved for the purpose shall be permitted for underplaster extensions.

Exception No. 2: As permitted in Section 645-2(c)(2).

See definition of "Exposed—(As applied to wiring methods)" in Article 100.

352-2. Other Articles. Metal surface raceways shall comply with the applicable provisions of Article 300.

▲ **In every type of wiring having a metal enclosure around the conductors, it is important that the metal shall be mechanically continuous in order to provide protection for the conductors and that the metal shall form a continuous electrical conductor of low impedance from the last outlet on the run to the cabinet or cutout box. A path to ground is thus provided through the box or cabinet, in case any conductor** comes in contact with the metal enclosure, an outlet box, or any other fitting. See Sec. 250-91(b).

352-3. Size of Conductors. No conductor larger than that for which the raceway is designed shall be installed in metal surface raceway.

▲ The manufacturers of metal surface raceways have provided the following illustrations and details (Figs. 352-1 through 352-4) on their products.

† Typical number of wires in one raceway

Type of raceway	Wire size gage No.	Type RH	Types T, TW	Types THWN
No. 200 (1¹¹/₃₂" × ½")	14 12	3 2	3 3	3 3
No. 500 (1⁷/₃₂" × ¾")	14 12 10 8	5 4 2	6 6 4 2	8 7 4 2
No. 700 (2¹/₃₂" × ¾")	14 12 10 8	7 6 3 2	8 8 6 3	11 10 8 5
No. 1000 (15⁄16" × 15⁄16")	14 12 10 8 6	10 10 6 5 4	10 10 8 8 5	21 18 10 10 6
No. 1500 (1⁹/₁₆" × 11⁄32")	14 12 10 8 6	4 4	8 6 4 4	10 8 5 3 2

Type of raceway	Wire size gage No.	Type RH – With receptacles	Type RH – Without receptacles	Types T, TW – With receptacles	Types T, TW – Without receptacles	Types THWN – Without receptacles
No. 1900 (9⁄16" × 13⁄16")	14 12	3 3	3 3	3 3	3 3	3 3
No. 2000 (1⁹/₃₂" × ¾")	14 12	3 3	3 3	3 3	3 3	3 3
No. 2100 (1¼" × ⅞")	14 12 10 8 6	* *	17 14 10 6 4	* * * * *	17 14 10 8 5	23 18 12 10 7

* See wiremold catalog

Type of raceway	Wire size gage No.	With receptacles	Without receptacles	With receptacles	Without receptacles	Without receptacles
No. 2200 (2⅜" × ¾")	14 12 10 8 6	10 10 6 4		10 10 10 7 3	10 10 10 8 5	14 13 12 10 7
				Types RU, T, TW		
No. 3000 (2¾" × 17⁄16")	14 12 10 8 6	* * * * *	44 40 20 14 10	* * * * *	56 42 20 16 14	75 55 24 18 13

* Type RH, T, TW with devices in place with standard flush-mounted snap switches and attachment-plug receptacles of a type not having pilot lights. 10 No.6; 10 No. 8; 10 No. 10; 10 No. 12; 10 No. 14.

† Recommended only for straight runs with no bends nor elbows.

Fɪɢ. 352-1. Wiremold metal surface raceway. (*The Wiremold Co.*)

Number of wires in one raceway			
Type of raceway	Wire size gage No.	Number of wires Type RH	Type T
No. 111 (17/64, 35/64")	14 12	3 2	3 3
No. 333 (7/16, 1")	14 12 10 8 6	7 6 3 2	9 8 6 3 2
No. 888 (11/16, 1 33/64")	14 12 10 8 6	10 10 9 7 4	10 10 10 10 5
No. 711-A (3/8, 1 1/8")	14 12 10 8	7 4 2 2	9 5 4 3
No. 733-A (11/16, 2 3/32")	14 12 10 8 6	10 10 10 7 4	10 10 10 10 6

Type of raceway	Wire size gage No.	With devices	Without devices	With devices	Without devices
No. 1700 (1 5/8, 2 1/8")	14 12 10 8 6	10 10 10 10 8	38 34 18 12 8	10 10 10 10 10	54 34 18 16 12

No. 3400	Catalog No. 3400 is a raceway consisting of two No. 1700 housings in a common cover. Each channel has the same wire fill as 1700.

FIG. 352-2. Types of metal surface raceways. (*National Electric Division, H. K. Porter Company, Inc.*)

FIG. 352-3. Typical use of small metal surface raceway for extensions from existing receptacle outlets. (*National Electric Division, H. K. Porter Company, Inc.*)

FIG. 352-4. Shallow switch and receptacle box with 500 Wiremold raceway. (*The Wiremold Co.*)

352-4. Number of Conductors in Raceways. The number of conductors installed in any raceway shall be no greater than the number for which the raceway is designed.

352-5. Extension through Walls and Floors. It shall be permissible to extend unbroken lengths of metal surface raceways through dry walls, dry partitions, and dry floors.

See Section 353-3 for multioutlet assemblies.

352-6. Combination Raceways. Where combination metal surface raceways are used both for signaling and for lighting and power circuits, the different systems shall be run in separate compartments identified by sharply contrasting colors of the interior finish, and the same relative position of compartments shall be maintained throughout the premises.

352-7. Splices and Taps. Splices and taps shall be permitted in metal surface raceway having a removable cover that is accessible after installation. The conductors, including splices and taps, shall not fill the raceway to more than 75 percent of its area at that point. Splices and taps in metal surface raceways without removable covers shall be made only in junction boxes. All splices and taps shall be made by approved methods.

352-8. Construction. Metal surface raceways shall be of such construction as will distinguish them from other raceways. Metal surface raceways and their elbows, couplings, and similar fittings shall be so designed that the sections can be electrically and mechanically coupled together without subjecting the wires to abrasion. Holes for screws or bolts inside the raceway shall be so designed that when screws or bolts are installed the heads will be flush with the metal surface.

Where covers and accessories of nonmetallic materials are used on metal raceways, they shall be approved for the purpose for which they are used.

▲ See Wiremold catalog No. 23 for additional information.

B. Nonmetallic Surface Raceways

352-21. Description. Part B of this Article shall apply to a type of nonmetalic surface raceway and fittings of suitable nonmetallic material that is resistant to moisture and chemical atmospheres. It shall also be flame-retardant, resistant to impact and crushing, resistant to distortion from heat under conditions likely to be encountered in service, and resistant to low-temperature effects.

352-22. Use. The use of nonmetallic surface raceways shall be permitted in dry locations. They shall not be used (1) where concealed; (2) where subject to severe physical damage unless approved for the purpose; (3) where 300 volts or more between conductors; (4) in hoistways; (5) in any hazardous location; (6) where subject to ambient temperatures exceeding 50°C; nor (7) for conductors whose insulation temperature exceeds 75°C.

352-23. Other Articles. Nonmetallic surface raceways shall comply with the applicable provisions of Article 300.

352-24. Size of Conductors. No conductor larger than that for which the raceway is designed shall be installed in nonmetallic surface raceway.

352-25. Number of Conductors in Raceways. The number of conductors installed in any raceway shall be no greater than the number for which the raceway is designed.

352-26. Combination Raceways. Where combination nonmetallic surface raceways are used both for signaling and for lighting and power circuits, the different systems shall be run in separate compartments, identified by printed legend or by sharply contrasting colors of the interior finish, and the same relative position of compartments shall be maintained throughout the premises.

352-27. General. Nonmetallic surface raceways shall be of such construction as will distinguish them from other raceways. Nonmetallic surface raceways and their elbows, couplings, and similar fittings shall be so designed that the sections can be mechanically coupled together without subjecting the wires to abrasion. Holes for screws or bolts inside the raceway shall be so designed that when screws or bolts are installed the heads will be flush with the nonmetallic surface.

ARTICLE 353. MULTIOUTLET ASSEMBLY

353-1. Other Articles. A multioutlet assembly shall comply with applicable provisions of Article 300.

See definition in Article 100.

▲ These assemblies are intended for surface mounting except that the metal type may be surrounded by the building finish or recessed so long as the front is not covered.

The nonmetallic type may be recessed in baseboards. In calculating the load for branch circuits supplying multioutlet assembly, see Sec. 220-2(c), Exception 1.

353-2. Use. The use of multioutlet assembly shall be permitted in dry locations. It shall not be installed: (1) where concealed, except that it shall be permissible to surround the back and sides of a metal multioutlet assembly by the building finish or recess a nonmetallic multioutlet assembly in a baseboard; (2) where subject to severe physical damage unless approved for the purpose; (3) where 300 volts or more between conductors unless the assembly is of metal having a thickness of not less than .040 inch; (4) where subject to corrosive vapors; (5) in hoistways; nor (6) in any hazardous locations.

353-3. Metal Multioutlet Assembly Through Dry Partitions. It shall be permissible to extend a metal multioutlet assembly through (not run within) dry partitions, if arrangements are made for removing the cap or cover on all exposed portions and no outlet is located within the partitions.

ARTICLE 354. UNDERFLOOR RACEWAYS

354-1. Other Articles. Underfloor raceways shall comply with the applicable provisions of Article 300.

354-2. Use. The installation of underfloor raceways shall be permitted beneath the surface of concrete or other flooring material or in office occupancies, where laid flush with the concrete floor and covered with linoleum or equivalent floor covering. Underfloor raceways shall not be installed (1) where subject to corrosive vapors, nor (2) in any hazardous location. Unless made of a material judged suitable for the condition or unless corrosion protection approved for the condition is provided, ferrous or nonferrous metal underfloor raceways, junction boxes, and fittings shall not be installed in concrete; or in areas subject to severe corrosive influences.

▲ Underfloor raceway was developed to provide a practical means of bringing conductors for lighting, power, and signaling systems to office desks and tables. It is also used in large retail stores, making it possible to secure connections for display-case lighting at any desired location.

This wiring method makes it possible to place a desk or table in any location where it will always be over, or very near to, a duct line. The wiring method for lighting and power between cabinets and the raceway junction boxes may be conduit, underfloor raceway, wall elbows and cabinet connectors.

354-3. Covering. Raceway coverings shall comply with (a) through (d) below.

(a) Raceways Not Over 4 Inches Wide. Half-round and flat-top raceways not over 4 inches in width shall have not less than $\frac{3}{4}$ inch of concrete or wood above the raceway.

Exception: As permitted in (c) below for flat-top raceways.

(b) Raceways Over 4 Inches Wide But Not Over 8 Inches Wide. Flat top raceways over 4 but not over 8 inches wide with a minimum of one inch spacing between raceways shall be covered with concrete to a depth of not less than one inch. Raceways spaced less than one inch apart shall be covered with concrete to a depth of $1\frac{1}{2}$ inches.

(c) Trench-Type Raceways Flush with Concrete. Trench-type flush raceways with removable covers shall be permitted to be laid flush with the floor surface. Such approved raceways shall be so designed that the cover plates will provide adequate mechanical protection and rigidity equivalent to junction box covers.

(d) Other Raceways Flush with Concrete. In office occupancies, approved metal flat-top raceways, if not over 4 inches in width, shall be permitted to be laid flush with the concrete floor surface provided they are covered with substantial linoleum not less than $\frac{1}{16}$ inch in thickness or with equivalent floor covering. Where more than one and not more than three single raceways are each installed flush with the concrete they shall be contiguous with each other and joined to form a rigid assembly.

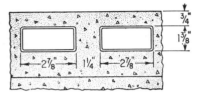

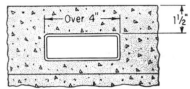

Fig. 354-1. Nepcoduct metal raceway. A $\frac{3}{4}$-in. wood or concrete covering is required. See Sec. 354-3(a). (*National Electric Division, H. K. Porter Company, Inc.*)

Fig. 354-2. Any flat-top raceway over 4 in. wide and spaced less than 1 in. from another raceway must be covered with concrete at least $1\frac{1}{2}$ in. in thickness. See Sec. 354-3(b). (*National Electric Division, H. K. Porter Company, Inc.*)

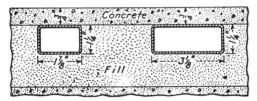

Fig. 354-3. Walker All-Steel metal raceway. A $\frac{3}{4}$-in. wood or concrete covering is required except for trench-type flush raceways covered in Sec. 354-3(c). (*Walker Bros.*)

▲ The intent in paragraphs (a) and (b) is to provide a sufficient amount of concrete over the ducts to prevent cracks in a cement, tile, or similar floor finish.

354-4. Size of Conductors. No conductor larger than that for which the raceway is designed shall be installed in underfloor raceways.

354-5. Maximum Number of Conductors in Raceway. The combined cross-sectional area of all conductors or cables shall not exceed 40 percent of the interior cross-sectional area of the raceway.

354-6. Splices and Taps. Splices and taps shall be made only in junction boxes. For the purposes of this Section, so-called loop wiring (continuous, unbroken conductor connecting the individual outlets) shall not be considered to be a splice or tap.

▲ The second paragraph recognizes "loop wiring" where "unbroken" wires extend from underfloor raceways to terminals of attached receptacles, and then back into the raceway to the other outlets. See Fig. 354-4.

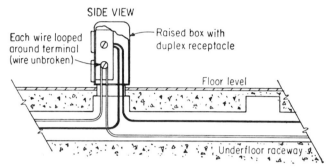

FIG. 354-4. "Loop" method permitted at outlets supplied from underfloor raceways.

354-7. Discontinued Outlets. When an outlet is abandoned, discontinued, or removed, the sections of circuit conductors supplying the outlet shall be removed from the raceway. No splices or reinsulated conductors, such as would be the case with abandoned outlets on loop wiring, shall be allowed in raceways.

354-8. Laid in Straight Lines. Underfloor raceways shall be laid so that a straight line from the center of one junction box to the center of the next junction box will coincide with the center line of the raceway system. Raceways shall be firmly held in place to prevent disturbing this alignment during construction.

354-9. Markers at Ends. A suitable marker shall be installed at or near each end of each straight run of raceways to locate the last insert.

354-10. Dead Ends. Dead ends of raceways shall be closed.

354-13. Junction Boxes. Junction boxes shall be leveled to the floor grade and sealed to prevent the free entrance of water or concrete. Junction boxes used with metal raceways shall be metal and shall be electrically continuous with the raceways.

354-14. Inserts. Inserts shall be leveled and sealed to prevent the entrance of concrete. Inserts used with metal raceways shall be metal and shall be electrically continuous with the raceway. Inserts set in or on fiber raceways before the floor is laid shall be mechanically secured to the raceway. Inserts set in fiber raceways after the floor is laid shall be screwed into the raceway. In cutting through the raceway wall and setting inserts, chips and other dirt shall not be allowed to remain in the raceway, and tools shall be used that are so designed as to prevent the tool from entering the raceway and injuring conductors that may be in place.

354-15. Connections to Cabinets and Wall Outlets. Connections between raceways and distribution centers and wall outlets shall be made by means of flexible metal conduit when not installed in concrete, rigid metal conduit, intermediate metal conduit, electrical metallic tubing, or fittings approved for the purpose.

ARTICLE 356. CELLULAR METAL
FLOOR RACEWAYS

356-1. Definitions. For the purposes of this Article, a "cellular metal floor raceway" shall be defined as the hollow spaces of cellular metal floors, together with suitable fittings, which may be approved as enclosures for electric conductors; a "cell" shall be defined as a single, enclosed tubular space in a cellular metal floor member, the axis of the cell being parallel to the axis of the metal floor member; a "header" shall be defined as a transverse raceway for electric conductors, providing access to predetermined cells of a cellular metal floor, thereby permitting the installation of electric conductors from a distribution center to the cells.

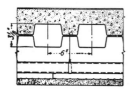

Fig. 356-1. Cross section of floor showing one type of cellular metal floor construction. (*H. H. Robertson Co.*)

▲ This is a type of floor construction designed for use in steel-frame buildings in which the members supporting the floor between the beams consist of sheet steel rolled into shapes which are so combined as to form cells, or closed passageways, extending across the building. The cells are of various shapes and sizes, depending upon the structural strength required.

The cellular members in this type of floor construction form raceways. A cross-sectional view of one type of cellular metal floor is shown in Fig. 356-1. Figure 356-2 shows a part of a building under construction, with the cellular metal floor in place and before the concrete covering over the steel members has been applied. See Fig. 356-5 for a typical installation of trench header duct.

356-2. Use. Conductors shall not be installed in cellular metal floor raceways (1) where subject to corrosive vapor; (2) in any hazardous location; nor (3) in commercial garages, other than for supplying ceiling outlets or extensions to the area below the floor but not above. No electric conductors shall be installed in any cell or header that contains a pipe for steam, water, air, gas, drainage, or any service other than electrical.

356-3. Other Articles. Cellular metal floor raceways shall comply with the applicable provisions of Article 300.

A. Installation

356-4. Size of Conductors. No conductor larger than No. 1/0 shall be installed, except by special permission.

356-5. Maximum Number of Conductors in Raceway. The combined cross-

FIG. 356-2. Cellular metal floor in place in a building under construction. (*H. H. Robertson Co.*)

sectional area of all conductors or cables shall not exceed 40 percent of the interior cross-sectional area of the cell or header.

▲ Connections to the ducts are made by means of *headers* extending across the cells. A header connects only to those cells which are to be used as raceways for conductors. Two or three separate headers, connecting to different sets of cells, may be used for different systems; for example, for light and power, signaling systems, and public telephones.

Figure 356-3 shows the cells, or ducts, with a header in place. By means of a special elbow fitting the header is extended up to a cabinet or distribution center on a wall or column. A junction box or access fitting is provided at each point where the header crosses a cell to which it connects.

356-6. Splices and Taps.   Splices and taps shall be made only in header access units or junction boxes.

For the purposes of this Section, so-called loop wiring (continuous unbroken conductor connecting the individual outlets) shall not be considered to be a splice or tap.

▲ See Fig. 354-4.

356-7. Discontinued Outlets.   When an outlet is abandoned, discontinued, or removed, the sections of circuit conductors supplying the outlet shall be removed from the raceway. No splices or reinsulated conductors, such as would be the case with abandoned outlets on loop wiring, shall be allowed in raceways.

356-8. Markers.   A suitable number of markers shall be installed for the future locating of cells.

▲ The markers used with this system consist of special flat-head brass screws, screwed into the upper side of the cells and with their heads flush with the floor finish.

Fig. 356-3. Header connecting to cells, junction boxes, and special fitting for connecting the header to a cabinet. (*H. H. Robertson Co.*)

356-9. Junction Boxes. Junction boxes shall be leveled to the floor grade and sealed against the free entrance of water or concrete. Junction boxes used with these raceways shall be of metal and shall be electrically continuous with the raceway.

▲ The fittings with round covers shown in Figs. 356-2 and 356-3 are termed "access fittings" by the manufacturer but actually serve as junction boxes. Where additional junction boxes are needed, a similar fitting of larger size is provided which may be attached to a cell at any point.

356-10. Inserts. Inserts shall be leveled to the floor grade and sealed against the entrance of concrete. Inserts shall be of metal and shall be electrically continuous with the raceway. In cutting through the cell wall and setting inserts, chips and other dirt shall not be allowed to remain in the raceway, and tools shall be used that are designed to prevent the tool from entering the cell and injuring the conductors.

▲ The construction of an insert is shown in Fig. 356-4. A $1\frac{5}{8}$-in.-diameter hole is cut in the top of the cell with a special tool. The lower end of the insert is provided with coarse threads of such form that the insert can be screwed into the hole in the cell, thus forming a substantial mechanical and electrical connection.

The fitting used for connecting a header to a cabinet is shown in Fig. 356-3. Junction boxes can be obtained with integral hubs to receive rigid conduit so that, if desired, the connections to cabinets can be made with conduit, or conduit may be run from junction boxes to wall outlets.

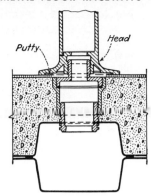

FIG. 356-4. Construction of insert used with cellular metal floor raceway. (*H. H. Robertson Co.*)

356-11. Connection to Cabinets and Extensions from Cells. Connections between raceways and distribution centers and wall outlets shall be made by means of flexible metal conduit when not installed in concrete, rigid metal conduit, intermediate metal conduit, electrical metallic tubing, or fittings approved for the purpose.

B. Construction Specifications

356-12. General. Cellular metal floor raceways shall be so constructed that adequate electrical and mechanical continuity of the complete system will be secured. They shall provide a complete enclosure for the conductors. The interior surfaces shall be free from burrs and sharp edges, and surfaces over which conductors are drawn shall be smooth. Suitable bushings or fittings having smooth rounded edges shall be provided where conductors pass.

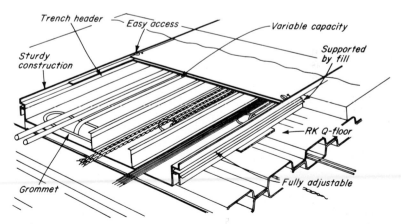

FIG. 356-5. Trench header duct used for cellular-metal-floor raceway. (*American Electricians' Handbook.*)

ARTICLE 358. CELLULAR CONCRETE
FLOOR RACEWAYS

358-1. Scope. Approved precast cellular concrete floor raceways shall comply with the applicable provisions of Article 300. For the purpose of this Article, "precast cellular concrete floor raceways" shall be defined as the hollow spaces in floors constructed of precast cellular concrete slabs, together with suitable metal fittings designed to provide access to the floor cells in an approved manner. A "cell" shall be defined as a single, enclosed tubular space in a floor made of precast cellular concrete slabs, the direction of the cell being parallel to the direction of the floor member. A "header" shall be defined as transverse metal raceways for electric conductors, providing access to predetermined cells of a precast cellular concrete floor, thereby permitting the installation of electric conductors from a distribution center to the floor cells.

▲ The term *precast cellular concrete floor* refers to a type of floor construction designed for use in steel frame, concrete frame, and wall bearing construction, in which the monolithically precast reinforced concrete floor members form the structural floor and are supported by beams or bearing walls. The floor members are precast with hollow voids which form smooth round cells. The cells are of various sizes depending on the size of floor member used.

The cells form raceways which by means of suitable fittings can be adapted for use as underfloor raceways. Figure 358-1 shows a building under construction with precast cellular concrete floor in place. This floor is fire-resistant and requires no additional fireproofing.

The trench header duct shown in Fig. 356-5 is similar to those used with cellular concrete floor raceways.

Fig. 358-1. Precast cellular concrete floor erected on steel frame. (*The Flexicore Co., Inc.*)

358-2. Use. Conductors shall not be installed in precast cellular concrete floor raceways (1) where subject to corrosive vapor; (2) in hazardous locations; nor (3) in commercial garages, other than for supplying ceiling outlets or extensions to the area below the floor but not above. No electric conductors shall be installed in any cell or header that contains a pipe for steam, water, air, gas, drainage, or any service other than electrical.

358-3. Header. The header shall be installed in a straight line, at right angles to the cells. The header shall be mechanically secured to the top of the precast cellular concrete floor. The end joints shall be closed by a metallic closure fitting and sealed against the entrance of concrete. The header shall be electrically continuous throughout its entire length and shall be electrically bonded to the enclosure of the distribution center.

358-4. Connection to Cabinets and Other Enclosures. Connections from headers to cabinets and other enclosures shall be made by means of metal raceways and fittings approved for the purpose.

358-5. Junction Boxes. Junction boxes shall be leveled to the floor grade and sealed against the free entrance of water or concrete. Junction boxes shall be of metal and shall be mechanically and electrically continuous with the header.

▲ Connections to the cells are made by means of *headers* extending from cabinets and across the cells. A header connects only those cells which are used as raceways for conductors. Two or three separate headers, connected to different sets of cells, may be used for different systems; for example, for light and power, signaling, and telephones.

Figure 358-2 shows three headers installed, each header connecting a cabinet with separate groups of cells. Special elbows extend the header to the cabinet.

Figure 358-3 shows a junction box where a header connects to a cell.

358-6. Markers. A suitable number of markers shall be installed for the future locating of cells.

▲ Markers used with this system are special flat-head brass screws which are installed level with the finished floor. One type of marker marks the location of an access point between a header and a spare cell reserved for, but not connected to, the header. A junction box can be installed at the point located by the marker if the spare cell is needed in the future. The screw for this type marker is installed in the center of a special knockout provided in the top of the header at the access point. The second type of marker is installed over the center of cells at various points on the floor to locate and identify the cells below. Screws with specially designed heads identify the type of service in the cell.

358-7. Inserts. Inserts shall be leveled and sealed against the entrance of concrete. Inserts shall be of metal and shall be fitted with receptacles of the grounded type. A grounding conductor shall connect the insert receptacles to a positive ground connection provided on the header. In cutting through the cell wall for setting inserts or other purposes (such as providing access openings between header and cells), chips and other dirt shall not be allowed to remain in the raceway, and the tool used shall be so designed as to prevent the tool from entering the cell and injuring the conductors.

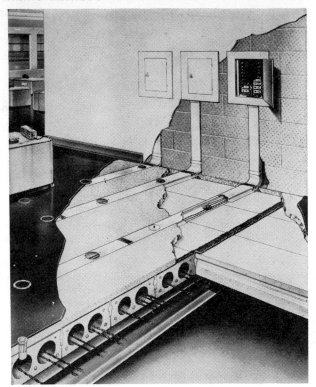

FIG. 358-2. Headers connecting wall cabinets to cells in floor. (*The Conduflor Corporation.*)

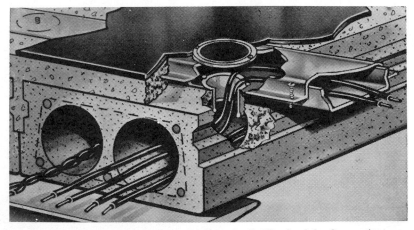

FIG. 358-3. Junction box connecting header and cell. (*The Conduflor Corporation.*)

▲ A 1⅞-in.-diameter hole is cut through the floor and into the center of a cell with a concrete drill bit. A plug is driven into the hole and a nipple is screwed into the plug. The nipple is designed to receive an outlet with a duplex electrical receptacle or an outlet designed for a telephone or signal system.

358-8. Size of Conductors. No conductor larger than No. 1/0 shall be installed, except by special permission.

358-9. Maximum Number of Conductors. The combined cross-sectional area of all conductors or cables shall not exceed 40 percent of the cross-sectional area of the cell or header.

358-10. Splices and Taps. Splices and taps shall be made only in header access units or junction boxes.

For the purpose of this Section, so-called loop wiring (continuous unbroken conductor connecting the individual outlets) shall not be considered to be a splice or tap.

358-11. Discontinued Outlets. When an outlet is abandoned, discontinued, or removed, the sections of circuit conductors supplying the outlet shall be removed from the raceway. No splices or reinsulated conductors, such as would be the case with abandoned outlets on loop wiring, shall be allowed in raceways.

ARTICLE 362. WIREWAYS

362-1. Definition. Wireways are sheet-metal troughs with hinged or removable covers for housing and protecting electric wires and cable and in which conductors are laid in place after the wireway has been installed as a complete system.

▲ Wireways are sheet-metal troughs in which conductors are laid in place after the wireway has been installed as a complete system. Figure 362-1 shows a length of wireway, as made by one manufacturer, furnished in lengths of 5 ft. Sections 1 and 2 ft long may also be obtained, so that runs of any exact number of feet can be made up without cutting the duct. The cover may be a hinged or removable type. Unlike auxiliary gutters, wireways represent a type of wiring, because they are used to carry conductors between points located considerable distances apart.

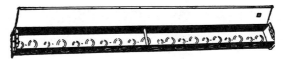

Fig. 362-1. A length of wireway with hinged cover. (*Square D Co.*)

The purpose of a wireway is to provide a flexible system of wiring in which the circuits can be changed to meet changing conditions, and one of its principal uses is for exposed work in industrial plants. Wireways are also used to carry control wires from the control board to remotely controlled stage switchboard equipment. A wireway

FIG. 362-2. An installation of wireway.

is approved for any voltage not exceeding 600 V between conductors or 600 V to ground. See comments following Sec. 374-1. An installation of wireway is shown in Fig. 362-2.

362-2. Use.   Wireways shall be permitted only for exposed work. Wireways intended for outdoor use shall be of approved raintight construction. Wireways shall not be installed: (1) where subject to severe physical damage or corrosive vapor; nor (2) in any hazardous location, except Class II, Division 2 locations as permitted in Section 502-4(b).

362-3. Other Articles.   Installations of wireways shall comply with the applicable provisions of Article 300.

362-4. Size of Conductors.   No conductor larger than that for which the wireway is designed shall be installed in any wireway.

362-5. Number of Conductors.   Wireways shall not contain more than 30 current-carrying conductors at any cross section. The sum of the cross-sectional areas of all contained conductors at any cross section of a wireway shall not exceed 20 percent of the interior cross-sectional area of the wireway.

Exception No. 1: As provided in Section 620-32 for elevators, dumb-waiters, etc. The correction factors specified in Note 8 to Tables 310-16 through 310-19 shall not be considered applicable to the foregoing.

Exception No. 2: Conductors for signaling circuits or controller conductors between a motor and its starter and used only for starting duty shall not be considered as current-carrying conductors.

Exception No. 3: When the correction factors specified in Note 8 of Tables 310-16 through 310-19 are applied, the number of current-carrying conductors shall not be limited, but the sum of the cross-sectional areas of all contained conductors at any cross section of the wireway shall not exceed 20 percent of the interior cross-sectional area of the wireway.

Exception No. 4: As provided in Section 520-5 for theaters and similar locations.

362-6. Splices and Taps. Splices and taps shall be permitted within a wireway provided they are accessible. The conductors, including splices and taps, shall not fill the wireway to more than 75 percent of its area at that point.

▲ The conductors should be reasonably accessible so that any circuit can be replaced with conductors of a different size if necessary and so that taps can readily be made to supply motors or other equipment. Accessibility is ensured by limiting the number of conductors and the space they occupy as provided in Secs. 362-5 and 362-6.

The cross-sectional areas of rubber- and thermoplastic-insulated conductors of all common sizes are given in Table 5, Chap. 9.

362-7. Supports. Wireways shall be securely supported at intervals not exceeding 5 feet, unless specially approved for supports at greater intervals, but in no case shall the distance between supports exceed 10 feet.

Exception: Vertical runs of wireways shall be securely supported at intervals not exceeding 15 feet and shall have not more than one joint between supports. Adjoining wireway sections shall be securely fastened together to provide a rigid joint.

362-8. Extension Through Walls. Unbroken lengths of wireway shall be permitted to pass transversely through walls if in unbroken lengths where passing through.

362-9. Dead Ends. Dead ends of wireways shall be closed.

362-10. Extensions From Wireways. Extensions from wireways shall be made with rigid or flexible metal conduit, intermediate metal conduit, electrical metallic tubing, metal surface raceway, or metal-clad cable.

▲ Knockouts are provided so that circuits can be run to motors or other apparatus at any point.

Sections of wireways are joined to one another by means of flanges which are bolted together, thus providing rigid mechanical connection and electrical continuity. Fittings with bolted flanges are provided for elbows, tees, and crosses, and for connections to cabinets. See Sec. 250-91(b).

362-11. Marking. Wireways shall be marked so that their manufacturer's name or trademark will be visible after installation.

ARTICLE 363. FLAT CABLE ASSEMBLIES

Type FC

363-1. Definition.   Type FC, a flat cable assembly, is an assembly of parallel conductors formed integrally with an insulating material web specifically designed for field installation in metal surface raceway approved for the purpose.

▲ Type FC cable is a flat assembly with three or four parallel No. 10 special stranded copper conductors. The assembly is installed in an approved U-channel surface metal raceway with one side open. Then tap devices can be inserted anywhere along the run. Connections from tap devices to the flat cable assembly are made by "pin-type" contacts when the tap devices are fastened in place. The pin-type contacts penetrate the insulation of the cable assembly and contact the multistranded conductors in a matched phase sequence (phase 1 to neutral, phase 2 to neutral, and phase 3 to neutral).

Covers are required when the installation is less than 8 ft from the floor. The maximum branch-circuit rating is 30 A.

Figures 363-1 and 363-2 show the basic components of this wiring method.

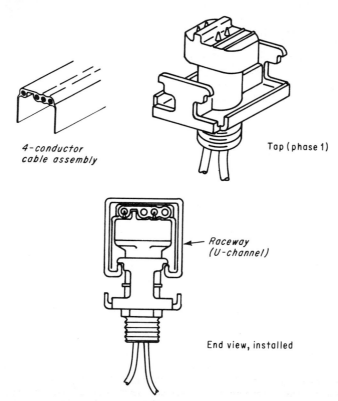

4-conductor cable assembly

Tap (phase 1)

Raceway (U-channel)

End view, installed

Fɪɢ. 363-1. Basic components of flat cable assembly system. (*Insul-8-Corp.*)

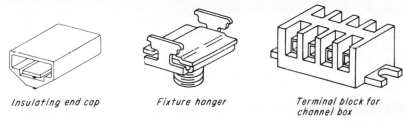

Insulating end cap   *Fixture hanger*   *Terminal block for channel box*

Fig. 363-2. Miscellaneous fittings for use with flat cable assemblies. (*Insul-8-Corp.*)

363-2. Other Articles. In addition to the provisions of this Article, installation of Type FC cable shall conform with the applicable provisions of Articles 210, 220, 250, 300, 310 and 352.

363-3. Uses Permitted. Flat cable assemblies shall be permitted only as branch circuits to supply suitable tap devices for lighting, small appliances, or small power loads. Flat cable assemblies shall be installed for exposed work only. Flat cable assemblies shall be installed in locations where they will not be subjected to severe physical damage.

363-4. Uses Not Permitted. Flat cable assemblies shall not be installed: (1) where subject to corrosive vapors unless specifically approved for the purpose; (2) in hoistways; (3) in any hazardous location; or (4) outdoors or in wet or damp locations unless specifically approved for the purpose.

363-5. Installation. Flat cable assemblies shall be installed in the field only in metal surface raceways approved for the purpose. The channel portion of the metal surface raceway systems shall be installed as complete systems before the flat cable assemblies are pulled into the raceways.

363-6. Number of Conductors. The flat cable assemblies shall consist of either 2, 3, or 4 conductors.

363-7. Size of Conductors. Flat cable assemblies shall have conductors of No. 10 special stranded copper wires.

363-8. Conductor Insulation. The entire flat cable assembly shall be formed to provide a suitable insulation covering all of the conductors and using one of the materials recognized in Table 310-13 for general branch-circuit wiring.

363-9. Splices. Splices shall be made in approved junction boxes using approved terminal blocks.

363-10. Taps. Taps shall be made only between any phase conductor and the neutral by means of devices and fittings approved for the purpose. Tap devices shall be rated at not less than 15 amperes or more than 300 volts, and they shall be color-coded in accordance with the requirements of Section 363-20.

363-11. Dead Ends. Each flat cable assembly dead end shall be terminated in an end-cap device approved for the purpose.

The dead-end fitting for the enclosing metal surface raceway shall be approved for the purpose.

363-12. Fixture Hangers. Fixture hangers installed with the flat cable assemblies shall be approved for the purpose.

363-13. Fittings. Fittings to be installed with flat cable assemblies shall be designed and installed to prevent physical damage to the cable assemblies.

363-14. Extensions. All extensions from flat cable assemblies shall be made from the terminal blocks enclosed within the junction boxes, installed at either end of the flat cable assembly runs.

All extensions shall be made with wiring methods approved for the purpose.

363-15. Supports. The flat cable assemblies shall be supported by means of their special design features, within the metal surface raceways with which they are specifically approved to be used.

The metal surface raceways shall be supported as required for the specific raceway to be installed.

363-16. Rating. The rating of the branch circuit shall not exceed 30 amperes.

363-17. Marking. In addition to the provisions of Section 310-11, Type FC cable shall have the temperature rating durably marked on the surface at intervals not exceeding 24 inches.

363-18. Protective Covers. When a flat cable assembly is installed less than 8 feet from the floor, it shall be protected by a metal cover approved for the purpose.

363-19. Identification. The neutral conductor shall be identified throughout its length by means of a distinctive and durable white or natural gray marking.

363-20. Terminal Block Identification. Terminal blocks approved for the purpose shall have distinctive and durable markings for color or word coding. The neutral section shall have a white marking or other suitable designation. The next adjacent section of the terminal block shall have a black marking or other suitable designation. The next section shall have a red marking or other suitable designation. The final or outer section, opposite the neutral section of the terminal block, shall have a blue marking or other suitable designation.

ARTICLE 364. BUSWAYS

A. General Requirements

364-1. Other Articles. Installations of busways shall comply with the applicable provisions of Article 300.

▲ A busway consists of a sheet-metal trough containing busbars of copper or aluminum insulated from each other and the enclosure. With some busways provision is made for plug-in units for taking current from the busbars.

Figure 364-2 is a cross-sectional view of a small busway known as "Trol-E-Duct," with a trolley in place. The duct is formed from a single piece of sheet steel. This type of busway has an ampacity of 50 A and is used for the supply of portable motor-driven tools or portable lamps through a cord connected to the busway by means of the trolley. Connection may also be made by means of the stationary plug-in device shown in Fig. 364-3 where lamps or motor need not be portable but flexibility in location is desirable.

Busways are necessarily made up in the shop or factory as a complete assembly in sections ready to be bolted together. The sections are commonly 10 ft or longer. Special sections are made to exact dimensions for terminals at switchboards and cabinets and where changes in direction are necessary.

364-2. Use.

(a) Use Permitted. Busways may be installed only where located in the open and are visible.

Exception: Busways shall be permitted to be installed behind panels if means of access are provided and if all the following conditions are met:

(1) No overcurrent devices are installed on the busway other than for an individual fixture.

(2) The space behind the access panels is not used for air handling purposes.

(3) The busway is totally enclosed, non-ventilating type.

(4) Busway is so installed that the joints between sections and fittings are accessible for maintenance purposes.

(b) Use Prohibited. Busways shall not be installed: (1) where subject to severe physical damage or corrosive vapors; (2) in hoistways; (3) in any hazardous location, unless specifically approved for such use (see Section 501-4(b); nor (4) outdoors or in wet or damp locations unless specifically approved for the purpose.

Where secondary systems are operated ungrounded, a combination ground detector and potentializer plug shall be permitted to be used as an auxiliary fitting for busway systems to establish a definite potential difference between the busbars and the grounded casing of the busways. This will serve to drain off any static or other charge from the entire busway system, including its connected apparatus, supply, and branch-circuit conductors.

▲ Busways are to be installed only where they will be open and visible. The Exception notes the conditions under which busways may be located behind panels. This requirement is not only to ensure that the busway is accessible but also that the heat developed by the busway can be properly dissipated. Because busway ampacity is based on the allowable temperature rise of the conductors, it is necessary to ascertain whether the space in which the busway is to be installed is suitable for the intended application. The maximum rating of listed busway is 600 V. Busway is marked for its intended use, for example, Lighting Busway, Continuous Plug-in Busway, Trolley Busway, etc.

The principal use for busways is in industrial plants, but they are also used in lieu of conduit and insulated conductors for feeders in high rise and commercial buildings.

On ungrounded power systems it has been found that in some cases an abnormal potential is built up on one of the conductors, which may be high enough to cause a flashover at some point on the system. To overcome this difficulty, a device has been developed known as a *potentializer plug,* which is designed as a complete assembly in a sheet metal enclosure with suitable contacts so that it can be plugged into a busway. The assembly contains three 18,000-ohm resistors connected as shown in Fig. 364-1. This serves to maintain each of the conductors at a normal potential to ground.

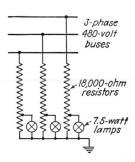

FIG. 364-1. Potentializer plug—
diagram of connections. (*I-T-E
Imperial Corp.*)

Each resistor is tapped at the proper point to provide 120 V between the tap and the ground, and three 7.5-W incandescent lamps, connected as shown in the diagram, serve as ground detectors.

364-3. Support. Busway shall be securely supported at intervals not exceeding 5 feet.

Exception No. 1: Horizontally mounted busway approved for the purpose and so marked shall be securely supported at intervals not exceeding 10 feet.

Exception No. 2: Vertically mounted busway approved for the purpose and so marked shall be securely supported at each floor but in no case at intervals exceeding 16 feet.

364-4. Through Walls and Floors. It shall be permissible to extend unbroken lengths of busway through dry walls. It shall be permissible to extend busways vertically through dry floors if totally enclosed (unventilated) where passing through and for a minimum distance of 6 feet above the floor to provide adequate protection from physical damage.

364-5. Dead Ends. A dead end of a busway shall be closed.

364-7. Branches from Busways. Branches from busways shall be made with busways, rigid or flexible metal conduit, electrical metallic tubing, metal surface raceway or metal-clad cable; or with suitable cord assemblies approved for hard usage for the connection of portable equipment or for the connection of stationary equipment to facilitate their interchange.

364-8. Overcurrent Protection. Overcurrent protection shall be provided in accordance with Sections 364-9 through 364-13.

364-9. Rating of Overcurrent Protection—Feeders and Sub-Feeders. Where the allowable current rating of the busway does not correspond to a standard rating of the overcurrent device, the next higher rating shall be permitted.

▲ The rated ampacity of a busway is fixed by the allowable temperature rise of the conductors. The ampacity can be determined in the field only by reference to the nameplate.

364-10. Reduction in Size of Busway. Omission of overcurrent protection shall be permitted at points where busways are reduced in size, provided that the smaller busway does not extend more than 50 feet and has a current rating at least equal to 1/3 the rating or setting of the overcurrent device next back on the line, and provided further that such busway is free from contact with combustible material.

▲ Where the smaller busway is kept within the limits specified, the hazards involved are very slight and the additional cost of providing overcurrent protection at the point where the size is changed is not considered as being warranted.

364-11. Sub-Feeder or Branch Circuits. Where a busway is used as a feeder, devices or plug-in connections for tapping off sub-feeder or branch circuits from the busway shall contain the overcurrent devices required for the protection of the sub-feeder or branch circuits. The plug-in device shall consist of an externally operable circuit breaker or an externally operable fusible switch. Where such devices are mounted out of reach and contain disconnecting means, suitable means such

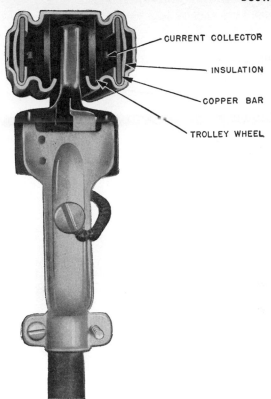

CURRENT COLLECTOR

INSULATION

COPPER BAR

TROLLEY WHEEL

FIG. 364-2. Cross-sectional view of Trol-E-Duct 50-A busway with trolley in place. (*I-T-E Imperial Corp.*)

as ropes, chains or sticks shall be provided for operating the disconnecting means from the floor.

Exception No. 1: As permitted in Section 240-21 for taps.

Exception No. 2: For fixed or semi-fixed lighting fixtures, where the branch-circuit overcurrent device is part of the fixture cord plug on cord-connected fixtures.

Exception No. 3: Where fixtures without cords are plugged directly into the busway and the overcurrent device is mounted on the fixture.

▲ **The busway shown in Fig. 364-2 has an ampacity of 50 and can therefore be used as a 15-, 20-, 30-, 40-, or 50-A branch circuit, depending upon the rating or setting of the overcurrent device protecting the conductors of the busway. Appliances may be connected directly to the busway without individual overcurrent protection where permitted by Sec. 210-23, provided that, in the case of motor-driven appliances, all applicable rules of Art. 430 are complied with.**

SUPPORT BRACKET

CURRENT COLLECTOR

INSULATION

COPPER BAR

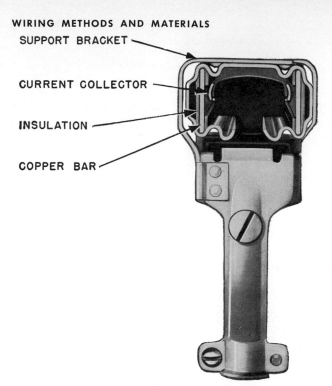

FIG. 364-3. Stationary plug-in device for use in place of trolley shown in Fig. 364-2. (*I-T-E Imperial Corp.*)

364-12. Rating of Overcurrent Protection—Branch Circuits. A busway shall be permitted as a branch circuit of any one of the types described in Artcle 210. When so used, the rating or setting of the overcurrent device protecting the busway shall determine the ampere rating of the branch circuit, and the circuit shall in all respects conform with the requirements of Article 210 that apply to branch circuits of that rating.

364-13. Length of Busways Used As Branch Circuits. Busways which are used as branch circuits and which are so designed that loads can be connected at any point shall be limited to such lengths as will provide that in normal use the circuits will not be overloaded.

▲ A busway used as a branch circuit is usually installed for a specific purpose, and the probable maximum load to be supplied by the circuit can be estimated without difficulty.

364-14. Marking. Busways shall be marked with the voltage and current rating for which they are designed, and with the manufacturer's name or trademark in such manner as to be visible after installation.

B. Requirements For Over 600 Volts, Nominal

364-21. Identification. Each bus run shall be provided with a permanent nameplate on which the following information shall be provided:

(a) Rated voltage.

(b) Rated continuous current; if bus is forced-cooled, both the normal forced-cooled rating and the self-cooled (not forced-cooled) rating for the same temperature rise shall be given.

(c) Rated frequency.

(d) Rated impulse withstand voltage.

(e) Rated 60-Hz withstand voltage (dry).

(f) Rated momentary current.

(g) Manufacturer's name or trademark.

Metal-enclosed buses shall be constructed and tested in accordance with ANSI C37.20 1969.

364-22. Grounding. Metal-enclosed bus shall be grounded in accordance with Article 250.

364-23. Adjacent and Supporting Structures. Metal-enclosed busways shall be installed so that temperature rise from induced circulating currents in any adjacent metallic parts will not be hazardous to personnel or constitute a fire hazard.

364-24. Neutral. Neutral bus, where required, shall be sized to carry all neutral load current, including harmonic currents, and shall have adequate momentary and short-circuit rating consistent with system requirements.

364-25. Barriers and Seals. Bus runs having sections located both inside and outside of buildings shall have a vapor seal at the building wall to prevent interchange of air between indoor and outdoor sections.

Exception: Vapor seals not required in forced-cooled bus. Fire barriers shall be provided where fire walls, floors, or ceilings are penetrated.

364-26. Drain Facilities. Drain plugs, filter drains, or similar methods shall be provided to remove condensed moisture from low points in bus run.

364-27. Ventilated Bus Enclosures. Ventilated bus enclosures shall be installed in accordance with Article 710 Part D, unless designed so that foreign objects inserted through any opening will be deflected from energized parts.

364-28. Terminations and Connections. Where bus enclosures terminate at machines cooled by flammable gas, seal-off bushings, baffles, or other means shall be provided to prevent accumulation of flammable gas in the bus enclosures.

Flexible or expansion connections shall be provided in long, straight runs of bus to allow for temperature expansion or contraction, or where the bus run crosses building vibration insulation joints.

All conductor termination and connection hardware shall be accessible for installation, connection, and maintenance.

364-29. Switches. Switching devices or disconnecting links provided in the bus run shall have the same momentary rating as the bus. Disconnecting links shall be plainly marked to be removable only when bus is de-energized. Switching devices which are not load break shall be interlocked to prevent operation under load and disconnecting link enclosures shall be interlocked to prevent access to energized parts.

364-30. Low-Voltage Wiring. Secondary control devices and wiring which are provided as part of the metal-enclosed bus run shall be insulated by fire-retardant barriers from all primary circuit elements with the exception of short lengths of wire, such as at instrument transformer terminals.

ARTICLE 365. CABLEBUS

365-1. Definition. Cablebus is an approved assembly of insulated conductors with fittings and conductor terminations in a completely enclosed, ventilated protective metal housing. The assembly is designed to carry fault current and to withstand the magnetic forces of such current. Cablebus shall be permitted at any voltage or current for which the spaced conductors are rated.

Cablebus is ordinarily assembled at the point of installation from components furnished or specified by the manufacturer in accordance with instructions for the specific job.

▲ Cablebus framework is installed in a manner similar to cable tray support systems. Insulated conductors are supported on special insulating blocks at specified intervals in the framework. Finally, a removable (ventilated) top is attached to the framework. See Fig. 365-1.

365-2. Use. Cablebus shall be installed only for exposed work. Cablebus installed outdoors or in corrosive, wet, or damp locations shall be approved for the purpose. Cablebus shall not be installed in hoistways or in hazardous locations unless specifically approved for such use. Cablebus may be used for branch circuits, feeders, and services.

Cablebus framework, where adequately bonded, shall be permitted as the equipment grounding conductor for branch circuits and feeders.

365-3. Conductors.

(a) Types of Conductors. The current-carrying conductors in cablebus shall have an insulation rating of 75°C or higher of an approved type and suitable for the application in accordance with Articles 310 and 710.

(b) Ampacity of Conductors. The ampacity of conductors in cablebus shall be in accordance with Tables 310-17 and 319-19.

(c) Size and Number of Conductors. The size and number of conductors shall be that for which the cablebus is designed, and in no case smaller than No. 1/0.

(d) Conductor Supports. The insulated conductors shall be supported on blocks or other mounting means designed for the purpose.

The individual conductors in a cablebus shall be supported at intervals not greater than 3 feet for horizontal runs and $1\frac{1}{2}$ feet for vertical runs. Vertical and horizontal spacing between supported conductors shall not be less than one conductor diameter at the points of support.

365-5. Overcurrent Protection. When the allowable ampacity of cablebus conductors does not correspond to a standard rating of an overcurrent device, the next higher ampere rated overcurrent device shall be permitted.

365-6. Support and Extension Through Walls and Floors.

(a) Cablebus shall be securely supported at intervals not exceeding 12 feet.

Exception: Where spans longer than 12 feet are required, the structure shall be specifically designed for the required span length.

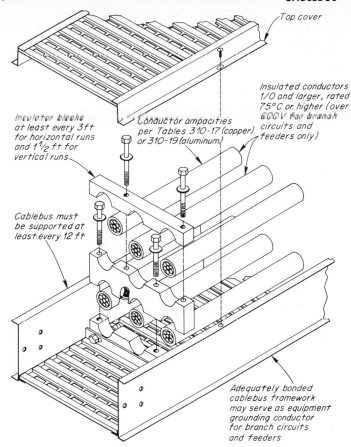

Top cover

Insulated conductors
1/0 and larger, rated
75°C or higher (over
600 V for branch
circuits and
feeders only)

Insulator blocks
at least every 3 ft
for horizontal runs
and 1½ ft for
vertical runs

Conductor ampacities
per Tables 310-17 (copper)
or 310-19 (aluminum)

Cablebus must
be supported at
least every 12 ft

Adequately bonded
cablebus framework
may serve as equipment
grounding conductor
for branch circuits
and feeders

FIG. 365-1. Cablebus.

(b) It shall be permissible to extend cablebus transversely through partitions or walls, other than fire walls, provided the section within the wall is continuous, protected against physical damage, and unventilated.

(c) Except where fire stops are required, it shall be permissible to extend cablebus vertically through dry floors and platforms, provided the cablebus is totally enclosed at the point where it passes through the floor or platform and for a distance of 6 feet above the floor or platform.

(d) Except where fire stops are required, it shall be permissible to extend cablebus vertically through floors and platforms in wet locations where (1) there are curbs or other suitable means to prevent waterflow through the floor or platform opening, and (2) where the cablebus is totally enclosed at the point where it passes through the floor or platform and for a distance of 6 feet above the floor or platform.

365-7. Fittings.   A cablebus system shall include approved fittings for:

(a) Changes in horizontal or vertical direction of the run.

(b) Dead ends.

(c) Terminations in or on connected apparatus or equipment or the enclosures for such equipment.

(d) Additional physical protection where required, such as guards for severe mechanical exposure.

365-8. Conductor Terminations.   Terminating means approved for the purpose shall be used for connections to cablebus conductors.

365-9. Grounding.   Sections of cablebus shall be electrically bonded either by inherent design of the mechanical joints or by applied bonding means.

See Section 250-75 for bonding of metal noncurrent-carrying parts.

A cablebus installation shall be grounded in accordance with Sections 250-32 and 250-33.

365-10. Marking.   Each section of cablebus shall be marked with the manufacturer's name or trade designation and the maximum diameter, number, voltage rating, and ampacity of the conductors to be installed. Markings shall be so located as to be visible after installation.

Fɪɢ. 365-2. A typical installation of cablebus. (*Husky Cabl-Bus.*)

ARTICLE 366. ELECTRICAL FLOOR ASSEMBLIES

A. General

366-1. Scope.   This Article covers a field-installed wiring system using electrically conductive panels and receptacle housing units for branch circuits, signaling circuits and communication circuits. The wiring system provides access into the panels and simultaneous conduction of power, signaling and communication.

▲ This article covers a field-installed wiring system using laminated panels containing sheets of electrical conducting and dielectric material. The electrical floor assembly is designed to provide random access for separate, or combinations of, power and signaling/communication systems. Receptacle units are installed and removed using special tools approved for the purpose.

The features of this total system's package provide power (120 V, 20 A, 60 Hz) and signal (telephone, audio, data control) on a random basis as required. Flexibility is the biggest advantage of this system. The electrical floor assembly uses modular panels, located beneath the floor covering, to carry both power and signal. The panels contain four conductive planes: two ground planes, a neutral plane, and a phase (hot) plane, insulated from each other in the form of a "sandwich" (see Fig. 366-1). The panels, sealed on all sides by a metallic, electrically grounded sheet, are connected to a standard 120 V, 20 A, 60 Hz branch-circuit panelboard power source, through a panel input unit located at the start of the string of panels.

Panels are electrically interconnected using screw-type terminations to form "power areas." Each power area is protected by a standard 20-A fuse or circuit breaker. The power areas typically are from 200 to 1,000 sq ft each, depending on individual needs.

366-2. Other Articles. In addition to the provisions of this Article, installation of the assembly shall conform with the applicable provisions of Articles 210, 220, 250, and 310.

The signaling and communication circuits used in conjunction with this assembly shall also conform to Article 725 and to Article 800.

366-3. Definitions.

(a) Panels. Laminated panels containing sheets of electrical conducting material separated by insulating material(s).

(b) Receptacle Housing Unit. A special housing designed for insertion into the panels and containing power and/or signaling/communication outlets and filtering as required.

(c) Signaling/Communications Receptacle Outlet. An outlet whose use is specifically limited to signaling and/or communications circuits.

(d) Termination Unit. A special unit which presents the proper impedance to the high-frequency signaling and communication circuits within the electrical floor assemblies without affecting the 60 Hertz power.

(e) Base Unit. That portion of the receptacle housing unit which contains terminal probes and means for terminating the various receptacle outlets.

(f) Terminal Probe. A special probe which makes contact only with the conductive sheet(s) with which it is designed to do so.

(g) Inter-Panel Connector. Connectors specifically designed with three conductors, one each for phase, neutral and grounding connections to interconnect the panels, and/or panel input units to panels, and/or termination units to panels.

(h) Panel Input Unit. A unit specifically designed to permit connections between panels and the power branch circuit and the signaling/communication circuits or for only power branch circuits whenever signaling/communications circuits are not used.

(i) Holddown Bar. A bar designed specifically to secure the floor panels in place on the floor.

366-4. Uses Permitted. Electrical floor assemblies shall be used only: (1) as branch circuits to supply lighting, small appliances, and small power loads; (2) to supply signaling circuits; and (3) to supply communication circuits.

366-5. Uses Not Permitted. Electrical floor assemblies shall not be installed: (1) where subject to corrosive vapors; (2) outdoors or in a wet or damp location; or (3) in any hazardous location.

366-6. Branch Circuit. The rating of the branch circuit shall not exceed 20 amperes, 120 volts, 2 wire, single phase.

B. Installation

366-10. Panels. The panels shall be installed on surfaces which are flat and smooth. The panels shall be installed in a secure fashion. The holdown bar shall be permitted for this purpose.

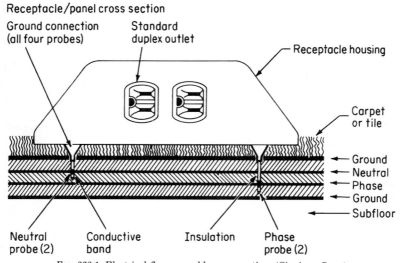

FIG. 366-1. Electrical floor assembly cross section. (*Sippican Corp.*)

366-11. All Circuits.

(a) From the Distribution Panelboards. All 15- and 20-ampere branch circuits shall be extended from their respective branch-circuit panelboards.

(b) From Signaling and/or Communication Equipment. All circuits for signaling and/or communication shall be extended from Class 2 sources.

(c) Wiring. The branch circuit conductors shall be installed in rigid metal conduit or raceways specifically approved for grounding purposes.

(d) Terminations. Termination for combination of 15- or 20-ampere branch circuits and signaling and/or communications circuits shall be within a panel input unit.

366-12. Circuits.

(a) Branch Circuits. A maximum length of 200 feet of panels shall be permitted to be connected in series. Any number of panels shall be permitted to be connected to form a single branch circuit provided the total area does not exceed 1024 square feet.

(b) Signaling/Communication Circuits. Signaling/communication circuits shall be permitted to feed any number of panels. A termination unit shall be permitted at the end of each series set of panels.

366-13. Receptacle Units. All receptacle units shall be installed or removed using suitable tools.

366-14. Grounding. The section of the branch circuit extended from the branch-circuit panelboard to the panel input unit shall have an equipment grounding conductor. This shall be a separate, continuous, copper equipment grounding conductor, not smaller than No. 12. This equipment grounding conductor shall be installed with the branch-circuit conductors in the approved metal raceway. The equipment grounding conductor shall be connected to a properly identified terminal screw in the panel input unit and in the branch-circuit panelboard.

C. Construction

366-20. Marking.

(a) All markings shall be durable and shall be placed on the surface of all components in a readily recognizable location.

(b) All panels, receptacle housing units, base units, panel input units, and tools shall be marked to indicate the following information:

(1) The maximum working voltage and current.

(2) The manufacturer's name, trademark, or other distinctive marking by which the organization responsible for the component can be readily identified.

366-21. Identification.

(a) Neutral. All neutral connections points and terminations shall be identified by means of a distinctive, durable white or natural gray marking.

(b) Grounding. All grounding connection points and terminations shall be identified as required by Section 200-10.

ARTICLE 370. OUTLET, SWITCH AND JUNCTION BOXES, AND FITTINGS

A. Scope and General

370-1. Scope. This Article covers the installation and use of boxes containing outlets, receptacles, switches or devices; junction or pull boxes and conduit bodies as required by Section 300-15. Fittings referred to in Section 300-15 used as outlet, junction or pull boxes shall conform with the provisions of this Article depending on their use.

Installations in hazardous locations shall conform to Articles 500 through 517.

For systems over 600 volts, nominal, see Part D of this Article.

370-2. Round Boxes. Round boxes shall not be used where conduits or connectors requiring the use of locknuts or bushings are to be connected to the side of the box.

▲ The purpose of this rule is to require the use of rectangular or octagonal boxes having at each knockout or opening a flat bearing surface for the locknut or bushing.

370-3. Nonmetallic Boxes. Nonmetallic boxes approved for the purpose shall be permitted only with open wiring on insulators, concealed knob-and-tube wiring, nonmetallic-sheathed cable, and with approved rigid nonmetallic conduit.

370-4. Metal Boxes. Where used with knob-and-tube wiring or nonmetallic-sheathed cable, and mounted on or in contact with metal or metal lath ceilings, walls, or metallic surfaces, metal boxes shall be grounded.

▲ With a metal box in contact with metal walls or ceilings covered with metal, or with metal lath or with conductive thermal insulation, a stray current may flow to ground through an unknown path if a "hot" wire should accidentally become grounded on the box. To prevent this, the box must be effectively grounded by means of a separate grounding conductor.

B. Installation

370-5. Damp or Wet Locations. In damp or wet locations, boxes and fittings shall be so placed or equipped as to prevent moisture from entering or accumulating within the box or fitting. Boxes and fittings installed in wet locations shall be approved for the purpose.

For boxes in floors, see Section 370-17(b).
For protection against corrosion, see Section 300-6.

▲ *Weatherproof* is defined as meaning "so constructed or protected that exposure to the weather will not interfere with its successful operation." A box or fitting may be considered weatherproof when so made and installed that it will exclude rain and snow. Such a box or fitting need not necessarily be sealed against the entrance of moisture.

Figure 370-1 shows a fitting which is considered as weatherproof because the openings for the conductors are so placed that rain or snow cannot enter the fitting.

Figure 370-2 shows a fitting made weatherproof by means of a metal cover that slides under flanges on the face of the fitting, and, as required by Sec. 230-53, an opening is provided through which any moisture condensing in the conduit can drain out.

See definition of "Wet and Damp Locations" in Art. 100.

370-6. Number of Conductors in Switch, Outlet, Receptacle, Device, and Junction Boxes. Boxes shall be of sufficient size to provide free space for all conductors enclosed in the box.

The provisions of this Section shall not apply to terminal housings supplied with motors. (See Section 430-12.)

Boxes and conduit bodies containing conductors, size #4 or larger, shall also comply with the provisions of Section 370-18.

(a) Standard Boxes. The maximum number of conductors, not counting fixture wires permitted in standard boxes, shall be as is listed in Table 370-6(a). See Section 370-18 where boxes or conduit bodies are used as junction or pull boxes.

(1) Table 370-6(a) shall apply where no fittings or devices, such as fixture studs, cable clamps, hickeys, switches, or receptacles, are contained in the box and where

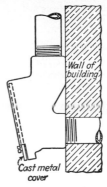

FIG. 370-1. Fitting for use at the outer end of a service conduit.

FIG. 370-2. Type LB conduit fittting used where a service conduit passes through a building wall. See Sec. 370-18.

no grounding conductors are part of the wiring within the box. Where one or more fixture studs, cable clamps, or hickeys are contained in the box, the number of conductors shall be one less than shown in the Tables; an additional deduction of one conductor shall be made for each strap containing one or more devices; and a further deduction of one conductor shall be made for one or more grounding conductors entering the box. A conductor running through the box shall be counted as one conductor, and each conductor originating outside of the box and terminating inside the box is counted as one conductor. Conductors, no part of which leaves the box, shall not be counted. The volume of a wiring enclosure (box) shall be the total volume of the assembled sections, and where used, the space provided by plaster rings, domed covers, extension rings, etc. that are marked with their volume in cubic inches.

(2) For combinations of conductor sizes shown in Table 370-6(a), the volume per conductor listed in Table 370-6(b) shall apply. The maximum number and size of conductors listed in Table 370-6(a) shall not be exceeded.

▲ In paragraph (a), one or more grounding conductors are counted as one conductor in determining the number of conductors permitted in a box.

Figure 370-3 illustrated a nonmetallic sheathed cable with three No. 14 copper conductors supplying a 15-A duplex receptacle (one ungrounded conductor, one grounded conductor and one "bare" grounding conductor).

After supplying the receptacle, these conductors are extended to other outlets and the conductor count would be as follows:

Circuit conductors	4
Grounding conductors	1
For internal cable clamps	1
For receptacle	1
Total	7

The No. 14 conductor column of the table indicates that a device box not less than

Table 370-6(a). Boxes

Box Dimension, Inches Trade Size or Type	Min. Cu. In. Cap.	Maximum Number of Conductors				
		#14	#12	#10	#8	#6
4 × 1¼ Round or Octagonal	12.5	6	5	5	4	0
4 × 1½ Round or Octagonal	15.5	7	6	6	5	0
4 × 2⅛ Round or Octagonal	21.5	10	9	8	7	0
4 × 1¼ Square	18.0	9	8	7	6	0
4 × 1½ Square	21.0	10	9	8	7	0
4 × 2⅛ Square	30.3	15	13	12	10	6*
4¹¹⁄₁₆ × 1¼ Square	25.5	12	11	10	8	0
4¹¹⁄₁₆ × 1½ Square	29.5	14	13	11	9	0
4¹¹⁄₁₆ × 2⅛ Square	42.0	21	18	16	14	6
3 × 2 × 1½ Device	7.5	3	3	3	2	0
3 × 2 × 2 Device	10.0	5	4	4	3	0
3 × 2 × 2¼ Device	10.5	5	4	4	3	0
3 × 2 × 2½ Device	12.5	6	5	5	4	0
3 × 2 × 2¾ Device	14.0	7	6	5	4	0
3 × 2 × 3½ Device	18.0	9	8	7	6	0
4 × 2⅛ × 1½ Device	10.3	5	4	4	3	0
4 × 2⅛ × 1⅞ Device	13.0	6	5	5	4	0
4 × 2⅛ × 2⅛ Device	14.5	7	6	5	4	0
3¾ × 2 × 2½ Masonry Box/gang	14.0	7	6	5	4	0
3¾ × 2 × 3½ Masonry Box/gang	21.0	10	9	8	7	0
FS—Minimum Internal Depth 1¾ Single Cover/Gang	13.5	6	6	5	4	0
FD—Minimum Internal Depth 2⅜ Single Cover/Gang	18.0	9	8	7	6	3
FS—Minimum Internal Depth 1¾ Multiple Cover/Gang	18.0	9	8	7	6	0
FD—Minimum Internal Depth 2⅜ Multiple Cover/Gang	24.0	12	10	9	8	4

* Not to be used as a pull box. For termination only.

3 × 2 × 2¾ in. is required. Where a square box with plaster ring is used, a 4 × 1½ in. size is required. (See Sec. 370–14.)

It should be noted that the total usable volume includes the space provided by plaster rings, domed covers, extension rings, etc., if marked with their volume in cubic inches.

Table 370-6(a) includes the most popular types of metal "trade-size" boxes used with wires No. 14 to No. 6. Cubic-inch capacities are listed for each box shown in the table. According to paragraph (b), boxes other than those shown in Table 370-6(a) are required to be marked with the cubic inch content so wire combinations can be readily computed.

(b) Other Boxes. Boxes 100 cubic inches or less other than those described in Table 370-6(a) and conduit bodies having provision for more than two conduit entries shall be durably and legibly marked by the manufacturer with their cubic inch capacity and the maximum number of conductors permitted shall be computed using the volume per conductor listed in Table 370-6(b). Boxes described in Table 370-6(a) that have a larger cubic inch capacity than is designated in the Table shall be

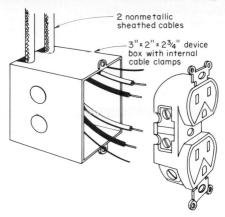

2 nonmetallic
sheathed cables

3"× 2"× 2¾" device
box with internal
cable clamps

FIG. 370-3. Device box illustrating compliance
with Section 370-6(a) by including *one* equipment
grounding conductor in determining box size.

permitted to have their cubic inch capacity marked as required by this Section and
the maximum number of conductors permitted shall be computed using the volume
per conductor listed in Table 370-6(b).

Where #6 conductors are installed the minimum wire bending space required
in Table 373-6(a) shall be provided.

▲ **The purpose of these provisions is to prevent the excessive crowding of wires and
splices in outlet and junction boxes. A wire passing through the box without a splice
or tap is counted as one wire.**

(c) Conduit Bodies.   Conduit bodies enclosing #6 conductors or smaller shall
have a cross-sectional area not less than twice the cross-sectional area of the largest
conduit to which it is attached. The maximum number of conductors permitted
shall be the maximum number permitted by Table I, Chapter 9, for the conduit
to which it is attached.

Conduit bodies having provisions for no more than two conduit entries shall not
contain splices, taps, or devices.

▲ **Conduit bodies having provisions for more than two conduit entries shall be durably
and legibly marked by the manufacturer with their cubic-inch capacity, and the
maximum number of conductors permitted shall be computed using the volume per
conductor listed in Table 370-6(b).**

Conduit bodies used as pull and junction boxes shall also conform to the requirements of Sec. 370-18.

370-7. Conductors Entering Boxes or Fittings.   Conductors entering boxes or
fittings shall be protected from abrasion, and shall comply with (a) through (d)
below.

(a) Openings to Be Closed.   Openings through which conductors enter shall be
adequately closed.

Table 370-6(b). Volume Required Per Conductor

Size of Conductor	Free Space Within Box for Each Conductor
No. 14	2. cubic inches
No. 12	2.25 cubic inches
No. 10	2.5 cubic inches
No. 8	3. cubic inches
No. 6	5. cubic inches

(b) Metal Boxes and Fittings. Where metal outlet boxes or fittings are installed with open wiring or concealed knob-and-tube wiring, conductors shall enter through insulating bushings or, in dry places, through flexible tubing extending from the last insulating support and firmly secured to the box or fitting. Where raceway or cable is installed with metal outlet boxes or fittings, the raceway or cable shall be secured to such boxes and fittings.

(c) Nonmetallic Boxes. Where nonmetallic boxes are used with open wiring or concealed knob-and-tube wiring, the conductors shall enter through individual holes. Where flexible tubing is used to encase the conductor, the tubing shall extend from the last insulating support and may be run into the box or terminate at the wall of the box. If nonmetallic-sheathed cable is used, the cable assembly shall enter the box through a knockout opening. Clamping of individual conductors or cables to the box shall not be required where supported within 8 inches of the box. Where rigid nonmetallic conduit is installed with nonmetallic boxes or fittings, the conduit shall be secured to such boxes and fittings in an approved manner.

▲ When used with open wiring on insulators, knob-and-tube work, or nonmetallic sheathed cable, nonmetallic boxes have the advantage that an accidental contact between a "hot" wire and the box will not ordinarily create a hazard.

(d) Conductors No. 4 AWG or Larger. Installation shall comply with Section 373-6(c).

370-8. Unused Openings. Unused openings in boxes and fittings shall be effectively closed to afford protection substantially equivalent to that of the wall of the box or fitting. Metal plugs or plates used with nonmetallic boxes or fittings shall be recessed at least $\frac{1}{4}$ inch from the outer surface.

370-9. Boxes Enclosing Flush Devices. Boxes used to enclose flush devices shall be of such design that the devices will be completely enclosed on back and sides, and that substantial support for the devices will be provided. Screws for supporting the box shall not be used in attachment of the device contained therein.

▲ If the screws used for attaching the receptacles and switches to boxes were used also for the mounting of boxes, a poor mechanical job would result, since the boxes would be insecurely held whenever the devices were not installed and the screws loosened for adjustment of the device position. Hence the prohibition.

370-10. In Wall or Ceiling. In walls or ceilings of concrete, tile, or other non-combustible material, boxes and fittings shall be so installed that the front edge of the box or fitting will not set back of the finished surface more than $\frac{1}{4}$ inch. In walls and ceilings constructed of wood or other combustible material, outlet boxes and fittings shall be flush with the finished surface or project therefrom.

370-11. Repairing Plaster. Plaster surfaces that are broken or incomplete shall be repaired so there will be no gaps or open spaces at the edge of the box or fitting. *Exception: On walls or ceilings of concrete, tile, or other noncombustible material.*

▲ The purpose of Sec. 370-10 and 370-11 is to prevent openings around the edge of the box through which fire could be readily communicated to combustible material in the wall or ceiling. For this reason inspection authorities do not allow square or hexagonal boxes in ceilings, finished with sheetrock, without the use of "mud rings."

370-12. Exposed Surface Extensions. In making an exposed surface extension from an existing outlet of concealed wiring, a box or an extension ring shall be mounted over the original box and electrically and mechanically secured to it.

▲ The extension should be made as illustrated in Fig. 370-4. The extension ring is secured to the original box by two screws passing through ears attached to the box.

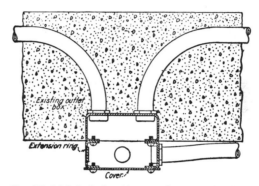

Fig. 370-4. Method of making a surface extension from concealed wiring.

370-13. Supports. Boxes shall be securely and rigidly fastened to the surface upon which they are mounted, or securely and rigidly embedded in concrete or masonry. Boxes shall be supported from a structural member of the building either directly or by using a substantial and approved metal or wooden brace, or shall be supported as is otherwise provided in this Section. If of wood, the brace shall not be less than nominal one-inch thickness. If of metal it shall be corrosion-resistant and shall not be less than No. 24 MSG.

Where mounted in new walls in which no structural members are provided or in existing walls in previously occupied buildings, boxes not over 100 cubic inches in size, specifically approved for the purpose, shall be affixed with approved anchors or clamps so as to provide a rigid and secure installation.

Threaded boxes or fittings not over 100 cubic inches in size that do not contain devices or support fixtures shall be considered adequately supported if two or more conduits are threaded into the box wrenchtight and are supported within 3 feet of the box on two or more sides as is required by this Section.

Threaded boxes or fittings not over 100 cubic inches in size shall be considered to be adequately supported if two or more conduits are threaded into the box wrenchtight and are supported as required by this Section within 18 inches of the box.

▲ Where locknut and bushing connections are used, the box must be independently fastened in place.

The requirement of metal or wood supports for boxes applies to concealed work in walls and floors of wood-frame construction and other types of construction having open spaces in which the wiring is installed. In walls or floors of concrete, brick, or tile where conduit and boxes are solidly built into the wall or floor material, special box supports are not usually necessary.

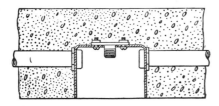

FIG. 370-5. Outlet box built into a concrete ceiling.

An outlet box built into a concrete ceiling as shown in Fig. 370-5 seldom needs any special support. At such an outlet, if it is intended for a fixture of too great weight to be safely hung on an ordinary $\frac{3}{8}$-in. fixture stud, a special fixture support consisting of a threaded pipe or rod is required, such as is shown in Fig. 370-6.

In a tile arch floor (Fig. 370-6) a large opening must be cut through the tile to receive the conduit and outlet box.

In an existing building, where any type of wiring is installed either exposed or concealed, the boxes may be mounted on plaster or any other ceiling or wall finish, the only requirement being that they must be securely fastened in place. Where no structural members are provided for, boxes not over 100 cubic inches in size, specifically approved for the purpose, shall be affixed with approved anchors or clamps. Figures 370-7 and 370-8 illustrate the intent of "specifically approved for the purpose."

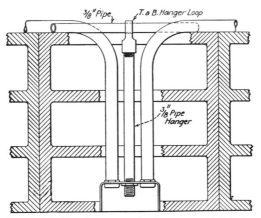

FIG. 370-6. Box hanger used where an outlet is installed in a tile arch ceiling.

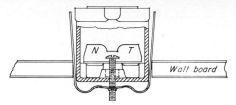

Fig. 370-7. Inserting box and bracket through wall board. (*Union Insulating Co., Inc.*)

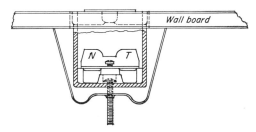

Fig. 370-8. Box anchored to wall. (*Union Insulating Co., Inc.*)

Figures 370-7 and 370-8 illustrate the use of approved mounting brackets as required in the second paragraph of Section 370-13.

The last paragraph of Sec. 370-13 permits two or more conduits to be threaded into threaded boxes or fittings (not over 100 cu in. in size) where such conduits are properly supported within 18 in. of the box. This recognizes the support of elevated threaded-hub junction boxes by conduits emerging from the earth, such as those used near swimming pools, patios, or shrubbery. Support by a single conduit is not recognized.

370-14. Depth of Outlet Boxes. No box shall have an internal depth of less than $\frac{1}{2}$ inch. Boxes intended to enclose flush devices shall have an internal depth of not less than $\frac{15}{16}$ inch.

▲ Sufficient space should be provided inside the box so that the wires do not have to be jammed together or against the box, and the box should provide enough of an enclosure so that in case of trouble, burning insulation cannot readily ignite flammable material outside the box.

370-15. Covers and Canopies. In completed installations each outlet box shall have a cover, faceplate, or fixture canopy.

(a) Nonmetallic or metal covers and plates shall be permitted with nonmetallic outlet boxes. Where metal covers or plates are used, they shall comply with the grounding requirements of Section 250-42.

See Section 410-18 for metal faceplates.

(b) Where a fixture canopy or pan is used, any combustible wall or ceiling finish exposed between the edge of the canopy or pan and the outlet box shall be covered with noncombustible material.

▲ If the ceiling or wall finish is of combustible material, the canopy and box must form a complete enclosure. The chief purpose of this rule is to require that no open space be left between the canopy and the edge of the box where the finish is wood or other combustible material. Where the wall or ceiling finish is plaster the requirement does not apply, since plaster is not classed as a combustible material; however, the plaster must be continuous up to the box, leaving no openings around the box.

(c) Covers of outlet boxes having holes through which flexible cord pendants pass shall be provided with bushings designed for the purpose or shall have smooth, well-rounded surfaces on which the cords may bear. So-called hard-rubber or composition bushings shall not be used.

▲ See Figs. 370-9 and 370-10.

Fig. 370-9. Steel box cover with bushed hole for cord.

Fig. 370-10. Porcelain box cover with hole for cord.

370-16. Fastened to Gas Pipes.   Outlet boxes used where gas outlets are present shall be so fastened to the gas pipes as to be mechanically secure.

370-17. Outlet Boxes.

(a) Boxes at Lighting Fixture Outlets.   Boxes used at lighting fixture outlets shall be designed for the purpose. At every outlet used exclusively for lighting, the box shall be so designed or installed that a lighting fixture may be attached.

(b) Floor Boxes.   Floor boxes especially approved for the purpose shall be used for receptacles located in the floor.

Exception: Standard approved types of flush receptacle boxes shall be permitted where receptacles are located in elevated floors of show windows or other locations when the authority having jurisdiction judges them to be free from physical damage, moisture, and dirt.

370-18. Pull and Junction Boxes.   Boxes and conduit bodies used as pull or junction boxes shall comply with (a) through (d) of this Section.

(a) Minimum Size.   For raceways $\frac{3}{4}$ inch trade size or larger, containing conductors of #4 or larger, and for cables containing conductors of #4 or larger, the minimum dimensions of pull or junction boxes installed in a raceway or cable run shall comply with the following:

(1) Straight Pulls.   In straight pulls the length of the box shall not be less than 8 times the trade diameter of the largest raceway.

(2) Angle or U Pulls.   Where angle or U pulls are made, the distance between each raceway entry inside the box and the opposite wall of the box shall not be less than 6 times the trade diameter of the largest raceway. This distance shall be increased for additional entries by the amount of the sum of the diameters of all other raceway entries on the same wall of the box. The distance between raceway entries enclosing the same conductor shall not be less than 6 times the trade diameter of the larger raceway.

Exception: Where a conduit or cable entry is in the wall of a box or conduit body opposite to a removable cover and where the distance from that wall to the cover is in conformance with the Column for one wire per terminal in Table 373-6(a).

When transposing cable size into raceway size in (a)(1) and (a)(2) above, the minimum trade size raceway required for the number and size of conductors in the cable shall be used.

(3) Boxes of dimensions less than those required in (a)(1) and (a)(2) above shall be permitted for installations of combinations of conductors that are less than the maximum conduit fill (of conduits being used) permitted by Table 1, Chapter 9, provided the box has been approved for and is permanently marked with the maximum number and maximum size of conductors permitted.

Exception: Terminal housings supplied with motors which shall comply with the provisions of Section 430-12.

(b) Conductors in Pull or Junction Boxes. In pull boxes or junction boxes having any dimension over 6 feet, all conductors shall be cabled or racked up in an approved manner.

See Section 373-6(c) for insulation of conductors at bushings.

(c) Covers. All pull boxes, junction boxes, and fittings shall be provided with covers approved for the purpose. Where metal covers are used, they shall comply with the grounding requirements of Section 250-42.

(d) Where permanent barriers are installed in a box, each section shall be considered as a separate box.

▲ In computing pull-box sizes, all raceways smaller than $\frac{3}{4}$ in. and cables containing conductors smaller than size No. 4 may be neglected.

Example 1. Straight Pull.

A pull box is to be installed in a group of straight runs of conduit in which the largest size is 3 in., which we must multiply by 8. 8 × 3 in. = 24 in., which is the minimum length of the pull box.

A 3-in. conduit could contain three 500,000 CM conductors, and practical considerations dictate a minimum length of about 30 in.

Example 2. Right-angle Pull.

A pull box is to be installed to make a right-angle turn in a group of conduits consisting of two 3-in., two $2\frac{1}{2}$-in., and four 2-in. conduits.

Subparagraph 2 gives two methods for computing the box dimensions, and both must be met.

First method:

$$6 \times 3 \text{ in.} = 18 \text{ in.}$$
$$1 \times 3 \text{ in.} = 3$$
$$2 \times 2\frac{1}{2} \text{ in.} = 5$$
$$4 \times 2 \text{ in.} = \underline{8}$$
$$\text{Total} = 34 \text{ in.}$$

Second method:

Assuming that the conduits are to leave the box in the same order in which they enter, the arrangement is shown in Fig. 370-11 and the distance A between the ends of the two conduits must be not less that 6×2 in. $= 12$ in. It can be assumed that this measurement is to be made between the centers of the two conduits. By calculation, or by laying out the corner of the box, it is found that the distance C should be about $8\frac{1}{2}$ in.

The distance B should be not less than $30\frac{1}{2}$ in., approximately, as determined by applying practical data for the spacing between centers of conduits,

$$30\frac{1}{2} \text{ in.} + 8\frac{1}{2} \text{ in.} = 39 \text{ in.}$$

which is the minimum allowable dimension.

In this case the box dimensions are governed by the second method. The largest dimension computed by either of the two methods is of course the one to be used.

The most practical method of determining the proper size of a pull box is to sketch the box layout with its contained conductors on a paper.

Section 370-18 applies particularly to the pull boxes commonly placed above distribution switchboards and which are often, and with good reason, termed *tangle boxes*. In such boxes, all conductors of each circuit should be cabled together by serving them with twine so as to form a self-supporting assembly that can be formed into shape, or the conductors should be supported in an orderly manner on racks. The conductors should not rest directly on any metalwork inside the box, and insulating bushings should be provided wherever required by Sec. 373-6(c).

For example, the box illustrated in Fig. 370-11 could be approximately 5 in. deep and accommodate one horizontal row of conduits.

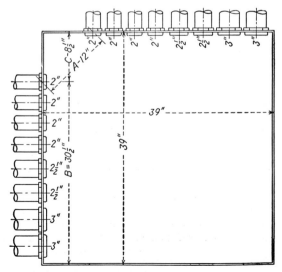

FIG. 370-11. Pull box used for right-angle turn.

By making it twice as deep, two horizontal rows or twice the number of conduits could be installed.

Insulating racks are usually placed between conductor layers, and space must be allowed for them.

Paragraph (a) provides the necessary guidance for determining the minimum dimensions of boxes based on the size and number of conduit and cable entries and the bending space to the opposite wall.

370-19. Junction, Pull and Outlet Boxes to Be Accessible. Junction, pull and outlet boxes shall be so installed that the wiring contained in them can be rendered accessible without removing any part of the building or in underground circuits without excavating sidewalks, paving earth or other substance that is to be used to establish the finished grade.

Exception: Boxes approved for the purpose shall be permitted where covered by gravel, light aggregate, or noncohesive granulated soil if their location is effectively identified and accessible for excavation.

▲ The term *box* may be considered as a covered box used at any point where it is necessary to tap a run of conduit, tubing, or cable and where the box is used for this purpose. See also comments under Sec. 300-15.

C. Construction Specifications

370-20. Metal Outlet, Switch and Junction Boxes, and Fittings. Metal outlet, switch and junction boxes, and fittings shall comply with (a) through (c) below.

(a) Corrosion Resistant. Metal boxes and fittings shall be corrosion-resistant or shall be well galvanized, enameled, or otherwise properly coated inside and out to prevent corrosion.

See Section 300-6 for limitation in the use of boxes and fittings protected from corrosion solely by enamel.

(b) Thickness of Metal. Sheet metal boxes and fittings not over 100 cubic inches in size shall be made from metal not less than No. 14 MSG. Cast-metal boxes of other than malleable iron shall have a wall thickness not less than $\frac{1}{8}$ inch. Boxes of malleable iron shall have a wall thickness of not less than $\frac{3}{32}$ inch.

(c) Boxes Over 100 Cubic Inches. Boxes of over 100 cubic inches in size shall be composed of metal and shall comply with the requirements for cabinets and cutout boxes.

Exception: It shall be permissible for covers to consist of single flat sheets secured to the box proper by screws or bolts instead of hinges. Boxes having covers of this form shall be used only for enclosing joints in conductors or to facilitate the drawing in of wires and cables. They shall not be used to enclose switches, cutouts, or other control devices.

370-21. Covers. Metal covers shall be of a thickness not less than that specified for the walls of the box or fitting of the same material and with which they are designed to be used, or shall be lined with firmly attached insulating material not less than $\frac{1}{32}$ inch in thickness. Covers of porcelain or other approved insulating material shall be permitted if of such form and thickness as to afford the required protection and strength.

370-22. Bushings. Covers of outlet boxes and outlet fittings having holes through which flexible cord pendants may pass, shall be provided with approved bushings or shall have smooth, well-rounded surfaces, upon which the cord may bear. Where conductors other than flexible cord may pass through a metal cover, a separate hole equipped with a bushing of suitable insulating material shall be provided for each conductor.

370-23. Nonmetallic Boxes. Provisions for supports or other mounting means for nonmetallic boxes shall be outside of the box, or the box shall be so constructed as to prevent contact between the conductors in the box and the supporting screws.

370-24. Marking. All boxes and conduit bodies, covers, extension rings, plaster rings, and the like shall be durably and legibly marked with the manufacturer's name or trademark.

D. Pull and Junction Boxes for Use on Systems Over 600-Volts, Nominal

370-50. General. In addition to the generally applicable provisions of Article 370, the rules in 370-51 and 370-52 shall apply.

370-51. Size of Pull and Junction Boxes. Pull and junction boxes shall provide adequate space and dimensions for the installation of conductors in accordance with the following:

(a) For Straight Pulls. The length of the box shall be not less than 48 times the outside diameter, over sheath, of the largest conductor or cable entering the box.

(b) For Angle or U Pulls. The distance between each cable or conductor entry inside the box and the opposite wall of the box shall not be less than 36 times the outside diameter, over sheath, of the largest cable or conductor. This distance shall be increased for additional entries by the amount of the sum of the outside diameters, over sheath, of all other cables or conductor entries through the same wall of the box.

The distance between a cable or conductor entry and its exit from the box shall be not less than 36 times the outside diameter, over sheath, of that cable or conductor.

Exception No. 1: Where a conductor or cable entry is in the wall of a box opposite to a removable cover and where the distance from that wall to the cover is in conformance with the provisions of 300-34.

Exception No. 2: Terminal housings supplied with motors which shall comply with the provisions of Section 430-12.

(c) One or more sides of any pull box shall be removable.

370-52. Construction and Installation Requirements.

(a) Boxes shall be made of material inherently resistant to corrosion or shall be suitably protected, both internally and externally, by enameling, galvanizing, plating or other means.

(b) Suitable bushing, shields, or fittings having smooth rounded edges shall be provided where conductors or cables pass through partitions and at other locations where necessary.

(c) Boxes shall provide a complete enclosure for the contained conductors or cables.

(d) Boxes shall be so installed that the wiring is accessible without removing any part of the building. Working space shall be provided in accordance with Section 110-34.

(e) Boxes shall be closed by suitable covers securely fastened in place. Underground box covers that weigh over one hundred pounds shall be considered as meeting this requirement. Covers for boxes shall be permanently marked "HIGH VOLTAGE." The marking shall be on the outside of the box cover and shall be readily visible. Letters shall be block type at least ½ inch in height.

(f) Boxes and their covers shall be capable of withstanding the handling to which they may be subjected.

ARTICLE 373. CABINETS AND CUTOUT BOXES

373-1. Scope. This Article covers the installation of cabinets and cutout boxes. Installations in hazardous locations shall comply with Articles 500 through 517.

▲ Cabinets and cutout boxes, according to the definitions, must have doors and are thus distinguished from large boxes with covers consisting of plates attached with screws or bolts.

Article 373 applies to all boxes used to enclose operating apparatus, i.e., apparatus having moving parts or requiring inspection or attention, such as panelboards, cutouts, switches, circuit breakers, or control apparatus.

A. Installation

373-2. Damp or Wet Locations. In damp or wet locations, cabinets and cutout boxes of the surface type shall be so placed or equipped as to prevent moisture or water from entering and accumulating within the cabinet or cutout box, and shall be mounted so there is at least ¼-inch air space between the enclosure and the wall or other supporting surface. Cabinets or cutout boxes installed in wet locations shall be weatherproof.

For protection against corrosion, see Section 300-6.

373-3. Position in Wall. In walls of concrete, tile, or other noncombustible material, cabinets shall be so installed that the front edge of the cabinet will not set back of the finished surface more than ¼ inch. In walls constructed of wood or other combustible material, cabinets shall be flush with the finished surface or project therefrom.

373-4. Unused Openings. Unused openings in cabinet or cutout boxes shall be effectively closed to afford protection substantially equivalent to that of the wall of the cabinet or cutout box. Where metal plugs or plates are used with nonmetallic cabinets or cutout boxes, they shall be recessed at least ¼ inch from the outer surface.

373-5. Conductors Entering Cabinets or Cutout Boxes. Conductors entering cabinets or cutout boxes shall be protected from abrasion and shall comply with (a) and (c) below.

(a) **Openings to Be Closed.** Openings through which conductors enter shall be adequately closed.

(b) **Metal Cabinets and Cutout Boxes.** Where metal cabinets or cutout boxes are installed with open wiring or concealed knob-and-tube wiring, conductors shall enter through insulating bushings or, in dry places, through flexible tubing extending from the last insulating support and firmly secured to the cabinet or cutout box.

(c) Cables. Where cable is used, each cable shall be secured to the cabinet or cutout box.

373-6. Deflection of Conductors. Conductors at terminals or conductors entering or leaving cabinets or cutout boxes and the like shall comply with (a) through (c) below.

(a) Width of Wiring Gutters. Conductors shall not be deflected within a cabinet or cutout box unless a gutter having a width in accordance with Table 373-6(a) is provided. Conductors in parallel in accordance with Section 310-4 shall be judged on the basis of the number of conductors in parallel.

(b) Wire Bending Space at Terminals. Conductors shall not be deflected at a terminal unless bending space in accordance with Table 373-6(a) is provided.

Table 373-6(a). Minimum Wire Bending Space at Terminals and Minimum Width of Wiring Gutters in Inches

AWG or Circular-Mil Size of Wire	Wires per Terminal				
	1	2	3	4	5
14–8	Not Specified	—	—	—	—
6	$1\frac{1}{2}$	—	—	—	—
4–3	2	—	—	—	—
2	$2\frac{1}{2}$	—	—	—	—
1	3	—	—	—	—
0–00	$3\frac{1}{2}$	5	7	—	—
000–0000	4	6	8	—	—
250 MCM	$4\frac{1}{2}$	6	8	10	—
300–350 MCM	5	8	10	12	—
400–500 MCM	6	8	10	12	14
600–700 MCM	8	10	12	14	16
750–900 MCM	8	12	14	16	18
1,000–1,250 MCM	10	—	—	—	—
1,500–2,000 MCM	12	—	—	—	—

Bending space at terminals shall be measured in a straight line from the end of the lug or wire connector (in the direction that the wire leaves the terminal) to the wall or barrier.

(c) Insulated Bushings. Where ungrounded conductors of No. 4 or larger enter a raceway in a cabinet, pull box, junction box, or auxiliary gutter, the conductors shall be protected by a substantial bushing providing a smoothly rounded insulating surface, unless the conductors are separated from the raceway fitting by substantial insulating material securely fastened in place. Where conduit bushings are constructed wholly of insulating material, a locknut shall be installed both inside and outside the enclosure to which the conduit is attached. The insulating bushing or insulating material shall have a temperature rating not less than the insulation temperature rating of the installed conductors.

▲ Paragraph (c) applies to all conductors of size No. 4 or larger entering a cabinet or box from rigid metal conduit, flexible metal conduit, electrical metallic tubing, etc.

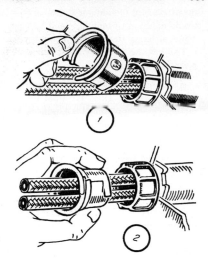

FIG. 373-1. Insulating sleeve. (*The Thomas & Betts Co., Inc.*)

To protect the conductors a smoothly rounded insulating surface is required. While many fittings are provided with insulated sleeves or linings, it is also possible to use a separate insulating lining or sleeve to meet the requirements of the Code. Figure 373-1 shows an approved sleeve which may be used to separate the conductors from the raceway fitting.

373-7. Space in Enclosures. Cabinets and cutout boxes shall have sufficient space to accommodate all conductors installed in them without crowding.

373-8. Enclosures for Switches or Overcurrent Devices. Enclosures for switches or overcurrent devices shall not be used as junction boxes, auxiliary gutters, or raceways for conductors feeding through or tapping off to other switches or overcurrent devices.

Exception: Where adequate space is provided so that the conductors do not fill the wiring space at any cross section to more than 40 percent of the cross-sectional area of the space, and so that the conductors, splices, and taps do not fill the wiring space at any cross section to more than 75 percent of the cross-sectional area of the space.

▲ Most enclosures for switches and/or overcurrent devices have been designed to accommodate only those conductors intended to be connected to terminals within such enclosures. And in designing such equipment it would be virtually impossible for manufacturers to anticipate various types of "foreign" circuits, feed-through circuits or numerous splices or taps.

In general, the most satisfactory way to connect various enclosures together is through the use of properly sized auxiliary gutters (Secs. 374-5 and 374-8) or junction boxes (Secs. 370-6 and 370-18). Following this concept enclosures for switches and/or overcurrent devices will not be overcrowded.

There are cases where large enclosures for switches and/or overcurrent devices will accommodate additional small conductors (No. 10 and less) and this is generally where the 40 percent (conductor space) and 75 percent (splices or taps) at one cross section would apply. An example would be control circuits tapped off or extending through 200-A or larger fusible switches or circuit-breaker enclosures.

The cross-sectional area within such enclosures is the *free gutter wiring space* intended for conductors.

Example: If an enclosure has a gutter space of 3 in. × 3 in. the cross-sectional area would be 9 sq in. Thus, the total conductor fill (use Table 5, Chap. 9) at any cross section could not exceed 3.6 sq in. (9 × 0.4), and the maximum space for splices at any cross section (including conductors) could not exceed 6.75 sq in. (9 × 0.75).

In the case of large conductors, a splice other than a wire-to-wire "C" or "tube" splice would not be acceptable if the conductors at the cross section are near a 40 percent fill because this would leave only a 35 percent space for the splice. Most splices for larger conductors with split-bolt connectors or similar types are usually twice the size of the conductors being spliced. Accordingly, where larger conductors are to be spliced within enclosures, the total conductor fill should not exceed *20 percent* to allow for any bulky splice at a cross section.

373-9. Side or Back Wiring Spaces or Gutters. Cabinets and cutout boxes shall be provided with back wiring spaces, gutters, or wiring compartments as required by Sections 373-11(c) and (d).

B. Construction Specifications

373-10. Material. Cabinets and cutout boxes shall comply with (a) through (c) below.

(a) Metal Cabinets and Cutout Boxes. Metal cabinets and cutout boxes shall be protected both inside and outside against corrosion and shall be approved for the purpose.

For protection against corrosion, see Section 300-6.

(b) Strength. The design and construction of cabinets and cutout boxes shall be such as to secure ample strength and rigidity. If constructed of sheet steel, the metal shall be of not less than No. 16 MSG.

(c) Nonmetallic Cabinets. Nonmetallic cabinets shall be submitted for approval prior to installation.

373-11. Spacing. The spacing within cabinets and cutout boxes shall comply with (a) through (d) below.

(a) General. Spacing within cabinets and cutout boxes shall be sufficient to provide ample room for the distribution of wires and cables placed in them, and for a separation between metal parts of devices and apparatus mounted within them as follows:

(1) Base. Other than at points of support, there shall be an air space of at least $\frac{1}{16}$ inch between the base of the device and the wall of any metal cabinet or cutout box in which the device is mounted.

(2) Doors. There shall be an air space of at least one inch between any live metal part, including live metal parts of enclosed fuses, and the door.

Exception: Where the door is lined with an approved insulating material or is of a thickness of metal not less than No. 12 MSG, the air space shall not be less than ½ inch.

(3) Live Parts. There shall be an air space of at least ½ inch between the walls, back, gutter partition, if of metal, or door of any cabinet or cutout box and the nearest exposed current-carrying part of devices mounted within the cabinet where the voltage does not exceed 250. This spacing shall be increased to at least one inch where the voltage exceeds 250.

Exception: As permitted in (1) or (2) above.

(b) Switch Clearance. Cabinets and cutout boxes shall be deep enough to allow the closing of the doors when 30-ampere branch-circuit panelboard switches are in any position; when combination cutout switches are in any position; or when other single-throw switches are opened as far as their construction will permit.

(c) Wiring Space. Cabinets and cutout boxes that contain devices or apparatus connected within the cabinet or box to more than 8 conductors, including those of branch circuits, meter loops, sub-feeder circuits, power circuits, and similar circuits, but not including the supply circuit or a continuation thereof, shall have back-wiring spaces or one or more side-wiring spaces, side gutters, or wiring compartments.

(d) Wiring Space—Enclosure. Side-wiring spaces, side gutters, or side-wiring compartments of cabinets and cutout boxes shall be made tight enclosures by means of covers, barriers, or partitions extending from the bases of the devices, contained in the cabinet to the door, frame, or sides of the cabinet.

Exception: Where the enclosure contains only those conductors that are led from the cabinet at points directly opposite their terminal connections to devices within the cabinet.

Partially enclosed back-wiring spaces shall be provided with covers to complete the enclosure. Wiring spaces that are required by (c) above, and that are exposed when doors are open, shall be provided with covers to complete the enclosure. Where adequate space is provided for feed-through conductors and for splices as required in Section 373-8 Exception, additional barriers shall not be required.

▲ See comments following Sec. 373-8.

ARTICLE 374. AUXILIARY GUTTERS

374-1. Use. Auxiliary gutters shall be permitted to supplement wiring spaces at meter centers, distribution centers, switchboards, and similar points of wiring systems and may enclose conductors or busbars, but shall not be used to enclose switches, overcurrent devices, appliances, or other similar equipment.

▲ Auxiliary gutters are sheet-metal troughs in which conductors are laid in place after the gutter has been installed. Auxiliary gutters are used as parts of complete assemblies of apparatus such as switchboards, distribution centers, and control equipment, and are not permitted to extend more than 30 ft beyond the equipment which they supplement, except in elevator work. Where an extension beyond 30 ft is necessary, Art. 362 for Wireways must be complied with. The label of Underwriters' Laboratories, Inc., on each length of trough bears the legend "Wireways or Auxiliary Gutters," which indicates that they may be identical troughs but are distinguished one from the other only by their use. See comments following Sec. 362-1.

374-2. Extension Beyond Equipment.   An auxiliary gutter shall not extend a greater distance than 30 feet beyond the equipment which it supplements.

Exception: As provided in Section 620-35 for elevators.

For wireways, see Article 362. For busways, see Article 364.

374-3. Supports.   Gutters shall be supported throughout their entire length at intervals not exceeding 5 feet.

374-4. Covers.   Covers shall be securely fastened to the gutter.

374-5. Number of Conductors.   Auxiliary gutters shall not contain more than 30 current-carrying conductors at any cross section. The sum of the cross-sectional areas of all contained conductors at any cross section of an auxiliary gutter shall not exceed 20 percent of the interior cross-sectional area of the auxiliary gutter.

Exception No. 1: As provided in Section 620-35 for elevators.

Exception No. 2: Conductors for signaling circuits or controller conductors between a motor and its starter and used only for starting duty shall not be considered as current-carrying conductors.

Exception No. 3: Where the correction factors specified in Note 8 to Tables 310-16 through 310-19 are applied, there shall be no limit on the number of current-carrying conductors, but the sum of the cross-sectional area of all contained conductors at any cross section of the auxiliary gutter shall not exceed 20 percent of the interior cross-sectional area of the auxiliary gutter.

▲ No limit is placed on the size of conductors that may be installed in an auxiliary gutter.

The cross-sectional area of rubber-covered and thermoplastic-covered conductors given in Table 5, Chap. 9, may be used in computing the size of gutters required to contain a given combination of such conductors.

374-6. Ampacity of Conductors.   Where the number of current-carrying conductors contained in the auxiliary gutter is 30 or less, the correction factors specified in Note 8 of Tables 310-16 through 310-19 shall not apply. The current carried continuously in bare copper bars in auxiliary gutters shall not exceed 1000 amperes per square inch of cross section of the conductor. For aluminum bars, the current carried continuously shall not exceed 700 amperes per square inch of cross section of the conductor.

374-7. Clearance of Bare Live Parts.   Bare conductors shall be securely and rigidly supported so that the minimum clearance between bare current-carrying metal parts of opposite polarities mounted on the same surface will not be less than 2 inches, nor less than one inch for parts that are held free in the air. A clearance not less than one inch shall be secured between bare current-carrying metal parts and any metal surface. Adequate provisions shall be made for the expansion and contraction of busbars.

374-8. Splices and Taps.   Splices and taps shall comply with (a) through (d) below.

(a) Splices or taps shall be permitted within gutters when they are accessible by means of removable covers or doors. The conductors, including splices and taps, shall not fill the gutter to more than 75 percent of its area.

(b) Taps from bare conductors shall leave the gutter opposite their terminal connections and conductors shall not be brought in contact with uninsulated current-carrying parts of opposite polarity.

(c) All taps shall be suitably identified at the gutter as to the circuit or equipment which they supply.

(d) Tap connections from conductors in auxiliary gutters shall be provided with overcurrent protection as required in Section 240-21.

▲ The insulation might be cut by resting on the sharp edge of the bar or the bar might become hot enough to injure the insulation. When taps are made to bare conductors in a gutter, care should be taken so as to place and form the wires in such a manner that they will remain permanently separated from the bare bars.

All taps shall be suitably identified at the gutter as to the circuit or equipment which they supply.

Identification shall be provided wherever it is not clearly evident what apparatus is supplied by the tap. Thus if a single set of tap conductors are carried through a short length of conduit from a gutter to a switch and the conduit is in plain view, the tap is fully identified and needs no special marking; but if two or more sets of taps are carried in a single conduit to two or more different pieces of apparatus, each tap should be identified by some marking such as a small tag secured to each wire.

Tap connections from conductors in auxiliary gutters shall be provided with overcurrent protection in conformity with the provisions of Sec. 240-21.

374-9. Construction and Installation. Auxiliary gutters shall comply with (a) through (f) below.

(a) Gutters shall be so constructed and installed that adequate electrical and mechanical continuity of the complete system will be secured.

(b) Gutters shall be of substantial construction and shall provide a complete enclosure for the contained conductors. All surfaces, both interior and exterior, shall be suitably protected from corrosion. Corner joints shall be made tight and where the assembly is held together by rivets or bolts, these shall be spaced not more than 12 inches apart.

(c) Suitable bushings, shields, or fittings having smooth rounded edges shall be provided where conductors pass between gutters, through partitions, around bends, between gutters and cabinets or junction boxes, and at other locations where necessary to prevent abrasion of the insulation of the conductors.

(d) Gutters shall be constructed of sheet metal of a thickness not less than is specified in Table 374-9(d).

(e) Where insulated conductors are deflected within an auxiliary gutter, either at the ends or where conduits, fittings, or other raceways enter or leave the gutter, or where the direction of the gutter is deflected greater than 30 degrees, dimensions corresponding to Section 373-6 shall apply.

(f) Auxiliary gutters intended for outdoor use shall be of approved raintight construction.

Table 374-9(d). Maximum Width of the Widest Surface of Gutters Thickness (Manufacturers Standard Gage)

Up to and including 6 inches	No. 16
Over 6 in. and not over 18 in.	No. 14
Over 18 in. and not over 30 in.	No. 12
Over 30 inches	No. 10

ARTICLE 380. SWITCHES

A. Installation

380-1. Scope. The provisions of this Article shall apply to all switches, switching devices, and circuit breakers where used as switches.

380-2. Switch Connections.

(a) Three-Way and Four-Way Switches. Three-way and four-way switches shall be so wired that all switching is done only in the ungrounded circuit conductor. Where in metal enclosures, wiring between switches and outlets shall be run with both polarities in the same enclosure.

▲ Three-way and four-way switches are actually single-pole switches and must not be used to disconnect the grounded circuit wire, because this would be a violation of Sec. 380-2(b).

(b) Grounded Conductors. Switches or circuit breakers shall not disconnect the grounded conductor of a circuit.

Exception No. 1: Where the switch or circuit breaker simultaneously disconnects all conductors of the circuit.

Exception No. 2: Where the switch or circuit breaker is so arranged that the grounded conductor cannot be disconnected until all the ungrounded conductors of the circuit have been disconnected.

▲ Switches having a suitable number of poles for controlling three of the more common types of circuits are shown in Figs. 380-1, 380-2, and 380-3.

Opening only the grounded wire of a two-wire circuit would leave all devices that are connected to the circuit alive and at a voltage to ground equal to the voltage between wires on the mains, and in case of an accidental ground on the grounded wire, the circuit would not be controlled by the single-pole switch.

In either of the circuits shown in Figs. 380-2 and 380-3, if the load consists of lamps connected between the neutral and the two or three outer wires and is not balanced, opening the neutral while the other wires are connected would cause the voltages to become unbalanced and might burn out all lamps on the more lightly loaded side.

In any case a switch may be arranged to open the grounded conductor if it simultaneously opens all the other conductors of the circuit. Thus a two-pole switch may be used to control the circuit of Fig. 380-1, a three-pole switch for the circuit of Fig. 380-2, and a four-pole switch for the circuit of Fig. 380-3.

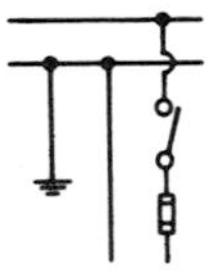

2 − Wire single−phase or
D. C. Circuit with one
conductor grounded

Fig. 380-1

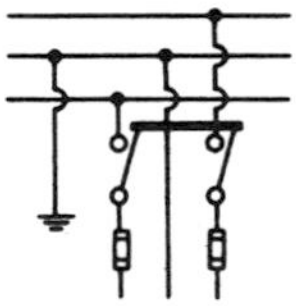

3 − Wire single − phase
or D.C. Circuit with
grounded neutral

Fig. 380-2

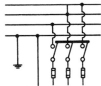

4 − Wire 3 − phase circuit with
grounded neutral

Fig. 380-3

Figs. 380-1, 380-2, and 380-3. Number of poles required for switches to control three common types of circuits.

380-3. Enclosure. Switches and circuit breakers shall be of the externally operable type enclosed in boxes or cabinets approved for the purpose.

Exception: Pendant- and surface-type snap switches and knife switches mounted on an open-face switchboard or panelboard.

380-4. Wet Locations. A switch or circuit breaker in a wet location or outside of a building shall be enclosed in a weatherproof enclosure or cabinet that shall comply with Section 373-2.

380-5. Time Switches, Flashers, and Similar Devices. Time switches, flashers and similar devices need not be of the externally operable type. They shall be enclosed in metal boxes or cabinets.

Exception No. 1: Where mounted on switchboards or control panels.

Exception No. 2: Where enclosed in approved individual housings.

▲ Any automatic switching device should be enclosed in a metal box unless it is a part of a switchboard or control panel which is located as required for live-front switchboards.

380-6. Position of Knife Switches. Single-throw knife switches shall be so placed that gravity will not tend to close them. Double-throw knife switches shall be permitted to be mounted so that the throw will be either vertical or horizontal. Where the throw is vertical, a locking device shall be provided that will insure the blades remaining in the open position when so set.

380-7. Connection of Knife Switches. Single-throw knife switches shall be so connected that the blades are dead when the switch is in the open position.

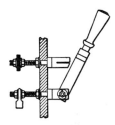

Fig. 380-4. A single-throw switch, if mounted vertically, must be mounted as here shown so that gravity will not tend to close it. A single-throw switch may also be mounted horizontally.

380-8. Accessibility and Grouping.

(a) All switches and circuit breakers used as switches shall be located that they may be operated from a readily accessible place. They shall be so installed that the center of the grip of the operating handle of the switch or circuit breaker, when in its highest position, will not be more than $6\frac{1}{2}$ feet above the floor or working platform.

Exception No. 1: On busway installations, fused switches and circuit breakers shall be permitted to be located at the same level as the busway. Suitable means shall be provided to operate the handle of the device from the floor.

Exception No. 2: Switches installed adjacent to motors, appliances or other equipment which they supply shall be permitted to be located higher than specified in the foregoing and to be accessible by portable means.

Exception No. 3: Hookstick operable isolating switches shall be permitted at heights of more than 6 feet, 6 inches.

(b) Snap switches shall not be grouped or ganged in outlet boxes unless they can be so arranged that the voltage between adjacent switches does not exceed 300, or unless they are installed in boxes equipped with permanently installed barriers between adjacent switches.

380-9. Faceplates for Flush-Mounted Snap Switches. Flush snap switches, that are mounted in ungrounded metal boxes and located within reach of conducting floors or other conducting surfaces, shall be provided with faceplates of nonconducting, noncombustible material. Metal faceplates shall be of ferrous metal not less than 0.030 inch in thickness or of nonferrous metal not less than 0.040 inch in thickness. Faceplates of insulating material shall be noncombustible and not less than 0.10 inch in thickness but they shall be permitted to be less than 0.10 inch in thickness if formed or reinforced to provide adequate mechanical strength.

▲ A metal switch plate, if not grounded, may become "alive" by reason of contact of the ungrounded circuit wire with the plate or switch box, and a hazard is thus created if the plate is within reach from any conductive object. The hazard still exists, however, if a plate of insulating material is attached by means of metal screws with exposed metal heads. Insulated screws and metal screws with insulated heads are available.

380-10. Mounting of Snap Switches.

(a) Surface-Type. Snap switches used with open wiring on insulators shall be mounted on insulating material that will separate the conductors at least $\frac{1}{2}$ inch from the surface wired over.

(b) Box Mounted. Flush-type snap switches mounted in boxes that are set back of the wall surface as permitted in Section 370-10 shall be installed so that the extension plaster ears are seated against the surface of the wall. Flush-type snap switches mounted in boxes that are flush with the wall surface or project therefrom shall be so installed that the mounting yoke or strap of the switch is seated against the box.

▲ The purpose of paragraph (b) is to prevent "loose switches" where openings around *recessed* boxes provide no means of seating the switch "ears" properly. It also permits the maximum projection of switch handles through the installed switch plate. The cooperation of other crafts, such as dry-wall installers, will be required to satisfy this rule.

380-11. Circuit Breakers as Switches. A hand-operable circuit breaker equipped with a lever or handle, or a power-operated circuit breaker capable of being opened by hand in the event of a power failure, shall be permitted to serve as a switch if it has the required number of poles.

▲ Molded-case circuit breakers are intended to be mounted on a vertical surface in an upright position or on their side. Thier use in any other position requires their evaluation for such use.

ON and OFF legends on circuit breakers and switches are not intended to be mounted upside down.

380-12. Grounding of Enclosures. Enclosures for switches or circuit breakers on circuits of over 150 volts to ground shall be grounded as specified in Article 250. Where nonmetallic enclosures are used with metal-sheathed cables or metallic conduits, provision shall be made for grounding continuity.

380-13. Knife Switches.

(a) Knife switches rated at over 1200 amperes at 250 volts or less, and at over 600 amperes at 251 to 600 volts, shall be used only as isolating switches and shall not be opened under load.

(b) To interrupt currents over 1200 amperes at 250 volts or less, or over 600 amperes at 251 to 600 volts, a circuit breaker or a switch of special design approved for such purpose shall be used.

(c) Knife switches of ratings less than specified in (a) and (b) above shall be considered general-use switches.

See definition of general-use switch in Article 100.

(d) Motor-circuit switches shall be permitted to be of the knife-switch type.

See definition of a motor-circuit switch in Article 100.

380-14. Rating and Use of Snap Switches.
Snap switches shall be used within their ratings and as follows:

(a) AC General-Use Snap Switch. A form of general-use snap switch suitable only for use on alternating-current circuits for controlling the following:

(1) Resistive and inductive loads, including electric-discharge lamps, not exceeding the ampere rating of the switch at the voltage involved.

(2) Tungsten-filament lamp loads not exceeding the ampere rating of the switch at 120 volts.

(3) Motor loads not exceeding 80 percent of the ampere rating of the switch at its rated voltage.

(b) AC-DC General-Use Snap Switch. A form of general-use snap switch suitable for use on either AC or DC circuits for controlling the following:

(1) Resistive loads not exceeding the ampere rating of the switch at the voltage applied.

(2) Inductive loads not exceeding 50 percent of the ampere rating of the switch at the applied voltage. Switches rated in horsepower are suitable for controlling motor loads within their rating at voltage applied.

(3) Tungsten-filament lamp loads not exceeding the ampere rating of the switch at the applied voltage if "T" rated.

For switches on signs and outline lighting, see Section 600-2.
For switches controlling motors, see Sections 430-83, 430-109, and 430-110.

▲ For a noninductive load not including any tungsten-filament lamps, a snap switch is merely required to have an ampere rating at least equal to the ampere rating of the load it controls. Electrically heated appliances are about the only common examples of such loads.

For the control of loads consisting of tungsten lamps alone, or tungsten lamps combined with any other noninductive load, snap switches should be "T" rated or for alternating current circuits, a general-use AC snap switch should be used.

The term *snap switch* as used here and elsewhere in the Code is intended to include, in general, the common types of flush and surface-mounted switches used for the control of lighting equipment and small appliances and the switches used to control branch circuits on lighting panelboards. These switches are now usually of the tumbler or toggle type but can be the rotary-snap or pushbutton type. The term is not applied to circuit breakers or to switches of the type that are commonly known as *knife switches.* See definition of "Switches" in Art. 100.

B. Construction Specifications

380-15. Marking. Switches shall be marked with the current and voltage and, if horsepower rated, the maximum rating for which they are designed.

380-16. 600-Volt Knife Switches. Auxiliary contacts of a renewable or quick-break type or the equivalent, shall be provided on all 600-volt knife switches designed for use in breaking currents over 200 amperes.

380-17. Fused Switches. A fused switch shall not have fuses in parallel.

ARTICLE 384. SWITCHBOARDS AND PANELBOARDS

384-1. Scope. This Article covers (1) all switchboards, panelboards, and distribution boards installed for the control of light and power circuits, and (2) battery-charging panels supplied from light or power circuits.

Exception: Switchboards or portions thereof used exclusively to control signaling circuits operated by batteries.

384-2. Other Articles. Switches, circuit breakers, and overcurrent devices used on switchboards, panelboards, and distribution boards, and their enclosures, shall comply with the requirements of Articles 240, 250, 370, 380, and other Articles that apply. Switchboards and panelboards in hazardous locations shall comply with the requirements of Articles 500 through 517.

384-3. Support and Arrangement of Busbars and Conductors.

(a) Conductors and busbars on a switchboard, panelboard, or control board shall be so located as to be free from physical damage and shall be held firmly in place. Other than the required interconnections and control wiring, only those conductors that are intended for termination in a vertical section of a switchboard shall be located in that section.

▲ This requirement, that only those conductors intended for termination in a vertical section of a switchboard shall be located at such section other than required inner connections for control wiring, was put into the Code because of the many cases on record of damage to switchboards having been caused by termination failures in one section being transported to other parts of the switchboard. In order to comply with this new requirement in the Code, it will be necessary in some cases to provide auxiliary gutters.

(b) The arrangement of busbars and conductors shall be such as to avoid overheating due to inductive effects.

(c) Each switchboard, switchboard section, or panelboard, if used as service equipment, shall be provided with a main bonding jumper sized in accordance with Section 250-79(c) or the equivalent placed within the service disconnect section for connecting the grounded service conductor on its supply side to the switchboard or panelboard frame. All sections of a switchboard shall be bonded together using an equipment grounding conductor sized in accordance with Table 250-95.

(d) Load terminals in switchboards and panelboards shall be so located that it will be unnecessary to reach across or beyond an ungrounded line bus in order to make load connections.

(e) On a switchboard or a panelboard supplied from a 4-wire delta-connected system, where the mid-point of one phase is grounded, that phase busbar or conductor having the higher voltage to ground shall be marked.

(f) The phase arrangement on three phase buses shall be A, B, C from front to back, top to bottom, or left to right, as viewed from the front of the switchboard or panelboard. The B phase shall be that phase having the higher voltage to ground. Other busbar arrangements shall be permitted for additions to existing installations and shall be marked.

▲ The reason for requiring the conductor having the higher voltage to ground to be marked and located in the center (B phase) is a consequence of the innumerable accidents resulting from attempts to insert single-phase breakers for lighting circuits off the high leg. This standardization of location will require basic phase identification throughout the electrical system.

A. Switchboards

384-4. Location of Switchboards. Switchboards that have any exposed live parts shall be located in permanently dry locations and then only where under competent supervision and accessible only to qualified persons. Switchboards shall be so located that the probability of damage from equipment or processes is reduced to a minimum.

384-5. Wet Locations. Where a switchboard is in a wet location or outside of a building, it shall be enclosed in a weatherproof enclosure or cabinet installed to comply with Section 373-2.

384-6. Location Relative to Easily Ignitible Material. Switchboards shall be so placed as to reduce to a minimum the probability of communicating fire to adjacent combustible materials.

384-7. Clearance From Ceiling. A space of 3 feet or more shall be provided between the top of any switchboard and any nonfireproof ceiling.

Exception: Where a fireproof shield is provided between the switchboard and the ceiling.

▲ This restriction does not apply to metal-enclosed dead-front switchboards which are commonly used today. At the time this rule was put in the Code as a recommendation in 1897, it was the practice to fabricate the switchboard on the job. These were mostly open-top live-front switchboards with open-type switches, etc.

384-8. Clearances Around Switchboards. Clearances around switchboards shall comply with the provisions of Section 110-16.

▲ Accessibility and working space are very necessary to avoid possible shock hazards and to provide easy access for maintenance, repair, operation, and housekeeping. It is preferable to increase the minimum space behind a switchboard where space will permit.

384-9. Conductor Covering. Insulated conductors where closely grouped, as on the rear of switchboards, shall each have a flame-retardant outer covering. The conductor covering shall be stripped back to avoid contact with the terminals. Insulated conductors used for instrument and control wiring on the rear of switchboards shall be flame-retardant, either inherently or by means of an outer covering, such as one of the following types: RH, RHH, RHW, V, ALS, AVA, AVB, SIS, T, TA, TBS, TW, THHN, THWN, THW, MI, XHHW, or other types approved for the purpose.

384-10. Clearance for Conductors Entering Bus Enclosures. Where conduits or other raceways enter a switchboard, floor standing panelboard, or similar enclosure at the bottom, sufficient space shall be provided to permit installation of conductors in the enclosure. The wiring space shall not be less than shown in the following table where the conduit or raceways enter or leave the enclosure below the busbars, their supports, or other obstructions. The conduit or raceways, including their end fittings shall not rise more than 3 inches above the bottom of the enclosure.

*Minimum Spacing Between
Bottom of Enclosure and
Busbars, their Supports, or other
Obstructions (Inches)*

Conductor
Insulated busbars, their supports, or other obstructions 8
Noninsulated busbars 10

384-11. Grounding Switchboard Frames. Switchboard frames and structures supporting switching equipment shall be grounded.

Exception: Frames of direct-current single-polarity switchboards shall not be required to be grounded if effectively insulated.

384-12. Grounding of Instruments, Relays, Meters, and Instrument Transformers on Switchboards. Instruments, relays meters, and instrument transformers located on switchboards shall be grounded as specified in Sections 250-121 through 250-125.

B. Panelboards

384-13. General. All panelboards shall have a rating not less than the minimum feeder capacity required for the load computed in accordance with Article 220. Panelboards shall be durably marked by the manufacturer with the voltage and the current rating and the number of phases for which they are designed and with the manufacturer's name or trademark in such a manner as to be visible after installation, without disturbing the interior parts or wiring.

▲ While marking may appear on the individual terminals, terminals can often be changed in the field, and wiring space and the means of mounting the terminals may not be suitable. Therefore, the panelboards should be marked independently of the marking on the terminals to identify the terminals and switch or circuit-breaker units which may be used with aluminum wire. If all terminals are suitable for use with aluminum conductors as well as with copper conductors, the panelboard will be marked "use copper or aluminum wire." A panelboard marked "use copper wire only" indicates that wiring space or other factors make the panelboard unsuitable for any aluminum conductors.

384-14. Lighting and Appliance Branch-Circuit Panelboard. For the purposes of this Article, a lighting and appliance branch-circuit panelboard is one having more than 10 percent of its overcurrent devices rated 30 amperes or less, for which neutral connections are provided.

▲ This definition is intended to describe the types of panelboards to which the requirements in Sec. 384-15 and 384-16(a) are applied.

Even though a panelboard may be used largely for other than lighting purposes, it is to be judged under the requirements for lighting and appliance branch circuit panelboards if it conforms to a specific condition stated in the definition. On the other hand, a panelboard which feeds only lighting but has no provision for neutrals is not so classified.

384-15. Number of Overcurrent Devices on One Panelboard. Not more than 42 overcurrent devices (other than those provided for in the mains) of a lighting and appliance branch-circuit panelboard shall be installed in any one cabinet or cutout box.

A lighting and appliance branch-circuit panelboard shall be provided with physical means to prevent the installation of more overcurrent devices than that number for which the panelboard was designed, rated, and approved.

For the purposes of this Article, a 2-pole circuit breaker shall be considered two overcurrent devices; a 3-pole breaker shall be considered three overcurrent devices.

▲ Figure 384-1 illustrates a panelboard with a 200-A main which provides for the insertion of class CTL* overcurrent devices. The top three stab receivers are of an F-slot configuration. Each F slot will receive only one breaker pole. The remainder of the slots are of an E configuration which will receive two breaker poles per slot. Thus there is provision for installing not more than 42 overcurrent devices, which does not include the main circuit breaker. This panelboard may also be supplied without main overcurrent protection (see Fig. 384-2), where such overcurrent protection is supplied elsewhere, as shown in Fig. 384-3.

* Class CTL is the Underwriters' Laboratories, Inc., designation for the code requirement for circuit limitation within a lighting and appliance branch-circuit panelboard. It means "circuit-limiting."

384-16. Overcurrent Protection.

(a) Each lighting and appliance branch-circuit panelboard shall be individually protected on the supply side by not more than two main circuit breakers or two sets of fuses having a combined rating not greater than that of the panelboard.

Exception No. 1: Individual protection for a lighting and appliance panelboard shall not be required if the panelboard feeder has overcurrent protection not greater than that of the panelboard.

▲ The main fuses or main circuit breakers may be mounted either in the panelboard or ahead of the panelboard. In Fig. 384-3 the 200-A overcurrent device ahead of panelboard A protects the panelboard because it is rated 200 A. The 200-A overcurrent device ahead of panelboards B and C protects both panelboards because each is rated 200 A. Exception No. 1 is complied with in both cases.

Exception No. 2: Individual protection for lighting and appliance branch-circuit panelboards is not required where such panelboards are used as service equipment in supplying an individual residential occupancy and where any bus supplying 15- or 20-ampere circuits is protected on the supply side by an overcurrent device.

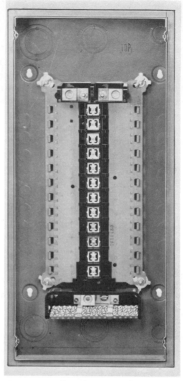

Fig. 384-1. Main circuit breakers service equipment panel. (*Federal Pacific Electric Company.*)

Fig. 384-2. Panelboard without main breaker. (*Federal Pacific Electric Company.*)

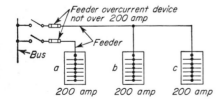

Fig. 384-3. Lighting and appliance branch-circuit panelboards.

▲ Individual residential occupancy means a single-family dwelling or an individual apartment in a multifamily dwelling.

Exception No. 2 must be taken in conjunction with Sec. 230-71 in order to have a complete picture. In effect the intent is to permit the use of a lighting and appliance branch-circuit panelboard as the service equipment in an individual residential occupancy provided that no switch or circuit breaker rated at 20 A or less may serve as one of the six permissible disconnecting means. Such 20-A or smaller devices must have an overcurrent device of larger rating on the supply side as shown in Fig. 384-4.

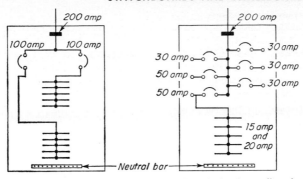

Fig. 384-4. 200-A lighting and appliance branch-circuit panelboards.

(b) Panelboards equipped with snap switches rated at 30 amperes or less, shall have overcurrent protection not in excess of 200 amperes.

▲ In this case the limitation on snap switches does not apply to circuit breakers.

(c) The total load on any overcurrent device located in a panelboard shall not exceed 80 percent of its rating where in normal operation the load will continue for 3 hours or more.

Exception: Where the assembly including the overcurrent device is approved for continuous duty at 100 percent of its rating.

(d) Where a panelboard is supplied through a transformer, the overcurrent protection required in (a) and (b) above shall be located on the secondary side of the transformer.

Exception: A panelboard supplied by the secondary side of a single-phase transformer having a two-wire (single-voltage) secondary shall be considered as protected by overcurrent protection provided on the primary (supply) side of the transformer, provided this protection is in accordance with Section 450-3(b)(1) and does not exceed the value determined by multiplying the panelboard rating by the secondary-to-primary voltage ratio.

384-17. Panelboards in Damp or Wet Locations. Panelboards in damp or wet locations shall be installed to comply with Section 373-2.

384-18. Enclosure. Panelboards shall be mounted in cabinets, cutout boxes, or enclosures approved for the purpose and shall be dead front.

Exception: Panelboards other than of the dead front externally operable type shall be permitted where accessible only to qualified persons.

384-19. Relative Arrangement of Switches and Fuses. In panelboards, fuses of any type shall be installed on the load side of any switches.

Exception: As provided in Section 230-94 for use as service equipment.

▲ For service equipment, switches are permitted on either the supply side or the load side of the fuses. In all other cases if the panelboards are accessible to other than qualified persons, Sec. 240-40 requires that the switches shall be on the supply side so that when replacing fuses all danger of shock or short circuit can be eliminated by opening the switch.

C. Construction Specifications

384-20. Panels. The panels of switchboards shall be made of moisture-resistant, noncombustible material.

384-21. Busbars. Bare busbars shall be permitted if they are rigidly mounted.

384-22. Protection of Instrument Circuits. Instruments, pilot lights, potential transformers, and other switchboard devices with potential coils shall be supplied by a circuit that is protected by standard overcurrent devices rated 15 amperes or less.

Exception No. 1: Where the operation of the overcurrent device might introduce a hazard in the operation of devices.

Exception No. 2: For ratings of 2 amperes or less, special types of enclosed fuses shall be permitted.

384-23. Component Parts. Switches, fuses, and fuseholders used on panelboards shall comply with the applicable requirements of Articles 240 and 380.

384-24. Knife Switches. Exposed blades of knife switches shall be dead when open.

384-25. Color Coding. On switchboards or panelboards that are provided with color markings to indicate the main busbars to which branch-circuit busbars are connected, the colors shall conform to the color coding of Section 210-5.

384-26. Minimum Spacings. The distance between bare metal parts, busbars, etc., shall not be less than specified in Table 384-26.

Exception No. 1: At switches or circuit breakers.

Exception No. 2: Inherent spacings in listed components.

Where close proximity does not cause excessive heating, parts of the same polarity at switches, enclosed fuses, etc. shall be permitted to be placed as close together as convenience in handling will allow.

Table 384-26. Minimum Spacings Between Bare Metal Parts

	Opposite Polarity Where Mounted on the Same Surface	Opposite Polarity Where Held Free in Air	* Live Parts to Ground
Not over 125 volts..............	$\frac{3}{4}$ inch	$\frac{1}{2}$ inch	$\frac{1}{2}$ inch
Not over 250 volts..............	$1\frac{1}{4}$ inch	$\frac{3}{4}$ inch	$\frac{1}{2}$ inch
Not over 600 volts..............	2 inches	1 inch	1 inch

* For spacing between live parts and doors of cabinets, see Section 373-11(a) (1), (2), and (3).

384-27. Grounding of Panelboards. Panelboard cabinets shall be grounded in the manner specified in Article 250 or Section 384-3(c). An approved terminal bar for equipment grounding conductors shall be provided and secured inside of the cabinet for the attachment of all the feeder and branch-circuit equipment grounding conductors, where the panelboard is used with nonmetallic raceway or cable, or where separate grounding conductors are provided. The terminal bar shall be bonded to the cabinet or panelboard frame and shall not be connected to the neutral bar in other than service equipment.

▲ A terminal bar for connecting equipment grounding conductors may be an inherent part of a panelboard, or terminal bar kits may be obtained for simple installation in any panelboard.

Exception: When an isolated ground conductor is provided as in Section 250-74, Exception No. 4, the insulated ground conductor which is run with the circuit conductors shall be permitted to pass through the panelboard without being connected to the panelboard grounding terminal bar.

▲ This exception allows an isolated ground-conductor run with the circuit conductors to pass through the panelboard without being connected to the panelboard grounding-terminal bar, in order to provide for the reduction of electrical noise (electro-magnetic interference) on the grounding circuit as provided for in Sec. 250-74, Exception No. 4.

In order to maintain the isolation of the grounding wire necessary for a low-noise ground, the grounding wire must be connected directly to the grounding-terminal bar in the service-entrance equipment. To do this it may be necessary for the grounding wires to pass through one or more panelboards.

Sensitive electronic equipment utilized in hospitals, laboratories and similar locations may malfunction due to electrical noise (electromagnetic interference) present in the electrical supply. This effect can be reduced by the proper use of an isolated grounding wire which connects directly to the service-entrance panel grounding-terminal bar. Such systems are being used in increasing numbers where computers are in use.

CHAPTER FOUR

Equipment for General Use

ARTICLE 400. FLEXIBLE CORDS AND CABLES

A. General

400-1. Scope. This Article covers general requirements, applications, and construction specifications for flexible cords and flexible cables.

400-2. Other Articles. Flexible cords and flexible cables shall comply with this Article and with the applicable provisions of other Articles of this Code.

400-3. Suitability. Flexible cords and cables and their associated fittings shall be suitable for the conditions of use and location.

400-4. Types. Flexible cords and flexible cables shall conform to the description in Table 400-4. Types of flexible cords and flexible cables other than those listed in the Table shall be the subject of special investigations and shall not be used before being approved.

400-5. Ampacity of Flexible Cords and Cables. Table 400-5 gives the allowable ampacity for not more than 3 current-carrying conductors in a cord. If the number of current-carrying conductors in a cord is from 4 to 6, the allowable ampacity of each conductor shall be reduced to 80 percent of the values for not more than 3 current-carrying conductors in the Table. A conductor used for equipment grounding and a neutral conductor which carries only the unbalanced current from other conductors, as in the case of normally balanced circuits of 3 or more conductors, shall not be considered as current-carrying conductors.

Where a single conductor is used for both equipment grounding and to carry unbalanced current from other conductors, as provided for in Section 250-60 for electric ranges and electric clothes dryers, it shall not be considered as a current-carrying conductor.

▲ The "Underwriters' knot" (Fig. 400-1) has been used for many years and is a good method for taking the strain from the socket terminals where lamp cord is used for the pendant. For reinforced cords and junior hard-service cords, sockets with cord grips such as shown in Fig. 400-2 provide an effective means of relieving the terminals of all strain.

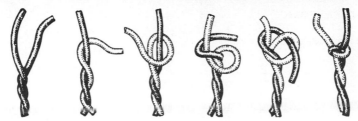

FIG. 400-1. Underwriters' knot.

FIG. 400-2. Lampholder with cord grip.

Notes to Table 400-4

1. Except for Types SP-1, SP-2, SP-3, SPT-1, SPT-2, SPT-3, HPN, TP, TPT, SRD (3-conductor) and SRDT (3-conductor) individual conductors are twisted together.

2. Cables constructed differently than specified herein and listed as component parts of a data processing system shall be permitted.

3. Types TP, TPT, TS, and TST shall be permitted in lengths not exceeding 8 feet when attached directly, or by means of a special type of plug, to a portable appliance rated at 50 watts or less and of such nature that extreme flexibility of the cord is essential.

4. Rubber-filled or varnished cambric tapes shall be permitted as a substitute for the inner braids.

5. Types S, SO, ST, and STO shall be permitted for use on theater stages, in garages, and elsewhere where flexible cords are permitted by this Code.

6. Traveling cables for operating, control and signaling circuits shall have one or more nonmetallic fillers or shall have a supporting filler of stranded steel wires having its own protective braid or cover. Cables exceeding 100 feet between supports shall have steel supporting fillers, except in locations subject to excessive moisture or corrosive vapors or gases. Where steel supporting fillers are used, they shall run straight through the center of the cable assembly and shall not be cabled with the copper strands of any conductor.

Types E, EO, EN, ET, ETP, ETLB, and ETT cables shall be permitted to incorporate in the construction No. 20 conductors formed as a pair, and covered with suitable shielding for telephone and other audio or higher frequency communication circuits. The insulation of the conductors shall be rubber or thermoplastic of thickness specified for the other conductors of the particular type of cable. The shield shall have its own protective covering. Where used, this component shall be permitted to be incorporated in any layer of the cable assembly, and shall not run straight through the center.

7. A third conductor in these cables is for grounding purposes only.

8. The individual conductors of all cords, except those of heat-resistant cords (Types AFC, AFPD, AFS, AFSJ, and CFPD), shall have a rubber or thermoplastic insulation, except that the grounding conductor where used shall be in accordance with Section 400-23(b). A rubber compound shall be vulcanized, except for heater cords (Types HPD and HSJ).

9. Where the voltage between any two conductors exceeds 300, but does not exceed 600, flexible cord of No. 10 and smaller shall have rubber or thermoplastic insulation on the individual conductors at least 45 mils in thickness, unless Type S, SO, ST, or STO cord is used.

Table 400-4. Flexible Cords and Cables (See Section 400-4)

Trade Name	Type Letter	Size AWG	No. of Conductors	Insulation	Nominal *Insulation Thickness AWG	Mils	Braid on Each Conductor	Outer Covering		Use	
Parallel Tinsel Cord	TP See Note 3	27	2	Rubber	27	30	None	Rubber	Attached to an Appliance	Damp Places	Not Hard Usage
	TPT See Note 3	27	2	Thermoplastic			None	Thermoplastic	Attached to an Appliance	Damp Places	Not Hard Usage
Jacketed Tinsel Cord	TS See Note 3	27	2	Rubber	27	15	None	Rubber	Attached to an Appliance	Damp Places	Not Hard Usage
	TST See Note 3	27	2	Thermoplastic			None	Thermoplastic	Attached to an Appliance	Damp Places	Not Hard Usage
Asbestos-Covered Heat-Resistant Cord	AFC	18-10	2 or 3	Impregnated Asbestos	18-14	30	Cotton or Rayon	None	Pendant	Dry Places	Not Hard Usage
	AFPD		2 / 2 or 3		12-10	45	None	Cotton, Rayon or Saturated Asbestos			

Trade Name	Type Letter	Size AWG	Number of Conductors	Insulation	Nominal Insulation Thickness AWG	Nominal Insulation Thickness (Mils)	Braid on Each Conductor	Outer Covering	Use		
Cotton-Covered Heat-Resistant Cord	CFPD	18-10	2 or 3 / 2	Impregnated Cotton	18-14 / 12-10	30 / 45	Cotton or Rayon	None	Pendant	Dry Places	Not Hard Usage
All Rubber Parallel Cord	SP-1 See Note 7	18		Rubber	18	30	None	Rubber	Pendant or Portable	Damp Places	Not Hard Usage
	SP-2 See Note 7	18-16	2 or 3	Rubber	18-16	45	None	Rubber	Pendant or Portable	Damp Places	Not Hard Usage
	SP-3 See Note 7	18-12	2 or 3	Rubber	18-16 / 14 / 12 / 10	60 / 80 / 95 / 110	None	Rubber	Refrigerators or Room Air Conditioners	Damp Places	Not Hard Usage
All Plastic Parallel Cord	SPT-1 See Note 7	18		Thermoplastic	18	30	None	Thermoplastic	Pendant or Portable	Damp Places	Not Hard Usage
	SPT-2 See Note 7	18-16	2 or 3	Thermoplastic	18-16	45	None	Thermoplastic	Pendant or Portable	Damp Places	Not Hard Usage
	SPT-3 See Note 7	18-10		Thermoplastic	18-16 / 14 / 12 / 10	60 / 80 / 95 / 110	None	Thermoplastic	Refrigerator or Room Air Conditioners	Damp Places	Not Hard Usage

*See Note 9.

See Notes 1 through 9 preceding table.

Table 400-4 (Continued)

Trade Name	Type Letter	Size AWG	No. of Conductors	Insulation	Nominal *Insulation Thickness		Braid on Each Conductor	Outer Covering	Use		
					AWG	Mils					
Lamp Cord	C	18-10	2 or more	Rubber	18-16	30	Cotton	None	Pendant or Portable	Dry Place	Not Hard Usage
Twisted Portable Cord	PD	18-10	2 or more	Rubber	14-10	45	Cotton	Cotton or Rayon	Pendant or Portable	Dry Places	Not Hard Usage
Vacuum Cleaner Cord	SV See Note 7	18		Rubber	18	15	None	Rubber	Pendant or Portable	Damp Places	Not Hard Usage
	SVO, SVT See Note 7	18-17		Thermopl'	18-17	15		Oil-Resistant Thermoplastic Compound			
	SVTO See Note 7	18	2 or 3		18	15		Oil-Resistant Thermoplastic			
Junior Hard Service Cord	SJ	18-14	2, 3, or 4	Rubber	18-14 (Rubber) 18-14 (Latex)	30 15	None	Rubber	Pendant or Portable	Damp Places	Hard Usage
	SJO							Oil-Resistant Compound			
	SJT			Thermopl' or Rubber	18-14	30		Thermoplastic			
	SJTO							Oil-Resistant Thermoplastic			

Trade Name	Type Letter	Size AWG	Nominal No. of Conductors	Insulation	AWG	Thickness	Braid on Each Conductor	Outer Covering	Use		
Hard Service Cord	S See Note 5	18-2	2 or more	Rubber	18-16 (Rubber)	30	None	Rubber	Pendant or Portable	Damp Places	Extra Hard Usage
	SO				18-16 (Latex)	15		Oil Resist. Compound			
					14-10 (Rubber)	45					
					14-10 (Latex)	18					
					8-2 (Rubber)	60					
	ST			Thermopl' or Rubber	18-16	30		Thermoplastic			
	STO				14-10	45		Oil Resistant Thermoplastic			
					8-2	60					
Rubber-Jacketed Heat-Resistant Cord	AFSJ	18-16	2 or 3	Impregnated Asbestos	18-14	30	None	Rubber	Portable Heater	Damp Places	Hard Usage
	AFS	18-16-14									Extra Hard Usage
Heater Cord	HPD	18-12	2, 3, or 4	Rubber or thermoplastic with Asbestos or All Neoprene	(Rubber or Thermoplastic)		None	Cotton or Rayon	Portable Heater	Dry Places	Not Hard Usage
					18-16	15					
					14-12	30					

See Notes 1 through 9 preceding table.

*See Note 9.

Table 400-4 (Continued)

Trade Name	Type Letter	Size AWG	No. of Conductors	Insulation	Nominal *Insulation Thickness AWG	Mils	Braid on Each Conductor	Outer Covering		Use	
Rubber Jacketed Heater Cord	HSJ	18-16	2, 3 or 4	Rubber or thermoplastic with Asbestos or All Neoprene	(All Neoprene)		None	Cotton and Rubber	Portable Heaters	Damp Places	Hard Usage
Jacketed Heater Cord	HSJO	18-16	2, 3 or 4	Rubber with Asbestos or All Neoprene	18-16	30	None	Cotton and Oil Resistant Compound			Hard Usage
	HS	14-12			14-12	45		Cotton and Rubber or Neoprene	Portable	Damp Places	Extra Hard Usage
	HSO	14-12						Cotton and Oil Resistant Compound			
Parallel Heater Cord	HPN See Note 7	18-12	2 or 3	Thermosetting	18-16 14 12	45 80 95	None	Thermosetting	Portable	Damp Places	Not Hard Usage
Range, Dryer Cable	SRD	10-4	3 or 4	Rubber	10-4	45	None	Rubber or Neoprene	Portable	Damp Places	Ranges, Dryers
	SRDT	10-4	3 or 4	Thermoplastic			None	Thermoplastic	Portable	Damp Places	Ranges, Dryers

Trade Name	Type	AWG	No. of Conductors	Insulation	AWG	Number	Braid on Each Conductor	Outer Covering	Use		
									Data Processing Systems	Dry Places	Power and Signaling Circuits
Data Processing Cable	DP See Note 2	32 Min.	2 or more	Thermoplastic, Rubber or Cross-linked Synthetic Polymer	32–27 (50V) 26–23 (50V) 22–20 (50V) 32–16 (300V) 14–10 (300V) 8– 2 (300V)	8 12 16 20 30 60	None	Thermoplastic, Rubber or Cross-linked Synthetic Polymer	Data Processing Systems	Dry Places	Power and Signaling Circuits
Elevator Cable	E See Note 6	18–14	2 or more	Rubber	18–16	20	Cotton	Three Cotton, Outer one Flame-Retardant & Moisture-Resist. See Note 4	Elevator Lighting and Control	Non-Hazardous Locations	
Elevator Cable	EO See Note 6	18–14	2 or more	Rubber	14	30	Cotton	One Cotton and a Neoprene Jacket See Note 4	Elevator Lighting and Control	Hazardous Locations	
Elevator Cable	EN See Note 6	18–14	2 or more	Rubber	18–16	20	Flexible Nylon Jacket	Three Cotton, Outer one Flame-Retardant & Moisture-Resist. See Note 4 — One Cotton and a Neoprene or Thermoplastic Jacket See Note 4	Elevator Lighting and Control	Non-Hazardous Locations — Hazardous Locations	

See Notes 1 through 9 preceding table.

* See Note 9.

Table 400-4 (Continued)

Trade Name	Type Letter	Size AWG	No. of Conductors	Insulation	Nominal *Insulation Thickness AWG	Mils	Braid on Each Conductor	Outer Covering	Use
	ET See Note 6			Thermo-plastic			Rayon	Three Cotton, Outer one Flame-Retardant & Moisture-Resist. See Note 4	Non-Hazardous Locations
	ETLB See Note 6			Thermo-plastic	14	30	None		
Elevator Cable	ETP See Note 6			Thermo-plastic			Rayon	Thermoplastic	
	ETT See Note 6			Thermo-plastic			None	One Cotton and a Thermoplastic Jacket	Hazardous Locations

See Notes 1 through 9 preceding table.
* See Note 9.

400-6. Marking. Flexible cords and cables shall be marked by means of a printed tag attached to the coil reel or carton. The tag shall contain the information required in Section 310-11(a).

Types SJ, SJO, SJT, SJTO, S, SO, ST, and STO flexible cords shall be durably marked on the surface at intervals not exceeding 24 inches with the type designation, size, and number of conductors.

400-7. Uses Permitted.

(a) Flexible cords and cables shall be used only for (1) pendants; (2) wiring of fixtures; (3) connection of portable lamps or appliances; (4) elevator cables; (5) wiring of cranes and hoists; (6) connection of stationary equipment to facilitate their frequent interchange; or (7) prevention of the transmission of noise or vibration; or (8) fixed or stationary appliances where the fastening means and mechanical connections are designed to permit removal for maintenance and repair; or (9) data processing cables as permitted by Section 645-2.

(b) Where used as permitted in sub-sections **(a)**(3), **(a)**(6), and **(a)**(8) of this Section, each flexible cord shall be equipped with an attachment plug and shall be energized from an approved receptacle outlet.

▲ It should be noted that the cords referred to are the cords attached to the appliance and not extension cords supplementing or extending the regular supply cords. The use of an extension cord would represent a conflict with the requirements of the Code in that it would serve as a substitute for a receptacle to be located near the appliance.

Extension cords are intended for temporary use with portable appliances, tools, and similar equipment which are not normally used at one specific location.

400-8. Uses Not Permitted. Flexible cords and cables shall not be used (1) as a substitute for the fixed wiring of a structure; (2) where run through holes in walls, ceilings, or floors; (3) where run through doorways, windows, or similar openings; (4) where attached to building surfaces; or (5) where concealed behind building walls, ceilings, or floors.

400-9. Splices. Flexible cord shall be used only in continuous lengths without splice or tap when initially installed in applications permitted by Section 400-7(a). The repair of hard-service flexible cords No. 12 and larger shall be permitted if conductors are spliced in accordance with Section 110-14(b) and the completed splice retains the insulation, outer sheath properties, flexibility, and usage characteristics of the cord being spliced.

400-10. Pull at Joints and Terminals. Flexible cords shall be so connected to devices and to fittings that tension will not be transmitted to joints or terminal screws. This shall be accomplished by a knot in the cord, winding with tape, by a special fitting designed for that purpose, or by other approved means which will prevent a pull on the cord from being directly transmitted to joints or terminal screws.

400-11. In Show Windows and Show Cases. Flexible cords used in show windows and show cases shall be Type S, SO, SJ, SJO, ST, STO, SJT, SJTO, or AFS.

Exception No. 1: For the wiring of chain-supported lighting fixtures.

Exception No. 2: As supply cords for portable lamps and other merchandise being displayed or exhibited.

▲ On account of the flammable material nearly always present in show windows,

Table 400-5. **Ampacity of Flexible Cords and Cables**
(Based on Ambient Temperature of 30°C (86°F) See Section 400-13 and Table 400-4)

Size AWG	Rubber Types TP, TS / Thermoplastic Types TPT, TST	Rubber Types C, PD, E, EO, EN, S, SO, SRD, SJ, SJO, SV, SVO, SP / Thermoplastic Types ET, ETT, ETLB, ETP, ST, STO, SRDT, SJT, SJTO, SVT, SVTO, SPT		Types AFS, AFSJ, HPD, HSJ, HSJO, HS, HSO, HPN	Cotton Types CFPD* / Asbestos Types AFC* AFPD*
		A†	B†		
27**	0.5	..	..	..	..
18	..	7	10	10	6
17	..	..	12	..	..
16	..	10	13	15	8
15	..	..	..	17	..
14	..	15	18	20	17
12	..	20	25	30	23
10	..	25	30	35	28
8	..	35	40	..	..
6	..	45	55	..	..
4	..	60	70	..	..
2	..	80	95	..	..

*These types are used almost exclusively in fixtures where they are exposed to high temperatures and ampere ratings are assigned accordingly.

**Tinsel Cord.

† The ampacities under sub-heading A apply to 3-conductor cords and other multiconductor cords connected to utilization equipment so that only 3 conductors are current carrying. The ampacities under sub-heading B apply to 2-conductor cords and other multiconductor cords connected to utilization equipment so that only 2 conductors are current carrying.

NOTE. Ultimate Insulation Temperature. In no case shall conductors be associated together in such way with respect to the kind of circuit, the wiring method used, or the number of conductors that the limiting temperature of the conductors will be exceeded.

great care should be taken to ensure that only approved types of cords are used and that they are maintained in good condition.

400-12. Minimum Size. The individual conductors of a flexible cord or cable shall not be smaller than the sizes in Table 400-4.

400-13. Overcurrent Protection. Flexible cords not smaller than No. 18, and tinsel cords or cords having equivalent characteristics of smaller size approved for use with specific appliances, shall be considered as protected against overcurrent by the overcurrent devices described in Section 240-4.

B. Construction Specifications

400-20. Labels. Flexible cords shall be examined and tested at the factory and labeled before shipment.

400-21. Nominal Insulation Thickness. The nominal thickness of insulation for conductors of flexible cords and cables shall not be less than specified in Table 400-4.

400-22. Grounded-Conductor Identification. One conductor of flexible cords which is intended to be used as a grounded circuit conductor shall have a continuous marker readily distinguishing it from the other conductor or conductors. The identification shall consist of one of the methods indicated in (a) through (f) below.

(a) Colored Braid. A braid finished to show a white or natural gray color and the braid on the other conductor or conductors finished to show a readily distinguishable solid color or colors.

(b) Tracer in Braid. A tracer in a braid of any color contrasting with that of the braid and no tracer in the braid of the other conductor or conductors. No tracer shall be used in the braid of any conductor of a flexible cord which contains a conductor having a braid finished to show white or natural gray.

Exception: In the case of Types C and PD, and cords having the braids on the individual conductors finished to show white or natural gray. In such cords the identifying marker shall be permitted to consist of the solid white or natural gray finish on one conductor, provided there is a colored tracer in the braid of each other conductor.

(c) Colored Insulation. A white or natural gray insulation on one conductor and insulation of a readily distinguishable color or colors on the other conductor or conductors for cords having no braids on the individual conductors.

Exception: Cords which have insulation on the individual conductors integral with the jacket.

It shall be permissible to cover the insulation with an outer finish to provide the desired color.

(d) Colored Separator. A white or natural gray separator on one conductor and a separator of a readily distinguishable solid color on the other conductor or conductors of cords having insulation on the individual conductors integral with the jacket.

(e) Tinned Conductors. One conductor having the individual strands tinned and the other conductor or conductors having the individual strands untinned for cords having insulation on the individual conductors integral with the jacket.

For jacketed cords furnished with appliances, one conductor having the individual strands tinned and its insulation colored light blue, with the other conductors having their individual strands untinned and insulation of a readily distinguishable color other than white or natural gray.

(f) Surface Marking. One or more stripes, ridges, or grooves so located on the exterior of the cord as to identify one conductor for cords having insulation on the individual conductors integral with the jacket.

400-23. Grounding-Conductor Identification. A conductor intended to be used as a grounding conductor shall have a continuous identifying marker readily distinguishing it from the other conductor or conductors. Conductors having a continuous green color or a continuous green color with one or more yellow stripes shall not be used for other than grounding purposes. The identifying marker shall consist of one of the methods in (a) or (b) below.

(a) Colored Braid. A braid finished to show a continuous green color or a continuous green color with one or more yellow stripes.

(b) Colored Insulation or Covering. For cords having no braids on the individual conductors, an insulation of a continuous green color or a continuous green color with one or more yellow stripes.

400-24. Attachment Plugs. Where a flexible cord is provided with a grounding conductor and equipped with an attachment plug, the attachment plug shall comply with Sections 250-59(a) and (b).

C. Portable Cables Over 600 Volts, Nominal

400-30. Scope. This part applies to multiconductor portable cables used to connect mobile equipment and machinery.

400-31. Construction.

(a) Conductors. The conductors shall be No. 8 or larger and shall employ flexible stranding.

(b) Shields. Cables operated at over 2000 volts shall be shielded. Shielding shall be for the purpose of confining the voltage stresses to the insulation.

(c) Grounding Conductor(s). Grounding conductor(s) shall be provided. The total area shall be not less than that of the size of conductor required in Section 250-95.

400-32. Shielding. All shields shall be grounded.

400-33. Grounding. Grounding conductors shall be connected in accordance with Part K of Article 250.

400-34. Minimum Bending Radii. The minimum bending radii for portable cables during installation and handling in service shall be adequate to prevent damage to the cable.

400-35. Fittings. Connectors used to connect lengths of cable in a run shall be of a type which lock firmly together. Provisions shall be made to prevent opening or closing these connectors while energized. Suitable means shall be used to eliminate tension at connectors and terminations.

400-36. Splices and Terminations. Portable cables shall not be operated with splices unless the splices are of the permanent molded, vulcanized, or other approved type. Terminations on high-voltage portable cables shall be accessible only to authorized and qualified personnel.

ARTICLE 402. FIXTURE WIRES

402-1. Scope. This Article covers general requirements and construction specifications for fixture wires.

402-2. Other Articles. Fixture wires shall comply with this Article and also with the applicable provisions of other Articles of this Code.

For application in lighting fixtures see Article 410.

402-3. Approved Types. Fixture wires shall be of a type listed in Table 402-3, and they shall comply with all requirements of that Table.

402-4. Insulation. The rubber insulations include those made from natural and synthetic rubber, neoprene, and other vulcanized materials.

Thermoplastic insulation may stiffen at temperatures colder than minus 10°C (plus 14°F), requiring care be exercised during installation at such temperatures. Thermoplastic insulation may also be deformed at normal temperatures where subjected to pressure, requiring care be exercised during installation and at points of support.

402-5. Ampacity of Fixture Wires. The ampacity of fixture wire shall not exceed the following:

Table 402-5

Size (AWG)	Ampacity
18	6
16	8
14	17

No conductor shall be used under such conditions that its operating temperature will exceed the temperature specified in Table 402-3 for the type of insulation involved.

402-6. Minimum Size. Fixture wires shall not be smaller than No. 18.

402-7. Number of Conductors in Conduit. The number of fixture wires permitted in a single conduit shall be as given in Table 2 of Chapter 9.

402-8. Grounded-Conductor Identification. One conductor of fixture wires which is intended to be used as a grounded conductor shall be identified by means of stripes or by the means described in Sections 400-22(a) through (e).

402-9. Marking.

(a) Required Information. All fixture wires shall be marked to indicate the information required in Section 310-11(a).

(b) Method of Marking. Thermoplastic-insulated fixture wire shall be durably marked on the surface at intervals not exceeding 24 inches. All other fixture wire shall be marked by means of a printed tag attached to the coil, reel, or carton.

402-10. Uses Permitted. Fixture wires shall be permitted: (1) for installation in lighting fixtures and in similar equipment where enclosed or protected and not subject to bending or twisting in use; or (2) for connecting lighting fixtures to the branch-circuit conductors supplying the fixtures.

402-11. Uses Not Permitted. Fixture wires shall not be used as branch-circuit conductors.

Exception: As permitted by Section 725-16 for Class 1 circuits.

402-12. Overcurrent Protection. Overcurrent protection for fixture wires shall be as specified in Section 240-4.

ARTICLE 410. LIGHTING FIXTURES, LAMPHOLDERS, LAMPS, RECEPTACLES, AND ROSETTES

A. General

410-1. Scope. This Article covers lighting fixtures, lampholders, pendants, receptacles, and rosettes, incandescent filament lamps, arc lamps, electric-discharge lamps, the wiring and equipment forming part of such lamps, fixtures and lighting installations which shall conform to the provisions of this Article.

Exception: As otherwise provided in this Code.

Table 402-3. Fixture Wire

Trade Name	Type Letter	Insulation	Thickness of Insulation AWG	Mils	Outer Covering	Max. Operating Temp.	Application Provisions
Heat Resistant Rubber-Covered Fixture Wire Solid or 7-Strand	RFH-1	Heat-Resistant Rubber	18	15	Nonmetallic Covering	75°C 167°F	Fixture wiring. Limited to 300 volts.
	RFH-2	Heat-Resistant Rubber	18-16	30	Nonmetallic Covering	75°C 167°F	Fixture wiring, and as permitted in Section 725-16.
		Heat-Resistant Latex Rubber	18-16	18			
Heat Resistant Rubber-Covered Fixture Wire Flexible Stranding	FFH-1	Heat-Resistant Rubber	18	15	Nonmetallic Covering	75°C 167°F	Fixture wiring. Limited to 300 volts.
	FFH-2	Heat-Resistant Rubber	18-16	30	Nonmetallic Covering		
		Heat-Resistant Latex Rubber	18-16	18		75°C 167°F	Fixture wiring, and as permitted in Section 725-16.
Thermoplastic-Covered Fixture Wire —Solid or Stranded	TF	Thermoplastic	18-16	30	None	60°C 140°F	Fixture wiring, and as permitted in Section 725-16.

					Temperature	
Thermoplastic-Covered Fixture Wire —Flexible Stranding	TFF	Thermoplastic	18-16..........30	None	60°C 140°F 140°F	Fixture wiring, and as permitted in Section 725-16.
Heat Resistant Thermoplastic-Covered Fixture Wire —Solid or Stranded	TFN	Thermoplastic	18-16..........15	Nylon Jacketed	90°C 194°F	Fixture wiring, and as permitted in Section 725-16.
Heat Resistant Thermoplastic-Covered Fixture Wire —Flexible Stranded	TFFN	Thermoplastic	18-16..........15	Nylon Jacketed	90°C 194°F	Fixture wiring, and as permitted in Section 725-16.
Cotton-Covered, Heat-Resistant, Fixture Wire	CF	Impregnated Cotton	18-14..........30	None	90°C 194°F	Fixture wiring. Limited to 300 volts.
Asbestos-Covered, Heat-Resistant, Fixture Wire	AF	Impregnated Asbestos	18-14..........30	None	150°C 302°F	Fixture wiring. Limited to 300 volts and Indoor Dry Location.

Table 402-3 (Continued)

Trade Name	Type Letter	Insulation	Thickness of Insulation AWG	Mils	Outer Covering	Max. Operating Temp.	Application Provisions
Silicone Insulated Fixture Wire Solid or 7-Strand	SF-1	Silicone Rubber	18	15	Nonmetallic Covering	200°C 392°F	Fixture wiring. Limited to 300 volts.
	SF-2	Silicone Rubber	18–14	30	Nonmetallic Covering	200°C 392°F	Fixture wiring, and as permitted in Section 725-16.
Silicone Insulated Fixture Wire Flexible Stranding	SFF-1	Silicone Rubber	18	15	Nonmetallic Covering	150°C 302°F	Fixture wiring. Limited to 300 volts.
	SFF-2	Silicone Rubber	18–14	30	Nonmetallic Covering	150°C 302°F	Fixture wiring, and as permitted in Section 725-16.
Fluorinated Ethylene Propylene Fixture Wire Solid or 7 Strand	PF	Fluorinated Ethylene Propylene	18–14	20	None	200°C 392°F	Fixture wiring, and as permitted in Section 725-16.
	PGF		18–14	14	Glass Braid		
Fluorinated Ethylene Propylene Fixture Wire Flexible Stranding	PFF	Fluorinated Ethylene Propylene	18–14	20	None	150°C 302°F	Fixture wiring, and as permitted in Section 725-16.
	PGFF		18–14	14	Glass Braid		

Table 402-3 (Continued)

Extruded Polytetra-fluoroethylene Solid or 7-Strand (Nickel or Nickel Coated Copper)	PTF	Extruded Polytetra-fluoroethylene	18-14 20	None	250°C 482°F	Fixture wire, and as permitted in Section 725-16. (Nickel or nickel-coated copper)
Extruded Polytetra-fluoroethylene Flexible Stranding (No. 26-36 AWG Silver or Nickel Coated Copper)	PTFF	Extruded Polytetra-fluoroethylene	18-14 20	None	150°C 302°F	Fixture wire, and as permitted in Section 725-16. (Silver or nickel-coated copper)

410-2. Application to Other Articles. Equipment for use in hazardous locations shall conform to Articles 500 through 517.

410-3. Live Parts. Fixtures, lampholders, lamps, rosettes, and receptacles shall have no live parts normally exposed to contact. Exposed accessible terminals in lampholders, receptacles, and switches shall not be installed in metal fixture canopies or in open bases of portable table or floor lamps.

Exception: Cleat-type lampholders, receptacles, and rosettes located at least 8 feet above the floor shall be permitted to have exposed contacts.

B. Fixture Locations

410-4. Fixtures in Specific Locations.

(a) Wet and Damp Locations. Fixtures installed in wet or damp locations shall be approved for the purpose and shall be so constructed or installed that water cannot enter or accumulate in wireways, lampholders, or other electrical parts. All fixtures installed in wet locations shall be marked, "Suitable for Wet Locations." All fixtures installed in damp locations shall be marked, "Suitable for Wet Locations" or "Suitable for Damp Locations."

Installations underground or in concrete slabs or masonry in direct contact with the earth, and locations subject to saturation with water or other liquids, such as locations exposed to weather and unprotected, vehicle washing areas, and like locations, shall be considered to be wet locations with respect to the above requirement.

Interior locations protected from weather but subject to moderate degrees of moisture, such as some basements, some barns, some cold storage warehouses and the like, the partially protected locations under canopies, marquees, roofed open porches, and the like, shall be considered to be damp locations with respect to the above requirement.

See Article 680 for lighting fixtures in swimming pools, fountains, and similar installations.

(b) Corrosive Locations. Fixtures installed in corrosive locations shall be of a type approved for such locations.

See Section 210-7 for receptacles in fixtures.

▲ An enclosed and gasketed fixture would fulfill the requirement that water shall be prevented from entering the fixture, though under some conditions water vapor might enter and a small amount of water might accumulate in the bottom of the globe.

Fixtures in the form of post lanterns, fixtures for use on service-station islands, and fixtures which are marked to indicate that they are intended for outdoor use have been investigated for outdoor installation.

An example of fixtures in "damp" locations would be those installed under canopies of stores in shopping centers where they would be protected against exposure to rain but would be subject to outside temperature variation and corresponding high humidity and condensation. Thus the internal parts of the fixture need to be of nonhygroscopic materials which will not absorb moisture and which will function under conditions of high humidity.

(c) In Ducts or Hoods. Fixtures in nonresidential occupancies shall not be installed in ducts or hoods used for removal of cooking smoke or grease-laden vapors or located in the path of travel of such exhaust products unless approved for the purpose.

Fixtures in nonresidential occupancies having approved metal enclosures mounted on the outer surface of the hood and separated from exhaust products by tight fitting glass shall be permitted. Fixtures on hoods in nonresidential occupancies shall not be located in concealed spaces unless part of an approved grease extractor.

▲ This requirement has been taken from NFPA No. 96—Vapor Removal from Commercial Equipment. It is extremely important that lighting fixtures on hoods be located out of the path of travel of exhaust products (smoke or grease-laden vapors), unless the entire hood assembly including fixtures have been tested and approved for such applications.

The use of enclosed-and-gasketed fixtures, unless located out of the path of travel of exhaust products, is not acceptable because a fire could result from high temperatures of lamps within an enclosed glass bowl coated with grease on the outer surface. In addition, grease can cause shorts or grounds in wiring within such areas.

410-5. Fixtures Near Combustible Material.   Fixtures shall be so constructed, or installed, or equipped with shades or guards that combustible material will not be subjected to temperatures in excess of 90°C (194°F).

410-6. Fixtures Over Combustible Material.   Lampholders installed over highly combustible material shall be of the unswitched type. Unless an individual switch is provided for each fixture, lampholders shall be located at least 8 feet above the floor, or shall be so located or guarded that the lamps cannot be readily removed or damaged.

▲ This refers to pendants and fixed lighting equipment, not to portable lamps. Where the lamp cannot be located out of reach, the requirement can be met by equipping the lamp with a guard.

410-7. Fixtures in Show Windows.   Externally wired fixtures shall not be used in a show window.

Exception: Fixtures of the chain-supported type may be externally wired.

410-8. Fixtures in Clothes Closets.

(a) **Location.**   A fixture in a clothes closet shall be installed:

(1) On the wall above the closet door, provided the clearance between the fixture and a storage area where combustible material may be stored within the closet is not less than 18 inches, or

(2) On the ceiling over an area which is unobstructed to the floor, maintaining an 18-inch clearance horizontally between the fixture and a storage area where combustible material may be stored within the closet.

A flush recessed fixture equipped with a solid lens shall be considered outside the closet area.

(b) **Pendants.**   Pendants shall not be installed in clothes closets.

▲ The intent is to prevent lamps from coming in contact with cartons or boxes stored on shelves and clothing hung in the closet, which would, of course, constitute a fire hazard.

It is quite obvious from the drawing in Fig. 410-1 that fixtures other than flush recessed types with solid lens cannot be located in *small* clothes closets that seem to prevail in building construction these days.

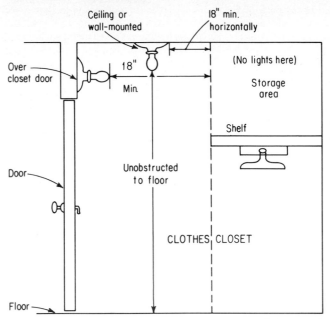

Fig. 410-1. Requirements for lighting fixtures (other than flush recessed types with a solid lens) in clothes closets.

These requirements apply to incandescent and fluorescent lighting and all types of occupancies.

For small clothes closets proper lighting may be achieved by locating fixtures on the outside ceiling in front of the closet door—especially in hall-ways where such fixtures can serve a dual function. Flush recessed fixtures with a solid lens are considered outside of the closet because the lamp is recessed behind the wall or ceiling line.

410-9. Space for Cove Lighting.   Coves shall have adequate space and shall be so located that lamps and equipment can be properly installed and maintained.

▲ Adequate space also improves ventilation, which is equally important for such equipment.

C. Provisions at Fixture Outlet Boxes, Canopies, and Pans

410-10. Space for Conductors.   Canopies and outlet boxes taken together shall provide adequate space so that fixture conductors and their connecting devices can be properly installed.

410-11. Temperature Limit of Conductors in Outlet Boxes.   Fixtures shall be of such construction or so installed that the conductors in outlet boxes shall not be subjected to temperatures greater than that for which the conductors are approved.

Branch-circuit wiring shall not be passed through an outlet box that is an integral part of an incandescent fixture unless the fixture is approved for the purpose.

▲ Fixtures equipped with incandescent lamps may cause the temperature in the outlet boxes to become excessively high. The remedy is to use fixtures of improved design, or in some special cases to use circuit conductors having insulation that will withstand the high temperature.

The second paragraph applies mainly to "prewired" recessed incandescent fixtures which have been designed to permit 90°C supply conductors in a junction box equipped with the fixture. Some of these fixtures have been listed by Underwriters' Laboratories, Inc., only on the basis of the heat contribution by the supply conductors at not more than the maximum permitted lamp load of the fixture (see Fig. 410-2).

Other fixtures have been investigated and listed for "feed-through" circuit wiring (see Fig. 410-3).

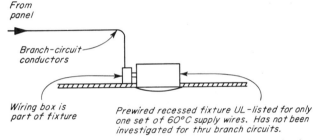

From panel

Branch-circuit conductors

Wiring box is part of fixture

Prewired recessed fixture UL–listed for only one set of 60°C supply wires. Has not been investigated for thru branch circuits.

Fɪɢ. 410-2. Fixture with attached junction box suitable for terminating branch-circuit conductors only.

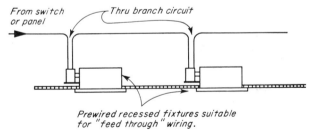

From switch or panel

Thru branch circuit

Prewired recessed fixtures suitable for "feed through" wiring.

Fɪɢ. 410-3. Fixtures with attached junction boxes suitable for "feeding through."

The following paragraph is an excerpt from the Underwriters' Laboratories, Inc., Electrical Construction Materials List (1974).

With the exception of fluorescent-lamp fixtures, recessed fixtures are marked with the required minimum temperature rating of wiring supplying the fixture. Unless marked "Maximum of _____ No. _____ AWG branch-circuit conductors suitable for at least _____°C (_____°F) permitted in junction box," no allowance has been made for any heat contributed by branch-circuit conductors which pass through, or supply and pass through, an outlet box or other splice compartment which is part of the fixture.

410-12. Outlet Boxes to be Covered. In a completed installation, each outlet box shall be provided with a cover unless covered by means of a fixture canopy, lampholder, receptacle, rosette, or similar device.

▲ The canopy may serve as the box cover, but if the ceiling or wall finish is of combustible material, the canopy and box must form a complete enclosure. The chief purpose of this is to require that no open space be left between the canopy and the edge of the box where the finish is wood or fibrous or any similar material. Where the wall or ceiling finish is plaster the requirement does not apply, since plaster is not classed as a combustible material; however, the plaster must be continuous up to the box, leaving no openings around the box.

410-13. Covering of Combustible Material at Outlet Boxes. Any combustible wall or ceiling finish exposed between the edge of a fixture canopy or pan and an outlet box shall be covered with noncombustible material.

▲ See comment following Sec. 410-12.

410-14. Connection of Electric-Discharge Lighting Fixtures. Where electric-discharge lighting fixtures are supported independently of the outlet box, they shall be connected through metal raceways, metal-clad cables, or nonmetallic-sheathed cables. It shall be permissible to suspend cord-equipped fixtures directly below the outlet box, if the cord is continuously visible for its entire length outside the fixture and is not subject to strain or physical damage. Such cord-equipped fixtures shall terminate at the outer end of the cord in a grounding-type attachment plug (cap) or busway plug.

Electric-discharge lighting fixtures provided with mogul-base screw-shell lamp-holders shall be permitted to be connected to branch circuits of 50 amperes or less by cords complying with Section 240-4. Receptacles and attachment plugs shall be permitted to be of lower ampere rating than the branch circuit but not less than 125 percent of the fixture full-load current.

Fixtures shall be permitted to be connected in accordance with Section 364-11.

▲ This permits the fixtures to be connected by means of cords only when such cords are not used as the supporting means, and when the fixture is suspended directly below the outlet boxes supplying such fixtures. Cord-connected fixtures are not permitted in lift-out-type ceilings. The second paragraph recognizes smaller receptacle ratings for certain types of mercury vapor or metal halide fixtures.

D. Fixture Supports

410-15. Supports—General. Fixtures, lampholders, rosettes, and receptacles shall be securely supported. A fixture that weighs more than 6 pounds or exceeds 16 inches in any dimension shall not be supported by the screw-shell of a lampholder.

410-16. Means of Support.

(a) Outlet Boxes. Where the outlet box or fitting will provide adequate support, a fixture shall be attached thereto or be supported as required by Section 370-13 for boxes. A fixture that weighs more than 50 pounds shall be supported independently of the outlet box.

(b) Suspended Ceilings. Framing members of suspended ceiling systems used to support fixtures shall be securely fastened to each other and shall be securely attached to the building structure at appropriate intervals. Fixtures so supported shall be securely fastened to the ceiling framing member.

(c) Raceway Fittings. Raceway fittings used to support lighting fixtures shall be approved for the purpose.

▲ The most common method of supporting fixtures is by means of fixture bars or straps bolted to the outlet boxes, as shown in Fig. 410-4. A fixture weighing over 50 lb can be supported on a hanger such as is shown in Fig. 370-6. Care should be taken to see that the pipe used in the construction of the hanger is of such size that the threads will have ample strength to support the weight.

E. Grounding

410-17. General. Fixtures and lighting equipment shall be grounded as provided in Part E of this Article.

410-18. Exposed Fixture Parts.

(a) The exposed conductive parts of lighting fixtures and equipment directly wired or attached to outlets supplied by a wiring method which provides an equipment ground shall be grounded.

(b) Fixtures directly wired or attached to outlets supplied by a wiring method which does not provide a ready means for grounding shall be made of insulating material and shall have no exposed conductive parts.

Exception: Fixtures mounted on electrically nonconductive ceilings or walls where located not less than 8 feet vertically or 5 feet horizontally from grounded surfaces.

410-19. Equipment Over 150 Volts to Ground.

(a) Metal fixtures, transformers, and transformer enclosures on circuits operating at over 150 volts to ground shall be grounded.

(b) Other exposed metal parts shall be grounded or insulated from ground and other conducting surfaces and inaccessible to unqualified persons.

Exception: Lamp tie wires, mounting screws, clips, and decorative bands on glass lamps spaced not less than $1\frac{1}{2}$ inches from lamp terminals shall not be required to be grounded.

410-21. Methods of Grounding. Equipment shall be considered grounded where mechanically connected in a permanent and effective manner to metal raceway, the armor of armored cable, mineral-insulated metal-sheathed cable, and aluminum-sheathed cable, copper-sheathed cable, the grounding conductor in nonmetallic-sheathed cable, or to a separate grounding conductor sized in accordance with Table 250-95, provided that the raceway, armor, or grounding conductor is grounded in a manner specified in Article 250.

F. Wiring of Fixtures

410-22. Fixture Wiring—General. Wiring on or within fixtures shall be neatly arranged and shall not be exposed to physical damage. Excess wiring shall be avoided. Conductors shall be so arranged that they shall not be subjected to temperatures above those for which they are approved.

410-23. Conductor Size. Fixture conductors shall not be smaller than No. 18.

410-24. Conductor Insulation.

(a) Fixtures shall be wired with conductors having insulation suitable for the current, voltage, and temperature to which the conductors will be subjected.

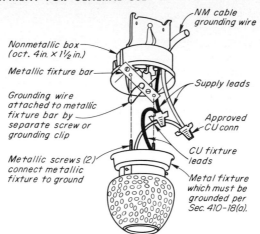

FIG. 410-4. Fixture and outlet box.

(b) Where fixtures are installed in damp, wet, or corrosive locations, conductors shall be of a type approved for the purpose.

For ampacity of fixture wire, see Table 402-5.
For maximum operating temperature and voltage limitation of fixtures wires, see Section 402-3.

410-25. Conductors for Certain Conditions.

(a) Mogul-Base Lampholders. Fixtures provided with mogul-base screw-shell lampholders and operating at not over 300 volts between conductors shall be wired with Type AF, SF-1, SF-2, SFF-1, SFF-2, PF, PGF, PFF, PGFF, PTF, or PTFF fixture wire.

(b) Other Than Mogul-Base Screw-Shell Lampholders. Fixtures provided with other than mogul-base screw-shell lampholders and operating at not over 300 volts between conductors shall be wired with Type AF, SF-1, SF-2, PF, PGF, PFF, PGFF, PTF, or PTFF fixture wire or Type AFC or AFPD flexible cord.

Exception No. 1: Where temperatures do not exceed 90°C (194°F), Types CF, TFN and TFFN fixture wire or Type CFPD flexible cord shall be permitted.

Exception No. 2: Where temperatures exceed 60°C (140°F) but are not higher than 75°C (167°C), Types RH and RHW rubber-covered wire and Type RFH-1, RFH-2, FFH-1, and FFH-2 fixture wires shall be permitted.

Exception No. 3: Where temperatures do not exceed 60°C (140°F), Type T thermoplastic wire, Type TF, TFF fixture wires shall be permitted, including fixtures of decorative types on which lamps of not over 60-watt rating are used in connection with imitation candles.

See Table 402-3 and Section 402-3 for fixture wires and conductors; and Table 400-5 for flexible cords.

410-26. Conductors for Movable Parts.

(a) Stranded conductors shall be used for wiring on fixture chains and on other movable or flexible parts.

(b) Conductors shall be so arranged that the weight of the fixture or movable parts will not put a tension on the conductors.

410-27. Pendant Conductors for Incandescent Filament Lamps.

(a) Pendant lampholders with permanently attached leads, where used for other than festoon wiring, shall be hung from separate stranded rubber-covered conductors that are soldered directly to the circuit conductors but supported independently thereof.

(b) Such pendant conductors shall not be smaller than No. 14 for mogul-base or medium-base screw-shell lampholders, nor smaller than No. 18 for intermediate or candelabra-base lampholders.

Exception: Approved Christmas tree and decorative lighting outfits shall be permitted to be smaller than No. 18.

(c) Pendant conductors longer than 3 feet shall be twisted together where not cabled in an approved assembly.

410-28. Protection of Conductors and Insulation.

(a) Properly Secured. Conductors shall be secured in a manner that will not tend to cut or abrade the insulation.

(b) Protection Through Metal. Conductor insulation shall be protected from abrasion where it passes through metal.

(c) Cord-Connected Showcases. Individual showcases, other than fixed, shall be permitted to be connected by flexible cord to permanently installed receptacles, and groups of not more than six such showcases shall be permitted to be coupled together by flexible cord and separable locking-type connectors with one of the group connected by flexible cord to a permanently installed receptacle.

The installation shall comply with the following requirements:

(1) Flexible cord shall be hard-service type, having conductors not smaller than the branch-circuit conductors, having ampacity at least equal to the branch-circuit overcurrent device, and having an equipment grounding conductor.

See Table 250-95 for size of grounding conductor.

(2) Receptacles, connectors, and attachment plugs shall be of an approved grounding type rated 15 or 20 amperes.

(3) Flexible cords shall be secured to the undersides of showcases so that: (1) wiring will not be exposed to mechanical damage; (2) a separation between cases not in excess of 2 inches, nor more than 12 inches between the first case and the supply receptacle will be assured; and (3) the free lead at the end of a group of showcases will have a female fitting not extending beyond the case.

(4) Equipment other than showcases shall not be electrically connected to showcases.

(5) Standpipes of floor receptacles shall allow floor-cleaning equipment to be operated without damage to receptacles.

410-29. Conductor Protection at Lampholders. Where a metal lampholder is attached to a flexible cord, the inlet shall be equipped with an insulating bushing which, if threaded, shall not be smaller than nominal $\frac{3}{8}$-inch pipe size. The cord hole shall be of a size appropriate for the cord, and all burrs and fins shall be removed in order to provide a smooth bearing surface for the cord.

Bushings having holes 9/32 inch in diameter shall be permitted for use with plain pendant cord and holes 13/32 inch in diameter with reinforced cord.

▲ Lampholders for cord pendants, if of the brass-shell type, should preferably have caps with insulating bushings permanently secured in place, or they may be of the nonmetallic type requiring no bushings.

410-30. Connections, Splices, and Taps.

(a) Inspection. Fixtures shall be so installed that the connections between the fixture conductors and the circuit conductors can be inspected without requiring the disconnection of any part of the wiring.

Exception: Fixtures connected by attachment plugs and receptacles.

(b) Fixture Stems. Splices and taps shall not be located within fixture arms or stems.

(c) Splices and Taps. No unnecessary splices or taps shall be made within or on a fixture.

For approved means of making connections, see Section 110-14.

(d) Electric discharge lighting fixtures surface mounted over concealed outlet, pull, or junction boxes shall be installed with suitable openings in back of the fixture to provide access to the boxes.

410-31. Fixtures As Raceways. Fixtures shall not be used as a raceway for circuit conductors.

Exception No. 1: Fixtures that meet the requirements for raceways.

▲ Fixtures meeting the requirements for "approved raceways" are labeled by Underwriters' Laboratories as "Fixtures Suitable for Use as Raceways."

Exception No. 2: Conductors of a two wire or multiwire branch circuit supplying the fixtures shall be permitted to be carried through:

a. Fixtures designed for end-to-end assembly to form a continuous raceway; or

b. Fixtures connected together by recognized wiring methods.

See Article 100 for definition of multiwire branch circuit.

Branch-circuit conductors within 3 inches of a ballast within the ballast compartment shall be recognized for use at temperatures not lower than 90°C (194°F), such as Types RHH, THW, THHN, FEP, FEPB, SA, XHHW and AVA.

410-32. Polarization of Fixtures. Fixtures shall be so wired that the screw-shells of lampholders will be connected to the same fixture or circuit conductor or terminal. The identified grounded conductor, where connected to a screw shell lampholder, shall be connected to the screw shell.

▲ This method of wiring fixtures is required in order to ensure that the screw shells of sockets will be connected to the grounded circuit wire.

G. Construction of Fixtures

410-34. Combustible Shades and Enclosures. Adequate air space shall be provided between lamps and shades or other enclosures of combustible material.

410-35. Fixture Rating.

(a) Marking. All fixtures requiring ballasts or transformers shall be plainly marked with their electrical rating and the manufacturer's name, trademark, or other suitable means of identification.

(b) Electrical Rating. The electrical rating shall include the voltage and frequency and shall indicate the current rating of the unit, including the ballast, transformer, or autotransformer.

410-36. Design and Material. Fixtures shall be constructed of metal, wood, or other approved material and shall be so designed and assembled as to secure requisite mechanical strength and rigidity. Wireways, including their entrances, shall be such that conductors may be drawn in and withdrawn without injury.

410-37. Nonmetallic Fixtures. In all fixtures not made entirely of metal or noncombustible material, wireways shall be lined with metal.

Exception: Where armored or lead-covered conductors with suitable fittings are used.

410-38. Mechanical Strength.

(a) Tubing for Arms. Tubing used for arms and stems where provided with cut threads shall not be less than 0.040 inch in thickness and where provided with rolled (pressed) threads shall not be less than 0.025 inch in thickness. Arms and other parts shall be fastened to prevent turning.

(b) Metal Canopies. Metal canopies supporting lampholders, shades, etc., exceeding 8 pounds, or incorporating attachment-plug receptacles, shall not be less than 0.020 inch in thickness. Other canopies shall not be less than 0.016 inch if made of steel and not less than 0.020 inch if of other metals.

(c) Canopy Switches. Pull-type canopy switches shall not be inserted in the rims of metal canopies that are less than 0.025 inch in thickness unless the rims are reinforced by the turning of a bead or the equivalent. Pull-type canopy switches, whether mounted in the rims or elsewhere in sheet metal canopies, shall not be located more than $3\frac{1}{2}$ inches from the center of the canopy. Double set-screws, double canopy rings, a screw ring, or equal method shall be used where the canopy supports a pull-type switch or pendant receptacle.

The above thickness requirements shall apply to measurements made on finished (formed) canopies.

410-39. Wiring Space. Bodies of fixtures, including portable lamps, shall provide ample space for splices and taps and for the installation of devices, if any. Splice compartments shall be of nonabsorbent, noncombustible material.

410-40. Fixture Studs. Fixture studs that are not a part of outlet boxes, hickeys, tripods, and crowfeet shall be made of steel, malleable iron, or other approved material.

410-41. Insulating Joints. Insulating joints shall be composed of materials especially approved for the purpose. Those that are not designed to be mounted with screws or bolts shall have a substantial exterior metal casing, insulated from both screw connections.

410-42. Portable Lamps. Portable table and floor lamps shall be wired with flexible cord approved for the purpose as listed in Article 400.

410-43. Portable Handlamps. Handlamps of the portable type supplied through flexible cords shall be of the molded composition or other type approved for the purpose. Metal-shell paper-lined lampholders shall not be used. Handlamps shall be equipped with a handle. Where subject to physical damage or where lamps are likely to come in contact with combustible material, handlamps shall be equipped with a substantial guard attached to the lampholder or the handle.

For garages, see Section 511-2(f).

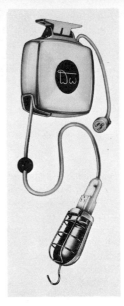

Fig. 410-5. This portable lamp is equipped with a grounded metallic guard and reflector. The rigid plastic handle provides protection for side outlet contacts. The swivel-type hook permits positioning in any location. (*Daniel Woodhead Co.*)

410-44. Cord Bushings. A bushing or the equivalent shall be provided where flexible cord enters the base or stem of a portable lamp. The bushing shall be of insulating material unless a jacketed-type of cord is used.

410-45. Tests. All wiring shall be free from short circuits and grounds and shall be tested for these defects prior to being connected to the circuit.

410-46. Live Parts. Exposed live parts within porcelain fixtures shall be suitably recessed and so located as to make it improbable that wires will come in contact with them. There shall be a spacing of at least $\frac{1}{2}$ inch between live parts and the mounting plane of the fixture.

H. Installation of Lampholders

410-47. Screw-Shell Type. Lampholders of the screw-shell type shall be installed for use as lampholders only.

▲ This warns against the previously common practice of installing screw-shell lampholders with screw-plug adapters in baseboards and walls for the connecting of cord-connected appliances and lighting equipment and thereby exposing live parts to contact by persons when the adapters were moved from place to place. See Sec. 410-56(a).

410-48. Double-Pole Switched Lampholders. Where used on unidentified 2-wire circuits tapped from the ungrounded conductors of multiwire circuits, the switching device of lampholders of the switched type shall simultaneously disconnect both conductors of the circuit in accordance with Section 210-10.

▲ On a circuit having one wire grounded, the grounded wire must always be connected to the screw shell of the socket, and sockets having a single-pole switching mechanism may be used. (See Sec. 410-52.) On a two-wire circuit tapped from the outside (ungrounded) wires of a three-wire or four-wire system, if sockets having switching mechanisms are used, these must be double-pole so that they will disconnect both of the ungrounded wires.

410-49. Lampholders in Wet or Damp Locations. Lampholders installed in wet or damp locations shall be of the weatherproof type.

J. Construction of Lampholders

410-50. Insulation. The outer metal shell and the cap shall be lined with insulating material which shall prevent the shell and cap from becoming a part of the circuit. The lining shall not extend beyond the metal shell more than $\frac{1}{8}$ inch, but shall prevent any current-carrying part of the lamp base from being exposed when a lamp is in the lampholding device.

410-51. Lead Wires. Lead wires, furnished as a part of weatherproof lampholders and intended to be exposed after installation, shall be of approved stranded, rubber-covered conductors not less than No. 14 and shall be sealed in place or otherwise made raintight.

Exception: No. 18 rubber-covered conductors shall be permitted for candelabra sockets.

410-52. Switched Lampholders. Switched lampholders shall be of such construction that the switching mechanism interrupts the electrical connection to the center contact. The switching mechanism shall also be permitted to interrupt the electrical connection to the screw-shell if the connection to the center contact is simultaneously interrupted.

K. Lamps and Auxiliary Equipment

410-53. Bases, Incandescent Lamps. An incandescent lamp for general use on lighting branch circuits shall not be equipped with a medium base if rated over 300 watts, nor with a mogul base if rated over 1500 watts. Special bases or other devices shall be used for over 1500 watts.

410-54. Enclosures for Electric-Discharge Lamp Auxiliary Equipment. Auxiliary equipment for electric-discharge lamps shall be enclosed in noncombustible cases and treated as sources of heat.

410-55. Arc Lamps. Arc lamps used in theaters shall comply with Section 520-61, and arc lamps used in projection machines shall comply with Section 540-20. Arc lamps used on constant-current systems shall comply with the general requirements of Article 710.

L. Receptacles, Cord Connectors, and Attachment Plugs (Caps)

410-56. Rating and Type.

    (a) Receptacles. Receptacles installed for the attachment of portable cords shall be rated at not less than 15 amperes, 125 volts, or 15 amperes, 250 volts, and shall be of a type not suitable for use as lampholders.

Exception: The use of receptacles of 10 ampere 250 volt rating used in nonresidential occupancies for the supply of equipment other than portable hand tools, portable hand lamps, and extension cords shall be permitted.

(b) Faceplates. Metal faceplates shall be of ferrous metal not less than 0.030 inch in thickness or of nonferrous metal not less than 0.040 inch in thickness. Faceplates of insulating material shall be noncombustible and not less than 0.10 inch in thickness but shall be permitted to be less than 0.10 inch in thickness if formed or reinforced to provide adequate mechanical strength.

(c) Position of Receptacle Faces. After installation, receptacle faces shall be flush with or project from faceplates of insulating material and shall project a minimum of 0.015 inch from metal faceplates. Faceplates shall be installed so as to seat against mounting surfaces. Boxes shall be installed in accordance with Section 370-10.

(d) Attachment Plugs. All 15- and 20-ampere attachment plugs and connectors shall be so constructed that there are no exposed current-carrying parts except the prongs, blades, or pins. The cover for wire terminations shall be a part, which is essential for the operation of an attachment plug or connector (dead-front construction).

Exception: A separate insulating disc which is mechanically secured in place shall be permitted to be used until January 1, 1978.

▲ Section 410-56(c), concerning receptacle faces, is necessary to assure a solid backing for receptacles so that attachment plugs can be inserted without difficulty. The requirement for receptacle faces to project at least 0.015 inch from installed metal faceplates is to prevent faults caused by countless existing attachment plugs with exposed bare terminal screws. The design requirements for attachment plugs and connectors in Sec. 410-56(d) should prevent such faults at metal plates, but the problem of existing attachment plugs in this regard will be around for many years.

With receptacle faces and faceplates installed according to Sec. 410-56(c), attachment plugs can be fully inserted into receptacles and will provide a better contact. The cooperation of other crafts, such as plasterers or dry-wall applicators, will be required to satisfy the requirements of Sec. 410-56(c).

(e) Noninterchangeability. Receptacles, cord connectors and attachment plugs shall be constructed so that the receptacle or cord connectors will not accept an attachment plug with a different voltage or current rating than that for which the device is intended. Nongrounding type receptacles and connectors shall not accept grounding type attachment plugs.

▲ See comments following Sec. 210-7(f) for ANSI C73 configuration chart.

Exception: A 20-ampere T-slot receptacle or cord connector shall be permitted to accept a 15-ampere attachment plug of the same voltage rating.

410-57. Receptacles in Damp or Wet Locations.

(a) Damp Locations. A receptacle installed outdoors in a location protected from the weather or in other damp locations shall have an enclosure for the receptacle that is weatherproof when the receptacle is covered (attachment plug cap not inserted and receptacle covers closed).

An installation suitable for wet locations shall also be considered suitable for damp locations.

A receptacle shall be considered to be in a location protected from the weather where located under roofed open porches, canopies, marquees, and the like, and will not be subjected to a beating rain or water run-off.

(b) Wet Locations. A receptacle installed outdoors where exposed to weather or in other wet locations shall be in a weatherproof enclosure, the integrity of which is not affected when the receptacle is in use (attachment plug cap inserted).

Exception: An enclosure that is weatherproof only when a self-closing receptacle cover is closed shall be permitted to be used for a receptacle installed outdoors where the receptacle is not likely to be used with other than portable tools or other portable equipment not usually left connected to the outlet indefinitely.

(c) Flush Mounting with Faceplate. The enclosure for a receptacle installed in an outlet box flush-mounted on a wall surface shall be made weatherproof by means of a weatherproof faceplate assembly that provides a watertight connection between the plate and the wall surface.

(d) Installation. A receptacle outlet installed outdoors shall be located so that water accumulation is not likely to touch the outlet cover or plate.

▲ In *damp* locations [Sec. 410-57(a)] most existing receptacle covers with hinged covers or screw caps (see Fig. 410-6) for receptacle faces will suffice.

In *wet* locations [Sec. 410-57(b)] receptacles with attachment plugs inserted must form a weatherproof connection. The exception permits outdoor receptacles to have *self-closing* receptacle covers to accommodate temporary uses of attachment plugs with portable tools and similar equipment which are not intended or designed to be connected to the receptacle for other than short periods of time.

Section 410-57(c) pertains to flush-mounted boxes in which receptacles are installed in wet locations, and Sec. 410-57(d) requires an elevation of outdoor receptacles to prevent accumulation of water.

410-58. Grounding-Type Receptacles, Adapters, Cord Connectors, and Attachment Plugs.

(a) Grounding Poles. Grounding-type receptacles, cord connectors, and attachment plugs shall be provided with one fixed grounding pole in addition to the circuit poles.

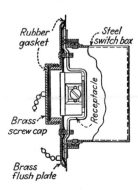

Fig. 410-6. Weatherproof receptacle suitable for installation in damp locations. (*Bryant Electric Co.*)

Exception: The grounding contacting pole of grounding-type attachment plugs on the power supply cords of portable hand-held, hand-guided or hand-supported tools or appliances shall be permitted to be of the movable self-restoring type on circuits operating at not over 150 volts between any two conductors nor over 150 volts between any conductor and ground.

(b) Grounding-Pole Identification. Grounding-type receptacles, adapters, cord connectors, and attachment plugs shall have a means for connection of a grounding conductor to the grounding pole. A terminal for connection to the grounding pole shall be designated by:

(1) A green-colored hexagonal headed or shaped terminal screw or nut, not readily removable; or

(2) A green-colored pressure wire connector body (a wire barrel); or

(3) A similar green-colored connection device in the case of adapters. The grounding terminal of a grounding adapter shall be a green-colored rigid ear, lug, or similar device. The grounding connection shall be so designed that it cannot make contact with current-carrying parts of the receptacle, adapter, or attachment plug. The adapter shall be polarized.

▲ **Subparagraph 3 removes the recognition of adapters with pigtail grounding leads.**

(4) If the terminal for the equipment grounding conductor is not visible, the conductor entrance hole shall be marked with the word "Green" or otherwise identified by a distinctive green color.

(c) Grounding Terminal Use. A grounding terminal or grounding-type device shall not be used for purposes other than grounding.

(d) Grounding-Pole Requirements. Grounding-type attachment plugs and mating cord connectors and receptacles shall be so designed that the grounding connection is made before the current-carrying connections. Grounding-type devices shall be designed so grounding poles of attachment plugs cannot be brought into contact with current-carrying parts of receptacles or cord connectors.

▲ **See Fig. 250-9.**

M. Rosettes

410-59. Unapproved Types.

(a) Fusible rosettes shall not be installed.

(b) Separable rosettes that may change polarity shall not be used.

410-60. Rosettes in Damp or Wet Locations. Rosettes installed in damp or wet locations shall be of the weatherproof type.

410-61. Rating. Rosettes shall be rated at 660 watts, 250 volts, with a maximum current rating of 6 amperes.

410-62. Rosettes for Exposed Wiring. Rosettes for exposed wiring shall be provided with bases that shall have at least two holes for supporting screws, shall be high enough to keep the wires and terminals at least $\frac{1}{2}$ inch from the surface wired over, and shall have a lug of insulating material under each terminal to prevent the rosette from being placed over projections that would reduce the separation to less than $\frac{1}{2}$ inch.

410-63. Rosettes for Use with Boxes or Raceways. Rosettes for use with conduit boxes or raceways shall have bases high enough to keep wires and terminals at least $\frac{3}{8}$ inch from the surface wired over.

N. Special Provisions for Flush and Recessed Fixtures

410-64. Approved Type. Fixtures installed in recessed cavities in walls or ceilings shall be of an approved type and shall comply with Sections 410-65 through 410-72.

410-65. Temperature.

(a) Combustible Material. Fixtures shall be so constructed or installed that adjacent combustible material will not be subjected to temperatures in excess of 90°C (194°F).

(b) Fire-Resistant Construction. Where a fixture is recessed in fire resistant material in a building of fire-resistant construction, a temperature higher than 90°C (194°F), but not higher than 150°C (302°F), shall be considered acceptable if the fixture is plainly marked that it is approved for that service.

410-66. Clearance. Recessed portions of enclosures, other than at points of support, shall be spaced at least ½ inch from combustible material. Thermal insulation shall not be installed within 24 inches of the top or within 3 inches of the side of a recessed fixture enclosure, wiring compartment or ballast unless labeled for the purpose.

410-67. Wiring.

(a) General. Conductors having insulation suitable for the temperature encountered shall be used.

(b) Over 60°C. Fixtures having branch-circuit terminal connections that operate at temperatures higher than 60°C (140°F) shall comply with (1) or (2) below.

(1) Branch-circuit conductors having an insulation suitable for the temperature encountered shall be permitted to be run directly to the fixture.

(2) Tap conductors having an insulation suitable for the temperature encountered shall be run from the fixture terminal connection to an outlet box placed at least one foot from the fixture. Such a tap shall be in a suitable metal raceway which shall extend for at least 4 feet but not more than 6 feet.

▲ Recessed fixtures are, in all cases, marked with the required minimum-temperature rating of wiring supplying the fixture. This marking does not allow for any heat contributed by a branch circuit passing through the fixture enclosure or through a splice compartment (outlet box or otherwise) that is part of the fixture construction. An insulation with a temperature rating higher than that indicated on the fixture may be required for such branch-circuit conductors. See Sec. 410-11.

The requirements given in Sec. 410-67(b)(2) are special provisions that apply to recessed fixtures and take precedence over the general requirements. This means that the tap conductors (usually in flexible conduit) connecting an unwired recessed fixture to the outlet box must be in metal raceway of at least 4 ft in length and not over 6 ft. The box is required to be at least 1 ft away from the fixture and the flexible conduit may be looped to use up the excess length (see Sec. 350-4, Exception 3). This rule does not apply to "prewired" fixtures designed for connection to 60°C supply wires.

The purpose of this requirement is to allow the heat to dissipate so that heat from the fixture will not cause an excessive temperature in the outlet box and thus overheat the branch-circuit conductors which could be of the general-use type limited to 60°C or 75°C temperatures.

P. Construction of Flush and Recessed Fixtures

410-68. Temperature. Fixtures shall be so constructed that adjacent combustible material will not be subject to temperatures in excess of 90°C (194°F).

410-69. Enclosure. Sheet metal enclosures shall be protected against corrosion and shall not be less than No. 22 MSG.

Exception: Where a wireway cover is within the No. 22 MSG enclosure, it shall be permitted to be of No. 24 MSG metal.

410-70. Lamp Wattage Marking. Incandescent lamp fixtures shall be marked to indicate the maximum allowable wattage of lamps. The markings shall be permanently installed, in letters at least $\frac{1}{4}$ inch high, and shall be located where visible during relamping.

410-71. Solder Prohibited. No solder shall be used in the construction of a fixture box.

410-72. Lampholders. Lampholders of the screw-shell type shall be of porcelain or be approved for the purpose. Where used, cements shall be of the high-heat type.

Q. Special Provisions for Electric-Discharge Lighting Systems of 1000 Volts or Less

410-73. General.

(a) Equipment for use with electric-discharge lighting systems and designed for an open-circuit voltage of 1000 volts or less shall be of a type intended for such service.

(b) The terminals of an electric-discharge lamp shall be considered as alive where any lamp terminal is connected to a supply of over 300 volts.

(c) Transformers of the oil-filled type shall not be used.

(d) In addition to complying with the general requirements for lighting fixtures, such equipment shall comply with Part Q of this Article.

(e) Integral ballast protection shall be provided for fluorescent fixtures installed indoors.

Exception to (e) above: Fluorescent fixtures with simple reactance ballasts.

▲ Paragraph (e) pertains only to fluorescent lamp ballasts used indoors. The protection called for must be a part of the ballast. Underwriters' Laboratories, Inc., has made an extensive investigation of various types of protective devices for use within such ballasts, and ballasts found to meet U/L requirements for these applications are listed and marked as "Class P." The protective devices are thermal trip devices or thermal fuses, which are responsive to abnormal heat developed within the ballast because of a fault in components such as autotransformers, capacitors, reactors, etc.

Simple reactance-type ballasts are equipped with two leads only, and are connected as shown in Fig. 410-7. These series reactors are used with preheat-type fluorescent lamp circuits for lamps rated less than 30 W. Also, a manual (momentary-contact) or automatic-type starter is used to start the lamp. The simple reactor-type ballast supplies one lamp only, has no autotransformer or capacitor, and can be readily identified by the presence of only two external leads.

Preheat lamps of 30 W and larger use an autotransformer in series with one or more reactors in typical preheat circuits with auxiliary starting devices.

410-74. Direct-Current Equipment. Fixtures installed on direct-current circuits shall be equipped with auxiliary equipment and resistors especially designed and for direct-current operation, and the fixtures shall be so marked.

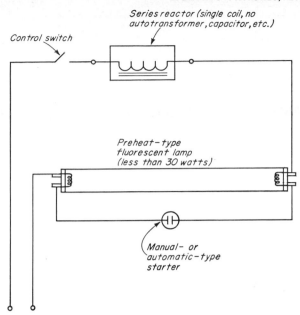

Series reactor (single coil, no
autotransformer, capacitor, etc.)

Control switch

Preheat-type
fluorescent lamp
(less than 30 watts)

Manual- or
automatic-type
starter

Fɪɢ. 410-7. A simple reactance-type ballast circuit.

410-75. Voltages—Dwelling Occupancies.

(a) Equipment having an open-circuit voltage exceeding 1000 volts shall not be installed in dwelling occupancies.

(b) Equipment having an open-circuit voltage exceeding 300 volts shall not be installed in dwelling occupancies unless such equipment is so designed that there will be no exposed live parts when lamps are being inserted, are in place, or are being removed.

▲ Fixtures which are intended for use in other than dwelling occupancies are so marked. This usually indicates that the fixture has maintenance features which are considered to be beyond the capabilities of the ordinary householder, or involves voltages in excess of those permitted by the National Electrical Code for dwelling occupancies.

410-76. Fixture Mounting.

(a) **Exposed Ballasts.** Fixtures having exposed ballasts or transformers shall be so installed that such ballasts or transformers will not be in contact with combustible material.

(b) **Combustible Low-Density Cellulose Fiberboard.** Where a surface-mounted fixture containing a ballast is to be installed on combustible low-density cellulose fiberboard, it shall be approved for this condition or shall be spaced not less than $1\frac{1}{2}$ inches from the surface of the fiberboard. Where such fixtures are partially or wholly recessed, the provisions of Sections 410-64 through 410-72 shall apply.

Combustible low-density cellulose fiberboard includes sheets, panels, and tiles that have a density of 20 pounds per cubic foot or less, and that are formed of bonded plant fiber material; but does not include solid or laminated wood, nor fiberboard that has a density in excess of 20 pounds per cubic foot or is a material that has been integrally treated with fire-retarding chemicals to the degree that the flame spread in any plane of the material will not exceed 25 determined in accordance with tests for surface burning characteristics of building materials. See Method of Test for Surface Burning Characteristics of Building Materials, ANSI A2.5-1970.

▲ Material meeting these requirements is listed in Underwriters' Laboratories, Inc., Building Materials List and in addition to other pertinent information includes the following: "This material has been found to comply with the flame spread requirements stipulated in Section 410-76 of the National Electrical Code as described therein."

Electric-discharge lamp fixtures which have been investigated for mounting directly on combustible low-density cellulose fiberboard ceilings are marked "Suitable for Surface Mounting on Combustible Low-Density Cellulose Fiberboard."

It should be noted that these fixtures have been investigated and found to operate within applicable temperature limits only with the ballast or ballasts specified by the marking in the fixture.

410-77. Equipment Not Integral with Fixture.

(a) Metal Cabinets. Auxiliary equipment, including reactors, capacitors, resistors, and similar equipment, where not installed as part of a lighting fixture assembly, shall be enclosed in accessible, permanently installed metal cabinets.

(b) Display Cases. Where display cases are not permanently installed, no portion of a secondary circuit shall be permitted in more than a single case.

(c) Separate Mounting. Separately mounted ballasts that are intended for direct connection to a wiring system shall not be required to be separately enclosed.

410-78. Autotransformers. An autotransformer which is used to raise the voltage to more than 300 volts, as part of a ballast for supplying lighting units, shall be supplied only by a grounded system.

410-79. Switches. Snap switches shall comply with Section 380-14.

R. Special Provisions for Electric-Discharge Lighting Systems of More Than 1000 Volts

410-80. General.

(a) Equipment for use with electric-discharge lighting systems and designed for an open-circuit voltage exceeding 1000 volts shall be of a type intended for such service.

(b) The terminal of an electric-discharge lamp shall be considered as alive when any lamp terminal is connected to a supply of over 300 volts.

(c) In addition to complying with the general requirements for lighting fixtures, such equipment shall comply with Part R of this Article.

For signs and outline lighting, see Article 600.

▲ These sections apply to interior neon-tube lighting, lighting with long fluorescent tubes requiring more than 1,000 V, and cold-cathode fluorescent-lamp installations arranged to operate with several tubes in series.

410-81. Control.

(a) Disconnection. Fixtures or lamp installations shall be controlled either singly or in groups by an externally operable switch or circuit breaker that opens all ungrounded primary conductors.

(b) Within Sight or Locked Type. The switch or circuit breaker shall be located within sight from the fixtures or lamps, or it shall be permitted elsewhere if it is provided with a means for locking in the open position.

▲ When any part of the equipment is being serviced, the primary circuit should be opened and the serviceman should have assurance that the disconnecting means will not be closed without his knowledge.

410-82. Lamp Terminals and Lampholders. Parts that must be removed for lamp replacement shall be hinged or fastened by an approved means. Lamps or lamp-holders will be so designed that there shall be no exposed live parts when lamps are being inserted or are being removed.

410-83. Transformer Ratings. Transformers and ballasts shall have a secondary open-circuit voltage of not over 15,000 volts with an allowance on test of 1000 volts additional. The secondary-current rating shall not be more than 120 milliamperes if the open-circuit voltage is over 7500 volts, and not more than 240 milliamperes if the open-circuit voltage is 7500 volts or less.

410-84. Transformer Type. Transformers shall be of an approved enclosed type. Transformers of other than the askarel-insulated or dry-type shall not be used.

410-85. Transformer Secondary Connections.

(a) The high-voltage windings of transformers shall not be connected in series or in parallel.

Exception: Two transformers, each having one end of its high-voltage winding grounded and connected to the enclosure, shall be permitted to have their high-voltage windings connected in series to form the equivalent of a mid-point grounded transformer.

(b) The grounded ends of paralleled transformers as permitted in (a) above shall be connected by an insulated conductor not smaller than No. 14.

410-86. Transformer Locations.

(a) Transformers shall be accessible after installation.

(b) Transformers shall be installed as near to the lamps as practicable to keep the secondary conductors as short as possible.

(c) Transformers shall be so located that adjacent combustible materials will not be subjected to temperatures in excess of 90°C (194°F).

410-87. Transformer Loading. The lamps connected to any transformer shall be of such length and characteristics as not to cause a condition of continuous over-voltage on the transformer.

▲ See comments following Sec. 600-32.

410-88. Wiring Method—Secondary Conductors. Approved gas-tube sign cable suitable for the voltage of the circuit shall be used. Conductors shall be installed in accordance with Section 600-31.

▲ This type of cable is not included in the table in Chap. 3 listing various types of insulated conductors, but Underwriters' Laboratories, Inc., have standards for such cables. The following information is an excerpt from the Underwriters' Laboratories, Inc., Electrical Construction Materials List:

"Gas tube sign and ignition cable is classified as Type GTO-5 (5,000 volts), GTO-10 (10,000 volts), or GTO-15 (15,000 volts), and is labeled in sizes Nos. 18-10 AWG copper

Underwriters' Laboratories, Inc.
®
L I S T E D
GAS TUBE SIGN
AND IGNITION CABLE

and Nos. 12-10 AWG aluminum and copper-clad aluminum. This material is intended for use with gas tube signs, oil burners, and inside lighting.

"L-used as a suffix in combination with any of the preceding type letter designations indicates that an outer covering of lead has been applied.

"The label of Underwriters' Laboratories, Inc., (illustrated above) on the product is the only method provided by Underwriters' Laboratories, Inc., to identify Gas Tube Sign and Ignition Cable which has been produced under the Label Service."

410-89. Lamp Supports. Lamps shall be adequately supported as required in Section 600-33.

410-90. Exposure to Damage. Lamps shall not be located where normally exposed to physical damage.

410-91. Marking. Each fixture or each secondary circuit of tubing having an open-circuit voltage of over 1000 volts shall have a clearly legible marking in letters not less than $\frac{1}{4}$-inch high reading "Caution . . . . volts." The voltage indicated shall be the rated open-circuit voltage.

410-92. Switches. Snap switches shall comply with Section 380-14.

ARTICLE 422. APPLIANCES

A. General

422-1. Scope. This Article covers electric appliances used in any occupancy. Equipment shall be of a type approved for the purpose and location.

▲ See definition for "Appliance," Art. 100.

For purposes of the Code, the definition for an appliance indicates that it is utilization equipment other than industrial and generally means small equipment such as may be used in a dwelling or office (clothes washer, clothes dryer, air conditioner, food mixer, coffee maker, etc.). See also definition for "Utilization Equipment" in Art. 100.

422-2. Live Parts. Appliances shall have no live parts normally exposed to contact.

Exception: Toasters, grills, or other appliances in which the current-carrying parts at high temperatures are necessarily exposed.

422-3. Other Articles. All requirements of this Code shall apply where applicable. Appliances for use in hazardous locations shall comply with Articles 500 through 517.

The requirements of Article 430 shall apply to the installation of motor-operated appliances and the requirements of Article 440 shall apply to the installation of appliances containing hermetic-refrigerant motor-compressor(s), except as specifically amended in this Article.

B. Branch-Circuit Requirements

422-5. Branch-Circuit Sizing. This Section specifies sizes of conductors capable of carrying appliance current without overheating under the conditions specified. This Section shall not apply to conductors that form an integral part of an appliance.

(a) Individual Circuits. The rating of an individual branch circuit shall not be less than the marked rating of the appliance or the marked rating of an appliance having combined loads as provided in Section 422-32.

Exception No. 1: For motor-operated appliances not having a marked rating the branch-circuit size shall be in accordance with Part B of Article 430.

Exception No. 2: For an appliance, other than a motor-operated appliance that is continuously loaded, the branch-circuit rating shall not be less than 125 percent of the marked rating; or not less than 100 percent if the branch-circuit device and its assembly is approved for continuous loading at 100 percent of its rating.

Exception No. 3: Branch circuits for household cooking appliances shall be permitted to be in accordance with Table 220-19.

(b) Circuits Supplying Two or More Loads. For branch circuits supplying appliance and other loads, the rating shall be determined in accordance with Section 210-23.

422-6. Branch-Circuit Overcurrent Protection. Branch circuits shall be protected in accordance with Section 240-3.

If a protective device rating is marked on an appliance, the branch-circuit overcurrent device rating shall not exceed the protective device rating marked on the appliance.

C. Installation of Appliances

422-7. General. All appliances shall be installed in an approved manner.

422-8. Flexible Cords.

(a) Heater Cords. All smoothing irons and portable electrically heated appliances that are rated at more than 50 watts and produce temperatures in excess of 121°C (250°F) on surfaces with which the cord is likely to be in contact shall be provided with one of the types of approved heater cords listed in Table 400-4.

(b) Other Heating Appliances. All other portable electrically heated appliances shall be connected with one of the approved types of cord listed in Table 400-4, selected in accordance with the usage specified in that Table.

(c) Other Appliances. Flexible cord shall be permitted (1) for connection of portable appliances; (2) for connection of stationary appliances to facilitate their frequent interchange or to prevent the transmission of noise or vibration; or (3) to facilitate the removal or disconnection of fixed appliances for maintenance or repair.

422-9. Portable Immersion Heaters. Electric heaters of the portable immersion type shall be so constructed and installed that current-carrying parts are effectively insulated from electrical contact with the substance in which they are immersed. The authority having jurisdiction may make exceptions for special applications of apparatus if suitable precautions are taken.

422-10. Protection of Combustible Material. Each electrically heated appliance that is intended by size, weight, and service to be located in a fixed position shall be so placed as to provide ample protection between the appliance and adjacent combustible material.

422-11. Stands for Portable Appliances. Each smoothing iron and other portable electrically heated appliance intended to be applied to combustible material shall be equipped with an approved stand, which shall be permitted to be a separate piece of equipment or a part of the appliance.

422-12. Signals for Heated Appliances. In other than dwelling-type occupancies, each electrically heated appliance or group of appliances intended to be applied to combustible material shall be provided with a signal.

Exception: If an appliance is provided with an integral temperature-limiting device.

▲ The standard form of signal is a red light so connected that the lamp remains lighted as long as the appliance is connected to the circuit. No signal lamp is required if the appliance is equipped with a thermostatic switch which automatically opens the circuit after the appliance has been heated to a certain temperature.

422-13. Flatirons. Electrically heated smoothing irons intended for use in residences shall be equipped with approved temperature-limiting means.

422-14. Water Heaters.

(a) Storage and Instantaneous Type Water Heaters. Each storage- or instantaneous-type water heater shall be equipped with a temperature-limiting means in addition to its control thermostat to disconnect all ungrounded conductors, and such means shall be: (1) installed to sense maximum water temperature; (2) either a trip-free, manually reset type or a type having a replacement element. Such water heaters shall be marked to require the installation of a temperature and pressure relief valve.

See Listing Requirements for Relief Valves and Automatic Gas Shutoff Devices for Hot Water Supply Systems. (ANSI Z 21.22-1972.)

Exception: Water heaters with supply water temperature of 180° F or above and capacity of 60 kW or above, and water heaters with a capacity of one gallon or less, approved for the purpose.

(b) Storage Type Water Heaters. All fixed storage water heaters having a capacity of 120 gallons or less shall be considered a continuous duty load.

Exception: The assembly including the overcurrent device protecting the branch circuit that is approved for continuous operation at 100 percent of its rating shall be permitted to supply its full rated load as provided in Section 210-22(c), Exception No. 3.

422-15. Infrared Lamp Industrial Heating Appliances.

(a) Infrared heating lamps rated at 300 watts or less shall be permitted with lampholders of the medium-base, unswitched porcelain type or other types approved for the purpose.

(b) Screw-shell lampholders shall not be used with infrared lamps over 300 watts rating.

Exception: Lampholders approved for the purpose.

(c) Lampholders shall be permitted to be connected to any of the branch circuits of Article 210 and, in industrial occupancies, shall be permitted to be operated in series on circuits of over 150 volts to ground provided the voltage rating of the lampholders is not less than the circuit voltage.

Each section, panel, or strip carrying a number of infrared lampholders (including the internal wiring of such section, panel, or strip) shall be considered an appliance. The terminal connection block of each such assembly shall be considered an individual outlet.

▲ So-called "infrared" lamps are tungsten-filament incandescent lamps, similar to lamps used for lighting, except that they are designed for operation with the filaments at a lower temperature, resulting, for a given wattage, in more heat radiation and less light output, also in a much longer lamp life.

Figure 422-1 is a view of an oven of medium size. The lampholders are mounted on panels which are hinged so that they can be swung out for inspection and relamping. The lampholders are so placed that the axis of each lamp is at an angle of about 45° from the surface of the panel, the object of this being to ensure that all sides of an object passing through the oven will receive a uniform amount of heat radiation.

Fig. 422-1. Oven heated by infrared lamps.

422-16. Grounding. Metal frames of portable, stationary, and fixed electrically heated appliances, operating on circuits over 150 volts to ground, shall be grounded in the manner specified in Article 250.

Exception: Where this is impracticable, grounding may be omitted by special permission, in which case the frames shall be permanently and effectively insulated from the ground.

Refrigerators and freezers shall comply with the requirements of Sections 250-42, 250-43, and 250-45. Electric ranges, wall-mounted ovens, counter-mounted cooking units and clothes dryers shall comply with the requirements of Sections 250-57 and 250-60.

422-17. Wall-Mounted Ovens and Counter-Mounted Cooking Units.

(a) Wall-mounted ovens and counter-mounted cooking units complete with provisions for mounting and for making electrical connections shall be considered as fixed appliances.

(b) A separable connector or a plug and receptacle combination in the supply line to an oven or cooking unit used only for ease in servicing or for installation shall:

(1) Not be installed as the disconnecting means required by Section 422-20;

(2) Be approved for the temperature of the space in which it is located.

422-18. Other Installation Methods.   Appliances employing methods of installation other than covered by this Article may be used only by special permission.

D. Control and Protection of Appliances

422-20. Disconnecting Means.   A means shall be provided to disconnect each appliance from all ungrounded conductors as required by the following Sections of Part D. If an appliance is supplied by more than one source, the disconnecting means shall be grouped and identified.

422-21. Disconnection of Fixed Appliances.

(a) For fixed appliances rated at not over 300 volt amperes or $\frac{1}{8}$ hp, the branch-circuit overcurrent device shall be permitted to serve as the disconnecting means.

(b) For fixed appliances of greater rating the branch-circuit switch or circuit breaker may, where readily accessible to the user of the appliance, serve as the disconnecting means.

422-22. Disconnection of Portable Appliances.

(a) For portable appliances, a separable connector or an attachment plug and receptacle shall be permitted to serve as the disconnecting means.

(b) The rating of a receptacle or of a separable connector shall not be less than the rating of any appliance connected thereto.

Exception: Demand factors authorized elsewhere in this Code shall be permitted to be applied.

(c) Attachment plugs and connectors shall conform to the following:

(1) Live Parts.   They shall be so constructed and installed as to guard against inadvertent contact with live parts.

(2) Interrupting Capacity.   They shall be capable of interrupting their rated current without hazard to the operator.

(3) Interchangeability.   They shall be so designed that they will not fit into receptacles of lesser rating.

422-23. Disconnection of Stationary Appliances.

(a) For stationary appliances rated at not over 300 volt amperes or $\frac{1}{8}$ horsepower, the branch-circuit overcurrent device shall be permitted to serve as the disconnecting means.

(b) For stationary appliances of greater rating, the branch-circuit switch or circuit breaker shall be permitted to serve as the disconnecting means where readily accessible to the user of the appliance.

(c) For cord-connected appliances, such as free-standing household-type ranges and clothes dryers, a separable connector or an attachment plug and receptacle shall be permitted to serve as the disconnecting means. Attachment plugs and connectors shall comply with Section 422-22(c).

For household electric ranges, an attachment plug and receptacle connection at the rear base of a range, if it is accessible from the front by removal of a drawer, shall be considered as meeting the intent of this rule.

▲ Examples of the application of this section for disconnecting means for appliances are found in the installation of household electric ranges and clothes dryers. The purpose of these requirements is to provide that for every such appliance there will be some means for opening the circuit to the appliance when it is to be serviced or repaired or when it is to be removed.

422-24. Unit Switches As Disconnecting Means. Unit switches that are a part of an appliance shall require additional means for disconnection as specified in (a), (b), (c), or (d) below to be acceptable as the disconnecting means required by Part D.

(a) Multifamily Dwellings. In multifamily (more than two) dwellings, the disconnecting means shall be within the apartment, or on the same floor as the apartment in which the appliance is installed, and shall be permitted to control lamps and other appliances.

(b) Two-Family Dwellings. In two-family dwellings, the disconnecting means shall be permitted to be outside the apartment in which the appliance is installed. In this case an individual switch for the apartment shall be permitted.

(c) Single-Family Dwellings. In single-family dwellings, the service disconnecting means shall be permitted to be used.

(d) Other Occupancies. In other occupancies, the branch-circuit switch or circuit breaker, where readily accessible to the user of the appliance, shall be permitted for this purpose.

422-25. Switch and Circuit Breaker to Be Indicating. Switches and circuit breakers used as disconnecting means shall be of the indicating type.

422-26. Disconnecting Means for Motor-Driven Appliances. If a switch or circuit breaker serves as the disconnecting means for a stationary or fixed motor-driven appliance of more than $\frac{1}{8}$ horsepower, it shall be located within sight from the motor controller and shall comply with Part H of Article 430.

422-27. Overcurrent Protection.

(a) Appliances shall be considered as protected against overcurrent if supplied by branch circuits as specified in (e) below and in Sections 422-5 and 422-6.

Exception: Motors of motor-operated appliances shall be provided with overload protection in accordance with Part C of Article 430. Hermetic refrigerant motor-compressors in air conditioning or refrigerating equipment shall be provided with overload protection in accordance with Part F of Article 440. When appliance overcurrent protective devices separate from the appliance are required, data for selection of these devices shall be marked on the appliance. The minimum marking shall be that specified in Sections 430-7 and 440-3.

(b) A household-type appliance with surface heating elements having a maximum demand of more than 60 amperes computed in accordance with Table 220-19 shall have its power supply subdivided into two or more circuits, each of which is provided with overcurrent protection rated at not over 50 amperes.

(c) Infrared lamp commercial and industrial heating appliances shall have overcurrent protection not exceeding 50 amperes.

(d) Open-coil or exposed sheathed-coil types of surface heating elements in commercial-type heating appliances shall be protected by overcurrent protective devices rated at not over 50 amperes.

(e) If the branch circuit supplies a single nonmotor-operated appliance, rated at 10 amperes or more, the overcurrent device rating shall not exceed 150 percent of the appliance rating.

(f) Electric heating appliances employing resistance type heating elements rated more than 48 amperes shall have the heating elements subdivided. Each subdivided load shall not exceed 48 amperes and shall be protected at not more than 60 amperes.

These overcurrent protective devices shall be: (1) factory installed within or on the heater enclosure or provided as a separate assembly by the heater manufacturer; and (2) accessible, but need not be readily accessible; and (3) suitable for branch-circuit protection.

The main conductors supplying these overcurrent protective devices shall be considered branch-circuit conductors.

Exception: Household type appliances with surface heating elements as covered in Section 422-27(b) and commercial type heating appliances as covered in Section 422-27(d).

E. Marking of Appliances

422-30. Nameplate.

(a) Each electric appliance shall be provided with a nameplate, giving the identifying name and the rating in volts and amperes, or in volts and watts. If the appliance is to be used on a specific frequency or frequencies, it shall be so marked.

When motor overload protection external to the appliance is required, the appliance shall be so marked.

See Section 422-27(a) Exception for overcurrent protection requirements.

(b) Marking shall be located so as to be visible or easily accessible after installation.

422-31. Marking of Heating Elements. All heating elements that are rated over one ampere, replaceable in the field, and a part of an appliance shall be legibly marked with the ratings in volts and amperes, or in volts and watts, or with the manufacturer's part number.

422-32. Appliances Consisting of Motors and Others Loads. Appliances shall be marked in accordance with (a) or (b) below.

(a) In addition to the marking required in Section 422-30, the marking on an appliance consisting of a motor with other load(s) or motors with or without other load(s) shall specify the minimum circuit size and the maximum rating of the circuit overcurrent protective device.

Exception No. 1: Portable appliances and other appliances, factory-equipped with cords and attachment plugs, complying with Section 422-30.

Exception No. 2: An appliance where both the minimum circuit size and maximum rating of the circuit overcurrent protective device are not more than 15 amperes and complies with Section 422-30.

(b) An alternate marking method shall be permitted to specify the rating of the largest motor in volts and amperes, and the additional load(s) in volts and amperes, or volts and watts in addition to the marking required in Section 422-30.

Exception No. 1: Portable appliances and other appliances, factory-equipped with cords and attachment plugs, complying with Section 422-30.

Exception No. 2: The ampere rating of a motor ⅛ hp or less or a nonmotor load one ampere or less shall be permitted to be omitted unless such loads constitute the principal load.

ARTICLE 424. FIXED ELECTRIC SPACE HEATING EQUIPMENT

A. General

424-1. Scope. This Article covers fixed electric equipment used for space heating. Equipment shall be of a type approved for the purpose and location where installed. For the purpose of this Article, heating equipment shall include heating cable, unit heaters, boilers, central systems, or other approved fixed electric space heating equipment. This Article shall not apply to process heating and room air conditioning.

424-2. Other Articles. All requirements of this Code shall apply where applicable. Fixed electric space heating equipment for use in hazardous locations shall comply with Articles 500 through 517. Fixed electric space heating equipment incorporating a hermetic-refrigerant motor-compressor shall also comply with Article 440.

424-3. Branch Circuits.

(a) Branch-Circuit Requirements. Individual branch circuits shall be permitted to supply any size fixed electric space heating equipment.

Branch circuits supplying two or more outlets for fixed electric space heating equipment shall be rated 15, 20, or 30 amperes.

Exception: In other than residential occupancies, fixed infrared heating equipment shall be permitted to be supplied from branch circuits rated not more than 50 amperes.

(b) Branch-Circuit Sizing. The size of branch-circuit conductors and overcurrent protective devices supplying fixed electric space heating equipment consisting of resistance elements with or without a motor shall be computed on the basis of 125 percent of the total load of the motors and the heaters. A contactor, thermostat, relay, or similar device, approved for continuous operation at 100 percent of its rating, shall be permitted to supply its full rated load as provided in Section 210-22(c), Exception No. 3.

The size of the branch-circuit conductors and overcurrent protective devices supplying fixed electric space heating equipment consisting of mechanical refrigeration with or without resistance units shall be computed in accordance with Sections 440-34 and 440-35.

The provisions of this Section shall not apply to conductors which form an integral part of approved fixed electric space heating equipment.

▲ The 125 percent requirement in paragraph (b) means that branch circuits for electric space heating equipment cannot be loaded to more than 80 percent of the branch-circuit *rating* unless the branch-circuit overcurrent devices and their assemblies are approved for 100 percent load.

Many line thermostats and contactors are approved for 100 percent load, and derating of such devices is not required.

B. Installation

424-9. General. All fixed electric space heating equipment shall be installed in an approved manner.

424-10. Special Permission. Fixed electric space heating equipment and systems installed by methods other than covered by this Article may be used only by special permission.

424-11. Supply Conductors. Fixed electric space heating equipment requiring supply conductors with over 60°C insulation shall be clearly and permanently marked. This marking shall be plainly visible after installation and shall be permitted to be adjacent to the field-connection box.

424-12. Locations.

(a) Fixed electric space heating equipment shall not be used where exposed to severe physical damage unless adequately protected.

(b) Heaters and related equipment installed in damp or wet locations shall be approved for such locations and shall be constructed and installed so that water cannot enter or accumulate in or on wired sections, electrical components, or duct work.

See Section 110-11 for equipment exposed to deteriorating agencies.

424-13. Spacing from Combustible Materials. Fixed electric space heating equipment shall be installed to provide the required spacing between the equipment and adjacent combustible material, unless it has been found to be acceptable where installed in direct contact with combustible material.

424-14. Grounding. All exposed metal parts of fixed electric space heating equipment likely to become energized shall be grounded as required in Article 250.

C. Control and Protection of Fixed Electric Space Heating Equipment

424-19. Disconnecting Means. Means shall be provided to disconnect the heater, controller(s), and overcurrent protective device(s) of all fixed electric space heating equipment from all ungrounded conductors. Where heating equipment is supplied by more than one source, the disconnecting means shall be grouped and identified.

(a) In Sight. The disconnecting means for fixed electric space heating equipment covered under Section 424-22(c) shall be in sight of the supplementary overcurrent protective device(s). This disconnecting means shall be permitted to serve as the required disconnecting means for the controller(s) and heater under the following conditions:

(1) The disconnecting means provided is also in sight from the controller(s) and the heater, or

(2) The disconnecting means provided shall be capable of being locked in the open position.

Exception: Where a motor(s) is part of the fixed electric space heating and the motor(s) is part of the fixed electric space heating and the motor(s) is not within sight of its controller(s), a disconnecting means for the motor(s) in accordance with Section 430-86 shall be permitted.

(b) Not Over 300 VA or ⅛ HP. For fixed electric space heating equipment rated at not over 300 volt-amperes or ⅛ horsepower, the branch-circuit overcurrent device shall be permitted to serve as the disconnecting means.

(c) Over 300 VA or ⅛ HP. For fixed electric space heating equipment rated over 300 volt-amperes or ⅛ horsepower, the branch-circuit switch or circuit breaker shall be permitted to serve as the disconnecting means, where readily accessible to the user of the equipment.

(d) Motor-Driven Heating Equipment. A switch or circuit breaker that serves as the disconnecting means for a motor-driven heater having a motor more than ⅛ horsepower shall be located within sight of the motor controller.

(e) Unit Switches as Disconnecting Means. Unit switches with a marked off position that are part of a fixed heater and disconnect all ungrounded conductors shall be permitted as the disconnecting means required by this Article where other means for disconnection are provided in the following types of occupancies:

(1) Multifamily Dwellings. In multifamily (more than two) dwellings, the other disconnecting means shall be within the apartment, or on the same floor as the apartment in which the fixed heater is installed, and shall also be permitted to control lamps and appliances.

(2) Two-Family Dwellings. In two-family dwellings, the other disconnecting means shall be permitted either inside or outside of the apartment in which the fixed heater is installed.

(3) Single-Family Dwellings. In single-family dwellings, the service disconnecting means shall be permitted to be the other disconnecting means.

(4) Other Occupancies. In other occupancies, the branch-circuit switch or circuit breaker, where readily accessible to the user of the fixed heater, shall be permitted as the other disconnecting means.

424-20. Controllers and Disconnecting Means.

(a) Thermostats and thermostatically controlled switching devices that indicate an off position and interrupt line current shall open all ungrounded conductors when the control device is in this off position.

(b) Thermostats and thermostatically controlled switching devices that do not have an off position shall not be required to open all ungrounded conductors.

(c) Remote-control thermostats shall not be required to meet the requirements of (a) and (b) above. These devices shall not be considered as the disconnecting means.

(d) Switching devices consisting of combined thermostats and manually controlled switches that serve both as controllers and disconnecting means shall.

(1) Open all ungrounded conductors when manually placed in the off position.

(2) Be so designed that the circuit cannot be energized automatically after the device has been manually placed in the off position.

424-21. Switch and Circuit Breaker to Be Indicating. Switches and circuit breakers used as disconnecting means shall be of the indicating type.

424-22. Overcurrent Protection.

(a) Branch-Circuit Devices. Electric space heating equipment, other than such motor-operated equipment as required by Articles 430 and 440 to have additional overcurrent protection, shall be considered as protected against overcurrent where supplied by one of the branch circuits in Article 210.

(b) Resistance Elements. Electric space heating equipment employing resist-heating elements rated more than 48 amperes shall have the heating elements subdivided. Each subdivided load shall not exceed 48 amperes and shall be protected at not more than 60 amperes.

Exception: As provided in Section 424-72(a).

(c) Overcurrent Protective Devices. The overcurrent protective devices specified in (b) above shall be: (1) factory-installed within or on the heater enclosure or provided as a separate assembly by the heater manufacturer; (2) accessible, but shall not be required to be readily accessible; and (3) suitable for branch-circuit protection.

Where cartridge fuses are used to provide this overcurrent protection, a single disconnecting means shall be permitted to be used for the several subdivided loads. See Section 240-40.

▲ The purpose of paragraph (c) is to require the heating manufacturer to furnish the necessary overcurrent protective devices where subdivided loads are required.

Main conductors supplying overcurrent protective devices for subdivided loads are considered as branch circuits to avoid controversies about applying the 125 percent requirement in Sec. 424-3(b) to branch circuits *only.* It is not the intent, however, to deny the use of the *feeder tap* rules in Sec. 240-21 for these *main* conductors.

(d) Branch-Circuit Conductors.   The conductors supplying the supplementary overcurrent protective devices shall be considered branch-circuit conductors.

Exception: For heaters rated 50 kW or more, the conductors supplying the supplementary overcurrent protective devices specified in (c) above shall be permitted to be sized at not less than 100 percent of the nameplate rating of the heater provided all of the following conditions are met:

1. The heater is marked with a minimum conductor size, and

2. The conductors are not smaller than the marked minimum size, and

3. A temperature actuated device controls the cyclic operation of the equipment.

D. Marking of Heating Equipment

424-28. Nameplate.

(a) Marking Required.   Each unit of fixed electric space heating equipment shall be provided with a nameplate giving the identifying name and the normal rating in volts and amperes, or in volts and watts.

Electric space heating equipment intended for use on alternating current only or direct current only shall be marked to so indicate. The marking of equipment consisting of motors over $\frac{1}{8}$ horsepower and other loads shall specify the rating of the motor in volts, amperes, and frequency, and the heating load in volts and watts, or volts and amperes.

(b) Location.   This nameplate shall be located so as to be visible or easily accessible after installation.

424-29. Marking of Heating Elements.   All heating elements that are replaceable in the field and are a part of an electric heater shall be legibly marked with the ratings in volts and amperes, or in volts and watts.

E. Electric Space Heating Cables and Panels

424-34. Heating Cable Construction.   Heating cable shall be furnished complete with factory-assembled nonheating leads at least 7 feet in length.

424-35. Marking of Heating Cables and Panels.   Each unit shall be marked with the identifying name or identification symbol, catalog number, ratings in volts and watts, or volts and amperes.

(a) Heating Cables. Each unit length of heating cable shall have a permanent legible marking on each nonheating lead located within 3 inches of the terminal end. The lead wire shall have the following color identification: 120-volt nominal, yellow; 208-volt nominal, blue; 240-volt nominal, red; and 277-volt nominal, brown.

(b) Heating Panels. Heating panels shall be permanently marked in a location that is readily visible prior to application of panel finish..

424-36. Clearances of Wiring in Ceilings. Wiring located above heated ceilings shall be spaced not less than 2 inches above the heated ceiling and shall be considered as operating at an ambient of 50°C. The ampacity of conductors shall be computed on the basis of the correction factors given in Note 13 to Tables 310-16 through 310-19.

Exception: Wiring above heated ceilings and located above thermal insulation having a minimum thickness of 2 inches shall not require correction for temperature.

424-37. Clearances of Branch-Circuit Wiring in Walls.

(a) Exterior Walls. Where located in exterior walls, wiring shall be located outside the thermal insulation.

(b) Interior Walls. Where located in interior walls or partitions, wiring shall be considered as operating at an ambient of 40°C (104°F); and the ampacity of conductors shall be computed on the basis of the correction factors given in Note 13 to Tables 310-16 through 310-19.

424-38. Area Restrictions.

(a) Heating cables and panels shall not extend beyond the room or area in which they originate.

(b) Cables and panels shall not be installed in closets, over walls or partitions that extend to the ceiling, or over cabinets whose clearance from the ceiling is less than the minimum horizontal dimension of the cabinet to the nearest cabinet edge that is open to the room or area.

Exception: Isolated single runs of cable shall be permitted to pass over partitions where they are embedded.

(c) This provision shall not prevent the use of cable or panels in closet ceilings as low temperature heat sources to control relative humidity, provided they are used only in those portions of the ceiling that are unobstructed to the floor by shelves or other permanent fixtures.

424-39. Clearance from Other Objects and Openings Panels and cables shall be separated at least 8 inches from the edge of outlet boxes and junction boxes that are to be used for mounting surface lighting fixtures. A clearance of not less than two inches shall be provided from recessed fixtures and their trims, ventilating openings, and other such openings in room surfaces. Sufficient area shall be provided to assure that no heating cable or panel will be covered by any surface mounted lighting units.

424-40. Splices. Embedded cables shall be spliced only where necessary and only by approved means, and in no case shall the length of the heating cable be altered.

424-41. Installation of Heating Cables on Dry Board, in Plaster and on Concrete Ceilings.

(a) Cables shall not be installed in walls.

Exception: Isolated single runs of cable shall be permitted to run down a vertical surface to reach a dropped ceiling.

(b) Adjacent runs of cable not exceeding $2\frac{3}{4}$ watts per foot shall be installed not less than $1\frac{1}{2}$ inches on centers.

(c) Heating cables shall be applied only to gypsum board, plaster lath or other fire-resistant material. With metal lath or other electrically conductive surfaces, a coat of plaster shall be applied to completely separate the metal lath or conductive surface from the cable.

See also (f) below.

(d) All heating cables, the splice between the heating cable and nonheating leads, and 3-inch minimum of the nonheating lead at the splice shall be embedded in plaster or dry board in the same manner as the heating cable.

(e) The entire ceiling surface shall have a finish of thermally noninsulating sand plaster having a nominal thickness of $\frac{1}{2}$ inch, or other noninsulating material approved for the purpose and applied according to specified thickness and directions.

(f) Cables shall be secured at intervals not exceeding 16 inches by means of approved stapling, tape, plaster, nonmetallic spreaders, or other approved means. Staples or metal fasteners that straddle the cable shall not be used with metal lath or other electrically conductive surfaces.

Exception: Cables approved for the purpose shall be permitted to be secured at intervals not to exceed six feet by approved means.

(g) In dry board installations, the entire ceiling below the heating cable shall be covered with gypsum board not exceeding $\frac{1}{2}$-inch thickness. The void between the upper layer of gypsum board, plaster lath, or other fire-resistant material and the surface layer of gypsum board shall be completely filled with thermally conductive nonshrinking plaster or other approved material of equivalent thermal conductivity.

(h) Cables shall be kept free from contact with metal or other electrical conductive surfaces.

(i) In dry-board applications, cable shall be installed parallel to the joist, leaving a clear space centered under the joist of $2\frac{1}{2}$ inches (width) between centers of adjacent runs of cable. Crossing of joist by cable shall be kept to a minimum. Surface layer of gypsum board shall be mounted so that the nails or other fasteners do not pierce the heating cable.

Where impracticable, cables shall cross joists only at the ends of a room.

424-42. Finished Ceilings. Finished ceilings shall not be covered with decorative panels or beams constructed of materials which have thermal insulating properties, such as wood, fiber, or plastic. Finished ceilings shall be permitted to be covered with paint, wallpaper, or other approved surface finishes.

424-43. Installation of Nonheating Leads of Cables and Panels.

(a) Free nonheating leads of cables and panels shall be installed in accordance with approved wiring methods from the junction box to a location within the ceiling. Such installations shall be permitted to be single conductors in approved raceways, single or multiconductor Type UF, Type NMC, or Type MI, or other approved conductors.

(b) Not less than 6 inches of free nonheating lead shall be within the junction box. The marking of the leads shall be visible in the junction box.

(c) Excess leads shall not be cut but shall be secured to the underside of the ceiling and embedded in plaster or other approved material, leaving only a length sufficient to reach the junction box with not less than 6 inches of free lead within the box.

424-44. Installation of Panels or Cables in Concrete or Poured Masonry Floors.

(a) Panels or heating units shall not exceed 33 watts per square foot of heated area or $16\frac{1}{2}$ watts per linear foot of cable.

(b) The spacing between adjacent runs of cable shall not be less than one inch on centers.

(c) Cables shall be secured in place by nonmetallic frames or spreaders or other approved means while the concrete or other finish is applied.

Cables, units, and panels shall not be installed where they bridge expansion joints unless protected from expansion and contraction.

(d) Spacings shall be maintained between the heating cable and metal embedded in the floor.

Exception: Grounded metal-clad cable shall be permitted to be in contact with metal embedded in the floor.

(e) Leads shall be protected where they leave the floor by rigid metal conduit, electrical metallic tubing, or by other approved means.

(f) Bushings or approved fittings shall be used where the leads emerge within the floor slab.

424-45. Inspection and Tests.   Cable installations shall be made with due care to prevent damage to the cable assembly and shall be inspected and approved before cables are covered or concealed.

424-46. Panels—General.   Sections 424-46 through 424-48 cover only heating panels of less than 25 watts per square foot assembled together in the field to form a heating installation in one room or area using approved methods of interconnection. Such an installation shall be connected by a recognized wiring method.

424-47. Panels to Be Complete Units.   Panels shall be installed as complete units unless approved for field cutting in a recognized manner.

424-48. Installation.   Panels shall be installed in an approved manner. Nails, staples, or other electrically conductive fasteners shall not be used where they penetrate current-carrying parts.

Exception: Insulated fasteners shall be permitted with systems for which they are recognized.

F. Duct Heaters

424-57. General.   Part F shall apply to any heater mounted in the air stream of a forced-air system where the air moving unit is not provided as an integral part of the equipment.

424-58. Approved.   Heaters installed in an air duct shall be approved for the purpose and installed in the approved manner.

424-59. Air Flow.   Means shall be provided to assure uniform and adequate air flow over the face of the heater.

Heaters installed within 4 feet of a fan outlet, elbows, baffle plates, or other obstruction in duct work may require turning vanes, pressure plates, or other devices on the inlet side of the duct heater to assure an even distribution of air over the face of the heater.

424-60. Elevated Inlet Temperature.   Duct heaters intended for use with elevated inlet air temperature (such as heat pumps) shall be approved for the purpose and so marked.

424-61. Installation of Duct Heaters with Heat Pumps and Air Conditioners. Heat pumps and air conditioners having duct heaters closer than 4 feet to the heat pump or air conditioner shall have both the duct heater and heat pump or air conditioner approved for such installation and so marked.

424-62. Condensation. Duct heaters used with air conditioners or other air-cooling equipment that may result in condensation of moisture shall be approved for use with air conditioners.

424-63. Fan Circuit Interlock. Means shall be provided to insure that the fan circuit is energized when the first heater circuit is energized. However, time or temperature controlled delay in energizing the fan motor shall be permitted.

424-64. Limit Controls. Each duct heater shall be provided with an approved, integral, automatic-reset temperature-limiting control or controllers to de-energize the circuit or circuits.

In addition, an integral independent supplementary control or controllers shall be provided in each duct heater that will disconnect a sufficient number of conductors to interrupt current flow. This device shall be manually resettable or replaceable.

424-65. Location of Disconnecting Means. Duct heater controller equipment shall be accessible with the disconnecting means installed at or within sight from the controller.

424-66. Installation. Duct heaters shall be installed in accordance with the manufacturer's instructions in a manner so that operation will not create a hazard to persons or property. Furthermore, duct heaters shall be located with respect to building construction and other equipment so as to permit access to the heater. Sufficient clearance shall be maintained to permit replacement of controls and heating elements and for adjusting and cleaning of controls and other parts requiring such attention. See Section 110-16.

For additional installation information, see Air Conditioning and Ventilating Systems (NFPA No. 90A-1973) and Warm Air Heating and Air Conditioning Systems (NFPA No. 90B-1973).

G. Resistance-Type Boilers

424-70. Scope. The provisions in Part G of this article shall apply to boilers employing resistance-type heating elements. Electrode-type boilers shall not be considered as employing resistance-type heating elements. See Part H of this Article.

424-71. Approved. Resistance-type boilers shall be approved for the purpose and installed in the approved manner.

424-72. Overcurrent Protection.

(a) A boiler employing resistance-type immersion heating elements contained in an ASME rated and stamped vessel shall have the heating elements subdivided into loads not exceeding 120 amperes and protected at not more than 150 amperes.

(b) A boiler employing resistance-type heating elements rated more than 48 amperes and not contained in an ASME rated and stamped vessel, shall have the heating elements subdivided into loads not exceeding 48 amperes and protected at not more than 60 amperes.

(c) The supplementary overcurrent protective devices as required by Section 424-72(a) and Section 424-72(b) shall be: (1) factory-installed within or on the boiler enclosure or provided as a separate assembly by the boiler manufacturer, and (2) accessible, but need not be readily accessible, and (3) suitable for branch-circuit protection.

Where cartridge fuses are used to provide this overcurrent protection, a single disconnecting means shall be permitted for the several subdivided circuits. See Section 240-40.

(d) The conductors supplying these supplementary overcurrent protective devices shall be considered branch-circuit conductors.

Exception: The heaters rated 50 kW or more, the conductors supplying the overcurrent protective device specified in (c) above, shall be permitted to be sized at not less than 100 percent of the nameplate rating of the heater provided all of the following conditions are met.

1. The heater is marked with a minimum conductor size, and

2. The conductors are not smaller than the marked minimum size, and

3. A temperature or pressure actuated device controls the cyclic operation of the equipment.

424-73. Over-Temperature Limit Control. Each boiler designed so that in normal operation there is no change in state of the heat transfer medium shall be equipped with a temperature sensitive limiting means. It shall be installed to limit maximum liquid temperature and shall directly or indirectly disconnect all ungrounded conductors to the heating elements. Such means shall be in addition to a temperature regulating system and other devices protecting the tank against excessive pressure.

424-74. Over-Pressure Limit Control. Each boiler designed so that in normal operation there is a change in state of the heat transfer medium from liquid to vapor shall be equipped with a pressure sensitive limiting means. It shall be installed to limit maximum pressure and shall directly or indirectly disconnect all ungrounded conductors to the heating elements. Such means shall be in addition to a pressure regulating system and other devices protecting the tank against excessive pressure.

424-75. Grounding. All non-current carrying metal parts shall be grounded in accordance with Article 250. Means for connection of equipment grounding conductor(s) sized in accordance with Table 250-95 shall be provided.

H. Electrode-Type Boilers

424-80. Scope. The provisions in Part H of this article shall apply to boilers in which heat is generated by the passage of current between electrodes through the liquid being heated.

424-81. Approved. Electrode-type boilers shall be approved for the purpose and installed in the approved manner.

424-82. Branch-Circuit Requirements. The size of branch-circuit conductors and overcurrent protective devices shall be calculated on the basis of 125 percent of the total load (motors not included). A contactor, relay or other device, approved for continuous operation at 100 percent of its rating, shall be permitted to supply its full rated load. See Section 210-22(c) Exception No. 3. The provisions of this Section shall not apply to conductors that form an integral part of an approved boiler.

Exception: For an electrode boiler 50 kW or more, the conductors supplying the boiler electrode(s) shall be permitted to be sized at not less than 100 percent of the nameplate rating of the electrode boiler provided all the following conditions are met:

1. The electrode boiler is marked with a minimum conductor size; and,

2. The conductors are not smaller than the marked minimum size; and,

3. A temperature or pressure actuated device controls the cyclic operation of the equipment.

424-83. Over-Temperature Limit Control. Each boiler designed so that in normal operation there is no change in state of the heat transfer medium shall be equipped with a temperature sensitive limiting means. It shall be installed to limit maximum liquid temperature and shall directly or indirectly interrupt all current flow through the electrodes. Such means shall be in addition to the temperature regulating system and other devices protecting the tank against excessive pressure.

424-84. Over-Pressure Limit Control. Each boiler designed so that in normal operation there is a change in state of the heat transfer medium from liquid to vapor shall be equipped with a pressure sensitive limiting means. It shall be installed to limit maximum pressure and shall directly or indirectly interrupt all current flow through the electrodes. Such means shall be in addition to a pressure regulating system and other devices protecting the tank against excessive pressure.

424-85. Grounding. All exposed non-current carrying metal parts including the supply and return connecting piping shall be grounded in accordance with Article 250. The pressure vessel containing the electrodes shall be isolated and electrically insulated from ground.

424-86. Markings. All electrode-type boilers shall be marked to show: (1) the manufacturer's name; (2) the normal rating in volts, amperes and kilowatts; (3) the electrical supply required specifying frequency, number of phases and number of wires; (4) the marking: "Electrode-Type Boiler;" (5) a warning marking—"ALL POWER SUPPLIES SHALL BE DISCONNECTED BEFORE SERVICING INCLUDING SERVICING THE PRESSURE VESSEL."

The nameplate shall be located so as to be visible after installation.

ARTICLE 426. FIXED OUTDOOR ELECTRIC DE-ICING AND SNOW MELTING EQUIPMENT

A. General

426-1. Scope. This Article covers electrically energized heating units, panels, and cables where embedded in driveways, walks, steps, and other areas.

426-2. Other Articles. All requirements of this Code shall apply where applicable.

426-3. Branch-Circuit Requirements. Fixed outdoor electric de-icing and snow melting equipment shall be considered as a continuous load for sizing branch circuits. Fixed outdoor electric de-icing and snow melting installations shall be permitted to be supplied by 15-, 20-, 25-, 30-, 40-, or 50-ampere branch circuits if the circuit supplies no other load.

▲ Being classified as a continuous load, branch circuits for fixed outdoor electric de-icing and snow-melting systems must be sized so that the load will not exceed 80 percent of the branch-circuit rating.

B. Installation

426-9. General. Equipment for use with fixed outdoor electric de-icing and snow melting systems shall be of a type approved for such service and for the location where installed.

426-10. Use.

(a) De-icing and snow melting equipment shall be installed only in the specific materials for which they are approved.

(b) De-icing and snow melting units shall be protected from physical damage.

426-11. Complete Units.

(a) Units, panels, and cables shall be installed in their complete sizes or lengths as supplied by the manufacturer.

Exception: Nonheating leads shall be permitted to be shortened if the marking specified in Section 426-26 is retained.

(b) Units without nameplates shall not be installed.

(c) Units shall be suitable for use with approved wiring systems.

426-12. Special Permission. Fixed outdoor electric de-icing and snow melting equipment employing methods of construction or installation other than that covered by this Article may be used only by special permission.

C. Control and Protection

426-20. Disconnecting Means. All fixed outdoor electric de-icing and snow melting equipment shall be provided with a means for disconnection from all ungrounded conductors. Where readily accessible to the user of the equipment, the branch-circuit switch or circuit breaker shall be permitted to serve as the disconnecting means. Switches used as disconnecting means shall be of the indicating type.

426-21. Controllers.

(a) Thermostats and thermostatically controlled switching devices that indicate an off position and interrupt line current shall open all ungrounded conductors when the control device is in the off position, and shall be permitted as the disconnecting means.

(b) Thermostats and thermostatically controlled switching devices shall be so designed that the circuit cannot be energized automatically after the device has been manually placed in the off position.

(c) Thermostats and thermostatically controlled switching devices that do not have an off position shall not be required to open all ungrounded conductors, but they shall not be used as the disconnecting means required in Section 426-20.

426-22. Overcurrent Protection. Fixed outdoor electric de-icing and snow melting equipment shall be considered as protected against overcurrent when supplied by one of the branch circuits specified in Section 426-3.

426-23. Nonheating Leads. Nonheating leads on the cables, panels, or units shall be furnished as part of the factory assembly. The leads shall consist of conductors and wiring approved for general use, or other wiring approved for the purpose.

426-24. Installation of Heating Cables, Units, or Panels.

(a) The operating characteristics of embedded assemblies of fixed outdoor electric de-icing and snow melting equipment depend upon the specific materials involved, and, therefore, embedded equipment shall be installed as designed for use in such materials.

(b) Panels or units shall not exceed 120 watts per square foot of heated area.

(c) The spacings between adjacent cable runs is dependent upon the rating of the cable, and shall not be less than one inch on centers.

(d) Units, panels, and cables shall be installed:

(1) On a substantial asphalt or masonry base at least 2 inches thick and have at least 1½ inches of asphalt or masonry applied over the units, panels, or cables; or

(2) They shall be permitted to be installed over other approved bases and embedded within 3½ inches of masonry or asphalt but not less than 1½ inches from the top surface; or

(3) Equipment that has been specially investigated for other forms of installation shall be installed only in the manner for which it has been investigated.

(e) Cables shall be secured in place by frames or spreaders or other approved means while the masonry or asphalt finish is applied.

(f) Cables, units, and panels shall not be installed where they bridge expansion joints unless adequately protected from expansion and contraction.

426-25. Installation of Nonheating Leads.

(a) Nonheating leads having a grounding sheath or braid shall be permitted to be embedded in masonry or asphalt in the same manner as the heating cable without additional protection.

(b) All but one to 6 inches of nonheating leads of Type TW and other approved types not having a grounding sheath shall be enclosed in conduit, electrical metallic tubing, or other raceways within the asphalt or masonry; and the distance from the factory splice to the raceway shall not be less than one inch nor more than 6 inches.

(c) Insulating bushings shall be used in the asphalt or masonry where leads enter conduit, tubing, or raceway.

(d) Leads shall be protected in expansion joints and where they emerge from masonry or asphalt by conduit, electrical metallic tubing, other raceways, or other approved means.

(e) Not less than 6 inches of free nonheating lead shall be within the junction box.

426-26. Marking. Each heating unit, panel, and cable shall be legibly marked within 3 inches of each end of the nonheating leads with the identification symbol, catalog number, and ratings in volts and watts, or volts and amperes.

426-27. Junction Boxes. All splices other than factory splices shall be made in properly installed boxes approved for the location.

426-28. Grounding.

(a) All exposed metal parts of fixed outdoor electric de-icing and snow melting equipment, raceways, boxes, etc., likely to become energized shall be grounded as required in Article 250.

(b) Grounding means, such as copper braid, lead or copper sheath, or other approved means, shall be provided as part of the heating section of the approved cable, panel, or unit.

(c) All noncurrent-carrying metal parts that are likely to become energized shall be bonded together and positively connected to a continuous (unbroken) No. 14 or larger covered copper wire sized in accordance with Table 250-95 extending to the distribution panelboard. Where the bonding conductor is subject to physical damage, it shall be at least No. 10 copper.

426-29. Inspection. Installations shall be inspected and approved before being covered.

ARTICLE 427. FIXED ELECTRIC HEATING EQUIPMENT FOR PIPELINES AND VESSELS

A. General

427-1. Scope. The requirements of this Article shall apply to electrically energized heating systems and the installation of these systems used with pipelines and/or vessels. This Article covers electrical heating of pipelines and/or vessels by separate external heating elements, other than the skin electric current tracing or impedance methods.

427-2. Definitions. For the purpose of this Article:

(a) A pipeline is a length of pipe including pumps, valves, flanges, control devices, strainers and/or similar equipment for conveying fluids.

(b) A vessel is a container such as a barrel, drum, or tank for holding fluids or other material.

(c) An integrated heating system is a complete system consisting of components such as pipelines, vessels, heating elements, heat transfer medium, thermal insulation, moisture barrier, nonheating leads, temperature controller, safety signs, junction boxes, conduit and fittings.

427-3. Application of Other Articles. All requirements of this Code shall apply except as specifically amended in this Article. Cord-connected pipe heating assemblies intended for specific uses and approved for the purpose shall be installed according to Article 422. Fixed electric pipeline and vessel heating equipment for use in hazardous locations shall comply with Articles 500 through 516.

427-4. Branch-Circuit Requirements. The minimum size of branch-circuit conductors and overcurrent protective devices supplying fixed electric pipeline and vessel heating equipment shall be calculated on the basis of 125 percent of the total load of the heaters.

B. Installation

427-10. General. Equipment for pipeline and vessel electrical heating shall be of a type compatible with the chemical, thermal and physical environment.

427-11. Use. Electric heating equipment shall be installed in such a manner as to be afforded protection from physical damage.

427-12. Integrated Electrical Heating System.

(a) Accessible external surfaces of pipeline and vessel heating equipment which operate at surface temperatures exceeding 60°C (140°F) shall be physically guarded, isolated, or thermally insulated to protect against contact by personnel in the area. In addition, the area utilizing the pipeline and vessel heating equipment shall be marked as specified in (b) below.

(b) The presence of electric pipeline and vessel heating equipment shall be evident by the posting of appropriate signs or other markings at frequent intervals in the area involved.

(c) Heating element assemblies shall be secured to the surfaces being heated in an approved manner by means other than thermal insulation. The securement means shall employ materials suitable for the environment and temperature involved and be located at not more than 12 inch intervals.

(d) Where the heating element is not in direct contact with the pipeline or vessel being heated, means shall be provided to prevent overtemperature of the heating element unless the design of the heater assembly is such that its temperature limitations will not be exceeded.

(e) Heating elements and assemblies shall not be installed where they bridge expansion joints unless provision is made for expansion and contraction.

(f) Where installed on flexible pipelines, the heater elements and assemblies shall have a flexural capability compatible with the pipeline.

C. Control and Protection

427-20. Disconnecting Means.

(a) Means shall be provided to disconnect all fixed electric pipeline or vessel heating equipment from all ungrounded conductors. The branch-circuit switch or circuit breaker, where readily accessible to the user of the equipment, shall be permitted to serve as the disconnecting means. Switches used as disconnecting means shall be of the indicating type, and shall be provided with a positive lockout in the off position.

(b) The factory-installed attachment plug of cord-connected equipment rated 20 amperes or less and 150 volts or less to ground is an acceptable means of disconnection.

427-21. Controls.

(a) Temperature-controlled switching devices which indicate an off position and which interrupt line current shall open all ungrounded conductors when the control device is in this off position. These devices shall not serve as disconnecting means unless provided with a positive lockout in the off position.

(b) Temperature-controlled switching devices which do not have an off position are not required to open all ungrounded conductors and shall not serve as disconnecting means.

(c) Remote-controlled temperature actuated devices shall not be required to meet the requirements of paragraphs (a) and (b) above. These devices shall not serve as the disconnecting means.

(d) Switching devices consisting of combined temperature actuated devices and manually controlled switches which serve both as controllers and disconnecting means shall:

(1) Open all ungrounded conductors when manually placed in the off position.

(2) Be so designed that the circuit cannot be energized automatically after the device has been manually placed in the off position.

(3) Be provided with a positive lockout in the off position.

427-22. Overcurrent Protection.
Heaters shall be protected against overcurrent in accordance with Section 210-20.

427-23. Nonheating Leads.

(a) Power supply nonheating leads (cold leads) for the electric heating elements shall be suitable for the temperature encountered and shall be supplied by the heating element manufacturer. Preassembled nonheating leads on approved heaters may be shortened if the markings specified in Section 427-24 are retained. Not less than 6 inches of nonheating leads shall be provided within the junction box.

(b) Nonheating power supply leads shall be protected where they emerge from electric pipeline or vessel heating units by metallic conduit or metallic tubing.

(c) Interconnecting nonheating leads connecting portions of the heating system shall be permitted to be covered by thermal insulation in the same manner as the heater.

427-24. Markings. Each factory-assembled heating unit shall be legibly marked within 3 inches of the end of each power supply nonheating lead with the permanent identification symbol, catalog number, and ratings in volts and watts, or volts and amperes.

427-25. Electrical Connections.

(a) Nonheating interconnections where required under thermal insulation, shall be made with properly installed insulated connectors approved for the purpose.

(b) Splice connections and terminations outside the thermal insulation shall be installed in a box or fitting in accordance with Sections 110-14 and 300-15.

427-26. Grounding. Exposed noncurrent-carrying metal parts of electric heating equipment which are likely to become energized shall be grounded as required in Article 250.

ARTICLE 430. MOTORS, MOTOR CIRCUITS, AND CONTROLLERS

A. General

430-1. Motor Feeder and Branch Circuits. The following general requirements cover provisions for motors, motor circuits, and controllers that do not properly fall into the other parts of this Article.

See Article 440 for air-conditioning and refrigerating equipment.
See Diagram 430-1.

430-2. Adjustable Speed Drive Systems. The incoming branch circuit or feeder to power conversion equipment included as a part of an adjustable speed drive system shall be based on the rated input to the power conversion equipment. If the power conversion equipment provides overload protection for the motor, additional protection is not required.

The disconnecting means shall be permitted to be in the incoming line to the conversion equipment and shall have a rating not less than 115 percent of the rated input current of the conversion unit.

430-3. Part-Winding Motors. A part-winding-start induction or synchronous motor is one arranged for starting by first energizing part of its primary (armature) winding and, subsequently, energizing the remainder of this winding in one or more steps. The purpose is to reduce the initial values of the starting current drawn or the starting torque developed by the motor. A standard part-winding-start induction motor is arranged so that one-half of its primary winding can be energized initially and, subsequently, the remaining half can be energized, both halves then carrying equal current. A hermetic refrigerant compressor motor shall not be considered a standard part-winding-start induction motor.

Diagram 430-1

To Supply

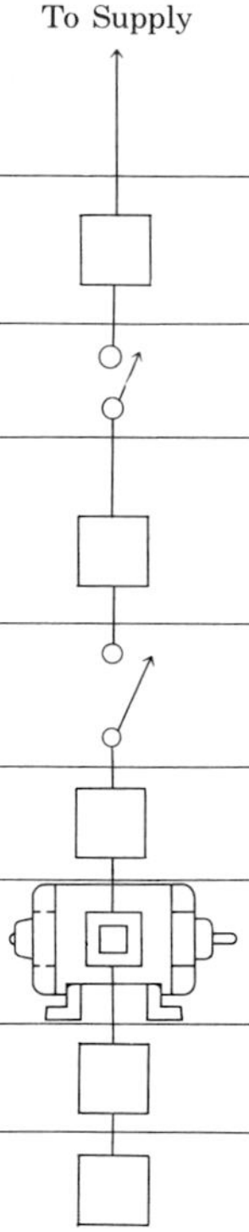

Motor Feeder	Part B
	Sec. 430-23 and 430-24
	430-25 and 430-26
Motor Feeder	Part E
Overcurrent protection	Part E
Motor Disconnecting Means	Part H
Motor Branch-Circuit Overcurrent protection	Part D
Motor Circuit Conductor	Part B
Motor Controller	Part G
Motor Control Circuits	Part F
Motor Running Overcurrent protection	Part C
Motor	Part A
Inherent Protection	Part C
Secondary Controller Secondary Conductors	Part B Sec. 430-23
Secondary Resistor	Sec. 430-23 and Art 470

Where separate running overcurrent devices are used with a standard part-winding-start induction motor, each half of the motor winding shall be individually protected in accordance with Sections 430-32 and 430-37 with a trip current one-half that specified.

Each motor-winding connection shall have branch-circuit short-circuit and ground-fault protection rated at not more than one-half that specified by Section 430-52.

Exception: A single device having this half rating shall be permitted for both windings if it will allow the motor to start. Where a time-delay (dual-element) fuse is used as a single device for both windings, it shall be permitted to have a rating not exceeding 150 percent of motor full-load current.

430-4. In Sight From. Where this Article specifies that one equipment shall be "in sight from" another equipment, one of the equipments specified shall be visible and not more than 50 feet distant from the other.

430-5. Other Articles. Motors and controllers shall also comply with the applicable provisions of the following:

430-6. Ampacity and Motor Rating Determination. Conductor ampacity and motor ratings shall be determined as specified in (a) and (b) below.

(a) General Motor Applications. Other than as specified for torque motors in (b) below, where the current rating of a motor is used to determine the ampacity of conductors or ampere ratings of switches, branch-circuit overcurrent devices, etc., the values given in Tables 430-147, 430-148, 430-149, and 430-150, including notes, shall be used instead of the actual current rating marked on the motor nameplate. Separate motor-running overcurrent protection shall be based on the motor nameplate current rating. Where a motor is marked in amperes, but not horsepower, the horsepower rating shall be assumed to be that corresponding to the value given in Tables 430-147, 430-148, 430-149, and 430-150, interpolated if necessary.

Exception No. 1: Multispeed motors shall be in accordance with Sections 430-22(a) and 430-52.

Exception No. 2: For equipment employing a shaded-pole or permanent-split-capacitor-type fan or blower motor that is marked with the motor type, the full-load current for such motor marked on the nameplate of the equipment in which the fan or blower motor is employed shall be used instead of the horse power rating to determine the ampacity or rating of the disconnecting means, the branch-circuit conductors, the controller, the branch-circuit short-circuit and ground-fault protection, and the separate overload protection. This marking on the equipment nameplate shall not be less than the current marked on the fan or blower motor nameplate.

(b) Torque Motors. For torque motors the rated current shall be locked-rotor current, and this nameplate current shall be used to determine the ampacity of the branch-circuit conductors covered in Sections 430-22 and 430-24 and the ampere rating of the motor running overcurrent protection.

For motor controllers and disconnecting means, see Section 430-83, Exception No. 3 and Section 430-110.

(c) A-C Adjustable Voltage Motors. For motors used in alternating-current, adjustable voltage, variable torque drive systems, the ampacity of conductors, or ampere ratings of switches, branch-circuit overcurrent devices, etc., shall be based on the maximum operating current marked on the motor and/or control nameplate.

If the maximum operating current does not appear on the nameplate, the ampacity determination shall be based on 150 percent of the values given in Tables 430-149 and 430-150.

430-7. Marking on Motors and Multimotor Equipment.

(a) **Usual Motor Applications.** A motor shall be marked with the following information:

(1) Maker's name.

(2) Rated volts and full-load amperes.

(3) Rated frequency and number of phases, if an alternating-current motor.

(4) Rated full-load speed.

(5) Rated temperature rise or the insulation system class and rated ambient temperature.

(6) Time rating.

(7) Rated horsepower if $\frac{1}{8}$ horsepower or more.

(8) Code letter if an alternating-current motor rated $\frac{1}{2}$ horsepower or more.

See (b) below.

(9) Secondary volts and full-load amperes if a wound-rotor induction motor.

(10) Field current and voltage for direct-current excited sychronous motors.

(11) Winding: straight shunt, stabilized shunt, compound, or series, if a direct-current motor.

A multispeed motor shall be marked with the amperes and horsepower for each speed. A motor provided with the thermal protector complying with Section 430-32(a)(2) or 430-32(c)(2) shall be marked "Thermally Protected." A motor complying with Section 430-32(c)(4) shall be marked "Impedance Protected." The time rating shall be 5, 15, 30, or 60 minutes, or continuous.

Exception No. 1: On polyphase wound-rotor motors the code letter shall be omitted.

Exception No. 2: Motors of arc welders are not required to be marked with the horsepower rating.

Exception No. 3: A shaded-pole or permanent-split capacitor motor shall not be required to have ampere or hp ratings marked for each speed.

Exception No. 4: Thermally protected motors rated 100 watts or less and complying with 430-32(c)(2) shall be permitted to use the abbreviated marking, "T.P."

Exception No. 5: Impedance protected motors rated 100 watts or less and complying with 430-32(c)(4) shall be permitted to use the abbreviated marking, "Z.P."

(b) **Locked-Rotor Indicating Code Letters.** Code letters marked on motor nameplates to show motor input with locked rotor shall be in accordance with Table 430-7(b).

The code letter indicating motor input with locked rotor shall be in an individual block on the nameplate, properly designated. This code letter shall be used for determining branch-circuit overcurrent protection by reference to Table 430-152, as provided in Section 430-52.

(1) Multispeed motors shall be marked with the code letter designating the locked-rotor kVA per horsepower for the highest speed at which the motor can be started.

Exception: Constant-horsepower multispeed motors shall be marked with the code letter giving the highest locked-rotor kVA per horsepower.

Table 430-7(b). Locked-Rotor Indicating Code Letters

Code Letter	Kilovolt-Amperes per Horsepower with Locked Rotor
A	0— 3.14
B	3.15— 3.54
C	3.55— 3.99
D	4.0 — 4.49
E	4.5 — 4.99
F	5.0 — 5.59
G	5.6 — 6.29
H	6.3 — 7.09
J	7.1 — 7.99
K	8.0 — 8.99
L	9.0 — 9.99
M	10.0 —11.19
N	11.2 —12.49
P	12.5 —13.99
R	14.0 —15.99
S	16.0 —17.99
T	18.0 —19.99
U	20.0 —22.39
V	22.4 —and up

(2) Single-speed motors starting on Y connection and running on delta connections shall be marked with a code letter corresponding to the locked-rotor kVA per horsepower for the Y connection.

(3) Dual-voltage motors that have a different locked-rotor kVA per horsepower on the two voltages shall be marked with the code letter for the voltage giving the highest locked-rotor kVA per horsepower.

(4) Motors with 60- and 50-Hertz ratings shall be marked with a code letter designating the locked rotor kVA per horsepower on 60 hertz.

(5) Part-winding-start motors shall be marked with a code letter designating the locked-rotor kVA per horsepower that is based upon the locked-rotor current for the full winding of the motor.

(c) Torque Motors. Torque motors are rated for operation at standstill and shall be marked in accordance with (a) above.

Exception: Locked rotor torque shall replace horsepower.

(d) Multimotor and Combination-Load Equipment. Multimotor and combination-load equipment shall be provided with a visible nameplate marked with the maker's name, the rating in volts, frequency, number of phases, minimum supply circuit conductor ampacity, and the maximum ampere rating of the circuit overcurrent device. The conductor ampacity shall be computed in accordance with Section 430-25 and counting all of the motors and other loads that will be operated at the same time. The overcurrent device rating shall not exceed the value computed in accordance with Section 430-53. Multimotor equipment for use on two or more circuits shall be marked with the above information for each circuit.

Where the equipment is not factory-wired and the individual nameplates of motors and other loads are visible after assembly of the equipment, the individual nameplates shall be permitted to serve as the required marking.

430-8. Marking on Controllers. A controller shall be marked with the maker's name or identification, the voltage, the current or horsepower rating, and such other necessary data to properly indicate the motors for which it is suitable. A controller that includes motor-running overcurrent protection suitable for group motor application shall be marked with the motor-running overcurrent protection and the maximum branch-circuit overcurrent protection for such applications.

Combination controllers employing adjustable instantaneous trip circuit breakers shall be clearly marked to indicate the ampere settings of the adjustable trip element.

Where a controller is built in as an integral part of a motor or of a motor-generator set, individual marking of the controller shall not be required if the necessary data are on the nameplate. For controllers that are an integral part of equipment approved as a unit, the above marking shall be permitted on the equipment nameplate.

430-9. Marking at Terminals. Terminals of motors and controllers shall be suitably marked or colored where necessary to indicate the proper connections.

430-10. Wiring Space in Enclosures. Enclosures for motor controllers and disconnecting means shall not be used as junction boxes, auxiliary gutters, or raceways for conductors feeding through or tapping off to the other apparatus unless designs are employed which provide adequate space for this purpose.

See Section 373-8 for switch and overcurrent-device enclosures.

▲ The standard types of enclosures for motor controllers provide space that is sufficient only for the branch-circuit conductors entering and leaving the enclosure and any control-circuit conductors that may be required. No additional conductors should be brought into the enclosure. For switches, see comments following Sec. 373-8.

430-11. Protection Against Liquids. Suitable guards or enclosures shall be provided to protect exposed current-carrying parts of motors and the insulation of motor leads where installed directly under equipment, or in other locations where dripping or spraying oil, water, or other injurious liquid may occur, unless the motor is designed for the existing conditions.

▲ Excessive moisture, steam, dripping oil, etc., on the exposed current-carrying parts of a motor may cause an insulation breakdown which in turn may be the cause of a fire.

430-12. Motor Terminal Housings.

(a) Material. Where motors are provided with terminal housings, the housings shall be of metal and of substantial construction.

Exception: In other than hazardous locations, substantial nonmetallic, non-burning housings shall be permitted on motors larger than 34 inches in diameter provided internal grounding means between the machine frame and the conduit connection is incorporated within the housing.

See Method of Test for Flammability of Self-Supporting Plastics (ANSI K65.21—1969) for over 0.127 CM (0.050 inch) in thickness, for nonburning test.

(b) Dimensions and Space—Wire-to-Wire Connections. When these terminal housings enclose wire-to-wire connections, they shall have minimum dimensions and usable volumes in accordance with the following:

Table 430-12(b). Terminal Housings—Wire-to-Wire Connections
Motors 11 Inches in Diameter or Less

HP	Cover Opening, Minimum Dimension, Inches	Usable Volume, Minimum, Cubic Inches
1 and smaller*	$1\frac{5}{8}$	$7\frac{1}{2}$
$1\frac{1}{2}$, 2 and 3†	$1\frac{3}{4}$	12
5 and $7\frac{1}{2}$	2	16
10 and 15	$2\frac{1}{2}$	26

*For motors rated one horsepower and smaller and with the terminal housing partially or wholly integral with the frame or end shield, the volume of the terminal housing shall be not less than 0.8 cubic inch per wire-to-wire connection. The minimum cover opening dimension is not specified.

†For motors rated $1\frac{1}{2}$, 2 and 3 horsepower and with the terminal housing partially or wholly integral with the frame or end shield, the volume of the terminal housing shall be not less than 1.0 cubic inch per wire-to-wire connection. The minimum cover opening dimension is not specified.

Motors over 11 Inches in Diameter
Alternating-Current Motors

Max. Full-load Current for Three-phase Motors with Max. of Twelve Leads	Terminal Box Minimum Dimension Inches	Usable Volume Minimum Cubic Inches	Typical Maximum Horsepower Three Phase	
			230 Volt	460 Volt
45	2.5	26	15	30
70	3.0	44	25	50
110	3.6	72	40	75
160	4.5	130	60	125
250	5.6	250	100	200
400	7	500	150	300
600	8.2	900	250	500

Direct-Current Motors

Maximum Full-load Current for Motors with Maximum of Six Leads	Terminal Box Minimum Dimensions Inches	Usable Volume, Minimum Cubic Inches
68	2.5	26
105	3.0	44
165	3.6	72
240	4.5	130
375	5.6	250
600	7	500
900	8.2	900

Auxiliary leads for such items as brakes, thermostats, space heater, exciting fields, etc., may be neglected if their current-carrying area does not exceed 25 percent of the current-carrying area of the machine power leads.

Table 430-12(c)(1). Terminal Spacings—Fixed Terminals

	Minimum Spacing, Inches	
Volts	Between Line Terminals	Between Line Terminals and Other Uninsulated Metal Parts
250 or less	$\frac{1}{4}$	$\frac{1}{4}$
251 through 600	$\frac{3}{8}$	$\frac{3}{8}$

Table 430-12(c)(2). Usable Volumes—Fixed Terminals

Power-Supply Conductor Size, AWG	Minimum Usable Volume per Power-Supply Conductor, Cubic Inches
14	1.0
12 and 10	$1\frac{1}{4}$
8 and 6	$2\frac{1}{4}$

(c) Dimensions and Space—Fixed Terminal Connections. Where these terminal housings enclose rigidly mounted motor terminals, the terminal housing shall be of sufficient size to provide minimum terminal spacings and usable volumes in accordance with Tables 430-12(c)(1) and (c)(2).

(d) Large Wire or Factory Connections. For motors with larger ratings, greater number of leads, or larger wire sizes, or where motors are installed as a part of factory-wired equipment, without additional connection being required at the motor terminal housing during equipment installation, the terminal housing shall be of ample size to make connections, but the foregoing provisions for the volumes of terminal housings shall not be considered applicable.

430-13. Bushing. Where wires pass through an opening in an enclosure, conduit box, or barrier, a bushing shall be used to protect the conductors from the edges of openings having sharp edges. The bushing shall have smooth well-rounded surfaces where it may be in contact with the conductors. If used where oils, greases, or other contaminants may be present, the bushing shall be made of material not deleteriously affected.

For conductors exposed to deteriorating agents, see Section 310-8.

430-14. Location of Motors.

(a) Ventilation and Maintenance. Motors shall be located so that adequate ventilation is provided and so that maintenance, such as lubrication of bearings and replacing of brushes, can be readily accomplished.

(b) Open Motors. Open motors having commutators or collector rings shall be located or protected so that sparks cannot reach adjacent combustible material, but this shall not prohibit the installation of these motors on wooden floors or supports.

430-16. Exposure to Dust Accumulations. In locations where dust or flying material will collect on or in motors in such quantities as to seriously interfere with the ventilation or cooling of motors and thereby cause dangerous temperatures, suitable types of enclosed motors that will not overheat under the prevailing conditions shall be used. Especially severe conditions may require the use of enclosed pipe-ventilated motors, or enclosure in separate dust-tight rooms, properly ventilated from a source of clean air.

▲ The conditions described in this section could make the location a Class II, Division 2 location; the types of motors required are specified in Art. 502.

430-17. Highest Rated (Largest) Motor. In determining compliance with Sections 430-24, 430-53(b), 430-53(c), and 430-62(a), the highest rated (largest) motor shall be considered to be that motor having the highest rated full-load current. The full-load current used to determine the highest rated motor shall be the equivalent value corresponding to the motor horsepower rating selected from Tables 430-147, 430-148, 430-149, and 430-150.

B. Motor Circuit Conductors

430-21. General. Part B specifies sizes of conductors capable of carrying the motor current without overheating under the conditions specified.

Exception: The provisions of Section 430-124 shall apply over 600 volts, nominal.

The provisions of Articles 250, 300, and 310 shall not apply to conductors that form an integral part of approved equipment, or to integral conductors of motors, motor controllers, and the like.

See Sections 300-1(b) and 310-1.

430-22. Single Motor.

(a) General. Branch-circuit conductors supplying a single motor shall have an ampacity not less than 125 percent of the motor full-load current rating.

In case of a multispeed motor, the selection of branch-circuit conductors on the line side of the controller shall be based on the highest of the full-load current ratings shown on the motor nameplate; selection of branch-circuit conductors between the controller and the motor, which are energized for that particular speed, shall be based on the current rating for that speed.

Exception: Conductors for a motor used for short-time, intermittent, periodic, or varying duty shall have an ampacity not less than the percentage of the motor nameplate current rating shown in Table 430-22(a) Exception unless the authority having jurisdiction grants special permission for conductors of smaller size.

(b) Separate Terminal Enclosure. The conductors between a stationary motor rated one horsepower or less and the separate terminal enclosure permitted in Section 430-145(b) shall be permitted to be smaller than No. 14 but not smaller than No. 18, provided they have an ampacity as specified in (a) above.

▲ *Types of Layouts*

Figures 430-1 through 430-4 indicate the use of cartridge-type fuses, and Sec. 240-40 requires a switch ahead of each set of fuses.

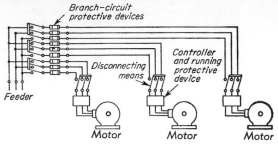

Fig. 430-1. Type 1 layout. Individual branch circuit to each motor from a distribution center.

Type 1

An individual branch circuit leads to each motor from a distribution center. This type of layout can be used under any conditions and is the one most commonly used.

Type 2

A feeder or subfeeder with branch circuits tapped on at convenient points. This is the same as Type 1 except that the branch-circuit overcurrent protective devices are mounted individually at the points where taps are made to the subfeeder, instead of being assembled at one location in the form of a branch-circuit distribution center. Under certain conditions, the branch-circuit protective devices may be located at any point not more than 25 ft distance from the point where the branch circuit is tapped to the feeder.

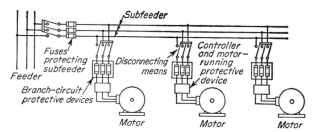

Fig. 430-2. Type 2 layout. Individual branch circuit to each motor from a subfeeder, no distribution center.

Type 3

Small motors, lamps, and appliances may be supplied by a 15- or 20-A circuit as described in Art. 210. Motors connected to these circuits must be provided with running overcurrent protective devices in most cases.

Motor Branch Circuits

Data are provided in this article governing three essential parts of a typical motor branch circuit, as employed in a Type 1 or Type 2 layout: (1) branch-circuit conductors, (2) branch-circuit overcurrent protective devices, and (3) motor-running protective devices. These three parts of a motor circuit are shown in Fig. 430-4.

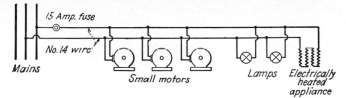

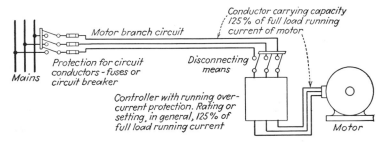

FIG. 430-3. Type 3 layout. 15-A branch circuit supplying small motors and other loads.

FIG. 430-4. The essential parts of a typical motor branch circuit.

The branch-circuit overcurrent protective device may be fuses or a circuit breaker. A motor-running protective device is always required, except for some small motors. This device is frequently combined with the motor controller.

In general, it is required that every motor shall be provided with a running protective device that will open the circuit on any current exceeding prescribed percentages of the full-load motor current, the percentage depending upon the type of motor. The running protective device is intended primarily to protect the windings of the motor, but by providing that the circuit conductors shall have an ampacity not less than 125 percent of the full-load motor current, it is obvious that these conductors are reasonably protected by the running protective device against any overcurrent caused by an overload on the motor.

When a motor is used for one of the classes of service listed in Table 430-22 (a)-Exception, the necessary ampacity of the branch-circuit conductors depends upon the class of service and upon the rating of the motor. A motor having a 5-min rating is designed to deliver its rated horsepower during periods of approximately 5 min each, with cooling intervals between the operating periods. The branch-circuit conductors have the advantage of the same cooling intervals and hence can safely be smaller than for a motor of the same horsepower but having a 60-min rating.

In the case of elevator motors, the many considerations involved in determining the smallest permissible size of the branch-circuit conductors make this a complex problem, and it is always the safest plan to be guided by the recommendations of the manufacturer of the equipment. This applies also to feeders supplying two or more elevator motors and to circuits supplying non-continuous-duty motors used for driving some other machines.

Table 430-22(a) Exception. Duty-Cycle Service

Classification of Service	Percentages of Nameplate Current Rating			
	5-Minute Rated Motor	15-Minute Rated Motor	30 & 60 Minute Rated Motor	Continuous Rated Motor
Short-Time Duty Operating valves, raising or lowering rolls, etc..........	110	120	150	...
Intermittent Duty Freight and passenger elevators, tool heads, pumps, drawbridges, turntables, etc. For arc welders, see Section 630-21.............	85	85	90	140
Periodic Duty Rolls, ore and coal-handling machines, etc............................	85	90	95	140
Varying Duty.................	110	120	150	200

Any motor application shall be considered as continuous duty unless the nature of the apparatus it drives is such that the motor will not operate continuously with load under any condition of use.
See Example No. 8, Chapter 9 and Diagram 430-1.

430-23. Wound-Rotor Secondary.

(a) Continuous Duty. For continuous duty, the conductors connecting the secondary of a wound-rotor alternating-current motor to its controller shall have an ampacity not less than 125 percent of the full-load secondary current of the motor.

(b) Other Than Continuous Duty. For other than continuous duty, these conductors shall have an ampacity, in percent of full-load secondary current, not less than that specified in Table 430-22(a) Exception.

(c) Resistor Separate from Controller. Where the secondary resistor is separate from the controller, the ampacity of the conductors between controller and resistor shall not be less than that given in Table 430-23(c).

Table 430-23(c). Secondary Conductor

Resistor Duty Classification	Ampacity of Wire in Percent of Full-Load Secondary Current
Light starting duty	35
Heavy starting duty	45
Extra-heavy starting duty...	55
Light intermittent duty	65
Medium intermittent duty	75
Heavy intermittent duty...	85
Continuous duty...	110

▲ The full-load secondary current of a wound-rotor or slip-ring motor must be obtained from the motor nameplate or from the manufacturer.

The starting, or starting and speed-regulating, portion of the controller for a wound-rotor motor usually consists of two parts—a dial-type or drum controller and a resistor bank. These two parts must, in many cases, be assembled and connected by the installer. (See Fig. 430-5.)

The conductors from the slip rings on the motor to the controller are in circuit continuously while the motor is running and hence, for a continuous-duty motor, must be large enough to carry the secondary current of the motor continuously.

If the controller is used for starting only and is not used for regulating the speed of the motor, the conductors between the dial or drum and the resistors are in use only during the starting period and are cut out of the circuit as soon as the motor has come up to full speed. These conductors may therefore be of a smaller size than would be needed for continuous duty.

If the controller is to be used for speed regulation of the motor, some part of the resistance may be left in circuit continuously and the conductors between the dial or drum and the resistors must be large enough to carry the continuous load without overheating. In Table 430-23(c) the term *continuous duty* applies to this condition.

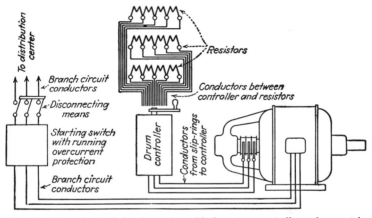

FIG. 430-5. Wound-rotor induction motor with drum-type controller and separately mounted resistors.

430-24. Conductors Supplying Several Motors. Conductors supplying two or more motors shall have an ampacity equal to the sum of the full-load current rating of all the motors plus 25 percent of the highest rated motor in the group.

Where one or more motors of the group are used on short-time, intermittent, periodic, or varying duty, the ampacity of the conductors shall be computed as follows:

(1) Determine the needed ampere rating for each motor used for other than continuous duty from Table 430-22(a) Exception.

(2) Determine the needed ampere rating for each continuous-duty motor based on 100 percent motor full-load current rating.

(3) Multiply the largest single motor ampere rating determined from (1) or (2) above by 1.25. Add all other motor ampere ratings from (1) and (2) above and select the conductor ampacity for this total ampere rating.

Exception: Where the circuitry is so interlocked as to prevent the starting and running of a second motor or group of motors, the conductor size shall be determined from the larger motor or group of motors that is to be operated at a given time.

See Example No. 8, Chapter 9.

▲ For the overcurrent protection of feeder conductors of the minimum size permitted by this section, the highest permissible rating or setting of the protective device is specified in Sec. 430-62. Where a feeder protective device of higher rating or setting is used because two or more motors must be started simultaneously, the size of the feeder conductors shall be increased correspondingly.

These requirements and those of Sec. 430-62 for the overcurrent protection of power feeders are based upon the principle that a power feeder should be of such size that it will have an ampacity equal to that required for the starting current of the largest motor supplied by the feeder, plus the full-load running currents of all other motors supplied by the feeder. Except under the unusual condition where two or more motors may be started simultaneously, the heaviest load that a power feeder will ever be required to carry is the load under the condition where the largest motor is started at a time when all the other motors supplied by the feeder are running and delivering their full-rated horsepower.

430-25. Conductors Supplying Motors and Other Loads.
(a) Combination Load. Conductors supplying a motor load and in addition a lighting or appliance load shall have an ampacity sufficient for the lighting or appliance load computed in accordance with Article 220 and other applicable Sections plus the motor load determined in accordance with Section 430-24, or, for a single motor, in accordance with Section 430-22.

Exception: The ampacity of conductors supplying motor-operated fixed electric space heating equipment shall conform with Section 424-3(b).

▲ For computing the minimum allowable conductor size for a combination lighting and power feeder, the required ampacity for the lighting load is to be determined according to the rules for feeders carrying lighting (or lighting and appliance) loads only. Where the motor load consists of one motor only, the required ampacity for this load is the capacity for the motor branch circuit, or 125 percent of the full-load motor current, as specified in Sec. 430-22. Where the motor load consists of two or more motors, the required ampacity for the motor load is the capacity computed according to Sec. 430-24.

(b) Multimotor and Combination-Load Equipment. The ampacity of the conductors supplying multimotor and combination-load equipment shall not be less than the minimum circuit ampacity marked on the equipment in accordance with Section 430-7(d).
430-26. Feeder Demand Factor. Where reduced heating of the conductors results from motors operating on duty-cycle, intermittently, or from all motors not operating at one time, the authority having jurisdiction may grant permission for feeder

conductors to have an ampacity less than specified in Sections 430-24 and 430-25, provided the conductors have sufficient ampacity for the maximum load determined in accordance with the sizes and number of motors supplied and the character of their loads and duties.

▲ **A demand factor of less than 100 percent may be applied in the case of some industrial plants where the nature of the work is such that there is never a time when all the motors are operating at one time.**

430-27. Capacitors with Motors. Where capacitors are installed in motor circuits, conductors shall comply with Sections 460-7, 460-8, and 460-9.

430-28. Feeder Taps. Feeder tap conductors shall have an ampacity not less than that required by Part B, shall terminate in a branch-circuit protective device and, in addition, shall meet one of the following requirements:

(1) be enclosed by either an enclosed controller or by a raceway and be not more than 10 feet in length; or

▲ **In applying Subsection 1 the conductor may be less than one-third that of the feeder conductors but must be limited to not more than ten ft in length and be enclosed within a controller or raceway.**

(2) have an ampacity of at least one-third that of the feeder conductors, be protected from physical damage and be not more than 25 feet in length; or

(3) have the same ampacity as the feeder conductors.

▲ **If conductors equal in size to the conductors of a feeder are connected to the feeder, no fuses or other overcurrent protection are needed at the point where the tap is made, since the tap conductors will be protected by the fuses or circuit breaker protecting the feeder.**

The more important circuit arrangement permitted by the above rule is shown in Fig. 430-6. This is another example of the Type 2 layout shown in Fig. 430-2.

Instead of placing the fuses or other branch-circuit protective device at the point where the connections are made to the feeder, conductors having at least one-third the ampacity of the feeder are tapped solidly to the feeder and may be run any distance not exceeding 25 ft to the branch-circuit protective device. From this point on to the motor-running protective device and thence to the motor, conductors are run having the standard ampacity, i.e., 125 percent of the full-load motor current, as specified in Sec. 430-22.

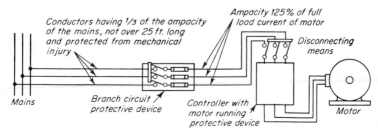

FIG. 430-6. Branch-circuit protective devices located at a distance not exceeding 25 ft. from the point where the connection is made to the feeder.

Example

A 15-hp 230-V three-phase motor with autotransformer starter is to be supplied by a tap made to a 250,000 CM feeder. All conductors are to be Type THW.

The feeder has an ampacity of 255 A; one-third of 255 A equals 85 A. Therefore the tap cannot be smaller than No. 4, which has an ampacity of 85 A for 75°C ratings.

The full-load current of the motor is 40 A and, according to Part D of Art. 430, assuming that the motor is not marked with a Code letter, the branch-circuit fuses should be rated at 125 A or less. With the motor-running protection set at 50 A the tap conductors are well protected from overload.

The conductors tapped solidly to the feeder must never be smaller than the size of branch-circuit conductors required by Sec. 430-22.

C. Motor and Branch-Circuit Running Overcurrent and Overload Protection

430-31. General.   Part C specifies overload devices intended to protect motors, motor-control apparatus, and motor branch-circuit conductors against excessive heating due to motor overloads and failure to start.

Overload in electrical apparatus is an operating overcurrent which, when it persists for a sufficient length of time, would cause damage or dangerous overheating of the apparatus. It does not include short circuits or ground faults.

These provisions shall not be interpreted as requiring overload protection where it might introduce additional or increased hazards, as in the case of fire pumps.

See Installation of Centrifugal Fire Pumps (NFPA No. 20-1972).

The provisions of Part C shall not apply to motor circuits rated over 600 volts nominal. See Part J.

▲ Detailed requirements for the installation of fire pumps is not included in the National Electrical Code, but this is covered in NFPA Pamphlet No. 20.

As intended by Sec. 430-52, the motor branch-circuit protective device provides short-circuit protection for the circuit conductors. In order to carry the starting current of the motor, this device must have a rating or setting so high that it cannot protect the motor against overload.

For a squirrel-cage induction motor it shall be of the inverse time type with a setting of not over 20 sec at 600 percent of the motor full-load current. It is the intent that the fire-pump motor attempt to run under any condition of loading and not be automatically disconnected by an overcurrent protection device. It will be noted that modern installations generally employ straight induction motors.

Pamphlet No. 20 requires a circuit breaker instead of a fuse as the short-circuit protection for the branch circuit and also requires an unfused isolating switch ahead of the circuit breaker.

Except where the special types of fuses described in Sec. 430-55 are used, in practically all cases where motor-running overcurrent protection is provided the motor controller consists of two parts: (1) a switch or contactor to control the circuit to the motor and (2) the motor-running protective device. Most of the protective devices make use of a heater coil, usually consisting of a few turns of high-resistance metal, though the heater may be of other form.

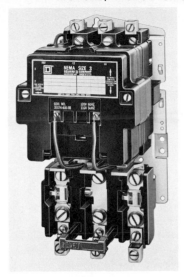

FIG. 430-7. Line-voltage magnetic
starter. (*Square D Co.*)

FIG. 430-8. Fustat
fuse. (*Bussmann
Mfg. Co.*)

Figure 430-7 shows a typical starter of the full-voltage or "across-the-line" type.

430-32. Continuous-Duty Motors.

(a) More Than One Horsepower. Each continuous-duty motor rated more than one horsepower shall be protected against overload by one of the following means:

(1) A separate overload device that is responsive to motor current. This device shall be selected to trip or rated at no more than the following percent of the motor nameplate full-load current rating:

Motors with a marked service factor not less than 1.15 . . . . 125%
Motors with a marked temperature rise not over 40°C 125%
All other motors 115%

For a multispeed motor, each winding connection shall be considered separately. This value may be modified as permitted by Section 430-34.

Where a separate motor-running overload device is so connected that it does not carry the total current designated on the motor nameplate, such as for wye-delta starting, the proper percentage of nameplate current applying to the selection or setting of the overload device shall be clearly designated on the equipment, or the manufacturer's selection table shall take this into account.

(2) A thermal protector integral with the motor, approved for use with the motor it protects on the basis that it will prevent dangerous overheating of the motor due to overload and failure to start. The ultimate trip current of a thermally protected motor shall not exceed the following percentage of motor full-load current given in Tables 430-148, 430-149, and 430-150:

Motor full-load current not exceeding 9 amperes 170%
Motor full-load current 9.1 to and including 20 amperes 156%
Motor full-load current greater than 20 amperes 140%

If the motor current-interrupting device is separate from the motor and its control circuit is operated by a protective device integral with the motor, it shall be so arranged that the opening of the control circuit will result in interruption of current to the motor.

(3) A motor shall be considered as being properly protected if it is a part of an approved assembly that does not normally subject the motor to overloads and if there is a protective device integral with the motor that will protect the motor against damage due to failure to start.

(4) For motors larger than 1500 horsepower, a protective device having embedded temperature detectors that cause current to the motor to be interrupted when the motor attains a temperature rise greater than marked on the nameplate in an ambient of 40°C.

(b) One Horsepower or Less, Manually Started.

(1) Each continuous-duty motor rated at one horsepower or less that is not permanently installed, is manually started, and is within sight from the controller location shall be considered as protected against overload by the branch-circuit short-circuit and ground-fault protective device. This branch-circuit protective device shall not be larger than that specified in Part D of Article 430.

Exception: Any such motor shall be permitted at 125 volts or less on a branch circuit protected at not over 20 amperes.

(2) Any such motor that is not in sight from the controller location shall be protected as specified in Section 430-32(c). Any motor rated at one horsepower or less that is permanently installed shall be protected in accordance with Section 430-32(c).

(c) One Horsepower or Less, Automatically Started.   Any motor of one horsepower or less that is started automatically shall be protected against overload by one of the following means:

(1) A separate overload device that is responsive to motor current. This device shall be selected to trip or rated at no more than the following percent of the motor nameplate full-load current rating:

Motors with a marked service factor not less than 1.15 . . . . 125%
Motors with a marked temperature rise not over 40°C 125%
All other motors 115%

For a multispeed motor, each winding connection shall be considered separately. Modification of this value shall be permitted as provided in Section 430-34.

(2) A thermal protector integral with the motor, approved for use with the motor which it protects on the basis that it will prevent dangerous overheating of the motor due to overload and failure to start. Where the motor current interrupting device is separate from the motor and its control circuit is operated by a protective device integral with the motor, it shall be so arranged that the opening of the control circuit will result in interruption of current to the motor.

(3) A motor shall be considered as being properly protected if it is part of an approved assembly that does not normally subject the motor to overloads and if there is a protective device integral with the motor that will protect the motor against damage due to failure to start, or if the assembly is also equipped with other safety controls (such as the safety combustion controls of a domestic oil burner) that protect the motor against damage due to failure to start. Where the assembly has safety controls that protect the motor, it shall be so indicated on the nameplate of the assembly where it will be visible after installation.

(4) In case the impedance of the motor windings is sufficient to prevent overheating due to failure to start, the motor shall be permitted to be protected as specified in Section 430-32(b)(1) for manually started motors if the motor is part of an approved assembly in which the motor will limit itself so that it will not be dangerously overheated.

Many alternating-current motors of less than $\frac{1}{20}$ horsepower, such as clock motors, series motors, etc., and also some larger motors such as torque motors, come within this classification. It does not include split-phase motors having automatic switches that disconnect the starting windings.

(d) Wound-Rotor Secondaries. The secondary circuits of wound-rotor alternating-current motors, including conductors, controllers, resistors, etc., shall be considered as protected against overload by the motor-running overload device.

▲ The term *rating or setting* as here used means the current at which the device will open the circuit if this current continues for a considerable length of time.

A motor having a temperature rise of 40°C when operated continuously at full load can carry a 25 percent overload for some time without injury to the motor. Other types of motors, such as enclosed types, do not have so high an overload capacity and the running protective device should therefore open the circuit on a prolonged overload which causes the motor to draw 115 percent of its rated full-load current.

A protective device integral with the motor as used for the protection of motors is shown in Figs. 430-9 and 430-10. This device is placed inside the motor frame and is connected in series with the motor winding. It contains a bimetallic disk carrying two contacts, through which the circuit is normally closed. If the motor is overloaded and its temperature is raised to a certain limiting value, the disk snaps to the "open" position and opens the circuit. The device also includes a heating coil in series with

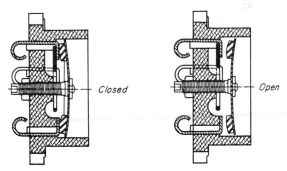

Closed   *Open*

FIG. 430-9. Klixon integral running protective device. (*Spencer Thermostat Co.*)

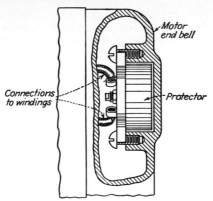

FIG. 430-10. Mounting of integral protective device shown in Fig. 430-9. (*Spencer Thermostat Co.*)

the motor windings which causes the disk to become heated more rapidly in case of a sudden heavy overload.

Single-phase motors equipped with integral protective devices of the general type shown in Figs. 430-9 and 430-10 are obtainable in ratings of 1 hp and less and in a few larger ratings. For motors of larger size a similar device is used which serves as a relay to actuate a separate contactor through a control circuit.

After opening the circuit on an overload, the integral device shown here will automatically reclose and start the motor after the motor has cooled. For some applications this may not be desirable and for such cases the device is so designed that after it has opened, it must be manually returned to the closed position by means of a reset button. (See Sec. 430-43.)

The motor and the integral device should be tested together as a complete assembly and the protective device should open the circuit on an overcurrent as specified in Sec. 430-32(a)(2).

Where the circuit-interrupting device is separate from the motor and is actuated by a device integral with the motor, the two devices must be so designed and connected that any accidental opening of the control circuit will stop the motor, otherwise the motor would be left operating without any overcurrent protection.

There is special need for running protection on an automatically started motor because, if the motor is stalled when the starter operates, the motor will probably burn out if it has no running protection.

430-33. Intermittent and Similar Duty. A motor used for a condition of service that is inherently short-time, intermittent, periodic, or varying duty, as illustrated by Table 430-22(a) Exception, shall be considered as protected against overload by the branch-circuit short-circuit and ground-fault protective device, provided the protective device rating or setting does not exceed that specified in Table 430-152.

Any motor application shall be considered to be for continuous duty unless the nature of the apparatus it drives is such that the motor cannot operate continuously with load under any condition of use.

▲ Where a motor is used for one of the "conditions of service" on account of the character of the machine or other apparatus which the motor drives, long-continued overloads are not likely to occur, except that some trouble in the driven machine or apparatus might stall the motor, and in this case the branch-circuit protective device would open the circuit. Running overcurrent protection for such motors is therefore not considered necessary. It should be noted that omission of the running protection is based upon the type of "duty" and is not in any way dependent upon the time rating of the motor.

430-34. Selection of Overload Relay. Where the overload relay selected in accordance with Sections 430-32(a-1) and 430-32(c-1) is not sufficient to start the motor or to carry the load, the next higher size overload relay shall be permitted to be used provided the trip current of the overload relay does not exceed the following percent of motor full-load current rating:

Motors with marked service factor not less than 1.15 . . . . 140%
Motors with a marked temperature rise not over 40°C 140%
All other motors 130%

If not shunted during the starting period of the motor as provided in Section 430-35, the overload device shall have sufficient time delay to permit the motor to start and accelerate its load.

430-35. Shunting During Starting Period.

(a) Manually Started. For a manually started motor (including starting with a magnetic starter having pushbutton control), the running overload protection may be shunted or cut out of circuit during the starting period of the motor if the device by which the overload protection is shunted or cut out cannot be left in the starting position and if fuses or inverse time circuit breakers rated or set at not over 400 percent of the full-load current of the motor are so located in the circuit as to be operative during the starting period of the motor.

(b) Automatically Started. The motor-running overload protection shall not be shunted or cut out during the starting period if the motor is automatically started.

▲ Where fuses are used as the motor-running protection, they may be cut out of the circuit during the starting period. (See Fig. 430-11.) This leaves the motor protected

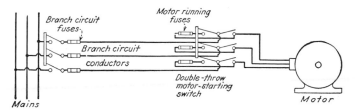

FIG. 430-11. Double-throw switch arranged for across-the-line starting. The switch is thrown to the right to start the motor, thus cutting the running fuses out of the circuit. The switch must be so made that it cannot be left in the starting position.

only by the branch-circuit fuses, but the rating of these fuses will always be well within the limits specified in the above rule. If the branch-circuit fuses are omitted, as allowed by the rules in Sec. 430-53, it is not permitted to use a starter that cuts out the motor fuses during the starting period unless the protection of the feeder is within the limits set by this rule.

430-36. Fuses—In Which Conductor.   Where fuses are used for motor-running protection, a fuse shall be inserted in each ungrounded conductor.

A fuse shall also be inserted in the grounded conductor if the supply system is 3-wire, 3-phase AC with one conductor grounded.

430-37. Devices Other Than Fuses—In Which Conductor.   Where devices other than fuses are used for motor-running overload protection, Table 430-37 shall govern the minimum allowable number and location of overload units such as trip coils, relays, or thermal cutouts.

▲ Three-element protection must be provided for all three-phase motors unless protected by other approved means (such as specially designed embedded detectors with or without supplementary external protective devices).

430-38. Number of Conductors Opened by Overload Device.   Motor-running overload devices other than fuses, thermal cutouts, or thermal protectors shall simultaneously open a sufficient number of ungrounded conductors to interrupt current flow to the motor.

430-39. Motor Controller As Running Overload Protection.   A motor controller

Table 430-37. Running Overload Units

Kind of Motor	Supply System	Number and location of overload units, such as trip coils, relays, or thermal cutouts
1-phase AC or DC	2-wire, 1-phase AC or DC ungrounded	1 in either conductor
1-phase AC or DC	2-wire, 1-phase AC or DC, one conductor grounded	1 in ungrounded conductor
1-phase AC or DC	3-wire, 1-phase AC or DC, grounded-neutral	1 in either ungrounded conductor
2-phase AC	3-wire, 2-phase AC, ungrounded	2, one in each phase
2-phase AC	3-wire, 2-phase AC, one conductor grounded	2 in ungrounded conductors
2-phase AC	4-wire, 2-phase AC, grounded or ungrounded	2, one per phase in ungrounded conductors
2-phase AC	5-wire, 2-phase AC, grounded neutral or ungrounded	2, one per phase in any ungrounded phase wire
3-phase AC	Any 3-phase	*3, one in each phase

Exception: Where protected by other approved means.

shall also be permitted to serve as a running overload device if the number of overload units complies with Table 430-37 and if these units are operative in both the starting and running position in the case of a direct-current motor, and in the running position in the case of an alternating-current motor.

▲ If fuses are used as the running protective device, Sec. 430-36 requires a fuse in each ungrounded conductor. If the protective device consists of an automatically operated contactor or circuit breaker, the device must open a sufficient number of conductors to stop the current flow to the motor and must be equipped with the number of overcurrent units specified in Table 430-37.

430-40. Thermal Cutouts and Overload Relays. Thermal cutouts, overload relays, and other devices for motor-running overload protection that are not capable of opening short circuits shall be protected by fuses or circuit breakers with ratings or settings in accordance with Section 430-52 or by a motor short-circuit protector in accordance with Section 430-52.

Exception No. 1: Where approved for group installation and marked to indicate the maximum size of fuse or inverse time circuit breaker by which they must be protected.

Exception No. 2: The fuse or circuit breaker ampere rating shall be permitted to be marked on the nameplate of approved equipment in which the thermal cutout or overload relay is used.

For instantaneous trip circuit breakers or motor short-circuit protectors, see Section 430-52.

430-42. Motors on General-Purpose Branch Circuits. Overload protection for motors used on general-purpose branch circuits as permitted in Article 210 shall be provided as specified in (a), (b), (c), or (d) below.

(a) Not Over One HP. One or more motors without individual running overload protection shall be permitted to be connected to general-purpose branch circuits only where the installation complies with all the limiting conditions specified in Section 430-53(a).

(b) Over One HP. Motors of larger ratings than specified in Section 430-53(a) shall be permitted to be connected to general-purpose branch circuits only where each motor is protected by running overload protection selected to protect the motor as specified in Section 430-32. Both the controller and the motor-running overload device shall be approved for group installation with the short-circuit and ground-fault protective device selected in accordance with Section 430-53.

(c) Cord- and Plug-Connected. Where a motor is connected to a branch circuit by means of an attachment plug and receptacle and individual running overload protection is omitted as provided in (a) above, the rating of the attachment plug and receptacle shall not exceed 15 amperes at 125 volts or 10 amperes at 250 volts. Where individual overload protection is required as provided in (b) above for a motor or motor-operated appliance that is attached to the branch circuit through an attachment plug and receptacle, the running overload device shall be an integral part of the motor or of the appliance. The rating of the attachment plug and receptacle shall determine the rating of the circuit to which the motor may be connected, as provided in Article 210.

(d) Time Delay. The branch-circuit short-circuit and ground-fault protective device protecting a circuit to which a motor or motor-operated appliance is connected shall have sufficient time delay to permit the motor to start and accelerate its load.

▲ Branch circuits supplying lamps are usually 115-V single-phase circuits, and on such a circuit the effect of subparagraph (a) is that any motor larger than 6 A must be provided with a starter that is approved for group operation.

It is provided in Sec. 210-24 that receptacles on a 20-A branch circuit may have a rating of 20 A, and in such case subparagraph (c) requires that any motor or motor-driven appliance connected through a plug and receptacle must have running overcurrent protection. If the motor rating exceeds 1 hp or 6 A, the protective device must be permanently attached to the motor and subparagraph (b) must be complied with.

The requirements of Sec. 430-32 for the running overcurrent protection of motors must be complied with in all cases, regardless of the type of branch circuit by which the motor is supplied and regardless of the number of motors connected to the circuit.

430-43. Automatic Restarting. A motor-running overload device that can restart a motor automatically after overload tripping shall not be installed unless approved for use with the motor it protects. A motor that can restart automatically after shutdown shall not be installed if its automatic restarting can result in injury to persons.

▲ As noted in the comments to Sec. 430-32, an integral motor-running protective device may be of the type which will automatically restart, or it may be so constructed that after tripping out it must be closed by means of a reset button.

D. Motor Branch-Circuit Short-Circuit and Ground-Fault Protection

430-51. General. Part D specifies devices intended to protect the motor branch-circuit conductors, the motor control apparatus, and the motors against overcurrent due to short circuits or grounds. They add to or amend the provisions of Article 240.

The provisions of Part D do not apply to motor circuits rated over 600 volts, nominal. See Part J.

430-52. Rating or Setting for Individual Motor Circuit. The motor branch-circuit short-circuit and ground-fault protective device shall be capable of carrying the starting current of the motor. The required protection shall be considered as being obtained where the protective device has a rating or setting not exceeding the values given in Table 430-152.

An instantaneous trip circuit breaker shall be used only if adjustable, if part of a combination controller having motor-running overload and also short-circuit and ground-fault protection in each conductor, and if the combination is especially approved for the purpose. A motor short-circuit protector shall be permitted in lieu of devices listed in Table 430-152 if the motor short-circuit protector is part of a combination controller having both motor-running overload protection and short-circuit and ground-fault protection in each conductor if it will operate at not more than 1300 percent of full-load motor current and if the combination is especially approved for the purpose.

Where the values for branch-circuit protective devices determined by Table

430-152 do not correspond to the standard sizes or ratings of fuses, nonadjustable circuit breakers, or thermal protective devices, or possible settings of adjustable circuit breakers adequate to carry the load, the next higher size, rating, or setting shall be permitted.

See Section 240-6 for standard ratings of fuses and circuit breakers.

Exception: Where the rating or setting specified in Table 430-152 is not sufficient for the starting current of the motor:

a. The rating of a nontime-delay fuse not exceeding 600 amperes shall be permitted to be increased but shall in no case exceed 400 percent of the full-load current.

b. The rating of a time-delay (dual-element) fuse shall be permitted to be increased but shall in no case exceed 225 percent of the full-load current.

c. The setting of an instantaneous trip circuit breaker shall be permitted to be increased but shall in no case exceed 1300 percent of the motor full-load current.

d. Torque motor branch circuits shall be protected at the motor nameplate current rating in accordance with Section 240-3, Exception No. 1.

e. The rating of an inverse time circuit breaker shall be permitted to be increased but shall in no case exceed (1) 400 percent for full-load currents of 100 amperes or less, or (2) 300 percent for full-load currents greater than 100 amperes.

f. The rating of a fuse of 601-6000 ampere classification shall be permitted to be increased but shall in no case exceed 300 percent of the full-load current.

For a multispeed motor, a single short-circuit and ground-fault protective device shall be permitted for two or more windings of the motor, provided the rating of the protective device does not exceed the above applicable percentage of the nameplate rating of the smallest winding protected.

Where maximum branch-circuit protective device ratings are shown in the manufacturer's overload relay table for use with a motor controller or are otherwise marked on the equipment, they shall not be exceeded even if higher values are allowed as shown above.

See Example No. 8, Chapter 9 and Diagram 430-1.

▲ Where a motor is supplied by an individual branch circuit, having branch-circuit protection, the circuit protective devices may be either fuses or a circuit breaker and the rating or setting of these devices must not exceed the values specified in Table 430-152 (exceptions noted). (See Fig. 430-1.)

Section 430-6 permits the rating or setting of these overcurrent devices to be based on the values of full-load motor current given in Tables 430-147 to 430-150.

In Fig. 430-4, the fuses or circuit breaker at the panelboard must carry the starting current of the motor, and in order to carry this current the fuse rating or circuit-breaker setting may be 150 to 300 percent of the running current of the motor, depending on the size and type of motor. It is evident that to install motor-circuit conductors having an ampacity of 150 to 300 percent of the motor full-load current would be unnecessary. See Sec. 430-52 for instantaneous-trip circuit breakers or motor short-circuit protectors.

There are three possible causes of excess current in the conductors between the panelboard and the motor controller, viz., a short circuit between two of these conductors, a ground on one conductor that forms a short circuit, and an overload on the motor. A short circuit would draw so heavy a current that the fuses or breaker at the panelboard would immediately open the circuit, even though the rating or setting is in excess of the conductor ampacity. Any excess current due to an overload on the motor must pass through the protective device at the motor controller, causing this device to open the circuit. Therefore with circuit conductors having an ampacity equal to 125 percent of the motor-running current and with the motor-protective device set to operate at or near the same current, the conductors are reasonably protected.

Section 430-7 provides for marking the nameplates of AC motors, $\frac{1}{2}$ hp and larger, to show the kilovoltampere input per horsepower with locked rotor. The use of the Code letters provides a more accurate and satisfactory means of determining the correct rating or setting of the protective devices than is otherwise possible. Motors without the Code letters will, however, be in use for a number of years, and the data in Table 430-152 apply to such motors and also to motors smaller than $\frac{1}{2}$ hp.

Certain types of motor controllers provide protection for the motors they control against all ordinary overloads but are not intended to open short circuits. Fuses, circuit breakers, or motor short-circuit protectors used as the branch-circuit protective device will open short circuits and therefore provide short-circuit protection for both the motor and the running protective device.

Under exceptionally severe starting conditions where the nature of the load is such that an unusually long time is required for the motor to accelerate to full speed, the fuse or circuit-breaker rating or setting recommended in Table 430-152 may not be high enough to allow the motor to start. It is desirable to keep the branch-circuit protection at as low a rating as possible, but in unusual cases, it is permissible to use a higher rating or setting, up to the maximum values stated in the Exception to Sec. 430-52.

It should be noted that for No. 14 branch-circuit conductors the branch-circuit fuse ratings given in Part D of Art. 430 are in no case less than 15 A. The ampacity of the wire is 15 A, and the wire is therefore protected by overcurrent devices of this rating.

The supply of two or more small motors by one branch circuit is mentioned in Sec. 430-42. In such cases the rating or setting of the overcurrent protection should not be less than the rating or setting for the protection of power feeders as given in Sec. 430-62, i.e., the highest rating or setting of the branch-circuit overcurrent protection for any one of the motors as given in Part D of Art. 430, plus the sum of the full-load current ratings for all the other motors.

430-53. Several Motors or Loads on One Branch Circuit. Two or more motors or one or more motors and other loads shall be permitted to be connected to the same branch circuit under the conditions specified in (a), (b), or (c) below.

(a) **Not Over One HP.** Several motors each not exceeding one horsepower in rating shall be permitted on a branch circuit protected at not over 20 amperes at 125 volts or less, or 15 amperes at more than 125 volts but no more than 600 volts, if all of the following conditions are met:

(1) The full-load rating of each motor does not exceed 6 amperes.

(2) The rating of the branch-circuit protective device marked on any of the controllers is not exceeded.

(3) Individual running overload protection conforms to Section 430-32.

(b) **If Smallest Motor Protected.** If the branch-circuit protective device is selected not to exceed that allowed by Section 430-52 for the motor of the smallest rating, two or more motors or one or more motors and other load(s), with each motor having individual running overload protection, shall be permitted to be connected to a branch circuit where it can be determined that the branch-circuit protective device will not open under the most severe normal conditions of service that might be encountered.

▲ The reference to Sec. 430-52 pertains to overcurrent protection not exceeding the values given in Table 430-152.

(c) Other Group Installation.   Two or more motors of any rating or one or more motors and other load(s), with each motor having individual running overload protection, shall be permitted to be connected to one branch circuit if all of the following conditions are complied with:

(1) Each motor-running overload device is approved for group installation with a specified maximum rating of fuse and/or inverse time circuit breaker.

(2) Each motor controller is approved for group installation with a specified maximum rating of fuse and/or circuit breaker.

(3) Each circuit breaker is of the inverse time type and approved for group installation.

(4) The branch circuit shall be protected by fuses or inverse time circuit breakers having a rating not exceeding that specified in Section 430-52 for the largest motor connected to the branch circuit plus an amount equal to the sum of the full-load current ratings of all other motors and the ratings of other loads connected to the circuit. Where this calculation results in a rating less than the ampacity of the supply conductors, it shall be permitted to increase the maximum rating of the fuses or circuit breaker to a value not exceeding that permitted by Section 240-3 Exception No. 1.

(5) The branch-circuit fuses or inverse time circuit breakers are not larger than allowed by Section 430-40 for the thermal cutout or overload relay protecting the smallest motor of the group.

(d) Single Motor Taps.   For group installations described above, the conductors of any tap supplying a single motor shall not be required to have an individual branch-circuit protective device, provided they comply with either of the following: (1) no conductor to the motor shall have an ampacity less than that of the branch-circuit conductors; or (2) no conductor to the motor shall have an ampacity less than $\frac{1}{3}$ that of the branch-circuit conductors, with a minimum in accordance with Section 430-22; the conductors to the motor-running overload device being not more than 25 feet long and being protected from physical damage.

▲ *Omission of Branch-Circuit Protective Device*

Case A

Motor branch-circuit protective devices may be omitted at each motor if the taps to each motor-running protective device have the same ampacity as the main branch-circuit conductors, as illustrated by Fig. 430-12. Such conductors are in fact a part of the circuit and it is evident that there is no need for any fuses or circuit breaker at the point where the conductors are connected together to the feeder. In this case the conductors between the motor-running protective device and the motor are branch-circuit conductors, and their size is governed by Sec. 430-22. The motor starter must be of the type approved for group installation.

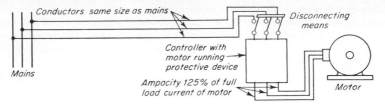

FIG. 430-12. Omission of branch-circuit protective devices. Case A—conductors to motor controller same size as feeder conductors.

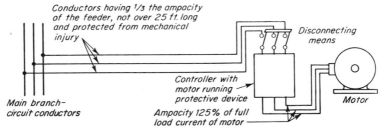

FIG. 430-13. Omission of branch-circuit protective devices. Case B—conductors to motor controller having one-third the ampacity of the mains.

Case B

Motor branch-circuit protective devices may be omitted provided that the tap conductors from the mains to the motor-running protective device have at least one-third the ampacity of the feeder, are not more than 25 ft long, are suitably protected from physical damage, and have at least the ampacity required by Sec. 430-22.

The conditions of Case B are illustrated by Fig. 430-13. As in Case A, the size of the conductors from the motor protective device to the motor is determined by the rule for the conductors of motor branch circuits in Sec. 430-22, and the starter or controller must be of the type approved for group installation.

The principle applied here is that, since the conductors are short and protected from physical damage, it is unlikely that trouble will occur in the run between the mains and the motor protection which will cause the conductors to be overloaded, except some accident resulting in an actual short circuit. A short circuit will blow the fuses or trip the circuit breaker protecting the mains. An overload on the conductors caused by overloading the motor or trouble in the motor itself will cause the motor protective device to operate and so protect the conductors.

It should be noted that the tap conductors should never be of smaller size than the branch-circuit conductors required by Sec. 430-22. Thus if a 20-hp 230-V three-phase squirrel-cage motor is to be supplied from a No. 000 circuit, assuming the use of Type T conductors, the branch-circuit tap conductors must not be smaller than No. 4 and conductors tapped solidly to the mains as permitted in the above rule must be not smaller than this size.

430-54. Multimotor and Combination-Load Equipment. The rating of the branch-circuit protective device for multimotor and combination-load equipment shall not exceed the rating marked on the equipment in accordance with Section 430-7(d).

430-55. Combined Overcurrent Protection. Motor branch-circuit short-circuit and ground-fault protection and motor-running overload protection shall be permitted to be combined in a single protective device where the rating or setting of the device provides the running overload protection specified in Section 430-32.

▲ Circuit breakers can be made having inverse time characteristics such that a single breaker can serve as both the branch-circuit protective device and the motor-running protective device, but this use of circuit breakers is not common.

The special time-delay fuses shown in Figs. 430-8, 430-14, and 430-15 are examples of devices which combine in a single unit the functions of a motor branch-circuit protective device and a motor-running protective device.

FIG. 430-14. Fusetron cartridge-type fuse. (*Bussmann Mfg. Co.*)

FIG. 430-15. Trion time-delay cartridge-type fuse. (*Chase-Shawmut Co.*)

The "Fustat" (Fig. 430-8) consists of two elements, (1) a fuse link which operates the same as any standard types of fuse, opening the circuit almost instantaneously on a short circuit or heavy overload, and (2) a heater element which, under a continued overload which would injure the motor, melts the solder retaining one end of the fuse link, thus permitting the spring to open the circuit by withdrawing the link from the melted solder.

These fuses may be used on circuits where the use of plug fuses is permitted. [See Sec. 240-50(a).] They are obtainable in ratings up to 30 A. To provide running protection for a motor, for ordinary service, the rating should be selected which is about 110 percent of the full-load current rating of the motor.

The cartridge-type fuses shown in Figs. 430-14 and 430-15 are available in all standard fuse ratings up to 600 A at 250 and 600 V. These fuses have sufficient time delay so that if used for the protection of a motor branch circuit, and if fuses are selected having a rating close to the full-load current of the motor, in most cases the fuses will not blow on the starting current of the motor but will blow on a continued overload.

430-56. Branch-Circuit Protective Devices—In Which Conductor. Branch-circuit protective devices shall comply with the provisions of Section 240-20.

▲ Motor branch circuits are to be protected in the same way as other circuits with regard to the number of fuses and the number of poles and overcurrent units of circuit breakers. If fuses are used, a fuse is required in each ungrounded conductor. If a circuit breaker is used, there must be an overcurrent unit in each ungrounded conductor.

430-57. Size of Fuseholder. Where fuses are used for motor branch-circuit short-circuit and ground-fault protection, the fuseholders shall not be of a smaller size than required to accommodate the fuses specified by Table 430-152.

Exception: Where fuses having time delay appropriate for the starting characteristics of the motor are used, fuseholders of smaller size than specified in Table 430-152 shall be permitted.

▲ Special time-delay fuses can be of lower ratings than the maximum ratings specified in part D of Art. 430, and better protection is secured by the use of fuses having the lower ratings. Where such fuses are used, it is possible to use smaller cutout bases, or smaller fusible switches, than would be required for fuses of the standard type. (See Table 430-152.)

430-58. Rating of Circuit Breaker. A circuit breaker for motor branch-circuit short-circuit and ground-fault protection shall have a current rating in accordance with Sections 430-52 and 430-110.

▲ In the case of a circuit breaker having an adjustable trip point, this rule refers to the capacity of the circuit breaker to carry current without overheating and has nothing to do with the setting of the breaker. The breaker most commonly used as a motor branch-circuit protective device is the nonadjustable circuit breaker (see Sec. 240-6), and any breaker of this type having a rating in conformity with the requirements of Sec. 430-52 will have an ampacity considerably in excess of 115 percent of the full-load motor current.

E. Motor Feeder Short-Circuit and Ground-Fault Protection

430-61. General. Part E specifies protective devices intended to protect feeder conductors supplying motors against overcurrents due to short circuits or grounds.

430-62. Rating or Setting—Motor Load.

(a) **Specific Load.** A feeder supplying a specific fixed motor load(s) and consisting of conductor sizes based on Section 430-24 shall be provided with a protective device having a rating or setting not greater than the largest rating or setting of the branch-circuit short-circuit and ground-fault protective device for any motor of the group (based on Table 430-152), plus the sum of the full-load currents of the other motors of the group.

Where two or more motors of equal horsepower rating are the largest in the group, one of these motors shall be considered as the largest for the above calculations.

See Example No. 8, Chapter 9.

(b) Future Additions. For large-capacity installations, where heavy-capacity feeders are installed to provide for future additions or changes, the rating or setting of the feeder protective devices shall be permitted to be based on the rated ampacity of the feeder conductors.

430-63. Rating or Setting—Power and Light Loads. Where a feeder supplies a motor load, and in addition a lighting or a lighting and appliance load, the feeder protective device shall be permitted to have a rating or setting sufficient to carry the lighting or the lighting and appliance load as determined in accordance with Articles 210 and 220, plus, for a single motor, the rating permitted by Section 430-52, and for two or more motors, the rating permitted by Section 430-62.

F. Motor Control Circuits

430-71. General. Part F contains modifications of the general requirements and applies to the particular conditions of motor control circuits.

Definition of Control Circuit: The circuit of a control apparatus or system that carries the electric signals directing the performance of the controller, but does not carry the main power current.

Control circuits tapped from the load side of the motor branch-circuit short-circuit protective devices shall not be considered to be branch circuits and shall be permitted to be protected by either supplementary or branch-circuit overcurrent protective devices.

430-72. Overcurrent Protection.

(a) In Equipment Enclosure. Conductors of control circuits which do not extend beyond the control equipment enclosure shall be considered to be protected by the motor branch-circuit short-circuit and ground-fault protective device(s).

(b) Extending Beyond Equipment Enclosure. Conductors of control circuits extending beyond the control equipment enclosure shall be protected against overcurrent in accordance with their ampacities.

Exception No. 1: Where a control circuit transformer is provided, overcurrent protection shall be in accordance with Section 430-72(c).

Exception No. 2: The conductors shall be considered to be protected by the motor branch-circuit short-circuit and ground-fault protective device(s) under either of the following conditions:

(a) Where the rating or setting of the protective device(s) is not more than 300 percent of the ampacity of the control circuit conductors.

(b) Where the opening of the control circuit would create a hazard, as for example, the control circuit of a fire pump motor, and the like.

(c) Control Circuit Transformer. Where a control circuit transformer is provided and its secondary circuit extends beyond the control equipment enclosure, an overcurrent protective device(s) shall be provided in the secondary circuit. This device(s) shall be rated or set at not more than 200 percent of the rated secondary current of the transformer and not more than 200 percent of the ampacity of the control circuit conductors extending beyond the control equipment enclosure.

Exception No. 1: Where the transformer supplies a Class 2 circuit, overcurrent protection shall conform with Part C of Article 725.

Exception No. 2: Where protection is provided by other approved means.

Exception No. 3: Overcurrent protection shall be omitted where the opening of the control circuit would create a hazard, as for example, the control circuit of a fire pump motor, and the like.

430-73. Mechanical Protection of Conductor. Where damage to a control circuit would constitute a hazard, all conductors of such a remote-control circuit that are outside the control device itself shall be installed in a raceway or be otherwise suitably protected from physical damage.

Where one side of the control circuit is grounded, the control circuit shall be so arranged that an accidental ground in the remote-control devices will not start the motor.

▲ The condition under which physical protection of the control circuit conductor becomes necessary is where damage to the conductors would constitute either a fire or an accident hazard. Damage to the control-circuit conductors resulting in short-circuiting two or more of the conductors or breaking one of the conductors would result either in causing the device to operate or in rendering it inoperative, and in some cases either condition would constitute a hazard either to persons or to property; hence, in such cases the conductors should be installed in rigid or other metal conduit. On the other hand, damage to the conductors of the low-voltage control circuit of a domestic oil burner or automatic stoker does not constitute a hazard, because the boiler or furnace is equipped with an automatic safety control.

430-74. Disconnection.

(a) General. Control circuits shall be so arranged that they will be disconnected from all sources of supply when the disconnecting means is in the open position. The disconnecting means shall be permitted to consist of two or more separate devices, one of which disconnects the motor and the controller from the source(s) of power supply for the motor, and the other(s), the control circuit(s) from its power supply. Where separate devices are used, they shall be located immediately adjacent one to each other.

(b) Control Transformer in Controller. Where a transformer or other device is used to obtain a reduced voltage for the control circuit and is located in the controller, such transformer or other device shall be connected to the load side of the disconnecting means for the control circuit.

▲ The control circuit of a remote-control motor controller shall always be so connected that it will be cut off when the disconnecting means is opened, unless a separate disconnecting means is provided for the control circuit.

G. Motor Controllers

430-81. General. Part G is intended to require suitable controllers for all motors.

(a) Definition. For definition of "Controller," see Article 100. For the purpose of this Article, the term "Controller" includes any switch or device normally used to start and stop a motor.

(b) Stationary Motor of $\frac{1}{8}$ **Horsepower or Less.** For a stationary motor rated at $\frac{1}{8}$ horsepower or less that is normally left running and is so constructed that it cannot be damaged by overload or failure to start, such as clock motors and the like, the branch-circuit protective device shall be permitted to serve as the controller.

(c) Portable Motor of $\frac{1}{3}$ **Horsepower or Less.** For a portable motor rated at $\frac{1}{3}$ horsepower or less, the controller shall be permitted to be an attachment plug and receptacle.

430-82. Controller Design.

(a) Starting and Stopping. Each controller shall be capable of starting and stopping the motor it controls, and shall be capable of interrupting the stalled-rotor current of the motor.

(b) Autotransformer. An autotransformer starter shall provide an off position, a running position, and at least one starting position. It shall be so designed that it cannot rest in the starting position or in any position that will render the overload device in the circuit inoperative.

(c) Rheostats. Rheostats shall be in compliance with the following:

(1) Motor-starting rheostats shall be so designed that the contact arm cannot be left on intermediate segments. The point or plate on which the arm rests when in the starting position shall have no electrical connection with the resistor.

(2) Motor-starting rheostats for direct-current motors operated from a constant voltage supply shall be equipped with automatic devices that will interrupt the supply before the speed of the motor has fallen to less than $\frac{1}{3}$ its normal value.

430-83. Rating. The controller shall have a horsepower rating not lower than the horsepower rating of the motor.

Exception No. 1: For a stationary motor rated at 2 horsepower or less, and 300 volts or less, the controller shall be permitted to be a general-use switch having an ampere rating not less than twice the full-load current rating of the motor.

On AC circuits, general-use snap switches suitable only for use on AC (not general-use AC-DC snap switches) shall be permitted to control a motor rated at 2 horsepower or less and 300 volts or less having a full-load current rating not more than 80 percent of the ampere rating of the switch.

Exception No. 2: A branch-circuit inverse time circuit breaker rated in amperes only shall be permitted as a controller. Where this circuit breaker is also used for overload protection, it shall conform to the appropriate provisions of this Article governing overload protection.

Exception No. 3: The motor controller for a torque motor shall have a continuous-duty full-load current rating not less than the nameplate current rating of the motor. For a motor controller rated in horsepower but not marked with the foregoing current rating, the equivalent current rating shall be determined from the horsepower rating by using Table 430-147, 430-148, 430-149, or 430-150.

▲ If used only as a controller, i.e., as a device for starting and stopping the motor, a circuit breaker is entirely suitable. In general, however, circuit breakers of the branch-circuit type are not well adapted for use as running protective devices for motors.

430-84. Need Not Open All Conductors. The controller shall not be required to open all conductors to the motor.

Exception: Where the controller serves also as a disconnecting means, it shall open all ungrounded conductors to the motor as provided in Section 430-111.

▲ A motor controller need open only as many of the conductors of the motor circuit as may be necessary to stop the motor. Thus for a DC or single-phase motor the controller need open only one conductor; for a three-phase motor, two conductors; and for a two-phase motor, three conductors.

430-85. In Grounded Conductors. One pole of the controller shall be permitted to be placed in a permanently grounded conductor, provided the controller is so designed that the pole in the grounded conductor cannot be opened without simultaneously opening all conductors of the circuit.

▲ Generally, one conductor of a 115-V circuit is grounded, and on such a circuit a single-pole controller may be used if connected in the ungrounded conductor, or a two-pole controller is permitted if both poles are opened together. In a 230-V circuit there is usually no grounded conductor, but if one conductor is grounded the rule applies.

430-86. Motor Not in Sight from Controller. Where a motor and the driven machinery are not in sight from the controller location, the installation shall comply with one of the following conditions:

(1) The controller disconnecting means shall be capable of being locked in the open position.

(2) A manually operable switch that will disconnect the motor from its source of supply shall be placed within sight from the motor location.

▲ The intent in paragraph (1) is to permit a workman to lock the disconnecting means in the open position and keep the key in his possession so that the circuit cannot be energized while he is working on it. This does not mean that a cabinet enclosing several switches could be locked to accomplish this purpose, because the other switches would be rendered inaccessible. Also it does not mean that removing a "pull out"-type switch serves the purpose, because a "spare" could be inserted in the opening.

Figures 430-16 through 430-18 illustrate arrangements that may be used where the motor is installed at a point that is not within sight from the controller location. See also Sec. 430-102.

The pushbutton station in Fig. 430-18 operates only the holding coil in the magnetic

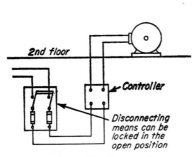

Fig. 430-16. Controller disconnecting means capable of being locked in the open position. See paragraph (1).

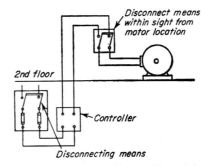

Fig. 430-17. A manually operable switch which will disconnect the motor from its source of supply is placed within sight from the motor location. See paragraph (2).

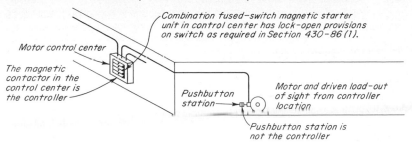

FIG. 430-18. Control center with lock-open provisions and pushbutton station at motor.

starter. The magnetic starter "controls" the current to the motor; for example, the control wires to a pushbutton station could become shorted after the motor is in operation and pushing the STOP button would not release the holding coil in the magnetic starter and the motor would continue to run. This is the reason that a disconnecting means is required to be within sight from the controller. In this case operating the disconnecting means will open the supply to the controller and shut off the motor.

430-87. Number of Motors Served by Each Controller. Each motor shall be provided with an individual controller.

Exception: For motors of 600 volts or less, a single controller rated at not less than the sum of the horsepower ratings of all of the motors of the group shall be permitted to serve the group of motors under any one of the following conditions:

a. Where a number of motors drive several parts of a single machine or piece of apparatus, such as metal and woodworking machines, cranes, hoists, and similar apparatus.

b. Where a group of motors is under the protection of one overcurrent device as permitted in Section 430-53(a).

c. Where a group of motors is located in a single room within sight from the controller location.

▲ These conditions are the same as those under which a single disconnecting means can be used for a group of motors. (See Sec. 430-112.)

430-88. Adjustable-Speed Motors. Adjustable-speed motors that are controlled by means of field regulation shall be so equipped and connected that they cannot be started under weakened field.

Exception: Where the motor is designed for such starting.

▲ Field weakening is quite commonly used as a method of controlling the speed of DC motors. If such a motor were started under a weakened field, the starting current would be excessive unless the motor is specially designed for starting in this manner.

430-89. Speed Limitation. Machines of the following types shall be provided with speed limiting devices:

(1) Separately excited direct-current motors.

(2) Series motors.

(3) Motor-generators and converters that can be driven at excessive speed from the direct-current end, as by a reversal of current or decrease in load.

Exception No. 1: When the inherent characteristics of the machines, the system, or the load and the mechanical connection thereto are such as to safely limit the speed.

Exception No. 2: When the machine is always under the manual control of a qualified operator.

▲ A common example of a separately excited DC motor is found in the Ward Leonard speed control system, which is widely used for electric elevators, hoists, and other applications where smooth control of speed from standstill to full speed is necessary. In the diagram, Fig. 430-19, G_1 and G_2 are two generators having their armatures

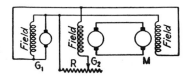

FIG. 430-19. Ward Leonard speed control system.

mounted on a shaft which is driven by a motor, not shown in the diagram. M is a motor driving the elevator drum or other machine. The fields of generator G_1 and motor M are excited by G_1. By adjusting the rheostat R, the voltage generated by G_2 is varied, and this in turn varies the speed of motor M. It is evident that if the field circuit of motor M should be accidentally opened while the motor is lightly loaded, the motor would reach an excessive speed. In many applications of this system the motor is always loaded and no speed-limiting device is required.

The speed of a series motor depends upon its load and will become excessive at no load or very light loads. Traction motors are commonly series motors, but such a motor is geared to the drive wheels of the car or locomotive and hence is always loaded.

Where a motor generator, consisting of a motor driving a compound-wound DC generator, is operated in parallel with a similar machine or is used to charge a storage battery, if the motor circuit is accidentally opened while the generator is still connected to the DC buses or battery, the generator will be driven as a motor and its speed may become dangerously high. A synchronous converter operating under similar conditions may also reach an excessive speed if the AC supply is accidentally cut off.

A safeguard against overspeed is provided by a centrifugal device on the shaft of the machine, arranged to close (or open) a contact at a predetermined speed, thus tripping a circuit breaker which cuts the machine off from the current supply.

430-90. Combination Fuseholder and Switch As Controller. The rating of a combination fuseholder and switch used as a motor controller shall be such that the fuseholder will accommodate the size of fuse specified in Part C of this Article for motor-running overload protection.

Exception: Where fuses having time delay appropriate for the starting characteristics of the motor are used, fuseholders of smaller size than specified in Part C of this Article shall be permitted.

▲ The use of a fusible switch as a motor controller with fuses as motor-running protective devices is seldom practicable unless special types of fuses are used. The rating of the fuses must not exceed 125 percent, or in some cases 115 percent, of the full-load motor current, and fuses of this rating would, in most cases, be blown by the starting current drawn by the motor, particularly where the motor turns on and off frequently. (See Sec. 430-35.)

H. Disconnecting Means

430-101. General. Part H is intended to require disconnecting means capable of disconnecting motors and controllers from the circuit.

See Diagram 430-1.
See Section 110-22 for identification of disconnecting means.

430-102. In Sight From Controller Location. A disconnecting means shall be located in sight from the controller location.

Exception: For motor circuits over 600 volts, nominal, the controller disconnecting means shall be permitted to be out of sight of the controller, provided the controller is marked with a warning label giving the location and identification of the disconnecting means to be locked in the open position.

▲ See comment following Sec. 430-86.

430-103. To Disconnect Both Motor and Controller. The disconnecting means shall disconnect the motor and the controller from all ungrounded supply conductors and shall be so designed that no pole can be operated independently. The disconnecting means shall be permitted in the same enclosure with the controller.

See Section 430-113 for equipment receiving energy from more than one source.

▲ The foregoing rule defines the meaning of the term *disconnecting means.*

In order that the necessary periodical inspection and servicing of motors and their controllers may be done with safety, the Code requires that a switch, circuit breaker or other device shall be provided for this purpose. Since the disconnecting means must disconnect the controller as well as the motor, it must be a separate device and cannot be a part of the controller, though it could be mounted on the same panel or enclosed in the same box with the controller.

The disconnecting means may be a motor-circuit switch, a general-use switch, an isolating switch, a circuit breaker, an attachment plug and receptacle, or the branch-circuit overcurrent protective device, the type depending upon the size of the motor and other conditions.

In case the motor controller fails to open the circuit if the motor is stalled, or under other conditions of heavy overload, the disconnecting means can be used to open the circuit. It is therefore required that a switch used as the disconnecting means shall be capable of interrupting a very heavy current. An exception is made in the case of motors larger than 100 hp. Switches rated up to 100 hp are readily available.

430-104. To Be Indicating. The disconnecting means shall plainly indicate whether it is in the open (off) or closed (on) position.

430-105. Grounded Conductors. One pole of the disconnecting means shall be permitted to disconnect a permanently grounded conductor, provided the disconnecting means is so designed that the pole in the grounded conductor cannot be opened without simultaneously disconnecting all conductors of the circuit.

430-106. Service Switch As Disconnecting Means. Where an installation consists of a single motor, the service switch may serve as the disconnecting means if it complies with this Article and is within sight from the controller location.

430-107. Readily Accessible. One of the disconnecting means shall be readily accessible.

430-108. Every Switch. Every switch in the motor branch circuit within sight from the controller location shall comply with the requirements of Part H of this Article.

430-109. Type. The disconnecting means shall be a motor-circuit switch rated in horsepower or a circuit breaker.

Exception No. 1: For stationary motors of $\frac{1}{8}$ horsepower or less, the branch-circuit overcurrent device shall be permitted to serve as the disconnecting means.

Exception No. 2: For stationary motors rated at 2 horsepower or less and 300 volts or less, the disconnecting means shall be permitted to be a general-use switch having an ampere rating not less than twice the full-load current rating of the motor.

On AC circuits, general-use snap switches suitable only for use on AC (not general-use AC-DC snap switches) shall be permitted to disconnect a motor having a full-load current rating not exceeding 80 percent of the ampere rating of the switch.

Exception No. 3: For motors of over 2 horsepower to and including 100 horsepower, the separate disconnecting means required for a motor with an autotransformer-type controller shall be permitted to be a general-use switch where all of the following provisions are met:

a. The motor drives a generator that is provided with overload protection.

b. The controller (1) is capable of interrupting the locked-rotor current of the motor, (2) is provided with a no-voltage release, and (3) is provided with running overload protection not exceeding 125 percent of the motor full-load current rating.

c. Separate fuses or an inverse time circuit breaker rated or set at not more than 150 percent of the motor full-load current are provided in the motor branch circuit.

Exception No. 4: For stationary motors rated at more than 100 horsepower, the disconnecting means shall be permitted to be a motor-circuit switch also rated in amperes, a general-use switch, or an isolating switch.

Isolating switches shall be plainly marked "Do not open under load."

Exception No. 5: For portable motors, an attachment plug and receptacle shall be permitted to serve as the disconnecting means.

▲ If in addition to the disconnecting means there is any other switch in the motor circuit and it is at all likely that this switch might be opened in case of trouble, this switch must have the interrupting capacity required for a switch intended for use as the disconnecting means.

For a motor larger than 2 hp, not larger than 100 hp, and not portable, a motor-circuit switch or a circuit breaker must be used as the disconnecting means, if a disconnecting means is required. A motor-circuit switch is a horsepower-rated switch.

(See definition, Art. 100.) The exceptions to the general rule are shown in Figs. 430-20 through 430-23.

It may be found that a switch having the required horsepower rating is not provided with fuse terminals of the size required to accommodate the branch-circuit fuses. For example, assume a $7\frac{1}{2}$-hp 230-V three-phase motor started at full line voltage. A switch used as the disconnecting means for this motor must be rated at not less than $7\frac{1}{2}$ hp, but this would probably be a 60-A switch and therefore, if fusible, would be equipped with terminals to receive 35- to 60-A fuses. Section 430-90 provides that fuse terminals must be installed that will receive fuses of 70-A rating. In any such case a switch of the next higher rating must be provided.

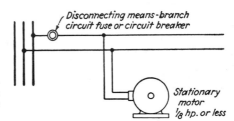

FIG. 430-20. Exception 1—for a stationary motor of $\frac{1}{8}$ hp or less, the branch-circuit overcurrent device may serve as the disconnecting means.

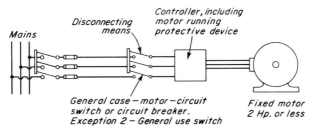

FIG. 430-21. Exception 2—for a 2-hp or smaller motor operating at 300 V or less, the disconnecting means may be a general-use switch rated at twice the full-load current rating of the motor.

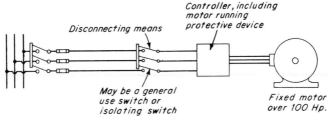

FIG. 430-22. Exception 4—for a fixed motor of over 100 hp the disconnecting means may be either a general-use switch or an isolating switch.

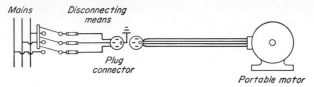

FIG. 430-23. Exception 5—for any portable motor a plug and receptacle may serve as the disconnecting means.

Exception: Where fuses having time delay appropriate for the starting characteristics of the motor are used, fuseholders of smaller size than specified in part C of Art. 430 may be used. (See Sec. 430-57.)

Horsepower-rated enclosed fusible switches usually have a marking within the switch which permits a dual horsepower rating. A larger horsepower rating for such switches is generally permitted where time-delay fuses are used as the branch-circuit overcurrent protection.

430-110. Ampere Rating and Interrupting Capacity.

(a) General. The disconnecting means for motor circuits rated 600 volts, nominal or less shall have an ampere rating of at least 115 percent of the full-load current rating of the motor.

(b) For Torque Motors. The disconnecting means for a torque motor shall be selected on the basis of the motor nameplate current as follows:

(1) The ampacity shall be at least 115 percent of the motor nameplate current.

(2) To determine the equivalent horsepower in complying with the requirements of Section 430-109, select the horsepower rating from Table 430-147, 430-148, 430-149, or 430-150 corresponding to the motor current. Where the motor nameplate current does not correspond to a current shown in the Table, the horsepower rating corresponding to the next higher value shall be selected.

(c) For Combination Loads. Where two or more motors are used together or where one or more motors are used in combination with other loads, such as resistance heaters, and where the combined load may be simultaneous on a single disconnecting means, the ampere and horsepower ratings of the combined load shall be determined as follows:

(1) The rating of the disconnecting means shall be determined from the summation of all currents, including resistance loads, at the full-load condition and also at the locked-rotor condition. The combined full-load current and the combined locked-rotor current so obtained shall be considered as a single motor for the purpose of this requirement as follows:

The full-load current equivalent to the horsepower rating of each motor shall be selected from Table 430-148, 430-149, or 430-150. These full-load currents shall be added to the rating in amperes of other loads to obtain an equivalent full-load current for the combined load.

The locked-rotor current equivalent to the horsepower rating of each motor shall be selected from Table 430-151. The locked-rotor currents shall be added to the rating in amperes of other loads to obtain an equivalent locked-rotor current for the combined load. Where two or more motors and/or other loads cannot be started simultaneously, appropriate combinations of locked-rotor and full-load current shall be permitted to be used to determine the equivalent locked-rotor current for the simultaneous combined loads.

Exception: Where part of the concurrent load is resistance load, and where the disconnecting means is a switch rated in horsepower and amperes, the horsepower rating of the switch shall not be less than the combined load of the motor(s), and the ampere rating shall not be less than the locked-rotor current of the motor(s) plus the resistance load.

(2) The ampere rating of the disconnecting means shall not be less than 115 percent of the summation of all currents at the full-load condition determined in accordance with (c)(1) above.

(3) For small motors not covered by Table 430-147, 430-148, 430-149, or 430-150, the locked-rotor current shall be assumed to be 6 times the full-load current.

▲ A general-use switch, circuit breaker, plug and receptacle, or fuse, used as a disconnecting means, must have an ampacity of not less than 115 percent of the full-load current of the motor.

430-111. Switch or Circuit Breaker As Both Controller and Disconnecting Means. A switch or circuit breaker complying with Section 430-83 shall be permitted to serve as both controller and disconnecting means if it opens all ungrounded conductors to the motor, if it is protected by an overcurrent device (which may be the branch-circuit fuses) that opens all ungrounded conductors to the switch or circuit breaker, and if it is of one of the following types:

(1) An air-break switch, operable directly by applying the hand to a lever or handle.

(2) An inverse time circuit breaker operable directly by applying the hand to a lever or handle.

(3) An oil switch used on a circuit whose rating does not exceed 600 volts or 100 amperes, or by special permission on a circuit exceeding this capacity where under expert supervision.

The oil switch or circuit breaker specified above shall be permitted to be both power and manually operable.

The overcurrent device protecting the controller shall be permitted to be part of the controller assembly or shall be permitted to be separate.

An autotransformer-type controller shall be provided with a separate disconnecting means.

▲ *Paragraph (1) Manually Operable Air-Break Switch.*

The intention in this case is to permit omission of the disconnecting means only where all other specified conditions are met and where the controller consists of, or includes, a manually operable switch, except that a separate disconnecting means must always be provided if the controller is of the autotransformer or "compensator" type. The switch may be combined with a motor-running protective device.

Where the controller consists of a manually operable air-break switch, a manually operable circuit breaker, or, for a motor operating at 600 V or less, an oil switch of 100 A rating (or of higher rating by special permission), the controller itself is considered as a satisfactory disconnecting means, and no additional device to serve as a disconnecting means is required. The switch or circuit breaker used as the controller must meet all requirements for controllers and must be protected by an overcurrent device that opens all ungrounded conductors.

The condition that the switch or circuit breaker shall be protected by an overcurrent device which opens all ungrounded conductors will always be fulfilled if branch-circuit overcurrent protective devices (fuses or a circuit breaker) are installed. The only cases where this condition will not be fulfilled are those where the branch-circuit protection is omitted, as permitted by Sec. 430-53.

The conditions under which the controller may serve also as the disconnecting means, or, in other words, where no disconnecting means is required, are shown in Fig. 430-24.

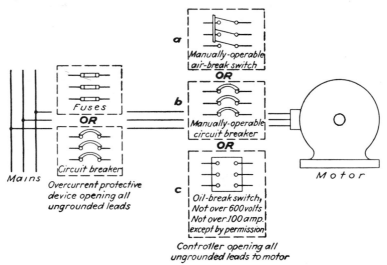

Fig. 430-24. Conditions where no disconnecting means in addition to the controller are required.

430-112. Motors Served by Single Disconnecting Means. Each motor shall be provided with an individual disconnecting means.

Exception: A single disconnecting means shall be permitted to serve a group of motors under any one of the following conditions:

a. Where a number of motors drive several parts of a single machine or piece of apparatus, such as metal and woodworking machines, cranes, and hoists.

b. Where a group of motors is under the protection of one set of branch-circuit protective devices as permitted by Section 430-53(a).

c. Where a group of motors is in a single room within sight from the location of the disconnecting means.

The single disconnecting means shall have a rating not less than is required by Section 430-110 for a single motor, the rating of which equals the sum of the horsepowers or currents of all the motors of the group.

▲ *Exception a*

In Sec. 610-31 it is required that the main collector wires of a traveling crane shall be controlled by a switch located within sight of the wires and readily operable from the floor or ground. This switch would serve as the disconnecting means for the motors on the crane. When repair or maintenance work is to be done on the electrical equipment of the crane, it is safer to cut off the current from all this equipment by opening one switch, rather than to use a separate switch for each motor. Also, in the case of a machine tool driven by two or more motors, a single disconnecting means for the group of motors is more serviceable than an individual switch for each motor, because repair and maintenance work can be done with greater safety when the entire electrical equipment is "dead."

Exception b

Such groups may consist of motors having full-load currents not exceeding 6 A each, with circuit fuses not exceeding 20 A at 125 V or less, or 15 A at 600 V or less. Because the expense of providing an individual disconnecting means for each motor is not always warranted for motors of such small size, and also because the entire group of small motors could probably be shut down for servicing without causing inconvenience, a single disconnecting means for the entire group is permitted.

Exception c

"Within sight" should be interpreted as meaning so located that there will always be an unobstructed view of the disconnecting switch from the motor, and Sec. 430-4 limits the distance in this case between the disconnecting means and any motor to a maximum of 50 ft.

These conditions are the same as those under which the use of a single controller is permitted for a group of motors. (See Sec. 430-87.) The use of a single disconnecting means for two or more motors is quite common, but in the majority of cases the most practicable arrangement is to provide an individual controller for each motor.

If a switch is used as the disconnecting means, it must be of the type and rating required by Sec. 430-109 for a single motor having a horsepower rating equal to the sum of the horsepower ratings of all the motors it controls. Thus, for six 5-hp motors the disconnecting means should be a motor-circuit switch rated at not less than 30 hp. If the total of the horsepower ratings is over 2 hp, a horsepower-rated switch must be used.

430-113. Energy From More Than One Source. Equipment receiving electrical energy from more than one source shall be provided with disconnecting means from each source of electrical energy immediately adjacent to the equipment served. Each source shall be permitted to have a separate disconnecting means.

J. Over 600 Volts, Nominal

430-121. General. Part J recognizes the additional hazard due to the use of high voltage. It adds to or amends the other provisions of this Article. Other requirements for circuits and equipment operating at over 600 volts, nominal are in Article 710.

430-122. Marking on Controllers. In addition to the marking required by Section 430-8, a controller shall be marked with the control voltage.

430-123. Conductor Enclosures Adjacent to Motors. Flexible metal conduit not exceeding 6 feet in length shall be permitted to be employed for raceway connection to a motor terminal enclosure.

430-124. Size of Conductors. Conductors supplying motors shall have an ampacity not less than the current at which the motor overload protective device is selected to trip.

430-125. Motor Circuit Overcurrent Protection.

(a) General. The high-voltage circuit for each motor shall include coordinated protection to automatically interrupt motor running overcurrent (overload) and fault currents in the motor, the motor circuit conductors, and the motor control apparatus.

Exception: Where a motor is vital to operation of the plant and the motor should operate to failure if necessary to prevent a greater hazard to persons, the sensing device(s) is permitted to be connected to a supervised annunciator or alarm instead of interrupting the motor circuit.

(b) Overload Protection.

(1) Each motor shall be protected against dangerous heating due to motor overloads and failure to start by a thermal protector integral with the motor or external current sensing devices, or both.

(2) The secondary circuits of wound-rotor alternating-current motors including conductors, controllers, and resistors rated for the application, shall be considered as protected against overcurrent by the motor overload protection means.

(3) Operation of the overload interrupting device shall simultaneously disconnect all ungrounded conductors.

(4) Overload sensing devices shall not automatically reset after trip unless resetting of the overload sensing device does not cause automatic restarting of the motor or there is no hazard to persons created by automatic restarting of the motor and its connected machinery.

(c) Fault Current Protection.

(1) Fault current protection shall be provided in each motor circuit by one of the following means:

a. A circuit breaker of suitable type and rating so arranged that it can be serviced without hazard. The circuit breaker shall simultaneously disconnect all ungrounded conductors. The circuit breaker shall be permitted to sense the fault current by means of integral or external sensing elements.

b. Fuses of a suitable type and rating placed in each ungrounded conductor. Fuses shall be used with suitable disconnecting means or they shall be of a type that can also serve as the disconnecting means. They shall be so arranged that they cannot be serviced while they are energized.

(2) Fault current interrupting devices shall not reclose the circuit automatically.

Exception: Where circuits are exposed to transient faults and where automatic reclosing of the circuit does not create a hazard to persons.

(3) Overload protection and fault current protection shall be permitted to be provided by the same device.

430-126. Rating of Motor Control Apparatus. Motor controllers and motor branch-circuit disconnecting means shall have a continuous ampere rating not less than the current at which the overload protective device is selected to trip.

430-127. Disconnecting Means. The controller disconnecting means shall be capable of being locked in the open position.

K. Protection of Live Parts—All Voltages

430-131. General. Part K specifies that live parts shall be protected in a manner judged adequate to the hazard involved.

430-132. Where Required. Exposed live parts of motors and controllers operating at 50 volts or more between terminals shall be guarded against accidental contact by enclosure or by location as follows:

(1) By installation in a room or enclosure that is accessible only to qualified persons.

(2) By installation on a suitable balcony, gallery, or platform, so elevated and arranged as to exclude unqualified persons.

(3) By elevation 8 feet or more above the floor.

Exception: Stationary motors having commutators, collectors, and brush rigging located inside of motor end brackets and not conductively connected to supply circuits operating at more than 150 volts to ground.

430-133. Guards for Attendants. Where live parts of motors or controllers operating at over 150 volts to ground are guarded against accidental contact only by location as specified in Section 430-132, and where adjustment or other attendance may be necessary during the operation of the apparatus, suitable insulating mats or platforms shall be provided so that the attendant cannot readily touch live parts unless standing on the mats or platforms.

For working space, see Sections 110-16 and 110-34.

L. Grounding

430-141. General. Part L specifies the grounding of motor and controller frames to prevent a potential above ground in the event of accidental contact between live parts and frames. Insulation, isolation, or guarding are suitable alternatives to grounding of motors under certain conditions.

430-142. Stationary Motors. The frames of stationary motors shall be grounded under any of the following conditions:

(1) Where supplied by metal-enclosed wiring.

(2) Where in a wet location and not isolated or guarded.

(3) If in a hazardous location as covered in Articles 500 through 517.

(4) If the motor operates with any terminal at over 150 volts to ground.

Where the frame of the motor is not grounded, it shall be permanently and effectively insulated from the ground.

▲ Usually stationary motors are supplied by wiring in metal raceway or metal-clad cable. The motor frames of such motors must be grounded, the raceway or cable armor being attached to the frame and serving as the grounding conductor. [See Sec. 250-91(b).]

Any motor in a wet location constitutes a serious hazard to persons and should be grounded unless it is so located or guarded that it is out of reach.

430-143. Portable Motors. The frames of portable motors that operate at over 150 volts to ground shall be guarded or grounded.

See Section 250-45(d) for grounding of portable appliances in other than residential occupancies.
See Section 250-59(b) for color of grounding conductor.

430-144. Controllers. Controller enclosures shall be grounded regardless of voltage.

Exception No. 1: Enclosures attached to ungrounded portable equipment.

Exception No. 2: Lined covers of snap switches.

430-145. Method of Grounding. Where required, grounding shall be done in the manner specified in Article 250.

(a) Grounding Through Terminal Housings. Where the wiring to fixed motors is Type AC metal-clad cable or in metal raceways, junction boxes to house motor terminals shall be provided, and the armor of the cable or the metal raceways shall be connected to them in the manner specified in Article 250.

(b) Separation of Junction Box from Motor. The junction box required by (a) above shall be permitted to be separated from the motor not more than 6 feet, provided the leads to the motor are Type AC metal-clad cable or armored cord or are stranded leads enclosed in flexible or rigid metal conduit or electrical metallic tubing not smaller than ⅜-inch electrical trade size, the armor or raceway being connected both to the motor and to the box. Where stranded leads are used, protected as specified above, they shall not be larger than No. 10, and shall comply with other requirements of this Code for conductors to be used in raceways.

(c) Grounding of Controller Mounted Devices. Instrument transformer secondaries and exposed noncurrent-carrying metal or other conductive parts or cases of instrument transformers, meters, instruments, and relays shall be grounded as specified in Sections 250-121 through 250-125.

▲ Good practice requires in nearly all cases that the wiring to motors which are not portable shall, at the motor, be installed in rigid or flexible metal conduit, electrical metallic tubing, or metal-clad cable and that such motors should be equipped with terminal housings. The method of connecting the conduit to the motor where some flexibility is necessary is shown in Fig. 430-25. The motor shown drives a compressor by means of a V belt, and the motor must be movable on its base so that the belt tension can be adjusted. The motor circuit is installed in rigid conduit extending about 12 in. above a concrete foundation, and a short length of flexible conduit is provided between the end of the rigid conduit and the terminal housing on the motor.

Fig. 430-25. Use of flexible conduit for connection to a motor.

This section permits the use of fixed motors without terminal housings. If a motor has no terminal housing, the branch-circuit conductors must be brought to a junction box not over 6 ft from the motor. Between the junction box and the motor, the following provisions apply:

1. The conductors must either be in the form of metal-clad cable or armored cord, or be installed in rigid or flexible metal conduit or electrical metallic tubing. See Sec. 350-5 for flexible metal conduit.

2. The conductors may be as small as No. 18; however, they must always have the ampacity required by Sec. 430-22.

3. If installed in ⅜-in. rigid or flexible conduit or tubing, conductors must not be larger than No. 10 and must be stranded. See Table 350-3.

According to Sec. 300-16, the conduit, tubing, or metal-clad cable must terminate close to the motor in a fitting having a separable bushed hole for each wire. The method of making the connection to the motor is not specified; presumably, it is the intention that the wires brought out from the terminal fitting shall be connected to binding posts on the motor or spliced to the motor leads. The conduit, tubing, or cable must be rigidly secured to the frame of the motor.

Table 430-147. Full-Load Current in Amperes, Direct-Current Motors

The following values of full-load currents* are for motors running at base speed.

HP	Armature Voltage Rating*					
	90V	120V	180V	240V	500V	550V
¼	4.0	3.1	2.0	1.6		
⅓	5.2	4.1	2.6	2.0		
½	6.8	5.4	3.4	2.7		
¾	9.6	7.6	4.8	3.8		
1	12.2	9.5	6.1	4.7		
1½		13.2	8.3	6.6		
2		17	10.8	8.5		
3		25	16	12.2		
5		40	27	20		
7½		58		29	13.6	12.2
10		76		38	18	16
15				55	27	24
20				72	34	31
25				89	43	38
30				106	51	46
40				140	67	61
50				173	83	75
60				206	99	90
75				255	123	111
100				341	164	148
125				425	205	185
150				506	246	222
200				675	330	294

*These are average direct-current quantities.

**Table 430-148. Full-Load Currents in Amperes Single-Phase
Alternating-Current Motors**

The following values of full-load currents are for motors running at usual speeds and motors with normal torque characteristics. Motors built for especially low speeds or high torques may have higher full-load currents, and multispeed motors will have full-load current varying with speed, in which case the nameplate current ratings shall be used.

To obtain full-load currents of 208- and 200-volt motors, increase corresponding 230-volt motor full-load currents by 10 and 15 percent, respectively.

The voltages listed are rated motor voltages. The currents listed shall be permitted for system voltage ranges of 110 to 120 and 220 to 240.

HP	115V	230V
$\frac{1}{6}$	4.4	2.2
$\frac{1}{4}$	5.8	2.9
$\frac{1}{3}$	7.2	3.6
$\frac{1}{2}$	9.8	4.9
$\frac{3}{4}$	13.8	6.9
1	16	8
$1\frac{1}{2}$	20	10
2	24	12
3	34	17
5	56	28
$7\frac{1}{2}$	80	40
10	100	50

ARTICLE 440. AIR-CONDITIONING AND REFRIGERATING EQUIPMENT

A. General

440-1. Scope.

The provisions of this Article apply to electric motor-driven air-conditioning and refrigerating equipment, and to the branch circuits and controllers for such equipment. It provides for the special considerations necessary for circuits supplying hermetic refrigerant motor-compressors and for any air-conditioning and/or refrigerating equipment which is supplied from an individual branch circuit which supplies a hermetic refrigerant motor-compressor.

Hermetic Refrigerant Motor-Compressor: A combination consisting of a compressor and motor, both of which are enclosed in the same housing, with no external shaft or shaft seals, the motor operating in the refrigerant.

440-2. Other Articles.

(a) These provisions are in addition to, or amendatory of, the provisions of Article 430 and other Articles in this Code, which apply except as modified in this Article.

(b) The rules of Articles 422, 424, or 430, as applicable, shall apply to air-conditioning and refrigerating equipment which does not incorporate a hermetic refriger-

Table 430-149. Full-Load Current Two-Phase Alternating-Current Motors (4-Wire)

The following values of full-load current are for motors running at speeds usual for belted motors and motors with normal torque characteristics. Motors built for especially low speeds or high torques may require more running current, and multispeed motors will have full-load current varying with speed, in which case the nameplate current rating shall be used. Current in the common conductor of a 2-phase, 3-wire system will be 1.41 times the value given.

The voltages listed are rated motor voltages. The currents listed shall be permitted for system voltage ranges of 110 to 120, 220 to 240, 440 to 480, and 550 to 600 volts.

HP	Induction Type Squirrel-Cage and Wound Rotor Amperes					Synchronous Type †Unity Power Factor Amperes			
	115V	230V	460V	575V	2300V	220V	440V	550V	2300V
½	4	2	1	.8					
¾	4.8	2.4	1.2	1.0					
1	6.4	3.2	1.6	1.3					
1½	9	4.5	2.3	1.8					
2	11.8	5.9	3	2.4					
3		8.3	4.2	3.3					
5		13.2	6.6	5.3					
7½		19	9	8					
10		24	12	10					
15		36	18	14					
20		47	23	19					
25		59	29	24		47	24	19	
30		69	35	28		56	29	23	
40		90	45	36		75	37	31	
50		113	56	45		94	47	38	
60		133	67	53	14	111	56	44	11
75		166	83	66	18	140	70	57	13
100		218	109	87	23	182	93	74	17
125		270	135	108	28	228	114	93	22
150		312	156	125	32		137	110	26
200		416	208	167	43		182	145	35

†For 90 and 80 percent power factor, the above figures shall be multiplied by 1.1 and 1.25 respectively.

ant motor-compressor. Examples of such equipment are devices which employ refrigeration compressors driven by conventional motors, furnaces with air-conditioning evaporator coils installed, fan-coil units, remote forced air-cooled condensers, remote commercial refrigerators, etc.

(c) Devices such as room air conditioners, household refrigerators and freezers, drinking-water coolers, and beverage dispensers shall be considered appliances and the provisions of Article 422 shall also apply.

Table 430–150. Full-Load Current* (Three-Phase Alternating-Current Motors)

	Induction Type Squirrel-Cage and Wound Rotor Amperes					Synchronous Type †Unity Power Factor Amperes			
HP	115V	230V	460V	575V	2300V	220V	440V	550V	2300V
½	4	2	1	.8					
¾	5.6	2.8	1.4	1.1					
1	7.2	3.6	1.8	1.4					
1½	10.4	5.2	2.6	2.1					
2	13.6	6.8	3.4	2.7					
3		9.6	4.8	3.9					
5		15.2	7.6	6.1					
7½		22	11	9					
10		28	14	11					
15		42	21	17					
20		54	27	22					
25		68	34	27		54	27	22	
30		80	40	32		65	33	26	
40		104	52	41		86	43	35	
50		130	65	52		108	54	44	
60		154	77	62	16	128	64	51	12
75		192	96	77	20	161	81	65	15
100		248	124	99	26	211	106	85	20
125		312	156	125	31	264	132	106	25
150		360	180	144	37		158	127	30
200		480	240	192	49		210	168	40

For full-load currents of 208- and 200-volt motors, increase the corresponding 230-volt motor full-load current by 10 and 15 percent, respectively.

*These values of full-load current are for motors running at speeds usual for belted motors and motors with normal torque characteristics. Motors built for especially low speeds or high torques may require more running current, and multispeed motors will have full-load current varying with speed, in which case the nameplate current rating shall be used.

†For 90 and 80 percent power factor the above figures shall be multipled by 1.1 and 1.25 respectively.

The voltages listed are rated motor voltages. The currents listed shall be permitted for system voltage ranges of 110 to 120, 220 to 240, 440 to 480, and 550 to 600 volts.

(d) Hermetic refrigerant motor-compressors, circuits, controllers, and equipment shall also comply with the applicable provisions of the following:

▲ Article 440 is patterned after Art. 430, and many rules, such as disconnecting means, controllers, conductor sizes, and group installation, are identical or quite similar in both articles.

Table 430-151. Locked-Rotor Current Conversion Table

As Determined from Horsepower and Voltage Rating For Use Only With Sections 430-110, 440-12, and 440-41.

Conversion Table

Max HP Rating	Single Phase		Two or Three Phase				
	115V	230V	115V	200V	230V	460V	575V
½	58.8	29.4	24	14	12	6	4.8
¾	82.8	41.4	33.6	19	16.8	8.4	6.6
1	96	48	42	24	21	10.8	8.4
1½	120	60	60	34	30	15	12
2	144	72	78	45	39	19.8	15.6
3	204	102	—	62	54	27	24
5	336	168	—	103	90	45	36
7½	480	240	—	152	132	66	54
10	600	300	—	186	162	84	66
15	—	—	—	276	240	120	96
20	—	—	—	359	312	156	126
25	—	—	—	442	384	192	156
30	—	—	—	538	468	234	186
40	—	—	—	718	624	312	246
50	—	—	—	862	750	378	300
60	—	—	—	1035	900	450	360
75	—	—	—	1276	1110	558	444
100	—	—	—	1697	1476	738	588
125	—	—	—	2139	1860	930	744
150	—	—	—	2484	2160	1080	864
200	—	—	—	3312	2880	1440	1152

New concepts for hermetic refrigerant motor-compressors are the terms "rated-load current" and "branch-circuit selection current." Definitions of these terms are in notes following Secs. 440-3(a) and (c).

When the equipment is marked with the branch-circuit selection current, this greatly simplifies the sizing of motor-branch-circuit conductors, disconnecting means, controllers, and overcurrent devices for circuit conductors and motors.

440-3. Marking on Hermetic Refrigerant Motor-Compressors and Equipment.

(a) A hermetic refrigerant motor-compressor shall be provided with a nameplate which shall give the manufacturer's name, trademark or symbol; identifying designation; the phase; voltage; and frequency. The rated load current in amperes of the motor-compressor, shall be marked by the equipment manufacturer on either or both the motor-compressor nameplate and the nameplate of the equipment in which the motor-compressor is used. The locked-rotor current of each single-phase motor-compressor having a rated-load current of more than 9 amperes at 115 volts or more than 4.5 amperes at 230 volts and each polyphase motor-compressor shall be marked on the motor-compressor nameplate. Where a thermal protector com-

Table 430-152. Maximum Rating or Setting of Motor Branch-Circuit
Protective Devices

	Percent of Full-Load Current			
Type of Motor	Nontime Delay Fuse	Dual-Element (Time-Delay) Fuse	Instan-taneous Trip Breaker	*Inverse Time Breaker
Single-phase, all types				
No code letter.................	300	175	700	250
All AC single-phase and polyphase squirrel-cage and synchronous motors† with full-voltage, resistor or reactor starting:				
No code letter.................	300	175	700	250
Code letter F to V.............	300	175	700	250
Code letter B to E.............	250	175	700	200
Code letter A.................	150	150	700	150
All AC squirrel-cage and synchronous motors† with autotransformer starting:				
Not more than 30 amps				
No code letter	250	175	700	200
More than 30 amps				
No code letter	200	175	700	200
Code letter F to V.............	250	175	700	200
Code letter B to E.............	200	175	700	200
Code letter A	150	150	700	150
High-reactance squirrel-cage				
Not more than 30 amps				
No code letter	250	175	700	250
More than 30 amps				
No code letter	200	175	700	200
Wound-rotor—No code letter......................	150	150	700	150
Direct-current (constant voltage)				
No more than 50 hp				
No code letter	150	150	250	150
More than 50 hp				
No code letter	150	150	175	150

For explanation of Code Letter Marking, see Table 430-7(b).

For certain exceptions to the values specified, see Sections 430-52 through 430-54.

*The values given in the last column also cover the ratings of nonadjustable inverse time types of circuit breakers that may be modified as in Section 430-52.

†Synchronous motors of the low-torque, low-speed type (usually 450 rpm or lower), such as are used to drive reciprocating compressors, pumps, etc. that start unloaded, do not require a fuse rating or circuit-breaker setting in excess of 200 percent of full-load current.

plying with Sections 440-52(a)(2) and (b)(2) is used, the motor-compressor nameplate on the equipment nameplate shall be marked with the words "Thermally Protected." Where a protective system, complying with Sections 440-52(a)(4) and 440-52(b)(4), is used and is furnished with the equipment, the equipment nameplate shall be marked with the words, "Thermally Protected System." Where a protective system complying with Sections 440-52(a)(4) and 440-52(b)(4) is specified, the equipment nameplate shall be appropriately marked.

Definition: The rated-load current for a hermetic refrigerant motor-compressor is the current resulting when the motor-compressor is operated at the rated load, rated voltage and rated frequency of the equipment it serves.

(b) Multimotor and combination-load equipment shall be provided with a visible nameplate marked with the maker's name, the rating in volts, frequency and number of phases, minimum supply circuit conductor ampacity, and the maximum rating of the branch-circuit short-circuit and ground-fault protective device. The ampacity shall be calculated by using Part D and counting all the motors and other loads which will be operated at the same time. The branch-circuit short-circuit and ground-fault protective device rating shall not exceed the value calculated by using Part C. Multimotor or combination-load equipment for use on two or more circuits shall be marked with the above information for each circuit.

Exception No. 1: Multimotor and combination-load equipment which is suitable under the provisions of this Article for connection to a single 15- or 20-ampere, 120-volt, or a 15-ampere, 208- or 240-volt single-phase branch circuit shall be permitted to be marked as a single load.

Exception No. 2: Room air conditioners as provided in Part G of Article 440.

(c) Hermetic refrigerant motor-compressors or equipment containing such compressor(s) in which the protection system, approved for use with the motor-compressor which it protects, permits continuous current in excess of the specified percentage of nameplate rated-load current given in Section 440-52(b)(2) or (b)(4) shall also be marked with a branch-circuit selection current that complies with Section 440-52(b)(2) or (b)(4). This marking shall be provided by the equipment manufacturer and shall be on the nameplate(s) where the rated-load current(s) appear.

Definition: Branch-circuit selection current is the value in amperes to be used instead of the rated-load current in determining the ratings of motor branch-circuit conductors, disconnecting means, controllers and branch-circuit short-circuit and ground-fault protective devices wherever the running overload protective device permits a sustained current greater than the specified percentage of the rated-load current. The value of branch-circuit selection current will always be greater than the marked rated-load current.

440-4. Marking on Controllers. A controller shall be marked with the maker's name, trademark, or symbol; identifying designation; the voltage; phase; full-load and locked-rotor current (or horsepower) rating; and such other data as may be needed to properly indicate the motor-compressor for which it is suitable.

440-5. Ampacity and Rating. Ampacity of conductors and rating of equipment shall be determined as follows:

(a) For a hermetic refrigerant motor-compressor, the rated-load current marked on the nameplate of the equipment in which the motor-compressor is employed shall be used in determining the rating or ampacity of the disconnecting means, the branch-circuit conductors, the controller, the branch-circuit short-circuit and ground-fault protection, and the separate motor overload protection. Where no rated-load current is shown on the equipment nameplate, the rated-load current shown on the compressor nameplate shall be used. For disconnecting means and controllers, see also Sections 440-12 and 440-41.

Exception No. 1: When so marked, the branch-circuit selection current shall be used instead of the rated-load current to determine the rating or ampacity of the disconnecting means, the branch-circuit conductors, the controller, and the branch-circuit short-circuit and ground-fault protection.

Exception No. 2: As permitted in Section 440-22(b) for branch-circuit short-circuit and ground-fault protection of cord- and plug-connected equipment.

(b) For multimotor equipment employing a shaded-pole or permanent split-capacitor-type fan or blower motor, the full-load current for such motor marked on the nameplate of the equipment in which the fan or blower motor is employed shall be used instead of the horsepower rating to determine the ampacity or rating of the disconnecting means, the branch-circuit conductors, the controller, the branch-circuit short-circuit and ground-fault protection, and the separate overload protection. This marking on the equipment nameplate shall not be less than the current marked on the fan or blower motor nameplate.

440-6. Highest Rated (Largest) Motor. In determining compliance with this Article and with Sections 430-24, 430-53(b), 430-53(c), and 430-62(a), the highest rated (largest) motor shall be considered to be that motor which has the highest rated-load current. Where two or more motors have the same rated-load current, only one of them shall be considered as the highest rated (largest) motor. For other than hermetic refrigerant motor-compressors, and fan or blower motors as covered in Section 440-5(b), the full-load current used to determine the highest rated motor shall be the equivalent value corresponding to the motor horsepower rating selected from Table 430-148, 430-149, or 430-150.

Exception: When so marked the branch-circuit selection current shall be used instead of the rated-load current in determining the highest rated (largest) motor-compressor.

440-7. Single Machine. An air-conditioning or refrigerating system shall be considered to be a single machine under the provisions of Section 430-87 Exception and Section 430-112 Exception. The motors shall be permitted to be located remotely from each other.

B. Disconnecting Means

440-11. General. The provisions of Part B are intended to require disconnecting means capable of disconnecting air-conditioning and refrigerating equipment including motor-compressors, and controllers, from the circuit feeder. See Diagram 430-1(a).

440-12. Rating and Interrupting Capacity.

(a) A disconnecting means serving a hermetic refrigerant motor-compressor shall be selected on the basis of the nameplate rated-load current or branch-circuit selection current, whichever is greater, and locked-rotor current, respectively, of the motor-compressor as follows:

(1) The ampere rating shall be at least 115 percent of the nameplate rated-load current or branch-circuit selection current, whichever is greater.

(2) To determine the equivalent horsepower in complying with the requirements of Section 430-109, the horsepower rating shall be selected from Tables 430-148, 430-149, or 430-150 corresponding to the rated-load current or branch-circuit selection current, whichever is greater, and also the horsepower rating from Table 430-151 corresponding to the locked-rotor current. In case the nameplate rated-load current or branch-circuit selection current and locked-rotor current do not correspond to the currents shown in Tables 430-148, 430-149, 430-150, or 430-151, the horsepower rating corresponding to the next higher value shall be selected. In case different horsepower ratings are obtained when applying these Tables, a horsepower rating at least equal to the larger of the values obtained shall be selected.

(b) Where one or more hermetic refrigerant motor-compressors are used together or are used in combination with other motors and/or loads such as resistance heaters and where the combined load may be simultaneous on a single disconnecting means, the rating for the combined load shall be determined as follows:

(1) The horsepower rating of the disconnecting means shall be determined from the summation of all currents, including resistance loads, at the rated-load condition and also at the locked-rotor condition. The combined rated-load current and the combined locked-rotor current so obtained shall be considered as a single motor for the purpose of this requirement as follows:

a. The full-load current equivalent to the horsepower rating of each motor, other than a hermetic refrigerant motor-compressor, and fan or blower motors as covered in Section 440-5(b) shall be selected from Tables 430-148, 430-149, or 430-150. These full-load currents shall be added to the motor-compressor rated-load current(s) or branch-circuit selection current(s), whichever is greater, and to the rating in amperes of other loads to obtain an equivalent full-load current for the combined load.

b. The locked-rotor current equivalent to the horsepower rating of each motor, other than a hermetic refrigerant motor-compressor, shall be selected from Table 430-151, and for fan and blower motors of the shaded-pole or permanent split-capacitor type marked with the locked-rotor current, the marked value shall be used. The locked-rotor currents shall be added to the motor-compressor locked-rotor current(s) and to the rating in amperes of other loads to obtain an equivalent locked-rotor current for the combined load. Where two or more motors and/or other loads cannot be started simultaneously, appropriate combinations of locked-rotor and rated-load current or branch-circuit selection current, whichever is greater, shall be an acceptable means of determining the equivalent locked-rotor current for the simultaneous combined load.

Exception: Where part of the concurrent load is a resistance load and the disconnecting means is a switch rated in horsepower and amperes, the horsepower rating of the switch shall be not less than the combined load of the motor-compressor(s) and other motor(s) at the locked-rotor condition and the ampere rating shall be not less than this locked-rotor load plus the resistance load.

(2) The ampere rating of the disconnecting means shall be at least 115 percent of the summation of all currents at the rated-load condition determined in accordance with Section 440-12(b)(1).

(c) For small motor-compressors not having the locked-rotor current marked on the nameplate, or for small motors not covered by Tables 430-147, 430-148, 430-149, or 430-150, the locked-rotor current shall be assumed to be 6 times the rated-load current. See Section 440-3(a).

(d) Where the rated-load or locked-rotor current as determined above would indicate a disconnecting means rated in excess of 100 hp, the provisions of Section 430-109, Exception No. 4, shall apply.

440-13. Cord-Connected Equipment. For cord-connected equipment such as room air conditioners, household refrigerators and freezers, drinking water coolers and beverage dispensers, a separable connector or an attachment plug and receptacle shall be permitted to serve as the disconnecting means. See also Section 440-63.

440-14. Location. A disconnecting means shall be located within sight from and readily accessible from the air-conditioning or refrigerating equipment.

See Parts G and H of Article 430 for additional requirements.

C. Branch-Circuit Short-Circuit and Ground-Fault Protection

440-21. General. The provisions of Part C specify overcurrent devices intended to protect the branch-circuit conductors, control apparatus and motors in circuits supplying hermetic refrigerant motor-compressors against overcurrent due to short circuits and grounds. They are in addition to or amendatory of the provisions of Article 240.

440-22. Application and Selection.

(a) Rating or Setting for Individual Motor-Compressor. The motor-compressor branch-circuit short-circuit and ground-fault protective device shall be capable of carrying the starting current of the motor. The required protection shall be considered as being obtained when this device has a rating or setting not exceeding 175 percent of the motor-compressor rated-load current or branch-circuit selection current, whichever is greater (15 amperes size minimum); provided that where the protection specified is not sufficient for the starting current of the motor, it shall be permitted to be increased, but shall not exceed 225 percent of the motor rated-load current or branch-circuit selection current, whichever is greater.

(b) Rating or Setting for Equipment. The equipment branch-circuit short-circuit and ground-fault protective device shall be capable of carrying the starting current of the equipment. Where the hermetic refrigerant motor-compressor is the only load on the circuit, the protection shall conform with Section 440-22(a). Where the equipment incorporates more than one hermetic refrigerant motor-compressor or a hermetic refrigerant motor-compressor and other motors or other loads, the equipment protection shall conform with Section 430-53 and the following:

(1) Where a hermetic refrigerant motor-compressor is the largest load connected to the circuit, the rating or setting of the protective device shall not exceed the value specified in Section 440-22(a) for the largest motor-compressor plus the sum of the rated-load current or branch-circuit selection current, whichever is greater, of the other motor-compressor(s) and the ratings of the other loads supplied.

(2) Where a hermetic refrigerant motor-compressor is not the largest load connected to the circuit, the rating or setting of the protective device shall not exceed a value equal to the sum of the rated-load current or branch-circuit selection current, whichever is greater, rating(s) for the motor-compressor(s) plus the value specified in Section 430-53(c)(4) where other motor loads are supplied, or the value specified in Section 240-3 where only nonmotor loads are supplied in addition to the motor-compressor(s).

Exception No. 1: Equipment which will start and operate on a 15- or 20-ampere,

120-volt or 15-ampere, 208- or 240-volt, single-phase branch circuit shall be considered as protected by the 15- or 20-ampere overcurrent device protecting the branch circuit, but if the maximum circuit protective device rating marked on the equipment is less than these values, the circuit protective device shall not exceed the value marked on the equipment nameplate.

Exception No. 2: The nameplate marking of cord- and plug-connected equipment rated not greater than 250 volts, single-phase, such as household refrigerators and freezers, drinking-water coolers, and beverage dispensers shall be used in determining the branch-circuit requirements, and each unit shall be considered as a single motor unless the nameplate is marked otherwise.

(c) Where maximum protective device ratings shown on a manufacturer's heater table for use with a motor controller are less than the rating or setting selected in accordance with Sections 440-22(a) and (b), the protective device rating shall not exceed the manufacturer's values marked on the equipment.

D. Branch-Circuit Conductors

440-31. General. The provisions of Part D and Articles 300 and 310 specify sizes of conductors required to carry the motor current without overheating under the conditions specified, except as modified in Section 440-5(a), Exception no. 1.

The provisions of these Articles shall not apply to integral conductors of motors, motor controllers and the like, or to conductors which form an integral part of approved equipment.

See Sections 300-1(b) and 310-1 for similar requirements.

440-32. Single Motor-Compressor. Branch-circuit conductors supplying a single motor-compressor shall have an ampacity not less than 125 percent of either the motor-compressor rated-load current or the branch-circuit selection current, whichever is greater.

440-33. Motor-Compressor(s) With or Without Additional Motor Loads. Conductors supplying one or more motor-compressor(s) with or without additional motor load(s) shall have an ampacity not less than the sum of the rated-load or branch-circuit selection current ratings, whichever are larger, of all the motor-compressor(s) plus the full-load currents of the other motor(s), plus 25 percent of the highest motor or motor-compressor rating in the group.

Exception No. 1: When the circuitry is so interlocked as to prevent the starting and running of a second motor-compressor or group of motor-compressors, the conductor size shall be determined from the largest motor-compressor or group or motor-compressors that is to be operated at a given time.

Exception No. 2: Room Air Conditioners as provided in Part G of Article 440.

440-34. Combination Load. Conductors supplying a motor-compressor load in addition to a lighting or appliance load as computed from Article 220 and other applicable Articles, shall have an ampacity sufficient for the lighting or appliance load plus the required ampacity for the motor-compressor load determined in accordance with Section 440-33, or, for a single motor-compressor, in accordance with Section 440-32.

Exception: When the circuitry is so interlocked as to prevent simultaneous operation of the motor-compressor(s) and all other loads connected, the conductor size shall be determined from the largest size required for the motor-compressor(s) and other loads to be operated at a given time.

440-35. Multimotor and Combination-Load Equipment. The ampacity of the conductors supplying multimotor and combination-load equipment shall not be less than the minimum circuit ampacity marked on the equipment in accordance with Section 440-3(b).

E. Controllers for Motor-Compressors

440-41. Rating.

(a) A motor-compressor controller shall have both a continuous-duty full-load current rating, and a locked-rotor current rating, not less than the nameplate rated-load current or branch-circuit selection current, whichever is greater, and locked-rotor current, respectively (see Sections 440-5 and 440-6) of the compressor. In case the motor controller is rated in horsepower, but is without one or both of the foregoing current ratings, equivalent currents shall be determined from the ratings as follows: Use Table 430-148, 430-149, or 430-150 to determine the equivalent full-load current rating. Use Table 430-151 to determine the equivalent locked-rotor current rating.

(b) A controller, serving more than one motor-compressor or a motor-compressor and other loads, shall have a continuous-duty full-load current rating, and a locked-rotor current rating not less than the combined load as determined in accordance with Section 440-12(b).

F. Motor-Compressor and Branch-Circuit Overload Protection

440-51. General. The provisions of Part F specify devices intended to protect the motor-compressor, the motor-control apparatus, and the branch-circuit conductors against excessive heating due to motor overload and failure to start. (See Section 240-3(a), Exception No. 3.)

Note: Overload in electrically driven apparatus is an operating overcurrent which, when it persists for a sufficient length of time, would cause damage or dangerous overheating. It does not include short circuits or ground faults.

440-52. Application and Selection.

(a) Protection of Motor-Compressor. Each motor-compressor shall be protected against overload and failure to start by one of the following means:

(1) A separate overload relay which is responsive to motor-compressor current. This device shall be selected to trip at not more than 140 percent of the motor-compressor rated-load current.

(2) A thermal protector integral with the motor-compressor, approved for use with the motor-compressor which it protects, on the basis that it will prevent dangerous overheating of the motor-compressor due to overload and failure to start. If the current-interrupting device is separate from the motor-compressor and its control circuit is operated by a protective device integral with the motor-compressor, it shall be so arranged that the opening of the control circuit will result in interruption of current to the motor-compressor.

(3) A fuse or inverse time circuit breaker responsive to motor current, which

shall also be permitted to serve as the branch-circuit short-circuit and ground-fault protective device. This device shall be rated at not more than 125 percent of the motor-compressor rated-load current. It shall have sufficient time delay to permit the motor-compressor to start and accelerate its load. The equipment or the motor-compressor shall be marked with this maximum branch-circuit fuse or inverse time circuit breaker rating.

(4) A protective system, furnished or specified and approved for use with the motor-compressor which it protects on the basis that it will prevent dangerous overheating of the motor-compressor due to overload and failure to start. If the current interrupting device is separate from the motor-compressor and its control circuit is operated by a protective device which is not integral with the current-interrupting device, it shall be so arranged that the opening of the control circuit will result in interruption of current to the motor-compressor.

(b) Protection of Motor-Compressor Control Apparatus and Branch-Circuit Conductors. The motor-compressor controller(s), the disconnecting means and branch-circuit conductors shall be protected against overcurrent due to motor overload and failure to start by one of the following means which may be the same device or system protecting the motor-compressor in accordance with Section 440-52(a):

Exception: For motor-compressors and equipment on 15- or 20-ampere single-phase branch circuits as provided in Sections 440-54 and 440-55.

(1) An overload relay selected in accordance with Section 440-52(a)(1).

(2) A thermal protector applied in accordance with Section 440-52(a)(2) and which will not permit a continuous current in excess of 156 percent of the marked rated-load current or branch-circuit selection current.

(3) A fuse or inverse time circuit breaker selected in accordance with Section 440-52(a)(3).

(4) A protective system in accordance with Section 440-52(a)(4) and which will not permit a continuous current in excess of 156 percent of the marked rated-load current or branch-circuit selection current.

440-53. Overload Relays. Overload relays and other devices for motor overload protection, which are not capable of opening short circuits, shall be protected by fuses or inverse time circuit breakers with ratings or settings in accordance with Part C unless approved for group installation or for part-winding motors and marked to indicate the maximum size of fuse or inverse time circuit breaker by which they shall be protected.

Exception: The fuse or inverse time circuit breaker-size marking shall be permitted on the nameplate of approved equipment in which the overload relay or other overload device is used.

440-54. Motor-Compressors and Equipment on 15- or 20-Ampere Branch Circuits—Not Cord- and Attachment Plug-Connected. Overload protection for motor-compressors and equipment used on 15- or 20-ampere 120 volt, or 15-ampere 208- or 240-volt, single-phase branch circuits as permitted in Article 210, shall be permitted as indicated in (a) and (b) below:

(a) The motor-compressor shall be provided with overload protection selected as specified in Section 440-52(a). Both the controller and motor overload protective device shall be approved for installation with the short-circuit and ground-fault protective device for the branch circuit to which the equipment is connected.

(b) The short-circuit and ground-fault protective device protecting the branch circuit shall have sufficient time delay to permit the motor-compressor and other motors to start and accelerate their loads.

440-55. Cord-and-Attachment Plug-Connected Motor-Compressors and Equipment on 15- or 20-Ampere Branch Circuits. Overload protection for motor-compressors and equipment that are cord-and-attachment plug-connected and used on 15- or 20-ampere 120-volt, or 15-ampere 208- or 240-volt, single-phase branch circuits as permitted in Article 210, shall be permitted as indicated in (a), (b), and (c) below.

(a) The motor-compressor shall be provided with overload protection as specified in Section 440-52(a). Both the controller and the motor overload protective device shall be approved for installation with the short-circuit and ground-fault protective device for the branch circuit to which the equipment is connected.

(b) The rating of the attachment plug and receptacle shall not exceed 20 amperes at 125 volts or 15 amperes at 250 volts.

(c) The short-circuit and ground-fault protective device protecting the branch circuit shall have sufficient time delay to permit the motor-compressor and other motors to start and accelerate their loads.

G. Provisions For Room Air Conditioners

440-60. General. The provisions of Part G shall apply to electrically energized room air conditioners that control temperature and humidity. For the purpose of Part G, a room air conditioner (with or without provisions for heating) shall be considered as an alternating current appliance of the air cooled window, console, or in-wall type, that is installed in the conditioned room and which incorporates a hermetic refrigerant motor-compressor(s). The provisions of Part G cover equipment rated not over 250 volts, single phase, and such equipment shall be permitted to be cord-and-attachment plug-connected.

A room air conditioner that is rated 3 phase or rated over 250 volts shall be directly connected to a wiring method recognized in Chapter 3, and provisions of Part G shall not apply.

440-61. Grounding. Room air conditioners shall be grounded in accordance with Sections 250-42, 250-43, and 250-45.

440-62. Branch Circuit Requirements.

(a) A room air conditioner shall be considered as a single motor unit in determining its branch circuit requirements when all the following conditions are met:

(1) It is cord-and-attachment plug-connected.

(2) Its rating is not more than 40 amperes and 250 volts, single phase.

(3) Total rated-load current is shown on the room air conditioner nameplate rather than individual motor currents, and

(4) The rating of the branch-circuit short-circuit and ground-fault protective device does not exceed the ampacity of the branch-circuit conductors or the rating of the receptacle, whichever is less.

(b) The total marked rating of a cord-and-attachment plug-connected room air conditioner shall not exceed 80 percent of the rating of a branch circuit where no other loads are supplied.

(c) The total marked rating of a cord-and-attachment plug-connected room air conditioner shall not exceed 50 percent of the rating of a branch circuit where lighting units or other appliances are also supplied.

440-63. Disconnecting Means. An attachment plug and receptacle shall be permitted to serve as the disconnecting means for a single phase room air conditioner rated 250 volts or less if: (1) the manual controls on the room air conditioner are readily accessible and located within 6 feet of the floor, or (2) an approved manually operable switch is installed in a readily accessible location within sight from the room air conditioner.

440-64. Supply Cords. Where a flexible cord is used to supply a room air conditioner, the length of such cord shall not exceed: (1) 10 foot for a nominal 120 volt rating, or (2) 6 feet for a nominal 208 or 240 volt rating.

ARTICLE 445. GENERATORS

445-1. Scope. Generators and their associated wiring and equipment shall be considered to be separately derived systems and shall comply with the applicable provisions of Article 230, 250, 700, and 750.

445-2. Location. Generators shall be of a type suitable for the locations in which they are installed. They shall also meet the requirements for motors in Section 430-14. Generators installed in hazardous locations as described in Articles 500 through 503, or in other locations as described in Articles 510 through 517, and in Articles 520, 530, and 665 shall also comply with the applicable provisions of those Articles.

445-3. Marking. Each generator shall be provided with a nameplate giving the maker's name, the rated frequency, power factor, number of phases if of alternating current, the rating in kilowatts or kilovolt amperes, the normal volts and amperes corresponding to the rating, rated revolutions per minute, insulation system class and rated ambient temperature or rated temperature rise, and time rating.

445-4. Overcurrent Protection.

(a) Constant-Voltage Generators. Constant-voltage generators, except alternating-current generator exciters, shall be protected from overloads by inherent design, circuit breakers, fuses, or other acceptable current-limiting means, suitable for the conditions of use.

(b) Two-Wire Generators. Two-wire, direct-current generators shall be permitted to have overcurrent protection in one conductor only if the overcurrent device is actuated by the entire current generated other than the current in the shunt field. The overcurrent device shall not open the shunt field.

(c) 65 Volts or Less. Generators operating at 65 volts or less and driven by individual motors shall be considered as protected by the overcurrent device protecting the motor if these devices will operate when the generators are delivering not more than 150 percent of their full-load rated current.

(d) Balancer Sets. Two-wire, direct-current generators used in conjunction with balancer sets to obtain neutrals for 3-wire systems shall be equipped with overcurrent devices that will disconnect the 3-wire system in case of excessive unbalancing of voltages or currents.

(e) 3-Wire, Direct-Current Generators. Three-wire, direct-current generators, whether compound or shunt wound, shall be equipped with overcurrent devices, one in each armature lead, and so connected as to be actuated by the entire current from the armature. Such overcurrent devices shall consist either of a double-pole, double-coil circuit breaker, or of a 4-pole circuit breaker connected in the main and equalizer leads and tripped by two overcurrent devices, one in each armature lead. Such protective devices shall be so interlocked that no one pole can be opened without simultaneously disconnecting both leads of the armature from the system.

▲ Alternating-current generators can be so designed that on excessive overload the voltage falls off sufficiently to limit the current and power output to values that will not injure the generator during a short period of time. Whether or not automatic overcurrent protection of a generator should be omitted in any particular case is a question that can best be answered by the manufacturer of the generator. It is common practice to operate an exciter without overcurrent protection, rather than to risk the shutdown of the main generator due to accidental opening of the exciter fuse or circuit breaker.

Figure 445-1 shows the connections of a two-wire DC generator with a single-pole protective device. If the machine is operated in multiple with one or more other generators, and so has an equalizer lead connected to the positive terminal, the current may divide at the positive terminal, part passing through the series field and positive lead and part passing through the equalizer lead. The entire current generated passes through the negative lead; therefore the fuse or circuit breaker, or at least the operating coil of a circuit breaker, must be placed in the negative lead.

The protective device should not open the shunt-field circuit, because if this circuit were opened with the field at full strength, a very high voltage would be induced which might break down the insulation of the field winding.

Paragraph (c) is intended to apply particularly to generators used in electrolytic work. Where such a generator forms part of a motor-generator set, no fuse or circuit breaker is necessary in the generator leads if the motor-running protective device will open when the generator delivers 150 percent of its rated full-load current.

Each of the two generators used as a balancer set carries approximately one-half the unbalanced load; hence these two machines are always much smaller than the main generator. In case of an excessive unbalance of the load, the balancer set might

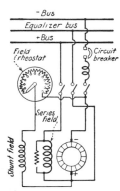

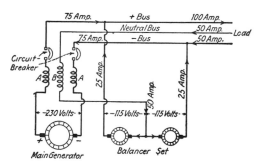

Fig. 445-1. Connections of a two-wire direct-current generator protected by a single-pole circuit breaker.

Fig. 445-2. Connection diagram of a balancer set used with a two-wire 230-volt generator to supply a three-wire system, showing (approximately) the currents flowing when the system supplies an unbalanced load of 100 amp on one side and 50 amp on the other side.

be overloaded while there is no overload on the main generator. This condition may be guarded against by installing a double-pole circuit breaker with one pole connected in each lead of the main generator and with the operating coil properly designed to be connected in the neutral of the three-wire system. (See Fig. 445-2. In this diagram, the circuit breaker is arranged so as to be operated by either one of the coils A in the leads from the main generator or by coil B in the neutral lead from the balancer set.)

445-5. Ampacity of Conductors. The conductors of the generator shall have an ampacity not less than 115 percent of the nameplate current rating of the generator. Neutral conductors shall be the same size as the conductors of the outside legs.

445-6. Protection of Live Parts. Live parts of generators of more than 150 volts to ground shall not be exposed to accidental contact where accessible to unqualified persons.

▲ As a general rule, no generator should be "accessible to unqualified persons." If necessary to place a generator operating at over 150 V to ground in a location where it is so exposed, the commutator or collector rings, brushes, and any exposed terminals should be provided with guards which will prevent any accidental contact with these live parts.

445-7. Guards for Attendants. Where necessary for the safety of attendants, the requirements of Section 430-133 shall apply.

445-8. Grounding. The frames of generators shall be grounded as specified in Section 250-26 when the system is required to be grounded by Section 250-5(d) and 250-6.

445-9. Bushings. Where wires pass through an opening in an enclosure, conduit box, or barrier, a bushing shall be used to protect the conductors from the edges of an opening having sharp edges. The bushing shall have smooth, well-rounded surfaces where it may be in contact with the conductors. If used where oils, grease, or other contaminants may be present, the bushing shall be made of a material not deleteriously affected.

ARTICLE 450. TRANSFORMERS AND TRANSFORMER VAULTS
(Including Secondary Ties)

450-1. Scope. This Article covers the installation of all transformers.

Exception No. 1: Current transformers.

Exception No. 2: Dry-type transformers that constitute a component part of other apparatus and comply with the requirements for such apparatus.

Exception No. 3: Transformers which are an integral part of an X-ray, high-frequency, or electrostatic-coating apparatus.

Exception No. 4: Transformers used with Class 2 and Class 3 circuits that comply with Article 725.

Exception No. 5: Transformers for sign and outline lighting that comply with Article 600.

Exception No. 6: Transformers for electric-discharge lighting that comply with Article 410.

Exception No. 7: Transformers used for power-limited fire protective signaling circuits that comply with Part C of Article 760.

This Article also covers the installation of transformers in hazardous locations as modified by Articles 501 through 503.

A. General Provisions

450-2. Location. Transformers and transformer vaults shall be readily accessible to qualified personnel for inspection and maintenance.

Exception No. 1: Dry-type transformers 600 volts or less, located in the open on walls, columns, or structures, shall not be required to be readily accessible.

Exception No. 2: Dry-type transformers not exceeding 600 volts and 50 kVA shall be permitted in fire-resistant hollow spaces of buildings not permanently closed in by structure and provided they meet the ventilation requirements of Section 450-8.

The location of oil-insulated transformers and transformer vaults is covered in Sections 450-24, 450-25, and 450-41; dry-type transformers, in Section 450-21; and askarel-insulated transformers, in Section 450-23.

450-3. Overcurrent Protection. Overcurrent protection shall comply with (a) through (c) below. As used in this section, the word "transformer" shall mean a transformer or polyphase bank of two or three single-phase transformers operating as a unit.

(a) Transformers Over 600 Volts.

(1) Primary. Each transformer over 600 volts shall be protected by an individual overcurrent device on the primary side. Where fuses are used, they shall be rated at not more than 150 percent of the rated primary current of the transformer. Where circuit breakers are used, they shall be set at not more than 300 percent of the rated primary current of the transformer.

Exception No. 1: Where 150 percent of the rated primary current of the transformer does not correspond to a standard rating of a fuse, the next higher standard rating shall be permitted.

Exception No. 2: An individual overcurrent device shall not be required where the primary circuit overcurrent device provides the protection specified in this Section.

Exception No. 3: As provided in (a)(2) below.

(2) Primary and Secondary. A transformer over 600 volts having an overcurrent device on the secondary side rated or set to open at not more than the values noted in Table 450-3(a)(2), or a transformer equipped with a coordinated thermal overload protection by the manufacturer, shall not be required to have an individual overcurrent device in the primary connection provided the primary feeder overcurrent device is rated or set to open at not more than the values noted in Table 450-3(a)(2).

(b) Transformers 600 Volts or Less.

(1) Primary. Each transformer 600 volts or less shall be protected by an individual overcurrent device on the primary side, rated or set at not more than 125 percent of the rated primary current of the transformer.

Exception No. 1: Where the rated primary current of a transformer is 9 amperes

Table 450-3(a)(2). Transformers Over 600 Volts.
Having Overcurrent Protection on the Primary and Secondary Sides.

	Maximum Overcurrent Device				
	Primary		Secondary		
	Over 600 Volts		Over 600 Volts		600 Volts or Below
Transformer Rated Impedance	Circuit Breaker Setting	Fuse Rating	Circuit Breaker Setting	Fuse Rating	Circuit Breaker Setting or Fuse Rating
Not more than 6%	600%	300%	300%	150%	250%
More than 6% and not more than 10%	400%	200%	250%	125%	250%

or more and 125 percent of this current does not correspond to a standard rating of a fuse or nonadjustable circuit breaker, the next higher standard rating described in Section 240-6 shall be permitted. Where the rated primary current is less than 9 amperes, an overcurrent device rated or set at not more than 167 percent of the primary current shall be permitted.

Where the rated primary current is less than 2 amperes, an overcurrent device rated or set at not more than 300% shall be permitted.

Exception No. 2: An individual overcurrent device shall not be required where the primary circuit overcurrent device provides the protection specified in this Section.

Exception No. 3: As provided in (b)(2) below.

(2) Primary and Secondary. A transformer 600 volts or less having an overcurrent device on the secondary side rated or set at not more than 125 percent of the rated secondary current of the transformer shall not be required to have an individual overcurrent device on the primary side if the primary feeder overcurrent device is rated or set at a current value not more than 250 percent of the rated primary current of the transformer.

A transformer 600 volts or less, equipped with coordinated thermal overload protection by the manufacturer and arranged to interrupt the primary current, shall not be required to have an individual overcurrent device on the primary side if the primary feeder overcurrent device is rated or set at a current value not more than 6 times the rated current of the transformer for transformers having not more than 6 percent impedance and not more than 4 times the rated current of the transformer for transformers having more than 6 but not more than 10 percent impedance.

Exception: Where the rated secondary current of a transformer is 9 amperes or more and 125 percent of this current does not correspond to a standard rating of a fuse or nonadjustable circuit breaker, the next higher standard rating described in Section 240-6 shall be permitted.

Where the rated secondary current is less than 9 amperes, an overcurrent device rated or set at not more than 167 percent of the rated secondary current shall be permitted.

(c) Potential (Voltage) Transformers. Potential transformers installed indoors or enclosed shall be protected with primary fuses.

▲ It should be understood that the overcurrent protection stated in Sec. 450-3 is for the transformers *only*. Such overcurrent protection will not necessarily protect the primary or secondary conductors or equipment connected on the secondary side of the transformer. Using overcurrent protection to the maximum values shown in Figs. 450-1 and 450-2 would require much larger conductors than the full-load current rating of the transformer (other than permitted in the 25-ft tap rule in Sec. 240-21, Exception 8). Accordingly, to avoid using oversized conductors, overcurrent devices should be selected at about 110 to 125 percent of the transformer full-load current rating. And when using such smaller overcurrent protection, devices should be of the time-delay type (on the primary side) to compensate for inrush currents which reach eight to ten times the full-load primary current of the transformer for about $\frac{1}{10}$ sec when energized initially.

In approaching a transformer installation it is best to use a one-line diagram, such as shown in Fig. 240-3. Then by applying the tap rules in Sec. 240-21 proper protection

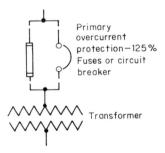

Primary overcurrent protection—125% Fuses or circuit breaker

Transformer

Fig. 450-1. Overcurrent protection of transformers 600 V or less with primary protection. See Section 450-3(b)(1).

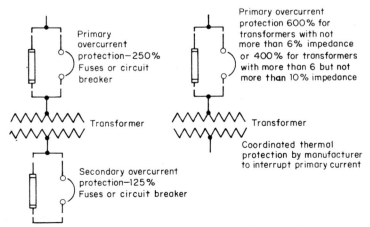

Primary overcurrent protection—250% Fuses or circuit breaker

Transformer

Secondary overcurrent protection—125% Fuses or circuit breaker

Primary overcurrent protection 600% for transformers with not more than 6% impedance or 400% for transformers with more than 6 but not more than 10% impedance

Transformer

Coordinated thermal protection by manufacturer to interrupt primary current

FIG. 450-2. Overcurrent protection of transformers 600 V or less with primary and secondary protection. See Section 450-3(b)(2).

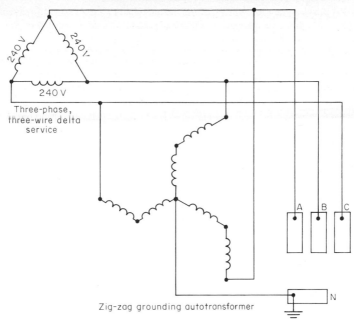

FIG. 450-3. Zig-zag autotransformer for establishing a ground reference.

of the conductors and equipment, which are part of the system, will be achieved. See comments following Sec. 240-21.

Sections 230-207 and 240-3, Exception 5 are the only code rules that consider properly sized primary overcurrent devices to protect the secondary conductors without secondary protection and no limit to the length of secondary conductors. The strict requirements in Sec. 230-207 apply where the transformers are in a *vault*, the primary load-interrupter switch is manually operable from outside the vault, and large secondary conductors are provided to achieve reflected protection through the transformer to the primary overcurrent protection.

Exception 5 to Sec. 240-3 applies where the primary and secondary each have a two-wire winding. (See comments following this exception and Sec. 240-21.)

450-4. Grounding Autotransformers.   Grounding autotransformers covered in this Section are zig-zag or T-connected transformers connected to 3-phase 3-wire ungrounded systems for the purpose of creating a 3-phase 4-wire distribution system or to provide a neutral reference for grounding purposes. Such transformers shall have a continuous per phase current rating and a continuous neutral current rating.

The phase current in a grounding autotransformer is one-third the neutral current.

(a) Three-Phase 4-Wire System.   A grounding autotransformer used to create a 3-phase 4-wire distribution system for a 3-phase 3-wire ungrounded system shall conform to the following:

(1) Connections.   The transformer shall be directly connected to the ungrounded phase conductors and shall not be switched or provided with overcurrent protection which is independent of the main switch and common-trip overcurrent protection for the 3-phase 4-wire system.

(2) Overcurrent Protection. An overcurrent sensing device shall be provided that will cause the main switch or common-trip overcurrent protection referred to in (a)(1) above to open if the load on the autotransformer reaches or exceeds 125 percent of its continuous current per phase or neutral rating. Delayed tripping for temporary overcurrents sensed at the autotransformer overcurrent device shall be permitted for the purpose of allowing proper operation of branch or feeder protective devices on the 4-wire system.

(3) Transformer Fault Sensing. A fault sensing system that will cause the opening of a main switch or common trip overcurrent device for the 3-phase 4-wire system shall be provided to guard against single-phasing or internal faults.

This can be accomplished by the use of two subtractive-connected donut-type current transformers installed to sense and signal when an unbalance occurs in the line current to the autotransformer of 50 percent or more of rated current.

(4) Rating. The autotransformer shall have a continuous neutral current rating sufficient to handle the maximum possible neutral unbalanced load current of the 4-wire system.

(b) Ground Reference for Fault Protection Devices. A grounding autotransformer used to make available a specified magnitude of ground fault current for operation of a ground responsive protective device on a 3-phase 3-wire ungrounded system shall conform to the following requirements:

(1) Rating. The autotransformer shall have a continuous neutral current rating sufficient for the specified ground fault current.

(2) Overcurrent Protection. An overcurrent protective device of adequate short-circuit rating that will open simultaneously all ungrounded conductors when it operates shall be applied in the grounding autotransformer branch circuit and rated or set at a current not exceeding 125 percent of the autotransformer continuous per phase current rating or 42 percent of the continuous current rating of any series connected devices in the autotransformer neutral connection. Delayed tripping for temporary overcurrents to permit the proper operation of ground responsive tripping devices on the main system shall be permitted, but shall not exceed values which would be more than the short-time current rating of the grounding autotransformer or any series connected devices in the neutral connection thereto.

(c) Ground Reference for Damping Transitory Overvoltages. A grounding autotransformer used to limit transitory overvoltages shall be of suitable rating and connected in accordance with (a)(1) above.

450-5. Secondary Ties. A secondary tie is a circuit operating at 600 volts or less between phases that connects two power sources or power supply points, such as the secondaries of two transformers. The tie may consist of one or more conductors per phase.

As used in this Section, the word "transformer" means a transformer or a bank of transformers operating as a unit.

(a) Tie Circuits. Tie circuits shall be provided with overcurrent protection at each end as required in Article 240.

Exception: Under the conditions described in (a)(1) and (a)(2) below, the over-current protection shall be permitted to be in accordance with (a)(3) below.

(1) Loads at Transformer Supply Points Only. Where all loads are connected at the transformer supply points at each end of the tie and overcurrent protection is not provided in accordance with Article 240, the rated ampacity of the tie shall not be less than 67 percent of the rated secondary current of the largest transformer connected to the secondary tie system.

(2) Loads Connected Between Transformer Supply Points. Where load is connected to the tie at any point between transformer supply points and overcurrent protection is not provided in accordance with Article 240, the rated ampacity of the tie shall not be less than 100 percent of the rated secondary current of the largest transformer connected to the secondary tie system.

Exception: As otherwise provided in (a)(4) below.

(3) Tie Circuit Protection. Under the conditions described in (a)(1) and (a)(2) above, both ends of each tie conductor shall be equipped with a protective device that will open at a predetermined temperature of the tie conductor under short-circuit conditions. This protection shall consist of one of the following: (1) a fusible link cable connector, terminal, or lug, commonly known as a limiter, each being of a size corresponding with that of the conductor and of construction and charac-teristics according to the operating voltage and the type of insulation on the tie conductors, or (2) automatic circuit breakers actuated by devices having comparable current-time characteristics.

(4) Interconnection of Phase Conductors Between Transformer Supply Points. Where the tie consists of more than one conductor per phase, the conductors of each phase shall be interconnected in order to establish a load supply point, and the protection specified in (a)(3) above shall be provided in each tie conductor at this point.

Exception: Loads shall be permitted to be connected to the individual conductors of a paralleled conductor tie without interconnecting the conductors of each phase and without the protection specified in (a)(3) above at load connection points provided the tie conductors of each phase have a combined capacity of not less than 133 percent of the rated secondary current of the largest transformer connected to the secondary tie system; the total load of such taps does not exceed the rated secondary current of the largest transformer; and the loads are equally divided on each phase and on the individual conductors of each phase as far as practicable.

(5) Tie Circuit Control. Where the operating voltage exceeds 150 volts to ground, secondary ties provided with limiters shall have a switch at each end, that when open, will de-energize the associated tie conductors and limiters. The current rating of the switch shall not be less than the rated current of the conductors connected to the switch. It shall be capable of opening its rated current, and it shall be constructed so that it will not open under the magnetic forces resulting from short-circuit current.

(b) Overcurrent Protection for Secondary Connections. Where secondary ties are used, an overcurrent device rated or set at not more than 250 percent of the rated secondary current of the transformers shall be provided in the secondary connections of each transformer. In addition, an automatic circuit breaker actuated by a reverse-current relay set to open the circuit at not more than the rated secondary current of the transformer shall be provided in the secondary connection of each transformer.

▲ In industrial plants having very heavy power loads it is usually economical to install a number of large transformers at various locations within each building, the transformers being supplied by primary feeders operating at voltages up to 13,800 V. One of the secondary systems that may be used in such cases is the network system.

The term *network system* as commonly used is applied to any secondary distribution system in which the secondaries of two or more transformers at different locations are connected together by secondary ties. The purpose of the system is to equalize the loading of the transformers, to reduce voltage drop, and to ensure continuity of service. The use of this system introduces certain complications, and, to ensure successful operation, the system must be designed by an experienced electrical engineer.

The protection required at each transformer is shown in Fig. 450-4. The provisions of Sec. 450-3 govern the protection in the primary.

The network protector consists of a circuit breaker and a reverse-power relay. The protector is necessary because without this device, if a fault develops in the transformer, or, in some cases, in the primary feeder, power will be fed back to the fault from the other transformers through the secondary ties. The relay is set to trip the breaker on a reverse-power current not greater than the rated secondary current of the transformer. This breaker is not arranged to be tripped by an overload on the secondary of the transformer.

Section 450-5(a)(3) provides that:

1. Where two or more conductors are installed in parallel, an individual protective device is provided at each end of each conductor.

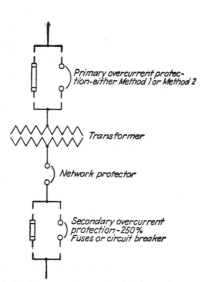

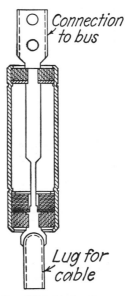

FIG. 450-4. Overcurrent protection of a transformer—network system.

FIG. 450-5. Limiter for protection of secondary ties in a network system. (*Westinghouse Electric Corp.*)

2. The protective device (fusible link or circuit breaker) does not provide overload protection, but provides short-circuit protection only.

In case of a short circuit, the protective device must open the circuit before the conductor reaches a temperature that would injure its insulation. The principles involved are that the entire system is so designed that the tie conductors will never be continuously overloaded in normal operation—hence protection against overloads of less severity than short circuits is not necessary—and that the protective devices should not open the circuit and thus cause an interruption of service on load peaks of such short duration that the conductors do not become overheated.

A limiter is a special type of fuse having a very high interrupting capacity. Figure 450-5 is a cross-sectional view of one type of limiter. The cable lug, the fusible section, and the extension for connection to the bus are all made in one piece from a length of copper tubing, and the enclosing case is also copper. It is stated that this device will interrupt a current of 50,000 A without perceptible noise and without the escape of flame or gases from the case.

Figure 450-6 is a single-line diagram of a simple three-phase industrial-plant network

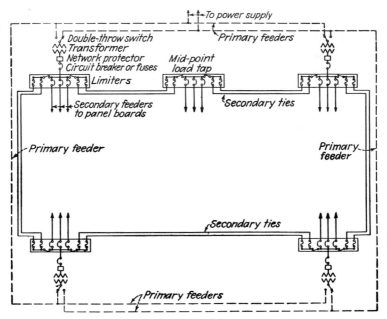

Fig. 450-6. A simple industrial-plant network system.

system. The primary feeders may operate at any standard voltage up to 13,800 V, and the secondary voltage would commonly be 480 V. The rating of the transformers used in such a system would usually be within the range of 300 to 1,000 kVA. The diagram shows two primary feeders, both of which are carried to each transformer so that by means of a double-throw switch each transformer can be connected to either feeder. Each feeder would be large enough to carry the entire load. It is assumed that the feeders are protected in accordance with Sec. 450-3(b)(2) so that no primary overcurrent devices are required at the transformers. The secondary ties consist of two conductors in multiple per phase and it will be noted that these conductors form a closed loop. Switches are provided so that any section of the loop, including the limiters protecting that section, can be isolated in case repairs or replacements should be necessary.

450-6. Parallel Operation. Transformers shall be permitted to be operated in parallel and switched as a unit provided that the overcurrent protection for each transformer meets the requirements of Section 450-3.

▲ To operate satisfactorily in parallel, transformers should have the same percentage impedance and the same ratio of reactance to resistance. Information on these characteristics should be obtained from the manufacturer of the transformers.

450-7. Guarding. Transformers shall be guarded as specified in (a) through (d) below.

(a) Mechanical Protection. Appropriate provisions shall be made to minimize the possibility of damage to transformers from external causes where the transformers are exposed to physical damage.

(b) Case or Enclosure. Dry-type transformers shall be provided with a noncombustible moisture-resistant case or enclosure that will provide reasonable protection against the accidental insertion of foreign objects.

(c) Exposed Live Parts. Transformers shall be so installed that live parts are guarded in accordance with Section 110-17.

(d) Voltage Warning. The operating voltage of exposed live parts of transformer installations shall be indicated by signs or visible markings on the equipment or structures.

450-8. Ventilation. The ventilation shall be adequate to dispose of the transformer full-load losses without creating an excessive ambient temperature.

See ANSI C57.12.00-1968—General Requirements for Distribution, Power, and Regulating Transformers and Shunt Reactors.

450-9. Grounding. Exposed noncurrent-carrying metal parts of transformer installations, including fences, guards, etc., shall be grounded where required under the conditions and in the manner specified for electric equipment and other exposed metal parts in Article 250.

450-10. Marking. Each transformer shall be provided with a nameplate giving the name of the manufacturer; rated kilovolt-amperes; frequency; primary and secondary voltage; impedance of transformers 25 kVA and larger; and the amount and kind of insulating liquid where used. In addition, the nameplate of each dry-type transformer shall include the temperature class for the insulation system.

▲ Article 220 provides a means of establishing the loads in buildings, and where the supply is derived from a transformer, it must be assumed that the transformer would need to be of sufficient capacity to carry this connected load.

B. Specific Provisions Applicable to Different Types of Transformers

450-21. Dry-Type Transformers Installed Indoors. Transformers installed indoors and rated $112\frac{1}{2}$ kVA or less shall have a separation of at least 12 inches from combustible material unless separated therefrom by a fire-resistant heat-insulating barrier, or unless of a rating not over 600 volts and completely enclosed except for ventilating openings.

Transformers of more than $112\frac{1}{2}$ kVA rating shall be installed in a transformer room of fire-resistant construction.

Exception No. 1: Transformers constructed with Class 80°C rise or higher insulation and separated from combustible material by a fire-resistant heat-insulating barrier or by not less than 6 feet horizontally and 12 feet vertically.

Exception No. 2: Transformers constructed with Class 80°C rise or higher insulation and of completely enclosed and ventilated type construction.

Transformers rated over 35,000 volts shall be installed in a vault complying with Part C of this Article.

▲ Dry-type transformers are those in which the windings are not immersed in any liquid. Transformers of this type of less than $112\frac{1}{2}$ kVA rating are quite commonly used in large industrial plants to supply lighting at 115 V, the primaries being connected to a power system operating at 480 V.

Where transformers of larger sizes are installed indoors and the primary voltage is not over 35,000 V, either the dry type or the askarel-filled type (see Sec. 450-23) is often preferred because no transformer vault is required.

Figure 450-7 shows the core and coil assembly of a 500-kVA three-phase dry-type transformer having a primary voltage rating of 13,800 V with a secondary voltage of 480 V. Figure 450-8 is a view of the transformer with the outside casing in place. The coils are cooled by circulation of air through the open spaces at the bottom of the casing and the louvers near the top. The lever shown in Fig. 450-8 operates a primary

FIG. 450-7. Core and coil assembly of a 500-kVA dry-type transformer. (*Westinghouse Electric Corp.*)

feeder-selector switch, i.e., a three-pole double-throw switch by means of which the primary of the transformer can be connected to either one of two feeders.

Dry-type transformers of over 112½ kVA rating are usually constructed with a 220° insulation system rated 150° average rise by resistance, which consists of mica, asbestos, fiberglass, and similar inorganic materials in built-up form, having organic building substances. Although mica, asbestos, and fiberglass are practically noncombustible, in using these materials as transformer insulation it is necessary to use some binder material, such as varnish, which may be combustible. If a fault should develop in the transformer, it is possible that some flame might escape from the enclosure for a short time. It is therefore necessary that the transformers be kept well away from any combustible part of the building structure or that a barrier of noncombustible material be provided.

FIG. 450-8. Dry-type transformer shown in Fig. 450-7 with outside casing in place. (*Westinghouse Electric Corp.*)

450-22. Dry-Type Transformers Installed Outdoors.   Dry-type transformers installed outdoors shall have a weatherproof enclosure.

450-23. Askarel-Insulated Transformers Installed Indoors.   Askarel-insulated transformers installed indoors and rated over 25 kVA shall be furnished with a pressure-relief vent. Where installed in a poorly ventilated place, they shall be furnished with a means for absorbing any gases generated by arcing inside the case, or the pressure relief vent shall be connected to a chimney or flue that will carry such gases outside the building. Askarel-insulated transformers rated over 35,000 volts shall be installed in a vault.

▲ See definition of "askarel" in Art. 100.

The use of oil-filled transformers involves some fire hazard, which can be avoided by using a nonflammable liquid in place of oil. As in the case of dry-type transformers, no vault is required for an askarel-filled transformer if the primary voltage is not over 35,000 V. Considerable economy can often be effected by locating a transformer of one or the other of these two types close to a heavy load, thus avoiding the use of long secondary feeders of large size.

450-24. Oil-Insulated Transformers Installed Indoors. Oil-insulated transformers installed indoors shall be installed in a vault constructed as specified in Part C of this Article.

Exception No. 1: Where the total capacity does not exceed 112½ kVA, the vault specified in Part C of this Article shall be permitted to be constructed of reinforced concrete not less than 4 inches thick.

Exception No. 2: Where the voltage does not exceed 600, a vault shall not be required if suitable arrangements are made to prevent a transformer oil fire from igniting other materials; and the total capacity in one location does not exceed 10 kVA in a section of the building classified as combustible, or 75 KVA where the surrounding structure is classified as fire-resistant construction.

Exception No. 3: Electric furnace transformers having a total rating not exceeding 75 kVa shall be permitted to be installed without a vault in a building or room of fire-resistant construction provided suitable arrangements are made to prevent a transformer oil fire from spreading to other combustible material.

Exception No. 4: Transformers shall be permitted to be installed in a detached building that does not comply with Part C of this Article if neither the building nor its contents present a fire hazard to any other building or property, and if the building is used only in supplying electric service and the interior is accessible only to qualified persons.

450-25. Oil-Insulated Transformers Installed Outdoors. Combustible material, combustible buildings and parts of buildings, fire escapes, and door and window openings shall be safeguarded from fires originating in oil-insulated transformers installed on roofs, attached to, or adjacent to a building or combustible material.

Space separations, fire-resistant barriers, automatic water spray systems, and enclosures that confine the oil of a ruptured transformer tank are recognized safeguards. One or more of these safeguards shall be applied according to the degree of hazard involved in cases where the transformer installation presents a fire hazard.

Oil enclosures shall be permitted to consist of fire-resistant dikes, curbed areas or basins, or trenches filled with coarse crushed stone. Oil enclosures shall be provided with trapped drains where the exposure and the quantity of oil involved are such that removal of oil is important. Transformers installed on poles or structures or underground shall conform to the National Electrical Safety Code, ANSI C2-1973.

C. Transformer Vaults

450-41. Location. Vaults shall be located where they can be ventilated to the outside air without using flues or ducts wherever such an arrangement is practicable.

450-42. Walls, Roof and Floor. The walls and roofs of vaults shall be constructed of materials which have adequate structural strength for the conditions with a minimum fire resistance of 3 hours according to ASTM Standard E119-71; Fire Tests of Building Construction and Materials; (NFPA No. 251-1972, also Methods of Fire Tests of Building Construction and Materials, ANSI A2.1-1972). The floors of vaults in contact with the earth shall be of concrete not less than 4 inches thick, but when the vault is constructed with a vacant space or other stories below it, the floor shall have adequate structural strength for the load imposed thereon and a minimum fire resistance of 3 hours.

Six inch thick reinforced concrete is a typical 3-hour construction.

450-43. Doorways. Vault doorways shall be protected as follows:

(a) Type of Door. Each doorway leading into a vault from the building interior shall be provided with a tight fitting door having a minimum fire rating of 3 hours as defined in the Standard for the Installation of Fire Doors and Windows (NFPA No. 80-1973). The authority having jurisdiction shall be permitted to require such a door for an exterior wall opening where conditions warrant.

For further information, see Standard for the Installation of Fire Doors and Windows (NFPA No. 80-1970) for definition of Class A situations.

(b) Sills. A door sill or curb of sufficient height to confine within the vault the oil from the largest transformer shall be provided, and in no case shall the height be less than 4 inches.

(c) Locks. Entrance doors shall be equipped with locks, and doors shall be kept locked, access being allowed only to qualified persons. Locks and latches shall be so arranged that the door can be readily and quickly opened from the inside.

▲ **The purpose of a transformer vault is to isolate the transformers and other apparatus. and to confine any fire that might be caused by the failure of any of the apparatus. It is important that the door as well as the remainder of the enclosure be of proper construction and that a substantial lock be provided.**

450-45. Ventilation Openings. Where required by Section 450-8, openings for ventilation shall be provided in accordance with (a) through (f) below.

(a) Location. Ventilation openings shall be located as far away as possible from doors, windows, fire escapes, and combustible material.

(b) Arrangement. A vault ventilated by natural circulation of air shall be permitted to have roughly half of the total area of openings required for ventilation in one or more openings near the floor and the remainder in one or more openings in the roof or in the sidewalls near the roof; or all of the area required for ventilation shall be permitted in one or more openings in or near the roof.

(c) Size. For a vault ventilated by natural circulation of air to an outdoor area, the combined net area of all ventilating openings after deducting the area occupied by screens, gratings, or louvers shall not be less than 3 square inches per kVA of transformer capacity in service, and in no case shall the net area be less than one square foot for any capacity under 50 kVA.

(d) Covering. Ventilation openings shall be covered with durable gratings, screens, or louvers, according to the treatment required in order to avoid unsafe conditions.

(e) Dampers. All ventilation openings to the indoors shall be provided with automatic closing dampers of not less than No. 10 MSG steel that operate in response to a vault fire.

(f) Ducts. Ventilating ducts shall be constructed of fire-resistant material.

450-46. Drainage. Where practicable, vaults containing more than 100-kVA transformer capacity shall be provided with a drain or other means that will carry off any accumulation of oil or water in the vault unless local conditions make this impracticable. The floor shall be pitched to the drain where provided.

450-47. Water Pipes and Accessories. Any pipe or duct system, foreign to the electrical installation shall not enter or pass through a transformer vault. Piping or other facilities provided for fire protection or for water cooled transformers shall not be considered foreign to the electrical installation.

Exception: By special permission, pipe or duct systems foreign to the electrical installation that do not contain appurtenances thereto that require maintenance shall be permitted to be installed in the transformer vault.

450-48. Storage in Vaults. Materials shall not be stored in transformer vaults.

ARTICLE 460. CAPACITORS

460-1. Scope. This Article covers the installation of capacitors on electric circuits.

Surge capacitors or capacitors included as a component part of other apparatus and conforming with the requirements of such apparatus are excluded from these requirements.

This Article also covers the installation of capacitors in hazardous locations as modified by Articles 501 through 503.

▲ The following sections apply chiefly to capacitors used for the power-factor correction of electric-power installations in industrial plants and for correcting the power factors of individual motors. These provisions apply only to capacitors used for surge protection, as such capacitors are not component parts of other apparatus.

In an industrial plant using induction motors, the power factor may be considerably less than 100 percent, particularly when all or part of the motors operate most of the time at much less than their full load. The lagging current can be counteracted and the power factor improved by installing capacitors across the line. By raising the power factor, for the same actual power delivered the current is decreased in the generator, transformers, and lines, up to the point where the capacitor is connected.

Figure 460-1 shows a capacitor assembly designed for connection to the main power circuit of a small industrial plant. Figure 460-2 is a diagram of the connections. An externally operable switch mounted on the wall is used as the disconnecting means and the discharge device required by Sec. 460-6 consists of two high-impedance coils inside the switch enclosure which consume only a small amount of power, but, having a comparatively low DC resistance, permit the charge to drain off rapidly after the capacitor assembly has been disconnected from the line.

460-2. Enclosing and Guarding.

(a) Capacitors containing more than 3 gallons of flammable liquid shall be enclosed in vaults or outdoor fenced enclosures complying with Article 710.

(b) Capacitors shall be enclosed, located, or guarded so that persons cannot come into accidental contact or bring conducting materials into accidental contact with exposed energized parts, terminals, or buses associated with them.

Exception: No additional guarding is required for enclosures accessible only to authorized and qualified persons.

FIG. 460-1. Three-phase capacitor assembly rated at 45 kVA, 230 V, or 90 kVA, 460 V, with front cover plate removed. (*General Electric Co.*)

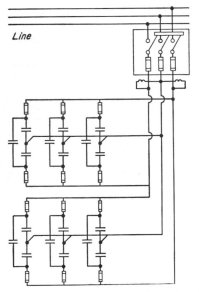

FIG. 460-2. Diagram of connections of capacitor assembly shown in Fig. 460-1.

FIG. 460-3. One unit of the capacitor assembly shown in Fig. 460-1. Each unit is internally delta-connected three-phase.

460-6. Drainage of Stored Charge. Capacitors shall be provided with a means of draining the stored charge.

(a) Time of Discharge. The residual voltage of a capacitor shall be reduced to 50 volts or less within one minute after the capacitor is disconnected from the source of supply.

(b) Means of Discharge. The discharge circuit shall be either permanently connected to the terminals of the capacitor or capacitor bank, or provided with automatic means of connecting it to the terminals of the capacitor bank on removal of voltage from the line. Manual means of switching or connecting the discharge circuit shall not be used.

▲ If no means were provided for draining off the charge stored in a capacitor after it is disconnected from the line, a severe shock might be received by a person servicing the equipment or the equipment might be damaged by a short circuit.

If a capacitor is permanently connected to the windings of a motor, as in Fig. 460-4, the stored charge will drain off rapidly through the windings when the circuit is opened. Reactors or resistors used as discharge devices must either be permanently connected across the terminals of the capacitor or a device must be provided that will automatically connect the discharge devices when the capacitor is disconnected from the source of supply.

460-7. Power Factor Correction—Motor Circuit. The total kVAr rating of capacitors that are connected on the load side of a motor controller shall not exceed the value required to raise the no-load power factor of the motor to unity.

460-8. Conductors.

(a) Ampacity. The ampacity of capacitor circuit conductors shall not be less than 135 percent of the rated current of the capacitor. The ampacity of conductors that connect a capacitor to the terminals of a motor or to motor circuit conductors shall not be less than $\frac{1}{3}$ the ampacity of the motor circuit conductors and in no case less than 135 percent of the rated current of the capacitor.

(b) Overcurrent Protection.

(1) An overcurrent device shall be provided in each ungrounded conductor for each capacitor bank.

Exception: A separate overcurrent device shall not be required for a capacitor connected on the load side of a motor-running overcurrent device.

(2) The rating or setting of the overcurrent device shall be as low as practicable.

(c) Disconnecting Means.

(1) A disconnecting means shall be provided in each ungrounded conductor for each capacitor bank.

Exception: Where a capacitor is connected on the load side of a motor running overcurrent device.

(2) The disconnecting means shall not be required to open all ungrounded conductors simultaneously.

(3) The disconnecting means shall be permitted to disconnect the capacitor from the line as a regular operating procedure.

(4) The rating of the disconnecting means shall not be less than 135 percent of the rated current of the capacitor.

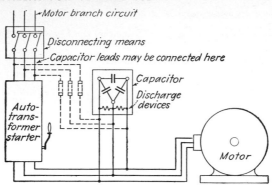

FIG. 460-4. Individual capacitor used to correct the power factor of a motor.

▲ Figure 460-4 shows a capacitor used to correct the power factor of a single motor. The capacitor may be connected to the motor circuit between the starter and the motor or may be connected between the disconnecting means and the starter, as indicated by the dotted lines in the diagram, and in either case no switch is required in the capacitor leads; however, if connected as shown by the dotted lines, an overcurrent device must be provided in these leads. The capacitor is shown as having discharge devices consisting in this case of resistors, though when connected as shown by the solid lines in the diagram, no discharge coils or resistors are required because the capacitor discharges through the motor windings.

Capacitors of the type to which Sec. 460-8 applies are commonly rated in kilovoltamperes, or the rating may be in "kilovars," meaning "reactive kilovoltamperes," abbreviated kvar. The capacitors are usually designed for connection to a three-phase system and constructed as a unit with three leads brought out.

The current corresponding to the kilovoltampere rating of a capacitor is computed in the same manner as for a motor or other load having the same rating in kilovoltamperes. Thus, the capacitor assembly shown in Fig. 460-1, used at 460 V, has a rating of 90 kVA and the current rating is $90,000/(460 \times 1.73) = 113$ A. The minimum required ampacity of the conductors would be 1.35×113 A, or 153 A.

The manufacturing standards for capacitors for power-factor correction call for a rating tolerance of " -0, $+15$ percent," meaning that the actual rating in kilovoltamperes is never below the nominal rating and may be as much as 15 percent higher. Thus, a capacitor having a nameplate rating of 100 kVA might actually draw a current corresponding to 115 kVA. The current drawn by a capacitor varies directly with the line voltage, so that, if the line voltage is higher than the rated voltage, the current will be correspondingly increased. Also, any variation of the line voltage from a pure sine wave form will cause a capacitor to draw an increased current. It is for these reasons that the conductors leading to a capacitor are required to have an ampacity not less than 135 percent of the rated current of the capacitor.

When a capacitor is thrown on the line, it may momentarily draw an excess current. A rating or setting of 250 percent of the capacitor current rating will provide short-circuit protection. Being a fixed load, a capacitor does not need overload protection such as is necessary for a motor.

A capacitor is a good example of a "continuous" load; i.e., it will draw at least its full rated current all the time it is connected to the line. If the rated current of a capacitor is 74 A, to comply with the rule, a switch used as the disconnecting means would have to be capable of carrying a load of 100 A continuously without overheating.

460-9. Rating or Setting of Motor-Running Overcurrent Device. Where a motor installation includes a capacitor connected on the load side of the motor-running overcurrent device, the rating or setting of the motor overcurrent device shall be determined in accordance with Section 430-32.

Exception: Instead of using the full-load rated current of the motor as provided in Section 430-32, a lower value corresponding with the improved power factor of the motor circuit shall be used. Section 430-22 applies with respect to the rating of the motor circuit conductors.

▲ If a capacitor is connected to a motor circuit as shown by the full lines in Fig. 460-4, the current passing through the overcurrent units, or relays, in the autotransformer starter is the reduced current corresponding with the improved power factor; and if the relays are rated at 125 percent of the full-load motor current (see Sec. 430-32), the motor will not be properly protected.

460-10. Grounding. Capacitor cases shall be grounded in accordance with Article 250.

Exception: Where the capacitor units are supported on a structure which is designed to operate at other than ground potential.

460-12. Marking. Each capacitor shall be provided with a nameplate giving the name of the manufacturer, rated voltage, frequency, kVAr or amperes, number of phases, and, if filled with a combustible liquid, the amount of liquid in gallons. When filled with a nonflammable liquid, the nameplate shall so state. The nameplate shall also indicate if a capacitor has a discharge device inside the case.

B. Over 600 Volts, Nominal

460-24. Switching.

(a) Load Current. Group-operated switches shall be used for capacitor switching and shall be capable of (1) carrying continuously not less than 135 percent of the rated current of the capacitor installation; (2) interrupting the maximum continuous load current of each capacitor, capacitor bank, or capacitor installation that will be switched as a unit; (3) withstanding the maximum inrush current, including contributions from adjacent capacitor installations; (4) carrying currents due to faults on capacitor side of switch.

(b) Isolation.

(1) A means shall be installed to isolate from all sources of potential each capacitor, capacitor bank, or capacitor installation that will be removed from service as a unit.

(2) The isolating means shall provide a visible gap in the electrical circuit adequate for the operating voltage.

(3) Isolating or disconnecting switches (with no interrupting rating) shall be interlocked with the load interrupting device or shall be provided with prominently displayed caution signs in accordance with Section 710-22 to prevent switching load current.

(c) Additional Requirements for Series Capacitors. The proper switching sequence shall be assured by use of one of the following: (1) mechanically sequenced isolating and bypass switches; (2) interlocks, or (3) switching procedure prominently displayed at the switching location.

460-25. Overcurrent Protection.

(a) A means shall be provided to detect and interrupt fault current likely to cause dangerous pressure within an individual capacitor.

(b) Single-phase or multiphase devices shall be permitted for this purpose.

(c) Capacitors may be protected individually or in groups.

(d) Protective devices for capacitors or capacitor equipment shall be rated or adjusted to operate within the limits of the Safe Zone for individual capacitors as defined by ANSI Standard for Shunt Power Capacitors, C-55.1-1968.

Exception: If the protective devices are rated or adjusted to operate within the limits of the ANSI Standard for Zone 1 or Zone 2, the capacitors shall be enclosed or isolated.

In no event shall the rating or adjustment of the protective devices exceed the maximum limit of the ANSI Standard, Zone 2.

460-26. Identification. Each capacitor shall be provided with a permanent nameplate giving the maker's name, rated voltage, frequency, kVAr or amperes, number of phases, and the amount of liquid in gallons identified as flammable, if such is the case.

460-27. Grounding. Capacitor neutrals and cases, if grounded, shall be grounded in accordance with Article 250.

Exception: Where the capacitor units are supported on a structure which is designed to operate at other than ground potential.

460-28. Means for Discharge.

(a) A means shall be provided to reduce the residual voltage of a capacitor to 50 volts or less within 5 minutes after the capacitor is disconnected from the source of supply.

(b) A discharge circuit shall be either permanently connected to the terminals of the capacitor or provided with automatic means of connecting it to the terminals of the capacitor bank after disconnection of the capacitor from the source of supply. The windings of motors, or transformers, or of other equipment directly connected to capacitors without a switch or overcurrent device interposed must meet the requirements of (a) above.

ARTICLE 470. RESISTORS AND REACTORS

For Rheostats, See Section 430-82

A. 600 Volts, Nominal and Under

470-1. Scope. This Article covers the installation of separate resistors and reactors on electric circuits.

Exception: Resistors and reactors that are component parts of other apparatus.

This Article also covers the installation of resistors and reactors in hazardous locations as modified by Articles 501 through 503.

470-2. Location. Resistors and reactors shall not be placed where exposed to physical damage.

470-3. Space Separation. A thermal barrier shall be required if the space between the resistors and reactors and any combustible material is less than 12 inches.

470-4. Conductor Insulation. Insulated conductors used for connections between resistance elements and controllers shall be suitable for an operating temperature of not less than 90°C (194°F).

Exception: Other conductor insulations shall be permitted for motor starting service.

▲ Except when installed in connection with switchboards or control panels that are so located that they are suitably guarded from physical damage and accidental contact with live parts, resistors should always be completely enclosed in properly ventilated metal boxes.

Large reactors are commonly connected in series with the main leads of large generators or the supply conductors from high-capacity network systems to assist in limiting the current delivered on short circuit. Small reactors are used with lightning arresters, the object here being to offer a high impedance to the passage of a high-frequency lightning discharge and so to aid in directing the discharge to ground. Another type of reactor, having an iron core and closely resembling a transformer, is used as a remote-control dimmer for stage lighting. Reactors as well as resistors are sources of heat and should therefore be mounted in the same manner as resistors.

B. Over 600 Volts, Nominal

470-18. General.

(a) Resistors and reactors shall be protected against physical damage.

(b) Resistors and reactors shall be isolated by enclosure or elevation to protect personnel from accidental contact with energized parts.

(c) Resistors and reactors shall not be installed in close enough proximity to combustible materials to constitute a fire hazard and in no case closer than within one foot of combustible materials.

(d) Clearances from resistors and reactors to grounded surfaces shall be adequate for the voltage involved.

See Article 710.

(e) Metallic enclosures of reactors and adjacent metal parts shall be installed so that the temperature rise from induced circulating currents will not be hazardous to personnel or constitute a fire hazard.

470-19. Grounding. Resistor and reactor cases or enclosures shall be grounded in accordance with Article 250.

470-20. Oil-Filled Reactors. Installation of oil-filled reactors, in addition to the above requirements, shall comply with applicable requirements of Article 450.

ARTICLE 480. STORAGE BATTERIES

480-1. Scope. The provisions of this Article shall apply to all stationary installations of storage batteries.

▲ Storage cells are of two general types: the so-called lead-acid type, in which the positive plates consist of lead grids having openings filled with a semisolid compound, commonly lead peroxide, and the negative plates are covered with sponge lead, the plates being immersed in dilute sulfuric acid; and the alkali type, in which the active materials are nickel peroxide for the positive plate and iron oxide for the negative plate, and the electrolyte is chiefly potassium hydroxide.

480-2. Definition of Nominal Battery Voltage: The voltage computed on the basis of 2.0 volts per cell for the lead-acid type, and 1.2 volts per cell for the alkali type.

▲ The voltage of each cell of a storage battery varies according to its condition of charge or discharge. It is therefore necessary to base the rules on a nominal voltage per cell for each type of battery.

480-3. Wiring and Equipment Supplied From Batteries. Wiring and equipment supplied from storage batteries shall be subject to the requirements of this Code applying to wiring and equipment operating at the same voltage.

Exception: As otherwise provided for communication systems in Article 800.

480-4. Grounding. The requirements of Article 250 shall apply.

480-5. Insulation of Batteries of Not Over 250 Volts. This Section shall apply to storage batteries having cells so connected as to operate at a nominal battery voltage of not over 250 volts.

(a) Lead-Acid Batteries. Cells and multicompartment batteries with covers sealed to containers of nonconductive heat-resistant material shall not require additional insulating support.

(b) Alkali-Type Batteries. Cells with covers sealed to jars of nonconductive heat-resistant material shall require no additional insulation support. Cells in jars of conductive material shall be installed in trays of nonconductive material with not more than 20 cells (24 volts) in the series circuit in any one tray.

(c) Sealed Rubber Jars. Cells in sealed rubber or composition containers shall require no additional insulating support where the total nominal voltage of all cells in series does not exceed 150. Where the total voltage exceeds 150, batteries shall be sectionalized into groups of 150 volts or less and each group shall have the individual cells installed in trays or on racks.

(d) Sealed Glass or Plastic Jars. Cells in sealed glass jars or in sealed jars of approved heat-resistant plastic, with or without wood trays, shall not require additional insulation.

480-6. Insulation of Batteries of Over 250 Volts. The provisions of Section 480-5 shall apply to storage batteries having the cells so connected as to operate at a nominal voltage exceeding 250 volts, and, in addition, the provisions of this Section shall also apply to such batteries. Cells shall be installed in groups having a total nominal voltage of not over 250 volts on any one rack. Insulation, which can be air, shall be provided between racks. Maximum protection can be secured by sectionalizing high-voltage batteries into groups.

480-7. Racks and Trays. Racks and trays shall conform to the following:

(a) Racks. Racks, as required in this Article, are rigid frames designed to support cells or trays. They shall be substantial and made of:

(1) Metal, so treated as to be resistant to deteriorating action by the electrolyte and provided with nonconducting members directly supporting the cells or with continuous insulating material other than paint or conducting members; or

(2) Other construction such as fiberglass or other suitable nonmetallic materials.

(b) Trays. Trays are frames, such as crates or shallow boxes usually of wood or other nonconductive material, so constructed or treated as to be resistant to deteriorating action by the electrolyte.

480-8. Battery Locations. Battery locations shall conform to (a) and (b) below:

(a) Ventilation. Provisions shall be made for sufficient diffusion and ventilation of the gases from the battery to prevent the accumulation of an explosive mixture.

(b) Live Parts. Guarding of live parts shall comply with Section 110-17.

▲ Because the fumes given off by a storage battery are very corrosive, the type of wiring must be such that it will withstand the corrosive action, and special precautions are necessary as to the type of insulation used, as well as protection of all metalwork.

It is stated by the respective manufacturers that conduit made of aluminum or Everdur (silicon-bronze) is well suited to withstand the corrosive effects of the fumes in battery rooms. If steel conduit is used, it is recommended that the conduit be zinc-coated and that it be kept well painted with asphaltum paint.

Batteries of the lead-acid type sometimes throw off a fine spray of the dilute acid which fills the air around the cells; hence steel conduit or tubing should not be brought close to any cell. On overcharge hydrogen and oxygen are given off, and the mixture of these two gases may be explosive.

There are no special requirements on the type of fixtures or other electrical equipment used in the battery room. Proper ventilation of the room will prevent explosions. See Secs. 300-6 and 410-4(b).

480-9. Vents.

(a) Vented Cells. Each vented cell shall be equipped with a safety vent designed to prevent destruction of the cell due to ignition of gases within the cell by an external spark or flame under normal operating conditions.

(b) Sealed Cells. Sealed (nonvented) cells shall be equipped with a pressure-release vent to prevent excessive accumulation of gas pressure or the battery cell shall be designed to prevent scatter of cell parts in event of a cell explosion.

CHAPTER FIVE.

Special Occupancies

ARTICLE 500. HAZARDOUS (CLASSIFIED) LOCATIONS

500-1. Scope—Articles 500 Through 503. Articles 500 through 503 cover locations in which the authority having jurisdiction judges the equipment and wiring to be subject to the conditions indicated by the classifications covered in this Article. Each room, section, or area (including motor and generator rooms and rooms for the enclosure of control equipment) shall be considered individually in determining its classification.

Exception: Except as modified in Articles 500 through 503, all other applicable rules contained in this Code shall apply to electric equipment and wiring installed in hazardous locations.

For definitions of "approved" and "explosion-proof" as used in these Articles, see Article 100; "dust-ignition-proof" is defined in Section 502-1.

Equipment and associated wiring approved as intrinsically safe shall be permitted in any hazardous (classified) location for which it is approved, and the provisions of Articles 500 through 517 shall not be considered applicable to such installations. Means shall be provided to prevent the passage of gases and vapors. Intrinsically safe equipment and wiring shall not be capable of releasing sufficient electrical or thermal energy under normal or abnormal conditions to cause ignition of a specific hazardous atmospheric mixture in its most easily ignited concentration.

Abnormal conditions shall include accidental damage to any field installed wiring, failure of electrical components, application of overvoltage, adjustment and maintenance operations, and other similar conditions.

For further information, see Intrinsically Safe Process Control Equipment for Use in Class I Hazardous Locations (NFPA No. 493-1969).

Through the exercise of ingenuity in the layout of electrical installations for hazardous locations, it is frequently possible to locate much of the equipment in less hazardous or in nonhazardous locations and thus to reduce the amount of special equipment required. In some cases, hazards may be reduced or hazardous locations limited or eliminated by adequate positive-pressure ventilation from a source of clean air in conjunction with effective safeguards against ventilation failure. For further information see Purged and Pressurized Enclosures for Electrical Equipment in Hazardous Locations (NFPA No. 496-1972).

It is important that the authority having jurisdiction be familiar with such recorded industrial experience as well as with such standards of the National Fire Protection Association as may be of use in the classification of various areas with respect to hazard.

For further information, see Flammable and Combustible Liquids Code (NFPA No. 30-1973); Dry Cleaning Plants (NFPA No. 32-1972); Manufacture of Organic Coatings (NFPA No. 35-1971); Solvent Extraction Plants (NFPA No. 36-1973); Storage and Handling of Liquefied Petroleum Gases (NFPA No. 58-1972); and Storage and Handling of Liquefied Petroleum Gases at Utility Gas Plants (NFPA No. 59-1968).

For protection against static electricity hazards, see Recommended Practice on Static Electricity (NFPA 77-1972).

All conduit referred to herein shall be threaded with a standard conduit cutting die that provides ³⁄₄-inch taper per foot. Such conduit shall be made up wrench tight to minimize sparking when fault current flows through the conduit system. Where it is impractical to make a threaded joint tight, a bonding jumper shall be utilized. **500-2. Special Precaution.** Articles 500 through 503 require a form of construction of equipment and of installation that will insure safe performance under conditions of proper use and maintenance.

It is important that inspection authorities and users exercise more than ordinary care with regard to installation and maintenance.

The explosion characteristics of air mixtures of hazardous gases, vapors, or dusts vary with the specific material involved. For Class I locations, Group A, B, C, and D, the classification involves determinations of maximum explosion pressure, maximum safe clearance between parts of a clamped joint in an enclosure, and the minimum ignition temperature of the atmospheric mixture. For Class II locations, Groups E, F, and G, the classification involves the tightness of the joints of assembly and shaft openings to prevent entrance of dust in the dust-ignition-proof enclosure, the blanketing effect of layers of dust on the equipment that may cause overheating, electrical conductivity of the dust, and the ignition temperature of the dust. It is necessary, therefore, that equipment be approved not only for the class, but also for the specific group of the gas, vapor, or dust that will be present.

For purposes of testing and approval, various air mixtures (not oxygen enriched) have been grouped on the basis of their hazardous characteristics and facilities have been made available for testing and approving equipment for use in the following atmospheric groups:

For Groups A, B, C, and D, see Table 500-2.

Group E: Atmospheres containing metal dust, including aluminum, magnesium, and their commercial alloys, and other metals of similarly hazardous characteristics.

Group F: Atmospheres containing carbon black, charcoal, coal or coke dusts which have more than 8 percent total volatile material (carbon black per ASTM D1620, charcoal, coal and coke dusts per ASTM D271) or atmospheres containing these dusts sensitized by other materials so that they present an explosion hazard.

Group G: Atmospheres containing flour, starch, or grain dust.

Certain chemical atmospheres may have characteristics that require safeguards beyond those required for any of the above groups. Carbon disulfide is one of these chemicals because of its low ignition temperature, 100°C (212°F), and the small joint clearance required to arrest its flame. For a complete list noting properties of flammable liquids, gases, and solids, see Fire-Hazard Properties of Flammable Liquids, Gases, Volatile Solids (NFPA No. 325M-1969).

(a) Approval for Class and Properties. Equipment shall be approved not only for the class of location but also for the explosion properties of the specific gas, vapor, or dust that will be present. In addition, equipment shall not have exposed any surface that operates at a temperature in excess of the ignition temperature of the specific gas, vapor, or dust.

The characteristics of various atmospheric mixtures of hazardous gases, vapors, and dusts depend on the specific hazardous material involved.

(b) Marking. Approved equipment shall be marked to show the Class, Group, and operating temperature, or temperature range, based on operation in a 40°C ambient, for which it is approved.

The temperature range, if provided, shall be indicated in identification numbers, as shown in Table 500-2(b).

Identification numbers marked on equipment nameplates shall be in accordance with Table 500-2(b).

Exception No. 1: Equipment of the nonheat-producing type, such as junction boxes, conduit, and fittings and equipment of the heat producing type having a maximum temperature not more than 100° C (212° F), shall not be required to have a marked operating temperature or temperature range.

Exception No. 2: Fixed lighting fixtures marked for use in Class I Division 2 locations only, need not be marked to indicate the Group.

For purposes of testing and approval, various atmospheric mixtures (not oxygen-enriched) have been grouped on the basis of their hazardous characteristics, and facilities have been made available for testing and approving equipment for use in the atmospheric groups listed in Table 500-2. Since there is no consistent relationship between explosion properties and ignition temperature, the two are independent requirements.

(c) Temperature. The temperature marking specified in (b) above shall not exceed the ignition temperature of the specific gas or vapor to be encountered.

For information regarding ignition temperatures of gases and vapors, see Fire-Hazard Properties of Flammable Liquids, Gases, Volatile Solids (NFPA No. 325M-1969).

Formerly the temperature limit of each Group was assumed to be the lowest ignition temperature of any material in the Group, i.e., 280°C for Group D, 180°C for Group C.

To avoid revising this limit as new gases are added (see hexane in Group D and acetaldehyde in Group C), temperature will be specified in future markings.

The ignition temperature for which equipment was approved prior to this requirement shall be assumed to be as follows:

Group A-280°C (536°F)
Group B-280°C (536°F)
Group C-180°C (356°F)
Group D-280°C (536°F)

Maximum surface temperatures for equipment in Class II hazardous locations are covered in Section 502-1.

▲ While the Code rules for Class I locations do not differ for different kinds of gas or vapor contained in the atmosphere, it is to be noted that it is necessary to select equipment designed for use in the particular atmospheric group to be encountered. This is necessary for the reason that explosive mixtures of the different groups have different flash points and explosion pressures; also, because the ignition temperatures vary with the groups.

Underwriters' Laboratories, Inc., lists fittings and equipment as suitable for use in all groups of Class I, although the listings for Groups A and B are not as complete as those for Groups C and D.

In Class II locations the Code, in a few cases, differentiates between the different kinds of dust, particularly dusts which are electrically conductive and those which are not conductive. Here again, as in Class I locations, care must be used to determine that the equipment selected is suitable for use where a particular kind of dust is present.

In addition to the use of more than ordinary care in selecting equipment for use in hazardous locations, special attention should be given to installation and maintenance details in order that the installations will be permanently free from electrical hazards. In making subsequent additions or changes, the high standards of the original installation must be maintained.

For a more thorough knowledge of specific hazardous areas and equipment selection and location it is essential to obtain copies of the various NFPA and ANSI standards referenced in Arts. 500 through 517.

500-3. Specific Occupancies. Articles 510 through 517 cover garages, aircraft hangars, gasoline dispensing and service stations, bulk storage plants, finishing processes, and health care facilities.

▲ At the suggestion of CMP14, NFPA No. 70C, Hazardous Locations Classification, was developed to supplement the NEC. This manual contains information on classifying locations for the purpose of determining the types of wiring systems and electrical equipment to be used. Material from 47 NFPA and ANSI standards are contained in this document.

It should be noted that Arts. 500 through 517 of the National Electrical Code refer to various NFPA and ANSI standards. In view of these references, which of necessity are broad in nature, it was felt that specific extracted material placed in a single document would provide a much greater convenience to users of the National Electrical Code, and NFPA No. 70C was developed for this purpose. Another benefit is that this composite document will be updated when changes are made to existing NFPA or ANSI standards, or when new standards are developed.

Copies of this manual may be obtained from the Publications Department of the National Fire Protection Association, 470 Atlantic Ave., Boston, Mass. 02210.

500-4. Class I Locations. Class I locations are those in which flammable gases or vapors are or may be present in the air in quantities sufficient to produce explosive or ignitible mixtures. Class 1 locations shall include those specified in (a) and (b) below.

▲ The requirements of Sec. 500-2 and Tables 500-2 and 500-2(b) provide the means of properly identifying and classifying equipment for use in hazardous locations. The identification numbers in Table 500-2(b) pertain to temperature-range classifications as used by Underwriters' Laboratories, Inc., in UL Hazardous Location Standards.

(a) Class I, Division 1. A Class I, Division 1 location is a location: (1) in which hazardous concentrations of flammable gases or vapors exist continuously, intermittently, or periodically under normal operating conditions; or (2) in which hazardous concentrations of such gases or vapors may exist frequently because of repair or maintenance operations or because of leakage; or (3) in which breakdown or faulty operation of equipment or processes that might release hazardous concentrations of flammable gases or vapors, and might also cause simultaneous failure of electric equipment.

This classification usually includes locations where volatile flammable liquids or liquefied flammable gases are transferred from one container to another; interiors of spray booths and areas in the vicinity of spraying and painting operations where volatile flammable solvents are used; locations containing open tanks or vats of volatile flammable liquids; drying rooms or compartments for the evaporation of flammable solvents; locations

Table 500-2. Chemicals by Groups

Group A Atmospheres	Group D Atmospheres
Chemical:	*Chemical:*

Chemical:

acetylene

Group B Atmospheres

butadiene[1]
ethylene oxide[2]
hydrogen
manufactured gases containing more
  than 30% hydrogen (by volume)
propylene oxide[2]

Group C Atmospheres

acetaldehyde
cyclopropane
diethyl ether
ethylene
unsymmetrical dimethyl hydrazine
  (UDMH 1, 1-dimethyl hydrazine)

Chemical:

acetone
acrylonitrile
ammonia[3]
benzene
butane
1-butanol (butyl alcohol)
2-butanol (secondary butyl alcohol)
n-butyl acetate
isobutyl acetate
ethane
ethanol (ethyl alcohol)
ethyl acetate
ethylene dichloride
gasoline
heptanes
hexanes
isoprene
methane (natural gas)
methanol (methyl alcohol)
3-methyl-1-butanol (isoamyl alcohol)
methyl ethyl ketone
methyl isobutyl ketone
2-methyl-1-propanol
  (isobutyl alcohol)
2-methyl-2-propanol
  (tertiary butyl alcohol)
petroleum naphtha[4]
octanes
pentanes
1-pentanol (amyl alcohol)
propane
1-propanol (propyl alcohol)
2-propanol (isopropyl alcohol)
propylene
styrene
toluene
vinyl acetate
vinyl chloride
xylenes

[1] Group D equipment shall be permitted for this atmosphere if such equipment is isolated in accordance with Section 501-5(a) by sealing all conduit $\frac{1}{2}$-inch size or larger.

[2] Group C equipment shall be permitted for this atmosphere if such equipment is isolated in accordance with Section 501-5(a) by sealing all conduit $\frac{1}{2}$-inch size or larger.

[3] For Classification of areas involving ammonia atmosphere, see Safety Code for Mechanical Refrigeration (ANSI B9.1-1971) and Safety Requirements for the Storage and Handling of Anhydrous Ammonia (ANSI K61.1-1972).

[4] A saturated hydrocarbon mixture boiling in the range 20-135°C (68-275°F). Also known by the synonyms benzine, ligroin, petroleum ether, or naphtha.

Table 500-2(b). Identification Numbers

Maximum Temperature		Identification Number
Degrees C	Degrees F	
450	842	T1
300	572	T2
280	536	T2A
260	500	T2B
230	446	T2C
215	419	T2D
200	392	T3
180	356	T3A
165	329	T3B
160	320	T3C
135	275	T4
120	248	T4A
100	212	T5
85	185	T6

containing fat and oil extraction equipment using volatile flammable solvents; portions of cleaning and dyeing plants where hazardous liquids are used; gas generator rooms and other portions of gas manufacturing plants where flammable gas may escape; inadequately ventilated pump rooms for flammable gas or for volatile flammable liquids; the interiors of refrigerators and freezers in which volatile flammable materials are stored in open, lightly stoppered, or easily ruptured containers; and all other locations where hazardous concentrations of flammable vapors or gases are likely to occur in the course of normal operations.

(b) Class I, Division 2. A Class I, Division 2 location is a location: (1) in which volatile flammable liquids or flammable gases are handled, processed, or used, but in which the hazardous liquids, vapors, or gases will normally be confined within closed containers or closed systems from which they can escape only in case of accidental rupture or breakdown of such containers or systems, or in case of abnormal operation of equipment; or (2) in which hazardous concentrations of gases or vapors are normally prevented by positive mechanical ventilation, but which might become hazardous through failure or abnormal operation of the ventilating equipment; or (3) that is adjacent to a Class I, Division 1 location, and to which hazardous concentrations of gases or vapors might occasionally be communicated unless such communication is prevented by adequate positive-pressure ventilation from a source of clean air, and effective safeguards against ventilation failure are provided.

This classification usually includes locations where volatile flammable liquids or flammable gases or vapors are used, but which, in the judgment of the authority having jurisdiction, would become hazardous only in case of an accident or of some unusual operating condition. The quantity of hazardous material that might escape in case of accident, the adequacy of ventilating equipment, the total area involved, and the record of the industry or business with respect to explosions or fires are all factors that merit consideration in determining the classification and extent of each location.

Piping without valves, checks, meters, and similar devices would not ordinarily introduce a hazardous condition even though used for hazardous liquids or gases. Locations used for the storage of hazardous liquids or of liquefied or compressed gases in sealed containers would not normally be considered hazardous unless subject to other hazardous conditions also.

Electrical conduits and their associated enclosures separated from process fluids by a single seal or barrier shall be classed as a Division 2 location if the outside of the conduit and enclosures is a nonhazardous location.

500-5. Class II Locations. Class II locations are those that are hazardous because of the presence of combustible dust. Class II locations shall include those specified in (a) and (b) below.

(a) Class II, Division 1. A Class II, Division 1 location is a location: (1) in which combustible dust is or may be in suspension in the air continuously, intermittently, or periodically under normal operating conditions, in quantities sufficient to produce explosive or ignitible mixtures; or (2) where mechanical failure or abnormal operation of machinery or equipment might cause such explosive or ignitible mixtures to be produced, and might also provide a source of ignition through simultaneous failure of electric equipment, operation of protection devices, or from other causes; or (3) in which combustible dusts of an electrically conductive nature may be present.

This classification usually includes the working areas of grain handling and storage plants; rooms containing grinders or pulverizers, cleaners, graders, scalpers, open conveyors or spouts, open bins or hoppers, mixers or blenders, automatic or hopper scales, packing machinery, elevator heads and boots, stock distributors, dust and stock collectors (except all-metal collectors vented to the outside), and all similar dust-producing machinery and equipment in grain-processing plants, starch plants, sugar-pulverizing plants, malting plants, hay-grinding plants, and other occupancies of similar nature; coal-pulverizing plants (except where the pulverizing equipment is essentially dust-tight); all working areas where metal dusts and powders are produced, processed, handled, packed, or stored (except in tight containers); and all other similar locations where combustible dust may, under normal operating conditions, be present in the air in quantities sufficient to produce explosive or ignitible mixtures.

Combustible dusts which are electrically nonconductive include dusts produced in the handling and processing of grain and grain products, pulverized sugar and cocoa, dried egg and milk powders, pulverized spices, starch and pastes, potato and woodflour, oil meal from beans and seed, dried hay, and other organic materials which may produce combustible dusts when processed or handled. Electrically conductive nonmetallic dusts include dusts from pulverized coal, coke, carbon black, and charcoal. Dusts containing magnesium or aluminum are particularly hazardous and the use of extreme precaution will be necessary to avoid ignition and explosion.

(b) Class II, Division 2. A Class II, Division 2 location is a location in which combustible dust will not normally be in suspension in the air or will not be likely to be thrown into suspension by the normal operation of equipment or apparatus in quantities sufficient to produce explosive or ignitible mixtures, but: (1) where deposits or accumulations of such combustible dust may be sufficient to interfere with the safe dissipation of heat from electric equipment or apparatus; or (2) where such deposits or accumulations of combustible dust on, in, or in the vicinity of electric equipment might be ignited by arcs, sparks, or burning material from such equipment.

Locations where dangerous concentrations of suspended dust would not be likely, but where dust accumulations might form on, or in the vicinity of electric equipment, would include rooms and areas containing only closed spouting and conveyors, closed bins or hoppers, or machines and equipment from which appreciable quantities of dust would escape only under abnormal operating conditions; rooms or areas adjacent to a Class II, Division 1 location as described in (a) above, and into which explosive or ignitible concentrations of suspended dust might be communicated only under abnormal operating conditions; rooms or areas where the formation of explosive or ignitible concentrations of suspended dust is prevented by the operation of effective dust control equipment; warehouses and shipping rooms where dust-producing materials are stored or handled only in bags or containers; and other similar locations.

500-6. Class III Locations. Class III locations are those that are hazardous because of the presence of easily ignitible fibers or flyings, but in which such fibers or flyings are not likely to be in suspension in the air in quantities sufficient to produce ignitible mixtures. Class III locations shall include those specified in (a) and (b) below.

(a) Class III, Division 1. A Class III, Division 1 location is a location in which easily ignitible fibers or materials producing combustible flyings are handled, manufactured, or used.

Such locations usually include some parts of rayon, cotton, and other textile mills; combustible fiber manufacturing and processing plants; cotton gins and cotton-seed mills; flax-processing plants; clothing manufacturing plants; wood-working plants; and establishments and industries involving similar hazardous processes or conditions.

Easily ignitible fibers and flyings include rayon, cotton (including cotton linters and cotton waste), sisal or henequen, istle, jute, hemp, tow, cocoa fiber, oakum, baled waste kapok, Spanish moss, excelsior, and other materials of similar nature.

(b) Class III, Division 2. A Class III, Division 2 location is a location in which easily ignitible fibers are stored or handled.

Exception: In process of manufacture.

▲ In each of the three classes of hazardous locations discussed in Secs. 500-4, 500-5, and 500-6, the Code recognizes varying degrees of hazard; hence under each class two divisions are defined. In the installation rules that follow, the requirements for Division 1 of each class are more rigid than the requirements for Division 2.

Briefly, the hazards in the three classes of locations are due to the following causes:

Class I, Highly flammable gases or vapors

Class II, Combustible dust

Class III, Combustible fibers or flyings

The classifications are easily understood, and, if a given location is to be classed as hazardous, it should not be difficult to determine in which of the three classes it belongs. However, it is obviously impossible to make rules that will in every case determine positively whether the location is or is not hazardous; considerable common sense and good judgment must be exercised in determining whether the location under consideration should be considered as hazardous or likely to become hazardous because of a change in the processes carried on, and if so, what portion of the premises should be classed as coming under Division 1 and what part may safely be considered as being in Division 2.

ARTICLE 501. CLASS I LOCATIONS

501-1. General. The general rules of this Code shall apply to the electric wiring and equipment in locations classified as Class I in Section 500-4.

Exception: As modified by this Article.

▲ *Installations in Class 1 Locations*

The more common Class I locations are those where some process is carried on involving the use of a highly volatile and flammable liquid, such as gasoline, petroleum naphtha, benzene, diethyl ether, or acetone, or flammable gases.

In any Class I location an explosive mixture of air and flammable gas or vapor may be present which can be caused to explode by an arc or spark. To avoid the danger of explosions all electrical apparatus which may create arcs or sparks should

FIG. 501-1. Explosionproof
junction box and cover.
(*Crouse-Hinds Co.*)

FIG. 501-2. Explosionproof
junction box and cover.
(*Appleton Electric Co.*)

if possible be kept out of the rooms where the hazardous locations exist, or, if this is not possible, such apparatus must be "of types approved for use in explosive atmospheres."

All equipment such as switches, circuit breakers, or motors must have some movable operating part projecting through the enclosing case, and any such part, as for example the operating lever of a switch or the shaft of a motor, must have sufficient clearance so that it will work freely; hence the equipment cannot be hermetically sealed. Also, the necessity for subsequent opening of the enclosures for servicing makes hermetic sealing impracticable. Furthermore, the enclosure of the equipment must be entered by a run of conduit, and it is practically impossible to make conduit joints absolutely air- and gastight. Due to slight changes in temperature, the conduit system and the apparatus enclosures "breathe"; that is, any flammable gas in the room may gradually find its way inside the conduit and enclosures and form an explosive mixture with air. Under this condition, when an arc occurs inside the enclosure an explosion may take place.

When the gas and air mixture explodes inside the enclosing case, the burning mixture must be confined entirely within the enclosure, so as to prevent the ignition of flammable gases in the room. In the first place it is necessary that the enclosing case be so constructed that it will have sufficient strength to withstand the high pressure generated by an internal explosion. The pressure in pounds per square inch produced by the explosion of a given gas-and-air mixture has been quite definitely determined, and the enclosure can be designed accordingly.

Since the enclosures for apparatus cannot be made absolutely tight, when an internal explosion occurs some of the burning gas will be forced out through any openings that exist. It has been found that the flame will not be carried out through an opening that is quite long in proportion to its width. This principle is applied in the design of so-called explosionproof enclosures for apparatus by providing a wide flange at the joint between the body of the enclosure and grinding these flanges to a definitely determined fit. In this case the flanges are so ground that when the cover is in place the clearance between the two surfaces will at no point exceed 0.0015 in. Thus, if an explosion occurs within the enclosure, in order to escape from the enclosure the burning gas must travel a considerable distance through an opening not more than 0.0015 in. wide. The same result may be accomplished by the use of a screwed-on cover having five full threads engaged as shown in Figs. 501-1 and 501-2. The fundamental principle of this construction is the same as has been used for many years in miners' safety lamps.

501-2. Transformers and Capacitors.

(a) Class I, Division 1. In Class I, Division 1 locations, transformers and capacitors shall comply with the following:

(1) Containing Liquid That Will Burn. Transformers and capacitors containing a liquid that will burn shall be installed only in approved vaults that comply with Sections 450-41 through 450-48, and in addition: (1) there shall be no door or other communicating opening between the vault and the hazardous area; and (2) ample ventilation shall be provided for the continuous removal of hazardous gases or vapors; and (3) vent openings or ducts shall lead to a safe location outside of buildings; and (4) vent ducts and openings shall be of sufficient area to relieve explosion pressures within the vault, and all portions of vent ducts within the buildings shall be of reinforced concrete construction.

(2) Not Containing Liquid That Will Burn. Transformers and capacitors that do not contain a liquid that will burn shall: (1) be installed in vaults complying with (a)(1) above, or (2) be approved for Class I locations.

(b) Class I, Division 2. In Class I, Division 2 locations, transformers and capacitors shall comply with Sections 450-21 through 450-25.

501-3. Meters, Instruments, and Relays.

(a) Class I, Division 1. In Class I, Division 1 locations, meters, instruments, and relays, including kilowatt-hour meters, instrument transformers, resistors, rectifiers, and thermionic tubes, shall be provided with enclosures approved for Class I locations.

(b) Class I, Division 2. In Class I, Division 2 locations, meters, instruments, and relays shall comply with the following:

(1) Contacts. Switches, circuit breakers, and make-and-break contacts of pushbuttons, relays, alarm bells, and horns, shall have enclosures approved for Class I locations.

Exception: General-purpose enclosures shall be permitted, if current-interrupting contacts are:

  a. Immersed in oil; or,

  b. Enclosed within a chamber hermetically sealed against the entrance of gases or vapors; or,

  c. In circuits that under normal conditions do not release sufficient energy to ignite a specific hazardous atmosphere mixture; i.e., are nonincendive.

(2) Resistors and Similar Equipment. Resistors, resistance devices, thermionic tubes, rectifiers, and similar equipment that are used in or in connection with meters, instruments, and relays shall comply with (a) above.

Exception: General-purpose type enclosures shall be permitted if such equipment is without make-and-break or sliding contacts (other than as provided in (b)(1) above) and if the maximum operating temperature of any exposed surface will not exceed 80 percent of the ignition temperature in degrees Celsius of the gas or vapor involved or has been tested and found incapable of igniting the gas or vapor.

(3) Without Make-or-Break Contacts. Transformer windings, impedance coils, solenoids, and other windings that do not incorporate sliding or make-and-break contacts shall be provided with enclosures that may be of the general-purpose type.

(4) General-Purpose Assemblies. Where an assembly is made up of components for which general-purpose enclosures are acceptable as provided in (b)(1), (b)(2), and (b)(3) above, a single general-purpose enclosure shall be acceptable for the assembly. Where such an assembly includes any of the equipment described in (b)(2) above, the maximum obtainable surface temperature of any component of the assembly shall be clearly and permanently indicated on the outside of the enclosure. Alternatively, approved equipment shall be permitted to be marked to indicate the temperature range for which it is suitable using the identification numbers of Table 500-2(b).

(5) Fuses. Where general-purpose enclosures are permitted in (b)(1), (b)(2), (b)(3), and (b)(4) above, fuses for overcurrent protection of the instrument circuits shall be permitted to be mounted in general-purpose enclosures if such fuses do not exceed a 3-ampere rating at 120 volts and if each such fuse is preceded by a switch complying with (b)(1) above.

(6) Connections. To facilitate replacements, process control instruments shall be permitted to be connected through flexible cord, attachment plug, and receptacle, provided: (1) a switch complying with (b)(1) above is provided so that the attachment plug is not depended on to interrupt current; and (2) the current does not exceed 3 amperes at 120 volts; and (3) the power-supply cord does not exceed 3 feet, is of a type approved for extra-hard usage or for hard usage if protected by location, and is supplied through an attachment plug and receptacle of the locking and grounding type; and (4) only necessary receptacles are provided; and (5) the receptacle carries a label warning against unplugging under load.

501-4. Wiring Methods. Wiring methods shall comply with (a) and (b) below.

(a) Class I, Division 1. In Class I, Division 1 locations, threaded rigid metal conduit or Type MI cable with termination fittings approved for the location shall be the wiring method employed. All boxes, fittings, and joints shall be threaded for connection to conduit or cable terminations, and shall be explosion-proof. Threaded joints shall be made up with at least 5 threads fully engaged. Type MI cable shall be installed and supported in a manner to avoid tensile stress at the termination fittings. Where necessary to employ flexible connections, as at motor terminals, flexible fittings approved for Class I locations shall be used.

▲ The term "approved for the location" in paragraph (a) means that approval is to be based on the performance of a fitting or equipment when subjected to a specific atmosphere.

As applied to rigid metal conduit, to be explosionproof, threaded joints must be used at couplings and for connection to fittings, the threads must be cleanly cut, five full threads must be engaged, and each joint must be made up tight.

All fittings, such as outlet boxes, junction boxes, and switch boxes, also all enclosures for apparatus, should have threaded hubs to receive the conduit and must be provided with suitable covers. The box and cover must be of sufficient strength to withstand an internal explosion, the method of securing the cover to the box must likewise provide sufficient strength, and the joint between the cover and the box must be explosionproof.

Explosionproof junction boxes are available in a wide variety of types. Figure 501-1 shows one of a series of boxes designed for general use in hazardous locations. The opening to receive the cover is threaded internally, and the cover is made of the same material as the box. Figure 501-2 shows a larger type of box having 10 threaded hubs, making it adaptable to a variety of conditions. Unused openings are closed with threaded plugs. The body of this box is malleable iron and the cover is brass, the cover being threaded internally in this design.

Box covers may have threaded connections with the boxes as shown in Figs. 501-1 and 501-2, or the cover may be attached with machine screws, in which case a carefully ground flanged joint is required.

A flexible fitting suitable for use in Class I hazardous locations is shown in Fig. 501-3. The flexible portion consists of a tube of bronze having deeply corrugated walls and reinforced by a braid of fine bronze wires. A heavy threaded fitting is securely joined to each end of the flexible tube, and a fibrous tubular lining, similar to "circular loom," is provided in order to prevent abrasion of the enclosed conductors that might result from long-continued vibration. The complete assembly is obtainable in various lengths up to a maximum of 3 ft.

In Class I, Division 2 locations explosionproof outlet boxes are not required at lighting outlets nor at junction boxes containing no arcing device; however, where conduit is used, it should enter the box through threaded openings as shown in Fig. 501-1, or if locknut-bushing attachment is used, a bonding jumper and/or fittings must be provided between the boxes and conduits.

(b) Class I, Division 2. In Class I, Division 2 locations, threaded rigid metal conduit, enclosed gasketed busways, or Type MI, MC, ALS, TC, or SNM cable with approved termination fittings shall be the wiring method employed. Type MI, MC, ALS, CS, TC, or SNM cable shall be installed in a manner to avoid tensile stress at the termination fittings. Boxes, fittings, and joints shall not be required to be explosion-proof except as required by Sections 501-5(b)(1) and (b)(2). Where provision must be made for limited flexibility, as at motor terminals, flexible metal fittings, flexible metal conduit with approved fittings, liquidtight flexible metal conduit with approved fittings, or flexible cord approved for extra-hard usage and provided with approved bushed fittings shall be used. An additional conductor for

Fig. 501-3. Pyle-o-flex flexible explosionproof fitting. (*The Pyle-National Co.*)

grounding shall be included in the flexible cord unless other acceptable means of grounding are provided.

Exception: Wiring, which under normal conditions cannot release sufficient energy to ignite a specific hazardous atmospheric mixture by opening, shorting or grounding, shall be permitted using any of the methods suitable for wiring in ordinary locations.

For voltages over 600 volts and where adequately protected from physical damage, metallic shielded high voltage cable shall be accepted in cable trays when installed in accordance with Article 318.

▲ Flexible connections permitted in Class I, Division 2 locations may consist of flexible conduit with approved fittings, and such fittings are not required to be specifically approved for Class I locations. It should be noted that a separate grounding conductor is necessary to bond across such flexible connections as required in Sec. 501-16(b).

Ordinary knockout-type boxes may be installed in such locations, but Sec. 501-16(b) rules out the use of locknuts and bushings for bonding purposes, and the requirement specifies either bonding jumpers or other approved means to assure adequate grounding from the hazardous area to the point of grounding at the service.

501-5. Sealing and Drainage. Seals in conduit and cable systems shall comply with (a) through (f) below. Sealing compound shall be of a type approved for the conditions and use. Sealing compound shall be used in Type MI cable termination fittings to exclude moisture and other fluids from the cable insulation.

Seals are provided in conduit and cable systems to prevent the passage of gases, vapors, or flames from one portion of the electrical installation to another through the conduit. Such communication through Type MI cable is inherently prevented by construction of the cable.

(a) Conduit Seals Class I, Division 1. In Class I, Division 1 locations, conduit seals shall be located as follows:

(1) In each conduit run entering an enclosure for switches, circuit breakers, fuses, relays, resistors, or other apparatus that may produce arcs, sparks, or high temperatures. Seals shall be placed as close as practicable and in no case more than 18 inches from such enclosures. There shall be no junction box or similar enclosure in the conduit run between the sealing fitting and the apparatus enclosure.

(2) In each conduit run of 2-inch size or larger entering an enclosure or fitting housing terminals, splices, or taps and within 18 inches of such enclosure or fitting.

See notes under Group B in Table 500-2.

(3) Where two or more enclosures for which seals are required under (a)(1) and (a)(2) above are connected by nipples or by runs of conduit not more than 36 inches long, a single seal in each such nipple connection or run of conduit shall be considered sufficient if located not more than 18 inches from either enclosure. Conduit fittings approved for Class 1 locations and similar to the "L," "T," or "Cross" type shall not be classed as enclosures where not larger than the trade size of the conduit.

(4) In each conduit run leaving the Class I, Division 1 hazardous area. The sealing fitting shall be permitted on either side of the boundary of such hazardous location, but shall be so designed and installed that any gases or vapors that may enter the conduit system within the Division 1 hazardous location will not enter or be communicated to the conduit beyond the seal. There shall be no union, coupling, box, or fitting in the conduit between the sealing fitting and the point at which the conduit leaves the Division 1 hazardous location.

Exception: Unbroken rigid metal conduit that passes completely through a Class I, Division 1 location with no fittings less than 12 inches beyond each boundary shall not be required to be sealed if the termination points of the unbroken conduit are in nonhazardous locations.

(b) Conduit Seals Class I, Division 2. In Class I, Division 2 locations, conduit seals shall be located as follows:

(1) For connections to enclosures that are required to be approved for Class I locations, seals shall be provided in accordance with (a)(1) and (a)(2) above. All portions of the conduit run or nipple between the seal and such enclosure shall comply with Section 501-4(a).

(2) In each conduit run passing from a Class I, Division 2 location into a nonhazardous location. The sealing fitting shall be permitted on either side of the boundary of such location, but shall be so designed and installed that any gases or vapors that may enter the conduit system within the Division 2 location will not enter or be communicated to the conduit beyond the seal. Rigid metal conduit shall be used between the sealing fitting and the point at which the conduit leaves the hazardous location, and a threaded connection shall be used at the sealing fitting. There shall be no union, coupling, box, or fitting in the conduit between the sealing fitting and the point at which the conduit leaves the hazardous location.

Exception: Unbroken rigid metal conduit that passes completely through a Class I, Division 2 location with no fittings less than 12 inches beyond each boundary shall not be required to be sealed if the termination points of the unbroken conduit are in nonhazardous locations.

(c) Class I, Divisions 1 and 2. Where required, seals in Class I, Division 1 and 2 locations shall comply with the following:

(1) Fittings. Enclosures for connections or equipment shall be provided with an approved integral means for sealing, or sealing fittings approved for Class I locations shall be used. Sealing fittings shall be accessible.

(2) Compound. Sealing compound shall be approved for the purpose, shall not be affected by the surrounding atmosphere or liquids, and shall not have a melting point of less than $93°C$ ($200°F$).

(3) Thickness of Compounds. In a completed seal, the minimum thickness of the sealing compound shall not be less than the trade size of the conduit, and in no case less than $\frac{5}{8}$ inch.

(4) Splices and Taps. Splices and taps shall not be made in fittings intended only for sealing with compound, nor shall other fittings in which splices or taps are made be filled with compound.

(5) Assemblies. In an assembly where equipment that may produce arcs, sparks, or high temperatures is located in a compartment separate from the compartment containing splices or taps, and an integral seal is provided where conductors pass from one compartment to the other, the entire assembly shall be approved for Class I locations. Seals in conduit connections to the compartment containing splices or taps shall be provided in Class I, Division 1 locations where required by (a)(2) above.

(d) Cable Seals, Class I, Division 1. In Class I, Division 1 locations, each multiconductor cable in rigid conduit shall be considered as a single conductor, and sealed in accordance with (a) above.

Cables with an impervious continuous sheath capable of transmitting gases or vapors through the cable core shall be sealed in the hazardous location in such a manner as to prevent passage of gases or vapors into a nonhazardous location.

(e) Cable Seals, Class I, Division 2.   In Class I, Division 2 locations, cable seals shall be located as follows:

(1) Cables entering enclosures which are required to be approved for Class I locations shall be sealed at the point of entrance. The sealing fitting shall comply with (b)(1) above. Multi-conductor cables shall be sealed after removing the jacket and any other coverings so that the sealing compound will surround each individual insulated conductor and the outer jacket.

(2) Cables with an impervious continuous sheath which will not transmit gases or vapors through the cable core shall not be required to be sealed except as required in (e)(1) above.

(3) Cables with an impervious continuous sheath capable of transmitting gases or vapors through the cable core shall be sealed in the hazardous location in such a manner as to prevent passage of gases or vapors into a nonhazardous location.

Exception: Cables with an unbroken impervious continuous sheath shall be permitted to pass through a Class I, Division 2 location without seals.

(4) Cables which do not have an impervious continuous sheath shall be sealed at the boundary of the hazardous and nonhazardous location in such a manner as to prevent passage of gases or vapors into a nonhazardous location.

(f) Drainage.

(1) Control Equipment.   Where there is a probability that liquid or other condensed vapor may be trapped within enclosures for control equipment or at any point in the raceway system, approved means shall be provided to prevent accumulation or to permit periodic draining of such liquid or condensed vapor.

(2) Motors and Generators.   Where the authority having jurisdiction judges that there is a probability that liquid or condensed vapor may accumulate within motors or generators, joints and conduit systems shall be arranged to minimize entrance of liquid. If means to prevent accumulation or to permit periodic draining are judged necessary, such means shall be provided at the time of manufacture and shall be considered an integral part of the machine.

(3) Canned Pumps, Etc.   For canned pumps, process connections for flow, pressure, or analysis measurement, etc., that depend upon a single seal diaphragm or tube to prevent process fluids from entering the electrical conduit system, an additional approved seal or barrier shall be provided with an adequate drain between the seals in such a manner that leaks would be obvious.

See also the last paragraph of Section 500-4(b).

▲ The proper sealing of conduits in Class I locations is an important matter. In Class I, Division 1 and Division 2 locations, each piece of apparatus such as a motor controller, switch, or receptacle should be isolated from all other apparatus by sealing so that an explosion in one enclosure cannot be communicated through the conduit to any other enclosure. Where two such pieces of apparatus are connected by a run of conduit not over 3 ft long, a single seal in this run is considered satisfactory if located at the center of the run. For runs of 2 in. or larger it is required that a seal be provided within 18 in. of each enclosure that is required to be explosionproof if the enclosure contains terminals, splices, or taps.

Each run of conduit from a hazardous location to a nonhazardous location should also be sealed, preferably just outside the hazardous area. The purpose of this sealing is twofold: (1) The conduit usually terminates in some enclosure in the nonhazardous area containing an arc-producing device, such as a switch or fuse. If not sealed, the conduit and apparatus enclosure are likely to become filled with an explosive mixture and the ignition of this mixture may cause local damage in the nonhazardous location. (2) An explosion or ignition of the mixture in the conduit in the nonhazardous area would probably travel back through the conduit to the hazardous area and might cause an explosion there if due to some defective fitting or poor workmanship the installation is not completely explosionproof.

In Class I, Division 2 locations a seal is required in each run of conduit entering an enclosure that is required to be explosionproof; also in each conduit run leaving the hazardous area.

The necessary sealing may be accomplished by inserting in the conduit runs special sealing fittings such as those shown in Figs. 501-4 through 501-6, or provision may be made for sealing in the enclosure for the apparatus. Thus an explosionproof motor is made with the leads sealed where they pass from the terminal housing to the interior of the motor, and no other seal is needed where a conduit terminates at the motor, except that if the conduit is 2 in. or larger in size, a seal must be provided not more than 18 in. from the motor terminal housing.

The sealing compound used must be one which has a melting point of not less than 200°F and is not affected by the liquid or gas which causes the location to be hazardous. Most of the insulating compounds commonly used in cable splices and potheads are soluble in gasoline and lacquer solvents and hence are unsuitable for sealing conduits in locations where these liquids are used. A mixture of litharge and glycerin is insoluble in nearly all liquids and gases found in Class I locations and meets all other requirements, though this mixture is open to the objection that it becomes very hard and is difficult to remove if the wires must be pulled out. No sealing compounds are listed by Underwriters' Laboratories, Inc., as suitable for this use except in connection with the explosionproof fittings of specific manufacturers.

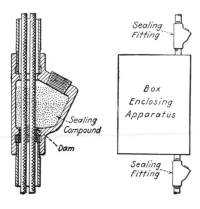

FIG. 501-4. A fitting providing means for sealing off a run of conduit to prevent the passage of gases. (*Crouse-Hinds Co.*)

FIG. 501-5. Sealing
fitting for horizontal
conduit runs and a
drain seal fitting.
(*Crouse-Hinds Co.*)

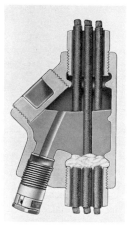

FIG. 501-6. Sealing fitting
with provision for drainage.
(*Crouse-Hinds Co.*)

Where conduit is run overhead and is brought down vertically to an enclosure for apparatus, any condensation of moisture in the vertical run would be trapped by the seal above the apparatus enclosure.

Figure 501-6 shows a sealing fitting designed to provide drainage for a vertical conduit run. Any water coming down from above runs over the surface of the sealing compound and down to an explosionproof drain, through which the water is automatically drained off. The construction of the drain is shown in Fig. 501-7, which illustrates a separate fitting that may be screwed into a tapped opening to drain any explosionproof enclosure.

Figure 501-8 shows an explosionproof "breather valve," designed to be screwed into a tapped opening in the top of an explosionproof enclosure; its purpose is to permit the escape of hot, moisture-laden air, which might otherwise cause the formation of mildew on the insulation of conductors within the enclosure.

Where either of the fittings shown in Figs. 501-7 and 501-8 is used, the metal into which the fitting is inserted must be of sufficient thickness so that five full threads will be engaged, in order to fulfill the requirements for an explosionproof joint.

Figure 501-9 is a wiring layout for a Class I, Division 1 location. The wiring is all rigid metal conduit with threaded joints. All fittings and equipment are explosionproof; this includes the motors, the motor controller for motor No. 1 (lower part of drawing), the pushbutton control station for motor No. 2 (upper part of drawing), and all outlet

Fig. 501-7. Drainage fitting. (*Crouse-Hinds Co.*)

Fig. 501-8. Breather valve.(*Crouse-Hinds Co.*)

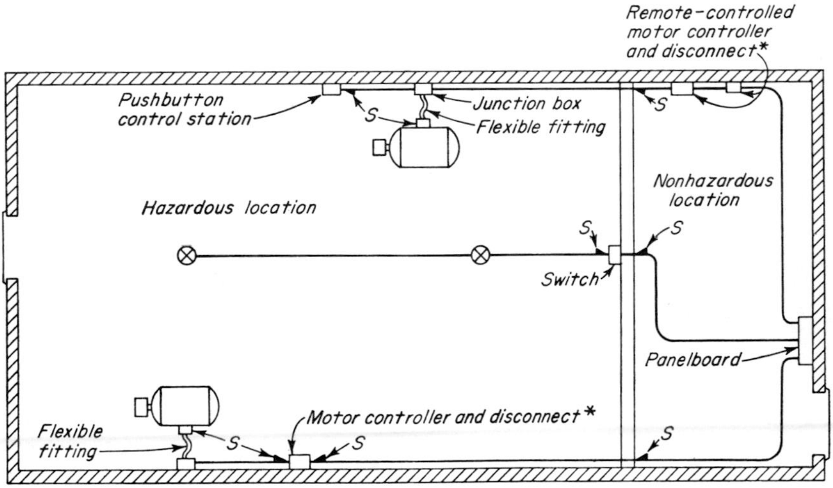

Fig. 501-9. Wiring layout for power and light in a Class I, Division 1 location. S indicates a point where conduit or equipment is sealed.

* Disconnecting means may be in same enclosure. See Sec. 430-103.

and junction boxes. The cabinet and a remote controller for motor No. 2 are placed outside the hazardous area and hence need not be explosionproof.

Each of the three runs of conduit from the cabinet is sealed just outside the hazardous area. A sealing fitting is provided in the conduit each side of the controller for motor No. 1 (lower part of drawing). The leads are sealed where they pass through the frame of the motor into the terminal housing, and no other seal is needed at this point provided that the conduit and flexible fitting enclosing the leads to the motor are smaller than 2 in. The pushbutton control station for motor No. 2 (upper part of drawing) is considered an arc-producing device, even though the contacts may be oil-immersed, and hence the conduit is sealed where it terminates at this device.

A seal is provided on each side of the switch controlling the lighting fixtures; one of these seals is in the nonhazardous room. The lighting fixtures are hung on rigid conduit stems threaded to the covers of explosionproof boxes on the ceiling.

501-6. Switches, Circuit Breakers, Motor Controllers, and Fuses.

(a) Class I, Division 1. In Class I, Division 1 locations, switches, circuit breakers, motor controllers, and fuses, including pushbuttons, relays, and similar devices, shall be provided with enclosures; and the enclosure in each case, together with the enclosed apparatus, shall be approved as a complete assembly for use in Class I locations.

(b) Class I, Division 2. Switches, circuit breakers, motor controllers, and fuses in Class I, Division 2 locations shall comply with the following:

(1) Type Required. Circuit breakers, motor controllers, and switches intended to interrupt current in the normal performance of the function for which they are installed shall be provided with enclosures approved for Class I locations, unless general-purpose enclosures are provided and (1) the interruption of current occurs within a chamber hermetically sealed against the entrance of gases and vapors, or (2) the current make-and-break contacts are oil-immersed, and of the general-purpose type having a two-inch minimum immersion for power and a one-inch minimum immersion for control.

(2) Isolating Switches. General-purpose-type enclosures containing no fuses shall be permitted to enclose disconnecting and isolating switches that are not intended to interrupt current.

(3) Fuses. For the protection of motors, appliances, and lamps, other than as provided in (b)(4) below, standard plug or cartridge fuses shall be permitted, provided they are placed within enclosures approved for the purpose and for the location; or fuses shall be permitted if they are within general-purpose enclosures, if they are approved for the purpose, and if they are of a type in which the operating element is immersed in oil or other approved liquid or the operating element is enclosed within a chamber hermetically sealed against the entrance of gases and vapors.

(4) Fuses or Circuit Breakers for Overcurrent Protection. Where not more than 10 sets of approved enclosed fuses or not more than 10 circuit breakers that are not intended to be used as switches for the interruption of current are installed for branch-circuit or feeder protection in any one room, area, or section of the Class I, Division 2 location, general-purpose-type enclosures for such fuses or circuit breakers shall be permitted if the fuses or circuit breakers are for the protection of circuits or feeders supplying lamps in fixed positions only.

FIG. 501-10. Twelve-circuit explosionproof panelboard. (*Crouse-Hinds Co.*)

A set of fuses is all the fuses required to protect all the ungrounded conductors of a circuit. For example, a group of 3 fuses protecting an ungrounded 3-phase circuit, and a single fuse protecting the ungrounded conductor of an identified 2-wire single-phase circuit, is a set of fuses in each instance.

Fuses complying with (b)(3) above shall not be required to be included in counting the ten sets of fuses permitted in general-purpose enclosures.

▲ Figure 501-10 shows a 12-circuit explosionproof panelboard. This device consists of an assembly of branch-circuit circuit breakers, each pair of circuit breakers being enclosed in a cast-metal explosionproof housing. Access to the circuit breakers and to the wiring compartment is through handholes with threaded covers, and threaded hubs are provided for the conduits.

A motor control starter and branch-circuit breaker is shown in Fig. 501-11.

Figure 501-12 shows a magnetically operated motor starter control switch enclosed in a cast-iron box, so as to be suitable for use in Class I, Group D, locations. The wide flanges on the box form a metal-to-metal joint with the cover plate. The cover is secured in place with 24 bolts in order to ensure a flame-tight joint between the box and cover. The illustration shows a starter that is designed for use with a separate pushbutton station; however, similar starters are available with START and STOP pushbuttons mounted in the cover.

Housings similar to that shown in Fig. 501-11 can be obtained which are designed to contain any one of quite a wide variety of across-the-line types of motor starters, either manually or magnetically operable and in ratings up to 25 hp at 220 V three-phase, or 50 hp at 440 V three-phase.

A snap switch in an explosionproof enclosure is shown in Fig. 501-13.

With reference to subparagraph (b)(4), it is assumed that fuses will very seldom blow, or circuit breakers will very seldom open, if used to protect feeders or branch circuits that supply only lamps in fixed positions. In Division 2 locations the conditions are not normally hazardous but may sometimes become so. There is very little probability that one of the overcurrent devices will operate at the same time that the hazardous conditions exist; hence it is not considered necessary to require that these overcurrent devices be in explosionproof enclosures.

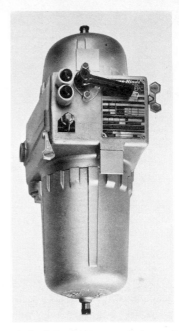

Fig. 501-11. A motor control starter and circuit breaker in an explosionproof housing (open and closed views). (*Crouse-Hinds Co.*)

Fig. 501-12. Magnetic motor starter for use in a Class I, Group D location. (*General Electric Co.*)

501-7. Control Transformers and Resistors. Transformers, impedance coils, and resistors used as, or in conjunction with, control equipment for motors, generators, and appliances shall comply with (a) and (b) below.

(a) Class I, Division 1. In Class I, Division 1 locations, transformers, impedance coils, and resistors, together with any switching mechanism associated with them, shall be provided with enclosures approved for Class I locations.

(b) Class I, Division 2. In Class I, Division 2 locations, control transformers and resistors shall comply with the following:

(1) Switching Mechanisms. Switching mechanisms used in conjunction with

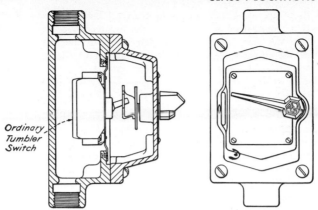

FIG. 501-13. Tumbler-type snap switch in an explosionproof housing.
(*Crouse-Hinds Co.*)

transformers, impedance coils, and resistors shall comply with Section 501-6(b).

(2) Coils and Windings. Enclosures for windings of transformers, solenoids, or impedance coils shall be permitted to be of the general-purpose type.

(3) Resistors. Resistors shall be provided with enclosures; and the assembly shall be approved for Class I locations, unless resistance is nonvariable and maximum operating temperature, in degrees Celsius, will not exceed 80 percent of the ignition temperature of the gas or vapor involved, or has been tested and found incapable of igniting the gas or vapor.

▲ The term *control transformer* is commonly applied to a small dry-type transformer used to supply the control circuits of one or more motors, stepping down the voltage of a 480-V power circuit to 120 V.

501-8. Motors and Generators.

(a) Class I, Division 1. In Class I, Division 1 locations, motors, generators, and other rotating electric machinery shall be: (1) approved for Class I locations; or (2) of the totally enclosed type supplied with positive-pressure ventilation from a source of clean air with discharge to a safe area, so arranged to prevent energizing of the machine until ventilation has been established and the enclosure has been purged with at least 10 volumes of air, and also arranged to automatically de-energize the equipment when the air supply fails; or (3) of the totally enclosed inert-gas-filled type supplied with a suitable reliable source of inert gas for pressuring the enclosure, with devices provided to insure a positive pressure in the enclosure and arranged to automatically de-energize the equipment when the gas supply fails; or (4) of a type designed to be submerged in a liquid which is flammable only when vaporized and mixed with air, or in a gas or vapor at a pressure greater than atmospheric and which is flammable only when mixed with air; and the machine is so arranged to prevent energizing it until it has been purged with the liquid or gas to exclude air, and also arranged to automatically de-energize the equipment when the supply of liquid, or gas or vapor, fails or the pressure is reduced to atmospheric. Totally enclosed motors of Types (2) or (3) shall have no external surface with an operating temperature in degrees Celsius in excess of 80 percent of the ignition temperature of the gas or vapor involved.

Appropriate devices shall be provided to detect and automatically de-energize the motor or provide an adequate alarm if there is any increase in temperature of the motor beyond designed limits. Auxiliary equipment shall be of a type approved for the location in which it is installed.

See ASTM Test Procedure (Designation D 2155-69).

(b) Class I, Division 2.   In Class I, Division 2 locations, motors, generators, and other rotating electric machinery in which are employed sliding contacts, centrifugal or other types of switching mechanism (including motor overcurrent devices), or integral resistance devices, either while starting or while running, shall be approved for Class I locations, unless such sliding contacts, switching mechanisms, and resistance devices are provided with enclosures approved for such locations.

In Class I, Division 2 locations, the installation of open or nonexplosion-proof enclosed motors, such as squirrel-cage induction motors without brushes, switching mechanisms, or similar arc-producing devices shall be permitted.

▲ A motor of a type approved for use in explosive atmospheres is shown in Figs. 501-14 and 501-15. This motor is of the totally enclosed, fan-cooled type. The main frame and end housings are made with sufficient strength to withstand internal pressures due to ignition of a combustible mixture inside the motor. Wide metal-to-metal joints are provided between the frame and housings. Circulation of the air is maintained inside the inner enclosure by fan blades on each end of the rotor. At the left side of the sectional view (Fig. 501-15) a fan is shown in the space between the inner and outer housings. This fan draws in air through a screen and drives it across the surface of the stator punchings and out through openings at the drive end of the motor.

Fig. 501-14. Totally enclosed fan-cooled motor of special type approved for use in explosive atmospheres. (*General Electric Co.*)

Fig. 501-15. View showing internal construction of motor shown in Fig. 501-14. (*General Electric Co.*)

Standard open-type squirrel-cage induction motors may be used in Division 2 locations. Motors having commutators or integral switching or control equipment must be explosionproof.

501-9. Lighting Fixtures.   Lighting fixtures shall comply with (a) or (b) below.

(a) Class I, Division 1.   In Class I, Division 1 locations, lighting fixtures shall comply with the following:

(1) Approved Fixtures.   Each fixture shall be approved as a complete assembly for the Class I, Division 1 location and shall be clearly marked to indicate the maximum wattage of lamps for which it is approved. Fixtures intended for portable use shall be specifically approved as a complete assembly for that use.

(2) Physical Damage.   Each fixture shall be protected against physical damage by a suitable guard or by location.

Fig. 501-16. Lighting fixture suitable for Class I, Group C and D locations. (*Crouse-Hinds Co.*)

(3) Pendant Fixtures. Pendant fixtures shall be suspended by and supplied through threaded rigid metal conduit stems, and threaded joints shall be provided with set-screws or other effective means to prevent loosening. For stems longer than 12 inches, permanent and effective bracing against lateral displacement shall be provided at a level not more than 12 inches above the lower end of the stem, or flexibility in the form of a fitting or flexible connector approved for the purpose and for the Class I, Division 1 location shall be provided not more than 12 inches from the point of attachment to the supporting box or fitting.

(4) Supports. Boxes, box assemblies, or fittings used for the support of lighting fixtures shall be approved for the purpose and for Class I locations.

(b) Class I, Division 2. In Class I, Division 2 locations, lighting fixtures shall comply with the following:

(1) Portable Lamps. Portable lamps shall comply with (a)(1) above.

(2) Fixed Lighting. Lighting fixtures for fixed lighting shall be protected from physical damage by suitable guards or by location. Where there is danger that falling sparks or hot metal from lamps or fixtures might ignite localized concentrations of flammable vapors or gases, suitable enclosures or other effective protective means shall be provided. Where lamps are of a size or type that may, under normal operating conditions, reach surface temperatures exceeding 80 percent of the ignition temperature in degrees Celsius of the gas or vapor involved, fixtures shall comply with (a)(1) above or shall be of a type which has been tested and found incapable of igniting the gas or vapor if the ignition temperature is not exceeded.

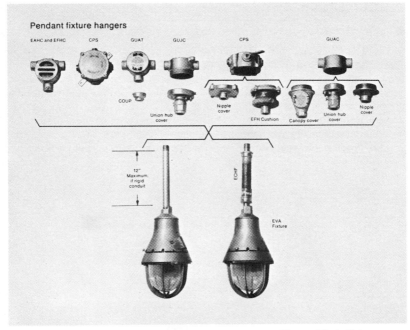

Fig. 501-17. Parts for a lighting fixture installation. (*Crouse-Hinds Co.*)

(3) Pendant Fixtures. Pendant fixtures shall be suspended by threaded rigid metal conduit stems or by other approved means. For rigid stems longer than 12 inches, permanent and effective bracing against lateral displacement shall be provided at a level not more than 12 inches above the lower end of the stem, or flexibility in the form of a fitting or flexible connector approved for the purpose shall be provided not more than 12 inches from the point of attachment to the supporting box or fitting.

(4) Supports. Boxes, box assemblies, or fittings used for the support of lighting fixtures shall be approved for the purpose.

(5) Switches. Switches that are a part of an assembled fixture or of an individual lampholder shall comply with Section 501-6(b)(1).

(6) Starting Equipment. Starting and control equipment for electric-discharge lamps shall comply with Section 501-7(b).

Exception: A thermal protector potted into a thermally protected fluorescent lamp ballast if the lighting fixture is approved for locations of this Class and Division.

▲ Typical parts for a complete lighting-fixture assembly for a Class I, Division 1 location are shown in Figs. 501-16 and 501-17.

Figure 501-17(a) shows an outlet box having an internally threaded opening designed to receive the canopy cover shown in Fig. 501-17(b). A flexible fixture support (c) makes a threaded connection with the canopy and by means of a coupling (d) is connected to the desired length of $^3/_4$-in. rigid conduit extending to the lighting fixture shown in Fig. 501-16. The flexible support is required if the total length of the fixture stem exceeds 12 in. All threaded connections are provided with set-screws to prevent any possible loosening when the fixture is being cleaned or relamped.

The body of the fixture, Fig. 501-16, is provided with a threaded hub to receive the $^3/_4$-in. rigid-conduit stem. A globeholder is threaded to the outside of the body and supports a heavy glass globe, guard, and reflector. This fixture can be obtained in sizes suitable for lamps of any size from 40 to 500 W.

Any desired type of lighting fixture may be installed in a Division 2 location if provided with a guard as specified. A stem, if used, must comply with subparagraph 3.

An explosionproof hand lamp is shown in Fig. 501-18. The construction of this device

FIG. 501-18. Hand lamp suitable for use in Class I locations. (*Crouse-Hinds Co.*)

is in general similar to that of the lighting fixture shown in Fig. 501-16. Section 501-11 requires that a three-conductor cord shall be used and that the device be provided with a terminal for the third, or grounding conductor, which serves to ground the exposed metal parts.

501-10. Utilization Equipment.

(a) Class I, Division 1.   In Class I, Division 1 locations, all utilization equipment shall be approved for Class I locations.

(b) Class I, Division 2.   In Class I, Division 2 locations, all utilization equipment shall comply with the following:

(1) Heaters.   Electrically heated utilization equipment shall be approved for Class I locations, unless it conforms with one of the following:

(a) If the maximum operating temperature of any exposed surface will not exceed 80 percent of the ignition temperature in degrees Celsius of the gas or vapor involved when: (1) continuously energized, (2) maximum ambient temperature, and (3) 20 percent over voltage, it shall be acceptable to omit the temperature controller for the particular heater involved.

(b) If the maximum operating temperature of any exposed surface will not exceed 80 percent of the ignition temperature in degrees Celsius of the gas or vapor involved when: (1) continuously energized, (2) maximum ambient temperature, and (3) normal or rated voltage applied, a temperature controller shall be required on each heater.

(2) Motors.   Motors of motor-driven utilization equipment shall comply with Section 501-8(b).

(3) Switches, Circuit Breakers, and Fuses.   Switches, circuit breakers, and fuses shall comply with Section 501-6(b).

▲ It is seldom necessary to use an appliance in a Class I location. The requirements are practically the same for Division 1 and Division 2 locations.

501-11. Flexible Cords, Class I, Divisions 1 and 2.   A flexible cord shall be permitted only for connection between a portable lamp or other portable utilization equipment and the fixed portion of its supply circuit; and where used shall: (1) be of a type approved for extra-hard usage; and (2) contain, in addition to the conductors of the circuit, a grounding conductor complying with Section 400-23; and (3) be connected to terminals or to supply conductors in an approved manner; and (4) be supported by clamps or by other suitable means in such a manner that there will be no tension on the terminal connections; and (5) be provided with suitable seals where the flexible cord enters boxes, fittings, or enclosures of the explosion-proof type.

Exception: As provided in Sections 501-3(b)(6) and 501-4(b).

See Section 501-13 for flexible cords exposed to liquids having a deleterious effect on the conductor insulation.

501-12. Receptacles and Attachment Plugs, Class I, Divisions 1 and 2.   Receptacles and attachment plugs shall be of the type providing for connection to the grounding conductor of a flexible cord and shall be approved for Class I locations.

Exception: As provided in Section 501-3(b)(6).

▲ A unit device consisting of a receptacle and plug interlocked with an explosionproof switch is shown in Fig. 501-19. The plug cannot be inserted or withdrawn unless the

FIG. 501-19. Explosionproof receptacle and attachment plug with interlocking switch. (*Appleton Electric Co.*)

FIG. 501-20. Explosionproof receptacle and attachment plug. (*Crouse-Hinds Co.*)

switch is open, and the switch cannot be closed until the plug has been inserted. An additional pole is provided in the plug and receptacle for connection to a grounding conductor in the cord.

Figure 501-20 shows a three-pole 30-A receptacle and the attachment plug which is so designed as to seal the arc when the circuit is broken, and therefore is suitable for use without a switch.

The circuit conductors are brought into the base or body through rigid conduit screwed into a tapped opening and are spliced to pigtail leads from the receptacle. The receptacle housing is then attached to the base, the joint being made at wide flanges ground to a suitable fit. All necessary sealing is provided in the device itself, and no additional sealing is required when it is installed.

The parts are so constructed that the plug must first be partially withdrawn, which breaks each pole of the circuit in a closed chamber, and the resulting arcs are quickly smothered. A sleeve on the receptacle must then be rotated through a small angle before the plug can be fully withdrawn; thus, the action is delayed so that the arcs are always extinguished before the contacts are withdrawn from the closed chamber.

The plug is designed to receive a three-conductor cord for a two-wire circuit or a four-conductor cord for a three-wire three-phase circuit, and is provided with a clamping device to relieve the terminals from any strain. The extra conductor is used to ground the equipment supplied.

501-13. Conductor Insulation Class I, Divisions 1 and 2. Where condensed vapors or liquids may collect on, or come in contact with, the insulation on conductors, such insulation shall be of a type approved for use under such conditions; or the insulation shall be protected by a sheath of lead or by other approved means.

▲ Because of economics and greater ease in handling, nylon-jacketed types TW and THWN wires suitable for use where exposed to gasoline have in most cases replaced lead-covered conductors.

An excerpt from Underwriters' Laboratories, Inc., Electrical Construction Materials List states as follows:

Wires, Thermoplastic.
Gasoline Resistant TW—Indicates a TW conductor with a jacket of extruded nylon suitable for use in wet locations, and for exposure to mineral oil, and to liquid gasoline and gasoline vapors at ordinary ambient temperature. It is identified by tag marking and by printing on the insulation or nylon jacket with the designation "Type TW Gasoline and Oil Resistant I."

Also listed for the above use is "Gasoline Resistant THWN" with the designation "Type THWN Gasoline and Oil Resistant II."

It should be noted that other thermoplastic wires may be suitable for exposure to mineral oil; but with the exception of those marked "Gasoline and Oil Resistant," reference to mineral oil does not include gasoline or similar light-petroleum solvents.

The conductor itself must bear the marking legend designating its use as suitable for gasoline exposure; such designation on the tag alone is not sufficient.

501-14. Signaling, Alarm, Remote-Control, and Communication Systems.
(a) Class I, Division 1. In Class I, Division 1 locations, all apparatus and equipment of signaling, alarm, remote-control, and communication systems, regardless of voltage, shall be approved for Class I locations, and all wiring shall comply with Sections 501-4(a) and 501-5(a) and (c).

(b) Class I, Division 2. In Class I, Division 2 locations, signaling, alarm, remote-control, and communication systems shall comply with the following:

(1) Contacts. Switches, circuit breakers, and make-and-break contacts of pushbuttons, relays, alarm bells, and horns shall have enclosures approved for Class I locations.

Exception: General-purpose enclosures shall be permitted if current interrupting contacts are:

a. Immersed in oil; or

b. Enclosed within a chamber hermetically sealed against the entrance of gases or vapors; or

c. In circuits that under normal conditions do not release sufficient energy to ignite a specific hazardous atmospheric mixture, i.e., are non-incendive.

(2) Resistors and Similar Equipment. Resistors, resistance devices, thermionic tubes, rectifiers, and similar equipment shall comply with Section 501-3(b)(2).

(3) Protectors. Enclosures shall be provided for lightning protective devices and for fuses. Such enclosures shall be permitted to be of the general-purpose type.

(4) Wiring and Sealing. All wiring shall comply with Sections 501-4(b) and 501-5(b) and (c).

▲ Nearly all signaling, remote-control, and communication equipment involves make or break contacts; hence in Division 1 locations all devices must be explosion-proof, and the wiring must comply with the requirements for light and power wiring in such locations, including seals.

Figure 501-21 shows a telephone signal bell having the operating mechanism mounted in an explosionproof housing. Similar equipment may be obtained for operating horns or sirens.

Referring to subparagraph (1), it would usually be the more simple method to use explosionproof devices, rather than devices having contacts immersed in oil or devices in hermetically sealed enclosures, though mercury switches, which are hermetically sealed, may be used for some purposes.

FIG. 501-21. Telephone signal bell for use in Class I hazardous locations. (*Crouse-Hinds Co.*)

501-15. Live Parts, Class I, Divisions 1 and 2. There shall be no exposed live parts.

501-16. Grounding, Class I, Divisions 1 and 2. Wiring and equipment shall be grounded as specified in (a) through (f) below.

(a) Exposed Parts. The exposed noncurrent-carrying metal parts of equipment, such as the frames or metal exteriors of motors, fixed or portable lamps, lighting fixtures, or other utilization equipment, and cabinets, cases, and conduit, shall be grounded as specified in Article 250.

(b) Bonding. The locknut-bushing and double-locknut types of contacts shall not be depended upon for bonding purposes, but bonding jumpers with proper fittings or other approved means shall be used. Such means of bonding shall apply to all intervening raceways, fittings, boxes, enclosures, etc., between hazardous areas and the point of grounding for service equipment. Where flexible conduit is used as permitted in Section 501-4(b), bonding jumpers with proper fittings shall be provided around such conduit.

(c) Lightning Protection. Each ungrounded service conductor of a wiring system in a Class I location, where supplied from an overhead line in an area where lightning disturbances are prevalent, shall be protected by a lightning protective device of proper type. Lightning protective devices shall be connected to the service conductors on the supply side of the service disconnecting means, and shall be bonded to the raceway system at the service entrance.

See Section 502-3 for surge protection.

(d) Grounded Service Conductor Bonded to Raceway. Wiring in a Class I location, where supplied from a grounded alternating-current supply system in which a grounded conductor is a part of the service, shall have the grounded service conductor bonded to the raceway system and to the grounding conductor for the raceway system. The bonding connection to the grounded service conductor shall be made on the supply side of the service disconnecting means.

(e) Transformer Ground Bonded to Raceway. Wiring in a Class I location, where supplied from a grounded alternating-current supply system in which no grounded conductor is a part of the service, shall be provided with a metal connection between the supply system ground and the service-equipment enclosure. The metal connection shall comply with Section 250-23(b).

(f) Multiple Grounds. Where, in the application of Section 250-21, it is necessary to abandon one or more grounding connections to avoid objectionable passage of current over the grounding conductors, the connection required in (d) and (e) above shall not be abandoned while any other grounding connection remains connected to the supply system.

▲ Special care in the grounding of all equipment is necessary in order to prevent the possibility of arcs or sparks when any grounded metal comes in contact with the frame or case of the equipment. All connections of conduit to boxes, cabinets, enclosures for apparatus, and motor frames must be so made as to secure permanent and effective electrical connections. To be effective, this form of construction is not only necessary in the spaces that are classed as hazardous, but should also be carried out back to the point where the connection for grounding the conduit is made to the water-piping system. Outside the space where the hazardous conditions exist, threaded connections should be used for conduit.

Lightning arresters are spark-producing devices and should be installed outside the building. For services less than 1,000 V the arresters must have grounding connections as provided in Sec. 250-131, and in addition, the grounding connection must be bonded to the service entrance conduit.

If the service voltage is not over 600 V, the supply system is a secondary system and the provisions of Art. 250 apply; hence the grounded service conductor will always be bonded to the equipment grounding conductor. It might be possible to install a system operating at over 600 V in a Class I, Division 2 location, but this would be an unusual case.

The conditions described in paragraph (e) would seldom be met in practice. The conductor used for making the connection would usually be an outdoor overhead conductor, in which case, according to Sec. 225-6, the conductor should not be smaller than No. 10. If the supply system has a grounded conductor, connection of this conductor to the equipment ground will help to provide proper operation of over-current protective devices.

ARTICLE 502. CLASS II LOCATIONS

502-1. General. The general rules of this Code shall apply to the electric wiring and equipment in locations classified as Class II locations in Section 500-5.

Exception: As modified by this Article.

"Dust-ignition-proof," as used in this Article shall mean enclosed in a manner that will exclude ignitible amounts of dusts or amounts that might affect performance or rating and that, where installed and protected in accordance with this Code, will not permit arcs, sparks, or heat otherwise generated or liberated inside of the enclosure to cause ignition of exterior accumulations or atmospheric suspensions of a specified dust on or in the vicinity of the enclosure.

▲ Referring to Sec. 500-5, the hazards in Class II locations are due to the presence of combustible dust. These locations are subdivided into three groups, as follows:

Group E, Atmospheres containing metal dust;

Group F, Atmospheres containing carbon black, coal dust, or coke dust;

Group G, Atmospheres containing grain dust.

It is important to note that some equipment that is suitable for Class II, Group G, is not suitable for Class II, Groups E and F.

Any one of four hazards, or a combination of two or more, may exist in a Class II location: (1) an explosive mixture of air and dust, (2) the collection of conductive dust on and around live parts, (3) overheating of equipment because deposits of dust interfere with the normal radiation of heat, and (4) the possible ignition of deposits of dust by arcs or sparks. A large number of processes which may produce combustible dusts are listed in Sec. 500-5. Most of the equipment listed as suitable for Class I locations is also dust-tight, but it should not be taken for granted that all explosionproof equipment is suitable for use in Class II locations. Some explosionproof equipment may reach too high a temperature if blanketed by a heavy deposit of dust. Grain dust will ignite at a temperature below that of many of the flammable vapors.

Location of service equipment, switchboards, and panelboards in a separate room away from the dusty atmosphere is always preferable.

Equipment installed in Class II locations shall be able to function at full rating without developing surface temperatures high enough to cause excessive dehydration or gradual carbonization of any organic dust deposits that may occur.

Dust that is carbonized or excessively dry is highly susceptible to spontaneous ignition.

In general, the maximum surface temperatures under actual operating conditions shall not exceed 165°C (329°F) for equipment that is not subject to overloading and 120°C (248°F) for equipment (such as motors or power transformers) that may be overloaded.

Equipment and wiring of the type defined in Article 100 as explosion-proof shall not be required and shall not be acceptable in Class II locations unless approved for such locations.

502-2. Transformers and Capacitors.

(a) Class II, Division 1. In Class II, Division 1 locations, transformers and capacitors shall comply with the following:

(1) Containing Liquid That Will Burn. Transformers and capacitors containing a liquid that will burn shall be installed only in approved vaults complying with Sections 450-41 through 450-48, and in addition: (1) doors or other openings communicating with the hazardous location shall have self-closing fire doors on both sides of the wall, and the doors shall be carefully fitted and provided with suitable seals (such as weather stripping) to minimize the entrance of dust into the vault, and (2) vent openings and ducts shall communicate only with the outside air; and (3) suitable pressure-relief openings communicating with the outside air shall be provided.

(2) Not Containing Liquid That Will Burn. Transformers and capacitors that do not contain a liquid that will burn shall: (1) be installed in vaults complying with Sections 450-41 through 450-48; or (2) be approved as a complete assembly, including terminal connections for Class II locations.

(3) Metal Dusts. No transformer or capacitor shall be installed in a location where dust from magnesium, aluminum, aluminum bronze powders, or other metals of similarly hazardous characteristics may be present.

(b) Class II, Division 2. In Class II, Division 2 locations, transformers and capacitors shall comply with the following:

(1) Containing Liquid That Will Burn. Transformers and capacitors containing a liquid that will burn shall be installed in vaults complying with Sections 450-41 through 450-48.

(2) Containing Askarel. Transformers containing askarel and rated in excess of 25 kVA shall: (1) be provided with pressure-relief vents; and (2) be provided with a means for absorbing any gases generated by arcing inside the case, or the pressure-relief vents shall be connected to a chimney or flue that will carry such gases outside the building; and (3) have an air space of not less than 6 inches between the transformer cases and any adjacent combustible material.

(3) Dry-Type Transformers. Dry-type transformers shall be installed in vaults or shall: (1) have their windings and terminal connections enclosed in tight metal housings without ventilating or other openings; and (2) operate at not over 600 volts.

▲ So far as can be learned, no askarel-insulated or dry-type transformers can be obtained which are dust-tight.

Capacitors of the type used for the correction of the power factor of individual motors are of sealed construction, but must be provided with dust-tight terminal enclosures if installed in these locations.

It would no doubt be possible to construct a small, low-voltage dry-type transformer without ventilating openings, but transformers having a primary voltage rating of over 600 V must either be askarel-filled or must be installed in vaults. It would seldom be necessary to install any transformer in a Class II, Division 2 location.

There are no special requirements for capacitors in Division 2 locations except that they must not contain oil or any other "liquid that will burn."

502-3. Surge Protection, Class II, Divions 1 and 2. In geographical locations where lightning disturbances are prevalent and where supplied from overhead lines, wiring systems in Class II locations shall be suitably protected against high-voltage surges. This protection shall include suitable lightning protective devices, interconnection of all grounds, and surge-protective capacitors.

Interconnection of all grounds shall include grounds for primary and secondary lightning protective devices, secondary system grounds, if any, and grounds of conduit and equipment of the interior wiring system.

For ungrounded secondary systems, secondary lightning protective devices may be provided both at the service and at the point where the secondary system receives its supply. The intervening secondary conductors shall be permitted as the metallic connection between the secondary protective devices, if grounds for the primary and secondary devices are metallically interconnected at the supply end of the secondary system, and if the secondary devices are grounded to the raceway system at the load end of the secondary system.

Surge-protective capacitors shall be of a type designed for the specific duty, shall be connected to each ungrounded service conductor, and shall be grounded to the interior conduit system. Capacitors shall be protected by 30-ampere fuses of suitable type and voltage rating, or by automatic circuit breakers of suitable type and rating, and shall be connected to the supply conductors on the supply side of the service disconnecting means.

▲ A common application of this requirement is found in grain-handling properties in localities where severe lightning storms are prevalent. Assuming a building supplied through a bank of transformers located a short distance from the building, the recommendations are, in general, as shown in the single-line diagram in Fig. 502-1.

The surge-protective equipment consists of primary lightning arresters at the transformers and surge-protective capacitors connected to the supply side of the service equipment. The lightning-arrester ground and the secondary system ground should be solidly connected together. All grounds should be bonded together and to the service conduit and to all boxes enclosing the service equipment, metering equipment, and capacitors.

Complete information on methods of providing surge protection may be obtained from the Mill Mutual Fire Prevention Bureau, 2 North Riverside Plaza, Chicago, Ill. 60606.

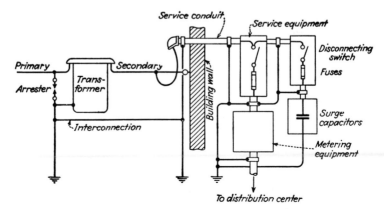

Fig. 502-1. Method of providing surge protection.

502-4. Wiring Methods. Wiring methods shall comply with (a) and (b) below.

(a) Class II, Division 1. In Class II, Division 1 locations, threaded rigid metal conduit or Type MI cable with termination fittings approved for the location shall be the wiring method employed. Type MI cable shall be installed and supported in a manner to avoid tensile stress at the termination fittings.

(1) Fittings and Boxes. Fittings and boxes shall be provided with threaded bosses for connection to conduit or cable terminations, shall have close fitting covers, and shall have no openings (such as holes for attachment screws) through which dust might enter or through which sparks or burning material might escape. Fittings and boxes in which taps, joints, or terminal connections are made, or that are used in locations where dusts are of a combustible electrically conductive nature, shall be approved for Class II locations.

(2) Flexible Connections. Where necessary to employ flexible connections, dust-tight flexible connectors, liquidtight flexible metal conduit with approved fittings, or flexible cord approved for extra-hard usage and provided with bushed fittings shall be used, except that where dusts are of an electrically conducting nature flexible cords shall be provided with dust-tight seals at both ends. An additional conductor for grounding shall be provided in the flexible cord unless other acceptable means of grounding is provided. Where flexible connections are subject to oil or other corrosive conditions, the insulation of the conductors shall be of a type approved for the condition or shall be protected by means of a suitable sheath.

▲ Where a flexible connection is necessary, it would usually be preferable to use a flexible fitting as shown in Fig. 501-17(c). Standard flexible conduit may be used except where combustible conductive dust is present, but in such case Sec. 502-16(b) requires that a bonding jumper must be provided around the conduit. The use of a hard-service cord having one conductor serving as a grounding conductor is permitted.

In Division 1 locations, threaded connections must be used for connecting rigid conduit to boxes and fittings. If any combustible conducting dust is present or if tape or joints are contained, boxes and fittings must be dust-tight, such as the type shown in Fig. 502-2.

In Division 2 locations, in order to provide adequate bonding, threaded fittings such as those shown in Figs. 502-2 and 502-3 should be used with rigid conduit. The requirement for close-fitting covers could best be taken care of by using the dust-tight

FIG. 502-2. Fitting for use in Class II locations where conducting dust is present. (*Appleton Electric Co.*)

FIG. 502-3. An explosion-proof and dust-tight switch. (*Appleton Electric Co.*)

fitting shown in Fig. 502-2. The standard types of pressed steel boxes cannot be used in any case where the box contains taps or splices, and even if no taps or splices are contained, a bonding jumper must be provided around any such box. In runs of conduit, seals can be provided by using any of the sealing fittings designed for use in Class I locations.

(b) Class II, Division 2. In Class II, Division 2 locations, rigid metal conduit, electrical metallic tubing, dust-tight wireways, or Type MI, MC, ALS, CS, or SNM cable with approved termination fittings shall be the wiring method employed.

(1) Wireways, Fittings, and Boxes. Wireways, fittings, and boxes in which taps, joints, or terminal connections are made shall be designed to minimize the entrance of dust, and: (1) shall be provided with telescoping or close fitting covers or other effective means to prevent the escape of sparks or burning material, and (2) shall have no openings (such as holes for attachment screws) through which, after installation, sparks or burning material might escape or through which adjacent combustible material might be ignited.

(2) Flexible Connections. Where flexible connections are necessary, (a)(2) above shall apply.

502-5. Sealing, Class II, Divisions 1 and 2. Where a raceway provides communication between an enclosure that is required to be dust-ignition-proof and one that is not, suitable means shall be provided to prevent the entrance of dust into the dust-ignition-proof enclosure through the raceway. One of the following means shall be permitted: (1) a permanent and effective seal; (2) a horizontal raceway not less than 10 feet long; or (3) a vertical raceway not less than 5 feet long and extending downward from the dust-ignition-proof enclosure. Sealing fittings shall be accessible.

▲ Dust-tight enclosures are required in many cases in Division 1 locations and under some conditions in Division 2 locations. Where a raceway connects two enclosures, only one of which is required to be dust-tight, three alternative methods are provided for preventing the travel of dust through the raceway into the dust-tight enclosure.

502-6. Switches, Circuit Breakers, Motor Controllers, and Fuses.

(a) Class II, Division 1. In Class II, Division 1 locations, switches, circuit breakers, motor controllers, and fuses shall comply with the following:

(1) Type Required. Switches, circuit breakers, motor controllers, and fuses, including pushbuttons, relays, and similar devices that are intended to interrupt current during normal operation or that are installed where dusts of a combustible electrically conductive nature may be present shall be provided with dust-ignition-proof enclosures, which, together with the enclosed equipment in each case, shall be approved as a complete assembly for Class II locations.

(2) Isolating Switches. Disconnecting and isolating switches containing no fuses and not intended to interrupt current and not installed where dusts may be of an electrically conductive nature shall be provided with tight metal enclosures that shall be designed to minimize the entrance of dust, and that shall: (1) be equipped with telescoping or close fitting covers or with other effective means to prevent the escape of sparks or burning material, and (2) have no openings (such as holes for attachment screws) through which, after installation, sparks or burning material might escape or through which exterior accumulations of dust or adjacent combustible material might be ignited.

(3) Metal Dusts.   In locations where dust from magnesium, aluminum, aluminum bronze powders, or other metals of similarly hazardous characteristics may be present, fuses, switches, motor controllers, and circuit breakers shall have enclosures specifically approved for such locations.

(b) Class II, Division 2.   In Class II, Division 2 locations, enclosures for fuses, switches, circuit breakers, and motor controllers, including pushbuttons, relays, and similar devices, shall comply with (a)(2) above.

FIG. 502-4. Panelboard in a dust-tight cabinet, suitable for use in Class II, Groups E, F, and G locations. (*Crouse-Hinds Co.*)

▲ Figure 502-4 shows a panelboard in a dust-tight cabinet which is approved for use in Class II locations.

Most of the switches and circuit breakers approved for Class I, Division 1 locations are also approved for use in Class II locations.

Switches conforming with the definition of the term *isolating switch* would seldom be used in any hazardous location. Such switches are permitted for use as the disconnecting means for motors larger than 100 hp.

502-7. Control Transformers and Resistors.

(a) Class II, Division 1.   In Class II, Division 1 locations, control transformers, solenoids, impedance coils, resistors, and any overcurrent devices or switching mechanisms associated with them shall have dust-ignition-proof enclosures approved for Class II locations. No control transformer, impedance coil, or resistor shall be installed in a location where dust from magnesium, aluminum, aluminum bronze powders, or other metals of similarly hazardous characteristics may be present unless provided with an enclosure approved for the specific location.

(b) Class II, Division 2.   In Class II, Division 2 locations, transformers and resistors shall comply with the following:

(1) Switching Mechanisms.   Switching mechanisms (including overcurrent devices) associated with control transformers, solenoids, impedance coils, and resistors shall be provided with enclosures complying with Section 502-6(a)(2).

(2) Coils and Windings.   Where not located in the same enclosure with switching mechanisms, control transformers, solenoids, and impedance coils shall be provided with tight metal housings without ventilating openings.

(3) Resistors. Resistors and resistance devices shall have dust-ignition-proof enclosures approved for Class II locations.

Exception: Where the maximum normal operating temperature of the resistor will not exceed 120°C (248°F), nonadjustable resistors or resistors that are part of an automatically timed starting sequence shall be permitted to have enclosures complying with (b)(1) above.

502-8. Motors and Generators.

(a) Class II, Division 1. In Class II, Division 1 locations, motors, generators, and other rotating electric machinery shall be dust-ignition-proof or totally enclosed pipe-ventilated and shall be approved for Class II locations.

(b) Class II, Division 2. In Class II, Division 2 locations, motors, generators, and other rotating electric machinery shall be dust-ignition-proof or totally enclosed pipe-ventilated, for which maximum surface temperatures shall not exceed 120°C (248°F).

Exception: If the authority having jurisdiction believes accumulations of non-conductive nonabrasive dust will be moderate; and if machines can be easily reached for routine cleaning and maintenance, the following may be installed:

a. Standard open-type machines without sliding contacts, centrifugal or other types of switching mechanism (including motor overcurrent devices), or integral resistance devices.

b. Standard open-type machines with such contacts, switching mechanisms, or resistance devices enclosed within tight metal housings without ventilating or other openings.

c. Self-cleaning textile motors of the squirrel-cage type.

▲ Figure 502-5 is a totally enclosed pipe-ventilated motor. A motor of this type is cooled by clean air forced through a pipe by a fan or blower. The cut shows the intake

Fig. 502-5. Totally enclosed pipe-ventilated motor. (*Westinghouse Electric Corp.*)

opening, where air is delivered to the motor through the pipe from the blower. The exhaust opening is on the opposite side; this should be connected to a pipe terminating outside the building, so that dust will not collect inside the motor while it is not running.

Motors of the common totally enclosed type without special provision for cooling may be used in Class II locations, but to deliver the same horsepower, a plain totally enclosed motor must be considerably larger and heavier than a motor of the open type or an enclosed fan-cooled or pipe-ventilated motor.

502-9. Ventilating Piping. Ventilating pipes for motors, generators, or other rotating electric machinery, or for enclosures for electric equipment shall be of metal not lighter than No. 24 MSG, or of equally substantial noncombustible material, and shall comply with the following: (1) lead directly to a source of clean air outside of buildings; (2) be screened at the outer ends to prevent the entrance of small animals or birds; and (3) be protected against physical damage and against rusting or other corrosive influences.

Ventilating pipes shall also comply with (a) and (b) below.

(a) Class II, Division 1. In Class II, Division 1 locations, ventilating pipes, including their connections to motors or to the dust-ignition-proof enclosures for other equipment, shall be dust-tight throughout their length. For metal pipes, seams and joints shall comply with one of the following: (1) be riveted and soldered; (2) be bolted and soldered; (3) be welded, or (4) be rendered dust-tight by some other equally effective means.

(b) Class II, Division 2. In Class II, Division 2 locations, ventilating pipes and their connections shall be sufficiently tight to prevent the entrance of appreciable quantities of dust into the ventilated equipment or enclosure, and to prevent the escape of sparks, flame, or burning material that might ignite dust accumulations or combustible material in the vicinity. For metal pipes, lock seams and riveted or welded joints shall be permitted; and tight-fitting slip joints shall be permitted where some flexibility is necessary, as at connections to motors.

502-10. Utilization Equipment.

(a) Class II, Division 1. In Class II, Division 1 locations, all utilization equipment shall be approved for Class II locations. Where dust from magnesium, aluminum, aluminum bronze powders, or other metals of similarly hazardous characteristics may be present, such equipment shall be approved for the specific location.

(b) Class II, Division 2. In Class II, Division 2 locations, all utilization equipment shall comply with the following:

(1) Heaters. Electrically heated utilization equipment shall be approved for Class II locations.

(2) Motors. Motors of motor-driven utilization equipment shall comply with Section 502-8(b).

(3) Switches, Circuit Breakers, and Fuses. Enclosures for switches, circuit breakers, and fuses shall comply with Section 502-6(a)(2).

(4) Transformers, Impedance Coils, and Resistors. Transformers, solenoids, impedance coils, and resistors shall comply with Section 502-7(b).

502-11. Lighting Fixtures. Lighting fixtures shall comply with (a) and (b) below.

(a) Class II, Division 1. In Class II, Division 1 locations, lighting fixtures for fixed and portable lighting shall comply with the following:

(1) Approved Fixtures. Each fixture shall be approved for Class II locations and shall be clearly marked to indicate the maximum wattage of the lamp for which it is approved. In locations where dust from magnesium, aluminum, aluminum bronze powders, or other metals of similarly hazardous characteristics may be present, fixtures for fixed or portable lighting and all auxiliary equipment shall be approved for the specific location.

(2) Physical Damage. Each fixture shall be protected against physical damage by a suitable guard or by location.

(3) Pendant Fixtures. Pendant fixtures shall be suspended by threaded rigid metal conduit stems, by chains with approved fittings, or by other approved means. For rigid stems longer than 12 inches, permanent and effective bracing against lateral displacement shall be provided at a level not more than 12 inches above the lower end of the stem, or flexibility in the form of a fitting or a flexible connector approved for the purpose and for the location shall be provided not more than 12 inches from the point of attachment to the supporting box or fitting. Threaded joints shall be provided with set-screws or other effective means to prevent loosening. Where wiring between an outlet box or fitting and a pendant fixture is not enclosed in conduit, flexible cord approved for hard usage shall be used, and suitable seals shall be provided where the cord enters the fixture and the outlet box or fitting. Flexible cord shall not serve as the supporting means for a fixture.

(4) Supports. Boxes, box assemblies, or fittings used for the support of lighting fixtures shall be approved for the purpose and for Class II locations.

(b) Class II, Division 2. In Class II, Division 2 locations, lighting fixtures shall comply with the following:

(1) Portable Lamps. Portable lamps shall be approved for Class II locations. They shall be clearly marked to indicate the maximum wattage of lamps for which they are approved.

(2) Fixed Lighting. Lighting fixtures for fixed lighting, where not of a type approved for Class II locations, shall provide enclosures for lamps and lampholders that shall be designed to minimize the deposit of dust on lamps and to prevent the escape of sparks, burning material, or hot metal. Each fixture shall be clearly marked to indicate the maximum wattage of the lamp that shall be permitted without exceeding an exposed surface temperature of 165°C (329°F) under normal conditions of use.

(3) Physical Damage. Lighting fixtures for fixed lighting shall be protected from physical damage by suitable guards or by location.

(4) Pendant Fixtures. Pendant fixtures shall be suspended by threaded rigid metal conduit stems, by chains with approved fittings, or by other approved means. For rigid stems longer than 12 inches, permanent and effective bracing against lateral displacement shall be provided at a level not more than 12 inches above the lower end of the stem, or flexibility in the form of a fitting or a flexible connector approved for the purpose shall be provided not more than 12 inches from the point of attachment to the supporting box or fitting. Where wiring between an outlet box or fitting and a pendant fixture is not enclosed in conduit, flexible cord approved for hard usage shall be used. Flexible cord shall not serve as the supporting means for a fixture.

(5) Supports. Boxes, box assemblies, or fittings used for the support of lighting fixtures shall be approved for the purpose.

(6) Electric-Discharge Lamps. Starting and control equipment for electric-discharge lamps shall comply with the requirement of Section 502-7(b).

Fig. 502-6. Lighting fixture for use in Class II, Division 1 locations. (*Crouse-Hinds Co.*)

▲ Where metal dusts are present, lighting fixtures must be approved for use in Group E atmospheres. The fixture shown in Fig. 502-6 is listed by Underwriters' Laboratories, Inc., as suitable for use in all three of the locations classed as Groups E, F, and G.

The purpose of the latter part of subparagraph (a)(3) is to specify the type of cord to be used for wiring a chain-suspended fixture. It is not the intention to permit a fixture to be suspended by means of a cord pendant or drop cord.

The only special requirements for lighting fixtures in Class II, Division 2 locations are that the lamp must be enclosed in a suitable glass globe and that a guard must be provided unless the fixture is so located that it will not be exposed to physical damage. The enclosing globe should be tight enough so that it will practically exclude dust, though dust-tight construction is not called for.

The portable handlamp shown in Fig. 501-18 is approved for use in any Class II, Group G location, i.e., where the hazards are due to grain dust.

502-12. Flexible Cords, Class II, Division 1 and 2.   Flexible cords used in Class II locations shall comply with the following: (1) be of a type approved for extra-hard usage; (2) contain, in addition to the conductors of the circuit, a grounding conductor complying with Section 400-23; (3) be connected to terminals or to supply conductors in an approved manner; (4) be supported by clamps or by other suitable means in such a manner that there will be no tension on the terminal connections; and (5) be provided with suitable seals to prevent the entrance of dust where the flexible cord enters boxes or fittings that are required to be dust-ignition-proof.

502-13. Receptacles and Attachment Plugs.

(a) Class II, Division 1.   In Class II, Division 1 locations, receptacles and attachment plugs shall be of the type providing for connection to the grounding conductor of the flexible cord and shall be approved for Class II locations.

(b) Class II, Division 2.   In Class II, Division 2 locations, receptacles and attachment plugs shall be of the type providing for connection to the grounding conductor of the flexible cord and shall be so designed that connection to the supply circuit cannot be made or broken while live parts are exposed.

502-14. Signaling, Alarm, Remote-Control, and Local Loud-Speaker Intercommunication Systems.

See Article 800 for rules governing the installation of communication circuits as defined in Article 100.

(a) Class II, Division 1.   In Class II, Division 1 locations, signaling, alarm, remote-control, and local loud-speaker intercommunication systems shall comply with the following:

(1) Wiring Methods.   Where accidental damage or breakdown of insulation might cause arcs, sparks, or high temperatures, the wiring method shall be rigid metal conduit, electrical metallic tubing, or Type MI cable with approved termination fittings. For conduit or electrical metallic tubing, the number of conductors shall be limited only by the requirement that the cross-sectional area of all conductors shall not exceed 40 percent of the area of the raceway. Where limited flexibility is desirable or where exposure to physical damage is not severe, flexible cord approved for extra-hard usage shall be permitted.

(2) Contacts. Switches, circuit breakers, relays, contactors, and fuses that may interrupt other than voice currents, and current-breaking contacts for bells, horns, howlers, sirens, and other devices in which sparks or arcs may be produced shall be provided with enclosures approved for a Class II location.

Exception: Where current-breaking contacts are immersed in oil, or where the interruption of current occurs within a chamber sealed against the entrance of dust, enclosures shall be permitted to be of the general-purpose type.

(3) Resistors and Similar Equipment. Resistors, transformers, choke coils, and similar equipment that may carry other than voice currents, and rectifiers, thermionic tubes, and other heat-generating equipment shall be provided with enclosures approved for Class II locations.

(4) Rotating Machinery. Motors, generators, and other rotating electric machinery shall comply with Section 502-8(a).

(5) Combustible Electrically Conductive Dusts. Where dusts are of a combustible electrically conductive nature, all wiring and equipment shall be approved for Class II locations.

(6) Metal Dusts. Where dust from magnesium, aluminum, aluminum bronze powders, or other metals of similarly hazardous characteristics may be present, all apparatus and equipment shall be approved for the specific conditions.

(b) Class II, Division 2. In Class II, Division 2 locations, signaling, alarm, remote-control, and local loudspeaker intercommunication systems shall comply with the following:

(1) Contacts. Enclosures shall comply with (a)(2) above; or contacts shall have tight metal enclosures designed to minimize the entrance of dust, and shall have telescoping or tight-fitting covers and no openings through which, after installation, sparks or burning material might escape.

(2) Transformers and Similar Equipment. The windings and terminal connections of transformers, choke coils, and similar equipment shall be provided with tight metal enclosures without ventilating openings.

(3) Resistors and Similar Equipment. Resistors, resistance devices, thermionic tubes, rectifiers, and similar equipment shall comply with (a)(3) above.

Exception: Enclosures for thermionic tubes, nonadjustable resistors, or rectifiers for which maximum operating temperature will not exceed 120° C (248° F) shall be permitted to be of the general-purpose type.

(4) Rotating Machinery. Motors, generators, and other rotating electric machinery shall comply with Section 502-8(b).

502-15. Live Parts, Class II, Divisions 1 and 2. Live parts shall not be exposed.

502-16. Grounding, Class II, Divisions 1 and 2. Wiring and equipment shall be grounded in accordance with (a) through (f) below.

(a) Exposed Parts. Exposed noncurrent-carrying metal parts of equipment, such as the frames or metal exteriors of motors, fixed or portable lamps, lighting fixtures, or other utilization equipment, or cabinets, cases, and conduit shall be grounded as specified in Article 250.

(b) Bonding. The locknut-bushing and double-locknut type of contact shall not be depended upon for bonding purposes; but bonding jumpers with proper fittings or other approved means shall be used. Such means of bonding shall apply to all intervening raceways, fittings, boxes, enclosures, etc., between hazardous areas and the point of grounding for service equipment. Where flexible conduit is used as permitted in Section 502-4, bonding jumpers with proper fittings shall be provided around such conduit.

▲ Paragraph (b) prohibits the use of locknuts and bushings and double locknuts and bushings for any of the raceways, boxes, fittings, enclosures, etc., between the hazardous area and the grounding electrode conductor connection at the service equipment. Bonding jumpers, with approved bonding fittings, are required for such intervening raceway and enclosures all the way to the grounding electrode conductor. See Sec. 250-79.

(c) **Lightning Protection.** Each ungrounded service conductor of a wiring system in a Class II location, where supplied from an ungrounded overhead electric supply system in an area where lightning disturbances are prevalent, shall be protected by a lightning protective device of proper type. Lightning protective devices shall be connected to the service conductors on the supply side of the service disconnecting means, and shall be bonded to the raceway system at the service entrance.

(d) **Grounded Service Conductor Bonded to Raceway.** Wiring in a Class II location, where supplied from a grounded alternating-current supply system in which a grounded conductor is a part of the service, shall have the grounded service conductor bonded to the raceway system and to the grounding conductor for the raceway system. The bonding connection to the grounded service conductor shall be made on the supply side of the service disconnecting means.

(e) **Transformer Ground Bonded to Raceway.** Wiring in a Class II location, where supplied from a grounded alternating-current supply system in which no grounded conductor is a part of the service, shall be provided with a metallic connection between the supply system ground and the service-equipment enclosure. The metallic connection shall comply with Section 250-23(b).

(f) **Multiple Grounds.** Where, in the application of Section 250-21, it is necessary to abandon one or more grounding connections to avoid objectionable passage of current over the grounding conductors, the connection required in (d) or (e) above shall not be abandoned while any other grounding connection remains connected to the supply system.

ARTICLE 503. CLASS III LOCATIONS

503-1. General. The general rules of this Code shall apply to electric wiring and equipment in locations classified as Class III locations in Section 500-6.

Exception: As modified by this Article.

Equipment installed in Class III locations shall be able to function at full rating without developing surface temperatures high enough to cause excessive dehydration or gradual carbonization of accumulated fibers or flyings. Organic material that is carbonized or excessively dry is highly susceptible to spontaneous ignition. The maximum surface temperatures under operating conditions shall not exceed 165°C

(329°F) for equipment that is not subject to overloading, and 120°C (248°F) for equipment (such as motors or power transformers) that may be overloaded.

For Electric Trucks see, Type Designation, Areas of Use, Maintenance, and Operation of Powered Industrial Trucks (NFPA No. 505-1973).

▲ The small fibers of cotton that are carried everywhere by air currents in some parts of cotton mills and the wood shavings that collect around planers in woodworking plants are common examples of the combustible flyings or fibers that cause the hazards in Class III, Division 1 locations. A cotton warehouse is a common example of a Class III, Division 2 location.

503-2. Transformers and Capacitors, Class III, Divisions 1 and 2. Transformers and capacitors shall comply with Section 502-2(b).

503-3. Wiring Methods. Wiring methods shall comply with (a) and (b) below.

(a) Class III, Division 1. In Class III, Division 1 locations, the wiring method shall be threaded rigid metal conduit or approved Type MI, MC, CS, or ALS cables.

(1) Boxes and Fittings. Fittings and boxes in which taps, joints, or terminal connections are made shall: (1) be provided with telescoping or close fitting covers or other effective means to prevent the escape of sparks or burning material, and (2) shall have no openings (such as holes for attachment screws) through which, after installation, sparks or burning material might escape, or through which adjacent combustible material might be ignited.

(2) Flexible Connections. Where flexible connections are necessary, Section 502-4(a)(2) shall apply.

(b) Class III, Division 2. In Class III, Division 2 locations, the wiring method shall comply with (a) above.

Exception: In sections, compartments, or areas used solely for storage and containing no machinery, open wiring on insulators shall be permitted where installed in accordance with Article 320, but only on condition that protection as required by Section 320-14 be provided where conductors are not run in roof spaces and are well out of reach of sources of physical damage.

503-4. Switches, Circuit Breakers, Motor Controllers, and Fuses, Class III, Divisions 1 and 2. Switches, circuit breakers, motor controllers, and fuses, including pushbuttons, relays, and similar devices, shall be provided with tight metal enclosures designed to minimize entrance of fibers and flyings, and which shall: (1) be equipped with telescoping or close fitting covers or with other effective means to prevent escape of sparks or burning material, and (2) have no openings (such as holes for attachment screws) through which, after installation, sparks or burning material might escape, or through which exterior accumulations of fibers or flyings or adjacent combustible material might be ignited.

503-5. Control Transformers and Resistors, Class III, Divisions 1 and 2. Transformers, impedance coils, and resistors used as or in conjunction with control equipment for motors, generators, and appliances shall comply with Section 502-7(b).

Exception: In Class III, Division 1 locations where these devices are in the same enclosure with switching devices of such control equipment and are used only for starting or short-time duty, the enclosure shall comply with Section 503-4.

503-6. Motors and Generators.

(a) Class III, Division 1. In Class III, Division 1 locations, motors, generators, and other rotating electric machinery shall be totally enclosed nonventilated, totally enclosed pipe-ventilated, or totally enclosed fan-cooled.

Exception: In locations where, in the judgment of the authority having jurisdiction, only moderate accumulations of lint or flyings will be likely to collect on, in, or in the vicinity of a rotating electric machine, and where such machine is readily accessible for routine cleaning and maintenance, one of the following shall be permitted:

a. Self-cleaning textile motors of the squirrel-cage types;

b. Standard open-type machines without sliding contacts, centrifugal or other types of switching mechanism, including motor overload devices; or

c. Standard open-type machines having such contacts, switching mechanisms, or resistance devices enclosed within tight metal housings without ventilating or other openings.

(b) Class III, Division 2.   In Class III, Division 2 locations, motors, generators, and other rotating electric machinery shall be totally enclosed nonventilated, totally enclosed pipe-ventilated, or totally enclosed fan-cooled.

(c) Types Not Permitted, Class III, Divisions 1 and 2.   Motors, generators, or other rotating electric machinery of the partially enclosed or splash-proof type shall not be installed in Class III locations.

503-7. Ventilating Piping, Class III, Divisions 1 and 2.   Ventilating pipes for motors, generators, or other rotating electric machinery, or for enclosures for electric equipment shall be of metal not lighter than No. 24 MSG, or of equally substantial noncombustible material, and shall comply with the following: (1) lead directly to a source of clean air outside of buildings; (2) be screened at the outer ends to prevent the entrance of small animals or birds; and (3) be protected against physical damage and against rusting or other corrosive influences.

Ventilating pipes shall be sufficiently tight, including their connections, to prevent the entrance of appreciable quantities of fibers or flyings into the ventilated equipment or enclosure and to prevent the escape of sparks, flame, or burning material that might ignite accumulations of fibers or flyings or combustible material in the vicinity. For metal pipes, lock seams and riveted or welded joints shall be permitted; and tight-fitting slip joints shall be permitted where some flexibility is necessary, as at connections to motors.

503-8. Utilization Equipment, Class III, Divisions 1 and 2.

(a) Heaters.   Electrically heated utilization equipment shall be approved for Class III locations.

(b) Motors.   Motors of motor-driven utilization equipment shall comply with Section 503-6.

(c) Switches, Circuit Breakers, Motor Controllers, and Fuses.   Switches, circuit breakers, motor controllers, and fuses shall comply with Section 503-4.

503-9. Lighting Fixtures, Class III, Divisions 1 and 2.

(a) Fixed Lighting.   Lighting fixtures for fixed lighting shall provide enclosures for lamps and lampholders that are designed to minimize entrance of fibers and flyings and to prevent the escape of sparks, burning material, or hot metal. Each fixture shall be clearly marked to show the maximum wattage of the lamps that shall be permitted without exceeding an exposed surface temperature of 165°C (329°F) under normal conditions of use.

(b) Physical Damage.   A fixture that may be exposed to physical damage shall be protected by a suitable guard.

(c) Pendant Fixtures.   Pendant fixtures shall be suspended by stems of threaded rigid metal conduit or threaded metal tubing of equivalent thickness. For stems longer than 12 inches, permanent and effective bracing against lateral displacement shall be provided at a level not more than 12 inches above the lower end of the stem, or flexibility in the form of a fitting or a flexible connector approved for the purpose shall be provided not more than 12 inches from the point of attachment to the supporting box or fitting.

(d) Supports. Boxes, box assemblies, or fittings used for the support of lighting fixtures shall be of a type approved for the purpose.

(e) Portable Lamps. Portable lamps shall be equipped with handles and protected with substantial guards, and lampholders shall be of the unswitched type with no exposed metal parts and without provision for receiving attachment plugs. In all other respects, portable lamps shall comply with (a) above.

503-10. Flexible Cords, Class III, Divisions 1 and 2. Flexible cords shall comply with Section 502-12.

503-11. Receptacles and Attachment Plugs, Class III, Divisions 1 and 2. Receptacles and attachment plugs shall comply with Section 502-13(b).

503-12. Signaling, Alarm, Remote-Control, and Local Loud-Speaker Intercommunication Systems, Class III, Divisions 1 and 2. Signaling, alarm, remote-control, and local loud-speaker intercommunication systems shall comply with Section 502-14(a).

503-13. Electric Cranes, Hoists, and Similar Equipment, Class III, Divisions 1 and 2. Where installed for operation over combustible fibers or accumulations of flyings, traveling cranes and hoists for material handling, traveling cleaners for textile machinery, and similar equipment shall comply with (a) through (d) below.

(a) Power Supply. Power supply to contact conductors shall be isolated from all other systems, shall be ungrounded, and shall be equipped with an acceptable recording ground detector that will give an alarm and automatically de-energize the contact conductors in case of a fault to ground, or with an acceptable ground-fault indicator that will give a visual and audible alarm, and maintain the alarm as long as power is supplied to the system and the ground fault remains.

(b) Contact Conductors. Contact conductors shall be so located or guarded as to be inaccessible to other than authorized persons and shall be protected against accidental contact with foreign objects.

(c) Current Collectors. Current collectors shall be so arranged or guarded as to confine normal sparking and prevent escape of sparks or hot particles. To reduce sparking, two or more separate surfaces of contact shall be provided for each contact conductor. Reliable means shall be provided to keep contact conductors and current collectors free of accumulations of lint or flyings.

(d) Control Equipment. Control equipment shall comply with Sections 503-4 and 503-5.

▲ A crane operating in a Class III location and having rolling or sliding collectors making contact with bare conductors introduces two hazards:

1. Any arcing between a collector and a conductor rail or wire may ignite flyings of combustible fibers that have collected on or near to the bare conductor. This danger may be guarded against by proper alignment of the bare conductor and by using a collector of such form that contact is always maintained, and by the use of guards or barriers which will confine the hot particles of metal that may be thrown off when an arc is formed.

2. Dust and flyings collecting on the insulating supports of the bare conductors

may form a conducting path between the conductors or from one conductor to ground and permit enough current to flow to ignite the fibers. This condition is much more likely to exist if moisture is present. Operation on a system having no grounded conductor makes it somewhat less likely that a fire will be started by a current flowing to ground. A recording ground detector will show when the insulation resistance is being lowered by an accumulation of dust and flyings on the insulators, and a relay actuated by excessively low insulation resistance and arranged to trip a circuit breaker provides automatic disconnection of the bare conductors when the conditions become dangerous.

503-14. Storage-Battery Charging Equipment, Class III, Divisions 1 and 2. Storage-battery charging equipment shall be located in separate rooms built or lined with substantial noncombustible materials so constructed as to adequately exclude flyings or lint and shall be well ventilated.

503-15. Live Parts, Class III, Divisions 1 and 2.   Live parts shall not be exposed. *Exception: As provided in Section 503-13.*

503-16. Grounding, Class III, Divisions 1 and 2.   Wiring and equipment shall be grounded in accordance with Section 502-16.

ARTICLE 510. HAZARDOUS (CLASSIFIED) LOCATIONS—SPECIFIC

510-1. Scope.   Articles 511 through 517 cover occupancies or parts of occupancies that are or may be hazardous because of atmospheric concentrations of flammable liquids, gases, or vapors, or because of deposits or accumulations of materials that may be readily ignitible.

510-2. General.   The general rules of this Code shall apply to electric wiring and equipment in occupancies within the scope of Articles 511 through 517, except as such rules are modified in those Articles. Where unusual conditions exist in a specific occupancy, the authority having jurisdiction shall judge with respect to the application of specific rules.

▲ Copies and price lists of the National Fire Protection Association Standards may be obtained from the NFPA offices at 470 Atlantic Ave., Boston, Mass. 02210.

ARTICLE 511. COMMERCIAL GARAGES, REPAIR AND STORAGE

511-1. Scope.   These occupancies shall include locations used for service and repair operations in connection with self-propelled vehicles (including passenger automobiles, buses, trucks, tractors, etc.) in which volatile flammable liquids are used for fuel or power. Areas in which flammable fuel is transferred to vehicle fuel tanks shall conform to Article 514. Parking garages used for parking or storage and where no repair work is done except exchange of parts and routine maintenance requiring no use of electrical equipment, open flame, welding, or the use of volatile flammable liquids are not classified as hazardous areas, but they shall be adequately ventilated to carry off the exhaust fumes of the engines.

For further information, see Parking Structures NFPA 88A-1973 and Repair Garages 88B-1973.

▲ Heating equipment may be installed in motor vehicle repair or parking areas where there is no dispensing or transferring of Class I or II flammable liquids (as defined in the Flammable and Combustible Liquids Code, NFPA 30-1973) or liquefied petroleum gas, provided the bottom of the combustion chamber is not less than 18 in. above the floor, the heating equipment is protected from physical damage by vehicles, and continuous mechanical ventilation is provided at the rate of 0.75 cfm/sq ft of floor area. The heating system and the ventilation system shall be suitably interlocked to ensure operation of the ventilation system when the heating system is in operation.

Approved suspended unit heaters may be used provided they are located not less than eight ft above the floor and are installed in accordance with the conditions of their approval.

Below-grade areas occupied for repairing, or communicating areas located below a repair garage, shall be continuously ventilated by a mechanical ventilating system having positive means for exhausting indoor air at a rate of not less than 0.75 cfm/sq ft of floor area. An approved means shall be provided for introducing an equal amount of outdoor air.

Operations involving open flame or electric arcs, including fusion, gas, and electric welding, shall be restricted to areas specifically provided for such purposes.

All enclosed, basement, and underground parking structures shall be continuously ventilated by a mechanical system capable of providing a minimum of six air changes per hour.

511-2. Hazardous Areas. Classification under Article 500.

(a) For each floor the entire area up to a level of 18 inches above the floor shall be considered to be a Class I, Division 2 location except where the enforcing agency determines that there is mechanical ventilation providing a minimum of four air changes per hour.

(b) Any pit or depression below floor level shall be considered to be a Class I, Division 1 location which shall extend up to said floor level, except that any pit or depression in which six air changes per hour are exhausted at the floor level of the pit shall be permitted to be judged by the enforcing agency to be a Class I, Division 2 location.

(c) Areas adjacent to defined locations in which hazardous vapors are not likely to be released such as stock rooms, switchboard rooms and other similar locations shall not be classed as hazardous when mechanically ventilated at a rate of four or more air changes per hour or when effectively cut off by walls or partitions.

(d) Adjacent areas, which by reason of ventilation, air pressure differentials or physical spacing are such that in the opinion of the authority enforcing this code no hazard exists, shall be classified as nonhazardous.

(e) When fuel dispensing units (other than liquid petroleum gas which is prohibited) are located within buildings, the requirements of Article 514 shall govern.

When mechanical ventilation is provided in the dispensing area, the controls shall be interlocked so that the dispenser cannot operate without ventilation as prescribed in Section 500-4(b).

(f) Portable lamps shall be equipped with handle, lampholder, hook and substantial guard attached to the lampholder or handle. All exterior surfaces which might come in contact with battery terminals, wiring terminals, or other objects shall be of nonconducting material or shall be effectively protected with insulation. Lampholders shall be of unswitched type and shall not provide means for plug-in of attachment plugs. Outer shell shall be of moulded composition or other material approved for the purpose. Unless the lamp and its cord are supported or arranged in such a manner that they cannot be used in the hazardous areas classified in Section 511-2 they shall be of a type approved for such hazardous locations.

▲ *Paragraph a*

Above grade: The hazardous area extends up to 18 in. above each floor.

Paragraph b

Below grade: Where positive-pressure ventilation is provided, the hazardous area extends up to 18 in. above each floor. Where it is not provided, the hazardous area extends from floor to ceiling.

In order to assure positive-pressure ventilation at all times, the authority making this decision may do this on the basis of having suitable interlocking provided between the electrical and ventilating systems.

511-3. Wiring and Equipment in Hazardous Areas.   Within hazardous areas as defined in Section 511-2 wiring and equipment shall conform to applicable provisions of Article 501. Raceways embedded in a masonry wall or buried beneath a floor shall be considered to be within the hazardous area above the floor if any connections or extensions lead into or through such areas.

511-4. Sealing.   Approved seals conforming to the requirements of Section 501-5 shall be provided, and Section 501-5(b)(2) shall apply to horizontal as well as vertical boundaries of the defined hazardous areas.

511-5. Wiring in Spaces Above Hazardous Areas.

(a) All fixed wiring above hazardous areas shall be in metallic raceways or shall be Type MI, TC, SNM, MC, CS, or Type ALS cable. Cellular metal floor raceways shall be permitted to be used only for supplying ceiling outlets or extensions to the area below the floor, but such raceways shall have no connections leading into or through any hazardous area above the floor. No electrical conductor shall be installed in any cell, header, or duct which contains a pipe for any service except electrical or compressed air.

(b) For pendants, flexible cord suitable for the type of service and approved for hard usage shall be used.

(c) When a circuit which supplies portables or pendants includes an identified grounded conductor as provided in Article 200, receptacles, attachment plugs, connectors, and similar devices shall be of polarized type, and the identified conductor of the flexible cord shall be connected to the screw shell of any lampholder or to the identified terminal of any utilization equipment supplied.

(d) Attachment plug receptacles in fixed position shall be located above the level of any defined hazardous area, or be approved for the location.

511-6. Equipment Above Hazardous Locations.

(a) Arcing Equipment.   Equipment that is less than 12 feet above the floor level and that may produce arcs, sparks, or particles of hot metal, such as cutouts, switches, charging panels, generators, motors, or other equipment (excluding receptacles, lamps and lampholders) having make-and-break or sliding contacts, shall be of the totally enclosed type or so constructed as to prevent escape of sparks or hot metal particles.

(b) Fixed Lighting. Lamps and lampholders for fixed lighting that is located over lanes through which vehicles are commonly driven or that may otherwise be exposed to physical damage shall be located not less than 12 feet above floor level, unless of the totally enclosed type or so constructed as to prevent escape of sparks or hot metal particles.

511-7. Battery Charging Equipment. Battery chargers and their control equipment, and batteries being charged shall not be located within hazardous areas classified in Section 511-2.

511-8. Electric Vehicle Charging.

(a) Cords. Flexible cords used for charging shall be suitable for the type of service and approved for extra-hard usage. Their ampacity shall be adequate for the charging current.

(b) Connector Rating. Connectors shall have an ampere rating not less than the ampacity of the cord, and in no case less than 50 amperes.

(c) Connector Design and Location. Connectors shall be so designed and installed that they will disconnect readily at any position of the charging cable, and live parts shall be guarded from accidental contact. No connector shall be located within a hazardous location as defined in Section 511-2.

(d) Plug Connections to Vehicles. Where plugs are provided for direct connection to vehicles, the point of connection shall not be within a hazardous location as defined in Section 511-2, and where the cord is suspended from overhead, it shall be so arranged that the lowest point of sag is at least 6 inches above the floor. Where the vehicle is equipped with an approved plug that will disconnect readily, and where an automatic arrangement is provided to pull both cord and plug beyond the range of physical damage, no additional connector shall be required in the cable or at the outlet.

▲ Equipment located in a suitable room or enclosure provided for the purpose or in a showroom separated from the garage proper by a partition which is reasonably tight up to 18 in. need not conform to the requirements of this section. Also, see Sec. 511-2(e).

In all garages within the scope of this chapter, because of the possible presence of gasoline vapor near the floor, any equipment which in its normal operation may cause arcs or sparks, if less than 18 in. above the floor, is considered as in a hazardous location.

It is seldom necessary to make use of devices having exposed live parts, but where this is unavoidable, even though the device is 18 in. above the floor, any such device should be well guarded.

The requirements for battery-charging cables and connectors are similar to the requirements for outlets for the connection of portable appliances, except that when hanging free the battery-charging cables and connectors may hang within 6 in. from the floor. The common form is a plug which is inserted into a receptacle on the vehicle, and, since the prongs are "alive," they must be covered by a protecting hood.

ARTICLE 513. AIRCRAFT HANGARS

513-1. Definition. An aircraft hangar is a location used for storage or servicing of aircraft in which gasoline, jet fuels, or other volatile flammable liquids or flammable gases are used. It shall not include locations used exclusively for aircraft that have never contained such liquids or gases, or that have been drained and properly purged.

513-2. Classification of Locations.

(a) **Below Floor Level.** Any pit or depression below the level of the hangar floor shall be classified as a Class I, Division 1 location that shall extend up to said floor level.

(b) **Areas Not Cut Off or Ventilated.** The entire area of the hangar, including any adjacent and communicating areas not suitably cut off from the hangar, shall be classified as a Class I, Division 2 location up to a level 18 inches above the floor.

(c) **Vicinity of Aircraft.** The area within 5 feet horizontally from aircraft power plants or aircraft fuel tanks shall be classified as a Class I, Division 2 location that shall extend upward from the floor to a level 5 feet above the upper surface of wings and of engine enclosures.

(d) **Areas Suitably Cut Off and Ventilated.** Adjacent areas in which flammable liquids or vapors are not likely to be released, such as stock rooms, electrical control rooms, and other similar locations, shall not be classified as hazardous where adequately ventilated and where effectively cut off from the hangar itself by walls or partitions.

513-3. Wiring and Equipment in Hazardous Areas. All wiring and equipment that is or may be installed or operated within any of the hazardous locations defined in Section 513-2 shall comply with the applicable provisions of Article 501. All wiring installed in or under the hangar floor shall comply with the requirements for Class I, Division 1 hazardous locations. Where such wiring is located in vaults, pits, or ducts, adequate drainage shall be provided; and the wiring shall not be placed within the same compartment with any service other than piped compressed air.

Attachment plugs and receptacles in hazardous locations shall be approved for Class I locations or shall be so designed that they cannot be energized while the connections are being made or broken.

513-4. Wiring Not Within Hazardous Areas.

(a) **Fixed Wiring.** All fixed wiring in a hangar, but not within a hazardous location as defined in Section 513-2, shall be installed in metallic raceways or shall be Type MI, TC, SNM, MC, CS, or Type ALS cable.

Exception: Wiring in nonhazardous locations as defined in Section 513-2(d) shall be of a type recognized in Chapter 3.

(b) **Pendants.** For pendants, flexible cord suitable for the type of service and approved for hard usage shall be used. Each such cord shall include a separate grounding conductor.

(c) **Portable Equipment.** For portable utilization equipment and lamps, flexible cord suitable for the type of service and approved for extra-hard usage shall be used. Each such cord shall include a separate grounding conductor.

(d) **Grounded and Grounding Conductors.** Where a circuit supplies portables or pendants and includes an identified grounded conductor as provided in Article 200, receptacles, attachment plugs, connectors, and similar devices shall be of the polarized type, and the grounded conductor of the flexible cord shall be connected to the screw-shell of any lampholder or to the grounded terminal of any utilization equipment supplied. Acceptacle means shall be provided for maintaining continuity of the grounding conductor between the fixed raceway system and the noncurrent-carrying metal portions of pendant fixtures, portable lamps, and portable utilization equipment.

513-5. Equipment Not Within Hazardous Locations.

(a) Arcing Equipment. In locations other than those described in Section 513-2, equipment that is less than 10 feet above wings and engine enclosures of aircraft and that may produce arcs, sparks or particles of hot metal, such as lamps and lampholders for fixed lighting, cutouts, switches, receptacles, charging panels, generators, motors, or other equipment having make-and-break or sliding contacts, shall be of the totally enclosed type or so constructed as to prevent escape of sparks or hot metal particles.

Exception: Equipment in areas described in Section 513-2(d) shall be permitted to be of the general-purpose type.

(b) Lampholders. Lampholders of metal-shell, fiber-lined types shall not be used for fixed incandescent lighting.

(c) Portable Lamps. Portable lamps that are or may be used within a hangar shall be approved for Class I locations.

(d) Portable Equipment. Portable utilization equipment that is or may be used within a hangar shall be of a type suitable for use in Class I, Division 2 locations.

513-6. Stanchions, Rostrums, and Docks.

(a) In Hazardous Location. Electric wiring, outlets, and equipment (including lamps) on or attached to stanchions, rostrums, or docks that are located or likely to be located in a hazardous location as defined in Section 513-2(c) shall comply with the requirements for Class I, Division 2 locations.

(b) Not in Hazardous Location. Where stanchions, rostrums, or docks are not located or likely to be located in a hazardous location as defined in Section 513-2(c), wiring and equipment shall comply with Sections 513-4 and 513-5, except that such wiring and equipment not more than 18 inches above the floor in any position shall comply with (a) above. Receptacles and attachment plugs shall be of locking type that will not readily disconnect.

(c) Mobile Type. Mobile stanchions with electric equipment complying with (b) above shall carry at least one permanently affixed warning sign to read: "WARN-ING—KEEP 5 FEET CLEAR OF AIRCRAFT ENGINES AND FUEL TANK AREAS."

513-7. Sealing. Approved seals shall be provided in accordance with Section 501-5. Sealing requirements specified in Sections 501-5(a)(4) and 501-5(b)(2) shall apply to horizontal as well as to vertical boundaries of the defined hazardous locations. Raceways embedded in a masonry floor or buried beneath a floor shall be considered to be within the hazardous location above the floor where any connections or extensions lead into or through such location.

513-8. Aircraft Electrical Systems. Aircraft electrical systems shall be de-energized when the aircraft is stored in a hangar, and, whenever possible, while the aircraft is undergoing maintenance.

513-9. Aircraft Battery—Charging and Equipment. Aircraft batteries shall not be charged when installed in an aircraft located inside or partially inside a hangar.

Battery chargers and their control equipment shall not be located or operated within any of the hazardous areas defined in Section 513-2, and shall preferably be located in a separate building or in an area such as defined in Section 513-2(d). Mobile chargers shall carry at least one permanently affixed warning sign to read: "WARNING—KEEP 5 FEET CLEAR OF AIRCRAFT ENGINES AND FUEL TANK AREAS." Tables, racks, trays, and wiring shall not be located within a hazardous location, and, in addition, shall comply with Article 480.

513-10. External Power Sources for Energizing Aircraft.

(a) Not Less Than 18 Inches Above Floor. Aircraft energizers shall be so designed and mounted that all electric equipment and fixed wiring will be at least 18 inches above floor level and shall not be operated in a hazardous location as defined in Section 513-2(c).

(b) Marking for Mobile Units. Mobile energizers shall carry at least one permanently affixed warning sign to read: "WARNING—KEEP 5 FEET CLEAR OF AIRCRAFT ENGINES AND FUEL TANK AREAS."

(c) Cords. Flexible cords for aircraft energizers and ground support equipment shall be approved for the type of service and extra-hard usage and shall include an equipment grounding conductor.

513-11. Mobile Servicing Equipment with Electric Components.

(a) General. Mobile servicing equipment (such as vacuum cleaners, air compressors, air movers, etc.) having electric wiring and equipment not suitable for Class I, Division 2 locations shall be so designed and mounted that all such fixed wiring and equipment will be at least 18 inches above the floor. Such mobile equipment shall not be operated within the hazardous location defined in Section 513-2(c) and shall carry at least one permanently affixed warning sign to read: "WARNING—KEEP 5 FEET CLEAR OF AIRCRAFT ENGINES AND FUEL TANK AREAS."

(b) Cords and Connectors. Flexible cords for mobile equipment shall be suitable for the type of service and approved for extra-hard usage, and shall include an equipment grounding conductor. Attachment plugs and receptacles shall be approved for the location in which they are installed, and shall provide for connection of the grounding conductor to the raceway system.

(c) Restricted Use. Equipment not suitable for Class I, Division 2 locations shall not be operated in locations where maintenance operations likely to release flammable liquids or vapors are in progress.

513-12. Grounding. All metal raceways and all noncurrent-carrying metal portions of fixed or portable equipment, regardless of voltage, shall be grounded as provided in Article 250.

ARTICLE 514. GASOLINE DISPENSING AND SERVICE STATIONS

514-1. Definition. A gasoline dispensing and service station is a location where gasoline or other volatile flammable liquids or liquefied flammable gases are transferred to the fuel tanks (including auxiliary fuel tanks) of self-propelled vehicles.

Other areas used as lubritoriums, service rooms, repair rooms, offices, salesrooms, compressor rooms, and similar locations shall comply with Articles 510 and 511 with respect to electric wiring and equipment.

Where the authority having jurisdiction can satisfactorily determine that flammable liquids having a flash point below 38°C (100°F), such as gasoline, will not be handled, he may classify such a location as nonhazardous.

Fur further information regarding safeguards for gasoline dispensing and service stations, see Flammable and Combustible Liquids Code (NFPA No. 30-1969).

514-2. Hazardous Locations.

(a) Vicinity of Dispenser. The space within the dispenser up to 4 feet from its base and the space within 18 inches extending horizontally from the dispenser up to 4 feet from its base shall be considered a Class I, Division 1 location. This classification shall also apply to any space below the dispenser that may contain electric wiring or equipment.

(b) Within 20 Feet of Dispenser. In an outside location, any area (excluding Class I, Division 1, but including buildings not suitably cut off) within 20 feet horizontally from the exterior enclosure of any dispensing pump shall be classified as a Class I, Division 2 location, which shall extend to a level 18 inches above driveway or ground level.

(c) Vicinity of Tank Fill-Pipe. In an outside location, any area (excluding Class I, Division 1, but including buildings not suitably cut off) within 10 feet horizontally from any tank fill-pipe shall be classified as a Class I, Division 2 location, which shall extend upward to a level 18 inches above driveway or ground level.

(d) Below Surface. Electric wiring and equipment, any portion of which is below the surface of locations defined as Class I, Division 1 or Division 2 in (a), (b), or (c) above shall be classified as a Class I, Division 1 location, which shall extend at least to the point of emergence above grade.

(e) Overhead Dispensing Units. Where the dispensing unit, including the hose and hose nozzle valve, is suspended from a canopy, ceiling, or structural support, the Class I, Division 1 location shall include the volume within the enclosure and shall also extend 18 inches in all directions from the enclosure where not suitably cut off by a ceiling or wall. The Class I, Division 2 location shall extend 2 feet horizontally in all directions beyond the Division 1 classified location and extend to grade below this classified location. In addition, the horizontal area 18 inches above grade for a distance of 20 feet, measured from a point vertically below the edge of any dispenser enclosure, shall be classified as a Division 2 location. All electric equipment integral with the dispensing hose or nozzle shall be approved for Class I locations.

(f) Vicinity of Tank Vent-Pipe. The spherical volume within a 3-foot radius from point of discharge of any tank vent-pipe shall be classified as a Class I, Division 1 location, and the volume between 3-foot to 5-foot radius from point of discharge of a vent shall be classified as a Class I, Division 2 location. For any vent that does not discharge upward, the cylindrical volume below both the Division 1 and 2 locations extending to the ground shall be classified as a Class I, Division 2 location. The hazardous location shall not extend beyond an unpierced wall.

(g) Pits Below Grade. In addition to the requirements of Section 514-1, the space within any pit, or space below grade in a lubrication room shall be classified as a Class I, Division 1 location. The area within the entire lubrication room up to 18 inches above the floor or grade, and the space within 3 feet measured in any direction from the dispensing point of a hand-operated unit dispensing Class I liquids shall be classified as a Class I, Division 2 location.

514-3. Wiring and Equipment Within Hazardous Locations. All electric equipment and wiring within hazardous locations defined in Section 514-2 shall comply with the applicable provisions of Article 501.

Exception: As permitted in Section 514-8.

For special requirements for conductor insulation, see Section 501-13.

514-4. Wiring and Equipment Above Hazardous Locations. Wiring and equipment above the hazardous locations defined in Section 514-2 shall comply with Sections 511-5 and 511-6.

514-5. Circuit Disconnects. Each circuit leading to or through a dispensing pump shall be provided with a switch or other acceptable means to disconnect simultaneously from the source of supply all conductors of the circuit, including the grounded neutral, if any.

514-6. Sealing.

(a) At Dispenser. An approved seal shall be provided in each conduit run entering or leaving a dispenser or any cavities or enclosures in direct communication therewith. The sealing fitting shall be the first fitting after the conduit emerges from the earth or concrete.

(b) At Boundary. Additional seals shall be provided in accordance with Section 501-5. Sections 501-5(a)(4) and 501-5(b)(2) shall apply to horizontal as well as to vertical boundaries of the defined hazardous locations.

514-7. Grounding. Metal portions of dispensing pumps, metal raceways, and all noncurrent-carrying metal parts of electric equipment, regardless of voltage, shall be grounded as provided in Article 250.

514-8. Underground Wiring. Underground wiring shall be installed in rigid metal conduit, or, where buried under not less than 2 feet of earth, it shall be permitted in rigid nonmetallic conduit complying with Article 347. Where rigid nonmetallic conduit is used, an equipment grounding conductor shall be included to provide electrical continuity of the raceway system and for grounding of noncurrent-carrying metal parts.

Exception: Type MI cable shall be permitted where it is installed in accordance with Article 330.

▲ Article 514 not only covers wiring in the pumps, it also specifies the type of wiring for the areas considered to be hazardous that extend to within 20 ft horizontally from any dispensing pump or 10 ft from any tank fill pipe. It should be noted that sealing is required where the conduit enters the pump and that additional seals are required in all conduits leaving a hazardous area.

In Fig. 514-1, four seals are shown. Normally panelboards are located in a nonhazardous location so that a seal is shown where the conduit is leaving the hazardous location. According to Sec. 514-6(a) there must also be a seal where the conduit enters or leaves the dispenser.

When the electrical equipment of a pump is being serviced or repaired, it is very important that there shall be no "hot" wire or wires inside the pump. Since it is always possible that the polarity of the circuit wires may have been accidentally reversed at the panelboard, control switches or circuit breakers must open all conductors. If these circuits are controlled at a panelboard, a special panelboard arrangement is required.

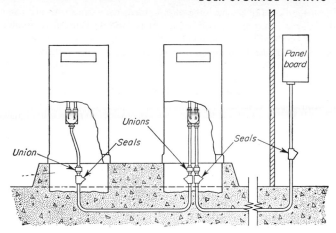

FIG. 514-1. Installation at a gasoline dispensing station.

For "gasoline and oil resistant" insulated conductors, see comments following Sec. 501-13.

Section 514-2(e) describes the Class I, Division 1 and 2 boundaries for overhead types of gasoline dispensing units.

ARTICLE 515. BULK-STORAGE PLANTS

515-1. Definition. A bulk-storage plant is a location where gasoline or other volatile flammable liquids are stored in tanks having an aggregate capacity of one carload or more, and from which such products are distributed (usually by tank truck).

515-2. Hazardous Locations.

   (a) Pumps, Bleeders, Withdrawal Fittings, Meters, and Similar Devices.

   (1) Adequately ventilated indoor locations containing pumps, bleeders, withdrawal fittings, meters, and similar devices that are located in pipe lines handling flammable liquids under pressure shall be classified as a Class I, Division 2 location within a 5-foot distance extending in all directions from the exterior surface of such devices. The Class I, Division 2 location shall also extend 25 feet horizontally from any surface of these devices and extend upward to 3 feet above floor or grade level.

See Flammable and Combustible Liquids Code (NFPA No. 30-1973) for discussion of factors influencing adequacy of ventilation required to prevent formation of hazardous vapor-air mixtures.

   (2) Inadequately ventilated indoor locations containing pumps, bleeders, withdrawal fittings, meters, and similar devices that are located in pipe lines handling flammable liquids under pressure shall be classified as a Class I, Division 1 location within a 5-foot distance extending in all directions from the exterior surface of such devices. The Class I, Division 1 location shall also extend 25 feet horizontally from any surface of the devices and extend upward to 3 feet above floor or grade level.

(3) Outdoor locations containing pumps, bleeders, withdrawal fittings, meters, and similar devices that are located in pipe lines handling flammable liquids under pressure shall be classified as Class I, Division 2 locations within a 3-foot distance extending in all directions from the exterior surface of such devices. The Class I, Division 2 location shall also extend up to 18 inches above grade level within 10 feet horizontally from any surface of the devices.

(b) Transfer of Flammable Liquids to Individual Containers.

(1) In outdoor locations or wherever positive and reliable mechanical ventilation is provided in indoor locations in which flammable liquids are transferred to individual containers, such locations shall be classified as a Class I, Division 1 location within 3 feet of the vent or fill opening extending in all directions. A Class I, Division 2 location shall be within the space extending between a 3-foot and 5-foot radius from the vent or fill opening extending in all directions, and including the area within a horizontal radius of 10 feet from the vent or fill opening and extending to a height of 18 inches above floor or grade levels.

See Flammable and Combustible Liquids Code (NFPA No. 30-1973) for discussion of factors pertaining to positive and reliable mechanical ventilation required to prevent formation of hazardous vapor-air mixtures.

(2) Indoor locations, in which flammable liquids are transferred to containers and where positive and reliable mechanical ventilation is not provided, shall be classified as Class I, Division 1 locations.

(c) Loading and Unloading of Tank Vehicles and Tank Cars in Outside Locations.

(1) The space extending 3 feet in all directions from the dome when loading through an open dome or from the vent when loading through a closed dome with atmospheric venting shall be classified as a Class I, Division 1 location.

(2) The space extending between a 3-foot and 5-foot radius from the dome when loading through an open dome or from the vent when loading through a closed dome with atmospheric venting shall be classified as a Class I, Division 2 location.

(3) The space extending within 3 feet in all directions from a fixed connection used in bottom loading or unloading, loading through a closed dome with atmospheric venting, or loading through a closed dome with a vapor recovery system, shall be classified as a Class I, Division 2 location. In the case of bottom loading or unloading, this classification shall also be applied to the area within a 10-foot radius from the point of connection and extending 18 inches above grade.

(d) Aboveground Tanks

(1) The space above the roof and within the shell of a floating roof type tank shall be classified as a Class I, Division 1 location.

(2) For all types of aboveground tanks, the space within 10 feet from the shell, ends, and roof of other than a floating roof shall be classified as a Class I, Division 2 location. Where dikes are provided, the space inside the dike and extending upward to the top of the dike shall be classified as a Class I, Division 2 location.

(3) The space within 5 feet of a vent opening and extending in all directions shall be classified as a Class I, Division 1 location.

(4) The space between 5 and 10 feet of a vent opening and extending in all directions shall be classified as a Class I, Division 2 location.

For underground tanks, see Article 514.

(e) Pits.

(1) Any pit or depression, any part of which lies within a Division 1 or Division 2 location as defined herein, shall be classified as a Class I, Division 1 location unless provided with positive and reliable mechanical ventilation.

(2) Any such location that is provided with positive and reliable mechanical ventilation shall be classified as a Class I, Division 2 location.

See Flammable and Combustible Liquids Code (NFPA No. 30-1973) for discussion of factors pertaining to positive and reliable mechanical ventilation required to prevent formation of hazardous vapor-air mixtures.

(3) Any pit or depression not within a Division 1 or Division 2 location as defined herein, but that contains piping, valves, or fittings, shall be classified as a Class I, Division 2 location.

(f) Garages for Tank Vehicles. Storage and repair garages for tank vehicles shall be classified as a Class I, Division 2 location up to 18 inches above floor or grade level.

Exception: Where in the judgment of the authority having jurisdiction, conditions warrant more severe classification or a greater extent of the hazardous location.

(g) Adjacent Locations. Office buildings, boiler rooms, and similar locations, that are outside the limits of hazardous locations as defined herein and are not used for handling or storage of volatile flammable liquids or containers for such liquids, shall not be classified as hazardous locations.

515-3. Wiring and Equipment Within Hazardous Locations. All electric wiring and equipment within the hazardous locations defined in Section 515-2 shall comply with the applicable provisions of Article 501.

Exception: As permitted in Section 515-5.

515-4. Wiring and Equipment Above Hazardous Locations. All fixed wiring above hazardous locations shall be in metallic raceways or be Type ALS, CS, MI, TC, SNM, or Type MC cable. Fixed equipment that may produce arcs, sparks, or particles of hot metal, such as lamps and lampholders for fixed lighting, cutouts, switches, receptacles, motors, or other equipment having make-and-break or sliding contacts, shall be of the totally enclosed type or be so constructed as to prevent escape of sparks or hot metal particles. Portable lamps or other utilization equipment and their flexible cords shall comply with the provisions of Article 501 for the class of location above which they are connected or used.

515-5. Underground Wiring.

(a) Wiring Method. Underground wiring shall be installed in rigid metal conduit, or where buried under not less than 2 feet of earth, shall be permitted in rigid nonmetallic conduit or in the form of cable approved for the purpose. Where cable is used, it shall be enclosed in rigid metal conduit from the point of lowest buried cable level to the point of connection to the aboveground raceway.

(b) Insulation. Conductor insulation shall comply with Section 501-13.

(c) Nonmetallic Wiring. Where rigid nonmetallic conduit or cable with a non-metallic sheath is used, an equipment grounding conductor shall be included to provide for electrical continuity of the raceway system and for grounding of non-current-carrying metal parts.

515-6. Sealing. Approved seals shall be provided in accordance with Section 501-5. Sealing requirements in Sections 501-5(a)(4) and 501-5(b)(2) shall apply to horizontal

as well as to vertical boundaries of the defined hazardous locations. Buried raceways under defined hazardous locations shall be considered to be within such locations.
515-7. Gasoline Dispensing. Where gasoline dispensing is carried on in conjunction with bulk station operations, the applicable provisions of Article 514 shall apply.
515-8. Grounding. All metal raceways and all noncurrent-carrying metal parts of electric equipment shall be grounded as provided in Article 250.

ARTICLE 516. FINISHING PROCESSES

516-1. Definition. This Article covers locations where paints, lacquers, or other flammable finishes are regularly or frequently applied by spraying, dipping, brushing, or by other means; where volatile flammable solvents or thinners are used; and where readily ignitible deposits or residues from such paints, lacquers, or finishes may occur.

For further information regarding safeguards for finishing processes, such as guarding, fire protection, posting of warning signs, and maintenance, see NFPA Standard for Spray Application Using Flammable and Combustible Materials, No. 33-1973, Dip Tanks Containing Flammable or Combustible Liquids (NFPA No. 34-1971). For additional information regarding ventilation, see Blower and Exhaust Systems, Dust, Stock and Vapor Removal, or Conveying. (NFPA No. 91-1973).

516-2. Hazardous Locations. Classification is with respect to the effects of and exposure to flammable vapors, and in some cases, deposits of paint spray residue.

For deposits and residues, see Sections 516-3(b) and (c).

(a) Class I, Division 1 Locations. The interiors of spray booths and their exhaust ducts; all space within 20 feet horizontally in any direction and 10 feet vertically from spraying operations more extensive than touch-up spraying and not conducted within spray booths; all space within 20 feet horizontally in any direction from dip tanks and their drain boards; and all other spaces where hazardous concentrations of flammable vapors are likely to occur shall be classified as Class I, Division 1 locations.
(b) Class I, Division 2 Locations. The following spaces shall be considered Class I, Division 2 locations unless the authority having jurisdiction judges otherwise.
(1) For extensive open spraying, all space outside of but within 20 feet horizontally and 10 feet vertically of the Class I, Division 1 location as defined in Section 516-2(a), and not separated from it by partitions. See Figure 1.
(2) For spraying operations conducted within a closed top, open face or front spray booth, the space shown in Figures 2 and 3, and the space within 3 feet in all directions from openings other than the open face or front.
The Class I, Division 2 location shown in Figures 2 and 3 shall extend from the open face or front of the spray booth in accordance with the following:
(a) If the ventilation system is interlocked with the spraying equipment so as to make the spraying equipment inoperable when the ventilation system is not in operation, the space shall extend 5 feet from the open face or front of the spray booth, and as otherwise shown in Figure 2.
(b) If the ventilation system is not interlocked with the spraying equipment

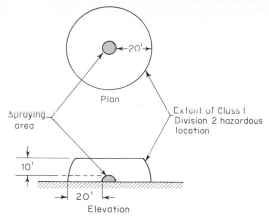

Plan

Spraying
area

Extent of Class I
Division 2 hazardous
location

10'

20'

Elevation

FIG. 1

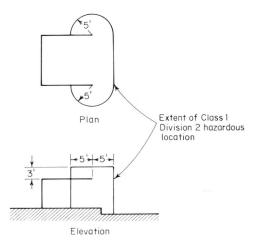

5'

5'

Plan

Extent of Class 1
Division 2 hazardous
location

5' 5'

3'

Elevation

FIG. 2

so as to make the spraying equipment inoperable when the ventilation system is not in operation, the space shall extend 10 feet from the open face or front of the spray booth, and as otherwise shown in Figure 3.

(3) For spraying operations conducted within an open top spray booth, the space 5 feet above the booth and within the space shown in Figure 3 as a Class I, Division 2 location adjacent to openings.

(4) For spraying operations confined to an enclosed spray booth, the space within 3 feet in all directions from any openings in the spray booth.

(5) All space within the room but beyond the limits for Class I, Division 1 as defined in Section 516-2(a) for dip tanks and drain boards, and for other hazardous operations.

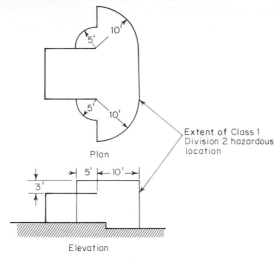

Plan

Extent of Class 1
Division 2 hazardous
location

Elevation

Fig. 3

(c) Adjacent Locations. Adjacent locations that are cut off from the defined hazardous locations by tight partitions without communicating openings, and within which hazardous vapors are not likely to be released, shall be classified as non-hazardous unless the authority having jurisdiction judges otherwise.

(d) Nonhazardous Locations. Locations utilizing drying, curing, or fusion apparatus and provided with positive mechanical ventilation adequate to prevent formation of flammable concentrations of vapors, and provided with effective interlocks to de-energize all electric equipment (other than equipment approved for Class I locations) in case the ventilating equipment is inoperative, may be classified as nonhazardous where the authority having jurisdiction so judges.

For further information regarding safeguards, see Ovens and Furnaces, Design, Location and Equipment (NFPA No. 86A-1973).

516-3. Wiring and Equipment in Hazardous Locations.

(a) Wiring and Equipment—Vapors. All electric wiring and equipment within the hazardous location (containing vapor only—not residues) defined in Section 516-2 shall comply with the applicable provisions of Article 501.

(b) Wiring and Equipment—Vapors and Residues. Unless approved for both readily ignitible deposits and the flammable vapor location, no electric equipment shall be installed or used where it may be subject to hazardous accumulations of readily ignitible deposits or residues, as the susceptibility to spontaneous heating and ignition of some residues may be greatly increased at temperatures above normal. Type MI cable and wiring in threaded rigid metal conduit may be installed in such locations, if the explosion-proof boxes or fittings contain no taps, splices, or terminal connections that may possibly become loose in service and thereby cause abnormal temperatures on external surfaces of boxes or fittings.

▲ **Only rigid metal conduit and Type MI cable and threaded boxes or fittings containing no taps, splices, or terminal connections may be installed in such locations.**

However, for that part of the hazardous area where the fixtures or equipment may not be subject to readily ignitible deposits or residues, fixtures and equipment approved for Class I, Division 1 locations may be installed. The authority having jurisdiction may decide that because of adequate positive-pressure ventilation the possibility of the hazard referred to in paragraph (b) has been eliminated.

(c) Illumination. Illumination of readily ignitible areas through panels of glass or other transparent or translucent material shall be permitted only if it complies with the following: (1) fixed lighting units are used as the source of illumination; (2) the panel effectively isolates the hazardous location from the area in which the lighting unit is located; (3) the lighting unit is approved for its specific location; (4) the panel is of a material or is so protected that breakage will be unlikely; and (5) the arrangement is such that normal accumulations of hazardous residue on the surface of the panel will not be raised to a dangerous temperature by radiation or conduction from the source of illumination.

(d) Portable Equipment. Portable electric lamps or other utilization equipment shall not be used within a hazardous location during operation of the finishing process. When such lamps or utilization equipment are used during cleaning or repairing operations, they shall be of a type approved for Class I, Group D, Division 1 locations, and all exposed metal parts shall be effectively grounded.

(e) Electrostatic Equipment. Electrostatic spraying or detearing equipment shall be installed and used only as provided in Section 516-4.

For further information, see NFPA Standard for Spray Application Using Flammable and Combustible Materials (NFPA No. 33-1973).

516-4. Fixed Electrostatic Equipment. This Section shall apply to any equipment using electrostatically charged elements for the atomization, charging, and/or precipitation of hazardous materials for coatings on articles or for other similar purposes in which the charging or atomizing device is attached to a mechanical support and is not hand-held or manipulated. Where fixed electrostatic spraying and detearing equipment is installed, such equipment shall be of an approved type and shall comply with (a) through (h) below.

(a) Power and Control Equipment. Transformers, power packs, control apparatus, and all other electric portions of the equipment shall be installed outside of the hazardous location as defined in Section 516-2 or be of a type approved for the location.

Exception: High-voltage grids, electrodes, electrostatic atomizing heads, and their connections shall be permitted within the hazardous location.

(b) Electrostatic Equipment. Electrodes and electrostatic atomizing heads shall be: (1) located in suitable noncombustible booths or enclosures provided with adequate mechanical ventilation; (2) adequately supported in permanent locations; and (3) effectively insulated from ground. Electrodes and electrostatic atomizing heads that are permanently attached to their bases, supports, or reciprocators shall be considered as complying with this Section. Insulators shall be nonporous.

Fine-wire elements, where used, shall be under tension at all times and be of unkinked hardened steel or material of comparable strength.

(c) High-Voltage Leads. High-voltage leads shall be properly insulated and protected from mechanical injury or exposure to destructive chemicals. Any exposed element at high voltage shall be effectively and permanently supported on suitable insulators and shall be effectively guarded against accidental contact or grounding. An automatic means shall be provided for grounding the electrode system when the primary of its high voltage supply is electrically de-energized for any reason.

(d) Separation of Goods From Electrostatic Equipment. A safe distance of at least twice the sparking distance shall be maintained between goods being painted and electrodes or electrostatic atomizing heads or conductors. A suitable sign indicating this safe distance shall be conspicuously posted near the assembly.

(e) Support of Goods. Goods being coated using this process shall be supported on conveyors or hangers. The conveyors or hangers shall be so arranged as to assure that the parts being coated are electrically connected to ground and to maintain safe distances between goods and the electrodes or electrostatic atomizing heads at all times. Goods shall be supported to prevent such swinging or movement which would reduce the clearance to less than that specified in (d) above.

(f) Automatic Controls. Electrostatic apparatus shall be equipped with automatic means which will rapidly de-energize the high voltage elements under any of the following conditions: (1) stoppage of ventilating fans or failure of ventilating equipment from any cause; (2) stoppage of the conveyor carrying goods through the high-voltage field; (3) occurrence of a ground or excessive current leakage at any point in the high-voltage system; (4) reduction of clearances below that specified in (d) above.

(g) Grounding. All electrically conductive objects within the charging influence of the electrodes except those required by the process to be at high voltage shall be adequately grounded. This requirement shall apply to paint containers, wash cans, guards, and any other electrically conductive objects or devices in the area. The equipment shall carry a prominent permanently installed warning regarding the necessity for grounding these objects.

(h) Isolation. Safeguards such as adequate booths, fencing, railings or other means shall be placed about the equipment so that they, either by their location or character or both, assure that a safe isolation of the process is maintained from plant storage or personnel. If mechanical guards are used, such guards shall be at least 5 feet from processing equipment.

516-5. Electrostatic Hand-Spraying Equipment. This Section shall apply to any equipment using electrostatically charged elements for the atomization, charging, and/or precipitation of materials for coatings on articles, or for other similar purposes in which the atomizing device is hand-held or manipulated during the spraying operation. Electrostatic hand-spraying equipment and devices used in connection with paint-spraying operations shall be of approved types and shall comply with (a) through (f) below.

(a) General. The high-voltage circuits shall be designed so as not to produce a spark of sufficient intensity to ignite the most hazardous of those vapor-air mixtures likely to be encountered, nor result in appreciable shock hazard upon coming in contact with a grounded object under all normal operating conditions. The electrostatically charged exposed elements of the hand gun shall be capable of being energized only by an actuator which also controls the paint supply.

(b) Power Equipment. Transformers, power packs, control apparatus, and all other electric portions of the equipment shall be located outside of the hazardous location or be approved for the location.

Exception: The hand gun itself and its connections to the power supply shall be permitted within the hazardous area.

(c) Handle. The handle of the spraying gun shall be electrically connected to ground by a metallic connection and be so constructed that the operator in normal operating position is in intimate electrical contact with the grounded handle to prevent build-up of a static charge on the operator's body. Signs indicating the necessity for grounding other persons entering the spray area shall be conspicuously posted.

(d) Electrostatic Equipment. All electrically conductive objects in the spraying area shall be adequately grounded. This requirement shall apply to paint containers, wash cans, and any other electrically conductive objects or devices in the area. The equipment shall carry a prominent, permanently installed warning regarding the necessity for this grounding feature.

(e) Support of Objects. Objects being painted shall be maintained in metallic contact with the conveyor or other grounded support. Hooks shall be regularly cleaned to insure this contact, and areas of contact shall be sharp points or knife edges where possible. Points of support of the object shall be concealed from random spray where feasible; and where the objects being sprayed are supported from a conveyor, the point of attachment to the conveyor shall be so located as to not collect spray material during normal operation.

(f) Ventilation. The spraying operation shall take place within a spray area that is adequately ventilated to remove solvent vapors released from the operation. The electric equipment shall be interlocked with the spraying area ventilation so that the equipment cannot be operated unless the ventilating fans are in operation.

516-6. Powder Coating. This Section shall apply to processes in which combustible dry powders are applied. The hazards associated with combustible dusts are present in such a process to a degree, depending upon the chemical composition of the material, particle size, shape, and distribution.

The hazards associated with combustible dusts are inherent in this process. Generally speaking, the hazard rating of the powders employed is dependent upon the chemical composition of the material, particle size, shape and distribution.

(a) Electric Equipment and Sources of Ignition. Electric equipment and other sources of ignition shall conform to the requirements of Article 502. Portable electrical lamps and other utilization equipment shall not be used within a hazardous area during operation of the finishing processes. When such lamps or utilization equipment are used during cleaning or repairing operations, they shall be of a type approved for Class II, Division 1 locations, and all exposed metal parts shall be effectively grounded.

(b) Fixed Electrostatic Spraying Equipment. The provisions of Sections 516-4 and (a) above shall apply to fixed electrostatic spraying equipment.

(c) Electrostatic Hand-Spraying Equipment. The provisions of Sections 516-5 and (a) above shall apply to electrostatic hand-spraying equipment.

(d) Electrostatic Fluidized Beds. Electrostatic fluidized beds and associated equipment shall be of approved types. The high-voltage circuits shall be so designed that any discharge produced when the charging electrodes of the bed are approached or contacted by a grounded object shall not be of sufficient intensity to ignite any powder-air mixture likely to be encountered nor to result in an appreciable shock hazard.

(1) Transformers, power packs, control apparatus, and all other electric portions of the equipment shall be located outside the powder-coating area or shall otherwise comply with the requirements of (a) above.

Exception: The charging electrodes and their connections to the power supply shall be permitted within the powder-coating area.

(2) All electrically conductive objects within the powder-coating area shall be adequately grounded. The powder-coating equipment shall carry a prominent, permanently installed warning regarding the necessity for grounding these objects.

(3) Objects being coated shall be maintained in electrical contact with the conveyor or other support in order to insure proper grounding. Hangers shall be regularly cleaned to insure effective electrical contact, and areas of electrical contact shall be sharp points or knife edges where possible.

(4) The electric equipment shall be interlocked with a ventilation system so that the equipment cannot be operated unless the ventilating fans are in operation.

516-7. Wiring and Equipment Above Hazardous Locations.

(a) Wiring. All fixed wiring above the hazardous locations shall be in metal raceways or shall be Type MI, TC, SNM, MC, CS, or Type ALS cable. Cellular metal floor raceways shall be permitted only for supplying ceiling outlets or extensions to the area below the floor of a hazardous location, but such raceways shall have no connections leading into or through the hazardous location above the floor unless suitable seals are provided. No electric conductor shall be installed in any cell or header that contains a pipe for steam, water, air, gas, drainage, or for other than the electrical service.

(b) Equipment. Equipment that may produce arcs, sparks, or particles of hot metal, such as lamps and lampholders for fixed lighting, cutouts, switches, receptacles, motors, or other equipment having make-and-break or sliding contacts, where installed above a hazardous location or above a location where freshly finished goods are handled, shall be of the totally enclosed type or be so constructed as to prevent escape of sparks or hot metal particles.

516-8. Grounding. All metal raceways and all noncurrent-carrying metal parts of fixed or portable equipment, regardless of voltage, shall be grounded as provided in Article 250.

▲ The safety of life and property from fire or explosion in the spray application of flammable paints and finishes depends upon the extent, arrangement, maintenance, and operation of the process.

An analysis of actual experience in industry demonstrates that largest fire losses and fire frequency have occurred where good practice standards were not observed.

Definitions—See NFPA Standard for Spray Finishing Using Flammable Materials (No. 33).

Spraying Area. Any area in which dangerous quantities of flammable vapors or mists, or combustible residues, dusts, or deposits are present due to the operation of spraying processes.

A spraying area includes:

(a) The interior of spray booths (with certain exceptions).

(b) The interior of ducts exhausting from spraying processes.

(c) Any area in the direct path of spray or any area containing dangerous quantities of air-suspended powder or combustible residue, dust, deposits, mists, or vapor as a result of spraying operations.

The inspection department having jurisdiction may, for the purpose of this standard, define the limits of the spraying area in any specific case.

Note: The "spraying area" in the vicinity of spraying operations will necessarily vary with the design and arrangement of equipment and method of operation.

When spraying operations are strictly confined to predetermined spaces which are provided with adequate and reliable ventilation, such as a properly constructed spray booth, the "spraying area" should ordinarily not extend beyond the booth enclosure.

When, however, spraying operations are not confined to adequately ventilated spaces, the "spraying area" may extend throughout the entire room containing spraying operations.

Spray Booth. A power-ventilated structure provided to enclose or accommodate a spraying operation, to confine and limit the escape of spray, vapor, and residue, and to safely conduct or direct them to an exhaust system.

Waterwash Spray Booth. A spray booth equipped with a waterwashing system designed to minimize dusts or residues entering exhaust ducts and to permit the recovery of overspray finishing material.

Dry Spray Booth. A spray booth not equipped with a waterwashing system as described above. A dry spray booth may be equipped with (1) distribution or baffle plates to promote an even flow of air through booth or cause deposit of overspray before it enters exhaust duct; or (2) overspray dry filters to minimize dusts or residues entering exhaust ducts; or (3) overspray dry filter rolls designed to minimize dusts or residues entering exhaust ducts; or (4) where dry powders are being sprayed, with powder collection systems arranged in the exhaust to capture oversprayed material.

Notes on Electrical Installations

As stipulated in Definitions, the inspection department having jurisdiction may, for any specific installation, determine the extent of the hazardous "spraying area."

From Sec. 516-3(b) it will be noted that in general electrical equipment is not permitted inside any spray booth, in the exhaust duct from a spray booth, in the entrained air of an exhaust system from a spraying operation, or in the direct path of spray, unless such equipment is specifically approved for both readily ignitible deposits and flammable vapor. Electric motors driving exhaust fans are specifically prohibited inside spray booths and exhaust ducts.

From the above, it will be noted that when electrical equipment is installed in locations not subject to deposits of combustible residues but, due to inadequate ventilation, is subject to explosive concentrations of flammable vapors or mists, only approved explosionproof equipment is permitted.

When spraying operations are confined to adequately ventilated spray booths there should be no dangerous concentrations of flammable vapors or mists, nor deposits of combustible residues outside of the spray booth under normal operation conditions.

In the interest of safety, however, it will be noted that unless separated by partitions, the area within 20 ft of the hazardous "spraying area" is considered Division 2; that is, it should contain no equipment which produces sparks under normal operation. Furthermore, within this 20-ft distance electric lamps must be enclosed to prevent hot particles falling on freshly painted stock or other readily ignitible material and if subject to physical damage must be properly guarded.

Electrical and Other Sources of Ignition

It is obvious that there should be a total absence of open flames or spark-producing equipment in any area where, because of inadequate ventilation, explosive vapor-air mixtures or mists are present. Obviously, no open flames or spark-producing equipment should be so located that there will be deposited on them highly combustible spray residues. Because some residues may be ignited at very low temperatures, additional consideration must be given to operating temperatures of equipment subject to residue deposits. Many deposits may be ignited at temperatures produced by incandescent light bulbs, even of the explosionproof type, or low-pressure steam pipes.

The area in the vicinity of spraying operations which may contain dangerous quantities of flammable vapors, mists, or residue deposits will vary with design and arrangement of equipment and methods of operation.

For the usual cabinet spray booth it has been generally considered that limited areas not separated by partitions and in the front of a booth may be dangerous. When, however, ventilation is inadequate and spraying is not strictly confined to the inside of the booth, the dangerous area may extend throughout the entire room.

On the other hand, when adequate, reliable, supervised ventilation is provided and spraying operations strictly confined to the predetermined designated spaces, the hazardous areas may not extend beyond the booth enclosure.

When areas of spraying with hazardous quantities of vapor or mists or residue under normal operation have been determined, the unpartitioned-off areas adjacent to hazardous areas which are safe under normal operating conditions but which may become dangerous due to accident or careless operation should be considered. In these adjacent areas, equipment known to produce sparks or flames under normal operating conditions should not be installed.

Sufficient lighting for operations, booth cleaning, and repair should be provided at the time of equipment installation in order to avoid the unjustified use of "temporary" or "emergency" electric lamps connected to ordinary extension cords. A satisfactory and practical method of lighting is the use of $\frac{1}{4}$-in.-thick wired or tempered glass panels in the top or sides of spray booths with electrical light fixtures outside the booth, hence not in the direct path of the spray.

Areas adjacent to a spray booth, particularly where paint stocks are located, should be provided with ventilation sufficiently adequate and reliable to prevent the presence of flammable vapors or deposits. It is nevertheless advisable that electric lamps be totally enclosed to prevent the falling of hot particles in any area where there may be freshly painted stock, accidentally spilled flammable or combustible liquids, or readily ignitible refuse or flammable or combustible liquid containers accidentally left open.

Where electric lamps are in areas subject to atmospheres of flammable vapor, the replacing of lamp bulbs should only be done when electricity is off; otherwise there may be a spark from this source.

The determination of the extent of hazardous areas involved in spray application requires an understanding of the dual hazards of flammable vapors or mists and highly combustible deposits together with intelligent judgment of the objectives, applied to each individual installation.

Automobile undercoating spray operations in garages, conducted in areas having adequate natural or mechanical ventilation, may be exempt from the requirements pertaining to spray finishing operations, when using undercoating materials not more hazardous than kerosene (as listed by Underwriters' Laboratories in respect to fire hazard rating 30–40) or undercoating materials using only solvents listed as having a flash point in excess of 100°F. There should be no open flames or other sources of ignition within 20 ft while such operations are conducted.

ARTICLE 517. HEALTH CARE FACILITIES

A. General

517-1. Scope. The provisions of this Article shall apply to health care facilities. For additional requirements see Article 660 for medical X-ray equipment and Article 665 for therapeutic high-frequency equipment.

▲ It should be noted that the provisions of this article apply to hospitals, nursing homes, residential custodial care facilities, and other health-care facilities serving patients who are unable to provide for their own safety. They also apply to the medical wiring and equipment wiring systems in mobile health-care units and doctors' and dentists' offices.

The diagram gives the minimum requirements for the essential electrical system for a hospital. As outlined under part C the requirements for nursing homes and similar facilities are slightly different, and this diagram therefore does not apply to them. It should be noted that the diagram does not require a life support branch; however, when it is installed it must be a part of the emergency system.

517-2. Definitions.

Alternate Power Source. One or more generator sets intended to provide power during the interruption of the normal electrical service or the public utility electrical service intended to provide power during interruption of service normally provided by the generating facilities on the premises.

Anesthetizing Location. Any area in which it is intended to administer any flammable or nonflammable inhalation anesthetic agents in the course of examination or treatment and includes operating rooms, delivery rooms, emergency rooms, anesthetizing rooms, corridors, utility rooms and other areas when used for induction of anesthesia with flammable or nonflammable anesthetizing agents.

Anesthetizing-Location Receptacle. A receptacle designed to accept the attachment plugs listed for use in such locations.

▲ The figures associated with this receptacle in the 1971 NEC have been deleted from this code. It should be understood that the deletion of these figures does not imply nonacceptability of such devices. Devices of the pin-and-sleeve style and also the parallel "U" blade style, both listed for Class I, Group C locations, have become a standard with many hospitals. The new definition in this article now permits the use of any device which is listed for use in such locations.

Continuous Power System. An electrical system, independent of the alternate source which supplies power without appreciable interruption (1-cycle or less).

Critical Branch. A sub-system of the emergency system consisting of feeders and branch circuits supplying energy to task illumination and selected receptacles serving areas and functions related to patient care, and which can be connected to alternate power sources by one or more transfer switches.

Critical Patient Care Area. A section (rooms, wards or portions of wards) designated for the treatment of critically ill patients.

Critical System. A system of feeders and branch circuits in Nursing Homes and Residential Custodial Care Facilities arranged for connection to the alternate power

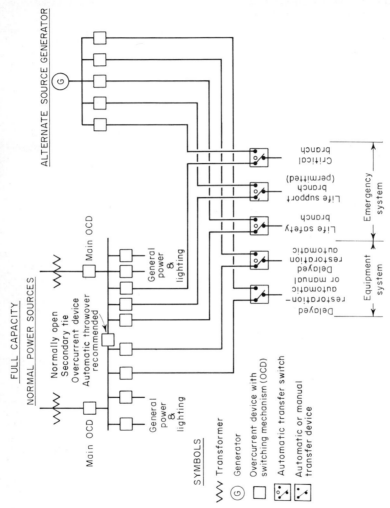

DIAGRAM 517-1. Typical Diagram for Essential Electrical Systems.

source to restore service to certain critical receptacles, task illumination and equipment.

Emergency System. A system of feeders and branch circuits meeting the requirements of Article 700, connected to alternate power sources by a transfer switch and supplying energy to an extremely limited number of prescribed functions vital to the protection of life and patient safety, with automatic restoration of electrical power within 10 seconds of power interruption.

Equipment System. A system of feeders and branch circuits arranged for delayed, automatic or manual connection to the alternate power source and which serves primarily 3-phase power equipment.

See Appendix A of Essential Electrical Systems for Health Care Facilities, NFPA No. 76A-1973.

Essential Electrical Systems. Systems comprised of alternate sources of power, transfer switches, overcurrent protective devices, distribution cabinets, feeders, branch circuits, motor controls, and all connected electrical equipment, designed to provide designated areas with continuity of electrical service during disruption of normal power sources, and also designed to minimize the interruptive effects of disruption within the internal wiring system.

Flammable Anesthetics. Gases or vapors such as fluroxene, cyclopropane, divinyl ether, ethyl chloride, ethyl ether, and ethylene, which may form flammable or explosive mixtures with air, oxygen, or reducing gases such as nitrous oxide.

Flammable Anesthetizing Location. Any operating room, delivery room, anesthetizing room, corridor, utility room, or any other area if used or intended for the application of flammable anesthetics.

Health Care Facilities. Buildings or parts of buildings that contain, but are not limited to, hospitals, nursing homes, extended-care facilities, clinics, and medical and dental offices, whether fixed or mobile.

Immediate Restoration of Service. Automatic restoration of operation with an interruption of not more than 10 seconds as applied to those areas and functions served by the Emergency System, except for areas and functions for which Article 700 otherwise makes specific provisions.

Life Safety Branch. A sub-system of the Emergency System consisting of feeders and branch circuits, meeting the requirements of Article 700 and intended to provide adequate power needs to insure safety to patients and personnel, and which can be connected to alternate power sources by one or more transfer switches.

Life Support Branch. A system of feeders and branch circuits connected to the alternate power source by a transfer switch and functioning as a component of the Emergency System that serves only selected receptacles or fixed equipment in critical patient care areas where electrical service may be necessary for patient survival.

Line Isolation Monitor. A test instrument designed to continually check the balanced and unbalanced impedance from each line of an isolated circuit to ground and equipped with a built-in test circuit to exercise the alarm without adding to the leakage current hazard.

"Line isolation monitor" was formerly known as "ground contact indicator."

Nurses' Stations. Areas intended to provide a center of nursing activity for a group of nurses working under one nurse supervisor and serving bed patients, where the patient calls are received, nurses are dispatched, nurses' notes written, inpatient charts prepared, and medications prepared for distribution to patients. Where such activities are carried on in more than one location within a nursing unit, all such separate areas are considered a part of the nurses' station.

Patient Grounding Point. A jack or terminal bus which serves as the collection point for redundant grounding of electric appliances serving a patient vicinity, and for grounding conductive furniture or nonelectric equipment within reach of a patient or a person who may touch him.

Patient Vicinity. The space with surfaces likely to be contacted by the patient or an attendant who can touch him. This represents a space 6 feet beyond the reach of the patient.

▲ This term now provides a definite value for limiting the area wherein special grounding requirements are to be observed in patient care areas.

Reference Grounding Point. A terminal bus which is an extension of the equipment grounding bus and is a convenient collection point for grounding all electric appliances, equipment and exposed conductive surfaces in a patient vicinity.

Room Bonding Point. A grounding terminal bus which serves as a collection point for grounding exposed metal or conductive building surfaces in a room.

Task Illumination. Provision for the minimum lighting required to carry out necessary tasks in the described areas, including safe access to supplies and equipment, and access to exits.

B. General Area Wiring Systems

517-3. Grounding. In locations intended for occupancy by patients at any time, all noncurrent-carrying conductive surfaces of electrical equipment that are subject to personal contact shall be grounded by an insulated copper conductor, sized in accordance with Table 250-95, installed with the circuit conductors supplying these receptacles and equipment.

▲ This section requires the use of a separate, insulated equipment-grounding-conductor run with the circuit conductors. Although they may be used as a redundant means, neither the conduit, nor the use of jumpers and box clips, nor the use of a receptacle as permitted in Sec. 250-74 Exception No. 2 may be used by themselves in order to provide the grounding intended. It should also be noted that the locations where this rule is to be observed now include not only patient rooms but corridors, waiting rooms, admitting rooms, solariums, and patient recreation areas. Such accessible items as television sets, clocks, floor and table lamps, and the like, when used in such areas, must be equipped with a power supply cord having an equipment grounding conductor grounded to all non-current-carrying conductive surfaces of the device. Unless specifically approved for insulating purposes, paints or anodizing and similar finishes do not render the device insulated.

517-4. Wiring Methods. Except as modified in this Article, wiring methods shall comply with the applicable requirements of Chapters 1 through 4 of this Code.

C. Essential Electrical Systems

For additional information, see Essential Electrical Systems for Health Care Facilities; NFPA 76A-1973 and Installation of Centrifugal Fire Pumps. NFPA No. 20-1972.

517-10. General.

(a) Part C applies to hospitals, nursing homes, residential custodial care facilities and other health care facilities serving patients who are unable to provide for their own safety.

(b) Essential Electrical Systems shall consist of two parts:

(1) In Hospitals, the Emergency System and the Equipment System. The systems shall be capable of supplying a limited amount of power and lighting service considered essential for life safety, life support and effective operation during the time the normal electrical service is interrupted for any reason.

See Diagram 517-1.

(2) In Nursing Homes and Residential Custodial Care Facilities, the Emergency System and the Critical System. The systems shall be capable of supplying an amount of power and lighting service considered essential for life safety and effective operation during the time the normal service is interrupted for any reason.

(c) Each essential system shall have adequate capacity and rating for the operation of all lighting and equipment it serves.

▲ The requirements of this section make it clear that essential electrical systems are to be installed in all hospitals as well as all nursing homes and similar facilities. However, it should be pointed out that essential electrical systems in hospitals are subdivided into the emergency system (consisting of the life safety, life support, and critical branches) and the equipment system, whereas the essential electrical systems for nursing homes and the like are subdivided into the emergency system and the critical system. It should be noted that the critical branch in hospitals comprises different equipment and connections than does the critical system in nursing homes. A summary of the requirements of essential electrical systems for these two types of occupancies is provided in Figs. 517-2, 517-3, and 517-4, which show these differences.

517-11. Emergency System—Hospitals.

(a) The Emergency System shall be permitted to consist of three parts: the life safety branch, the critical branch, and the life support branch. These branches shall be limited to circuits essential to specified functions.

(b) A life safety branch and a critical branch shall be required in all hospitals.

(1) The life safety branch shall serve illumination, alarm and alerting equipment which shall be operable at all times for protection of life during emergencies.

(2) The critical branch shall serve lighting and receptacles in critical patient care areas.

(3) The life support branch shall be permitted to be installed as a component of the emergency system. When provided, it shall serve only selected receptacles or fixed equipment in critical patient care areas where electrical service may be necessary for patient survival.

(c) The feeders for the emergency system shall be physically separated from the normal wiring or protected in such a way as to minimize the possibility of simultaneous interruption.

(d) The life safety branch, life support branch, and critical branch of the Emergency System shall be run in metal raceways.

These branches shall be kept entirely independent of all other wiring and equipment and shall not enter the same raceways, boxes or cabinets with each other or other wiring.

Exception No. 1: As permitted in 517-11(b)(3).

Fig. 517-2. Plug/receptacle types for use in health-care facilities.

	Class I Group C	Enclosed type	"Hospital grade"	Listed general purpose	"EMI" type per sec. 250-74, Exc. 4°
Hazardous locations	Required				
Above hazardous locations	Permitted	Required			
Nonhazardous locations	Permitted	Permitted			
Other than hazardous locations	Permitted	Permitted			
Critical care areas	Permitted	Permitted	Permitted	Permitted	
General care areas	Permitted	Permitted	Permitted	Permitted	Permitted
All other areas	Permitted	Permitted	Permitted	Permitted	Permitted

°See comments on insulating-type (electromagnetic interference) receptacles following Sec. 250-74, Exception No. 4.

Exception No. 2: In transfer switches.

Exception No. 3: In exit or emergency lighting fixtures supplied from two sources.

(e) Only those functions utilizing illumination or equipment which are listed in Sections 517-12, -13, and -14 shall be connected to the Emergency System.

(f) All branches of the Emergency System shall be so installed and connected to the alternate source of power that all lighting and equipment shall be automatically restored to operation within 10 seconds after interruption of the normal source.

517-12. Life Safety Branch—Hospitals. The life safety branch of the Emergency System shall serve the lighting, receptacles and other equipment which are related to the safety of life as follows:

For additional information see Essential Electrical Systems for Health Care Facilities, NFPA No. 76A-1973.

(1) Illumination of means of egress, such as lighting required for corridors, passageways, stairways and landings at exit doors, and all necessary ways of approach to exits.

See Life Safety Code, NFPA No. 101-1973, Section 5-10.

(2) Exit signs and directional signs.

See Life Safety Code, NFPA No. 101-1973, Section 5-11.

(3) Alarm systems, including: fire alarms actuated at manual stations, electric water-flow alarm devices in connection with sprinkler systems, automatic fire or smoke or products of combustion detection devices.

See Life Safety Code, NFPA No. 101-1973, Sections 6-3, 10-1 and 10-2.

(4) Alarms required for systems used for the piping of nonflammable medical gases.

See Nonflammable Medical Gas Systems, NFPA No. 56F-1973.

(5) Hospital communication systems when these are intended for issuing instructions during emergency conditions, including local power requirements for the telephone system.

(6) Generator-set location, including task illumination and selected receptacles.

517-13. Critical Branch—Hospitals. The critical branch of the Emergency System shall serve only the following areas and functions related to patient care:

(1) Isolating transformers serving anesthetizing locations.

(2) Task illumination and selected receptacles in: (a) infant nurseries; (b) medication preparation areas; (c) pharmacy dispensing areas; (d) selected acute nursing areas; (e) psychiatric bed areas (task illumination only); (f) nurses' stations (unless adequately lighted by corridor luminaires); (g) ward treatment rooms; (h) surgical and obstetrical suites; (i) angiographic labs; (j) cardiac catheterization labs; (k) coronary care units; (l) delivery rooms; (m) dialysis units; (n) emergency room treatment areas; (o) human physiology labs; (p) intensive care units; (q) operating rooms; (r) post-operative recovery rooms.

517-14. Life Support Branch—Hospitals.

(a) The life support branch when installed shall supply selected receptacles or fixed equipment in critical patient care areas where electrical service may be necessary for patient survival as designated by the governing authority of the hospital.

(b) The power systems in the above locations shall be permitted to be served by an uninterruptible power supply.

517-15. Equipment Systems—Hospitals.

(a) The Equipment System shall be so installed and connected to the alternate source that equipment listed in Section 517-15(d) shall be automatically restored to operation at appropriate time-lag intervals following the restoration of the emergency system to operation. This arrangement shall also provide for reconnection of equipment listed in Sections 517-15(e) and (f) by either delayed, automatic, or manual operation.

(b) The Equipment Systems shall be permitted in raceways and boxes with general wiring.

(c) The Equipment System shall be connected to equipment listed in Sections 517-15(d) and (e). Connection to equipment listed in Section 517-15(f) shall be permitted.

(d) The following components of the Equipment System shall be arranged for automatic restoration of operation: (1) central vacuum and medical air systems serving medical and surgical functions; (2) sump pumps and other equipment including associated control systems and alarms required to operate for the safety of essential apparatus.

(e) The following required components of the Equipment System shall be arranged for either automatic or manual connection to the alternate power source:

(1) Heating equipment for heating of operating, delivery, labor, recovery, and patient rooms, and intensive care units and nurseries.

Exception: Patient room heating during disruption of normal source under either of the following conditions:

a. The outside air design temperature is higher than $-7°C$, $(+20°F)$.

This is based on the median of extremes as shown in the 1967 edition of the American Society of Heating, Air Conditioning and Refrigeration Engineers Handbook of Fundamentals.

b. The hospital is served by at least two utility services, each supplied by separate generating sources or a network distribution system fed by two or more generators. The utility services shall be routed, connected, and protected so that a fault any place between the generators and the hospital will not likely cause an interruption of more than one of the utility services.

(2) Elevator service that reaches every patient floor, ground floors, and floors on which surgical suites and obstetrical delivery suites are located. This shall include connections for cab lighting and control and signal systems.

In instances where interruption of power results in an elevator stopping between floors, the provision of throw-over facilities permits the temporary operation of any elevator to release patients or other persons who may be trapped between floors.

(3) Supply and exhaust ventilating systems for laboratory fume hoods, and surgical suites, obstetrical suites, infant nurseries, and emergency treatment spaces where such areas contain no windows.

(f) The following components of the equipment systems shall be permitted to be arranged for either automatic or manual connection to the alternate source:

(1) Selected autoclaving equipment if electrically heated or controlled.

FIG. 517-3. Essential electrical systems for hospitals* (Secs. 517-11 through 517-15).

Emergency system [immediate (10 second) restoration]		Life support branch (permitted)	Equipment (all delayed restoration)
Life safety branch	Critical branch		
Lighting and receptacles for: —Means of egress illumination —Exit and directional signs —Alarm systems 　·Manual fire stations 　·Sprinklers 　·Fire & smoke detection —Alarms for nonflammable medical gas —Communications for emergency use —Generator—set location	—Isolating transformers in anesthetizing locations —Task illumination and selected receptacles in: 　·Nurseries 　·Medication preparation 　·Pharmacy 　·Acute nursing 　·Psychiatric beds (no receptacles) 　·Nurses stations 　·Ward treatment rooms 　·Surgery and obstetrics 　·Angiographic labs 　·Cardiac catheter labs 　·Coronary care 　·Delivery 　·Dialysis 　·Emergency 　·Human physiology labs 　·Intensive care 　·Operating rooms 　·Post-operative 　·Recovery rooms	(Uninterruptible power supply permitted) Selected receptacles and fixed equipment necessary for patient survival. Such locations may be, but are not limited to, the areas listed opposite.	Automatic restoration —Vacuum and air systems serving medical and surgical —Sump pumps and associated controls serving essential apparatus Automatic or manual restoration —Heating for O.R., delivery, labor, recovery, patient, ICU, and nursery —Elevator service to all patient floors, O.R., and ground floor —Ventilating for lab hoods and windowless surgery, obstetrics, nurseries, and emergency rooms —Selected autoclaving —Selected equipment in kitchens, laundries, radiological, and central refrigeration

*For nursing homes, see Fig. 517-4.

(2) Other selected equipment in locations such as kitchens, laundries, radiological and central refrigeration rooms.

Where heavy interruption currents can be anticipated, the transferred load may be reduced by use of multiple transfer devices. For example, elevator feeders may cause less hazard to electrical continuity if they are fed through individual transfer devices.

517-20. Systems—Nursing Homes and Residential Custodial Facilities.

(a) The requirements of this paragraph shall apply to any nursing home or residential custodial care facility.

Exception: Any freestanding building used for health care other than inpatient hospital care which meets all the requirements of (1), (2), and (3) below inclusive.

1. Maintains admitting and discharge policies that preclude the provision of care for any patient or resident who may need to be sustained by line-operated electro-mechanical means such as electric respirators, suction apparatus, external heart pacers and other life support apparatus.

2. Offers no surgical treatment requiring general anesthesia.

3. Provides automatic battery operated systems or equipment that will be effective for 4 or more hours and is otherwise in accordance with Section 700-6(e) and will be capable of supplying power for lighting for exit signs, exit corridors, stairways, nursing stations, medication preparation areas, boiler rooms, and communication areas and supplies battery power to operate all alarm systems.

(b) The Emergency System in nursing homes and residential custodial care facilities shall be so installed and connected to the alternate power source so that all functions specified herein shall be automatically restored to operation within ten seconds after interruption of the normal source. The Emergency System shall supply only the following lighting, receptacles, and equipment which are related to the safety of life:

(1) Illumination of means of egress as necessary for corridors, passageways, stairways, landings, and exit doors, and all ways of approach to exits.

See Life Safety Code, NFPA No. 101-1973, Section 5-10.

(2) Exit signs and exit directional signs.

See Life Safety Code, NFPA No. 101-1973, Section 5-11.

(3) Sufficient lighting in dining and recreation areas to provide illumination to exit ways.

(4) Alarm systems including:

(a) Fire alarms activated at manual stations, by electric water flow alarm devices in connection with sprinkler systems, and by automatic fire or smoke or products of combustion detection devices.

See Life Safety Code, NFPA No. 101-1973, Sections 6-3 and 10-136.

(b) Alarms required for systems used for the piping of nonflammable medical gas.

See Standard for Nonflammable Medical Gas systems, NFPA No. 56F-1973.

(5) Communication systems where these are used for issuing instructions during emergency conditions.

(6) Generator set location, task illumination, and selected receptacles.

(c) The critical system shall be so installed and connected to the alternate power source that equipment listed in 517-20(c)(1) shall be automatically restored to operation at appropriate time lag intervals following the restoration of the Critical System to operation. Its arrangement shall also provide for the additional connection of equipment listed in 517-20(c)(2) by either delayed automatic or manual operation.

(1) The following equipment shall be arranged for automatic connection to the alternate power source:

(a) Patient Care Areas—task illumination and selected receptacles in: (1) Medication preparation areas; (2) Pharmacy dispensing areas; (3) Nurses' stations (unless adequately lighted by corridor luminaries).

(b) Sump pumps and other equipment required to operate for the safety of major apparatus including associated control systems and alarms.

(c) Elevator cab lighting and communication systems.

(2) The following equipment shall be arranged for either automatic or manual connection to the alternate power source:

(a) Heating equipment to provide heating for patient rooms.

Exception: Heating of patient rooms during disruption of the normal source shall not be required under either of the following conditions:

(1) The design temperature is higher than +20°F, based on the Median of Extremes as shown in the current edition of the ASHRAE Handbook of Fundamentals.

(2) The facility is served by two or more electrical services supplied from separate generators or a utility distribution network having multiple power input sources and arranged to provide mechanical and electrical separation so that a fault between the facility and the generating sources is not likely to cause an interruption of more than one of the facility service feeders.

(b) Where provided, elevator service that reaches every patient floor and ground floor. This shall include connections for cab lighting and control and signal systems. In instances where interruption of power would result in elevators stopping between floors, it may be desirable to provide throw-over facilities to allow the temporary operation of any elevator for the release of patients or other persons who may be confined between floors.

517-30. Power Sources.

(a) Essential electrical systems shall have a minimum of two independent sources of power: a normal source generally supplying the entire health care facility and an alternate source(s) for use when the normal source is interrupted.

(b) The alternate source of power shall be a generator set(s) driven by some form of prime mover, and located on the premises.

Exception: Where the normal source consists of generating units on the premises, the alternate source shall be either another generating set or an external utility service.

(c) All equipment shall be located to minimize the hazards that might cause complete failure of the equipment, such as floods, fires and icing.

(d) Electrical characteristics of the generator set(s) shall be suitable for the operation of all lighting and equipment to be served.

A higher degree of electrical service continuity will be provided where facilities are two separate full-capacity external services (Section 700-6(c)), connected in such a manner as to pick up the load automatically and so arranged that the load will not be transferred to the generator set(s) if either external service is energized.

Fig. 517-4. Essential electrical systems for nursing homes and the like (Sec. 517-20).

Emergency system [immediate (10 second) restoration]	Critical system (delayed restoration)
Lighting, receptacles, and equipment related to life safety:	Automatic restoration
—Means of egress illumination	—Patient care areas
—Exit and directional signs	—Task illumination and selected receptacles in:
—Exit illumination in dining and recreational areas	·Medication preparation ·Pharmacy ·Nurses stations
—Alarm systems ·Manual fire stations ·Sprinklers ·Fire and smoke detection	—Sump pumps and associated controls serving major apparatus
—Alarms for nonflammable medical gas	—Elevator cab lighting and communication systems
—Communications for emergency use	Automatic or manual restoration
—Generator set location	—Heating for patient rooms
	—Elevators reaching every patient floor and ground floor

517-40. Switching and Overcurrent Protection.

(a) The emergency system and the equipment system in hospitals shall be so arranged that in the event of interruption of the normal power source, an alternate power source shall be automatically connected within 10 seconds to the distribution panels connected to the emergency system and to the time-delay and/or manually operated switches connected to the equipment system. The emergency system and critical system in Nursing Homes and Residential Custodial Care Facilities shall be so arranged that in the event of interruption of the normal power source, an alternate power source shall be automatically connected within 10 seconds to the distribution panels connected to the emergency system and to the time delay and/or manually operated switches connected to the critical system. Where one or more generators are provided in addition to one or more external services as alternate sources, the automatic connection sequence shall connect either the alternate external service or the generator(s), whichever is arranged for automatic connection.

If the external service and the generator(s) are both arranged for automatic connection, the order of connection to these alternate power sources is an optional design choice.

(b) Automatic switching equipment shall be approved for emergency service and shall be designed and installed with interlocking provisions that will prevent interconnection of normal and alternate sources or any two separate sources of power in any operation of the automatic switching equipment. The equipment shall be so connected that the load is served by the normal power source, except when the normal source is interrupted. Controls and switching equipment shall be so arranged that interruption of the normal sources automatically starts an alternate source generator, automatically disconnects the interrupted normal source of power, and connects the alternate source of power in proper sequence. If a generator is the only alternate source of power time shall be allowed, but not more than 10 seconds, for the generator to attain rated voltage before its connection. Upon transfer from the normal power source to the alternate power source, the loads connected to the emergency system shall be automatically energized immediately. The loads connected onto the equipment system in hospitals and critical systems in nursing homes and residential custodial care facilities shall be connected either automatically or manually after a time delay in such sequential manner as not to overload the generator.

When the normal power source is restored, the automatic transfer devices shall disconnect the alternate source and restore service connection to the normal power source, permitting the operation of manual switches to reconnect the normal power source.

For automatic operation, the provision of a 15-minute or longer time-delay will avoid short-time re-establishment of the normal service and the possibility of erratic operation of the transfer switch.

▲ It should be pointed out that, although this note is advisory in nature, the provisions of 700-6(b)(1) now contain a mandatory requirement for a time-delay feature with a 15-min minimum setting to avoid short-time re-establishment of the normal source.

(c) The provisions of Section 700-18 shall apply to switches installed in exit lighting circuits.

Exception: As provided in Section 700-20(b) switching arrangements to transfer corridor lighting in patient areas to fixtures designed for night lighting.

For more details, see Life Safety Code, NFPA No. 101-1973.

(d) The provisions of Section 700-18, with respect to the location and installation of switches in lighting circuits other than those controlling exit lighting and exit directional signs, shall apply. Personnel ordinarily assigned to work in an area illuminated by fixtures connected to the Emergency System shall be considered as authorized personnel.

This paragraph applies particularly to ungrounded circuits in anesthetizing locations connected to emergency systems.

(e) The life safety branch, the life support branch, the critical branch and the equipment system in hospitals and critical systems in nursing homes and residential custodial care facilities shall be protected by overcurrent devices so that interruption of service in other wiring systems, due to internal failure shall not interrupt supply to these branches or systems.

It is extremely important that the various overcurrent devices in the essential electrical systems be coordinated to protect against cascading operation on short circuit faults. Primary consideration should also be given to prevent overloading of equipment by limiting the possibilities of large current inrushes due to instantaneous re-establishment of connections to heavy loads.

(f) The electrical characteristics of the transfer switches shall be suitable for the connected load.

The capacity of transfer switches shall be adequate to carry full-load currents and to withstand the thermal and electromagnetic effects of short circuit currents.

517-41. Ground Fault Protection.

(a) When ground-fault protection is provided in the normal service disconnecting means, at least one more step of ground-fault protection, downstream toward the load, in each feeder shall be provided. Such protection shall consist of overcurrent devices and current transformers or other equivalent protective equipment which shall cause the feeder disconnecting devices to open.

(b) Main and feeder ground-fault protection shall be fully selective such that the feeder device and not the main device shall open on ground faults on the load side of the feeder device. A 6-cycle minimum separation between the main and feeder ground-fault tripping bands shall be provided. Operating time of the disconnecting devices shall be considered in selecting the time spread between these two bands to achieve 100 percent selectivity.

▲ At least one additional level of ground-fault protection is now required for health care facilities where required by Sec. 230-95. Where the provisions of Sec. 230-95 require the installation of ground-fault protection on the normal service-disconnecting means, then each feeder must be provided with similar protective means. This requirement was added in order to prevent a catastrophic outage. By applying appropriate selectivity at each level, the ground fault can be limited to a single feeder, and thereby service may be maintained to the balance of the health-care facility.

D. Patient Care Areas

517-50. General.

(a) It is the purpose of Part D to specify the performance criteria and/or wiring methods which will minimize electrical hazards by the maintenance of adequately low-potential differences between conductive surfaces which could be contacted by a patient.

In a health care facility, it is difficult to prevent the occurrence of a conductive or capacitive path from the patient's body to some grounded object, because that path may be established accidentally or through instrumentation directly connected to the patient. Other electrically conductive surfaces which may make an additional contact with the patient, or instruments which may be connected to the patient, then become possible sources of electric currents which can traverse the patient's body. The hazard is increased as more apparatus is associated with the patient, and therefore more intensive precautions must be taken. A special problem is presented by the patient with an externalized electric conductor connected to his heart. He may be electrocuted at current levels so low that special consideration must be given to the design of the patient electrical environment. He requires additional protection in the design of appliances, insulation of his catheter and control of medical practice.

(b) Patient Care areas shall be classified into one of the three following categories:

(1) General Care Area. Areas where patients ordinarily have only incidental contact with electrical devices.

(2) Critical Care Area, Controlled. Areas where patients ordinarily are intentionally exposed to electrical devices, and where the governing body requires protection (insulation) of externalized cardiac conductors from contact with conductive surfaces other than those designed for connection to such cardiac conductors.

(3) Critical Care Area, Uncontrolled. Areas where patients ordinarily are intentionally exposed to electrical devices and where the governing body makes no requirements for protection of externalized cardiac conductors from contact with conductive surfaces other than those designed for the purpose.

(c) The designation of areas in the health care facility in accordance with the classification of patients shall be the responsibility of the governing body of the facility.

▲ This section now deals with patient care areas in general rather than the electrically susceptible patient himself. It also reserves the designation of the various types of areas to the governing body of the health-care facility. With these two changes the Code now recognizes responsibility for evaluation of patient medical conditions, and the consequent placement of patients within specific areas is reserved to the medical staff and governing body of that health-care facility. On the other hand, it now provides specific electrical rules for systems and areas which are the proper concern of architects, engineers, and maintenance staff.

The general care area would include all ward areas in most cases. Occasional exposure to such items as an electrocardiograph, portable x-ray, a nebulizer, and the like would not warrant exceptional electrical precautions. Basically, any electrodes applied to the patient in a general care area should be of short duration and should be noninvasive. The designation of a critical care area as "controlled" presumes that the hospital has a written policy which prohibits the use of cardiac conductors having uninsulated external terminals. This rule does recognize the conductive connection necessary between the external cardiac conductors and the device with which the conductors are intended to be used. Absence of such a policy for insulation automatically classifies a critical care area as "uncontrolled."

517-51. Performance.

(a) Any two exposed conductive surfaces in the patient vicinity shall not exceed the following potential differences at frequencies of 1000 Hertz or less measured across a 1000 ohm resistance.

(1) General Care Areas. 500 mv under normal operation.

(2) Critical Care Areas, Controlled. 100 mv under normal operation.

Fig. 517-5. Assembly with isolation transformer, dynamic-type line isolation monitor, and reference grounding bus receptacles of the plug-in-jack type. (*Sorgel Electric Corp., Subsidiary of Square D. Co.*)

(3) Critical Care Areas, Uncontrolled.   100 mv under normal operation or under conditions of line-to-ground fault.

Exception: Permanently installed x-ray equipment.

▲ Initial studies of the problem which has come to be categorized as "microshock" indicated that current values as low as 20 microamperes applied directly to the interior surfaces of the heart could produce ventricular fibrillation. These studies utilized dogs as their subjects, and by comparison with human data it was determined that 10 microamperes should be the maximum allowable current leakage in critical care areas. More recent studies actually utilizing human subjects now indicate that there is a wider margin between dogs and humans than was initially anticipated. The new values for permissible potential differences within patient care areas now reflect studies which have been performed both in the United States and abroad on this subject.

In most cases it will be found that the limits for potential differences permitted in general care areas and controlled critical care areas can be maintained using only the grounding requirements which are set forth in this article. However, inasmuch as uncontrolled critical care areas permit a maximum of 100 mV potential difference

FIG. 517-6. Module with 120-V power receptacles (lower) and grounding plugs. (*Sorgel Electric Corp., Subsidiary of Square D. Co.*)

to be maintained under conditions of line-to-ground fault as well as normal operations, the use of an isolated power system or some equivalent means will have to be employed in order to limit the rise of potential difference under fault conditions.

Permanently installed x-ray equipment is exempted from the above potential limits, since their high power requirements generally take them beyond the capacity of listed isolated power supplies which are presently available. Additional grounding requirements do apply to this type of equipment, however, under Sec. 517-51(c), and it is felt that the observance of these requirements together with the presence of qualified personnel during its use with the patient provides a reasonable level of safety.

Figure 517-7 shows a transparent, fused attachment plug that permits a constant visual check of wiring connections, and a small fuse, sized according to the rating of an equipment, which will disconnect a faulty unit without opening the entire branch circuit. Such attachment plugs have been developed to protect delicate biomedical equipment, which has no internal fuse protection. Figure 517-8 shows a portable field probe that will detect leakage currents as low as 5 microamperes. Equipment such

FIG. 517-7. Transparent, fused attachment plug for use with biomedical equipment. (*Daniel Woodhead Co.*)

Fig. 517-8. Portable field probe to detect leakage currents, static electricity, and open grounds. (*Daniel Woodhead Co.*)

as this is extremely useful in a well-planned hospital preventative maintenance program.

(b) Special Requirements. The following requirements in both categories shall not apply to small portable nonelectric devices such as bed pans, chairs, and the like.

(1) General Care Areas. Each patient bed location shall be provided with a minimum of four single or two duplex receptacles, each receptacle shall be grounded by means of an insulated copper conductor sized in accordance with Table 250-95.

Each patient bed location shall be supplied by at least two branch circuits of either the normal system and/or the essential electrical system.

The equipment grounding terminal bars of the normal and essential electrical system panelboards shall be bonded together with an insulated continuous, stranded copper bonding jumper not smaller than No. 10.

(2) Critical Care Areas. Each patient bed location shall be provided with a minimum of six single or three duplex receptacles, and grounded to the reference grounding point by means of an insulated copper equipment grounding conductor.

Each patient bed location shall be supplied by at least two branch circuits at least one of which shall be an individual branch circuit from a single panelboard of either the normal system and/or the essential electrical system.

Each patient bed location shall be provided with a patient grounding point, grounded to the reference grounding point by means of an insulated continuous, stranded copper conductor, not smaller than No. 10. The patient grounding point shall contain one or more jacks, approved for the purpose to facilitate the grounding of nonelectric portable equipment.

All exposed conductive surfaces of portable equipment used in the patient vicinity, including those on double-insulated and nonelectric beds shall be grounded to the reference grounding point.

The equipment grounding terminal bars of the normal and essential electrical system panelboards shall be bonded together with an insulated continuous, stranded copper conductor, not smaller than No. 10.

One or more room bonding points shall be provided, and shall be grounded to the reference point by means of an insulated continuous, stranded copper conductor, not smaller than No. 10.

All exposed conductive surfaces in the patient vicinity shall be bonded to the room bonding point(s) by means of an insulated continuous, stranded copper conductor, not smaller than No. 10, run in either a centric or looped manner, or combinations thereof.

Any of the grounding and bonding points in Section 517-51(b)(2) shall be permitted to be combined into a single point.

One patient bed location shall not be served by more than one reference grounding point.

(3) When a grounded electrical distribution system is used, grounding of all metallic raceways shall be assured by means of grounding bushings on all conduit terminations at the panelboard and by means of an insulated, continuous, stranded, copper conductor, not smaller than No. 12, extended from the grounding bus in the panelboard to the conduit grounding bushings.

(4) When an isolated ungrounded system is used to supply power to any area other than anesthetizing locations, it shall conform to the requirements of Sections 517-63(b) and (d), except that the audible and visual indicators of the line isolation monitor shall be permitted to be remotely located if desired.

(5) The use of an isolated ungrounded power source limits the first-fault ground current to a low magnitude; therefore, it shall not be necessary to provide a low ground circuit impedance by running the grounding conductor in the same enclosure as the circuit conductors.

(6) Means of frequent, periodic testing for continuity between the patient ground and any grounded surface shall be provided. The continuity tester shall be permitted to be either permanently mounted or portable and shall be approved for the purpose.

(7) The equipment grounding conductor for special purpose receptacles such as the operation of mobile x-ray equipment shall be extended to the reference grounding points for all locations likely to be served from such receptacles. When such a circuit is served from an isolated ungrounded system, the grounding conductor need not be run with the power conductors; however, the equipment grounding terminal of the special purpose receptacle shall be connected to the reference grounding point.

▲ Patient bed locations in general care areas must be supplied by four single or two duplex receptacles, whereas critical care area patient beds must be supplied by six single or three duplex receptacles. In both cases, at least two branch circuits must supply these receptacles; these two branch circuits may originate in either the normal system panelboard or the essential electrical system panelboard, or one branch circuit may be taken from each of these two panelboards. In the case of general care areas additional receptacles serving other patient locations may be served by these branch circuits, but in the case of critical care areas at least one of these branch circuits is required to be an individual branch having no other receptacles on it except those of a single bed location. Normal and essential electrical system panelboards serving either type of patient locations must have their equipment grounding terminal bars bonded together with an insulated, continuous-stranded copper bonding jumper not smaller than No. 10 AWG.

Regardless of what additional methods are employed, in order to keep potential differences within the required limits, equipotential grounding is essential to the electrical safety of critical care areas. Some of the earliest equipotential grounding installations consisted of copper busbars run around the walls of patient rooms to which furniture and equipment were attached by means of grounding jumpers. Based on experience obtained through these early installations as well as the refinements produced by the NFPA Committee on Hospitals, the National Electrical Code now contains the requirements which correlate with the pertinent NFPA standards on the subject. At the same time these new requirements also permit the achievement of the desired end with a minimum of expenditure in labor and materials.

Each patient bed location is to be served by only one reference grounding point; however, one reference grounding point can serve more than one patient bed location. This reference grounding point is an extension of the grounding terminal bus in either of the two previously mentioned panelboards. The reference grounding point is connected to the panelboard by means of an equipment grounding conductor not smaller than No. 10 AWG. The reference grounding point then serves two additional points at the patient location. The first point is the patient grounding point, which contains one or more jacks which are intended to facilitate the grounding of all nonelectric portable equipment in the patient vicinity. This would include such things as nonelectric beds and bedside tables, but would not include metal chairs, overbed tables, bedpans, and the like.

The second type of point which is to be served by the reference grounding point is the room bonding point. From the room bonding point, grounding connections are made to all exposed conductive surfaces in the patient vicinity which are a part of the building structure and the like. Such surfaces would include window frames, door frames, permanently installed metal shelving, metal sinks and plumbing, and oxygen and vacuum outlets. Either these connections can be run from the room bonding point to each individual item as individual conductors, or the conductor may be looped from item to item, whichever may be more practical.

All these points, the reference grounding point, the patient grounding point, and the room bonding point, may be combined into one point, and indeed this is most desirable when the room layout is small enough to permit it. None of the grounding connections to the building structure need to be run in conduit; however, all grounding connections made within the room must conform to the provisions of Sec. 250-113.

When testing ground continuity under the provisions of subparagraph (6) of this section, it will be helpful to maintain a written record of such tests so that longer intervals between tests can eventually be used, providing the record warrants it.

(c) Permanently Installed X-Ray Equipment.

(1) In addition to the grounding requirements of Article 660, permanently installed X-ray systems shall have a patient grounding point as described in (b) above, located as close as possible to the patient support, and be connected to the metal frame of the patient support by a separate, insulated, continuous, stranded, copper conductor, not smaller than No. 4.

(2) The patient grounding point shall be connected to the grounding conductor serving the X-ray equipment by an insulated, stranded, copper conductor not smaller than No. 10.

(3) The permanently installed X-ray system including all equipment powered from the X-ray generator power supply shall not be required to be powered by an isolated system. The equipment grounding conductors associated with the equipment shall have a maximum DC resistance of 0.025 ohms, as measured between the chassis and the patient ground point.

517-52. Additional Protective Techniques.

(a) An isolated power system, comprising an isolating transformer or its equivalent, with a line isolation monitor, to supply ungrounded circuits, shall be permitted as part of a system to improve electrical safety, provided that the components of the system are so designed and installed that they meet the requirements for similar systems specified for anesthetizing locations in Section 517-63.

(b) 125-volt, single-phase, 15- and 20-ampere receptacles supplying locations which are commonly subject to wet conditions shall be provided with Ground-Fault Circuit-Interrupters if interruption of power under fault conditions can be tolerated, or an isolated power system if such interruption cannot be tolerated.

▲ The locations intended for ground-fault protection under this section are limited to patient care areas. So, even though the governing body of the hospital may wish to extend this form of protection to such areas as laundries, boiler rooms, and kitchens, the fact that these are not considered patient care areas does not make GFCI protection mandatory in such locations. Locations which are intended for protection would include hydrotherapy, dialysis facilities, selected wet laboratories, and special-purpose rooms.

E. Inhalation Anesthetizing Locations

For further information regarding safeguards for anesthetizing locations, see Inhalation Anesthetics Standard, NFPA No. 56A-1973.

517-60. Anesthetizing Locations Classifications.

(a) Hazardous Location.

(1) Any room or space in which flammable anesthetics or volatile flammable disinfecting agents are stored shall be considered to be a Class I, Division 1 location throughout.

(2) In a flammable anesthetizing location, the entire area shall be considered to be a Class I, Division 1 location which shall extend upward to a level 5 feet above the floor.

(b) Other Than Hazardous Locations. The term "other than hazardous locations" shall apply to any operating rooms, delivery rooms, anesthesia rooms, corridors, utility rooms, and other areas permanently used for or intended for the exclusive use of nonflammable anesthetizing agents.

Confirmation of other than hazardous locations shall be accomplished by a written policy by the hospital administration prohibiting the use of flammable anesthetics and posting of rooms. In such cases, the rooms are excluded from the requirements of Section 517-61, 517-62, 517-63(f)(2), and 517-63(f)(3) as applied to X-ray systems only.

517-61. Wiring and Equipment Within Hazardous Areas.

(a) In hazardous areas referred to in Section 517-60, all fixed wiring and equipment, and all portable equipment, including lamps and other utilization equipment, operating at more than 8 volts between conductors, shall conform to the requirements of Sections 501-1 through 501-15 and Sections 501-16(a) and (b) for Class I, Division 1 locations. All such equipment shall be specifically approved for the hazardous atmospheres involved.

(b) Where a box, fitting or enclosure is partially, but not entirely, within a hazardous area, the hazardous area shall be considered to be extended to include the entire box, fitting or enclosure.

(c) Flexible cords, which are or may be used in hazardous areas for connection to portable utilization equipment, including lamps operating at more than 8 volts between conductors, shall be of a type approved for extra-hard usage, shall be of ample length, and shall include an additional conductor for grounding. A storage device for the flexible cord shall be provided, and shall not subject the cord to bending at a radius of less than 3 inches.

(d) Receptacles and attachment plugs in hazardous areas shall be listed for use in Class I, Group C hazardous locations, and shall have provision for the connection of a grounding conductor.

517-62. Wiring and Equipment in Nonhazardous or Above Hazardous Anesthetizing Areas.

(a) Wiring above a hazardous area as referred to in Section 517-60 or in a nonflammable anesthetizing area shall be installed in rigid raceways or shall be Type MI cable, Type ALS cable, Type CS cable, or Type MC cable which employs a continuous, impervious metallic sheath.

(b) Equipment which may produce arcs, sparks or particles of hot metal, such as lamps and lampholders for fixed lighting, cutouts, switches, receptacles, generators, motors, or other equipment having make-and-break or sliding contacts, shall be of the totally enclosed type or so constructed as to prevent escape of sparks or hot metal particles.

(c) Surgical and other lighting fixtures shall conform to Section 501-9(b).

Exception No. 1: The surface temperature limitations set forth in Section 501-9(b)(2) shall not apply.

Exception No. 2: Integral or pendant switches which are located above and cannot be lowered into the hazardous area shall not be required to be explosion-proof.

(d) Approved seals shall be provided in conformance with Section 501-5, and Section 501-5(a)(4) shall apply to horizontal as well as to vertical boundaries of the defined hazardous areas.

Exception: Seals shall be permitted within 18 inches of the point at which a conduit emerges from a wall forming the boundary of an anesthetizing location if all of the following conditions are met:

a. The junction box, switch or receptacle contains a seal-off device between the arcing contacts and the conduit.

b. The conduit is continuous (without coupling or fitting) between the junction box and the sealing fitting within 18 inches of the point where the conduit emerges from the wall.

(e) Anesthetizing-location receptacles and attachment plugs in nonhazardous or above hazardous anesthetizing areas shall be listed for hospital use for services of prescribed voltage, frequency, rating, and number of conductors with provision for the connection of the grounding conductor. This requirement shall apply to attachment plugs and receptacles of the two-pole, 3-wire grounding-type for single-phase 125-volt AC service.

(f) Plugs and receptacles for connection of 250V, 50-ampere and 60-ampere AC medical equipment for use in nonhazardous areas of flammable anesthetic Anesthetizing Locations and in nonflammable Anesthetizing Locations shall be so arranged that the 60-ampere receptacle will accept either the 50-ampere or the 60-ampere

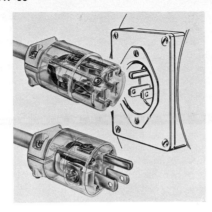

Fig. 517-9. "Hospital Grade" wiring devices provide additional assurance of serviceability in abusive hospital environments. Plastic construction eliminates hazards of accidental energization of exposed conductive parts. (*Daniel Woodhead Co.*)

plug. 50-ampere receptacles shall be designed so as not to accept the 60-ampere attachment plug. The plugs shall be of the two-pole, 3-wire design with a third contact connecting to the (green or green with yellow stripe) equipment grounding conductor of the electrical system.

▲ In the past few years Underwriters' Laboratories, Inc., has devised a special series of tests for wiring devices intended for hospital use. These tests are substantially more abusive than those performed on general-purpose devices and are designed to ensure the reliability of the grounding connection in particular, when used in the hospital environment. Devices which pass this test are listed as "Hospital Grade" and are identified with these words and a green dot, both of which are visible after installation. At the time of this writing, UL listings include 15- and 20-A 125-V grounding, nonlocking-type plugs, receptacles, and connectors. This class of device is acceptable for use in any nonhazardous anesthetizing location; however, their use would not be acceptable above hazardous anesthetizing areas, inasmuch as they are not totally enclosed and might permit the escape of sparks or hot metal particles which could fall into the hazardous area. The use of this special type of device will permit wider use of some equipment which may be needed not only in a nonhazardous anesthetizing location but also in certain critical care areas, inasmuch as an adapter will no longer be required in going from one room to another.

517-63. Circuits in Anesthetizing Locations.

(a) Except as provided in Section 517-63(f) and (g), each circuit within, or partially within, an anesthetizing location as referred to in Section 517-60 shall be controlled by a switch having a disconnecting pole in each circuit conductor, and shall be isolated from any distribution system supplying areas other than anesthetizing locations. Such isolation shall be acceptable by means of one or more transformers having no electrical connection between primary and secondary windings, by means of motor-generator sets, or by means of suitably isolated batteries.

(b) Circuits supplying primaries of isolating transformers shall operate at not more than 300 volts between conductors, and shall be provided with proper overcurrent protection. Secondary voltage of such transformers shall not exceed 300 volts between conductors, and all circuits supplied from such secondaries shall be ungrounded and shall have an approved overcurrent device of proper rating in each conductor. Circuits supplied from batteries or from generators or motor-generator sets shall be ungrounded, and shall be protected against overcurrent in the same manner as transformer-fed secondary circuits.

(c) Transformers, motor-generator sets, batteries and battery chargers, together with their overcurrent devices, shall be installed in nonhazardous locations, and shall conform to the requirements of this Code for such locations.

(d) Line Isolation Monitor.

(1) In addition to the usual control and overcurrent protective devices, each isolated power system shall be provided with a continually operating line isolation monitor, approved for the purpose, that indicates possible leakage or fault currents from either isolated conductor to ground. The monitor shall be designed so that a green signal lamp, conspicuously visible to persons in the anesthetizing location, remains lighted when the system is adequately isolated from ground; an adjacent red signal lamp and an audible warning signal (remote if desired) shall be energized when the total hazard index (consisting of possible resistive and capacitive leakage currents) from either isolated conductor to ground reaches a threshold value of 2 milliamperes under nominal line voltage conditions. The line isolation monitor is not to alarm for a fault hazard index of less than 0.7 milliamperes.

Exception: A system may be designed to operate at a lower threshold value of total hazard index. A line isolation monitor for such a system may be approved with the provision that the fault hazard index may be reduced but not to less than 35 percent of the corresponding threshold value of the total hazard index, and the monitor hazard index is to be correspondingly reduced to no more than 50 percent of the alarm threshold value of the total hazard index.

Such systems contribute little additional electrical safety and are used for special applications.

(2) The line isolation monitor shall be designed to have sufficient internal impedance such that when properly connected to the isolated system the maximum internal current that can flow through the line isolation monitor, when any point of the isolated system is grounded, shall be one milliampere.

Reduction of the monitor hazard index, provided this reduction results in an increased "not alarm" threshold value for the fault hazard index, will increase circuit capacity.

(3) An ammeter calibrated in the total hazard index of the system (contribution of the fault hazard index plus monitor hazard index) shall be mounted in a plainly visible place on the line isolation monitor with the "alarm on" (total hazard index = 2 milliamperes) zone at approximately the center of the scale. It is desirable to locate the ammeter so that it is conspicuously visible to persons in the anesthetizing location.

Exception: The line isolation monitor may be a composite unit, with a sensing section cabled to a separate display panel section on which the alarm and/or test functions are located.

(e) A branch circuit supplying an anesthetizing location shall supply no other location. The insulation of the branch circuit conductors on the secondary side of isolated power supplies shall have a dielectric constant of 3.5 or less. Wire pulling compounds that increase the dielectric constant shall not be used on the secondary conductors of the isolated power supplies.

(f) Branch circuits supplying only fixed lighting fixtures in nonhazardous areas of anesthetizing locations other than surgical lighting fixtures, or supplying only approved permanently installed X-ray equipment shall be permitted to be supplied by a conventional grounded system, provided: (1) wiring for grounded and ungrounded circuits does not occupy the same raceways; (2) the lighting fixtures and the X-ray equipment (except the enclosed X-ray tube and the metal-enclosed high-voltage leads to the tube) are located at least 8 feet above the floor or outside the anesthetizing location; and (3) switches for the grounded circuits are located outside of the anesthetizing location.

(g) Components of an isolated power center approved for the purpose and its grounded primary feeder shall be permitted to be located in an anesthetizing location provided it is located in an other than hazardous area.

Note 1: For a description of approved permanently installed X-ray equipment, see Sections 3384, 3385, 3432, 3433, 4435, and 4437 of the Inhalation Anesthetics Standard, NFPA No. 56A-1973.

Note 2: Remote-control stations for remote-control switches shall be permitted in the anesthetizing location if the remote-control circuit is energized from the ungrounded distribution system.

517-64. Low-Voltage Equipment and Instruments.

(a) Low-voltage equipment which is frequently in contact with the bodies of persons or has exposed current-carrying elements shall:

(1) Operate on an electrical potential of 8 volts or less, or

(2) Be approved as intrinsically safe or double-insulated equipment,

(3) Be moisture resistant.

(b) Power shall be supplied to low-voltage equipment from:

(1) An individual isolating transformer (autotransformers shall not be used) connected to an outlet receptacle by means of an anesthetizing location cord and attachment plug, or

(2) A common isolating transformer installed in a nonhazardous location, or

(3) Individual dry-cell batteries, or

(4) Common batteries made up of storage cells located in a nonhazardous location.

(c) Isolating-type transformers for supplying low-voltage circuits shall:

(1) Have approved means for insulating the secondary circuit from the primary circuit, and

(2) Have the core and case grounded in an approved manner.

(d) Resistance or impedance devices shall be permitted to control low-voltage equipment but shall not be used to limit the maximum input voltage.

(e) Battery-powered appliances shall not be capable of being charged while in operation unless their charging circuitry incorporates an integral isolating-type transformer.

(f) Any receptacle or attachment plug used on low-voltage circuits shall be of a type which does not permit interchangeable connection with circuits of higher voltage.

Any interruption of the circuit, even circuits as low as 8 volts, either by any switch, or loose or defective connections anywhere in the circuit, may produce a spark sufficient to ignite flammable anesthetic agents. (See Section 352 of the Inhalation Anesthetics Standard. NFPA No. 56A-1973.)

517-65. Other Equipment.

(a) Suction, pressure, or insufflation equipment involving electrical elements, and located or used within a hazardous area shall be approved for Class I locations.

(b) X-ray equipment installed or operated in an anesthetizing location as defined in Section 517-2 shall be provided with approved means for preventing accumulation of electrostatic charges. All X-ray control devices, switches, relays, meters, and transformers shall be totally enclosed, and where installed or operated within a hazardous area, shall be approved for Class I, Group C locations. High-voltage wiring shall be effectively insulated from ground and adequately guarded against accidental contact. The entire installation shall comply with Article 660.

(c) Equipment for generating high-frequency currents or voltages used in electrocautery, diathermy, television, etc., where installed or used in an anesthetizing location, shall conform to Sections 517-61 and 517-62.

517-66. Grounding. In any anesthetizing area, all metallic raceways, and all noncurrent-carrying conductive portions of fixed or portable equipment including the conductive floor shall be grounded.

Exception: Equipment operating at not more than 8 volts between conductors shall not be required to be grounded.

F. Communications, Signaling Systems, and Data Systems

517-80. Critical Patient Care Areas. Isolation and grounding equivalent to that required for the electrical distribution systems in this Article for these areas shall also be provided. See also Articles 725 and 800.

An acceptable alternate means of providing isolation for patient/nurse call systems is by the use of only nonelectrified signaling, communication or control devices held by the patient or within reach of the patient.

ARTICLE 518. PLACES OF ASSEMBLY

518-1. Scope. This Article covers all buildings or that part of a building or structure designed or intended for use by 100 or more persons for assembly purposes, such as dining, meetings, entertainment, lectures, bowling, worship, dancing or exhibition, and includes museums, gymnasiums, armories, group rooms, mortuaries, skating rinks, pool rooms, places of awaiting transportation, places for deliberation (court rooms), places for sporting events, and similar purposes.

When any such building structures or portion thereof contain a projection booth or stage platform or area for the presentation of theatrical or musical production, either fixed or portable, the wiring for that area shall comply with all applicable provisions of Article 520.

For methods of determining population capacity, see local building code or in its absence Life Safety Code (NFPA No. 101-1973).

▲ **The following information is found in NFPA No. 101, Life Safety Code, for determining occupant load in places of assembly.**

Occupant Load. The occupant load permitted in any assembly building, structure, or portion thereof shall be determined by dividing the net floor area or space assigned to that use by the square feet per occupant as follows:

(a) An assembly area of concentrated use without fixed seats such as an auditorium, church, chapel, dance floor, and lodge room—7 square feet per person.

(b) An assembly area of less concentrated use such as a conference room, dining room, drinking establishment, exhibit room, gymnasium, or lounge—15 square feet per person.

(c) Standing room or waiting space—3 square feet per person.

The occupant load of an area having fixed seats shall be determined by the number of fixed seats installed. Required aisle space serving the fixed seats shall not be used to increase the occupant load.

The occupant load permitted in a building or portion thereof may be increased above that specified in "Occupant Load" if the necessary aisles and exits are provided subject to the approval of the authority having jurisdiction. An approved aisle, exit, and/or seating diagram may be required by the authority having jurisdiction to substantiate an increase in occupant load.

518-2. Other Articles.

(a) Hazardous areas located in any assemblage occupancy shall be installed in accordance with Article 500—Hazardous Locations.

(b) In exhibition halls used for display booths, as in trade shows, the temporary wiring shall be installed in accordance with Article 305—Temporary Wiring, except that approved portable cables and cords shall be permitted to be laid on floors where protected from contact by the general public.

FIG. 518-1. Rubber cord protectors provide a treadle to prevent cord abuse when laid across aisles and walkways. (*Daniel Woodhead Co.*)

518-3. Wiring Methods.
The fixed wiring methods shall be metal raceways, nonmetallic raceways encased in not less than 2 inches of concrete, Type ALS cable, Type CS cable, mineral-insulated metal-sheathed cable, or Type MC cable.

Exception No. 1: Nonmetallic-sheathed cable, Type AC metal-clad cable, and rigid nonmetallic conduit shall be permitted to be installed in those buildings or portions thereof that are not required to be fire rated construction by the applicable building code.

Exception No. 2: As provided in Article 640, Sound Reproduction and Similar Equipment, in Article 800, Communication Circuits, and in Article 725 for Class 2 and Class 3 remote control and signaling circuits, and in Article 760 for fire protective signaling circuits.

Fire rated construction is the fire-resistive classification used in building codes.

ARTICLE 520. THEATERS AND SIMILAR LOCATIONS

A. General

520-1. Scope.
This Article covers all buildings or that part of a building or structure designed or intended to be used for dramatic, musical, motion picture projection, or similar purposes and to areas of motion picture and television studios which incorporate assembly areas.

▲ Where only a part of a building is used as a theater or similar location, these special requirements apply only to that part and do not necessarily apply to the entire building. A common example is a school building in which there is an auditorium used for dramatic or other performances. All special requirements of this chapter would apply to the auditorium, stage, dressing rooms, and main corridors leading to the auditorium, but not to other parts of the building that do not pertain to the use of the auditorium for performances or entertainments.

520-2. Motion-Picture Projectors. Motion-picture equipment and its installation and use shall comply with Article 540.

520-3. Sound Reproduction. Sound-reproducing equipment and its installation shall comply with Article 640.

520-4. Wiring Methods. The fixed wiring method shall be metal raceways, nonmetallic raceways encased in at least 2 inches of concrete, Type ALS cable, Type CS cable, mineral-insulated metal-sheathed, or Type MC cable.

Exception No. 1: As provided in Article 640 for sound reproduction, in Article 800 for communication circuits, and in Article 725 for Class 2 and Class 3 remote-control and signaling circuits, and in Article 760 for fire protective signaling circuits.

Exception No. 2: The wiring for stage set lighting and stage effects and other wiring that is not fixed as to location shall be permitted with approved portable cables and approved flexible cords.

▲ Building laws usually require theaters and motion-picture houses to be of fireproof construction; hence practical considerations limit the types of concealed wiring for light and power chiefly to those included in Sec. 520-4.

Much of the stage lighting in a modern theater is provided by floodlights and projectors mounted in the ceiling or on the balcony front. In order that the projectors may be adjustable in position, they may be connected by plugs and short cords to suitable receptacles or "pockets."

520-5. Number of Conductors in Raceway. The number of conductors permitted in any metal conduit or electrical metallic tubing for border or stage pocket circuits or for remote-control conductors shall not exceed the percentage fill shown in Table 1 of Chapter 9. Where contained within an auxiliary gutter or a wireway, the sum of the cross-sectional areas of all contained conductors at any cross section shall not exceed 20 percent of the interior cross-sectional area of the auxiliary gutter or wireway. The 30-conductor limitation of Sections 362-5 and 374-5 shall not apply.

520-6. Enclosing and Guarding Live Parts. Live parts shall be enclosed or guarded to prevent accidental contact by persons and objects. All switches shall be of the externally operable type. Dimmers, including rheostats, shall be placed in cases or cabinets that enclose all live parts.

B. Fixed Stage Switchboard

520-21. Dead Front. Stage switchboards shall be of the dead-front type and shall comply with Part C of Article 384 unless approved for the purpose.

520-22. Guarding Back of Switchboard. Stage switchboards having exposed live parts on the back of such boards shall be enclosed by the building walls, wire mesh grills, or by other methods approved for the purpose. The entrance to this enclosure shall be by means of a self-closing door.

520-23. Control and Overcurrent Protection of Receptacle Circuits. Means shall be provided at a stage lighting switchboard to which load circuits are connected for individual overcurrent protection of stage lighting branch circuits and stage and gallery receptacles used for portable stage equipment. Where the stage switchboard contains dimmers to control nonstage lighting, the locating of the overcurrent protective devices for these branch circuits at the stage switchboard shall be permitted.

▲ The term *gallery receptacles* should be understood as including all receptacles, wherever they may be located, that are intended for the connection of stage lighting equipment. Circuits to such receptacles must of necessity be controlled at the same location as other stage lighting circuits.

520-24. Metal Hood. A stage switchboard that is not completely enclosed dead-front and dead-rear or recessed into a wall shall be provided with a metal hood extending the full length of the board to protect all equipment on the board from falling objects.

▲ Because of the large amount of flammable material always present on a stage, and because of the crowded space, a stage switchboard must have no live parts on the front, and the back must be so guarded as to keep unauthorized persons away from the space in back of the board. The best form of construction is a sheet-steel enclosure for the space between the back of the board and the wall, with a door at one end of the enclosure.

The more important stage switchboards are commonly of the remote-control type. Pilot switches mounted on the stage board control the operation of contactors installed in any convenient location where space is available, usually below the stage. The contactors in turn control the lighting circuits.

Figure 520-1 is the front view of a small stage switchboard of the partial remote-control type. The small handles at the lower part of the small panels operate 30-A switches for direct control of all low-capacity circuits. For the control of heavier loads, the same type of switch is used to control magnetically operated contactors located at any convenient point, usually in a special room on a floor below the stage. The egg-shaped handles operate dimmers for individual circuits. The three large levers in a vertical row are for master operation of the dimmers for the three colors, while by means of the single lever at the left all or any desired part of the dimmers may be operated simultaneously.

The stage switchboard is usually built into a recess in the proscenium wall, as shown in the plan view, Fig. 520-2. After passing through the switches and dimmers, many of the main circuits must be subdivided into branch circuits so that no branch circuit will be loaded to more than 20 A. Where the board is of the remote-control type, the branch-circuit fuses are often mounted on the same panels as the contactors. Where a direct-control type of board is used, and sometimes where the board is remotely controlled, the branch-circuit fuses are mounted on special panelboards known as *magazine panels*, which are installed in the space back of the switchboard, usually in the location of the junction box shown in Fig. 520-2.

520-25. Dimmers. Dimmers shall comply with (a) through (d) below.

(a) Disconnection and Overcurrent Protection. Where dimmers are installed in ungrounded conductors, each dimmer shall have overcurrent protection not greater than 125 percent of the dimmer rating, and shall be disconnected from all ungrounded conductors when the master or individual switch or circuit breaker supplying such dimmer is in the open position.

FIG. 520-1. Small stage switchboard of the partial remote-control type.

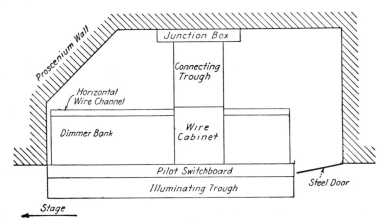

FIG. 520-2. Plan showing location of a stage switchboard in a recess in the proscenium wall.

(b) Resistance- or Reactor-Type Dimmers. Resistance- or series reactor-type dimmers may be placed in either the grounded or the ungrounded conductor of the circuit. Where designed to open either the supply circuit to the dimmer or the circuit controlled by it, the dimmer shall then comply with Section 380-1. Resistance or reactor type dimmers placed in the grounded neutral conductor of the circuit shall not open the circuit.

(c) Autotransformer-Type Dimmers. The circuit supplying an autotransformer-type dimmer shall not exceed 150 volts between conductors. The grounded conductor shall be common to the input and output circuits.

(d) Solid-State Type Dimmers. The circuit supplying a solid-state dimmer shall not exceed 150 volts between conductors unless the dimmer is specifically approved for higher voltage operation. When a grounded conductor supplies a dimmer, it shall be common to the input and output circuits. Dimmer chassis shall be connected to the equipment ground conductor.

See Section 210-9 for circuits derived from autotransformers.

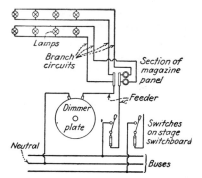

FIG. 520-3. Stage switchboard. Typical connections of control switch, dimmer plate, and one section of magazine panel for the control of two branch circuits.

▲ Figure 520-3 shows typical connections of two branch circuits arranged for control by one switch and one dimmer plate or section. The single-pole switch on the stage switchboard is connected to one of the outside buses, and from this switch a wire runs to a short bus on the magazine panel. The magazine panel is similar to an ordinary panelboard, except that it contains no switches and the circuits are divided into many sections, each section having its own separate buses. One terminal of the dimmer plate, or variable resistor, is connected to the neutral bus at the switchboard, and from the other terminal of the dimmer a wire runs to the neutral bus on the magazine panel. This neutral bus must be well insulated from ground and must be separate from other neutral buses on the panel; otherwise the dimmer would be shunted and would fail to control the brightness of the lamps.

While the dimmer is permanently connected to the neutral of the wiring system, this neutral is presumed to be thoroughly grounded and hence the dimmer is dead.

Figure 520-4 shows an autotransformer used as a dimmer. By changing the position of the movable contact, any desired voltage may be supplied to the lamps, from full line voltage to a voltage so low that the lamps are "black out." As compared with a resistance-type dimmer, a dimmer of this type has the advantages that it operates at a much higher efficiency, generates very little heat, and, within its maximum rating, the dimming effect is not dependent upon the wattage of the load it controls.

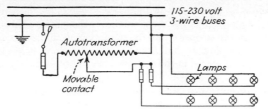

FIG. 520-4. Autotransformer dimmer.

520-26. Type of Switchboard. Stage switchboard shall be either one or a combination of the following types:

(a) Manual. Dimmers and switches are operated by handles mechanically linked to the control devices.

(b) Remotely Controlled. Devices are operated electrically from a pilot type control console or panel. Pilot control panels shall either be part of the switchboard or shall be permitted to be at another location.

520-27. Stage Switchboard Feeders. Feeders supplying stage switchboards shall be one of the following:

(a) A single feeder disconnected by a single disconnect device.

(b) Multiple feeders disconnected and/or protected by separate devices in an intermediate stage switchboard, provided that all feeders are part of a single system. Where multiple feeders are used, all conductors are to be of the same length. Neutral conductors of multiple feeders shall be combined; however, neutral conductors shall be arranged so that the sum of the neutral conductors in a given wireway is of adequate ampacity to carry the maximum unbalanced phase current which shall be permitted to be supplied by other feeder conductors in the same wireway.

C. Stage Equipment—Fixed

520-41. Circuit Loads. Footlights, border lights, and proscenium side lights shall be so arranged that no branch circuit supplying such equipment will carry a load exceeding 20 amperes.

Exception: Where heavy-duty lampholders only are used, such circuits shall be permitted to comply with Article 210 for circuits supplying heavy-duty lampholders.

520-42. Conductor Insulation. Foot, border, proscenium, or portable strip light fixtures and connector strips shall be wired with conductors having insulation suitable for the temperatures at which the conductors will be operated and not less than 125°C (257°F).

See Table 310-13 for conductor types.

520-43. Footlights.

(a) Where metal trough construction is employed for footlights, the trough containing the circuit conductors shall be made of sheet metal not lighter than No. 20 MSG treated to prevent oxidation. Lampholder terminals shall be kept at least ½ inch from the metal of the trough. The circuit conductors shall be soldered to the lampholder terminals.

(b) Where the metal trough construction specified in Section 520-43(a) is not used, footlights shall consist of individual outlets with lampholders, wired with rigid or flexible metal conduit, Type ALS cable, Type CS cable, or mineral-insulated metal-sheathed cable. The circuit conductors shall be soldered to the lampholder terminals. Disappearing footlights shall be so arranged that the current supply will be automatically disconnected when the footlights are replaced in the recess designed for them.

520-44. Borders and Proscenium Sidelights.

(a) General. Borders and proscenium sidelights shall be: (1) constructed as specified in Section 520-43; (2) suitably stayed and supported; and (3) so designed that the flanges of the reflectors or other adequate guards will protect the lamps from mechanical injury and from accidental contact with scenery or other combustible material.

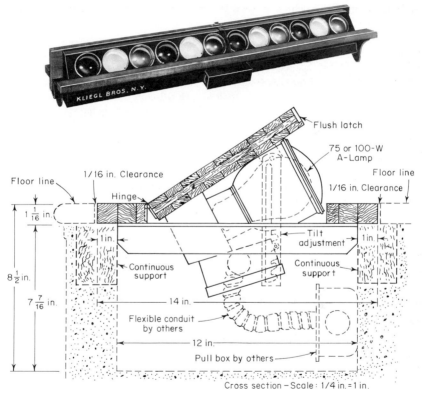

FIG. 520-5. Footlight with individual reflector for each lamp. (*Kliegl Bros.*)

▲ A footlight of the disappearing type might produce so high a temperature as to be a serious fire hazard if the lamps should be left burning after the footlight is closed.

There is no restriction on the number of lamps that may be supplied by one branch circuit. The lamp wattage supplied by one circuit should be such that the current will be slightly less than 20 A.

Individual outlets as described here are seldom used for footlights, as such construction would be much more expensive than the standard trough type.

A modern type of footlight is shown in Fig. 520-5. The wiring is carried in a sheet-iron wire channel in the face of which lamp receptacles are mounted. Each lamp is provided with an individual reflector and glass color screen or "roundel." The circuit wires are usually brought to the wire channel in rigid conduit. In the older type of footlight, still used to some extent, the lamps are placed vertically or nearly so, and an extension of one side of the wire channel is shaped so as to form a reflector to direct the light toward the stage.

(b) Cables for Border Lights. Cables for supply to border lights shall be Type S, SO, ST, or STO flexible cable as provided in Table 400-4. The cables shall be suitably supported. Such cables shall be employed only where flexible conductors are necessary.

▲ Figure 520-6 shows a border light of modern type as it appears when installed in place over the stage. Figure 520-7 is a cross section showing the construction of the border. This particular type is intended for the use of 200-W lamps. An individual reflector is provided for each lamp so as to secure the highest possible efficiency of light utilization. A glass roundel is fitted to each reflector; these may be obtained in any desired color, commonly white, red, and blue for three-color equipment and white, red, blue, and amber for four-color equipment. A splice box is provided on top of the housing for enclosing the connections between the border-light cable and the wiring of the border. From this splice box, the wires are carried to the lamp sockets in a trough extending the entire length of the border.

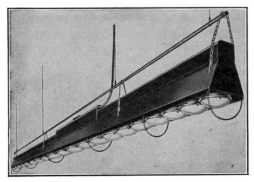

Fɪɢ. 520-6. Modern type of border light. (*Major Equipment Co.*)

Border lights are usually hung on steel cables so that their height may be adjusted and so that they may be lowered to the stage for cleaning and replacing lamps and color screens; hence the circuit conductors supplying the lamps must be carried to the border through a flexible cable. The individual conductors of the cable may be of No. 14, though No. 12 is more commonly used.

520-45. Receptacles. Receptacles intended for the supply of arc lamps shall be rated at not less than 50 amperes and shall be supplied by conductors not smaller

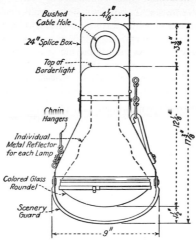

FIG. 520-7. Construction of border light shown in Fig. 520-6. (*Major Equipment Co.*)

than No. 6. Receptacles intended for the supply of incandescent lamps shall be rated at not less than 20 amperes and shall be supplied by conductors not smaller than No. 12. Attachment plugs for arc and incandescent receptacles shall not be interchangeable.

520-46. Stage Pockets. Receptacles intended for the connection of portable stage lighting equipment shall be mounted in suitable pockets or enclosures and shall comply with Section 520-45.

FIG. 520-8. Stage floor pocket with a single receptacle. (*Kliegl Bros.*)

FIG. 520-9. A four-gang stage wall pocket designed for flush mounting. (*Major Equipment Co.*)

▲ Figure 520-8 shows a common form of stage pocket. A separate circuit of No. 6 should be installed to supply each arc receptacle and a separate circuit of No. 12 or larger to supply each incandescent receptacle.

Figure 520-9 shows a wall pocket designed for flush mounting and equipped with receptacles to receive the standard type of plug, the same as is used with floor pockets.

520-47. Lamps in Scene Docks. Lamps installed in scene docks shall be so located and guarded as to be free from physical damage and shall provide an air space of not less than 2 inches between such lamps and any combustible material.

520-48. Curtain Motors. Curtain motors having brushes or sliding contacts shall comply with one of the conditions in (a) through (f) below.

(a) Be of the totally enclosed, enclosed-fan-cooled, or enclosed-pipe-ventilated type.

(b) Be enclosed in separate rooms or housings built of noncombustible material so constructed as to exclude flyings or lint, and properly ventilated from a source of clean air.

(c) Have the brush or sliding-contact end of motor enclosed by solid metal covers.

(d) Have brushes or sliding contacts enclosed in substantial, tight metal housings.

(e) Have the upper half of the brush or sliding contact end of the motor enclosed by a wire screen or perforated metal and the lower half enclosed by solid metal covers.

(f) Have wire screens or perforated metal placed at the commutator or brush ends. No dimension of any opening in the wire screen or perforated metal shall exceed .05 inch, regardless of the shape of the opening and of the material used.

520-49. Flue Damper Control. Where stage flue dampers are released by an electrical device, the circuit operating the device shall be normally closed and shall be controlled by at least two externally operable switches, one switch being placed at the electrician's station and the other where designated by the authority having jurisdiction. The device shall be designed for the full voltage of the circuit to which it is connected, no resistance being inserted. The device shall be located in the loft above the scenery and shall be enclosed in a suitable metal box having a tight, self-closing door.

▲ A normally-closed-circuit device has the inherent safety feature that in case the control circuit is accidentally opened by the blowing of a fuse, or in any other way, the device immediately operates to open the flue dampers.

D. Portable Switchboards on Stage

520-51. Supply. Portable switchboards shall be supplied only from outlets provided for the purpose. Such outlets shall include externally operable, enclosed fused switches or circuit breakers mounted on the stage wall or at the permanent switchboard in locations readily accessible from the stage floor.

520-52. Overcurrent Protection. Circuits from portable switchboards directly supplying equipment containing incandescent lamps of not over 300 watts shall be protected by overcurrent devices having a rating or setting of not over 20 amperes. Circuits for lampholders over 300 watts shall be permitted where overcurrent protection complies with Article 210. Other circuits shall be provided with overcurrent devices with a rating or setting not higher than the current required for the connected load.

520-53. Construction. Portable switchboards for use on stages shall comply with (a) through (j) below.

(a) Enclosure. Portable switchboards shall be placed within an enclosure of substantial construction, which shall be permitted to be so arranged that the enclosure is open during operation. Enclosures of wood shall be completely lined with sheet metal of not less than No. 24 MSG and shall be well galvanized, enameled, or otherwise properly coated to prevent corrosion or be of a corrosion-resistant material.

(b) Live Parts. There shall be no exposed live parts within the enclosure. *Exception: For dimmer faceplates as provided in (e) below.*

(c) Switches and Circuit Breakers. All switches and circuit breakers shall be of the externally operable, enclosed type.

(d) Circuit Protection. Overcurrent devices shall be provided in each ungrounded conductor of every circuit supplied through the switchboard. Enclosures shall be provided for all overcurrent devices in addition to the switchboard enclosure.

(e) Dimmers. The terminals of dimmers shall be provided with enclosures, and dimmer faceplates shall be so arranged that accidental contact cannot be readily made with the faceplate contacts.

(f) Interior Conductors. All conductors within the switchboard enclosure shall be stranded and shall be asbestos-covered Type AA or other types approved for an operating temperature of 200°C (392°F).

Each conductor shall have an ampacity at least equal to the rating of the circuit breaker, switch, or fuse which it supplies.

Exception: Conductors for incandescent lamp circuits having overcurrent protection of not over 20 amperes.

Conductors shall be enclosed in metal wireways or be securely fastened in position and shall be bushed where they pass through metal.

(g) Pilot Light. A pilot light shall be provided within the enclosure and shall be so connected to the circuit supplying the board that the opening of the master switch will not cut off the supply to the lamp. This lamp shall be on an independent circuit having overcurrent protection rated or set at not over 15 amperes.

(h) Supply Connections. The supply to a portable switchboard shall be by means of Type S, SO, ST, or STO flexible cord terminating within the switchboard enclosure or in an externally operable fused master switch or circuit breaker. The supply cable shall have sufficient ampacity to carry the total load connected to the switchboard and shall be protected by overcurrent devices.

(i) Cable Arrangement. Cables shall be protected by bushings where they pass through enclosures and shall be so arranged that tension on the cable will not be transmitted to the connections.

(j) Terminals. Terminals to which stage cables are connected shall be so located as to permit convenient access to the terminals.

E. Stage Equipment—Portable

520-61. Arc Lamps. Arc lamps shall be listed.

520-62. Portable Plugging Boxes. Portable plugging boxes shall comply with (a) through (c) below.

(a) Enclosure. The construction shall be such that no current-carrying part will be exposed.

(b) Receptacles and Overcurrent Protection. Each receptacle shall have a rating of not less than 30 amperes, and shall have overcurrent protection installed in an enclosure equipped with self-closing doors.

(c) Busbars and Terminals. Busbars shall have an ampacity equal to the sum of the ampere ratings of all the receptacles. Lugs shall be provided for the connection of the master cable.

520-63. Bracket Fixture Wiring.

(a) Bracket Wiring. Brackets for use on scenery shall be wired internally, and the fixture stem shall be carried through to the back of the scenery where a bushing shall be placed on the end of the stem.

Exception: Externally wired brackets or other fixtures shall be permitted where wired with cords designed for hard usage that extend through scenery and without joint or splice in canopy of fixture back and terminate in an approved type stage connector located, where practical, within 18 inches of the fixture.

(b) Mounting. Fixtures shall be securely fastened in place.

Fig. 520-10. Portable plugging box for stage use. (*Kliegl Bros.*)

520-64. Portable Strips. Portable strips shall be constructed in accordance with the requirements for border lights and proscenium side lights in Section 520-44(a). The supply cable shall be protected by bushings where it passes through metal and shall be so arranged that tension on the cable will not be transmitted to the connections.

See Section 520-42 for wiring of portable strips.

520-65. Festoons. Joints in festoon wiring shall be staggered where practicable. Lamps enclosed in lanterns or similar devices of combustible material shall be equipped with guards.

▲ "Lanterns or similar devices" are very likely to be made of paper or other flammable material, and the lamps should be prevented from coming in contact with such material.

520-66. Special Effects. Electrical devices used for simulating lightning, waterfalls, and the like shall be so constructed and located that flames, sparks, or hot particles cannot come in contact with combustible material.

520-67. Cable Connectors. Cable connectors for flexible conductors shall be so constructed that tension on the cord or cable will not be transmitted to the connections. The female half of the connector shall be attached to the line end of the cord or cable.

See Section 400-10 for pull at terminals.

520-68. Conductors for Portables. Flexible conductors used to supply portable stage equipment shall be Type S, SO, ST, or STO

Exception: Reinforced cord shall be permitted to supply stand lamps where the cord is not subject to severe physical damage and is protected by an overcurrent device rated at not over 20 amperes.

F. Dressing Rooms

520-71. Pendant Lampholders. Pendant lampholders shall not be installed in dressing rooms.

520-72. Lamp Guards. All incandescent lamps in dressing rooms, where less than 8 feet from the floor, shall be equipped with open-end guards riveted to the outlet box cover or otherwise sealed or locked in place.

▲ **Lamps in dressing rooms should be provided with guards that cannot easily be removed to prevent them from coming in contact with flammable material.**

520-73. Switches Required. All lights and receptacles in dressing rooms shall be controlled by wall switches installed in the dressing rooms. Each switch controlling receptacles shall be provided with a pilot light to indicate when the receptacles are energized.

G. Grounding

520-81. Grounding. All metal raceways shall be grounded. The metal frames and enclosures of equipment, including border lights, shall be grounded.

Exception: The frames and enclosures of portable equipment on grounded circuits operating at not over 150 volts to ground and not within reach of grounded surfaces need not be grounded.

Grounding, where employed, shall be in accordance with Article 250.

ARTICLE 530. MOTION-PICTURE
STUDIOS AND
SIMILAR LOCATIONS

A. General

530-1. Scope. The requirements of this Article shall apply to television studios (except as covered in Section 520-1), motion-picture studios, exchange, factory, laboratory, stage, or a portion of the building in which motion-picture films more than $7/8$ inch in width are manufactured, exposed, developed, printed, cut, edited, rewound, repaired, or stored.

For the purpose of this Article, a motion-picture studio is one in which photographic film is used to record action. A television studio shall mean one which employs the use of electronic cameras only.

For methods of protecting against cellulose nitrate film hazards, see Standard for the Storage and Handling of Cellulose Nitrate Motion Picture Film (NFPA No. 40-1967).

▲ The term *motion-picture studio* is commonly used as meaning a large space, sometimes 100 acres or more in extent, enclosed by walls or fences within which are several "stages," a number of spaces for outdoor setups, warehouses, storage sheds, separate buildings used as dressing rooms, a large substation, a restaurant, and other necessary buildings. The so-called "stages" are large buildings containing numerous temporary and semipermanent setups for both indoor and outdoor views.

The Code rules for motion-picture studios are intended to apply only to those locations where special hazards exist. Such special hazards are confined to the buildings in which films are handled or stored, the stages, and the outdoor spaces where flammable temporary structures and equipment are used. Some of these special hazards are due to the presence of a considerable quantity of highly flammable film; otherwise, the conditions are much the same as on a theater stage and, in general, the same rules should be observed as in the case of theater stages.

B. Stage or Set

530-11. Permanent Wiring. The permanent wiring shall be Type ALS cable, Type CS cable, Type MI cable, or in approved metal raceways.

Exception: Communication circuits, and sound recording and reproducing equipment shall be permitted to be wired as permitted by Articles 640 and 800.

530-12. Portable Wiring. The wiring for stage set lighting, stage effects, and other wiring not fixed as to location shall be done with portable cables and flexible cords approved for the purpose. This requirement shall not apply to portable lamps or other electric equipment used as properties in a motion picture set, on a studio stage or lot, or on location.

530-13. Stage Lighting and Effects Control. Switches used for studio stage set lighting and effects (on the stages and lots and on location) shall be of the externally operable type. Where contactors are used as the disconnecting means for fuses, an individual externally operable switch, such as a tumbler switch, for the control of each contactor shall be located at a distance of not more than 6 feet from the contactor, in addition to remote-control switches.

Exception: A single externally operable switch shall be permitted to simultaneously disconnect all the contactors on any one location board, where located at a distance of not more than 6 feet from the location board.

530-14. Plugging Boxes. Each receptacle of plugging boxes shall be rated at not less than 30 amperes.

530-15. Enclosing and Guarding Live Parts.

(a) Live parts shall be enclosed or guarded to prevent accidental contact by persons and objects.

(b) All switches shall be of the externally operable type.

(c) Rheostats shall be placed in approved cases or cabinets that enclose all live parts, having only the operating handles exposed.

(d) Current-carrying parts of "bull-switches," "location boards," "spiders," and plugging boxes shall be so enclosed, guarded, or located that persons cannot accidentally come into contact with them or bring conductive material into contact with them.

530-16. Portable Lamps. Portable lamps and work lights shall be equipped with portable cords, composition or metal-sheathed porcelain sockets, and substantial guards.

Exception: Portable lamps used as properties in a motion picture set or television stage set, on a studio stage or lot, or on location.

530-17. Portable Arc Lamps. Portable arc lamps shall be substantially constructed. The arc shall be provided with an enclosure designed to retain sparks and carbons and to prevent persons or materials from coming into contact with the arc or bare live parts. The enclosures shall be ventilated. All switches shall be of the externally operable type.

530-18. Overcurrent Protection—Short-Time Rating.*

General. Automatic overcurrent protective devices (circuit breakers or fuses) for motion-picture studio stage set lighting and the stage cables for such stage set lighting shall be as given in (a) through (e) below.

Note: *Special consideration is given to motion-picture studios and similar locations because filming periods are of short duration.

(a) Stage Cables. Stage cables for stage set lighting shall be protected by means of overcurrent devices set at not more than 400 percent of the values given in Tables 310-16 through 310-19 and Table 400-5.

(b) Feeders. In buildings used primarily for motion-picture production, the feeders from the substations to the stages shall be protected by means of overcurrent devices (generally located in the substation) having suitable ampere rating. The overcurrent devices shall be permitted to be multipole or single-pole gang-operated. No pole or overcurrent device shall be required in the neutral conductor. The overcurrent device setting for each feeder shall not exceed 400 percent of the ampacity of the feeder, as given in Table 310-16 for the kind of insulation used.

(c) Location Boards. Overcurrent protection (fuses or circuit breakers) shall be provided at the "location boards." Fuses in the "location boards" shall have an ampere rating of not over 400 percent of the ampacity of the cables between the "location boards" and the plugging boxes.

(d) Plugging Boxes. Where plugging boxes are not provided with overcurrent devices, each cable or cord smaller than No. 8 supplied through a plugging box shall be attached to the plugging box by means of a plug containing two cartridge fuses or a circuit breaker. The rating of the fuses or the setting of the circuit breaker shall not be over 400 percent of the safe ampacity of the cables or cords as given in Tables 310-16, 310-17, and 400-5 for the kind of insulation used.

(e) Lighting. Work lights, stand lamps, and fixtures shall be connected to plugging boxes by means of plugs containing two cartridge fuses not larger than 20 amperes, or they shall be permitted to be connected to special outlets on circuits protected by fuses or circuit breakers rated at not over 20 amperes. Plug fuses shall not be used unless they are on the load side of the fuse or circuit breakers on the "location boards."

530-19. Sizing of Feeder Conductors for Television Studio Sets.

(a) General. It shall be permissible to apply the demand factors listed in Table

530-19(a) to that portion of the maximum possible connected load for studio or stage set lighting for all permanently installed feeders between substations and stages and to all permanently installed subfeeders between the main stage switchboard and stage distribution centers or location boards.

Table 530-19(a). Demand Factors for Stage Set Lighting

Total Stage Set Lighting Load (Wattage)	Feeder Demand Factor
First 50,000 or less at	100%
Next 50,001 to 100,000 at	75%
Next 100,001 to 200,000 at	60%
All over 200,000	50%

(b) Portable Feeders. A demand factor of 50 percent of maximum possible connected load shall be permitted for all portable feeders.

530-20. Grounding. Metal-clad cable, metal raceways, and all noncurrent-carrying metal parts of appliances, devices, and equipment shall be grounded as specified in Article 250. This shall not apply to pendant and portable lamps, to stage lighting and stage sound equipment, nor to other portable or semiportable special stage equipment operating at not over 150 volts to ground.

C. Dressing Rooms

530-31. Dressing Rooms. Fixed wiring in dressing rooms shall be installed in accordance with wiring methods covered in Chapter 3. Wiring for portable dressing rooms shall be approved for the purpose.

D. Viewing, Cutting, and Patching Tables

530-41. Lamps at Tables. Only composition or metal-sheathed, porcelain, keyless lampholders equipped with suitable means to guard lamps from physical damage and from film and film scrap shall be used at patching, viewing, and cutting tables.

E. Film Storage Vaults

530-51. Lamps in Cellulose Nitrate Film Storage Vaults. Lamps in cellulose nitrate film storage vaults shall be rigid fixtures of the glass enclosed and gasketed type. Lamps shall be controlled by a switch having a pole in each ungrounded conductor. This switch shall be located outside of the vault and provided with a pilot light to indicate whether the switch is on or off. This switch shall disconnect from all sources of supply all ungrounded conductors terminating in any outlet in the vault.

530-52. Motors and Other Equipment in Cellulose Nitrate Film Storage Vaults. No receptacles outlets, electric motors, heaters, portable lights, or other portable electric equipment shall be located in film storage vaults.

F. Substations

530-61. Substations. Wiring and equipment of over 600 volts shall comply with Article 710.

530-62. Low-Voltage Switchboards. On 600 volts or less, switchboards shall comply with Article 384.

530-63. Overcurrent Protection of DC Generators. Three-wire DC generators shall have protection consisting of overcurrent devices having an ampere rating or setting in accordance with the generator ampere rating. Single-pole or double-pole overcurrent devices shall be permitted, and no pole or overcurrent coil shall be required in the neutral lead (whether it is grounded or ungrounded).

530-64. Working Space and Guarding. Working space and guarding in permanent fixed substations shall comply with Sections 110-16 and 110-17.

For guarding of live parts on motors and generators, see Sections 430-11 and 430-14.

Exception: Switchboards of not over 250 volts DC between conductors, when located in substations or switchboard rooms accessible to qualified persons only, shall not be required to be dead-front.

530-65. Portable Substations. Wiring and equipment in portable substations shall conform to the Sections applying to installations in permanent fixed substations, but, due to the limited space available, the working spaces shall be permitted to be reduced, provided that the equipment shall be so arranged that the operator can do his work safely, and so that other persons in the vicinity cannot accidentally come into contact with current-carrying parts or bring conducting objects into contact with them while they are energized.

530-66. Grounding at Substations. Noncurrent-carrying metal parts shall be grounded.

Exception: Frames of DC circuit breakers installed on switchboards.

ARTICLE 540. MOTION-PICTURE PROJECTORS

A. General

540-1. Scope. This Article covers motion-picture projectors and associated equipment of the professional and nonprofessional types.

For further information, see Storage and Handling of Cellulose Nitrate Motion Picture Film (NFPA No. 40-1967).

B. Equipment and Projectors of the Professional Type

540-10. Professional Projector—Definition. The professional projector employs a 35-millimeter film which is $1\frac{3}{8}$ inch wide and has on each edge 5.4 perforations per inch. Wider film, such as 70-millimeter, shall be permitted.

▲ According to the definitions of hazardous locations in Art. 500, a motion-picture booth is not classed as a hazardous location, even though the film is highly flammable. The film is not volatile at ordinary temperatures and hence no flammable gases are present, and the wiring installation need not be explosionproof but should be made with special care to guard against fire hazards.

540-11. Enclosure. The professional type of projector, such as is commonly used in theaters and motion-picture houses, shall be located in an enclosure approved for the purpose. Such enclosure shall not be considered as a hazardous location as defined in Article 500.

540-12. Motor-Driven Projectors. Motor-driven projectors shall be approved for the purpose as an assembly or shall comply with all of the following conditions:

(a) A listed projector shall be used.

(b) A listed projector lamp shall be used.

(c) Motors shall be so designed or guarded as to prevent ignition of film by sparks or arcs.

(d) Projectors shall be in charge of a qualified operator.

▲ Figure 540-1 shows the arrangement of the apparatus and wiring in the projection room of a large modern motion-picture theater. This room, or booth, contains three motion-picture projectors *P*, one stereopticon or "effect machine" *L*, and two spot machines *S*.

The light source in each of the six machines is an arc lamp operated on DC. The DC supply is obtained from two motor-generator sets which are installed in the basement in order to avoid any possible interference with the sound-reproducing apparatus. The two motor-generators are remotely controlled from the generator panel in the projection room. From each generator a feeder consisting of two 500,000-CM cables is carried to the DC panelboard in the projection room.

From the DC panelboard to each picture machine and to each of the two spot machines a branch circuit is provided consisting of two No. 00 cables. One of these conductors leads directly to the machine; the other side of the circuit is led through the auxiliary gutter to the bank of resistors in the rheostat room and from its rheostat to the machine. The resistors are provided with short-circuiting switches so that the total resistance in series with each arc may be preadjusted to any desired value.

Two circuits consisting of No. 1 conductors are carried to the stereopticon or "effect machine," since this machine contains two arc lamps.

The conduit leading to each machine is brought up through the floor.

It is provided in Sec. 540-13 that the wires to the projector outlet shall not be smaller than No. 8, but in every case the maximum current drawn by the lamp should be ascertained and conductors should be installed of sufficient size to carry this current. In this case, when suitably adjusted for the large pictures, the arc in each projector takes a current of nearly 150 A.

In addition to the main outlet for supplying the arc, four other outlets are installed at each projector-machine location for auxiliary circuits.

Outlets *F* are for foot switches which control the shutters in front of the lenses for changeover from one projector to another.

Outlets *G* are for a No. 8 grounding conductor which is connected to the frame of each projector and to the water-piping system.

From outlets *C* a circuit is brought up to each machine for a small incandescent lamp inside the lamp house and a lamp to illuminate the turntable. Outlets *M* are for power circuits to the motors used to operate the projector machines.

Ventilation is provided by two exhaust fans and two duct systems, one exhausting

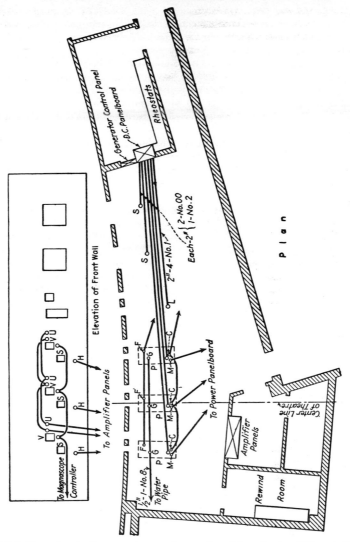

Fig. 540-1. Plan of projection room in a modern motion-picture theater. (*Edwards Electric Construction Co.*)

from the ceiling of the projection room and one connected to the arc-lamp housing of each machine.

A separate room is provided for rewinding films, but as this room opens only into the projection room, it may be considered that the rewinding is performed in the projection room.

540-13. Conductors Size. Conductors supplying outlets for arc projectors of the professional type shall not be smaller than No. 8 and shall be of sufficient size for the projector employed. Conductors for incandescent-type projectors shall conform to normal wiring standards as provided in Section 210-24.

540-14. Conductors on Lamps and Hot Equipment. Asbestos-covered conductors Type AA or other types of insulated conductors having a maximum operating temperature of 200°C (392°F) shall be used on all lamps or other equipment where the ambient temperature at the conductors as installed will exceed 50°C (122°F).

540-15. Flexible Cords. Cords approved for hard service in Table 400-4 shall be used on portable equipment.

540-16. Lamp Guards. Incandescent lamps in projection rooms or booths shall be provided with an approved lamp guard unless otherwise protected by noncombustible shades or other enclosures.

540-17. Location of Equipment. Motor-generator sets, transformers, rectifiers, rheostats, and similar equipment for the supply or control of current to arc lamps on projectors shall, if practicable, be located in separate rooms. Where placed in the projector room, they shall be so located or guarded that arcs or sparks cannot come in contact with film, and motor-generator sets shall have the commutator end or ends protected as provided in Section 520-48.

540-19. Equipment Prohibited. Switches, overcurrent devices, or other equipment not normally required or used for projectors, sound reproduction, flood, or other special-effect lamps or other equipment shall not be installed in such booths or rooms.

Exception: Remote-control switches for the control of auditorium lights or a switch for the motor operating the curtain at the motion-picture screen.

▲ **All necessary equipment may be located in a projector booth, but equipment which is not necessary in the normal operation of the motion-picture projectors, stage-lighting projectors, and control of the auditorium lighting and stage curtain must be located elsewhere. Equipment such as service equipment and panelboards for the control and protection of circuits for signs, outside lighting, and lighting in the lobby and box office must not be located in the booth.**

540-20. Approval. Projectors and enclosures for arc or incandescent lamps, rectifiers, transformers, rheostats, and similar equipment shall be listed.

540-21. Marking. Projectors and other equipment as set forth in Section 540-20 shall be marked with the name or trademark of the maker and with the voltage and current for which they are designed.

C. Nonprofessional-Type Projectors

540-30. Definition. The nonprofessional projector employs film other than that used on professional-type projectors.

540-31. Booth Not Required. Projectors of the nonprofessional or miniature type, when employing only approved slow-burning (cellulose acetate or equivalent) film, shall be permitted to be operated without a booth.

540-32. Approval. Projectors, lamp enclosures, and current-controlling devices and similar devices shall be listed as component parts of the projector equipment.

540-33. Source of Illumination. The source of illumination shall be a lamp or a type listed for stereopticon use or for motion-picture projection.

540-34. Marking. Projectors shall be marked with: (1) the name or trademark of the maker; (2) the current and voltage for which they are designed; and (3) for projectors of this type using the standard 35-millimeter film, the wording "For use with slow-burning films only."

540-35. Nonprofessional Film Marking. The slow-burning (cellulose acetate or equivalent) film shall have a permanent distinctive marker for its entire length identifying the manufacturer and the slow-burning character of the film stock.

D. Sound Recording and Reproduction

540-50. Sound Recording and Reproduction. Sound recording and reproduction equipment shall comply with Article 640.

ARTICLE 545. MANUFACTURED BUILDING

A. General

545-1. Scope. This Article covers requirements for a manufactured building and/or building components as herein defined.

545-2. Other Articles. Wherever the requirements of other Articles of this Code and Article 545 differ, the requirements of Article 545 shall apply.

545-3. Definitions.

(a) **Manufactured Building:** "Manufactured Building" means any building which is of closed construction and which is made or assembled in manufacturing facilities on or off the building site for installation, or assembly and installation, on the building site, other than mobile homes or recreational vehicles.

(b) **Building Component:** "Building Component" means any subsystem, subassembly, or other system designed for use in or integral with or as part of a structure, which can include structural, electrical, mechanical, plumbing and fire protection systems and other systems affecting health and safety.

(c) **Building System:** "Building System" means plans, specifications and documentation for a system of manufactured building or for a type or a system of building components, which can include structural, electrical, mechanical, plumbing, and fire protection systems, and other systems affecting health and safety, and including such variations thereof as are specifically permitted by regulation, and which variations are submitted as part of the building system or amendment thereto.

(d) **Closed Construction:** "Closed Construction" means any building, building component, assembly or system manufactured in such a manner that all concealed parts or processes of manufacture cannot be inspected before installation at the building site without disassembly, damage, or destruction.

545-4. Wiring Methods. All raceway and cable wiring methods included in this Code and such other wiring systems specifically intended and approved for use in manufactured building shall be permitted with approved fittings and with fittings approved for manufactured building. Where wiring devices with integral enclosures are used, sufficient length of conductor shall be provided to facilitate replacement.

545-5. Service-Entrance Conductors: Service-entrance conductors shall meet the requirements of Article 230. Provisions shall be made to route the service-entrance conductors from the service equipment to the point of attachment of the service.

545-6. Installation of Service-Entrance Conductors: Service-entrance conductors shall be installed after erection at the building site.

Exception: Where point of attachment is known prior to manufacture.

545-7. Service-Equipment Location: The service equipment shall be located at a readily accessible point nearest to the entrance of the conductors either inside or outside the building.

545-8. Protection of Conductors and Equipment: Protection shall be provided for exposed conductors and equipment during processes of manufacturing, packaging, in transit, and erection at the building site.

545-9. Outlet Boxes: Outlet boxes of dimensions other than those required in Table 370-6(a)(1) shall be permitted to be installed when tested and approved to applicable standards.

Where mounted in walls of closed construction, boxes not over 100 cubic inches in size approved for the purpose shall be affixed with approved anchors or clamps so as to provide a rigid and secure installation.

545-10. Receptacle or Switch with Integral Enclosure: A receptacle or switch with integral enclosure and mounting means, when tested and approved to applicable standards, shall be permitted to be installed.

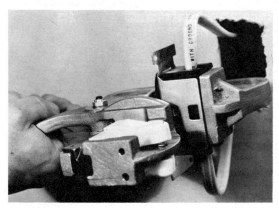

FIG. 545-1. A tool which is used to connect integral switch and receptacle enclosures to nonmetallic-sheathed cable. (*Amp Inc.*)

545-11. Bonding and Grounding: Prewired panels and/or building components shall provide for the bonding and/or grounding of all exposed metals likely to become energized, in accordance with Article 250, Part E, F, and G.

545-12. Grounding Electrode Conductor: The grounding electrode conductor shall meet the requirements of Article 250, Part J. Provisions shall be made to route the grounding electrode conductor from the service equipment to the point of attachment of the grounding electrode.

545-13. Component Interconnections: Fittings and connectors which are intended to be concealed at the time of on-site assembly, when tested and approved to applicable standards shall be permitted for on-site interconnection of modules or other building components. Such fittings and connectors shall be equal to the wiring method employed in insulation, temperature rise, fault-current withstand and shall be capable of enduring the vibration and minor relative motions occurring in the components of manufactured building.

Fig. 545-2. NM cable connector parts before mating together. (*Burndy.*)

Fig. 545-3. NM cable connector after being mated. (*Burndy.*)

▲ Figures 545-2 and 545-3 depict a UL-listed device that is intended to be used to meet the requirements of Sec. 545-13 for component interconnections at the time of on-site assembly. This device eliminates the chance for do-it-yourself wiremen to incorrectly wire component parts. These connectors, once mated, cannot be disconnected. Standard plug-and-cap connections do not satisfy the requirements of Sec. 545-13.

ARTICLE 550. MOBILE HOMES AND MOBILE HOME PARKS

550-1. Scope.

(a) The provisions of this Article cover the electrical conductors and equipment installed within or on mobile homes, the conductors that connect mobile homes to a supply of electricity, and the installation of electrical wiring, fixtures, equipment and appurtenances related to electrical installations within a mobile home park up to the mobile home service-entrance conductors or, if none, the mobile home service equipment.

Wherever the requirements of other Articles of this Code and Article 550 differ, the requirements of Article 550 shall apply.

For requirements on body and frame design, construction, and the installation of plumbing and heating systems in mobile homes, refer to Standard for Mobile Homes (NFPA No. 501B-1973).

(b) A mobile home not intended as a dwelling unit, as for example, equipped for sleeping purposes only, contractor's on-site offices, construction job dormitories, mobile studio dressing rooms, banks, clinics, mobile stores, or intended for the display or demonstration of merchandise or machinery, shall not be required to meet the provisions of this Article pertaining to the number or capacity of circuits required. It shall, however, meet all other applicable requirements of this Article if provided with an electrical installation intended to be energized from a 115-volt or 115/230-volt AC power supply system.

(c) Mobile homes installed in other than mobile home parks shall comply with the provisions of this Article.

(d) The provisions of this Article apply to mobile homes intended for connection to a wiring system nominally rated 115/230-volts, 3-wire AC, with grounded neutral.

▲ Several states have laws that require factory inspection of mobile homes by state inspectors, and some states require that mobile homes be inspected by a nationally recognized independent testing laboratory. Underwriters' Laboratories now lists a number of mobile home manufacturers, and such listings are acceptable in many areas of the country.

In setting up any factory inspection program it is in the interest of public safety to adopt the latest edition of NFPA No. 501B—Standard for Mobile Homes. This standard contains electrical requirements identical to those in Art. 550, and in addition, contains requirements on body and frame design, construction, exits, interior-finish flame spread, and installation of plumbing and heating systems. Inspection of only the wiring will not ensure complete protection for purchasers or users of mobile homes.

550-2. Definitions.

Distribution Panelboard: See definition of panelboard in Article 100.

Feeder Assembly: The overhead or under-chassis feeder conductors, including the grounding conductor, together with the necessary fittings and equipment or a power-supply cord approved for mobile home use, designed for the purpose of delivering energy from the source of electrical supply to the distribution panelboard within the mobile home.

Mobile Home: A factory-assembled structure or structures equipped with the necessary service connections and made so as to be readily movable as a unit or units on their own running gear and designed to be used as a dwelling unit(s) without a permanent foundation.

The phrase "without a permanent foundation" indicates that the support system is constructed with the intent that the mobile home placed thereon will be moved from time to time at the convenience of the owner.

Mobile Home Accessory Building or Structure: Any awning, cabana, ramada, storage cabinet, carport, fence, windbreak or porch established for the use of the occupant of the mobile home upon a mobile home lot.

Mobile Home Lot: A designated portion of a mobile home park designed for the accommodation of one mobile home and its accessory buildings or structures for the exclusive use of its occupants.

Mobile Home Park: A contiguous parcel of land which is used for the accommodation of occupied mobile homes.

Mobile Home Service Equipment: The equipment containing the disconnecting means, overcurrent protective devices, and receptacles or other means for connecting a mobile home feeder assembly.

Park Electrical Wiring Systems: All of the electrical wiring, fixtures, equipment and appurtenances related to electrical installations within a mobile home park, including the mobile home service equipment.

A. Mobile Homes

550-3. Power Supply.

(a) The mobile home service equipment shall be located adjacent to the mobile home and not mounted in or on the mobile home. The power supply to the mobile home shall be a feeder assembly consisting of not more than 3 mobile home power-supply cords, each rated 50 amperes or a permanently installed circuit.

Exception: A mobile home that is factory-equipped with gas or oil-fired central heating equipment and cooking appliances shall be permitted to be provided with a mobile home power-supply cord rated 40 amperes.

(b) If the mobile home has a power-supply cord, it shall be permanently attached to the distribution panelboard or to a junction box permanently connected to the distribution panelboard, with the free end terminating in an attachment plug cap.

(c) Cords with adapters and pigtail ends, extension cords, and similar items shall not be attached to, or shipped with, a mobile home.

(d) A suitable clamp or the equivalent shall be provided at the distribution panelboard knockout to afford strain relief for the cord to prevent strain from being transmitted to the terminals when the power supply cord is handled in its intended manner.

(e) The cord used shall be of an approved type with four conductors, one of which shall be identified by a continuous green color or a continuous green color with one or more yellow stripes for use as the grounding conductor.

(f) The attachment plug cap shall be a 3-pole 4-wire grounding type, rated 50 amperes, 125/250 volts with a configuration as shown in Figure 550-3(f) and intended for use with the 50-ampere, 125/250 receptacle configuration shown in Figure 550-3(f). It shall be molded of butyl rubber, neoprene, or other approved materials which have been found suitable for the purpose, and shall be molded to the flexible cord so that it adheres tightly to the cord at the point where the cord enters the attachment plug cap. If a right-angle cap is used, the configuration shall be so oriented that the grounding member is farthest from the cord.

Complete details of the 50-ampere plug and receptacle shown in Figure 550-3(f) can be found in ANSI Standard Dimensions of Caps, Plugs and Receptacles, C73.17-1972.

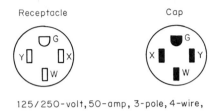

125/250-volt, 50-amp, 3-pole, 4-wire,
grounding type

Figure 550-3(f). 50-ampere 125/250 volt receptacle and attachment-plug-cap configurations, 3-pole 4-wire grounding types, used for mobile home supply cords and mobile home parks.

(g) The overall length of a power-supply cord, measured from the end of the cord, including bared leads, to the face of the attachment plug cap shall not be less than 21 feet and shall not exceed $36\frac{1}{2}$ feet. The length of the cord from the face of the attachment plug cap to the point where the cord enters the mobile home shall not be less than 20 feet.

(h) The power-supply cord shall bear the following marking: "For use with mobile homes—40 amperes" or "For use with mobile homes—50 amperes."

(i) The point of entrance of the feeder assembly to the mobile home shall be in the exterior wall, floor, or roof, in the rear third section (away from the coupler) of the mobile home.

(j) Where a separately metered appliance is installed in the mobile home, or where the calculated load of the mobile home is between 50 amperes and 150 amperes, up to three 50-ampere power-supply cords may be installed when permitted by the authority having jurisdiction, or a feeder assembly as provided for in Section 550-3(a) or 550-3(k) shall be permitted. The additional power-supply cords shall be located not more than 12 inches away from the point of entrance of the main power-supply cord. They shall not be interconnected on either the line side or the load side, except that the grounding means shall be electrically interconnected.

▲ The reason special permission is required to permit two or three 50-A power-supply cords is that most mobile home parks are not presently equipped to handle more than one such power-supply cord for each mobile home lot. However, in areas where mobile home parks are being wired with three 50-A receptacles at each mobile home lot, special permission will usually be permitted to accept mobile homes equipped with two or three 50-A power-supply cords.

In some areas mobile homes are permanently connected as permitted in paragraph (k) below. Accordingly, local requirements must be checked in regard to the approved method of installing feeder assemblies.

(k) Where the calculated load exceeds 150 amperes or where a permanent feeder is used, the supply shall be by means of:

(1) One mast weatherhead installation installed in accordance with Article 230 containing 4 continuous, insulated, color-coded, feeder conductors, one of which shall be an equipment grounding conductor; or,

(2) An approved metal raceway from the disconnecting means in the mobile home to the underside of the mobile home with provisions for the attachment to a suitable junction box or fitting to the raceway on the underside of the mobile home (with or without conductors as in Section 550-3(k)(1)).

▲ Sometimes a raceway is stubbed to the underside of a mobile home from the distribution panelboard. It is optional as to whether the feeder conductors are installed in the raceway by the mobile home manufacturer or by field installers. When installed, four continuous, insulated, color-coded conductors, as indicated in Sec. 550-3(k)(1), are required. The feeder conductors may be spliced in a suitable junction box, but in no case within the raceway proper.

550-4. Disconnecting Means and Branch-Circuit Protective Equipment. The branch-circuit equipment shall be permitted to be combined with the disconnecting means as a single assembly. Such a combination shall be permitted to be designated as a distribution panelboard. If a fused distribution panelboard is used, the maximum fuse size for the mains shall be plainly marked, with lettering at least $\frac{1}{4}$ inch high and visible when fuses are changed.

Plug fuses and fuseholders shall be tamper-resistant, Type "S," enclosed in dead-front fuse panelboards.

See Section 110-22 concerning identification of each disconnecting means and each service, feeder, or branch circuit at the point where it originated and the type marking needed.

(a) Disconnecting Means. A single disconnecting means shall be provided in each mobile home consisting of a circuit breaker, or a switch and fuses and their accessories installed in a readily accessible location near the point of entrance of the supply cord or conductors into the mobile home. The main circuit breakers or fuses shall be plainly marked "Main." This equipment shall contain a solderless type of grounding connector or bar for the purposes of grounding with sufficient terminals for all grounding conductors. The neutral bar termination of the grounded circuit conductors shall be insulated. The disconnecting equipment shall have a rating suitable for the connected load. The distribution equipment, either circuit breaker or fused type, shall be located a minimum of 24 inches from the bottom of such equipment to the floor level of the mobile home.

Where more than one power-supply cord is installed, disconnecting means shall be provided for each cord and shall be permitted to be combined in a single equipment but without electrical interconnections other than for grounding purposes.

A distribution panelboard main circuit breaker shall be rated 50 amperes and employ a 2-pole circuit breaker rated 40 amperes for a 40-ampere supply cord, or 50 amperes for a 50-ampere supply cord. A distribution panelboard employing a disconnect switch and fuses shall be rated 60 amperes and shall employ a single 20-pole 60-ampere fuseholder with 40- or 50-ampere main fuses for 40- or 50-ampere supply cords, respectively. The outside of the distribution panelboard shall be plainly marked with the fuse size.

The distribution panelboard shall be permitted just inside a closet entry if the location is such that a clear space of 6 inches to easily ignitible materials is maintained in front of the distribution panelboard, and the distribution panelboard door can be extended to its full open position (at least 90 degrees). A clear working space at least 30 inches wide and 30 inches in front of the distribution panelboard shall be provided. This space shall extend from floor to the top of the distribution panelboard.

(b) Branch-Circuit Protective Equipment. Branch-circuit distribution equipment shall be installed in each mobile home and shall include overcurrent protection for each branch circuit consisting of either circuit breakers or fuses.

The branch-circuit overcurrent devices shall be rated: (1) not more than the circuit conductors; and (2) not more than 150 percent of the rating of a single appliance rated 10 amperes or more which is supplied by an individual branch circuit; but (3) not more than the fuse size marked on the air conditioner or other motor-operated appliance.

A 15-ampere multiple receptacle shall be acceptable when connected to a 20-ampere laundry circuit.

(c) Two-Pole Circuit Breakers. When circuit breakers are provided for branch-circuit protection, 230-volt circuits shall be protected by a 2-pole common or companion trip, or handle-tied paired circuit breakers.

(d) Electrical Nameplates. A metal nameplate on the outside adjacent to the feeder assembly entrance shall read: "This Connection for 120/240-Volt, 3-Pole, 4-Wire, 60 Hertz, . . . Ampere Supply." The correct ampere rating shall be marked in the blank space.

550-5. Branch Circuits. The number of branch circuits required shall be determined in accordance with (a) through (c) below.

(a) Lighting. Based on 3 watts per square foot times outside dimensions of the mobile home (coupler excluded) divided by 115 volts to determine the number of 15- or 20-ampere lighting area circuits, e.g.,

$$\frac{3 \times \text{Length} \times \text{Width}}{115 \times 15 \text{ (or 20)}} = \text{No. of 15- (or 20-) ampere circuits.}$$

(b) Portable Appliances. For the small appliance load in kitchen, pantry, family room, dining room, and breakfast rooms of mobile homes, two or more 20-ampere appliance branch circuits in addition to the branch circuits specified in Section 550-5(a) shall be provided for all receptacle outlets in these rooms, and such circuits shall have no other outlets. Receptacle outlets supplied by at least two appliance receptacle branch circuits shall be installed in the kitchen.

(c) General Appliances. (Including furnace, water heater, range, and central or room air conditioner, etc.) There shall be one or more circuits of adequate rating in accordance with the following:

(1) Ampere rating of fixed appliances not over 50 percent of circuit rating if lighting outlets (receptacles, other than kitchen, dining area, and laundry, considered as lighting outlets) are on the same circuit;

(2) For fixed appliances on a circuit without lighting outlets, the sum of rated amperes shall not exceed the branch-circuit rating for other than motor loads or 80 percent of the branch-circuit rating for air conditioning or other motor loads;

(3) The rating of a single portable appliance on a circuit having no other outlets shall not exceed 80 percent of the circuit rating;

(4) The rating of range branch circuit shall be based on the range demand as specified for ranges in Section 550-11(b)(5).

For the laundry branch circuit, see Section 220-3(c).
For central air conditioning, see Article 440.

550-6. Receptacle Outlets.

(a) All receptacle outlets: (1) shall be of grounding type; (2) shall be installed according to Section 210-7; and (3) except when supplying specific appliances, receptacles shall be parallel-blade, 15-ampere, 125-volt, either single or duplex.

For ground-fault circuit-interrupter requirements, refer to Section 210-8(a).

(b) There shall be an individual outlet of the grounding type for each cord-connected fixed appliance installed.

(c) Receptacle Outlets Required. Except in the bath and hall areas, receptacle outlets shall be installed at all wall spaces 2 feet wide or more, so that no point along the floor line is more than 6 feet, measured horizontally, from an outlet in that space. Except as explained in the following, receptacle outlets are not required for wall spaces occupied by kitchen or wardrobe cabinets.

In addition, a receptacle outlet shall be installed: (1) Over or adjacent to counter tops in the kitchen (at least one on each side of the sink if counter tops are on each side and 12 inches or more in width); (2) Adjacent to the refrigerator and free-standing gas-range space; (3) At counter top spaces for built-in vanities; (4) At counter top spaces under wall-mounted cabinets.

(d) Receptacle outlets shall not be installed within or adjacent to a shower or bathtub space.

550-7. Fixtures and Appliances.

(a) Electrical materials, devices, appliances, fittings, and other equipment installed, intended for use in, or attached to the mobile home shall be approved for the application and shall be connected in an approved manner when in service. Facilities shall be provided to securely fasten appliances when the mobile home is in transit. (See Section 550-9 for provisions on grounding.)

(1) Specifically approved pendant-type fixtures or pendant cords shall be permitted in mobile homes.

(2) If a lighting fixture is provided over a bathtub or in a shower stall, it shall be of the approved enclosed and gasketed type.

(3) The switch for shower lighting fixtures and exhaust fans located over a tub or in a shower stall shall be located outside the tub or shower space.

(b) Every appliance shall be accessible for inspection, service, repair, or replacement without removal of permanent construction.

550-8. Wiring Methods and Materials. Except as specifically limited in this Section, the wiring methods and materials included in this Code shall be used in mobile homes.

(a) Nonmetallic outlet boxes shall be acceptable only with nonmetallic cable.

(b) Nonmetallic cable located 15 inches or less above the floor, if exposed, shall be protected from physical damage by covering boards, guard strips, or conduit. Cable likely to be damaged by stowage shall be so protected in all cases.

(c) Metal-clad and nonmetallic cables shall be permitted to pass through the centers of the wide side of 2-inch by 4-inch studs. However, they shall be protected where they pass through 2-inch by 2-inch studs or at other studs or frames where the cable or armor would be less than $1\frac{1}{2}$ inches from the inside or outside surface. Steel plates on each side of the cable, or a tube, with not less than No. 16 MSG wall thickness, shall be required to protect the cable. These plates or tubes shall be securely held in place.

(d) Where metallic faceplates are used, they shall be effectively grounded.

(e) If the range, clothes dryer, or similar appliance is connected by metal-clad cable or flexible conduit, a length of free cable or conduit should be provided to permit moving the appliance. The cable or flexible conduit should be adequately secured to the wall. If the range, clothes dryer, or similar appliance is connected by metal-clad cable or flexible conduit, a length of not less than three feet of free cable or conduit shall be provided to permit moving the appliance. Type NM or type SE cable shall not be used to connect a range or dryer. This shall not prohibit the use of type NM or type SE cable between the branch circuit overcurrent protective device and a junction box or range or dryer receptacle.

This does not prohibit the use of Type NM cable between the branch-circuit overcurrent protective device and a range or dryer receptacle.

(f) Threaded rigid conduit shall be provided with a locknut inside and outside the box, and a conduit bushing shall be used on the inside. Rigid nonmetallic conduit shall be permitted. Inside ends of the conduit shall be reamed.

(g) Switches shall be rated as follows:

(1) For lighting circuits, switches shall have a 10-ampere 120-125-volt rating; or higher, if needed for the connected load.

(2) For motors or other loads, switches shall have ampere or horsepower ratings, or both, adequate for loads controlled. (An "AC general-use" snap switch shall be permitted to control a motor 2 horsepower or less with full-load current not over 80 percent of the switch ampere rating.)

(h) At least 4 inches of free conductor shall be left at each outlet box except where conductors are intended to loop without joints.

(i) Under-Chassis Wiring. (Exposed to Weather).

(1) When outdoor or under-chassis line-voltage wiring is exposed to moisture or physical damage, it shall be protected by rigid metal conduit. The conductors shall be suitable for wet locations.

Exception: Electrical metallic tubing shall be permitted when closely routed against frames and equipment enclosures.

(2) The cables or conductors shall be Type NMC, TW, or equivalent.

(j) Outlet boxes of dimensions less than those required in Table 370-6(a) shall be permitted provided the box has been tested and approved for the purpose.

▲ **The smaller-dimensional box mentioned in this rule would usually be a box designed for a special switch or receptacle, or a combination box and wiring device. Such combinations can be properly evaluated and tested with a limited number of conductors and connections and a specific lay of conductors to ensure adequate wiring space in the spirit of the first paragraph in Sec. 370-6.**

(k) Boxes, fittings and cabinets shall be securely fastened in place.

Exception: Snap-in type boxes or boxes provided with special wall or ceiling brackets that securely fasten boxes in walls or ceilings shall be permitted.

(l) Appliances having branch-circuit terminal connections which operate at temperatures higher than 60°C (140°F) shall have circuit conductors as described in (1) and (2) below:

(1) Branch-circuit conductors having an insulation suitable for the temperature encountered shall be permitted to be run directly to the appliance.

(2) Conductors having an insulation suitable for the temperature encountered shall be run from the appliance terminal connection to a readily accessible outlet box placed at least one foot from the appliance. These conductors shall be in a suitable raceway which shall extend for at least 4 feet.

550-9. Grounding. Grounding of both electrical and nonelectrical metal parts in a mobile home shall be through connection to a grounding bus in the mobile home distribution panelboard. The grounding bus shall be grounded through the green-colored conductor in the supply cord or the feeder wiring to the service ground in the service-entrance equipment located adjacent to the mobile home location. Neither the frame of the mobile home nor the frame of any appliance shall be connected to the neutral conductor in the mobile home.

▲ The white (neutral) conductor is required to be run from the "insulated busbar" in the mobile-home panel to the service-entrance equipment, where it is connected to the terminal at the point of connection to the grounding electrode conductor.

The green-colored conductor is required to be run from the "panel grounding bus" in the mobile home to the service-entrance equipment, where it is connected to the neutral conductor at the point of connection to the grounding electrode conductor.

The requirements provide that the grounded (white) conductor and the grounding (green) conductor be kept separate within the mobile-home structure in order to secure the maximum protection against electric-shock hazard if the supply neutral conductor should become open.

(a) Insulated Neutral.

(1) The grounded circuit conductor (neutral) shall be insulated from the grounding conductors and from equipment enclosures and other grounded parts. The grounded (neutral) circuit terminals in the distribution panelboard and in ranges, clothes dryers, counter-mounted cooking units, and wall-mounted ovens shall be insulated from the equipment enclosure. Bonding screws, straps, or buses in the distribution panelboard or in appliances shall be removed and discarded.

(2) Connections of ranges and clothes dryers with 115/230-volt, 3-wire ratings shall be made with 4-conductor cord and 3-pole, 4-wire grounding-type plugs, or by Type AC metal-clad cable or conductors enclosed in flexible metal conduit.

For 115 volt rated devices, a 3-conductor cord and a 2-pole, 3-wire grounding-type plug shall be permitted.

(b) Equipment Grounding Means.

(1) The green-colored grounding wire in the supply cord or permanent feeder wiring shall be connected to the grounding bus in the distribution panelboard or disconnecting means.

(2) In the electrical system, all exposed metal parts, enclosures, frames, lamp fixture canopies, etc., shall be effectively bonded to the grounding terminal or enclosure of the distribution panelboard.

(3) Cord-connected appliances, such as washing machines, clothes dryers, refrigerators, and the electrical system of gas ranges, etc., shall be grounded by means of an approved cord with grounding conductor and grounding-type attachment plug.

(c) Bonding of Noncurrent-Carrying Metal Parts.

(1) All exposed noncurrent-carrying metal parts that may become energized shall be effectively bonded to the grounding terminal or enclosure of the distribution panelboard. A bonding conductor shall be connected between each distribution panelboard and an accessible terminal on the chassis.

(2) Grounding terminals shall be of the solderless type and approved as pressure-terminal connectors recognized for the wire size used. The bonding conductor shall be solid or stranded, insulated or bare, and shall be No. 8 copper minimum, or equal. The bonding conductor shall be routed so as not to be exposed to physical damage.

(3) Metallic gas, water, and waste pipes and metallic air circulating ducts shall be considered bonded if they are connected to the terminal on the chassis (see Section 550-9(c)(1)) by clamps, solderless connectors, or by suitable grounding-type straps.

(4) Any metallic roof and exterior covering shall be considered bonded if (a) the metal panels overlap one another and are securely attached to the wood or metal frame parts by metallic fasteners, and (b) if the lower panel of the metallic exterior covering is secured by metallic fasteners at a cross member of the chassis by two metal straps per mobile home unit or section at opposite ends.

The bonding strap material shall be a minimum of 4 inches in width of material equivalent to the skin or a material of equal or better electrical conductivity. The straps shall be fastened with paint-penetrating fittings, such as screws and star-washers or equivalent.

550-10. Testing. Dielectric Strength Test. The wiring of each mobile home shall be subjected to a 1-minute, 900-volt, dielectric strength test (with all switches closed) between live parts (including neutral) and the mobile home ground. Alternatively, the test shall be permitted to be performed at 1,080 volts for 1 second. This test shall be performed after branch circuits are complete and after fixtures or appliances are installed.

Exception: Fixtures or appliances which are approved shall not be required to withstand the dielectric strength test.

550-11. Calculations. The following method shall be employed in computing the supply-cord and distribution-panelboard load for each feeder assembly for each mobile home in lieu of the procedure shown in Article 220 and shall be based on a 3-wire, 115/230-volt supply with 115-volt loads balanced between the two legs of the 3-wire system.

(a) Lighting and Small Appliance Load:

Lighting Watts: Length times width of mobile home (outside dimensions, exclusive of coupler) times 3 watts per square foot; e.g., Length × width × 3 = _____ lighting watts.

Small Appliance Watts: Number of circuits times 1,500 watts for each 20-ampere appliance receptacle circuit (see definition of Appliance, Portable with note); e.g., Number of circuits × 1,500 = _____ small appliance watts.

Total: Lighting watts plus small appliance = _____ total watts.

First 3,000 total watts at 100 percent plus remainder at 35 percent = _____ watts to be divided by 230 volts to obtain current (amperes) per leg.

(b) Total load for determining power supply is the summation of:

(1) Lighting and small appliance load as calculated in Section 550-11(a).

(2) Nameplate amperes for motors and heater loads (exhaust fans, air conditioners,* electric, gas, or oil heating).**

*Omit smaller of these two, except include blower motor if used as air conditioner evaporator motor.

**When an air conditioner is not installed and a 40-ampere power supply cord is provided, allow 15 amperes per leg for air conditioning.

(3) 25 percent of current of largest motor in (2).

(4) Total of nameplate amperes for: disposal, dishwasher, water heater, clothes dryer, wall-mounted oven, cooking units.

Where number of these appliances exceeds 3, use 75 percent of total.

(5) Derive amperes for free-standing range (as distinguished from separate ovens and cooking units) by dividing values below by 230 volts.

Nameplate Rating	Use
10,000 watts or less	80 percent of rating
10,001–12,500 watts	8,000 watts
12,501–13,500 watts	8,400 watts
13,501–14,500 watts	8,800 watts
14,501–15,500 watts	9,200 watts
15,501–16,500 watts	9,600 watts
16,501–17,500 watts	10,000 watts

(6) If outlets or circuits are provided for other than factory-installed appliances, include the anticipated load.

See following Example for illustration of application of this calculation.

Example

A mobile home is 70 × 10 feet and has two portable appliance circuits, a 1000-watt 230-volt heater, a 200-watt 115-volt exhaust fan, a 400-watt 115-volt dishwasher and a 7000-watt electric range.

Lighting and small appliance load

Lighting 70 × 10 × 3 =	2100 watts
Small appliance 1500 × 2 =	3000 watts
	5100 watts
1st 3000 watts at 100%........................	3000
Remainder (5,100 − 3,000 = 2,100) at 35%..............	735
	3735

$$\frac{3735}{230} = 16 \text{ amperes per leg}$$

1000 watt (heater) ÷ 230 =	4.4 amp
200 watt (fan) ÷ 115 =	1.7 amp
400 watt (dishwasher) ÷ 115 =	3.5 amp
7000 watt (range) × .8 ÷ 230 =	24. amp

| | Amperes per leg | |
	A	B
Lighting and appliances	16	16
Heater (230 volt)	4	4
Fan (115 volt)	2	–
Dishwasher (115 volt)	–	4
Range	24	24
	Totals 46	48

Based on the higher current calculated for either leg, use one 50-ampere supply cord.

(c) Optional Method of Calculation for Lighting and Appliance Load.

For mobile homes, the optional method for calculating lighting and appliance load shown in Section 220-30 and Table 220-30 shall be permitted.

550-12. Wiring of Expandable Units and Dual Units.

(a) Expandable or dual-unit mobile homes shall use fixed-type wiring methods and materials for connecting such units to each other.

(b) Expandable or dual-unit mobile homes not having permanently installed feeders, and which are to be moved from one location to another, shall be permitted to have disconnecting means with branch-circuit protective equipment in each unit when so located that after assembly or joining together of units, the requirements of Section 550-3(j) are met.

550-13. Outdoor Outlets, Fixtures, Air-Cooling Equipment, Etc.

(a) Outdoor fixtures and equipment shall be recognized for outdoor use. Outdoor receptacle or convenience outlets shall be of a gasketed-cover type.

(b) A mobile home provided with a receptacle outlet designed to energize heating and/or air-conditioning equipment located outside the mobile home, shall have permanently affixed, adjacent to the outlet receptacle, a metal tag which reads:

> This Connection is for Air-Conditioning Equipment Rated at Not More Than . . . . Amperes, at . . . . Volts, 60 Hertz.

The correct voltage and ampere rating shall be given. The tag shall be not less than 0.020 inch, etched brass, stainless steel, anodized or alclad aluminum or equivalent. The tag shall not be less than 3 inches by $1\frac{3}{4}$ inches minimum size.

B. Mobile Home Parks

550-21. Distribution System. The mobile home park secondary electrical distribution system to mobile home lots shall be single-phase, 115/230 volts, nominal. For the purpose of Part B, where the park service exceeds 240 volts, transformers and secondary distribution panelboards shall be treated as services.

See Table 550-22 for calculation of load.

▲ The mobile home park supply is limited to nominal 115/230-V, single-phase, three-wire to accommodate appliances rated at nominal 230 V or a combination nominal voltage of 115/230 V. Accordingly, a three-wire 120/208-V supply, derived from a four-wire 208Y/120-V supply, would not be acceptable.

While the demand factor for a single mobile home lot is computed at 16,000 W, it should be noted that Sec. 550-22(c) requires the feeder circuit conductors extending to each mobile home lot to be not less than 100 A.

550-22. Calculated Load.

(a) Park electrical wiring systems shall be calculated on the basis of not less than 16,000 watts (at 115/230 volts) per each mobile home service. The demand factors which are set forth in Table 550-22 shall be considered the minimum allowable demand factors which shall be permitted in calculating load on feeders and service. No demand factor shall be allowed for any other load, except as provided in this Code.

Table 550-22. Demand Factors for Feeders and Service-Entrance Conductors

Number of Mobile Home Lots	Demand Factor (Percent)
1	100
2	55
3	44
4	39
5	33
6	29
7–9	28
10–12	27
13–15	26
16–21	25
22–40	24
41–60	23
61 and over	22

(b) The demand factor for a given number of lots shall apply to all lots indicated.

Example: 20 lots calculated at 25 percent of 16,000 watts result in a permissible demand of 4,000 watts per lot or a total of 80,000 watts for 20 lots.

(c) Mobile home lot feeder circuit conductors shall have adequate capacity for the loads supplied, and shall be rated at not less than 100 amperes at 115/230 volts.

▲ See comments following Sec. 550-21.

550-23. Mobile Home Service Equipment.

(a) Mobile home service equipment shall be rated at not less than 100 amperes, and provision shall be made for connecting a mobile home feeder assembly by a permanent wiring method. Power outlets used as mobile home service equipment shall also be permitted to contain receptacles rated up to 50 amperes with appropriate overcurrent protection. Fifty-ampere receptacles shall conform to the configuration shown in Figure 550-3(f).

Complete details on the 50-ampere attachment plug cap configuration can be found in American National Standard Dimensions of Caps, Plugs and Receptacles, ANSI C73.17-1972.

(b) Mobile home service equipment shall also contain a means for connecting a mobile home accessory building or structure or additional electrical equipment located outside a mobile home by a fixed wiring method.

(c) Additional receptacles shall be permitted for connection of electrical equipment located outside the mobile home, and all such 120-volt, single-phase, 15- and 20-ampere receptacles shall be protected by approved ground-fault circuit protection for personnel.

ARTICLE 551. RECREATIONAL VEHICLES AND RECREATIONAL VEHICLE PARKS

A. Recreational Vehicles

551-1. Scope.

(a) The provisions of Part A cover the electrical conductors and equipment installed within or on recreational vehicles and also the conductors that connect them to a supply of electricity. Wherever the requirements of other Articles of this Code and Article 551 differ, the requirements of Article 551 shall apply.

For requirements on the installation of plumbing and heating systems in recreational vehicles, refer to Standard for Recreational Vehicles (NFPA No. 501C-1972).

(b) A recreational vehicle not used for the purposes as defined in Section 551-2 shall not be required to meet the provisions of Part A pertaining to the number or capacity of circuits required. It shall, however, meet all other applicable requirements of this Article if the recreational vehicle is provided with an electrical installation intended to be energized from a 115- or 115/230-volt, AC power-supply system.

(c) Part A covers battery and direct-current power (12-volt or less) systems, combination electrical systems, generator installations, and nominal 115- or 115/230-volt systems.

▲ Some states have laws that require factory inspection of recreational vehicles by state inspectors. Such laws closely follow NFPA No. 501C, Standard for Recreational Vehicles. This standard contains electrical requirements in accordance with part A of Art. 551. It also contains requirements for plumbing and heating systems.

551-2. Definitions.   (See Article 100 for other definitions.)

Air-Conditioning or Comfort-Cooling Equipment: All of that equipment intended or installed for the purpose of processing the treatment of air so as to control simultaneously its temperature, humidity, cleanliness and distribution to meet the requirements of the conditioned space.

Camping Trailer: A vehicular portable unit mounted on wheels and constructed with collapsible partial side walls which fold for towing by another vehicle and unfold at the campsite to provide temporary living quarters for recreational, camping, or travel use. (See "Recreational Vehicle.")

Converter: A device which changes electrical energy from one form to another, as from alternating current to direct current.

Dead Front (As applied to switches, circuit breakers, switchboards, and distribution panelboards):   So designed, constructed and installed that no current-carrying parts are normally exposed on the front.

Disconnecting Means: The necessary equipment usually consisting of a circuit breaker or switch and fuses, and their accessories, located near the point of entrance of supply conductors in a recreational vehicle and intended to constitute the means of cutoff for the supply to that recreational vehicle.

Receptacles used as disconnecting means shall be accessible (as applied to wiring methods) and capable of interrupting their rated current without hazard to the operator.

Distribution Panelboard: A single panel or group of panel units designed for assembly in the form of a single panel; including buses, and with or without switches and/or automatic overcurrent protective devices for the control of light, heat or power circuits of small individual as well as aggregate capacity; designed to be placed in a cabinet or cutout box placed in or against a wall or partition and accessible only from the front.

Low-Voltage: An electromotive force rated nominal 24 volts, nominal or less, supplied from a transformer, converter, or battery.

Motor Home: A vehicular unit designed to provide temporary living quarters for recreational, camping or travel use built on or permanently attached to a self-propelled motor vehicle chassis or on a chassis cab or van which is an integral part of the completed vehicle. (See "Recreational Vehicle.")

Power-Supply Assembly: The conductors, including the grounding conductors, insulated from one another, the connectors, attachment plug caps, and all other fittings, grommets, or devices installed for the purpose of delivering energy from the source of electrical supply to the distribution panel within the recreational vehicle.

Recreational Vehicle: A vehicular type unit primarily designed as temporary living quarters for recreational, camping, or travel use, which either has its own motive power or is mounted on or drawn by another vehicle. The basic entities are: travel trailer, camping trailer, truck camper and motor home.

Transformer: A device, which when used, will raise or lower the voltage of alternating current of the original source.

Travel Trailer: A vehicular unit mounted on wheels, designed to provide temporary living quarters for recreational, camping, or travel use, of such size or weight as not to require special highway movement permits when drawn by a motorized vehicle, and with a living area of less than 220 square feet, excluding built-in equipment (such as wardrobes, closets, cabinets, kitchen units or fixtures) and bath and toilet rooms. (See "Recreational Vehicle.")

Truck Camper: A portable unit constructed to provide temporary living quarters for recreational, travel, or camping use, consisting of a roof, floor, and sides, designed to be loaded onto and unloaded from the bed of a pick-up truck. (See "Recreational Vehicle.")

551-3. Low-Voltage Systems.

▲ Sections 551-3, 551-4, and 551-5 concern 12-V systems for running and signal lights similar to those in conventional automobile systems. Also, many recreational vehicles use 12-V systems for interior lighting or other small loads. The 12-V system is derived from an on-board battery or through a transfer switch from a 120/12-V transformer often equipped with a full-wave rectifier.

(a) Low-Voltage Circuits. Low-voltage circuits furnished and installed by the recreational vehicle manufacturer, other than those related to braking, are subject to this Code. Circuits supplying lights subject to Federal or State regulations shall be in accordance with applicable government regulations, but shall not be lower than provided by this Code.

(b) Low-Voltage Wiring Materials.

(1) Copper conductors shall be used for low-voltage circuits.

(2) The insulation of low-voltage conductors shall be rated at least 60°C.

(3) Conductors furnished and installed by the recreational vehicle manufacturer shall have a minimum of 30 mils thermoplastic insulation or equal.

(4) The insulation of outdoor or under-chassis wire shall be moisture and heat resistant, Type THW or equivalent.

(5) Single-wire, low-voltage conductors shall be of the stranded type.

Exception: Metal chassis or frame shall be permitted as the return path for exterior lighting. Terminals for connection to the chassis or frame shall be of the solderless type and approved for the size and type wire used. Mechanical connections to the frame or chassis shall be made secure.

(c) Low-Voltage Wiring Methods.

(1) Conductors shall be protected against physical damage and shall be secured. Where insulated conductors are clamped to the structure, the conductor insulation shall be supplemented by an additional wrap or layer of equivalent material, except that jacketed cables need not be so protected. Wiring shall be routed away from sharp edges, moving parts or heat sources.

(2) Conductors shall be spliced or joined with approved splicing devices or by brazing, welding, or soldering with a fusible metal or alloy. Soldered splices shall first be so spliced or joined as to be mechanically and electrically secure without solder and then soldered. All splices, joints, and free ends of conductors shall be covered with an insulation equivalent to that on the conductors.

(3) Battery and direct-current circuits shall be physically separated by at least a ½-inch gap or other approved means, from circuits of a different power source. Acceptable methods shall be by clamping, routing, or equivalent means which ensure permanent total separation.

(d) Battery Installations. Storage batteries subject to the provisions of this Code shall be securely attached to the vehicle and installed in an area vaportight to the interior and ventilated directly to the exterior of the vehicle. When batteries are installed in a compartment, the compartment shall be ventilated with openings of not less than 2 square inches at the top and 2 square inches at the bottom. Batteries shall not be installed in a compartment containing spark or flame producing equipment.

(e) Overcurrent Protection.

(1) Low-voltage circuit wiring shall be protected by overcurrent protective devices rated not in excess of the ampacity of copper conductors, as follows:

Wire Size	Ampacity	Wire Type
18	6	Stranded only
16	8	Stranded only
14	15	Stranded or Solid
12	20	Stranded or Solid
10	30	Stranded or Solid

(2) Circuit breakers or fuses shall be of an approved type, including automotive types. Fuseholders shall be clearly marked with maximum fuse size.

For further information, see Society of Automotive Engineers (SAE) Standard J554-1968, and Standard for Electric Fuses, ANSI C118.1-1973 and Underwriters' Laboratories, Inc. Standard for Automotive Glass Tube Fuses, UL 275b-1973.

(3) Higher current-consuming direct-current appliances such as pumps, compressors, heater blowers and similar motor-driven appliances shall be installed in accordance with the manufacturer's instructions.

Motors which are controlled by automatic switching or by latching-type manual switches shall be protected in accordance with Section 430-32(c).

(4) The overcurrent protective device shall be installed in an accessible location on the vehicle as close as practical to the point where the power supply connects to the vehicle circuits. If located outside the recreational vehicle, the device shall be protected against weather and physical damage.

(f) Switches. Switches shall be rated at not less than the connected load.

551-4. Combination Electrical Systems.

(a) General. Vehicle wiring suitable for connection to a battery or direct-current supply source shall be permitted to be connected to a 115-volt source provided that the entire wiring system and equipment are rated and installed in full conformity with Part A requirements covering 115-volt electrical systems. Circuits fed from alternating-current transformers shall not supply direct-current appliances.

(b) Voltage Converters (115-Volts Alternating Current to Low-Voltage Direct Current). The 115-volt alternating current side of voltage converters shall be wired in full conformity with Part A requirements for 115-volt electrical systems. Converters supplied as an integral part of an approved appliance shall not be subject to the above. All converters and transformers shall be listed and shall be used within their marked electrical ratings.

(c) Dual-Voltage Fixtures or Appliances. Fixtures or appliances having both 115-volt and low-voltage connections shall be approved for dual voltage.

▲ Such fixtures must have barriers to separate 115-V and 12-V wiring and connections.

(d) Autotransformers. Autotransformers shall not be used.

(e) Receptacles and Plug Caps. When a recreational vehicle is equipped with a 120-volt or 120/240-volt alternating-current system and/or a low-voltage system, receptacles and plug caps of the low-voltage system shall differ in configuration from those of the 120- or 120/240-volt system.

(f) Identification.

(1) When a vehicle equipped with a battery or direct-current system has an external connection for low-voltage power, the receptacle shall have a configuration that will not accept 120-volt power. The vehicle shall have permanently affixed on the outside wall, adjacent to the point of entrance of the power supply conductors, a tag which reads:

THIS CONNECTION IS FOR LOW-VOLTAGE BATTERY OR DIRECT CURRENT ONLY. DO NOT CONNECT TO 120 OR 240 VOLTS AC.

(2) The tag shall be 3 inches by $1\frac{3}{4}$ inches minimum size, made of etched, metal-stamped or embossed brass, stainless steel, anodized or alclad aluminum not less than 0.020 inch thick, or other approved material (e.g., 0.005-inch plastic laminates).

551-5. Generator Installations.

(a) Mounting. Generators shall be mounted in such a manner as to be effectively bonded to the recreational vehicle chassis.

(b) Generator Protection. Equipment shall be installed to ensure that the generator is disconnected when the vehicle is energized from an outside source and to ensure that the outside source is disconnected when the vehicle is energized by the generator. The generator field shall be protected by appropriately rated, approved equipment.

(c) Installation of Storage Batteries and Generators. Storage batteries and internal-combustion-driven generator units (subject to the provisions of this Code) shall be secured in place to avoid displacement from vibration and road shock and shall be installed in a compartment which is vaportight to the interior of the vehicle.

(d) Ventilation of Generator Compartments. Compartments accommodating internal-combustion-driven generator units shall be provided with approved ventilation in accordance with instructions provided by the manufacturer of the generator unit.

(e) Location of Internal-Combustion-Engine Generator Exhaust. Exhaust from generator internal-combustion engines shall not terminate adjacent to the vehicle gasoline-tank filler-spout inlet.

(f) Supply Conductors. Supply conductors from the generators to the junction box (having a blank cover) on the compartment wall shall be of the stranded type installed in flexible conduit.

551-6. 115- or 115/230-Volt, Nominal Systems.

(a) General Requirements. The electrical equipment and material of recreational vehicles indicated for connection to a wiring system nominally rated 115 volts, 2-wire with ground, or a wiring system nominally rated 115/230 volts, 3-wire with ground, shall be approved and installed in accordance with the requirements of Part A.

(b) Materials and Equipment. Electrical materials, devices, appliances, fittings, and other equipment installed, intended for use in, or attached to the recreational vehicle shall be approved for the purpose. All products shall be used only in the manner in which they have been tested and found suitable for the intended use.

551-7. Receptacle Outlets Required.

(a) Receptacle outlets shall be installed at wall spaces 2 feet wide or more so that no point along the floor line is more than 6 feet, measured horizontally, from an outlet in that space.

Exception No. 1: Bath and hall areas.

Exception No. 2: Wall spaces occupied by kitchen cabinets, wardrobe cabinets, built-in furniture, behind doors which may open fully against a wall surface, or similar facilities.

(b) Receptacle outlets shall be installed:

(1) Adjacent to counter tops in the kitchen (at least one on each side of the sink if counter tops are on each side and are 12 inches or over in width).

(2) Adjacent to the refrigerator and gas range space, except when a gas-fired refrigerator or cooking appliance, requiring no external electrical connection, is factory-installed.

(3) Adjacent to counter top spaces (and built-in vanities) which cannot be reached from a receptacle required in Section 551-7(b)(1) by a cord of 6 feet without crossing a traffic area, cooking appliance or sink.

(c) When installed adjacent to a bathroom lavatory, the receptacle outlet shall be a minimum of 30 inches from the floor. The receptacle outlet shall be permitted in an approved lighting fixture. A receptacle outlet shall not be installed in a tub or combination shower compartment.

(d) A receptacle shall not be installed in a face-up position in any counter top or similar horizontal surfaces within the living area.

551-8. Branch Circuits Required. The branch circuits required in a recreational vehicle shall conform to Section 551-19 and be determined in accordance with subparagraphs (a), (b), (c) or (d) below, When provisions are made to facilitate future installations of an electrical appliance, the anticipated load of such appliance shall be counted in the total rating of fixed appliances (e.g., air-conditioning prewiring).

(a) Recreational vehicles with not more than 8 lighting and receptacle outlets combined shall have either:

(1) One 15-ampere general-purpose branch circuit to supply these outlets, provided the total rating of fixed appliances connected to this circuit does not exceed 600 watts, or

(2) One 20-ampere general-purpose branch circuit to supply these outlets, provided the total rating of fixed appliances connected to this circuit does not exceed 1,000 watts.

Vehicles wired in accordance with (a)(1) or (a)(2) above shall not be equipped with electrical heating or cooking appliances.

(b) Recreational vehicles with more than 8 lighting and receptacle outlets combined shall have one 20-ampere appliance branch circuit, and either:

(1) One 15-ampere branch circuit to supply these outlets, provided this circuit does not supply receptacles in the cooking and dining area(s) or electrical heating or cooking appliances, and provided the total rating of fixed appliances connected to this circuit does not exceed 600 watts, or

(2) One 20-ampere branch circuit, to supply these outlets, provided this circuit does not supply receptacles in the cooking and dining area(s) or electrical heating or cooking appliances, and provided the total rating of fixed appliances connected to this circuit does not exceed 1,000 watts.

(c) Recreational vehicles having a distribution panelboard and a feeder assembly rated not less than 30 amperes shall be permitted to serve the following circuits:

(1) One 20-ampere circuit for use with air conditioner rated not more than 16 amperes.

(2) One 20-ampere portable appliance circuit and/or;

(3) One 15-ampere branch circuit for lights and receptacles and fixed appliances rated not more than 600 watts.

(d) Calculations for Lighting and Appliance Load. When Section 551-8(b) (relative to recreational vehicles with more than 8 lighting and receptacle outlets combined) is not applied, the following method shall be employed in computing the power-supply assembly and distribution panelboard load for the recreational vehicle:

A. Lighting. Length times width of vehicle (outside dimensions, exclusive of hitch and cab) times 3 watts per square foot, e.g.,

$$\text{Length} \times \text{width} \times 3 = \underline{\hspace{2cm}} \text{ lighting watts.}$$

B. Small Appliance. Number of circuits times 1,500 watts for each 20-ampere appliance receptacle circuit, e.g.,

$$\text{Number of Circuits} \times 1,500 \underline{\hspace{2cm}} \text{ small appliance watts.}$$

C. Total. Lighting watts plus small appliance watts = _____ total watts.

D. First 3,000 total watts at 100 percent plus remainder at 35 percent = _____ watts to be divided by voltage to obtain current (amperes) per leg.

	Amperes per Leg	
	A	B

Lighting and small appliance current (amperes) per leg (from D above) = _____

E. Add nameplate amperes for motors and heater loads (exhaust fans, air conditioners*, electric, gas, or oil heating*) = _____
  *Omit smaller of these two except include any motor common to both functions.

F. Add 25 percent of amperes of largest motor in E = _____

G. Add nameplate amperes for:** _____

Disposal	_____	_____
Water Heater	_____	_____
Wall-Mounted Ovens	_____	_____
Cooking Units	_____	_____

TOTAL   _____   _____ = _____

**When number of appliances is four or more, use 75 percent of total.

H. Add amperes for free-standing range as distinguished from separate ovens and cooking units. Derive from following table by dividing watts by 230 volts.

Range	Nameplate Rating (watts)	Use (watts)
(Free-standing range	10,000 or less	80 percent of rating
as distinguished	10,001–12,500	8,000
from separate oven	12,501–13,500	8,400
and cooking units)	13,501–14,500	8,800
	14,501–15,500	9,200
	15,501–16,500	9,600
	16,501–17,500	10,000

	Amperes per Leg	
	A	B

I. If outlets or circuits are provided for other than factory-installed major appliances, the anticipated load shall be added for each.

TOTAL = _____

When the total for Legs A and B are unequal, use the larger to determine the distribution panelboard and supply cord rating. (Service amperes shall not exceed supply cord rating. See Section 551-10.)

551-9. Branch-Circuit Protection.

(a) The branch-circuit overcurrent devices shall be rated:

(1) Not more than the circuit conductors; and

(2) Not more than 150 percent of the rating of a single appliance rated 10 amperes or more and supplied by an individual branch circuit; but

(3) Not more than the fuse size marked on an air conditioner or other motor-operated appliances.

(b) A 20-ampere fuse or circuit breaker shall be considered adequate protection for fixture leads, cords, or portable appliances, and No. 14 tap conductors, not over 6 feet long for recessed lighting fixtures.

(c) If more than one outlet or load is on a branch circuit, a 15-ampere receptacle shall be considered protected by a 20-ampere fuse or circuit breakers.

551-10. Power-Supply Assembly.

(a) Recreational vehicles wired in accordance with Section 551-8(a)(1) shall use an approved 15-ampere, or larger, main power-supply assembly.

(b) Recreational vehicles wired in accordance with Section 551-8(a)(2) shall use an approved 20-ampere, or larger, main power-supply assembly.

(c) Recreational vehicles wired in accordance with Section 551-8(b) or 551-8(c) shall use an approved 30-ampere, or larger, main power-supply assembly.

(d) In accordance with Section 551-8(c), any recreational vehicle with a rating in excess of 30 amperes, 115 volts, shall use an approved 40-ampere or 50-ampere 115/230-volt power-supply assembly.

Exception No. 1: When the calculated load of the recreational vehicle exceeds 30 amperes, 115 volts, a second power-supply cord shall be permitted. Where a two-cord supply system is installed, they shall not be interconnected on either the line side or the load side. The grounding circuits and grounding means shall be electrically interconnected.

Exception No. 2: For a dual-supply source consisting of a generator and a power supply cord, see Section 551-12.

551-11. Distribution Panelboard.

(a) A listed and appropriately rated distribution panelboard or other equipment specifically listed for the purpose shall be used. The distribution panelboard shall be of the insulated neutral type, with the grounding bar attached to the metal frame of the panelboard or other approved grounding means.

(b) The distribution panelboard shall be installed in a readily accessible location and shall be permitted in a closet.

(c) The distribution panelboard shall be of the dead-front type and shall consist of one or more circuit breakers or Type S fuseholders. A main disconnecting means shall be provided where fuses are used or where more than two circuit breakers are employed.

551-12. Dual-Supply Source.

(a) Where a dual-supply system, consisting of a generator and a power-supply cord is installed, the feeder from the generator shall be protected by an overcurrent protective device. Installation shall be in accordance with Sections 551-5(a) and 551-5(b).

(b) Calculation of loads shall be in accordance with Section 551-8(d).

(c) The two supply sources shall not be required to be of the same capacity.

(d) If the AC generator source exceeds 30 amperes, 115 volts, it shall be permissible to wire either as a 115-volt system or a 115/230-volt system, providing an overcurrent protective device of the proper rating is installed in the feeder.

(e) The external power-supply assembly shall be permitted to be less than the calculated load but not less than 30 amperes and shall have overcurrent protection not greater than the capacity of the external power-supply assembly.

551-13. Means for Connecting to Power Supply.

(a) Assembly. The power-supply assembly or assemblies shall be factory-supplied or factory-installed when of the permanently connected type as specified herein:

(1) Separable. When a separable power-supply assembly consisting of a cord with a female connector and molded attachment plug cap is provided, the vehicle shall be equipped with a permanently mounted, approved, male-recessed-type motor-base receptacle wired directly to the distribution panelboard by an approved wiring method. The attachment plug cap shall be of an approved type.

(2) Permanently Connected. Each power-supply assembly shall be connected directly to the terminals of the distribution panelboard or conductors within an approved junction box and provided with means to prevent strain from being transmitted to the terminals. The ampacity of the conductors between each junction box and the terminals of each distribution panelboard shall be at least equal to the ampacity of the power-supply cord. The supply end of the assembly shall be equipped with an attachment plug of the type described in Section 551-13(c). Where the cord passes through the walls or floors, it shall be protected by means of conduit and bushings or equivalent.

(b) Cord. The cord set shall be approved for use with recreational vehicles. The cord shall be not less than 20 feet as measured from the point of entrance to the recreational vehicle or the face of the motorbase attachment plug nor more than $26\frac{1}{2}$ feet in length overall to the face of the attachment plug at the supply end.

(c) Attachment Plugs.

(1) Recreational vehicles having only one 15-ampere branch circuit as permitted by Section 551-8(a)(1) shall have an attachment plug which shall be 2-pole, 3-wire, grounding-type, rated 15 amperes, 125 volts, conforming to the configuration shown in Figure 551-13(c).

Complete details of this configuration can be found in American National Standard ANSI C73.11-1972.

(2) Recreational vehicles having only one 20-ampere branch circuit as permitted in Section 551-8(a)(2) shall have an attachment plug which shall be 2-pole, 3-wire, grounding-type, rated 20 amperes, 125 volts, conforming to the configuration shown in Figure 551-13(c).

Complete details of this configuration can be found in American National Standard ANSI C73.12-1972.

(3) Recreational vehicles wired in accordance with Sections 551-8(b) or 551-8(c) shall have an attachment plug which shall be 2-pole, 3-wire, grounding-type, rated 30 amperes, 125 volts, conforming to the configuration shown in Figure 551-13(c) intended for use with units rated at 30 amperes, 125 volts.

Complete details of this configuration can be found in American National Standard Dimensions of Caps, Plugs and Receptacles, ANSI C73.13-1972.

(4) Recreational vehicles having a power-supply assembly rated 40 amperes or 50 amperes as permitted by Section 551-8(c) shall have a 3-pole, 4-wire, grounding-type attachment plug rated 50 amperes, 125/250 volts, conforming to the configuration shown in Figure 551-13(c).

Complete details of this configuration can be found in American National Standard Dimensions of Caps, Plugs and Receptacles, ANSI C73.13-1972.

Figure 551-13(c). Configurations for grounding-type receptacles and attachment plug caps used for recreational vehicle supply cords and recreational vehicle lots.

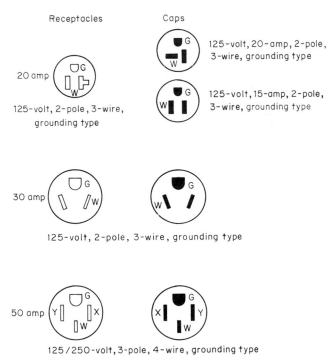

Receptacles   Caps

125-volt, 20-amp, 2-pole, 3-wire, grounding type

20 amp

125-volt, 2-pole, 3-wire, grounding type

125-volt, 15-amp, 2-pole, 3-wire, grounding type

30 amp

125-volt, 2-pole, 3-wire, grounding type

50 amp

125/250-volt, 3-pole, 4-wire, grounding type

(d) Labeling at Electrical Entrance. Each recreational vehicle shall have permanently affixed to the exterior skin at or near the point of entrance of the power-supply cord(s) a tag 3 inches by 1¾ inches minimum size, made of etched, metal-stamped or embossed brass, stainless steel, anodized or alclad aluminum not less than 0.020 inch thick, or other approved material (e.g., 0.005 inch plastic laminates), which reads, as appropriate, either:

"This connection is for 110-125-volt AC, 60-Hz (Cycles) service. Do not connect to higher voltage"; or

"This connection is for 3-wire 120/240-volt AC, 60-Hz (Cycles) _____ ampere service." The correct ampere rating shall be marked in the blank space.

(e) Location. The point of entrance of a power-supply assembly shall be located within 25 feet of the rear, on the left (road) side or at the rear, left of the longitudinal center of the vehicle, within 18 inches of the outside wall.

Exception: A trailer having a gross vehicle weight rating of 1,500 pounds or less, a motor home, or a truck camper shall be permitted to have the electrical point of entrance located on either side provided the main drain outlet is located on the same side.

551-14. Wiring Methods.

(a) Electrical metallic tubing, flexible metal conduit, metal-clad cable, and nonmetallic-sheathed cable with a grounding conductor, shall terminate by means of fittings, clamps or connectors approved for the purpose. Flexible metal conduit shall be permitted as a grounding means where both the conduit and the fittings are approved for the purpose.

(b) Rigid metal conduit shall be provided with a locknut inside and outside the box, and a conduit bushing shall be used on the inside. Inside ends of the conduit shall be reamed.

(c) Nonmetallic outlet boxes shall be acceptable only with nonmetallic-sheathed cable.

(d) In walls and ceilings constructed of wood or other combustible material, outlet boxes and fittings shall be flush with the finished surface or project therefrom.

(e) Wall and ceiling outlets shall be mounted in accordance with Article 370.

Exception: Snap-in type boxes or boxes provided with special wall or ceiling brackets that securely fasten boxes in walls or ceilings shall be permitted.

(f) The sheath of nonmetallic cable or the armor of metal-clad cable shall be continuous between outlet boxes and other enclosures.

(g) Metal-clad and nonmetallic cables shall be permitted to pass through the centers of the wide side of 2-inch by 4-inch studs. However, they shall be protected where they pass through 2-inch by 2-inch studs or at other studs or frames where the cable would be less than $1\frac{1}{2}$ inches from the inside or outside surface. Steel plates on each side of the cable, or a steel tube, with not less than No 16 MSG wall thickness, shall be installed to protect the cable. These plates or tubes shall be securely held in place.

(h) No bend shall have a radius of less than 5 times the cable diameter.

(i) When connected with cable connectors or clamps, cables shall be supported within 12 inches of outlet boxes, distribution panelboards, and splice boxes on appliances. Supports shall be provided every $4\frac{1}{2}$ feet at other places.

(j) Nonmetallic-sheathed cables shall be supported within 8 inches of a nonmetallic outlet box without cable clamps.

Exception: Where approved devices of insulating material are employed with a loop of extra cable to permit future replacement of the device, the cable loop shall be considered as an integral portion of the device.

(k) Where subject to physical damage, exposed nonmetallic cable shall be protected by covering boards, guard strips, or conduit.

(l) Metallic faceplates shall be of ferrous metal not less than 0.030 inch in thickness or of nonferrous metal not less than 0.040 inch in thickness. Nonmetallic faceplates shall be of an approved type.

(m) Where metallic faceplates are used, they shall be effectively grounded.

(n) Where outdoor or underchassis wiring is 115 volts (nominal) or over and is exposed to moisture or physical damage, the wiring shall be protected by rigid metal conduit, or by electrical metallic tubing that is closely routed against frames and equipment enclosures.

551-15. Conductors and Outlet Boxes.

(a) The maximum number of conductors permitted in outlet and junction boxes, shall be in accordance with Section 370-6.

Exception: Outlet boxes of dimensions less than those required in Table 370-6(a) of this Code shall be permitted provided the box has been tested and approved for the purpose.

▲ See comments following Sec. 550-8(j).

(b) At least 4 inches of free conductor shall be left at each outlet box except where conductors are intended to loop without joints.

551-16. Grounded Conductors.   The identification of grounded conductors shall be in accordance with Section 200-6.

551-17. Connection of Terminals and Splices.   Conductor splices and connections at terminals shall be in accordance with Section 110-14. If splices of the grounding wire in nonmetallic-sheathed cable are made in outlet boxes, the splices shall be insulated.

551-18. Switches.   Switches shall be rated as follows:

(a) For lighting circuits, switches shall be rated not less than 10 amperes, 120-125 volts and in no case less than the connected load.

(b) For motors or other loads, switches shall have ampere or horsepower ratings, or both, adequate for loads controlled. (An AC general-use snap switch shall be permitted to control a motor 2 horsepower or less with full-load current not over 80 percent of the switch ampere rating.)

551-19. Receptacles.   All receptacle outlets shall be: (1) of the grounding type; and (2) installed in accordance with Sections 210-21 and 210-25.

551-20. Lighting Fixtures.

(a) General.   Any combustible wall or ceiling finish exposed between the edge of a fixture canopy, or pan and the outlet box, shall be covered with noncombustible material of either metal equal to the thickness of the fixture or asbestos of $\frac{1}{16}$ inch.

(b) Shower Fixtures.   If a lighting fixture is provided over a bathtub or in a shower stall, it shall be of the enclosed and gasketed type and approved for the type of installation.

The switch for shower lighting fixtures and exhaust fans, located over a tub or in a shower stall, shall be located outside the tub or shower space.

(c) Outdoor Outlets, Fixtures, Air-Cooling Equipment, Etc.   Outdoor fixtures and other equipment shall be approved for outdoor use.

551-21. Grounding.   (See also Section 551-23 on bonding of noncurrent-carrying metal parts.)

(a) Power-Supply Grounding.   The grounding conductor in the supply cord or feeder shall be connected to the grounding bus or other approved grounding means in the distribution panelboard.

(b) Distribution Panelboard.   The distribution panelboard shall have a grounding bus with sufficient terminals for all grounding conductors or other approved grounding means.

(c) Insulated Neutral.

(1) The grounded circuit conductor (neutral) shall be insulated from the equipment grounding conductors and from equipment enclosures and other grounded parts. The grounded (neutral) circuit terminals in the distribution panelboard and in ranges, clothes dryers, counter-mounted cooking units, and wall-mounted ovens shall be insulated from the equipment enclosure. Bonding screws, straps or buses in the distribution panelboard or in appliances shall be removed and discarded.

(2) Connection of electric ranges and electric clothes dryers utilizing a grounded (neutral) conductor, if cord-connected, shall be made with 4-conductor cord and 3-pole, 4-wire grounding-type plug caps and receptacles.

551-22. Interior Equipment Grounding.

(a) In the electrical system, all exposed metal parts, enclosures, frames, lighting fixture canopies, etc., shall be effectively bonded to the grounding terminals or enclosure of the distribution panelboard.

(b) Bare wires, green-colored wires, or green wires with yellow stripe(s) shall be used for equipment grounding conductors only.

(c) Where grounding of electrical equipment is specified, it shall be permitted as follows:

(1) Connection by metallic raceway (conduit or electrical metallic tubing) or the sheath of metal-clad cable to metallic outlet boxes.

(2) A connection between the one or more grounding conductors and a metallic box by means of a grounding screw, which shall be used for no other purpose, or an approved grounding device.

(3) The grounding wire in nonmetallic-sheathed cable shall be permitted to be secured under a screw threaded into the fixture canopy other than a mounting screw or cover screw; or attached to an approved grounding means (plate) in a nonmetallic outlet box for fixture mounting (grounding means shall also be permitted for fixture attachment screws).

(d) A connection between the one or more grounding conductors brought into a nonmetallic outlet box shall be so arranged that a connection can be made to any fitting or device in that box that requires grounding.

(e) Where more than one equipment grounding conductor of a branch circuit enters a box, all such conductors shall be in good electrical contact with each other, and the arrangement shall be such that the disconnection or removal of a receptacle, fixture, or other device fed from the box will not interfere with or interrupt the grounding continuity.

(f) Cord-connected appliances, such as washing machines, clothes dryers, refrigerators, and the electrical system of gas ranges, etc., shall be grounded by means of an approved cord with grounding conductor and grounding-type attachment plug.

551-23. Bonding of Noncurrent-Carrying Metal Parts.

(a) All exposed noncurrent-carrying metal parts that may become energized shall be effectively bonded to the grounding terminal or enclosure of the distribution panelboard.

(b) A bonding conductor shall be connected between any distribution panelboard and an accessible terminal on the chassis.

Exception: Any recreational vehicle which employs a unitized metal chassis-frame construction to which the distribution panelboard is securely fastened with a bolt(s) and nut(s) or by welding or riveting shall be considered to be bonded.

(c) Grounding terminals shall be of the solderless type and approved as pressure terminal connectors recognized for the wire size used. The bonding conductor shall be solid or stranded, insulated or bare, and shall be No. 8 copper minimum, or equal.

(d) The metallic roof and exterior covering shall be considered bonded if:

(1) The metal panels overlap one another and are securely attached to the wood or metal frame parts by metallic fasteners, and

(2) The lower panel of the metallic exterior covering is secured by metallic fasteners at each cross member of the chassis, or the lower panel is bonded to the chassis by a metal strap.

(e) The gas, water and waste pipes shall be considered grounded if they are bonded to the chassis.

See Section 551-23(b) for chassis bonding.

(f) Furnace and metallic circulating air ducts shall be bonded.

551-24. Appliance Accessibility. Every appliance shall be accessible for inspection, service, repair and replacement without removal of permanent construction.

551-25. Factory Tests (Electrical).

Electrical Factory Test. Each recreational vehicle shall be subjected to the following tests:

(a) Circuits of 115 Volts or 115/230 Volts. Each recreational vehicle designed with a 115-volt or a 115/230-volt electrical system shall withstand the applied potential without electrical breakdown of a one-minute, 900-volt dielectric strength test, or a one-second, 1080-volt dielectric strength test, with all switches closed, between current-carrying conductors, including neutral, and the recreational vehicle ground. During the test, all switches and other controls shall be in the "on" position. Fixtures and permanently installed appliances shall not be required to withstand this test.

Each recreational vehicle shall be subjected to:

(1) a continuity test to assure that all metallic parts are properly bonded,

(2) operational tests to demonstrate that all equipment is properly connected and in working order, and

(3) polarity checks to determine that connections have been properly made.

(b) Low-Voltage Circuits. Low-voltage circuit conductors in each recreational vehicle shall withstand the applied potential without electrical breakdown of a one-minute, 500-volt or a one second, 600-volt dielectric strength test. The potential shall be applied between live and grounded conductors.

The test shall be permitted on running light circuits before the lights are installed provided the vehicle's outer covering and interior cabinetry has been secured. The braking circuit shall be permitted to be tested before being connected to the brakes, provided the wiring has been completely secured.

B. Recreational Vehicle Parks

551-40. Application and Scope. Part B covers electrical systems on recreational vehicle parks. It does not apply to the electrical systems of recreational vehicles or the conductors that connect them to the park electrical supply facilities. Wherever the requirements of other Articles of this Code and Article 551 differ, the requirements of Article 551 shall apply.

551-41. Definitions.

Lot: The area in a recreational park intended for the connection of one recreational vehicle.

Power-Supply Assembly: The conductors, including the grounding conductors, insulated from one another, the connectors, attachment plug caps, and all other fittings, grommets, or devices installed for the purpose of delivering energy from the source of electrical supply to the distribution panelboard within the recreational vehicle.

Recreational Vehicle Lot Electric Supply Equipment: The necessary equipment, usually a power outlet, consisting of a circuit breaker or switch and fuse and their accessories, located near the point of entrance of supply conductors to a recreational vehicle lot and intended to constitute the disconnecting means for the supply to that lot.

Recreational Vehicle Park: Recreational vehicle park is the contiguous parcel of land which is used for the accommodation of occupied recreational vehicles.

551-42. Receptacles Required. A minimum of 75 percent of all lots with electrical supply shall each be equipped with a 20-ampere and 30-ampere 125-volt receptacle conforming to Figure 551-13(c). The remainder of all lots with electrical supply shall each be equipped with a 20-ampere 125-volt receptacle conforming to Figure 551-13(c).

Exception: Where the type of lot justifies, special permission may be given to alter the percentage of lots to be equipped with both 20-ampere and 30-ampere receptacles, as specified herein.

Complete details of these receptacle configurations can be found in American National Standard Dimensions of Caps, Plugs, and Receptacles, ANSI C73.12-1972 (20 ampere) and ANSI C73.13-1972 (30 ampere).

551-43. Distribution System. The recreational vehicle park secondary electrical distribution system to recreational vehicle lots shall be derived from a single-phase 120/240-volt, 3-wire system.

▲ See comments in first paragraph following Sec. 550-21.

551-44. Calculated Load.

(a) Electrical service and feeders shall be calculated on the basis of not less than 3,600 watts per lot equipped with both 20-ampere and 30-ampere supply facilities and 2,400 watts per lot equipped with only 20-ampere supply facilities. The demand factors set forth in Table 551-44 shall be the minimum allowable demand factors that shall be permitted in calculating load for service and feeders.

Table 551-44. Demand Factors for Feeders and Service-Entrance Conductors for Park Lots

Number of Recreational Vehicle Lots	Demand Factor (percent)	Number of Recreational Vehicle Lots	Demand Factor (percent)
1	100	10–12	29
2	100	13–15	28
3	70	16–18	27
4	55	19–21	26
5	44	22–40	25
6	39	41–100	24
7–9	33	101 and over	23

(b) For the purpose of this Code, where the park service exceeds 240 volts, transformers and secondary distribution panelboards shall be treated as services.

(c) The demand factor for a given number of lots shall apply to all lots indicated. For example: 20 lots calculated at 26 percent of 3,600 watts result in a permissible demand of 936 watts per lot or a total of 18,720 watts for 20 lots.

(d) Recreational vehicle lot feeder circuit conductors shall have adequate ampacity for the loads supplied, and shall be rated at not less than 30 amperes.

551-45. Overcurrent Protection. Overcurrent protection shall be provided in accordance with Article 240.

551-46. Grounding. All electrical equipment and installations in recreational vehicle parks shall be grounded as required by Article 250.

551-47. Recreational Vehicle Lot Electric Supply Equipment.

(a) Disconnecting Means. A disconnecting switch or circuit breaker shall be provided in the lot supply equipment for disconnecting the power supply to the recreational vehicle.

(b) Access. All lot supply equipment shall be accessible by an unobstructed entrance or passageway not less than two feet wide and 6½ feet high.

(c) Mounting Height. Lot supply equipment shall be located not less than 2 feet nor more than 6½ feet above the ground.

(d) Working Space. Sufficient space shall be provided and maintained about all electrical equipment to permit ready and safe operation, in accordance with Section 110-16.

551-48. Grounding, Recreational Vehicle Lot Supply Equipment.

(a) Exposed noncurrent-carrying metal parts of fixed equipment, metal boxes, cabinets and fittings, which are not electrically connected to grounded equipment shall be grounded by a continuous grounding conductor run with the circuit conductors from the service equipments or from the transformer of a secondary distribution system.

(b) Each secondary distribution system shall be grounded at the transformer.

(c) The neutral conductor shall not be used as an equipment ground for recreational vehicles or equipment within the recreational vehicle park.

(d) No connection to a grounding electrode shall be made to the neutral conductor on the load side of the service disconnecting means or transformer distribution panelboard.

551-49. Protection of Outdoor Equipment.

(a) Wet Locations. All switches, circuit breakers, receptacles, control equipment and metering devices located in wet places or outside of a building shall be rainproof equipment.

(b) Meters. If secondary meters are installed, meter sockets without meters installed shall be blanked off with an approved blanking plate.

551-50. Overhead Conductors.

(a) Vertical Clearance. Open conductors of not over 600 volts shall have a vertical clearance of not less than 18 feet in all areas subject to recreational vehicle movement. In all other areas, vertical clearances shall conform to Section 225-18.

For clearance of conductors of over 600 volts, see National Electrical Safety Code (ANSI C2-1973).

(b) Horizontal Clearance. The horizontal clearance from structures and recreational vehicles for overhead conductors shall be not less than 3 feet for 600 volts or less.

551-51. Underground Service, Feeder, Branch-Circuit and Recreational Vehicle Lot Feeder Circuit Conductors.

(a) General. All direct-burial conductors, including the equipment grounding conductor if of aluminum, shall be insulated and specifically approved for the purpose. All conductors shall be continuous from fitting to fitting. All splices shall be made in approved junction boxes.

(b) Mechanical Protection. Where underground conductors enter or leave a building or trench, they shall have mechanical protection in the form of rigid metal conduit, electrical metallic tubing or other approved mechanical means, extending a minimum of 18 inches into the trench from the finished grade.

See Section 310-6 and Article 339 for conductors or Type UF cable used underground or in direct burial in earth.

551-52. Receptacles. A receptacle to supply electric power to a recreational vehicle shall be one of the configurations shown in Figure 551-13(c) in the following ratings:

(a) 125/250 volts, 50-ampere, 3-pole, 4-wire, grounding type for 115/230-volt systems.

(b) 125-volt, 30-ampere, 2-pole, 3-wire grounding type for 115-volt systems.

(c) 125-volt, 20-ampere, 2-pole, 3-wire, grounding type for 115-volt systems.

Complete details of these configurations can be found in American National Standard Dimensions of Caps, Plugs and Receptacles, ANSI C73.17-1972; ANSI C73.13-1972; and C73.12-1972.

ARTICLE 555. MARINAS AND BOATYARDS

555-1. Scope. This Article covers the installation of wiring and equipment in the areas comprising fixed or floating piers, wharfs, and docks, and other areas in marinas, boatyards, boat basins, and similar establishments that are used, or intended for use for the purpose of repair, berthing, launching, storage, or fueling of small craft.

555-2. Application of Other Articles. Wiring and equipment for marinas and boatyards shall comply with this Article and also with the applicable provisions of other Articles of this Code.

See notes following Sections 210-19(a) and 215-2(c) for voltage drop on branch circuits and feeders respectively.

555-3. Receptacles. Receptacles that provide shore power for boats shall be rated not less than 20 amperes and shall be single and of the locking and grounding types.

For various configurations and ratings of locking- and grounding-type receptacles and caps, see Dimensions of Caps, Plugs, and Receptacles (ANSI C73-1972).

▲ Figure 555-1 shows typical configurations of locking- and grounding-type receptacles and attachment plugs used in marinas and boatyards. A complete chart of these devices can be obtained from the National Electrical Manufacturers Association or various wiring-device manufacturers. Locking-type receptacles and caps are required to provide proper contact and assurance that attachment plugs will not fall out easily and disconnect on-board equipment such as bilge pumps or refrigerators.

Receptacle   *Cap*

125 volt, 2 pole, 3 wire, grounding type

20 amp

30 amp

Receptacle   *Cap*

125 / 250 volt, 3 pole, 4 wire, grounding type

30 amp

Fig. 555-1. Typical configurations for receptacles and attachment plug caps of the locking and grounding types used in marinas and boatyards.

According to Sec. 555-4 each of these single receptacles must be installed on an individual branch circuit.

See configuration chart following Sec. 210-7(f).

555-4. Branch Circuits. Each single receptacle that supplies shore power to boats shall be supplied from a power outlet or panelboard by an individual branch circuit of the voltage class and rating corresponding to the rating of the receptacle.

555-5. Feeders and Services. The load for each ungrounded feeder and service conductor supplying receptacles that supply shore power for boats shall be calculated as follows:

For 1 to 4 receptacles—100 percent of the sum of the rating of the receptacles.

For 5 to 8 receptacles—90 percent of the sum of the rating of the receptacles.

For 9 to 13 receptacles—80 percent of the sum of the rating of the receptacles.

For 14 or more receptacles—70 percent of the sum of the rating of the receptacles.

555-6. Wiring Methods. Where exposed to the weather or water, the wiring method shall be one or more of the following:

(1) Rigid nonmetallic conduit approved for the purpose.

(2) Mineral-insulated metal-sheathed cable.

(3) Nonmetallic cable approved for the purpose.

(4) Corrosion-resistant rigid metal conduit approved for the purpose.

(5) Underground wiring that complies with the requirements of this Code.

Exception No. 1: Where flexibility is required, other types approved for the purpose.

Exception No. 2: Open wiring shall be permitted by special permission.

In granting special permission, major factors include possible contact of open wires with masts, cranes, or similar structures or equipment.

See Fire Protection Standard for Marinas and Boatyards (NFPA No. 303-1969) for further information on wiring methods for various locations.

555-7. Grounding.

(a) Equipment to Be Grounded. The following items shall be connected to an equipment grounding conductor run with the circuit conductors in a raceway or cable:

(1) Boxes, cabinets, and all other metal enclosures.

(2) Metal frames of utilization equipment.

(3) Grounding terminals of grounding-type receptacles.

(b) Type of Equipment Grounding Conductor. The equipment grounding conductor shall be an insulated copper conductor with a continuous outer finish that is either green or green with one or more yellow stripes.

(c) Size of Equipment Grounding Conductor. The insulated copper equipment grounding conductor shall be sized in accordance with Section 250-95 but not smaller than No. 12.

(d) Branch-Circuit Equipment Grounding Conductor. The insulated equipment grounding conductor for branch circuits shall terminate at a grounding terminal in a remote panelboard or the grounding terminal in the main service equipment.

(e) Feeder Equipment Grounding Conductors. Where a feeder supplies a remote panelboard, an insulated equipment grounding conductor shall extend from a grounding terminal in the service equipment to a grounding terminal in the remote panelboard.

▲ **The purpose of Sec. 555-7 is to require an insulated equipment grounding wire that will ensure a grounding circuit of high integrity. Due to the corrosive influences around marinas and boatyards, metal raceways and boxes are not permitted to serve as equipment grounding conductors.**

555-8. Wiring Over and Under Navigable Water. Wiring over and under navigable water shall be subject to approval by the authority having jurisdiction.

▲ **There are some federal and local agencies that have specific control over navigable waterways. Accordingly, any proposed installations over or under such waterways should be cleared with the appropriate authorities.**

555-9. Gasoline Dispensing Stations-Hazardous
         (Classified) Locations.

(a) The following spaces shall be considered a Class I, Division 1 location:

(1) The space within the dispenser from its base to a level measured 4 feet vertically from its base.

(2) The space outside the dispenser for a distance measured 4 feet horizontally from all points of the dispenser and measured vertically upwards for a distance of 18 inches from the base of the dispenser.

(3) The entire space between the base of the dispenser and the lowest water surface for a distance of 4 feet measured horizontally from any point on the outside of the dispenser.

(b) In an outside location, the following space shall be considered a Class I, Division 2 location (spaces which are Class I, Division 1 as defined above are excluded. Buildings within the following space which are not suitably cut off shall be included). This space shall include the entire volume enveloped within the following limits:

(1) A horizontal limit of 20 feet from all points on the exterior enclosure of a dispenser.

(2) An upper limit of 18 inches measured vertically from the base of the dispenser.

(3) A lower limit which shall be the lowest water surface.

555-11. Sealing.

(a) At Dispenser. An approved seal shall be provided in each conduit run entering or leaving a dispenser or any cavities or enclosures in direct communication therewith.

(b) At Boundary. Additional seals shall be provided in accordance with Section 501-5. Sections 501-5(a)(4) and 501-5(b)(2) shall apply to horizontal as well as to vertical boundaries of the defined hazardous (classified) locations.

CHAPTER SIX

Special Equipment

ARTICLE 600. ELECTRIC SIGNS AND OUTLINE LIGHTING

A. General

600-1. Scope. This Article covers the installation of conductors and equipment for electric signs and outline lighting as defined in Article 100.

▲ In the case of signs that are constructed at a shop or factory and sent out complete and ready for erection, the inspection department must require listing and installation in conformance with the listing. In the case of outline lighting and signs that are constructed at the location where they are installed, the inspection department must make a detailed inspection to make sure that all requirements of this article are complied with. In some cities, inspection departments inspect signs in local shops.

600-2. Disconnect Required. Each outline lighting installation, and each sign of other than the portable type, shall be controlled by an externally operable switch or breaker which will open all ungrounded conductors.

(a) In Sight of Sign. The disconnecting means shall be within sight of the sign or outline lighting which it controls.

Exception: Signs operated by electronic or electromechanical controllers located external to the sign shall have a disconnecting means located within sight from the controller location. The disconnecting means shall disconnect the sign and the controller from all ungrounded supply conductors and shall be so designed that no pole can be operated independently. The disconnecting means shall be permitted to be in the same enclosure with the controller. The disconnecting means shall be capable of being locked in the open position.

▲ Figures 600-1 and 600-2 depict the disconnecting means that shall be within sight of the sign, outline lighting, or remote controller. However, the term "within sight"

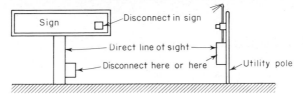

Fig. 600-1. Depicts the disconnecting means placement to satisfy the requirements of Section 600-2(a).

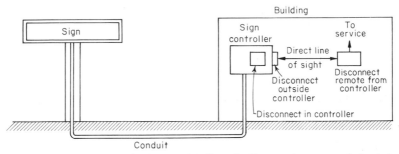

Fig. 600-2. The exception to Section 600-2(a) allows the disconnecting means to be located within sight of the controller where the signs are operated by electronic or electromechanical controllers located external to the sign.

is not clearly defined. It has been well understood that the term "in sight from" specifies that it shall be visible and not more than 50 ft distant from the other as indicated in Sec. 430-4.

(b) Control Switch Rating. Switches, flashers and similar devices controlling transformers shall be either a type approved for the purpose or have an ampere rating not less than twice the ampere rating of the transformer.

Exception: For other than motors, AC general use snap switches shall be permitted to be used on alternating-current circuits to control inductive loads not exceeding the ampere rating of the switch.

See Section 380-14 for rating of Snap Switches.

▲ Any switching device controlling the primary of a transformer that supplies a luminous gas tube operates under unusually severe conditions. In order to avoid rapid deterioration of the switch or flasher due to arcing at the contacts, the device must be a general-use AC snap switch or have a current rating of at least twice the current rating of the transformer it controls.

600-3. Enclosures As Pull Boxes. The wiring method used to supply signs and outline lighting shall terminate in the sign or transformer enclosures.

Exception: Such signs and transformer boxes shall be permitted to be used as pull or junction boxes for conductors supplying other adjacent signs, outline lighting systems and floodlights that are part of signs provided the conductors extending from the equipment are protected by an overcurrent device rated 20 amperes or less.

600-4. Listing Required. Every electric sign of any type, fixed or portable, shall be listed and installed in conformance with that listing.

600-5. Grounding. Signs, troughs, tube terminal boxes, and other metal frames shall be grounded in the manner specified in Article 250.

Exception No. 1: Insulated and Inaccessible. Where they are insulated from ground and from other conducting surfaces and are inaccessible to unauthorized persons, they need not be grounded.

Exception No. 2: Isolated Parts. Isolated noncurrent-carrying metal parts of outline lighting may be bonded by No. 14 conductors and grounded in accordance with Article 250.

Exception No. 3: Portable Signs. Signs of the portable incandescent or fluorescent lamp type in which the open-circuit voltage does not exceed 150 volts to ground are not required to be grounded.

600-6. Branch Circuits.

(a) Rating. Circuits which supply lamps, ballasts, and transformers, or combinations shall be rated not to exceed 20 amperes. Circuits containing electric-discharge lighting transformers exclusively shall not be rated in excess of 30 amperes.

(b) Required Branch Circuit. Each commercial building and each commercial occupancy with ground floor footage shall be provided at an accessible location outside the occupancy, with at least one outlet for sign or outline lighting use. This outlet shall be supplied by an individual 20-ampere branch circuit.

▲ **No limit is placed on the number of outlets that may be connected on one circuit on a sign or for outline lighting, except that the total load shall not exceed the rating of the circuit. Where in normal operation the load will continue for 3 hr or more, the load shall not exceed 80 percent of the branch circuit rating. See Sec. 210-22(c).**

600-7. Marking.

(a) Signs. Signs shall be marked with the maker's name; and, for incandescent lamp signs, with the number of lampholders; and, for electric-discharge-lamp signs, with input amperes at full load and input voltage. The marking of the sign shall be visible after installation.

(b) Transformers. Transformers shall be marked with the maker's name; and transformers for electric-discharge-lamp signs shall be marked with the input rating in amperes or volt-amperes, the input voltage, and the open-circuit output voltage.

600-8. Enclosures.

(a) Conductors and Terminals. Conductors and terminals in sign boxes, cabinets, and outline troughs shall be enclosed in metal or other noncombustible material.

Exception: The supply leads shall not be required to be enclosed.

(b) Cutouts, Flashers, etc. Cutouts, flashers, and similar devices shall be enclosed in metal boxes, the doors of which shall be arranged so they can be opened without removing obstructions or finished parts of the enclosure.

(c) Strength. Enclosures shall have ample strength and rigidity.

(d) Material. Signs and outline lighting shall be constructed of metal or other noncombustible material. Wood shall be permitted for external decoration if placed not less than 2 inches from the nearest lampholder or current-carrying part.

Exception: Portable signs of the indoor type shall not be required to meet this requirement.

(e) Minimum Thickness—Enclosure Metal. Sheet copper shall be at least 20 ounce (0.028 inch). Sheet steel shall be of No. 28 MSG.

Exception: For outline lighting and for electric-discharge signs, sheet steel shall be of No. 24 MSG if not ribbed, corrugated, or embossed over its entire surface and of No. 26 MSG if it is so ribbed, corrugated, or embossed.

(f) Protection of Metal. All steel parts of enclosures shall be galvanized or otherwise protected from corrosion.

(g) Enclosures Exposed to Weather. Enclosures for outdoor use shall be weatherproof and shall have an ample number of drain holes, each not larger than ½ inch or smaller than ¼ inch. Wiring connections shall not be made through the bottoms of nonraintight enclosures exposed to the weather.

600-9. Portable Letters. Portable letters, fixtures, symbols and similar displays used in conjunction with fixed outdoor signs shall only be used when in compliance with all applicable provisions of this Code and, in addition, shall meet all of the following requirements:

(a) A weatherproof receptacle and attachment plug having one pole for grounding shall be provided for each individual letter, fixture, or sign.

(b) All cords shall be Type SJ, SO, or ST 3-conductor, with one conductor grounded as provided in the foregoing.

(c) No cord shall be less than 10 feet from the ground level directly underneath.

600-10. Clearances.

(a) Vertical and Horizontal. Signs and outline system enclosures shall have not less than the vertical and horizontal clearances from open conductors specified in Article 225.

(b) Elevation. The bottom of sign and outline lighting enclosures shall not be less than 16 feet above areas accessible to vehicles.

Exception: The bottom of such enclosures may be less than 16 feet above areas accessible to vehicles where such enclosures are protected from physical damage.

B. 600 Volts, Nominal or Less

600-21. Installation of Conductors.

(a) Wiring Method. Conductors shall be installed in rigid metal conduit, intermediate metal conduit, flexible metal conduit, liquidtight flexible metal conduit, electrical metallic tubing, metal-clad cable, metal troughing, aluminum-sheathed cable, copper-sheathed cable, and mineral-insulated metal-sheathed cable.

(b) Insulation and Size. Conductors shall be of a type approved for general use and shall not be smaller than No. 14.

Exception: Conductors not smaller than No. 18 of a type approved for the purpose shall be permitted:

a. In portable signs.

b. As short leads permanently attached to lampholders or electric-discharge ballasts.

c. As leads not more than 8 feet long permanently attached to electric-discharge lampholders or electric-discharge ballasts if the leads are enclosed in wiring channels.

d. For signs with multiple incandescent lamps requiring one conductor from a control to one or more lamps whose total load does not exceed 250 watts, if in an approved cable assembly of two or more conductors.

(c) Exposed to Weather. Conductors in raceways, metal-clad cable, or enclosures exposed to the weather shall be of the lead-covered type or other type specially approved for the conditions.

Exception: This shall not apply when rigid conduit, electrical metallic tubing, or enclosures are made raintight and arranged to drain.

(d) Number of Conductors in Raceway. The number of conductors in a raceway for sign fixtures shall be in accordance with Table 1 of Chapter 9.

(e) Conductors Soldered to Terminals. Where the conductors are fastened to lampholders other than of the pin type, they shall be soldered to the terminals or made with wire connectors approved for the purpose; and the exposed parts of conductors and terminals shall be treated to prevent corrosion. Where the conductors are fastened to pintype lampholders that protect the terminals from the entrance of water, and that have been found acceptable for sign use, the conductors shall be of the stranded type but shall not be required to be soldered to the terminals.

▲ Portable signs are nearly always small and may be considered as in the same class as portable lighting equipment, and hence No. 16 or 18 wire may be used inside the sign enclosure, provided that the size used shall always have sufficient ampacity for the load.

600-22. Lampholders. Lampholders shall be of the unswitched type having bodies of suitable insulating material and shall be so constructed and installed as to prevent turning. Miniature lampholders shall not be employed for outdoor signs and outline lighting. The screw-shell contact of all sign lampholders in grounded circuits shall be connected to the grounded conductor of the circuit.

600-23. Conductors Within Signs and Troughs. Wires within the sign and outline lighting troughs shall be installed as to be mechanically secure.

600-24. Protection of Leads. Bushings shall be employed to protect wires feeding through enclosures.

C. Over 600 Volts, Nominal

600-31. Installation of Conductors.

(a) Wiring Method. Conductors shall be installed as concealed conductors on insulators, in rigid metal conduit, in flexible metal conduit, in liquidtight flexible metal conduit, or in electrical metallic tubing.

(b) Insulation and Size. Conductors shall be of a type approved for the purpose and for the voltage of the circuit and shall not be smaller than No. 14.

Exception: Conductors not smaller than No. 18 of a type approved for the purpose shall be permitted:

a. As leads not more than 8 feet long permanently attached to electric-discharge lampholders or electric-discharge ballasts if the leads are enclosed in wiring channels.

b. In show window displays or small portable signs, as leads not more than 8 feet long that run from the line ends of the tubing to the secondary windings of transformers if the leads are permanently attached within the transformer enclosure.

(c) Bends in Conductors. Sharp bends in the conductors shall be avoided.

(d) Concealed Conductors on Insulators—Indoors. Concealed conductors on insulators shall be separated from each other and from all objects other than the insulators on which they are mounted by a spacing of not less than 1½ inches for voltages above 10,000 and not less than one inch for voltages of 10,000 or less. They shall be installed in channels lined with noncombustible material and used for no other purpose, except that the primary circuit conductors shall be permitted to be in the same channel. The insulators shall be of noncombustible, non-absorbent material. Concealed conductors on insulators shall not be allowed outside the sign enclosure.

(e) Conductors in Raceways. Where the conductors are covered with lead or other metal sheathing, the covering shall extend beyond the end of the raceway, and the surface of the cable shall not be injured where the covering terminates.

(1) In damp or wet locations, the insulation on all conductors shall extend beyond the metal covering or raceway not less than 4 inches for voltages over 10,000, 3 inches for voltages over 5000 but not exceeding 10,000, and 2 inches for voltages of 5000 or less.

(2) In dry locations the insulation shall extend beyond the end of the metal covering or raceways not less than 2½ inches for voltages over 10,000, 2 inches for voltages over 5000 but not exceeding 10,000, and 1½ inches for voltages of 5000 or less.

(3) For conductors at grounded midpoint terminals, no spacing shall be required.

(4) A metal raceway containing a single conductor from one secondary terminal of a transformer shall not exceed 20 feet in length.

(f) Show Windows and Similar Locations. Conductors that hang freely in the air, away from combustible material, and where not subject to physical damage, as in some show window displays, shall not be required to be otherwise protected.

(g) Between Tubing and Grounded Midpoint. Conductors shall be permitted to be run from the ends of tubing to the grounded midpoint of transformers specifically designed for the purpose and provided with terminals at the midpoint. Where such connections are made to the transformer grounded midpoint, the connections between the high-voltage terminals of the transformer and the line ends of the tubing shall be as short as possible.

600-32. Transformers.

(a) Voltage. The transformer secondary open-circuit voltage shall not exceed 15,000 volts with an allowance on test of 1,000 volts additional. For end-grounded transformers, the secondary open-circuit voltage shall not exceed 7500 volts with an allowance on test of 500 volts additional.

(b) Type. Transformers shall be of a type approved for the purpose and shall be limited in rating to a maximum of 4500 volt-amperes.

Open core-and-coil type transformers shall be limited to 5000 volts with an allowance on test of 500 volts and to indoor applications in small portable signs.

Transformers for outline lighting installations shall have secondary current ratings not more than 30 milliamperes.

Exception: Where the transformers and all wiring connected to them are installed in accordance with Article 410 for electric-discharge lighting of the same voltage.

(c) Exposed to Weather. Transformers used outdoors shall be of the weatherproof type or shall be protected from the weather by enclosure in the sign body or in a separate metal box.

(d) Transformer Secondary Connections. The high voltage windings of transformers shall not be connected in parallel or in series.

Exception No. 1: Two transformers each having one end of its high-voltage winding connected to the metal enclosure shall be permitted to have their high-voltage windings connected in series to form the equivalent of a midpoint-grounded transformer. The grounded ends shall be connected by insulated conductors not smaller than No. 14.

Exception No. 2: Transformers for small portable signs, show windows, and similar locations that are equipped with leads permanently attached to the secondary winding within the transformer enclosure and that do not extend more than 8 feet beyond the enclosure for attaching to the line ends of the tubing, but shall not be smaller than No. 18 and shall be of a type approved for the purpose.

(e) Accessibility. Transformers shall be located where accessible and shall be securely fastened in place.

(f) Working Space. A work space at least three feet high and measuring at least three feet by three horizontally shall be provided about each transformer or its enclosure where not installed in a sign.

(g) Attic Locations. Transformers may be located in attics provided there is a passageway at least 3 feet in height and at least 2 feet in width, provided with a suitable permanent fixed walkway or catwalk at least 12 inches in width extending from the point of entry into the attic to each transformer.

▲ The transformers used to supply luminous gas tubes are, in general, constant-current devices and, up to a certain limit, the voltage delivered by the transformer increases as the impedance of the load increases. The impedance of the tube increases as the length increases and is higher for a tube of small diameter than for one of larger diameter. Hence a transformer should be selected which is designed to deliver the proper current and voltage for the tube; if the tube is too long or of too small a diameter, the voltage of the transformer may rise to too high a value.

600-33. Electric-Discharge Tubing.

(a) Design. The tubing shall be of such length and design as not to cause a continuous overvoltage on the transformer.

(b) Support. Tubing shall be adequately supported on noncombustible, nonabsorbent supports. Tubing supports shall, where practicable, be adjustable.

(c) Contact with Flammable Material and Other Surfaces. The tubing shall be free from contact with flammable material and shall be located where not normally exposed to physical damage. Where operating at over 7500 volts, the tubing shall be supported on noncombustible, nonabsorbent insulating supports that maintain a spacing of not less than $\frac{1}{4}$ inch between the tubing and the nearest surface.

600-34. Terminals and Electrode Receptacles for Electric-Discharge Tubing.

(a) Terminals. Terminals of the tubing shall be inaccessible to unqualified persons and isolated from combustible material and grounded metal or shall be enclosed. Where enclosed, they shall be separated from grounded metal and combustible material by noncombustible, nonabsorbent insulating material approved for the purpose or by not less than $1\frac{1}{2}$ inches of air. Terminals shall be relieved from stress by the independent support of the tubing.

(b) Tube Connections Other Than with Receptacles. Where tubes do not terminate in receptacles designed for the purpose, all live parts of tube terminals and conductors shall be supported so as to maintain a separation of not less than $1\frac{1}{2}$ inches between conductors or between conductors and any grounded metal.

(c) **Receptacles.** Electrode receptacles for the tubing shall be of noncombustible, nonabsorbent insulating material approved for the purpose.

(d) **Bushings.** Where electrodes enter the enclosure of outdoor signs or of an indoor sign operating at a voltage in excess of 7500 volts, bushings shall be used unless receptacles are provided. Electrode terminal assemblies shall be supported not more than 6 inches from the electrode terminals.

(e) **Show Windows.** In the exposed type of show-window signs, terminals shall be enclosed by receptacles.

(f) **Receptacles and Bushing Seals.** A flexible, nonconducting seal shall be permitted to close the opening between the tubing and the receptacle or bushing against the entrance of dust or moisture. This seal shall not be in contact with grounded conductive material and shall not be depended upon for the insulation of the tubing.

(g) **Enclosures of Metal.** Enclosures of metal for electrodes shall not be less than No. 24 MSG sheet metal.

(h) **Enclosures of Insulating Material.** Enclosures of insulating material shall be noncombustible, nonabsorbent, and approved for the voltage of the circuit.

(i) **Live Parts.** Live parts shall be enclosed or suitably guarded to prevent contact.

▲ The component parts of a gas-tube sign or lighting system are:

1. A transformer having a 115- or 230-V primary and a high-voltage secondary. Most primaries are 115 V.

2. High-voltage leads from the transformer to the tube.

3. The tube terminals, by means of which the leads are connected to the electrodes at the ends of the tube.

4. The tube itself.

Aside from the high-voltage leads and the tube terminals, the tube of a gas-tube system involves little accident hazard except that with high voltages a discharge may take place from the tube to conductive objects. The tube should be kept away from flammable material since such material might be slightly conductive, and the tube should not be located where it is likely to be broken.

In outdoor signs the tube terminals usually project within the sign enclosure. They may, however, be contained in separate enclosures of sheet metal or insulating material or may be without any enclosure if kept away from combustible material and inaccessible to unauthorized persons.

For exposed signs in show windows, the tube terminals must be enclosed in sleeves of insulating material and the high-voltage leads may consist of conductors insulated for the operating voltage and hanging free in air, if kept away from combustible or conductive material and not subject to physical damage.

600-35. Switches on Doors. Doors or covers giving access to uninsulated parts of indoor signs or outline lighting exceeding 600 volts and accessible to the general public shall either be provided with interlock switches that on the opening of the doors or covers disconnect the primary circuit, or shall be so fastened that the use of other than ordinary tools will be necessary to open them.

600-36. Fixed Outline Lighting and Skeleton-Type Signs for Interior Use.

(a) **Tube Support.** Gas tubing shall be supported independently of the conductors by means of insulators of noncombustible, nonabsorptive materials such as glass or porcelain or by suspension from suitable wires or chains.

(b) Transformers. Transformers shall be installed in metal enclosures and as near as practicable to the gas tubing system.

(c) Supply Conductors. The supply conductors for the transformers shall be enclosed in grounded metallic raceway.

(d) High-Tension Conductors. High-tension conductors shall be insulated for the voltage of the circuit and shall be enclosed in grounded metallic raceway.

Exception: Conductors not exceeding 4 feet in length between gas tubing and adjacent metallic enclosures shall be permitted to be enclosed in continuous glass or other insulating sleeves.

600-37. Portable Gas Tube Signs for Show Windows and Interior Use.
This Section shall apply to the installation and use of portable gas tube signs.

(a) Location. Portable gas tube signs shall be for indoor use only.

(b) Transformer. The transformer shall be of the window type or shall be within a metal enclosure.

(c) Supply Conductors. Supply conductors shall consist of hard or extra-hard usage type cord containing a grounding conductor. The cord shall not exceed more than 10 feet in length.

(d) High-Voltage Conductors. High-voltage conductors shall not be more than 6 feet long and shall be located where not subject to mechanical injury, and shall be insulated for the voltage of the circuit and be protected by continuous glass or other insulating sleeves or tubing.

(e) Grounding. Transformers and attached noncurrent-carrying metal parts shall be grounded in accordance with Article 250.

(f) Support. Portable indoor signs shall be held in place by not to exceed two open hooks attached to the transformer case.

ARTICLE 610. CRANES AND HOISTS

A. General

610-1. Scope. This Article covers the installation of electrical equipment and wiring used in connection with cranes, monorail hoists, hoists, and all runways.

For further information, see Safety Code for Cranes, Derricks, Hoists, Jacks, and Slings, ANSI B-30.

610-2. Special Requirements for Particular Locations.

(a) Hazardous Locations. All equipment which operates in a hazardous location shall conform to Article 500.

(1) Equipment used in locations which are hazardous because of the presence of flammable gases or vapors shall conform to Article 501.

(2) Equipment used in locations which are hazardous because of combustible dust shall conform to Article 502.

(3) Equipment used in locations which are hazardous because of the presence of easily ignitable fibers or flyings shall conform to Article 503.

(b) Combustible Materials. Where a crane, hoist, or monorail hoist operates over readily combustible material, the resistors shall be placed in a well-ventilated cabinet composed of noncombustible material so constructed that it will not emit flames or molten metal.

Exception: Resistors shall be permitted to be located in a cage or cab constructed of noncombustible material which encloses the sides of the cage or cab from the floor to a point at least 6 inches above the top of the resistors.

B. Wiring

610-11. Wiring Method. Conductors shall be enclosed in raceway or be Type ALS cable, Type CS cable, or Type MI cable.

Exception No. 1: Contact conductors.

Exception No. 2: Short lengths of open conductors at resistors, collectors, and other equipment.

Exception No. 3: Where flexible connections are necessary to motors and similar equipment, flexible stranded conductors shall be installed in flexible metal conduit, liquidtight flexible metal conduit, metal-clad cable, multiconductor cable, or an approved nonmetallic enclosure.

Exception No. 4: Where multiconductor cable is used with a suspended push-button station, the station shall be supported in some satisfactory manner that protects the electric conductors against strain.

▲ In general, the wiring on a crane or a hoist should be rigid-conduit work or electrical metallic tubing. Short lengths of flexible conduit or metal-clad cable may be used for connections to motors, brake magnets, or other devices where a rigid connection is impracticable because the devices are subject to some movement with respect to the bases to which they are attached. In outdoor or wet locations liquidtight flexible metal conduit should be used for flexible connections.

610-12. Raceway Terminal Fittings. Conductors leaving raceways shall comply with one of the following:

(a) A box or terminal fitting having a separately bushed hole for each conductor shall be used wherever a change is made from conduit, electrical metallic tubing, nonmetallic-sheathed cable, metal-clad cable, aluminum-sheathed cable, or mineral-insulated cable or surface raceway wiring to open wiring. A fitting used for this purpose shall contain no taps or splices and shall not be used at fixture outlets.

(b) A bushing shall be permitted to be used in lieu of a box at the end of a conduit or electrical metallic tubing where the raceway terminates at DC split frame motors, unenclosed control, or similar equipment including contact conductors, collectors, resistors, DC series wound brakes, and power circuit limit switches.

610-13. Types of Conductors. Conductors shall be of the rubber-covered or the thermoplastic-insulated type or Type MI cable.

Exception No. 1: Conductors exposed to external heat or connected to resistors shall have an insulation suitable for the temperature and location. Where conductors not having flame-resistant outer covering are grouped together, the group shall be covered with a flame-resistant tape.

Exception No. 2: Contact conductors along runways, crane bridges, and monorails shall be permitted to be bare, but shall be guarded in an approved manner where accidental contact can occur, and shall be copper, aluminum, steel, or other alloys or combinations thereof in the form of hard drawn wire, tees, angles, tee rails, or other stiff shapes.

Exception No. 3: Flexible conductors shall be permitted to be used to convey current and, where practicable, cable reels or take-up devices shall be employed.

Table 610-14(a). Ampacities of Insulated Conductors up to Four Conductors in Raceway or Cable Used with Short-Time Rated Crane and Hoist Motors**

Max. Operating Temp. Size AWG MCM	75°C Type MTW, RH, RHW, THW, THWN, XHHW		90°C Type AVB, FEP, FEPB, RHH, SA, TA, THHN, XHHW*		110°C Type AVA	
	60 min	30 min	60 min	30 min	60 min	30 min
16	10	12				
14	25	26	31	32	38	40
12	30	33	36	40	45	50
10	40	43	49	52	60	65
8	55	60	63	69	73	80
6	76	86	83	94	93	105
5	85	95	95	106	109	121
4	100	117	111	130	126	147
3	120	141	131	153	145	168
2	137	160	148	173	163	190
1	143	175	158	192	177	215
0	190	233	211	259	239	294
00	222	267	245	294	275	331
000	280	341	305	372	339	413
0000	300	369	319	399	352	440
250	364	420	400	461	447	516
300	455	582	497	636	554	707
350	486	646	542	716	616	809
400	538	688	593	760	666	856
450	600	765	660	836	740	930
500	660	847	726	914	815	1004

Other insulations shown in Table 310-13 and approved for the temperatures and location shall be permitted to be substituted for those shown in Table 610-14(a).

The allowable ampacities of conductors used with 15-minute motors shall be the 30-minute ratings increased by 12 percent.

* For dry locations only. See Table 310-13.

** For 5 or more power conductors in raceway or cable, the ampacity of each power conductor shall be reduced to a value of 80 percent of that shown in the table.

Exception No. 4: Varnished-cambric insulated conductors (Type V) or asbestos varnished-cambric insulated conductors (Type AVA and AVB) shall be permitted in dry locations.

610-14. Rating and Size of Conductors.

(a) Ampacity. The allowable ampacities of conductors shall be as shown in Table 610-14(a).

For the ampacities of conductors between controllers and resistors, see Section 430-23.

(b) Secondary Resistor Conductors. Where the secondary resistor is separate from the controller, the minimum size of the conductors between controller and resistor shall be calculated by multiplying the motor secondary current by the appropriate factor from Table 610-14(b) and selecting a wire from Table 610-14(a).

Table 610-14(b). Secondary Conductor Rating Factors

Time in Seconds		Ampacity of Wire in Percent of Full-Load Secondary Current
On	Off	
5	75	35
10	70	45
15	75	55
15	45	65
15	30	75
15	15	85
Continuous Duty		110

(c) Minimum Size. Conductors external to motors and controls shall not be smaller than No. 16.

Exception No. 1: No. 18 wire in multiple conductor cord shall be permitted for control circuits at not over 7 amperes.

Exception No. 2: Wires not smaller than No. 20 shall be permitted for electronic circuits.

(d) Contact Conductors. Contact wires shall have an ampacity not less than that required by Table 610-14(a) for 75°C wire, and in no case shall they be smaller than the following:

Distance Between End Strain Insulators or Clamp-Type Intermediate Supports	Size of Wire
0–30 feet	No. 6
30–60 feet	No. 4
Over 60 feet	No. 2

(e) Calculation of Motor Load.

(1) For one motor, use 100 percent of motor nameplate full-load ampere rating.

(2) For multiple motors on a single crane or hoist, the minimum circuit ampacity of the power supply conductors on a crane or hoist shall be the nameplate full-load ampere rating of the largest motor or group of motors for any single crane motion, plus 50 percent of the nameplate full-load ampere rating of the next largest motor or group of motors, using that column of Table 610-14(a) which applies to the longest time rated motor.

(3) For multiple cranes and/or hoists supplied by a common conductor system, compute the motor minimum ampacity for each crane as defined in Section 610-14(e), add them together, and multiply the sum by the appropriate demand factor from Table 610-14(e).

Table 610-14(e). Demand Factors

Number of Cranes or Hoists	Demand Factor
2	0.95
3	0.91
4	0.87
5	0.84
6	0.81
7	0.78

(f) Other Loads. Additional loads, such as heating, lighting, and air conditioning, shall be provided for by application of the appropriate Sections of this Code.

(g) Nameplate. Each crane, monorail, or hoist shall be provided with a visible nameplate marked with the maker's name, the rating in volts, frequency, number of phases, and circuit ampacity as calculated in Section 610-14(e) and (f).

610-15. Common Return. Where a crane or hoist is operated by more than one motor, a common-return conductor of proper ampacity shall be permitted.

C. Contact Conductors

610-21. Installation of Contact Conductors. Contact conductors shall comply with (a) through (h) below:

(a) Locating or Guarding Contact Conductors. Runway contact conductors shall be guarded and bridge contact conductors shall be located or guarded in a manner that persons cannot inadvertently touch energized current-carrying parts.

(b) Contact Wires. Wires that are used as contact conductors shall be secured at the ends by means of approved strain insulators and shall be so mounted on approved insulators that the extreme limit of displacement of the wire will not bring the latter within less than $1\frac{1}{2}$ inches from the surface wired over.

(c) Support Along Runways. Main contact conductors carried along runways shall be supported on insulating supports placed at intervals not exceeding 20 feet.

Exception: Supports for grounded rail conductors as provided in (f) below shall not be required to be of the insulating type.

Such conductors shall be separated not less than 6 inches other than for monorail hoists where a spacing of not less than 3 inches shall be permitted. Where necessary, intervals between insulating supports shall be permitted to be increased up to 40 feet, the separation between conductors being increased proportionately.

(d) Support on Bridges. Bridge wire contact conductors shall be kept at least $2\frac{1}{2}$ inches apart, and where the span exceeds 80 feet, insulating saddles shall be placed at intervals not exceeding 50 feet.

(e) Supports for Rigid Conductors. Conductors along runways and crane bridges, which are of the rigid type specified in Section 610-13, Exception No. 2, and not contained within an approved enclosed assembly, shall be carried on insulating supports spaced at intervals of not more than 80 times the vertical dimension of the conductor, but in no case greater than 15 feet, and spaced apart sufficiently to give a clear electrical separation of conductors or adjacent conductors of not less than one inch.

(f) Track As Circuit Conductor. Monorail, tramrail, or crane-runway tracks shall be permitted as a conductor of current for one phase of a 3-phase alternating-current system furnishing power to the carrier, crane, or trolley, provided all of the following conditions are met:

(1) The conductors supplying the other two phases of the power supply are insulated.

(2) The power for all phases is obtained from an insulating transformer.

(3) The voltage does not exceed 300 volts.

(4) The rail serving as a conductor is effectively grounded at the transformer and also shall be permitted to be grounded by the fittings used for the suspension or attachment of the rail to a building or structure.

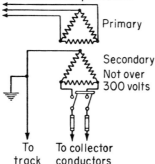

To power supply disconnecting means and overcurrent protection.

Primary

Secondary
Not over
300 volts

To   To collector
track   conductors

FIG. 610-1. Three-phase isolating transformer for crane service.

▲ In some cases, particularly where a monorail crane or conveyer is used for handling light loads, for the sake of convenience and simplicity it may be desirable to use the track as one conductor of a three-phase system. Where this arrangement is used the power must be supplied through a transformer or bank of transformers so that there will be no electrical connection between the primary power supply and the crane circuit. (See Fig. 610-1.) The secondary voltage would usually be 220 V, and the primary of the transformer would usually be connected to the power-distribution system of the building or plant. The leg connected to the track must be grounded at the transformer only, except as permitted in Sec. 610-21(f) (4).

(g) Electrical Continuity of Contact Conductors. All sections of contact conductors shall be mechanically joined to provide a continuous electrical connection.

(h) Not to Supply Other Equipment. Contact conductors shall not be used as feeders for any equipment other than the crane or cranes which they are primarily designed to serve.

610-22. Collectors. Collectors shall be so designed as to reduce to a minimum sparking between them and the contact conductor; and where operated in rooms used for the storage of easily ignitible combustible fibers and materials, they shall comply with Section 503-13.

D. Disconnecting Means

610-31. Runway Conductor Disconnecting Means. A disconnecting means having a continuous ampere rating not less than that computed in Section 610-14(e) and (f) shall be provided between the runway contact conductors and the power supply. Such disconnecting means shall consist of a motor circuit switch or circuit breaker. This disconnecting means shall be readily accessible and operable from the ground, shall be arranged to be locked in the open position, shall open all ungrounded conductors simultaneously, and shall be placed within view of the crane or hoist and the runway contact conductors.

610-32. Disconnecting Means for Cranes and Monorail Hoists. A motor circuit switch or circuit breaker arranged to be locked in the open position shall be provided in the leads from the runway contact conductors or other power supply on all cranes and monorail hoists.

Exception: Where the crane or monorail hoist installation meets all of the following, the disconnect shall be permitted to be omitted:

(a) *The unit is floor controlled.*

(b) *Only one unit is supplied by the runway conductor system or other power supply.*

(c) *The unit is within view of the power supply disconnecting means.*

(d) *No fixed work platform has been provided for servicing the unit.*

Where the disconnecting means is not readily accessible from the crane operating station, means shall be provided at the crane operating station to open the power circuit to the crane motors.

▲ This switch is an emergency device provided for use in case trouble develops in any of the electrical equipment on the crane or monorail hoist, or to permit maintenance work to be done safely.

610-33. Rating of Disconnecting Means. The continuous ampere rating of the switch or circuit breaker required by Section 610-32 shall not be less than 50 percent of the combined short-time ampere rating of the motors, nor less than 75 percent of the sum of the short-time ampere rating of the motors required for any single motion.

▲ It is possible that all the motors on a crane might be in operation at one time, but this condition would continue for only a very short while. A switch or circuit breaker having a current rating not less than 50 percent of the sum of full-load current rating of all the motors will have ample capacity.

E. Overcurrent Protection

610-41. Feeders, Runway Conductors. The runway supply conductors and main contact conductors of a crane or monorail shall be protected by an overcurrent device(s) which shall not be greater than the largest rating or setting of any branch-circuit protective device, plus the sum of the nameplate ratings of all the other loads with application of the demand factors from Table 610-14(e).

610-42. Branch-Circuit Protection. Branch circuits shall be protected as follows:

(a) Fuse or Circuit Breaker Rating Crane, hoist, and monorail hoist motor branch circuits shall be protected by fuses or time-limit circuit breakers having a rating in accordance with Table 430-152. Taps to control circuits shall be permitted to be taken from the load side of a branch-circuit protective device, provided each tap and piece of equipment is properly protected.

Exception No. 1: When two or more motors operate a single motion, the sum of their nameplate current ratings shall be considered as a single motor current in the above calculations.

Exception No. 2: Two or more motors shall be permitted to be connected to the same branch circuit if no tap to an individual motor has an ampacity less than one-third that of the branch circuit and if each motor is protected for running overcurrent according to Section 610-43.

(b) Tap Conductors. Taps to brake coils do not require separate overcurrent protection.

610-43. Motor Running Overcurrent Protection. Each motor shall be protected from running overcurrent by one of the following means:

(1) A single motor shall be considered as protected when the branch-circuit overcurrent device meets the rating requirements of Section 610-42.

(2) Overload relay elements in each ungrounded circuit conductor, with all relay heaters protected from short circuit by the branch-circuit protection.

(3) Thermal sensing device(s), sensitive to motor temperature or to temperature and current which are thermally in contact with the motor winding(s). A hoist or trolley is considered to be protected if the sensing device is connected in the hoist's upper limit switch circuit so as to prevent further hoisting during an overcurrent condition of either motor.

Exception No. 1: If the motor is manually controlled, with spring return controls, the running overcurrent protective device need not protect the motor against stalled rotor conditions.

Exception No. 2: Where two or more motors drive a single trolley, truck, or bridge and are controlled as a unit by a single set of running overcurrent devices with a rating equal to the sum of their rated full-load currents. A hoist or trolley is considered to be protected if the sensing device is connected in the hoist's upper limit switch circuit so as to prevent further hoisting during an overtemperature condition of either motor.

Exception No. 3: Hoists and monorail hoists and their trolleys which are not used as part of an overhead traveling crane do not require individual motor running overcurrent protection provided the largest motor does not exceed $7\frac{1}{2}$ horsepower and all motors are under manual control of the operator.

F. Control

610-51. Separate Controllers. Each motor shall be provided with an individual controller.

Exception No. 1: Where two or more motors drive a single hoist, carriage, truck, or bridge, they shall be permitted to be controlled by a single controller.

Exception No. 2: One controller shall be permitted to be switched between motors provided,

    (a) The controller shall have a horsepower rating which shall not be lower than the horsepower rating of the largest motor.

    (b) Only one motor is operated at one time.

610-53. Overcurrent Protection. Conductors of control circuits shall be protected against overcurrent. Control circuits shall be considered as protected by overcurrent devices that are rated or set at not more than 500 percent of the ampacity of the control conductors.

Exception No. 1: Taps to control transformers shall be considered as protected when the secondary circuit is properly protected.

Exception No. 2: Such conductors shall be considered as being properly protected by the branch-circuit overcurrent devices where the opening of the control circuit would create a hazard, as for example, the control circuit of a hot metal crane.

610-55. Limit Switch. A limit switch or other device shall be provided to prevent the load block from passing the safe upper limit of travel of all hoisting mechanisms.

610-57. Clearance. The dimension of the working space in the direction of access to live parts which are likely to require examination, adjustment, servicing, or maintenance while alive shall be in accordance with Section 110-16. Where controls are enclosed in cabinets, the door(s) shall either open at least 90 degrees or be removable.

G. Grounding

610-61. Grounding. All exposed metal parts of cranes, monorail hoists and accessories including pendant controls shall be metallically joined together into a continuous electrical conductor so that the entire crane or hoist will be grounded on installation in accordance with Article 250. Moving parts, other than removable accessories or attachments having metal to metal bearing surfaces, shall be considered to be electrically connected to each other through the bearing surfaces for grounding purposes. The trolley frame and bridge frame shall be considered as electrically grounded through the bridge and trolley wheels and their respective tracks unless local conditions, such as paint or other insulating material, prevent reliable metal to metal contact. In this case a separate grounding conductor shall be provided.

ARTICLE 620. – ELEVATORS, DUMBWAITERS, ESCALATORS, AND MOVING WALKS

A. General

620-1. Scope. This Article covers the installation of electric equipment and wiring used in connection with elevators, dumbwaiters, escalators, and moving walks.

    For further information, see Safety Code for Elevators, Dumbwaiters, Escalators and Moving Walks (ANSI A17.1-1972).

▲ These provisions may also be considered as applying to console lifts, equipment for raising and lowering or rotating portions of theater stages, and all similar equipment.

620-2. Voltage Limitations. The nominal voltage used for elevator, dumbwaiter, escalator, and moving-walk operating control and signaling circuits, operating equipment, driving machine motors, machine brakes, and motor-generator sets shall not exceed the following:

(1) For operating control and signaling circuits and related equipment, including door operator motors. 300 volts.

Exception: Higher potentials shall be permitted for frequencies of 25-through 60-Hertz alternating current or for direct current provided the current in the system cannot, under any conditions, exceed 8 milliamperes for alternating current or 30 milliamperes for direct current.

(2) Driving machine motors, machine brakes, and motor-generator sets: 600 volts.

Exception: Higher potentials shall be permitted for driving motors of motor-generator sets.

620-3. Live Parts Enclosed. All live parts of electric apparatus in the hoistways, at the landings, or in or on the cars of elevators and dumbwaiters or in the wellways or the landings of escalators or moving walks shall be enclosed to protect against accidental contact.

B. Conductors

620-11. Insulation of Conductors. The insulation of conductors installed in connection with elevators, dumbwaiters, escalators, and moving walks shall comply with (a) through (d) below.

(a) Control Panel Wiring. Conductors from panels to main circuit resistors shall be flame-retardant and suitable for a temperature of not less than 90°C (194°F). All other wiring on control panels shall be flame-retardant and moisture-resistant.

(b) Traveling Cables. Traveling cables used as flexible connections between the elevator or dumbwaiter car and the raceway shall be of the types of elevator cable listed in Table 400-4 or other approved types.

(c) Other Wiring. All conductors in raceways; in or on the cars of elevators and dumbwaiters; in the wellways of escalators and moving walks; and in the machine room of elevators, dumbwaiters, escalators, and moving walks shall have flame-retardant and moisture-resistant insulation.

(d) Thickness of Insulation. The thickness of the insulation of all conductors shall be suitable for the voltage to which the conductors are subjected.

▲ A distinction is made here between the conductors carrying the power current and the smaller wires of operating circuits, such as wires connected to the magnet coils of contactors. The operating current passing through the magnet coils may be quite small, and a small current leaking through damp slow-burning insulation where two insulated wires are in contact might be sufficient to operate a contactor.

620-12. Minimum Size of Conductors. The minimum size of conductors used for elevator, dumbwaiter, escalator, and moving-walk wiring, other than conductors that form an integral part of control equipment, shall be as follows:

(a) Traveling Cables.

(1) For lighting circuits: No. 14.

Exception: No 20 or larger conductors shall be permitted in parallel provided the ampacity is equivalent to at least that of No. 14 wire.

(2) Operating control and signaling circuits: No. 20.

(b) Other Wiring. All operating control and signaling circuits: No. 20.

▲ Tables 310-16 to 310-19 do not include the ampacity for No. 20 AWG copper conductors. However, it is generally considered that the ampacity for No. 20 conductors up to two conductors in cable or cord may safely carry 3 A.

The development of elevator control equipment, which has been taking place for many years, has resulted in the design and use of equipment including electronic unit contactors requiring very much smaller currents (milliamperes) for their operation.

As a result, the insistence on the use of No. 16 wire for elevator control and operating circuits requires the use of far larger wire than would be required if the size was based, as it should be, on the allowable ampacity of the wires. Even No. 18 wire is considerably larger than is required to safely handle the actual currents involved.

620-13. Motor Circuit Conductors. Conductors supplying elevator, dumbwaiter, escalator, or moving-walk motors shall have an ampacity in accordance with (a), (b), and (c) below based on the nameplate current rating of the motors. With generator field control, the ampacity shall be based on the nameplate current rating of the driving motor of the motor-generator set which supplies power to the elevator motor.

The heating of conductors depends on root-mean-square current values which, with generator field control, are reflected by the nameplate current rating of the motor-generator set driving motor rather than by the rating of the elevator motor, which represents actual but short-time and intermittent full-load current values.

(a) Conductors Supplying Single Motor. Conductors supplying a single motor shall have an ampacity in conformance with Section 430-22, Table 430-22(a) Exception.

(b) Conductors Supplying Several Motors. Conductors supplying two or more motors shall have an ampacity of not less than 125 percent of the nameplate current rating of the highest rated motor in the group plus the sum of the nameplate current ratings of the remainder of the motors in the group.

(c) Feeder Demand Factor. Feeder conductors of less ampacity than required by (b) above shall be permitted subject to the requirements of Section 430-26.

C. Wiring

620-21. Wiring Methods. Conductors located in hoistways, in escalator and moving-walk wellways, in or on cars, and in machine and control rooms, not including the traveling cables connecting the car and hoistway wiring, shall be installed in rigid conduit, intermediate metal conduit, electrical metallic tubing, wireways, or be Type ALS cable, Type CS cable, or Type MI cable.

Exception No. 1: Flexible metal conduit or Type AC metal-clad cable shall be permitted in hoistways and in escalator and moving-walk wellways between risers and limit switches, interlocks, operating buttons, and similar devices.

Exception No. 2: Short runs of flexible metal conduit or Type AC metal-clad cable shall be permitted on cars where so located as to be free from oil and if securely fastened in place.

Exception No. 3: Type S, SO, STO, or ST cords shall be permitted as flexible connections between the fixed wiring on the car and the switches on car doors or gates. Such cords shall be permitted as flexible connections for the top-of-car operating device or the car top work light. These devices or fixtures shall be grounded by means of a grounding conductor run with the circuit conductors.

Exception No. 4: Conductors between control panels and machine motors, machine brakes, and motor-generator sets, not exceeding 6 feet in length, shall be permitted to be grouped together and taped or corded without being installed in a raceway provided the taping or cording is painted with an insulating paint. Such cable groups shall be supported at intervals of not more than 3 feet and so located as to be free from physical damage.

Where motor-generators and machine motors are located adjacent to or underneath control equipment and are provided with extra length terminal leads not exceeding 6 feet in length, such leads shall be permitted to be extended to connect directly to controller terminal studs without regard to the carrying-capacity requirements of Articles 430 and 445. Auxiliary gutters shall be permitted in machine and control rooms between controllers, starters, and similar apparatus.

620-22. Car Light Source. On multi-car installations, a separate branch circuit shall supply the car lights for each elevator.

D. Installation of Conductors

620-31. Raceway Terminal Fittings. Conductors shall comply with Section 300-16(b). In locations where conduits project from the floor and terminate in other than a wiring enclosure, they shall extend at least 6 inches above the floor.

620-32. Wireways. Section 362-5 shall not apply to wireways. The sum of the cross-sectional area of the individual conductors in a wireway shall not be more than 50 percent of the interior cross-sectional area of the wireway.

Vertical runs of wireways shall be securely supported at intervals not exceeding 15 feet and shall have not more than one joint between supports. Adjoining wireway sections shall be securely fastened together to provide a rigid joint.

620-33. Number of Conductors in Raceways. The sum of the cross-sectional area of the operating and control circuit conductors in raceways shall not exceed 40 percent of the interior cross-sectional area of the raceway.

Exception: In wireways as permitted in Section 620-32.

620-34. Supports. Supports for cables or raceways in a hoistway or in an escalator or moving-walk wellway shall be securely fastened to the guide rail or to the hoistway or wellway construction.

620-35. Auxiliary Gutters (Wiring Troughs). Auxiliary gutters shall not be subject to the restrictions of Section 374-2 as to length or of Section 374-5 as to number of conductors.

620-36. Different Systems in One Raceway or Traveling Cable. Conductors for operating, control, power, signaling, and lighting circuits of 600 volts or less shall be permitted to be run in the same traveling cable or raceway system if all conductors are insulated for the maximum voltage found in the cables or raceway system and if all live parts of the equipment are insulated from ground for this maximum voltage. Such a traveling cable or raceway shall also be permitted to include a pair of telephone conductors for the car telephone, provided such conductors are insulated for the maximum voltage found in the cable or raceway system.

▲ It would be difficult, if not practically impossible, to keep the wires of each system completely isolated from the wires of every other system in the case of elevator control and signal circuits. Hence such wires may be run in the same conduits and cables if all wires are insulated for the highest voltage used and if all live parts of apparatus are insulated from ground for the highest voltage, provided that the signal system is an integral part of the elevator wiring system.

620-37. Wiring in Hoistways. Main feeders for supplying power to elevators and dumbwaiters shall be installed outside the hoistway. Only such electric wiring, conduit, and cable used directly in connection with the elevator or dumbwaiter, including wiring for signals, for communication with the car, for lighting and ventilating the car, and wiring for fire-detecting systems for the hoistways, shall be permitted inside the hoistway.

Exception: In existing structures, feeders for elevators or other purposes shall be permitted within a hoistway by special permission provided no conductors are spliced within the hoistway.

620-38. Electric Equipment in Garages and Similar Occupancies. Electric equipment and wiring used for elevators, dumbwaiters, escalators, and moving walks in garages shall comply with the requirements of Article 511. Wiring and equipment located on the underside of the car platform shall be considered as being located in the hazardous area.

620-39. Sidewalk Elevators. Sidewalk elevators with sidewalk doors located exterior to the building shall have all electric wiring in rigid metal conduit or electrical metallic tubing; and all electrical outlets, switches, junction boxes, and fittings shall be weatherproof.

E. Traveling Cables

620-41. Suspension. Traveling cables shall be so suspended at the car and hoistway ends as to reduce the strain on the individual copper conductors to a minimum.

Cables with an unsupported length exceeding 100 feet shall have steel supporting fillers and shall be suspended directly by the steel supporting fillers.

Where nonmetallic fillers are used, the cables shall be suspended by looping the cables around the supports, or shall be suspended from the support by a means that automatically tightens around the cable when tension is increased.

620-42. Hazardous Locations. In hazardous locations, traveling cables shall be of a type approved for hazardous locations and shall be secured to explosion-proof cabinets as provided in Section 501-11.

620-43. Location of and Protection for Cables. Traveling cable supports shall be so located as to reduce to a minimum the possibility of damage due to the cables coming in contact with the hoistway construction or equipment in the hoistway. Where necessary, suitable guards shall be provided to protect the cables against damage.

F. Control

620-51. Disconnecting Means. Elevators, dumb waiters, escalators, and moving walks shall have a single means for disconnecting all ungrounded main power supply conductors for each unit.

On single and multi-car installations where a separate power supply is used for signals or lights or other equipment (multi-car) common to the group, additional separate disconnecting means shall be provided to disconnect all such ungrounded conductors for these power supplies.

Where interconnections between control panels are necessary for operation of the system on multi-car installations that remain energized from a source other than the disconnecting means, a warning sign shall be mounted on or adjacent to the disconnecting means. The sign shall be clearly legible and shall read "Warning— Parts of the control panel are not de-energized by this switch."

(a) Type. The disconnecting means shall be an enclosed externally operable fused motor circuit switch or circuit breaker arranged to be locked in the open position. No provision shall be made to close this disconnecting means from any other part of the premises, nor shall circuit breakers be opened automatically by a fire alarm system.

(b) Location. The disconnecting means shall be located in a readily accessible location. Where practicable, the disconnecting means shall be located adjacent to the door of the machine room or enclosure.

(1) On AC control and rheostatic controlled elevators where the machine is not in the vicinity of the disconnecting means, an additional manually operated switch shall be provided at the machine, connected in the control circuit to prevent starting.

(2) On elevators with generator field control, the disconnecting means shall be located within sight of the motor starter for the driver motor of the motor generator set. When the disconnecting means is not within sight of the hoist machine, the control panel, or the motor generator set, an additional manually operated switch shall be installed adjacent to the remote equipment, connected in the control circuit to prevent starting.

620-53. Phase Protection. Electric elevators driven by polyphase alternating-current machine motors shall be provided with a means to prevent starting of the elevator motor when: (1) the phase rotation is in the wrong direction, or (2) there is a failure in any phase.

▲ If the connections of any two leads of a three-phase motor are interchanged, or if the connections of the two leads of one phase of a two-phase motor are interchanged, the direction of rotation of the motor will be reversed. This phase reversal is sometimes made unintentionally when repair work is being done on the motor or wiring system and, of course, has the effect of reversing the direction of travel of the car. The reverse-phase relay makes it impossible to operate the controller and start the motor under these conditions.

If one of the leads to the motor is disconnected, leaving the other leads connected, the motor winding that remains connected will draw an excessive current and a burnout will probably result unless the motor is completely disconnected at once.

G. Overcurrent Protection

620-61. Overcurrent Protection. Overcurrent protection shall be provided as follows:

(a) Control and Operating Circuits. Control and operating circuits and signaling circuits shall be protected against overcurrent in accordance with the requirements of Section 725-12.

(b) Motors.

(1) Duty on elevator and dumbwaiter driving machine motors and driving motors of motor-generators used with generator field control shall be classed as intermittent. Such motors shall be protected against overcurrent in accordance with Section 430-33.

(2) Duty on escalator and moving-walk driving machine motors shall be classed as continuous. Such motors shall be protected against overcurrent in accordance with Section 430-32.

(3) Escalator and moving-walk driving machine motors and driving motors of motor-generator sets shall be protected against running overcurrent as provided in Table 430-37.

H. Machine Room

620-71. Guarding Equipment. Elevator, dumbwaiter, escalator, and moving-walk driving machines, motor-generator sets, controllers, auxiliary control equipment, and disconnecting means shall be installed in a room or enclosure set aside for that purpose. The room or enclosure shall be secured against unauthorized access.

Exception: Dumbwaiter, escalator, or moving-walk controllers shall be permitted outside the spaces herein specified, provided they are enclosed in cabinets with doors or removable panels capable of being locked in the closed position and the disconnecting means is located adjacent to the controller. Such cabinets shall be permitted in the balustrading on the side away from the moving steps or moving treadway.

620-72. Clearance Around Control Panels. Sufficient clear working space shall be provided around control panels to provide safe and convenient access to all live parts of the equipment necessary for maintenance and adjustment. The minimum clear working space about live parts on control panels shall not be less than specified in Section 110-16.

Exception: Where an escalator or moving-walk control panel is mounted in the same space as the escalator or moving-walk drive machine and the clearances specified cannot be provided, the clearance requirements of Section 110-16 shall be permitted to be waived where the entire panel is arranged so that it can be readily removed from the machine space and is provided with flexible leads to all external connections.

Where control panels are not located in the same space as the drive machine, they shall be located in cabinets with doors or removable panels capable of being locked in the closed position. Such cabinets shall be permitted in the balustrading on the side away from the moving steps or moving treadway.

J. Grounding

620-81. Metal Raceways Attached to Cars. Conduit, Type ALS cable, Type CS cable, or Type AC metal-clad cable attached to elevator cars shall be bonded to grounded metal parts of the car with which they come in contact.

620-82. Electric Elevators. For electric elevators, the frames of all motors, elevator machines, controllers, and the metal enclosures for all electric devices in or on the car or in the hoistway shall be grounded.

620-83. Nonelectric Elevators. For elevators other than electric having any electric conductors attached to the car, the metal frame of the car, where normally accessible to persons, shall be grounded.

620-85. Inherent Ground. Equipment mounted on members of the structural metal frame of a building shall be considered to be grounded. Metal car frames supported by metal hoisting cables attached to or running over sheaves or drums of elevator machines shall be considered to be grounded where the machine is grounded in accordance with Article 250.

K. Overspeed

620-91. Overspeed Protection for Elevators. Under overhauling load conditions, a means shall be provided on the load side of each elevator power disconnecting means to prevent the elevator from attaining a speed equal to the governor tripping speed or a speed in excess of 125 percent of the elevator rated speed, whichever is the lesser.

620-92. Motor-Generator Overspeed Device. Motor-generators driven by direct-current motors and used to supply direct current for the operation of elevator machine motors shall be provided with speed-limiting devices as required by Section 430-89(3) that will prevent the elevator from attaining at any time a speed of more than 125 percent of its rated speed.

620-101. Emergency Power. An elevator can be powered by an emergency power system provided when operating on such emergency power there is conformance with Section 620-91. For passenger elevators, 125 percent of rated load shall be used in place of rated load.

Exception: Where the emergency power system is designed to operate only one elevator at a time, the energy absorption means, if required, shall be permitted on the power side of the disconnecting means, provided all other requirements of Section 620-91 are conformed to when operating any of the elevators the system might serve.

(a) Other building loads, such as power and light that can be supplied by the emergency power system, shall not be considered as means of absorbing the regenerated energy for the purpose of conforming to Section 620-91 unless such loads are using their normal power from the emergency power system when it is activated.

(b) The disconnecting means required by Section 620-51 shall disconnect the emergency power service and the normal power service.

ARTICLE 630. ELECTRIC WELDERS

A. General

630-1. Scope. This Article covers electric arc welding, resistance welding apparatus, and other similar welding equipment that is connected to an electric supply system.

▲ There are two general types of electric welding: arc welding and resistance welding. In arc welding, an arc is drawn between the metal parts to be joined together and a metal electrode (a wire or rod), and metal from the electrode is deposited on the joint. In resistance welding, the metal parts to be joined are pressed tightly together between two electrodes, and a heavy current is passed through the electrodes and the plates or other parts to be welded. The electrodes make contact on a small area—thus the current passes through a small cross section of metal having a high resistance—and sufficient heat is generated to raise the parts to be welded to a welding temperature.

In arc welding with AC, an individual transformer is used for each operator; i.e., a transformer supplies current for one arc only. When DC is used, there is usually an individual generator for each operator, though there are also "multioperator" arc-welding generators.

B. AC Transformer and DC Rectifier Arc Welders

630-11. Ampacity of Supply Conductors. The ampacity of conductors for AC transformer and DC rectifier arc welders shall be as follows:

(a) Individual Welders. The rated ampacity of the supply conductors shall not be less than the current values determined by multiplying the rated primary current in amperes given on the welder nameplate and the following factor based upon the duty cycle or time rating of the welder.

Duty Cycle (percent)	100	90	80	70	60	50	40	30	20	or less
Multiplier	1.00	.95	.89	.84	.78	.71	.63	.55	.45	

For a welder having a time rating of one hour, the multiplying factor shall be 0.75.

(b) Group of Welders. The rated ampacity of conductors that supply a group of welders shall be permitted to be less than the sum of the currents, as determined in accordance with (a) above, of the welders supplied. The conductor rating shall be determined in each case according to the welder loading based on the use to be made of each welder and the allowance permissible in the event that all the welders supplied by the conductors will not be in use at the same time. The load value used for each welder shall take into account both the magnitude and the duration of the load while the welder is in use.

Conductor ratings based on 100 percent of the current, as determined in accordance with (a) above, of the two largest welders, 85 percent for the third largest welder, 70 percent for the fourth largest welder, and 60 percent for all the remaining welders, can be assumed to provide an ample margin of safety under high-production conditions with respect to the maximum permissible temperature of the conductors. Percentage values lower than those given are permissible in cases where the work is such that a high operating duty cycle for individual welders is impossible.

▲ The term *transformer arc welder* is commonly used in the trade and hence is used in the Code, though the equipment might more properly be described as an *arc-welding transformer*. Reference should be made here to Sec. 630-31 where the term *duty cycle* is explained.

It is evident that the load on each transformer is intermittent. Where several transformers are supplied by one feeder, the intermittent loading will cause much less heating of the feeder conductors than would result from a continuous load equal to the sum of the full-load current ratings of all the transformers. The ampacity of the feeder conductors may therefore be reduced if the feeder supplies three or more transformers.

630-12. Overcurrent Protection. Overcurrent protection for AC transformer and DC rectifier arc welders shall be as provided in (a) and (b) below. Where the nearest standard rating of the overcurrent device used is under the value specified in this Section, or where the rating or setting specified results in unnecessary opening of the overcurrent device, the next higher rating or setting shall be permitted.

(a) For Welders. Each welder shall have overcurrent protection rated or set at not more than 200 percent of the rated primary current of the welder.

Exception: An overcurrent device shall not be required for a welder having supply conductors protected by an overcurrent device rated or set at not more than 200 percent of the rated primary current of the welder.

(b) For Conductors. Conductors that supply one or more welders shall be protected by an overcurrent device rated or set at not more than 200 percent of the conductor rating.

▲ Arc-welding transformers are so designed that as the secondary current increases, the secondary voltage decreases. This characteristic of the transformer greatly reduces the fluctuation of the load on the transformer as the length of the arc, and consequently the secondary current, is varied by the operator.

The rating or setting of the overcurrent devices specified in this section provides short-circuit protection. It has been stated that with the electrode "frozen" to the work the primary current will in most cases rise to about 170 percent of the current rating of the transformer. This condition represents the heaviest overload that can occur, and of course this condition would never be allowed to continue for more than a very short time.

630-13. Disconnecting Means. A disconnecting means shall be provided in the supply for each AC transformer and DC rectifier arc welder which is not equipped with a disconnect mounted as an integral part of the welder.

The disconnecting means shall be a switch or circuit breaker, and its rating shall not be less than that necessary to accommodate overcurrent protection as specified under Section 630-12.

630-14. Marking. A nameplate shall be provided for AC transformer and DC rectifier arc welders giving the following information: name of manufacturer; frequency; number of phases; primary voltage; rated primary current; maximum open-circuit voltage; rated secondary current; basis of rating, such as the duty cycle or time rating.

C. Motor-Generator Arc Welders

630-21. Ampacity of Supply Conductors. The ampacity of conductors for motor-generator arc welders shall be as follows:

(a) Individual Welders. The rated ampacity of the supply conductors shall not be less than the current values determined by multiplying the rated primary current in amperes given on the welder nameplate and the following factor based upon the duty cycle or time rating of the welder.

Duty Cycle (percent)	100	90	80	70	60	50	40	30	20	or less
Multiplier	1.00	.96	.91	.86	.81	.75	.69	.62	.55	

For a welder having a time rating of one hour, the multiplying factor shall be 0.80.

(b) Group of Welders. The rated ampacity of conductors that supply a group of welders shall be permitted to be less than the sum of the currents, as determined in accordance with (a) above, of the welders supplied. The conductor rating shall be determined in each case according to the welder loading based on the use to be made of each welder and the allowance permissible in the event that all the welders supplied by the conductors will not be in use at the same time. The load value used for each welder shall take into account both the magnitude and the duration of the load while the welder is in use.

Conductor ratings based on 100 percent of the current, as determined in accordance with (a) above, of the two largest welders, 85 percent for the third largest welder, 70 percent for the fourth largest welder, and 60 percent for all the remaining welders, can be assumed to provide an ample margin of safety under high-production conditions with respect to the maximum permissible temperature of the conductors. Percentage values lower than those given are permissible in cases where the work is such that a high operating duty cycle for individual welders is impossible.

630-22. Overcurrent Protection. Overcurrent protection for motor-generator arc welders shall be as provided in (a) and (b) below. Where the nearest standard rating of the overcurrent device used is under the value specified in this Section, or where the rating or setting specified results in unnecessary opening of the overcurrent device, the next higher rating or setting shall be permitted.

(a) For Welders. Each welder shall have overcurrent protection rated or set at not more than 200 percent of the rated primary current of the welder.

Exception: An overcurrent device shall not be required for a welder having supply conductors protected by an overcurrent device rated or set at not more than 200 percent of the rated primary current of the welder.

(b) For Conductors. Conductors that supply one or more welders shall be protected by an overcurrent device rated or set at not more than 200 percent of the conductor rating.

630-23. Disconnecting Means. A disconnecting means shall be provided in the supply connection of each motor-generator arc welder.

The disconnecting means shall be a circuit breaker or motor-circuit switch, and its rating shall not be less than that necessary to accommodate overcurrent protection as specified under Section 630-22.

630-24. Marking. A nameplate shall be provided for each motor-generator arc welder giving the following information: name of manufacturer; rated frequency; number of phases; input voltage; input current; maximum open-circuit voltage; rated output current; basis of rating, such as duty cycle or time rating.

D. Resistance Welders

630-31. Ampacity of Supply Conductors. The ampacity of the supply conductors for resistance welders necessary to limit the voltage drop to a value permissible for the satisfactory performance of the welder is usually greater than that required to prevent overheating as prescribed in (a) and (b) below.

(a) Individual Welders. The rated ampacity for conductors for individual welders shall comply with the following:

(1) The rated ampacity of the supply conductors for a welder that may be operated at different times at different values of primary current or duty cycle shall not be less than 70 percent of the rated primary current for seam and automatically fed welders, and 50 percent of the rated primary current for manually operated nonautomatic welders.

(2) The rated ampacity of the supply conductors for a welder wired for a specific operation for which the actual primary current and duty cycle are known and remain unchanged shall not be less than the product of the actual primary current and the multiplier given below for the duty cycle at which the welder will be operated.

Duty Cycle (percent)	50	40	30	25	20	15	10	7.5	5.0	or less
Multiplier	71	.63	.55	.50	.45	.39	.32	.27	.22	

(b) Groups of Welders. The rated ampacity of conductors that supply two or more welders shall not be less than the sum of the value obtained in accordance with (a) above for the largest welder supplied, and 60 percent of the values obtained for all the other welders supplied.

Explanation of Terms. (1) The rated primary current is the rated kVA multiplied by 1000 and divided by the rated primary voltage, using values given on the nameplate. (2) The actual primary current is the current drawn from the supply circuit during each welder operation at the particular heat tap and control setting used. (3) The duty cycle is the percentage of the time during which the welder is loaded. For instance, a spot welder supplied by a 60-Hertz system (216,000 cycles per hour) making four hundred 15-cycle welds per hour would have a duty cycle of 2.8 percent (400 multiplied by 15, divided by 216,000, multiplied by 100). A seam welder operating 2 cycles "on" and 2 cycles "off" would have a duty cycle of 50 percent.

▲ Subparagraph (a)(1) applies where a resistance welder is intended for a variety of different operations, such as for welding plates of different thicknesses or for welding different metals. In this case the branch-circuit conductors must have an ampacity sufficient for the heaviest demand that may be made upon them. Because the loading is intermittent, the ampacity need not be as high as the rated primary current. A value of 70 percent is specified for any type of welding machine which is fed automatically. For a manually operated welder, the duty cycle will always be lower and a conductor ampacity of 50 percent of the rated primary current is considered sufficient.

Example 1

A spot welder supplied by a 60-Hz system makes 400 welds per hour, and in making each weld, current flows during 15 cycles.

The number of cycles per hour is 60 × 60 × 60 = 216,000 cycles.

During 1 hr, the time during which the welder is loaded, measured in cycles, is 400 × 15 = 6,000 cycles.

The duty cycle is therefore $\dfrac{6,000}{216,000} \times 100 = 2.8$ percent.

Example 2

A seam welder operates 2 cycles "on" and 2 cycles "off" or in every 4 cycles the welder is loaded during 2 cycles.

The duty cycle is therefore $\dfrac{2}{4} \times 100 = 50$ percent.

Transformers for resistance welders are commonly provided with taps by means of which the secondary voltage, and consequently the secondary current, can be adjusted. The rated primary current is the current in the primary when the taps are adjusted for maximum secondary current.

When a resistance welder is set up for a specific operation, the transformer taps are adjusted to provide the exact heat desired for the weld; then in order to apply subparagraph (a)(2) the actual primary current must be measured. A special type of ammeter is required for this measurement because the current impulses are of very short duration, often a small fraction of a second. The duty cycle is controlled by the adjustment of the controller for the welder.

The procedure in determining conductor sizes for an installation consisting of a feeder and two or more branch circuits to supply resistance welders is first to compute the required ampacity for each branch circuit. Then the required feeder ampacity is 100 percent of the highest ampacity required for any one of the branch circuits, plus 60 percent of the sum of the ampacities of all the other branch circuits.

Some resistance welders are rated as high as 1,000 kVA and may momentarily draw loads of 2,000 kVA, or even more. Voltage drop must be held within rather close limits to ensure satisfactory operation.

630-32. Overcurrent Protection.   Overcurrent protection for resistance welders shall be as provided in (a) and (b) below. Where the nearest standard rating of the overcurrent device used is under the value specified in this Section, or where the rating or setting specified results in unnecessary opening of the overcurrent device, the next higher rating or setting shall be permitted.

(a) For Welders.   Each welder shall have an overcurrent device rated or set at not more than 300 percent of the rated primary current of the welder.

Exception: An overcurrent device shall not be required for a welder having a supply circuit protected by an overcurrent device rated or set at not more than 300 percent of the rated primary current of the welder.

(b) For Conductors.   Conductors that supply one or more welders shall be protected by an overcurrent device rated or set at not more than 300 percent of the conductor rating.

▲ In this case, as in the case of the overcurrent protection of arc-welding transformers (Sec. 630-12), the conductors are protected against short circuits. The conductors of motor branch circuits are protected against short circuits by the branch-circuit overcurrent devices and depend upon the motor-running protective devices for overload protection. Although the resistance welder is not equipped with any device similar to the motor-running protective device, satisfactory operation of the welder is a safeguard against overloading of the conductors. Overheating of the circuit could result only from so operating the welder that either the welds would be imperfect, or parts of the control equipment would be damaged, or both.

630-33. Disconnecting Means.   A switch or circuit breaker shall be provided by which each resistance welder and its control equipment can be isolated from the supply circuit. The ampere rating of this disconnecting means shall not be less than the supply conductor ampacity determined in accordance with Section 630-31. The supply circuit switch shall be permitted as the welder disconnecting means where the circuit supplies only one welder.

630-34. Marking. A nameplate shall be provided for each resistance welder giving the following information: name of manufacturer, frequency, primary voltage, rated kVA at 50 percent duty cycle, maximum and minimum open-circuit secondary voltage, short-circuit secondary current at maximum secondary voltage, and specified throat and gap setting.

ARTICLE 640. SOUND-RECORDING AND SIMILAR EQUIPMENT

640-1. Scope. This Article covers equipment and wiring for sound-recording and reproduction, centralized distribution of sound, public address, speech-input systems, and electronic organs.

▲ Centralized distribution systems consist of one or more radio receivers, the audio-frequency output of which is distributed to a number of reproducers or loudspeakers.

A public-address system includes one or more microphones, an amplifier, and any desired number of reproducers or speakers. A common use of such a system is to render the voice of a speaker clearly audible in all parts of a large assembly room.

640-2. Application of Other Articles.

(a) Wiring To and Between Devices. Wiring and equipment from source of power to and between devices connected to the interior wiring systems shall comply with the requirements of Chapters 1 through 4, except as modified by this Article.

(b) Wiring and Equipment. Wiring and equipment for public-address, speech-input, radio-frequency and audio-frequency systems, and amplifying equipment associated with radio receiving stations in centralized distribution systems shall comply with Article 725.

▲ In general, the power-supply wiring from the building light or power service to the special equipment named in Sec. 640-1, and between any parts of this equipment, should be installed as required for light and power systems of the same voltage. Certain variations from the standard requirements are permitted by the following sections. For radio and sound systems the requirements of Art. 810 apply except as otherwise permitted here.

640-3. Number of Conductors in Raceway. The number of conductors in a conduit or other raceway shall comply with Tables 1 through 7 of Chapter 9.

Exception No. 1: Special permission may be granted for the installation of two 2-conductor lead-covered cables in 3/4-inch conduit, provided the cross-sectional area of each cable does not exceed .11 square inch.

Exception No. 2: Special permission may be granted for the installation of two 2-conductor No. 19 lead-covered cables in 1/2-inch conduit, provided the sum of the cross-sectional areas of the cables does not exceed 32 percent of the internal cross-sectional area of the conduit.

640-4. Wireways and Auxiliary Gutters. Wireways shall comply with the requirements of Article 362, and auxiliary gutters shall comply with the requirements of Article 374.

Exception: Where used for sound-recording and reproduction, the following shall be complied with:

a. Conductors in wireways or gutters shall not fill the raceway to more than 75 percent of its depth.

b. Where the cover of auxiliary gutters is flush with the flooring and is subject to the moving of heavy objects, it shall be of steel at least $\frac{1}{4}$ inch in thickness; where not subject to moving of heavy objects, as in the rear of patch or other equipment panels, the cover shall be at least No. 10 MSG.

c. Wireways shall be permitted in concealed places provided they are run in a straight line between outlets or junction boxes. Covers of boxes shall be accessible. Edges of metal shall be rounded at outlet or junction boxes and all rough projections smoothed to prevent abrasion of insulation or conductors. Wireways made of sections shall be bonded and grounded as specified in Section 250-76.

d. Wireways and auxiliary gutters shall be grounded in accordance with the requirements of Article 250. Where the wireway or auxiliary gutter does not contain power-supply wires, the grounding conductor shall not be required to be larger than No. 14 copper or its equivalent. Where the wireway or auxiliary gutter contains power-supply wires, the grounding conductor shall not be smaller than specified in Section 250-95.

640-5. Conductors. Amplifier output circuits carrying audio-program signals of 70 volts or less and whose open-circuit voltage will not exceed 100 volts shall be permitted to employ Class 2 or Class 3 wiring as covered in Article 725.

The above is based on amplifiers whose open-circuit voltage will not exceed 100 volts when driven with a signal at any frequency from 60 to 100 Hertz sufficient to produce rated output (70.7 volts) into its rated load. This also accepts the known fact that the average program material is 12 db below the amplifier rating—thus the average rms voltage for an open-circuit 70-volt output would be only 25 volts.

640-6. Grouping of Conductors. Conductors of different systems grouped in the same conduit or other metal enclosure or in portable cords or cables shall comply with (a) through (c) below.

(a) Power-Supply Conductors. Power-supply conductors shall be properly identified and shall be used solely for supplying power to the equipment to which the other conductors are connected.

(b) Leads to Motor-Generator or Rotary Converter. Input leads to a motor-generator or rotary converter shall be run separately from the output leads.

(c) Conductor Insulation. The conductors shall be insulated individually, or collectively in groups, by insulation at least equivalent to that on the power supply and other conductors.

Exception: Where the power supply and other conductors are separated by a lead sheath or other continuous metallic covering.

640-7. Flexible Cords. Flexible cords and cables shall be of Types S, SJ, ST, SJO, and SJT or other types approved for the purpose for which they are to be used. The conductors of flexible cords, other than power-supply conductors, shall be permitted to be of a size not smaller than No. 26, provided such conductors are not in direct electrical connection with the power-supply conductors and are equipped with a current-limiting means so that the maximum power under any condition will not exceed 150 watts.

640-8. Terminals. Terminals shall be marked to show their proper connections.

Terminals for conductors other than power-supply conductors shall be separated from the terminals of the power-supply conductors by a spacing at least as great as the spacing between power-supply terminals of opposite polarity.

▲ In this class of work, the wires of different systems are in many cases closely associated in the apparatus itself; hence little would be gained by separating them elsewhere.

The input leads to a motor-generator set or to a rotary converter would commonly be 115- or 230-V power circuits; these wires are not a part of the sound recording or -reproducing system and should be kept entirely separate from all wires of the sound system.

640-9. Storage Batteries.   Storage batteries shall comply with (a) and (b) below.

(a) Installation.   Storage batteries shall be installed in accordance with Article 480.

(b) Conductor Insulation.   Storage-battery leads shall be rubber-covered or thermoplastic-covered.

640-10. Overcurrent Protection of "A," "B" and "C" Circuits.   Over-current protection shall be provided as follows:

(a) "A" circuit, where supplied by lighting branch circuits, or by storage batteries of more than 20-ampere-hour capacity, shall have overcurrent protection not exceeding 15 amperes.

(b) "B" circuits shall have overcurrent protection not exceeding one ampere. The overcurrent protection shall be placed in each positive lead.

(c) "C" circuits where supplied from lighting branch circuits or from storage batteries of more than 20-ampere-hour capacity shall have over-current protection not exceeding one ampere.

(d) Overcurrent devices shall be located as near as practicable to the battery.

▲ The terms used in the foregoing rule are those that have been adopted by engineers as applying to circuits used in electronics.

A 20 amp-hr battery is capable of delivering a heavy enough current to heat a No. 14 or smaller wire to a dangerously high temperature, and overcurrent protection is therefore quite necessary. A storage B battery might be capable of delivering enough current to overheat some part of the equipment. Several different positive connections may be made to the battery in order to obtain different voltages, and each such lead must be provided with overcurrent protection.

640-11. Amplifiers and Rectifiers—Type.

(a) Approved Type.   Amplifiers and rectifiers shall be suitably housed and shall be of a type approved for the purpose.

Exception: Where otherwise expressly permitted by the authority having jurisdiction.

(b) Readily Accessible.   Amplifiers and rectifiers shall be so located as to be readily accessible.

(c) Ventilation.   Amplifiers and rectifiers shall be so located as to provide sufficient ventilation to prevent undue temperature rise within the housing.

640-12. Hazardous Locations.   Equipment used in hazardous locations shall be approved for the purpose.

640-13. Protection Against Physical Damage. Amplifiers, rectifiers, loud-speakers, and other equipment shall be so located or protected as to guard against physical damage, such as might result in fire or personal hazard.

ARTICLE 645. DATA PROCESSING SYSTEMS

For further information, see Standard for the Protection of Electronic Computer/Data Processing Equipment (NFPA No. 75-1972).

645-1. Scope. This Article covers equipment, power-supply wiring, equipment interconnecting wiring, and grounding of data processing systems, including data communications equipment used as a terminal unit.

645-2. Supply Circuits and Interconnecting Cables.

(a) Branch-Circuit Conductors. The branch-circuit conductors to which one or more units of a data processing system are connected to a source of supply shall have an ampacity not less than 125 percent of the total connected load.

(b) Connecting Cables. The data processing system shall be permitted to be connected by means of computer cable or flexible cord and an attachment plug cap or cord-set assembly specifically approved as a part of the data processing system. Separate units shall be permitted to be interconnected by means of flexible cords and cables specifically approved as part of the data processing system. When run on the surface of the floor, they shall be protected against physical damage.

(c) Under Raised Floors. The power and communication supply cables and interconnecting cables shall be permitted under a raised floor provided:

(1) The raised floor is of suitable construction.

See Electronic Computer/Data Processing Equipment, NFPA No. 75-1972.

(2) The branch-circuit supply conductors to receptacles are in rigid conduit, electrical metallic tubing, metal surface raceway with metal cover, flexible metal conduit, liquidtight flexible conduit, Type MI mineral-insulated metal-sheathed cable, Type CS copper-sheathed cable, or Type ALS aluminum-sheathed cable.

Exception: Metal surface raceway, so long as the wiring method is exposed.

(3) Ventilation in the underfloor area is used for the data processing equipment and data processing area only.

645-3. Disconnecting Means. In addition to any integral individual disconnect switches for components or other units of the data processing system, disconnecting means shall comply with (a) and (b) below.

(a) In Data Processing Rooms. The disconnecting means shall disconnect the ventilation system serving that room and the power to all electric equipment in the room except lighting, and shall be controlled from locations readily accessible to the operator and at designated exit doors from the data processing room.

(b) In General Building Areas. The disconnecting means shall disconnect all interconnected data processing equipment in the area and shall be controlled from a location readily accessible to the operator.

645-4. Grounding. All exposed noncurrent-carrying metal parts of a data processing system shall be grounded in accordance with Article 250.

645-5. Marking. Each unit of a data processing system that is intended to be supplied by a branch circuit shall be provided with a manufacturer's nameplate, which shall also include the rating in volts, the operating frequency, and the total load in amperes.

ARTICLE 650. ORGANS

650-1. Scope. This Article covers those electric circuits and parts of electrically operated organs which are employed for the control of the sounding apparatus and keyboards. Electronic organs shall comply with the appropriate provisions of Article 640.

650-2. Source of Energy. The source of energy shall have a potential of not over 15 volts and shall be a self-excited generator, a two-coil transformer-type rectifier, or a battery.

650-3. Insulation—Grounding. The generator shall be effectively insulated from ground and from the motor driving it, or both the generator and the motor frames shall be grounded in the manner specified in Article 250.

▲ Organ control systems are usually supplied from a motor-generator set consisting of a 115- or 230-V motor driving a generator that operates at about 10 V. Neither the generator windings nor the control wires are necessarily insulated for the motor voltage. Assume that the frames of the two machines are electrically connected together by being mounted on the same base and that the frames are not grounded. If a wire of the motor winding becomes grounded to the frame of the motor, the frames of both machines may be raised to a potential of 115 or 230 V above ground, and this voltage may break down the insulation of the generator winding or of the circuit wiring. If the generator is insulated from the motor, or if both frames are well grounded, this trouble cannot occur.

650-4. Conductors. Conductors shall comply with (a) through (d) below.

(a) Size. No conductor shall be smaller than No. 26, and the common-return conductor shall not be smaller than No. 14.

(b) Insulation. Conductors shall have rubber, thermoplastic, asbestos, cotton, or silk insulation.

Exception: The common-return conductors shall be rubber-covered, thermoplastic, or asbestos-covered (Types AA, AI, or AIA).

The cotton or silk shall be permitted to be saturated with paraffin if desired.

(c) Conductors to Be Cabled. Except the common-return conductor and conductors inside the organ proper, the organ sections and the organ console conductors shall be cabled. The common-return conductor shall be permitted under an additional covering enclosing both cable and return conductor, or shall be permitted as a separate conductor and shall be permitted to be in contact with the cable.

(d) Cable Covering. The cable shall be provided with one or more braided outer coverings, or a tape shall be permitted in place of an inner braid. Where not installed in metal raceways, the outer braid shall be flame-retardant or shall be covered with a closely wound fire-proof tape.

▲ The wires of the cable are normally all of the same polarity and hence need not be heavily insulated from one another. The full voltage of the control system exists between the wires in the cable and the common return wire; therefore the common wire must be reasonably well insulated from the cable wires.

650-5. Installation of Conductors. Cables shall be securely fastened in place and shall be permitted to be attached directly to the organ structure without insulating supports. Cables shall not be placed in contact with other conductors.

▲ A 15-V system involves very little fire hazard, and the cable may be run in any manner desired, but for protection against injury and convenience in making repairs the cable should preferably be installed in a metal raceway.

650-6. Overcurrent Protection. Circuits shall be so arranged that all conductors shall be protected from overcurrent by an overcurrent device rated at not over 15 amperes.

Exception: The main supply conductors and the common-return conductor.

▲ The "main supply conductors" extend from the generator to a convenient point at which one conductor is connected through 15-A fuses to as many circuits as may be necessary, while the other main conductor is connected to the common return.

ARTICLE 660. X-RAY EQUIPMENT

A. General

660-1. Scope. This Article covers all X-ray equipment operating at any frequency or voltage for medical or industrial use, or for any other purpose.

Nothing in this Article shall be construed as specifying safeguards against the useful beam or stray X-ray radiation.

Radiation safety and performance requirements of several classes of X-ray equipment are regulated under Public Law 90-602 and are enforced by the Department of Health, Education, and Welfare.

In addition, information on radiation protection by the National Council on Radiation Protection and Measurements are published as Reports of the National Council on Radiation Protection and Measurement. These reports are obtainable from NCRP Publications, P.O. Box 30175, Washington, D.C. 20014.

660-2. Definitions:

Portable: X-ray equipment designed to be hand-carried.

Mobile: X-ray equipment mounted on a permanent base with wheels and/or casters for moving while completely assembled.

Transportable: X-ray equipment to be installed in a vehicle or that may be readily disassembled for transport in a vehicle.

Long-Time Rating: A rating based on an operating interval of five minutes or longer.

Momentary Rating: A rating based on an operating interval that does not exceed five seconds.

660-3. Hazardous Locations. Unless approved for the location, X-ray and related equipment shall not be installed or operated in hazardous locations.

See Article 517, Part E.

▲ An x-ray tube of the hot-cathode type, as now commonly used, is a two-element vacuum tube in which a tungsten filament serves as the cathode. Current is supplied to the filament at low voltage. In most cases unidirectional pulsating voltage is applied between the cathode and the anode. The applied voltage is measured or described in terms of the peak voltage, which may be anywhere within the range of 10,000 to 1,000,000 V, or even more. The current flowing in the high-voltage circuit may be as low as 5 mA or may be as much as 1 A, depending upon the desired intensity of radiation. The high voltage is obtained by means of a transformer, usually operating at 230 V primary, and usually is made unidirectional by means of two-element rectifying vacuum tubes, though in some cases an alternating current is applied to the x-ray tube. The x rays are radiations of an extremely high frequency (or short wave length) which are the strongest in a plane at right angles to the electron stream passing between the cathode and the anode in the tube.

As used by physicians and dentists, x rays have three applications: *fluoroscopy*, where a picture or shadow is thrown upon a screen of specially prepared glass by rays passing through some part of the patient's body; *radiography*, which is similar to fluoroscopy except that the picture is thrown upon a photographic film instead of a screen; and *therapy*, in which use is made of the effects of the rays upon the tissues of the human body.

660-4. Connection to Supply Circuit.

   (a) Fixed and Stationary Equipment.   Fixed and stationary X-ray equipment shall be connected to the power supply by means of a wiring method meeting the general requirements of this Code.

   Exception: Equipment properly supplied by a branch circuit rated at not over 30 amperes shall be permitted to be supplied through a suitable attachment plug cap and hard-service cable or cord.

   (b) Portable, Mobile, and Transportable Equipment.   Individual branch circuits shall not be required for portable, mobile, and transportable medical X-ray equipment requiring a capacity of not over 60 amperes. Portable and mobile types of X-ray equipment of any capacity shall be supplied through a suitable hard-service cable or cord. Transportable X-ray equipment of any capacity shall be permitted to be connected to its power supply by suitable connections and hard-service cable or cord.

   (c) Over 600-Volt Supply.   Circuits and equipment operated on a supply circuit of over 600 volts shall comply with Article 710.

660-5. Disconnecting Means.   A disconnecting means of adequate capacity for at least 50 percent of the input required for the momentary rating or 100 percent of the input required for the long-time rating of the X-ray equipment, whichever is greater, shall be provided in the supply circuit. The disconnecting means shall be operable from a location readily accessible from the X-ray control. For equipment connected to a 120-volt branch circuit of 30 amperes or less, a grounding-type attachment plug cap and receptacle of proper rating shall be permitted to serve as a disconnecting means.

660-6. Rating of Supply Conductors and Overcurrent Protection.

   (a) The ampacity of supply branch circuit conductors and the overcurrent protective devices shall not be less than 50 percent of the momentary rating or 100 percent of the long time rating, whichever is the greater.

(b) The rated ampacity of conductors and overcurrent devices of a feeder for two or more branch circuits supplying X-ray units shall not be less than 100 percent of the momentary demand rating (as determined by (a)) of the two largest medical diagnostic X-ray apparatus plus 20 percent of the momentary ratings of other medical diagnostic X-ray apparatus. Medical X-ray therapy equipment or industrial X-ray units shall be calculated at 100 percent.

The ampacity of the branch-circuit conductors and the ratings of disconnecting means and overcurrent protection for X-ray equipment are usually designated by the manufacturer for the specific installation.

660-7. Wiring Terminals. X-ray equipment shall be provided with suitable wiring terminals or leads for the connection of power supply conductors of the size required by the rating of the branch circuit for the equipment.

Exception: Where provided with a permanently attached cord or a cord set.

660-8. Number of Conductors in Raceway. The number of control circuit conductors installed in a raceway shall be determined in accordance with Section 300-17.

660-9. Minimum Size of Conductors. Sizes No. 18 or 16 fixture wires as specified in Section 725-16 and flexible cords shall be permitted for the control and operating circuits of X-ray and auxiliary equipment where protected by not larger than 20-ampere overcurrent devices.

660-10. Equipment Installations. All equipment for new X-ray installations and all used or reconditioned X-ray equipment moved to and reinstalled at a new location shall be of an approved type.

B. Control

660-20. Fixed and Stationary Equipment.

(a) Separate Control Device. A separate control device, in addition to the disconnecting means, shall be incorporated in the X-ray control supply or in the primary circuit to the high-voltage transformer. This device shall be a part of the X-ray equipment, but shall be permitted in a separate enclosure immediately adjacent to the X-ray control unit.

(b) Protective Device. A protective device, which shall be permitted to be incorporated into the separate control device, shall be provided to control the load resulting from failures in the high-voltage circuit.

660-21. Portable and Mobile Equipment. Portable and mobile equipment shall comply with Section 660-20, but the manually controlled device shall be located in or on the equipment.

660-23. Industrial and Laboratory Equipment.

(a) Radiographic and Fluoroscopic Types. All radiographic- and fluoroscopic-type equipment shall be effectively enclosed or shall have interlocks that de-energize the equipment automatically to prevent ready access to live current-carrying parts.

(b) Diffraction and Irradiation Types. Diffraction- and irradiation-type equipment shall be provided with a positive means to indicate when it is energized. The indicator shall be a pilot light, readable meter deflection, or equivalent means.

Exception: Equipment or installations effectively enclosed or provided with interlocks to prevent access to live current-carrying parts during operation.

660-24. Independent Control. Where more than one piece of equipment is operated from the same high-voltage circuit, each piece or each group of equipment as a unit shall be provided with a high-voltage switch or equivalent disconnecting means. This disconnecting means shall be constructed, enclosed, or located so as to avoid contact by persons with its live parts.

▲ In radiography it is important that the exposure be accurately timed, and for this purpose a switch is used which can be set to open the circuit automatically in any desired time after the circuit has been closed.

C. Transformers and Capacitors

660-35. General. Transformers and capacitors that are part of an X-ray equipment shall not be required to comply with Articles 450 and 460.

▲ A power transformer supplying electrical systems is usually supplied at a high primary voltage; hence in case of a breakdown of the insulation on the primary winding, a large amount of energy can be delivered to the transformer. An askarel-filled x-ray transformer involves much less fire hazard because the primary voltage is low, and it is therefore not required that such transformers be placed in vaults of fire-resistant construction.

660-36. Capacitors. Capacitors shall be mounted within enclosures of insulating material or grounded metal.

D. Guarding and Grounding

660-47. General.
(a) High-Voltage Parts. All high-voltage parts, including X-ray tubes, shall be mounted within grounded enclosures. Air, oil, gas, or other suitable insulating media shall be used to insulate the high voltage from the grounded enclosure. The connection from the high-voltage equipment to X-ray tubes and other high-voltage components shall be made with high-voltage shielded cables.

(b) Low-Voltage Cables. Low-voltage cables connecting to oil-filled units that are not completely sealed, such as transformers, condensers, oil coolers, and high-voltage switches, shall have insulation of the oil-resistant type.

▲ This section definitely requires that all new x-ray equipment shall be so constructed that all high-voltage parts, except leads to the x-ray tube, are in grounded metal enclosures, unless the equipment is in a separate room or enclosure and the circuit to the primary of the transformer is automatically opened by unlocking the door to the enclosure. Conductors leading to the x-ray tube are heavily insulated.

660-48. Grounding. Noncurrent-carrying metal parts of X-ray and associated equipment (controls, tables, X-ray tube supports, transformer tanks, shielded cables, X-ray tube heads, etc.) shall be grounded in the manner specified in Article 250. Portable and mobile equipment shall be provided with an approved grounding-type attachment plug cap. In areas designated as critical care areas, X-ray equipment shall be grounded in the manner prescribed in Section 517-51.
Exception: Battery-operated equipment.

ARTICLE 665. INDUCTION AND DIELECTRIC HEATING EQUIPMENT

A. General

665-1. Scope. This Article covers the construction and installation of induction and dielectric heating equipment and accessories for industrial, scientific, and medical applications, but not for appliances.

665-2. Definitions.

Dead Front: There are no live parts exposed to a person on the operating side of the equipment.

Dielectric Heating: Dielectric heating is the heating of a nominally insulating material due to its own dielectric losses when the material is placed in a varying electric field.

Heating Equipment: The term "heating equipment" as used in this Article includes any equipment used for heating purposes whose heat is generated by induction or dielectric methods.

Induction Heating: Induction heating is the heating of a nominally conductive material due to its own I^2R losses when the material is placed in a varying electromagnetic field.

Therapeutic High-Frequency Equipment: The term "therapeutic high-frequency equipment" as used in this Article means generating equipment capable of producing alternating currents having frequencies greater than those frequencies which elicit neuromuscular response. In order to comply with the above, the output frequency of the therapeutic high-frequency equipment shall not be less than 2 megahertz.

▲ Induction and dielectric heating are systems wherein a workpiece is heated by means of a rapidly alternating magnetic or electric field.

Induction Heating

Induction heating is used to heat materials that are good electrical conductors, for such purposes as soldering, brazing, hardening, and annealing. Induction heating, in general, involves frequencies ranging from 3 to about 500 kHz, and power outputs from a few hundred watts to several thousand kilowatts. In general, motor-generator sets are used for frequencies up to about 30 kHz; spark-gap converters, from 20 to 400 kHz; and vacuum-tube generators, from 100 to 500 kHz. Isolated special jobs may use frequencies as high as 60 to 80 MHz. Motor-generator sets normally supply power for heating large masses for melting, forging, deep hardening, and the joining of heavy pieces, whereas spark-gap and vacuum-tube generators find their best applications in the joining of smaller pieces and shallow case hardening, with vacuum-tube generators also being used where special high heat concentrations are required.

To heat a workpiece by induction heating, it is placed in a work coil consisting of one or more turns, which is the output circuit of the generator (Fig. 665-1). The high-frequency current which flows through this coil sets up a rapidly alternating magnetic field within it. By inducing a voltage in the workpiece, this field causes a current flow in the piece to be heated. As the current flows through the resistance of the workpiece, it generates heat (I^2R loss) in the piece itself. It is this heat that is utilized in induction heating.

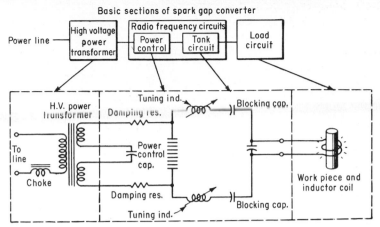

FIG. 665-1. Spark-gap converter for induction heating—simplified basic diagram. (*Westinghouse Electric Corp.*)

Dielectric Heating

In contrast, dielectric heating is used to heat materials that are nonconductors, such as wood, plastic, textiles, rubber, etc., for such purposes as drying, gluing, curing, and baking. It uses frequencies from 1 to 200 MHz, especially those from 1 to 50 MHz. Vacuum-tube generators are used exclusively to supply dielectric heating power, with outputs ranging from a few hundred watts to several hundred kilowatts.

Whereas induction heating uses a varying magnetic field, dielectric heating employs a varying electric field. This is done by placing the material to be heated between a pair of metal plates, called electrodes, in the output circuit of the generator. When high-frequency voltage is applied to the electrodes, a rapidly alternating electric field is set up between them, passing through the material to be heated. Because of the electrical charges within the molecules of this material, the field causes the molecules to vibrate in proportion to its frequency. This internal molecular action generates the heat used for dielectric heating.

Generators

In general, both spark-gap and vacuum-tube generators consist of a power-supply circuit, a voltage and/or frequency conversion circuit, a control circuit, and an output circuit. This combination is familiar in motor-generator operation, and can be easily understood in high-frequency generators by referring to Figs. 665-1 through 665-3.

In the spark-gap converter (Fig. 665-1), tank capacitors are alternately charged and discharged, to produce high-frequency oscillations in the output circuit. In vacuum-tube generators, these oscillations are produced by a vacuum-tube oscillator, which is fed by DC power from a high-voltage power supply. The induction heating generator (Fig. 665-2) and the dielectric heating generator (Fig. 665-3) differ chiefly in their output circuits. Typical control circuits are shown for each.

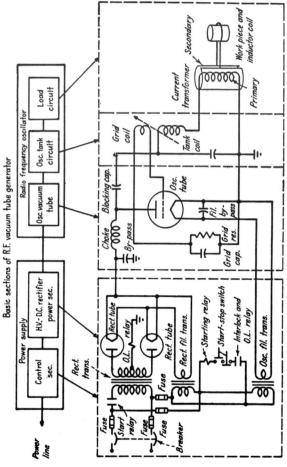

FIG. 665-2. Vacuum-tube generator for induction heating—simplified basic diagram. (*Westinghouse Electric Corp.*)

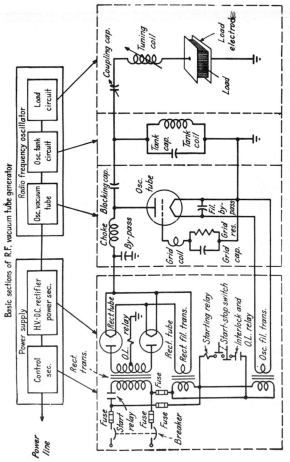

FIG. 665-3. Vacuum-tube generator for dielectric heating—simplified basic diagram. (*Westinghouse Electric Corp.*)

The actual work loads are shown disconnected from the rest of the output circuit, emphasizing the fact that external auxiliary equipment is often needed to ensure the most efficient transfer of power from generator to load.

Except in the case of motor-generator sets, low-power generators will probably contain enough control and cooling apparatus for normal operation. However, on installations of over 50 kW, external switchgear and cooling systems are usually required. Such equipment should comply with the appropriate articles of the Code.

665-3. Other Articles. Wiring from the source of power to the heating equipment shall comply with Chapters 1 through 4. Circuits and equipment operating on a supply circuit of over 600 volts shall comply with Article 710.

665-4. Hazardous Locations. Induction and dielectric heating equipment shall not be installed in hazardous locations as defined in Article 500.

Exception: Where the equipment and wiring are designed and approved for the hazardous locations.

B. Guarding, Grounding and Labeling

665-20. Enclosures. The converting apparatus (including the DC line) and high-frequency electric circuits (excluding the output circuits and remote-control circuits) shall be completely contained within an enclosure or enclosures of noncombustible material.

665-21. Panel Controls. All panel controls shall be of dead-front construction.

665-22. Access to Internal Equipment. Doors or detachable panels may be employed for internal access. Where doors are used giving access to voltages from 500 to 1000 volts AC or DC, either door locks shall be provided or interlocking shall be installed. Where doors are used giving access to voltages of over 1000 volts AC or DC, either mechanical lockouts with a disconnecting means to prevent access until voltage is removed from the cubicle, or both door interlocking and mechanical door locks shall be provided. Detachable panels not normally used for access to such parts shall be fastened in a manner that will make them inconvenient to remove.

▲ This section allows the manufacturer the option of using interlocked doors or detachable panels. Where panels are used and are not intended as normal access points, they shall be fastened with bolts or screws of sufficient number to discourage removal. They should not be held in place with any type of speed fastener.

665-23. Warning Labels. "Danger" labels shall be attached on the equipment, and shall be plainly visible even when doors are open or panels are removed from compartments containing voltages of over 250 volts AC or DC.

665-24. Capacitors. Where capacitors in excess of 0.1 microfarad are used in DC circuits, either as rectifier filter components or suppressors, etc., having circuit voltages of over 240 volts to ground, bleeder resistors or grounding switches shall be used as grounding devices. The time of discharge shall be in accordance with Section 460-6(a).

Where auxiliary rectifiers are used with filter capacitors in the output for bias supplies, tube keyers, etc., bleeder resistors shall be used even though the DC voltage may not exceed 240 volts.

665-25. Work Applicator Shielding. Protective cages or adequate shielding shall be used to guard work applicators other than induction heating coils. Induction heating coils shall be permitted to be protected by insulation and/or refractory materials. Interlock switches shall be used on all hinged access doors, sliding panels, or other easy means of access to the applicator. All interlock switches shall be connected in such a manner as to remove all power from the applicator when any one of the access doors or panels is open. Interlocks on access doors or panels shall not be required if the applicator is an induction heating coil at DC ground potential or operating at less than 150 volts AC.

▲ See discussion under Sec. 665-44. This section is intended primarily to apply to dielectric heating installations where it is absolutely essential that the electrodes and associated tuning or matching devices are properly shielded.

665-26. Grounding and Bonding. Grounding and/or inter-unit bonding shall be used wherever required for circuit operation, for limiting to a safe value radio frequency potentials between all exposed noncurrent-carrying parts of the equipment and earth ground, between all equipment parts and surrounding objects, and between such objects and earth ground. Such grounding and bonding shall be installed in accordance with Article 250.

▲ *Bonding*

At radio frequencies, and especially at dielectric-heating frequencies (1 to 200 MHz), it is very possible for differences in radio-frequency potential to exist between the equipment proper and other surrounding metal objects or other units of the complete installation. These potentials exist because of stray currents flowing between units of the equipment or to ground. Bonding is therefore essential, and such bonding must take the form of very wide copper or aluminum straps between units and to other surrounding metal objects such as conveyers, presses, etc. The most satisfactory bond is provided by placing all units of the equipment on a flooring or base consisting of copper or aluminum sheet, thoroughly joined where necessary by soldering, welding, or adequate bolting. Such bonding reduces the radio-frequency resistance and reactance between units to a minimum, and any stray circulating currents flowing through this bonding will not cause sufficient voltage drop to become dangerous.

Shielding

Shielding at dielectric-heating frequencies is a necessity to provide operator protection from the high radio-frequency potentials involved, and also to prevent possible interference with radio communication systems. Shielding is accomplished by totally enclosing all work circuit components with copper sheet, copper screening, or aluminum sheet.

665-27. Marking. Each heating equipment shall be provided with a nameplate giving the manufacturer's name and model identification and the following input data: line volts, frequency, number of phases, maximum current, full-load kVA, and full-load power factor.

C. Motor-Generator Equipment

665-40. General. Motor-generator equipment shall include all rotating equipment designed to operate from an AC or DC motor or by mechanical drive from a prime mover, producing an alternating current of any frequency for induction and/or dielectric heating.

665-41. Ampacity of Supply Conductors. The ampacity of supply conductors shall be determined in accordance with Article 430.

665-42. Overcurrent Protection. Overcurrent protection shall be provided as specified in Article 430 for the electric supply circuit.

665-43. Disconnecting Means. The disconnecting means shall be provided as specified in Article 430.

A readily accessible disconnecting means shall be provided by which each heating equipment can be isolated from its supply circuit. The ampere rating of this disconnecting means shall not be less than the nameplate current rating of the equipment. The supply circuit disconnecting means shall be permitted as a heating equipment disconnecting means where the circuit supplies only one equipment.

665-44. Output Circuit. The output circuit shall include all output components external to the generator, including contactors, transformers, busbars, and other conductors, and shall comply with (a) and (b) below.

(a) Generator Output. The output circuit shall be isolated from ground.

Exception: Where the capacitive coupling inherent in the generator causes the generator terminals to have voltages from terminal to ground that are equal.

Where rated at over 500 volts, the output circuit shall incorporate a DC ground protector unit. The DC impressed on the output circuit shall not exceed 30 volts and shall not exceed a current capability of 5 milliamperes.

An isolating transformer for matching the load and the source shall be permitted in the output circuit if the output secondary is not at DC ground potential.

(b) Component Interconnections. The various components required for a complete induction heating equipment installation shall be connected by properly protected multiconductor cable, busbar, or coaxial cable. Cables shall be installed in nonferrous raceways. Busbars shall be protected, where required, by nonferrous enclosures.

▲ *RF Lines*

When it is necessary to transmit the high-frequency output of a generator any distance to the work applicator, a radio-frequency line is generally used. This usually consists of a conductor totally enclosed in a grounded metal housing. This central conductor is commonly supported by insulators, mounted in the grounded housing and periodically spaced along its length. Figure 665-4 shows such a line, rectangular in cross section, connecting two induction generators to the load.

While contact with high-voltage radio frequencies may cause severe burns, contact with high-voltage DC could be fatal. Therefore, it is imperative that generator output (directly, capacitively, or inductively coupled) be effectively grounded with respect to DC so that, should generator failure place high-voltage DC in the tank oscillating circuit, there will still be no danger to the operator. This grounding is generally internal in vacuum-tube generators, as shown in the accompanying diagrams. In all types of induction generators, one side of the work coil should usually be externally grounded.

In general, all high-voltage connections to the primary of a current transformer should be enclosed. The primary concern is the operator's safety. Examples would be interlocked cages around small dielectric electrodes, and interlocking safety doors.

Fig. 665-4. Two 20-kW, 450-MHz induction-heating generators used in hardening wristpins. Note the radio-frequency lines connecting the generators to the work applicator. (*Westinghouse Electric Corp.*)

On induction heating jobs, it is not always practical to completely house the work coil and obtain efficient production operation. In these cases, precautions should be taken to minimize the chance of operator contact with the coil.

665-46. Control Enclosures. Direct current or low-frequency AC shall be permitted in the control portion of the heating equipment. This shall be limited to not over 150 volts. Solid or stranded wire No. 18 or larger shall be used. A step-down transformer with proper overcurrent protection shall be permitted in the control enclosure to obtain an AC voltage of less than 150 volts. The higher voltage terminals shall be guarded to prevent accidental contact. Sixty-Hertz components shall be permitted to control high frequency where properly rated by the induction heating equipment manufacturer. Electronic circuits utilizing solid-state devices and tubes shall be permitted printed circuits or wires smaller than No. 18.

665-47. Remote Control.

(a) Selector Switch. Where remote controls are used for applying power, a selector switch shall be provided and interlocked to provide power from only one control point at a time.

(b) Foot Switches. Switches operated by foot pressure shall be provided with a shield over the contact button to avoid accidental closing of a switch.

D. Equipment Other Than Motor-Generator

665-60. General. Equipment other than motor-generators shall consist of all static multipliers and oscillator-type units utilizing vacuum tubes and/or solid-state devices. The equipment shall be capable of converting AC or DC to an AC frequency suitable for induction and/or dielectric heating.

665-61. Ampacity of Supply Conductors. The ampacity of supply conductors shall be determined in accordance with (a) and (b) below.

(a) The ampacity of the circuit conductors shall not be less than the nameplate current rating of the equipment.

(b) The ampacity of conductors supplying two or more equipments shall not be less than the sum of the nameplate current ratings on all equipments.

Exception: If simultaneous operation of two or more equipments supplied from the same feeder is not possible, the ampacity of the feeder shall not be less than the sum of the nameplate ratings for the largest group of machines capable of simultaneous operation, plus 100 percent of the stand-by currents of the remaining machines supplied.

▲ Quite often where several equipments are operated in a single plant it is possible to conserve on power-line requirements by taking into account the load or use factor of each equipment. The time cycles of operation on various machines may be staggered to allow a minimum of current to be taken from the line. In such cases the Code requires sufficient capacity to carry all full-load currents from those machines which will operate simultaneously, plus the standby requirements of all other units.

665-62. Overcurrent Protection. Overcurrent protection shall be provided as specified in Article 240 for the equipment as a whole. This overcurrent protection shall be provided separately or as a part of the equipment.

665-63. Disconnecting Means. A readily accessible disconnecting means shall be provided by which each heating equipment can be isolated from its supply circuit. The rating of this disconnecting means shall not be less than the nameplate rating of the equipment. The supply circuit disconnecting means shall be permitted for disconnecting the heating equipment where the circuit supplies only one equipment.

665-64. Output Circuit. The output circuit shall include all output components external to the converting device, including contactors, transformers, busbars, and other conductors and shall comply with (a) and (b) below.

(a) Converter Output. The output circuit (direct or coupled) shall be at DC ground potential.

(b) Converter and Applicator Connection. Where the connections between the converter and the work applicator exceed 2 feet in length, the connections shall be enclosed or guarded with noncombustible material.

665-66. Line Frequency in Converter Equipment Output. Commercial frequencies of 25- to 60-Hertz alternating-current output shall be permitted to be coupled for control purposes, but shall be limited to not over 150 volts during periods of circuit operation.

665-67. Keying. Where high-speed keying circuits dependent on the effect of "oscillator blocking" are employed, the peak radio frequency output voltage during the blocked portion of the cycle shall not exceed 100 volts in units employing radio frequency converters.

▲ Radio-frequency generators are often turned on and off by applying a blocking bias to the grid circuit of the oscillator tube, for the purpose of obtaining fast, accurate control of power. If this keying circuit does not completely block the tube oscillations, high-frequency power will appear at the work applicator, even though the operator thinks it has been turned off. However, if this residual output voltage is limited to a value of 100 V peak, the operator will be protected from any serious burns.

665-68. Remote Control.
(a) Selector Switch. Where remote controls are used for applying power, a selector switch shall be provided and interlocked to provide power from only one control point at a time.

(b) Foot Switches. Switches operated by foot pressure shall be provided with a shield over the contact button to avoid accidental closing of the switch.

▲ If interlocking were not provided, there would be a definite danger to an operator at the remote-control station. It might then be possible, if the operator had turned off the power and was doing some work in contact with a work coil, for someone else to apply power from another point, seriously injuring the operator.

E. Therapeutic Equipment

665-80. Installation.
(a) Portability Not Essential. Where portability is not essential, equipment shall be permanently installed in accordance with Chapters 1 through 3.

(b) Portability Is Essential. Where portability is essential, the power-supply cord shall be a 3-conductor hard-service type with an ampacity not less than the marked ampere rating of the equipment. One insulated conductor having a continuous green color or a continuous green color with one or more yellow stripes shall be used solely for equipment grounding. The cord shall terminate in an approved grounding-type attachment plug as provided in Section 250-59(b).

665-81. Applicators for Therapeutic Equipment. Application of the high-frequency power to the patient shall be permitted by means of an electric field or an induction field. Current-carrying parts of applicators shall be so insulated or enclosed that reliable isolation of the patient will be assured.

665-82. Enclosure. The converting apparatus, including the DC line and high-frequency electric circuits, but excluding the line cord for portable units and the output circuits, shall be contained in an enclosure of noncombustible material.

▲ This section is intended to include all generating equipment except rotating machines, as such machines are normally enclosed according to existing motor-generator set standards. The enclosure referred to is expected to enclose the generating apparatus to protect operating personnel from the high voltages encountered in this type of equipment. The enclosure need not comply with Art. 100 where the word "cabinet" is defined.

665-83. Panel Controls. All panel controls shall be of dead-front construction.
665-84. Access to Internal Equipment. Access shall be through panels not conveniently removable. Panels that must be removed to provide access for adjustments or to fuses, tubes, overload reset devices, internal tap switches, and the like shall be labeled to indicate danger if and when the panels are removed, or shall be provided with suitable electrical interlock devices.

ARTICLE 670. METALWORKING MACHINE TOOLS

For further information, see Electrical Metalworking Machine Tools (NFPA No. 79-1973).

670-1. Scope. This Article covers the size and overcurrent protection of supply conductors to metalworking machine tools and the nameplate data required on each such tool.

670-2. Definition: Metalworking Machine Tool. A power-driven machine not portable by hand, used to shape or form metal by cutting, impact, pressure, electrical techniques, or a combination of these processes.

▲ It should be noted that these provisions do not apply to woodworking machines or to any other type of motor-driven machine which is not included in this definition of machine tools. The provisions do not apply to any machine or tool which is not normally used in a fixed location and can be carried from place to place by hand.

670-3. Machine Tool Nameplate Data. A permanent nameplate listing supply voltage, phase, frequency, full-load currents (see notes below), ampere rating of largest motor, short-circuit interrupting capacity of the machine overcurrent protective device if furnished, and diagram number shall be attached to the control equipment enclosure or machine where plainly visible after installation.

NOTE 1. The full-load current shall not be less than the sum of the full-load currents required for all motors and other equipment which may be in operation at the same time under normal conditions of use. Where unusual type loads, duty cycles, etc., require oversized conductors, the required capacity shall be included in the marked "full-load current."

NOTE 2. Where more than one incoming supply circuit is to be provided, the nameplate shall state the above information for each circuit.

670-4. General.

(a) Circuit Conductors. The supply circuit conductors shall have an ampacity of not less than the marked full-load current rating plus 25 percent of the full-load current rating of the highest rated motor as indicated on the nameplate.

For the protection of supply conductors to the machine tool, see Section 240-3.

(b) Single Unit. A machine tool complying with NFPA No. 79-1974 shall be considered an individual unit equipment. It shall be provided with a disconnecting means and shall be permitted to be supplied by branch circuits protected by either fuses or circuit breakers.

(c) Overcurrent Protection. The disconnecting means shall not be required to incorporate overcurrent protection. Where the machine tool nameplate is marked "Overcurrent protection provided at machine supply terminals," the supply conductors shall be considered either as feeders or taps as covered by Section 240-21.

"Overcurrent protection provided at machine supply terminals" means that provision has been made in the machine tool for each set of supply conductors to terminate in a single circuit breaker or set of fuses.

▲ NFPA No. 79 states: "The center of the grip of the operating handle of the disconnecting means when in its highest position, shall not be more than 6½ feet above the floor. The operating handle shall be so arranged that it may be locked in the 'Off' position."

ARTICLE 675. ELECTRICALLY DRIVEN OR CONTROLLED IRRIGATION MACHINES

A. General

675-1. Scope. The provisions of this Article apply to electrically driven or controlled irrigation machines, and to the branch circuits and controllers for such equipment.

675-2. Definitions.

Irrigation Machines: An irrigation machine is an electrically driven or controlled machine, with one or more motors, not hand portable, and used primarily to transport and distribute water for agricultural purposes.

Center Pivot Irrigation Machines: A center pivot irrigation machine is a multi-motored irrigation machine which revolves around a central pivot and employs alignment switches or similar devices to control individual motors.

Collector Rings: A collector ring is an assembly of slip rings for transferring electrical energy from a stationary to a rotating member.

675-3. Other Articles. These provisions are in addition to, or amendatory of, the provisions of Article 430 and other Articles in this Code which apply except as modified in this Article.

675-4. Irrigation Cable.

(a) Construction. The cable used to interconnect enclosures on the structure of an irrigation machine shall be an assembly of stranded, insulated conductors with nonhygroscopic filler in a core of moisture and flame-resistant, nonmetallic material overlaid with a metallic covering and jacketed with a moisture, corrosion and sunlight-resistant, non-metallic material.

The conductor insulation shall be of a type listed in Table 310-13 for an operating temperature of 75° centigrade, and for use in wet locations. The core insulating material thickness shall be not less than 30 mils and the metallic overlay thickness shall be not less than 8 mils. The jacketing material thickness shall be not less than 50 mils.

A composite of power, control, and grounding conductors in the cable shall be permitted.

(b) Alternate Wiring Methods. Other cables approved for the purpose.

(c) Supports. Irrigation cable shall be secured by approved straps, hangers or similar fittings so designed and installed as not to injure the cable. Cable shall be supported at intervals not exceeding 4 feet.

(d) Fittings. Fittings shall be used at all points where irrigation cable terminates. The fittings shall be designed for use with the cable and shall be suitable for the conditions of service.

675-5. More Than Three Conductors in a Raceway or Cable. The signal and control conductors of a raceway or cable shall not be counted for the purpose of derating the conductors as required in Note 8 of Table 310-16.

675-6. Marking on Main Control Panel. The main control panel shall be provided with a nameplate which shall give the following information:

(a) The manufacturer's name; the rated voltage; the phase; and the frequency.

(b) The current rating of the machine.

(c) The rating of the main disconnecting means and size of overcurrent protection required.

675-7. Collector Rings.

(a) Collector rings shall have an ampacity not less than 125 percent of the full-load current of the largest device served plus the full-load current of all other devices served.

(b) Collector rings used for grounding shall be of the same ampacity as the largest collector ring in the assembly.

675-8. Grounding. The following equipment shall be grounded:

(a) All electrical equipment on the irrigation machine.

(b) All electrical equipment associated with the irrigation machine.

(c) Metallic junction boxes and enclosures.

(d) Control panels or control equipment that supply or control electrical equipment to the irrigation machine.

Exception: Grounding shall not be required on machines where all of the following provisions are met:

(a) The machine is electrically controlled but not electrically driven.

(b) The control voltage is 30 volts or less.

(c) The control or signal circuits are current limited as specified in Section 725-31.

675-9. Methods of Grounding. Machines which require grounding shall have a noncurrent carrying equipment grounding conductor provided as an integral part of each cord, cable or raceway. This grounding conductor shall be equal in size to the supply conductors, but not smaller than #14 copper.

675-10. Bonding. Where electrical grounding is required on an irrigation machine, the metallic structure of the machine, metallic conduit or metallic sheath of cable shall be bonded to the grounding conductor. Metal-to-metal contact with a part which is bonded to the grounding conductor and the noncurrent carrying parts of the machine shall be considered as an acceptable bonding path.

675-11. Lightning Protection. If an irrigation machine has a stationary point, a driven ground rod shall be connected to the machine at the stationary point for lightning protection.

675-12. Energy From More Than One Source. Equipment within an enclosure receiving electrical energy from more than one source shall not be required to have a disconnecting means for the additional source, provided that its voltage is 30 volts or less and meets the requirements of Section 725-31.

B. Center Pivot Irrigation Machines

675-21. General. The provisions of Part B are intended to cover additional special requirements which are peculiar to Center Pivot Irrigation Machines. See Section 675-2 for definition of Center Pivot Irrigation Machines.

675-22. Equivalent Current Ratings. In order to establish ratings of controllers, disconnecting means, conductors, and the like, for the inherent intermittent duty of Center Pivot Irrigation Machines, the following determination shall be used:

(a) The equivalent continuous current rating for the selection of branch-circuit conductors and branch-circuit devices, shall be equal to 125 percent of the full-load current of the largest motor plus 60 percent of the sum of the full load currents of all remaining motors on the circuit.

(b) The equivalent locked rotor current rating shall be equal to the numerical sum of 2 times the locked rotor current of the largest motor plus 80 percent of the sum of the full-load currents of all the remaining motors on the circuit.

675-23. Disconnecting Means.

(a) Main Controller. A controller which is used to start and stop the complete machine shall meet all of the following requirements:

(1) An equivalent continuous current rating not less than specified in 675-22(a).

(2) A horsepower rating not less than the value from Table 430-151 based on the equivalent locked rotor current specified in 675-22(b).

(b) Main Disconnecting Means. The main disconnecting means for the machine shall be located at the point of connection of electrical power to the machine and shall be readily accessible and capable of being locked in the open position. This disconnecting means shall have the same horsepower and current ratings as required for the main controller.

(c) Disconnecting Means for Individual Motors and Controllers. A disconnecting means shall be provided for each motor and controller and shall be located as required by Article 430, Part H. The disconnecting means shall not be required to be readily accessible.

675-24. Branch-Circuit Conductors. The branch-circuit conductors shall have an ampacity not less than specified in 675-22(a).

675-25. Several Motors on One Branch Circuit.

(a) Several motors, each not exceeding two horsepower rating, shall be permitted to be used on an irrigation machine circuit protected at not more than 30 amperes at 600 volts or less, provided all of the following conditions are met:

(1) The full-load rating of any motor is the circuit shall not exceed 6 amperes.

(2) Each motor in the circuit shall have individual running overcurrent protection in accordance with Section 430-32.

(3) Taps to individual motors shall not be smaller than #14 copper and not more than 25 feet in length.

(b) Individual branch-circuit short-circuit protection for motors and motor controllers shall not be required where the requirements of 675-25(a) are met.

675-26. Collector Rings.

(a) Collector rings transmitting current for power purposes shall have an ampacity not less than specified in Section 675-22(a).

(b) Collector rings for control and signal purposes shall have an ampacity not less than 125 percent of the full-load current of the largest device served plus the full-load current of all other devices served.

(c) The collector ring used for grounding shall be of the same ampacity as the largest collector ring in the assembly.

ARTICLE 680. SWIMMING POOLS, FOUNTAINS AND SIMILAR INSTALLATIONS

A. General

680-1. Scope. The provisions of this Article apply to the construction and installation of electric wiring for and equipment in or adjacent to all swimming, wading, therapeutic, and decorative pools and fountains whether permanently installed or storable, and to metallic auxiliary equipment, such as pumps, filters, and similar equipment.

▲ Research work conducted by Underwriters' Laboratories, Inc., and others, indicated that an electric shock could be received in two different ways. One of these involved the existence in the water of an electrical potential with respect to ground, and the other involved the existence of a potential gradient in the water itself.

A person standing in the pool and touching the energized enclosure of faulty equipment located at poolside would be subject to a severe electrical shock because of the good ground which his body would establish through the water and pool to earth. Accordingly, the provisions as given in this article apply to construction and installations in and adjacent to pools and fountains.

680-2. Approval of Equipment. All electric equipment installed in the water, walls or deck of swimming pools, fountains and similar installations shall comply with the provisions of this Article.

680-3. Other Articles. Except as modified by this Article, wiring and equipment in or adjacent to swimming pools shall comply with the applicable requirements of Chapters 1 through 4.

See Section 370-13 for junction boxes, Section 347-3 for rigid nonmetallic conduit, and Article 720 for low-voltage lighting.

680-4. Definitions.

Dry-Niche Lighting Fixture. A lighting fixture intended for installation in the wall of the pool in a niche that is sealed against the entry of pool water by a fixed lens.

Forming Shell: A metal structure designed to support a wet-niche lighting fixture assembly and intended for mounting in a swimming pool structure.

Ground-Fault Circuit-Interrupter: A device whose function is to interrupt the electric circuit to the load when a fault current to ground exceeds some predetermined value that is less than that required to operate the overcurrent protective device of the supply circuit.

Permanently Installed Decorative Fountains and Reflection Pools: Those that are constructed in the ground, on the ground, or in a building in such a manner that the pool cannot be readily disassembled for storage and are served by electrical circuits of any nature. These units are primarily constructed for their aesthetic value and not intended for swimming or wading.

Permanently Installed Swimming Pools, Wading and Therapeutic Pools: Those that are constructed in the ground, on the ground, or in a building in such a manner that the pool cannot be readily disassembled for storage and are served by electrical circuits of any nature.

Exception: Therapeutic pools in health care facilities shall be exempt from this Article.

Storable Swimming or Wading Pool: One that is so constructed that it may be readily disassembled for storage and reassembled to its original integrity.

Wet-Niche Lighting Fixture: A lighting fixture intended for installation in a metal forming shell mounted in a swimming pool structure where the fixture will be completely surrounded by pool water.

680-5. Transformers and Ground-Fault Circuit-Interrupters.

(a) Transformers. Transformers used for the supply of fixtures, together with the transformer enclosure, shall be approved for the purpose. The transformer shall be a two-winding type having a grounded metal barrier between the primary and secondary windings.

(b) Wiring. Conductors on the load side of a ground-fault circuit-interrupter or of a transformer, used to comply with the provisions of Section 680-20(a)(1), shall be kept entirely independent of all other wiring and electric equipment.

Exception: Ground-fault circuit-interrupters shall be permitted in a panelboard that contains circuits protected by other than ground-fault circuit-interrupters when supplementary insulation (such as nonmetallic sleeving or tubing) is provided on the load side of the ground-fault circuit-interrupter.

680-6. Lighting Fixtures and Lighting Outlets.

(a) Receptacles. Receptacles on the property shall be located at least 10 feet from the inside walls of a pool. Receptacles located within 15 feet of the inside walls of a pool shall be protected by a ground-fault circuit-interrupter.

In determining the above dimensions, the distance to be measured is the shortest path the supply cord of an appliance connected to the receptacle would follow without piercing a floor, wall or ceiling of a building or other effective permanent barrier.

(b) Lighting Fixtures and Lighting Outlets.

(1) Lighting fixtures and lighting outlets located not less than five feet nor more than 16 feet, measured horizontally from the inside walls of a pool, shall be protected by a ground-fault circuit-interrupter installed in the branch circuit supplying the fixture.

(2) Existing lighting fixtures and lighting outlets located less than five feet, measured horizontally, from the inside walls of a pool shall be at least five feet above the surface of the deck or the ground and shall be rigidly attached to the existing structure. They shall also be protected by a ground-fault circuit-interrupter installed in the branch circuit supplying the fixture.

(2) Lighting fixtures and lighting outlets installed within five feet of the inside wall of a pool or directly over the water surface shall be rigidly attached to the structure adjacent to or enclosing the pool. They must also be at least 12 feet above the ground or water surface.

(4) If any lighting fixture or any of its supporting parts are less than 16 feet from any point on the water surface, measured radially, the fixtures shall be protected by a ground-fault circuit-interrupter wired into the branch circuit supplying the fixture.

(5) Cord-connected lighting fixtures shall meet the same specifications as other cord and plug connected equipment as set forth in Section 680-7 when installed within 16 feet of any point on the water surface, measured radially.

See Section 400-8 for prohibited uses and Section 210-8(a) for outdoor residential receptacles.

680-7. Cord- and Plug-Connected Equipment. Fixed or stationary equipment rated 20 amperes or less, other than an underwater lighting fixture for a permanently installed pool, shall be permitted to be connected with a flexible cord to facilitate the removal or disconnection for maintenance or repair. For other than storable pools, the flexible cord shall not exceed 3 feet in length and shall have a copper equipment grounding conductor not smaller than No. 12 with a grounding-type attachment plug.

See Section 680-25(f) for connection with flexible cords.

▲ The three-foot cord limitation mentioned in this rule would not apply to swimming-pool filter pumps used with storable pools under part C of Art. 680, because these pumps are considered as portable instead of *fixed or stationary.* See comments following Sec. 680-30.

680-8. Overhead Conductor Clearances. The following parts of swimming pools shall not be placed under existing service-drop conductors or any other open overhead wiring; nor shall such wiring be installed above the following:

(c.) Swimming pool and the area extending 10 feet horizontally from the inside of the walls of the pool.

(b) Diving structure.

(c) Observation stands, towers or platforms.

B. Permanently Installed Pools

680-20. Underwater Lighting Fixtures

(a) **General.** Paragraphs (a) through (c) of this Section apply to all lighting fixtures installed below the normal water level of the pool.

(1) The design of an underwater lighting fixture supplied from a branch circuit either directly or by way of a transformer meeting the requirements of Section 680-5(a) shall be such that when the fixture is properly installed without a ground-fault circuit-interrupter, there is no shock hazard with any likely combination of fault conditions during normal use (not relamping).

In addition, a ground-fault circuit-interrupter shall be installed in the branch circuit supplying fixtures operating at more than 15 volts, so that there is no shock hazard during relamping. The installation of the ground-fault circuit-interrupter shall be such that there is no shock hazard with any likely fault-condition combination that involves a person in a conductive path from any ungrounded part of the branch circuit or the fixture to ground.

Compliance with this requirement shall be obtained by the use of an approved underwater lighting fixture and by installation of an approved ground-fault circuit-interrupter in the branch circuit.

(2) No lighting fixtures shall be installed for operation at over 150 volts between conductors.

(3) Lighting fixtures mounted in walls shall be installed with the top of the

fixture lens at least 18 inches below the normal water level of the pool. A lighting fixture facing upward shall have the lens adequately guarded to prevent contact by any person.

Exception: Lighting fixtures approved for the purpose shall be permitted at a depth of not less than 4 inches below the normal water level of the pool.

(b) Wet-Niche Fixtures.

(1) Approved metal forming shells shall be installed for the mounting of all wet-niche underwater fixtures and shall be equipped with provisions for threaded conduit entries. Rigid metal conduit of brass or other approved corrosion-resistant metal or rigid nonmetallic conduit shall extend from the forming shell to a suitable junction box or other enclosure located as provided in Section 680-21. Where rigid nonmetallic conduit is used, a No. 8 insulated, solid copper conductor shall be installed in this conduit with provisions for terminating in the forming shell junction box or transformer enclosure or ground-fault circuit-interrupter enclosure. The termination of the No. 8 conductor in the forming shell shall be covered with, or encapsulated in, a suitable potting compound to protect such connection from the possible deteriorating effect of pool water. Metal parts of the fixture and forming shell in contact with the pool water shall be of brass or other approved corrosion-resistant metal.

(2) The end of the flexible-cord jacket and the flexible-cord conductor terminations within a fixture shall be covered with or encapsulated in a suitable potting compound to prevent the entry of water into the fixture through the cord or its conductors. In addition, the grounding connection within a fixture shall be similarly treated to protect such connection from the deteriorating effect of pool water in the event of water entry into the fixture.

(3) The fixture shall be bonded to and secured to the forming shell by a positive locking device that assures a low-resistance contact and requires a tool to remove the fixture from the forming shell.

(c) Dry-Niche Fixtures. A dry-niche lighting fixture shall be provided with: (1) provision for drainage of water; and (2) means for accommodating one equipment grounding conductor for each conduit entry.

Approved rigid metal or rigid nonmetallic conduit shall be installed from the fixture to the service equipment or panelboard. A junction box shall not be required, but if used, shall not be required to be elevated or located as specified in Section 680-21(a)(4) if the fixture is specifically approved for the purpose.

▲ Some approved dry-niche fixtures are provided with an integral flush deck box used to change lamps. Such fixtures have a drain connection at the bottom of the fixture to prevent accumulation of water or moisture.

680-21. Junction Boxes and Enclosures for Transformers or Ground-Fault Circuit-Interrupters.

(a) Junction Boxes. A junction box connected to a conduit that extends directly to an underwater pool-light forming shell shall be:

(1) equipped with provisions for threaded conduit entries; and

(2) of copper, brass, suitable plastic, or other approved corrosion-resistant material; and

(3) provided with electrical continuity between every connected metal conduit

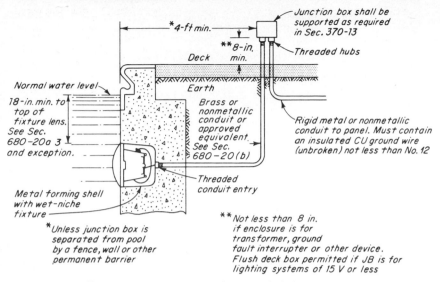

FIG. 680-1. Basic requirements for wet-niche lighting fixtures.

and the grounding terminals by means of copper, brass, or other approved corrosion-resistant metal that is integral with the box; and

(4) located not less than 8 inches, measured from the inside of the bottom of the box, above the ground level, pool deck, or maximum pool water level, whichever provides the greatest elevation, and located not less than 4 feet from the inside wall of the pool unless separated from the pool by a solid fence, wall, or other permanent barrier.

Exception: On lighting systems of 15 volts or less, a flush deck box shall be permitted provided:

a. An approved potting compound is used to fill the box to prevent the entrance of moisture; and

b. The flush deck box is located not less than 4 feet from the inside wall of the pool.

(b) Other Enclosures. An enclosure for a transformer, ground-fault circuit-interrupter, or a similar device connected to a conduit that extends directly to an underwater pool-light forming shell shall be:

(1) Equipped with provisions for threaded conduit entries; and

(2) Provided with an approved seal, such as duct seal at the conduit connection, that prevents circulation of air between the conduit and the enclosures; and

(3) Provided with electrical continuity between every connected metal conduit and the grounding terminals by means of copper, brass, or other approved corrosion-resistant metal that is integral with the enclosures; and

(4) Located not less than 8 inches, measured from the inside bottom of the enclosure to the ground level, pool deck, or maximum pool water level, whichever provides the greatest elevation, and located not less than 4 feet from the inside wall of the pool unless separated from the pool by a solid fence, wall, or other permanent barrier.

(c) Protection. Junction boxes and enclosures mounted above the grade of the finished walkway around the pool shall not be located in the walkway unless afforded additional protection, such as by location under diving boards, adjacent to fixed structures, and the like.

(d) Grounding Terminals. Junction boxes, transformer enclosures, and ground-fault circuit-interrupter enclosures connected to a conduit which extends directly to an underwater pool light forming shell shall be provided with a number of grounding terminals that shall be at least one more than the number of conduit entries.

(e) A strain relief shall be added to the flexible cord, furnished as part of an approved wet-niche lighting fixture at the termination of the cord within a junction box, transformer enclosure, or ground-fault circuit-interrupter.

680-22. Bonding.

(a) The following parts shall be bonded together:

(1) All metallic parts of the pool structure, including the reinforcing steel.

(2) All forming shells.

(3) All metal fittings within or attached to the pool structure.

(4) Metal parts of electric equipment associated with the pool water circulating system, including pump motors.

(5) Metal conduit and metal piping within 5 feet of the inside walls of the pool and that are not separated from the pool by a permanent barrier; and

(6) All fixed metal parts that are within 5 feet of the inside walls of the swimming pool and not separated from the pool area by a permanent barrier.

Exception No. 1: The usual steel tie wires shall be considered suitable for bonding the reinforcing steel together, and welding or special clamping shall not be required.

Exception No. 2: Structural reinforcing steel or the walls of welded metal pool structures shall be permitted as a common bonding grid for nonelectrical parts where connections can be made in accordance with Section 250-113.

(b) These parts shall be connected to a common bonding grid with a No. 8 solid, copper conductor and connection shall be made in accordance with Section 250-113. The common bonding grid may be any of the following:

(1) The structural reinforcing steel of a concrete pool where the reinforcing rods are bonded together by the usual steel tie wires or the equivalent; or,

(2) The wall of a welded metal pool; or,

(3) A solid, copper conductor not smaller than No. 8.

(c) For pool water heaters having a rating of more than 50 amperes and having specific instructions regarding the parts of the equipment to be bonded to the other pool components, and the parts of the equipment to be grounded, only those parts designated to be bonded shall be bonded, and only those parts designated to be grounded shall be grounded.

680-23. Underwater Audio Equipment. All underwater audio equipment shall be approved for the purpose.

680-24. Grounding. The following equipment shall be grounded: (1) wet-niche underwater lighting fixtures; (2) dry-niche underwater lighting fixtures; (3) all electric equipment located within 5 feet of the inside wall of the pool; (4) all electric equipment associated with the recirculating system of the pool; (5) junction boxes; (6) transformer enclosures; (7) ground-fault circuit-interrupters; (8) panelboards that are not part of the service equipment and that supply any electric equipment associated with the pool.

680-25. Methods of Grounding.

(a) General. The following provisions shall apply to the grounding of underwater lighting fixtures, metal junction boxes, metal transformer enclosures, and other metal enclosures:

(1) Wet-niche lighting fixtures that are supplied by a flexible cord or cable shall have all exposed noncurrent-carrying metal parts grounded by an insulated, copper equipment grounding conductor that is an integral part of the cord or cable. This grounding conductor shall be connected to a grounding terminal in the supply junction box, transformer enclosure, or other enclosure. The grounding conductor shall not be smaller than the supply conductors and not smaller than No. 16.

(2) The junction box, transformer enclosure, or other enclosure in the supply circuit to a wet-niche lighting fixture and the field-wiring chamber of a dry-niche lighting fixture shall be grounded to the equipment grounding terminal of the panelboard. This terminal shall be directly connected to the panelboard enclosure. The equipment grounding conductor shall be installed without joint or splice.

Exception No. 1: Where more than one underwater lighting fixture is supplied by the same branch circuit, the equipment grounding conductor, installed between the junction boxes, transformer enclosures, or other enclosures in the supply circuit to wet-niche fixtures or between the field-wiring compartments of dry-niche fixtures, shall be permitted to be terminated on grounding terminals.

Exception No. 2: Where the underwater lighting fixture is supplied from a transformer or a ground-fault circuit-interrupter which is located between the panelboard and a junction box connected to the conduit that extends directly to the underwater lighting fixture, the equipment grounding conductor shall be permitted to terminate on grounding terminals in the transformer or ground-fault circuit-interrupter enclosure.

(b) Other Equipment. Other electric equipment shall be grounded to the equipment grounding terminal of the panelboard.

(c) Panelboards. A panelboard, not part of the service equipment, shall have an equipment grounding conductor installed between its grounding terminal and the grounding terminal of the service equipment.

(d) Equipment Grounding Conductor—Size and Type. An equipment grounding conductor shall be sized in accordance with Table 250-95 but not smaller than No. 12. It shall be an insulated copper conductor and shall be installed with the circuit conductors in rigid metal conduit or rigid nonmetallic conduit.

Exception No. 1: The equipment grounding conductor specified in (a)(1) above.

Exception No. 2: The equipment grounding conductor between the wiring chamber of the secondary winding of a transformer and a junction box shall be sized in accordance with the overcurrent device in this circuit.

See (a)(2), Exception No. 2 above.

Exception No. 3: The equipment grounding conductor between an existing remote panelboard and the service equipment shall not be required to be in conduit if the interconnection is by means of (1) an approved cable assembly with an insulated or covered copper equipment grounding conductor; or (2) insulated copper conductors within an approved raceway.

Exception No. 4: Where necessary to employ flexible connections, flexible metal conduit with approved fittings shall be permitted.

(e) Equipment Grounding Conductor Between Panelboard and Service Equipment. The equipment grounding conductor between a remote panelboard and the service equipment shall be sized in accordance with the overcurrent devices protecting the conductors supplying the panelboard.

See Table 250-95 for sizing equipment grounding conductor.

(f) Cord-Connected Equipment. Where fixed or stationary equipment is connected with a flexible cord to facilitate removal or disconnection for maintenance, repair, or storage as provided in Section 680-7, the equipment grounding conductors shall be connected to a fixed metal part of the assembly. The removable part shall be mounted on or bonded to the fixed metal part.

▲ All fixed metallic parts located within this 5-ft area must be effectively bonded and tied together so as to provide a common grounding source with the metal which is otherwise installed in the enclosing walls and floor of the pool. This applies whether a grounded or isolated electrical system is used. See Fig. 680-2.

The bonding or interconnecting of circuits or equipment is covered in Sec. 250-113, and specifically names several commonly recognized means. Because it also recognizes "approved means," it includes any method which is acceptable to the authority having jurisdiction. Where bonding is required between reinforcing bars or wire mesh which is encased in concrete, the use of tie wires tightly applied and used in sufficient number to provide parallel paths is usually found to have adequate conductivity.

In considering the need to ground metal appurtenances in or within 5 ft of a

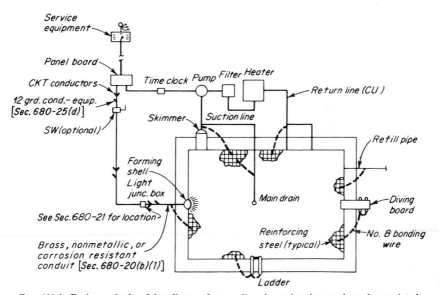

Fig. 680-2. Basic methods of bonding and grounding for swimming pools and associated equipment. See Secs. 680-20 through 680-25.

swimming pool, it should be realized that stray currents in the ground or in piping connected to the swimming pool can be hazardous to persons in the pool. Even where plastic piping is used, water which contains salt or chemicals used to provide sanitation may have a resistance so low as to permit dangerous currents to flow.

A protective ground placed on electrical equipment may be lost in time through corrosion which is normally associated with the wet conditions and dampness usually found around swimming pools, so wiring should be checked periodically.

C. Storable Pools

680-30. Pumps. A cord-connected swimming-pool filter pump shall incorporate an approved system of double insulation or its equivalent, and shall be provided with means for grounding only the internal and nonaccessible noncurrent-carrying metal parts of the appliance.

The means for grounding shall be an equipment grounding conductor run with the power-supply conductors in the flexible cord that is properly terminated in a grounding-type attachment plug having a fixed grounding contact member.

▲ There are portable filter pumps listed by Underwriters' Laboratories, Inc., and they comply with Sec. 680-30.

680-31. Ground-Fault Circuit-Interrupters Required. All electric equipment, including power supply cords, used with storable swimming pools shall be protected by ground-fault circuit-interrupters.

When flexible cords are used, see Section 400-4.

▲ Ground-fault circuit-interrupters must be installed so that all wiring used with storable pools will be protected. For various types of ground-fault circuit-interrupters see Figs. 210-1, 210-2, 210-3, and 210-4, and comments following Sec. 210-8.

D. Fountains

680-40. General. The provisions of Part D include fountains, fountain pools, ornamental display pools, and reflection pools. Fountains which have water common to a swimming pool shall comply with the swimming pool requirements of this Article.

680-41. Lighting Fixtures, Submersible Pumps and Other Submersible Equipment.

(a) Ground-Fault Circuit-Interrupter. A ground-fault circuit-interrupter shall be installed in the branch circuit supplying fountain equipment.

Exception: Ground-fault circuit-interrupters shall not be required for equipment operating at 15 volts or less and supplied by a transformer complying with Section 680-5(a).

(b) Operating Voltage. No lighting fixture shall be installed for operation at over 150 volts between conductors. Circuits supplying submersible pumps and other submersible equipment shall operate at not to exceed 300 volts between conductors.

(c) Lighting Fixture Lenses. Lighting fixtures shall be installed with the top of the fixture lens below the normal water level of the fountain unless approved for above water locations. A lighting fixture facing upward shall have the lens adequately guarded to prevent contact by any person.

(d) Overheating Protection. Electrical equipment which depends on submersion for safe operation shall be protected against overheating by a low-water cut-off or other approved means if the water level drops below normal.

(e) Wiring. Equipment shall be equipped with provisions for threaded conduit entries or be provided with a suitable flexible cord. The maximum length of exposed cord in the fountain shall be limited to 10 feet. Cords extending beyond the fountain perimeter shall be enclosed in approved wiring enclosures. Metal parts of equipment in contact with water shall be of brass or other approved corrosion-resistant metal.

(f) Servicing. All equipment shall be removable from the water for relamping or normal maintenance. Fixtures shall not be permanently imbedded into the fountain structure so that the water level must be reduced or the fountain drained for relamping, maintenance, or inspection.

(g) Stability. Equipment shall be inherently stable or be securely fastened in place.

680-42. Junction Boxes and Other Enclosures.

(a) General. Junction boxes and other enclosures used for other than underwater installation shall comply with Sections 680-21(a) (1), (2), (3); 680-21(b); Section 680-21(c) and 680-21(d).

(b) Underwater Junction Boxes and Other Underwater Enclosures. Junction boxes and other underwater enclosures immersed in water or exposed to water spray shall comply with the following:

(1) Shall be equipped with provisions for threaded conduit entries or compression glands or seals for cord entry; and

(2) Shall be of copper, brass, or other approved corrosion-resistant material; and

(3) Shall be located below the water level in the fountain wall or floor. An approved potting compound shall be used to fill the box to prevent the entry of moisture; and

(4) When the junction box is supported only by the conduit, the conduit shall be of copper, brass, or other approved corrosion-resistant metal. When the box is fed by nonmetallic conduit, it shall have additional supports and fasteners of copper, brass, or other approved corrosion-resistant material. The box must be firmly attached to the supports or directly to the fountain surface and bonded as required.

680-43. Bonding. All metallic piping systems associated with the fountain shall be bonded to the electrical system ground as required in Article 250.

680-44. Grounding. The following equipment shall be grounded: (1) all electric equipment located within 5 feet of the inside wall of the fountain; (2) all electric equipment associated with the recirculating system of the fountain; (3) panelboards that are not part of the service equipment and that supply any electric equipment associated with the fountain.

680-45. Methods of Grounding.

(a) The following provisions of Section 680-25 shall apply: Paragraph (a) and (d) excluding Exception 3.

(b) Electric equipment that is supplied by a flexible cord shall have all exposed noncurrent-carrying metal parts grounded by an insulated copper equipment grounding conductor that is an integral part of this cord. This grounding conductor shall be connected to a grounding terminal in the supply junction box, transformer enclosure or other enclosure.

680-46. Cord and Plug-Connected Equipment.

(a) Ground-Fault Circuit-Interrupter. All electric equipment, including power supply cords, shall be protected by ground-fault circuit-interrupters.

(b) Cord Type. Flexible cord immersed in or exposed to water shall be a water-resistant Type SO or ST.

(c) Sealing. The end of the flexible cord jacket and the flexible cord conductor termination within equipment shall be covered with or encapsulated in a suitable potting compound to prevent the entry of water into the equipment through the cord or its conductors. In addition, the ground connection within equipment shall be similarly treated to protect such connections from the deteriorating effect of water which may enter into the equipment.

(d) Terminations. Connections with flexible cord shall be permanent, except that grounding-type attachment plugs and receptacles shall be permitted to facilitate removal or disconnection for maintenance, repair, or storage of fixed or stationary equipment not located in any water-containing part of a fountain or pool.

680-47. Equipment Rooms. Electric equipment shall not be installed in rooms which do not have adequate drainage to prevent water accumulation during normal operation or filter maintenance.

CHAPTER SEVEN

Special Conditions

ARTICLE 700. EMERGENCY SYSTEMS

A. General

700-1. Scope. The provisions of this Article apply to the installation, operation, and maintenance of circuits, systems, and equipment intended to supply illumination and power in the event of failure of the normal supply or in the event of accident to elements of a system supplying power and illumination essential for safety to life and property where such systems or circuits are legally required and are classed as emergency by Municipal, State, Federal, or other Codes, or by any governmental agency having jurisdiction.

▲ The placement or location of exit lights is not a function of the National Electrical Code but is covered in the Life Safety Code, NFPA No. 101 (formerly Building Exits Code).

The National Electrical Code indicates how the installation will be made, not where the emergency lighting is required, except as specified in part C of Art. 517 for essential electrical systems in health-care facilities.

Emergency systems are generally installed in places of assembly where artificial illumination is required, such as buildings subject to occupancy by large numbers of persons, hotels, theaters, sports arenas, hospitals, and similar institutions. Emergency systems may provide power for such functions as essential refrigeration, operation of mechanical breathing apparatus, ventilation when essential to maintain life, illumination and power for hospital operating rooms, fire alarm systems, fire pumps, industrial processes where current interruption would produce serious hazards, public address systems, and similar functions.

See Life Safety Code (NFPA No. 101-1973) for specification of locations where emergency lighting is considered essential to life safety.

▲ An emergency lighting system in a theater or other place of public assemblage includes exit signs, the chief purpose of which is to indicate the location of the exits,

681

and lighting equipment commonly called "emergency lights," the purpose of which is to provide sufficient illumination in the auditorium, corridors, lobbies, passageways, stairways, and fire escapes to enable persons to leave the building safely.

These details, as well as the various classes of buildings in which emergency lighting is required, are left to be determined by state or municipal codes, and where such codes are in effect, the following provisions apply.

700-2. Application of Other Articles. Except as modified by this Article, all applicable Articles of this Code shall apply.

700-3. Equipment Approval. All equipment shall be approved for use on emergency systems.

700-4. Tests and Maintenance.

(a) The authority having jurisdiction shall conduct or witness a test on the complete system upon installation and periodically afterward.

(b) Systems shall be tested periodically on a schedule acceptable to the authority having jurisdiction to assure their maintenance in proper operating condition.

(c) Where battery systems or unit equipments are involved, including batteries used for starting or ignition in auxiliary engines, the authority having jurisdiction shall require periodic maintenance.

(d) A written record shall be kept of such tests and maintenance.

(e) Means for testing any emergency lighting or power system under load shall be provided at the location of the generator, transfer switch, central battery location, or other location satisfactory to the enforcing authority.

700-5. Capacity. An emergency system shall have adequate capacity and rating for the emergency operation of all equipment connected to the system.

▲ It is extremely important that the supply source be of adequate capacity. There are two main reasons for adequate capacity:

1. It is important that power be available for the necessary supply to exit lights, emergency and egress lighting, as well as to operate such equipment as required for elevators and other equipment connected to the emergency system.

2. In such occupancies as hospitals there may be a need for an emergency supply for lighting in hospital operating rooms, and also for such equipment as inhalators, iron lungs, incubators, and the like. See part C of Art. 517 for requirements in health-care facilities.

B. Sources of Power

700-6. Systems. Current supply shall be such that in event of failure of the normal supply to or within the building or group of buildings concerned, emergency lighting, emergency power, or both, will be immediately available. The supply system for emergency purposes shall be permitted to comprise one or more of the types of systems described in (a) through (d) below. Unit equipments in accordance with Section 700-6(e) shall satisfy the applicable requirements of this Article.

Consideration shall be given to the type of service to be rendered, whether of short time duration, as for exit lights of a theater, or of long duration, as for supplying emergency power and lighting due to a long period of current failure from trouble either inside or outside the building, as in the case of a hospital.

Assignment of degree of reliability of the recognized emergency supply system depends upon the careful evaluation of the variables at each particular installation.

(a) Storage Battery. One service, in accordance with Article 230, and a storage battery of suitable rating and capacity to supply and maintain at not less than $87\frac{1}{2}$ percent of system voltage the total load of the circuits supplying emergency lighting and emergency power for a period of at least $1\frac{1}{2}$ hours.

Batteries whether of the acid or alkali type shall be designed and constructed to meet the requirements of emergency service, and shall be compatible with the charger for that particular installation.

For the maintenance-free battery, the container shall not be required to be transparent. However, for the lead acid battery which requires water additions, transparent or translucent jars shall be furnished. Automotive type batteries shall not be used.

An automatic battery charging means shall be provided.

▲ Two separate services brought to different locations in the building are always preferable, and these services should at least receive their supply from separate transformers where this is practicable. In some localities, municipal ordinances require either two services from independent sources of supply, or auxiliary supply for emergency lighting from a storage battery or a generator driven by a steam turbine, internal-combustion engine, or other prime mover.

(b) Generator Set.

(1) One service in accordance with Article 230 and a generator set driven by a prime mover acceptable to the authority having jurisdiction and sized in accordance with Section 700-5. Means shall be provided for automatically starting the prime mover on failure of the normal service. Automatic means shall also be provided for transferring those loads necessary to protect human life from the normal supply to the emergency supply. For hospitals, the transition time from the instant of failure of the normal power source to the emergency generator source shall not exceed 10 seconds. A time delay feature with a 15 minute minimum setting shall be provided to avoid short time reestablishment of the normal source.

(2) When internal combustion engines are used as the prime mover, an on-site fuel supply shall be provided sufficient to operate the prime mover at full demand load for 90 minutes.

(3) Prime movers shall not be solely dependent upon a public utility gas system for their fuel supply. Means shall be provided for automatically transferring from one fuel supply to another where dual fuel supplies are used.

(4) Where the means of starting the prime mover is a storage battery, it shall be suitable for the purpose and shall be equipped with an automatic charging means.

See Section 700-4 for test and maintenance requirements.

▲ See comment following Sec. 700-6(e).

(c) Separate Service. Two services, each in accordance with Article 230, with separate service drops or laterals, widely separated electrically and physically to minimize the possibility of simultaneous interruption of supply.

▲ See comment following Sec. 700-6(e).

(d) Connection Ahead of Service Disconnecting Means. Connections on the line side of the main service disconnecting means if sufficiently separated from the main service disconnecting means to prevent simultaneous interruption of supply through an occurrence within the building or groups of buildings served.

See Section 230-82 for equipment permitted on the supply side of a service disconnecting means.

(e) Unit Equipment. Individual unit equipment for emergency illumination shall consist of: (1) a rechargeable battery; (2) a battery charging means; (3) provisions for one or more lamps mounted on the equipment and shall be permitted to have terminals for remote lamps; and (4) a relaying device arranged to energize the lamps automatically upon failure of the supply to the unit equipment. The batteries shall be of suitable rating and capacity to supply and maintain at not less than $87\frac{1}{2}$ percent of the nominal battery voltage for the total lamp load associated with the unit for a period of at least $1\frac{1}{2}$ hours, or the unit equipment shall supply and maintain not less than 60 percent of the initial emergency illumination for a period of at least $1\frac{1}{2}$ hours. Storage batteries whether of the acid or alkali type shall be designed and constructed to meet the requirements of emergency service.

Unit equipment shall be permanently fixed in place (i.e., not portable) and shall have all wiring to each unit installed in accordance with the requirements of any of the wiring methods in Chapter 3. Flexible cord and plug connection shall be permitted provided that the cord does not exceed 3 feet in length. The branch circuit feeding the unit equipment shall be the same branch circuit as that serving the normal lighting in the area and connected ahead of any local switches. Emergency illumination fixtures that obtain power from a unit equipment and are not part of the unit equipment shall be wired to the unit equipment as required by Section 700-17 and by one of the wiring methods of Chapter 3.

▲ The intent of the $87\frac{1}{2}$ percent value is to assure proper *lighting output* from lamps supplied by unit equipment. It is generally considered acceptable to design equipment that will produce acceptable lighting levels for the required $1\frac{1}{2}$ hours, even though the $87\frac{1}{2}$ percent rating of the battery would not be maintained during this period. The objective is adequate light output to permit safe egress from buildings in emergencies. Hence, the unit equipment shall supply and maintain not less than 60 percent of the initial emergency illumination for a period of at least $1\frac{1}{2}$ hours.

Even though the unit equipment is allowed to be hooked up with flexible cord-and-plug connections, it is still necessary that the unit equipment be permanently fixed in place. Individual unit equipment provides emergency illumination only for the area in which it is installed; therefore, it is not necessary to carry a circuit back to the service equipment to feed the unit. This section clearly indicates that the branch circuit feeding the normal lighting in the area to be served is the same circuit that should supply the unit equipment.

General Discussion of Requirements for Emergency Lighting Systems

Two sources of supply should be provided. These sources may be (1) two services from central-station supply, (2) one service and a storage battery (or battery/inverter), or (3) one service and a generator set.

Either *a single emergency lighting system* may be installed or *two complete systems,* each one of which will, when operated without the other, provide all required emergency illumination.

Single Emergency System

If a single emergency system is installed, a throw-over switch shall be provided which, in case of failure of the source of supply on which the system is operating, will automatically transfer the emergency system to the other source. Where the two sources of supply are two services, the single emergency system may normally operate on either source. Where the two sources of supply are one service and a storage battery, or one service and a generator set, the single emergency system would, as a general rule, be operated normally on the service, using the battery or generator only as a reserve in case of failure of the service.

Two Emergency Systems

If two emergency lighting systems are installed, each system shall operate on a separate source of supply. Either both systems shall be kept in operation, or switches shall be provided which will automatically place either system in operation upon failure of the other system.

Cases Arising under These Rules

Case 1. Single Emergency System and Two Services.

a. One service is to supply emergency lighting only, and one service is to supply the general lighting and must be capable of supplying the emergency lighting also. The emergency system is to be supplied from either service through an automatic throw-over switch.

The service arrangement for case 1*a* is shown in Fig. 700-1. The emergency-system feeder is small and would not be protected by the fuses or circuit breaker of the general

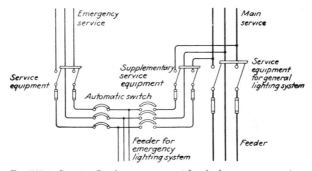

FIG. 700-1. *Case 1a.* Service arrangement for single emergency system with two services, one for emergency system only and one for both general lighting and emergency system.

lighting service. Taps to the general lighting service for supplying the emergency system should be made ahead of the main service equipment, and a supplementary service switch and fuses (or circuit breaker) must be installed in this line.

b. Each service is to carry a part of the general lighting load, with sufficient additional capacity to carry the emergency system also. The emergency system is to be supplied from either service through an automatic throw-over switch.

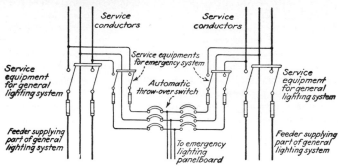

FIG. 700-2. *Case 1b.* Service arrangement for single emergency system with two services, each to supply a part of the general lighting system, with capacity to carry the emergency system also.

The service arrangement for this case is shown in Fig. 700-2. For the same reason as in case 1*a*, as explained above, taps to the two services must be made ahead of the general lighting service switches and two sets of service equipment must be provided for the emergency system.

Case 2. Single Emergency System with One Service and a Storage Battery or Generator Set.

The service is to supply the general lighting system and, normally, to supply the emergency system also. The emergency system is to be supplied either from the service or from the battery or generator through an automatic throw-over switch.

Figure 700-3 shows the service arrangement for case 2.

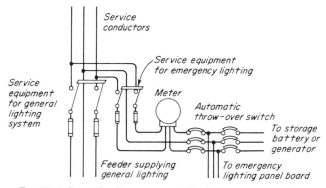

FIG. 700-3. *Case 2.* Service arrangement for single emergency system and a storage battery or generator set as reserve supply.

700-11. Auxiliary Source. The requirements of Sections 700-5 and 700-6 shall also apply to installations where the entire electrical load on a service or sub-service is arranged to be supplied from a second source.

700-12. Signals. Audible and visual signal devices shall be provided, where practicable, for the following purposes:

(1) To give warning of derangement of the emergency or auxiliary source.

(2) To indicate that the battery or generator set is carrying load.

(3) To indicate by a visual signal that a battery charger is functioning properly.

▲ In order to be effective, the signal devices should be located in some room where an attendant is on duty. Lamps may readily be used as signals to indicate the position of an automatic switching device. An audible signal in any place of public assemblage should not be so located or of such a character that it will cause a general alarm.

The standard signal equipment furnished by the Electric Storage Battery Co. with their 60-cell battery for emergency lighting includes an indicating lamp which is lighted when the charger is operating at the high rate, and a voltmeter marked in three colored sections indicates (1) that the battery is not being charged, or is discharging into the emergency system, (2) that the battery is being trickle charged, or (3) that the battery is being charged at the high rate. This last indication duplicates the indication given by the lamp.

C. Emergency Circuits for Lighting and Power

700-13. Loads on Emergency Branch Circuits. No appliances and no lamps, other than those specified as required for emergency use, shall be supplied by emergency lighting circuits.

700-14. Emergency Illumination. Emergency illumination shall include all required exit lights and all other lights specified as necessary to provide sufficient illumination.

Emergency lighting systems shall be so designed and installed that the failure of any individual lighting element, such as the burning out of a light bulb, cannot leave any space in total darkness.

700-15. Circuits for Emergency Lighting. Branch circuits intended to supply emergency lighting shall be so installed as to provide service immediately when the normal supply for lighting is interrupted. Such installations shall provide either one of the following:

(1) An emergency lighting supply, independent of the general lighting system, with provisions for automatically transferring, by means of devices approved for the purpose, the emergency lights upon the event of failure of the general lighting system supply; or

(2) Two or more separate and complete systems with independent power supply, each system providing sufficient current for emergency lighting purposes. Unless both systems are used for regular lighting purposes and are both kept lighted, means shall be provided for automatically energizing either system upon failure of the other. Either or both systems shall be permitted to be part of the general lighting system of the protected occupancy if circuits supplying lights for emergency illumination are installed in accordance with other Sections of this Article.

▲ *1. Location of Overcurrent Devices.*

The installation of an automatic transfer switch does not alter the basic code requirements regarding the location of the overcurrent devices as covered in Sec. 240-21.

Overcurrent devices must be furnished for both the normal and emergency sources of supply and must be so located as to conform to Sec. 240-21.

2. *Solid Neutral on AC and DC Systems.*

On AC to AC automatic transfer switches, solid neutrals can be used based on the grounding connections specified in Sec. 250-23. However, in some installations, objectionable ground-current flow may occur because of site conditions requiring corrective measures as outlined in Sec. 250-21.

On AC to DC automatic transfer switches, a solid neutral tie between the AC and DC neutrals is not permitted where both sources of supply are exterior distribution systems. Sec. 250-22 regarding location of grounds for DC exterior systems clearly specifies that the DC system can be grounded only at the supply station.

Where the DC system is an interior isolated system, such as a storage battery, solid neutral connection between the AC system neutral and the DC source is acceptable.

When the neutrals must be switched on AC to DC automatic transfer switches, the required capacity of the neutral switching pole must be properly evaluated on the basis of the service combination. Thus in an installation utilizing a three-phase four-wire normal source and a two-wire DC emergency source, with the neutral switched, a four-pole double-throw switch would be required. One pole on the DC emergency source would be required to carry three times the current of the remaining poles.

3. *Close Differential Voltage Supervision of Normal Source.*

Normally adequate voltage supervision of the normal source can be provided by relays adjusted to effect transfer to the emergency source when the normal source voltage is 70 percent or less on any phase. This value of voltage ensures reasonable lighting intensity as well as ensuring transfer when the overcurrent device in any branch or phase opens.

Consideration must be given to voltage supervision at close differential for many installations where the load circuits are critical to voltage.

As an example, starter-type fluorescent lighting is extremely voltage sensitive, starting becoming uncertain at voltages below 105 V. Close differential relay supervision providing 105 V transfer and 115 retransfer for a 120-V system is a requirement for this type of lighting.

Electronic equipment load is frequently voltage critical. Among such installations are television stations, microwave communications, telephone communications, and similar applications. To accommodate the broad requirements of this class of load, the transfer voltage setting should preferably be adjustable over a minimum range of 75 to 93 percent of normal rated voltage.

Automatic transfer switches applied to motor installations of the polyphase type also require close differential voltage supervision. A polyphase motor operating at partial load will tend to sustain terminal voltages despite the loss of line voltage on one phase. Close differential voltage relays capable of adjustment to within transfer and retransfer values of 2 percent will ensure detection of phase outage over a practical range of motor loading.

4. *Automatic Transfer Switches with Emergency Source on Automatically Started Power Plant.*

In these installations the normal source is usually a utility power line and the emergency source a power plant which starts upon failure of the normal source. To ensure maximum reliability, a minimum installation should be arranged to:

  a. Initiate starting of the power plant from a contact on relay SE. (See Fig. 700-5.)

Fig. 700-4. Automatic emergency lighting transfer switch. (*Automatic Switch Co.*)

b. Sustain connection of load circuits to the normal source during the starting period to provide utilization of any existing service on the normal source.

c. Measure output voltage and frequency of emergency source through use of voltage-frequency-sensitive LO relay (see Fig. 700-5) and to effect transfer of the load circuits to the power plant only when both voltage and frequency of the power plant are approximately normal.

d. Provide audible or visual signal when power plant is feeding the load.

5. *Time-Delay Devices on Automatic Transfer Switches.*

All distribution systems are subject to transient conditions which cause outages of the system often of extremely short duration. These momentary outages can usually be ignored, particularly if less than 1 sec duration (field experience indicates that outages less than 1 sec duration are transients and will not be sustained). A desirable addition to automatic transfer switches is the addition of a feature so that outages of less than 1 sec duration will be ignored.

This is readily accomplished by adding the feature to selector relay SE already existing in the transfer panel. (See Fig. 700-5.) The timing feature should be fixed and preferably not longer than 3 sec.

The advantages of this feature are realized in all types of automatic transfer installations. In standby plant installations the reduced number of false starts is especially important to minimize wear on the starting gear, battery, and associated equipment.

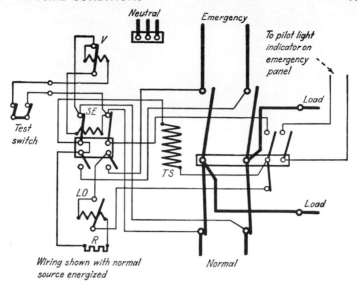

FIG. 700-5. Diagram of connections of the automatic transfer switch shown in Fig. 700-4.

A time-delay relay functioning upon retransfer to normal is also a requirement for transfer switch installations. The transfer to the emergency source is the result of unstable or outage conditions of the normal source. Obviously some means to determine sustained stability of the normal source is desirable.

A simple and effective means of accomplishing this is to install a time-delay relay, set at a minimum of 15 min, between relays V and SE. (See Fig. 700-5.) Upon restoration of the normal source, relay V operates to energize the time-delay relay. After the preselected timing period the timer contact closes to energize relay SE to effect the transfer to the normal source. This time delay should be connected so that if the emergency source of supply should fail while it is feeding the load, the time delay will be nullified, and retransfer to the normal source will be made instantaneously when normal source is again available.

700-16. Circuits for Emergency Power. For branch circuits that supply equipment classed as emergency, there shall be an emergency supply source to which the load will be transferred automatically and immediately upon the failure of the normal supply.

700-17. Independent Wiring. Emergency circuit wiring shall be kept entirely independent of all other wiring and equipment and shall not enter the same raceway, cable, box, or cabinet with other wiring.

Exception No. 1: In transfer switches.

Exception No. 2: In exit or emergency lighting fixtures supplied from two sources.

Exception No. 3: In a common junction box attached to exit or emergency lighting fixtures supplied from two sources.

▲ This section requires that the wiring for emergency systems be kept entirely independent of the regular wiring used for lighting and that it thus needs to be in separate raceways, cables, and boxes. This requirement is to ensure that where faults may occur on the regular wiring, they will not affect the emergency-system wiring, as it will be in a separate enclosure.

Exception No. 1 for transfer switches is intended to permit normal supply conductors to be brought into the transfer-switch enclosure and that these conductors would be the only ones within the transfer-switch enclosure which were not part of the emergency system. Exceptions Nos. 2 and 3 permit two sources supplying emergency or exit lighting to enter the fixture and its common junction box.

D. Control

700-18. Switch Requirements. The switch or switches installed in emergency lighting circuits shall be so arranged that only authorized persons will have control of emergency lighting.

Exception No. 1: Where two or more single-throw switches are connected in parallel to control a single circuit, at least one of these switches shall be accessible only to authorized persons.

Exception No. 2: Additional switches that act only to put emergency lights into operation but not disconnect them are permissible.

Switches connected in series or 3- and 4-way switches shall not be used.

700-19. Switch Location.

(a) All manual switches for controlling emergency circuits shall be in locations convenient to authorized persons responsible for their actuation. In places of assembly, such as theaters, a switch for controlling emergency lighting systems shall be located in the lobby or at a place conveniently accessible thereto.

(b) In no case shall a control switch for emergency lighting in a theater or motion-picture theater be placed in a motion-picture projection booth or on a stage.

Exception: Where multiple switches are provided, one such switch shall be permitted in such locations where so arranged that it can energize but not disconnect the circuit.

700-20. Other Switches.

(a) Exterior Lights. Those lights on the exterior of a building that are not required for illumination when there is sufficient daylight shall be permitted to be controlled by an automatic light-actuated device approved for the purpose.

(b) Hospital Corridors. Switching arrangements to transfer corridor lighting in patient areas of hospitals from overhead fixtures to fixtures designed to provide night lighting shall be permitted if the switching system is so designed that switches can only select between two sets of fixtures and cannot extinguish both sets at the same time.

E. Overcurrent Protection

700-21. Accessibility. The branch-circuit overcurrent devices in emergency circuits shall be accessible to authorized persons only.

ARTICLE 710. OVER 600 VOLTS, NOMINAL—GENERAL

A. General

710-1. Scope. This Article covers the general requirements for all circuits and equipment operated at more than 600 volts. For specific installations, see the Articles referred to in Section 710-2.

710-2. Other Articles. Provisions applicable to specific types of installations are included in Article 225, Outside Branch Circuits and Feeders; Article 230, Services; Article 346, Rigid Metal Conduit; Article 347, Rigid Nonmetallic Conduit; Article 365, Cablebus; Article 410, Lighting Fixtures, Lampholders, Lamps, Receptacles, and Rosettes; Article 430, Motors, Motor Circuits, and Controllers; Article 450, Transformers and Transformer Vaults; Article 460, Capacitors; Article 600, Electric Signs and Outline Lighting; Article 660, X-ray Equipment, and Article 665, Induction and Dielectric Heating Equipment and for construction and ampacities of high-voltage conductors, see Article 310, Part C.

710-3. Wiring Methods.

(a) Aboveground Conductors. Aboveground conductors shall be installed in rigid metal conduit, in cablebus, in other suitable raceways, or as open runs of metal-clad cable suitable for the use and purpose.

In locations accessible to qualified persons only, open runs of nonmetallic-sheathed cable, bare conductors and bare busbars shall also be permitted.

(b) Underground Conductors. Underground conductors shall be suitable for the voltage and conditions under which they are installed.

Direct burial cables shall be of the construction whereby the energized conductors are surrounded by effectively grounded, multiple concentric conductors, closely and evenly spaced, or conducting sheath of equivalent ampacity to meet requirements of Section 250-51.

Underground cables shall be permitted to be direct buried or installed in raceways approved for the purpose and shall meet the depth requirements of Table 710-3(b).

Exception No. 1: The above minimum cover requirements shall be permitted to be reduced 6 inches for each 2 inches of concrete or equivalent above the conductors.

Table 710-3(b). Minimum Cover Requirements (Cover Means the Distance in Inches between the Top Surface of Cable or Duct and the Grade)

Circuit Voltage	Direct Buried Cables	Rigid Nonmetallic Conduit Approved for Direct Burial*	Rigid Metal Conduit
Over 600-22kV	30	18	6
Over 22kV–40kV	36	24	6
Over 40kV	42	30	6

Unshielded cables shall be installed in rigid metal conduit or rigid nonmetallic conduit encased in not less than 3 inches of concrete.

* Listed by a nationally recognized testing agency as suitable for direct burial without encasement. All other nonmetallic systems shall require 2 inches of concrete or equivalent above conduit in addition to above depth.

Exception No. 2: Areas subject to heavy vehicular traffic, such as thoroughfares or commercial parking areas, shall have a minimum cover of 24 inches.

Exception No. 3: Lesser depths are permitted where cables and conductors rise for terminations or splices or where access is otherwise required.

Exception No. 4: In airport runways including adjacent defined areas where trespass is prohibited, cable shall be permitted to be buried not less than 18 inches deep and without raceways, concrete enclosement or equivalent.

Exception No. 5: Ducts installed in solid rock shall be permitted to be buried at lesser depth when covered by 2 inches of concrete which may extend to the rock surface.

(1) Protection From Damage. Conductors emerging from the ground shall be enclosed in approved raceway. Raceways installed on poles shall be of rigid metal conduit, PVC Schedule 80 or equivalent extending from the ground line up to a point 8 feet above finished grade. Conductors entering a building shall be protected by an approved enclosure from the ground line to the point of entrance. Metallic enclosures shall be grounded.

(2) Splices. Direct burial cables shall be permitted to be spliced or tapped without the use of splice boxes provided they are installed using materials suitable for the application. The taps and splices shall be watertight and protected from mechanical injury. Where cables are shielded, the shielding shall be continuous across the splice or tap.

(3) Backfill. Backfill containing large rock, paving materials, cinders, large or sharply angular substance, or corrosive material shall not be placed in an excavation where materials can damage ducts, cables, or other substructures or prevent adequate compaction of fill or contribute to corrosion of ducts, cables, or other substructures.

(4) Raceway Seal. Where a raceway or duct enters from an underground system the end within the building shall be sealed with suitable compound so as to prevent the entrance of moisture or gases, or it shall be so arranged to prevent moisture from contacting live parts.

▲ In locations accessible to qualified persons only there are no restrictions on the types of wiring that may be used. The types more commonly employed are open wiring on insulators with conductors either bare or insulated, and rigid metal conduit or nonmetallic rigid conduit containing lead-covered cable.

710-4. Braid-Covered Insulated Conductors—Open Installation. Open runs of braid-covered insulated conductors shall have a flame-retardant braid. If the conductors used do not have this protection, a flame-retardant saturant shall be applied to the braid covering after installation. This treated braid covering shall be stripped back a safe distance at conductor terminals, according to the operating voltage. This distance shall not be less than one inch for each kilovolt of the conductor-to-ground voltage of the circuit, where practicable.

710-6. Termination of Shielded Conductors. Metallic shielding components and any other conducting or semi-conducting static shielding components of shielded cable shall be stripped back to a safe distance according to the circuit voltage, at all terminations of the shielding. At such points, pot-heads, terminators, stress cones, or similar devices shall be installed for stress reduction.

Metallic shielding components such as tapes, wires or braids or combinations thereof and their associated conducting or semiconducting components shall be grounded.

▲ See Figs. 310-1, 310-2, and 310-3.

710-7. Grounding. Wiring and equipment installations shall be grounded in accordance with the applicable provisions of Article 250.

710-8. Moisture or Mechanical Protection for Metal-Sheathed Cables. Where cable conductors emerge from a metal sheath and where protection against moisture or physical damage is necessary, the insulation of the conductors shall be protected by a cable termination.

710-9. Protection of Service Equipment. Pipes or ducts foreign to the electrical installation which require periodic maintenance or whose malfunction would endanger the operation of the electrical system shall not be located in the vicinity of the service equipment. Arrangements shall be made where necessary to avoid possible trouble from condensation leaks and breaks in such foreign systems.

B. Equipment—General Provisions

710-11. Indoor Installations. See Section 110-31(a).

710-12. Outdoor Installations. See Section 110-31(b).

710-13. Metal-Enclosed Equipment. See Section 110-31(c).

710-14. Oil-Filled Equipment. Installation of electrical equipment, other than transformers, covered in Article 450, containing more than 10 gallons of flammable oil per unit shall meet the requirements of Parts B and C of Article 450.

C. Equipment—Specific Provisions

See also references to specific types of installations in Section 710-2.

710-20. Overcurrent Protection. Overcurrent protection shall be provided for each ungrounded conductor by one of the following:

(a) Overcurrent Relays and Current Transformers. Circuit breakers used for overcurrent protection of AC 3-phase circuits shall have a minimum of three overcurrent relays operated from three current transformers.

Exception No. 1: On 3-phase 3-wire circuits, an overcurrent relay in the residual circuit of the current transformers shall be permitted to replace one of the phase relays.

Exception No. 2: An overcurrent relay, operated from a current transformer which links all phases of a 3-phase, 3-wire circuit, shall be permitted to replace the residual relay and one of the phase conductor current transformers.

(b) Fuses. A fuse shall be connected in series with each ungrounded conductor.

710-21. Circuit Interrupting Devices.

(a) Circuit Breakers.

(1) Indoor installations shall consist of metal-enclosed units or fire-resistant cell-mounted units.

Exception: Open mounting of circuit breakers shall be permitted in locations accessible to qualified persons only.

(2) Circuit breakers shall be trip-free in all positions. In every installation, the circuit-breaker rating in respect to closing, carrying, or interrupting capabilities shall not be less than the short-circuit duty at the point of application.

Circuit breakers used to control oil-filled transformers shall be either located outside the transformer vault or be capable of operation from outside the vault.

(3) Circuit breakers shall have a means of indicating the open and closed position of the breaker at the point(s) from which they may be operated.

(4) Oil circuit breakers shall be so arranged or located that adjacent readily combustible structures or materials are safeguarded in an approved manner. Adequate space separation; fire-resistant barriers or enclosures; trenches containing sufficient coarse crushed stone; and properly drained oil enclosures, such as dikes or basins, shall be considered suitable for this purpose.

▲ A typical assembly of metal-enclosed switchgear is shown in Fig. 710-1. This assembly is designed for a maximum voltage of 5,000 V. Each unit is equipped with an oil circuit breaker having six contact pockets which, in the operating position, fit corresponding contact posts. When the breaker is in the open position, it can be lowered by means of a crank so that the disconnecting contacts are separated, and the assembly is thus an example of "automatic disconnecting switchgear equipment" for which no separate isolating switch is required. After being lowered, the breaker can be withdrawn from the metal enclosure for inspection or repairs. The circuit breakers are electrically remote-controlled. On the front of each panel are mounted indicating instruments, a wattmeter, two protective relays, and the operating lever of the switch for control of the circuit breaker. This assembly is designed for control of outgoing feeders from a substation.

(b) Fuseholders and Fuses.

(1) Fuses that expel flame in opening the circuit shall be so designed or arranged that they will function properly without hazard to persons or property.

(2) Fuseholders shall be designed so that they can be de-energized while replacing a fuse.

Exception: If the fuse and fuseholder are designed to permit fuse replacement by qualified persons using equipment designed for the purpose without de-energizing the fuseholder.

Metal-enclosed switchgear and substations that utilize high-voltage fuses shall be provided with a gang-operated disconnecting switch. Isolation of the fuses from the circuit shall be provided by either connecting a switch between the source and the fuses or providing roll-out switch and fuse type of construction. The switch shall be of the load-interrupter type, unless mechanically or electrically interlocked with a load-interrupting device arranged to reduce the load to the interrupting capability of the switch.

(3) If high-voltage fused cutouts are installed in a building or a transformer vault, they shall be of a type designed for use in buildings. If such cutouts are not suitable to interrupt the circuit manually while carrying full load, a switch or contactor shall be provided that is capable of interrupting the entire load. In addition, the cutouts shall be interlocked with the approved interrupter or bear a conspicuous sign reading "Do Not Open Cutout Under Load."

The cutouts shall be so located that they may be readily and safely operated and re-fused. Fuses shall be accessible from a clear floor space.

Fig. 710-1. An assembly of metal-enclosed switchgear with roll-out breakers. (*Westinghouse Electric Corp.*)

(c) Load Interrupters. Load-interrupter switches shall be permitted if suitable fuses or circuit breakers are used in conjunction with these devices to interrupt fault currents. Where these devices are used in combination, they shall be so coordinated electrically that they will safely withstand the effects of closing, carrying, or interrupting all possible currents up to the assigned maximum short-circuit rating.

710-22. Isolating Means. Means shall be provided to completely isolate an item of equipment. The use of isolating switches shall not be required where there are other ways of de-energizing the equipment for inspection and repairs, such as draw-out-type metal-enclosed switchgear units and removable truck panels.

Isolating switches not interlocked with an approved circuit-interrupting device shall be provided with a sign warning against opening them under load.

A fuseholder and fuse, designed for the purpose, shall be permitted as an isolating switch.

710-23. Voltage Regulators. Proper switching sequence for regulators shall be assured by use of one of the following:

(1) Mechanically sequenced regulator bypass switch(es).

(2) Mechanical interlocks.

(3) Switching procedure prominently displayed at the switching location.

D. Installations Accessible to Qualified Persons Only

710-31. Enclosure for Electrical Installations. See Section 110-31.

710-32. Circuit Conductors. Circuit conductors shall be permitted to be installed in conduit, in duct systems, as metal-clad cable, as bare wire, cable, and busbars, or as nonmetallic-sheathed cables, or conductors as provided in Sections 710-3 through 710-6. Bare live conductors shall conform with Sections 710-33 and 710-34.

Insulators, together with their mounting and conductor attachments, where used as supports for wires, single-conductor cables, or busbars, shall be capable of safely withstanding the maximum magnetic forces that would prevail when two or more conductors of a circuit were subjected to short-circuit current.

Open runs of insulated wires and cables having a bare lead sheath or a braided outer covering shall be supported in a manner designed to prevent physical damage to the braid or sheath. Supports for lead-covered cables shall be designed to prevent electrolysis of the sheath.

710-33. Minimum Space Separation. The minimum indoor air separation between bare live conductors and between such conductors and adjacent surfaces shall not be less than the values given in Table 710-33. The specified space separation shall

Table 710-33. Minimum Air Separation in Inches, Indoors*

Circuit Voltage, kV	Between Bare Live Conductors	Between Bare Live Conductors and Adjacent Surfaces
2.5	5	4
5.0	6	5
7.5	7	6
15.0	12	7
23.0	15	10
34.5	18	13
46.0	21	17
69.0	31	25

*The values given are the minimum permissible space separation under favorable service conditions. They shall be increased under unfavorable service conditions or wherever space limitations permit.

apply to interior wiring design and construction but not to the space separation provided within electric apparatus and wiring devices.

710-34. Work Space and Guarding. See Section 110-34.

E. Mobile and Portable Equipment

710-41. General.

(a) The provisions of this Part shall apply to installations and use of high-voltage power distribution and utilization equipment which is portable and/or mobile, such as substations and switch houses mounted on skids, trailers, or cars, mobile shovels, draglines, cranes, hoists, drills, dredges, compressors, pumps, conveyors, underground excavators, and the like.

(b) **Other Requirements.** The requirements of this Part shall be additional to, or amendatory of, those prescribed in Articles 100 through 725, of this Code. Special attention shall be paid to Article 250.

(c) **Protection.** Adequate enclosures and/or guarding shall be provided to protect portable and mobile equipment from physical damage.

710-42. Overcurrent Protection. Motors driving single or multiple DC generators supplying a system operating on a cyclic load basis do not require running overcurrent protection, provided that the thermal rating of the AC drive motor cannot be exceeded under any operating condition. However, the branch-circuit protective device(s), which may be external to the motor, must provide short-circuit and locked-rotor protection.

710-43. Enclosures. All energized switching and control parts shall be enclosed in effectively grounded metal cabinets or enclosures. These cabinets or enclosures shall be marked "WARNING—HIGH VOLTAGE" and shall be locked so that only authorized and qualified persons can enter. Circuit breakers and protective equipment shall have the operating means projecting through the metal cabinet or enclosure so these units can be reset without opening locked doors. With doors closed, reasonable safe access for normal operation of these units shall be provided.

710-44. Collector Rings. The collector ring assemblies on revolving type machines (shovels, draglines, etc.) shall be guarded to prevent accidental contact with energized parts by personnel on or off the machine.

710-45. Power Cable Connections to Mobile Machines. A metallic enclosure shall be provided on the mobile machine for enclosing the terminals of the power cable. The enclosure shall include provisions for a solid connection for the ground wire(s) terminal to effectively ground the machine frame. Ungrounded conductors shall be attached to insulators or terminated in approved high-voltage cable couplers (which include ground wire connectors) of proper voltage and ampere rating. The method of cable termination used shall prevent any strain or pull on the cable from stressing the electrical connections. The enclosure shall have provision for locking so only authorized and qualified persons may open, and shall be marked "WARNING— HIGH VOLTAGE."

710-46. High-Voltage Portable Cable for Main Power Supply. Flexible high-voltage cable supplying power to portable or mobile equipment shall comply with Articles 250 and 400.

710-47. Grounding. Mobile equipment shall be grounded in accordance with Article 250.

F. Tunnel Installations

710-51. General.

(a) The provisions of this Article shall apply to installation and use of high-voltage power distribution and utilization equipment which is portable and/or mobile, such as substations, trailers, or cars, mobile shovels, draglines, hoists, drills, dredges, compressors, pumps, conveyors, underground excavators, and the like.

(b) **Other Articles.** The requirements of this Article shall be additional to, or amendatory of, those prescribed in Articles 100 through 710 of this Code. Special attention shall be paid to Article 250.

(c) **Protection Against Physical Damage.** Conductors and cables in tunnels shall be located above the tunnel floor and so placed or guarded to protect them from physical damage.

710-52. Overcurrent Protection. Motor-operated equipment shall be protected from overcurrent in accordance with Article 430. Transformers shall be protected from overcurrent in accordance with Article 450.

710-53. Conductors. High-voltage conductors in tunnels shall be installed in (1) metal conduit or other metal raceway, (2) metal-armored or steel-taped cable, or (3) other approved multi-conductor cable. Multi-conductor portable cable shall be permitted to supply mobile equipment.

710-54. Bonding and Equipment Grounding Conductor.

(a) All nonenergized metal parts of electric equipment and all metal raceways and cable sheaths shall be effectively grounded and bonded to all metal pipes and rails at the portal and at intervals not exceeding 1000 feet throughout the tunnel.

(b) An equipment grounding conductor shall be run with circuit conductors inside the metal raceway or inside the multi-conductor cable jacket. The equipment grounding conductor shall be permitted to be insulated or bare.

710-55. Transformers, Switches, and Electric Equipment. All transformers, switches, motor controllers, motors, rectifiers, and other equipment installed below ground shall be protected from physical damage by location or guarding.

710-56. Energized Parts. Bare terminals of transformers, switches, motor controllers, and other equipment shall be enclosed to prevent accidental contact with energized parts.

710-57. Ventilation System Controls. Electrical controls for the ventilation system shall be so arranged that the air flow can be reversed.

710-58. Disconnecting Means. A switching device meeting the requirements of Article 430 or 450 shall be installed at each transformer or motor location for disconnecting the transformer or motor. The switching device shall open all ungrounded conductors of a circuit simultaneously.

710-59. Enclosures. Enclosures for use in tunnels shall be drip-proof, weather-proof, or submersible as required by the environmental conditions. Switch or contactor enclosures shall not be used as junction boxes or raceways for conductors feeding through or tapping off to other switches, unless special designs are used to provide adequate space for this purpose.

710-60. Grounding. Tunnel equipment shall be grounded in accordance with Article 250.

ARTICLE 720. CIRCUITS AND EQUIPMENT
OPERATING AT LESS
THAN 50 VOLTS

720-1. Scope. This Article covers installations operating at less than 50 volts, direct current or alternating current.

Exception: As covered in Articles 650, 725, and 760.

720-2. Hazardous Locations. Installations coming within the scope of this Article and installed in hazardous locations shall also comply with the appropriate provisions of Articles 500 through 517.

720-4. Conductors. Conductors shall not be smaller than No. 12 copper or equivalent. Conductors for appliance branch circuits supplying more than one appliance or appliance receptacle shall not be smaller than No. 10 copper or equivalent.

720-5. Lampholders. Standard lampholders having a rating of not less than 660 watts shall be used.

720-6. Receptacle Rating. Receptacles shall have a rating of not less than 15 amperes.

720-7. Receptacles Required. Receptacles of not less than 20-ampere rating shall be provided in kitchens, laundries, and other locations where portable appliances are likely to be used.

720-8. Overcurrent Protection. Overcurrent protection shall comply with Article 240.

720-9. Batteries. Installations of storage batteries shall comply with Article 480.

720-10. Grounding. Grounding shall comply with Sections 250-5(a) and 250-45.

ARTICLE 725. CLASS 1, CLASS 2, AND CLASS 3 REMOTE-CONTROL, SIGNALING, AND POWER-LIMITED CIRCUITS

A. Scope and General

725-1. Scope. This Article covers remote-control, signaling, and power-limited circuits that are not an integral part of a device or appliance.

The circuits described herein are characterized by usage and electrical power limitations which differentiate them from light and power circuits and, therefore, special consideration is given with regard to minimum wire sizes, derating factors, overcurrent protection, and conductor insulation requirements.

725-2. Locations and Other Articles. Circuits or equipment shall comply with (1), (2), and (3) below.

(1) Section 300-21.

(2) Articles 500 through 516, and Article 517 Part E where installed in hazardous locations.

(3) Section 300-22 where installed in ducts or plenums.

Exception to (3): Conductors of Class 2 and Class 3 having inherent fire-resistant and low-smoke producing characteristics approved for the purpose shall be permitted for ducts, hollow spaces used as ducts, and plenums other than those described in Section 300-22(a).

725-3. Classifications. A remote-control, signaling, or power-limited circuit is the portion of the wiring system between the load side of the overcurrent device or the power limited supply and all connected equipment, and shall be Class 1, Class 2, or Class 3 as defined in (a) and (b) below.

(a) Class 1 Circuits. Circuits that comply with Part B of this Article and in which the power is limited in accordance with Section 725-11.

(b) Class 2 and Class 3 Circuits. Circuits that comply with Part C of this Article and in which the power is limited in accordance with Section 725-31.

725-4. Safety Control Equipment. Remote-control circuits to safety control equipment shall be Class 1 if the failure of the equipment to operate introduces a direct fire or life hazard. Room thermostats, water temperature regulating devices, and similar controls used in conjunction with electrically controlled household heating and air conditioning shall not be considered safety-control equipment.

725-5. Communication Cables. Class 1 circuits shall not be run in the same cable with communication circuits. Class 2 and Class 3 circuit conductors shall be permitted in the same cable with communication circuits, in which case the Class 2 and Class 3 circuits shall be classified as communication circuits and shall meet the requirements of Article 800.

B. Class 1 Circuits

725-11. Power Limitations for Class 1 Circuits.

(a) Class 1 Power-Limited Circuits. These circuits shall be supplied from a source having a rated output of not more than 30 volts and 1000 volt-amperes. The source shall be protected by overcurrent devices rated at not more than 167 percent of the volt-ampere rating of the source divided by the rated voltage. The overcurrent devices and their mounting shall be approved for the purpose and shall not be interchangeable with overcurrent devices of a higher rating. The overcurrent device shall be permitted to be an integral part of the power supply.

(1) Transformers. Transformers used to supply power-limited Class 1 circuits shall comply with Article 450.

(2) Other Power Sources. To comply with the 1000 volt-ampere limitation, power sources other than transformers shall not exceed a maximum power output of 2500 volt-amperes, and the product of the maximum current and maximum voltage shall not exceed 10,000 volt-amperes with the overcurrent protection bypassed.

(b) Class I Remote-Control and Signaling Circuits. Class I remote-control and signaling circuits shall not exceed 600 volts; however, the power output of the source shall not be required to be limited.

725-12. Overcurrent Protection.

(a) Conductors Larger Than No. 14. Conductors larger than No. 14 shall be protected against overcurrent in accordance with the ampacities given in Tables 310-16 through 310-19.

(b) Conductors of Nos. 18, 16, and 14. Conductors of Nos. 18, 16, and 14 shall be considered as protected by overcurrent devices of not over 20 amperes rating.

Exception No. 1 for (a) and (b) above: Where other Articles of this Code permit or require other overcurrent protection.

See Section 430-72 for motors and Section 620-61 for elevators, escalators and moving walks.

Exception No. 2 for (a) and (b) above: In Class 1 power-limited circuits having main overcurrent protection, the branch circuits shall not be required to have individual overcurrent protection.

725-13. Location of Overcurrent Devices. Overcurrent devices shall be located at the point where the conductor to be protected receives its supply.

Exception: Where the overcurrent device protecting the larger conductor also protects the smaller conductor.

725-14. Wiring Method. Installations of Class 1 circuits shall be in accordance with the appropriate Articles in Chapter 3.

Exception No. 1: As provided in Sections 725-15 through 725-17.

Exception No. 2: Where other Articles of this Code permit or require other methods.

725-15. Conductors of Different Circuits in Same Enclosure, Cable, or Raceway. Class 1 circuits shall be permitted to occupy the same enclosure, cable, or raceway without regard to whether the individual circuits are alternating current or direct current, provided all conductors are insulated for the maximum voltage of any conductor in the enclosure, cable or raceway. Power supply and Class 1 circuit conductors shall be permitted in the same enclosure, cable, or raceway only when connected to the same equipment.

725-16. Conductors.

(a) Sizes and Use. Conductors of Nos. 18 and 16 shall be permitted to be used provided they supply loads that do not exceed the ampacities given in Section 402-5 and are installed in a raceway or a cable approved for the purpose. Conductors larger than No. 16 shall not supply loads greater than the ampacities given in Tables 310-16 through 310-19. Flexible cords shall comply with Article 400.

(b) Insulation. Insulation on conductors shall be suitable for 600 volts. Conductors larger than No. 16 shall comply with Article 310. Conductors in sizes No. 18 and 16 shall be Types RFH-2, FFH-2, TF, TFF, TFN, TFFN, PF, PFF, PGF, PGFF, PTF, PTFF, SF-2, SFF-2. Conductors with other types and thickness of insulation shall be permitted if approved for the purpose.

725-17. Number of Conductors in Raceways and Cables, and Derating.

(a) Where only Class 1 circuits are in a raceway, the number of conductors shall be determined in accordance with Section 300-17. The derating factors given in Note 8 to Tables 310-16 through 310-19 shall apply only if such conductors carry continuous loads.

(b) Where power-supply conductors and Class 1 circuit conductors are permitted in a raceway in accordance with Section 725-15, the number of conductors shall be determined in accordance with Section 300-17. The derating factors given in Note 8 to Tables 310-16 through 310-19 shall apply as follows:

(1) To all conductors when the Class 1 circuit conductors carry continuous loads and where the total number of conductors are more than three.

(2) To the power-supply conductors only, when the Class 1 circuit conductors do not carry continuous loads and where the number of power-supply conductors are more than three.

725-18. Physical Protection. Where damage to remote-control circuits of safety control equipment would introduce a hazard, as covered in Section 725-4, all conductors of such remote-control circuits shall be installed in rigid metal conduit, intermediate metal conduit, electrical metallic tubing, Type MI cable, Type ALS cable, Type CS cable, or be otherwise suitably protected from physical damage.

725-19. Circuits Extending Beyond One Building. Class 1 circuits that extend aerially beyond one building shall also meet the requirements of Article 225.

725-20. Grounding. Class 1 circuits and equipment shall be grounded in accordance with Article 250.

C. Class 2 and Class 3 Circuits

725-31. Power Limitations of Class 2 and Class 3 Circuits. The power for Class 2 and Class 3 circuits shall be either inherently limited requiring no overcurrent protection as specified in Table 725-31(a), or limited by a combination of a power source and overcurrent protection, as specified in Table 725-31(b).

725-32. Interconnection of Power Supplies. Class 2 or Class 3 power supplies shall not be paralleled or otherwise interconnected unless approved for the purpose.

Table 725-31(a). Power Limitations for Class 2 and Class 3 Circuits Supplied From an Inherently Limited Power Source

Class	Circuit Voltage V_{max} AC-DC (Volts)	Maximum Nameplate Ratings		Current Limitation I_{max} (Amps)
		VA (Volt-Amps)	Current (Amps)	
2	0 to 150	$0.005 \times V_{max}$	0.005	0.005
2 (note 3)	0 to 20	$5.0 \times V_{max}$	5.0	8.0
	over 20 to 30	100	$100/V_{max}$	8.0
	over 30 to 60 DC only	100	$100/V_{max}$	$150/V_{max}$
3	over 30 to 60 AC only	100	$100/V_{max}$	$150/V_{max}$
	over 60 to 100	100	$100/V_{max}$	$150/V_{max}$

Note 1. V_{max}: Maximum output voltage regardless of load with rated input applied. I_{max}: Maximum output current regardless of load.

Note 2. A dry cell battery shall be considered an inherently limited supply provided the voltage is 30 volts or less and the capacity is equal to or less than that available from series connected No. 6 carbon zinc cells.

Note 3. Voltage ranges shown are for sinusoidal AC and continuous DC in indoor locations or where wet contact is not likely to occur. For non-sinusoidal AC, V_{max} shall be not greater than 42.4 volts peak. For DC interrupted at a rate of 10 to 200 Hz, V_{max} shall be not greater than 24.8 volts.

Where wet contact (immersion not included) is likely to occur, V_{max} shall be not greater than: 15 volts for sinusoidal AC; 30 volts for continuous DC; 21.2 volts peak for nonsinusoidal AC and 12.4 volts for DC that is interrupted at a rate of 10 to 200 Hz.

725-33. Power Supply Leads. The input leads of a transformer or other power supply supplying Class 2 and Class 3 circuits shall be permitted to be smaller than No. 14, but not smaller than No. 18 if they are not over 12 inches long and if they have insulation that complies with Section 725-16(b).

725-34. Marking. A Class 2 or Class 3 power supply unit shall be durably marked where plainly visible to indicate the class of supply and its electrical rating.

725-35. Overcurrent Protection. Where overcurrent protection is required, such protection and its mounting shall be approved for the purpose and shall not be interchangeable with protection of higher rating. The overcurrent protection shall be permitted as an integral part of a transformer or other power supply devices approved for the purpose.

725-36. Location of Overcurrent Devices. Overcurrent devices shall be located at the point where the conductor to be protected receives its supply.

725-37. Wiring Methods on Supply Side. Conductors and equipment on the supply side of overcurrent protection, transformers, or current-limiting devices shall be installed in accordance with the appropriate requirements of Chapter 3. Transformers or other devices supplied from light or power circuits shall be protected by an overcurrent device rated not over 20 amperes.

725-38. Wiring Methods on Load Side. Conductors on the load side of overcurrent protection, transformers, and current-limiting devices shall be insulated in accordance with Section 725-40 and shall comply with (a) and (b) below.

(a) Separation from Light, Power, and Class 1 Conductors.

(1) Open Conductors. Conductors of Class 2 and Class 3 circuits shall be separated at least 2 inches from conductors of any light, power, and Class 1 circuits.

Table 725-31(b). Power Limitations for Class 2 and Class 3 Circuits Supplied From a Power Source with Overcurrent Protection

Class	Circuit Voltage V_{max} AC-DC (Volts)	Maximum Nameplate Ratings		Current Limitation I_{max} (Amps)	Power Limitation $(VA)_{max}$ (Volt Amps)	Maximum Overcurrent Protection (Amps)
		VA (Volts-Amps)	Current (Amps)			
2 (note 3)	0 to 20	$5.0 \times V_{max}$	5.0	$1000/V_{max}$	250	5.0
	over 20 to 30	100	$100/V_{max}$	$1000/V_{max}$	250 (or note 2)	$100/V_{max}$
	over 30 to 60 DC only	100	$100/V_{max}$	$1000/V_{max}$	250	$100/V_{max}$
3	over 30 to 60 AC only	100	$100/V_{max}$	$1000/V_{max}$	250	$100/V_{max}$
	over 60 to 100	100	$100/V_{max}$	$1000/V_{max}$	250	$100/V_{max}$
	over 100 to 150	100	$100/V_{max}$	1.0	NA	1.0

Note 1. V_{max}: Maximum output voltage regardless of load with rated input applied.
I_{max}: Maximum output current regardless of load with overcurrent protection by-passed. $(VA)_{max}$: Maximum volt-ampere output regardless of load with overcurrent protection by-passed.
Note 2. If the power source is a transformer, $(VA)_{max}$ is 350 or less when V_{max} is 15 or less.
Note 3. Voltage ranges shown are for sinusoidal AC and continuous DC in indoor locations or where wet contact is not likely to occur. For non-sinusoidal AC, V_{max} shall be not greater than 42.4 volts peak. For DC interrupted at a rate of 10 to 200 Hz, V_{max} shall be not greater than 24.8 volts.
  Where wet contact (immersion not included) is likely to occur, V_{max} shall be not greater than: 15 volts for sinusoidal AC; 30 volts for continuous DC; 21.2 volts peak for non-sinusoidal AC and 12.4 volts for DC that is interrupted at a rate of 10 to 200 Hz.

Exception No. 1: Where the light or power, and Class 1 circuit conductors are in a raceway or in metal-sheathed, metal-clad, nonmetallic-sheathed, or Type UF cables.

Exception No. 2: Where the conductors are permanently separated from the conductors of the other circuits by a continuous and firmly fixed nonconductor, such as porcelain tubes or flexible tubing in addition to the insulation on the wire.

(2) In Enclosures, Raceways and Cables. Conductors of Class 2 and Class 3 circuits shall not be placed in any enclosure, raceway, cable, compartment, outlet box, or similar fitting with conductors of light, power, and Class 1 circuits.

Exception No. 1: Where the conductors of the different circuits are separated by a partition.

Exception No. 2: Conductors in outlet boxes, junction boxes, or similar fittings, or compartments where power-supply conductors are introduced solely for supplying power to the equipment connected to Class 2 or Class 3 circuits to which the other conductors in the enclosure are connected.

(3) In Shafts. Class 2 or Class 3 conductors run in the same shaft with conductors for light, power, or Class 1 circuits shall be separated by not less than 2 inches from the light, power, and Class 1 conductors.

Exception No. 1: Where the conductors of either the light, power, or Class 1 circuits or the Class 2 or Class 3 circuits are encased in noncombustible tubing.

Exception No. 2: Where the light, power, or Class 1 circuit conductors are in a raceway, or are in metal-sheathed, metal-clad, nonmetallic-sheathed, or Type UF cables.

(4) In Hoistways. Class 2 or Class 3 conductors shall be installed in rigid conduit, intermediate metal conduit, or electrical metallic tubing in hoistways.

Exception: As provided for in Section 620-21, Exception Nos. 1 and 2 for elevators and similar equipment.

(b) Vertical Runs. Conductors in a vertical run in a shaft or partition shall have a fire-resistant covering capable of preventing the carrying of fire from floor to floor.

Exception: Where conductors are encased in noncombustible tubing or other outer covering of noncombustible materials or are located in a fireproof shaft having fire stops at each floor.

725-39. Conductors of Different Class 2 and Class 3 Circuits in Same Cable, Enclosure, or Raceway.

(a) Conductors of two or more Class 2 circuits shall be permitted within the same cable, enclosure, or raceway provided all conductors in the cable, enclosure, or raceway are insulated for the maximum voltage of any conductor.

(b) Conductors of two or more Class 3 circuits shall be permitted within the same cable, enclosure, or raceway.

(c) Conductors of one or more Class 2 circuits shall be permitted within the same cable, enclosure, or raceway with conductors of Class 3 circuits provided that the insulation of the Class 2 circuit conductors in the cable, enclosure, or raceway is at least that required for Class 3 circuits.

725-40. Conductors. Conductors shall comply with (a) and (b) below.

(a) Class 2 Circuits. The conductor size and insulation shall be suitable for the particular application.

The kind of insulation for the conductors is not specified in further detail as reliance is placed on current limitation to stop dangerous currents.

▲ Although any type of insulation is permitted for the conductors of Class 2 systems, in order to ensure continuity of service a type of insulation should be selected which is suitable for the conditions, such as the voltage to be employed and possible exposure to moisture.

There is a marked distinction between power-limited circuits supplied by limited power sources with overcurrent protection and those without; but within the same source category, little difference exists in the power limitation.

The significant distinction between Class 2 circuits and Class 3 circuits is the character and magnitude of the voltages. The classifications of Class 2 circuits recognize their acceptability from both fire and shock hazard. Class 3 circuits recognize fire hazard only; hence the reason for more restrictive conductor and insulation requirements.

(b) Class 3 Circuits. Class 3 circuit conductors shall be as described in (1), (2), or (3) below.

(1) Conductors of a multi-conductor cable shall be of solid or stranded copper not smaller than No. 22, and shall have thermoplastic insulation of not less than 12 mils nominal (10 mils minimum) thickness. The cable conductors shall have an overall thermoplastic jacket having a nominal thickness of not less than 35 mils (30 mils minimum). Where the number of conductors in a cable exceeds 4, the thickness of the thermoplastic jacket shall be increased so as to provide equivalent performance characteristics. Similarly, where the size of conductors in a cable exceeds No. 16, the thickness of the conductor insulation shall be increased so as to provide equivalent performance characteristics.

Exception No. 1: Where approved for the purpose, cables with smaller conductors and thinner insulations and jackets shall be permitted.

Exception No. 2: Two conductors assembled in a flat parallel construction with a 30-mil nominal integral insulation-jacket and a 47-mil minimum web shall be permitted.

(2) Single conductors shall not be smaller than No. 18 and shall be insulated in accordance with Section 725-16(b).

(3) Approved power-limited (low-energy) circuit cable, Class 3 circuit cable, or other equivalent cable.

▲ *General Discussion of Signaling and Remote-Control Systems*

The provisions of the preceding sections of this chapter divide all signaling and remote-control systems into three classes.

Class 1 includes all signaling and remote-control systems which do not have the special current limitations of Class 2 and Class 3 systems.

Class 2 and Class 3 systems are those systems in which the current is limited to certain specified low values by fuses or circuit breakers, and by supply through transformers which will deliver only very small currents on short circuit, or by other means which are considered satisfactory. The current values depend upon the voltage at which the system operates and range from 5 mA. All Class 2 and Class 3 circuits must have a power source with the power-limiting characteristics assigned in the tables in addition to the overcurrent device.

Class 1 Systems

Class 1 systems may operate at any voltage not exceeding 600 V. They are, in many cases, merely extensions of light and power systems, and, with a few exceptions, are subject to all the installation rules for light and power systems. The following exceptions are made:

1. No. 14, No. 16, or No. 18 conductors may be used under certain conditions.
2. No. 16 and No. 18 conductors may have special types of insulation.
3. Mechanical protection for the conductors is required in certain cases.
4. In certain cases the general rules for overcurrent protection are modified.
5. Some exceptions are made to the general requirements for system grounding.

A very common example of a Class 1 remote-control system is the circuit wiring and devices used for the operation of a magnetically operated motor controller. Section 430-72 provides that under certain conditions the control-circuit conductors need not have overcurrent protection in accordance with their ampacity; however, Sec. 725-12(b) requires overcurrent protection of not over 20-A rating or setting if No. 14, No. 16, or No. 18 conductors are used. Conductors of these sizes are often used where a considerable number of control conductors must be provided between two outlets, as in the case of some printing-press control systems.

The term *remote-control switch* is used in various code references to designate a switch or contactor used for the remote control of a feeder or branch circuit. The control conductors and devices are usually Class 1 control systems. As in the case of the circuits of remote-control motor controllers, special provisions apply to the overcurrent protection of the conductors; No. 14, No. 16, or No. 18 conductors may be used, and for these sizes the overcurrent protection is limited to a maximum of 20 A.

The signaling systems which are included in Class 1 in many cases operate at 115 V with 20-A overcurrent protection, though they are not necessarily limited to this voltage and current. Some of the signaling systems which may be so operated are some electric clocks, bank alarm systems, and factory call systems. No. 14, No. 16, or No. 18 conductors may be used for any of these systems when provided with 20-A overcurrent protection.

An example of a lower voltage Class 1 signaling system is a nurses' call system, as used in hospitals. Such systems commonly operate at not over 25 V.

Class 2 and Class 3 Systems

Class 2 and Class 3 signaling, remote-control, and power-limited systems are used where the current and voltage requirements are such that it is not necessary to comply with the general requirements for light and power systems.

Current supply from primary batteries is considered as providing satisfactory current limitation as indicated by Note 2 to Table 725-31(a).

Where batteries are employed to supply small bell, buzzer, or annunciator systems, it is the usual practice to use several No. 6 dry cells in series. One of these cells will deliver 25 to 30 A on short circuit but the current falls off very rapidly. It would be possible to provide a dry-cell battery that would deliver a fairly heavy current for several hours; however, such batteries are not needed for these systems, and it is therefore safe to assume that they will not be installed and that, in any practical case, supply of the system from a primary battery will provide sufficient current limitation.

Wherever AC service is available, current limitation can be provided by using so-called "current-limiting" transformers. These are transformers having so high a secondary impedance that, even on short circuit, they cannot deliver a current higher than a certain maximum.

It is probable that a doorbell type of transformer will provide the required current limitation for a Class 2 system. In the NEMA Specialty Transformer Standards it is stated that the open-circuit secondary voltage for a doorbell transformer shall not exceed 25 V and that the maximum input with the secondary short-circuited shall be 50 W. U/L lists energy-limiting transformers suitable for Class 2 systems.

The NEMA Standards include the following data applying to the type known as signaling transformers.

Output ratings: 50 and 100 VA.
Secondary open-circuit voltages for either rating: 4.4, 8.8, 13.2, 17.6, 22.0, and 26.4 volts.
Secondary short-circuit current at maximum voltage: 50-VA rating, 2.1 amp, 100-VA rating, 4.2 amp. The secondary short-circuit current at any lower voltage is proportional to the voltage.

The great majority of small bell, buzzer, and annunciator systems come under Class 2 classification, 0 to 20 V, 5 A. This will also include small intercommunicating telephone systems in which the talking circuit is supplied by a primary battery and the ringing circuit by a transformer.

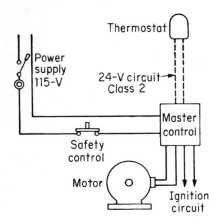

Fig. 725-1. Automatic control for a domestic oil burner.

The application of Sec. 725-4 is illustrated by Fig. 725-1, which is a simplified diagram of a common type of automatic control for a domestic oil burner. Assuming a steam boiler, the safety control is a switch that opens automatically when the steam pressure reaches a predetermined value and, preferably, also opens if the water level is allowed to fall too low. The master control includes a transformer of the current-limiting type which supplies the thermostat circuit at a voltage of 24 V. When the thermostat contacts close, a relay closes the circuits to the motor and to the ignition transformer.

Failure of the safety control or ignition to operate would introduce a direct hazard; hence, the circuits to this equipment are Class 1. The thermostat circuit fulfills all requirements of a Class 2 circuit and can be short-circuited or broken without introducing any hazard. The wiring of this circuit can therefore be done with any type of wire or cable that is sufficiently protected from physical damage to ensure serviceability.

725-41. Circuits Extending Beyond One Building. Class 2 or Class 3 circuits that extend beyond one building and are so run as to be subject to accidental contact

with light or power conductors operating at over 300 volts to ground shall also meet the requirements of Sections 800-2, 800-11, and 800-12 for communication circuits.
725-42. Grounding. Class 2 and Class 3 circuits and equipment shall be grounded in accordance with Article 250.

ARTICLE 750. STAND-BY POWER GENERATION SYSTEMS

750-1. Scope. This Article covers the installation, operation, and maintenance of circuits, systems, and equipment intended to supply on-site generated power to selected loads (other than those of Article 700, Emergency Systems), automatically or manually, in the event of failure of the normal source of electric service including those systems legally required and classed as standby power systems by Municipal, State, Federal or other Codes or by any governmental agency having jurisdiction. The systems covered by this Article consist only of those that are permanently installed in their entirety, including the prime movers.

Stand-by systems are generally installed to provide an alternate source of electric energy to serve loads, such as heating and refrigeration systems, communications systems, and industrial processes that, when stopped during any power outage, could cause discomfort, serious interruption of the process, or damage to the product or process, or the like.

▲ The intent here is to recognize a permanently installed standby system that is not considered to be an "Emergency System" as covered in Arts. 517 or 700 of the National Electrical Code, or "Essential Electrical Systems for Health Care Facilities" as covered in NFPA Pamphlet No. 76A.

750-2. Other Articles. Except as modified by this Article, all applicable Articles of this Code shall apply.
750-3. Equipment Approval. All equipment shall be approved for the use intended.
750-6. Capacity of the System. The stand-by system shall have adequate capacity and rating for the operation of all equipment to be supplied at one time.
750-7. Controls and Transfer Equipment. Equipment shall be suitable for its intended use and be so designed and installed as to prevent the inadvertent interconnection of normal and stand-by sources of supply in any operation of the transfer equipment.

A time-delay will avoid short-time operation of the stand-by system.

750-8. Systems Protection. Transfer equipment and wiring associated with the stand-by system shall be provided with suitably rated protective devices.
750-9. Wiring. The stand-by system wiring shall not be subject to the provisions of Section 700-17, and the wiring of this system shall be permitted to occupy the same raceways, boxes, cabinets, and panelboards with other wiring. The stand-by wiring shall not occupy the same raceways, boxes, or cabinets as wiring for emergency systems.
750-10. Legally Required Stand-by Power Generation Systems. Legally required stand-by power systems shall conform to all other provisions of this Article and, in addition, the systems shall (a) be equipped with suitable means for automatically

starting the generator set upon failure of the normal electrical service and for automatic transfer and operation of all required electrical functions at full power within sixty seconds of such normal service failure; (b) be provided with an on-premise fuel supply sufficient for not less than two hours full demand operation of the system; (c) be tested at completion and periodically thereafter, on a schedule and in a manner acceptable to the authority having jurisdiction, to assure the maintenance of the system in proper operating condition.

ARTICLE 760. FIRE PROTECTIVE SIGNALING SYSTEMS

A. Scope and General

760-1. Scope. This Article covers the installation of wiring and equipment of fire-protective signaling systems operating at 600 volts or less.

For further information for fire alarm, guard tour, sprinkler waterflow, and sprinkler supervisory systems, refer to the following:
NFPA Standard No. 71 -1974—Central Station Signaling Systems.
NFPA Standard No. 72A-1974—Local Protective Signaling Systems.
NFPA Standard No. 72B-1974—Auxiliary Protective Signaling Systems.
NFPA Standard No. 72C-1974—Remote Station Protective Signaling Systems.
NFPA Standard No. 72D-1974—Proprietary Protective Signaling Systems.
NFPA Standard No. 72E-1974—Automatic Fire Detectors.
NFPA Standard No. 74 -1974—Household Fire Warning Equipment.
Class 1, 2 and 3 circuits are defined in Article 725.

▲ Signaling Systems Prologue

NFPA No. 71, Central Station Signaling Systems, pertains to fire protective signaling alarm services which are transmitted to a privately owned central station building from whence the fire department is notified or other action is taken as deemed adequate. The types of services provided include manual fire alarm service, guard tour supervisory service, automatic fire detection and alarm service, sprinkler system waterflow alarm, and supervisory signal service.

NFPA No. 72A, Local Protective Signaling Systems, covers provisions for supervised systems providing fire alarm or supervisory signals within the protected premises. These systems are primarily for the protection of life by indicating the necessity for evacuation of the building and secondarily for the protection of the property. The systems may provide for (1) manual fire alarm service; (2) automatic fire alarm service; (3) automatic detection of alarm or abnormal conditions in extinguishing systems, such as sprinkler and carbon dioxide; (4) watchmen's supervisory service; and (5) automatic detection of abnormal conditions in industrial processes which could result in a fire or explosion hazard affecting safety to life.

NFPA No. 72B, Auxiliary Protective Signaling Systems, provides protection to an individual occupancy or building or to a group of buildings of a single occupancy and utilizes the municipal fire alarm facilities to transmit an alarm to the fire department. An auxiliary alarm system deals with equipment and circuits in the protected property and is connected to a municipal fire alarm system to summon the fire department.

There are three types of auxiliary alarm systems, which include (1) local energy type, which provides its own power supply and is electrically isolated from the municipal alarm systems; (2) shunt type, which is electrically connected to and is an integral part of the municipal alarm system; and (3) a direct circuit, in which the alarms are transmitted over a circuit directly connected to the annunciating switchboard at the fire department headquarters.

Proprietary and local systems may be auxiliarized, in which case NFPA No. 72B would apply to the circuitry between the proprietary or local system and the transmitting device.

NFPA No. 72C, Remote Station Protective Signaling Systems, pertains to a system of electrically supervised circuits employing a direct circuit connection between signaling devices at the protected premises and signal receiving equipment at a remote station, such as a municipal fire alarm headquarters, a fire station, or another location acceptable to the authority having jurisdiction. The type of signaling services include (1) automatic fire detection and alarm service; (2) sprinkler system waterflow alarm and supervisory signal service; (3) manual fire alarm service; and (4) automatic smoke alarm service.

NFPA No. 72D, Proprietary Protective Signaling Systems, deals with electrically operated circuits designed to transmit alarms and supervisory and trouble signals for the protection of life and property to a central supervising station at the property to be protected. This system shall be maintained and tested by owner personnel or an organization satisfactory to the authority having jurisdiction.

NFPA No. 73, Public Fire Service Communications, covers the municipal fire alarm system, telephone facilities, and fire department radio facilities, all of which fulfill two principal functions: that of receiving fire alarms or other emergency calls from the public and that of retransmitting these alarms and emergency calls to fire companies and other interested agencies.

Fire alarm systems on private premises from which signals are received directly or indirectly by the communications center are covered by other NFPA standards.

NFPA No. 74, Household Fire Warning Equipment, covers the proper selection, installation, operation, and maintenance of fire warning equipment. The primary intent of this standard is to alert occupants for protection of life. This consists of a system or device which produces an audible alarm indicating the need to evacuate the premises. The types of detection devices used to sense fires are heat detectors and smoke detectors. Heat detectors should never be used by themselves, but must be used in conjunction with smoke detectors. Many building codes and others (such as NFPA No. 501B, Mobile Homes) require at least one smoke detector located between the sleeping areas and other parts of the residence. Obviously a full-protection system, consisting of heat detectors and/or smoke detectors in each major area of the home, will give the best protection; however, one or more smoke detectors will provide a degree of protection. NFPA No. 74 should be consulted for placement and number of detection devices to be used; in addition, local building codes may require the use of full systems or individual smoke detectors.

760-2. Classifications. Fire protective signaling circuits shall be classified as non-power limited or power limited. All fire protective signaling circuits shall comply with Part A and, in addition, non-power limited circuits shall comply with Part B and power limited circuits with Part C.

760-3. Identification. Fire protective signaling circuits shall be identified at terminal and junction locations, in a manner which will prevent unintentional interference with the signaling circuit during testing and servicing.

Fig. 760-1. An ionization-type smoke detector. (*Statitrol.*)

Fig. 760-2. A single zone fire alarm control unit that mounts in a 4 gang box. (*Edwards.*)

760-4. Location. Equipment and its associated wiring installed in hazardous locations shall also comply with Articles 500 through 516 and 517 Part E.

Equipment and its associated wiring installed in corrosive, damp, or wet locations shall also comply with Sections 110-11, 300-6, and 310-8.

760-5. Signaling Line Circuits Extending Beyond One Building. Fire protective signaling line circuits that extend aerially beyond one building shall either meet the requirements of Article 800 and be classified as communications circuits, or shall meet the requirements of Article 225.

760-6. Grounding. Fire protective signaling circuits and equipment shall be grounded in accordance with Article 250.

Exception: DC power limited fire protective signaling circuits having a maximum current of 0.030 amperes.

760-7. Supervision. The circuit shall be electrically supervised so that a trouble signal shall indicate the occurrence of a single open or a single ground fault on any installation wiring circuit that would prevent proper alarm operation.

See Articles on electrical supervision in NFPA Standards 71, 72A, 72B, 72C and 72D for more information about electrical supervision.

B. Nonpower Limited Fire Protective
   Signaling Circuits

760-11. Power Limitations. The power supply of non-power limited fire protective signaling circuits shall comply with Chapters 1 through 4 and the output voltage shall not exceed 600 volts.

FIG. 760-3. A large fire alarm control unit, consisting of several cabinets, combined with an emergency communications system for use in high-rise buildings. It is not unusual to combine security systems with fire protective signaling systems, provided a fault in the security systems will not interfere with the operation of the fire protective signaling circuits. (*Edwards.*)

760-12. Overcurrent Protection.

(a) **Conductors Larger Than No. 14.** Conductors larger than No. 14 shall be protected against overcurrent in accordance with the ampacities given in Tables 310-16 through 310-19.

(b) **Conductors of Nos. 18, 16 and 14.** Conductors of Nos. 18, 16 and 14 shall be considered as protected by overcurrent devices of not over 20 amperes rating.

Exception for (a) and (b) above: Where other Articles of this Code require other overcurrent protection.

760-13. Location of Overcurrent Devices. Overcurrent devices shall be located at the point where the conductor to be protected receives its supply.

Exception: Where the overcurrent device protecting the larger conductor also protects the smaller conductor.

760-14. Wiring Method. Wiring installation shall be in accordance with the appropriate articles in Chapter 3.

Exception No. 1: As provided in Sections 760-15 through 760-18.

Exception No. 2: Where other Articles of this Code require other methods.

760-15. Conductors of Different Circuits in Same Enclosure, Cable or Raceway.
Class 1 and nonpower limited fire protective signaling circuits shall be permitted

to occupy the same enclosure, cable or raceway without regard to whether the individual circuits are alternating current or direct current, provided all conductors are insulated for the maximum voltage of any conductor in the enclosure or raceway. Power supply and fire protective signaling circuit conductors shall be permitted in the same enclosure, cable or raceway only when connected to the same equipment.

760-16. Conductors.

(a) Sizes and Use. Conductors of Nos. 18 and 16 shall be permitted to be used provided they supply loads that do not exceed the ampacities given in Table 402-5 and are installed in a raceway or a cable approved for the purpose. Conductors larger than No. 16 shall not supply loads greater than the ampacities given in Tables 310-16 through 310-19.

(b) Insulation. Insulation on conductors shall be suitable for 600 volts. Conductors larger than No. 16 shall comply with Article 310. Conductors in sizes Nos. 18 and 16 shall be Types RFH-2, FFH-2, TF, TFF, TFN, TFFN, PF, PGF, PFF, PGFF, PTF, PTFF, SF-2, or SFF-2. Conductors with other type and thickness of insulation shall be permitted if approved for the purpose.

760-17. Multi-Conductor Cable for Circuits Operating at 150V or Less. A multi-conductor cable of 2 or more Nos. 16 or 18 solid copper conductors approved for the purpose shall be permitted to be used on fire protective signaling circuits operating at 150 volts or less. The multi-conductor cable shall be installed in raceway or exposed in accordance with the requirements of Chapter 3 except that surface mounted cable shall not be permitted within seven feet of the floor.

760-18. Number and Ampacity of Conductors in Raceways and Cables, and Derating.

(a) Where only nonpower limited fire protective signaling circuits and Class 1 circuits are in a raceway, the number of conductors shall be determined in accordance with Section 300-17. The derating factors given in Note 8 to Tables 310-16 through 310-19 shall apply if such conductors carry continuous loads.

(b) Where power-supply conductors and fire protective signaling circuit conductors are permitted in a raceway in accordance with Section 760-15, the number of conductors shall be determined in accordance with Section 300-17. The derating factors given in Note 8 to Tables 310-16 through 310-19 shall apply as follows:

(1) To all conductors when the fire protective signaling circuit conductors carry continuous loads and where the total number of conductors are more than three.

(2) To the power-supply conductors only, when the fire protective signaling circuit conductors do not carry continuous loads and where the number of power-supply conductors are more than three.

C. Power Limited Fire Protective Signaling Circuits

760-21. Power Limitations. The power for power limited fire protective signaling circuits shall be either inherently limited, as specified in Table 760-21(a), requiring no overcurrent protection, or limited by a combination of a power source and overcurrent protection, as specified in Table 760-21(b).

760-22. Supervision. In addition to the requirements of Section 760-7 either a trouble or alarm signal shall indicate the occurrence of a multiple ground fault or any short circuit fault that would prevent proper alarm operation.

760-23. Marking. The circuit shall be durably marked where plainly visible at terminations to indicate that it is a power limited fire protective signaling circuit.

Table 760-21(a). Power Limitations for Power Limited Fire Protective Signaling Circuits Supplied From an Inherently Limited Power Source

Circuit Voltage V_{max} AC-DC (Volts)	Maximum Nameplate Ratings		Current Limitation I_{max} (Amperes)
	VA (Volt Amperes)	Current (Amperes)	
0 to 20	5.0 × V_{max}	5.0	0.0
over 20 to 30	100	100/V_{max}	8.0
over 30 to 100	100	100/V_{max}	150/V_{max}
over 100 to 250 DC only	0.030 × V_{max}	0.030	0.030

Note. V_{max}: Maximum output voltage regardless of load with rated input applied.
I_{max}: Maximum output current regardless of load.

760-24. Power Supply Leads. The input leads of a transformer or other power supply supplying power limited fire protective signaling circuits shall be permitted to be smaller than No. 14 but not smaller than No. 18, if they are not over 12 inches long and if they have insulation at least equal to 600 volt fixture wire or approved equivalent.

760-25. Overcurrent Protection. Where overcurrent protection is required, such protection and its mounting shall be approved for the purpose and shall not be interchangeable with protection of higher rating. The overcurrent protection shall be permitted as an integral part of a transformer or other power supply device approved for the purpose.

760-26. Location of Overcurrent Device. Overcurrent devices shall be located at the point where the conductor to be protected receives its supply.

760-27. Wiring Methods on Supply Side. Conductors and equipment on the supply side of overcurrent protection, transformers, or current-limiting devices shall be installed in accordance with the appropriate requirements of Part B and Chapter 3. Transformers or other devices supplied from power supply conductors shall be protected by an overcurrent device rated not over 20 amperes.

760-28. Wiring Methods on Load Side. Conductors on the load side of overcurrent protection, transformers and current-limiting devices shall be insulated in accordance with 760-30 and shall comply with (a), (b) and (c) below.

(a) Separation from Light, Power, Class 1 and Non-Power Limited Fire Protective Signaling Circuits.

(1) Power limited circuits shall be separated at least two inches from open conductors of any light, power, Class 1 and nonpower limited fire protective signaling circuits.

Exception No. 1: Where the light, power, Class 1 and nonpower limited fire protective signaling circuit conductors are in raceway or in metal-sheathed, metal-clad, nonmetallic-sheathed or Type UF cables.

Exception No. 2: Where the power-limited circuit conductors are permanently separated from the conductors of the other circuits by a continuous and firmly fixed nonconductor, such as porcelain tubes or flexible tubing in addition to the insulation on the wire.

(2) Power limited circuits shall not be placed in any enclosure, raceway, cable,

Table 760-21(b). Power Limitations for Power Limited Fire Protective Signaling Circuits Supplied From a Power Source With Overcurrent Protection

Circuit Voltage V_{max} AC-DC (Volts)	Maximum Nameplate Ratings		Current Limitation I_{max} (Amperes)	Power Limitation $(VA)_{max}$ (Volt Amps)	Maximum Overcurrent Protection (Amperes)
	VA (Volt Amperes)	Current (Amperes)			
0 to 20	$5.0 \times V_{max}$	5.0	$1000/V_{max}$	250 (or note 2)	5.0
over 20 to 100	100	$100/V_{max}$	$1000/V_{max}$	250	$100/V_{max}$
over 100 to 150	100	$100/V_{max}$	1.0	NA	1.0

Note 1. V_{max}: Maximum output voltage regardless of load with rated input applied.
I_{max}: Maximum output current regardless of load with overcurrent protection by-passed.
$(VA)_{max}$: Maximum volt-ampere output regardless of load with overcurrent protection by-passed.
Note 2. If the power source is a transformer $(VA)_{max}$ is 350 or less when V_{max} is 15 or less.

compartment, outlet box, or similar fitting containing conductors of light, power, Class 1 and nonpower limited fire protective signaling circuits.

Exception No. 1: Where the conductors of the different systems are separated by a partition.

Exception No. 2: Conductors in outlet boxes, junction boxes, or similar fittings, or compartments where power supply conductors are introduced solely for supplying power to the power limited fire protective signaling system to which the other conductors in the enclosure are connected.

(0) Power limited circuits shall be separated by not less than two inches from light, power, Class 1 and nonpower limited fire protective signaling circuit conductors run in the same shaft.

Exception No. 1: Where the conductors of either the light, power, Class 1 or the nonpower limited fire protective signaling circuits or the power limited fire protective signaling circuit are encased in noncombustible tubing.

Exception No. 2: Where the light, power, Class 1, or the nonpower limited fire protective signaling circuit conductors are in a raceway, or are in metal-sheathed, metal-clad, nonmetallic-sheathed, or Type UF cables.

(4) Power limited circuit cable shall be installed in rigid conduit, intermediate metal conduit or electrical metallic tubing in hoistways.

Exception: As provided for in Section 620-21, exception Nos. 1 and 2 for elevators and similar equipment.

(b) Vertical Runs. Power limited circuit conductors shall have a fire-resistant covering capable of preventing the carrying of fire from floor to floor when installed in a vertical run in a shaft or partition.

Exception: Where conductors are encased in noncombustible tubing or other outer covering of noncombustible materials or are located in a fireproof shaft having fire stops at each floor.

(c) Conductors of Different Power Limited Fire Protective Signaling Circuits and Class 2 and Class 3 Circuits in Same Cable, Enclosure, or Raceway.

(1) Cables and conductors of two or more power limited fire protective signaling circuits or Class 3 circuits shall be permitted in the same cable, enclosure or raceway.

(2) Conductors of one or more Class 2 circuits shall be permitted within the same cable, enclosure, or raceway with conductors of power limited fire protective signaling circuits provided that the insulation of the Class 2 circuit conductors in the cable, enclosure or raceway is at least that required for the power limited fire protective signaling circuits.

760-29. Physical Protection. Power limited circuit conductors described in 760-30 shall be permitted to be installed as follows:

(a) Exposed on surface of ceiling and sidewalls or "fished" in concealed spaces. Cable shall be adequately supported and terminated in approved fittings and installed in such a way that maximum protection against physical injury is afforded by building construction such as baseboards, door frames, ledges, etc. When located within 7 feet of the floor, cable shall be securely fastened in an approved manner, such as insulated stapling at intervals of not more than 18 inches.

(b) As protection against physical injury, conductors and cables shall be installed in metal raceway when passing through a floor or wall to a height of 7 feet above the floor unless adequate protection can be afforded by building construction such as detailed in (a) above, or unless an equivalent solid guard is provided.

760-30. Conductors and Cables. Conductors and cables for use with power limited fire protective signaling circuits shall be approved for the purpose and meet the requirements of (a), (b), (c), (d) and (e) below.

(a) Conductors shall be solid copper or bunch-tinned (bonded) stranded copper.

(b) Conductors shall be not smaller than No. 16 for single conductor, No. 19 for 2 or more conductor and No. 22 for 5 or more conductor multi-conductor cables.

(c) Conductors of a multi-conductor cable shall be covered by approved thermoplastic insulation of not less than 12 mils nominal (10 mils minimum) thickness. The cable conductor shall have an overall thermoplastic jacket having a nominal thickness of not less than 35 mils (30 mils minimum). Where the number of conductors in a cable exceeds 4, the thickness of the thermoplastic jacket shall be increased so as to provide equivalent performance characteristics. Similarly, where the size of conductors in a cable exceed No. 16, the thickness of the conductor insulation shall be increased so as to provide equivalent performance characteristics.

Exception: Two conductors assembled in a flat parallel construction with a 30 mils nominal integral insulation-jacket and a 47 mils minimum web shall be permitted.

(d) Single conductors shall be covered by approved thermoplastic insulation of not less than 30 mils nominal (28 mils minimum) thickness.

(e) The cable shall have a voltage rating of not less than 300V and the jacket compound shall have a high degree of abrasion resistance.

760-31. Current-Carrying Continuous Line Type Fire Detectors.

(a) **Application.** Continuous line type fire detectors approved for the purpose, including insulated copper tubing of pneumatically operated detectors, employed for both detection and carrying signaling currents shall be permitted to be used in circuits having power limiting characteristics in accordance with 760-21.

(b) **Insulation.** Continuous line type fire detectors shall be insulated in accordance with Section 760-30(c) through (e), or with an equivalent type of insulation approved for the purpose.

(c) **Installation.** Continuous line type fire detectors shall be installed in accordance with Section 760-22 through 760-29.

CHAPTER EIGHT

Communication Systems

ARTICLE 800. COMMUNICATION CIRCUITS

A. General

800-1. Scope. This Article covers telephone, telegraph (except radio), district messenger, outside wiring for fire alarm and burglar alarms, and similar central station systems; and telephone systems not connected to a central station system but using similar types of equipment, methods of installation, and maintenance.

For further information for fire alarm, sprinkler, supervisory, or watchman systems, see Article 760.

▲ The sections of this chapter apply basically to those systems which are connected to a central station and operate as parts of a central-station system.

The paragraph titled "Code Arrangement" of the "Introduction to the Code" states that Chap. 8, which includes Art. 800, Communication Systems, is independent of the preceding chapters except as they are specifically referred to.

B. Protection

800-2. Protective Devices. A protector approved for the purpose shall be provided on each circuit run partly or entirely in aerial wire or aerial cable not confined within a block. Also, a protector approved for the purpose shall be provided on each circuit, aerial or underground, so located within the block containing the building served as to be exposed to accidental contact with light or power conductors operating at over 300 volts to ground.

The word "block" as used in this Article means a square or portion of a city, town, or village enclosed by streets and including the alleys so enclosed but not any street.

The word "exposed" as used in this Article means that the circuit is in such a position that in case of failure of supports or insulation, contact with another circuit may result.

(a) Location. The protector shall be located in, on, or immediately adjacent to the structure or building served and as close as practicable to the point at which the exposed conductors enter or attach.

(b) Hazardous Locations. The protector shall not be located in any hazardous location as defined in Article 500, nor in the vicinity of easily ignitible material.

(c) Protector Requirements. The protector shall consist of an arrester connected between each line conductor and ground in an appropriate mounting. Protector terminals shall be marked to indicate line and ground as applicable.

(1) Fuseless type protectors shall be permitted under any of the following conditions:

a. Where circuits enter a building through metallic-sheathed cable or through a nonmetallic-sheathed cable having a metallic grounding shield between the sheath and the conductor assembly, if the metallic sheath or shield of the cable is effectively grounded, and if the conductors in the cable safely fuse on all currents greater than the current-carrying capacity of the protector, and the ampacity of the protector grounding conductor.

b. Where insulated conductors in accordance with Section 800-11(c)(1) or (c)(2) are used to extend circuits to a building from a metallic-sheathed cable or from a nonmetallic-sheathed cable having a metallic grounding shield between the sheath and the conductor assembly, if the metallic sheath or shield is effectively grounded and if the conductors in the cable or cable stub, or the connections between the insulated conductors and the exposed plant safely fuse on all currents greater than the current-carrying capacity of the protector, and the ampacity of the associated insulated conductors and the protector grounding conductor.

c. Where insulated conductors in accordance with Section 800-11(c)(1) or (c)(2) are used to extend circuits to a building from other than a grounded metallic-sheathed or shielded cable, if (1) the protector is approved for this purpose; (2) the protector grounding conductor is connected to a water pipe electrode or the grounding conductor or grounding electrode of a multigrounded neutral power system; and (3) the connections of the insulated conductors to the exposed plant or the conductors of the exposed plant safely fuse on all currents greater than the current-carrying capacity of the protector, and the ampacity of the associated insulated conductors and the protector grounding conductor.

d. Where insulated conductors in accordance with Section 800-11(c)(1) or (c)(2) are used to extend circuits aerially to a building from an unexposed buried or underground circuit.

Effectively grounded means permanently connected to earth through a ground connection of sufficiently low impedance and having sufficient ampacity to prevent the building up of voltages that may result in undue hazard to connected equipment or to persons.

(2) Where the requirements listed under (c)(1)a, (1)b, (1)c, or (1)d above are not met, fused-type protectors shall be used, Fused-type protectors shall consist of an arrester connected between each line conductor and ground, a fuse in series with each line conductor, and an appropriate mounting arrangement. Protector terminals shall be marked to indicate line, instrument, and ground, as applicable.

800-3. Installation of Conductors. Conductors from the protector to the equipment or, where no protector is required, conductors attached to the outside or inside of the building shall comply with (a) through (d) below.

(a) Separation from Other Conductors.

(1) Open Conductors. Conductors shall be separated at least 2 inches from conductors of any light or power circuits or Class 1 circuits.

Exception No. 1: Where the light or power or Class 1 circuit conductors are in a raceway or in metal-sheathed, metal-clad, nonmetallic-sheathed, or Type UF cables.

Exception No. 2: Where the conductors are permanently separated from the conductors of the other circuit by a continuous and firmly fixed nonconductor, such as porcelain tubes or flexible tubing, in addition to the insulation on the wire.

(2) In Raceways and Boxes. Communication conductors shall not be placed in any raceway, compartment, outlet box, junction box, or similar fitting with conductors of light or power circuits or Class 1 circuits.

Exception No. 1: Where the conductors of the different systems are separated by a partition.

Exception No. 2: Conductors in outlet boxes, junction boxes, or similar fittings or compartments where such conductors are introduced solely for power supply to communication equipment or for connection to remote-control equipment.

(3) In Shafts. Conductors run in the same shaft with conductors of light or power shall be separated from light or power conductors by not less than 2 inches.

Exception No. 1: Where the conductors of either system are encased in noncombustible tubing.

Exception No. 2: Where the light or power conductors are in a raceway, or in metal-sheathed, metal-clad, nonmetallic-sheathed, or Type UF cables.

(b) Vertical Runs. Conductors bunched together in a vertical run in a shaft shall have a fire-resistant covering capable of preventing the carrying of fire from floor to floor.

Exception: Where conductors are encased in noncombustible tubing or are located in a fireproof shaft having fire stops at each floor.

The conductors referred to in this Section would ordinarily be insulated, but the kind of insulation is not specified as reliance is placed on the protective device to stop all dangerous voltages and currents.

(c) Prevention of Spread of Fire or Smoke. Installations shall be so made that the possible spread of fire or products of combustion through fire-rated, fire-resistant or fire-stopped walls, partitions, ceilings and floors; hollow spaces; vertical shafts; and ventilating or air-handling ducts will not be substantially increased.

(d) Location. Circuits and equipment installed in ducts and plenums shall also comply with Section 300-22 as to wiring methods.

Exception: Conductors having inherent fire-resistant and low-smoke producing characteristics approved for the purpose, shall be permitted for ducts, hollow spaces used as ducts, and plenums other than those described in Section 300-22(a).

▲ It should be noted that the addition of "products of combustion" in Sec. 800-3(c) and the requirements of Sec. 800-3(d) Exception now give authorities enforcing the Code the tools whereby they can judge whether the types of cables used in communication circuits substantially contribute to the hazards during fire conditions where fire fighters must of necessity be subjected to these products of combustion. Statistics show that most people die from smoke and products of combustion and not from the heat of fires. Because of this fact it is imperative that electrical materials which contribute products of combustion be held to a minimum. The requirements in Sec. 800-3 now give electrical inspectors and fire marshals the tools whereby they can judge the hazards which conductors contribute to fire problems.

C. Outside Conductors

800-11. Overhead Conductors. Overhead conductors entering buildings shall comply with (a) through (c) below.

(a) On Poles. Where communication conductors and light or power conductors are supported by the same pole, the following conditions shall be met:

(1) Relative Location. Where practicable, the communications conductors shall be located below the light or power conductors.

(2) Attachment to Crossarms. Conductors shall not be attached to a crossarm that carries light or power conductors.

(3) Climbing Space. The climbing space through communication conductors shall comply with the requirements of Section 225-14(d).

(b) On Roofs. Conductors passing over buildings shall be kept at least 8 feet above any roof that may be readily walked upon.

Exception: Auxiliary buildings, such as garages and the like.

(c) Circuits Requiring Protectors. Circuits that require protectors as provided in Section 800-2 shall comply with the following:

(1) Insulation, Single or Paired Conductors. Each conductor from the last outdoor support to the protector shall have 30-mil rubber insulation, except that where such conductors are entirely within a block the insulation on the conductor may be less than 30 mils, but not less than 25 mils in thickness. In addition, the conductor, either individually or over the pair, shall be covered with a substantial fibrous covering or equivalent protection. Conductors approved for the purpose having rubber insulation of a thickness less than specified above, or having other kinds of insulation, shall be permitted.

(2) Insulation, Cables. Conductors within a cable of the metal-sheathed type or within a cable having a rubber sheath of at least 30-mil thickness and covered with a substantial fibrous covering shall be permitted to have paper or other suitable insulation. Where the metal or rubber sheath is omitted, each conductor shall be insulated as required in (c)(1) above, and the bunched conductors shall be covered with a substantial fibrous covering or equivalent covering.

(3) On Buildings. Open conductors shall be separated at least 4 inches from light or power conductors not in conduit or cable, or be permanently separated from conductors of the other system by a continuous and firmly fixed nonconductor in addition to the insulation on the wires, such as porcelain tubes or flexible tubing. Open conductors exposed to accidental contact with light and power conductors operating at over 300 volts to ground and attached to buildings shall be separated from woodwork by being supported on glass, porcelain, or other insulating material approved for the purpose.

Exception: Separation from woodwork shall not be required where fuses are omitted as provided for in Section 800-2(c)(1), or where conductors approved for the purpose are used to extend circuits to a building from a cable having a grounded metal sheath.

(4) Entering Buildings. Where a protector is installed inside the building, the conductors shall enter the building either through a noncombustible, nonabsorbent insulating bushing, or through a metal raceway. The insulating bushing shall not be required where the entering conductors (1) are in metal-sheathed cable; (2) pass through masonry; (3) are approved for the purpose and fuses are omitted as provided in Section 800-2(c)(1); or (4) are approved for the purpose and are used to extend circuits to a building from a cable having a grounded metal sheath. Raceways or bushings shall slope upward from the outside or, where this cannot be done, drip loops shall be formed in the conductors immediately before they enter the building. Raceways shall be equipped with an approved service head. More than one conductor shall be permitted to enter through a single raceway or bushing. Conduits or other metal raceways located ahead of the protector shall be grounded.

800-12. Lightning Conductors. Where practicable, a separation of at least 6 feet shall be maintained between open conductors of communication systems on buildings and lightning conductors.

D. Underground Circuits

800-21. Underground Circuits Entering Buildings. Underground conductors of communication circuits entering buildings shall comply with (a) and (b) below.

(a) With Electric Light or Power Conductors. Underground conductors in a duct, handhole, or manhole containing electric light or power conductors shall be in a section separated from such conductors by means of brick, concrete, or tile partitions.

(b) Underground Block Distribution. Where the entire street circuit is run underground and the circuit within the block is so placed as to be free from likelihood of accidental contact with electric light or power circuits of over 300 volts to ground, the insulation requirements of Section 800-11(c)(1) and (c)(4) shall not apply, insulating supports shall not be required for the conductors, and bushings shall not be required where the conductors enter the building.

E. Grounding

800-31. Grounding. Equipment shall be grounded as specified in (a) and (b) below.

(a) Cable Sheath. Where exposed to contact with electric light or power conductors, the metal sheath of aerial cables entering buildings shall be grounded or shall be interrupted close to the entrance to the building by an insulating joint or equivalent device.

(b) Protector Ground. The protector ground shall comply with the following:

(1) Insulation. The grounding conductor shall have a 30-mil rubber insulation and shall be covered by a substantial fibrous covering. Conductors approved for the purpose having less than 30-mil rubber insulation or having other kinds of insulation shall be permitted.

(2) Size. The grounding conductor shall not be smaller than No. 18 copper or equivalent.

(3) Run in Straight Line. The grounding conductor shall be run to the grounding electrode in as straight a line as practicable.

(4) Physical Damage. Where necessary, the grounding conductor shall be guarded from physical damage.

(5) Electrode. The grounding conductor shall be connected as follows:

    a. To an available water pipe electrode; or

    b. To the power service conduit, service-equipment enclosure, or grounding electrode conductor where the grounded conductor of the power service is connected to a water pipe electrode at the building; or

    c. Where the grounding means in (b)(5)a or (5)b above are not available to the service conduit, service-equipment enclosure, grounding electrode conductor, or grounding electrode of the power service of a multigrounded neutral power system; or

d. Where the grounding means in (b)(5)a, (5)b, or (5)c above are not available to: (1) a concrete-encased electrode of not less than 20 feet of bare copper conductor not smaller than No. 4 encased by at least 2 inches of concrete and located within and near the bottom of a concrete foundation footing that is in direct contact with the earth; (2) an effectively grounded metal structure; (3) a continuous and extensive underground gas piping system where acceptable to both the serving gas supplier and to the authority having jurisdiction; or (4) to a ground rod or pipe driven into permanently damp earth. Steam or hot-water pipes, lighting-rod conductors, or pipe or rod electrodes grounding other than multigrounded neutral power circuits shall not be employed as electrodes for protectors.

(6) Electrode Connection. The grounding conductor shall be attached to a pipe electrode by means of a bolted clamp to which the conductor is connected in an effective manner. Where a gas pipe electrode is used, connection shall be made between the gas meter and the street main. In every case the connection to the grounding electrode shall be made as close to the earth as practicable.

(7) Bonding of Electrodes. A bonding jumper not smaller than No. 6 copper or equivalent shall be connected between the communication and the power grounding electrodes where the requirements of (5) above result in the use of separate electrodes. Bonding together of all separate electrodes shall be permitted.

See Section 250-86 for use of lightning rods.
Bonding together of all separate electrodes will limit potential differences between them and between their associated wiring systems.

ARTICLE 810. RADIO AND TELEVISION EQUIPMENT

A. General

810-1. Scope. This Article covers radio and television receiving equipment and amateur radio transmitting and receiving equipment, but not equipment and antennas used for coupling carrier current to power line conductors.

▲ For service drops and conductors on the exteriors of buildings, the requirements for insulating covering and methods of installation depend upon the likelihood of crosses occurring between signal conductors and light or power conductors. Where communication wires are run on poles in streets, it is assumed that they are exposed to contact with other wires, and in Sec. 800-11, 30-mil insulation is required. But where the overhead wires are run in an alley or from building to building and kept away from streets, lighter insulation is permitted.

Where a communication system is connected to a distribution system that is entirely underground except within the block in which the building is located, and any overhead wires in alleys or attached to buildings are not likely to become crossed with light or power wires, nearly all restrictions as to insulating covering and methods of installation are eliminated. The minimum thickness of insulation called for in Sec. 800-21 and the bushings specified in Sec. 800-11 are not required under these conditions.

810-2. Other Articles. Wiring from the source of power to and between devices connected to the interior wiring system shall comply with Chapters 1 through 4 other than as modified by Sections 640-3, 640-4, and 640-5. Wiring for radio-frequency and audio-frequency equipment and loud speakers shall comply with Article 640.

810-3. Community Television Antenna. The antenna shall comply with this Article. The distribution system shall comply with Article 820.

810-4. Radio Noise Suppressors. Radio interference eliminators, interference capacitors, or noise suppressors connected to power-supply leads shall be of a type approved for the purpose. They shall not be exposed to physical damage.

B. Receiving Equipment—Antenna Systems

810-11. Material. Antennas and lead-in conductors shall be of hard-drawn copper, bronze, aluminum alloy, copper-clad steel or other high-strength, corrosion-resistant material.

Exception: Soft-drawn or medium-drawn copper shall be permitted for lead-in conductors where the maximum span between points of support is less than 35 feet.

810-12. Supports. Outdoor antennas and lead-in conductors shall be securely supported. The antennas shall not be attached to the electric service mast. They shall not be attached to poles or similar structures carrying electric light or power wires or trolley wires of over 250 volts between conductors. Insulators supporting the antenna conductors shall have sufficient mechanical strength to safely support the conductors. Lead-in conductors shall be securely attached to the antennas.

810-13. Avoidance of Contacts with Conductors of Other Systems. Outdoor antennas and lead-in conductors from an antenna to a building shall not cross over electric light or power circuits and shall be kept well away from all such circuits so as to avoid the possibility of accidental contact. Where proximity to electric light or power service conductors of less than 250 volts between conductors cannot be avoided, the installation shall be such as to provide a clearance of at least 2 feet.

Where practicable, antenna conductors shall be so installed as not to cross under electric light or power conductors.

▲ It is obviously important that all possible precautions be taken to prevent the possibility of a cross between a radio antenna and a light or power conductor.

810-14. Splices. Splices and joints in antenna spans shall be made mechanically secure with approved splicing devices or by such other means as will not appreciably weaken the conductors.

▲ The antenna may unavoidably be so located that in case of a break in the wire it may come in contact with electric light or power wires. For this reason, the wire should be of sufficient size to have considerable mechanical strength, and the joints should be as reliable as the wire. Joints will have sufficient mechanical strength if properly made with the standard double-tube connectors used in telephone and telegraph work.

810-15. Grounding. Masts and metal structures supporting antennas shall be permanently and effectively grounded without splice or connection in the grounding conductor.

Table 810–16(a). Size of Receiving-Station Outdoor Antenna Conductors

Material	Minimum Size of Conductors		
	When Maximum Open Span Length is		
	Less than 35 feet	35 feet to 150 feet	Over 150 feet
Aluminum alloy, hard-drawn copper... 19		14	12
Copper-clad steel, bronze, or other high strength material... 20		17	14

810-16. Size of Wire-Strung Antenna—Receiving Station.

(a) **Size of Antenna Conductors.** Outdoor antenna conductors for receiving stations shall be of a size not less than given in Table 810-16(a).

(b) **Self-Supporting Antennas.** Outdoor antennas, such as vertical rods or dipole structures, shall be of noncorrodible materials and of strength suitable to withstand ice and wind loading conditions, and shall be located well away from overhead conductors of electric light and power circuits of over 150 volts to ground, so as to avoid the possibility of the antenna or structure falling into or making accidental contact with such circuits.

810-17. Size of Lead-In—Receiving Station. Lead-in conductors from outside antennas for receiving stations shall, for various maximum open span lengths, be of such size as to have a tensile strength at least as great as that of the conductors for antennas as specified in Section 810-16. Where the lead-in consists of two or more conductors that are twisted together, are enclosed in the same covering, or are concentric, the conductor size shall, for various maximum open span lengths, be such that the tensile strength of the combination will be at least as great as that of the conductors for antennas as specified in Section 810-16.

810-18. Clearances—Receiving Stations.

(a) **On Outside of Buildings.** Lead-in conductors attached to buildings shall be so installed that they cannot swing closer than 2 feet to the conductors of circuits of 250 volts or less between conductors, or 10 feet to the conductors of circuits of over 250 volts between conductors, except that in the case of circuits not over 150 volts between conductors, where all conductors involved are supported so as to insure permanent separation, the clearance shall be permitted to be reduced but shall not be less than 4 inches. The clearance between lead-in conductors and any conductor forming a part of a lightning rod system shall not be less than 6 feet unless the bonding referred to in Section 250-86 is accomplished.

(b) **Antennas and Lead-Ins—Indoors.** Indoor antennas and indoor lead-ins shall not be run nearer than 2 inches to conductors of other wiring systems in the premises.

Exception No. 1: Where such other conductors are in metal raceways or cable armor.

Exception No. 2: Where permanently separated from such other conductors by a continuous and firmly fixed nonconductor, such as porcelain tubes or flexible tubing.

810-19. Electric Supply Circuits Used in Lieu of Antenna—Receiving Stations. Where an electric supply circuit is used in lieu of an antenna, the device by which the radio receiving set is connected to the supply circuit shall be approved for the purpose.

▲ The device referred to usually consists of a small fixed condenser connected between one wire of the lighting circuit and the antenna terminal of the receiving set. As most receiving sets are arranged, a breakdown in this condenser would result in a short circuit to ground through the antenna coil of the set, and the condenser should therefore be one that is designed for operation at 300 V or higher in which mica is used as the dielectric so that it will have a high factor of safety.

810-20. Antenna Discharge Units—Receiving Stations.
(a) Where Required. Each conductor of a lead-in from an outdoor antenna shall be provided with an antenna discharge unit approved for the purpose.
Exception: Where the lead-in conductors are enclosed in a continuous metallic shield that is either permanently and effectively grounded, or is protected by an antenna discharge unit.
(b) Location. Antenna discharge units shall be located outside the building or inside the building between the point of entrance of the lead-in and the radio set or transformers, and as near as practicable to the entrance of the conductors to the building. The antenna discharge unit shall not be located near combustible material nor in a hazardous location as defined in Article 500.

▲ Where the lead-in is enclosed in a continuous metallic shield, i.e., is run in rigid conduit or electrical metallic tubing, or consists of a lead-covered conductor or pair of conductors, and the metallic enclosure is well grounded, a lightning discharge will usually jump from the lead-in conductor to the metallic shield, because this path to ground offers a much lower impedance than the path through the antenna coil of the receiving set. A lightning arrester is therefore not required where the lead-in is so shielded.

810-21. Grounding Conductors—Receiving Stations. Grounding conductors shall comply with (a) through (i) below.
(a) Material. The grounding conductor shall be of copper, aluminum, copper-clad steel, bronze, or similar corrosion-resistant material.
(b) Insulation. Insulation on grounding conductors shall not be required.
(c) Supports. The grounding conductors shall be securely fastened in place and shall be permitted to be directly attached to the surface wired over without the use of insulating supports.
Exception: Where proper support cannot be provided, the size of the grounding conductors shall be increased proportionately.
(d) Mechanical Protection. The grounding conductor shall be protected where exposed to physical damage, or the size of the grounding conductors shall be increased proportionately to compensate for the lack of protection.
(e) Run in Straight Line. The grounding conductor for an antenna mast or antenna discharge unit shall be run in as straight a line as practicable from the mast or discharge unit to the grounding electrode.
(f) Connection to Grounding Electrode. The grounding conductor shall be connected to a metal underground water piping system as specified in Section 250-81. Where the building is not supplied with a metal underground water piping system, the connection shall be made to the metal frame of the building if the frame is

effectively grounded, or to a grounding electrode as specified in Section 250-83. At a penthouse or similar location, the grounding conductor shall be permitted to be connected to a grounded water pipe or rigid metal conduit.

▲ In order to avoid potential differences between various masses of metal, in or on buildings, and lead-in conductors, the metal portions of antenna masts should never be grounded to soil pipes, soil vent pipes, metal gutters, downspouts, etc.; in other words, grounding must be done in accordance with Art. 250, and it is required to use the same grounding electrode for the grounding of masts as for the electrical system in the building.

(g) Inside or Outside Building. The grounding conductor shall be permitted to be run either inside or outside the building.

(h) Size. The grounding conductor shall not be smaller than No. 10 copper or No. 8 aluminum or No. 17 copper-clad steel or bronze.

(i) Common Ground. A single grounding conductor shall be permitted for both protective and operating purposes.

C. Amateur Transmitting and Receiving Stations—Antenna Systems

810-51. Other Sections. In addition to complying with Part C, antenna systems for amateur transmitting and receiving stations shall also comply with Sections 810-11 through 810-15.

810-52. Size of Antenna. Antenna conductors for transmitting and receiving stations shall be of a size not less than given in Table 810-52.

Table 810-52. Size of Amateur Station Outdoor Antenna Conductors

	Minimum Size of Conductors	
	Where Maximum Open Span Length Is	
	Less Than	Over
Material	150 feet	150 feet
Hard-drawn copper	14	10
Copper-clad steel, bronze or other high-strength material	14	12

810-53. Size of Lead-in Conductors. Lead-in conductors for transmitting stations shall, for various maximum span lengths, be of a size at least as great as that of conductors for antennas as specified in Section 810-52.

810-54. Clearance on Building. Antenna conductors for transmitting stations, attached to buildings, shall be firmly mounted at least 3 inches clear of the surface of the building on nonabsorbent insulating supports, such as treated pins or brackets equipped with insulators having not less than 3-inch creepage and airgap distances. Lead-in conductors attached to buildings shall also comply with these requirements.

Exception: Where the lead-in conductors are enclosed in a continuous metallic shield that is permanently and effectively grounded, they shall not be required to comply with these requirements. Where grounded, the metallic shield shall also be permitted to be used as a conductor.

▲ The creepage distance is the distance from the conductor to the building measured on the surface of the supporting insulator. The air gap is the distance measured straight across from the conductor to the building.

810-55. Entrance to Building. Except where protected with a continuous metallic shield that is permanently and effectively grounded, lead-in conductors for transmitting stations shall enter buildings by one of the following methods: (1) through a rigid, noncombustible, nonabsorbent insulating tube or bushing; (2) through an opening provided for the purpose in which the entrance conductors are firmly secured so as to provide a clearance of at least 2 inches; or (3) through a drilled window pane.

810-56. Protection Against Accidental Contact. Lead-in conductors to radio transmitters shall be so located or installed as to make accidental contact with them difficult.

810-57. Antenna Discharge Units—Transmitting Stations. Each conductor of a lead-in for outdoor antennas shall be provided with an antenna discharge unit or other suitable means that will drain static charges from the antenna system.

Exception No. 1: Where protected by a continuous metallic shield that is permanently and effectively grounded.

Exception No. 2: Where the antenna is permanently and effectively grounded.

▲ A transmitting station should be protected against lightning, either by an arrester or by a switch that connects the lead-in to ground and is kept closed at all times when the station is not in operation.

810-58. Grounding Conductors—Amateur Transmitting and Receiving Stations. Grounding conductors shall comply with (a) through (c) below.

(a) Other Sections. All grounding conductors for amateur transmitting and receiving stations shall comply with Sections 810-21(a) through (g).

(b) Size of Protective Grounding Conductor. The protective grounding conductor for transmitting stations shall be as large as the lead-in, but not smaller than No. 10 copper, bronze, or copper-clad steel.

(c) Size of Operating Grounding Conductor. The operating grounding conductor for transmitting stations shall not be less than No. 14 copper or its equivalent.

D. Interior Installation—Transmitting Stations

810-70. Clearance From Other Conductors. All conductors inside the building shall be separated at least 4 inches from the conductors of any lighting or signaling circuit.

Exception No. 1: As provided in Article 640.

Exception No. 2: Where separated from other conductors by conduit or some firmly fixed nonconductor, such as porcelain tubes or flexible tubing.

810-71. General. Transmitters shall comply with (a) through (d) below.

(a) Enclosing. The transmitter shall be enclosed in a metal frame or grille, or separated from the operating space by a barrier or other equivalent means, all metallic parts of which are effectively connected to ground.

(b) Grounding of Controls. All external metal handles and controls accessible to the operating personnel shall be effectively grounded.

(c) Interlocks on Doors. All access doors shall be provided with interlocks that will disconnect all voltages of over 350 volts between conductors when any access door is opened.

(d) Audio-Amplifiers. Audio-amplifiers that are located outside the transmitter housing shall be suitably housed and shall be so located as to be readily accessible and adequately ventilated.

ARTICLE 820. COMMUNITY ANTENNA TELEVISION AND RADIO DISTRIBUTION SYSTEMS

A. General

820-1. Scope. This Article covers coaxial cable distribution of radio frequency signals typically employed in community antenna television (CATV) systems. Where the wiring system employed is other than coaxial, Article 800 shall apply.

The coaxial cable shall be permitted to deliver low-energy power to equipment directly associated with this radio frequency distribution system if the voltage is not over 60 volts and if the current supply is from a transformer or other device having energy-limiting characteristics.

820-2. Material. Coaxial cable used for radio frequency distribution systems shall be suitable for the application.

B. Protection

820-7. Ground of Outer Conductive Shield of a Coaxial Cable. Where coaxial cable is exposed to lightning or to accidental contact with lightning arrester conductors or power conductors operating at a potential of over 300 volts to ground, the outer conductive shield of the coaxial cable shall be grounded at the building premises as close to the point of cable entry as practicable.

Where the outer conductive shield of a coaxial cable is grounded, no other protective devices shall be required.

C. Installation of Cable

820-11. Outside Conductors. Coaxial cables, prior to the point of grounding, as defined in Section 820-7, shall comply with (a) through (e) below.

(a) On Poles. Where practicable, conductors on poles shall be located below the light or power conductors and shall not be attached to a cross arm that carries light or power conductors.

(b) Lead-in Clearance. Lead-in or aerial-drop cables from a pole or other support, including the point of initial attachment to a building or structure, shall be kept away from electric light or power circuits so as to avoid the possibility of accidental contact.

Exception: Where proximity to electric light or power service conductors cannot be avoided, the installation shall be such as to provide clearances of not less than 12 inches from light or power service drops.

(c) Over Roofs. Cables passing over buildings shall be at least 8 feet above any roof that is accessible for pedestrian traffic.

(d) Between Buildings. Cables extending between buildings and also the supports or attachment fixtures shall be acceptable for the purpose and shall have sufficient strength to withstand the loads to which they may be subjected.

Exception: Where a cable does not have sufficient strength to be self-supporting, it shall be attached to a supporting messenger cable that, together with the attachment fixtures or supports, shall be acceptable for the purpose and shall have sufficient strength to withstand the loads to which they may be subjected.

(e) On Buildings. Where attached to buildings, cables shall be securely fastened in such a manner that they will be separated from other conductors as follows:

(1) Light or Power. The coaxial cable shall have a separation of at least 4 inches from light or power conductors not in conduit or cable, or be permanently separated from conductors of the other system by a continuous and firmly fixed nonconductor in addition to the insulation on the wires.

(2) Other Communication Systems. Coaxial cable shall be installed so that there will be no unnecessary interference in the maintenance of the separate systems. In no case shall the conductors, cables, messenger strand, or equipment of one system cause abrasion to the conductors, cable, messenger strand, or equipment of any other system.

(3) Lightning Conductors. Where practicable, a separation of at least 6 feet shall be maintained between any coaxial cable and lightning conductors.

820-12. Entering Buildings. Coaxial cable shall slope upward from the outside where entering a building; or where this is impracticable, drip loops shall be formed in the cable at the point of entrance.

820-13. Conductors Inside Buildings. Beyond the point of grounding, as defined in Section 820-7, the cable installation shall comply with (a) through (e) below.

(a) Light or Power. Coaxial cable shall be separated at least 2 inches from conductors of any light or power circuits or Class 1 circuits.

Exception No. 1: Where the light or power or Class 1 circuit conductors are in a raceway, or in metal-sheathed, metal-clad, nonmetallic-sheathed, or Type UF cables.

Exception No. 2: Where the conductors are permanently separated from the conductors of the other circuit by a continuous and firmly fixed nonconductor, such as porcelain tubes or flexible tubing, in addition to the insulation on the wire.

(b) In Raceways and Boxes. Coaxial cable shall not be placed in any raceway, compartment, outlet box, junction box, or other enclosures with conductors of light or power circuits or Class 1 circuits.

Exception No. 1: Where the conductors of the different systems are separated by a permanent partition.

Exception No. 2: Conductors in outlet boxes, junction boxes, or similar fittings or compartments where such conductors are introduced solely for power supply to the coaxial cable system distribution equipment or for power connection to remote-control equipment.

(c) In Shafts. Coaxial cable installed in the same shaft with conductors for light or power shall be separated from the light or power conductors by not less than 2 inches.

Exception No. 1: Where the conductors of either system are encased in non-combustible tubing.

Exception No. 2: Where the light or power conductors are in a raceway, or in metal-sheathed, metal-clad, nonmetallic-sheathed, or Type UF cables.

(d) Vertical Runs. Coaxial cables bunched together in a vertical run in a shaft shall have a fire-resistant covering capable of preventing the carrying of flame from floor to floor.

Exception: Where cables are encased in noncombustible tubing or are located in a fireproof shaft having fire stops at each floor.

There is no specific separation requirement between Class 2 or Class 3 circuits, wired distribution system cables, and communication cables or conductors, other than the clearance necessary to prevent conflict or abrasion.

820-14. Prevention of Spread of Fire. Installations shall be so made that the possible spread of fire through fire walls, fire partitions, or fire-resistive floors is reduced to a minimum.

D. Underground Circuits

820-18. Entering Buildings. Underground coaxial cables in a duct, pedestal, handhole, or manhole containing electric light or power conductors shall be in a section permanently separated from such conductors by means of a suitable barrier.

E. Grounding

820-22. Cable Grounding. Coaxial cable shall be grounded as specified in (a) through (h) below.

(a) Insulation. The grounding conductor shall have a rubber or other suitable kind of insulation.

(b) Material. The grounding conductor shall be copper or other corrosion-resistant conductive material, stranded or solid.

(c) Size. The grounding conductor shall not be smaller than No. 18; it shall have an ampacity approximately equal to that of the outer conductor of the coaxial cable.

(d) Run in Straight Line. The grounding conductor shall be run to the grounding electrode in as straight a line as practicable.

(e) Physical Protection. Where necessary, the grounding conductor shall be guarded from physical damage.

(f) Electrode. The grounding conductor shall be connected as follows:

(1) To an available water pipe electrode; or

(2) To the power service conduit, service-equipment enclosure, or grounding electrode conductor where the grounded conductor of the power service is connected to a water pipe electrode at the building; or

(3) Where the grounding means in (1) or (2) above are not available, to the service conduit, service-equipment enclosure, grounding electrode conductor, or grounding electrode of the power service of a multigrounded neutral power system; or

(4) Where the grounding means in (1), (2), or (3) above are not available to: (a) a concrete-encased electrode of not less than 20 feet of bare copper conductor not smaller than No. 4 encased by at least 2 inches of concrete and located within and near the bottom of a concrete foundation footing that is in direct contact with

the earth, (b) an effectively grounded metal structure; (c) a continuous and extensive underground gas piping system where acceptable to both the serving gas supplier and to the authority having jurisdiction; or (d) to a ground rod or pipe driven into permanently damp earth. Steam or hot-water pipes, lightning-rod conductors, or pipe or rod electrodes grounding other than multigrounded neutral power circuits shall not be employed as electrodes.

(g) Electrode Connection. Connections to grounding electrodes shall comply with Section 250-115. Where a gas pipe electrode is used, connection shall be made between the gas meter and the street main. In every case the connection to the grounding electrode shall be made as close to the earth as practicable.

(h) Bonding of Electrodes. A bonding jumper not smaller than No. 6 copper or equivalent shall be connected between the antenna systems and the power grounding electrodes where the requirements of (f) above result in the use of separate electrodes. Bonding together of all separate grounding electrodes shall be permitted.

See Section 250-86 for use of lightning rods.

820-23. Equipment Grounding. Unpowered equipment and enclosures or equipment powered by the coaxial cable shall be considered grounded where connected to the metallic cable shield.

CHAPTER NINE

Tables and Examples

A. Tables

Notes to Tables

1. Tables 3A, 3B and 3C apply only to complete conduit or tubing systems and are not intended to apply to short sections of conduit or tubing used to protect exposed wiring from physical damage.

2. Equipment grounding conductors, when installed, shall be included when calculating conduit or tubing fill. The actual dimensions of the equipment grounding conductor (insulated or bare) shall be used in the calculation.

3. When conduit nipples having a maximum length not to exceed 24 inches are installed between boxes, cabinets, and similar enclosures, the nipple shall be permitted to be filled to 60 percent of its total cross-sectional area, and Note 8 of Tables 310-16 through 310-19 does not apply to this condition.

4. For conductors not included in Chapter 9, the actual dimensions shall be used.

5. See Table 1 for allowable percentage of conduit or tubing fill.

▲ Tables 1, 3A, 3B, and 3C do not apply where short conduit sleeves are used to protect various types of cables from physical damage.

While Note 2 mentions only bare equipment grounding conductors, Note 4 to Table 1 applies to all forms of *bare* conductors (equipment grounding conductors and neutral or grounded conductors). Where any bare conductors are used in conduit or tubing, the dimensions given in Table 8 may be used. Since *all* wires utilize space in raceways, they must be counted in calculating raceway sizes whether the conductors are insulated or bare. The only exception to this is in Table 350-3 for short lengths of ³⁄₈-in. flexible metal conduit.

In regard to Note 4 there are conductors (particularly high-voltage types) that do not have dimensions listed in Chap. 9. Conduit sizes for such conductors may be determined by computing the cross-sectional area of each conductor as follows:

$D^2 \times 0.7854$ = cross-sectional area, where D = outside diameter of conductor, including insulation. Then the proper conduit size can be determined by applying Tables 1 and 4 for the appropriate number of conductors.

Table 1. Percent of Cross Section of Conduit and Tubing for Conductors (See Table 2 for Fixture Wires)

Number of Conductors	1	2	3	4	Over 4
All conductor types except lead-covered (new or rewiring)	53	31	40	40	40
Lead-covered conductors	55	30	40	38	35

Note 1. See Tables 3A, 3B and 3C for number of conductors all of the same size in trade sizes of conduit ½ inch through 6 inch.

Note 2. For conductors larger than 750 MCM or for combinations of conductors of different sizes, use Tables 4 through 8, Chapter 9, for dimensions of conductors, conduit and tubing.

Note 3. Where the calculated number of conductors, all of the same size, includes a decimal fraction, the next higher whole number shall be used where this decimal is 0.8 or larger.

Note 4. When bare conductors are permitted by other Sections of this Code, the dimensions for bare conductors in Table 8 of Chapter 9 shall be permitted.

Note 5. A multi-conductor cable of three or more conductors shall be treated as a single conductor cable for calculating percentage conduit fill area.

Example: Three single-conductor 5-kV cables are to be installed in conduit. The outside diameter (*D*) of each conductor is 0.750 in. Then $0.750^2 \times 0.7854 \times 3 = 1.3253$ sq in. From Tables 1 and 4 (40 percent fill) a 2-in. conduit would be required. Tables 3A, 3B, and 3C are based on Table 1 allowable percentage fills, and have been provided for the sake of convenience. In any calculation, however, Table 1 is the table to be used where any conflict may occur in Tables 3A, 3B, or 3C.

Table 1 is also used for computing conduit sizes where various sizes of conductors or conductor types are to be used in the same conduit. Tables 1, 3A, 3B, and 3C apply to new work or rewiring, exposed or concealed.

An example of Note 3 would be to determine how many No. 14 Type TW conductors would be permitted in a ½-in. conduit. For three or more such conductors Table 1 permits a 40 percent fill. From Table 4, 40 percent of the internal cross-sectional area of a ½-in. conduit is 0.12 sq in. From Table 5 (column 5) the cross-sectional area of a No. 14 Type TW conductor is 0.0135 sq in. Thus 0.12/0.0135 = 8.8, or 9 such conductors would be permitted in a ½-in conduit. Where the decimal is less than 0.8 (such as 0.7), the decimal would be dropped and the whole number would be the maximum number of equally sized conductors permitted; e.g., 8.7 would be 8 conductors.

The following is an example for computing a conduit size for various conductor sizes:

Number	Wire size and type	Table 5 Cross-sectional area (ea.)	Subtotal Cross-sectional area
3	No. 10 TW	0.0224	0.0672
3	No. 12 TW	0.0172	0.0516
3	No. 6 TW	0.0819	0.2457
		Total cross-sectional area	0.3645

Table 1 permits a 40 percent fill for three or more conductors. Following the 40 percent column in Table 4, 1¼-in. conduit or tubing would be required for these nine conductors, which have a combined cross-sectional area of 0.3645 sq in.

Table 2. Maximum Number of Fixture Wires in Trade Size of Conduit or Tubing (40 Percent Fill Based on Individual Diameters)

Conduit Trade Size (Inches) Wire Types	½			¾			1			1¼			1½			2		
	18	16	14	18	16	14	18	16	14	18	16	14	18	16	14	18	16	14
PTF, PTFF, PGFF, PGF, PFF, PF	23	18	14	40	31	24	65	50	39	115	90	70	157	122	95	257	200	156
TFFN, TFN	19	15		34	26		55	43		97	76		132	104		216	169	
SF-1	16			29			47			83			114			186		
SFF-1, FFH-1	15			26			43			76			104			169		
CF	13	10	8	23	18	14	38	30	23	66	53	40	91	72	55	149	118	90
TF	11	10		20	18		32	30		57	53		79	72		129	118	
RFH-1	11			20			32			57			79			129		
TFF	11	10		20	17		32	27		56	49		77	66		126	109	
AF	11	9	7	19	16	12	31	26	20	55	46	36	75	63	49	123	104	81
SFF-2	9	7	6	16	12	10	27	20	17	47	36	30	65	49	42	106	81	68
SF-2	9	8	6	16	14	11	27	23	18	47	40	32	65	55	43	106	90	71
FFH-2	9	7		15	12		25	19		44	34		60	46		99	75	
RFH-2	7	5		12	10		20	16		36	28		49	38		80	62	

Table 3A. Maximum Number of Conductors in Trade Sizes of Conduit or Tubing (Based on Table 1, Chapter 9)

Type Letters	Conductor Size AWG, MCM	½	¾	1	1¼	1½	2	2½	3	3½	4	4½	5	6
TW, T, RUH, RUW, XHHW (14 thru 8)	14	9	15	25	44	60	99	142	171					
	12	7	12	19	35	47	78	111	131	176				
	10	5	9	15	26	36	60	85						
	8	2	4	7	12	17	28	40	62	84	108			
RHW and FHH (without outer covering), THW	14	6	10	16	29	40	65	93	143	192				
	12	4	8	13	24	32	53	76	117	157	163			
	10	4	6	11	19	26	43	61	95	127				
	8	1	3	5	10	13	22	32	49	66	85	106	133	
TW, T, THW, RUH (6 thru 2), RUW (6 thru 2)	6	1	2	4	7	10	16	23	36	48	62	78	97	141
	4	1	1	3	5	7	12	17	27	36	47	58	73	106
	3	1	1	2	4	6	10	15	23	31	40	50	63	91
	2	1	1	2	4	5	9	13	20	27	34	43	54	78
	1		1	1	3	4	6	9	14	19	25	31	39	57
FEPB (6 thru 2), RHW and RHH (without outer covering)	0		1	1	2	3	5	8	12	16	21	27	33	49
	00		1	1	1	3	5	7	10	14	18	23	29	41
	000		1	1	1	2	4	6	9	12	15	19	24	35
	0000			1	1	1	3	5	7	10	13	16	20	29
	250			1	1	1	2	4	6	8	10	13	16	23
	300			1	1	1	2	3	5	7	9	11	14	20
	350				1	1	1	3	4	6	8	10	12	18
	400				1	1	1	2	4	5	7	9	11	16
	500				1	1	1	1	3	4	6	7	9	14
	600					1	1	1	3	4	5	6	7	11
	700					1	1	1	2	3	4	5	7	10
	750					1	1	1	2	3	4	5	6	9

Table 3B. Maximum Number of Conductors in Trade Sizes of Conduit or Tubing (Based on Table 1, Chapter 9)

Type Letters	Conductor Size AWG, MCM	1/2	3/4	1	1 1/4	1 1/2	2	2 1/2	3	3 1/2	4	4 1/2	5	6
THWN,	14	13	24	39	69	94	154							
	12	10	18	29	51	70	114	164						
	10	6	11	18	32	44	73	104	160					
	8	3	5	9	16	22	36	51	79	106	136			
THHN,	6	1	4	6	11	15	26	37	57	76	98	125	154	
	4	1	2	4	7	9	16	22	35	47	60	75	94	137
FEP (14 thru 2),	3	1	1	3	6	8	13	19	29	39	51	64	80	116
FEPB (14 thru 8),	2	1	1	3	5	7	11	16	25	33	43	54	67	97
	1		1	1	3	5	8	12	18	25	32	40	50	72
XHHW (4 thru 500MCM)	0		1	1	3	4	7	10	15	21	27	33	42	61
	00		1	1	2	3	6	8	13	17	22	28	35	51
	000		1	1	1	3	5	7	11	14	18	23	29	42
	0000		1	1	1	2	4	6	9	12	15	19	24	35
	250			1	1	1	3	4	7	10	12	16	20	28
	300			1	1	1	3	4	6	8	11	13	17	24
	350			1	1	1	2	3	5	7	9	12	15	21
	400				1	1	1	3	5	6	8	10	13	19
	500				1	1	1	2	4	5	7	9	11	16
	600				1	1	1	1	3	4	5	7	9	13
	700					1	1	1	3	4	5	6	8	11
	750					1	1	1	2	3	4	6	7	11
XHHW	6	1	3	5	9	13	21	30	47	63	81	102	128	185
	600				1	1	1	1	3	4	5	7	9	13
	700					1	1	1	3	4	5	6	7	11
	750					1	1	1	2	3	4	6	7	10

Table 3C. Maximum Number of Conductors in Trade Sizes of Conduit or Tubing (Based on Table 1, Chapter 9)

Type Letters	Conductor Size AWG, MCM	½	¾	1	1¼	1½	2	2½	3	3½	4	4½	5	6
RHW,	14	3	6	10	18	25	41	58	90	121	155			
	12	3	5	9	15	21	35	50	77	103	132			
	10	2	4	7	13	18	29	41	64	86	110	138		
	8	1	2	4	7	9	16	22	35	47	60	75	94	137
RHH	6	1	1	2	5	6	11	15	24	32	41	51	64	93
	4	1	1	1	3	5	8	12	18	24	31	39	50	72
(with	3	1	1	1	3	4	7	10	16	22	28	35	44	63
outer	2		1	1	3	4	6	9	14	19	24	31	38	56
covering)	1		1	1	1	3	5	7	11	14	18	23	29	42
	0		1	1	1	2	4	6	9	12	16	20	25	37
	00			1	1	1	3	5	8	11	14	18	22	32
	000			1	1	1	3	4	7	9	12	15	19	28
	0000			1	1	1	2	4	6	8	10	13	16	24
	250				1	1	1	3	5	6	8	11	13	19
	300				1	1	1	3	4	5	7	9	11	17
	350				1	1	1	2	4	5	6	8	10	15
	400				1	1	1	1	3	4	6	7	9	14
	500				1	1	1	1	3	4	5	6	8	11
	600					1	1	1	2	3	4	5	6	9
	700					1	1	1	1	3	3	4	6	8
	750						1	1	1	3	3	4	5	8

Tables 4 through 8, Chapter 9. Tables 4 through 8 give the nominal size of conductors and conduit or tubing for use in computing size of conduit or tubing for various combinations of conductors. The dimensions represent average conditions only, and variations will be found in dimensions of conductors and conduits of different manufacture.

Table 4. Dimensions and Percent Area of Conduit and of Tubing

Areas of Conduit or Tubing for the Combinations of Wires Permitted in Table 1, Chapter 9.

Trade Size	Internal Diameter Inches	Total 100%	Not Lead Covered			Lead Covered				
			2 Cond. 31%	Over 2 Cond. 40%	1 Cond. 53%	1 Cond. 55%	2 Cond. 30%	3 Cond. 40%	4 Cond. 38%	Over 4 Cond. 35%
1/2	.622	.30	.09	.12	.16	.17	.09	.12	.11	.11
3/4	.824	.53	.16	.21	.28	.29	.16	.21	.20	.19
1	1.049	.86	.27	.34	.46	.47	.26	.34	.33	.30
1 1/4	1.380	1.50	.47	.60	.80	.83	.45	.60	.57	.53
1 1/2	1.610	2.04	.63	.82	1.08	1.12	.61	.82	.78	.71
2	2.067	3.36	1.04	1.34	1.78	1.85	1.01	1.34	1.28	1.18
2 1/2	2.469	4.79	1.48	1.92	2.54	2.63	1.44	1.92	1.82	1.68
3	3.068	7.38	2.29	2.95	3.91	4.06	2.21	2.95	2.80	2.58
3 1/2	3.548	9.90	3.07	3.96	5.25	5.44	2.97	3.96	3.76	3.47
4	4.026	12.72	3.94	5.09	6.74	7.00	3.82	5.09	4.83	4.45
4 1/2	4.506	15.94	4.94	6.38	8.45	8.77	4.78	6.38	6.06	5.56
5	5.047	20.00	6.20	8.00	10.60	11.00	6.00	8.00	7.60	7.00
6	6.065	28.89	8.96	11.56	15.31	15.89	8.67	11.56	10.98	10.11

Area—Square Inches

Table 5. Dimensions of Rubber-Covered and Thermoplastic-Covered Conductors

Size AWG MCM	Types RFH-2, RH, RHH,*** RHW,*** SF-2		Types TF, T, THW,† TW, RUH,** RUW**		Types TFN, THHN, THWN		Types**** FEP, FEPB, TFE, PF, PGF, PTF		Type XHHW	
	Approx. Diam. Inches	Approx. Area Sq. In.	Approx. Diam. Inches	Approx. Area Sq. In.	Approx. Diam. Inches	Approx. Area Sq. In.	Approx. Diam. Inches	Approx. Area Sq. Inches	Approx. Diam. Inches	Approx. Area Sq. In.
Col. 1	Col. 2	Col. 3	Col. 4	Col. 5	Col. 6	Col. 7	Col. 8	Col. 9	Col. 10	Col. 11
18	.146	.0167	.106	.0088	.089	.0064	.081	.0052	...	...
16	.158	.0196	.118	.0109	.100	.0079	.092	.0066	...	...
14	30 mils .171	.0230	.131	.0135	.105	.0087	.105 .105	.0087 .0087		
14	45 mils .204*	.0327*	.162†	.0206†					.129	.0131
14										
12	30 mils .188	.0278	.148	.0172	.122	.0117	.121. .121	.0115 .0115		
12	45 mils .221*	.0384*	.179†	.0251†					.146	.0167
12										
10	.242	.0460	.168	.0224	.153	.0184	.142 .142	.0159 .0159	.166	.0216
10			.199†	.0311†						
8	.328	.0854	.245	.0471	.218	.0373	.206 .186	.0333 .0272	.241	.0456
8			.276†	.0598†						
6	.397	.1238	.323	.0819	.257	.0519	.244 .302	.0467 .0716	.282	.0625
4	.452	.1605	.372	.1087	.328	.0845	.292 .350	.0669 .0962	.328	.0845
3	.481	.1817	.401	.1263	.356	.0995	.320 .378	.0803 .1122	.356	.0995
2	.513	.2067	.433	.1473	.388	.1182	.352 .410	.0973 .1316	.388	.1182
1	.588	.2715	.508	.2027	.450	.1590	.420	.1385	.450	.1590
0	.629	.3107	.549	.2367	.491	.1893	.462	.1676 ...	.491	.1893
00	.675	.3578	.595	.2781	.537	.2265	.498	.1974 ...	.537	.2265
000	.727	.4151	.647	.3288	.588	.2715	.560	.2463 ...	.588	.2715
0000	.785	.4840	.705	.3904	.646	.3278	.618	.2999 ...	.646	.3278

Table 5 (Continued)

Size AWG MCM	Types RFH-2, RH, RHH, RHW,*** SF-2		Types TF, T, THW,† TW, RUH,** RUW**		Types TFN, THHN, THWN		Types**** FEP, FEPB, PF, PGF, TFE, PTF		Type XHHW	
	Approx. Diam. Inches	Approx. Area Sq. In.	Approx. Diam. Inches	Approx. Area Sq. In.	Approx. Diam. Inches	Approx. Area Sq. In.	Approx. Diam. Inches	Approx. Area Sq. Inches	Approx. Diam. Inches	Approx. Area Sq. In.
Col. 1	Col. 2	Col. 3	Col. 4	Col. 5	Col. 6	Col. 7	Col. 8	Col. 9	Col. 10	Col. 11
250	.868	.5917	.788	.4877	.716	.4026	...	...	.716	.4026
300	.933	.6837	.843	.5581	.771	.4669	...	...	.771	.4669
350	.985	.7620	.895	.6291	.822	.5307	...	...	.822	.5307
400	1.032	.8365	.942	.6969	.869	.5931	...	...	.869	.5931
500	1.119	.9834	1.029	.8316	.955	.7163	...	...	.955	.7163
600	1.233	1.1940	1.143	1.0261	1.058	.8792	...	...	1.073	.9043
700	1.304	1.3355	1.214	1.1575	1.129	1.0011	...	...	1.145	1.0297
750	1.339	1.4082	1.249	1.2252	1.163	1.0623	...	...	1.180	1.0936
800	1.372	1.4784	1.282	1.2908	1.196	1.1234	...	...	1.210	1.1499
900	1.435	1.6173	1.345	1.4208	1.259	1.2449	...	...	1.270	1.2668
1000	1.494	1.7531	1.404	1.5482	1.317	1.3623	...	...	1.330	1.3893
1250	1.676	2.2062	1.577	1.9532	...	...	...	...	1.500	1.7672
1500	1.801	2.5475	1.702	2.2748	...	...	...	...	1.620	2.0612
1750	1.916	2.8895	1.817	2.5930	...	...	...	...	1.740	2.3779
2000	2.021	3.2079	1.922	2.9013	...	...	...	...	1.840	2.6590

*The dimensions of Types RHH and RHW.

**No. 14 to No. 2.

†Dimensions of THW in sizes 14 to 8. No. 6 THW and larger is the same dimension as T.

***Dimensions of RHH and RHW without outer covering are the same as THW. No. 18 to No. 10, solid; No. 8 and larger, stranded.

****In Columns 8 and 9 the values shown for sizes No. 1 thru 0000 are for TFE only. The right-hand values in Columns 8 and 9 are for FEPB only.

Table 6. Dimensions of Lead-Covered Conductors

Types RL, RHL, and RUL

Size AWG-MCM	Single Conductor		Two Conductor		Three Conductor	
	Diam. Inches	Area Sq. Ins.	Diam. Inches	Area Sq. Ins.	Diam. Inches	Area Sq. Ins.
14	.28	.062	.28 × .47	.115	.59	.273
12	.29	.066	.31 × .54	.146	.62	.301
10	.35	.096	.35 × .59	.180	.68	.363
8	.41	.132	.41 × .71	.255	.82	.528
6	.49	.188	.49 × .86	.369	.97	.738
4	.55	.237	.54 × .96	.457	1.08	.916
2	.60	.283	.61 × 1.08	.578	1.21	1.146
1	.67	.352	.70 × 1.23	.756	1.38	1.49
0	.71	.396	.74 × 1.32	.859	1.47	1.70
00	.76	.454	.79 × 1.41	.980	1.57	1.94
000	.81	.515	.84 × 1.52	1.123	1.69	2.24
0000	.87	.593	.90 × 1.64	1.302	1.85	2.68
250	.98	.754	. . . .	. . . . .	2.02	3.20
300	1.04	.85	. . . .	. . . . .	2.15	3.62
350	1.10	.95	. . . .	. . . . .	2.26	4.02
400	1.14	1.02	. . . .	. . . . .	2.40	4.52
500	1.23	1.18	. . . .	. . . . .	2.59	5.28

The above cables are limited to straight runs or with nominal offsets equivalent to not more than two quarter bends.

Note–No. 14 to No. 8, solid conductors; No. 6 and larger, stranded conductors.

Table 7. Dimensions of Asbestos-Varnished-Cambric Insulated Conductors

Types AVA, AVB, and AVL

Size AWG MCM	Type AVA		Type AVB		Type AVL	
	Approx. Diam. Inches	Approx. Area Sq. Ins.	Approx. Diam. Inches	Approx. Area Sq. Ins.	Approx. Diam. Inches	Approx. Area Sq. Ins.
14	.245	.047	.205	.033	.320	.080
12	.265	.055	.225	.040	.340	.091
10	.285	.064	.245	.047	.360	.102
8	.310	.075	.270	.057	.390	.119
6	.395	.122	.345	.094	.430	.145
4	.445	.155	.395	.123	.480	.181
2	.505	.200	.460	.166	.570	.255
1	.585	.268	.540	.229	.620	.300
0	.625	.307	.580	.264	.660	.341
00	.670	.353	.625	.307	.705	.390
000	.720	.406	.675	.358	.755	.447
0000	.780	.478	.735	.425	.815	.521
250	.885	.616	.855	.572	.955	.715
300	.940	.692	.910	.649	1.010	.800
350	.995	.778	.965	.731	1.060	.885
400	1.040	.850	1.010	.800	1.105	.960
500	1.125	.995	1.095	.945	1.190	1.118
550	1.165	1.065	1.135	1.01	1.265	1.26
600	1.205	1.140	1.175	1.09	1.305	1.34
650	1.240	1.21	1.210	1.15	1.340	1.41
700	1.275	1.28	1.245	1.22	1.375	1.49
750	1.310	1.35	1.280	1.29	1.410	1.57
800	1.345	1.42	1.315	1.36	1.440	1.63
850	1.375	1.49	1.345	1.43	1.470	1.70
900	1.405	1.55	1.375	1.49	1.505	1.78
950	1.435	1.62	1.405	1.55	1.535	1.85
1000	1.465	1.69	1.435	1.62	1.565	1.93

Note: No. 14 to No. 8, solid, No. 6 and larger, stranded; except AVL where all sizes are stranded.

Varnished-Cambric Insulated Conductors
Type V

The insulation thickness for varnished-cambric conductors, Type V, is the same as for rubber-covered conductors, Type RHH, except for No. 8 which has 45-mil insulation for varnished-cambric, and 60-mil insulation for rubber-covered conductors. See Table 310-13. Therefore, Table 3C shall be permitted to be used for the number of varnished-cambric insulated conductors in a conduit or tubing.

Table 8. Properties of Conductors

Size AWG MCM	Area Cir. Mils	Concentric Lay Stranded Conductors No. Wires	Concentric Lay Stranded Conductors Diam. Each Wire Inches	Bare Conductors Diam. Inches	Bare Conductors *Area Sq. Inches	DC Resistance Ohms/M Ft. At 25°C. 77°F. Copper Bare Cond.	DC Resistance Ohms/M Ft. At 25°C. 77°F. Copper Tin'd. Cond.	DC Resistance Ohms/M Ft. At 25°C. 77°F. Aluminum
18	1620	Solid	.0403	.0403	.0013	6.51	6.79	10.7
16	2580	Solid	.0508	.0508	.0020	4.10	4.26	6.72
14	4110	Solid	.0641	.0641	.0032	2.57	2.68	4.22
12	6530	Solid	.0808	.0808	.0051	1.62	1.68	2.66
10	10380	Solid	.1019	.1019	.0081	1.018	1.06	1.67
8	16510	Solid	.1285	.1285	.0130	.6404	.659	1.05
6	26240	7	.0612	.184	.027	.410	.427	.674
4	41740	7	.0772	.232	.042	.259	.269	.424
3	52620	7	.0867	.260	.053	.205	.213	.336
2	66360	7	.0974	.292	.067	.162	.169	.266
1	83690	19	.0664	.332	.087	.129	.134	.211
0	105600	19	.0745	.372	.109	.102	.106	.168
00	133100	19	.0837	.418	.137	.0811	.0843	.133
000	167800	19	.0940	.470	.173	.0642	.0668	.105
0000	211600	19	.1055	.528	.219	.0509	.0525	.0836
250	250000	37	.0822	.575	.260	.0431	.0449	.0708
300	300000	37	.0900	.630	.312	.0360	.0374	.0590
350	350000	37	.0973	.681	.364	.0308	.0320	.0505
400	400000	37	.1040	.728	.416	.0270	.0278	.0442
500	500000	37	.1162	.813	.519	.0216	.0222	.0354
600	600000	61	.0992	.893	.626	.0180	.0187	.0295
700	700000	61	.1071	.964	.730	.0154	.0159	.0253
750	750000	61	.1109	.998	.782	.0144	.0148	.0236
800	800000	61	.1145	1.030	.833	.0135	.0139	.0221
900	900000	61	.1215	1.090	.933	.0120	.0123	.0197
1000	1000000	61	.1280	1.150	1.039	.0108	.0111	.0177
1250	1250000	91	.1172	1.289	1.305	.00863	.00888	.0142
1500	1500000	91	.1284	1.410	1.561	.00719	.00740	.0118
1750	1750000	127	.1174	1.526	1.829	.00616	.00634	.0101
2000	2000000	127	.1255	1.630	2.087	.00539	.00555	.00885

*Area given is that of a circle having a diameter equal to the over-all diameter of a stranded conductor.

The values given in the Table are those given in Handbook 100 of the National Bureau of Standards except that those shown in the 8th column are those given in Specification B33 of the American Society for Testing and Materials, and those shown in the 9th column are those given in Standard No. S-19-81 of the Insulated Power Cable Engineers Association and Standard No. WC3-1964 of the National Electrical Manufacturers Association.

The resistance values given in the last three columns are applicable only to direct current. When conductors larger than No. 4/0 are used with alternating current, the multiplying factors in Table 9 compensate for skin effect.

Table 9. Multiplying Factors for Converting DC Resistance to 60-Hertz AC Resistance

Size	Multiplying Factor			
	For Nonmetallic Sheathed Cables in Air or Nonmetallic Conduit		For Metallic Sheathed Cables or all Cables in Metallic Raceways	
	Copper	Aluminum	Copper	Aluminum
Up to 3 AWG	1.	1.	1.	1.
2	1.	1.	1.01	1.00
1	1.	1.	1.01	1.00
0	1.001	1.000	1.02	1.00
00	1.001	1.001	1.03	1.00
000	1.002	1.001	1.04	1.01
0000	1.004	1.002	1.05	1.01
250 MCM	1.005	1.002	1.06	1.02
300 MCM	1.006	1.003	1.07	1.02
350 MCM	1.009	1.004	1.08	1.03
400 MCM	1.011	1.005	1.10	1.04
500 MCM	1.018	1.007	1.13	1.06
600 MCM	1.025	1.010	1.16	1.08
700 MCM	1.034	1.013	1.19	1.11
750 MCM	1.039	1.015	1.21	1.12
800 MCM	1.044	1.017	1.22	1.14
1000 MCM	1.067	1.026	1.30	1.19
1250 MCM	1.102	1.040	1.41	1.27
1500 MCM	1.142	1.058	1.53	1.36
1750 MCM	1.185	1.079	1.67	1.46
2000 MCM	1.233	1.100	1.82	1.56

B. Examples

Selection of Conductors. In the following examples, the results are generally expressed in amperes. To select conductor sizes, refer to Tables 310-16 through 310-19 and the Notes that pertain to such tables.

Voltage. For uniform application of the provisions of Articles 210, 215 and 220, a nominal voltage of 115 and 230 volts shall be used in computing the ampere load on the conductor.

Fractions of an Ampere. Except where the computations result in a major fraction of an ampere (larger than 0.5), such fractions may be dropped.

Ranges. For the computation of the range loads in these examples, Column A of Table 220-19 has been used. For optional methods, see Columns B and C of Table 220-19.

▲ It is assumed that the loads in the following examples are properly balanced on the system. If they are not properly balanced on the system, additional feeder capacity may be required.

Example No. 1. Single-Family Dwelling

Dwelling has a floor area of 1500 sq. ft. exclusive of unoccupied cellar, unfinished attic, and open porches. It has a 12-kw range.

▲ *Example:* A two-story dwelling 30 by 25 ft. First and second floors 30 by 25 ft by 2 = 1,500 sq ft. The "floor" area is computed from the "outside" dimensions of the building and multiplied by the number of floors. [Sec. 220-2(b).]

Computed Load (see Section 220-10(a)):
General Lighting Load:
  1500 sq. ft. at 3 watts per sq. ft. = 4500 watts.
Minimum Number of Branch Circuits Required (see Section 220-3):
General Lighting Load:
  4500 ÷ 115 = 39.1 amperes: or three 15-ampere 2-wire circuits; or two 20-ampere 2-wire circuits
Small Appliance Load: Two 2-wire 20-ampere circuits (Section 220-3(b))
Laundry Load: One 2-wire 20-ampere circuit (Section 220-3(c))
Minimum Size Feeders Required (see Section 220-10(a)):
Computed Load

General Lighting	4500 watts
Small Appl. Load	3000 watts
Laundry	1500 watts
Total (without range)	9000 watts
3000 watts at 100%	3000 watts
9000 − 3000 = 6000 watts at 35% =	2100 watts
Net computed load (without range)	5100 watts
Range Load (see Table 220-19)	8000 watts
Net computed load (with range)	13,100 watts

For 115/230-volt 3-wire system feeders, 13,100 ÷ 230 = 57 amperes
Net computed load exceeds 10 kW. so service conductors shall be 100 amperes (see Section 230-41(b)(2).

Reduced size neutral shall be permitted, usually two trade sizes smaller than the ungrounded conductors.

Feeder and Service Neutral

Lighting and small appliance load	5100 watts
Range load 8000 watts at 70%	5600 watts
Total	10,700 watts

10,700 W ÷ 230 = 46.5 = 46 amperes

Example No. 1(a). Single-Family Dwelling

Same conditions as Example No. 1, plus addition of one 6-ampere 230-volt room air-conditioning unit and three 12-ampere 115-volt room air-conditioning units.* See Article 440, Part G.

From Example No. 1, feeder current is 57 amperes (3 wire, 230 volt)

Line A	Neutral	Line B	
57	46	57	amperes from Example No. 1
6	—	6	one 230-volt air cond. motor
12	12	12	two 115-volt air cond. motors
—	12	12	one 115-volt air cond. motor
3	3	3	25% of largest motor (Section 430-24)
78	73	90	amperes per line

* For feeder neutral, use load of one air cond. motor for unbalanced condition.

Example No. 1(b). Single-Family Dwelling
Optional Calculation for Single-Family Dwelling (Section 220-30)

Dwelling has a floor area of 1500 sq. ft. exclusive of unoccupied cellar, unfinished attic and open porches. It has a 12-kW range, a 2.5-kW water heater, a 1.2-kW dishwasher, 9 kW of electric space heating installed in five rooms, a 5-kW clothes dryer, and a 6-amp. 230-volt room air-conditioning unit.

$$\text{Air conditioner kW is } 6 \times 230 \div 1000 = 1.38 \text{ kW}$$

1.38 kW is less than the connected load of 9 kW of space heating; therefore, the air conditioner load need not be included in the service calculation (see Section 220-21).

1500 sq. ft. at 3 watts	4.5 kW
Two 20-amp. appliance outlet circuits at 1500 watts each	3.0 kW
Laundry circuit	1.5 kW
Range (at nameplate rating)	12.0 kW
Water heater	2.5 kW
Dishwasher	1.2 kW
Space heating	9.0 kW
Clothes dryer	5.0 kW
	38.7 kW

First 10 kW at 100% = 10.00 kW
Remainder at 40% (28.7 kW × .4) = 11.48 kW
Calculated load for service size 21.48 kW = 21,480 watts

$$21,480 \div 230 = 93 \text{ amperes}$$

Therefore, this dwelling may be served by a 100-ampere service.

Feeder Neutral Load, per Section 220-22:

1500 sq. ft. @ 3 watts	4500 watts
3-20 amp. circuits @ 1500 watts	4500 watts
Total	9000 watts
3000 watts @ 100%	3000 watts
9000 W − 300 W = 6000 watts @ 35%	2100 watts
	5100 watts
Range −8 kW @ 70%	5600 watts
Dishwasher	1200 watts
Total	11,900 watts

$$11,900 \text{ W} \div 230 \text{ V} = 51.7 = 52 \text{ amp.}$$

Example No. 1(c). Single-Family Dwelling
Optional Calculation for Single-Family Dwelling (See Section 220-30)

Dwelling has a floor area of 1,500 sq. ft. exclusive of unoccupied cellar, unfinished attic and open porches. It has two 20-ampere small appliance circuits, one 20-ampere laundry circuit, two 4-kW wall-mounted ovens, one 5.1-kW counter-mounted cooking unit, a 4.5-kW water heater, a 1.2-kW dishwasher, a 5-kW combination clothes washer and dryer, six 7-ampere 230-volt room air-conditioning units and a 1.5-kW permanently installed bathroom space heater.

Air Conditioning kW Calculation:
$$\text{Total amperes } 6 \times 7 = 42.00 \text{ amperes}$$
$$42 \times 230 \div 1000 = 9.7 \text{ kW of air-conditioned load}$$

Load Included at 100%:

Air conditioning	9.7 kW
Space heater (omit, see Section 220-21)	

Other Load: kW

1,500 sq. ft. at 3 watts	4.5
Two 20-amp small appliance circuits	
at 1500 watts	3.0
Laundry circuit	1.5
2 ovens	8.
1 cooking unit	5.1
Water heater	4.5
Dishwasher	1.2
Washer/dryer	5.0
Total other load	32.8
1st 10 kW at 100% . . . . 10.0 kW	
Remainder at 40% (22.8 kW × .4) . . . . 9.12 kW	
Total calculated load . . . . 28.82 kW	= 28,820 watts

$$28,820 \div 230 = 125 \text{ amperes (service rating)}$$

▲ **All the air-conditioning load is counted at 100 percent, as stated in Table 220-30, and this load as calculated in Example 1(c) is figured separately from the "other loads" in order to comply with the requirements.**

Feeder Neutral Load, per Section 220-22:
(It is assumed that the 2-4 kW wall-mounted ovens are supplied by one branch circuit, the 5.1 kW counter-mounted cooking unit by a separate circuit.)

1500 sq. ft. @ 3 watts	4500 watts
3-20 amp. circuits @ 1500 watts	4500 watts
Total	9000 watts
3000 watts @ 100%	3000 watts
9000 W − 3000 W = 6000 watts @ 35%	2100 watts
	5100 watts
2.4 kW ovens = 8000 watts @ 65% =	
5200 watts @ 70% (for neutral load)	3640 watts
1-5.1 kW cooking unit @ 80% =	
4080 watts @ 70% (for neutral load)	2856 watts
(See Table 220-19, Note 4)	
Dishwasher	1200 watts
Total	12,796 watts

12,796 watts ÷ 230 V − 55.6 − 56 amperes

Example No. 2. Small Roadside Fruitstand with No Show Windows

A small roadside fruitstand with no show windows has a floor area of 150 square feet. The electrical load consists of general lighting and a 1,000-watt flood light. There are no other outlets.

Computed Load (Section 220-10(a)):
　* General Lighting
　　150 sq. ft. at 3 watts/sq. ft. × 1.25 = 562 watts
　　(3 watts/sq. ft. for stores)
　　562 watts ÷ 115 = 4.88 amperes
　　One 15-ampere 2-wire branch circuit required (Section 220-3)
Minimum Size Service Conductor Required (Section 230-41(b) Exception No. 1):
　Computed load . . . . 562 watts
　Floodlight load . . . . <u>1000 watts</u>
　Total load . . . . 1562 watts
　　1562 ÷ 115 = 13.6 amperes
　Use No. 8 service conductor (Section 230-41(b) Exception No. 1)
　Use a 30-ampere service switch or breaker (Section 230-79(b))

Example No. 3. Store Building

A store 50 feet by 60 feet, or 3,000 square feet, has 30 feet of show window.

Computed Load (Section 220-10(a)):
　* General lighting load:
　　3,000 square feet at 3 watts per square foot × 1.25 . . . . 11,250 watts
　** Show window lighting load:
　　30 feet at 200 watts per foot . . . . 6,000 watts
Minimum Number of Branch Circuits Required (Section 220-3):
　*** General lighting load: 11,250 ÷ 230 = 49 amperes for 3-wire, 115/230 volts; or 98 amperes for 2-wire, 115 volts:
　　Three 30-ampere, 2-wire; and one 15-ampere, 2-wire circuits; or
　　Five 20-ampere, 2-wire circuits; or
　　Three 20-ampere, 2-wire, and three 15-ampere, 2-wire circuits; or
　　Seven 15-ampere, 2-wire circuits; or
　　Three 15-ampere, 3-wire, and one 15-ampere, 2-wire circuits.
　Special lighting load (show window): (Sections 220-2(c) Exception No. 3 and 220-12): 6,000 ÷ 230 = 26 amperes for 3-wire, 115/230 volts; or 52 amperes for 2-wire, 115 volts:
　　Four 15-ampere, 2-wire circuits; or
　　Three 20-ampere, 2-wire circuits; or
　　Two 15-ampere, 3-wire circuits.
Minimum Size Feeders (or Service Conductors) Required (Section 215-2):
　For 115/230-volt, 3-wire system:
　　Ampere load: 49 plus 26 = 75 amperes. (Section 220-2)
　For 115-volt system:
　　Ampere load: 98 plus 52 = 150 amperes. (Section 220-2)

* The above examples assume that the entire general lighting is a continuous load and the load is therefore increased by 25 percent in accordance with Section 220-2. The 25 percent increase is not applicable to any portion of the load that is not continuous.

** If show window load is computed as per Section 220-2, the unit load per outlet shall be increased 25 percent.

*** The load on each general lighting branch circuit shall not exceed 80 percent of the branch-circuit rating (Section 210-23(a)).

Example No. 4. Multi-Family Dwelling

Multi-family dwelling having a total floor area of 32,000 square feet with 40 apartments. Meters in two banks of 20 each and individual sub-feeders to each apartment.

One-half of the apartments are equipped with electric ranges of not exceeding 12 kW each. Area of each apartment is 800 square feet.

Laundry facilities on premises available to all tenants. Add no circuit to individual apartment. Add 1,500 watts for each laundry circuit to house load and add to the example as a "house load."

Computed Load for Each Apartment (Article 220):
General lighting load:
800 square feet at 3 watts per square foot . . . . 2,400 watts
Special appliance load:
Electric range . . . . 8,000 watts

Minimum Number of Branch Circuits Required for Each Apartment
(Section 220-3):
General lighting load: 2,4000 ÷ 115 = 21 amperes or two 15-ampere, 2-wire circuits; or two 20-ampere, 2-wire circuits.
Small appliance load: Two 2-wire circuits of No. 12 wire. (See Section 220-3(b)).
Range circuit: 8,000 ÷ 230 = 35 amperes or a circuit of two No. 8's and one No. 10 as permitted by Section 210-19(b).

Minimum Size Sub-Feeder Required for Each Apartment (Section 215-2):
Computed load (Article 220):

General Lighting load	2,400 watts
Small appliance load, two 20-ampere circuits	3,000 watts
Total computed load (without ranges)	5,400 watts

Application of Demand Factor:

3,000 watts at 100%	3,000 watts
2,400 watts at 35%	840 watts
Net computed load (without ranges)	3,840 watts
Range load	8,000 watts
Net computed load (with ranges)	11,840 watts

For 115/230-volt, 3-wire system (without ranges):
Net computed load, 3,840 ÷ 230 = 16.7 amperes.
Size of each sub-feeder (see Section 215-2).
For 115/230-volt, 3-wire system (with ranges):
Net computed load, 11,840 ÷ 230 = 51.5 amperes.
Sub-Feeder Neutral:

Lighting and small appliance load	3,840 watts
Range load, 8,000 watts at 70% (see Section 220-22)	5,600 watts
Net computed load (neutral)	9,440 watts

9,440 ÷ 230 = 41 amperes

Minimum Size Feeders Required from Service Equipment to Meter Bank
(For 20 Apartments—10 with Ranges):
Total Computed Load:

Lighting and small appliance load, 20 × 5,400	108,000 watts

Application of Demand Factor:

3,000 watts at 100%	3,000 watts
105,000 watts at 35%	36,750 watts
Net computed lighting and small appliance load	39,750 watts
Range load, 10 ranges (less than 12 kW; Col. A, Table 220-19	25,000 watts
Net computed load (with ranges)	64,750 watts

For 115/230-volt, 3-wire system:
Net computed load, 64,750 ÷ 230 = 282 amperes.
Feeder Neutral:

Lighting and small appliance load	39,750 watts
Range load: 25,000 watts at 70% (see Section 220-22)	17,500 watts
Computed load (neutral)	57,250 watts

57,250 ÷ 230 = 249 amperes.
Further Demand Factor (Section 220-22):

200 amperes at 100%	− 200 amperes	
49 amperes at 70%	= 34 amperes	
Net computed load (neutral)	234 amperes	

Minimum Size Main Feeder (or Service Conductors) Required
(For 40 Apartments—20 with Ranges):
Total Computed Load:
Lighting and small appliance load, 40 × 5,400 . . . . 216,000 watts

Application of Demand Factor:

3,000 watts at 100%	3,000 watts
117,000 watts at 35%	40,950 watts
96,000 watts at 25%	24,000 watts
Net computed lighting and small appliance load	67,950 watts
Range load, 20 ranges (less than 12 kW, Col. A, Table 220-19)	35,000 watts
Net computed load	102,950 watts

For 115/230-volt, 3-wire system:

Net computed load, 102,950 ÷ 230 = 448 amperes.

Feeder Neutral:

Lighting and small appliance load	67,950 watts
Range load, 35,000 watts at 70% (see Section 220-22)	24,500 watts
Computed load (neutral)	92,450 watts

92,450 ÷ 230 = 402 amperes.

Further Demand Factor (see Section 220-22):

200 amperes at 100%	= 200 amperes
202 amperes at 70%	= 141 amperes
Net computed load (neutral)	341 amperes

See Tables 310-16 through 310-19, Notes 8 and 10.

Example No. 4(a). Optional Calculation for Multi-Family Dwelling

Multi-family dwelling equipped with electric cooking and space heating or air conditioning and having a total floor area of 32,000 square feet with 40 apartments.

Meters in two banks of 20 each plus house metering and individual subfeeders to each apartment.

Each apartment is equipped with an electric range of 8-kW nameplate rating, four 1.5-kW separately controlled 230-volt electric space heaters, and a 2.5-kW 230-volt electric water heater. A common laundry facility is available to all tenants (Section 210-25(b), Exception No. 1). Area of each apartment is 800 square feet.

Computed Load for each Apartment (Article 220):

General Lighting Load:

800 square ft. at 3 watts per sq. ft.	2,400 watts
Electric range	8,000 watts
Electric heat 6 kW	6,000 watts
(or air conditioning if larger)	
Electric water heater	2,500 watts

Minimum Number of Branch Circuits Required for Each Apartment:

General lighting load 2400 watts ÷ 115 = 21 amperes or two 15-ampere 2-wire circuits or two 20 amp 2-wire circuits.

Small appliance load: Two 2-wire circuits of No. 12 (See Section 220-3(b))

Range circuit 8000 watts × 80% ÷ 230 = 28 amperes on a circuit of three No. 10 as permitted in Column C of Table 220-19

Space Heating 6000 watts ÷ 230 = 26 amperes

No. of circuits (See Section 220-3)

Minimum Size Sub-Feeder Required for Each Apartment (Section 215-2):

Computed Load (Article 220):

General lighting load	2,400 watts
Small appliance load, two 20-amp. circuits	3,000 watts
Total computed load (without range and space heating)	5,400 watts

Application of Demand Factor:

3,000 watts at 100%	3,000 watts
2,400 watts at 35%	840 watts
Net computed load (without range and space heating)	3,840 watts
Range load	6,400 watts
Space heating, Section 220-15	6,000 watts

Water heater . . . .   <u>2,500 watts</u>
Net computed load for individual apartment . . . .   18,740 watts
For 115/230-volt 3-wire system
Net computed load 18,740 ÷ 230 = 81 amperes
Sub-Feeder Neutral (Section 220-22)
Lighting and small appliance load . . . .   3,840 watts
Range load 6,400 watts at 70% (see Section 220-22) . . . .   4,480 watts
Space and water heating (no neutral) 230 volt . . . .   <u>0 watts</u>
Net computed load (neutral) . . . .   8,320 watts
8320 ÷ 230 = 36 amperes

Minimum Size Feeder Required from Service Equipment to Meter Bank for 20 Apartments:
Total Computed Load:
Lighting and small appliance load 20 × 5400 . . . .   108,000 watts
Water and space heating load 20× 8500 . . . .   170,000 watts
Range load 20 × 8000 . . . .   160,000 watts
Net computed load (20 apartments) . . . .   438,000 watts
Net Computed using Optional Calculation (Table 220-32)
438,000 × .38 . . . .   166,440 watts
166,440 ÷ 230 = 724 amperes

Minimum Size Mains Feeder Required (less house load)
(For 40 Apartments):
Total Computed Load:
Lighting and small appliance load 40 × 5400 . . . .   216,000 watts
Water and space heating 40 × 8500 . . . .   340,000 watts
Range load 40 × 8000 . . . .   <u>320,000 watts</u>
Net computed load (40 apartments) . . . .   876,000 watts
Net computed using Optional Calculation (Table 220-32)
876,000 × 28% . . . .   245,280 watts
245,280 ÷ 230 = 1066 amperes

Feeder Neutral Load for Feeder from Service Equipment to Meter Bank for 20 Apartments:
Lighting and small appliance load
20 × 5400 watts   = 108,000 watts
1st 3000 watts @ 100%   =   3,000 watts
105,000 watts @ 35%   = <u>36,750</u> watts
Sub-Total . . . .   39,750 watts
20 Ranges = 35,000 watts @ 70% . . . .   <u>24,500</u> watts
(See Table 220-19 and Sec. 220-22)
Total . . . .   64,250 watts
64,250 watts ÷ 230 volts = 279 amperes
Further Demand Factor (Sec. 220-22)
First 200 amperes@ 100%   = 200 amperes
Balance: 79 amperes @ 70%   = 55
Total . . . .   255 amperes

Feeder Neutral Load for Mains Feeder (less house load):
Lighting and small appliance load
40 × 5400 watts . . . .   216,000 watts
1st 3000 watts @ 100% . . . .   3,000 watts
216,000 watts − 3000 watts = 213,000 watts @ 35% . . . .   <u>74,550</u> watts
77,550 watts
40 Ranges = 55,000 watts @ 70% . . . .   <u>38,500</u> watts
(See Table 220-19 and Sec. 220-22)
Total . . . .   116,050 watts
116,050 watts ÷ 230 volt = 504.5 − 504 amperes
Further demand factor (220-22)

First 200 amp. @ 100%   = 200 amperes
Balance: 304 amperes @ 70%   = 213 amperes

Total . . . . 413 amperes

Example No. 5. Calculation of Feeder Neutral

(See Section 220-22)

The following example illustrates the method of calculating size of a feeder neutral for the computed load of a 5-wire, 2-phase system, where it is desired to modify the load in accordance with provisions of Sections 220-22.

An installation consisting of a computed load of 250 amperes connected between the feeder neutral and each ungrounded feeder conductor.

Feeder Neutral (maximum unbalance of load 250 amp. $\times$ 140% = 350 amperes):
200 amperes (first)   at 100% = 200 amperes
150 amperes (excess) at   70% = 105 amperes

Computed load . . . . 305 amperes

Example No. 6. Maximum Demand for Range Loads

Table 220-19, Column A applies to ranges not over 12 kW. The application of Note 1 to ranges over 12 kW (and not over 27 kW) is illustrated in the following examples:

A. Ranges all of same rating.
Assume 24 ranges each rated 16 kW.
From Column A the maximum demand for 24 ranges of 12 kW rating is 39 kW.
16 kW exceeds 12 kW by 4.
5% $\times$ 4 = 20% (5% increase for each kW in excess of 12).
39 kW $\times$ 20% = 7.8 kW increase.
39 + 7.8 = 46.8 kW: value to be used in selection of feeders.

B. Ranges of unequal rating.
Assume 5 ranges each rated 11 kW.
2 ranges each rated 12 kW.
20 ranges each rated 13.5 kW.
3 ranges each rated 18 kW.
5 $\times$ 12   = 60 Use 12 kW for range rated less than 12.
2 $\times$ 12   = 24
20 $\times$ 13.5 = 270
3 $\times$ 18   = 54
30   408 kW
408 $\div$ 30 = 13.6 kW (average to be used for computation)
From Column A the demand for 30 ranges of 12 kW rating is 15 + 30 = 45 kW.
13.6 exceeds 12 by 1.6 (use 2).
5% $\times$ 2 = 10% (5% increase for each kW in excess of 12).
45 kW $\times$ 10% = 4.5 kW increase.
45 + 4.5 = 49.5 kW = value to be used in selection of feeders.

Example No. 7. Ranges on a 3-Phase System

(Section 220-19)

Thirty ranges rated at 12 kW each are supplied by a 3-phase, 4-wire, 120/208-volt feeder, 10 ranges on each phase.

As there are 20 ranges connected to each ungrounded conductor, the load should be calculated on the basis of 20 ranges (or in case of unbalance, twice the maximum number between any two phase wires), since diversity applies only to the number of ranges connected to adjacent phases and not the total.

The current in any one conductor will be one-half the total watt load of two adjacent phases divided by the line-to-neutral voltage. In this case, 20 ranges, from Table 220-19, will have a total watt load of 35,000 watts for two phases; therefore, the current in the feeder conductor would be:

17,500 ÷ 120 = 146 amperes.

On a 3-phase basis the load would be:

3 × 17,500 = 52,500 watts

and the current in each feeder conductor—

$$\frac{52,500}{208 \times 1.73} = 146 \text{ amperes}$$

Example No. 8. Motors, Conductors, and Overcurrent Protection

(See Sections 430-22, 430-24, 430-32, 430-52, 430-62, and Tables 430-150, and 430-152.)

Determine the conductor size, the motor-running overcurrent protection, the branch-circuit protection, and the feeder protection, for one 25-h.p. squirrel-cage induction motor (full-voltage starting, service factor 1.15, Code letter F), and two 30-h.p. wound-rotor induction motors (40°C rise), on a 460-volt, 3-phase, 60-Hertz supply.

Conductor Loads

The full-load current of the 25-h.p. motor is 34 amperes (Table 430-150). A full-load current of 34 amperes × 1.25 = 42.5 amperes (Section 430-22). The full-load current of the 30-h.p. motor is 40 amperes (Table 430-150). A full-load current of 40 amperes × 1.25 = 50 amperes (Section 430-22).

The feeder ampacity will be 125 percent of 40 plus 40 plus 34, or 124 amperes (Section 430-24).

Overcurrent Protection

Running. The 25-h.p. motor, with full-load current of 34 amperes, must have running overcurrent protection of not over 42.5 amperes. The 30-h.p. motor with full-load current of 40 amperes must have running overcurrent protection of not over 50 amperes.

Branch Circuit. The branch circuit of the 25-h.p. motor must have branch-circuit overcurrent protection of not over 300 percent for a nontime-delay fuse (Table 430-152) or 3.00 × 34 = 102 amperes. The next larger size standard fuse is 110 amperes. (See Section 430-52.)

For the 30-h.p. motor, the branch-circuit overcurrent protection is 150 percent (Table 430-152) or 1.50 × 40 = 60 amperes. Where the maximum value of overcurrent protection is not sufficient to start the motor, the value for a nontime-delay fuse may be increased to 400 percent (Section 430-52 Exception (a)).

Feeder Circuit. The maximum rating of the feeder overcurrent protection device is based on the sum of the largest branch-circuit protective device (110-ampere fuse) plus the sum of the full-load currents of the other motors or 110 plus 40 plus 40 = 190 amperes. The nearest standard fuse which does not exceed this value is 175 amperes.

APPENDIX

Rules of Procedure for the NFPA Electrical Section and the National Electrical Code Committee

Adopted by the NFPA Board of Directors on January 23, 1964 and Amended June 28, 1967

The National Fire Protection Association is sponsor of the National Electrical Code (ANSI C1, NFPA No. 70) and other standards covering the safe use of electricity. In 1948, the NFPA Board of Directors authorized an Electrical Section of NFPA. The National Electrical Code Committee consists of a Correlating Committee and a number of Code-Making Panels. The Rules of Procedure for these organizations consist of:

Part A—Rules of Procedure for the NFPA Electrical Section

Part B—Rules of Procedure for the National Electrical Code Committee

Part C—Rules of Procedure—Tentative Interim Amendments to the National Electrical Code

Part D—Interpretation Procedure of the National Electrical Code Committee

PART A—RULES OF PROCEDURE FOR THE NFPA ELECTRICAL SECTION

Section 10. General

10. There are no dues or fees beyond the regular NFPA membership dues.

11. The Section provides particular opportunity for Section members to become informed and contribute to the development of NFPA electrical standards. It sponsors, for this purpose, open meetings where proposals for revisions or additions to these standards may be discussed.

12. Bulletins and reports on matters affecting the work of NFPA Technical Committees in this field are made available to members of the Section as the need indicates, through its Chairman, Secretary, or the NFPA Executive Office.

Section 20. Activities, Membership, Meetings, Officers

21. Activities, programs, and procedures not covered in these Rules for the NFPA Electrical Section shall be in accordance with the Regulations for NFPA Sections.

22. Membership in the NFPA Electrical Section is open to any Associate Member of the Association and up to four individuals designated by an Organization Member. To become a member of the NFPA Electrical Section, it is necessary to file a special application form with the NFPA Executive Office or the Electrical Section Secretary (forms available on request).

23. The Section shall meet at least annually at the time and place of the National Fire Protection Association Annual Meeting (unless omitted on the request of the Section with the consent of the NFPA Annual Meeting Program Committee). Other meetings of the Section may be held at times and places it may select.

24. The Chairman and Secretary of the National Electrical Code Committee shall be the Chairman and Secretary, respectively, of the Electrical Section. The Secretary of the Section shall keep a record of the membership, notify its members of Section meetings and keep members of the Section informed on matters of interest to them.

25. In order to transact business at any meeting of the Section, there shall be at least fifty members of the Section present. Robert's Rules of Order, Revised, shall govern the transactions of business at all meetings.

26. The Chairman of the National Electrical Code Committee (or his representative) shall report to the Annual Meeting of the Section on the work of that Committee and may take such other steps as he considers desirable to keep the Section informed on Committee matters. The Electrical Section may vote to request further consideration of a specific item by the Correlating Committee. Reports from other existing NFPA Technical Committees may be presented to the Annual Meeting of the Section when such action is considered appropriate by the officers of the Electrical Section.

27. The Section may recommend to the NFPA Board of Directors the establishment of other Technical Committees useful in promoting its objectives, other than as covered by the scope of the National Electrical Code. These Committees, if authorized, shall be organized and operated under the NFPA Regulations Governing Technical Committees or under such special rules as may be authorized by the NFPA Board of Directors. The Chairman of any such Committee so established shall follow the procedures outlined in Paragraph 26.

28. Reports of Technical Committees covering areas that are currently covered by the National Electrical Code, shall be submitted through the Correlating Committee of the National Electrical Code Committee when so directed by the NFPA Board of Directors. (See Paragraphs 54 and 55 of the NFPA Regulations Governing Technical Committees.)

29. The Section does not have authority to commit the Association nor does membership in the Section commit any individual or organization to a course of action.

PART B—RULES OF PROCEDURE FOR THE NATIONAL ELECTRICAL CODE COMMITTEE

Section 30. General

31. The National Electrical Code Committee shall consist of

a. A Correlating Committee, and

b. A number of Code-Making Panels.

32. The functions of the National Electrical Code Committee shall be established by the NFPA Board of Directors and shall include

a. Developing periodically revisions of the National Electrical Code (ANSI C1, NFPA No. 70) on a schedule to be announced to the public following issuance of each successive edition.

b. Processing proposals for Tentative Interim Amendments of the current edition of the National Electrical Code in accordance with the Rules of Procedure—Tentative Interim Amendments to the National Electrical Code (see Part C of these Rules).

c. Interpreting provisions of the current edition of the National Electrical Code in accordance with the Interpretation Procedure of the National Electrical Code Committee (see Part D of these Rules).

Section 40. Membership

41. The Chairman of the National Electrical Code Committee shall be the Chairman of the Correlating Committee of the National Electrical Code Committee and shall be appointed by the Board of Directors of the National Fire Protection Association. (See also Paragraph 24 of Part A—Rules of Procedure for the NFPA Electrical Section.)

42. Subject to approval by the Board of Directors of the National Fire Protection Association, the NFPA Electrical Field Engineer serves as the Secretary of the National Electrical Code Committee and as the Secretary of the Correlating Committee of the National Electrical Code Committee. He shall serve in this capacity as a nonvoting member, except as noted in Paragraphs 112 and 121.b. (See also Paragraph 24 of Part A—Rules of Procedure for the NFPA Electrical Section.)

43. Other members of the Correlating Committee shall also be appointed by the NFPA Board of Directors acting on recommendations of the Chairman of the Committee. Alternates for such individuals may be nominated when conditions warrant. The membership of the Correlating Committee shall be restricted to nine voting members

(Secretary and other nonvoting members excluded).

44. Groups concerned with various Articles of the Code may nominate qualified individuals to serve on the Code-Making Panels, submitting their recommendations to the Chairman of the Correlating Committee in such form as he may request. Alternates for such individuals may be nominated when conditions warrant. Individuals having an interest in only a portion of the scope of the work of a particular Panel may be nominated to limited membership covering their special field of interest. All appointments of members and alternates shall be made by the Chairman of the Correlating Committee acting with the advice and consent of the members of the

Correlating Committee acting in consideration of the items noted in Paragraph 46.

45. The Chairman of the Correlating Committee shall appoint the Chairman of each Code-Making Panel, acting with the advice and consent of the members of the Correlating Committee.

46. All appointments to the Correlating Committee and to the Code-Making Panels shall be based on the technical competence of the individuals selected. Proper balance of all interests concerned shall be made within the desired limits of effective committee size and in accordance with the objectives of the National Fire Protection Association and in accordance with procedures of the American National Standards Institute.

Section 50. Functions of the Correlating Committee

51. The Correlating Committee shall have the following functions:

a. Determine the steps and schedule for each revised edition of the National Electrical Code, subject to approval by the Board of Directors of the National Fire Protection Association.

b. Organize the Code-Making Panels in such a manner as to effectively cover the technical objectives of the National Electrical Code as set forth in Article 90 of the Code. The number of Code-Making Panels and the Code Articles assigned to each shall be determined by the Correlating Committee.

c. Appoint, as needed, Technical Subcommittees to assist in developing the National Electrical Code and such other Codes, Standards or Manuals which the NFPA Board of Directors recommends be handled by the National Electrical Code Committee.

d. Review all reports by the Code-Making Panels that recommend changes or additions to the National Electrical Code; determine whether a consensus exists warranting acceptance of such recommended changes or additions; and determine whether the proposals shall be approved for further processing, rejected, returned to the appropriate Code-Making Panel or Panels for further study, or submitted to a Technical Subcommittee for further consideration. Action to recommend amendments to the National Electrical Code for action at an NFPA Annual Meeting shall require at least seven

affirmative votes by the Correlating Committee provided that, if any absent member subsequently registers disapproval, the action must be reaffirmed by letter ballot or at a later meeting of the Committee.

e. Review all reports of other technical committees of the Electrical Section that normally submit such reports in accordance with Paragraph 28.

f. Establish that no conflict exists and satisfactory correlation is achieved between recommendations of the various Code-Making Panels and with other NFPA Technical Committees having an interest in the subjects under consideration.

g. Report to the Director of Engineering Services of the National Fire Protection Association any proposals for revisions or additions to the National Electrical Code.

h. Determine the Rules of Procedure for Tentative Interim Amendments of the National Electrical Code, subject to approval of the Board of Directors of the National Fire Protection Association (see Part C of these Rules).

i. Establish an Interpretation Procedure for the National Electrical Code, subject to approval of the Board of Directors of the National Fire Protection Association (see Part D of these Rules).

52. Meetings of the Correlating Committee shall be held at the call of the Chairman. Seven members shall constitute a quorum.

Section 60. Functions of the Code-Making Panels

61. A Code-Making Panel shall consider and report its recommendations on all matters referred to it by any of the methods outlined in Paragraph 91 of these Rules.

62. The program of each Code-Making Panel shall be directed by its Chairman as seems most appropriate for the efficient disposition of its business subject to the approval of the Correlating Committee. Code-Making Panel Meeting dates and places shall be coordinated through the Secretary of the National Electrical Code Committee to avoid conflicts of meetings and to assure that the established schedule is adhered to. Within this framework, each Code-Making Panel may develop its own working methods consistent with the objectives of the Association and the National Electrical Code Committee as herein established. A guide outline of "Manual of Procedure for Code-Making Panels" is available from the Secretary of the National Electrical Code Committee. Any proposed revision of the National Electrical Code recommended by a Panel shall represent, to a major degree, the consensus of the membership substantially concerned. (It shall be the responsibility of the Correlating Committee to determine if such a valid consensus exists.)

63. When reporting recommendations, the vote of each member of a Panel shall be recorded with the Correlating Committee by the Chairman of the Panel. This report shall identify affirmative voters, negative voters, those abstaining, and those whose ballots have not been returned, together with the reasons for negative votes and abstentions.

64. Each Panel shall report the consideration given to each proposal for Code changes that have been referred to it, whether it recommends a specific action, rejects the proposal, votes to retain the item on its docket for further study, refers the proposal to another Code-Making Panel, or takes any other course of action.

65. The various Panels are authorized to solicit from individuals or groups concerned with the scope of an Article such technical assistance and cooperation as will contribute to their work. The Chairman of the National Electrical Code Committee should be kept advised of such actions and those cooperating in this manner shall be mentioned in the report of the Panel to the Correlating Committee.

Section 70. Technical Subcommittees

71. Technical Subcommittees to consider any designated topic shall be appointed by the Chairman of the National Electrical Code Committee. Forming such Technical Subcommittees may result from a recommendation of the Correlating Committee or a request of a Code-Making Panel following approval by the Correlating Committee. Where the topic to be considered is wholly within a single Panel, the Chairman of the National Electrical Code Committee may request the Chairman of the Code-Making Panel to appoint the members of the Technical Subcommittee.

72. Those invited to serve on a Technical Subcommittee shall be chosen on the basis of familiarity with the problem or topic and need not be members of the National Electrical Code Committee.

73. Any report from a Technical Subcommittee, if containing proposals for changes or additions to the National Electrical Code, shall be referred to the Code-Making Panel or Panels to which the affected Articles of the Code have been assigned. Further processing shall follow the procedures indicated in Sections 91 to 93, inclusive, of these Rules.

Section 80. Revisions, Additions, and Deletions to the National Electrical Code

81. To be approved by the Correlating Committee, a revision of the National Electrical Code shall be either for:

a. A proposed revision for a new Edition of the Code, or

b. A Tentative Interim Amendment (see Part C of these Rules).

82. A new Edition of the National Electrical Code will be planned according to the following conditions:

a. Upon the initiative of the Correlating Committee on a three-year or four-year schedule, or

b. After a shorter interval when requested by the Correlating Committee or the Board of Directors of the National Fire Protection Association.

83. A Tentative Interim Amendment is a revision applied for and processed in accordance with the Rules of Procedure for Tentative Interim Amendments (see Part C of these Rules).

84. A schedule for each revised Edition of the Code shall be published by the Association and announced in suitable news releases to the technical press within six months following the issuance of each revised edition. This schedule shall include dates during which comments or recommendations from the public are to be received.

Section 90. Methods for Handling Proposed Code Revisions

91. The stages through which proposed changes in the Code are to be considered shall be as follows:

a. Proposal is prepared by any member of the National Electrical Code Committee, by any interested person, or by any interested organization and submitted to the Chairman of the National Electrical Code Committee with copies to the Secretary of the National Electrical Code Committee and to the Chairman of the responsible Code-Making Panel. If the submitter is not sure which Code-Making Panel has jurisdiction or if it involves a subject not previously assigned, an extra copy of the proposal should be sent to the Chairman of the National Electrical Code Committee for proper disposition.

b. The proposal is circulated to the members of the Code-Making Panel by its Chairman.

c. The Code-Making Panel considers the proposal and takes one or more of the following steps:

(1) Drafts or prepares a proposed revision or addition to the National Electrical Code, ballots on same, and forwards its recommendations, with a ballot statement (see Paragraphs 63 and 64) to the Correlating Committee for approval as a proposed revision for a new Edition of the Code.

(2) Requests coordination with any other affected Code-Making Panel through the Correlating Committee, looking forward to future submittal in accordance with Paragraph 91.c.(1).

(3) Rejects the proposal, submitting it and a vote statement explaining its action to the Correlating Committee.

(4) Reports to the Correlating Committee that the proposal has been placed on the Panel's docket pending further study.

(5) Refers the recommendation to a Technical Subcommittee for detailed consideration (see Section 70 of these Rules).

d. All proposals for revisions or changes made by the Code-Making Panels and referred to the Correlating Committee are reviewed and processed in accordance with Paragraphs 51.d. and 51.f.

e. For a new Edition of the National Electrical Code, the Committee Secretary prepares for public dissemination through the National Fire Protection Association the "Preprint of the Proposed Amendments for the . . . . .* National Electrical Code" for study and comment, announcing at that time a final date for receipt of such comment in accordance with the prearranged schedule (see Paragraphs 51.a. and 82).

f. Following action specified in Paragraph 91.e., all comments received are referred to the Code-Making Panels for their final consideration and vote. Their proposals are then resubmitted to the Correlating Committee, which reviews them and takes one of the actions indicated in Paragraph 91.d.

g. The Secretary of the National Electrical Code Committee then prepares for publication in the NFPA Technical Committee Reports the proposed . . . . .* National Electrical Code.

h. The Electrical Section (see Part A) is provided with the opportunity of reviewing these amendments or the revised edition at its Annual Meeting prior to Association action on the report. The Electrical Section may vote to request further consideration of a specific item by the Correlating Committee. The Correlating Committee in giving further consideration must either reaffirm its original position or refer the matter back to the Code-Making Panel involved for further study.

i. Following final consideration by the Correlating Committee, the report is submitted to the membership of the National Fire Protection Association in Annual Meeting for action in accordance with the NFPA Regulations Governing Technical Committees.

92. The NFPA submits each edition of the National Electrical Code (NFPA No. 70) to the American National Standards Institute for adoption as a ANSI Standard (ANSI Standard C1).

93. A new edition of the Code is published by the National Fire Protection Association.

* Next date of issue

PART C—RULES OF PROCEDURE—TENTATIVE INTERIM AMENDMENTS TO THE NATIONAL ELECTRICAL CODE

Section 100. Purpose and Scope of Tentative Interim Amendments

101. A Tentative Interim Amendment to the National Electrical Code is an amendment processed and promulgated separate and apart from a revised edition of the Code

in accordance with this Part.

102. The purpose of a Tentative Interim Amendment is to correct errors and conflicts or to accomplish recognition of advances in the art of safeguarding of persons and of buildings and their contents as set forth in Section 90-1 of the National Electrical Code.

103. This method of amending the Code shall be resorted to only when action is urgently needed and should not be deferred until the next scheduled revision.

Section 110. Handling Proposals for Tentative Interim Amendments

111. A proposal for such a Tentative Interim Amendment should include a full explanation of the proposal and an exact statement of the suggested solution supported by all pertinent data, together with a specific statement of what new text or amendment of the existing text of the National Electrical Code is recommended. Each proposal must be endorsed by a member of the National Electrical Code Committee and the proposer must be prepared to furnish as many copies of the proposal and supporting data as the Chairman of the National Electrical Code Committee may determine are needed for appropriate consideration.

112. The Chairman of the National Electrical Code Committee shall refer each proposal to a special Subcommittee appointed by him and consisting of two members of the Correlating Committee of the National Electrical Code Committee and the Chairman or Chairmen of the Code-Making Panel(s) concerned with the proposal. The Chairman and Secretary of the National Electrical Code Committee shall be voting members of this special Subcommittee. This special Subcommittee shall determine whether the proposal is within the stated purpose of the Tentative Interim Amendment Procedure set forth in Paragraphs 102 and 103.

a. If the proposal is found not to be within the stated purpose of this procedure, the Chairman of the National Electrical Code Committee shall so notify the submitter.

113. If the proposal is found to be within the stated purpose of this Procedure, the Chairman of the National Electrical Code Committee shall refer the proposal and all supporting data to the appropriate Code-Making Panel or Panels. The Panel or Panels shall report any recommendations to the Correlating Committee of the National Electrical Code Committee, following which the Chairman of the National Electrical Code Committee shall report the proposed Panel action to the submitter. If the submitter is not satisfied with the proposed Panel action, he shall be privileged to withdraw his proposal or submit a revision of the proposed amendment or new data in support of his original proposal. Such a submitter's revision, new data, or both, shall be referred to the Code-Making Panel or Panels for further consideration and report.

a. The Panel is not privileged to revise or amend the proposal as submitted, except for purely editorial content. If it is felt desirable to amend or revise the substantive content of the original proposal, such amendments or revisions shall be subject to the same criteria for handling as a Tentative Interim Amendment, as the original proposal, namely, the criteria specified in Paragraphs 102 and 103.

114. If the Panel recommends against adoption of the proposal and the Correlating Committee determines that the proposal has been processed in accordance with the procedures described herein, the Chairman of the National Electrical Code Committee shall notify the proposer that the National Electrical Code Committee has declined to accept the Tentative Interim Amendment as proposed.

115. If agreement is reached between the interested Panel or Panels and the proposer as to a specific Tentative Interim Amendment of the Code, it shall be submitted to the Correlating Committee for formal approval. If approved by both the Panel and the Correlating Committee with no more than one negative vote by either group, such a Tentative Interim Amendment shall be promulgated for the current edition of the National Electrical Code and will become effective immediately.

a. If the Panel approves the Tentative Interim Amendment by a consensus of voting, but with two or more negative votes or if there is more than one negative vote by the Correlating Committee, the Association shall publish in one of its publications distributed to all members the proposed Amendment with the notice that it is being considered for the current edition of the National Electrical Code, and those persons wishing to comment should file such comments with the Chairman of the National Electrical Code Committee within 60 days after the mailing date of the publication. Any comments so received shall be considered by the Code-Making Panel, which shall make a final report to the Correlating Committee. The latter will then reconsider the amendment, make a final decision regarding it, and notify the submitter of the action taken.

b. A Tentative Interim Amendment, when approved with or without the 60-day waiting period, shall be published by the Association in a manner or manners best designed to notify all interested parties and announced in a suitable NFPA news release to the technical press.

116. All Tentative Interim Amendments are subject to further consideration by the appropriate Code-Making Panel or Panels in preparing recommendations for a subsequent new edition of the National Electrical Code as though originating in accordance with the established regular procedure for revising the National Electrical Code.

PART D—INTERPRETATION PROCEDURE OF THE NATIONAL ELECTRICAL CODE COMMITTEE

Section 120. Personnel of Interpretations Committee

121. There shall be a standing committee of the National Electrical Code Committee to be known as the Interpretations Committee. This Committee shall consist of:

a. The Chairman of the Correlating Committee, who shall be the Chairman of the Interpretations Committee and a voting member.

b. The Secretary of the Correlating Committee, who shall be the Secretary of the Interpretations Committee and a voting member.

c. The Chairman of that Code-Making Panel which has charge of the affected Article of the Code for which an interpretation is requested, and

d. At least two other members or alternates of the National Electrical Code Committee selected by the Chairman depending upon the availability, experience, knowledge, and interest of the members. The Code-Making Panel Chairman and the two other members shall be selected for each specific interpretation and shall be discharged upon completion of each.

122. No member or alternate shall be eligible who is directly concerned with a controversial situation to which the specific question for interpretation applies.

Section 130. Method of Applying for Interpretations

131. Those desiring an interpretation shall direct their requests to the Chairman of the Interpretations Committee, National Electrical Code, National Fire Protection Association, 470 Atlantic Avenue, Boston, Mass. 02210, supplying five identical copies of a statement in which shall appear specific references to a single problem, Article or Section. Such a statement shall be on the business stationery of the inquirer and shall be duly signed.

132. When applications involve actual field situations, they shall so state and all parties involved shall be named.

Section 140. Forms of Interpretations Recognized

141. Two general forms of findings will be recognized:

a. Those making an interpretation of the literal text.

b. Those making an interpretation of the intent of the National Electrical Code Committee when a particular rule was adopted.

142. There are certain questions which arise in the application of the requirements of the National Electrical Code which are not subject to interpretation under the procedures described herein. These include degree and extent of a hazardous location area, interpretation of suitability of isolation or guarding, interpretation of equivalent protection—and such items which involve an intimate knowledge of the installation rather than a knowledge of the intent and meaning of the requirement.

Section 150. Methods of Handling and Issuing Interpretations

151. The findings of the Interpretations Committee will be in its name and for the National Electrical Code Committee as a whole. In any case, where there is more than one negative vote on any proposed interpretation, the interpretation shall be referred to the Correlating Committee. The Correlating Committee shall then make a judgment on the consensus of voting in the Committee to determine that a consensus does exist. If it is determined that a consensus does not exist, the request shall be referred to the proper Code-Making Panel or Panels.

152. The applicant will be informed of the

finding promptly following its having been determined. As soon as feasible, the Interpretation, serially numbered, but not otherwise identified, shall be published by the Association and announced in a suitable NFPA news release to the technical press.

153. When the Committee on Interpretations reports to the Electrical Correlating Committee at its regular meeting, a statement shall be made as to extent of concurrence of the members in the separate findings covered in their report. No other release shall be made of any minority views.

154. Each interpretation will be based on the best judgment of the Committee, but the Committee cannot be responsible for subsequent actions by authorities enforcing the National Electrical Code as to whether they accept or reject the findings.

155. Each Code-Making Panel will be expected to give appropriate consideration to the text of any Article or Section of the National Electrical Code which has produced an Interpretation finding to the end that a suitable revision of the text may be recommended to eliminate the difficulty which prompted the request.

TIME SCHEDULE FOR THE 1978 NATIONAL ELECTRICAL CODE

Adopted by the Correlating Committee of the National Electrical Code Committee, February 14, 1974

Dec. 1, 1975	Final date for receipt of proposals from the public for revision of the 1975 *National Electrical Code* preparatory to the issuance of a 1978 edition. Proposals should be forwarded to the Chairman, the Secretary, and the responsible Code Making Panel Chairmen. (Full names and addresses published on Pages 70-v to 70-xv of the 1975 NEC.)
Dec. 1, 1975 to April 1976	Code Making Panels consider proposals for Code changes and prepare reports for submittal to Correlating Committee.
April 14, 1976	Final Date for Code Making Panel reports to be submitted to the Correlating Committee
April 15, 1976 to May 1976	Correlating Committee reviews reports submitted by Code Making Panels. Advises Panels with respect to existence of consensus, correlates work among Panels, assigns Panel jurisdiction over new and borderline items. Submits reports of the Panels to the NFPA Executive Office for the *Preprint of the Proposed Amendments for the 1978 National Electrical Code.*
May 1976	Informal report to the NFPA Electrical Section by the Correlating Committee at the 1976 NFPA Annual Meeting.
July 1976	*Preprint of the Proposed Amendments for the 1978 National Electrical Code* published for distribution to the National Electrical Code Committee and other interested parties.
July 1976 to Nov. 15, 1976	Period for study by members of the National Electrical Code Committee, electrical inspectors, industry and others, and submittal of recommendations to Code Making Panel Chairmen* for changes.
Nov. 16, 1976 to Feb. 1, 1977	Code Making Panels reconsider all proposed recommendations for changes and prepare final report for submittal to the Correlating Committee.
Feb. 1, 1977	Final date for Code Making Panel reports to be submitted to the Correlating Committee.
Feb. 1977	Correlating Committee reviews Final Reports of Code Making Panels, accepts or rejects changes, determines existence of consensus, resolves conflicts between Code Making Panel Reports.
March 1, 1977	Final date for Correlating Committee to submit the final proposed changes to NFPA for printing in the *1977 NFPA Technical Committee Reports.*
April 1977	NFPA prints and distributes the *1977 NFPA Technical Committee Reports* containing the proposed 1978 National *Electrical Code* to members of the National Electrical Code Committee and to all other NFPA members who file requests therefor.
May 1977	Review by the NFPA Electrical Section and official action by NFPA Annual Meeting. Submittal by NFPA to American National Standards Institute for approval as ANSI Standard.
September 1977	Publication of the 1978 *National Electrical Code.*

---

* Copies should also be sent to the Chairman and the Secretary.

METHOD OF SUBMITTING PROPOSAL TO REVISE
THE NATIONAL ELECTRICAL CODE

A proposal to revise the 1975 Edition of the National Electrical Code must be submitted prior to December 1, 1975 as indicated in the time schedule for the 1978 National Electrical Code. The proposal shall be sent to the Chairman and Secretary of the National Electrical Code Committee in the form indicated below. The proposal is to be identified by Section number and paragraph letter, where applicable, and is to state the new or revised Code text. It is essential that the submitter fully understand the intent of an existing requirement before attempting to propose a revision of it.

The submitter is to identify the source of the proposal, indicating whether it is his own or is being submitted by a committee or organization.

The proposal needs to be accompanied by supporting comment explaining the need for the change and should include any available substantiating information or data. Where the submitter believes it imperative that the supporting comment shall provide considerable detailed information that cannot be accommodated on a single page, he is to provide 25 copies of this proposal on plain paper for subsequent use by the Panel Chairman in processing the proposal. An example of a properly submitted proposal is as follows:

Section 250-74

PROPOSAL:

Amend Section 250-74 to read:

250-74. Bonding at Grounding-Type Receptacles. Grounding continuity between a grounded outlet box and the grounding circuit of the receptacle shall be established by means of a bonding jumper between the outlet box and the receptacle grounding terminal.

Exception 1: When the box is surface-mounted, direct metal-to-metal contact between the device yoke and the box may be used to establish the grounding circuit.

Exception 2: Contact devices or yokes designed and approved for the purpose may be used in conjunction with the supporting screws to establish the grounding circuit between the device yoke and flush-type boxes installed in walls.

SUBMITTER:

International Association of Electrical Inspectors.

SUPPORTING COMMENT:

Direct contact between device yokes and boxes is seldom achieved between devices and boxes installed in walls, inasmuch as flush boxes are in practice seldom found flush, despite the provisions of Section 370-10. Screws and yokes currently in use were designed solely for the support of devices rather than as part of the grounding circuit. The intent of the amendment is to encourage the design of either a modified yoke or a supplemental conducting member to augment the supporting screw in the device-to-box grounding circuit.

Index